May 18–20, 2016
Boston, MA, USA

Association for
Computing Machinery

Advancing Computing as a Science & Profession

GLSVLSI'16

Proceedings of the 2016 ACM
Great Lakes Symposium on VLSI

Sponsored by:

ACM SIGSAC

Technical Sponsors:

IEEE & CEDA

Supported by:

BU - Department of Electrical & Computer Engineering, Cādence, and Living Computer Project

Association for
Computing Machinery

Advancing Computing as a Science & Profession

The Association for Computing Machinery
2 Penn Plaza, Suite 701
New York, New York 10121-0701

ISBN: 978-1-4503-4274-2 (Digital)

ISBN: 978-1-4503-4479-1 (Print)

Additional copies may be ordered prepaid from:

ACM Order Department
PO Box 30777
New York, NY 10087-0777, USA

Phone: 1-800-342-6626 (USA and Canada)
+1-212-626-0500 (Global)
Fax: +1-212-944-1318
E-mail: acmhelp@acm.org
Hours of Operation: 8:30 am – 4:30 pm ET

Printed in the USA

Foreword

Welcome to the 26th edition of the *Great Lakes Symposium on VLSI (GLSVLSI) 2016,* held at Boston University Department of Electrical and Computer Engineering in Boston, MA, USA. GLSVLSI is a premier venue for the dissemination of manuscripts of the highest quality in all areas related to VLSI, devices, and system-level design. The location of this year's GLSVLSI is Boston, which continues GLSVLSI's tradition of organizing meetings near noted bodies of water. While not a "great lake", the Charles River flows across the Greater Boston area, separating the city of Boston from Cambridge. The basin of the Charles River is located in Hopkinton, Massachusetts, and serves as the starting point of the Boston Marathon. While the marathoners run 26 miles to the city, the Charles River twists and turns for 80 miles before ending its journey in Boston Harbor, where it meets the Atlantic Ocean.

The Greater Boston area, consisting of Boston and its surrounding neighborhoods, is the 10th largest metropolitan area of the US. Boston is one of the oldest cities in the US, and was the first city to open a public school and a transportation system in the country. Boston is truly an intellectual, technological, and political hub. It is home to around 50 universities and colleges, making it one of the most prominent centers of higher education and medicine internationally. Boston is experiencing substantial industrial growth, particularly in the fields of computer and electrical engineering. Each year, millions of tourists visit Boston to explore the city's historic landmarks, to include Faneuil Hall, Fenway Park (home of the Boston Red Sox), Boston Common, and Harvard Square. Boston University, located along the Charles River, is in the heart of the city with easy access to all major tourist attractions, parks, concert venues, and museums. Boston is a great location for this high-quality symposium on VLSI, and we believe that you will enjoy the beautiful city as well as the symposium.

This year's special theme for GLSVLSI is *Hardware and System Design for Security and Privacy.* To support this theme, we have organized several keynote talks by recognized experts and dedicated three special sessions to this topic. On Wednesday we will open the symposium with Marc Witteman, the Chief Executive Officer of Riscure in the Netherlands, who will speak about building secure chips. Kevin Fu, professor at University of Michigan and the Chief Scientist of Virta Labs, will talk about medical device security on Thursday afternoon. On Friday, Ingrid Verbauwhede, professor at University of Leuven in Belgium and at UCLA, will deliver another keynote talk on low power embedded encryption. Special sessions on the hardware security theme cover Internet-of-Things security (Wednesday), emerging technologies and security (Thursday), and a panel on future of hardware security research with speakers from industry, government agencies, and academia (Friday).

In addition to including a substantial amount of focus on the hardware security theme, we made sure to provide perspectives on other cutting edge topics to enrich and diversify the symposium program. Yusuf Leblebici, professor at the Swiss Federal Institute of Technology, will talk about multi-sensor vision system design on Thursday. Also on Thursday, we have an exciting special session discussing synthetic biology research, explicitly targeting the VLSI and EDA communities.

As for the technical content, GLSVLSI 2016 had outstanding statistics: 197 papers were submitted, by authors from 25 different countries, of which 50 papers were accepted as full papers for oral presentation (with a **25%** acceptance rate). Including poster papers, a total of **71 papers** will be included in the symposium and published in the proceedings. Of the authors of these papers in the program, 53% are from the Americas, 28% from Asia, and 19% from Europe. The final technical program consists of 21 long presentations and 29 short presentations in 12 oral sessions, and 21 posters in two poster sessions. Special sessions add another 9 exciting papers to the proceedings of the symposium.

GLSVLSI 2016 starts on Wednesday, May 18th 2016, with an exciting line up of speakers on a broad range of issues including hardware security, encryption, new methods in CAD and network-on-chips (NoCs), low-power systems and emerging memory designs, and stochastic computing applications. On the second day, in addition to continuing the discussion on CAD and VLSI design challenges, we have technical sessions focused on error resilience and robustness, emerging technologies and post-CMOS VLSI. On the third day, further discussions are dedicated to the innovative solutions for emerging technologies, low-power systems, and VLSI design. The technical program of GLSVLSI 2016 contains two parallel tracks to allow the inclusion of more papers and extensive discussions during the three days of the symposium. Overall, there are 12 regular sessions, 4 special sessions, and 2 poster sessions in the technical program. Four outstanding papers have been selected as candidates for the best paper award and will be presented in different technical sessions (as marked in the program). The best paper award will be announced at the symposium banquet on Thursday evening.

The social events of GLSVLSI 2016 include two special events this year. The first event is a reception cocktail on Wednesday evening at the historic *Boston University Castle*. Then, on Thursday, May 19th, in a special version of the famous "Boston Duck Tour", attendees will get a chance to see various Boston monuments and neighborhoods, and enjoy a short trip on the river. The 1-hour tour will be followed by the symposium banquet that will be held at the *Boston University Trustees Ballroom*.

We would like to thank all the members of the Technical Program Committee and the secondary reviewers, who have done a rigorous and thorough job in evaluating the submissions and determining the final high quality technical program of GLSVLSI 2016. The Track Chairs have done outstanding work in ensuring that each submitted paper was consistently reviewed and in preparing the final program. In addition, we extend our strong appreciation to the other members of the Organizing Committee (Ajay Joshi, Sherief Reda, Emre Salman, Theocharis Theocharides, Miroslav Velev, Aida Todri-Sanial, and Brett Meyer) for their hard work and excellent service while organizing the proceedings, special sessions, publicity, registration, finances, organization of the event, and web presence to make this edition of GLSVLSI a great success.

We thank Boston University Electrical and Computer Engineering Department, especially Gabriella Mcnevin and Karen Hennessey, for their gracious support and tremendous assistance in the organization of GLSVLSI. Our corporate sponsors, BU ECE Department, Cadence, and the Living Computing Project, have enabled extending a larger number of travel and registration awards to students.

We trust that you will find GLSVLSI 2016 highly rewarding and exciting in terms of the technical quality, networking opportunities, as well as the content and diversity of the talks and sessions.

Ayse K. Coskun and Martin Margala
General Co-Chairs

Laleh Behjat and Jie Han
Program Co-Chairs

Table of Contents

Session 3: VLSI Design 1

Session Chairs: Himanshu Thapliyal & *(University of Kentucky)*, Houman Homayoun *(George Mason University)*

Session 4: CAD 1

Session Chairs: Tosiron Adegbija *(University of Arizona)* & Marisa López-Vallejo *(Universidad Politécnica de Madrid)*

Poster Session 1

Session Chair: Tali Moreshet *(Boston University)*

Session 5: Low Power 1

Session Chair: Ioannis Savidis *(Drexel University)*

Special Session 1: IoT Security: Issues, Innovations and Interplays

Session Chair: Swarup Bhunia *(University of Florida)*

Session 6: Test 2

Session Chair: Qiaoyan Yu *(University of New Hampshire)*

Session 7: VLSI Circuits 2

Session Chair: Hai Li *(University of Pittsburgh)*

Session 8: Emerging 1

Session Chair: Bo Yuan *(City University of New York)*

Session 9: CAD 2

Session Chair: Miroslav Velev *(Aries Design Automation)*

Special Session 3: Emerging Technology Devices and Security
Session Chair: JV Rajendran *(UT Dallas)*

Session 10: VLSI Design 2
Session Chair: Brett Meyer *(McGill University)*

Special Session 4: Emerging Frontiers in Hardware Security
Session Chairs: Ajay Joshi & *(Boston University)*, Gang Qu *(University of Maryland)*

Poster Session 2
Session Chair: Hamed Tabkhi *(Northeastern University)*

26th ACM Great Lakes Symposium on VLSI Organization

General Chairs: Ayse K. Coskun *(Boston University, USA)*
Martin Margala *(University of Massachusetts, Lowell, USA)*

Program Chairs: Laleh Behjat *(University of Calgary, Canada)*
Jie Han *(University of Alberta, Canada)*

Web Chair: Theocharis Theocharides *(University of Cyprus, Cyprus)*

Registration Chair: Emre Salman *(Stony Brook University, USA)*

Proceedings Chair: Miroslav N. Velev *(Aries Design Automation, USA)*

Finance Chair: Sherief Reda *(Brown University, USA)*

Publicity Chairs: Aida Todri-Sanial *(CNRS, LIRMM, France)*
Brett Meyer *(McGill University, Canada)*

Special Sessions Chair: Ajay Joshi *(Boston University, USA)*

Steering Committee: David Atienza *(EPFL, Switzerland)*
Jose Ayala *(Univ. Complutense Madrid, Spain)*
Iris Bahar *(Brown University, USA)*
Sanjukta Bhanja *(University of South Florida, USA)*
Erik Brunvand *(University of Utah, USA)*
Yehea Ismail *(American Uniersity in Cairo, Egypt)*
Alex K. Jones *(University of Pittsburgh, USA)*
Hai (Helen) Li *(University of Pittsburgh, USA)*
Fabrizio Lombardi *(Northeastern University, USA)*
Enrico Macii *(Politecnico di Torino, Italy)*
Gang Qu *(University of Maryland, USA)*
Ken Stevens *(University of Utah, USA)*
Yuan Xie *(University of California, Santa Barbara, USA)*
Zhiyuan Yan *(Lehigh University, USA)*
Hai Zhou *(Northwestern University, USA)*

Student Volunteers for Conference Organization Fulya Kaplan *(Boston University, USA)*
Yenai Ma *(Boston University, USA)*
Tiansheng Zhang *(Boston University, USA)*
Boyou Zhou *(Boston University, USA)*

Program Committee: Antonio Acosta-Jimenez *(IMSE-CNM/University of Seville, Spain)*
Iraklis Anagnostopoulos *(Southern Illinois University, USA)*
Jose Ayala *(Univ. Complutense Madrid, Spain)*
Giovanni Beltrame *(Ecole Polytechinque de Montreal, Canada)*
Youcef Bouchebaba *(Synopsys, USA)*
Eli Bozorgzadeh *(University of California, Irvine, USA)*
Andrea Calimera *(Politecnico di Torino, Italy)*
Xi Chen *(Qualcomm, USA)*
Philippe Coussy *(Universit de Bretagne Sud / Lab-STICC, France)*
Alfred Crouch *(SiliconAid and ASSET InterTech, USA)*
Jianwei Dai *(Intel, USA)*
Bishnu Prasad Das *(Indian Institute of Technology, Roorkee, India)*
Shamik Das *(The MITRE Corporation, USA)*
Jayita Das *(Intel, USA)*
Jason Doege *(Centaur Technology, USA)*
Rolf Drechsler *(University of Bremen, Germany)*
Liu Duo *(Chongqing University, China)*
Jennifer Dworak *(Southern Methodist University, USA)*
Fabrizio Ferrandi *(Politecnico di Milano, Italy)*
Pierre-Emmanuel Gaillardon *(LSI – EPFL, Switzerland)*
Dhruva Ghai *(Oriental University, India)*
Prasun Ghosal *(Indian Institute of Engineering Science & Technology, India)*
Swarup Ghosh *(University of South Florida, USA)*
Ann Gordon-Ross *(University of Florida, USA)*
Sumeet Gupta *(The Pennsylvania State University, USA)*
Mona Hella *(RPI, USA)*
Domenik Helms *(Oldenburger Institut fur Informatik, Germany)*
Houman Homayoun *(George Mason University, USA)*
Vinayak Honkote *(Intel, USA)*
Chih-Tsun Huang *(National Tsing-Hua University, Taiwan)*
Yier Jin *(The University of Central Florida, USA)*
Mehdi Kamal *(University of Tehran, Iran)*
Srinivas Katkoori *(University of South Florida, USA)*
Yong-Bin Kim *(Northeastern University, USA)*
Kyung Ki Kim *(Daegu University, Korea)*
Farinaz Koushafar *(Rice University, USA)*
Rene Krenz-Baath *(Hamm-Lippstadt Univ. of Applied Sciences, Germany)*
Dhireesha Kudithipudi *(Rochester Institute of Technology, USA)*
Akash Kumar *(Dresden University of Technology, Germany)*
Erik Larsson *(Lund University, Sweden)*
Sébastien Le Beux *(Lyon Institute of Nanotechnology (INL), France)*
Shuai Li *(Cadence Design Systems, USA)*
Karthikeyan Lingasubramanian *(Univ. of Alabama at Birmingham, USA)*
Mirko Loghi *(Universita' di Udine, Italy)*
Marisa López-Vallejo *(Universidad Politecnica Madrid, Spain)*

Program Committee (continued):

Xiaoqing Wen *(Kyushu Institute of Technology, Japan)*
James Wingfield *(AMD, USA)*
Tian Xia *(University of Vermont, USA)*
Sungjoo Yoo *(Seoul National University, Korea)*
Bei Yu *(The Chinese University of Hong Kong, Hong Kong)*
Qiaoyan Yu *(University of New Hampshire, USA)*
Shimeng Yu *(Arizona State University, USA)*
Joseph Zambreno *(Iowa State University, USA)*
Wei Zhang *(Hong Kong Univ. of Science and Technology, Hong Kong)*
Jishen Zhao *(University of California, Santa Cruz, USA)*
Geng Zheng *(Analog Devices, USA)*
Yong Zou *(Synopsys, USA)*

Additional reviewers:

Sonia Lopez Alarcon
Hassan Anwar
Paolo Burgio
Chun-Hsiang Chang
Hari Chauhan
Gengjie Chen
Pai-Yu Chen
Yi-Chung Chen
Yongsuk Choi
Wing-Kai Chow
Dharanidhar Dang
Marc Fyrbiak
Ping Gao
Vladimir Herdt
Chin Hau Hoo
Mahmoud Ibrahim
Sheikh Ariful Islam
Nicolas Jeanniot
Heungjun Jeon
In-Seok Jung
Charalampos Kalargaris
Amit Karel
Oliver Keszöcze
Youngbok Kim
Elias Kougianos
Jian Kuang
Vianney Lapotre
Hoang M. Le
Ho Joon Lee
Haitong Li
Rui Liu
Wei Liu
Manqing Mao
Cory Merkel
Jin Miao
Przemyslaw Mroszczyk
Jaewon Nam
Tuan Nguyen
Karl Ott
Hoda Pahlevanzadeh
Paolo Palmieri
Ioannis Papistas
Nam Khanh Pham
Ilia Polian
Subhendu Roy
Pablo Royer
Kenneth Schmitz
Dinesh Kumar Selvakumaran
Sophiane Senni
Saeideh Shirinzadeh
Mathias Soeken
Prabha Sundaravadivel
Kainan Wang
Wei Wei
Li Xu
Ni Xu
Venkata Prasanth Yanambaka
Jinghua Yang
Seyed Alireza Zahrai
Hang Zhang
Liuyang Zhang
Marina Zlochisti

GLSVLSI 2016 Sponsors & Supporters

Sponsors:

Technical Co-Sponsors:

Supporters:

Why Is It So Hard to Make Secure Chips?

Marc Witteman
Riscure

ABSTRACT

Chip security has long been the domain of smart cards. These microcontrollers are specifically designed to thwart many different attacks in order to deliver typical security functions as payment cards, electronic passports, and access cards.

With the advent of IoT everything is changing. Billions of devices will need security. We need access to our information sources and property. We expect our privacy to be respected and rely on the confidentiality of our sensitive information. We trust that our assets are well protected and cannot be manipulated by criminals. Can chip technology actually deliver on these demands?

In this presentation we start by looking at the security architecture of electronic devices and mechanisms to restrict access and protect information. Then we explain the threat landscape and explain different types of attacks. Next we zoom in to security properties of the chips, which are at the core of all electronic devices. Finally we show how attack resistance can be tested and how chip vendors can gain assurance about the security of their products.

Categories and Subject Descriptions

E.0 [General]

Keywords

Hardware security; Cybersecurity

GLSVLSI'16, May 18–20, 2016, Boston, MA, USA.
ACM 978-1-4503-4274-2/16/05.
DOI: http://dx.doi.org/10.1145/2902961.2902962

BIO

Marc Witteman has a long track record in the security industry. He has been involved with a variety of security projects for over two decades and worked on applications in mobile communications, payment industry, identification, and pay television. Recent work includes secure programming and mobile payment security issues.

He has authored several articles on smart card and embedded device security issues. Further, he has extensive experience as a trainer, lecturing security topics for audiences ranging from novices to experts.

As a security analyst he developed several tools for testing software and hardware security. This includes Inspector, a platform for conducting side-channel analysis and JCworkBench, a logical test tool.

Marc Witteman has an MSc in Electrical Engineering from the Delft University of Technology in the Netherlands. From 1989 till 2001 he worked for several telecom operators, the ETSI standardization body and a security evaluation facility.

In 2001 he founded Riscure, a security lab based in the Netherlands. Riscure offers test tools and services to manufacturers and issuers of advanced security technology.

Between 2001 and 2009 he raised the company to a leading security test lab, and side channel test tool vendor. In 2010 Marc Witteman started Riscure Inc, the US branch of Riscure, based in San Francisco. At present he is the Chief Executive Officer of Riscure.

Design and Implementation of Real-Time Multi-sensor Vision Systems

Yusuf Leblebici
Swiss Federal Institute of
Technology in Lausanne

ABSTRACT

Implementation of high performance multi-camera / multi-sensor imaging systems that are required to produce real-time video output pose a large number of unique challenges to conventional digital design based on general-purpose processors or GPUs. In potential application areas ranging from machine vision, automotive, and virtual reality, the need for real-time operation with very limited latency dictates customized architectures that are not readily implementable using conventional approaches. In this talk, we will discuss the algorithms that are utilized in such multi-sensor platforms, the specialized architectures that allow streaming video processing, and system-level integration issues. Problems such as light-field reconstruction, multi-band blending, pixel-level interpolation, and rectification are presented, with detailed circuit and system level examples.

Categories and Subject Descriptions

E.0 [General]

Keywords

VLSI Design; Real-Time Imaging

BIO

Yusuf Leblebici received the B.Sc. and M.Sc. degrees in electrical engineering from Istanbul Technical University, Istanbul, Turkey, in 1984 and 1986, respectively, and the Ph.D. degree in electrical and computer engineering from the University of Illinois, Urbana-Champaign (UIUC), in 1990. Since 2002, he is a Chair Professor at the Swiss Federal Institute of Technology in Lausanne (EPFL), and director of Microelectronic Systems Laboratory. His research interests include design of high-speed CMOS digital and mixed-signal integrated circuits, computer-aided design of VLSI systems, intelligent sensor interfaces, modeling and simulation of semiconductor devices, and VLSI reliability analysis. He is the coauthor of six textbooks, as well as more than 300 articles published in various journals and conferences. He is a Fellow of IEEE since 2010, and he has been elected as Distinguished Lecturer of the IEEE Circuits and Systems Society for 2010-2011.

GLSVLSI'16, May 18–20, 2016, Boston, MA, USA.
ACM 978-1-4503-4274-2/16/05.
http://dx.doi.org/10.1145/2902961.2902965

Medical Device Security: The First 165 Years

Kevin Fu
University of Michigan

ABSTRACT

Today, it would be difficult to find medical device technology that does not critically depend on computer software. Network connectivity and wireless communication has transformed the delivery of patient care. The technology often enables patients to lead more normal and healthy lives. However, medical devices that rely on software (e.g., drug infusion pumps, linear accelerators, pacemakers) also inherit the pesky cybersecurity risks endemic to computing. What's special about medical devices and cybersecurity? What's hype and what's real? What can history teach us? How are international standards bodies and regulatory cybersecurity requirements changing the global manufacture of medical devices? This talk will provide a glimpse into the risks, benefits, and regulatory issues for medical device cybersecurity and innovation of trustworthy medical device software.

Categories and Subject Descriptions

E.0 [General]

Keywords

Cybersecurity; Medical device security.

BIO

Kevin Fu is credited for establishing the field of medical device security beginning with the 2008 IEEE paper on defibrillator security. Kevin is Chief Scientist of Virta Labs, Inc. and Associate Professor in EECS at the University of Michigan where he directs the Archimedes Center for Medical Device Security and the Security and Privacy Research Group (SPQR).

Kevin has testified in the House and Senate on matters of information security and has written commissioned work on trustworthy medical device software for the Institute of Medicine of the National Academies. He is member of NIST Information Security and Privacy Advisory Board, the CRA Computing Community Consortium Council, and the ACM Committee on Computers and Public Policy. He was named MIT Technology Review TR35 Innovator of the Year. Kevin served as program chair of USENIX Security during a period of unprecedented growth. He co-chairs the AAMI Working Group on Medical Device Security. He served as a visiting scientist at the Food & Drug Administration, the Beth Israel Deaconess Medical Center of Harvard Medical School, Microsoft Research, and MIT CSAIL. Fu received his B.S., M.Eng., and Ph.D. from MIT. He earned a certificate of artisanal bread making from the French Culinary Institute.

GLSVLSI'16, May 18 20, 2016, Boston, MA, USA.
ACM 978-1-4503-4274-2/16/05.
DOI: http://dx.doi.org/10.1145/2902961.2902964

VLSI Design Methods for Low Power Embedded Encryption

Ingrid Verbauwhede
COSIC, KU Leuven and UCLA

ABSTRACT

Intelligent things, medical devices, vehicles and factories, all part of cyberphysical systems, will only be secure if we can build devices that can perform the mathematically demanding cryptographic operations in an efficient way. Unfortunately, many of devices operate under extremely limited power, energy and area constraints. Yet we expect that they can execute, often in real-time, the symmetric key, public key and/or hash functions needed for the application. At the same time, we request that the implementations are also secure against a wide range of physical attacks.

This presentation will focus on the design methods to realize cryptographic operations on resource constrained devices. To reach the extremely low power, low energy and area budgets, we need to consider in an integrated way the protocols, the algorithms, the architectures and the circuit aspects of the application. These concepts will be illustrated with the design of several cryptographic co-processors suitable for implementation in embedded context.

Categories and Subject Descriptions

E.0 [General]

Keywords

Hardware Security, Cryptography, Low Power Design

BIO

Dr. Ingrid Verbauwhede is a Professor in the research group COSIC of the Electrical Engineering Department of the KU Leuven in Belgium. At COSIC, she leads the embedded systems and hardware group. She is also adjunct professor at the EE department at UCLA, Los Angeles, CA. She joined COSIC in 2003 and UCLA in 1998. Before joining UCLA she worked at UC Berkeley as a post-doctoral researcher and visiting lecturer, and later at TCSI and Atmel Lab in Berkeley, CA. She is a Member of IACR and a fellow of IEEE. She was elected as member of the Royal Flemish Academy of Belgium for Science and the Arts in 2011.

She is a pioneer in the field of efficient and secure implementations of cryptographic algorithms in embedded context on ASIC, FPGA and embedded SW. It has been the main focus of her PhD and of her research at UCLA and KU Leuven. At COSIC she also supervises the hardware electronics lab to perform side-channel and fault-attacks.

She is the author and co-author of more than 300 publications at conferences, journals, book chapters and books. She graduated 27 PhD students between 2004 and 2015, which have positions in academia and in industry, all over the world.

Dr. Verbauwhede has been the general chair in 2012 and the program chair in 2007 of the IACR CHES (Cryptographic Hardware and Embedded Systems) workshop, which is the flagship venue for secure hardware design. She has been member of the program committee of a large number of conferences, including DAC, DATE, ISSCC, Usenix, SIPS, ISCAS, ISLPED, and more.

Prof. Verbauwhede has participated in several EU funded hardware and embedded systems security projects. Currently her research group participates in the H2020 projects HECTOR and ECRYPT-CSA. Her list of publications and patents is available at www.esat.kuleuven.be/cosic.

GLSVLSI'16, May 18–20, 2016, Boston, MA, USA.
ACM 978-1-4503-4274-2/16/05.
DOI: http://dx.doi.org/10.1145/2902961.2902963

High-Speed Polynomial Multiplier Architecture for Ring-LWE Based Public Key Cryptosystems

Chaohui Du
Department of Computer Science and Technology
Tsinghua University
Beijing, China
dch11@mails.tsinghua.edu.cn

Guoqiang Bai
Institute of Microelectronics
Tsinghua University
Beijing, China
baigq@tsinghua.edu.cn

Xingjun Wu
Institute of Microelectronics
Tsinghua University
Beijing, China
wuxj@tsinghua.edu.cn

ABSTRACT

Many lattice-based cryptosystems are based on the security of the Ring learning with errors (Ring-LWE) problem. The most critical and computationally intensive operation of these Ring-LWE based cryptosystems is polynomial multiplication. In this paper, we exploit the number theoretic transform to build a high-speed polynomial multiplier for the Ring-LWE based public key cryptosystems. We present a versatile pipelined polynomial multiplication architecture to calculate the product of two n-degree polynomials in about $((n \lg n)/4+n/2)$ clock cycles. In addition, we introduce several optimization techniques to reduce the required ROM storage. The experimental results on a Spartan-6 FPGA show that the proposed hardware architecture can achieve a speedup of on average 2.25 than the state of the art of high-speed design. Meanwhile, our design is able to save up to 47.06% memory blocks.

Keywords

lattice-based cryptography; post-quantum cryptography; Ring-LWE; number theoretic transform; polynomial multiplication

1. INTRODUCTION

The public key cryptosystems widely used today [9, 13, 18] are believed to withstand attacks by classical computers, which are based on hardness of the number theoretical problems that cannot be solved efficiently on classical computes. However, Shor's algorithm [21] can solve these number theoretical problems in polynomial time on a powerful quantum computer. The widely used public key cryptosystems will become insecure when powerful quantum computers become a reality. Therefore, it is important for the researchers to investigate post-quantum cryptography [3] that can withstand attacks by both classical computers and quantum computers.

Due to the seminal work of Ajtai [1], lattice-based cryptography is emerging as an important candidate for post-quantum cryptography. The security of lattice-based cryptography is based on the hardness of lattice problems that remain hard for both classical computers and quantum computers. The introduction of the *Ring learning with errors* (Ring-LWE) [12] makes it possible to build practical and efficient lattice-based cryptosystems, which has been proved to be at least as hard as solving certain lattice problems in the worst case [12]. Ring-LWE has served as the building block of many lattice-based cryptosystems, such as public key encryption [10], digital signature [11], fully homomorphic encryption (FHE) [7], "somewhat" homomorphic encryption scheme (SHE) [14] and much more.

The most critical and computationally intensive operation of these Ring-LWE based cryptosystems is polynomial multiplication. In recent years, the *number theoretic transform* (NTT) [15] has been exploited to speed up polynomial multiplication from quadratic to quasi-linear run-time, and several NTT based polynomial multiplication architectures have been published [2, 4, 8, 16, 19]. In [8], the authors presented a fully parallel NTT based hardware architecture. It improves the throughput of the Ring-LWE based public key cryptosystems [10] by a factor of 316 than the software implementation. However, the design costs too many hardware resources, which results in the cryptosystem with medium security cannot even fit on the largest FPGA of the Virtex 6 family. In order to reduce the hardware resources, several compact NTT based polynomial multipliers have been introduced [2, 16, 19]. These designs exploit only one butterfly operator to compute the NTT and inverse-NTT, which reduces the hardware usage significantly. However, the compact designs are too slow to meet the requirements of the high-speed applications. In [4], the authors have introduced a high-speed polynomial multiplication architecture. The design is consisted of two butterfly operators together with two modulo q multipliers. These processing units compute the two NTT computations concurrently and are reused to compute the one inverse-NTT computation. Compared with the compact design in [16], the high-speed design can achieve a speedup of approximately 3.5 times. However, the utilization rate of the main data processing units (four multipliers and four modulo q modules) is rather low. Therefore, a further speedup of polynomial multiplication is possible. Besides, one of the two polynomials in the Ring-LWE based public key cryptosystems is constant, which will be shown later. However, the existing high-speed design performs number theoretic transform of the constant polynomial on-line, which slows down the polynomial multiplication.

In this paper, we focus on the polynomial multiplication architecture for the Ring-LWE based public key cryptosystems [10]. We introduce several techniques to optimize the NTT based polynomial multiplication scheme. Then we present a versatile pipelined high-speed polynomial multiplication architecture based on the optimized scheme, which can calculate a n-degree polynomial multiplication in about $((n \lg n)/4 + n/2)$ clock cycles. In addition, we introduce several optimization techniques to reduce the ROM storage. In order to make a fair comparison with the state of the art of high-speed design [4], we have implemented the proposed polynomial multiplication architecture with the same secure parameter sets on the same FPGA. The experimental results show that our proposed hardware architecture can save 43.74% up to 61.01% clock cycles and reduce 25.00% up to 47.06% block RAMs. Furthermore, our design can achieve a speedup of 2.25 on average.

The rest of the paper is organized as follows. Section 2 presents a brief background. In Section 3, we show our high-speed polyno-

GLSVLSI '16, May 18-20, 2016, Boston, MA, USA

 ISBN 978-1-4503-4274-2/16/05... $15.00

DOI: http://dx.doi.org/10.1145/2902961.2902969

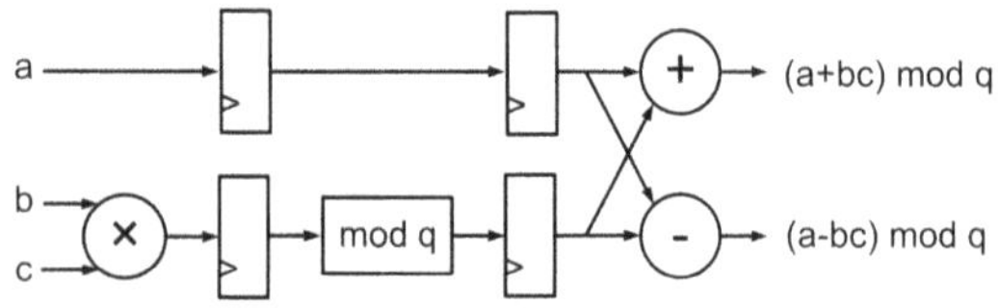

Figure 1: A butterfly operator. The addition and subtraction are modulo q.

mial multiplier architecture. Section 4 illustrates the experimental results. Finally, we conclude this paper in Section 5.

2. BACKGROUND

In this paper, lg represents the base-2 logarithm. We denote by n the degree of the lattice, where n is a power of 2. Z_q represents the set with the interval $[0, q)$. $Z_q[x]$ contains all polynomials with all coefficients in Z_q. The quotient ring $R_q = Z_q[x]/<x^n+1>$ contains all polynomials of degree less than n in $Z_q[x]$, where $q = 1 \bmod 2n$.

In [10], the authors introduced the Ring-LWE based public key cryptosystem. The cryptosystem uses a uniformly random ring element $\boldsymbol{a} \in R_q$, which can be generated by a trusted source or chosen by the user. The cryptosystem is defined as:

- **Gen($\boldsymbol{a}$)**: choose $\boldsymbol{r_1}$ and $\boldsymbol{r_2}$ from the error distribution, calculate $\boldsymbol{p} = \boldsymbol{r_1} - \boldsymbol{a} \cdot \boldsymbol{r_2} \in R_q$. The public key is $\boldsymbol{p}$ and the secret key is $\boldsymbol{r_2}$.
- **Enc($\boldsymbol{a}$, $\boldsymbol{p}$, $\boldsymbol{m} \in \{0,1\}^n$)**: choose error vectors $\boldsymbol{e_1}$, $\boldsymbol{e_2}$ and $\boldsymbol{e_3}$ from the error distribution. Let $\overline{\boldsymbol{m}} = encode(\boldsymbol{m}) \in R_q$, and calculate the ciphertext $[\boldsymbol{c_1} = \boldsymbol{a} \cdot \boldsymbol{e_1} + \boldsymbol{e_2}, \boldsymbol{c_2} = \boldsymbol{p} \cdot \boldsymbol{e_1} + \boldsymbol{e_3} + \overline{\boldsymbol{m}}] \in R_q \times R_q$.
- **Dec($\boldsymbol{c}$ =[$\boldsymbol{c_1}$, $\boldsymbol{c_2}$], $\boldsymbol{r_2}$)**: output $decode(\boldsymbol{c_1} \cdot \boldsymbol{r_2} + \boldsymbol{c_2}) \in \{0,1\}^n$.

The error distribution is usually a discrete Gaussian distribution. The message encoder encodes a vector in $\{0,1\}^n$ to a polynomial in R_q. The decoder decodes a polynomial in R_q to a vector in $\{0,1\}^n$.

The most critical and computational operation of Ring-LWE based public key cryptosystem is polynomial multiplication over a polynomial ring R_q. The *number theoretical transform* (NTT) [15] and the *negative wrapped convolution theorem* [22] can be exploited to compute polynomial multiplication efficiently.

NTT is the *fast Fourier transform* (FFT) [5] applied in a finite field. Algorithm 1 shows how to perform NTT. ω_n denotes the primitive n-th root of unity, which is defined as the smallest element in Z_q that satisfies the conditions $\omega_n^n = 1 \bmod q$ and $\omega_n^j \neq 1$ for $0 < j < n$. The NTT is composed of bit-reverse operation (line 1), which stores the coefficient at k to bit-reverse(k), and $\lg n$ stages of butterfly operations (line 3 – line 16). Figure 1 shows a butterfly operation, which operates on coefficient a, coefficient b and constant factor c to compute the new values of a and b.

Let ψ be the element in Z_q that satisfies the condition $\psi^2 = \omega_n \bmod q$. Let $\boldsymbol{a} = (a_0, a_1, \cdots, a_{n-1})$, $\boldsymbol{s} = (s_0, s_1, \cdots, s_{n-1})$, and $\boldsymbol{d} = (d_0, d_1, \cdots, d_{n-1})$ be elements in R_q. We denote by $\hat{\boldsymbol{a}}$, $\hat{\boldsymbol{s}}$, and $\hat{\boldsymbol{d}}$ the products of $\boldsymbol{a}$, $\boldsymbol{s}$, $\boldsymbol{d}$ component-wise multiplied with $(1, \psi^1, \cdots, \psi^{n-1})$ respectively. Then, we can calculate $\hat{\boldsymbol{d}}$ by the negative wrapped convolution theorem as follows:

$$\hat{\boldsymbol{d}} = NTT_{\omega_n}^{-1}(NTT_{\omega_n}(\hat{\boldsymbol{a}}) \odot NTT_{\omega_n}(\hat{\boldsymbol{s}})), \tag{1}$$

where $\odot$ denotes the component-wise multiplication and the inverse-NTT, $NTT_{\omega_n}^{-1}$, is determined by using ω_n^{-1} in Algorithm 1 and multiplying each coefficient of the result with n^{-1} over Z_q [22]. Notice that the coefficients of $\boldsymbol{d}$ can be calculated by component-wise multiplying $\hat{\boldsymbol{d}}$ with $(1, \psi^{-1}, \cdots, \psi^{-(n-1)})$. Algorithm 2 shows the details about how to perform polynomial multiplication by applying NTT and the negative wrapped convolution theorem.

Algorithm 1 Number Theoretical Transform

Input: $\boldsymbol{a} \in R_q$, $\omega_n \in Z_q$
Output: $\boldsymbol{A} = NTT_{\omega_n}(\boldsymbol{a})$
1: $\boldsymbol{A}$ = bit-reverse($\boldsymbol{a}$);
2: $n = \boldsymbol{A}$.length;
3: **for** ($s = 1$; $s \leq \lg n$; $s = s + 1$) **do**
4: $\quad m = 2^s$;
5: $\quad \omega_m = \omega_n^{n/m}$;
6: $\quad$ **for** ($k = 0$; $k < n$; $k = k + m$) **do**
7: $\quad\quad \omega = 1$;
8: $\quad\quad$ **for** ($i = 0$; $i < m/2$; $i = i + 1$) **do**
9: $\quad\quad\quad t = \omega\ \boldsymbol{A}[k + i + m/2] \bmod q$;
10: $\quad\quad\quad u = \boldsymbol{A}[k + i]$;
11: $\quad\quad\quad \boldsymbol{A}[k + i] = u + t \bmod q$;
12: $\quad\quad\quad \boldsymbol{A}[k + i + m/2] = u - t \bmod q$;
13: $\quad\quad\quad \omega = \omega\ \omega_m \bmod q$;
14: $\quad\quad$ **end for**
15: $\quad$ **end for**
16: **end for**
17: **return** $\boldsymbol{A}$;

Algorithm 2 Polynomial multiplication using NTT and the negative wrapped convolution theorem

Input: $\boldsymbol{a}, \boldsymbol{s} \in R_q$, $\omega_n \in Z_q$, $\psi \in Z_q$
Output: $\boldsymbol{d} = \boldsymbol{a} \cdot \boldsymbol{s} \in R_q$
1: **for** ($k = 0$; $k < n$; $k = k + 1$) **do**
2: $\quad \hat{\boldsymbol{a}}[k] = \boldsymbol{a}[k]\psi^k \bmod q$
3: $\quad \hat{\boldsymbol{s}}[k] = \boldsymbol{s}[k]\psi^k \bmod q$
4: **end for**
5: $\tilde{\boldsymbol{a}} = \text{NTT}_{\omega_n}(\hat{\boldsymbol{a}})$
6: $\tilde{\boldsymbol{s}} = \text{NTT}_{\omega_n}(\hat{\boldsymbol{s}})$
7: **for** ($k = 0$; $k < n$; $k = k + 1$) **do**
8: $\quad \tilde{\boldsymbol{d}}[k] = \tilde{\boldsymbol{a}}[k]\tilde{\boldsymbol{s}}[k] \bmod q$
9: **end for**
10: $\hat{\boldsymbol{d}} = NTT_{\omega_n}^{-1}(\tilde{\boldsymbol{d}})$
11: **for** ($k = 0$; $k < n$; $k = k + 1$) **do**
12: $\quad \boldsymbol{d}[k] = \hat{\boldsymbol{d}}[k]\psi^{-k} \bmod q$
13: **end for**
14: **return** $\boldsymbol{d}$;

3. HIGH-SPEED POLYNOMIAL MULTIPLICATION ARCHITECTURE

In this section, we first introduce several techniques to optimize the polynomial multiplication scheme for the Ring-LWE based public key cryptosystem. Then we present our high-speed polynomial multiplication architecture, which is based on the optimized scheme. Finally, we show the optimized ROM storage scheme.

3.1 Algorithm Level Optimization

Carefully examining the Ring-LWE based public key cryptosystem shown in Section 2, we can find that $\boldsymbol{a}$ is constant in **Gen($\boldsymbol{a}$)**, $\boldsymbol{a}$ and $\boldsymbol{p}$ are constant in **Enc($\boldsymbol{a}$, $\boldsymbol{p}$, $\boldsymbol{m} \in \{0,1\}^n$)**, and $\boldsymbol{r_2}$ is constant in **Dec($\boldsymbol{c}$ =[$\boldsymbol{c_1}$, $\boldsymbol{c_2}$], $\boldsymbol{r_2}$)**. Hence, one of the two polynomials in Algorithm 2 is constant and its number theoretical transform can be pre-computed. Thus, one pre-computation (line 2 or 3 of Algorithm 2) and a NTT computation (line 5 or 6 of Algorithm 2) can be reduced. For simplicity, in the rest of this paper, we suppose polynomial $\boldsymbol{a}$ is constant and polynomial $\boldsymbol{s}$ is variable in Algorithm 2.

Algorithm 2 still requires to perform a pre-computation (line 3) and a post-computation (line 12). The pre-computation can be merged into the NTT computation by simply changing line 7 of Algorithm 1 from $\omega = 1$ to $\omega = \omega_{2m}$ [19]. The post-computation can also be optimized. At the end of inverse-NTT, each coefficient should multiply by n^{-1}. Then, the post-computation is performed, which multiplies the k-th coefficient by constant factor ψ^{-k}. Therefore, the post-computation can be merged into the inverse-NTT computation by simply multiplying the k-th coefficient at the end of inverse-NTT computation by constant factor $n^{-1}\psi^{-k}$.

After computing the component-wise multiplication (line 8 of Algorithm 2), the first stage of butterfly operations of inverse-NTT is calculated (line 10 of Algorithm 2). Since the constant factor is always equals to 1 during the first stage of butterfly operations, the modulo q multiplication can be omitted. For instance, if c is equals to 1 in Figure 1, the new values of a and b can be simplified to calculate $(a + b) \bmod q$ and $(a - b) \bmod q$. Thus, we can calculate the component-wise multiplication and the first stage of butterfly operations in pipeline. The component-wise multiplication can be computed by the modulo q multiplier of the butterfly operator, and the results can be manipulated by the adder and subtractor of the butterfly operator to calculate the first stage of butterfly operations.

To sum up, the optimized scheme pre-computes the NTT of the constant polynomials, reduces the overhead of pre-computation by merging it into the NTT computation, reduces the cost of post-computation by merging it into the inverse-NTT computation, and merges the first stage of butterfly operations of inverse-NTT into the component-wise multiplication.

3.2 Hardware Architecture

To further speed up polynomial multiplication for the Ring-LWE based public key cryptosystem, we propose to exploit the parallel property of NTT. Recall that, during the s-th stage of butterfly operations, the k-th and $(k{+}2^{s-1})$-th coefficients are operated to calculate their corresponding new values (line 9–12 of Algorithm 1). During the $(s{+}1)$-th stage, the k'-th and $(k'{+}2^s)$-th coefficients are manipulated to compute their corresponding new values. For simplicity, we denote the pair of coefficients that a butterfly operator operates on as {*first-index,second-index*}. Notice that if two butterfly operators operate on $\{k,k{+}2^{s-1}\}$ and $\{k{+}2^s, k{+}2^s{+}2^{s-1}\}$ respectively in parallel during the s-th stage, the new coefficients $\{k,k{+}2^s\}$ and $\{k{+}2^{s-1}, k{+}2^s{+}2^{s-1}\}$ can be manipulated for the $(s{+}1)$-th stage in parallel. Therefore, we can configure four butterfly operators as 2×2 butterfly operators to perform the s-th and $(s{+}1)$-th stages of butterfly operations in pipeline. Two out of the total four butterfly operators operate on four coefficients to calculate their s-th stage of butterfly operations in parallel, the other two butterfly operators operate on the four new coefficients generated by the first two butterfly operators to compute their $(s{+}1)$-th stage of butterfly operations in parallel. Based on these observations, we propose to configure the extra two modulo q multipliers (two integer multipliers and two modulo q modules) in [4] as two butterfly operators by adding two adders and two subtractors. The four butterfly operators are exploited to compute consecutive two stages of butterfly operations on four coefficients in pipeline.

Based on these ideas, we propose a high-speed polynomial multiplication architecture for the Ring-LWE based public key cryptosystem, which is composed of the datapath and the controller. The datapath is shown in Figure 2. It consists of two dual-port RAM modules, ROM modules, four butterfly operators, and a buffer. The two dual-port RAM modules have a read-only port and a write-only port, which can be read and written concurrently. There are $n/4$ cells in each RAM module, and each cell is able to store two coefficients. The ROM modules in Figure 2 are exploited to store the constant factors. We will show the details of our optimized ROM storage scheme in next section. The four butterfly operators are exploited to compute butterfly operations and configured as modulo q multipliers to compute component-wise multiplications. The buffer buffers and shuffles the new generated coefficients. The controller generates the control signals for the datapath.

Since n is a power of 2, $\lg n$ is either an even integer or odd integer. The proposed high-speed polynomial multiplication architecture divides n into two subsets depending on $\lg n$ is even or odd. For each subset, it works in pipeline and performs several consecutive tasks to perform a n-degree polynomial multiplication.

3.2.1 $\lg n$ is even

In order to compute the product of two n-degree polynomials (a constant polynomial $\boldsymbol{a}$ and a variable polynomial $\boldsymbol{s}$), the proposed polynomial multiplication architecture works in pipelined fashion and partitions the goal into several consecutive tasks:

- *task1*: computes the first $(\lg n - 2)$ stages of butterfly operations of $NTT(\hat{\boldsymbol{s}})$.
- *task2*: computes the last 2 stages of butterfly operations of $NTT(\hat{\boldsymbol{s}})$.
- *task3*: computes the component-wise multiplications of $NTT(\hat{\boldsymbol{a}})$ and $NTT(\hat{\boldsymbol{s}})$ by the modulo q multipliers of the left two butterfly operators, computes the first stage of butterfly operations of inverse-NTT by the adders and subtractors of the left two butterfly operators, computes the second stage of butterfly operations of inverse-NTT by the right two butterfly operators.
- *task4*: computes the next $(\lg n - 4)$ stages of butterfly operations of inverse-NTT.
- *task5*: computes the last 2 stages of butterfly operations of inverse-NTT.
- *task6*: computes the component-wise multiplications by configuring the four butterfly operators as modulo q multipliers.

To calculate *task1*, the four butterfly operators are exploited to perform consecutive two stages of butterfly operations on four coefficients. For simplicity, we suppose the s-th and $(s + 1)$-th stages are calculated. At each clock cycle, the k-th, $(k + 2^{s-1})$-th, $(k + 2^s)$-th and $(k + 2^s + 2^{s-1})$-th coefficients are loaded from the two RAM modules. The left two butterfly operators operates on the four coefficients to perform the s-th stage of butterfly operations. The four new coefficients generated by the left two butterfly operators are manipulated by the right two butterfly operators to perform the $(s + 1)$-th stage of butterfly operations. Finally, the new coefficients are buffered and shuffled by the buffer, and stored back to the RAM modules in a way that the k'-th and $(k' + 2^{s+1})$-th coefficients are stored in the same cell. *task1* costs around $(\frac{\lg n - 2}{2} \times \frac{n}{4} = \frac{n(\lg n - 2)}{8})$ clock cycles.

During *task2*, the k-th, $(k + \frac{n}{4})$-th, $(k + \frac{n}{2})$-th and $(k + \frac{3n}{4})$-th coefficients are provided by the two RAM modules, the four butterfly operators perform the last 2 stages of butterfly operations on these coefficients, and the results are stored back to the RAM modules in a manner that the k'-th and $(k' + \frac{n}{2})$-th coefficients are stored in the same cell. *task2* takes around $\frac{n}{4}$ clock cycles.

task3 computes the component-wise multiplications of $NTT(\hat{\boldsymbol{a}})$ and $NTT(\hat{\boldsymbol{s}})$, and the first two stages of butterfly operations of inverse-NTT. Four coefficients are loaded from the two RAM modules at every two clock cycles. The modulo q multipliers of the left two butterfly operators perform component-wise multiplications on the four coefficients in two clock cycles. The results are manipulated by the adders and subtractors of the left two butterfly operators to perform the first stage of butterfly operations of inverse-NTT. Then, the right two butterfly operators operate on the new coefficients generated by the left two butterfly operators to perform the second stage of butterfly operations. The final results are buffered and shuffled and stored back to the RAM modules in a way that the k'-th and $(k' + 2^2)$-th coefficients are stored in the same cell. Since the left two butterfly operators consume 4 out of the total n coefficients at every two clock cycles, *task3* costs about $\frac{n}{2}$ clock cycles.

The proposed polynomial multiplication architecture performs *task4* in the similar way with *task1*. The four butterfly operators operate on four coefficients to perform consecutive two stages of butterfly operations. *task4* consumes about $(\frac{\lg n - 4}{2} \times \frac{n}{4} = \frac{n(\lg n - 4)}{8})$ clock cycles.

The polynomial multiplier computes *task5* in the same way with *task2*. The four butterfly operators perform the last 2 stages of butterfly operations of inverse-NTT. It takes around $\frac{n}{4}$ clock cycles.

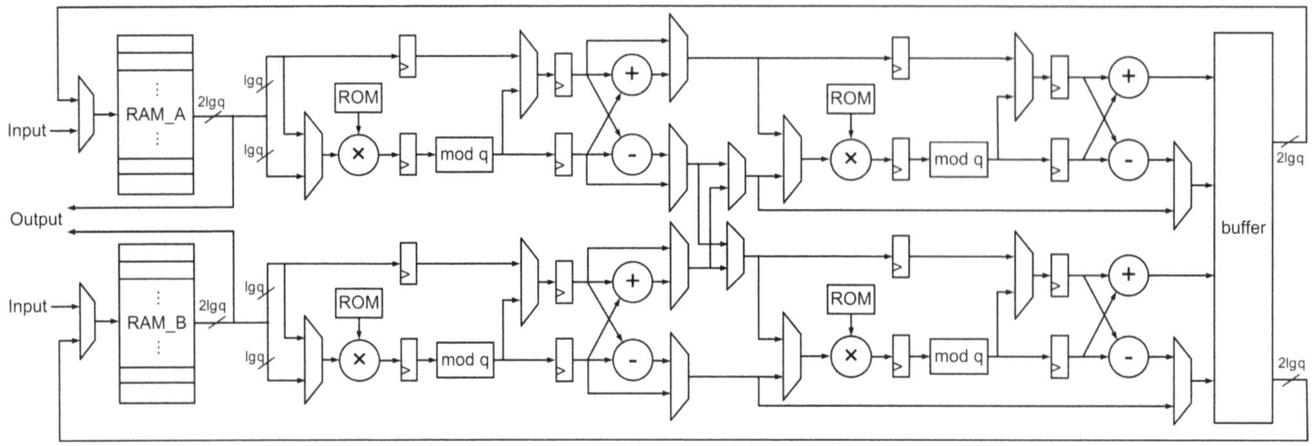

Figure 2: Datapath of the proposed high-speed polynomial multiplication architecture.

During *task6*, the four butterfly operators are configured as modulo q multipliers to multiply the k-th coefficient with constant factor $\psi^{-k}n^{-1}$ over Z_q. As 4 out of the total n coefficients are consumed at each clock cycle, *task6* takes around $\frac{n}{4}$ clock cycles.

To sum up, the proposed polynomial multiplication architecture performs consecutive six tasks to calculate the product of two n-degree polynomials with $\lg n$ being even. The required clock cycles are around $(\frac{n(\lg n-2)}{8}+\frac{n}{4}+\frac{n}{2}+\frac{n(\lg n-4)}{8}+\frac{n}{4}+\frac{n}{4}) = (\frac{n\lg n}{4}+\frac{n}{2})$.

3.2.2 $\lg n$ *is odd*

When $\lg n$ is odd, the proposed polynomial multiplication architecture also partitions the goal into several consecutive tasks:

task1: computes the first $(\lg n-3)$ stages of butterfly operations of $NTT(\hat{\boldsymbol{s}})$.

task2: computes the next 2 stages of butterfly operations of $NTT(\hat{\boldsymbol{s}})$.

task3: computes the last stage of butterfly operations of $NTT(\hat{\boldsymbol{s}})$ by the left two butterfly operators, computes the component-wise multiplications of $NTT(\hat{\boldsymbol{a}})$ and $NTT(\hat{\boldsymbol{s}})$ by the modulo q multipliers of the right two butterfly operators, computes the first stage of butterfly operations of inverse-NTT by the adders and subtractors of the right two butterfly operators.

task4: computes the next $(\lg n-3)$ stages of butterfly operations of inverse-NTT.

task5: computes the last 2 stages of butterfly operations of inverse-NTT.

task6: computes the component-wise multiplications by configuring the four butterfly operators as modulo q multipliers.

The calculation of *task1* is similar with the *task1* when $\lg n$ is even. The four butterfly operators in Figure 2 are exploited to perform consecutive two stages of butterfly operations on four coefficients at each clock cycle. It takes around $(\frac{\lg n-3}{2}\times\frac{n}{4}=\frac{n(\lg n-3)}{8})$ clock cycles.

task2 computes the $(\lg n-2)$-th and $(\lg n-1)$-th stages of butterfly operations of $NTT(\hat{\boldsymbol{s}})$. At each clock cycle, the k-th, $(k+\frac{n}{8})$-th, $(k+\frac{n}{4})$-th and $(k+\frac{3n}{8})$-th coefficients are loaded from the RAM modules, the left two butterfly operators perform $(\lg n-2)$-th stage of butterfly operations on the four coefficients and the right two perform $(\lg n-1)$-th stage. The final results are stored back to the RAM modules in a way that the k'-th and $(k'+\frac{n}{2})$-th coefficients are stored in the same cell. *task2* costs about $\frac{n}{4}$ clock cycles.

task3 computes the last stage of butterfly operations of $NTT(\hat{\boldsymbol{s}})$, the component-wise multiplications of $NTT(\hat{\boldsymbol{a}})$ and $NTT(\hat{\boldsymbol{s}})$, and the first stage of butterfly operations of inverse-NTT. At every two clock cycles, the k-th, $(k+\frac{n}{2})$-th, $(k+\frac{n}{4})$-th and $(k+\frac{3n}{4})$-th coefficients are loaded from the RAM modules, the left two butterfly operators perform the last stage of butterfly operations of $NTT(\hat{\boldsymbol{s}})$ on the four coefficients. The modulo q multipliers of the right two butterfly operators operate on the new coefficients generated by the left two butterfly operators to perform component-wise multiplications in two clock cycles. The results are manipulated by the adders and subtractors of the right two butterfly operators to perform the first stage of butterfly operations of inverse-NTT. The final results are buffered and shuffled by the buffer and stored back to the RAM modules in a way that the k'-th and $(k'+2^1)$-th coefficients are stored in the same cell. Since the butterfly operators consume 4 out of the total n coefficients at every 2 clock cycles, *task3* consumes about $\frac{n}{2}$ clock cycles.

task4 is similar to *task1*. At each clock cycle, the four butterfly operators operate on four coefficients to perform consecutive two stages of butterfly operations. It demands about $(\frac{\lg n-3}{2}\times\frac{n}{4}=\frac{n(\lg n-3)}{8})$ clock cycles.

The polynomial multiplication architecture performs *task5* in the similar way with *task5* when $\lg n$ is even. The four butterfly operators calculate the last 2 stages of butterfly operations of inverse-NTT. *task5* takes around $\frac{n}{4}$ clock cycles.

task6 is the same as *task6* with even $\lg n$. The four butterfly operators are configured as modulo q multipliers to multiply the k-th coefficient with constant factor $\psi^{-k}n^{-1}$ over Z_q. It consumes about $\frac{n}{4}$ clock cycles.

To sum up, our polynomial multiplication architecture performs consecutive six tasks to calculate the product of two n-degree polynomials with $\lg n$ being odd. It costs around $(\frac{n(\lg n-3)}{8}+\frac{n}{4}+\frac{n}{2}+\frac{n(\lg n-3)}{8}+\frac{n}{4}+\frac{n}{4})=(\frac{n\lg n}{4}+\frac{n}{2})$ clock cycles.

3.3 ROM Storage Scheme

The proposed polynomial multiplication architecture stores the constant factors in the ROM modules instead of generating them on-the-fly. Recall that, ψ^k $(0\le k<n)$ and $\omega_{2^s}^j$ $(1\le s\le\lg n, 0\le j<2^{s-1})$ are required for the computation of $NTT(\hat{\boldsymbol{s}})$, $(\omega_{2^s}^j)^{-1}$ $(1\le s\le\lg n, 0\le j<2^{s-1})$ is demanded for the inverse-NTT computation, ψ^{-k} $(0\le k<n)$ is needed for the post-computation. Besides, $NTT(\hat{\boldsymbol{a}})$ should be pre-computed and the coefficients should be stored at the ROM modules. As a result, each ROM module should store about $5n$ constant factors and each one occupies $\lceil\lg p\rceil$ bits. In order to decrease the demanded ROM storage, we introduce several techniques to optimize the constant factors.

During the computation of $NTT(\hat{\boldsymbol{s}})$, ψ^k $(0\le k<n)$ and $\omega_{2^s}^j$ $(1\le s\le\lg n, 0\le j<2^{s-1})$ are demanded. The cancellation lemma [6] can be exploited to optimize these constant factors. It states that:

$$\omega_{dn}^{dk} = \omega_n^k, \tag{2}$$

where n and k are non-negative integers and d is a positive integer. Therefore, we can derive the following equation by exploiting the cancellation lemma:

$$\omega_{2^s}^j = \omega_{2^{(\lg n - s)} 2^s}^{2^{(\lg n - s)} j} = \omega_n^{(n-2^s)j} = \psi^{2(n-2^s)j}, \tag{3}$$

where $1 \le s \le \lg n, 0 \le j < 2^{s-1}$. As a consequence, we can only store ψ^k $(0 \le k < n)$ in the ROMs, and derive ωs from ψs. When $\lg n$ is even, the last stage of butterfly operations are performed by the right two butterfly operators. So, the left two ROM modules only need to store ψ^{2k} $(0 \le k < n/2)$ instead of all ψs. Similarly, the last stage of butterfly operations are calculated by the left two butterfly operators when $\lg n$ is odd, and the right two ROM modules only need to store ψ^{2k} $(0 \le k < n/2)$.

When $\lg n$ is even, the left two butterfly operators compute the component-wise multiplications of $NTT(\hat{\boldsymbol{a}})$ and $NTT(\hat{\boldsymbol{s}})$. Therefore, only the left two ROM modules demand to store all coefficients of $NTT(\hat{\boldsymbol{a}})$. When $\lg n$ is odd, the right two butterfly operators compute the component-wise multiplications, and only the right two ROM modules need to store $NTT(\hat{\boldsymbol{a}})$.

During the computation of inverse-NTT, $(\omega_{2^s}^j)^{-1}$ $(1 \le s \le \lg n, 0 \le j < 2^{s-1})$ is demanded. By applying the cancellation lemma, we can derive the following equation to optimize the required storage:

$$(\omega_{2^s}^j)^{-1} = (\omega_{2^{(\lg n - s)} 2^s}^{2^{(\lg n - s)} j})^{-1} = (\omega_n^{(n-2^s)j})^{-1}, \tag{4}$$

where $1 \le s \le \lg n, 0 \le j < 2^{s-1}$. Hence, we can only store $(\omega_n^j)^{-1}$ $(0 \le j < n/2)$ in each ROM module, and derive the other constant factors by (4). Since the last stage of butterfly operations are calculated by the right two butterfly operators, the left two ROM modules only need to store $(\omega_{\frac{n}{2}}^j)^{-1}$ $(0 \le j < n/4)$.

Recall that, the optimized polynomial multiplication scheme requires to multiply the k-th coefficient by $n^{-1}\psi^{-k}$ at the end of inverse-NTT computation. So, each ROM module needs to store $n^{-1}\psi^{-k}$ $(0 \le k < n)$. However, each constant factor is only manipulated by a specific butterfly operator. Therefore, we can divide the n constant factors into four disjoint subsets, and each ROM module only needs to store one subset.

In practical applications, the ROM modules shown in Figure 2 can also be implemented with dual-port ROMs. Thus, constant factors for the left two butterfly operators can be loaded from one dual-port ROM module, and another dual-port ROM module can provide constant factors for the right two butterfly operators.

To sum up, the four ROM modules can be implemented with two dual-port ROM modules. When $\lg n$ is even, the left dual-port ROM module needs to store ψ^{2k} $(0 \le k < n/2)$, $NTT(\hat{\boldsymbol{a}})$, $(\omega_{\frac{n}{2}}^j)^{-1}$ $(0 \le j < n/4)$, and a subset of $n^{-1}\psi^{-k}$, the right dual-port ROM module needs to store ψ^k $(0 \le k < n)$, $(\omega_n^j)^{-1}$ $(0 \le j < n/2)$, and a subset of $n^{-1}\psi^{-k}$. When $\lg n$ is odd, the left dual-port ROM module needs to store ψ^k $(0 \le k < n)$, $(\omega_{\frac{n}{2}}^j)^{-1}$ $(0 \le j < n/4)$, and a subset of $n^{-1}\psi^{-k}$, the right dual-port ROM module needs to store ψ^{2k} $(0 \le k < n/2)$, $NTT(\hat{\boldsymbol{a}})$, $(\omega_n^j)^{-1}$ $(0 \le j < n/2)$, and a subset of $n^{-1}\psi^{-k}$.

4. EXPERIMENTAL RESULTS

Our hardware architecture is versatile. It can be used in different applications and implemented with different secure parameters. For the sake of making a fair comparison with the state of the art of high-speed design in [4], our experiments use the secure parameters proposed in [4] and the same Spartan-6 LX100 FPGA. The experimental results were obtained after post place-and-route analysis with the Xilinx ISE 14.7.

We have implemented the modulo q modules using the same technique presented in [4] to make a fair comparison. Table 1 shows the secure parameter sets proposed in [4] for different applications. How to choose the secure parameter set and design the modulo q module is out of the scope of this paper, the interested reader might refer to [4, 17].

Table 1: Secure parameter sets proposed in [4] for different applications.

Application	Degree of polynomial (n)	prime q
LWE [20]	256	1049089
LWE [20]	512	4206593
SHE [14]	1024	536903681
SHE [14]	2048	$2^{57} + 25 \cdot 2^{13} + 1$

Table 2 presents the hardware resource consumptions and performance of our implementation. The theoretic total clock cycles required to perform a polynomial multiplication of two n-degree polynomials are about $(\frac{n \lg n}{4} + \frac{n}{2})$. However, Table 2 reveals that our implementation takes on average 11.95% more clock cycles. This is mainly due to the idle clock cycles introduced to avoid read before write collisions between different stages of butterfly operations. Table 2 also presents the comparison of our implementation with the state of the art of high-speed design [4]. Our implementation takes on average 44.57% more slices than the high-speed design in [4]. However, our design reduces on average 32.87% BRAMs and saves on average 54.60% clock cycles. It outperforms the high-speed design in [4] by a factor of on average 2.25.

5. CONCLUSIONS AND FUTURE WORKS

This paper presents a pipelined high-speed polynomial multiplier architecture for the Ring-LWE based public key cryptosystems. The proposed hardware architecture can compute the product of two n-degree polynomials (a variable polynomial and a constant polynomial) in about $((n \lg n)/4 + n/2)$ clock cycles. Experimental results on a Spartan-6 FPGA show that our design outperforms the state of the art of high-speed design by a factor of on average 2.25 and reduce on average 32.87% block RAMs. Future works will explore techniques to reduce the overhead introduced by avoiding read/write collisions. We will also investigate how to integrate the proposed polynomial multiplier in the real applications, such as the Ring-LWE based public key cryptosystems and "somewhat" homomorphic encryption scheme.

Acknowledgment

This work was supported by the National Natural Science Foundation of China (Grants 61472208 and U1135004), and by the National Key Basic Research Program of China (Grant 2013CB338004).

6. REFERENCES

[1] M. Ajtai. Generating hard instances of lattice problems (extended abstract). *Proceedings of the Twenty-eighth Annual ACM Symposium on Theory of Computing*, pages 99–108, 1996.

[2] A. Aysu, C. Patterson, and P. Schaumont. Low-cost and area-efficient fpga implementations of lattice-based cryptography. *Hardware-Oriented Security and Trust (HOST), 2013 IEEE International Symposium on*, pages 81–86, June 2013.

[3] D. Bernstein. *Introduction to post-quantum cryptography.* Springer Berlin Heidelberg, 2009.

[4] D. Chen, N. Mentens, F. Vercauteren, S. Roy, R. Cheung, D. Pao, and I. Verbauwhede. High-speed polynomial multiplication architecture for ring-lwe and she cryptosystems. *Circuits and Systems I: Regular Papers, IEEE Transactions on*, 62(1):157–166, Jan 2015.

[5] J. W. Cooley and J. W. Tukey. An algorithm for the machine calculation of complex fourier series. *Math. Comp.*, 19:297–301, 1965.

Table 2: Comparison of our implementation with the high-speed design in [4] on a Spartan-6 LX100 FPGA.

Design	n	Slice	DSP	BRAM	Period (ns)	Cycles	Cycle Reduction	Latency (μs)	Speedup
Design in [4]	256	580	16	8.5	3.802	1630	–	6.197	–
This work	256	953	16	4.5	4.056	917	43.74%	3.719	×1.67
Design in [4]	512	870	16	8.5	3.946	3630	–	14.324	–
This work	512	1246	16	6	4.010	1690	53.44%	6.777	×2.11
Design in [4]	1024	915	16	14	4.050	7971	–	32.283	–
This work	1024	1387	16	10.5	4.247	3172	60.21%	13.471	×2.40
Design in [4]	2048	2374	64	50	4.751	17454	–	82.924	–
This work	2048	2829	64	35	5.399	6806	61.01%	36.746	×2.26

[6] T. H. Cormen, C. E. Leiserson, R. L. Rivest, and C. Stein. *Introduction to Algorithms, 3rd Edition*. The MIT Press, 3rd edition, 7 2009.

[7] C. Gentry. Fully homomorphic encryption using ideal lattices. *Proceedings of the Forty-first Annual ACM Symposium on Theory of Computing*, pages 169–178, 2009.

[8] N. Göttert, T. Feller, M. Schneider, J. Buchmann, and S. Huss. On the design of hardware building blocks for modern lattice-based encryption schemes. *Cryptographic Hardware and Embedded Systems – CHES 2012*, 7428:512–529, 2012.

[9] N. Koblitz. Elliptic curve cryptosystems. *Math. Comp.*, 48:203–209, 1987.

[10] R. Lindner and C. Peikert. Better key sizes (and attacks) for lwe-based encryption. Cryptology ePrint Archive, Report 2010/613, 2010. http://eprint.iacr.org/.

[11] V. Lyubashevsky. Lattice signatures without trapdoors. *Advances in Cryptology – EUROCRYPT 2012*, 7237:738–755, 2012.

[12] V. Lyubashevsky, C. Peikert, and O. Regev. On ideal lattices and learning with errors over rings. *Advances in Cryptology – EUROCRYPT 2010*, 6110:1–23, 2010.

[13] V. Miller. Use of elliptic curves in cryptography. *Advances in Cryptology – CRYPTO '85 Proceedings*, 218:417–426, 1986.

[14] M. Naehrig, K. Lauter, and V. Vaikuntanathan. Can homomorphic encryption be practical? *Proceedings of the 3rd ACM Workshop on Cloud Computing Security Workshop*, pages 113–124, 2011.

[15] J. M. Pollard. The fast Fourier transform in a finite field. *Math. Comp.*, 25:365–374, 1971.

[16] T. Pöppelmann and T. Güneysu. Towards efficient arithmetic for lattice-based cryptography on reconfigurable hardware. *Progress in Cryptology – LATINCRYPT 2012*, 7533:139–158, 2012.

[17] R. Lindner and C. Peikert. Better key sizes (and attacks) for lwe-based encryption. *Topics in Cryptology – CT-RSA 2011*, 6558:319–339, 2011.

[18] R. L. Rivest, A. Shamir, and L. Adleman. A method for obtaining digital signatures and public-key cryptosystems. *Commun. ACM*, 21(2):120–126, feb 1978.

[19] S. Roy, F. Vercauteren, N. Mentens, D. Chen, and I. Verbauwhede. Compact ring-lwe cryptoprocessor. *Cryptographic Hardware and Embedded Systems – CHES 2014*, 8731:371–391, 2014.

[20] M. RÃijckert and M. Schneider. Estimating the security of lattice-based cryptosystems. Cryptology ePrint Archive, Report 2010/137, 2010. http://eprint.iacr.org/.

[21] P. Shor. Algorithms for quantum computation: discrete logarithms and factoring. *Foundations of Computer Science, 1994 Proceedings., 35th Annual Symposium on*, pages 124–134, Nov 1994.

[22] F. Winkler. *Polynomial algorithms in computer algebra.* Texts and monographs in symbolic computation. Springer, Wien, New York, 1996.

Reduced Overhead Gate Level Logic Encryption

Kyle Juretus
Drexel University
Philadelphia, Pennsylvania 19104
kjj39@drexel.edu

Ioannis Savidis
Drexel University
Philadelphia, Pennsylvania 19104
isavidis@coe.drexel.edu

ABSTRACT

Untrusted third-parties are found throughout the integrated circuit (IC) design flow resulting in potential threats in IC reliability and security. Threats include IC counterfeiting, intellectual property (IP) theft, IC overproduction, and the insertion of hardware Trojans. Logic encryption has emerged as a method of enhancing security against such threats, however, current implementations of logic encryption, including the XOR or look-up table (LUT) techniques, have high per-gate overheads in area, performance, and power. A novel gate level logic encryption technique with reduced per-gate overheads is described in this paper. In addition, a technique to expand the search space of a key sequence is provided, increasing the difficulty for an adversary to extract the key value. A power reduction of 41.50%, an estimated area reduction of 43.58%, and a performance increase of 34.54% is achieved when using the proposed gate level logic encryption instead of the LUT based technique for an encrypted AND gate.

1. INTRODUCTION

The design of an integrated circuit (IC) typically focuses on methods to increase performance and reduce power and area. More importantly, an IC must function as intended. The current monetary and time constraints placed on semiconductor companies have introduced an increasing number of third-parties into the IC design flow, creating concern over the ability to trust the given hardware. As a result, the security of the IC against malicious adversaries is becoming a critical design consideration.

As more and more IC design firms utilize third party foundries, partially due to the $5 billion dollar investment required for an in-house fabrication facility [1], the threat of a malicious foundry has gained significant attention. The level of information a third party foundry is privy to further increases the threat, as a foundry typically has access to the GDS-II file and possesses the necessary tools and knowledge required to reverse engineer a design from the GDS II file alone [2].

GLSVLSI '16, May 18-20, 2016, Boston, MA, USA

 ISBN 978-1-4503-4274-2/16/05...$15.00

DOI: http://dx.doi.org/10.1145/2902961.2902972

The level of information possessed by the third party foundry allows for the theft of intellectual property (IP), the ability to counterfeit and overproduce ICs, and the ability to insert malicious circuitry (hardware Trojans) into an IC design. At the very least, these threats pose a serious concern in terms of monetary loss. Pirating and counterfeiting are expected to result in losses of $1.7 trillion dollars in 2015 [3], and a 2008 analysis estimated the IC industry lost $4 billion dollars in IP revenue alone [4]. The monetary concerns are overshadowed by the potential harm caused by an IC that does not function to design specifications. An IC that fails to meet the original specifications causes increased failure rates, produces logical errors, and/or includes hardware Trojans embedded in the IC. Hardware Trojans provide additional challenges as many different attack vectors, including denial of service, stealing information, and/or corrupting functionality, are possible [5]. The challenge in security then becomes protecting against the wide variety of possible threats.

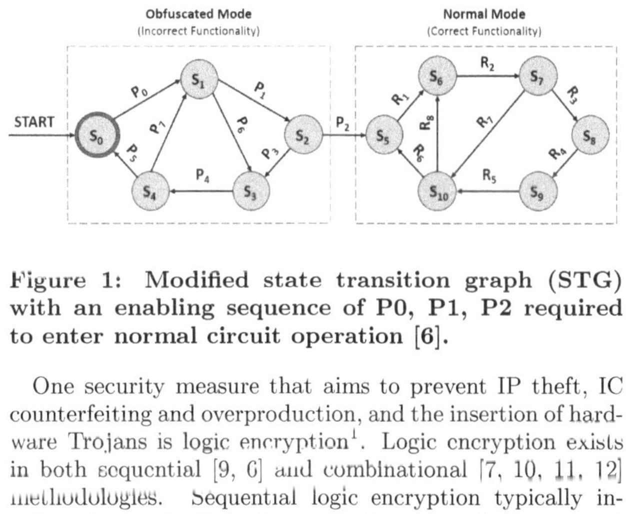

Figure 1: Modified state transition graph (STG) with an enabling sequence of P0, P1, P2 required to enter normal circuit operation [6].

One security measure that aims to prevent IP theft, IC counterfeiting and overproduction, and the insertion of hardware Trojans is logic encryption[1]. Logic encryption exists in both sequential [9, 6] and combinational [7, 10, 11, 12] methodologies. Sequential logic encryption typically involves the application of a required sequence before correct circuit operation is achieved. An example of sequential logic encryption is shown in Fig. 1, where the sequence of P_0, P_1, and P_2 must be entered before the IC operates correctly.

Combinational logic encryption adds key gates to the circuit, requiring the adversary to determine the key before correct functionality is obtained. In addition, combinational

[1] Researchers have previously referred to logic encryption as logic obfuscation [7], but [8] distinguishes between the two as logic encryption prevents black-box use of the design.

logic encryption changes the logic within the circuit, creating additional obfuscation over sequential logic encryption and therefore providing an advantage against IP theft. Without the key, it is also more difficult for an adversary to counterfeit or overproduce an IC, as the functionality of the circuit is unknown. Logic encryption also prevents the insertion of hardware Trojans, as the entire design is no longer known to an adversary, making it more difficult to insert a Trojan without causing unintended actions that are more readily detected.

While combinational logic encryption provides a method to increase IC security against a multitude of threats, current logic encryption techniques result in high overheads in performance, power, and area. A novel gate level implementation of logic encryption that significantly reduces the per-gate overhead of encrypting a gate is described in this paper. The reduction in per-gate overhead provides the ability to increase the key size without increasing the total overhead of current logic encryption methodologies, further deterring adversaries from detecting the key.

The paper begins with an introduction to current combinational logic encryption methodologies in Section 2. A per-gate overhead analysis of the described logic encryption techniques is provided in Section 3, followed by an explanation of the proposed gate topologies in Section 4. Circuit topologies to utilize key expansion, a methodology to potentially double the key search space for an adversary, are described in Section 5. A comparison between the proposed topologies and current techniques is described in Section 6. Finally, conclusions are offered in Section 7.

2. COMBINATIONAL LOGIC ENCRYPTION

Combinational logic encryption requires a key to enable the correct operation of an IC by altering the logic structure of the circuit to include key gates. The two prominent logic encryption techniques are: 1) the insertion of a LUT as a gate replacement [12], and 2) the utilization of XOR/XNOR gates [7, 10]. An additional technique is based on the insertion of 2x1 MUXes [11], which requires connecting the correct output to one MUX input and a net that carries the negated version of the correct net to the other input. The select signal of the MUX then serves as the key input, with either the correct or negated net passed to the next stage of logic. Finding a net that is always the negation of the correct input is difficult and limits the use of 2x1 MUX logic encryption.

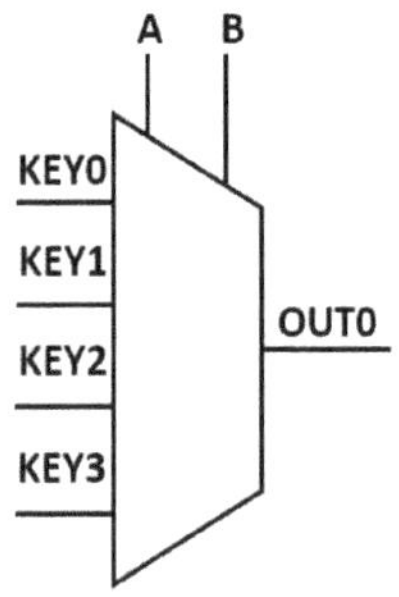

Figure 2: Logic encryption with the use of a 4x1 MUX.

2.1 LUT Based Encryption

The method proposed in [12] utilizes a MUX to encrypt a circuit in the form of a look-up table structure. The key is no longer applied to the select signals of the MUX directly. Instead the key values are passed as inputs to the MUX and set the functionality of the gate. The methodology to encrypt a single gate with a 4x1 MUX structure is shown in Fig. 2. Note that the illustration in Fig. 2 does not include any memory elements attached to the inputs of the 4x1 MUX, as memory is not explicitly required to encrypt the functionality of a gate. If memory elements are used in the circuit, the per-gate encryption overhead increases significantly.

An advantage of the 4x1 MUX based logic encryption method is that any 2-input function is realized, generating more functional combinations for an adversary to search before the correct key value is determined. In addition, the original gates are removed from the circuit and are replaced with 4x1 MUXes, leaving no remnants of the original functionality. Gate replacement with 4x1 MUXes is dissimilar to the XOR encryption discussed in Section 2.2, which requires the addition of inverters to the circuit to prevent adversaries from knowing the original gate functionality.

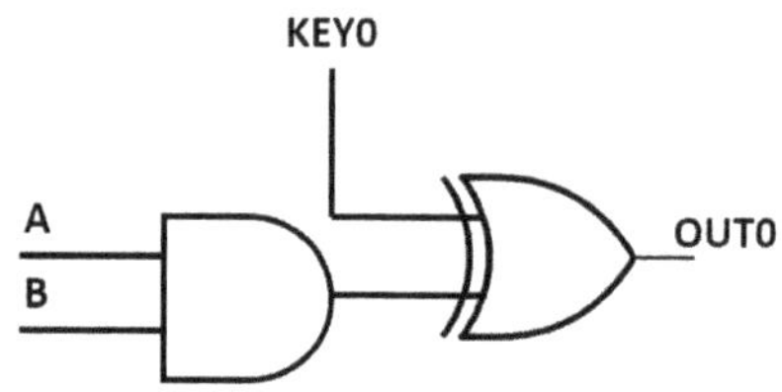

Figure 3: Logic encryption with the use of an XOR gate.

2.2 XOR Based Encryption

The XOR based encryption methodology connects the key value to one input of the XOR gate and the net to encrypt to the other input. By setting the value of the key, the output net OUT0 may either be left with the original or negated input value. An example of encrypting an AND gate with an XOR is shown in Fig. 3. The XOR behaves as an inverter when KEY0 is 1 and as a buffer when KEY0 is 0. Therefore, when KEY0 is 1, an incorrect value is obtained on OUT0. Unlike the 4x1 MUX based encryption, the original gate is not removed from the circuit. Inverters are added in select locations, essentially inverting the key, to deter adversaries from knowing the value of KEY0 that obtains the correct functionality [7]. While the additional inverters secure the key value, the area and power overhead increase.

3. OVERHEAD OF LOGIC ENCRYPTION

The per-gate overheads in performance, power, and area associated with encrypting a gate using the XOR and LUT based encryption techniques are described in this section. For comparison, the performance and area of the standard un-encrypted gates are listed in Table 1. In addition, both the average power and average leakage power of the un-encrypted standard cell gates are provided in Table 2.

The circuits presented in the paper are implemented in an IBM 180 nm technology. The power and performance were determined by matching the drive strength of the gates to ensure a fair analysis between the standard cells and the

Table 1: **Analysis of the propagation delay and area of standard cells from a 180 nm fabrication process.**

Standard Cell	Propagation Delay (ps)	Area (μm^2)
AND	69.79	30.73
NAND	36.71	23.25
OR	92.90	30.73
NOR	42.09	23.25
XOR	91.23	45.69
XNOR	106.7	41.62

equivalent encrypted topologies. The following simulation characteristics were applied:

1. All simulations were completed with a load capacitance of 5 fF.
2. The worst case propagation delay is determined from the low to high and high to low transient delays.
3. The area was obtained from a layout of the implemented topologies.
4. The average power is determined by matching the duration and input transitions for a given gate function.
5. The highest average leakage power is reported from all possible input combinations to a gate.

Table 2: Analysis of the average and leakage power of standard cells from a 180 nm fabrication process.

Standard Cell	Average Power (nW)	Average Leakage Power (pW)
AND	70.40	192.5
NAND	72.67	149.7
OR	64.52	252.3
NOR	96.85	193.6
XOR	148.0	455.3
XNOR	204.6	527.6

Note that for the analysis of the overhead for the XOR and LUT encryption techniques, no inverters were added after the XOR encryption gates and no memory elements were used for the LUT based approach. The values provided for the per-gate overhead of each method are therefore highly optimistic as compared to implementations that include the inverters and memory.

The per-gate overheads in power, performance, and area of the XOR based logic encryption technique are listed in Table 3. Similarly, the overheads of the LUT based logic encryption method are listed in Table 4. The leakage power for both the XOR and LUT encryption techniques is provided in Table 5.

The large overheads in power, area, and performance indicated by the results listed in Tables 3, 4, and 5 limit the use of the XOR and LUT logic encryption techniques in many IC applications. The large per-gate encryption overhead limits the acceptable signal paths to place gates without decreasing performance. In addition, the total number of encrypted gates placed in a circuit is limited by power and area constraints. As ICs must meet performance, power, and area constraints, the large per-gate overheads limit the added security when implementing the logic encryption techniques. It is therefore imperative to reduce the per-gate encryption overhead.

Table 3: Analysis of the propagation delay, power, and area of XOR based logic encryption. Per-gate overheads are provided as percent increases over the standard cell values in Tables 1 and 2.

Standard Cell	Prop. Delay (ps)	Power (nW)	Area (μm^2)
AND	151.3 (116.8%)	150.4 (113.6%)	63.73 (107.4%)
NAND	127.6 (247.6%)	142.2 (95.68%)	63.73 (174.1%)
OR	157.5 (69.54%)	174.6 (170.6%)	63.73 (107.4%)
NOR	134.3 (219.1%)	168.5 (73.98%)	63.73 (174.1%)
XOR	181.8 (99.27%)	219.3 (48.18%)	84.50 (84.94%)
XNOR	201.3 (88.66%)	226.3 (10.61%)	84.50 (101.4%)
Average	**140.2%**	**85.45%**	**124.9%**

Table 4: Analysis of the propagation delay, power, and area of 4x1 MUX based logic encryption. Per-gate overheads are provided as percent increases over the standard cell values in Tables 1 and 2.

Standard Cell	Prop. Delay (ps)	Power (nW)	Area (μm^2)
AND	122.5 (75.53%)	146.0 (107.4%)	90.58 (194.8%)
NAND	124.6 (239.4%)	157.0 (116.0%)	90.58 (289.6%)
OR	120.8 (30.03%)	142.2 (120.4%)	90.58 (194.8%)
NOR	126.8 (201.3%)	158.8 (63.96%)	90.58 (289.6%)
XOR	124.0 (35.92%)	191.8 (29.59%)	90.58 (98.25%)
XNOR	124.6 (16.78%)	191.7 (6.310%)	90.58 (115.9%)
Average	**99.82%**	**73.95%**	**197.2%**

Table 5: Analysis of the average leakage power of the XOR and LUT based logic encryption methods. Per-gate overheads are provided as percent increases over the standard cell values listed in Table 2.

Standard Cell	XOR Leakage (pW)	LUT Leakage (pW)
AND	673.8 (250.0%)	895.8 (365.3%)
NAND	581.0 (288.1%)	841.8 (462.3%)
OR	661.5 (162.2%)	863.4 (242.2%)
NOR	648.9 (235.2%)	973.7 (402.9%)

4. GATE LEVEL LOGIC ENCRYPTION

The motivation for gate level logic encryption is due to the large performance, power, and area overheads associated with the XOR (see Fig. 3) and LUT (see Fig. 2) based logic encryption methodologies. Consider an un-encrypted AND gate as a way to demonstrate the inefficiencies of current logic encryption methodologies. The XOR method shown in Fig. 3 adds an additional XOR gate after the AND gate to mask OUT0 with KEY0. However, the data must now propagate through both the AND and XOR gates, resulting in a reduction in performance. The added XOR gate also contributes power and area over the original un-encrypted AND gate.

The LUT based approach replaces the AND gate with a 4x1 MUX structure as shown in Fig. 2, which is used to implement any two input function. While the per-gate security is enhanced, the performance, power, and area are negatively affected by the additional transistors required to implement a given function. Two novel gate level logic encryption methodologies are described in this section that enhance the security of a gate while also reducing the power, performance, and area overheads as compared to both the LUT and XOR techniques.

4.1 Stack-based Topology

The first topology is termed *stack-based* (see Fig. 4) as portions, or stacks, of logic are turned off/on depending on the key input. The topology depicted in Fig. 4 functions as either a NAND or NOR gate depending on the value of KEY0. When KEY0 is 0, the PMOS stack is activated allowing the gate to behave as a NAND. When KEY0 is set to 1, the NMOS stack is activated and the gate behaves as a NOR. Placing the KEY0 transistors on the OUT net of the gate reduces the capacitance connected to OUT by essentially disconnecting one of the logic stacks during execution. A smaller output capacitance reduces the performance and power overhead of implementing the stack based logic encryption.

Truth Table

KEY0	A	B	OUT
0	0	0	1
0	0	1	1
0	1	0	1
0	1	1	0
1	0	0	1
1	0	1	0
1	1	0	0
1	1	1	0

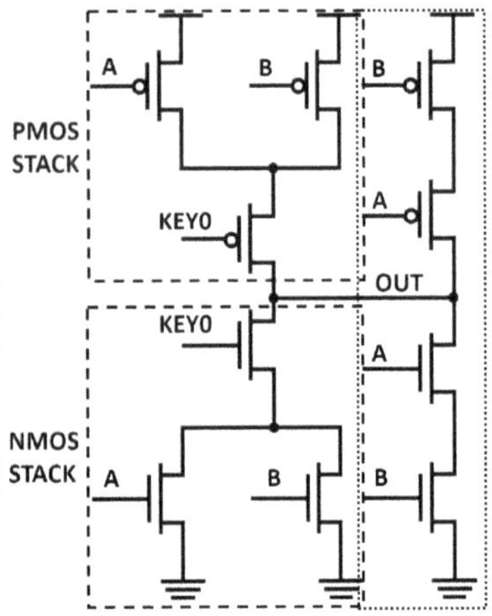

Figure 4: Stack-based topology implementing a NAND or NOR gate depending on the value of KEY0.

The NAND/NOR stack-based topology has two important characteristics: 1) The ability to share common input-output combinations between implemented logical functions, and 2) implementations that do not require negated inputs. For example, the NAND and NOR gates have the same logical output when inputs A and B are both 0 or 1, which permits shared functionality as indicated by the fine dashed box (*shared func.*) shown in Fig. 4. The shared logic does not require a key transistor as the NAND and NOR produce the same output for both the 00 and 11 input combinations. The ability to forgo the key transistor reduces the area, power, and performance overheads of utilizing the stack-based approach.

The second characteristic of the NAND/NOR topology, is not requiring negated inputs of A and B, which removes two additional inverters from the circuit and further reduces the overhead of the methodology. The negated inputs are required if a NAND/AND stack-based topology was implemented instead. The negated logic is needed as the same input combinations must either turn on a PMOS or NMOS stack depending on the key.

While both characteristics of the stack-based topology allow for the reduction in the overhead in performance, power, and area of the NAND/NOR gate, sharing the two common output cases when inputs A and B are both 0 or 1 reduces the percentage of inputs that produce incorrect outputs when an incorrect key is applied. Both characteristics that reduce the overhead must be ignored to achieve complete output corruption when an incorrect key is entered, which results in a larger overhead in power and performance.

Truth Table

KEY0	KEY1	A	B	OUT
0	0	X	X	0
0	1	0	0	0
0	1	0	1	0
0	1	1	0	0
0	1	1	1	1
1	0	0	0	1
1	0	0	1	1
1	0	1	0	1
1	0	1	1	0
1	1	X	X	1

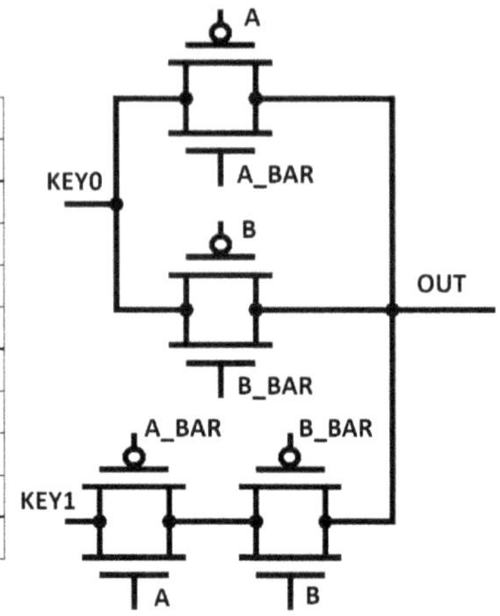

Figure 5: Transmission gate based topology implementing an AND/NAND depending on the values of KEY0 and KEY1.

4.2 Transmission Gate Topology

The transmission gate topology shown in Fig. 5 is better suited to completely corrupt the outputs of the implemented circuit functions. The key value is passed through the transmission gates, eliminating the additional key transistors required in the stack-based topology. The removal of the key transistors reduces the overhead in the performance, power, and area, making the transmission gate topology better suited to replicate the functionality of the XOR based logic encryption method.

The transmission gate topology shown in Fig. 5 implements either an AND or a NAND gate depending on the values of KEY0 and KEY1. When KEY0 is 0 and KEY1 is 1, the topology behaves as an AND gate. When KEY0 is 1 and KEY1 is 0, the topology behaves as a NAND gate. Note that if KEY0 and KEY1 are 0 the AND/NAND topology produces a constant low on OUT. Similarly, a constant high output is achieved when KEY0 and KEY1 are 1. The use cases for the two constant outputs are described in Section 5.

The transmission gate topology is modified slightly to implement an encrypted OR/NOR. For the AND/NAND topology, if logic low is applied to either input A or B the value of KEY0 is passed to OUT. Similarly, when inputs A and B are both logic high, the value of KEY1 is passed to OUT. An OR/NOR gate encryption is achieved by passing the value of KEY0 when input A or B is logic high, and the value of KEY1 when inputs A and B are both low.

While the implementation of a NAND, AND, OR, or NOR gate with transmission gate logic provides simplifications to reduce the power, performance, and area overhead, encrypting an XOR or XNOR gate does not include the same logic simplifications. The only simplification that is possible for the XOR or XNOR gates is to eliminate one of the key inputs by tying the KEY1 and KEY2 inputs in Fig. 2 together.

The reduction in the number of key values is beneficial when routing congestion is a concern.

5. KEY EXPANSION

The transmission gate topology shown in Fig. 5 has the ability to output a constant logic low or a constant logic high independent of the inputs A and B. The number of key combinations an adversary must consider effectively doubles when utilizing the constant outputs of the transmission gate topology, while still achieving the reduction in overhead provided by gate level logic encryption. The ability to utilize the constant outputs to expand the key search space of an adversary is coined key expansion. Circuit topologies that utilize the constant low and constant high output of the transmission gate logic encryption family to force an adversary to consider a larger key search space are provided in this section.

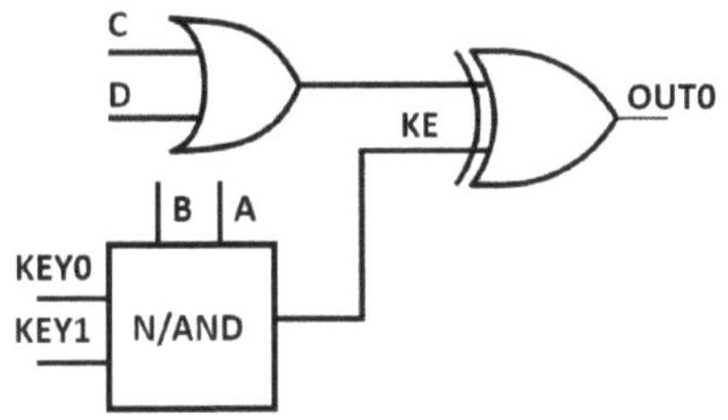

Figure 6: Key expansion utilizing net KE as a standard key input.

5.1 Key Expansion Topologies

Key expansion is successfully included into a circuit when the expanded key appears to be a standard case of logic encryption. As a result, one encrypted gate must not be directly connected to the key input of another encrypted gate. The first topology that encrypts the input keys is shown in Fig. 6, where the net labeled KE represents the key expanded net. For the topology shown in Fig. 6, A and B are inputted from nearby nets, providing the appearance that the encrypted gate is a NAND or AND. However, when KEY0 is equal to KEY1, a constant value is generated on KE, essentially replicating the XOR based encryption technique. The topology shown in Fig. 6 also functions when the XOR gate is replaced by another standard gate such as an AND or OR. For the case that the XOR is replaced with an OR, if a controlling value is generated on KE, then OUT0 is a corrupted version of the output of the OR gate.

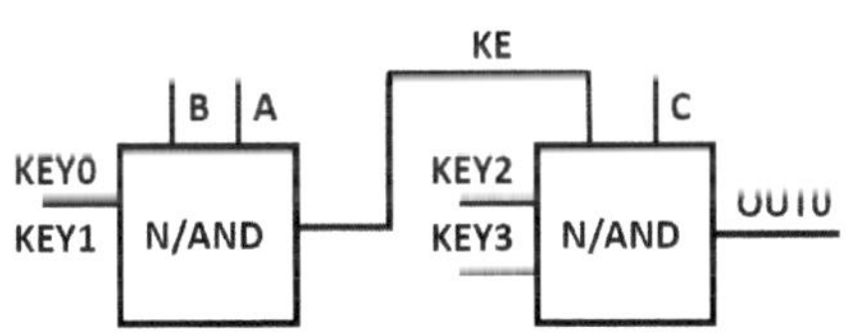

Figure 7: Key expansion topology with two NAND/AND gate level logic encryption gates.

Another topology that allows for key expansion is shown in Fig. 7. The output of a gate level logic encryption instance is connected to one of the logical inputs of another encrypted instance. The topology appears to be a standard logical connection within the circuit, however, key expansion is implemented by holding the KE net constant. When KE is held at a constant high, OUT0 is either C, the inversion of C, a constant 0, or a constant 1 depending on the values of KEY2 and KEY3. The AND/NAND structure no longer functions as an AND/NAND gate, forcing an adversary to explore more key input combinations.

The topology shown in Fig. 8 is an expanded use case of the topology in Fig. 7. Instead of directly connecting the output of one encrypted gate to another, a controllable path within the circuit is used to disguise the use of key expansion. The modified circuit makes it more difficult for an adversary to associate the given topology with key expansion.

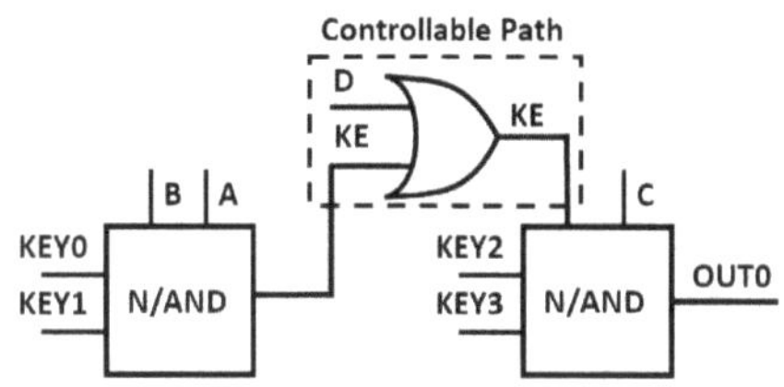

Figure 8: Controllable path insertion to mask key expansion.

While the presented key expansion topologies present opportunities to utilize the constant output cases of the transmission gate logic encryption, the overheads of the topologies are larger than a standard encrypted gate. As such, the ideal circuit candidate is one that already includes the budget for the implementation of the XOR or LUT based logic encryption techniques. For example, the c432 ISCAS benchmark implemented with the fault-based XOR logic encryption technique has a performance overhead of approximately 10%, a power overhead of 55%, and an area overhead of 57% [11]. Although the impact on performance requires further investigation, the use of gate level logic encryption reduces the power overhead to an estimated 32.3% and the area overhead to 45.7% for the same implementation. The 22.7% difference in the power overhead and 11.3% difference in the area overhead are available for key expansion. The reduced overhead of gate level logic encryption permits the addition of key expansion to further increase the key combinations an adversary must search while maintaining a similar overhead budget to current methodologies.

6. EVALUATION OF POWER, AREA, AND PERFORMANCE

The improvements in the power, propagation delay, and area for both the stack and transmission gate topologies are described in this section. As with the simulation described in Section 3, the drive strengths of the encrypted cells were matched with those of the XOR and LUT based logic encryption techniques. In order to match the drive strength, an inverter was added to the output of both the stack and transmission gate topologies. The functionality of the stack-based design is therefore an AND/OR gate as opposed to a NAND/NOR. The improvement in performance is described as a reduction in propagation delay. An analysis of the average power and average leakage power is provided for each gate. The area improvement is based on an area estimate determined from a layout of the encrypted gates as compared with layouts of the XOR and LUT encryption

Table 6: Propagation delay, power, and area analysis of the AND/OR implemented with stack-based encryption. Percent improvements over XOR and LUT logic encryption are listed.

Comp.	Standard Cell	Prop. Delay (ps)	Power (nW)	Area (μm^2)
XOR	AND	119.8 (20.82%)	80.72 (46.33%)	41.62 (34.77%)
	OR	116.7 (25.90%)	79.87 (54.26%)	
LUT	AND	119.8 (2.204%)	80.72 (44.71%)	41.62 (54.05%)
	OR	116.7 (3.394%)	79.87 (43.83%)	

methods. The improvements over the XOR and LUT based encryption techniques are listed in Tables 6, 7, and 8 for, respectively, an AND/OR, NAND/AND, and NOR/OR. The average leakage power of each of the topologies and the percentage improvement over the XOR based technique is listed in Table 9. A comparison with the LUT based technique results in larger improvements.

Table 7: Propagation delay, power, and area analysis of the NAND/AND implemented with transmission gate encryption. Percent improvements over XOR and LUT logic encryption are listed.

Comp.	Standard Cell	Prop. Delay (ps)	Power (nW)	Area (μm^2)
XOR	AND	80.19 (46.99%)	85.41 (43.21%)	51.10 (19.81%)
	NAND	98.54 (22.77%)	101.0 (28.97%)	
LUT	AND	80.19 (34.54%)	85.41 (41.50%)	51.10 (43.58%)
	NAND	98.54 (20.91%)	101.0 (35.67%)	

The results demonstrate a substantial reduction in the performance, power, and area overheads associated with encrypting a gate. The reductions allow for an expanded key search space to further deter adversaries without increasing the overheads of current logic encryption methods. In addition, the lower per-gate encryption overheads allow for the placement of encrypted gates closer to the critical timing path within a circuit.

Table 8: Propagation delay, power, and area analysis of the NOR/OR implemented with transmission gate encryption. Percent improvements over XOR and LUT logic encryption are listed.

Comp.	Standard Cell	Prop. Delay (ps)	Power (nW)	Area (μm^2)
XOR	OR	86.99 (44.77%)	91.44 (47.63%)	51.10 (19.81%)
	NOR	96.77 (27.94%)	88.00 (47.78%)	
LUT	OR	86.99 (27.99%)	91.44 (35.70%)	51.10 (43.58%)
	NOR	96.77 (23.68%)	88.00 (44.58%)	

7. CONCLUSIONS

A methodology to insert key control into a gate, referred to as gate level logic encryption, is described. Two gate level logic encryption topologies were described in the paper. Substantial reductions in the per-gate encryption overhead were achieved by utilizing gate level logic encryption. As an example, encrypting an AND gate resulted in a power reduction of 41.50%, an estimated area reduction of 43.58%, and a performance increase of 34.54% over the LUT based encryption technique. In addition, a methodology to expand the key search space of an adversary when utilizing gate level logic encryption (key expansion) was introduced. The techniques provided in the paper demonstrate the importance of considering security when designing a library of logic gates.

Table 9: Analysis of the average leakage power of the stack-based AND/OR and transmission gate based AND/NAND and OR/NOR topologies. Percent improvement over the XOR based topology are listed.

Standard Cell	Stack (pW)	Trans. Gate (pW)
AND	226.8 (66.34%)	405.1 (39.88%)
NAND	-	371.6 (36.04%)
OR	181.2 (68.81%)	528.2 (20.15%)
NOR	-	494.6 (23.78%)

8. REFERENCES

[1] DigiTimes, "Trends in the global IC design service market," www.digitimes.com/news/a20120313RS400.html?chid=2, March 2012.

[2] R. Torrance and D. James, "The State-of-the-Art in Semiconductor Reverse Engineering," *Proceedings of the IEEE Design Automation Conference*, pp. 333 – 338, June 2011.

[3] International Chamber of Commerce, "Impacts of counterfeiting and piracy to reach US $1.7 trillion by 2015," http://www.iccwbo.org/News/Articles/2011/Impacts-of-counterfeiting-and-piracy-to-reach-US$1-7-trillion-by-2015/, Feb. 2011.

[4] Semiconductor Equipment and Materials Industry, "Intellectual Property (IP) Challenges and Concerns of the Semiconductor Equipment and Materials Industry," http://www.semi.org/cms/groups/public/documents/web_content/p043701.pdf, April 2008.

[5] M. Tehranipoor and F. Koushanfar, "A Survey of Hardware Trojan Taxonomy and Detection," *IEEE Design and Test of Computers*, Vol. 27, No. 1, pp. 10 – 25, Feb. 2010.

[6] S. Chakraborty and S. Bhunia, "HARPOON: An Obfuscation-Based SoC Design Methodology for Hardware Protection," *IEEE Transactions on Computer-aided Design of Integrated Circuits and Systems*, Vol. 28, No. 10, pp. 1493 – 1502, Oct. 2009.

[7] J. Roy, F. Koushanfar, and I. Markov, "EPIC: Ending Piracy of Integrated Circuits," *Proceedings of the IEEE/ACM Design, Automation and Test in Europe*, pp. 1069 – 1074, Oct. 2008.

[8] Rajendran, J. and Sinanoglu, O. and Karri, R., "Regaining Trust in VLSI Design: Design-for-Trust Techniques," *Proceedings of the IEEE*, Vol. 102, No. 8, pp. 1266 – 1282, July 2014.

[9] Y. Alkabani and K. Farinaz, "Active Hardware Metering for Intellectual Property protection and Security," *Proceedings of the USENIX Security Symposium*, pp. 291 – 306, Aug. 2007.

[10] Rajendran, J. and Pino, Y. and Sinanoglu, O. and Karri, R., "Logic Encryption: A Fault Analysis Perspective," *Proceedings of the IEEE/ACM Design, Automation and Test in Europe*, pp. 953 – 958, Oct. 2012.

[11] Rajendran, J. and Zhang, H. and Zhang, C. and Rose, G. and Pino, Y. and Sinanoglu, O. and Karri, R., "Fault Analysis-Based Logic Encryption," *IEEE Transactions on Computers*, Vol. 64, No. 2, pp. 410 – 424, Feb. 2015.

[12] A. Baumgarten, A. Tyagi, and J. Zambreno, "Preventing IC Piracy Using Reconfigurable Logic Barriers," *IEEE Design and Test of Computers*, Vol. 27, No. 1, pp. 66 – 75, Feb. 2010.

A Design of a Non-Volatile PMC-Based (Programmable Metallization Cell) Register File

Salin Junsangsri,
ECE
ECE Dept, Northeastern University
Boston, MA 02115, USA
(1) 857-225-3755
Junsangsri.s@husky.neu.edu

Jie Han
ECE Dept, University of Alberta
Edmonton, Alberta, Canada T6G 2V4
(1) 780-492-1361
jhan8@ualberta.ca

Fabrizio Lombardi
ECE Dept, Northeastern University
Boston, MA 02115, USA
(1) 617-373-4854
lombardi@ece.neu.edu

ABSTRACT
This paper presents the design of a non-volatile register file using cells made of a SRAM and a Programmable Metallization Cell (PMC). The proposed cell is a symmetric 8T2P (8-transistors, 2PMC) design; it utilizes three control lines to ensure the correctness in its operations (i.e. Write, Read, Store and Restore). Simulation results using HSPICE are provided for the cell as well as the register file array (both one- and two-dimensional schemes). At cell level, it is shown that the off-state resistance has a limited effect on the Read time, because in the proposed circuit the transistor connecting the PMCs to the SRAM is off. While having no significant effect on the Store time, the time of the Restore operation depends on the value of the off-state resistance, i.e. an increase in off-state PMC resistance causes an increase in Restore time. Comparison between non-volatile register files utilizing either PMCs, or Phase Change Memories (PCMs) is provided.The register file using PMCs has a faster Store and Read times than the PCM-based counterpart; this is mostly caused by the difference in resistance values for these two non-volatile technologies. The lower delay involved in these operations confirms that the proposed PMC-based register file offers significant advantages in terms of delay performance.

Keywords
Register File; Non-volatile Operation; Emerging Technology

1. INTRODUCTION
Non-volatile memories (NVMs) have gained considerable attention due to the requirement of portable storage for many computer applications such as consumer electronics [1]. In the past, they have been used as secondary memory for long term persistent storage; however, technology advances have made possible to have NVMs operating higher in the memory hierarchy [2].

GLSVLSI '16, May 18-20, 2016, Boston, MA, USA
 ISBN 978-1-4503-4274-2/16/05…$15.00
DOI: http://dx.doi.org/10.1145/2902961.2903034

A register file is used at the top of the memory hierarchy. It is usually implemented by fast Static Random Access Memories (SRAMs); however, SRAMs are volatile circuits [3] and in many applications, non-volatile storage is required to meet both temporal and space localities in memory accesses [13]. PMC has been recently proposed as a candidate for the next-generation of non-volatile memory due to its simple structure, high resistance ratio, multilevel capability, low power consumption, favorable scalability and high operational speed [3]. This manuscript considers the Programmable Metallization Cell (PMC) (also referred to as the conducting bridge random access memory, CBRAM, or electrochemical metallization ECM) as non-volatile memory element; it deals with the design of a register file whose non-volatile operation is accomplished by using PMCs. The operations related to the SRAM and the non-volatile elements within a cell are analyzed in details for different figures of merit using an 8T2P (8 transistors, 2 PMCs) configuration. The cell operations are then extended to one- and two-dimensional array schemes for register-file implementation. Comparison with the same scheme but employing Phase Change Memories (PCMs) as non-volatile elements is presented.

2. REVIEW
This section presents a brief review of a register file and PMC as relevant to the proposed designs.

Register file: In a microprocessor, the memory architecture is hierarchically organized. On-chip memory is utilized for very fast access time; cache and register files are two of the most commonly used on-chip memories [5]. A register file is embedded in the central processing unit (CPU) and stores both data and mapping information (such as locations); these locations store specific addresses for loading programs, or data to meet spatial and temporal locality requirements [13].The register file is usually designed as a memory array with the fastest access time in the hierarchy. In the register file, two memory technologies are often used. (i) Static random access memory (SRAM): SRAMs are fast, but they are volatile and each cell requires at least 6 transistors. (ii) Dynamic random access memory (DRAM): DRAMs requires refresh and are slower than SRAMs; they require less area due to the reduced circuit complexity. DRAMs are also volatile. A SRAM consists of two crossed inverters with two additional transistors for data control; this configuration is generally known as 6T.

Programmable Metallization Cell: The SRAM is a volatile memory circuit; different devices and operations (such as Store and Restore) are commonly used for non-volatile storage. Some of the non-volatile storage operations are very important when *temporal and space locality considerations* are required in a register file for preserving crucial data at the highest level of the memory hierarchy [13]. The non-volatile property also permits continuous storage of data for improved performance. The Programmable Metallization Cell (PMC) is a non-volatile memory, whose resistance changes by modifying the biasing voltage across the cell. The change in resistance occurs by having metallic ions pass through a solid electrolyte and the subsequent formation and dissolution of a metallic conductive filament (CF) connecting the two electrodes [3].The PMC has two states: *set* (OFF to ON state transition) and the *reset (*ON to OFF state transition). The set state occurs when the positive voltage bias is higher than the positive threshold voltage; this will cause an electrochemical reaction to form a conducting link between the top and bottom electrodes such that ions can tunnel through the cell. Thus, the resistance will change from R_{off} (off state resistance) to R_{on} (on state resistance), as a set state. When the negative voltage is biased over the negative threshold voltage, there is no connection between the electrodes. Therefore, the resistance changes from R_{on} to R_{off} due to the reset state.

3. CELL DESIGN AND EVALUATION

The proposed cell for a register file is a symmetric circuit; two PMCs (storing data of opposite values) are utilized. The non-volatile elements are connected to a SRAM, such that data can be stored (from SRAM to non-volatile elements), or restored (from non-volatile elements to SRAM). The PMCs are connected to the storage nodes (D and DN) of the SRAM in a balanced (symmetric) scheme, as described in more detail next. This design is referred to as the shared control cell (Figure 1); the two PMCs are controlled by a single signal (given by Ctrl1). As this is an 8T2P symmetric cell, hence the times of the Store and Restore operations are the same for both values ('0' and '1'). The Store and Restore operations of the 8T2P cell are controlled by adjusting the voltages at nodes BL, BLN and WL using 3control signals described in more detail next.

Store Operation: The Store operation is used to transfer the data from the SRAM to the non-volatile elements (i.e. the two PMCs are directly connected to D and DN). In this 8T2P cell, the voltage at node Ctrl2 must be at 0V to allow the supply voltage to the SRAM. The voltage at node WL is high to allow the voltages at BL and BLN to the SRAM (through transistors M5 and M6). Moreover, Ctrl0 is high to allow the voltages at Ctrl1to affect the PMCs. Ctrl1 must be biased to change both PMCs, so the signal on Ctrl1 is (with a full swing from 0V to V_{dd}) reduces the Store time and allows only one PMC to '1' (thus forcing the other node of the SRAM to become '0' in a shorter time). The values of BL and BLN depend on the desired value to be stored.

Restore Operation: The Restore operation occurs when either the supply is restored and/or the data from the non-volatile element(s) is written to the SRAM. Instability in the final step (i.e. the voltage at the storage node D could be close to the voltage at node DN) must be avoided; this is accomplished by having BL, BLN and WL high. Moreover, a PMOS is used to connect or disconnect the supply voltage from the circuit by utilizing Ctrl2; also, Ctrl0 is low to isolate both PMCs from the SRAM. When the voltages at D and DN are close (at a time referred in this paper as the switching restore time, or SRT), Ctrl2 connects the supply voltage to the cell and Ctrl0 allows the voltages at Ctrl1 to the PMCs and restore the data.

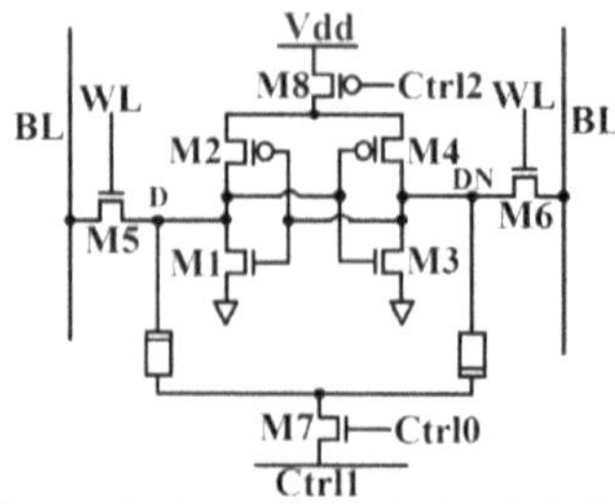

Figure 1. Shared control cell (8T2P)

Next, the proposed cell is evaluated with respect to its operations. For the Read and Write operations, only the SRAM is involved; due to lack of space these operations are not treated furthermore.

The two operations (Store and Restore) dealing with non-volatile storage are discussed in more detail next (the same process is applicable to both '0' and '1' for the value at nodes D and DN due to the symmetric nature of the proposed cell). Simulation is performed at 32-nm feature size using the Predictive Technology Model (PTM) [9] under the conditions of the parameters shown in Table 1. M7 and M8 allow the correct voltage values to the cell, while control is enforced by Ctrl0, Ctrl1 and Ctrl2 for the correct execution of the Store and Restore operations.

Store Operation: The Store operation is used to transfer the data from the SRAM to the non-volatile elements (i.e. the two PMCs are directly connected to D and DN). The Store operation requires a higher voltage than the other operations, because the resistances of both PMCs are changed by voltage biasing for state switching. The stored values at the PMCs are connected to D and DN, therefore the Store operation starts at the same time on both PMCs. The Store operation is similar to the Write operation for the SRAM; Ctrl0 and Ctrl1 are used as control signals to bias the voltage for storing the desired data in both PMCs. This operation requires an increase of the bias voltage to 3.5V. Moreover, a voltage pulse is needed at Ctrl1 to change the values stored in both PMCs. The timing diagrams of the relevant signals are shown in Figure 2.

The Store operation requires the PMCs to change state in a stable fashion; this process requires more time to change the resistive states from R_{on} to R_{off} than R_{off} to R_{on}. As the resistive states of both PMCs must be changed during this operation, then the proposed cell requires a square pulse signal as input. Figure 3 shows the relationship between the Store time (for the '0' value) and the PMC bias voltage in a semi-logarithm plot scale; the Store time is inversely proportional to the bias voltage, i.e. a smaller bias voltage causes a larger Store time. However, a larger voltage implies larger power dissipation too.

Restore Operation: The Restore operation occurs when either the supply is restored and/or the data from the non-volatile element(s) is written to the SRAM. For the Restore operation, 0.9V (same as the supply voltage at 32nm) is used as voltage value to keep a low power consumption in the circuit. A *switching restore time* (or STR) must be allowed to ensure that both D and DN have correct and stable values (for similar reason as in the Store operation). The values and corresponding timing diagrams of the proposed cell for BL, BLN, WL, Ctrl0, Ctrl1, Ctrl2 are given in Figure 4; the STR is given by 425ps.

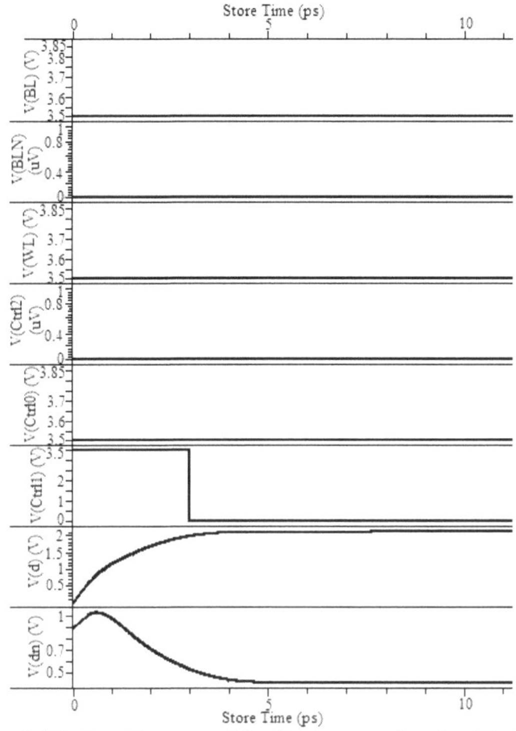

Figure 2. Timing diagram of the Store operation for BL, BLN, WL, Ctrl0, Ctrl1, Ctrl2, V(D) and V(DN).

Table 1. Parameters used in simulation [3]

Parameter	*Value*
R_{on} (Ω)	30.0625k
R_{off} (Ω)	99.9579M
NMOS (nm)	32
PMOS (nm)	32
V_{dd} (V)	0.9

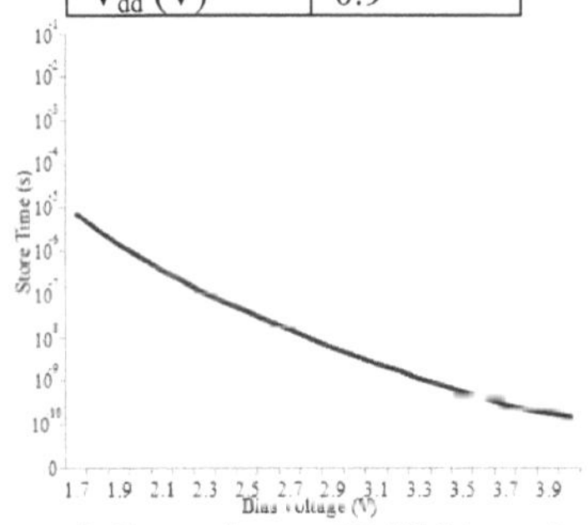

Figure 3. Store time vs.PMC bias voltage

In Figure 4, the voltages of BL, BLN, WL, and Ctrl2 are '1' for 425ps (i.e. the STR); then these voltages have a value of '0' to copy the data from the PMCs to the SRAM. The results (Figure 5) show that the Restore time for the proposed 8T2P cell is 470.73ps.

Consider next the relationship between the cell operations and the PMC resistance; Figure 6 shows the Read/Write times (for both '0' and '1') of the SRAM when varying the value of the off-state resistance of the PMC (and keeping the on-state resistance to its default value as in Table 1).

Figures 6 and 7 show the Store and Restore times (same for '0' and '1') by varying the off-state PMC resistance; while the value of this resistance has no significant effect on the Store time, the time of the Restore operation depends on the value of the off-state resistance. So, an increase in off-state PMC resistance causes an increase in Restore time. The simulation results show that the off-state resistance has a limited effect on the Read time, because the transistor connecting the PMCs to the SRAM is off.

Static Noise Margin (SNM): The static noise margin (SNM) is defined as the minimum static voltage capable of change the state of a memory cell, the SNM is widely used as a stability criterion [11]. It is well known that the presence of additional hardware (such as a non-volatile element) causes a reduction in the SNM [12]; simulation has found that the SNM for the proposed design is 0.22843V (the 6T (volatile) SRAM has a SNM of 0.2581V). This corresponds to a 15% reduction; this small reduction is due to the utilization of the two control signals Ctr0 and Ctr1 in the operation of the proposed cell.

Power Dissipation: Power dissipation and the power delay product (PDP) are also important metrics in the operations of the cell; the results are shown in Table 2.

Table 2. Power dissipation and PDP of proposed cell

Operation	*Power Dissipation*	*PDP (fWs)*
Write	45.405uW	1.106
Read	17.232uW	0.132
Store	46.98mW	185.631
Restore	96.061uW	44.711

As the proposed cell is a symmetric scheme, there is no difference in operation due to the data values; Table 2 shows that only Store incurs in a substantial power dissipation (and corresponding higher PDP); this is caused by the higher voltage level required for writing to the non-volatile elements. However, operationally critical data is preserved in the SRAMs by evoking a Store operation only in occasional cases [14]. Usually high performance computing utilizes very often the non-volatile Restore by which the data stored in the non-volatile elements is loaded into the SRAM, so avoiding data search in the lower memory levels (and incurring in longer latency delays).

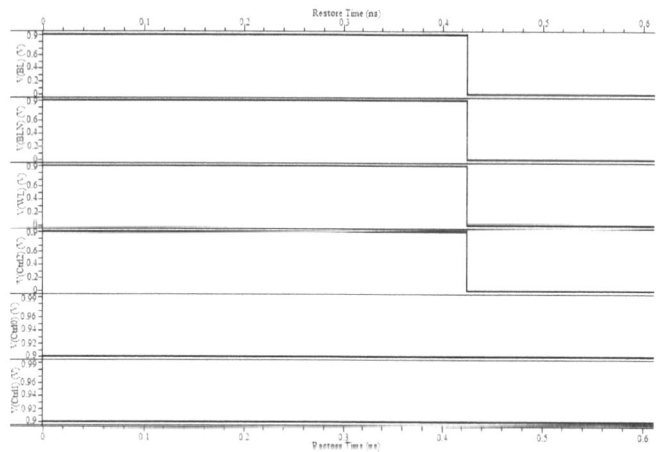

Figure 4. Timing diagram of the Restore operation for BL, BLN, WL, Ctrl0, Ctrl1, and Ctrl2.

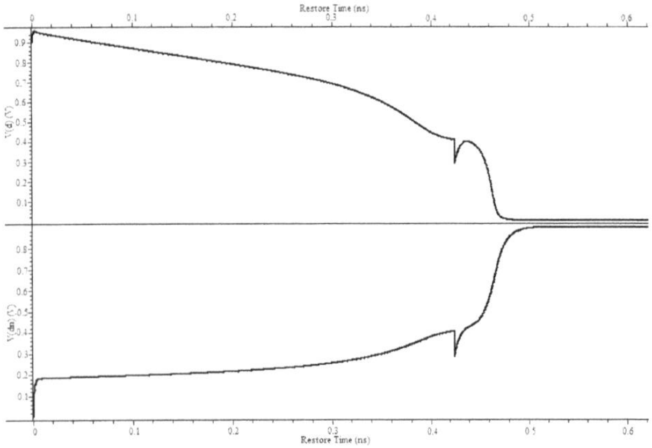

Figure 5. Restore time at nodes D and DN

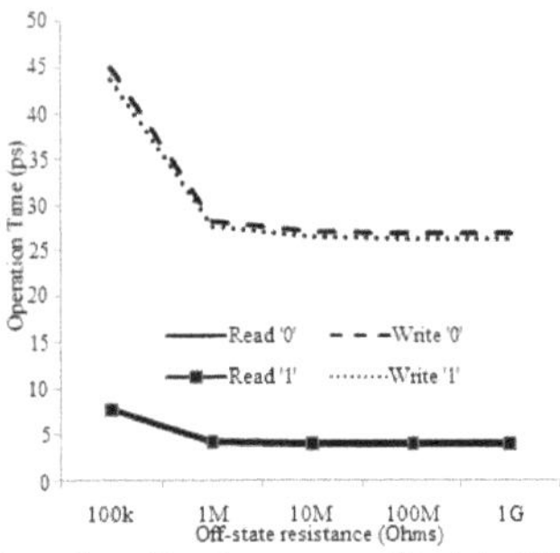

Figure 6. Read and write times vs. off-state PMC resistance.

4. REGISTER FILE EVALUATION

In this paper, the register file is designed as consisting of cells arranged in one-dimensional (1-D) and two dimensional (2-D) schemes.

One-Dimensional (1-D) Array: In the 1-D configuration, all register files are connected to common BL and BLN; moreover, simulation considers only one cell of the array to be selected (all other N-1 cells are left unselected).

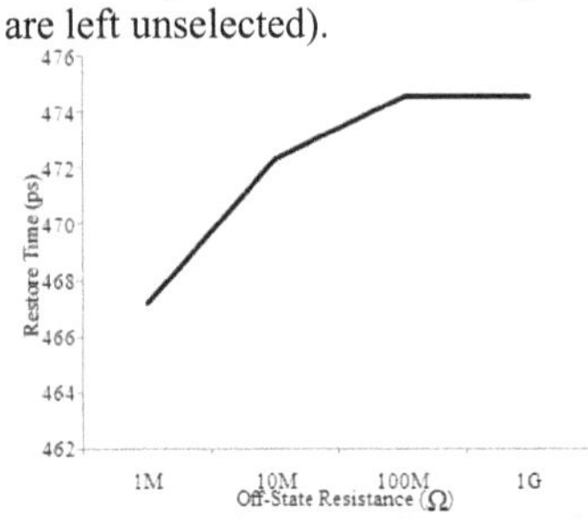

Figure 7. Restore time vs. off-state resistance.

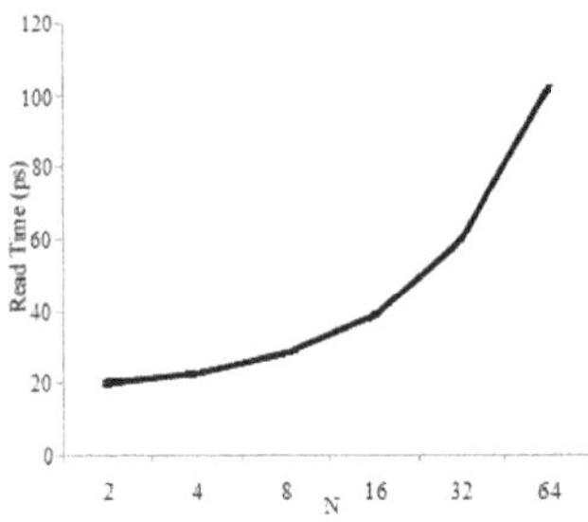

Figure 8. Read time vs. dimension N

As shown in Figure 8, a larger array size causes more parasitic capacitance resulting in a longer delay for the Read operation. Simulation has confirmed that N has no significant effect on the Write, Store and Restore times, i.e. nearly constant values. These results confirm that the parasitic capacitance has hardly any effect on the Write, Store and Restore operations due to the bias voltage at BL and BLN, i.e. only the Read operation (Figure 8) shows a dependency on N.

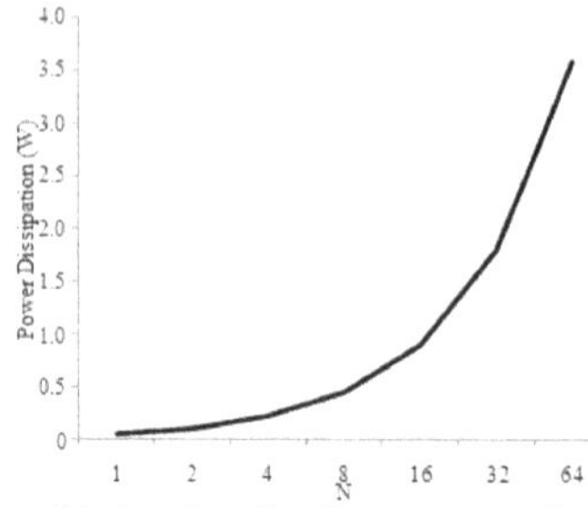

Figure 9. Power dissipation for Store operation vs. dimension N

Power dissipation of the operations of the proposed cell increases at a larger array size (Figures 9 and 10). The Store operation incurs in the highest power dissipation (Figure 9) due to the larger bias voltage. The power dissipation of the Write, Read and Restore operations are shown in Figure 10; all these operations show a dependency of power dissipation on N. The SRAM operations (Read and Write) show the largest increases (the pre-charging process required for the Read operation is the cause of the largest dissipation when N is increased).

Two-Dimensional (2-D) Array: A register file is usually implemented as a two-dimensional (2-D) array of dimension N; it is assumed that only one cell (the so-called center cell) is selected, all other cells are unselected. By varying the dimension of the 2-D array, simulation shows that the Write, Store and Restore times are only marginally affected because the bias voltages on BL and BLN are sufficiently high to overcome the parasitic capacitance; BL and BLN in the Read operation are not biased, so the effect of the parasitic capacitance makes the Read time longer at a larger array size (Figure 11).

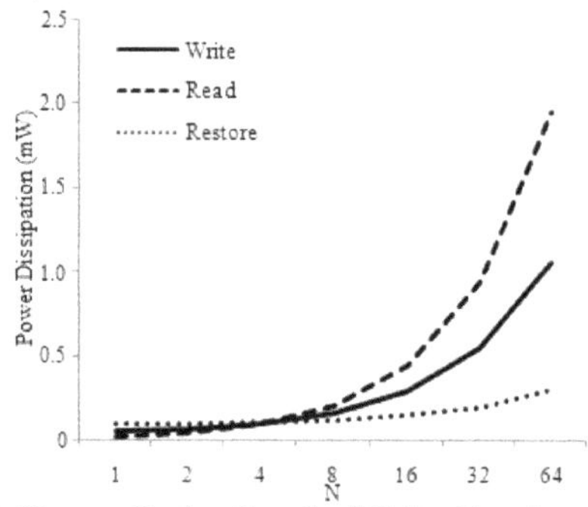

Figure 10. Power dissipation for Write, Read, and Restore operations vs. dimension N

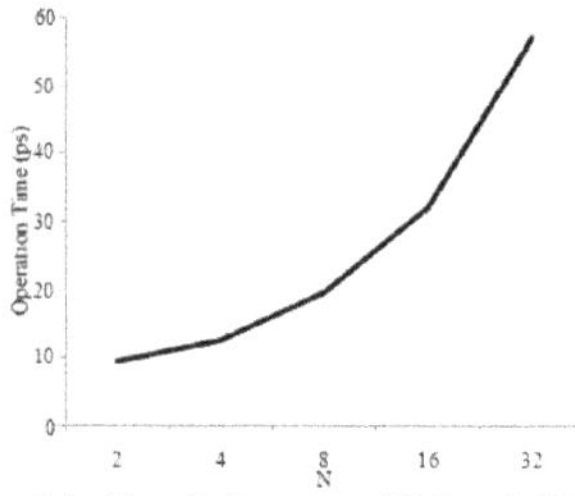

Figure 11. Read time vs. N for 2-D array

The Restore operation for a larger array size requires a longer time in the first step (due to the larger parasitic capacitances at the bit and word lines); a value of 500ps is found by simulation and used as STR, this corresponds to an increase of 75ps from the single cell case (i.e. nearly 15%).

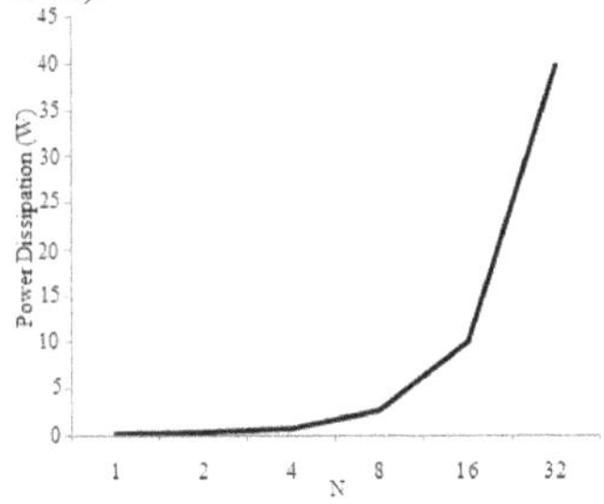

Figure 12. Power dissipation of Store operation vs. N

When considering power dissipation, a larger memory size causes a power dissipation higher than for example the 1-D array. The result for the Store operation of a 2-D array is shown in Figure 12; its trend is similar to the Store operation of a 1-D array. The power dissipation for the three other operations is shown in Figure 13.

5. COMPARATIVE EVALUATION

In this Section, the technology of the resistive non-volatile elements is changed and the corresponding register files are assessed. A PCM (phase change memory) element is also considered [6]. This comparison is performed using the parameters of Table 1; in particular the supply voltage is 0.9V (for the Read, Write and Restore operations) and a Store operation requires 3.5 V as bias voltage.

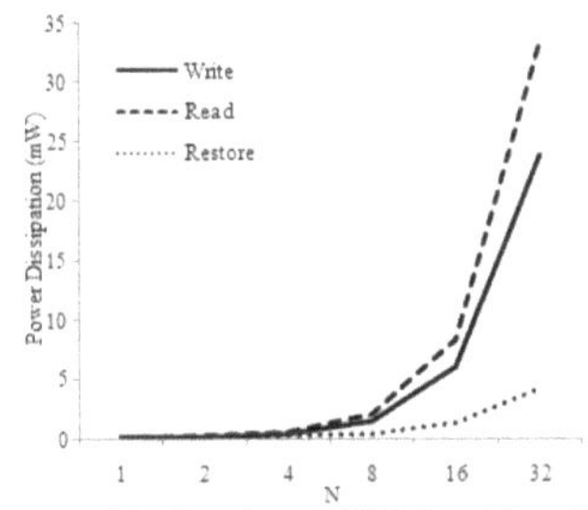

Figure 13. Power dissipation of Write, Read, and Restore operations vs. N

A MOSFET has a standard P/N width ratio of 2.5 (as used throughout the previous sections), so the W/L ratio must be increased to at least 9 to ensure that a PCM can perform a Store operation. The simulation results for the register file cells made of these two technologies are shown in Table 3 (bold entries denote the best values); the delay is the same for the '0' and '1' data values due to symmetry in the cell.

Table 3. Operation delays of PMC and PCM cells when W=9L, P/N ratio = 2.5

Operation	*PMC Cell*	*PCM Cell*
Write	26.16ps	**25.84ps**
Read	**0.07ps**	9.276ps
Store	**3.951ps**	287.10ns
Restore	470.73ps	**296.84ps**

Note that a 6T (non-volatile) SRAM cell incurs in delays of 24.583ps, and 6.8618ps for the Read and Write operations, respectively; so a penalty is incurred for the presence of non-volatile elements in a register-file cell. Table 3 shows that a PCM-based cell has worse performance in two out of four operations (so except for the Write and Restore). A state change in a PCM incurs in a more substantial delay than a PMC, especially for a Store operation (nearly two orders of dimensions); this occurs because the PCM requires a rather long time [6] to change the material structure of the GST compound (and hence its resistivity). The increase in W/L is needed for achieving the required bias voltage for the Store operation in a PCM-based cell.

Next, consider the 2-D level comparison for the register file; results are obtained for square register files of dimension 16 and 32. The results in Figure 14 show the Write and Read times for the PMC and PCM-based register files. These results show that the Write time is not significantly affected by the resistive element type and N; the Read time however, increases at a higher value of N and is substantially larger in a PCM-based register file.

Figures 15 and 16 show the Store and Restore times of the PMC- and PCM-based register files when N is 16 and 32. The increase in array size does not significantly affect the Store or Restore operations. Figure 15 shows the benefit of storing data into a PMC (rather than a PCM) due to the order of magnitude time difference between these non-volatile technologies. Figure 16 shows that the reverse (i.e. for a Restore operation), the register file made of PCM-based cells is significantly better than the PMC counterpart. This occurs due to the resistances at the on-/off- states for these technologies, a smaller resistance causes a faster Restore time due to the larger voltage across the cell.

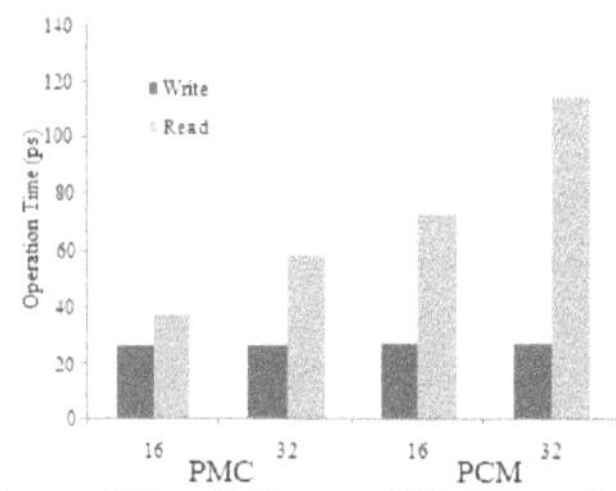

Figure 14. Write and Read times of PMC and PCM-based 2-D register files vs. N

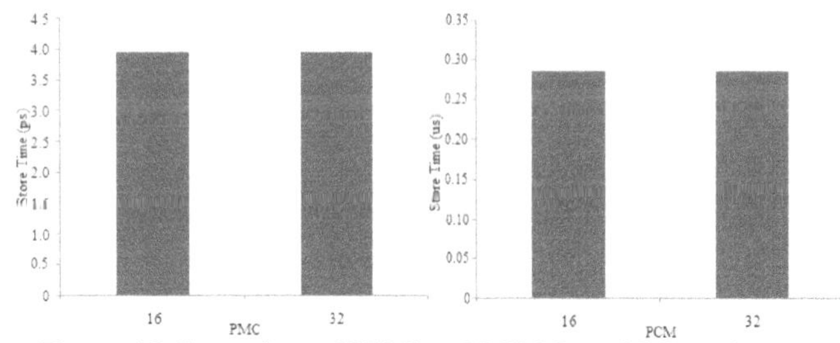

Figure 15. Store time of PMC and PCM-based 2-D register files vs. N

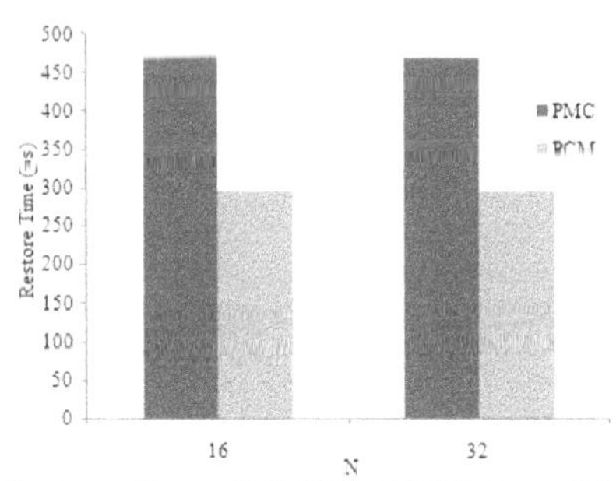

Figure 16. Restore time of PMC and PCM-based 2-D register files vs. N

6. CONCLUSION

This paper has presented the design and evaluation of a non-volatile register file; the cell in the register file consists of a SRAM and a Programmable Metallization Cell (PMC) in a symmetric 8T2P (8-transistors, 2PMC) design. Three control lines are utilized in the proposed cell to ensure the correctness in its four operations (i.e. Write, Read, Store and Restore. Simulation results using HSPICE have been provided for the cell as well as the register file array (both one- and two-dimensional schemes). Comparison in operation times between non-volatile register files utilizing either PMCs, or Phase Change Memories (PCMs) have also been assessed. Table 4 shows the ranking of these register files. The following features are evident. (i) The register file using PMCs has a faster Store and Read times than the PCM-based counterpart; this is mostly caused by the difference in resistance values for these two non-volatile technologies and the delay involved in these operations [6]. (ii) The Write and Restore times are better for a PCM-based register file; as these operations are not as frequent as the others at the highest level of a (non-volatile) memory hierarchy [2], then the proposed PMC-based register file offers significant advantages in terms of delay performance.

Table 4. Ranking of PMC- and PCM-based register files

Operation	PMC	PCM
Write time	2	1
Read time	1	2
Store time	1	2
Restore time	2	1

7. REFERENCES

[1] R. K. Gupta, S. Krishnamoorthy, D. Y. Kusuma, P. S. Lee, M. P. Srinivasan "Enhancing charge-storage capacity of non-volatile memory devices using template-directed assembly of gold nanoparticles" Nanoscale Issue 7 pp. 2296-2300, Jan. 2012

[2] H. Li, Y. Chen, L. Benini, G. De Micheli, B. Al-hashimi, W. Mueller "An Overview of Non-Volatile Memory Technology and the Implication for Tools and Architectures" Design, Automation and Test in Europe pp.731-736, 2009

[3] D. Liu, Nannan Wang, Guang Wang, ZhengZheng Shao, Xuan Zhu, ChaoyangZhang"Programmable metallization cell based on amorphous $La_{0.79}Sr_{0.21}MnO_3$ thin films for memory applications" Journal of Alloys and Compounds, vol. 580, pp. 354-357, Dec. 2013. doi: 10.1016/j.jallcom.2013.06.095

[4] P. Junsangsri, F, Lombardi and J. Han "HSPICE Macromodel of a Programmable Metallization Cell (PMC) and its application to memory Design" IEEE/ACM international Symposium on NANOARCH, pp. 45-50, July 2014, doi: 10.1109/NANOARCH.2014.6880477

[5] Hao YAN, Yan LIU, Dong-hui WANG, Chao-huan HOU "A Low-power 8-Read 4-Write Register File Design" IEEE Conference Publications. On Microelectronics and Electronics, pp. 178-181, Sept. 2010. doi: 10.1109/PRIMEASIA.2010.5604933

[6] P. Junsangsri and F. Lombardi "A New Comprehensive Model of a Phase Change Memory (PCM) Cell" IEEE Trans. On Nanotechnology, vol. 13, no. 6, pp. 1213–1225, Nov. 2014.

[7] M. H. Kaffashian, R. Lotfi, K. Mafinezhad, H. Mahmoodi "Impact of NBTI on performance of domino logic circuits in nano-scale CMOS " Microelectronics Journal, vol. 42, no. 12, pp. 1327-1334, Dec. 2011

[8] K. Osada (2011). Fundamental of SRAM Memory Cell. In K. Osada, K. Ishibashi (Eds.), Low Power and Reliable SRAM Memory Cell and Array Design (pp. 6) Springer Series in Advanced Microelectronics, vol. 31

[9] PTM Model, 32-nm MOSFETs. Retrieved from http://www.ptm.asu.edu

[10] P.E. Dodd, F.W. Sexton "Critical charge concepts for CMOS SRAMs" IEEE Trans. On Nuclear Science, vol. 42, no. 6, pp. 1764 – 1771, Dec. 1995.

[11] E. Seevinck, F. J List, J. Lohstroh "Static-Noise Margin Analysis of MOS SRAM Cells" IEEE Journal of Solid-state circuits, vol. 22, no. 5, pp. 748-754, Oct. 1987

[12] W. Wei, K. Namba, J. Han and F. Lombardi, "Design of a Non-Volatile 7T1R SRAM Cell for Instant-on Operation." IEEE Transactions on Nanotechnology, vol. 13, no. 5, pp. 905-916, 2014.

[13] Q. Zhu, K. Vaidyanathan, O. Shacham, M. Horowitz, L. Pileggi, F. Franchetti "Design Automation Framework for Application-Specific Logic in Memory Block" IEEE ASAP 23rd pp.125-132, July 2012.

[14] W. Wei, K. Namba, and F. Lombardi, "Design and Analysis of Non-Volatile Memory Cells for SEU Tolerance," Proc. 17th IEEE Symposium on Defect and Fault Tolerance in VLSI and Nanotechnology Systems, pp. 69-74, Amsterdam, October 2014

A Clockless Sequential PUF with Autonomous Majority Voting

Xiaolin Xu Daniel Holcomb
Department of Electrical and Computer Engineering
University of Massachusetts Amherst
{xiaolinx, holcomb}@engin.umass.edu

ABSTRACT

Physical unclonable functions (PUFs) leverage minute silicon process variations to produce device-tied secret keys. The energy and area costs of creating keys from PUFs can far exceed the costs of the basic PUF circuits alone. Minimizing the end-to-end cost of reliable key generation is critical to enable broader adoption of PUFs. In this work, we introduce a new style of PUF that employs autonomous majority voting to improve reliability. The novelty of this design, and the source of its efficiency, is that the inherently sequential majority voting procedure is carried out by a self-timed circuit without orchestration by a global clock. We use circuit simulation to evaluate the energy versus reliability tradeoffs achieved by different parameterizations of the design, to show that the design performs well across a range of supply voltages, and to quantify the robustness of the design across a broad range of operating temperatures.

1. INTRODUCTION

Physical Unclonable Functions (PUFs) are circuits that produce output values that depend on process variations and are therefore unique to each device. PUF-based secret keys offer security benefits over traditional cryptographic keys. More specifically, PUFs offer an increased resistance to cloning, and resistance to invasive attacks that aim to read out key values that are stored in non-volatile memories. The additional measure of security provided by PUF-based keys is important in ubiquitous electronics that operate in uncontrolled and untrusted environments.

The secret key generated by a PUF is derived from the intrinsic variations that are inherent in the manufacturing of each integrated circuit instance. Such a circuit is denoted in literature as a "weak" PUF, to distinguish it from the "strong" PUFs that perform challenge-response hashing such as the well-known arbiter PUF [8]. In this paper, as strong PUFs are not considered, we will refer to weak PUFs simply as PUFs. Because of noise, PUF outputs typically have a bit error rate of a few percent. Circuit level reliability techniques and error correcting codes are therefore used to produce reliable keys from the slightly-unreliable PUFs.

GLSVLSI '16, May 18-20, 2016, Boston, MA, USA
© 2016 ACM. ISBN 978-1-4503-4274-2/16/05...$15.00
DOI: http://dx.doi.org/10.1145/2902961.2903029

In this paper we propose a PUF that has the external interface of a simple weak PUF, but has an internal structure that autonomously performs majority voting to improve reliability. The specific contributions of this work as follows:

- We describe a novel clockless sequential PUF structure that performs autonomous majority voting.
- We evaluate using circuit simulation the reliability of the proposed PUF across a range of supply voltages and temperatures.
- We explore the tradeoffs of energy and reliability that can be accomplished using different parameterizations of the proposed PUF.

2. RELATED WORK

Secret key style PUFs generate n-bit outputs using n-instantiations of logically identical cells, each of which generates a single output bit. The cells used for these PUFs resemble memory cells, and in many cases actually are re-purposed memory cells. Such a cell has two stable states. The PUF output bit is generated by driving the cell to an unstable state and letting it transition to a stable state that is determined by process variation of the cell. Perhaps the best known PUF of this sort is based on the power-up state of SRAM cells [10, 9]; at power-up, an SRAM cell with both state nodes discharged becomes unstable and transitions to one of its two stable states. One variant of SRAM PUF is the DRV PUF proposed by Holcomb et al. [11, 19], that leverages the unique DRV value of SRAM cells. Other examples of cross-coupled PUF cells are ones based on resettable NOR latches [18], the butterfly PUF based on cross-coupled latches [13], and PUFs based on flip-flops [14] or sense amplifiers [4]. Yamamoto et al. [20] propose a PUF based on RS latches with inputs tied together, and this basic circuit is also a component of our proposed PUF. However, the manner in which the RS latch is used in our design differs substantially. Yamamoto's work is based on the location of RS latches with random output bits.

Secret keys used for cryptography must be highly repeatable over time, and given that PUFs are based on physical processes that are susceptible to noise, mechanisms are required to bridge the gap from unreliable circuits to reliable keys. These mechanisms can be broken into circuit-level techniques operating at the level of individual PUF bits, and error correction happening at the word level across many bits in aggregate. The two types of mechanisms can be used together, such that the circuit-level techniques reduce the bit-error-rate, and the reduced number of errors are then corrected using coding.

2.1 Reliability Enhancements in Secret Key PUFs

Bit-level reliability enhancements for PUFs decrease the error rate by reducing the impact of noise on the PUF outputs. Cells that are highly biased toward one output are largely immune to the small influence of noise, and bit errors happen in PUF cells that are approximately metastable. Directed accelerated aging techniques measure PUF outputs after manufacturing, and then reinforce cell tendencies using aging to increase the bias of each cell toward its more probable output [3]. Dark-bit masking [2] refers to precharacterizing cells to identify and then mask out unreliable bits. Dark-bit masking can either be applied as a post-silicon testing step, or performed on-line in the field by evaluating the PUF under various stress conditions [15, 17].

2.2 Temporal Majority Voting

Especially relevant to the work in this paper is temporal majority voting [2, 15]. In majority voting, a cell is evaluated n times in sequence, and the overall output is decided according to which value occurs in a majority of the n trials. Larger values of n improve the reliability of the PUF output. Effectively, majority voting across n trials counteracts the influence of noise that can cause a cell to produce its less likely value in a single trial. For example, consider a cell that has probability 0.1 of producing output value 0, and probability 0.9 of producing output value 1; this cell can be considered as having a error rate of 0.1 and nominal output value of 1. Using p to denote the error rate before majority voting, the error rate of the same bit after majority voting across n output observations is $p_{bit} = \sum_{i=\frac{n+1}{2}}^{n} \binom{n}{i} p^i (1-p)^{n-i}$. The relationship between p_{bit} and p for different values of n is shown in Fig. 1. For a bit as described above ($p = 0.1$), the error rate after majority voting is $p_{bit} = 0.028$ for $n = 3$, and $p_{bit} = 0.0027$ for $n = 7$.

Note that majority voting will not improve reliability of a cell that is equally likely to produce either output value ($p = 0.5$), or a cell for which the more likely output changes according to temperature or another environmental parameter. Reliability of these cells must be addressed through one of the other reliability mechanism such as dark-bit masking, directed aging, or error correcting codes with helper data.

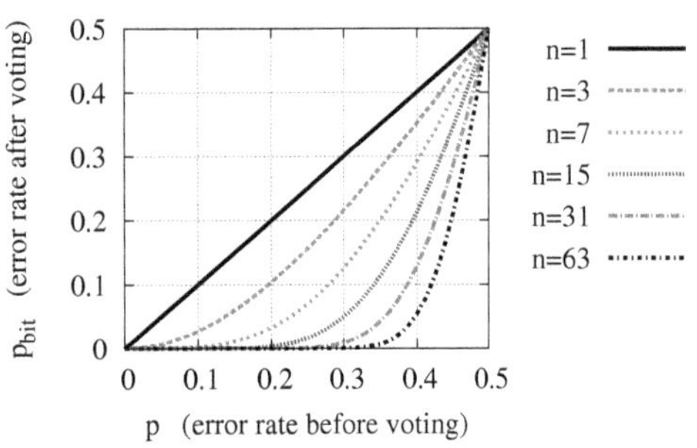

Figure 1: The impact of majority voting on reliability of a single bit. For any probability p of an output error in a single trial, p_{bit} is the corresponding probability of having an output error after using majority voting across n trials. Increasing n decreases the probability of error, except for cells with p equal to 0.5.

2.3 Error Correction using Helper Data

Reliability enhancements such as majority voting are complementary to the use of error correction. An example of error correction using the code-offset construction [12, 7] is shown in Fig. 2. An arbitrary secret key K is chosen for each PUF at enrollment and then encoded to a codeword $C(K)$ that is XORed with PUF response W to generate helper data. The unknowability of W prevents helper data $C(K) \oplus W$ from revealing secret $C(K)$, so helper data need not be protected against invasive attack and can be stored using any non-volatile memory, fuses, or antifuses. To regenerate the secret key in the field, a PUF produces a value W' that may differ slightly from W due to noise or environmental variations. Response W' is XORed with the helper data to produce a version of codeword $C(K)$ that is corrupted by the difference between W and W'. If the number of errors that can be corrected by the chosen code exceeds the Hamming distance between W and W', then key K is correctly recovered by decoding the noisy codeword. Note that more reliable PUFs will have smaller Hamming distances between W and W', and this reduces the number of errors that must be correctable by the error correcting code.

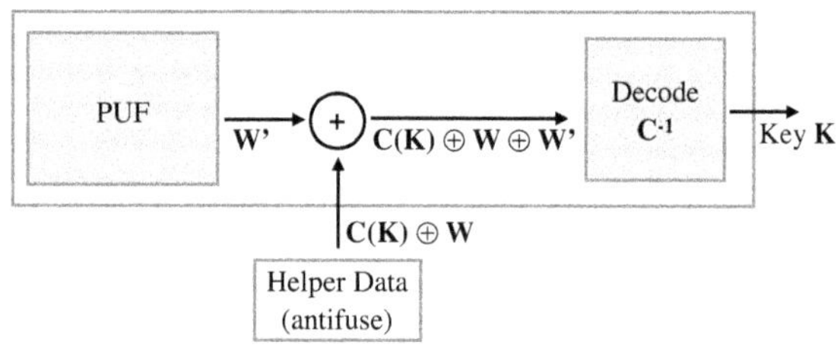

Figure 2: PUF-based secret key generation using helper data for error correction. The helper data is generated during a one-time enrollment process and is fixed over the life of the PUF.

3. DESIGN OF A CLOCKLESS SEQUENTIAL PUF

In this work we propose a clockless sequential PUF that performs majority voting as part of its sequential behavior. Fig. 4 shows the proposed PUF design; each bit of PUF output corresponds one instantiation of this design. The design uses two LFSRs to count oscillations on circuit nodes, and the PUF output is determined according to which LFSR is first to reach its final count. Because each oscillation is effectively a PUF observation, producing an output based on oscillation counts constitutes autonomous voting without orchestration by a global clock. In other words, the sequential behavior of the PUF is unrelated to the system clock, and in some configurations can occur within a single system clock. The evaluation of the PUF is initiated by asserting EVAL. When the PUF has completed its sequential evolution, signal READY is asserted, and the output is read from OUT. Note that READY can be neglected if sufficiently conservative time is waited between asserting EVAL and reading OUT.

3.1 Principle of Operation

Each PUF output bit is determined by the variation-induced behavior of an 8-transistor cross-coupled SR latch with its two inputs tied together. As shown in the shaded box in Fig. 4a, we denote the input X and the outputs Y1 and Y0. The SR latch is stable only when {X,Y1,Y0} takes the values {0,1,1}, {1,1,0} or {1,0,1}. If these signals have any other combination of values, the latch is unstable and its outputs will immediately transition to a stable latch configuration; for example {0,1,0} would transition to {0,1,1}.

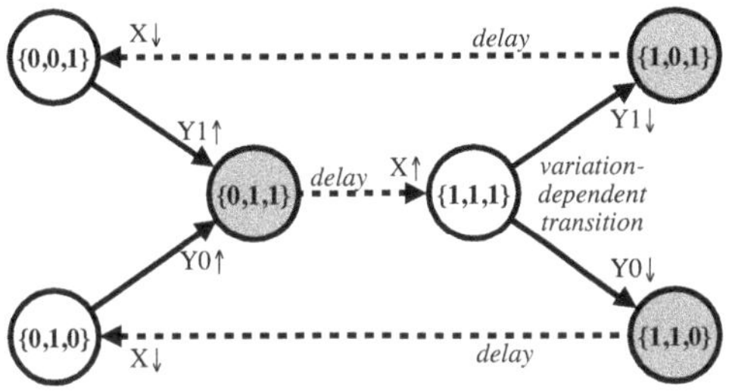

Figure 3: The evolution of SR latch state when embedded in the feedback circuit of Fig. 4a. The three values marking each state are assignments to {X,Y1,Y0}. The states that are shaded grey would be stable states if not for feedback. The unshaded states occur transiently when latch outputs propagate back to change the value of X. The successor state to {1,1,1} is determined by process variation and, to a lesser extent, by noise.

Our design implements feedback around the SR latch to ensure that there are no stable states of the overall PUF circuit during evaluation, and furthermore that there are two possible modes of oscillation. During evaluation, the RUN signal input to the AND3 gate is high, so that X is a logical AND of delayed versions of Y1 and Y0. Because of this logical AND, each stable state {X,Y1,Y0} will lead after a propagation delay to a successor state {X',Y1,Y0}, such that X' = AND(Y1,Y0). These successor states are all unstable and will immediately transition to a stable state and then again propagate back to an unstable state, continuing in this way indefinitely. This constant evolution of state is shown in Fig. 3, where all unstable states are shown as unshaded. The variation-sensitive state transition of the PUF is the choice of stable state that follows unstable state {1,1,1}. The state of the circuit will never settle until RUN is deasserted. If the evolution of circuit state tends to follow the upper loop of Fig. 3, then node Y1, and OSC1 in Fig. 4, will tend to oscillate. If the evolution of circuit state follows the lower loop, then Y0 and OSC0 will oscillate.

3.2 Linear Feedback Shift Register as Counter

To meet strict timing constraints, An LFSR instead of a binary counter is used to count oscillations. In any digital circuit, the delay of the critical path must be less than the clock period, so that the combinational logic will stabilize to its final value before the next clock edge comes. If this condition is not met, then a timing violation is said to occur, and the value that gets stored on the clock edge is unpredictable. In our circuit (Fig. 4a), the clock signal to each counter is in reality an oscillating signal from the PUF. The time between successive rising edges on the LFSR clock input is the oscillation period of PUF node OSC1 or OSC0, and is therefore determined by the time for a signal to propagate twice through an AND3 gate, a NAND2 gate, and two inverters. The oscillation periods of these nodes are shorter than the delay of carry chains in adder circuits, so adders cannot be used to count oscillations without causing timing violations. We resolve this concern by using an LFSR, which has a much shorter critical path delay, for the counter. Because the LFSR critical path delay is shorter than the oscillations of the PUF nodes (Fig. 8), it can be clocked using the oscillating PUF nodes without causing timing violations. An LFSR has previously been used as a round counter in the the KATAN block cipher by DeCanniere et al. [6]; as in our case here, DeCanniere chooses to use an LFSR for its short critical path, small implementation, and low power. An alternative solution to using LFSR counters is to lengthen the PUF oscillation period by increasing the propagation delay of the feedback structure, but this is avoided because it would incur area and power costs.

The size of the LFSR, in number of bits, is a parameter of the PUF that can be chosen at design time. In Fig. 4b we show a 3-bit counter as one particular choice of LFSR size. For any given LFSR size n, a maximum length polynomial must be chosen so that the LFSR will have $2^n - 1$ non-repeating states, and therefore $2^n - 2$ transitions between the initial state and the final state. The implications of LFSR size are discussed in the evaluation sections.

The proposed PUF architecture can be built from an industry gate library, and the synthesized PUF with 3-bit LFSR counters is shown in Fig. 4c. The area is 43 μm^2 in a 45nm technology node. The schematics of Fig. 4 imply that each PUF has two dedicated LFSR counters, and in this case all PUFs can be evaluated in parallel. It is also possible to design the PUF so that LFSR counters are shared across multiple PUF bits; PUF bits that share counters would be evaluated serially. Sharing of counters or other support circuits would reduce area cost but increase latency due to serialization. In this work, we assume the fully parallel solution, where each PUF has its own dedicated LFSR counters. Note that the area overhead of counters is not unique to our design and in fact any majority voting scheme must similarly have counters.

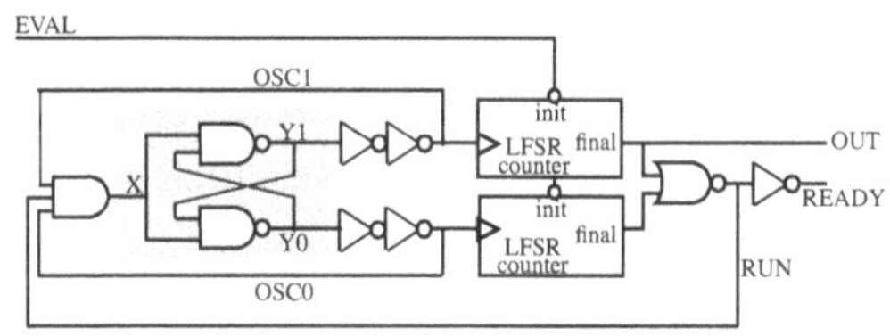

(a) Overall PUF circuit schematic including two LFSR counters

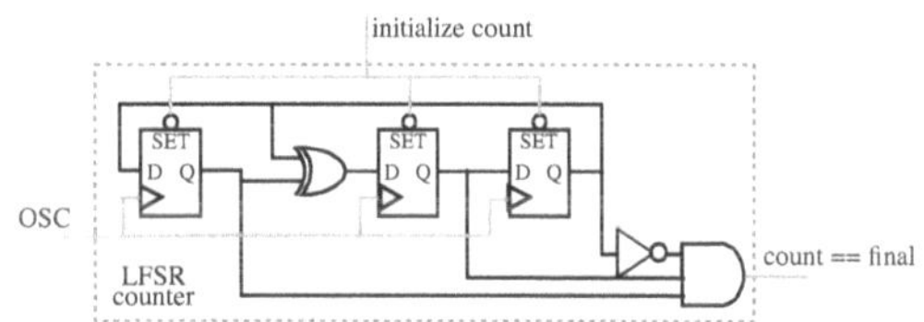

(b) Detailed schematic view of 3-bit LFSR counter

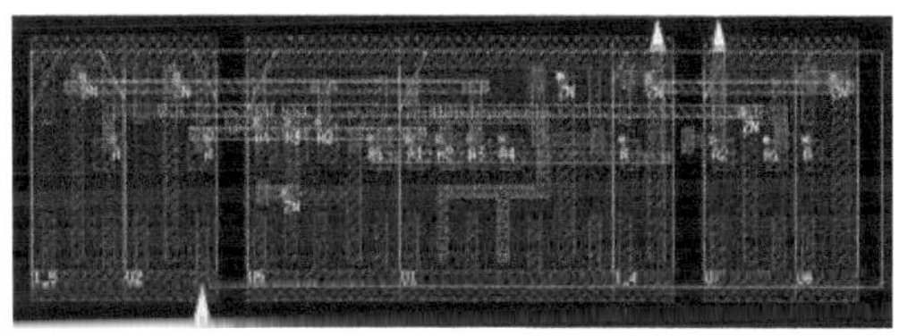

(c) Layout view of PUF with 3-bit LFSR counters (M1-M4 layers shown)

Figure 4: Schematic and layout view of the proposed PUF. The SR latch and feedback circuit together induce an oscillating behavior that favors OSC1 or OSC0. An LFSR advances its state at each rising edge of OSC1 or OSC0 to count the oscillations of that signal. When one LFSR reaches its final count value, RUN is deasserted, and the output is ready to read out.

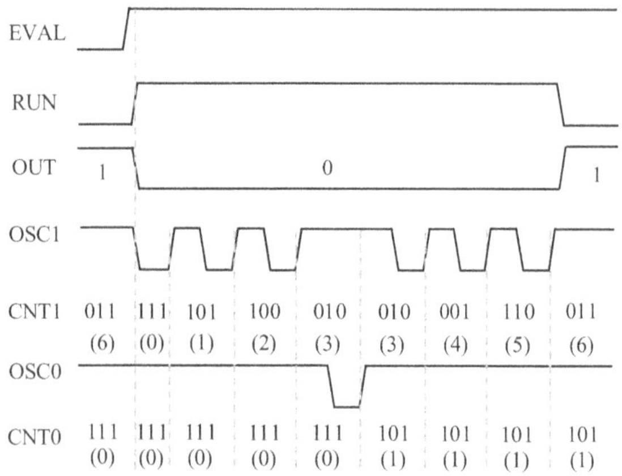

Figure 5: The transient waveforms of a single execution of the proposed PUF. The EVAL signal starts the evaluation by initializing the LFSR counter states (see Fig. 4), and everything thereafter happens autonomously. Once a counter (counter 1 in this case) reaches its sixth and final state, the oscillation is terminated, and the output is ready. In this example the PUF output is 1 because counter 1 reached its final state.

4. EXPERIMENTAL VALIDATION

We evaluate the proposed PUF design by simulating the circuit at different supply voltages and temperatures.

4.1 Simulation Methodology

The results in this paper are obtained from circuit simulation using Synopsys HSPICE, version E-2010.

Transistor Models and Sizing

Transistor and interconnect models are from the freely-available Predictive Technology Model (PTM). More specifically, the transistor models are PTM models for a 45 nm process [5]. The circuit behavior is sensitive to the transistors in the inverters and the NAND2 gates in the SR latch, so the relevant parameters for these transistors are shown in Tab. 1. The mean value μ for each variation-impacted parameter is the nominal value in the transistor model. The standard deviation (σ) of threshold voltage ($vth0$) depends on transistor size, and is calculated from Eq. 1 using a value of 1.8 $mV\ \mu m$ for A_{VT} [16]. The 3σ of transistor length is set to be 10% of the overall transistor length based on existing literature [1], and this is implemented using transistor parameter lint[1] as shown in Tab. 1.

$$\sigma_{VT} = \frac{A_{VT}}{\sqrt{WL}} \qquad (1)$$

		Sizing		Process Variation			
		W [nm]	L [nm]	vth0 [mV] μ	vth0 [mV] σ	lint [nm] μ	lint [nm] σ
NAND2	NMOS	180	50	468	19.0	5	1.7
	PMOS	180	50	-491	19.0	5	1.7
INV	NMOS	90	50	468	26.8	5	1.7
	PMOS	180	50	-491	19.0	5	1.7

Table 1: Transistor sizes and process variation parameters.

[1]lint, standing for internal length, represents the difference between nominal and effective transistor length

Noise

To evaluate the ability of majority voting to mitigate noise, we adopt two noise models in our simulation: flicker noise and channel thermal noise. Flicker noise is a frequency dependent noise caused by charge fluctuation in oxide traps, and results in fluctuations of both mobile carrier numbers and mobilities in the channel. Channel thermal noise reflects voltage fluctuations due to the random motion of electrons. The BSIM4[2] parameters *fnoimod* and *tnoimod* implement flicker and thermal noise respectively;[3] noise is therefore modeled on all transistors in the circuit. The simulation results of Fig. 6 obtained using the described variation and noise models shows the clear separation of between-class and within-class Hamming distances. The large between-class Hamming distance implies high uniqueness, and the relatively small within-class Hamming distance implies high reliability.

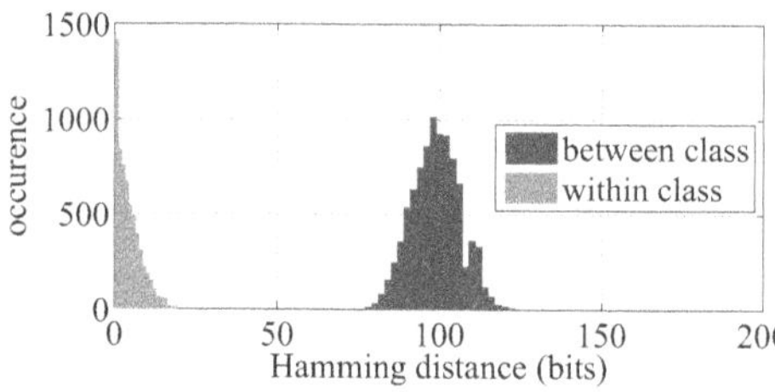

Figure 6: Hamming distances of the proposed PUF with 7-bit LFSR counters. Within-class data points are two outputs from the same PUF, and between class are from different PUFs. In addition to noise, the temperature is assigned randomly from the range of 0°C to 100°C in each trial for this plot.

4.2 Reliability

The reliability of the proposed PUF is evaluated at the nominal supply voltage of 1.1 V, and at voltages of 0.825 V and 0.55 V (Fig. 7). On each plot of Fig. 7, each line shows reliability across temperature of PUFs with a given size LFSR; correctness of the PUF output is determined by comparing each output value against an output from the same PUF at 25°C. Increasing the size of the LFSR improves the reliability of the PUF because it increases the number of majority voting trials that occur internally before an output is produced when one of the LFSR counters reaches its final value.

4.3 Error Correction

Error correcting codes are used to correct PUF output bit errors to produce reliable secret keys (see Sec. 2.3). The number of PUF output bits needed to generate a key is significantly larger than the key size, and this number increases when more errors must be correctable. For example, Guajardo et al. [9] show that reliably generating a 228-bit key requires 6,128 PUF output bits when conservatively assuming a bit-error-rate of 0.16. Our use of majority voting in the proposed PUF reduces bit-error-rate and reduces the number of PUF output bits used to generate a key. There are at least three benefits to reducing the required number

[2]BSIM4 model is based on the industry standard efforts of the Compact Modeling Counsel and the BSIM modeling group at UC Berkeley.

[3]the values assigned to the three parameters comprising *fnoimod* are noia = 6.25e41, noib = 3.125e26, noic = 8.75; the values assigned to the parameters comprising *tnoimod* are ntnoi = 1, tnoia = 1.5e6 and tnoib = 3.5e6

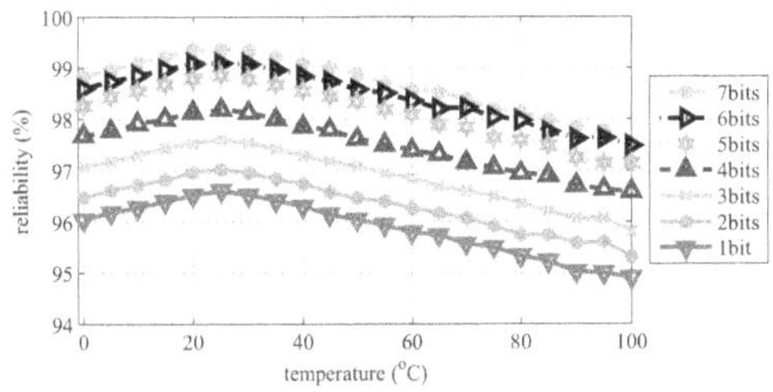

(a) Nominal Vdd of 1.1 V

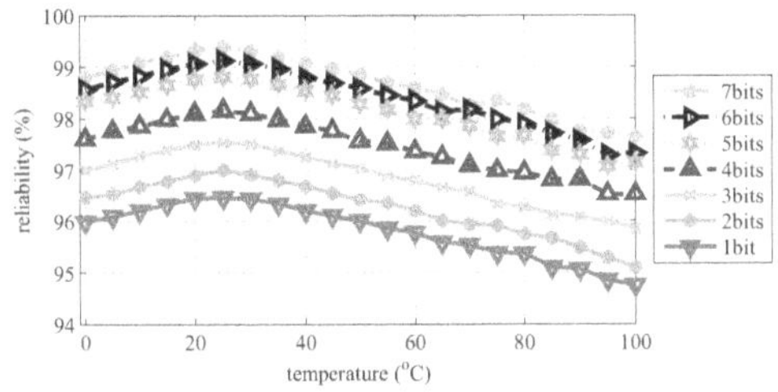

(b) Reduced Vdd of 0.825 V

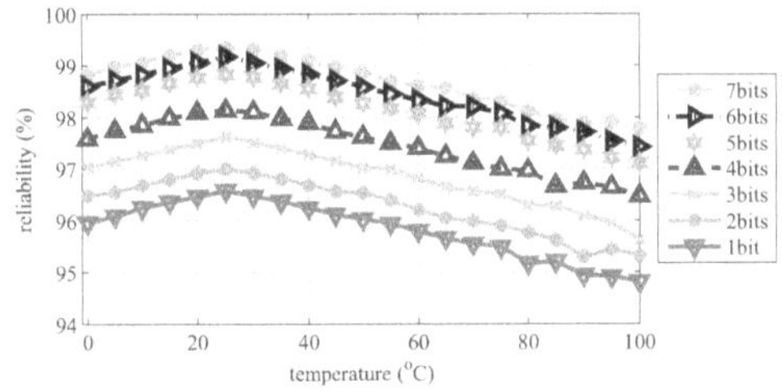

(c) Reduced Vdd of 0.55 V

Figure 7: Reliability evaluation of the proposed PUF across temperatures for various widths of LFSR counter. The results are averaged based on 1,000,000 PUF instances. For the result labeled as a 1-bit counter, no majority voting is performed.

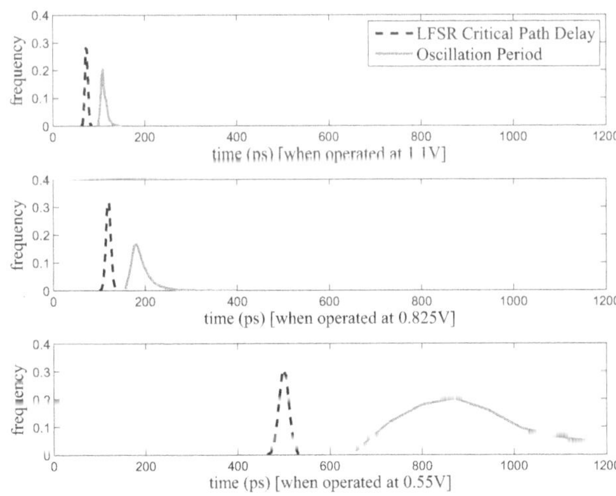

Figure 8: The distribution of LFSR critical path delays and PUF oscillation periods at three different supply voltages. Because LFSR critical path delay is shorter that the oscillation period even with process variation, the LFSR circuit can use the PUF oscillations as a clock without having timing violations.

of PUF output bits: *1*) the area cost of PUF circuitry is proportional to its number of output bits; *2*) the amount of helper data (see Fig. 2) is also proportional to its number of output bits; and *3*) the area and energy cost of the error correction algorithm increases with the number of bits used.

In this section, we quantify how the reliability improvement of the proposed PUF reduces the burden of error correction. We focus on binary BCH codes, which are a set of codes that can be adapted for their block size and for the number of correctable errors in each block. As the number of correctable errors per block increases, the number of useful bits in each block decreases.

For a PUF with bit error rate p_{bit}, we search for the BCH code that uses the minimum number of PUF output bits to generate a 2,048-bit key that will be incorrect fewer than once per billion uses. We find an optimal code for different values of p_{bit} by using exhaustive search of all BCH codes that have block length less than 511 bits. For a BCH code described by parameters b (block size in bits), k (useful key bits per block), and t (correctable errors per block), the following procedure calculates the probability (denoted p_{key}) of producing an incorrect 2,048-bit key. First, the probability (denoted p_{block}) of having an uncorrectable error in a single block is calculated as the probability of having more than t erroneous bits in the block (Eq. 2), under the assumption that bit errors are independent and identically distributed. Then, given that $n_{blocks} = \lceil 2,048/k \rceil$ blocks are needed to generate the entire key, the key error probability p_{key} is calculated as the probability that not all blocks are error-free (Eq. 3). If the p_{key} of a particular BCH code is less than 1E-9, then the BCH code is deemed suitably reliable for correcting a bit error rate of p_{bit}, and will be considered optimal if the number of bits used ($b * n_{blocks}$) is fewest among all BCH codes that satisfy the same condition of p_{key} being less than 1E-9.

$$p_{block} = \sum_{i=t+1}^{b} \binom{b}{i} p_{bit}^{i} (1 - p_{bit})^{b-i} \quad (2)$$

$$p_{key} = 1 - (1 - p_{block})^{n_{blocks}} \quad (3)$$

Based on the analysis described in the preceding paragraph, Table 2 shows the optimal BCH code for the p_{bit} values from different LFSR counter sizes. For each LFSR size, the value of p_{bit} is the bit error rate obtained in the worst-case scenario of 100°C and 0.55 V (see Fig. 7c). The improved reliability that comes from increasing LFSR size has a large impact on the number of PUF bits needed to generate the key.

4.4 Energy

Changing the LFSR counter size trades energy-per-bit against reliability. For an n-bit LFSR, a maximal length polynomial is chosen so that the evaluation will end after one counter has experienced $2^n - 2$ rising transitions on its oscillating input. When considering both counters, the total number of oscillations in the evaluation is between $2^n - 2$ and $2(2^n - 2) - 1$. The energy of a PUF evaluation is roughly linear in the number of oscillations and therefore exponential in LFSR size n (Fig. 9). Once the LFSR becomes sufficiently large, the small reliability gains from additional majority voting trials come at a high energy cost. In addition to changing the LFSR size at design time, another strategy to reduce energy-per-bit is lowering the operating voltage of the PUF. Note that both increasing LFSR size and lowering supply voltage increase the time required to complete each evaluation of the PUF.

Number of LFSR bits	p_{bit}	Optimal BCH code b	k	t	PUF bits required	Percent of bits saved
1	0.0519	255	47	42	11,220	-
2	0.0468	511	103	61	10,220	8.9%
3	0.0437	511	121	58	8,687	22.6%
4	0.0353	511	157	51	7,154	36.2%
5	0.0290	511	184	45	6,132	45.3%
6	0.0257	511	211	41	5,110	54.5%
7	0.0221	511	229	38	4,599	59.0%

Table 2: BCH codes that generate a 2,048-bit key using the minimal number of PUF outputs for different values of p_{bit}. The BCH codes are chosen such that the key will be generated incorrectly less than once per billion uses. The value of p_{bit} in each row corresponds to the observed bit-error-rate at 100°C at 0.55 V supply. Each BCH code block uses b bits to encode k key bits with capability to correct up to t errors.

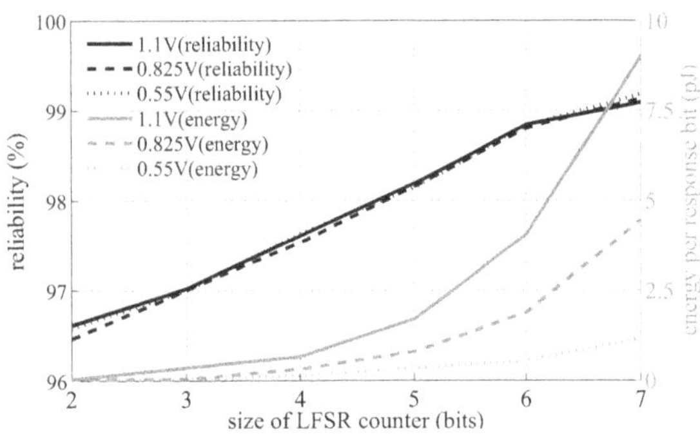

Figure 9: The energy-per-response-bit increases roughly linearly with the number of oscillations, which is exponential in the number of LFSR counter bits. Meanwhile, the reliability increases with the size of the LFSR counter due to the increased number of majority voting trials performed.

5. CONCLUSIONS AND FUTURE WORK

This paper proposes a novel PUF that uses autonomous majority voting without orchestration by a clock. The proposed design is parameterizable by its LFSR counter size, and this allows reliability to be traded off against energy and area. Our experiments show that the improved reliability of the design translates to as much as 59% savings in the number PUF bits needed for key generation when combined with error correcting codes. An interesting direction for future work is to minimize total energy of PUF key generation when using this design together with both dark bit masking and error correction. Future work will also pursue an FPGA implementation to provide silicon measurements of the proposed PUF design.

6. REFERENCES

[1] Anis, M., and Aburahma, M. H. Leakage current variability in nanometer technologies. In *System-on-Chip for Real-Time Applications, 2005. Proceedings. Fifth International Workshop on*, pp. 60–63.

[2] Armknecht, F., Maes, R., Sadeghi, A.-R., Sunar, B., and Tuyls, P. Memory leakage-resilient encryption based on physically unclonable functions. In *Towards Hardware-Intrinsic Security*, A.-R. Sadeghi and D. Naccache, Eds., Information Security and Cryptography. Springer Berlin Heidelberg, 2010, pp. 135–164.

[3] Bhargava, M., Cakir, C., and Mai, K. Reliability enhancement of bi-stable PUFs in 65nm bulk CMOS. *Hardware-Oriented Security and Trust, 2012 IEEE International Symposium on*, 25–30.

[4] Bhargava, M., Cakir, C., and Mai, K. Attack Resistant Sense Amplifier Based PUFs (SA-PUF) with Deterministic and Controllable Reliability of PUF Responses. *Hardware-Oriented Security and Trust, IEEE International Symposium on* (2010).

[5] Cao, Y., Sato, T., Sylvester, D., Orshansky, M., and Hu, C. Predictive technology model. *Internet: http://ptm.asu.edu* (2002).

[6] De Canniere, C., Dunkelman, O., and Knežević, M. Katan and ktantan:a family of small and efficient hardware-oriented block ciphers. In *Cryptographic Hardware and Embedded Systems-CHES*. Springer, 2009, pp. 272–288.

[7] Dodis, Y., Ostrovsky, R., Reyzin, L., and Smith, A. Fuzzy extractors: How to generate strong keys from biometrics and other noisy data. *SIAM journal on computing 38*, 1 (2008), 97–139.

[8] Gassend, B., Clarke, D., and Van Dijk, M. Silicon physical random functions. In *Proceedings of the IEEE Computer and Communications Society* (2002).

[9] Guajardo, J., Kumar, S. S., Schrijen, G.-J., and Tuyls, P. Physical unclonable functions and public-key crypto for fpga ip protection. In *Field Programmable Logic and Applications*. (2007), pp. 189–195.

[10] Holcomb, D. E., Burleson, W. P., and Fu, K. Power-up SRAM state as an identifying fingerprint and source of true random numbers. *IEEE Transactions on Computers* (2009).

[11] Holcomb, D. E., Rahmati, A., Salajegheh, M., Burleson, W. P., and Fu, K. DRV-Fingerprinting: using data retention voltage of SRAM cells for chip identification. In *RFIDSec'12: Proceedings of the 8th international conference on Radio Frequency Identification: security and privacy issues* (July 2012), Springer-Verlag.

[12] Juels, A., and Wattenberg, M. A fuzzy commitment scheme. In *Proceedings of the 6th ACM conference on Computer and communications security* (1999), pp. 28–36.

[13] Kumar, S. S., Guajardo, J., Maes, R., Schrijen, G. J., and Tuyls, P. The butterfly PUF protecting IP on every FPGA. *Hardware-Oriented Security and Trust.* (2008).

[14] Maes, R., Tuyls, P., and Verbauwhede, I. Intrinsic PUFs from flip-flops on reconfigurable devices. In *3rd Benelux workshop on information and system security (WISSec 2008)* (2008), vol. 17.

[15] Mathew, S. K., Satpathy, S. K., Anders, M. A., Kaul, H., Hsu, S. K., Agarwal, A., Chen, G. K., Parker, R. J., Krishnamurthy, R. K., and De, V. A 0.19pJ/b PVT-variation-tolerant hybrid physically unclonable function circuit for 100% stable secure key generation in 22nm CMOS. In *Solid-State Circuits Conference (ISSCC), 2014 IEEE International* (2014), pp. 278–279.

[16] Qazi, M., Tikekar, M., Dolecek, L., Shah, D., and Chandrakasan, A. Loop flattening & spherical sampling: highly efficient model reduction techniques for SRAM yield analysis. In *DATE '10: Proceedings of the Conference on Design, Automation and Test in Europe* (Mar. 2010).

[17] Satpathy, S., Mathew, S., Li, J., Koeberl, P., Anders, M., Kaul, H., Chen, G., Agarwal, A., Hsu, S., and Krishnamurthy, R. 13fj/bit probing-resilient 250k PUF array with soft darkbit masking for 1.94% bit-error in 22nm tri-gate CMOS. In *European Solid State Circuits Conference (ESSCIRC)* (2014), IEEE, pp. 239–242.

[18] Su, Y., Holleman, J., and Otis, B. A digital 1.6 pj/bit chip identification circuit using process variations. *IEEE Journal of Solid-State Circuits 43*, 1 (Jan. 2008), 69 –77.

[19] Xu, X., Rahmati, A., Holcomb, D. E., Fu, K., and Burleson, W. Reliable physical unclonable functions using data retention voltage of sram cells. *Computer-Aided Design of Integrated Circuits and Systems, IEEE Transactions on 34*, 6 (2015), 903–914.

[20] Yamamoto, D., Sakiyama, K., Iwamoto, M., Ohta, K., Ochiai, T., Takenaka, M., and Itoh, K. Uniqueness enhancement of PUF responses based on the locations of random outputting RS latches. In *Cryptographic Hardware and Embedded Systems-CHES 2011*. Springer, 2011, pp. 390–406.

Area-Efficient Error-Resilient Discrete Fourier Transformation Design using Stochastic Computing

Bo Yuan
City University of New York, City College
160 Convent Avenue, New York, NY 10031
byuan@ccny.cuny.edu

Yanzhi Wang
Syracuse University
900 South Crouse Ave, Syracuse, NY 13244
ywang393@syr.edu

Zhongfeng Wang
Nanjing University
22 Hankou Rd, Nanjing, China
zfwang@nju.edu.cn

ABSTRACT
Discrete Fourier Transformation (DFT)/Fast Fourier Transformation (FFT) are the widely used techniques in numerous modern signal processing applications. In general, because of their inherent multiplication-intensive characteristics, the hardware implementations of DFT/FFT usually require a large amount of hardware resource, which limits their applications in area-constraint scenarios. To overcome this challenge, this paper, for the first time, proposes area-efficient error-resilient DFT designs using stochastic computing. By leveraging low-complexity stochastic multipliers, two types of stochastic DFT design are presented with significant reduction in overall area. Analysis results show that compared with the conventional design, the proposed two 256-point stochastic DFT designs achieve 76% and 62% reduction in area, respectively. More importantly, these stochastic DFT designs also show much stronger error-resilience, which is very attractive in nanoscale CMOS era.

General Terms
Algorithms, Design

Keywords
DFT; FFT; Stochastic Computing; Error Resilience; VLSI

1. INTRODUCTION
Discrete Fourier Transformation (DFT) is one of the most important Fourier-related transformations in the digital signal processing and image processing fields, such as filter bank, data compression, to name a few. In practical systems, N-point DFT is usually performed with the Fast Fourier Transformation (FFT) algorithm, which enables significant reduction in computing complexity from $O(N^2)$ to $O(N\log N)$. However, from the perspective of hardware design, the computation-intensive FFT is still a resource-hungry block since an N-point FFT requires $0.5N\log N$ complex multiplications and $N\log N$ complex additions, which cause very high hardware resource consumption in large N cases. As a result, low-complexity FFT design is an important research topic for hardware implementation of signal processing systems, especially for resource-constraint wireless communication.

To date, many prior efforts have been made to develop area-efficient DFT/FFT. Various techniques, such as folding and resource sharing [1] were reported to alleviate the high-complexity problem of DFT/FFT design [2-4]. However, all of the existing works are based on the conventional 2's complement computing (referred as *binary computing*). Deviated from the binary computing that uses weight binary representation, the *stochastic computing* (SC) [5-6] utilizes a stream of bits to interpret the number. Here the portion of bit "1" over the entire stream represents the value of the number. Built on this type of redundant representation, the corresponding arithmetic units of stochastic computing is very simple. For instance, the multiplication can be performed using a single AND or XNOR gate in the stochastic computing scenario. Based on its encouraging simplicity, stochastic computing is expected to be a good candidate to address the high-complexity problem of DFT/FFT design.

This paper, *for the first time*, proposes area-efficient error-resilient DFT design using stochastic computing (SC). By leveraging low-complexity stochastic multipliers, two types of stochastic DFT design are presented with significant reduction in overall area. Analysis results show that compared with the conventional design, the proposed two 256-point stochastic DFT designs achieve 76% and 62% reduction in area, respectively. More importantly, these stochastic DFT designs also show much stronger error-resilience, which is very attractive in nanoscale CMOS era.

The rest of this paper is organized as below. Section 2 gives a brief review on DFT/FFT and stochastic computing. The proposed two stochastic DFT designs are presented in Section 3. Section 4 analyzes and discusses the error-resilient capability and hardware performance of the proposed stochastic designs. Conclusions are drawn in Section 5.

2. REVIEW OF DFT/FFT AND SC
2.1 DFT and FFT
In signal processing theory [7], DFT is a fundamental and powerful technique to perform time-to-frequency domain transformation for discrete signal. In general, an N-point DFT can be described in (1). Here $x[n]$ is the input discrete signal in the time domain and $X[k]$ is the output signal in the frequency domain. For details of DFT, the reader is referred to [7].

$$X[k] = \sum_{n=0}^{N-1} x[n]W_N^{kn}, \text{ where } W_N = e^{-j\frac{2\pi}{N}}. \quad (1)$$

A straightforward definition based computation of DFT is very inefficient since a large amount of complex multiplication and addition are required. Therefore, FFT, as a fast version of DFT, is usually adopted in the practical applications. Fig. 1 shows the architecture of a butterfly-style radix-2 8-point FFT. Here it can be seen that the total number of required multiplication and addition is significantly reduced. In general, by fully leveraging the symmetric characteristics of DFT, the overall computing complexity for an N-point FFT is reduced from $O(N^2)$ to $O(N\log N)$.

GLSVLSI '16, May 18-20, 2016, Boston, MA, USA
© 2016 ACM. ISBN 978-1-4503-4274-2/16/05…$15.00
DOI: http://dx.doi.org/10.1145/2902961.2902978

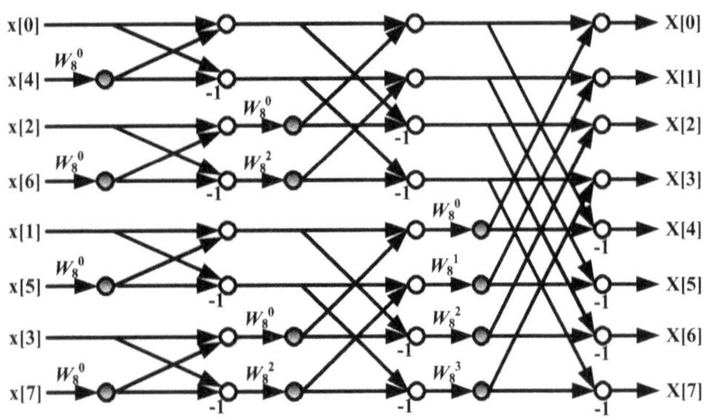

Fig. 1. Butterfly-style architecture of example 8-point FFT.

2.2 Stochastic Computing

As indicated in Section 1, stochastic computing (SC) utilizes bit-stream for number representation, where value of number is encoded via the probability of bit "1" over the stream. In general, an SC system can be either built on either unipolar form or bipolar form [5-6]. Here unipolar form only works for positive-number-only applications while bipolar form is suitable for processing both positive and negative numbers. Considering the targeted DFT/FFT applications are involved with negative number, this paper adopts the bipolar form as the underlying SC representation. Fig. 2(a) illustrates three different bipolar-based representation of -0.2 with length-10 bit-streams.

Fig. 2(b)(c)(e)(g) shows the stochastic circuits for some basic arithmetic functions, including multiplication, scaled addition, scaled subtraction and linear gain. In addition, Fig. 2(d) and Fig. 2(f) show the architecture of interface blocks between stochastic computing and binary computing domains, respectively. For the details of these basic SC circuits, the reader is referred to [5-6].

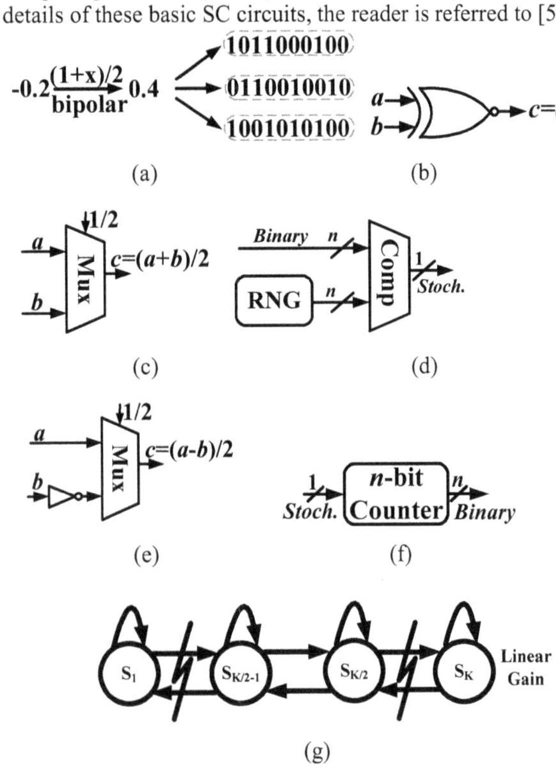

Fig. 2. Bipolar SC system: (a) Representation (b) Multiplication (c) Scaled addition (d) Binary to stochastic (B-to-S) block (e) Scaled subtraction (f) Stochastic to binary (S-to-B) block (g) Linear gain. Cited from [8].

3. Stochastic DFT Design

Fig. 1 and Fig. 2 in Section 2 describe the detailed architecture of FFT and fundamental arithmetic SC blocks, respectively. Intuitively, a stochastic FFT design can be developed by applying those basic blocks in Fig. 2 into Fig. 1. However, as to be discussed in Section 3.1, such straightforward design is inferior in computing accuracy, especially for large-scale case. To overcome this challenge, in Section 3.2 two new stochastic DFT designs are proposed to achieve high performance in both accuracy and hardware.

3.1 Straightforward FFT Design

As mentioned in the above paragraph, a stochastic FFT design can be developed by replacing the basic 2's complement arithmetic (addition, subtraction and multiplication) block in Fig. 1 with their stochastic counterparts. In particular, because those operations in Fig. 1 are performed in complex domain, the corresponding stochastic circuits for complex operations should be developed first. Recall that for two complex inputs $a = \mathbf{Re}(a) + j*\mathbf{Im}(a)$ and $b = \mathbf{Re}(b) + j*\mathbf{Im}(b)$, their complex multiplication and addition can be calculated as $out = (\mathbf{Re}(a)\mathbf{Re}(b) - \mathbf{Im}(a)\mathbf{Im}(b)) + j*(\mathbf{Re}(a)\mathbf{Im}(b) + \mathbf{Re}(b)\mathbf{Im}(a))$ and $\text{out} = ((\mathbf{Re}(a)+\mathbf{Re}(b)) + j*(\mathbf{Im}(a)+\mathbf{Im}(b))$, respectively. Therefore, the stochastic multiplication and additions can be constructed as shown in Fig. 3. It should be noted that here the output is scaled by 1/2 due to the inherent scaling characteristic of stochastic addition (see Fig. 2).

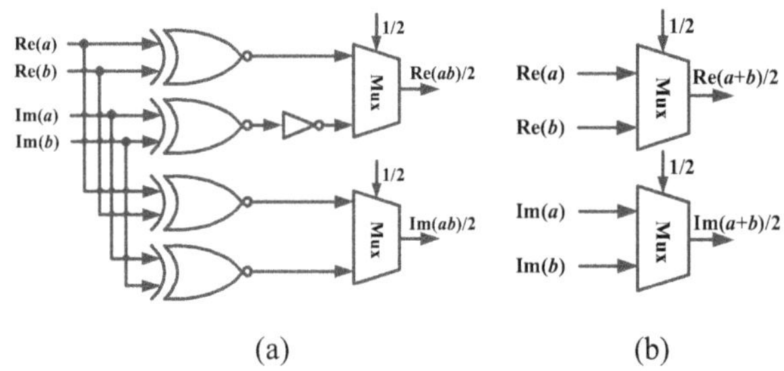

Fig. 3. Stochastic circuit for (a) complex multiplication (b) complex addition.

With the use of those basic blocks in Fig. 3, a stochastic FFT can be simply developed based on the traditional butterfly-style architecture in Fig. 1. However, such straightforward design suffers from high accuracy loss incurred by the multi-stage scaling operation. For instance, for a medium size N such as 64, the stochastic FFT design needs 6 stages of butterfly units that includes multiplication and addition, which corresponds to 6*2=12 times of scaling by 1/2. As a result, the actual output is downscaled by $(1/2)^{12}$. Consider the limited precision of SC systems, such aggressive downscaling will cause very high accuracy loss.

To address this challenge, two potential approaches can be applied to this scenario. The first one is to use the stochastic linear gain (LG) block to compensate the scaling effect at each stage of FFT (see Fig. 4(a)). The second one is to perform a one-time compensation at the output end of the last stage of FFT (see Fig. 4(b)). However, although these two approaches may alleviate the accuracy loss by the scaling, the accuracy loss for stochastic FFT is still high due to the inherent approximation of stochastic computing. In particular, for N-point stochastic FFT this drawback is very significant due to the inaccuracy propagation through the $2m$ levels of stochastic multiplications and additions, where

$m=\log_2 N$. Even worse, this type of accuracy loss cannot be compensated like Fig. 4 since it comes from the inherent property of stochastic computing and the multi-stage architecture of FFT. Fig. 5 shows the signal-to-noise ratio (SNR) for N-point stochastic FFT with 1024-length bit-stream. It is seen that the computing accuracy of stochastic FFT quickly decreases when N increases. In particular, even with a medium-size N=32 the accuracy loss of stochastic FFT is already very high (SNR<-50). Therefore, the straightforward design of stochastic FFT is not suitable for the practical applications that require medium or large size N.

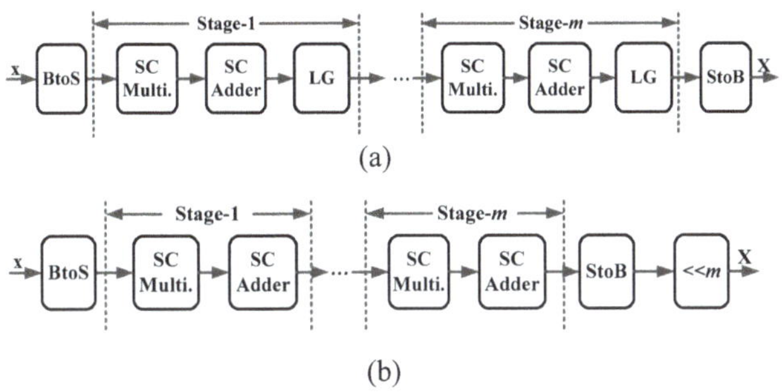

Fig. 4. (a) Compensation at each stage (b) One-time compensation.

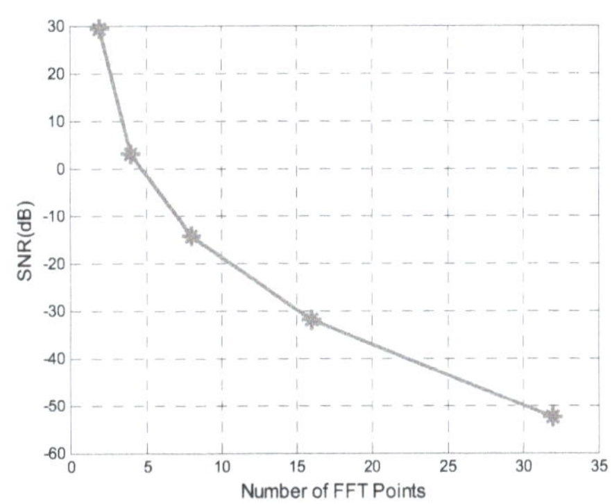

Fig. 5. SNR performance of stochastic FFT.

3.2 Dot-product-based Design

Section 3.1 shows that the multiple stages ($2N$) of stochastic multiplier and additions cause low computing accuracy for stochastic FFT. To address this challenge, the underlying architecture should be reformulated to reduce the number of stages of data-path, thereby mitigating the error propagation problem. However, since the computation procedure of FFT is inherently propagated in a multi-stage way, any FFT-based stochastic design always causes severe inaccuracy propagation. Therefore, in order to devise a high-accuracy stochastic design for DFT-embedded applications, the original definition of DFT should be revisited.

Recall that the inherent procedure of DFT is actually a vector-matrix multiplication which can be written as $\mathbf{X}=\mathbf{W}\mathbf{x}$, where $\mathbf{X}=[X[0], X[1],\dots, X[N-1]]^T$, $\mathbf{x}=[x[0], x[1],\dots, x[N-1]]^T$ and $\mathbf{W}$ is the transfer matrix as below:

$$\mathbf{W}=\begin{bmatrix} 1 & 1 & 1 & 1 & \cdots & 1 \\ 1 & \omega & \omega^2 & \omega^3 & \cdots & \omega^{N-1} \\ 1 & \omega^2 & \omega^4 & \omega^6 & \cdots & \omega^{2(N-1)} \\ 1 & \omega^3 & \omega^6 & \omega^9 & \cdots & \omega^{3(N-1)} \\ \vdots & \vdots & \vdots & \vdots & \ddots & \vdots \\ 1 & \omega^{N-1} & \omega^{2(N-1)} & \omega^{3(N-1)} & \cdots & \omega^{(N-1)(N-1)} \end{bmatrix}.$$

Accordingly, if we denote the j-th column of $\mathbf{W}$ as $\mathbf{Col}(j)=[1, \omega^j, \omega^{2j}, \dots\omega^{(N-1)j}]^T$, then $X[j] = \mathbf{Col}(j)\bullet\mathbf{x}$, which is just a dot-product of a constant vector $\mathbf{Col}(j)$ and an variable vector $\mathbf{x}$. This phenomenon inspires us to develop dot-product-based stochastic DFT design that requires much shorter data-path than butterfly-based stochastic FFT design since all the multiplications can now be performed in parallel. In the next two subsections, two types of stochastic DFT designs are discussed and presented.

3.2.1 Uneven-multiplexer-based Stochastic DFT

In [9], an uneven-weighted size-2 stochastic dot-product was introduced. Compared to the straightforward design of stochastic dot-product, the downscaling effect in this uneven-weighted design was mitigated. Fig. 6(a) shows its corresponding architecture, where the selection signal of the multiplexer is no longer 1/2 but configured unevenly according to the information of constant vector. As a result, the scaling coefficient of the output signal is $1/(|b_0|+|b_1|)$ instead of 1/2.

In this subsection we extend the original size-2 stochastic dot product to the general size-N case, and then apply it to the stochastic DFT design. Fig. 6(b) shows the architecture of the size-N uneven-multiplexer-based stochastic dot-product (DP) block. Its functional validity can be proved as below:

Proposition: With the input of variable vector $\mathbf{a}=[a_0, \dots, a_{N-1}]$ and constant vector $\mathbf{b}=[b_0, \dots, b_{N-1}]$, the architecture shown in Fig. 6(b) can generate output as $\frac{a_0b_0+\cdots+a_{N-1}b_{N-1}}{|b_0|+\cdots+|b_{N-1}|}$.

Proof: Consider the hierarchical architecture of Fig. 6(b), a mathematical induction can be used as below:

When $N=2^1$, because basic dot-product (DP) in Fig. 6(b) is just the dot-product block in Fig, 6(a). Therefore, in this case Fig. 6(b) is simplified to Fig. 6(a), which is consistent with conclusion of the proposition.

When $N=2^k$, the output of two k-stage is $in_1=\frac{a_0b_0+\cdots+a_{N-1}b_{N-1}}{|b_0|+\cdots+|b_{N-1}|}$ and $in_2=\frac{a_Nb_N+\cdots+a_{2N-1}b_{2N-1}}{|b_N|+\cdots+|b_{2N-1}|}$, respectively.

In addition, the selection signal for the $(k+1)$-stage of multiplexer is $sel=\frac{|b_0|+\cdots+|b_{2N/2-1}|}{|b_0|+\cdots+|b_{2N-1}|}=\frac{|b_0|+\cdots+|b_{N-1}|}{|b_0|+\cdots+|b_{2N-1}|}$.

As a result, the output of the $(k+1)$-stage of multiplexer is:

$$Out = sel * in_1 + (1-sel) * in_2$$

$$=\frac{|b_0|+\cdots+|b_{N-1}|}{|b_0|+\cdots+|b_{2N-1}|}\frac{a_0b_0+\cdots+a_{N-1}b_{N-1}}{|b_0|+\cdots+|b_{N-1}|}$$

$$+(1-\frac{|b_0|+\cdots+|b_{N-1}|}{|b_0|+\cdots+|b_{2N-1}|})\frac{a_Nb_N+\cdots+a_{2N-1}b_{2N-1}}{|b_N|+\cdots+|b_{2N-1}|}$$

$$=\frac{a_0b_0+\cdots+a_{2N-1}b_{2N-1}}{|b_0|+\cdots+|b_{2N-1}|},$$

which is also consistent with the conclusion of the proposition.

Based on the general size-N stochastic dot-product (SDP) block in Fig. 6(b), the overall stochastic DFT can now be developed. Fig. 6(c) shows the architecture of one processing element (PE) of the proposed stochastic DFT. Here its function is to calculate the real and imaginary part of scaled $X[j]$. In general, an N-point stochastic DFT has N copies of PEs that enable parallel output of $X[j]$.

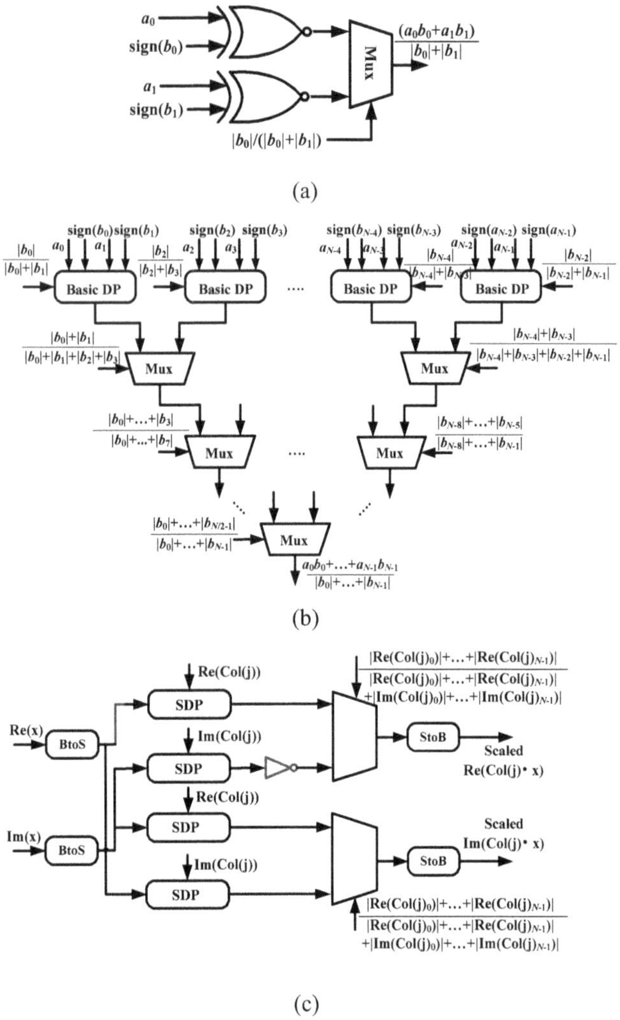

Fig. 6. Architecture for (a) Uneven-multiplexer-based size-2 dot-product (b) Uneven-multiplexer-based size-N dot-product (c) PE of stochastic DFT.

Fig. 7 shows the SNR performance of the proposed size-N uneven-multiplexer-based stochastic DFT design with different values of N. As compared to the straightforward stochastic FFT in Fig. 5, it is seen that the proposed stochastic DFT design has much higher computing accuracy, especially in the medium-size N range. In general, this improvement on accuracy comes from two sources. First, the non-2 scaling coefficient leads to less accuracy loss during the scaling procedure. Second, the total number of stages of stochastic units is reduced from $2N$ to N, which efficiently avoids severe error propagation.

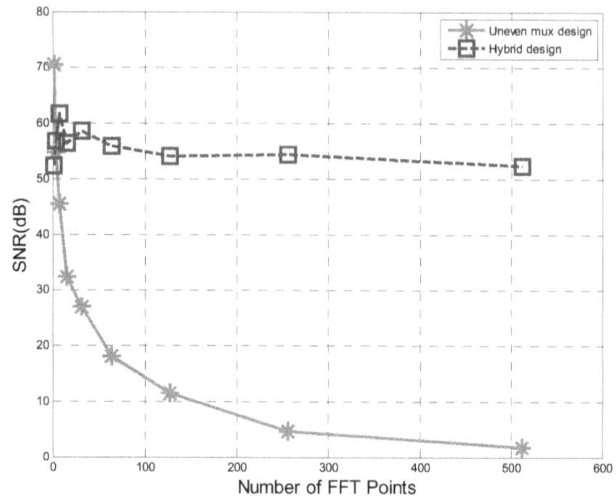

Fig. 7. SNR performance of two types of stochastic DFT.

3.2.2 *Hybrid Stochastic DFT*

A potential problem of the above uneven-multiplexer-based stochastic DFT is its relatively inferior SNR performance in large-scale N region. This because the error propagation through the N stages of stochastic multiplexers will become non-negligible when N becomes large. To address this challenge, a hybrid stochastic DFT design is proposed in this subsection.

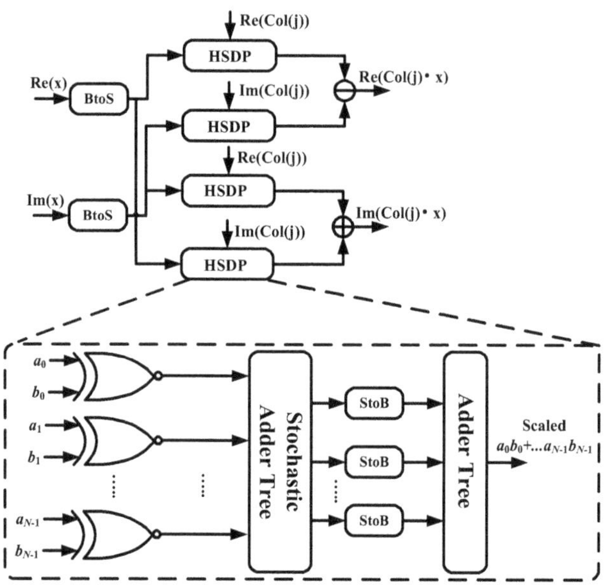

Fig. 8. PE of hybrid stochastic DFT.

The architecture of the PE of the hybrid stochastic and its component hybrid stochastic dot-product (HSDP) block are shown in Fig. 8. As seen in the Fig. 8, the multiplication is performed by stochastic multiplier (XNOR gate) and partial stochastic adder (Multiplexer) tree, and then the processed data is converted back to the 2's complement form for further addition operation. The goal of this allocation of stochastic and conventional blocks is to mitigate the accuracy loss incurred by the original multiple stages of stochastic addition in large N case. In general, built on this hybrid PE, the overall hybrid stochastic DFT can achieve very low computing inaccuracy. Fig. 7 shows the SNR performance of this hybrid stochastic DFT design with different values of N. From this figure it can be seen that the proposed hybrid design has very high SNR performance over the entire range, especially for large N region. As a result, this type of architecture is very suitable for the DFT in large-scale applications.

It should be noted that the proposed hybrid stochastic DFT contains N copies of PE in Fig. 8. In order to achieve low hardware complexity, all the stochastic components (XNOR gates) are fully parallel but the 2's complement components (adder) are shared by the PEs. This source sharing technique will not cause significant increase in latency for this stochastic computing scenario.

4. PERFORMANCE ANALYSIS

4.1 Error-resilient Performance

One of the attractive advantages of stochastic computing is their strong tolerance for errors, especially for soft errors (bit-flipping). Fig. 9 shows the error-resilient capability of the proposed two types of stochastic DFT with different N. Here the RBF is referred as ratio of bit flips, which corresponds to the flipping probability of each bit in the entire system.

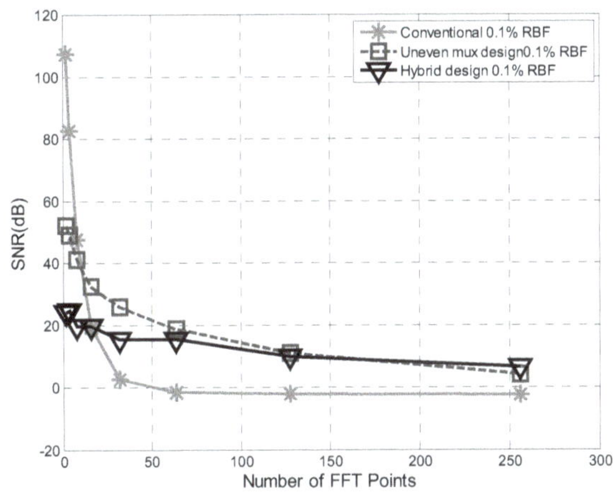

(a)

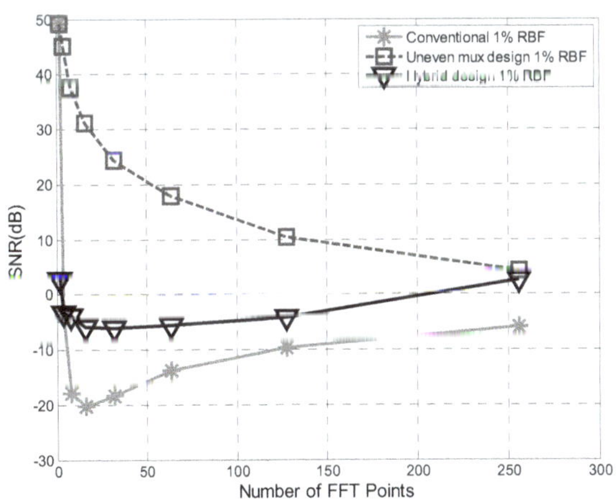

(b)

Fig. 9. SNR performance of DFT/FFT with different RBFs: (a) 0.1% RBF (b) 1% RBF.

From this figure it can be seen that, except very small N (=2 or 4) cases that are not used in practical applications, the SNR of the proposed two stochastic designs always achieve at least 10dB gain over their conventional 2's complement counterpart. This phenomenon indicates that in an environment where noise is at a medium (RBF=0.1%) or very high (RBF=1%) level, the proposed two stochastic designs are able to tolerance more errors and generate much more accurate results than the conventional FFT design.

It should be noted that at the right subfigure of Fig. 9, the SNR curves for conventional design and hybrid stochastic design show non-monotonicity as N increases. Interestingly, this behavior does not appear in left figure where RBF is relatively lower. A potential explanation for this phenomenon is that when RBF is high, the inaccuracy caused by the higher probability of bit flips may compensate the approximation effect of the stochastic computing system, and hence improve the overall computing accuracy. A detailed exploration and potential utilization of this phenomenon will be conducted in the future work.

4.2 Hardware Performance

Table 1 shows the estimated hardware performance of the proposed stochastic DFT designs. Here N is set as 256 and the length of bit-stream is 1024, which corresponds to 10-bit precision for conventional 2's complement design.

From the table it can be seen that the proposed stochastic DFT designs consumes much less hardware resource as compared to the conventional FFT design. For the same N=256 case, the proposed two designs can achieve 76% and 62% reduction in gate counts, respectively. The difference of gate counts in the proposed two designs comes from their different overall architecture. In general, the one with more gate counts has better computing accuracy but weaker error resilience. As a result, the system designers can choose appropriate architectures according to different requirements of practical applications in terms of area and fault-tolerance.

Table 1. Estimated Hardware Performance for 256-point DFT/FFT

Design	Uneven Mux-based	Hybrid	Conventional
DFT/FFT	DFT	DFT	FFT
Computing Style	Stochastic	Stochastic	2's complement
CMOS Technology	90nm		
Clock Frequency	600MHz		
Pipeline Strategy	Non pipeline	1-stage	Multi-stage
Gate Counts	196K	316K	830K

5. Conclusion

This paper presents two types of stochastic DFT design. With the use of stochastic circuits the proposed designs achieve significant reduction in area. In addition, the stochastic designs also achieve much stronger error-resilience as compared to the conventional design.

6. REFERENCES

[1] K. K. Parhi, VLSI Digital Signal Processing Systems: Design and Implementation, New York, NY: John Wiley & Sons Inc., 1999.

[2] M. Ayinala and K.K. Parhi, "FFT Architectures for Real-valued Signals based on Radix-2^3 and Radix-2^4 algorithms," *IEEE Trans. Circuits and Systems-I*: Regular Papers, 60(9), pp. 2422-2430, Sept. 2013

[3] M. Ayinala, M.J. Brown and K.K. Parhi, "Pipelined Parallel FFT Architectures via Folding Transformation," *IEEE Trans. VLSI Systems* , pp. 1068-1081, 20(6), June 2012

[4] C. Cheng and K.K. Parhi, "Hardware Efficient Fast Computation of the Discrete Fourier Transform," *Springer Journal of VLSI Signal Processing*, pp. 159-171, 42(2), Feb. 2006

[5] B. Gaines, "Stochastic computing systems," *Advances in Information Systems Science*, vol. 2, no. 2, pp. 37–172, 1969.

[6] B. Brown and H. Card, "Stochastic neural computation I: computational elements," *IEEE Trans. Comput.*, vol. 50, no. 9, pp. 891-905, Sept. 2001.

[7] Oppenheim, A. V. and Schafer, R. W. Discrete-Time Signal Processing. Prentice-Hall, Englewood Cliffs, NJ, 1989.

[8] B. Yuan, C. Zhang and Z. Wang, "Design space exploration for Hardware-efficient stochastic computing: A case study on discrete cosine transformation," accepted by *IEEE Intl. Conf. on Acoustics, Speech and Signal Processing (ICASSP) 2016*

[9] Y-N. Chang and K. K. Parhi, "Architectures for digital filters using stochastic computing," in *Proc. of 2013 IEEE International Conference on Acoustics, Speech and Signal Processing (ICASSP)*,pp. 2697-2701, 2013.

[10] A. Alaghi, Cheng Li and John P. Hayes. "Stochastic circuits for real-time image processing applications," in *Proc. of Design Automation Conference (DAC)*, pp. 1-6, 2013.

[11] A. Alaghi and J. P. Hayes, "Fast and accurate computation using stochastic circuits," in *Proc. of Design, Automation and Test Conference in Europe (DATE)*, pp. 1-4, 2014.

[12] P. Li, D. J. Lilja, W. Qian, and K. Bazargan, "Computation on stochastic bit streams: Digital image processing case studies," *IEEE Trans. on Very Large Scale Integrated (VLSI) Systems*, vol. 22, no. 3, pp. 449-462, April 2013.

[13] W. Qian, X. Li, Marc D. Riedel, K. Bazargan, and D. J. Lilja, "An architecture for fault-tolerant computation with stochastic logic," *IEEE Trans. on Computers*, vol. 60, no. 1, pp. 93-105, 2011.

[14] S. Sharifi Tehrani, W. Gross and S. Mannor, "Stochastic decoding of LDPC codes," *IEEE Commun. Lett.*, vol. 10, no. 10, pp. 716–718, Oct. 2006.

[15] S. Sharifi Tehrani, S. Mannor, and W. J. Gross, "Fully parallel stochastic LDPC decoders," *IEEE Trans. on Signal Processing*, vol. 56, no. 11, pp. 5692–5703, Nov.2008.

[16] T-H. Chen and J.P. Hayes, "Design of Stochastic Viterbi Decoders for Convolutional Codes," in *Proc. of IEEE Intl. Design and Diagnostics of Electronic Circuits. & Systems. (DDECS)*, pp. 66-71, April 2013.

[17] X-R Lee, C-L Chen, H-C Chang and C-Y Lee, "Stochastic decoding for LDPC convolutional codes," in *Proc. IEEE Int. Symp. Circuits Syst.(ISCAS)*, pp. 2621-2624, May 2012.

[18] A. Naderi, S. Mannor, M. Sawan and W. J. Gross, "Delayed stochastic decoding of LDPC Codes," *IEEE Trans.on Signal Processing*, vol. 59, no. 11, pp. 5617-5626, Nov. 2011.

[19] X. –R. Lee, C. –L. Chen, H. –C. Chang and C. –Y. Lee, "A 7.92 Gb/s 437.2 mW stochastic LDPC decoder chip for IEEE 802.15.3C applications," *IEEE Trans. Circuits and Systems-I: Regular Papers*, vol. 62, no. 2, Feb. 2015.

[20] B. Yuan and K.K. Parhi, "Successive Cancellation Decoding of Polar Codes Using Stochastic Computing," in *Proc. of 2015 IEEE International Symposium on Circuits and Systems (ISCAS)*, May 2015.

Concurrent Error Detection for Reliable SHA-3 Design

Pei Luo*, Cheng Li†, and Yunsi Fei*
* Electrical & Computer Engineering Department, Northeastern University, Boston, MA 02115 USA
† Electrical & Computer Engineering Department, University of Rochester, Rochester, NY 14627 USA
silenceluo@coe.neu.edu, lich.univ@gmail.com, yfei@ece.neu.edu

ABSTRACT

Cryptographic systems are vulnerable to random errors and injected faults. Soft errors can inadvertently happen in critical cryptographic modules and attackers can inject faults into systems to retrieve the embedded secret. Different schemes have been developed to improve the security and reliability of cryptographic systems. As the new SHA-3 standard, Keccak algorithm will be widely used in various cryptographic applications, and its implementation should be protected against random errors and injected faults. In this paper, we devise different parity checking methods to protect the operations of Keccak. Results show that our schemes can be easily implemented and can effectively protect Keccak system against random errors and fault attacks.

CCS Concepts

•**Networks** → **Error detection and error correction;** •**Hardware** → **Robustness;**

Keywords

SHA-3, Keccak, Random errors, Fault injection, Reliability

1. INTRODUCTION

Keccak is a new algorithm that can be used for hashing, stream encryption, pseudo-random sequence generation, message authentication codes (MAC), etc., and has been recently selected as SHA-3 standard [1]. As SHA-3 will be widely used in cryptographic applications, reliability and security of its implementations will be of vital importance to the SHA-3 based security engine.

Cryptographic systems are sensitive to random errors caused by aging, ambient environment such as temperature and X-ray radiation [9, 19]. For cryptographic systems used for encryption, authentication and integrity checking, etc., the random errors will cause incorrect results and make the cryptographic systems unreliable. Attackers can also inject faults temporarily to the system to retrieve the secret key or state. Analyzing the correct output and faulty output is called differential fault analysis (DFA), which has been shown to be very effective in cracking block ciphers including Data Encryption Standard (DES) and Advanced Encryption Standard (AES) [6, 17]. A recent work [3] shows that DFA can also be used to attack SHA-3 implementations to recover the internal states.

To protect cryptographic systems against random errors and injected faults, different error detection methods have been adopted in cryptographic systems [8, 9, 10, 11, 13, 14, 19]. Many schemes are based on redundancy - with another copy of the original implementation for outputs comparison so as to detect error occurring in either copy. To further improve the reliability, the second copy can have different implementation from the first copy [8]. To reduce the resource overhead, error detection coding is also widely used. Parity checking code has been used in the protection of AES [19] because of its efficient design and high error coverage. Besides parity checking, non-linear codes are also introduced to further improve system reliability with higher fault coverage [10].

Previous works on Keccak mainly focus on side-channel analysis and collisions attacks on Keccak [7, 12, 16, 18], while leaving its reliable design against injected faults and random errors almost blank. To the best of our knowledge, only one work about reliable Keccak design has been published [5]. In [5], the authors find a property of Keccak algorithm: each lane of the Keccak state can be rotated by a random number before each round operation, and then shifted back after Keccak operations without changing the results. Based on this property, they implement another copy of Keccak with this kind of rotation for comparison. Any error can cause output mismatch of the two copies and thus can be detected. With different implementations in the two copies, it is unlikely that same errors will appear in the two copies. However, this method has high resource overhead due to the extra copy.

In this paper, we propose a simple and efficient parity checking based error detection method for Keccak. Optimized designs are also proposed to further improve the efficiency of the proposed scheme. We implement the proposed scheme in VHDL and simulate fault injection at gate level to get the fault coverage of the proposed scheme. Results show that our scheme has a high fault coverage for hardware implementations with very small resource overhead.

The rest of this paper is organized as follows. In Section 2, some basic knowledge of Keccak and preliminaries of error detection are introduced. In Section 3, the mathemat-

GLSVLSI '16, May 18-20, 2016, Boston, MA, USA

DOI: http://dx.doi.org/10.1145/2902961.2902985

ical property of Keccak is analyzed and our parity checking scheme for Keccak operations is proposed. In Section 4, implementation and fault injection simulation results of the proposed schemes are given. Finally, the paper is concluded in Section 5.

2. PRELIMINARIES

2.1 Preliminaries of Keccak Hash Function

Keccak can work in different modes and have variable length [1]. In this paper, we use Keccak-1600 as an example to demonstrate our scheme. All of the 1600-bit states are organized in a 3-D array, as shown in Figure 1. Each bit is addressed by three coordinates, denoted as $S(x, y, z)$, $x, y \in \{0, 1, ..., 4\}$, $z \in \{0, 1, ..., 63\}$. 2-D entities, plane, sheet and slice, and 1-D entities, lane, column and row, are also defined in Keccak and shown in Figure 1.

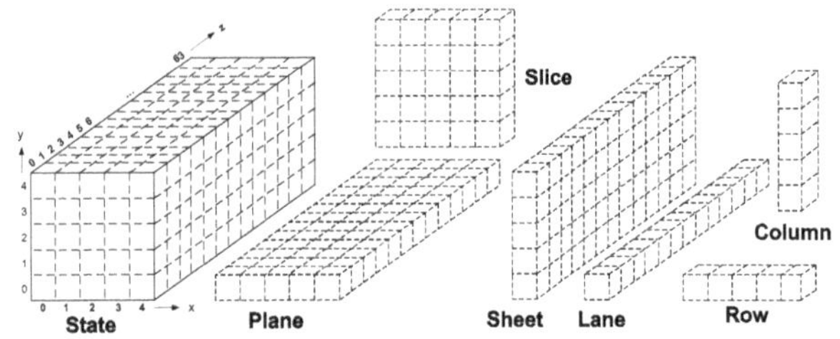

Figure 1: Terminology used in Keccak

Notations: We use 3-D coordinates x, y and z to locate each bit. We also define vectors $X = [0:4]$, $Y = [0:4]$ and $Z = [0:63]$ to stand for multiple bits in one row, column and lane, respectively. Note that coordinates x and y are modular 5 while z is modular 64.

Keccak relies on a Sponge architecture to iteratively absorb message inputs and squeeze out outputs by a f permutation function. The f function consists of 24 rounds, where each round has five sequential steps:

$$S_{i+1} = \iota \circ \chi \circ \pi \circ \rho \circ \theta(S_i),\ i \in \{0, 1, \cdots, 23\} \quad (1)$$

in which S_0 is the initial input. Details of each step are described below:

– θ is a linear operation which involves 11 input bits and outputs a single bit. Each output state bit is the XOR of the input state bit and two intermediate bits produced by its two neighbor columns. We denote the input to θ operation as θ_i while the output as θ_o, and the operation is given as follows:

$$\theta_o(x, y, z) = \theta_i(x, y, z) \oplus (\oplus_{y=0}^{4} \theta_i(x-1, y, z)) \oplus (\oplus_{y=0}^{4} \theta_i(x+1, y, z-1)). \quad (2)$$

– ρ is a permutation over the bits of the state along z-axis (in lanes), and the amount of shifted bits depend on the (x, y) coordinates.

– π is a permutation over the bits of the state within slices. Only the center bit ($x = 0$, $y = 0$) of the slice does not move. All other bits are permuted to other positions depending on their original coordinates.

– χ is a non-linear step that contains mixed binary operations. Every bit of the output state is the result of an XOR between the corresponding input state bit and its two neighboring bits along the x-axis (in a row):

$$\chi_o(x, y, z) = \chi_i(x, y, z) \oplus (\overline{\chi_i(x+1, y, z)} \cdot \chi_i(x+2, y, z)).$$

– ι is a binary XOR with a round constant which is publicly known.

Further details of Keccak can be found in [1].

2.2 Reliable Design with Error Detection

Reliable cryptographic modules rely on error detection to detect random errors and injected faults in systems. The basic structure of error detection is shown in Figure 2, in which the cryptographic module is protected by introducing another module, Protector. Protector is composed of three modules, which are Predictor, Compressor and Comparator.

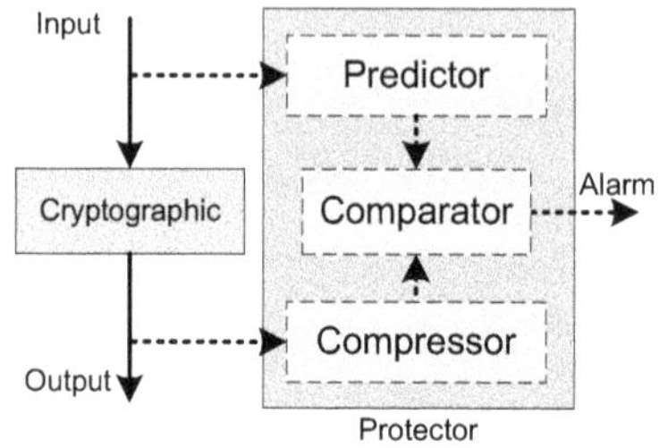

Figure 2: Conception of error detection

Predictor and Compressor read the input and output of cryptographic module respectively, and generate some intermediate computation results. Comparator compares the results of Predictor and Compressor for error detection. If errors happen in cryptographic module, results of Predictor and Compressor may not match, and errors will be detected. Design of predictor and compressor will significantly determine the resource overhead and fault coverage. For example, in redundancy-based error detection, predictor is another copy of the original implementation and there is no compressor.

3. PARITY CHECKING OF KECCAK

In this section, we will propose our parity checking based concurrent error detection scheme for Keccak. We take each operation of Keccak as a cryptographic module shown in Figure 2, and the goal is to design efficient and effective predictor and compressor suitable for each operation.

3.1 Analysis of the Protection of Keccak

Sponge function involves a lot of simple bitwise operations such as XOR, AND, NOT etc., rather than complex nonlinear operations such as S-box in block ciphers. Such bit-wise operations can be combined according to Boolean algebra for efficient predictor and compressor design. For each 3-D input and output state of a cryptographic operation, parity checking can be implemented at different granularities. For example, it can be implemented in row, column, or lane, or in 2-D entities, in unit of slice, sheet, or plane. This will result in different compression ratio, yielding different error coverage and resource overhead.

For concurrent error detection, usually some steps can be combined to achieve higher efficiency. For example, the error detection of ShiftRows, MixColumns and AddRoundKey of AES can be combined together to achieve lower overhead and higher efficiency [10]. Instead of protecting each operation of Keccak separately, we propose to combine the protections of some operations to improve the efficiency and save resource. For example, ι is a binary XOR operation with a constant number, and thus the protection of ι can be efficiently combined with the protection of χ. In this section, we show how to make use of the property of Keccak and combine parity checking of some steps to achieve higher efficiency.

The overall protection scheme is shown in Figure 3. The protections of χ and ι, ρ and π, are combined respectively for higher efficiency, with the combined operations denoted as χ' and ρ'.

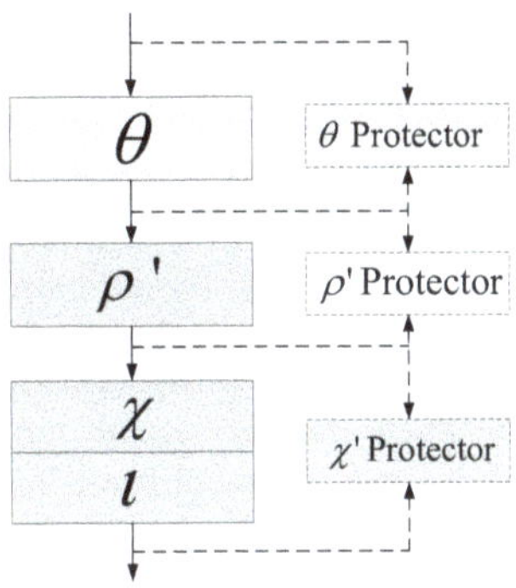

Figure 3: Error detection structure of Keccak

Note that depending on the implementation of Keccak, the ρ' protector may be optional. This is because both ρ and π are permutation operations and only change the position of bits without changing the values. If no storage (state register) is used in these operations, they will be synthesized as wires in FPGA or ASIC. Any errors (stuck-at-zero or stuck-at-one) will be detected by the previous θ protector or the following χ' protector. Nevertheless, we present protection on ρ and π in this section at the algorithm level, and leave the implementation to the next section.

3.2 Parity Checking of θ

3.2.1 Parity Checking of θ in 1-D Entities

As shown in formula (2), each θ operation works on one input bit θ_i and two nearby columns (each five bits). Operations on five bits in the same column of θ_i involve the same two nearby columns. Thus we propose to implement parity checking of θ along the y axis (in column). For each column of θ_o, the parity checking is as follows:

$$\bigoplus_{y=0}^{4} \theta_o(x,y,z) = \bigoplus_{y=0}^{4} \theta_i(x,y,z) \oplus \Big(\bigoplus_{y=0}^{4}\bigoplus_{y=0}^{4} \theta_i(x+1,y,z-1)\Big) \oplus \Big(\bigoplus_{y=0}^{4}\bigoplus_{y=0}^{4} \theta_i(x-1,y,z)\Big).$$

Due to the property of XOR operation ($a \oplus 0 = a$, $a \oplus a \oplus a = a$), we can simplify the above equation as:

$$\bigoplus_{y=0}^{4} \theta_o(x,y,z) = \bigoplus_{y=0}^{4} \theta_i(x,y,z) \oplus \Big(\bigoplus_{y=0}^{4} \theta_i(x+1,y,z-1)\Big) \oplus \Big(\bigoplus_{y=0}^{4} \theta_i(x-1,y,z)\Big). \quad (3)$$

Where the parity checking of each column of θ_o ($\theta_o(x,Y,z)$ on the left hand) is the parity checking of three θ_i columns ($\theta_i(x,Y,z)$, $\theta_i(x-1,Y,z)$ and $\theta_i(x+1,Y,z-1)$).

We denote the parity checking result of θ_i in each column as $P[\theta_i](x,z)$, which means to compress θ_i along the y direction. The parity checking of the input state is a plane ($X = [0:4]$, $Z = [0:63]$). Similarly, we denote the parity checking result of θ_o in each column as $P[\theta_o](x,z)$. We can represent (3) as follows:

$$P[\theta_o](x,z) = P[\theta_i](x,z) \oplus P[\theta_i](x+1,z-1) \oplus P[\theta_i](x-1,z). \quad (4)$$

The parity checking can also be done along the row. Similarly, we have:

$$P[\theta_o](y,z) = P[\theta_i](y,z) \oplus P[\theta_i](z) \oplus P[\theta_i](z-1), \quad (5)$$

in which $P[\theta_i](z)$ stands for the compression of each slice of θ_i and therefore the input state is compressed to a parity lane, and $P[\theta_i](y,z)$ is the parity of a row. Compared to (4), it involves multiple parity generations (both in row and in slice).

3.2.2 Parity Checking of θ in Slice

Equation (4) shows that parity checking in each column involves nearby columns (with one on the same slice). Equation (5) shows that parity checking in each row already involves two slices. We examine parity checking in 2-D entities too. Parity of each slice is denoted as:

$$\bigoplus_{x=0}^{4}\bigoplus_{y=0}^{4} \theta_o(x,y,z) = \Big(\bigoplus_{x=0}^{4}\bigoplus_{y=0}^{4} \theta_i(x,y,z)\Big) \oplus \Big(\bigoplus_{x=0}^{4}\bigoplus_{y=0}^{4}\bigoplus_{y=0}^{4} \theta_i(x-1,y,z)\Big) \oplus \Big(\bigoplus_{x=0}^{4}\bigoplus_{y=0}^{4}\bigoplus_{y=0}^{4} \theta_i(x+1,y,z-1)\Big). \quad (6)$$

Due to the property of XOR operation, we find a unique property for slice based parity checking of θ operation:

$$\bigoplus_{x=0}^{4}\bigoplus_{y=0}^{4} \theta_o(x,y,z) = \bigoplus_{x=0}^{4}\bigoplus_{y=0}^{4} \theta_i(x+1,y,z-1). \quad (7)$$

It means that the parity of each slice of θ_o is the parity of a nearby slice of θ_i. For the 1,600 bit state of Keccak, there are 64 slice-based parity checking bits for θ_i and θ_o respectively. Define $P[\theta_o](Z)$ and $P[\theta_i](Z)$ as following:

$$\begin{cases} P[\theta_i](z) = \oplus_{x=0}^{4} \oplus_{y=0}^{4} \theta_i(x,y,z) \\ P[\theta_o](z) = \oplus_{x=0}^{4} \oplus_{y=0}^{4} \theta_o(x,y,z) \end{cases},$$

then (7) can be represented as:

$$P[\theta_i](z) = P[\theta_o](z+1), \; Z = [0:63], \quad (8)$$

which means that the slice-based parity lane of θ_o is a round shift of the parity lane of θ_i. This makes the slice-based parity checking for θ very efficient.

For the three parity generation and checking schemes introduced in Section 3.2.1 and Section 3.2.2, we compare their resource overhead in terms of XOR2 gates. Take parity checking in slice as an example, the predictor compresses every slice into one bit, requiring 24 XOR gates, and the predictor needs 1536 (24 * 64) XOR gates in total. The XOR gates consumption of different protection schemes of θ are listed in Table 1.

Table 1: XOR gates overhead of θ protection

	Predictor	Compressor	Comparator	Total
Column	1920	1280	639	3839
Row	2176	1280	639	4095
Slice	1536	1536	127	3199
Duplicate	3520	0	3199	6719

For schemes with parity generation in row and column, they protect θ for every five bits, while the slice based scheme protect θ operation for every 25 bits. Thus the row and column based schemes have higher error coverage than the slice based scheme. Table 1 shows that the slice based parity checking scheme has lower area overhead than the other two schemes. A balance should be made between error coverage and resource overhead during design. Meanwhile, comparing with the proposed parity checking schemes, duplication based error detection requires much higher resource overhead. In this paper, we use slice-based parity generation to implement the parity checking of θ operation.

3.3 Parity Checking of ρ and π

As discussed in Section 3.1, ρ and π can be left unprotected if they are implemented using wires in circuit. For implementations in which ρ and π use registers (pipelined design, for example), the protections of ρ and π can be implemented either separately or combined together.

For ρ, the permutation is along z-axis, thus we propose to compress ρ operation along each lane, and the protection function is as following:

$$P[\rho_i](x,y) = P[\rho_o](x,y). \tag{9}$$

In (9), the left side is the predictor while the right side is the compressor design. Similarly, while π permutes the state bits inside each slice, we propose to compress the bits inside each slice:

$$P[\pi_i](z) = P[\pi_o](z). \tag{10}$$

The protection of ρ and π can both be implemented efficiently because of their simple operations. To further improve the implementation efficiency, we propose to combine ρ and π as a new operation ρ' and protect it instead. For the protection of ρ', parity checking can be efficiently implemented in z-axis. The protector of ρ' can be designed as following:

$$\pi(P[\rho_i'](x,y)) = P[\rho_o'](x,y), \tag{11}$$

in which the left-hand side is predictor and the right-hand side is for compressor design. For predictor design, the 1,600-bit state is firstly compressed to a slice $P[\rho_i'](x,y)$, and this slice is then permuted according to π operation. For this protection scheme, the predictor and compressor both require 1,575 XOR gates, and the comparator needs 49 XOR gates. Although θ can be also combined with ρ', the efficiency is not improved significantly, thus we protect them separately in this paper.

3.4 Parity Checking of χ and ι

3.4.1 *What Should We Avoid in Protection of χ?*

χ is the only non-linear step in Keccak and it involves both NOT and AND operations. This makes the parity checking of χ step different from previous operations. In this section, we first show a pitfall for the protection of χ which should be avoided in practical design.

We take one row of χ_i as an example here, we denote the five bits of this row as $\{a,b,c,d,e\}$. Then five bits of corresponding χ_o output row can be denoted as $a \oplus (\bar{b}\cdot c)$, $b \oplus (\bar{c}\cdot d)$, $c \oplus (\bar{d}\cdot e)$, $d \oplus (\bar{e}\cdot a)$ and $e \oplus (\bar{a}\cdot b)$. The parity bit of this single row is:

$$\begin{aligned} &a \oplus b \oplus c \oplus d \oplus e \oplus (\bar{b}\cdot c) \oplus (\bar{c}\cdot d) \oplus (\bar{d}\cdot e) \oplus (\bar{e}\cdot a) \oplus (\bar{a}\cdot b) \\ &= (a\cdot b) \oplus (b\cdot c) \oplus (c\cdot d) \oplus (d\cdot e) \oplus (e\cdot a). \end{aligned} \tag{12}$$

For equation (12), if one bit out of five bits in this row is flipped, the final result of equation (12) may not change. Take bit a as an example, the change of a will affect both $(e\cdot a)$ and $(a\cdot b)$. According to De Morgan's laws:

$$(e\cdot a) \oplus (a\cdot b) = a\cdot(b\oplus e). \tag{13}$$

When a flips, if $b\oplus e$ is already 0, the above result does not change, then the result of (12) will not change either. Assume all bits are independent, the probability of $b\oplus e = 0$ is 50% and therefore the fault coverage of this scheme is 50% for single bit errors. So parity checking in each row of χ should be avoided because of the non-linearity of χ operation, and thus parity checking in each slice will not be applicable for χ operation either.

3.4.2 *Parity Checking of χ in Each Lane*

In this section, we show how to build practical error detection module for χ operation. As x-axis compression of χ is not a good choice, we considering compressing χ results along either z-axis or y-axis. For parity generation along z-axis, 64 bits in each lane are compressed to one bit and thus the 1,600 bits are compressed to one slice. The parity generation can be denoted as following:

$$P[\chi_o](x,y) = \bigoplus_{z=0}^{63} \chi_o(x,y,z). \tag{14}$$

According to the definition of χ operation, we have:

$$\begin{aligned} P[\chi_o](x,y) = &\bigoplus_{z=0}^{63} (\chi_i(x,y,z) \oplus \chi_i(x+2,y,z) \\ &\oplus \chi_i(x+1,y,z)\cdot\chi_i(x+2,y,z)) \\ =&P[\chi_i](x,y) \oplus P[\chi_i](x+2,y) \\ &\oplus P[\chi_{and}](x,y), \end{aligned}$$

in which $\chi_{and}(x,y,z) = \chi_i(x+1,y,z)\cdot\chi_i(x+2,y,z)$. Thus the predictor design of parity checking for χ at z-axis is also easy to implement. It involves AND operations first, then it compresses the data in z-axis to generate the parity for checking.

Meanwhile, the parity of χ can also be generated in each column, along y-axis direction. For this scheme, five bits in each column are compressed to one bit, and the 1,600-bits state is compressed to one plane. The compressor works as follows:

$$P[\chi_o](x,z) = P[\chi_i](x,z) \oplus P[\chi_i](x,z) \oplus P[\chi_{and}](x,z).$$

In this scheme, the overhead is higher than the z-axis compression scheme due to its lower compression ratio, while it has higher fault coverage. Thus designers can choose the best scheme according to the system requirement. In this paper, we implement the protection of χ operation along

Table 2: Resource overhead and error coverage results

	Area		Timing		Power		Error
	(um^2)	Normalized	(ns)	Normalized	(mW)	Normalized	coverage
Original	41611.7	100.00%	3.892	100.00%	17.95	100.00%	0%
Proposed	52867.2	127.05%	4.500	115.62%	26.69	148.69%	83.60%
Design 2	62429.4	150.01%	5.476	140.70%	41.78	232.76%	83.34%
Design 3	66621.0	160.10%	4.381	112.56%	44.07	245.52%	89.89%

the z-axis direction (lane) for fault injection simulation and resource overhead evaluations.

3.4.3 Combination of χ and ι

While ι only adds a constant number to χ result, it can be easily combined with χ as discussed in previous section. If χ is checked at z-axis, the combined parity checking is

$$P[\iota_o](x,y) = P[\chi_i](x,y) \oplus P[\chi_i](x+2,y) \oplus P[\chi_{and}](x,y) \oplus P[\iota_c](x,y), \quad (15)$$

and parity checking of χ combining with ι at other directions are similar. Note here that $P[\iota_c](x,y)$ is computed at design stage to avoid computations for each run. This protection scheme requires 3,200 XOR gates and 1,600 AND gates for the predictor, 1,575 XOR gates for the compressor, and 49 XOR gates for the comparator.

4. IMPLEMENTATION AND FAULT INJECTION RESULTS

4.1 Implementation Results

To evaluate the proposed scheme, we implement the unprotected Keccak implementation (referring to the official implementation provided online [2]) and the proposed scheme in Figure 3 . We implement three variants of the proposed scheme:

- Proposed combines the protection of χ and ι as described in Section 3.4.3, and leaves ρ and π unprotected;
- Design 2 protects χ and ι separately, and leaves ρ and π unprotected;
- Design 3 combines the protection of χ and ι as described in Section 3.4.3, and protects ρ and π together referring to (11).

For the above three designs, we implement the protection of θ using the scheme in Section 3.2.2, which is to implement parity checking in each slice. Each protector is composed of three parts, as described in Figure 2. All the designs have five steps in each round within one clock cycle using combinational circuits. For the proposed schemes, we implement the original circuit and the protection circuits in parallel and they work simultaneously.

For integrated circuit resource evaluation, the implementations (with and without protections) are modeled in VHDL and synthesized in Cadence Encounter RTL Compiler with a 45nm Opencell library (NanGate FreePDK45 v1_3_v2009_07). The designs were placed and routed using Cadence Encounter. The power and area overhead of the protection schemes were estimated using Concurrent Current Source (CCS) model under typical operation conditions assuming a supply voltage of 1.1V and a temperature of 25 Celsius degree. The results including area, timing delay and power consumption are shown in Table 2.

Table 2 shows that Proposed has much higher performance while lower area and power consumption than Design 2 and Design 3.

Comparing with original implementation, Proposed has about 27.05% area resource overhead. Meanwhile, our proposed scheme maintains high performance because it has the protection modules works concurrently with Keccak module. What's more, the proposed scheme combines ρ and π, χ and ι together respectively, thus it has small timing delay overhead.

Comparing with Proposed, Design 2 does not optimize the protections of χ and ι and protect these two modules separately. It shows that Design 2 has much higher area resource overhead than the proposed design because of this separate protection design. Meanwhile, it has larger timing dealy and power consumption than the proposed design as well. Design 3 protects ρ and π together as described in Section 3.4.3, results show that it has much higher area resource overhead than the proposed scheme, as well as larger timing delay and power consumption. Thus the proposed optimization methods can help to save resources in the protection of Keccak.

4.2 Fault Coverage Analysis

Theoretically, for parity checking schemes, if odd number bits are flipped, the errors will be detected with 100% probability; while if even number bits are flipped, the errors will be always undetected. For real hardware systems, it will be very difficult for the attackers to precisely control the numbers and positions of faulty gates in the circuit [4]. What's more, the errors in the circuit will randomly propagate and cause different numbers of faulty bits in the output [15]. Thus, fault injection simulation results at gate level are required for error coverage evaluation.

In this paper, we randomly inject one to ten stuck-at-0 and stuck-at-1 faults into Keccak circuit for error coverage simulation. To get the fault coverage result, we give random plaintext input for one round of Keccak, then randomly inject one to ten stuck-at-0 or stuck-at-1 faults into the system. We check the results of the protected implementation and the alarm signals to see if we miss any errors. For each design, we run about 10^9 fault injection trials and the error coverage results are shown in Table 2.

Table 2 shows that the proposed scheme has error coverage about 83.60%. Meanwhile, results show that separate protections of χ and ι in Design 2 will not increase the error coverage. This is because ι module is very small and only occupies very small ratio of gates in the design. The probability of errors happening in ι is very small, and the error coverage of Design 2 is almost the same as the proposed design.

For Design 3, it has a large part of gates used for the protection of ρ and π, and errors happen in ρ' module with high probability. In such case, we can assume that a large part of errors are injected into the protection module of ρ' and this part of errors will be detected with high probability. Results show that the error coverage will increase to 89.89% for Design 3. Thus for pipelined designs which use registers to store the results of ρ and π, the protection method proposed in Section 3.3 should be implemented for higher error coverage.

In conclusion, according to the synthesis results in Section 4.1 and fault injection simulation results in Section 4.2, the proposed scheme has a small resource overhead and high performance, and it can detect the injected faults with a high probability. Thus our proposed scheme strikes a good balance between resource overhead and error coverage, and can be efficiently implemented for the protection of Keccak implementations.

5. CONCLUSION

In this paper, we look into the parity checking of Keccak to protect it against random errors and injected faults. We make use of the mathematical properties of Keccak to implement parity checking based error detection. We find that combining protections of some steps reduces the area overhead, timing delay, and power consumption significantly without sacrificing the error coverage. Results show that our scheme has small resource overhead, while the timing delay and power consumption are also very small. Under multiple bit random errors model, fault injection simulation results show that our method can detect 83.60% injected faults. The future work will be more efficient protection methods of Keccak against random errors and injected faults, and protections of Keccak against other kinds of attacks.

Acknowledgment: The authors would like to thank Dr. Rex Xiaofei Guo at Intel for his help. This work was supported in part by National Science Foundation under grants SaTC-1314655 and MRI-1337854.

6. REFERENCES

[1] DRAFT FIPS PUB 202: SHA-3 Standard: Permutation-Based Hash and Extendable-Output Functions, 2014. Federal Information Processing Standards Publication.

[2] *Keccak Hardware implementation in VHDL Version 3.1*, 2015 (accessed July 14, 2015).

[3] N. Bagheri, N. Ghaedi, and S. Sanadhya. Differential fault analysis of SHA-3. In *Progress in Cryptology – INDOCRYPT 2015*, volume 9462, pages 253–269. 2015.

[4] A. Barenghi, L. Breveglieri, I. Koren, and D. Naccache. Fault injection attacks on cryptographic devices: Theory, practice, and countermeasures. *Proceedings of the IEEE*, 100(11):3056–3076, Nov 2012.

[5] S. Bayat-sarmadi, M. Mozaffari-Kermani, and A. Reyhani-Masoleh. Efficient and concurrent reliable realization of the secure cryptographic SHA-3 algorithm. *IEEE Trans. on Computer-Aided Design of Integrated Circuits & Systems*, 33(7):1105–1109, July 2014.

[6] E. Biham and A. Shamir. Differential fault analysis of secret key cryptosystems. In *Advances in Cryptology – CRYPTO '97*, volume 1294, pages 513–525. 1997.

[7] I. Dinur, O. Dunkelman, and A. Shamir. Collision attacks on up to 5 rounds of SHA-3 using generalized internal differentials. In *Fast Software Encryption*, volume 8424, pages 219–240. 2014.

[8] X. Guo and R. Karri. Invariance-based concurrent error detection for Advanced Encryption Standard. In *Proc. IEEE Design Automation Conf.*, pages 573–578, 2012.

[9] X. Guo and R. Karri. Recomputing with permuted operands: A concurrent error detection approach. *IEEE Trans. on Computer-Aided Design of Integrated Circuits & Systems*, 32(10):1595–1608, Oct 2013.

[10] M. Karpovsky, K. Kulikowski, and A. Taubin. Differential fault analysis attack resistant architectures for the Advanced Encryption Standard. In *Smart Card Research and Advanced Applications VI*, volume 153, pages 177–192. 2004.

[11] R. Karri, K. Wu, P. Mishra, and Y. Kim. Concurrent error detection of fault-based side-channel cryptanalysis of 128-bit symmetric block ciphers. In *Proc. IEEE Design Automation Conf.*, pages 579–584, 2001.

[12] P. Luo, Y. Fei, X. Fang, A. Ding, D. Kaeli, and M. Leeser. Side-channel analysis of MAC-Keccak hardware implementations. In *Hardware & Architectural Support for Security & Privacy*, 2015.

[13] P. Luo, Y. Fei, L. Zhang, and A. Ding. Side-channel power analysis of different protection schemes against fault attacks on AES. In *Int. Conf. ReConFigurable Computing & FPGAs (ReConFig)*, pages 1–6, Dec 2014.

[14] P. Maistri and R. Leveugle. Double-data-rate computation as a countermeasure against fault analysis. *IEEE Trans. on Computers*, 57(11):1528–1539, Nov 2008.

[15] M. Mozaffari-Kermani and A. Reyhani-Masoleh. A lightweight high-performance fault detection scheme for the Advanced Encryption Standard using composite fields. *IEEE Trans. on Very Large Scale Integration Systems*, 19(1):85–91, Jan 2011.

[16] M. Naya-Plasencia, A. RÃűck, and W. Meier. Practical analysis of reduced-round keccak. In *Progress in Cryptology - INDOCRYPT 2011*, volume 7107, pages 236–254. 2011.

[17] G. Piret and J.-J. Quisquater. A differential fault attack technique against SPN structures, with application to the AES and Khazad. In *Cryptographic Hardware and Embedded Systems*, volume 2779, pages 77–88. 2003.

[18] M. Taha and P. Schaumont. Side-channel analysis of MAC-Keccak. In *IEEE Int. Symp. on Hardware-Oriented Security & Trust*, pages 125–130, June 2013.

[19] C.-H. Yen and B.-F. Wu. Simple error detection methods for hardware implementation of Advanced Encryption Standard. *IEEE Trans. on Computer*, 55(6):720–731, June 2006.

Secure Model Checkers for Network-on-Chip (NoC) Architectures

Travis Boraten, Dominic DiTomaso and Avinash Karanth Kodi
Department of Electrical Engineering and Computer Science
Ohio University
Athens, Ohio
tb286706@ohio.edu, dd292006@ohio.edu, kodi@ohio.edu

ABSTRACT

As chip multiprocessors (CMPs) are becoming more susceptible to process variation, crosstalk, and hard and soft errors, emerging threats from rogue employees in a compromised foundry are creating new vulnerabilities that could undermine the integrity of our chips with malicious alterations. As the Network-on-Chip (NoC) is a focal point of sensitive data transfer and critical device coordination, there is an urgent demand for secure and reliable communication. In this paper we propose Secure Model Checkers (SMCs), a real-time solution for control logic verification and functional correctness in the micro-architecture to detect Hardware Trojan (HT) induced denial-of-service attacks and improve reliability. In our evaluation, we show that SMCs provides significant security enhancements in real-time with only 1.5% power and 1.1% area overhead penalty in the micro-architecture.

CCS Concepts

•Security and privacy → Hardware security implementation; •Networks → Network on chip; *Denial-of-service attacks;*

Keywords

Hardware security; Network-on-Chip; Hardware trojan

1. INTRODUCTION

Network-on-Chip (NoC) architectures have emerged as the prevailing communication fabric for on-chip communication today that efficiently interconnect heterogeneous processing cores, last level of cache(s), memory controllers and I/O devices [2, 5]. As NoC coordinates and controls all data transfer on the chip, communication on the NoC must be both reliable and secure. However, the complex, globalized circuit design and fabrication process makes the NoC vulnerable to both device faults and security threats [3, 13, 14]. Reliability and security in the NoC control paths can be compromised by inadvertent errors, malicious hardware or a combination of both.

GLSVLSI '16, May 18-20, 2016, Boston, MA, USA

 ISBN 978-1-4503-4274-2/16/05...$15.00

DOI: http://dx.doi.org/10.1145/2902961.2903032

Inadvertent errors are unintentional bit corruptions caused by the failure or unexpected behavior of devices. Unreliability in devices can be caused by many factors including voltage, temperature, process variations, crosstalk, device wear-out, and electromigration. The combined effect of these factors results in transient and permanent faults on the links and the router microarchitecture of the NoC which adversely affects the energy-efficiency and performance of the NoC due to packet loss, misrouting, packet duplication, network disruptions, etc. NoCs are designed with fault-tolerant techniques that include both fault-recovery and fault detection techniques. To recover from errors, error correction codes (ECC), re-routing, modular redundancy and other techniques could be used. To detect the errors, Built-in-Self-Test (BIST), error-detection codes (EDC) or dynamic verification with model checkers could be employed. Invariant model checkers are light-weight error detection mechanisms that target both functional as well as runtime errors with minimal impact to power/performance of NoCs.

Malicious hardware, on the other hand, is purposefully injected into the system with the intent to deny service, steal information, slow traffic, bypass encryption/authentication, or corrupt data. A Hardware Trojan (HT) is a result of an untrusted third-party maliciously modifying hardware at some point during the integrated circuit (IC) design process. HTs can be inserted by an intellectual property (IP) vendor, untrusted CAD tool/designer, or at the foundry through reverse engineering [3, 13, 14]. While ICs are extensively tested and validated, HTs can still go undetected as billions of transistors from different IP vendors are integrated on chip which make physical inspection and reverse engineering difficult and costly process [14]. Furthermore, with the increase of inadvertent errors, HT can mask themselves as transient errors which can only be activated under very specific conditions to avoid detection.

As HTs manifest as transient errors that either corrupt data or steal data, HTs can exploit vulnerabilities created by the fault-tolerant techniques. For example, data corruption on the channel connecting adjacent routers can be recovered by ECC that may trigger a retransmission (multi-bit errors using single-error correction with double error detection (SECDED)). HTs may intentionally corrupt data to cause retransmissions which may lead to a Denial-of-Service (DoS) attack by creating false congestion between the routers by consuming network resources. While the error may appear as benign for the system, this is intentionally created by

HTs to create DoS attack and disrupt the system. Therefore we believe that both security and fault tolerance are intertwined issues and an integrated framework that simultaneously targets both is essential and focus of this paper.

In this paper, we propose **S**ecure **M**odel **C**heckers (**SMCs**) - in which we provide real-time security enhancements to reduce HT micro-architecture vulnerabilities through improved fault coverage for control logic with minimal power and area overhead. To achieve our objective, first we provide a design methodology that identifies vulnerabilities within the NoC which we define as *security points-of-interests* (SPOI) and discuss possible mitigation techniques. To improve the security of control logic, we propose *secure model checkers* (SMCs) to enhance dynamic verification employed by fault detection techniques by incorporating security features that were identified by SPOIs. Using our design methodology, SMCs provide erroneous execution coverage for invalid, and illegal output, but also for newly defined *inefficient* output to detect HT induced faults. SMCs differ from prior fault detection model checkers as they compare previous router pipeline stage computation with the next stage to validate and assert that the computation is legal and not malicious. Our major contributions are as follows:

1. **Security Points-of-Interest**: We define SPOI and their vulnerabilities in existing NoC micro-architectures and fault tolerant techniques. With SPOI identified, threats are examined and adequate mitigation techniques proposed to improve security and reliability.

2. **Secure Model Checkers**: We propose SMCs, which include enhancements over existing independent invariant model checkers to improve prevention of HT-enabled DoS attacks and malicious gaming of resources in a compromised NoC.

2. RELATED WORK

2.1 Fault Detection

The micro-architecture should identify, isolate, and recover from faults to ensure functional correctness in critical control logic and provide recovery mechanisms when faults are detected. One approach is to diagnose faults with BIST [7, 9, 11] that periodically evaluate the operational correctness of critical control logic. To minimize the performance impact of fault diagnosis, the authors in [12], proposed NoCAlert, a real-time fault detection mechanism implemented with light-weight invariant checkers. Unlike BIST, which requires putting devices under test, invariance rule checking can be executed concurrently and in real-time with simple hardware assertions. While invariance checkers detect faults that create rule violations through illegal outputs, faults that create legal but invalid outputs create outcomes where faults may go undetected and cause devices to operate in-efficiently. Careful consideration must be taken when defining rules such that when invalid outcomes occur, faults are benign or they are subsequently detected in downstream routers.

2.2 Security

In NoCs, several security papers have begun to address architectural concerns in quality of service [16], DoS attacks [8, 6], HTs [1, 8, 17], and obfuscation [1]. The focal point of recent work however, has been on prevention and mitigation, and little has been done in regards to HT detection. There are many reasons for this, as HTs are often dormant until activated, and when active, the diversity of HT triggers makes this task non-trivial because triggers may be combinational circuits and require rare excitation, sequential, ticking time bombs, or could be externally driven. If a HT can be triggered, logic testing [4, 13] can be used to detect the presence and location of the threat. Since uphill challenges exist in trying to detect HTs, authors in [1] proposed obfuscation of routing tables and data scrambling in an approach to reduce the chance of activating HTs triggered by snooping data in a compromised router.

More recently, a DoS attack was proposed in [8] that suppresses allocation requests and de-prioritizes arbiters within the micro-architecture to increase contention and flit latency. While the authors proposed a runtime latency auditor to systematically monitor the trustworthiness of the NoC, using delay to detect an attack is difficult as several factors influence packet latency during normal operation. While this technique to attack is new, other existing fault tolerant run-time invariant checkers proposed in [12] could easily detect and prevent the attack if invariant rules are violated, however many invariant rules fail to shield control units like arbitration from de-prioritization, starvation, flooding, or modulated attacks.

Since security can be compromised by injecting faults, one way to improve security is to identify the ways in which faults could be used to maliciously exploit architecture features, protocols, control logic, reconfiguring hardware, and mitigation responses. With SMCs, we enhance security by blanketing control logic with secure model checkers to detect HTs that would violate functional correctness in ways traditional random faults would not.

3. DESIGN METHODOLOGY

In this section we will present a design methodology that designers could use to evaluate their architectures and aid development of future NoCs with improved security. Next, we will use our methodology and describe in detail our proposed secure model checkers to enhance security for pipeline control logic. In the following section, we will discuss our performance evaluation and compare other state-of-the-art architectures to SMCs in terms of the reliability, network performance, and power and area overhead.

As hardware security emerges as a threat to undermine the reliability of future technologies, researchers need tools to evaluate the integrity of their designs, and develop hardware with fail-over mechanisms in a similar way we approach fault tolerance. A significant portion of that challenge starts by shifting the focus from porous post chip validation and offline side channel analysis [15, 10], to the architectural design phase. We now outline steps that should be exercised with each development phase.

Design phase: During the design phase, architects should critically analyze their implementations and thereby pinpoint single points of failure, or devices that could be maliciously *gamed*. Gaming of architectural features could starve, flood, or deny service of network resources, for example, exploitation of retransmission and cache coherency protocols, fairness of arbitration units, illegal VC allocations and inadvertent triggering of power-gating or dynamic voltage and frequency scaling (DVFS) technology. In a compromised

Table 1: SPOI for NoCs

Security Points-of-Interest		
Router	1	Buffers
	2	Pipeline stages (BW,RC,VA,SA,ST,LT)
	3	Status registers
Techniques	4	Asynchronous logic
	5	Cache
	6	DVFS
	7	Power-gating
	8	Reconfiguration
	9	Speculation
	10	Wear-out & aging
	11	Wireless
Links		
Memory Controllers		

Table 2: Security Threats for NoCs

Threat Types	
1	Hardware trojans (HT)
2	Denial-of-Service (DoS)
3	Covert Side-channels
4	Side-channel analysis
5	Fault tolerance

NoC, strategically placed HTs in any of those critical components within the delicate router micro-architecture could silently degrade performance unbeknownst to the user.

Security Points-of-Interest: In our methodology, we define vulnerable locations and exploitable architecture features as *security points-of-interest (SPOI)*. Accurately identifying SPOI is not trivial, HTs may inject faults locally that would traditionally be disregarded as benign, but cascade in a manner that violate global functional correctness. For control logic model checkers, this includes expanding the blanket of coverage to include the validation of inputs in previous steps to validate the result of the current step. For example, a HT could suppress or impair the result in early RC, VA, or SA stages, such that a flit that should take ST in the next stage, would be disallowed to move, but not create an invariance violation because the model checker for the ST stage is independent and unaware of the results in previous stages. In the micro-architecture, multiple violations that exhibit the same dependencies exist. Outside the pipeline, many SPOI exist as extensive research in NoCs has led to adaptive, reconfigurable and increasingly complex designs. In table 1, we include a number of locations we classify as SPOI for existing architectures. Techniques like power-gating, DVFS, and reconfiguration are SPOI because they could be maliciously modulated to covertly pass messages across security domains with covert side-channels or inadvertently switched to cause inefficient execution.

Identifying Threats: After SPOI have been identified, threats can be evaluated for the design in question. In table 2, we list a series of threats poised to challenge the reliability of future NoCs. It is important to determine the applicable threats because each type of threat could require a unique counter-measure. For example, a crypto-circuit that handles encrypt/decrypt transactions is more likely to face side-channel attacks to steal encryption key information, while a HT attack for router control logic would be more detrimental than a side-channel because the HT could not only steal information, but alter execution. Many of these threats have been recently explored for NoCs. In contrast, devices may face a combination of threats that are not guaranteed to be mutually exclusive. A HT on links, memory controllers, or control logic, could be engineered to create a control-driven DoS attack, unlike flood-based bandwidth depleting DoS. In NoCs, detection of a particular control-driven DoS attack was proposed in [8], but in this paper we will show how our proposed SMCs can prevent the attack, after identifying the porus holes with existing fault tolerant designs.

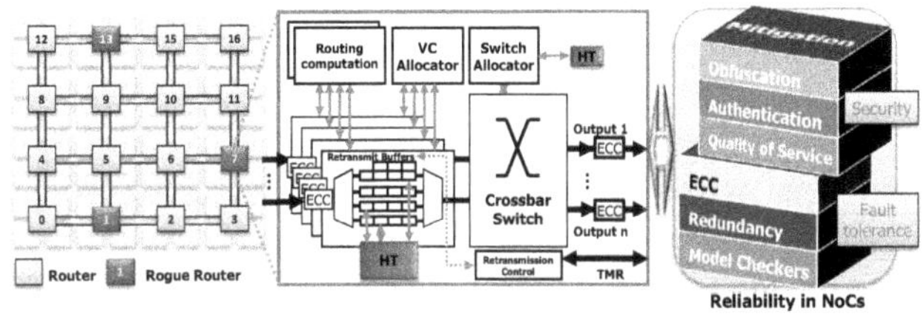

Figure 1: A secure fault tolerant stack to evaluate architectures during design time to identify HT points of interest, evaluate threats, and select adequate mitigation.

Mitigation Selection: While challenges continue to exist in off-line detection for integrated circuits, architects should develop designs with detection and mitigation techniques. Ignoring threats could facade performance and overall reliability. After carefully identifying SPOI and evaluating designs for vulnerabilities, selecting the proper detection and mitigation techniques to reinforce weak points in the design is the last step in the process. In Figure 1, we show a compromised NoC with multiple HTs embedded within the pipeline logic and buffers. The infected routers were chosen randomly but could be selected appropriately to target resources in different geographical locations of the chip. In this scenario, HTs have access to influence resource allocations and corrupt data. Currently, fault tolerance for faults in both locations is inadequate to prevent such an attack. For example, when flits are transmitted, switch-to-switch (s2s) ECC decodes for errors, after which the data is stored in buffers unprotected. Typically the data is not encoded until the flit progresses to the next router. A HT injecting faults in the buffer will bypass s2s detection. For a control logic HT, suppression of requests in VA logic for a flit could side-line a packet and create a DoS attack. Suppressing the request effectively masks the fault as a loss in arbitration and the fault would be undetected.

To improve reliability, we propose a two-fold approach involving fault tolerance and security. In Figure 1, we illustrate the reliability stack which consists of *Obfuscation, Authentication, Quality of Service, ECC, Redundancy, and Model Checkers*. Each of the SPOIs and threats presented above can be addressed with at least one element of the stack. In the next sections, we will describe how we use elements of the stack to improve coverage for control flow and data paths.

4. SECURE MODEL CHECKERS

To protect the critical micro-architecture pipeline and its control logic, light-weight invariant model checkers proposed in [12], provide near instantaneous concurrent fault detec-

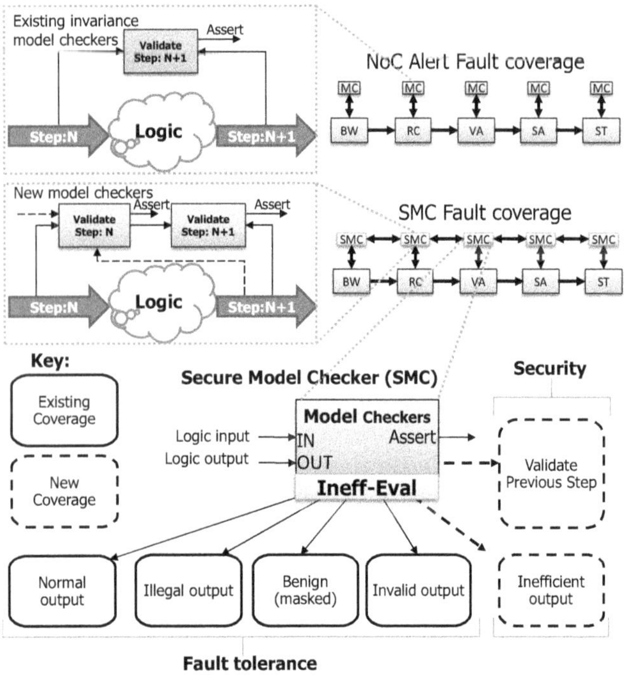

Figure 2: High level overview and the fault coverage enhancements for the proposed SMCs.

tion. Model checkers consist of hardware assertions with simple combinational logic, implemented to follow a set of invariant rules. The invariant rules are enforced by comparing the inputs of control logic to the output. Output for model checkers can be classified in the following ways: Normal, and Invalid. Invalid output can be benign, or illegal. Illegal output is output that violates an invariant rule. For example, if an arbiter receives one or more requests, at least one grant should be on the output. An assertion flag is raised when a violation occurs.

Inefficient Output: For SMCs we expand this model to include an additional classification of invalid output, namely, *inefficient output*. In Figure 2, we show a generic model checker, a proposed SMC, and the expansion of coverage. In Figure 3, we further expand the classification of inefficient output and provide example violations. For inefficient output, this includes the modulated, flooded, starved and de-prioritization of network resources. In this paper, we propose security through enhanced fault tolerance to detect malicious gaming of resources. In traditional fault tolerance, the threat of inefficient output exist through permanent faults but is minimal. When transient faults occur in this category, the faults will be detected downstream or result in benign violations. We will now discuss how our proposed SMCs include coverage for the new violations.

Starvation & Previous Step Validation: For existing model checkers shown in Figure 2, we define the output they validate as the *next step* (Step N+1). The input provided to the control logic, which came from the previous stage, is defined as the *previous step* (Step N). For example, Step N could be the execution of the RC stage and Step N+1 is the following VA stage. Between the time RC and VA was computed in adjacent cycles, the output of RC is stored for the flit and the state machine tracking pipeline progress is updated, allowing the flit to request VA in the next cycle.

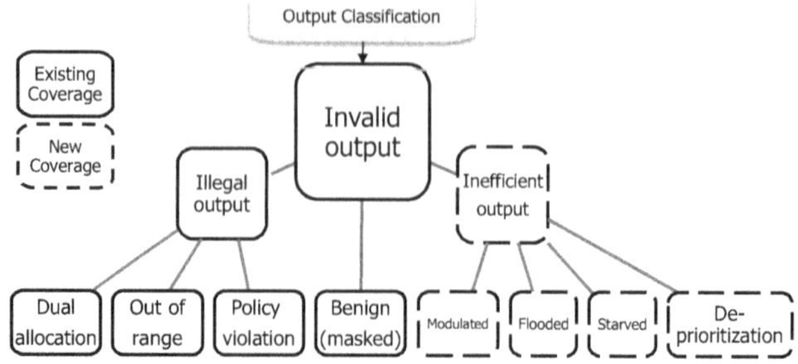

Figure 3: Threat identification and enhancements from traditional model checkers to the proposed SMCs.

While invariant rules cover the detection of faults on the inputs of control logic, generic model checkers are designed independently and Step N+1 is oblivious to output generated in the Step N. If a HT is maliciously suppressing a VA request, the generic model checker methodology would not raise an invariance violation and diagnose the fault as benign. Disallowing the flit to move and disguising the fault as a arbitration loss because the generic model checker is unaware of the results in the previous stage. We integrate our proposed SMCs and define new violations to detect HTs and prevent them from stalling flits by suppressing resource requests. The integration of SMCs is shown in Figure 2. Each SMC has access to adjacent SMCs and direct access to buffers and status registers. For a SMC blanketing a VA block, a HT suppressing a request would no longer go undetected. Other scenarios exist that include SA and credit counts and SA, ST integration. A complete list of violations will be provided later in the paper.

De-prioritization: In addition to suppressing requests and grants, arbiters are vulnerable to de-prioritization HT attacks. In a de-prioritization attack, a HT embedded within arbitration logic directly influences the allocation of resources. Flits could be permanently or periodically stalled to create a DoS attack. Depending on the implementation (round robin, weighted, FIFO) different approaches are required. For FIFO and round robin, no requester should win consecutive grants in the presence of multiple requesters. To capture the violation, previous inputs and outputs are stored to validate the next grant. For weighted, detection is longer because counters are needed to measure the arbitration fairness. In the performance evaluation section, we will evaluate the cost of each approach.

5. PERFORMANCE EVALUATION

In this section, we provide the results of the proposed SMCs and discuss our HT detection technique to address the SPOI presented earlier in this paper in terms of area, power, detection latency, and network performance. In our evaluation, we compare against NoCAlert [12], an existing fault tolerant detection framework that originally proposed light-weight invariant checkers for real-time fault detection in the router micro-architecture.

As a first order analysis, we assume only a single point of attack in the compromised NoC which is sufficient to provide significant network disruption but the number of compromised routers is orthogonal. Power and area were synthesized and optimized using the Synopsys Design Compiler

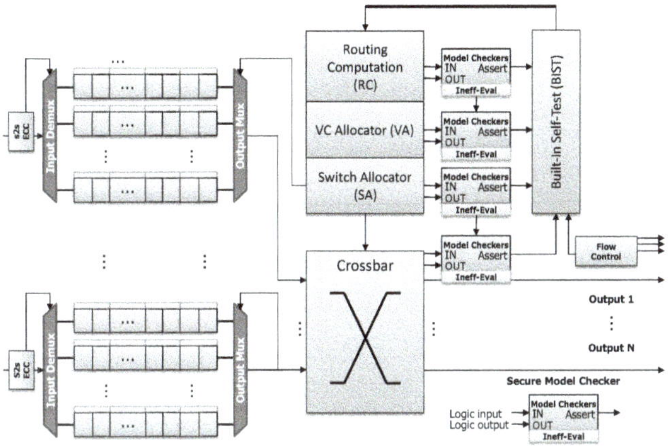

Figure 4: The SMC micro-architecture with the proposed enhancements in blue.

tool using the TSMC 40 nm technology libraries with a 1.0 V supply voltage and 2 GHz operating frequency. Network evaluation was conducted using an in-house cycle accurate network simulator and used real traffic distributions from the PARSEC and SPLASH-2 benchmark suites on a 64-core, 16 router mesh-based NoC with each router connected to 4 cores. Each router has two unidirectional links connecting adjacent routers with 4 VCs per port and a 5-stage router pipeline.

5.1 Micro-architecture Rules

In this section, we describe the proposed micro-architecture and a set of additional functional correctness rules obtained using our SPOI methodology. In Figure 4, we illustrate the modifications needed to implement SMCs (shown in blue) in a typical fault tolerant micro-architecture (shown in grey), and arrows between each model checker to relay previous state information between consecutive stages. In addition to previous state information, SMCs concurrently observe inputs and output values to verify the functional correctness of each pipeline stage without causing an interruption in performance during fault free operation. In Figure 5, we list a portion of invariance rules proposed in [12] (left), and the security enhancements provided by SMCs proposed in this paper (right) for a detail comparison. It is important to note NoCAlert was originally designed with naturally occurring faults in mind and not those injected to maliciously game network resources and produce in-efficient output or denial of service. With the expansion of coverage shown in Figure 5, we improve the reliability of NoCs by increasing our ability to verify functional correctness and detect HTs. When SMCs detect HTs our proposed design could complement mitigation techniques by enabling them or begin the shutdown of compromised components in a controlled manner.

5.2 Area overhead and power consumption

Our proposed design includes additions to the BW, RC, VA ,SA and ST stages of the router micro-architecture. The area overhead and power consumption for each stage is presented in Figure 6 and 7 respectively. While the overhead cost for area and power consumption is larger than that of NoCAlert, that is expected as the proposed SMCs include additional hardware assertions and are integrated together

	#	Existing Model Checkers (NoCAlert)	SMC enhancments	#
RC	1	Illegal turn	Inefficient route selection	1
	2	Invalid RC output direction	Deprioritization (if required)	2
	3	Non-minimal routing (if required)		
VA and SA	4	Grant w/o request	No VA requests w/ existing flits	3
	5	Grant to nobdy	No VA requests w/ mismatched credit count	4
	6	1-hot grant vector	Deprioritization of VA grants	5
	7	Grant to occupied or full VC	VA requets inconsistent with flits in previouc RC cycle	6
	8	One-to-One VC assignment	No SA requests w/ existing flits	7
	9	One-to-One port assignment	No SA requests w/ mismatched credit count	8
	10	VA agress with RC	Deprioritization of SA grants	9
	11	SA agrees with RC		
	12	Intra-VA stage order		
	13	Intra-SA stage order		
ST	14	1-hot column control vector	ST inconsistent with grants in previous VASA cycle	10
	15	1-hot row control vector		
	16	# of Incoming flits equals # of Outgoing flits		

Figure 5: List of invariant rules proposed in [12] (left), and security rule enhancements proposed in this paper with SMCs (right).

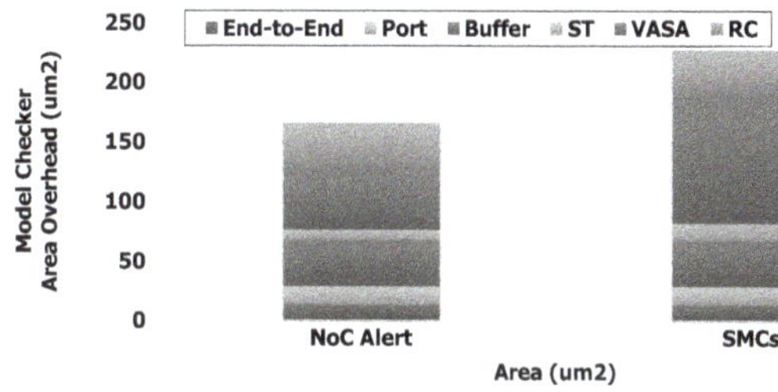

	NoC Alert	SMCs
RC	37.926	37.044
VASA	51.3324	107.604
ST	9.3492	15.1704
Buffer	38.2788	38.2788
Port	15.6996	15.6996
End-to-End	13.0536	13.0536

Figure 6: Comparison of area overhead for SMCs to traditional model checkers.

to expand coverage to malicious HTs. Results indicate a 35% increase in total area overhead, and 124% increase in power consumption to that of NoCAlert with round robin arbitration. This cost however, is only 1.1% area overhead and 1.5% power consumption of a single router. The majority of the SMC cost is due to the verification of arbitration units and the counters needed to detect de-prioritization. Since it is not uncommon for NoCs to implement other arbitration methods such as round robin and different weights for VA and SA, we provide a comprehensive look at the cost of arbitration shown in Figure 8. What we found was that verifying round robin is significantly cheaper than weighted units because of expensive multi-bit counters.

5.3 Detection latency

When protecting against HTs, time is of the essence since a single HT could cause denial of service, create routing dead-locks, or covertly leak sensitive information. To avoid detection, HTs can be implemented in a variety of ways and lay dormant until selectively enabled through combination logic, sequential clocks, or external signals. Fortunately, with our proposed SMCs, near instantaneous HT detection is possible within pipeline control logic. For rules involving previous state information, SMCs can detect each violation in the subsequent cycle. For de-prioritization, the detection latency depends on the size of counters needed to measure weighted values which could reach tens to hundreds of cycles. For round robin arbitration, detection time is near instantaneous.

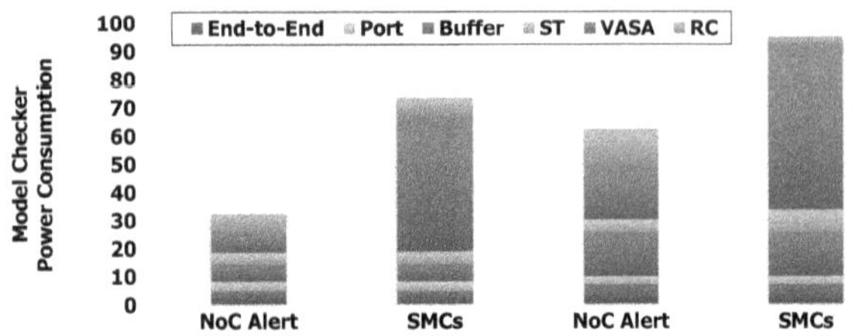

	Dynamic Power (uw)		Static Power (nw)	
	NoC Alert	SMCs	NoC Alert	SMCs
RC	6.9646	6.9739	13.7104	14.5054
VASA	6.9649	47.505	18.1341	46.7618
ST	4.1702	4.6024	4.6856	7.9891
Buffer	5.9119	5.9119	15.7099	15.7099
Port	3.4348	3.4348	2.8368	2.8368
End-to-End	4.9633	4.9633	7.2056	7.2056

Figure 7: Comparison of power consumption for SMCs to traditional model checkers.

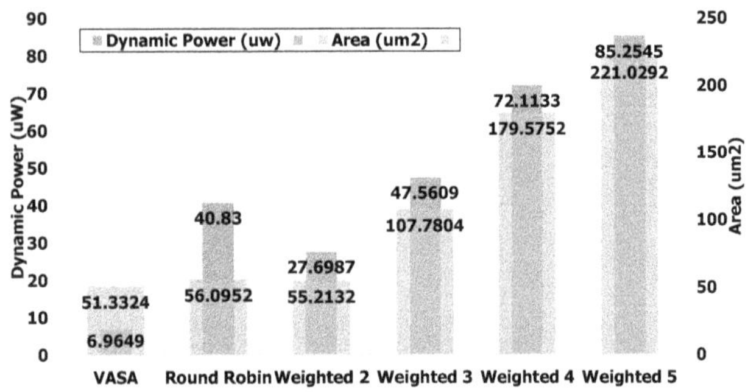

Figure 8: Comparison of area overhead and power consumption for arbitration model checker units.

6. CONCLUSION

In this paper, we proposed a design methodology that defined SPOI and their vulnerabilities in existing NoC microarchitectures and fault tolerant techniques. With SPOI identified, we then proposed SMCs to provide near instantaneous HT detection and prevent in-efficient gaming of network resources with only 1.1% and 1.5% total router area overhead and power consumption respectively. With identification of SPOI, SMCs could be tailored to future designs and improve on mitigation techniques complemented by our threat detectors.

Acknowledgement

This research was partially supported by NSF grants CCF-1054339 (CAREER), CCF-1420718, CCF-1318981, ECCS-1342657, and CCF-1513606.

7. REFERENCES

[1] D. M. Ancajas, K. Chakraborty, and S. Roy. Fort-nocs: Mitigating the threat of a compromised noc. In *Proceedings of the The 51st Annual Design Automation Conference on Design Automation Conference*, DAC '14, 2014.

[2] L. Benini and G. De Micheli. Networks on chips: a new soc paradigm. *Computer*, 35(1):70–78, 2002.

[3] S. Bhunia, M. Hsiao, M. Banga, and S. Narasimhan. Hardware trojan attacks: Threat analysis and countermeasures. *Proceedings of the IEEE*, 102(8):1229–1247, Aug 2014.

[4] R. S. Chakraborty, F. Wolff, S. Paul, C. Papachristou, and S. Bhunia. Mero: A statistical approach for hardware trojan detection. In *Proceedings of the 11th International Workshop on Cryptographic Hardware and Embedded Systems*, CHES '09, 2009.

[5] W. J. Dally and B. Towles. Route packets, not wires. In *Proceedings of the Design Automation Conference (DAC)*, Las Vegas, NV, USA, June 18-22 2001.

[6] D. Fang, H. Li, J. Han, and X. Zeng. Robustness analysis of mesh-based network-on-chip architecture under flooding-based denial of service attacks. In *Networking, Architecture and Storage (NAS), 2013 IEEE Eighth International Conference on*, pages 178–186, 2013.

[7] D. Fick, A. DeOrio, J. Hu, V. Bertacco, D. Blaauw, and D. Sylvester. Vicis: A reliable network for unreliable silicon. In *Design Automation Conference, 2009. DAC '09. 46th ACM/IEEE*, pages 812–817, 2009.

[8] R. JS, D. M. Ancajas, K. Chakraborty, and S. Roy. Runtime detection of a bandwidth denial attack from a rogue network-on-chip. In *Proceedings of the 9th International Symposium on Networks-on-Chip*, NOCS '15, pages 8:1–8:8, 2015.

[9] M. Kakoee, V. Bertacco, and L. Benini. A distributed and topology-agnostic approach for on-line noc testing. In *Networks on Chip (NoCS), 2011 Fifth IEEE/ACM International Symposium on*, pages 113–120, 2011.

[10] J. Li and J. Lach. At-speed delay characterization for ic authentication and trojan horse detection. In *Hardware-Oriented Security and Trust, 2008. HOST 2008. IEEE International Workshop on*, June 2008.

[11] R. Parikh and V. Bertacco. Forever: A complementary formal and runtime verification approach to correct noc functionality. *ACM Trans. Embed. Comput. Syst.*, 13(3s):104:1–104:30, Mar. 2014.

[12] A. Prodromou, A. Panteli, C. Nicopoulos, and Y. Sazeides. Nocalert: An on-line and real-time fault detection mechanism for network-on-chip architectures. In *Microarchitecture (MICRO), 2012 45th Annual IEEE/ACM International Symposium on*, pages 60–71, 2012.

[13] S. Sethumadhavan, A. Waksman, M. Suozzo, Y. Huang, and J. Eum. Trustworthy hardware from untrusted components. *Commun. ACM*, 58(9):60–71, Aug. 2015.

[14] M. Tehranipoor and F. Koushanfar. A survey of hardware trojan taxonomy and detection. *Design Test of Computers, IEEE*, 27(1):10–25, Jan 2010.

[15] X. Wang, H. Salmani, M. Tehranipoor, and J. Plusquellic. Hardware trojan detection and isolation using current integration and localized current analysis. In *Defect and Fault Tolerance of VLSI Systems, 2008. DFTVS '08. IEEE International Symposium on*, Oct 2008.

[16] H. M. G. Wassel, Y. Gao, J. K. Oberg, T. Huffmire, R. Kastner, F. T. Chong, and T. Sherwood. Surfnoc: A low latency and provably non-interfering approach to secure networks-on-chip. *SIGARCH Comput. Archit. News*, 41(3):583–594, June 2013.

[17] Q. Yu and J. Frey. Exploiting error control approaches for hardware trojans on network-on-chip links. In *Defect and Fault Tolerance in VLSI and Nanotechnology Systems (DFT), 2013 IEEE International Symposium on*, Oct 2013.

Parameter-importance based Monte-Carlo Technique for Variation-aware Analog Yield Optimization

Sita Kondamadugula
International Institute of Information Technology,Bangalore
26/C,Electronics City
Bangalore, India
sitakondamadugula@gmail.com

Srinath R Naidu
International Institute of Information Technology,Bangalore
26/C,Electronics City
Bangalore, India
srinathn@iiitb.ac.in

ABSTRACT

The Monte-Carlo method is the method of choice for accurate yield estimation. Standard Monte-Carlo methods suffer from a huge computational burden even though they are very accurate. Recently a Monte-Carlo method was proposed for the parametric yield estimation of digital integrated circuits [13] that achieves significant computational savings at no loss of accuracy by focusing on those statistical variables that have a significant impact on yield. We adapt this technique to the context of analog circuit yield estimation. The inputs to the proposed method are the designable parameters, the uncontrollable statistical variations, and the operating conditions of interest. The technique of [13] operates on a linear model of circuit variations. In our work we first convexify the nonlinear design constraints to obtain a convex feasible region. We then consider an accurate polytope-approximation of the convex feasible region by taking tangent hyperplanes at various points on the surface of the convex region. The hyperplanes give rise to a matrix of design variable sensitivities, which is then used to glean information about the importance of design variables for yield estimation. Finally the knowledge of which design variables are very important for yield estimation is used to allow the Monte-Carlo technique achieve a lower error compared to standard Monte-Carlo in the same amount of simulation time.

CCS Concepts

•**Hardware → Physical design (EDA); Design for manufacturability; Process variations; Yield and cost optimization;**

Keywords

Yield Optimization,Monte-Carlo, Variation-aware Analog Yield, Yield Estimation

GLSVLSI '16, May 18-20, 2016, Boston, MA, USA
© 2016 ACM. ISBN 978-1-4503-4274-2/16/05...$15.00
DOI: http://dx.doi.org/10.1145/2902961.2903018

1. INTRODUCTION

The ever shrinking size of analog circuits makes yield estimation difficult. Even a small analog circuit has tens to hundreds of real-valued design parameters that must be set in order to meet its specifications. Most of the analog circuit parameters are highly nonlinear. Process variations influence the difference between the values of the design variables set by the designer and what actually appear on the manufactured chip. This situation contributes to yield-loss, i.e manufactured chips which do not meet their specifications . These variations in the process technology have a large influence on the yield of a designed and manufactured circuit [3]. Given the continuous advancement of process technology, the effect of variation is likely to get worse for future technology nodes. For technologies larger than 180nm, variations are mostly in the below 10 percent range. For technologies down to 90nm, 65nm, 45nm and below, the variations can be more than 50 percent. The correlation between circuit yield and profit necessitates yield maximization in different design stages. Process variations include inter-die, intra-die and environmental variations and all of them need to be taken into account during the design process. A robust design is one which is capable of meeting its specifications in the presence of process variations. It is challenging to come up with a robust design methodology for analog circuits. Different methods have been introduced to address the robust design problem in the face of process variations [6]. Analytic modeling of yield optimization is addressed by constraint transformation and topology selections [8],[5].

Geometric programming methods for maximizing the yield cast circuit specifications as posynomials, and the objective function as yield. Since the formulation is convex after a variable transformation, very efficient techniques for convex optimization can be used to solve the problem. Geometric programming techniques can be used to compute globally optimal trade-off curves to reach specified performance constraints subjected to yield maximization [2]. Projection-based performance modeling starts with simplified models optimized based on the knowledge of experts and extends these models to large scale problems using a projection based scheme for performance modeling [9]. Casting specifications in the form of equations causes some inaccuracy in the modeling of higher order effects which becomes more and more significant as technologies are scaled to smaller feature sizes and subjected to higher performance ranges. Geometrical methods suffer from the trade-off between accuracy

and cost of modeling. Statistical methods target the maximization of the acceptability region by choosing optimum values for specific parameters based on probability distributions [14]. Statistical methods can be classified briefly as worst-case methods and Monte-Carlo methods. Worst-case methods use nonlinear optimization formulation to search for the worst-case point. These methods give the range of allowed values of process parameters that will still enable the circuit to satisfy the performance requirement. Some methods only can be trusted to give an approximate estimate of the yield. Worst-case methods are generally inaccurate [3]. Monte-Carlo techniques sample process parameters to simulate the circuit behavior for various settings of the design parameters [10]. Monte-Carlo based methods are generally accurate in estimating yield but not efficient enough as the complexity increases. Therefore, these methods generally face the disadvantage of being computationally expensive as the complexity of the design models increases. Several variants of Monte-Carlo methods have been proposed to increase efficiency like Acceptance Sampling and Latin Hypercube Sampling. These techniques are used to replace random sampling [7]. In order to compute yield with as few samples as possible, many variants of MC(Monte Carlo) method have been tried, but each of them lacks in one of robustness, accuracy, practicality or stability. The Monte-Carlo method is also used partially in the calculation of yield, sometimes this is used in different stages of different algorithms [11].
Yield analysis is performed using many different methods. One method to perform yield optimization is by directly considering yield as the objective function to maximize. Another method is design centring which indirectly maximizes yield by placing the nominal design in the center of the acceptability region by inclines of worst-case distances[1]. The design center is the best design point with regard to the feasible region in the sense that even a large deviation in the the values of design parameters caused by process and environmental variations will still prevent the design center from leaving the region of acceptability [9].

Definitions and Mathematical Representations of Yield: The performance space ϕ is described by n_p performance parameters, one for each circuit specification of interest ϕ.

$$\phi = (\phi_1, \phi_2 \cdots \phi_{n_p}) \tag{1}$$

The performance space can also be expressed as a feasible region in the space of design parameters p_i, also known as design space or parametric space. Each point in design space can be denoted as follows:

$$p = (p_1, p_2 \cdots p_n) \tag{2}$$

Note that the number of design variables is n.The acceptability region A_ϕ can be explained as the circuit performance region where performance and parameter values fall within their limits.

Yield is defined as the percentage of the total number of circuits manufactured that fulfill parametric performance requirements. The probability that a designed circuit will fall in the acceptable performance region can be expressed as follows:

$$Y = Prob\{\phi \in A_\phi\} = \int_{A_\phi} f_\phi(\phi) d\phi \tag{3}$$

To achieve DFY (Design For Yield) design parameters of circuit can be represented as function of nominal values p_0 and process variations. Let ξ be a vector containing process variation random variables. Then the vector of design parameters can be written as:

$$p = p(p_0, \xi) \tag{4}$$

1.1 Introduction to Yield Optimization

The performance values f of a circuit can be calculated for a given set of parameter values by feeding the vector (d, s, θ) to the circuit design models. Here
d is the vector of design parameters eg:nominal widths, lengths, currents, bias voltages, capacitances and resistances.
s is the vector of process variations in oxide thickness and threshold voltage of the transistors in the circuit.
and θ is the vector of environment parameters like supply voltage and temperature.
The goal of yield optimization is to choose a design point d where yield is maximum considering the effects of the process parameter variation vector s,and environment parameter variation vector θ.[11],[15].
The parametric yield Y can be given as

$$Y(d, \theta) = \int_{f(d,s,\theta)} pdf(s) ds \tag{5}$$

where d refers to a design point in the design space, and θ refers to a particular setting of the environment parameters. The above equation defines yield as a function of d and θ and is obtained by integrating the joint distribution of process parameters over the acceptable region of process parameters.

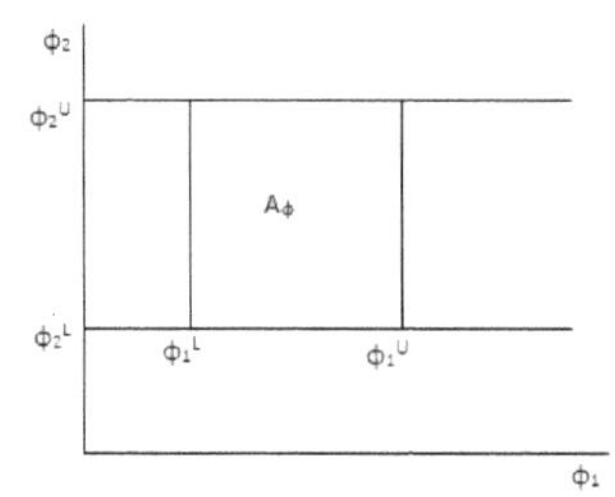

Figure 1: Acceptability region in performance space.

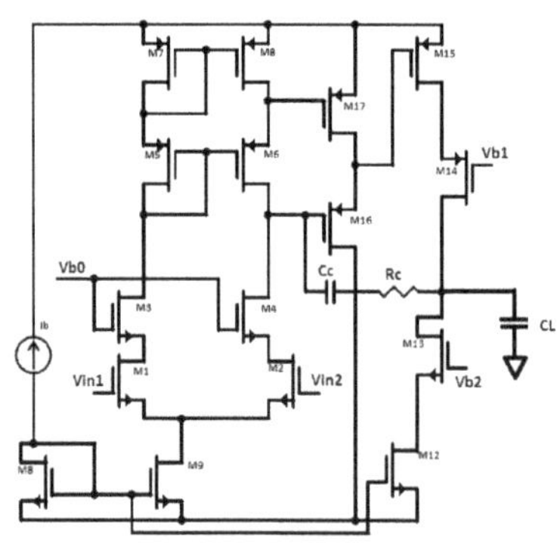

Figure 2: Two stage Op-amp Circuit

The circuit shown in Fig.2 is a two-stage op-amp consisting of an input stage, a second stage, and a compensating circuit. The input stage has three parts: a current source, a differential pair, and a current mirror. The second stage has two parts: a transconductance amplifier, and an active load. We use this circuit to calculate yield [16]. Constraints include design space constraints to keep transistors in saturation and to keep transistors lengths and widths within limits to meet the performance parameters mentioned in Table 1. A total of 24 constraints are used to calculate yield. This circuit is designed in 180nm CMOS process with VDD = 1.2V. The different steps of yield calculation are described using the example circuit shown in Fig.2. Transistor widths, lengths, biasing current, compensation capacitance and Vth are design parameters of the circuit. The performance specifications of the circuit such as gain A(0), Unity Gain Frequency, Slew Rate, Common Mode Ratio (CMR) are mentioned in Table 1. Also mentioned are the constraints on widths, lengths, and biasing currents of transistors. We set up design space constraints to keep transistors in saturation. There are additional constraints to ensure that the considered variable values are within specified limits.

Performance Parameters	Spec
Gain(A(0))(dB)	70
UGF(MHz)	10
PM(deg)	60
CMR(V)	-2.5,2.5
SR(V/μ sec)	20

Table 1: Specifications of performance parameters

2. PARAMETER-IMPORTANCE BASED MC TECHNIQUE

The state-of-art approaches to find the best design point for yield maximization considers parametric space(s) to be as important as performance space. We introduce a method to sample parametric space with reference to the "importance" of parameters in a system of equations used to model the acceptability region in parametric space. The design flow is shown in Fig.3. The importance of a parameter roughly translates into the impact of the parameter on the yield of the manufactured circuit. We expend more of the computational effort of sampling on those parameters which have more impact on yield at the expense of those that have lower impact on yield. This leads to a more efficient Monte-Carlo method as compared to conventional Monte-Carlo where all parameters are sampled equally, without regard to their estimated impact on yield.

Our method is inspired by the research contained in [13]. There it was noted in the context of digital circuit yield estimation, that gate delay parameters belonging to a lot of critical paths in the circuit had a greater impact on manufacturing yield compared to those that did not appear in many critical paths. For example gates close to primary outputs, or those with a large fan-out were seen to have a particularly large impact on yield. We translate this observation into our domain by asking which of the design parameters in an analog circuit have a disproportionate impact on yield. In our context, the feasible region is nonlinear unlike in [13]. We therefore linearise the non-linear feasible region so as to be able to apply an importance measure similar to[13]. Linearisation of the feasible region transforms the feasible region into a system of linear inequalities expressible in matrix terms as $Ad \leq b$, where d is the design vector. The importance of a design variable is determined by the sum of absolute values in the column of matrix A corresponding to the variable. The given feasible region in design space is described by nonlinear constraints and can be shown to be convex if we make an appropriate variable transformation. Our method is especially effective on convex feasible regions.

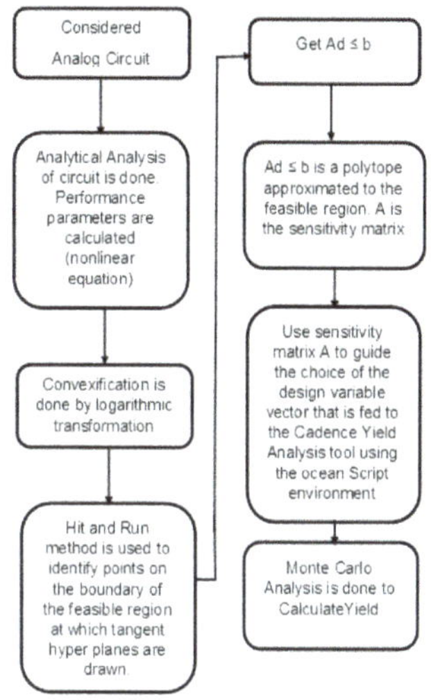

Figure 3: Flow diagram of implemented method.

Our method first approximates the feasible region using tangent hyperplanes drawn at random points selected on the boundary of the feasible region. The random points are selected using a hit-and-run procedure where we project an arbitrary point in space to the boundary of the feasible region. The tangent hyper planes taken together give a polytope approximation of the feasible region, i.e as a set of linear inequalities in the design parameters. For each variable in the design parameter space, we obtain a sensitivity value for the variable as the sum of absolute values of the coefficients of the variable in all the inequalities that feature the variable. The idea behind this is that the sensitivity of a variable is high if a small change in the value of the variable impacts the constraints significantly, and could cause yield loss by causing some critical constraints to be dissatisfied. On the other hand, if a variable has low sensitivity, an equivalent small change in the value of the variable will not have the same impact on yield. We illustrate below the various steps involved in our method, starting with a convex GP formulation of the feasible region, use of a hit-and-run strategy to obtain points on the boundary and the calculation of the tangent hyperplanes to obtain a polytope approximation of the feasible region.

2.1 Convexification of feasible region

Constraints for the design considered in this paper can be recast as posynomial constraints in a Geometric Programming (GP) formulation following [13]. The constraints g_i's are posynomials of V_{GT}, g_m, g_d, I_b of different transistors and V_T, V_{TSAT} and $(1 + \lambda V_{DS})$. I_D of the transistors, W,L, and I_b are design variables. It is known that the GP formulation is itself non-convex but a logarithmic transformation of the optimization problem, as shown below, makes the problem convex.

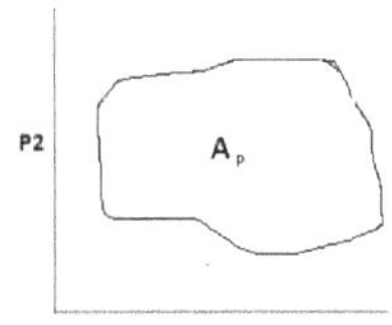

Figure 4: Feasible region

$$g_i = f(W, L, I_b) \leq 1$$

$y_1 = log(W), y_2 = log(L), y_3 = log(I_b), g_i$is transformed as $g_i = f(e^{y_1}, e^{y_2}, e^{y_3})$ Note that V_{TSAT}, g_{d1}, g_{d3} etc are expressed in terms of W,L,and I_b as product-of-power or PoP functions [12] and after substituting for them, every constraint in the original problem becomes a posynomial inW_i, L_i, I_b.

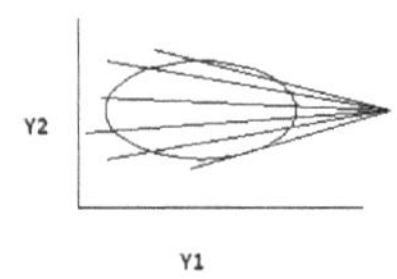

Figure 5: $\vec{v}_i$ are drawn to design space

We give below details of the hit-and-run algorithm used to obtain points on the feasible region boundary in design space. This algorithm is along the lines of the procedure described in [16] where it is used in the context of geometric random walks. Let d be an arbitrary point in design space which may or may not belong in the feasible region. Let $\vec{v}$ be a random vector which is drawn uniformly at random from the set of all possible directions. This is done using $v_i = N(0,1)$ where $N(0,1)$ is a sample of a Gaussian random variable with mean 0 and variance 1. The choice of a unit normal random variable for each component of the vector $\vec{v}$ ensures that we sample all directions uniformly. For each constraint i we let (t^i_{min}, t^i_{max}) represent the range for the scalar quantity t such that $d + t\vec{v}$ still satisfies the i-th constraint. Since the region is convex, we are guaranteed to find a single contiguous interval for the value of t for each constraint. Then we take the intersection of all the intervals to obtain a range (t_{min}, t_{max}) for all constraints. We note that the vectors $d + t_{min}\vec{v}$ and $d + t_{max}\vec{v}$ represent two points on the boundary of the feasible region. We repeat this procedure for different random vectors $\vec{v}$ to obtain different points on the boundary.

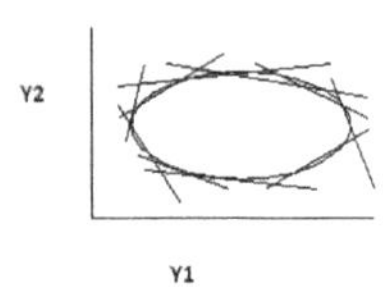

Figure 6: Tangents drawn to (log space)design space at t

The last step consists of drawing tangent hyperplanes at the points on the boundary selected by the hit-and-run procedure described above. The equation of a plane at the point $(u_0, u_1, u_2 \cdots u_n)$ on the surface where the normal vector is $\vec{(n)} = (a_0, a_1, a_2 \cdots a_n)$ is given by

$$\sum_{i=0}^{i=n} a_i(d_i - u_i) = 0 \tag{6}$$

The polytope approximation for the convex feasible region is given by

$$Ad \leq b \tag{7}$$

where each row of the matrix A represents a tangent hyper plane. We treat the matrix A as a "sensitivity" matrix and use its columns to obtain information about the importance of the variables. For a design variable d_i we define its importance to be the length of the ith column vector in the matrix A. The idea here is that if the ith column has a large length relative to the other variables, then d_i must be sampled much more carefully relative to the other variables in our search for the design point that maximizes yield. Here the length of a column is the sum of the absolute values of the elements in the column.

Monte-Carlo sampling for the design vector takes into account the importance of variables during the sampling procedure and samples variables according to their ratio of importance. For example, if we have a system of two variables where the importance of the first variable is 4 and that of the second two, we generate samples along the following lines: $(a_1, b_1), (a_2, b_1), (a_3, b_2), (a_4, b_2)$. In other words we generate two samples for variable 1 for every sample generated for variable 2. This allows us to explore variable 1 more carefully compared to variable 2.

3. YIELD ESTIMATION PROCEDURE AND SIMULATION BUDGET ALLOCATION

Algorithm 1 Method A

```
for i = 0 to n do
  FullDesignVector=RandSampleVector(g)
  :
  :
  yield=CalculateYield(FullDesignVector)
end for
```

In Algorithm 1 (Method A), we sample all g design variables n times and calculate yield. In Algorithm 2 (MethodB), we sample the u "low sensitivity" design variables k times and v "high sensitivity" design variables $km > n$ times, and calculate yield. Note that $u + v = g$, so we are partitioning the design variables in two categories. Here $km > n$.τ is time spent by both methods. Method A samples the g design variables n times, and performs only n simulations. Method B in contrast, spends less time sampling variables because only a small fraction of variables is sampled $km > n$ times, and all other variables are sampled very few times. Method B directs the savings in sampling time towards extra simulations. We hope that Method B explores design space more efficiently than Method A because it actually performs more simulations and scans through the most important variables more times than method A.

Algorithm 2 Method B

```
for j = 0 to k − 1 do
  LowSensitivityDesignVector=RandSampleVector(u)
  for k = 0 to m − 1 do
    HighSensitivityDesignVector=RandSampleVector(v)
    :
    :
    yield=CalculateYield(LowSensitivityDesignVector,
    HighSensitivityDesignVector)
  end for
end for
```

We now explore the tradeoffs involved between our method (Method B) and more conventional Monte-Carlo simulation (Method A). Let T be the number of design points that method A manages to explore in time τ. For each design point, it samples all g design variables once at a cost in time of $g\rho$ and then computes yield at a cost in time of M. The total time consumed by Method A is $\tau = T(g\rho + M)$. Method B samples $T + \alpha$ design points in time τ. It manages to simulate extra design points because it spends less time in sampling - it incurs a time cost of $p\rho$ where $p << g$ in sampling because it only samples a small number ($= v$) of design variables to the fullest extent, and for each design point incurs a cost of M while calculating yield. Therefore we have $\tau = (T + \alpha)(p\rho + M)$. Equating the two values for τ we have

$$T(g\rho + M) = (T + \alpha) * (p\rho + M) \quad (8)$$

Solving for α we have $\alpha = \frac{T(g-p)\rho}{p\rho+M}$. If we assume that p is very small, then we see that $\alpha = Tg/M$. Thus we can run many more simulations in our method (Method B) when the yield computing cost M is small. The sweet spot of our method will be when we can compute yield quickly, preferably through a non-Monte-Carlo procedure.

4. EXPERIMENTAL RESULTS

A two-stage amplifier circuit is chosen as the design example for the method described in Fig.2. There are 32 design variables in total including the lengths and widths of various transistors and bias currents. Process variations are considered for V_{th} and all the transistor lengths and widths. Yield calculation is performed with Cadence using 180nm technology. The results of a 50000 MC simulation analysis is provided to estimate yield. The reference value of yield from this simulation is 98.9% and the other methods are analyzed with respect to this "golden" simulation. The entire flow of our technique can be seen in the flow-chart given (Fig.3) above. The results of applying our technique and a conventional Monte-Carlo technique on the same circuit are shown in the tables below for different simulation times. Since the two techniques are quite different, we decided that an "apple-to-apple" comparison of the two methods would allocate the same amount of time τ to both methods and see which method performed better. The value of τ is 21 min in our experimental setup. We considered a 10%-30% process variation in each design variable. We selected design points according to a uniform distribution for conventional Monte-Carlo and for our technique, we generated design points taking into account the relative importance of design variables. For our method, we oversampled the "high-sensitivity" design vector 150 times more than the "low-sensitivity" design

Time	MC Yield	MMC Yield
τ	87.3%	91.2%
τ	86.4%	92.7%
τ	83.4%	91.4%
τ	85.1%	93.2%
τ	82.4%	91.6%

Table 2: Calculated Yield Results Obtained by Monte Carlo(MC)method and Modified Monte Carlo Method with given Importance Sampling(MMC). The simulation time for both methods is the same, i.e τ.

Time	MC Yield	MMC Yield
2τ	82.97%	93.4%
2τ	89.1%	96.2%
2τ	87.92%	95.1%
2τ	91.32%	94.5%
2τ	87.3%	95.8%

Table 3: Calculated Yield Results Obtained by Monte Carlo(MC)method and Modified Monte Carlo Method with given Importance Sampling(MMC). Here we have taken simulation time for both methods to be 2τ.

vector, i.e for every one sample of the low-sensitivity design vector we used 150 samples for the high-sensitivity design vector. For each design point in both methods, we used the Ocean script environment in Cadence to generate yield values,and reported the best design point found. As can be seen in the tables below, for the same simulation time τ and its multiples used in both methods, our method was able to consistently produce a better design point than conventional Monte-Carlo.

5. CONCLUSION AND FUTURE WORK

This paper demonstrates the efficacy of a special Monte-Carlo procedure to generate yield-maximizing design points for analog circuits considering the impact of design variables on yield. The work builds on a method proposed for yield estimation of digital integrated circuits . The nonlinear, non-convex constraints that describe the feasible region of acceptability for the analog circuit are first convexified, and then approximated by a polytope which is described by linear constraints. Information from these linear constraints is then used to devise a measure of importance of variables. The importance of variables is factored into a Monte-Carlo procedure to search the design space for a yield point that

Time	MC Yield	MMC Yield
3τ	90.2 %	97.46 %
3τ	89.12 %	95.32 %
3τ	91.4 %	98.14 %
3τ	92.32 %	94.62 %
3τ	90.45 %	96.57 %

Table 4: Calculated Yield Results Obtained by Monte Carlo(MC)method and Modified Monte Carlo Method with given Importance Sampling(MMC). Here we have taken simulation time for both methods to be 3τ.

TimeBudget	Error% of MC	Error% of MMC Yield
τ	5.2%	0.479%
2τ	4.9%	0.16%
3τ	4.68%	0.05 %

Table 5: Efficiency of Method A and Method B with reference to golden value

maximizes yield. The experimental results show that the method performs better than a conventional sampling procedure that is blind to the impact of design variables on yield. In future work, we propose to look at different kinds of sampling for the inner-loop of our method. Since our method partitions design space into more important and less important variables, we reduce the dimensionality of the set of variables to be carefully sampled. This will in turn enable us to use special Monte-Carlo techniques that work well for low-dimensions such as low-discrepancy sequences. Further, our current work uses design-space information only to explore the design space more efficiently. We propose to use design space information to speed up the Monte-Carlo procedure for the estimation of the yield integral.

6. REFERENCES

[1] Yukio Aoki, Hiroo Masuda, Shōzō Shimada, and Shoji Sato. A new design-centering methodology for vlsi device development. *Computer-Aided Design of Integrated Circuits and Systems, IEEE Transactions on*, 6(3):452–461, 1987.

[2] Stephen P Boyd, Thomas H Lee, et al. Optimal design of a cmos op-amp via geometric programming. *Computer-Aided Design of Integrated Circuits and Systems, IEEE Transactions on*, 20(1):1–21, 2001.

[3] Markus Bühler, Jürgen Koehl, Jeanne Bickford, Jason Hibbeler, Ulf Schlichtmann, Ralf Sommer, Michael Pronath, and Andreas Ripp. Dfm/dfy design for manufacturability and yield-influence of process variations in digital, analog and mixed-signal circuit design. In *Proceedings of the conference on Design, automation and test in Europe: Proceedings*, pages 387–392. European Design and Automation Association, 2006.

[4] Kalyanmoy Deb, Amrit Pratap, Sameer Agarwal, and TAMT Meyarivan. A fast and elitist multiobjective genetic algorithm: Nsga-ii. *Evolutionary Computation, IEEE Transactions on*, 6(2):182–197, 2002.

[5] Nagu R Dhanwada, Adrian Nunez-Aldana, and Ranga Vemuri. Automatic constraint transformation with integrated parameter space exploration in analog system synthesis. In *Design Automation Conference, 1999. Proceedings of the ASP-DAC'99. Asia and South Pacific*, pages 153–156. IEEE, 1999.

[6] Stephen W Director, Peter Feldmann, and Kannan Krishna. Optimization of parametric yield: A tutorial. *International Journal of High Speed Electronics and Systems*, 3(01):95–136, 1992.

[7] Norman J Elias. Acceptance sampling: An efficient, accurate method for estimating and optimizing parametric yield [ic manufacture]. *Solid-State Circuits, IEEE Journal of*, 29(3):323–327, 1994.

[8] Carlo Guardiani, Primo Scandolara, Jacques Benkoski, and Germano Nicollini. Yield optimization of analog ics using two-step analytic modeling methods. *Solid-State Circuits, IEEE Journal of*, 28(7):778–783, 1993.

[9] Xin Li, Padmini Gopalakrishnan, Yang Xu, and Lawrence T Pileggi. Robust analog/rf circuit design with projection-based performance modeling. *Computer-Aided Design of Integrated Circuits and Systems, IEEE Transactions on*, 26(1):2–15, 2007.

[10] Bo Liu, Francisco V Fernández, Dimitri De Jonghe, and Georges Gielen. Less expensive and high quality stopping criteria for mc-based analog ic yield optimization. In *Electronics, Circuits, and Systems, 2009. ICECS 2009. 16th IEEE International Conference on*, pages 267–270. IEEE, 2009.

[11] Bo Liu, Francisco V Fernández, and Georges GE Gielen. Efficient and accurate statistical analog yield optimization and variation-aware circuit sizing based on computational intelligence techniques. *Computer-Aided Design of Integrated Circuits and Systems, IEEE Transactions on*, 30(6):793–805, 2011.

[12] Pradip Mandal and V Visvanathan. Cmos op-amp sizing using a geometric programming formulation. *Computer-Aided Design of Integrated Circuits and Systems, IEEE Transactions on*, 20(1):22–38, 2001.

[13] Srinath R Naidu. Speeding up monte-carlo simulation for statistical timing analysis of digital integrated circuits. In *VLSI Design, 2007. Held jointly with 6th International Conference on Embedded Systems., 20th International Conference on*, pages 265–270. IEEE, 2007.

[14] Md Waliullah Khan Nomani, Mohab Anis, and Goutam Koley. Statistical approach for yield optimization for minimum energy operation in subthreshold circuits considering variability issues. *Semiconductor Manufacturing, IEEE Transactions on*, 23(1):77–86, 2010.

[15] Robert Schwencker, Frank Schenkel, Michael Pronath, and H Graeb. Analog circuit sizing using adaptive worst-case parameter sets. In *date*, page 0581. IEEE, 2002.

[16] Santosh Vempala. Geometric random walks: a survey. *Combinatorial and computational geometry*, 52(573-612):2, 2005.

Low Energy Sketching Engines on Many-Core Platform for Big Data Acceleration

Amey Kulkarni†, Tahmid Abtahi, Emily Smith and Tinoosh Mohsenin
Department of Computer Science & Electrical Engineering
University of Maryland, Baltimore County
†ameyk1@umbc.edu

ABSTRACT

Almost 90% of the data available today was created within the last couple of years, thus Big Data set processing is of utmost importance. Many solutions have been investigated to increase processing speed and memory capacity, however I/O bottleneck is still a critical issue. To tackle this issue we adopt Sketching technique to reduce data communications. Reconstruction of the sketched matrix is performed using Orthogonal Matching Pursuit (OMP). Additionally we propose Gradient Descent OMP (GD-OMP) algorithm to reduce hardware complexity. Big data processing at real-time imposes rigid constraints on sketching kernel, hence to further reduce hardware overhead both algorithms are implemented on a low power domain specific many-core platform called Power Efficient Nano Clusters (PENC). GD-OMP algorithm is evaluated for image reconstruction accuracy and the PENC many-core architecture. Implementation results show that for large matrix sizes GD-OMP algorithm is 1.3× faster and consumes 1.4× less energy than OMP algorithm implementations. Compared to GPU and Quad-Core CPU implementations the PENC many-core reconstructs 5.4× and 9.8× faster respectively for large signal sizes with higher sparsity.

Keywords

OMP;Compressive Sensing; Many-Core; High Performance and Reconfigurable Architecture

1. INTRODUCTION

In past decade one of challenges that the research community has faced is Big Data processing on hardware. Big Data is everywhere as sensors and servers produce large amount of data at every second. Three problems have been constantly discussed in Big Data hardware processing namely storage, processing and memory bandwidth bottleneck. Streaming applications generate a humongous amount of data and needs to be processed in real-time, however generated data sets require large memory storage and thus high processing times [7].

GLSVLSI '16, May 18-20, 2016, Boston, MA, USA

DOI: http://dx.doi.org/10.1145/2902961.2902984

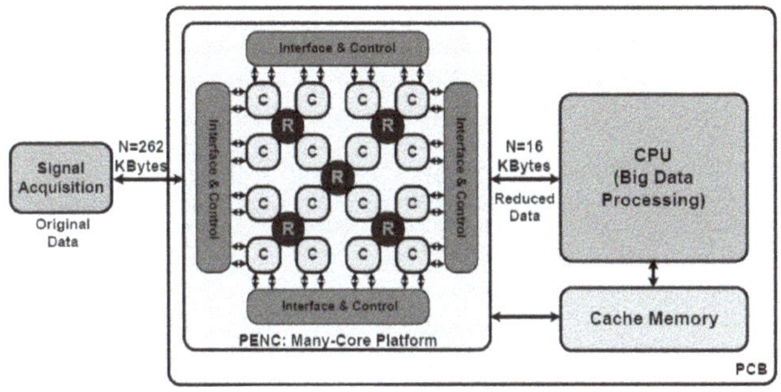

Figure 1: Low Energy Sketching Framework, where PENC Many-Core Platform acts as an accelerator and Big Data computations are performed on Host Platform

To solve these issues we propose to adopt sketching techniques. Sketching represents data set concisely, while keeping properties of data set intact. It can reduce the size of data set by upto 70%, however recovery of sketched data set should have less error rates with low computational complexity. Also, recovery algorithms should have lower hardware overhead in terms of energy and latency per operation.

Big data applications need to process large amount of data thus it increases processing time. Therefore, adopting sketching technique to reduce processor bandwidth, needs to perform real-time tasks with low hardware overhead and should be scalable. In this paper, we take advantage of a low power domain specific PENC many-core architecture in order to reduce hardware overhead of sketching module. The PENC many-core platform has shown efficiency in various DSP and Machine Learning applications. Domain specific many-core architectures are considered to be better than CPUs and GPUs since it has small and low power processing cores which can be operated in parallel to speed-up the application. The many-core architecture reduces processing time by implementing sketching kernels in parallel, whereas energy efficiency is increased by introducing low power processing cores with Globally Asynchronous Locally Synchronous (GALS) routing architecture.

Though adopting sketching techniques demonstrates various advantages, reconstruction of sketched signal is computationally complex [6]. The paper implements OMP algorithm as reconstruction kernel, which has three interdependent kernels namely Dot product, Sort and Least Square kernel. The least square kernel has the highest hardware complexity among all OMP kernels. Therefore we propose Gradient Descent OMP (GD-OMP) algorithm to reduce hardware complexity of OMP algorithm while keeping error rate

Algorithm 1 OMP Reconstruction Algorithm

1:**Initialization**

- $R_0 = y$, $\Lambda_0 = \emptyset$, $Q_0 = \emptyset$ and $t = 0$

2:**Identification**

- Find Index $\lambda_t = max_{j=1..n}$ subject to $| < \phi_j R_{t-1} > |$

3:**Augmentation**

- Update $\Lambda_t = \Lambda_{t-1} \bigcup \lambda_t$
- Update $Qt = [Q_{t-1}\ \phi_{\Lambda_t}]$

4:**Residual Update**

- Solve the Least Squares Problem $x_t = \min_x \|\ y - Q_y\ x\|^2$
- Calculate new approximation: $\alpha_t = Q_t\ x_t$
- Calculate new residual: $R_t = y - \alpha_t$

5: Increment t, and repeat from step 2 if $t < k$
After all the iterations, we can find correct sparse signals.

in satisfactory bounds. Figure 1 shows the proposed sketching framework on many-core platform for Big Data processing acceleration. The PENC many-core architecture acts as co-processor working in tandem with a general purpose CPU allowing it to accelerate Big Data processing.

The main contributions to the paper include:

- Adopting sketching framework to reduce I/O bottleneck.
- PENC: Power Efficient Nano Clusters, Many-Core platform.
- A Low hardware complexity GD-OMP Algorithm for reconstruction of sketched signal.
- Energy efficient implementations of OMP and GD-OMP algorithms.

2. BACKGROUND

2.1 Sketching Algorithms

In this section, we discuss OMP algorithm and proposed Gradient Descend (GD-OMP) technique. OMP is a greedy algorithm; it finds the sparsest solution iteratively by computing support of x and subtracting it from measurement vector y at every iteration. OMP has three different phases, Identification, Augmentation and Residual Update as explained in Algorithm 1. In Identification phase, index i of highest magnitude of $\phi * R$ is chosen as potential vector to find closest approximation to x. At each iteration, index i is added to the list of estimated support vectors in Augmentation phase. In the Residual update phase new estimation and residual are calculated for next iteration. In this phase first, formed Q augmented matrix is used in Least Square regression model to find linear relationship between augmented matrix Q and measured vector y. Finally, the amount of contribution that column y provides is subtracted to obtain a residue. The OMP algorithm takes k iterations to determine correct set of columns [9].

The Identification phase mainly contributes to latency of operations whereas computational complexity of OMP algorithm is dominated by Residual Update phase. Following section 2.2 discuss about proposed reduced hardware complexity modification to OMP.

Algorithm 2 Stochastic Gradient Descend Function

1:**Initialization**

- Inputs: Q_t, $\theta_{Initialize}$, y, α
- Output: θ

2: Gradient Update

- $\theta_i = \theta_i - \alpha \sum_{j=1}^{j=m} [\theta * (Q^j) - y^j] * Q_i^j;$

3: Check Convergence
Cost Computation using Mean Square Error analysis
4: If Cost $> \gamma$, Increment i, and repeat from step 2

Algorithm 3 GD-OMP Reconstruction Algorithm

1:**Initialization**

- $R_0 = y$, $\Lambda_0 = \emptyset$, $Q_0 = \emptyset$ and $t = 0$

2:**Identification**

- Find Index $\lambda_t = max_{j=1..n}$ subject to $| < \phi_j R_{t-1} > |$

3:**Augmentation**

- Update $\Lambda_t = \Lambda_{t-1} \bigcup \lambda_t$
- Update $Q_t = [Q_{t-1}\ \phi_{\Lambda_t}]$

4:**Residual Update**

- Function minimization using Gradient Descent $x_t = Stochastic\_Gradient\_Descent(Q_t, \theta_{Initialize}, y, \alpha)$
- Calculate new approximation: $\alpha_t = Q_t\ x_t$
- Calculate new residual: $R_t = y - \alpha_t$

5: Increment t, and repeat from step 2 if $t < k$ After all the iterations, we can find correct sparse signals.

2.2 Gradient Descend OMP

Least Square kernel is the most computationally intensive kernel among all in OMP algorithm. Least Square kernel consists of Matrix Inversion module which increases the hardware area and power. In this work, we propose to use Stochastic Gradient Descend technique to reduce hardware cost instead of Matrix Inversion based least square calculations. Gradient Descend is first order iterative based function minimizing technique in which α steps are taken towards positive gradient of the function. Khandekar et.al [3] shows that gradient descent function guarantees recovery under Restricted Isometric Property (RIP) conditions. Algorithm 3 shows the integration of gradient descent function (Algorithm 2) with OMP algorithm.

2.3 Proposed Many-Core Architecture:PENC

PENC is composed of 64 processing clusters (192 Cores) connected through routers in a three-level hierarchical tree. The lowest level consists of four clusters connected by a router with five ports: one for each cluster and one for communication to the next level. Three processing nodes and a shared memory compose a cluster and communicate with each other and a low-latency bus. Figure 2 shows PENC

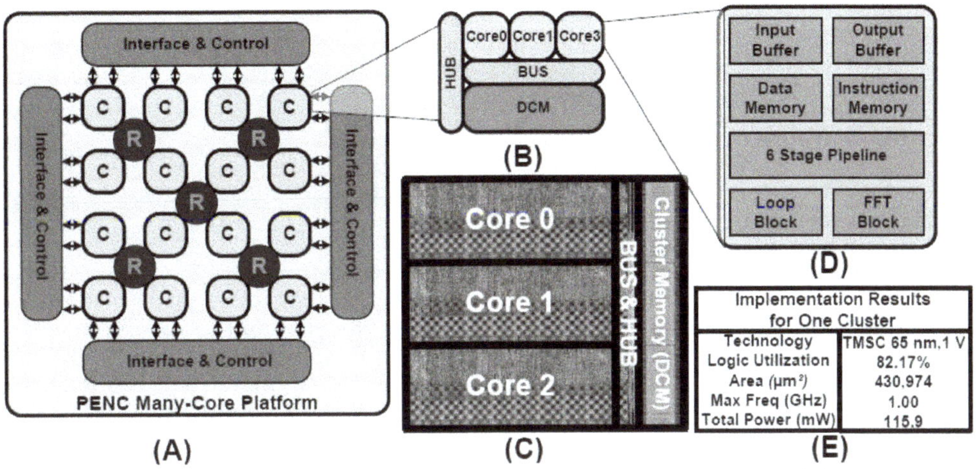

Figure 2: (A) PENC: Power Efficient Nano Clusters, Many-Core Architecture (B) Bus-based Cluster Architecture (C) Layout of Bus-based Cluster implemented in 65nm TSMC CMOS technology (D) Block Diagram of Core Architecture (E) Post Layout Implementation Results of Bus-based Cluster

architecture and its kernel with post layout analysis of bus-based cluster architecture on 65nm CMOS technology.

2.3.1 *Bus-Based Cluster*

Each 16-bit core consists of a six-stage processor pipeline, 128-deep instruction and data memories, and 16 registers. For all ALU instructions, the sources and destinations can be either registers or local data memory references. In either case, the read data is available before the execute stage, eliminating the need for separate `LD` and `ST` instructions for applications whose state fits in the local data memory. Register accesses are resolved in the Instruction-Decode stage, and accesses to a core's local data memory are resolved in the Memory-Decode stage. Cores use `IN` and `OUT` instructions to communicate with each other. When a core executes an `OUT` instruction, the data and relevant addressing information is packetized and sent to its output FIFO. When data is present in a core's output FIFO, it requests to use the bus. The bus then arbitrates between requests, only granting those whose transactions can be completed. Each core has an input FIFO, and if the input FIFO corresponding to the `OUT` is not full, the `OUT` can be completed. The processing core contains a 32-element content-addressable memory (CAM) to store packets from the bus and allow a finite state machine to find a word corresponding to the source core field in the IN instruction.

2.3.2 *Distributed Cluster Memory*

Within each cluster, three 1024×16 SRAM cells compose a Distributed Cluster Memory (DCM). The processor nodes within the cluster can all access the cluster memory via the bus. To access the memory, cores use two memory instructions: `LD` and `ST`. Using data memory as operands for instructions is still beneficial to using `LD` and `ST` from an efficiency standpoint because of the one-cycle read/write capability. Referencing data from the cluster memory has latency and requires a separate instruction, which reduces the overall instructions per cycle that the pipeline can complete. However, the `LD` and `ST` instructions enable the use of a much larger addressable space, which allows the PENC to support this application.

2.3.3 *Programming and Evaluation Methodology*

Our many-core development environment includes an architecture simulator written in Java. The simulator serves as a reference implementation of the architecture; its purpose is to make testing, refining, and enhancing the architecture easier. Each task of OMP algorithm is first implemented in assembly language on every processing core using many-core simulator. Binary files generated by many-core simulator are used to program each core individually. The simulator reads in the assembled code as well as an initial state for the register file and data memory in each core. It then models the functionality of the processor and calculates the final state of register files and data memories. For execution time and energy consumption analysis, both algorithms are implemented on the hardware model of the PENC many-core platform and simulated using Cadence NC-Verilog. The activity factor is then derived and is used by the Cadence Encounter tool for accurate power computation.The many-core simulator reports statistics such as the number of cycles required for ALU, branch, and communication instructions which are used for the throughput analysis of the PENC many-core architecture.

3. APPLICATION MAPPING

3.1 OMP Algorithm Mapping

Figure 3 shows the task graph for OMP mapping on PENC platform. In identification phase, Dot and Sort kernel performs dot product between the measurement matrix (Φ) and Residual vector (R). We preloaded the measurement matrix (ϕ) into Cluster Memory. The index of highest element of the dot product is stored on data memory of one of the cores. The index λ_t of the measurement matrix is fetched to obtain Q matrix in augmentation phase. The residue update phase consists of Least Square kernel, it performs matrix-matrix multiplication, matrix-vector multiplication and matrix inversion. The Q matrix is accessed from cluster memory. At each iteration size of (Q^t) matrix increments, hence reconfigurable matrix inversion is implemented using LU decomposition algorithm. OMP algorithm has interdependent kernels, thus cores can be reused to reduce resource consumption. We implement OMP algorithm mapping for three different image sizes i.e. 128×128, 256×256, and 512×512 with $2\times$, $4\times$, and $8\times$ parallelism among the kernels. For the serial implementation ($1\times$) of OMP algorithm for 128×128

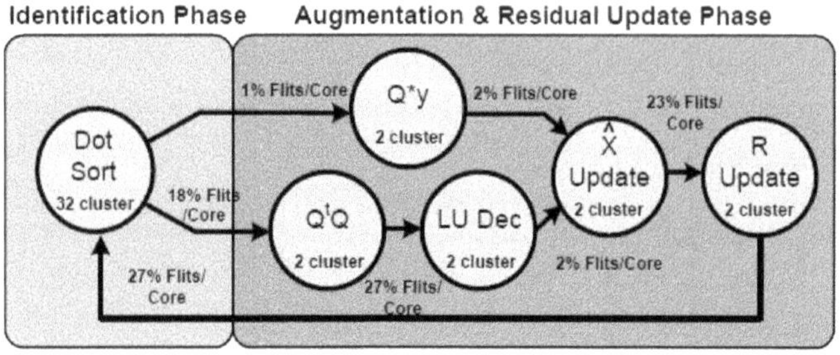

Figure 3: Task Graph for OMP algorithm mapping for 256×256 image size ($4\times$ implementation), requiring 108 cores and 32 cluster memories

image size with 16 sparsity (k), 9 cores are utilized with measurement matrix stored in 2 cluster memories. It has been observed that DS kernel residing in Identification phase is the bottleneck of the implementation, it needs 46% of overall clock cycles. The throughput of the $1\times$ implementation is 6760 clock cycles per column equaling 53 clock cycles per Byte. However for $2\times$ implementation 18 cores were utilized with measurement matrix stored in 4 cluster memories. For $2\times$ implementation DS kernel has been implemented on 16 cores, the cores are reused for matrix-matrix, matrix-vector and vector-vector operations. The throughput of the $2\times$ implementation is 3272 clock cycles per column equaling 25 clock cycles per Byte. Furthermore we experimented with $4\times$ and $8\times$ implementations to reduce execution time and increase throughput, the results shows $4\times$ implementation takes 14 clock cycles per Byte whereas $8\times$ implementation requires 9 clock cycles per Byte.

For image size of 256×256 with sparsity (k) of 32, the measurement matrix (Φ) is stored on 8 cluster memories. In serial implementation of 256×256, identification and residual update phase required 42% and 46% of overall clock cycles. The throughput for serial implementation is 36,455 clock cycles per column equaling 142 clock cycles per Byte. Whereas $2\times$ implementation of 256×256 image size requires 54 cores, achieving 15,156 clock cycles per column equaling 59 clock cycles per Byte throughput. Furthermore, $4\times$ and $8\times$ implementations show increase in throughput achieving 38 and 23 clock cycles per Byte respectively.

For image size of 512×512 with 64 sparsity, we could implement only till $2\times$ implementations as it requires 192 cores exhausting processing tiles. To store measurement matrix of 512×512, 28 cluster memories were required. In serial implementation of 512×512, residual update phase requires highest number of clock cycles (54%) among all phases. The throughput for serial implementation is 47098 clock cycles per column equaling 91 clock cycles per Byte whereas for $2\times$ implementation requires 37221 clock cycles per column equaling 72 clock cycles per Byte. The proposed implementations are scalable and can be reconfigured till 1024×1024 image sizes without using external cache to store measurement matrix. Executing time, area and energy efficiency of the algorithm is discussed in Section 4.

3.2 GD-OMP Algorithm Mapping

GD-OMP algorithm reduces hardware complexity of the OMP algorithm by replacing least square kernel residing in residual update phase with stochastic gradient descent function. Thus GD-OMP algorithm does not include LU decomposition, it only consist of simple matrix multiplication kernels. The stochastic gradient descent function is repeated for 100 iterations for best reconstruction quality. Identification and augmentation phase of the both OMP and GD-OMP algorithm is implemented in same way. In GD-OMP the residual phase consists of matrix-vector multiplications only, thus cores used for Identification phase are reused.

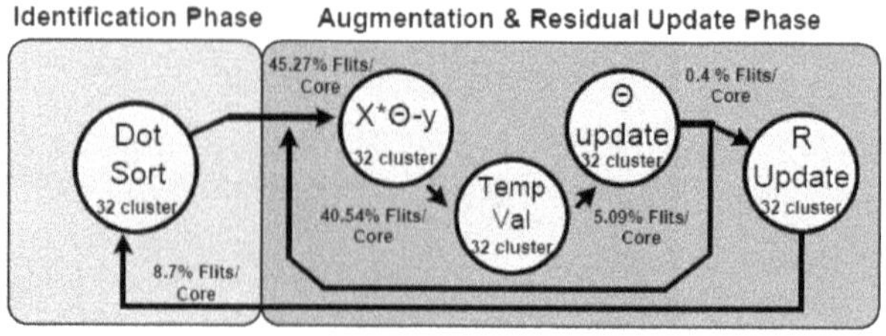

Figure 4: Task Graph for GD-OMP algorithm mapping for 256×256 image size ($4\times$ implementation), requiring 96 cores and 32 cluster memories, achieving $3.7\times$ improvement in Energy-Area-Delay Product as compared to similar OMP implementation

GD-OMP algorithm is also implemented for three different image sizes i.e. 128×128, 256×256, and 512×512 with $2\times$, $4\times$, and $8\times$ parallelism among the kernels. The GD-OMP can be mapped into one kernel, since its algorithmic complexity is less than the OMP algorithm. For 128×128 image size, the serial implementation requires 6 cores and 2 cluster memories. The results show that Residual update phase dominates the execution time and takes 58% of total clock cycles. The throughput of GD-OMP serial implementation is 19,783 clock cycles per column equaling 154 clock cycles per Byte. The $2\times$ implementation achieves throughput of 7,875 clock cycles per column, increasing by $2.4\times$ as compared to $2\times$ implementation of OMP for 128×128 image size. The core count is also reduced by $1.5\times$, requiring only 12 cores. For $4\times$ and $8\times$ implementations computation-to-communication ratio (CCR) decreases, hence reducing the performance of the GD-OMP algorithm. Throughput in terms of clock cycles per column reduces by $2.9\times$ and $3\times$ respectively.

For 256×256 image size with sparsity of 32, serial implementation of GD-OMP requires 24 cores with 8 cluster memories. The throughput of GD-OMP algorithm is 21,729 clock cycles per column equaling 84 clock cycles per Byte. The GD-OMP implementation shows $1.7\times$ improvement in clocks per column and achieves almost $2\times$ improvement in Area-Delay-Product (ADP) as compared to serial implementation of OMP algorithm for 256×256. Parallel implementation ($2\times$) also shows $1.2\times$ improvement in clock cycles per column and $1.4\times$. However for $4\times$ and $8\times$ implementation CCR reduces, thus curtailing throughput performance of GD-OMP algorithm by $1.5\times$ as compared to OMP algorithm for both $4\times$ and $8\times$ implementations.

4. IMPLEMENTATION RESULTS

Big Data processing establishes rigid constraints on processing time. In this paper sketching technique is introduced before Big Data processing to reduce I/O bandwidth i.e. data transfers between external memory and Big Data processing platform as shown in Figure 1. OMP and GD-OMP sketching algorithms are mapped on PENC, which works in tandem with general purpose CPU platform [5],[4]. Therefore sketching algorithms should have lower hardware over-

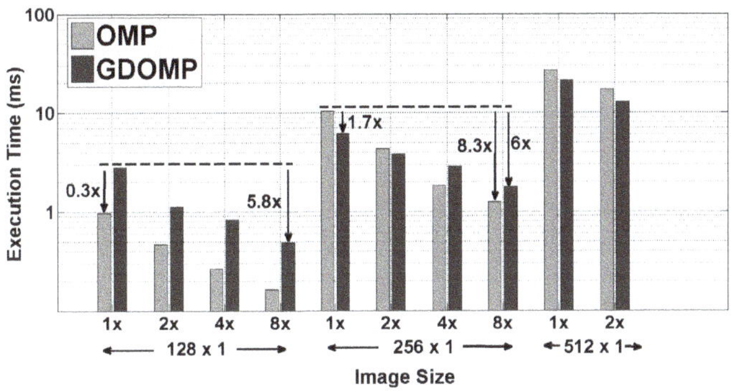

Figure 5: Single Column Execution Time Analysis of OMP and GD-OMP algorithm on PENC platform, experiments were performed on three image sizes and different level of parallelism

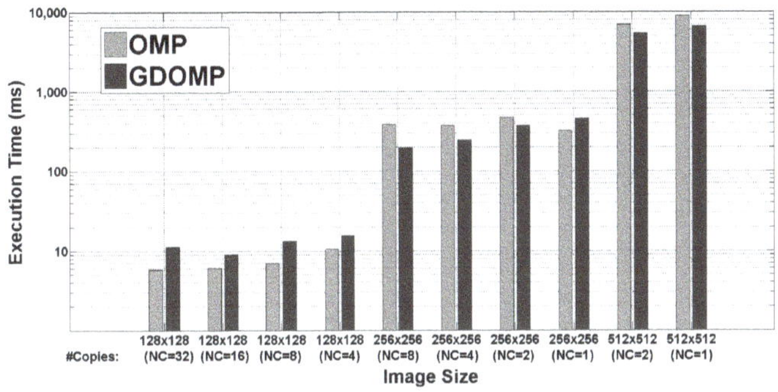

Figure 6: Execution Time Analysis with multiple copies of OMP and GD-OMP algorithm on PENC platform for different image sizes and level of parallelism, where NC= Number of Copies made

head i.e. area and energy efficient with lower execution time. In this section, we first perform hardware overhead analysis and later compare our work with previously published work on CPU and GPU platforms. We do not compare PENC many-core with FPGAs, ASICs, and ASIPs as they are application specific hardware.

4.1 Execution Time Analysis

Both OMP and GD-OMP algorithms are implemented on PENC in serial (1×), and parallel (2×, 4× and 8×). The serial implementation of the algorithm requires least number of cores but execution time is higher, whereas parallel implementations require higher number of cores with reduction in execution time. Figure 5 shows execution time analysis for single column of image size for both algorithms. We implemented multiple copies of implementation to reduce overall image reconstruction (execution) time. In case of serial implementation we could implement more copies as compared to parallel implementations, thus reducing execution time. Figure 6 execution time required to reconstruct complete image using 192 cores. For 128×128 image size least execution time is 5.7 ms using 32 copies of OMP algorithm, whereas for 256×256 image size least execution time is 197.7 ms using 8 copies of GD-OMP algorithm. Moreover, GD-OMP also achieves least execution time $5.4secs$ for 512×512 image size.

4.2 Energy Efficiency Analysis

Each core on the PENC platform can operate up to 1 GHZ

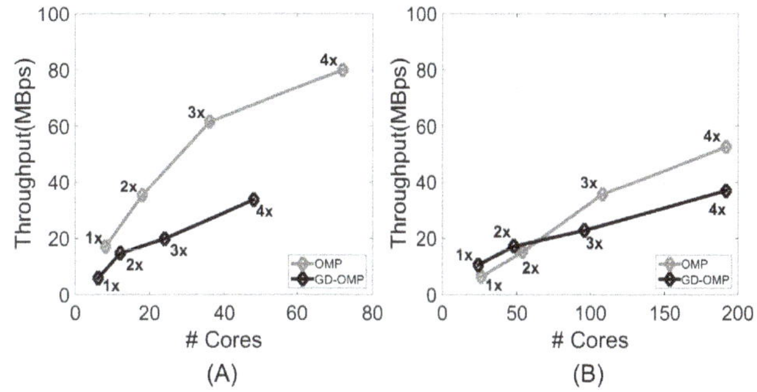

Figure 7: Throughput vs Number of Cores Analysis for OMP and GD-OMP algorithm (A) 128×128 (B) 256×256 image size

at 1 V. PENC is connected through GALS hierarchical tree routing architecture hence the un-used clusters can be shut off. The power of the processor drops to leakage power when the clocks is halted. Also, the processor power drops by almost 50% when its stalling. The GD-OMP implementation requires less number of cores as compared to OMP implementations, however execution time performance is best when implemented for large matrix sizes. Thus for 128×128 image size, OMP has lower energy consumption as compared to GD-OMP, of 0.49 mJ when mapped on 9 cores and 2 cluster memories. For 256×256 image size, GD-OMP consumes low energy 6.9 mJ, 2× less as compared to OMP algorithm. GD-OMP also consumes least energy 88 mJ among all 512×512 implementations.

4.3 Area Efficiency Analysis

In terms of our 64 cluster many-core architecture less modular area which is represented by number of cores implies we can map several modules to operate in parallel. To evaluate area efficiency we use *ThroughputPerCore* (TPC) metric. TPC is the ratio between the throughput of each design to the number of cores used for implementation. Figure 7 shows the throughput trend over cores for OMP and GD-OMP with 128×128 and 256×256 image size with different parallel mapping variations. The overall throughput increases with increased parallelism. Higher the TPC greater is the area efficiency. For 128×128 image size TPC is higher for OMP, however it needs 1.6× additional cores as compared to GD-OMP. On the other hand, for 256×256 and 512×512 implementations GD-OMP exhibits higher TDP as well as requires less number of cores as compared to OMP.

5. CONCLUSION

In this paper we adopt sketching framework to reduce I/O bottleneck for Big data acceleration. We propose PENC many-core architecture consisting of 192 small processing cores, which can work as a co-processor in tandem with a general purpose CPU to accelerate Big Data processing. We implemented OMP and GD-OMP algorithm for three different image sizes with four level of parallelism. The results shows that GD-OMP is efficient for large matrix sizes, for 512×512 image size it requires 1.4× less execution time, and 2× less Energy-Delay-Area product. However OMP works better for 128×128 matrix size, it requires 2.9× less execution time, and has 3.5× less Energy-Delay-Area product.

Table 1: Throughput and Energy-Delay-Area Product (EDAP) Analysis for Different Implementations

Implementations	OMP			GD-OMP		
	#Cores	Throughput (MBps)	EDAP	Cores	Throughput (MBps)	EDAP
128 × 128 (1×)	9	17	0.7	6	5.8	2.2
128 × 128 (2×)	18	35.2	0.9	12	14.6	1.2
128 × 128 (4×)	36	61.5	0.8	24	19.8	2.8
128 × 128 (8×)	72	99.9	1	48	33.7	3.7
256 × 256 (1×)	26	6.3	595.3	24	10.6	157.6
256 × 256 (2×)	54	15.2	411.7	48	17.2	227.4
256 × 256 (4×)	108	35.6	299.6	96	22.8	529.4
256 × 256 (8×)	192	52.6	393	192	37	795.6
512 × 512 (1×)	96	9.8	46103	90	12.4	25821
512 × 512 (2×)	192	15.2	75085	180	20.5	36973

Table 2: Comparison with Previous Work on OMP algorithm

Platforms	Signal Size	Sparsity	Tech (nm)	Area (mm^2)	Vdd (V)	Power (W)	Execution Time (ms)
GPU (Nvidia GeForce) [1]	1024 × 1	12	90	484	1.8	67.5	37.5
CPU (Core i7) [2]	1024 × 1	12	45	263	1.15	16.25	68
PENC **(This Work)**	128 × 128	16	65	5.5	1	6.1	6.9
	256 × 256	32				5.3	370.8
	512 × 512	64				8.7	8814

Compared to GPU and Quad-Core CPU implementations, the PENC many-core reconstructs 5.4× and 9.8× faster respectively for large signal sizes with higher sparsity.

6. REFERENCES

[1] M. Andrecut. Fast gpu implementation of sparse signal recovery from random projections, 2008.

[2] L. Bai, P. Maechler, M. Muehlberghuber, and H. Kaeslin. High-speed compressed sensing reconstruction on fpga using omp and amp. In *Electronics, Circuits and Systems (ICECS),19th IEEE International Conference on*, 2012.

[3] R. Garg and R. Khandekar. Gradient descent with sparsification: An iterative algorithm for sparse recovery with restricted isometry property. In *Proceedings of the 26th Annual International Conference on Machine Learning*, ICML '09, pages 337–344, 2009.

[4] M. Khavari Tavana, A. Kulkarni, A. Rahimi, T. Mohsenin, and H. Homayoun. Energy-efficient mapping of biomedical applications on domain-specific accelerator under process variation. In *Proceedings of the 2014 International Symposium on Low Power Electronics and Design*, ISLPED '14, pages 275–278, New York, NY, USA, 2014. ACM.

[5] A. Kulkarni, A. Jafari, C. Sagedy, and T. Mohsenin. Sketching-based high-performance biomedical big data processing accelerator. In *Circuits and Systems (ISCAS), 2016 IEEE International Symposium on*, 2016.

[6] A. Kulkarni, H. Homayoun, and T. Mohsenin. A parallel and reconfigurable architecture for efficient omp compressive sensing reconstruction. In *Proceedings of the 24th Edition of the Great Lakes Symposium on VLSI*, GLSVLSI '14, pages 299–304, 2014. ACM.

[7] K. Neshatpour, M. Malik, M. A. Ghodrat, A. Sasan, and H. Homayoun. Energy-efficient acceleration of big data analytics applications using fpgas. In *Big Data (Big Data), 2015 IEEE International Conference on*, pages 115–123, Oct 2015.

[8] A. Kulkarni and T. Mohsenin. Accelerating compressive sensing reconstruction OMP algorithm with CPU, GPU, FPGA and domain specific many-core. In *Circuits and Systems (ISCAS), 2015 IEEE International Symposium on*, pages 970–973, 2015.

[9] J. Tropp and A. Gilbert. Signal recovery from random measurements via orthogonal matching pursuit. *IEEE Trans. on Information Theory*, 53(12):4655–4666, 2007.

[10] F. Conti and L. Benini. A Ultra-low-energy Convolution Engine for Fast Brain-inspired Vision in Multicore Clusters. In *Proceedings of the 2015 Design, Automation Test in Europe Conference Exhibition.*, DATE'15, pages 683–688, 2015.

[11] J. Constantin, A. Dogan, O. Andersson, P. Meinerzhagen, J.N. Rodrigues, D. Atienza, and A. Burg. TamaRISC-CS: An ultra-low-power application-specific processor for compressed sensing. In *IEEE/IFIP 20th International Conference on VLSI and System-on-Chip.*, VLSI-SoC'12, pages 159–164, 2012

[12] J. Zhang, Y. Yan,L. J. Chen, M. Wang, T. Moscibroda, and Z.Zhang. Impression Store: Compressive Sensing-based Storage for Big Data Analytics. *USENIX Conference on Hot Topics in Cloud Computing*,2014.

[13] A. Stillmaker, L. Stillmaker, and B. Baas. Fine-Grained Energy-Efficient Sorting on a Many-Core Processor Array. *In IEEE 18th International Conference on Parallel and Distributed Systems (ICPADS)*, 2012.

[14] A. Kulkarni, Y. Pino, M. French and T. Mohsenin. Real-Time Anomaly Detection Framework for Many-Core Router through Machine Learning Techniques. *ACM Journal on Emerging Technologies in Computing (JETC)*, 2016.

[15] M. Malik, S. Rafatirah, A. Sasan, and H. Homayoun. System and architecture level characterization of big data applications on big and little core server architectures. *IEEE In International Conference on Big Data (Big Data)*, 2015.

[16] P. Meher, B. Mohanty, and T. Srikanthan. Area-delay efficient architecture for MP algorithm using reconfigurable inner-product circuits. *In IEEE International Symposium on Circuits and Systems (ISCAS), 2014.*

Low-Power Manycore Accelerator for Personalized Biomedical Applications

Adam Page
Dept. of Computer Science & Electrical Engineering
University of Maryland, Baltimore County
apage2@umbc.edu

Nasrin Attaran
Dept. of Computer Science & Electrical Engineering
University of Maryland, Baltimore County
attar1@umbc.edu

Colin Shea
Dept. of Computer Science & Electrical Engineering
University of Maryland, Baltimore County
cshea3@umbc.edu

Houman Homayoun
Dept. of Electrical & Computer Engineering
George Mason University
Fairfax, VA
hhomayou@gmu.edu

Tinoosh Mohsenin
Dept. of Computer Science & Electrical Engineering
University of Maryland, Baltimore County
tinoosh@umbc.edu

ABSTRACT

Wearable personal health monitoring systems can offer a cost effective solution for human healthcare. These systems must provide both highly accurate, secured and quick processing and delivery of vast amount of data. In addition, wearable biomedical devices are used in inpatient, outpatient, and at home e-Patient care that must constantly monitor the patient's biomedical and physiological signals 24/7. These biomedical applications require sampling and processing multiple streams of physiological signals with strict power and area footprint. The processing typically consists of feature extraction, data fusion, and classification stages that require a large number of digital signal processing and machine learning kernels. In response to these requirements, in this paper, a low-power, domain-specific manycore accelerator named Power Efficient Nano Clusters (PENC) is proposed to map and execute the kernels of these applications. Experimental results show that the manycore is able to reduce energy consumption by up to 80% and 14% for DSP and machine learning kernels, respectively, when optimally parallelized. The performance of the proposed PENC manycore when acting as a coprocessor to an Intel Atom processor is compared with existing commercial off-the-shelf embedded processing platforms including Intel Atom, Xilinx Artix 7 FPGA, and NVIDIA TK1 ARM-A15 with GPU SoC. The results show that the PENC manycore architecture reduces the energy by as much as 10X while outperforming all off-the-shelf embedded processing platforms across all studied machine learning classifiers.

CCS Concepts

•**Computer systems organization** → **Architectures;** •**Computing methodologies** → *Parallel computing methodologies, Machine learning algorithms;* •**Applied computing** → *Bioinformatics;*

GLSVLSI '16, May 18-20, 2016, Boston, MA, USA

DOI: http://dx.doi.org/10.1145/2902961.2902986

Keywords

Low power; biomedical; manycore; accelerator; digital signal processing; machine learning; FPGA; embedded processors.

Sensor	# Channels	Sampling Freq.	Description
HR	1 - 2	100 Hz	Heart Rate
SpO2	1 - 2	0.2 - 0.5 kHz	Blood Oxygen
ECG	3 - 12	0.2 - 1.0 kHz	Heart Elec Act.
EEG	6 - 64	0.1 - 1.0 kHz	Scalp Elec. Act.
GSR	1 - 4	50 - 100 Hz	Skin Conductance
EMG	4 >	1 - 2 kHz	Muscle Elec. Act.
RESP	1 - 3	50 - 100 Hz	Respiration

Table 1: Example sensors for biomedical applications with typical number of channels and sampling frequencies. Demonstrates the various sampling frequencies and multiple channels.

1. INTRODUCTION

Personalized biomedical applications primarily consist of three basic stages: 1. a sensor front-end to capture and digitize physiological signals, 2. a processing stage to analyze, classify, and potentially store the sensors' data, and 3. a RF module stage to transmit the data, classification, and/or diagnostics to the user or medical personnel [13, 16, 17, 10]. There has been an incredible amount of innovation and improvement in sensor design that has dramatically reduced power while maintaining high accuracy. This is the result of technologies such as MEMS sensors and specialized AFEs targeted for physiological signals, such as Texas Instruments medical AFEs like ADS129x and AFE44xx. There has also been a tremendous amount of work done on wireless RF modules ranging from specialized research modules to commercial modules such as Bluetooth Smart (17.9mA RX, 18.2mA TX, 1uA sleep). Still the relatively high amount of power required to transmit raw or even compressed data, makes it essential to perform local on-board processing [5]. The enterprise of this work is on the processor architecture that addresses the unique challenges and characteristics of biomedical applications. Most previous works have focused on modifications to existing microcontrollers/processors by reducing the instruction set architecture (ISA) or creating an SoC with specialized accelerator cores targeted for particular biomedical applications [7, 4, 15]. These approaches are often very expensive and require long development time to develop specialized chips. Furthermore, these modifications do not target the fundamental characteristics in-common with a majority of biomedical applications. Besides the major restrictions on power and area, the processor must be able to efficiently process several physiological signal streams. Table 1 provides some example sensors with typical number of channels and sampling frequencies. Processing the streams often includes feature extraction, data fusion, and classification stages that consist of both digital signal processing (DSP) and machine learning (ML) kernels that exhibit task-level and data-level parallelism.

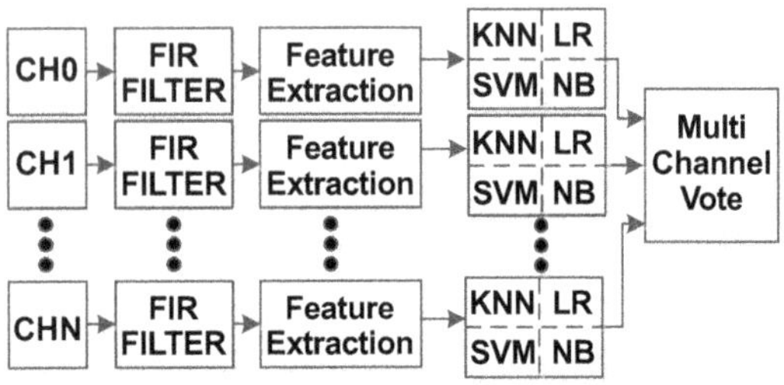

Figure 1: Block diagram of a parallel multi-channel seizure detection application containing feature extraction, classifier, multi-channel vote, and IO interface. The application also shows inherent data-level and task-level parallelism.

2. BIOMEDICAL APPLICATIONS

Among the many commonalities shared between personal biomedical applications, the need to process parallel streams of data in real-time is a dominating feature. The analysis of these multiple streams requires a mix of data-level and task-level parallel computation [3, 6, 2, 1]. In addition, these applications often require a large number of digital signal processing (DSP) and machine learning (ML) techniques. DSP is often used to extract useful representations of the input data while machine learning is needed to perform automated classification for diagnostic and detection purposes. In order to demonstrate these dominant commonalities, we investigated various common DSP and ML kernels. The examined DSP kernels include filtering (FIR), windowing, Fourier transform (FFT), and compressive sensing (CS), while the examined ML kernels include logistic regression (LR), naive Bayes (NB), support vector machine (SVM), and k-nearest neighbor (KNN) [6]. In addition to exploring these various DSP and ML kernels, a case study of seizure detection was also implemented on a number of hardware platforms. The main block diagram of the seizure detection application is presented in Fig. 1 [13, 12]. This case study is an ideal example of a biomedical application that exhibits multiple streams (up to 24 EEG channels) of real-time data that must be processed with DSP and ML kernels. In addition, the multiple streams allow for intuitive parallel processing. Each streams pipelined stages provide task-level parallelism, while within each stage there exists a large degree of potential data-level parallelism. Discussion of the case study along with comparison results are presented in Section 5.

3. PROCESSORS AND PLATFORMS

3.1 Off-the-shelf Processors

In order to study how embedded off-the-shelf processors can efficiently process biomedical applications, we conducted several experiments on two state-of-the-art low power architectures, Atom and ARM, which are substantially different in their core micro-architecture, memory subsystem, and instruction set architecture (ISA). ARM is using ARMs Thumb whereas ATOM is using Intel X86. A recent work has shown that each of these architectures offers a different power and performance trade-off for various applications [15, 11]. Although easy to program, these processors have limited flexibility and parallelism. Therefore, a field-programmable gate array (FPGA) is also explored which provides high flexibility but requires writing low-level logic.

3.1.1 ATOM

The Intel Atom is an ultra low-power processor architecture mainly used in mobile and portable platforms. In this paper we conduct our study on the Intel Edison platform, a system on chip (SoC), containing an IA-32 low-power dual core processor, 1 GB of DDR3, Wi-Fi, Bluetooth, and 4 GB eMMC. The cores are Intel's Silvermont architecture providing a standard x86 architecture, streaming SIMD extension (SSE) and running at a fixed clock of 500MHz.

3.1.2 ARM A15 CPU/NVIDIA K1 GPU

NVIDIA's Jetson TK1 is a System-on-Chip (SoC) combining the Kepler graphics processing unit (GPU) and a 4-Plus-1 ARM processor arrangement. The 4-plus-1 processor configuration, also known as variable Symmetric Multiprocessing (vSMP), consists of five Cortex A15 ARM processors, four high performance and one low power processor. Each ARM A15 CPU has a 32KB L1 data and instruction cache supporting 128-bit NEON™ general-purpose single instruction and SIMD instructions. All processors configuration have shared access to a 2MB L2 cache. The K1 GPU is available to either processor power configuration and consists of a single Streaming Multiprocessor (SMX). The SMX has a CUDA™ compute capability of 3.2, which provides a majority of the architectural benefits of the K20c only scaled down to a single SMX group. The Jetson TK1 has 2GB of DDR3 memory that is shared between the CPU and GPU and is rated up to 933MHz. In this paper we explored different combinations of the four high performance Cortex A15 ARM processors and the GPU for comparison.

3.1.3 FPGA

Field-programmable gate arrays (FPGA) are highly flexible allowing on-the-fly configuration to optimize bit resolution, clock frequency, and parallelization for a given application. In addition, modern FPGAs provide accelerators to boost the performance for operations such as multipliers, generic DSP cores, and embedded memories. The main disadvantages of FPGAs, however, are that they have substantially higher leakage power and require writing low level logic blocks. In this paper, we utilize Xilinx low-power Artix-7 FPGA platform (xc7a200tlfbg484). A very efficient implementation of the seizure detection application with different machine learning classifiers has previously been implemented [13]. This implementation is optimized on the bit-width resolution in addition to the level of parallelism and pipelining to meet the application deadline.

3.2 Domain-Specific PENC Manycore Accelerator

PENC manycore accelerator has a homogeneous architecture that consists of in-order processors with a 6 stage pipeline, a RISC-like DSP instruction set and a Harvard memory model [1, 2, 6, 9, 8]. The core operates on a 16-bit data-path with minimal instruction and data memory suitable for task-level parallelism. Furthermore, the cores have a low complexity, limited instruction set to further reduce area and power footprint. A processor can support up to 128 instructions, 128 data memory, and provides 16 quick-access registers. In the network topology, a cluster consists of three

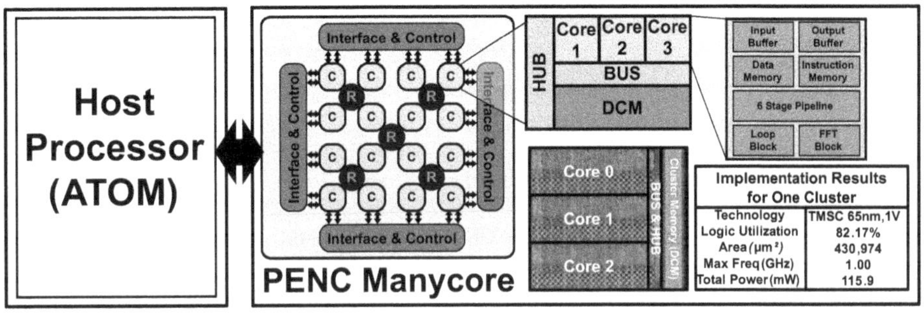

Figure 2: Block diagram of the PENC manycore acting as a coprocessor to the Intel Atom host. The manycore consists of 16 clusters (192 cores) routed through hierarchical routers. On the right, there is a detailed view and ASIC layout of a cluster which contains 3 lightweight cores, a shared bus and memory.

cores that can perform intra-cluster communication directly via a bus and inter-cluster communication through a hierarchical routing architecture. Each cluster also contains a shared memory. Figure 2 shows the block diagram of a 16 cluster version of the design, highlighting the processing cores in a cluster. Each core and router was synthesized and placed and routed in a 65 nm CMOS technology. Our manycore development environment and simulator provides cycle accurate results including completion time, instructions, and memory usage per core. The simulator also breaks down the instructions into groups such as ALU, branch, and communication.

This manycore architecture is ideally suited for most biomedical applications as it addresses the inherent characteristics and challenges. As previously discussed, biomedical applications process a number of physiological signals. Each signal can be processed in parallel in different designated clusters. Dynamic voltage and frequency scaling (DVFS) of the clusters can be used to align the sensor computation completion time, which can dramatically reduce energy usage. The lightweight cores also help to ensure that all used cores are fully utilized. While the lightweight cores are ideal for DSP kernels that require minimal static data [1, 2], ML kernels often require larger amounts of memory for their model data. This is addressed with the cluster-level shared memory that is interfaced to the bus. The shared memory can be accessed within the cluster using the bus and from other clusters through the router. The next section provides empirical results showing how these manycore features are well suited for biomedical applications.

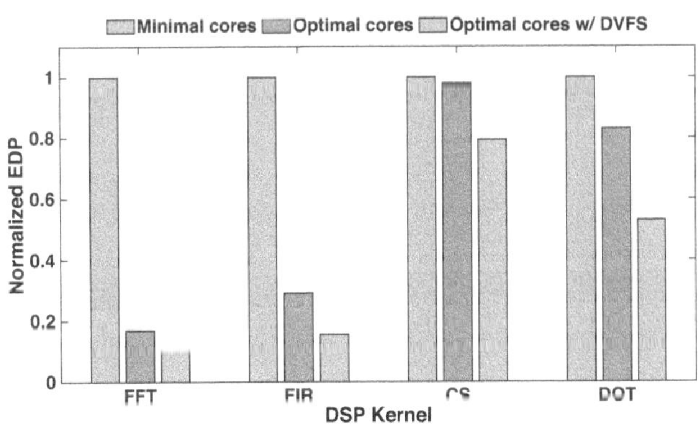

Figure 3: Mappings of DSP kernels including fast Fourier transform (FFT), FIR filter (FIR), compressive sensing (CS), and dot-product (DOT). First mapping uses the minimum cores needed. The second mapping utilizes maximum cores to leverage parallelism. The third is the same as second but with scaled frequency and voltage (DVFS).

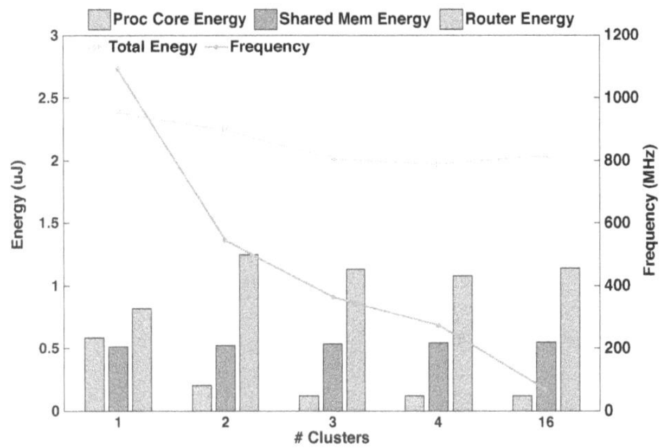

Figure 4: Comparison of different mappings of k-nearest neighbor (KNN) kernel on PENC manycore with voltage and frequency scaling to meet deadline. Additional clusters can be utilized to exploit KNN parallel structure allowing to reduce frequency and voltage. Energy dissipation (w/ core, router and memory breakdown), frequency, and voltage values are shown.

4. MANYCORE ANALYSIS

In order to demonstrate the manycore's effectiveness at targeting low-power biomedical applications, experiments were performed that highlight the unique characteristics of these applications. Specifically, the experiments map various DSP and ML kernels with performance measured in energy, execution time, and memory demands.

4.1 DSP Kernel Mapping with DVFS

In the first experiment, various digital signal processing kernels were mapped onto the manycore. The DSP kernels include fast Fourier transform (FFT), finite impulse response filter (FIR), compressive sensing (CS), and dot-product operation (DOT). An initial mapping was performed that used the minimum number of cores to act as a baseline. A second mapping was then performed that used the optimal amount of cores. This was done by selecting the best from a number of implementations. The final mapping is equivalent to the second mapping but scales the voltage and frequency to meet the execution time of the first mapping. Figure 3 shows all three of these mapping for the four DSP kernels with their corresponding energy-delay product (EDP). The plot shows that the manycore is able to efficiently parallelize all of the kernels and is able to achieve an energy reduction of up to 80%.

4.2 ML Kernel Mapping with DVFS

Many digital signal processing kernels require very little static and dynamic memory. For example, an 128-point FFT requires around 512 words of memory assuming twiddle factors are precomputed and the input is complex. On the other hand, many machine learning kernels can often require storing a large volume of model data. For example, k-nearest neighbor essentially requires storing all of the training data. This could correspond to thousands of values needing to be stored. This is accommodated for by having cluster-level shared memory accessible through the cluster's bus. Similar to the mappings of the DSP kernels, the mapping of a ML kernel onto the manycore is performed. The k-nearest neighbor algorithm with 3,000 model data is mapped using between 1 and 16 clusters. The results are depicted in Fig. 4. As can be seen, increasing the number of clusters to map KNN allows the frequency to be dramatically reduced. The optimal mapping is obtained using 4 clusters which was able to reduce energy by 14% and execution time by 30% compared to single cluster.

5. CASE STUDY COMPARISON

5.1 Seizure Detection Overview

Epilepsy is a common neurological disease that affects approximately 2.2 million Americans. According to a recent Institute of Medicine report, epilepsy is the 4th most common neurological disorder in the US with roughly 1 in 26 people being diagnosed with epilepsy in their lifetime [1]. The ability to monitor epileptic patients in an ambulatory setting is a crucial tool that has significant medical, psycho-social, cost, and safety advantages. For example, this device could help determine the minimal effective dosage as well as alert medical personnel when a seizure is detected to reduce the occurrences of sudden unexpected death in epilepsy (SUDEP).

In our previous work, a flexible seizure detection hardware system was implemented to detect the onset of a seizure by analyzing multiple channel, scalp-based EEG data in real time [13, 12, 5]. The developed system is capable of processing up to 24 channels of EEG electrodes that are digitized using specialized AFE ICs. Each stream of EEG sensor data is sampled at a rate of 256 Hz with 16-bit resolution. The processing consists of 4 main stages as previously shown in the diagram in Fig. 1. The EEG sensor data is first passed through a filter to remove high frequency and DC components. A feature extraction stage is then used to convert windows of time-series data into 5 temporal features per EEG channel. Each channel's features are then classified using one of four classifiers: k-nearest neighbor (KNN), support vector machine (SVM), naive Bayes (NB), or logistic regression (LR). A final stage is then used to produce a final decision based on a multi-channel voting scheme. For our study, the windows consist of 256 samples (1 second) with 50% overlapping windows. This means that a window will contain half-second of new data, which gives a 500 ms deadline to process each window. Figure 5 depicts the task graph for each classifier variant of the seizure detection system. The task graphs highlight the parallelism that exists within the stages and between the EEG channels.

5.2 Platform Implementation

In this comparison, three platforms were use to implement and evaluate 5 processor combinations. Great care was taken to ensure optimal implementation and consistency across all combinations.

5.2.1 *Intel Edison*

The Intel Edison platform was used to gather results for the Intel Atom processors and is the purposed interface with the PENC. When using the Atom processors, great care was done to efficiently utilize the low power x86 cores. The software was written as a single program, multiple thread (SPMT) execution model. With in each thread the math operations were optimized for single instruction, multiple data (SIMD) execution. This was accomplished by explicit exploitation of parallelism through multithreading across the EEG channels, where the total number of channels is divided equally between available cores. The GCC/G++ compiler was passed architecture appropriate flags to increase the compilers effort on performance such as -O3, mtune=native, and specification of the floating point unit of SSE 4.2. To enhance the SIMD further, Intel® Performance Primitives (IPP) were used when the compiler could not vectorize or correctly map the functions to SIMD instructions. When the manycore is interfaced as an accelerator, the Edison is used as the host to perform data marshalling. In this case, the system toggles between active mode to transfer window of EEG data and sleep mode otherwise.

5.2.2 *NVIDIA Jetson TK1*

The NVIDIA® Jetson TK1 platform was used to obtain results for the ARM A15 CPU processors as well as with the embedded GPU as an accelerator. The application development and testing is similar to [14]. The same application architecture used for the Intel Edison was employed for the ARM A15 CPUs. With a combination of SPMT for partitioning groups of channel processing between the multiple core configurations. Each thread also targets the use of SIMD through ARM's NEON architecture. As there is no commercial optimizations for ARM's Neon SIMD, these functions are accelerated using the ARM Ne10 project. When using the GPU, the CPU cluster only has two cores active. One is used to dispatch kernels to the GPU and perform data marshalling. Another A15 core was used to service the OS. The application architecture utilizes existing CUDA libraries, cuBLAS and CUDA Math Libraries, for the KNN, SVM, NB, and LR kernels. In order to extract the maximum amount of parallelism, by allowing for kernel overlap, from the implementations, each operation within uses up to sixteen CUDA streams.

5.2.3 *Xilinx Artix-7*

For the Artix-7 FPGA, the entire system was implemented in Verilog. Xilinx's proprietary synthesizer was used to generate the register transistor language (RTL) as well perform the optimal translation onto the Artix-7 FPGA. When synthesizing, a balance design approach was used to balance area, power, and latency. The classifier model data was also stored using the FPGAs block random access memories (BRAM). A number of designs were explored that looked to optimize in the form bit resolution, parallelism, and pipelining. Further details can be found in [12].

5.3 Experimental Setup

Consistency had to be ensured when collecting power and timing results of the platforms. The execution times for all implementations were found by averaging thousands of processed windows of EEG data. For the Intel Edison and Jetson TK1 platforms, the power consumption of the entire system was captured using TI INA219 voltage and power meter, which is shown in Fig. 6. As previously discussed, power and cycle accurate results for the manycore were obtained in simulation. The power metrics for the manycore are based on Cadence projections of the standard-cell layout of the cores and routers. The required power of the manycore when processing was added to the Intel Edison power which consisted of both active and sleep states. For the Artix-7 FPGA implementation, the power and timing results were obtained using Xilinx XPower and Timing analyzer, respectively. Since this only includes power dissipation of the chip, the power usage of the Intel Edison is also added when the Atom processor is idle.

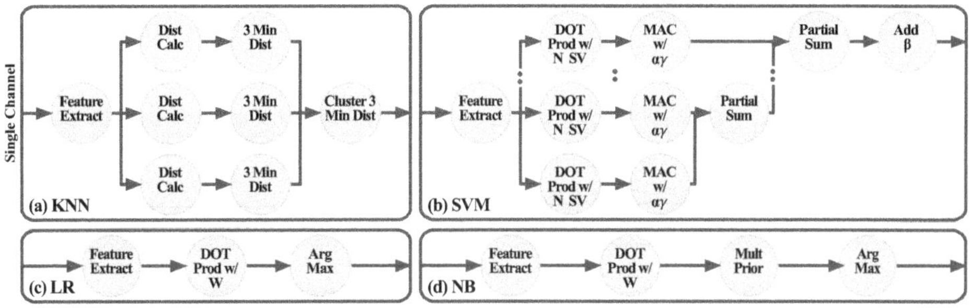

Figure 5: Task graphs of each classifier variation of the seizure detection case study. The task graphs highlight the task-level parallelism and interconnect between feature extraction and classification stage for single channel.

Figure 6: Experimental setup to obtain power and execution time measurements for TK1 using TI INA219 and Arduino. For this platform both ARM A15 cores & embedded GPU are targeted. The embedded GPU is used as an accelerator.

Design	KNN	SVM	NB	LR
Logic Slices	3788	4281	2987	2583
Memory (Kb)	2916.4	828.4	0.26	0.30
Max Freq (MHz)	131	152	101	134
Latency (cycle)	644,622	108,665	264	242
Nominal Freq (KHz)[1]	1286.01	217.33	0.53	0.48
Dynamic Power (uW)[1]	2697.76	192.96	0.171	0.098
Leakage Power (mW)	122	122	122	122
Dynamic Energy (uJ)[2]	1348.9	96.5	0.09	0.05
Total Energy (mJ)	62.35	61.10	61.00	61.00

Table 2: Artix-7 performance for seizure detection case study consisting of 5 features/channel and classifier. 1) The power results are for Nominal frequency to meet 0.5 sec interval, 2) The FPGA has large leakage power dominant compared to dynamic power, both dynamic and total results are presented.

5.4 Results

The FPGA platform is the most similar to the manycore in that it allows for the most flexibility in scaling frequency and targeting the data-level and task-level parallelism. Unfortunately, FPGA suffers from having very high leakage power. The results of the FPGA are summarized in Table 2. The leakage power is comparable to the dynamic power and therefore causes the total energy usage of the system to become much larger. Figure 7 compares the energy dissipation of the seizure detection application across four different processor combinations: Intel Atom, NVIDIA TK1, Artix-7 FPGA and Atom+PENC manycore. For the TK1, using the embedded GPU as an accelerator improved efficiency over using just the ARM A15 processors. Therefore, the combination is only provided for this platform. For all four classifier variants, the manycore accelerator consumes roughly 2-3X less energy than the

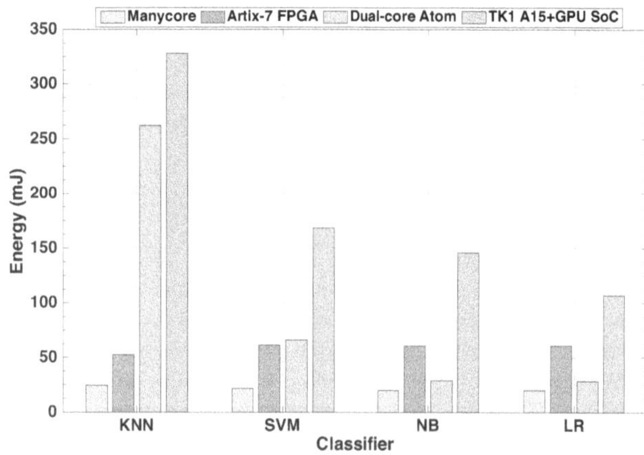

Figure 7: Comparison of different platforms' energy usage to process 1-sec window for the seizure detection case study. All four classifier variants are included. For PENC manycore, the Intel Edison platform power is included to perform data marshalling.

custom FPGA implementation. Besides consuming less energy, the manycore also has the advantage of faster development time compared to FPGA by enabling designs to be implemented in Assembly (and later C) with the ability to rapidly simulate designs on existing hardware. When compared to the TK1 and standalone Atom, the Atom+manycore is able to reduce energy usage by up to 10X. The greatest reduction in energy occurs for the KNN and SVM variants which contain significantly more computation and parallelism as highlighted in the task graphs. For the NB and LR variants, the manycore provides minimal reduction in energy, roughly 1.2X. This is due to the fact that NB and LR have very little computation which is negated by transfer time and long idle times for all processor combinations when not processing. This is corroborated by the fact that the Atom is able to have better energy efficiency than the TK1 with the GPU accelerator for these cases.

The execution time to process one window of EEG data for the seizure detection system is shown in Fig. 8. For all classifiers, the PENC manycore is able to meet the 500 ms deadline along with all other platforms. The manycore is faster than the Intel Atom processor and TK1 ARM+GPU SoC while also dissipating the least amount of energy. The biggest reduction in execution time is seen in KNN-based seizure detection which contains maximum amount of computation and parallelism. For this variant, the manycore is 10X, 15X, and 7X faster than FPGA, standalone Atom, and NVIDIA TK1 implementations, respectively. Only in the NB and LR variants does the FPGA implementation obtain lower execution times, however, the FPGA requires twice the amount of energy.

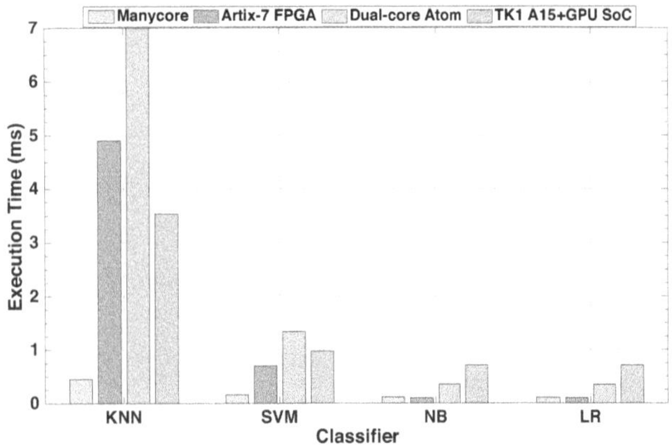

Figure 8: Comparison of different platforms' execution time to process 1-sec window for the seizure detection case study. All four classifier variants are also included. The seizure application assumes 50% overlapping windows which allots 500ms to process each window.

6. CONCLUSION

This paper explores the choice of embedded architectures for energy-efficient processing of biomedical applications. Biomedical applications share strong commonalities requiring sampling from a number of physiological signals and processing that contains various digital signal processing and machine learning kernels. The software as well as hardware implementations of machine learning biomedical kernels are compared. For the choice of software, state-of-the-art commercial off-the-shelf embedded processing platforms such as ARM and Atom are compared with the hardware implementation of these kernels on embedded low-power FPGA. To further push the energy-efficiency, a custom lightweight, symmetric GALS manycore architecture is proposed that enables not only exploiting the task-level and data-level parallelism that exists in biomedical kernels, but also perform dynamic voltage and frequency scaling to dramatically reduce the energy usage. By using the optimal number of cores with DVFS, we were able to reduce energy usage by up to 80% and 14% for DSP and ML tasks, respectively, relative to using the minimal number of cores. When compared to other commercial off-the-shelf platforms for the case study of seizure detection, the PENC manycore is able to reduce energy by up to 10X while having comparable execution time.

7. ACKNOWLEDGEMENT

This material is based upon work supported by the National Science Foundation under Grant No. 00008999 and 00010145.

8. REFERENCES

[1] J. Bisasky, D. Chandler, and T. Mohsenin. A many-core platform implemented for multi-channel seizure detection. In *Circuits and Systems (ISCAS), IEEE International Symposium on*, pages 564–567, May 2012.

[2] J. Bisasky, H. Homayoun, et al. A 64-core platform for biomedical signal processing. In *Quality Electronic Design (ISQED), 2013 14th International Symposium on*, pages 368–372, March 2013.

[3] H. Ghasemzadeh and R. Jafari. Ultra low-power signal processing in wearable monitoring systems: A tiered screening architecture with optimal bit resolution. *ACM Trans. Embed. Comput. Syst.*, 13(1):9:1–9:23, Sept. 2013.

[4] S.-Y. Hsu, Y. Ho, et al. A sub-100uw multi-functional cardiac signal processor for mobile healthcare applications. In *VLSI Circuits (VLSIC), 2012 Symposium on*, pages 156–157, June 2012.

[5] A. Jafari and T. Mohsenin. A low power seizure detection processor based on direct use of compressively-sensed data and employing a deterministic random matrix. In *IEEE Biomedical Circuits and Systems (Biocas) Conference*, Oct 2015.

[6] M. Khavari Tavana, A. Kulkarni, et al. Energy-efficient mapping of biomedical applications on domain-specific accelerator under process variation. In *Proceedings of the 2014 International Symposium on Low Power Electronics and Design*, ISLPED '14, pages 275–278, New York, NY, USA, 2014. ACM.

[7] C. Kim et al. Ulp-srp: Ultra low-power samsung reconfigurable processor for biomedical applications. *ACM Trans. Reconfigurable Tech. Syst.*, 7:22:1–22:15, Sept. 2014.

[8] A. Kulkarni, A. Jafari, et al. Sketching-based high-performance biomedical big data processing accelerator. In *Circuits and Systems (ISCAS), 2016 IEEE International Symposium on*, 2016.

[9] A. Kulkarni, Y. Pino, M. French, and T. Mohsenin. Real-time anomaly detection framework for many-core router through machine learning techniques. In *ACM Journal on Emerging Technologies in Computing (JETC)*, New York, NY, USA, 2016. ACM.

[10] K. H. Lee and N. Verma. A low-power processor with configurable embedded machine-learning accelerators for high-order and adaptive analysis of medical-sensor signals. *IEEE Journal of Solid-State Circuits*, 48:1625–37, July 2013.

[11] P. Otto, M. Malik, N. Akhlaghi, R. Sequeira, H. Homayoun, and S. Sikdar. Power and performance characterization, analysis and tuning for energy-efficient edge detection on atom and arm based platforms. In *Computer Design (ICCD), 2015 33rd IEEE International Conference on*, pages 479–482, Oct 2015.

[12] A. Page, S. Pramod, et al. An ultra low power feature extraction and classification system for wearable seizure detection. In *Engineering in Medicine and Biology Society (EMBC), 2015 37th Annual International Conference of the IEEE*, Sept 2015.

[13] A. Page, C. Sagedy, et al. A flexible multichannel eeg feature extractor and classifier for seizure detection. *Circuits and Systems II: Express Briefs, IEEE Transactions on*, 62(2):109–113, 2015.

[14] A. Page, C. Shea, and T. Mohsenin. Wearable seizure detection using convolutional neural networks with transfer learning. In *Circuits and Systems (ISCAS), 2016 IEEE International Symposium on*, 2016.

[15] A. Venkat and D. M. Tullsen. Harnessing ISA diversity: Design of a heterogeneous-isa chip multiprocessor. In *ACM/IEEE 41st International Symposium on Computer Architecture, ISCA 2014, Minneapolis, MN, USA, June 14-18, 2014*, pages 121–132, 2014.

[16] S. Viseh, M. Ghovanloo, and T. Mohsenin. Towards an ultra low power on-board processor for tongue drive system. *Circuits and Systems II: IEEE Transactions on, accepted*, 62(2):174–178, Feb 2015.

[17] J. Yoo, L. Yan, et al. An 8-channel scalable eeg acquisition soc with patient-specific seizure classification and recording processor. *Solid-State Circuits, IEEE Journal of*, 48(1):214–228, 2013.

Hardware Security Threats and Potential Countermeasures in Emerging 3D ICs

Jaya Dofe
Qiaoyan Yu
Department of Electrical and Computer Engineering
University of New Hampshire
Durham, NH 03824
<jhs49, qiaoyan.yu>
@unh.edu

Hailang Wang
Emre Salman
Department of Electrical and Computer Engineering
Stony Brook University
Stony Brook, NY 11794
<hailang.wang, emre.salman>
@stonybrook.edu

ABSTRACT

New hardware security threats are identified in emerging three-dimensional (3D) integrated circuits (ICs) and potential countermeasures are introduced. Trigger and payload mechanisms for future 3D hardware Trojans are predicted. Furthermore, a novel, network-on-chip based 3D obfuscation method is proposed to block the direct communication between two commercial dies in a 3D structure, thus thwarting reverse engineering attacks on the vertical dimension. Simulation results demonstrate that the proposed method effectively obfuscates the cross-plane communication by increasing the reverse engineering time by approximately 5× as compared to using direct through silicon via (TSV) connections. The proposed method consumes approximately one fifth the area and power of a typical network-on-chip designed in a 65 nm technology, exhibiting limited overhead.

Categories and Subject Descriptors

B.7 [**Integrated Circuits**]: VLSI (very large scale integration)

Keywords

3D ICs, hardware security, Network-on-Chip

1. INTRODUCTION

Three-dimensional (3D) integration has attracted significant attention during the past two decades to develop diverse computing platforms such as high performance processors, low power systems-on-chip (SoCs), and reconfigurable platforms such as FPGAs. Despite the well-understood advantages over 2D integrated circuits (ICs), 3D ICs introduce unique and unexplored challenges on managing hardware security. Unfortunately, existing work on hardware security of 3D ICs primarily focuses on methods to leverage 3D characteristics to resolve the security challenges of 2D ICs, rather than studying the security threats and corresponding countermeasures in 3D ICs.

One of the significant challenges is ensuring *inter-die security* within a heterogeneous 3D stack. For example, a 3D IC consisting of multiple dies from different vendors (as in the plug-and-play based 3D integration) suffers from trustworthiness since different intellectual property (IP) providers may not follow the same regulations and conduct the same degree of die authentication. Integrating dies from third-party vendors by utilizing an interposer based 2.5D technology is already a common practice. This trend is expected to grow, particularly for 3D SoCs where multiple functionalities coexist. Thus, inter-die security is expected to be a serious concern for emerging 3D ICs. These challenges are identified in this paper and potential solutions are proposed to enhance hardware security within 3D ICs.

The rest of the paper is organized as follows. Existing hardware security threats and typical countermeasures are summarized in Section 2. Three important security threats are introduced for 3D ICs in Section 3. A potential countermeasure is proposed in Section 4 to address reverse engineering attacks on vertical communication channels. Simulation results are provided in Section 5. The paper is concluded in Section 6.

GLSVLSI '16, May 18-20, 2016, Boston, MA, USA
 ISBN 978-1-4503-4274-2/16/05. . . $15.00
DOI: http://dx.doi.org/10.1145/2902961.2903014

2. BACKGROUND

2.1 Security Threats and Countermeasures in 2D ICs

Hardware security threats on traditional 2D ICs are primarily from hardware Trojan horse [1], side-channel analysis attacks [2], fault attacks [3], counterfeit chips [4], and reverse engineering induced loss of IP piracy [5]. Hardware Trojan models and general detection methods have been well studied in existing literature [1, 6, 7]

Side-channel analysis (SCA) attacks [2] aim to retrieve the secret key in cryptosystems by analyzing the power and delay characteristics of the IC. The most common countermeasures for SCA attacks are random masking techniques [8], insertion of dummy code, power consumption randomization, and balancing the data.

Fault attacks can compromise the cipher implementation and produce faulty ciphertexts for cryptanalysts to retrieve the secret key [3, 9]. White light, laser beams, voltage glitches, and temperature control are possible manipulation means to perform fault attacks [10]. Existing countermeasures for fault attacks are primarily based on error detection or/and correction codes [11, 12].

Methods to identify counterfeit chips and IP piracy have also been well studied [4, 5]. Vertical integration brings a new dimension to the counterfeit design. In addition to the protection of each die, the trustworthiness of the vertical connections/communication should also be ensured.

2.2 Existing Work on Hardware Security for 3D ICs

Majority of the existing work leverages the unique 3D characteristics to enhance security of 2D ICs rather than investigating hardware security within stand-alone 3D ICs. As indicated by leading 3D manufacturing foundries [13], the stacking process of 3D ICs conceals the details of the circuit design and therefore thwarts reverse engineering. Secondly, 3D ICs facilitate *split manufacturing* where the entire IC is distributed throughout multiple dies/planes. Thus, due to the incompleteness of each plane, design details of a functional block are not revealed.

Existing 3D split manufacturing approaches fall into two primary categories. In the first category, as investigated by Valamehr *et al.* [14], the entire design is separated into two tiers: one plane is dedicated as the primary computation plane whereas the second plane is an optional control plane that should be provided by a trusted foundry. This control plane is used to monitor possible malicious behavior within the computation plane and overwrites the malicious signals, if necessary.

The second category, as studied by Imeson *et al.* [15], relies on interconnects of a trusted die to obfuscate the entire 3D circuit. Thus, the circuit within the untrusted tier cannot be reverse engineered since interconnectivity is unknown. Similar studies have been performed to further enhance the obfuscation level achieved by split manufacturing [16–18].

As exemplified by these studies, existing approaches rely primarily on the presence of a trusted plane. While effective to enhance security, these existing techniques do not investigate the potential security weaknesses inherent to 3D ICs.

3. NEW SECURITY THREATS IN 3D ICS

One of the primary limitations of existing work is that the trustworthiness of the vertical communication process is taken for granted. This assumption leaves a critical component of 3D integration insecure. In this section, new security threats induced by 3D integration are introduced.

3.1 Trustworthiness of Vertical Communication

A nontrivial security weakness within 3D ICs is the trustworthiness of vertical communication. In a heterogeneous 3D stack with dies from different vendors, one of the dies can attempt to extract secret information such as an encryption key, authentication code, or certain IP characteristics. Thus, a die within a 3D stack should not only be protected from external attacks (as is the case in traditional 2D ICs), but also from attacks originating from a nearby die within the same 3D stack. Furthermore, since the authentication level of each die is different, the security of the overall 3D IC is dependent upon the weakest die. The overall 3D IC (including the die with a strong authentication level) can be compromised once an attacker succeeds in accessing the weak die. Note that due to high bandwidth inter-die vertical communication, an attacker has more access points to compromise security, producing additional security threats that do not exist in 2D ICs.

Another potential weakness is the leak of connectivity information from an untrusted 3D integration foundry. Existing approaches that rely on split manufacturing typically assume that the vertical communication is inherently secure. Unfortunately, this assumption is not always accurate. For example, the foundry that manufactures vertical interconnects may leak this connectivity information, resulting in weaker design obfuscation than what is assumed with split manufacturing. Existing work has indicated that the straightforward split manufacturing suffers from proximity attack [17].

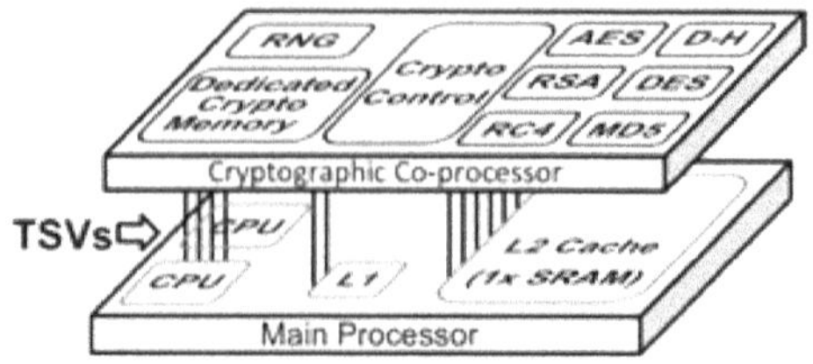

Figure 1: **Secure crypto plane in 3D ICs [21].**

3.2 Potential Trigger and Payload Mechanisms for Hardware Trojans

Due to limited and immature design-for-test techniques for 3D integration, it is more challenging to detect hardware Trojans in 3D ICs. Furthermore, attackers have new design space to hide hardware Trojans. For example, in 2.5D integration, an interposer plane can be exploited to generate a Trojan that is harder to detect. Assume a malicious interconnect within the interposer plane that connects two TSVs together through a switch transistor, fabricated within a die above the interposer. The switch transistor can be activated through a thermal sensor, short circuiting the two distinct TSVs. Thus, a payload mechanism can be as simple as a short wire and a switch transistor.

Another characteristic of 3D ICs that can be exploited by attackers is the poor thermal conductivity. Hardware aging induced metal disconnect and transistor threshold voltage shifting are well-known reliability concerns that accelerate at higher temperatures. Thus, an attacker can insert resistive based heat generation units that accelerate certain reliability mechanisms. This kind of Trojan triggering mechanism is highly challenging to be recognized at the die-level (pre-bond) test or at the final system test stage. Furthermore, due to the immaturity of 3D test mechanisms, hardware Trojan payloads such as voids and partially filled TSVs can generate denial-of-service.

3.3 Side-Channel Analysis Attacks

To retrieve the secret crypto key, side-channel attacks exploit the correlation between the measured side-channel signals (such as delay and power) and the suspected secret key to reduce the number of brute-force attempts. Studies in [19, 20] prove that key retrieval is possible through the analysis of crypto execution times. Side-channel attack can even be done remotely by merely invoking a crypto operation on another machine and measuring the varying execution time [20].

The variation characteristics of 3D ICs add noise to the side-channel signals, thereby blurring the relationship between side-channel signals and the real key. Split manufacturing technique suggests separating the system functions to multiple planes. For instance, as shown in Fig. 1, a separate layer is used for cryptographic operation. These mechanisms, however, cannot completely thwart side-channel attacks. If an attacker can perceive the power measurement of crypto engine by muting other system operations, the well-known power-based SCA methods [22] can be applied to 3D ICs. In another example [23], authors can retrieve the high nibble of key byte in both 2D and 3D cache configurations through delay measurement.

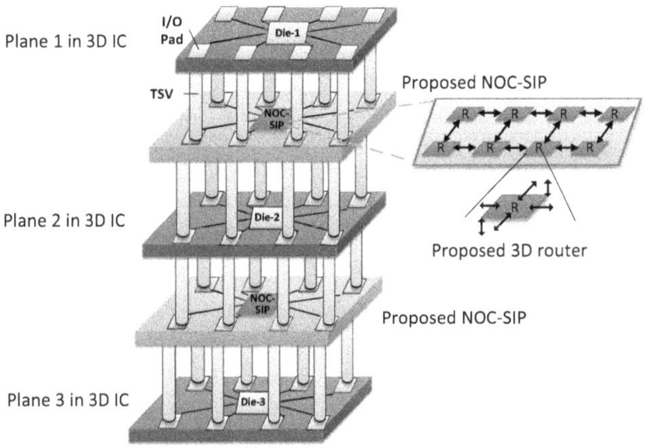

Figure 2: **Conceptual representation of the proposed countermeasure for 3D IC security.**

4. PROPOSED COUNTERMEASURE TO THWART REVERSE ENGINEERING IN 3D ICS: NOC-SIP

The proposed countermeasure is fundamentally different from the split manufacturing approach, where one of the dies and vertical connections must be manufactured by a trusted foundry. Without this assumption, split manufacturing cannot ensure the trustworthiness of a 3D SoC with dies from different vendors. It is predicted that commercial dies, rather than customized dies, will be vertically integrated to develop 3D ICs in the near future. Since the I/O definition and certain specifications of commercial dies are public, an attacker can reverse engineer the 3D SoC design, particularly if each die of the 3D IC can be separated from the stack using a debonding technique. To eliminate the need for at least one trusted foundry for 3D ICs, a secure cross-plane communication network is proposed.

4.1 Overview of the Proposed Method

The proposed method is based on the insertion of a *Network-on-Chip (NoC) based shielding plane* between two commercial dies to thwart reverse engineering attacks on the vertical dimension. As shown in Fig. 2, the proposed NoC shielding plane (NOC-SIP) obfuscates the communication among the adjacent dies.

As compared to the split manufacturing, this method provides higher flexibility and scalability when developing secure 3D ICs. This characteristic is due to the enhanced modularity and scalability of NoCs as compared to a bus centric communication network. Ad-hoc algorithms that split IC functionalities are not suitable for a large-scale system. Furthermore, additional wire lifting through split manufacturing leads to a larger number of TSVs, resulting in more area overhead and TSV capacitance (and therefore power).

The proposed countermeasure aims to address the reverse engineering attack in 3D ICs. We assume that the design in one of the dies could have utilized some obfuscation methods. However, as two dies are integrated in the same package through TSVs, we argue that it is easier to perform sniffing attacks through internal connection in 3D ICs than through external I/O pads. In practice, a 3D chip designer may combine both high-end and low-end dies to reduce the overall cost of a 3D stack. In 2D ICs, the security vulnerability is determined by a single die. Whereas in 3D ICs, the security of the entire system is determined by the weakest die. If the security of the cross-plane communication cannot be assured, the trustworthiness of the heterogeneous 3D stack cannot be guaranteed.

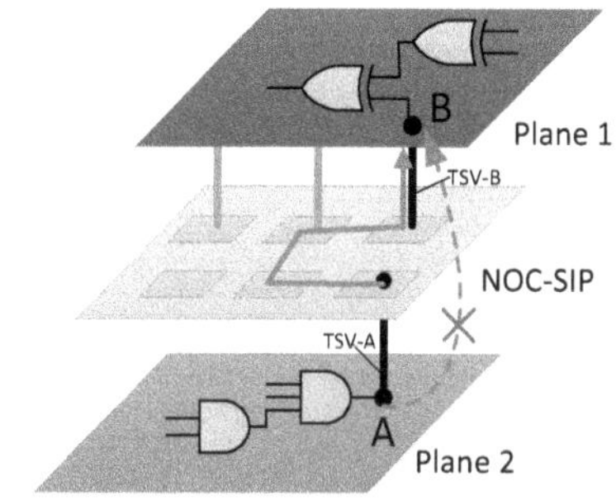

Figure 3: **An example of vertical communication through the proposed NOC-SIP.**

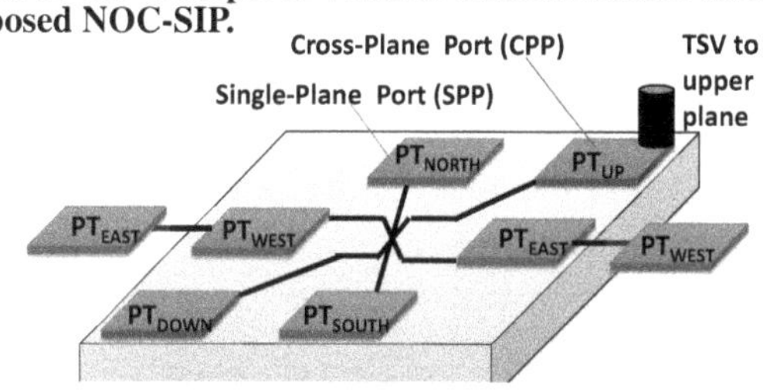

Figure 4: **Proposed 3D router architecture.**

The essence of the proposed NOC-SIP is to provide an obfuscated communication channel between two planes that host commercial dies. Our method makes it significantly more challenging to reverse engineer the 3D system. If the proposed shielding layer is sufficiently strong, the 3D system has more flexibility to use low-end dies without sacrificing the overall system's security assurance. We assume each commercial die has a regular I/O pad map. Those I/O pads are connected to the proposed NOC-SIP with a regular node array, as shown in Fig. 2. Therefore, the specific I/O connectivity information of the dies is hidden to the 3D foundry. As a result, the proximity attack [17] is less likely to help to reveal the design details from split dies.

An example of the proposed method is depicted in Fig. 3. Without the proposed NOC-SIP die, the node A in plane 2 would be connected to the node B in plane 1 directly through a TSV. If an attacker has the ability to reverse engineer debonded planes 1 and 2, the 3D IC would be compromised. Alternatively, the NOC-SIP plane redirects the signal from a TSV-A on A to several routing hops before the signal truly reaches TSV-B on B. Thus, the direct connection from A to B is removed. The proposed NOC-SIP enhances security for the following three reasons: (1) even if the adversary successfully separates planes 1 and 2, a scanning electron microscope (SEM) picture of the vertical connection does not reveal useful information for reverse engineers to retrieve the complete system design, (2) the inserted NOC-SIP facilitates the use of 2D security countermeasures to address 3D security threats, and (3) the inherent scalability of the NOC-SIP overcomes the limited flexibility and scalability concerns in the existing split manufacturing algorithms.

4.2 Proposed 3D Router Design

4.2.1 Difference between Typical 2D Router and Proposed 3D Router

The proposed 3D router is shown in Fig. 4. The single-plane ports (SPP) PT_{North}, PT_{East}, PT_{South}, and PT_{West} fulfill the communication function within the NOC-SIP. Alternatively, the two cross-

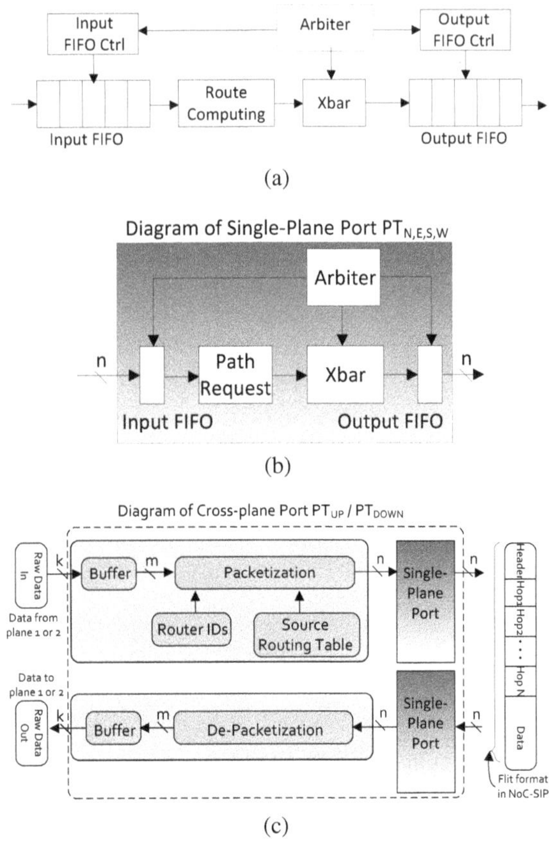

Figure 5: **Schematics of (a) one pair of input and output ports in a 2D router, (b) single-plane port in the proposed 3D router, and (c) cross-plane port in the proposed 3D router.**

plane ports (CPP) PT_{UP} and PT_{DOWN} are responsible for cross-plane communication. In contrast, a typical 2D router has five pairs of input and output ports. Fig. 5(a) shows the diagram of one input and one output port for a 2D router. The proposed 3D router in the NOC-SIP is different than the router in the traditional 2D NoC. As shown in Fig. 5(b), the logic of the input and output ports in our 3D router is much simpler than that of 2D router. Only single-depth input and output FIFO are required; FIFO controllers are removed; route computing unit is replaced with a simple routing path request unit (no computation inside); a simpler arbiter can fulfill the routing arbitration. Among the five ports in a 2D router, one port is connected with a network interface (NI) to reach a processing element (e.g. microprocessor or a memory core). However, in the NOC-SIP, no processing element is connected to any port of the 3D router. The packetization function executed in the NI of a 2D NoC is part of our vertical router's function.

4.2.2 Router Ports for Vertical Connection

In our 3D router, the cross-plane ports, PT_{UP} and PT_{DOWN}, are designed for vertical connection from/to other planes. The primary functions of these two ports include: (1) packetize/de-packetize the bit stream from/to the other plane, (2) assign a source-routing path for each data packet, and (3) buffer the bit stream if the previous packets do not have available bandwidth.

As shown in Fig. 5(c), k-bit data from plane 1 is stored in the buffer before packetization. The packet leaving the cross-plane port is formatted in a way that starts with header information, follows with the detailed routing hops, and ends with the real data. The uniqueness of this cross-plane port is the existence of a router identifier (that is programmable after fabrication) and source routing table, which are provided by the 3D chip designer through one-time read-only-memory (ROM) programming equipment. As the router identifier and routing table are initialized after fabrication, placing malicious hardware in the NOC-SIP during the design stage cannot guarantee system compromise. Similarly, the knowledge of the 3D router design does not help the reverse engineer, as the router identifier and source routing table are unknown before deployment. Once the router ID or the source routing table is changed, the secret information sniffed by the attack for one case would not be useful.

4.2.3 Dynamic Source Routing for Obfuscation

Source routing introduces unpredictability for the adversary who intends to insert hardware Trojans in the NOC-SIP. As there is no computation unit for route path preparation, the attacker cannot successfully execute a meaningful attack without the knowledge of router identifier assignment. Another advantage of source routing is to manually balance the latency for the transmission between different pairs of I/O pads on planes 1 and 2, shown in Fig. 2. To thwart the delay-based side-channel attacks, the source routing design in the 3D router further facilitates a dynamic routing, which varies the latency of the communication between source and destination ports within the NOC-SIP.

5. SIMULATION RESULTS

We implemented the proposed NOC-SIP in Verilog HDL and synthesized the HDL code in Synopsys Design Compiler with a 65 nm TSMC technology. The width of the raw data from a plane (other than NOC-SIP) is set to 5 bits, and the packet width for the NOC-SIP is 32 bits. The input and output FIFOs are 32-bit single-depth buffer. XY routing algorithm is applied to the 2D NoC design. Round-robin arbitration is used in both 2D NoC and NOC-SIP. The NI for the 2D mesh NoC is OCP-IP compatible [24]. The hardware cost of our NOC-SIP is compared with two typical 4×4 mesh NoCs.

5.1 Router Activity

The router switching activity of the NOC-SIP is used as a metric to evaluate the difficulty of identifying vertical connectivity through reverse engineering. Three cross-plane communication methods are compared: direct TSV, NOC-SIP with XY routing, and NOC-SIP with source routing. Direct TSV refers to the case where the I/O pads from different dies are statically connected during the 3D IC integration process. NOC-SIP with XY and source routing stand for the proposed shielding layer using XY packet routing and dynamic source routing, respectively.

First, we randomly select a single pair of I/O pads from two planes for vertical communication. The number of switching transitions of each 3D router is recorded in 5000 clock cycles. As shown in Fig. 6(a), the activity of the TSVs directly connected to two I/O pads indicates that the TSV nodes 4 and 9 are used in the cross-plane communication. Note that the color bar represents the number of node transitions in 5000 cycles. Alternatively, the router activity map [Fig. 6(b)] of the NOC-SIP with XY routing shows that the routers 4, 8, 9, 10, 11, and 12 are used in the cross-plane communication. A reverse engineer, however, cannot know which two TSVs in the routers are actually used for cross-plane communication. The use of source routing further increases the number of involved routers to 10, thereby increasing the degree of obfuscation, as shown in Fig. 6(c).

If two pairs of vertical communication are applied, the NOC-SIP achieves enhanced obfuscation performance. As shown in Fig. 7, the number of active routers in the NOC-SIP is always greater than the direct TSV method. The source routing for NOC-SIP has

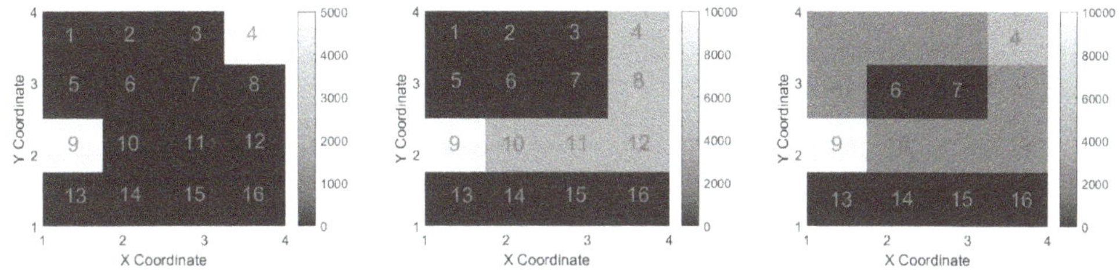

(a) (b) (c)

Figure 6: **Single pad-to-pad vertical communication. (a) Direct TSV, (b) NOC-SIP with XY routing, and (c) NOC-SIP with source routing.**

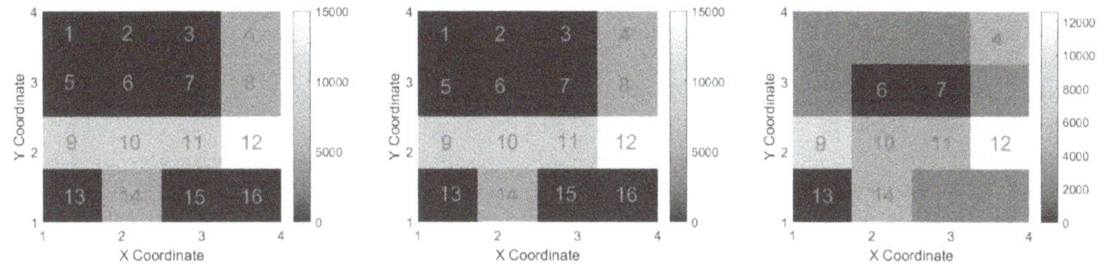

(a) (b) (c)

Figure 7: **Double pad-to-pad vertical communication. (a) Direct TSV, (b) NOC-SIP with XY routing, and (c) NOC-SIP with source routing.**

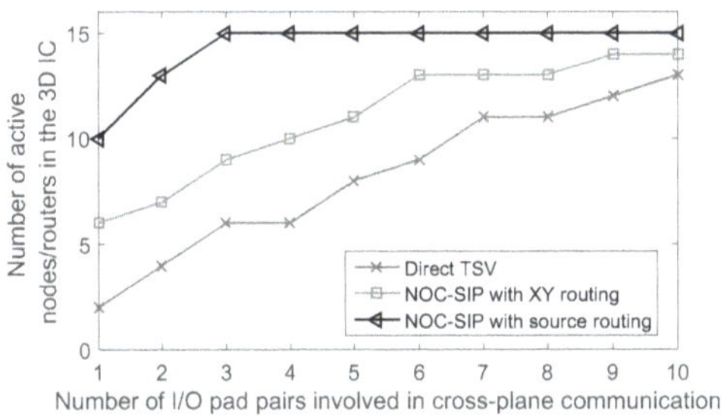

Figure 8: **The number of active routers versus the number of routers having incoming data.**

the ability to distribute the data transmission throughout the entire NOC-SIP. Thus, the proposed approach makes reverse engineering significantly more difficult.

The experiments shown by Figs. 6 and 7 are extended by increasing the number of communication pad pairs to 10. As shown in Fig. 8, the NOC-SIP with source routing engages 12 routers with two pairs of pads. In contrast, the direct TSV method involves 12 routers with 10 pairs of pads. This behavior demonstrates that the proposed NOC-SIP method effectively obfuscates the cross-plane communication by increasing the reverse engineering time by approximately 5× as compared to using direct TSV connections. The direct TSV is the most vulnerable method against reverse engineering on vertical connections.

5.2 Area, Delay and Power Comparison

Since the same topology (mesh) is used in the 2D NoC and NOC-SIP, the area and worst-case delay within a router (i.e. a single node) are compared. The conclusion obtained from this analysis is valid for the entire network. As listed in Table 1, the proposed NOC-SIP with source routing (XY routing) consumes 82% (86%) less area than the 2D NoC in [24]. We added the typical 2D router design and the NI presented in [25] as another reference point. Proposed NOC-SIP with source routing reduces the area overhead by 86% as compared to [25] . The source routing results in more area overhead because of the large source routing table in the cross-plane routers.

Table 1: Area and the Worst-case Delay Comparison, *: Source routing, #: XY routing.

	Single node at 2D NoC		Single node at 3D NoC-SIP	
Modules	Area (μm^2)	Critical Delay (ns)	Area (μm^2)	Critical Delay (ns)
Input FIFO	4122	0.09	288	0.07
Output FIFO	3323	0.33	262	0.07
Route computing	81	0.26	50	0.08
Arbiter	4257	0.69	5298	0.12
NI	19133 [24]	–	–	–
Packetization for cross plane communication	–	–	2962*	0.12*
			719#	0.12#
Total	60517 [24]	0.69	10916*	0.12*
	66508 [25]	0.69	8673#	0.12#

Table 2. Power Consumption Comparison.

On-chip communication network		Power Consumption	
		Dynamic (mW)	Leakage (μW)
Single node at 2D NoC	Router	30.6	187.9
	NI [24]	6.491	
Single node at 3D NOC-SIP with source routing		7.8	46.5
Single node at 3D NOC-SIP with XY routing		7.5	35.3

Since the worst-case delay for the 2D NoC is 0.69 ns, we set the clock frequency to 1.25 GHz for all designs under comparison. The comparison listed in Table 2 indicates that the power consumption of the proposed NOC-SIP with source routing (XY routing) is only 21% (20%) of the 2D NoC.

6. CONCLUSIONS

Existing works have demonstrated that 3D integration provides additional security defense to thwart hardware attacks in 2D ICs. The security threats that are inherent to true 3D ICs, however, have not received much attention. We identify three potential security threats in 3D ICs: (1) the trustworthiness of vertical communication channel, (2) new hardware Trojan mechanisms, and (3) new side-channel attacks. To thwart reverse engineering attacks on the cross-plane communication (i.e. vertical communication channel), a NOC-SIP layer is proposed. The proposed NOC-SIP obfuscates the vertical communication within a 3D stack. Simulation results demonstrate that the proposed approach engages all of the routers as long as more than two pairs of I/O pads from different planes are in use. Alternatively, direct TSV connection method requires ten pairs of I/O pads from two planes to reach the same level of obfuscation as the proposed method. Thus, the proposed NOC-SIP makes it significantly more challenging for a reverse engineer to retrieve the vertical connectivity information. The proposed NOC-SIP was implemented with Verilog HDL and synthesized with a 65 nm technology. Synthesis results demonstrate that the proposed 3D router consumes approximately 1/5 of the area and power of a typical 2D router. This reduced overhead is achieved by the simplified single-plane and cross-plane ports in the 3D router.

7. REFERENCES

[1] S. Bhunia, M. S. Hsiao, M. Banga, and S. Narasimhan, "Hardware Trojan Attacks: Threat Analysis and Countermeasures," *Proceedings of the IEEE*, Vol. 102, No. 8, pp. 1229–1247, 2014.

[2] P. Kocher, J. Jaffe, and B. Jun, "Differential power analysis," *Advances in Cryptology—CRYPTO'99*, pp. 388–397. Springer, 1999.

[3] A. Moradi, M. T. M. Shalmani, and M. Salmasizadeh, "A generalized method of differential fault attack against AES cryptosystem," *Cryptographic Hardware and Embedded Systems-CHES 2006*. Springer, 2006, pp. 91–100.

[4] U. Guin, *et al.*, "Counterfeit integrated circuits: a rising threat in the global semiconductor supply chain," *Proceedings of the IEEE*, Vol. 102, No. 8, pp. 1207–1228, 2014.

[5] M. Rostami, F. Koushanfar, and R. Karri, "A primer on hardware security: Models, methods, and metrics," *Proc. of the IEEE*, Vol. 102, No. 8, pp. 1283–1295, 2014.

[6] F. Courbon, P. Loubet-Moundi, J. J. Fournier, and A. Tria, "SEMBA: A SEM based acquisition technique for fast invasive Hardware Trojan detection," *Circuit Theory and Design (ECCTD), 2015 European Conference on*, pp. 1–4. IEEE, 2015.

[7] J. Zhang, H. Yu, and Q. Xu, "HTOutlier: Hardware Trojan detection with side-channel signature outlier identification," *Hardware-Oriented Security and Trust (HOST), 2012 IEEE International Symposium on*, pp. 55–58. IEEE, 2012.

[8] E. Prouff and M. Rivain, "Masking against side-channel attacks: A formal security proof," *Advances in Cryptology–EUROCRYPT 2013*. Springer, 2013, pp. 142–159.

[9] J. Blömer and J.-P. Seifert, "Fault based cryptanalysis of the advanced encryption standard (AES)," *Financial Cryptography*, pp. 162–181. Springer, 2003.

[10] H. Bar-El, *et al.*, "The sorcerer's apprentice guide to fault attacks," *Proceedings of the IEEE*, Vol. 94, No. 2, pp. 370–382, 2006.

[11] G. Di Natale, M. Doulcier, M.-L. Flottes, and B. Rouzeyre, "A reliable architecture for parallel implementations of the advanced encryption standard," *Journal of Electronic Testing*, Vol. 25, No. 4-5, pp. 269–278, 2009.

[12] M. Mozaffari-Kermani and A. Reyhani-Masoleh, "Concurrent structure-independent fault detection schemes for the advanced encryption standard," *Computers, IEEE Transactions on*, Vol. 59, No. 5, pp. 608–622, 2010.

[13] S. Bansal, "3D IC Design," *EETimes (Nov 14, 2011), http://www.eetimes.com/document.asp?doc_id=1279081*, 2011.

[14] J. Valamehr, *et al.*, "A 3-D Split Manufacturing Approach to Trustworthy System Development," *Computer-Aided Design of Integrated Circuits and Systems, IEEE Transactions on*, Vol. 32, No. 4, pp. 611–615, 2013.

[15] F. Imeson, A. Emtenan, S. Garg, and M. V. Tripunitara, "Securing Computer Hardware Using 3D Integrated Circuit (IC) Technology and Split Manufacturing for Obfuscation." *USENIX Security*, Vol. 13, 2013.

[16] K. Xiao, D. Forte, and M. M. Tehranipoor, "Efficient and secure split manufacturing via obfuscated built-in self-authentication," *Hardware Oriented Security and Trust (HOST), 2015 IEEE International Symposium on*, pp. 14–19. IEEE, 2015.

[17] J. Rajendran, O. Sinanoglu, and R. Karri, "Is split manufacturing secure?" *Design, Automation & Test in Europe Conference & Exhibition (DATE), 2013*, pp. 1259–1264. IEEE, 2013.

[18] Y. Xie, C. Bao, and A. Srivastava, "Security-Aware Design Flow for 2.5 D IC Technology," *Proceedings of the 5th International Workshop on Trustworthy Embedded Devices*, pp. 31–38. ACM, 2015.

[19] P. C. Kocher, "Timing Attacks on Implementations of Diffie-Hellman, RSA, DSS, and Other Systems," *Proceedings of the 16th Annual International Cryptology Conference on Advances in Cryptology*, ser. CRYPTO '96, pp. 104–113. London, UK, UK: Springer-Verlag, 1996. [Online]. Available: http://dl.acm.org/citation.cfm?id=646761.706156

[20] D. J. Bernstein, "Cache-timing attacks on AES," Tech. Rep., 2005.

[21] J. Valamehr, *et al.*, "A Qualitative Security Analysis of a New Class of 3-D Integrated Crypto Co-processors." *Cryptography and Security*, D. Naccache, Ed., pp. 364-382, 2012.

[22] S. Narasimhan, *et al.*, "Multiple-parameter side-channel analysis: A non-invasive hardware Trojan detection approach," *Hardware-Oriented Security and Trust (HOST), 2010 IEEE International Symposium on*, pp. 13–18. IEEE, 2010.

[23] C. Bao and A. Srivastava, "3D Integration: New opportunities in defense against cache-timing side-channel attacks," *Computer Design (ICCD), 2015 33rd IEEE International Conference on*, pp. 273-280, Oct 2015.

[24] J. Frey and Q. Yu, "Exploiting state obfuscation to detect hardware trojans in NoC network interfaces," *Circuits and Systems (MWSCAS), 2015 IEEE 58th International Midwest Symposium on*, pp. 1–4. IEEE, 2015.

[25] S. Saponara, *et al.*, "Design of an NoC Interface Macrocell with Hardware Support of Advanced Networking Functionalities," *Computer, IEEE Transactions on*, Vol. 63, No. 3, pp. 609-621, March 2014.

Real-Time Analysis for Wormhole NoC: Revisited and Revised

Qin Xiong[†], Zhonghai Lu[‡], Fei Wu[†,*] and Changsheng Xie[†]
[†]Wuhan National Laboratory for Optoelectronics, Huazhong University of Science and Technology, Wuhan, China
[‡]School of Information and Communication Technology, KTH Royal Institute of Technology, Stockholm, Sweden
{qinxiong, zhonghai}@kth.se, {wufei, Cs_xie}@hust.edu.cn

ABSTRACT

The network delay upper-bound analysis problem is of fundamental importance to real-time applications in Network-on-Chip (NoC). In the paper, we revisit a state-of-the-art analysis model for real-time communication in wormhole NoC with priority-based preemptive arbitration and show that the model may provide pessimistic or even incorrect network delay upper-bound. We then propose a revised analysis model to correct the flaws in the previous model by further classifying indirect interference as upstream and downstream indirect interferences according to the relative positions of traffic flows and taking buffer influence into consideration. Simulated evaluations show that our model provides tighter and correct network delay upper-bound compared with the state-of-the-art model.

Keywords

Wormhole NoC; Real-Time Communication; Network Delay

1. INTRODUCTION

As NoC is becoming the de facto mainstream interconnect for large scale MPSoCs, satisfying timing requirements of real-time communication becomes an increasing concern in order to support a wide range of timing-sensitive applications in embedded mobile platforms, automotive, aerospace and networking applications. For example, Kalray's MPPA manycore processor [5], uses a customized NoC to provide timing predictability for communication tasks.

Compared with non-realtime communication, aside from the requirement of correct logical results, real-time communication also demands timely delivery to guarantee Quality of Service (QoS). If all packets of a real-time traffic flow meet the deadline under any conditions, this traffic flow is termed feasible. However, packet delay is indeterminate since the packet may suffer various interferences caused by link and buffer sharing [11]. Few investigations have been performed to analyze the network delay upper-bounds of real-time traffic flows in wormhole NoC [12] with *virtual channels* (VCs) which makes efficient use of buffer space and achieves high throughput [4].

Employing real-time scheduling theory, Shi and Burns presented an analysis model which can calculate the network delay upper-bounds of real-time traffic flows in priority-based wormhole NoC [16]. However, the result of this model may be pessimistic and sometimes incorrect due to analysis flaws which do not consider relative positions of flows and buffering impact on delay propagation. In the paper, we propose a revised real-time analysis model for wormhole NoC with priority-based preemptive arbitration by taking relative position and buffer influence into consideration.

The rest of the paper is organized as follows. Section 2 discusses related works. In Section 3, the delay bound analysis problem is illustratively given and the Shi and Burns' model, called *SB's model*, is revisited. In Section 4, we propose a revised model for the SB's model, which corrects its problems. In Section 5, we conduct a detailed case to show quantitative results comparing the SB's model with ours in terms of tightness and correctness. Finally, we conclude in Section 6.

2. RELATED WORK

In wormhole NoC, real-time communication analysis has attracted research attentions recently. There exist two main techniques to compute end-to-end network delay upper-bound on wormhole NoC.

One method is the network calculus theory which has been proposed for Internet QoS [3][10] and employed in many other fields such as switched Ethernet network [6] and on-chip network [13], etc. Network calculus is a set of rules and results based on $(min, +)$ algebra and deals with queuing problems encountered in packet-switched network. Network calculus contains bounding constraints on packet arrival and service, and derives bounds of work backlogs and the packet delays, which can be used to quantify the real-time network delay upper-bound immediately [7]. In [13], Qian et al. proposed a delay bound analysis technique which considers link sharing, buffer sharing and credit-based flow control for best-effort communication flows in wormhole NoC. Recently, this technique [19] is incorporated into the delay bound analysis methodology which adopts a formalized router model based on Intel's eXtensible Micro-Architectural Specification (xMAS) as an intermediate model between an ad hoc router model and its network calculus analysis model.

As another approach for analyzing network delay bound for on-chip networks, the real-time scheduling theory has been borrowed from the uniprocessor scheduling area to address the problem. In [11], Lu et al. formulated a contention tree to express contentions among real-time traffic flows. However, no formula of delay upper-bound is derived. In [16], the approach raised by Shi and Burns can predict the worst-case network delay based on two quantifiable different interferences: direct interference and indirect interference. The formulas of network delay upper-bound are derived based on the works of processor scheduling theory [1]. In their flow-level model, links on a traffic flow's routing path is treated as one resource in calculation. In a series of publications [15][17][18], the ap-

*Corresponding author: wufei@hust.edu.cn

GLSVLSI '16, May 18-20, 2016, Boston, MA, USA

DOI: http://dx.doi.org/10.1145/2902961.2903023

plication scope of this method was extended by Shi et al. In [2], Burns et al. introduced this analysis model into the mixed criticality system and derived formulas for scheduling analysis of mixed criticality tasks [2]. In [9], Kashif and Patel noticed that the chain-blocking caused by back-pressure, which was ignored in the previous works, would affect network delays. In this work, minimum buffer space requirement for validating SB's model is bounded to prevent back-pressure from occurring. A stage-level analysis (SLA) model [8] was proposed for producing tighter network delay upper-bound under a key assumption that each VC has enough buffer space. SLA model analyzes a traffic flow using pipelined communication resource stage by stage and provides tighter delay bound at the cost of higher computational complexity. Nevertheless, due to the cost restrictions in NoC, buffer space of each VC in wormhole NoC is usually not large enough to eliminate back-pressure and SLA model cannot be employed in that more realistic situation.

To our knowledge, SB's model [16] represents the state-of-the-art for real-time communication delay bound analysis of on-chip wormhole networks. Nevertheless, some shortcomings still exist. Since important delay contributing factors such as the relative position of flows and buffer influence are ignored, the analysis results of SB's model may be pessimistic and when buffer size is not large enough, incorrect. The details about their analysis are introduced in Section 3.3. In order to address these problems, we propose a new model by taking relative position and buffer influence into consideration to improve the accuracy of results and break the restriction of minimal buffer size proposed in [9].

3. PROBLEM AND PREVIOUS ANALYSIS

3.1 Problem Illustration

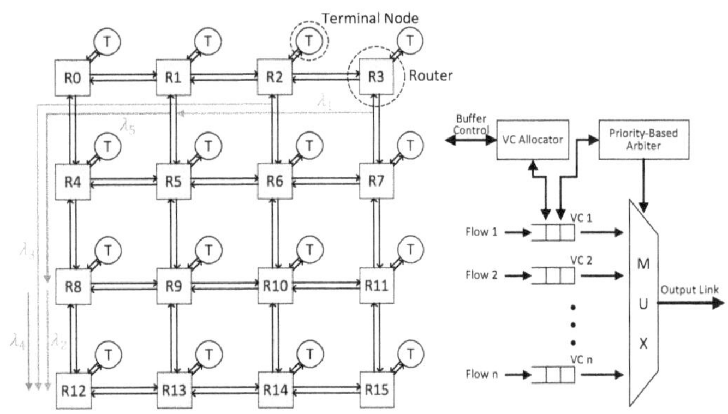

(a) (b)

Figure 1: (a) A 4×4 NoC example with five traffic flows. (b) Per-flow buffering and priority-based link arbitration.

Our real-time analysis problem is to analyze packet delay upper-bound of real-time flows in wormhole NoC. Fig.1(a) illustrates a 4×4 NoC example with five real-time flows. The packet-switching routers perform wormhole flow control, meaning pipelined packet delivery with Virtual Channels allocated at the packet level and the physical channels at the flit level (flit is the flow control unit). Each router has a terminal node (T) which processes computational tasks and communicates with other terminal nodes through the network. The dimension-order X-Y routing is employed for simplicity and deadlock freedom. A packet is routed first in X (horizontal) dimension until it arrives at the same column as destination router and then in Y (vertical) dimension to destination [14]. For example, λ_5 starts in R1 and is transmitted to R0 in the X dimension, then passes through R4 and terminates in R8 along the Y dimension. Fig. 1(b) shows per-flow VCs and priority-based preemptive arbitration for a link (physical channel).

3.2 Symbols, Assumptions and System Model

We globally use the symbols in Table 1 throughout the paper. The symbols for a specific definition, formula or proof are defined within their own section.

Table 1: Symbols and explanations

Symbol	Explanation
Λ	The set of real-time traffic flows in a NoC
λ_i	A real-time traffic flow
C_i	The maximum non-contentional network delay of λ_i
T_i	The period of λ_i
D_i	The end-to-end delay constraint of λ_i
J_i	The release jitter of λ_i
ℓ_i^n	The nth unidirectional link along the routing path of λ_i
$\mathcal{L}_i$	The set of unidirectional links along the routing path of λ_i
S_{D_i}	The set of traffic flows which directly contend with λ_i
S_{I_i}	The set of traffic flows which indirectly contend with λ_i
$S_{I_i}^{U_j}$	The set of traffic flows which indirectly contend with λ_i through $\lambda_j \in S_{D_i}$ at upstream position
$S_{I_i}^{D_j}$	The set of traffic flows which indirectly contend with λ_i through $\lambda_j \in S_{D_i}$ at downstream position
R_i	The network delay upper-bound of λ_i
I_i	The maximum interference (in time) suffered by λ_i
I_{ji}	The maximum interference (in time) suffered by λ_i from λ_j
IP_{ji}	The maximum interference (in time) suffered by λ_i from a packet of λ_j
IT_{ji}	The maximum number of packets from λ_j that can interfere with one packet of λ_i
I_{ji}^U	The maximum interference (in time) suffered by λ_j from flows in $S_{I_i}^{U_j}$
I_{ji}^D	The maximum interference (in time) suffered by λ_j from flows in $S_{I_i}^{D_j}$

We make the following basic assumptions:

1. We consider real-time communication in wormhole NoC with VCs and deterministic routing. Priority-based preemptive scheduling is used for link arbitration.
2. A flow λ_i is a stream of periodic packets, whose deadline is no larger than its period, i.e. $D_i \leq T_i$. Each flow λ_i has a unique priority, with a lower index indicating a higher priority.
3. The router uses per-flow buffering, meaning that the number of VCs at each port is no less than that of flow priority levels such that each VC is exclusively used by one flow.

A wormhole real-time network includes n periodic real-time traffic flows $\Lambda = \{\lambda_1, \lambda_2, \cdots, \lambda_n\}$. Each real-time flow can be characterized by four parameters $\lambda_i = \{C_i, T_i, D_i, J_i\}$. Every packet of λ_i should be delivered within D_i, and J_i is the upper-bound of deviation between the release interval of successive packets and the period. By definition, for an *observed* flow λ_i, the network delay upper-bound R_i of a packet is:

$$R_i = C_i + I_i \tag{1}$$

If $R_i \leq D_i$, λ_i can meet its deadline under any scenario. For simplicity, time unit is not explicitly given since the same time base is used throughout the paper.

3.3 Previous Analysis Model

Applying real-time scheduling theory, Shi and Burns presented an analysis method for the problem [16]. Next, we summarize and discuss the correctness of their model.

3.3.1 *Direct and Indirect Interference*

The analysis quantifies two distinct interferences from higher priority flows: *direct interference* and *indirect interference*. If flow λ_j has higher priority than λ_i and shares at least one link with λ_i, λ_j has direct interference relation with λ_i. If flow λ_j has no shared link with λ_i and directly contends with an intermediate flow which has direct interference relation with λ_i, λ_j has indirect interference relation with λ_i. The corresponding direct and indirect interference flow sets S_{D_i} and S_{I_i} of λ_i are defined as:

$$S_{D_i} = \{\lambda_j | \mathcal{L}_i \cap \mathcal{L}_j \neq \phi, i > j, \forall \lambda_j \in \Lambda\} \quad (2)$$

$$S_{I_i} = \{\lambda_j | \mathcal{L}_i \cap \mathcal{L}_j = \phi, \forall \lambda_k \in S_{D_i}, \forall \lambda_j \in S_{D_k}\} \quad (3)$$

3.3.2 *Analysis of Direct Interference*

The maximum direct interference suffered by a packet from λ_i when indirect interference is not considered is:

$$I_i = \sum_{\forall \lambda_j \in S_{D_i}} \lceil \frac{R_i + J_j}{T_j} \rceil C_j \quad (4)$$

3.3.3 *Analysis of Indirect Interference*

If S_{I_i} is a non-empty set, flows in S_{I_i} may cause interference to the observed flow λ_i through the intermediate flows in S_{D_i}. When considering the indirect interference, the upper-bound of interference from higher priority flows to a packet of λ_i is:

$$I_i = \sum_{\forall \lambda_j \in S_{D_i}} \lceil \frac{R_i + J_j + J_j^I}{T_j} \rceil C_j \quad (5)$$

where J_j^I means the deviation caused by higher priority flows between the release interval of consecutive packets and the period, and is called *interference jitter*. The upper-bound of the interference jitter is:

$$J_j^I = I_j = R_j - C_j \quad (6)$$

3.3.4 *The SB's delay bound model*

Using Eq. (5) to substitute I_i in Eq. (1), the formula of network delay upper-bound is:

$$R_i = \sum_{\forall \lambda_j \in S_{D_i}} \lceil \frac{R_i + J_j + J_j^I}{T_j} \rceil C_j + C_i \quad (7)$$

Note that in this formula, J_j^I exists and is equal to $R_j - C_j$ if and only if λ_j is an intermediate flow between λ_i and traffic flows in S_{I_i}, i.e. $S_{D_j} \cap S_{I_i} \neq \phi$. If $S_{D_j} \cap S_{I_i} = \phi$, on the contrary, J_j^I does not exist or can be regarded as 0.

3.4 Correctness Problem with the SB's Model

When analyzing the example in Fig. 1 using the SB's model and then simulating the network behavior, we found that the SB's model is not always correct. In Section 5, we will show detailed setups as well as analytic and simulation results. Here we give a short summary according to Table 3. For λ_3 which has only direct contention, the SB's model gives a correct delay bound (270). However, it computes either pessimistic or incorrect result for flows with indirect interference. Specifically, for λ_4, it calculates a correct but pessimistic delay bound (520 vs max. delay 300). The worst happens to λ_5. The model computes a incorrect delay bound (250 vs. max. delay 264).

While the analysis model for direct interference (Eq. (4)) is valid, we find that the treatment for indirect interference (Eq. (5)) is only partially correct in the sense that it works for indirect interference which is present at the *upstream* of the observed flow, but not for indirect interference which is present at the *downstream* of the observed flow. We call the former *upstream indirect interference* and the latter *downstream indirect interference*. In the next Section 4, we first illustrate the different behaviors of upstream and downstream indirect interferences before formally defining them, then give new formulas for the delay bound analysis.

4. REVISED ANALYSIS MODEL

4.1 Upstream and Downstream Indirect Interference

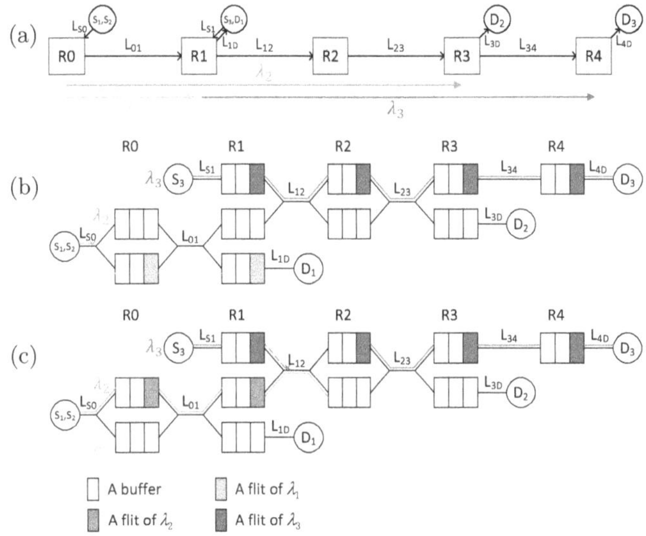

Figure 2: Illustration of upstream indirect contention.

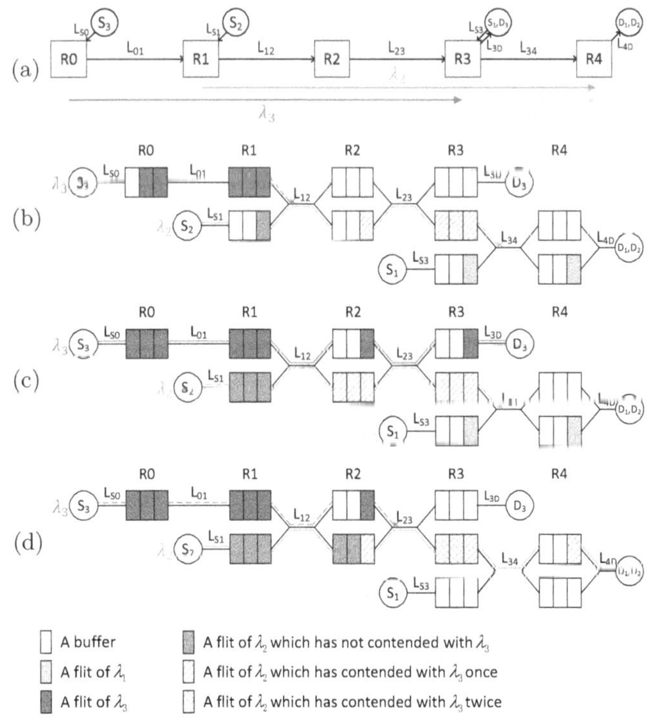

Figure 3: Illustration of downstream indirect contention.

Fig. 2(a) shows an upstream indirect interference. Flow λ_1 located at the *upstream* position of λ_3 indirectly interferes with λ_3 through λ_2. Fig. 2(b) shows that λ_1 blocks the intermediate flow λ_2 on link L_{s0}. After the blocking is released, Fig. 2(c) shows that λ_2 blocks λ_3 on L_{12}. The packet from λ_2 can be blocked by upstream indirect higher priority traffic flow λ_1, as shown in Fig. 2(b), before it arrives at R_1. This may lead to a deviation between the presumed periodic arrival time and the real arrival time of the packet from λ_2 reaching R_1. This deviation called *interference jitter* is handled properly by the SB's model. However, this analysis is *not applicable to downstream indirect interference* due to the different behavior, as we illustrate below.

Fig. 3(a) shows a downstream indirect interference, symmetric to Fig. 2(a). Flow λ_1 located at the *downstream* position of λ_3 indirectly interferes λ_3 through λ_2. Under this situation, one flit from the intermediate flow may block the observed flow multiple times at multiple shared channels when the intermediate flow progressively moves forward. We illustrate this phenomena step by step.

In Fig. 3(b), λ_1 blocks λ_2 on L_{34}. Flits of λ_2 are transmitted to and stored in R2 and R3, and λ_3 is interfered by those flits on L_{12}. After λ_2 has filled up its virtual channel buffers in R2 and R3, λ_3 cannot be blocked by λ_2 while λ_1 is still contending with λ_2 on L_{34}, like in Fig. 3(c). In Fig. 3(d), the transmission of λ_2 is resumed after the entire packet from λ_1 passes L_{34} and λ_2 wins arbitration of L_{23} against λ_3. Note that the flits which are stored in R2 in Fig. 3(c) and have contended with λ_3 once can interfere with λ_3 again, as the red grid rectangles shown in Fig. 3(d). This phenomenon leads to the result that the interference caused by a packet of λ_2 may exceed C_2.

As we can observe, this behavior largely differs from that of the upstream indirect interference. The SB's model fails to catch such *multi-point progressive blocking* behavior. This is the key reason for its flaw as it *incorrectly* handles the downstream indirect interference in the same way as the upstream indirect interference.

4.2 Analysis with Upstream/Downstream Indirect Interference

4.2.1 Definition

To handle indirect interference properly, we need to further divide indirect interference flows into upstream indirect interference flow set denoted $S_{I_i}^{U_j}$, and downstream indirect interference flow set denoted $S_{I_i}^{D_j}$. Let γ_{ji}^n indicate a shared link, which is the nth link in λ_j's routing path, between λ_j and λ_i. Γ_{ji} denotes the set of γ_{ji}^n. Since the superscripts of links in λ_j's routing path are in sequence, the link in Γ_{ji} with the minimum superscript is the first shared link between λ_i and λ_j. Let m_{ji} be the minimum superscript in Γ_{ji}. $S_{I_i}^{U_j}$ and $S_{I_i}^{D_j}$ are defined as:

$$S_{I_i}^{U_j} = \{\lambda_k | \exists \gamma_{jk}^n \in \Gamma_{jk} : n < m_{ji}, \lambda_i \in \Lambda, \lambda_j \in S_{D_i}, \forall \lambda_k \in S_{D_j} \cap S_{I_i}\} \tag{8}$$

$$S_{I_i}^{D_j} = \{\lambda_k | \exists \gamma_{jk}^n \in \Gamma_{jk} : n > m_{ji}, \lambda_i \in \Lambda, \lambda_j \in S_{D_i}, \forall \lambda_k \in S_{D_j} \cap S_{I_i}\} \tag{9}$$

and their relationship to S_{I_i} is:

$$S_{I_i} = \bigcup_{\forall \lambda_j \in S_{D_i}} (S_{I_i}^{U_j} \cup S_{I_i}^{D_j}) \tag{10}$$

Since indirect higher priority traffic flow $\lambda_k \in S_{I_i}$ shares no link with λ_i, $\nexists \gamma_{jk}^n \in \Gamma_{jk} : n = m_{ji}$. For some traffic flows in S_{I_i}, they may share links with intermediate traffic flows in S_{D_i} at both upstream and downstream positions. In this situation, they are in both upstream and downstream interference flow sets of λ_i.

4.2.2 Analysis

Traffic flows in $S_{I_i}^{U_j}$ and $S_{I_i}^{D_j}$ directly contend with λ_j, and indirectly contend with λ_i through λ_j at upstream and downstream positions, respectively. The maximum interferences suffered by λ_j from traffic flows in $S_{I_i}^{U_j}$ and $S_{I_i}^{D_j}$ are as follows:

$$I_{ji}^U = \sum_{\lambda_k \in S_{I_i}^{U_j}} I_{kj} \tag{11}$$

$$I_{ji}^D = \sum_{\lambda_k \in S_{I_i}^{D_j}} I_{kj} \tag{12}$$

The interference I_i suffered by the observed traffic flow λ_i is composed of all I_{ji}, which is caused by λ_j itself and indirect higher priority traffic flows in $S_{I_i}^{U_j} \cup S_{I_i}^{D_j}$. A packet of λ_i may be blocked by more than one packet from λ_j. The upper-bound of interference suffered by λ_i from λ_j can be expressed as the maximum interference caused by one packet of λ_j multiplied by the maximum number of λ_j's packets contending with the same packet of λ_i. I_i can thus be expressed as:

$$I_i = \sum_{\forall \lambda_j \in S_{D_i}} I_{ji} = \sum_{\forall \lambda_j \in S_{D_i}} (IT_{ji} \cdot IP_{ji}) \tag{13}$$

In the following we reason about the bounds for IT_{ji} and IP_{ji} through two theorems, one for each.

THEOREM 1. *The maximum number of packets from λ_j that can contend with a packet of λ_i is:*

$$IT_{ji} = \lceil \frac{R_i + J_j + I_{ji}^U}{T_j} \rceil \tag{14}$$

PROOF. According to Theorem 1 and its proof in [16], the largest number of packets from λ_j that can contend with a packet of λ_i is:

$$IT_{ji} = \lceil \frac{R_i + J_j + J_j^I}{T_j} \rceil \tag{15}$$

Note that, in [16], IT_{ji} is represented by g and J_j^I is equal to $R_j - C_j$. When considering the interference from λ_j to λ_i, J_j^I means the maximum interference suffered by the head flit of packet from λ_j before it contends with λ_i. But because of the inherent features of NoC, a flit is transmitted forward one router at a time. So λ_j can only suffer interference from traffic flows which share links at the upstream position before it starts to block λ_i. This means that the interference jitter is only caused by upstream indirect higher priority traffic flows, and downstream indirect contention cannot influence interference jitter. Hence, $J_j^I = I_{ji}^U$. Substitute I_{ji}^U for J_j^I in Eq. (15), we can get Eq. (14). □

THEOREM 2. *The maximum interference suffered by λ_i from a packet of λ_j is:*

$$IP_{ji} = C_j + I_{ji}^D \tag{16}$$

PROOF. According to the analysis of the case in Fig. 3, the multi-point progressive blocking is contributed by the flits of λ_j which interfere with λ_i more than once. For indirect higher priority traffic flow λ_k which can lead to the multi-point progressive blocking, a necessary condition is that the

λ_j's flits which are stored in buffer caused by the blocking of λ_k can contend with λ_i later. Hence, the shared links between λ_k and λ_j should be at the downstream of shared links between λ_j and λ_i, namely, λ_k must be at the downstream position, $\lambda_k \in S_{I_i}^{D_j}$. The traffic flows only in $S_{I_i}^{U_j}$ cannot cause the multi-point progressive blocking.

The interference from λ_j to λ_i is composed of two parts: 1) the interference when λ_j is not blocked by λ_k; 2) the interference when λ_j is blocked by λ_k. The upper-bound of these two parts are C_j and the summation of all interference from traffic flows in $S_{I_i}^{D_j}$ to λ_j, I_{ji}^D, respectively. Thus, the maximum IP_{ji} is $C_j + I_{ji}^D$. □

In summary, the upstream indirect interference is used to determine the number of times λ_j can interfere with a packet of λ_i (IT_{ji}) while the interference of each λ_j's packet (IP_{ji}) can be inflated by the downstream interference. Thus, with respect to Eq. (7), we are reducing J_i^I (using IT_{ji}) while increasing C_j (using IP_{ji}).

4.3 Our Analysis Model

A real-time flow may suffer one or more kinds of interference. Hence, using the combination of Eq. (13), (14) and (16) to substitute I_i in Eq. (1), we can get the network delay upper-bound of λ_i as follows:

$$R_i = \sum_{\forall \lambda_i \in S_{D_i}} \lceil \frac{R_i + J_j + I_{ji}^U}{T_j} \rceil (C_j + I_{ji}^D) + C_i \qquad (17)$$

In general, no analytic formula can solve this equation and numerical analysis should be used to solve it. Usually the iterative algorithm is used to obtain the network delay upper-bound. $R_i^{(n)}$ indicates the nth iterative value of R_i, the iterative initial value is $R_i^{(0)} = \sum_{\forall \lambda_j \in S_{D_i}} (C_j + I_{ji}^D) + C_i$ and the iteration terminates when $R_i^{(n+1)} = R_i^{(n)}$ or $R_i^{(n)} > D_i$ or the number of iteration exceeds the limitations. If the iteration terminates with $R_i^{(n+1)} = R_i^{(n)}$, the network delay upper-bound of λ_i is $R_i = R_i^{(n)}$.

We can now qualitatively compare our model in Eq. (17) with SB's model in Eq. (7) and summarize three cases:

1. For S_{D_i} only, both models are consistent.
2. For S_{D_i} plus *only* $S_{I_i}^{U_j}$ which causes I_{ji}^U ($I_{ji}^D = 0$), both models are correct, but our model gives equal or tighter delay bound.
3. For S_{D_i} plus *any* $S_{I_i}^{D_j}$ which causes I_{ji}^D (with or without I_{ji}^U), the SB's model may give incorrect delay bound. Our model gives correct result.

5. CASE STUDY

We conduct a case study with both analysis and simulation to 1) give a detailed analysis example; 2) quantitatively contrast the SB's and our model against simulated results; 3) discuss correctness and tightness in a concrete context.

5.1 Setup

We use the illustrative example in Fig. 1(a) as our case study, which is simple to understand and has necessary interference patterns to compare the two models. There are five periodic flows with their parameters listed in Table 2.

Given the flows and their interference patterns in the network, we can obtain per-flow delay upper bounds using the two models. To obtain simulation results, we build a network behavior simulator fulfilling the assumptions for the delay bound

Table 2: Flow parameters

Traffic Flow	C_i (L_i *, H_i **)	T_i	D_i	J_i
λ_1	30 (27, 4)	150	100	0
λ_2	30 (28, 3)	150	100	0
λ_3	150 (144, 7)	400	300	0
λ_4	100 (98, 3)	600	550	0
λ_5	100 (96, 5)	300	250	0

* L_i denotes the number of flits of λ_i's packets.
** H_i indicates the hop count of λ_i including from terminal to router and router to terminal, one hop each.

analysis problem. Specifically, the network performs wormhole switching, and the router uses flit-sized virtual channels, per-flow buffering and priority-based channel arbitration. The router is single-cycle router, meaning that switching any flit from one hop to the next hop takes one cycle. As a result of wormhole transmission, the non-contentional network delay C_i equals $L_i + H_i - 1$.

Traffic flows generate fixed-size packets periodically according to Table 2. All flows are injected synchronously. To simulate all possible contention scenarios, they are generated with phase shifts up to their corresponding periods. For example, flow λ_1 has an injection phase of 0 to 149 cycles, and flow λ_5 0 to 299 cycles. For each combination of the phase shifts under a particular buffer size setting, the simulation includes two basic phases: warm-up and measurement. Both phases are the least common multiple (1200) of the periods of the five flows in length. After the warm-up phase, the measurement phase begins and records the delay of each packet in this phase. We then use the statistics to compare with analytic results.

5.2 Basic Comparison

To show the direct and indirect interferences clearer, we draw the flow interference graph for the example in Fig. 4.

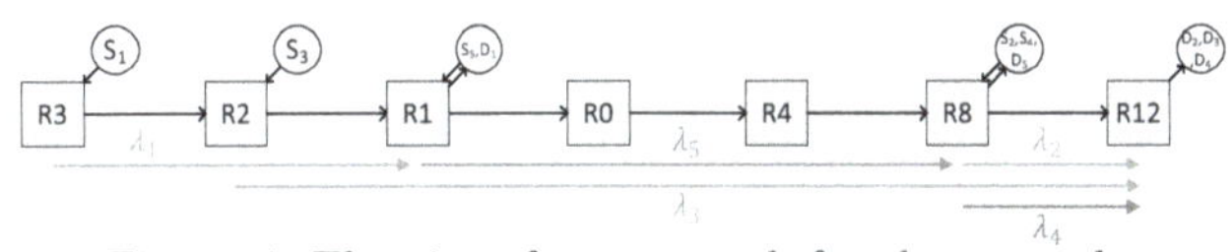

Figure 4: Flow interference graph for the example.

Table 3: Analysis and Simulation (Buffer Size = 10) Results

					Results		
λ_i	S_{D_i}	S_{I_i}	$S_{I_i}^{U_j}$	$S_{I_i}^{D_j}$	SB's	Our	Simulation
λ_1	ϕ	ϕ	ϕ	ϕ	30	30	30
λ_2	ϕ	ϕ	ϕ	ϕ	30	30	30
λ_3	$\{\lambda_1, \lambda_2\}$	ϕ	ϕ	ϕ	270	270	233
λ_4	$\{\lambda_2, \lambda_3\}$	$\{\lambda_1\}$	$\{\lambda_1\}$ (j=3)	ϕ	520	340	300
λ_5	$\{\lambda_3\}$	$\{\lambda_1, \lambda_2\}$	$\{\lambda_1\}$ (j=3)	$\{\lambda_2\}$ (j=3)	250	310	264

Table 3 gives the two analytic delay bounds (independent of buffer size), and the maximum simulated delay for each flow when the buffer size (B) is 10, implying that back-pressure may exist according to the analysis in [9]. To clearly associate this quantitative comparison with the qualitative comparison (Section 4.3), we also list the *direct*, *upstream indirect* and *downstream indirect interference sets*, i.e. S_{D_i}, $S_{I_i}^{U_j}$ and $S_{I_i}^{D_j}$, respectively, for all flows. Flow λ_1 and λ_2 have no interference, thus their delay bounds are equal to their ideal communication time. From this table, we observe matching results with the qualitative comparison. Specifically,

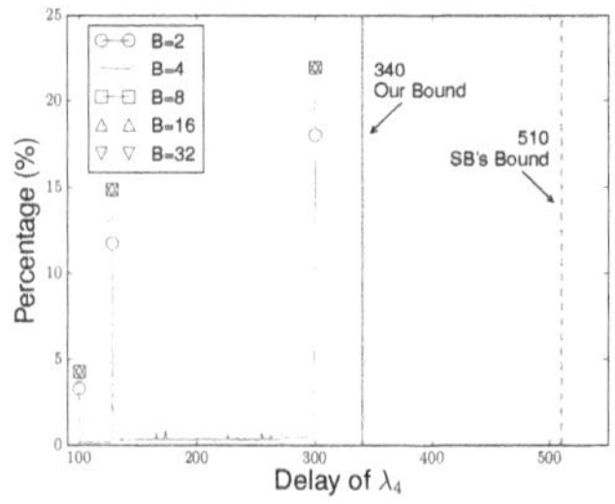

(a)

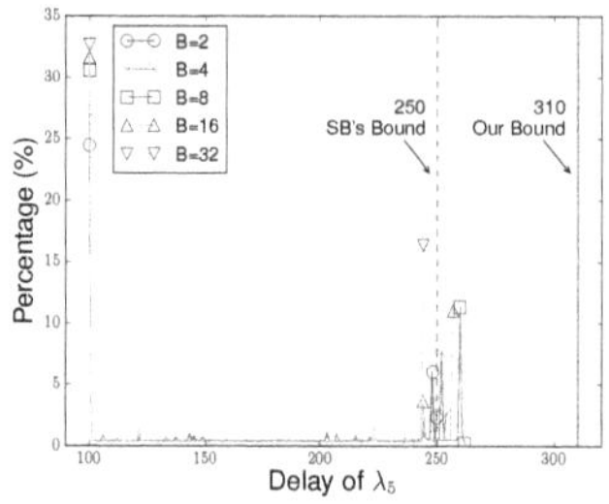

(b)

Figure 5: Delay distributions of (a) λ_4 and (b) λ_5.

1. λ_3 has only direct contention (non-empty S_{D_3}). Thus both models obtain the same correct delay bound.
2. λ_4 has direct (non-empty S_{D_4}) and only upstream indirect contention (non-empty $S_{I_4}^{U_3}$), both analytic delay bounds correctly bound the maximum simulated delay (300), and our delay bound (340 vs. 520) is much tighter.
3. λ_5 has direct (non-empty S_{D_5}) and downstream indirect interference (non-empty $S_{I_5}^{D_3}$), the SB's delay bound (250) is incorrect as exceeded by the simulated delay (264), and our delay bound (310) is correct.

5.3 Buffer Size Influence and Tightness

To further look into the impact of buffering on the maximum delay, we simulate with different buffer sizes.

Fig. 5(a) shows the distributions of λ_4's network delay when VC buffer size is 2, 4, 8, 16 and 32. All of the five distributions have the similar features and the worst-case network delays are the same, 300. Since the preemptive arbitration policy is employed and λ_4 has direct and only upstream indirect contention (no downstream indirect contention), the buffer size can only slightly influence the distributions. The worst-case delays are less than our delay bound (340) and SB's delay bound (520), and our delay bound is much tighter.

Fig. 5(b) gives the distributions of λ_5's delay under the same conditions as Fig. 5(a). Compared with the distributions of λ_4, the five curves are more irregular and the worst-case network delay varies with the buffer size. Since λ_5 has downstream indirect contention, the buffer size can have more influence on the distributions through the multi-point progressive blocking. From the statistics, there are 11.2%, 17% and 14.3% of packets exceeding the SB's delay bound (250) when the buffer size is 4, 8 and 16, respectively, which invalidate the SB's delay bound. Under the various buffer sizes, no packet's delay exceeds our delay bound (310).

6. CONCLUSION

We have presented a new delay bound analysis model for real-time communication in wormhole NoC with priority-based preemptive arbitration. This model corrects the flaws present in a state-of-the-art analysis model [16] called SB's model in the paper. The main cause of the flaws lies in the uniform treatment of *upstream* and *downstream* indirect interferences. The two different indirect interferences actually show very different blocking behaviors when packets move from one buffer to the next buffer. In particular, the downstream indirect interference exhibits a multi-point progressive blocking phenomenon which was not captured by the SB's model. We have given theorems to prove our analysis method. Furthermore, we have qualitatively and quantitatively compared our model with the SB's model. In summary, for flows with direct interference only, both models are consistent; for flows with upstream indirect interference only, our model gets either equally good or tighter delay bound than the SB's model; for flows with downstream indirect interference, the SB's model is flawed and ours is correct.

In our analysis, the buffering effect is qualitatively counted, and the delay bound formula is independent of the buffer size. In the future, we plan to include the buffer size in the analysis model in order to quantify its impact on the delay bound.

7. ACKNOWLEDGMENTS

This work was sponsored the National Natural Science Foundation of China No. 61300047, No. 61370063, and No. 61472152, and Natural Science Foundation of Hubei Province No. 2015CFB315.

8. REFERENCES

[1] N. Audsley, A. Burns, M. Richardson, K. Tindell, and A. J. Wellings. Applying new scheduling theory to static priority pre-emptive scheduling. *Software Engineering Journal*, 8(5):284–292, 1993.

[2] A. Burns, J. Harbin, and L. Indrusiak. A wormhole NoC protocol for mixed criticality systems. In *RTSS*, pages 184–195, 2014.

[3] R. Cruz. A calculus for network delay, part II: Networks analysis. *IEEE Trans. Inf. Theory*, 37(1):132–141, 1991.

[4] W. J. Dally and B. P. Towles. *Principles and practices of interconnection networks*. Elsevier, 2004.

[5] B. D. De Dinechin, Y. Durand, D. Van Amstel, and A. Ghiti. Guaranteed services of the NoC of a manycore processor. In *NoCArc*, pages 11–16, 2014.

[6] J.-P. Georges, E. Rondeau, and T. Divoux. Evaluation of switched ethernet in an industrial context by using the network calculus. In *WFCS*, pages 19–26, 2002.

[7] J. Jasperneite, P. Neumann, M. Theis, and K. Watson. Deterministic real-time communication with switched Ethernet. In *WFCS*, pages 11–18, 2002.

[8] H. Kashif, S. Gholamian, and H. Patel. SLA: A stage-level latency analysisfor real-time communicationin a pipelined resource model. *IEEE Trans. Comput.*, 64(4):1177–1190, 2015.

[9] H. Kashif and H. Patel. Bounding buffer space requirements for real-time priority-aware networks. In *ASP-DAC*, pages 113–118, 2014.

[10] J.-Y. Le Boudec and P. Thiran. *Network calculus: a theory of deterministic queuing systems for the internet*, volume 2050. Springer Science & Business Media, 2001.

[11] Z. Lu, A. Jantsch, and I. Sander. Feasibility analysis of messages for on-chip networks using wormhole routing. In *ASP-DAC*, volume 2, pages 960–964, 2005.

[12] L. M. Ni and P. K. McKinley. A survey of wormhole routing techniques in direct networks. *Computer*, 26(2):62–76, 1993.

[13] Y. Qian, Z. Lu, and W. Dou. Analysis of worst-case delay bounds for best-effort communication in wormhole networks on chip. In *NOCS*, pages 44–53, 2009.

[14] V. Rantala, T. Lehtonen, and J. Plosila. *Network on chip routing algorithms*. Citeseer, 2006.

[15] Z. Shi and A. Burns. Priority assignment for real-time wormhole communication in on-chip networks. In *RTSS*, pages 421–430, 2008.

[16] Z. Shi and A. Burns. Real-time communication analysis for on-chip networks with wormhole switching. In *NOCS*, pages 161–170, 2008.

[17] Z. Shi and A. Burns. Real-time communication analysis with a priority share policy in on-chip networks. In *ECRTS*, pages 3–12, 2009.

[18] Z. Shi, A. Burns, and L. S. Indrusiak. Schedulability analysis for real time on-chip communication with wormhole switching. *IJERTCS*, 1(2):1–22, 2010.

[19] X. Zhao and Z. Lu. Per-flow delay bound analysis based on a formalized microarchitectural model. In *NOCS*, pages 1–8, 2013.

A New Methodology for Noise Sensor Placement Based on Association Rule Mining

Yu-Hsiang Hung[1], Sheng-Hsin Fang[1], Hung-Ming Chen[1], Shen-Min Chen[2], Chang-Tzu Lin[2] and Chia-Hsin Lee[2]

[1]Institute of Electronics and SoC Center, National Chiao Tung University, Hsinchu, Taiwan
yhhung.ee03g@g2.nctu.edu.tw, vanessa_fangsh@hotmail.com, hmchen@mail.nctu.edu.tw
[2]Information and Communications Research Laboratories, Industrial Technology Research Institute, Taiwan
shenmin.nthu@gmail.com, ctzulin@itri.org.tw, JerryLee@itri.org.tw

ABSTRACT

Due to near-threshold computing nowadays, voltage emergency is threatening our design margins very seriously. Noise sensors are inserted in order to prevent various integrity issues from happening during runtime. In this work, we use a new technique based on association rule mining to plan and place noise sensors. This new methodology can consider the miss rate (the probability of any node occurring voltage emergency without any detection by placed sensors) and simultaneously minimize the number of sensors utilized. The results show that our approach is very effective in converging the miss rate to zero by the least number of sensors. Compared with the state-of-the-art, we can reduce the number of sensors by half in benchmarks while the miss rate is comparable or even smaller than the prior work.

Keywords

Noise sensor placement; Near threshold computing; Power integrity

1. INTRODUCTION

The power consumption from continued performance scaling is a major challenge in modern design. Owing to the advanced process technology and complex design, decreasing the power supply voltage even operating at near threshold voltage is the trend [1]. Besides, voltage fluctuations keep worsening since the low power techniques (e.g., power gating and clock gating) lead to instantaneous large current. Hence, power integrity issues have attracted more and more attentions in recent years. Noise margin violation, also called voltage emergency defined as the amplitude of the noise surpassing the threshold voltage for a duration of threshold time (T_t) [11], will cause unexpected results such as timing violations even the function incorrectness. It will also degrade overall performance.

Conventionally, solving the dynamic IR-Drop usually relied on the decoupling capacitance (Decap) insertion and metal sizing/filling. The previous work [3] claimed that if the decap can not be inserted at the dynamic IR-Drop hot spots, the improvement will not be obvious even the number of inserted decap is towards 200K instances. On the other hand, another work [12] presented that only 2% dynamic IR-Drop will be reduced while filling the metal connected to Power/Ground in the available tracks after design is frozen. Both aforementioned techniques will not only make negative effects such as large leakage current but are also very expensive in the advanced process technology.

In recent years, there are many researches proposed to prevent the undesired effects from voltage emergency in the architecture level. One such kind is prediction-based mechanism. It tries to track the patterns and recognize the signatures of voltage emergency according to the voltage/current profiles, and throttle the instruction immediately while detecting the imminent voltage emergencies [14][5]. The other kind is sensor-based mechanism, using the noise sensor to detect the voltage emergency. This mechanism is categorized into two types: throttling and rolling back system with conservative threshold voltage and aggressive threshold voltage respectively. While detecting the voltage emergency, the first tries to reduce the fluctuation of current by dynamic frequency voltage scaling (DVFS) [4][8] or pipeline muffling and damping [9][13], and the second allows the voltage emergency occurring, the recovery system will be actuated and roll back the correct state [6].

The sensor-based mechanism depends on the sensors to detect the voltage emergency. Therefore, performance of sensor-based mechanism is mainly dominated by the locations where sensors are placed to monitor. However, noise sensor placement has not been addressed much in the literature yet. Due to the sensor cost and overhead, we can only deploy a limited number of sensor in a chip. The prior work [15] proposed a statistical framework for the sensor placement, called Eagle-Eye. It only considered the miss rate. Another one [10] proposed a method to detect voltage emergency by predicting the noise in the function area based on the magnitude detected by the sensors placed in blank area without considering the extra time cost produced by the predicting step. However, how to find the correlations and importance between each node and optimize the number of sensors so that we can get an optimal balance among miss rate and overhead are still open problems.

In this paper, we propose an effective method for noise sensor placement based on the association rule mining, which will be used to extract the co-occurrence patterns effectively.

GLSVLSI '16, May 18-20, 2016, Boston, MA, USA

DOI: http://dx.doi.org/10.1145/2902961.2902973

We also analyze the miss rate versus the number of sensors. The main contributions of our work are summarized below:

- We propose a new formulation for noise sensor placement with considering both miss rate and number of sensors in the meantime.
- We propose a novel modeling which simplifies the noise sensor placement to the frequent pattern mining problem. The experimental results show that our modeling is very effective on identifying the nodes needed to be monitored.
- We propose a method for identifying the node based on the modeling which can optimize the miss rate and the number of sensors. The experimental results show that our method can achieve the minimum miss rate at zero. In addition, we can reduce the number of sensors by half in benchmarks while the miss rate is comparable or even smaller than the state-of-the-art.

The remainder of this paper is organized as follows. We present the preprocessing for noise waveform in Section 2.1 and formulate the objective for the noise sensor placement in Section 2.2. Our method based on FP-Tree and the node identification scheme are described in Section 3. The experimental results are shown in Section 4. Finally, the conclusions are given in Section 5.

2. PRELIMINARIES

In this section, we formulate the noise sensor placement problem while considering both miss rate and number of sensors. First, we pre-process the noise waveforms and transform the definition of voltage emergency based on [15]. Then, we derive the objective which should be optimized for noise sensor placement.

2.1 Binary Voltage Emergency

In order to simplify the identification of voltage emergency, we transform the definition of voltage emergency as Eq. (1):

$$E_i(t) = \begin{cases} 1, & \text{if } z_i(t) \geq V_t \\ 0, & \text{if } z_i(t) < V_t \end{cases} \tag{1}$$

where

$$z_i(t) = min_{t-T_t \leq t' \leq t} \Delta v_i(t')$$

V_t and T_t denote the threshold voltage and the threshold time respectively. As in Fig. 1, we extract the minimum value in each time window as a symbolic voltage for each duration [15]. With this transformation, we can simplify the identification of voltage emergency with only considering a binary variable, which implies whether there is a voltage emergency occurrence at a node during a time window. The result of transformation is also same as the output of the noise sensor which we adopt in [11].

2.2 Objective Derivation

Before describing the derivation, there are some given information as input:

1. In a power delivery network, there are m available candidate nodes with their respective information of voltage emergency for noise sensor to be placed.
2. Threshold voltage is assigned by designer. In this paper, we set 5% VDD reported as a hard value [6] and 1 ns as the threshold voltage and threshold time respectively for all sensors.

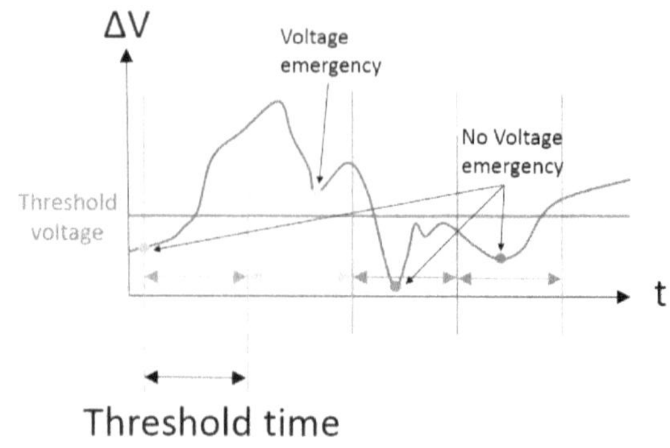

Figure 1: Simplified voltage emergency definition.

Our objective is to identify the *unknown number* of nodes needed to be monitored, including the nodes whose locations are not available to place sensors. In practice, the sensors can be placed in the area adjacent to the identified nodes and we say that the sensor placed at node i is to sense the voltage of node i for simplicity. Assume the number of nodes identified by our method is k. What we want to optimize is using only k sensors to minimize the miss rate defined as the probability of occurring voltage emergency among all nodes without any detection of voltage emergency by placed sensors. Miss rate can be formally represented as the following equation:

$$Miss\ Rate = P(E_{sensor} = 0 | E_{node} = 1) \tag{2}$$

where E_{sensor}, a binary variable defined previously, is the OR operation of variables corresponding to the nodes with placed sensor (E_{si}), as Eq. (3). Similarly, E_{node} is the OR operation of variables corresponding to all nodes (E_{ni}) as in Eq. (4). In the following discussion, we use E_{sensor}, E_{node}, E_{si} and E_{ni} to represent the set of voltage emergency scenarios of nodes in whole time steps for simplicity, for instance, $E_{si} = \int_0^{\#\ of\ all\ time\ steps} E_{si}(t)\, dt$.

$$E_{sensor} = E_{s1} \vee E_{s2} \vee \ldots \vee E_{sk} \tag{3}$$

$$E_{node} = E_{n1} \vee E_{n2} \vee \ldots \vee E_{nm} \tag{4}$$

By Baye's rule, we can transform Eq. (2) as follows:

$$P(E_{sensor} = 0 | E_{node} = 1)$$

$$= 1 - P(E_{sensor} = 1 | E_{node} = 1) \tag{5}$$

According to Eq. (5), it is straight-forward that if we optimize the miss rate, it is equivalent to the following equation:

$$Maximize\ P(E_{sensor} = 1 | E_{node} = 1) \tag{6}$$

Because the design is given, $P(E_{node} = 1)$ is a constant and independent to the noise sensor placement [15]. With this understanding, the objective can be simplified as:

$$Maximize\ P(E_{sensor} = 1) \tag{7}$$

Although the equation can archieve the least miss rate, it is not enough to consider the number of sensors at the same time. Therefore, we propose a constraint to Eq. (7) so that we can optimize the miss rate by using the least number of sensors. In fact, Eq. (3) provides a little insight in optimizing the number of sensor implicitly. For example, Fig. 2 depicts the coverage by 2 sensors. We can observe

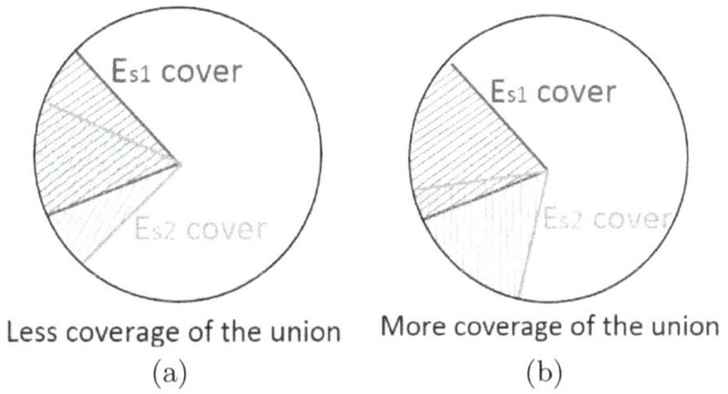

Figure 2: The coverage space of $P(E_{node} = 1)$ by 2 different selected nodes with (a) more intersection. (b) fewer intersection.

that if we can choose the least intersection between each node, we will get a bigger union under a fixed space since the $P(E_{node} = 1)$ is constant by the given design.

We then have the following objective:

$$Maximize\ P(E_{sensor} = 1) \quad (8)$$

$$s.\ t.\ \ P(E_{s1} \wedge E_{s2} \wedge \ldots \wedge E_{sk} = 1)\ is\ minimized$$

With Eq. (8), we can optimize the miss rate and number of sensors simultaneously. That is, the objective turns to identify the nodes with the highest frequency of occurring voltage emergency while these identified nodes will not co-occur voltage emergency at the same time.

3. ALGORITHM

3.1 Overview

Association rules mining is a method for discovering the strong rules in a huge database. There are many innovation algorithms proposed to solve the problem such as Apriori algorithm[2] and FP-Growth algorithm[7]. For instance, it is used to find the rules that will predict the occurrence of an item based on the occurrence of other items in a set of transactions. In other words, it is used to find the aforementioned co-occurring items (frequent patterns). On the contrary, the objective is to identify the nodes which will not co-occur voltage emergency (infrequent patterns) at the same time. In fact, the infrequent patterns are the patterns which are not identified as frequent patterns. Therefore, we use the association rule mining technique in our method.

FP-Growth algorithm [7] we try to adopt is one of the most popular and fastest algorithms for frequent patterns mining. There are two major steps in this algorithm. One is constructing the FP-Tree, the other is to find the frequent pattern in the set with all items. In this paper, we focus on the part of constructing FP-Tree since the existing throttling and rolling back mechanisms belong to a distributed sensors and central controlled system [15]. Besides, our objective has turned to identify the infrequent patterns. As a result, we do not need to extract the frequent patterns exhaustively. With this adoption, we can consider both frequency of voltage emergency and relations among nodes rather than considering the voltage drop of node only in the prior work[15].

The block diagram of our method is shown in Fig. 3. First, we construct the FP-Tree based on all voltage emergency information of all nodes. Then, we select the nodes in the FP-Tree until the miss rate is convergent.

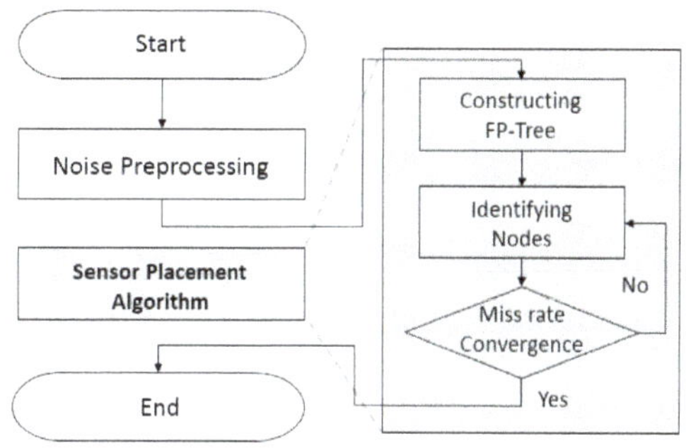

Figure 3: Block diagram of our method.

3.2 Problem Transformation

With the basic background about FP-Growth, we aim to model the noise sensor placement problem to the frequent pattern mining problem in this section. First, we change the terminologies as below:

$$Time\ step \Longrightarrow Transaction$$

$$Node \Longrightarrow Item$$

As Table 1(a), it is a simple example where T_n and E_i denote the nth time window and the binary variable of node i defined in Eq. (1) respectively. Each row is a time step with voltage emergency information of nodes. Then, we collect the nodes whose variables are equal to 1 represented in Table 1(b). With this transformation, we can model the nodes as items in transactions. Because nodes whose variables are equal to 1 during a time step is similar to items bought in a transaction, these two both belong to something occurring in an event. It is also the reason that we simplify the identification of voltage emergency as Eq. (1).

Table 1: Voltage emergency information in (a) variable form. (b) nodes form.

(a)

Time ID	Nodes				
	E_a	E_b	E_c	E_d	E_e
T_1	1	1	0	0	0
T_2	0	1	1	1	1
T_3	1	0	0	1	1
T_4	1	1	0	1	1
T_5	1	1	0	0	1

(b)

TID	Nodes
1	a,b
2	b,c,d,e
3	a,d,e
4	a,b,d,e
5	a,b,e

3.3 Constructing FP-Tree

FP-Tree is similar to the prefix tree which is an ordered tree data structure. The procedures of transforming the database of voltage emergency information into FP-Tree are summarized as follows:

1. **Counting**: Scan all time steps in the database, and sum the times of occurring voltage emergency for each node.

2. **Sorting and reordering**: Sort all nodes as a list with descending order according to the times of occurring voltage emergency. Then, reorder the nodes in each time step.

3. **Constructing**: Construct the FP-Tree based on the set of time steps with reordered nodes.

Table 2: Nodes with voltage emergency in time steps. (a) Example of original data. (b) The list of nodes vs. times of its occurrence of voltage emergency. (c) With descending ordering.

(a)

TID	Nodes
1	b,e,f
2	a,c,d,e
3	a,e
4	a,c,e
5	c,d
6	a,b,e
7	a,d,e
8	c,d,g
9	a,c,e,f
10	a,b,e

(b)

e → 8
a → 7
c → 5
d → 4
b → 3
f → 2
g → 1

(c)

TID	Nodes
1	e,b,f
2	e,a,c,d
3	e,a
4	e,a,c
5	c,d
6	e,a,b
7	e,a,d
8	c,d,g
9	e,a,c,f
10	e,a,b

Now, we show how to construct the FP-Tree. For example, there is a set of nodes with the details as in Table 2(a), where TID means the sequence number of time step, and the variables within the nodes column are the nodes occurring voltage emergency in corresponding time. After counting times of occurring voltage emergency for all nodes in all time steps, we sort the nodes by their times of occurring voltage emergency and generate a list in descending order, shown in Table 2(b). Then, we reorder the nodes in each time step according to the list sorted previous step as in Table 2(c).

Algorithm 1: Constructing FP-Tree

```
Input: All time steps with voltage emergency
       information of nodes in database
Output: Complete FP-Tree
Create a vertex V_root;
Create a vertex V_parent;
for each time step in the database do
    V_parent = V_root;
    for each reordered node n_scan do
        if V_parent has child vertex V_n_scan then
            Increase the occurrence of V_n_scan by 1;
        end
        else
            Create a vertex V_n_scan under V_parent;
            Set the occurrence of V_n_scan = 1;
        end
        V_parent = V_n_scan;
    end
end
```

Next, we construct the FP-Tree, the algorithm is shown in Algorithm 1. The node and vertex in the following discussion stand for the node in power network and the vertex in graph. We always start from the root vertex for each time step, and scan the reordered node one by one to construct the FP-Tree. Fig. 4(a) depicts the FP-Tree with one time step. By iteratively scanning each time step, we can get a complete FP-Tree shown as Fig. 4(c).

3.4 Planning Sensors for Minimal Miss Rate

The miss rate is mainly dominated by the nodes which are identified to be monitored. Therefore, it is important to decide the locations to place sensors.

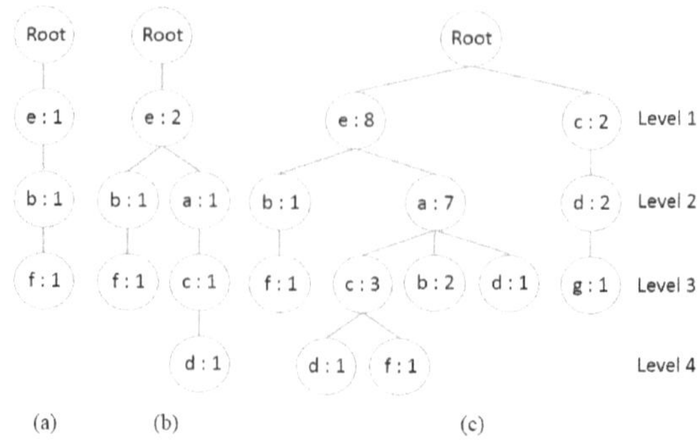

Figure 4: FP-Trees for the example in Table 2(c) with (a) one transaction. (b) two transactions. (c) all transactions.

We propose a node identification method based on the FP-Tree, which is able to optimize the objective derived in Eq. (8). The method is motivated by the following observations, as shown in Fig. 5(a), where S_i and the value next to S_i denote the ith identified node to place sensor and the frequency of occurring voltage emergency at the node respectively. It is needed about 6 sensors to converge the miss rate with only considering the frequency of occurring voltage emergency. However, only 3 sensors is needed to get a comparable miss rate in our approach. The main reason is that the identified nodes sense the voltage emergency with the least overlapping coverage while doing the activities of patterns learning, which also refers to Fig. 2.

In Fig. 5(b), there are three main functional blocks: F1, F2 and F3, where F1 has the most complex function and usually leads to large current. S_1, S_2 and S_3 all are with high frequency of occurring voltage emergency (around 50% or above) since they are located at the same hot region (F1). Once the function in F1 is actuated, there is a very high probability that these nodes in this region co-occur voltage emergency. In this case, if placing the sensor at S_2 and S_3, these two sensor can not make extra contribution on the miss rate while S_1 had been selected. It is because the coverage of these two sensors is covered by S_1. In addition, these two can not cover the voltage emergency caused by other functional blocks. As a result, we can achieve the least miss rate and the least number of sensors by learning the activities of patterns. By clustering the nodes based on learning the activities of patterns, we can identify the node S_1, S_4 and S_6 directly. These are all significant nodes

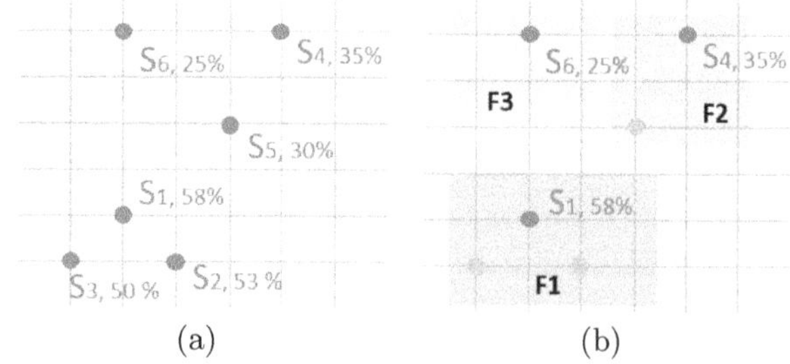

Figure 5: Planning minimal # of sensors (a) Without activities of pattern learning. (b) With activities of pattern learning.

identified from the clusters whose intersection between them is minimized.

As the motivation described previously, we need to use FP-Tree to help us find the clusters according to the activities of patterns. However, the clustering has been done implicitly while FP-Tree is constructed. Each subtree whose root is the child vertex at the first level of the FP-Tree is a cluster. In other words, the noise sensor placement problem turns to identify the child vertices at first level in a FP-Tree. The key idea is the step titled as sorting and reordering in Section 3.3. By sorting the nodes according to the times of occurring voltage emergency of each node, we can get a list of nodes in descending order, and reorder the nodes in each time step based on the list sorted previously. The reason behind this step is moving the node with the most frequent occurrence of voltage emergency in each time step to the vertex which will be created first in the FP-Tree. Therefore, the child vertices at first level are all with the highest frequency of occurring voltage emergency in each subtree.

On the other hand, the relations between each node in a time step will be constructed as a path from the root to the leaf. In a subtree, the vertices are with high correlations, meaning the probability of these nodes co-occurring voltage emergency is very high. However, in different subtree, the correlation will be minimized. As a result, we can minimize the miss rate and number of sensors by identifying all child vertices at first level in the FP-Tree. With the feature of FP-Tree, it is intuitive to optimize the noise sensor placement.

In addition, we can do a much better trade-off even the number of sensor is limited. If is, we can identify the vertices with more occurrences at first level in FP-Tree. If not, we can place the sensor to sense all nodes at first level in FP-Tree. Therefore, we can evaluate the number of sensors needed to be placed after constructing the FP-Tree. As in the example in Table 2(a), the nodes e, a and c will be identified with only considering the frequency. In our method, we select only two nodes e and c directly as the child vertices at the first level in the FP-Tree, shown in Fig. 4(c). Observed form FP-Tree, the occurrence of node a is always followed by the node e. Therefore, our method can optimize miss rate with the minimum number of sensors.

4. EXPERIMENTAL RESULTS

We present the experimental results of our method in C++ on a machine with 2.6 GHz Intel Xeon E5-2630 V2 CPUs and 32GB memories. First, we pre-process the noise information from simulated results of three benchmarks extracted from the industrial designs obtained from the authors of [15].

The objective in our work is to minimize the miss rate by the least number of sensors. The miss rate is calculated as the T_{miss}/T_{total}, where T_{miss} and T_{total} stand for the time steps of voltage emergency miss, which means an emergency occurring in any node without any detection by sensors and total time steps in the transient simulation respectively. The results in Table 3 show that the miss rate can be even optimized to zero while the number of placed sensors is not limited (sensing all nodes at first level in FP-Tree). In addition, our method can converge the miss rate more efficiently (as in Fig. 6) since we select the nodes with the most frequency of occurrence in each cluster whose intersection between each others is minimized. Therefore, every selected node by our method will make the positive contribution on the miss rate.

Due to the different setup of benchmarks in [10], we compare our work with the recent work [15] in Fig. 7. The convergent rate of our method is much faster than [15]. The

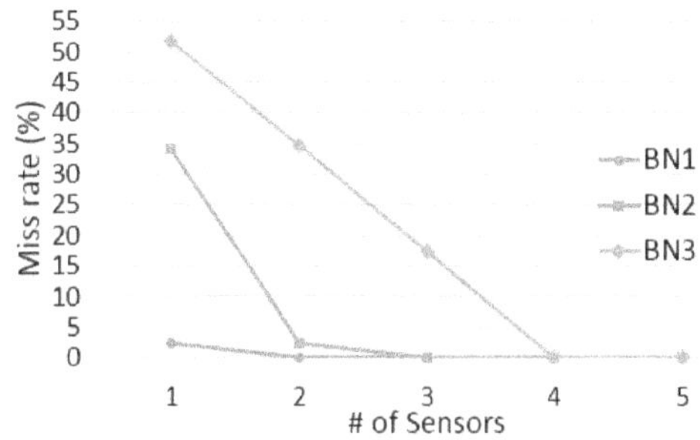

Figure 6: The miss rate vs. # of placed sensors with support rate = 0%. The miss rate can be decreased to zero by our method.

nodes identified in [15] do not make effective contribution on the miss rate when the number of sensors is very small. The reason is that they focus on identifying the nodes with the most severe drop. If they belong to the same cluster(subtree), these nodes will co-occur voltage emergency although the drops of these nodes are larger than others. However, we can extract the significant nodes in different clusters by learning the activities of patterns. Therefore, the miss rate will be decreased monotonously while increasing the number of selected nodes in our method.

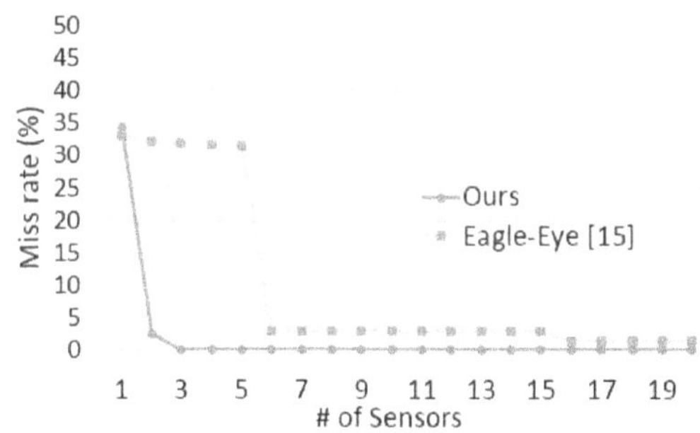

Figure 7: Comparison of our work with Eagle-Eye [15] ($V_t = 5\%VDD$, T_t=1ns). Obviously ours declines the miss rate much faster.

Fig. 8 depicts the information of identified nodes from the benchmark 3. Each node is identified from the first level vertices in FP-Tree. The occurrences in each subtree(cluster) and in complete FP-Tree(all time steps) are shown in Fig. 8(a) and Fig. 8(b) respectively. By observing the two figures, the occurrences (206) of third selected node in all time step are more than those (196) of second selected node. However only 97 occurrences of voltage emergency at third selected node are independent to other selected nodes. It is less than the occurrences (100) of second selected nodes. Therefore, we first select the node with more occurrences in a subtree, which can maximize the union of most coverage. It is proved that we can do an optimal trade-off while the number of noise sensors is limited.

On the other hand, the occurrences of fourth identified node in both figures are equal, meaning that the fourth identified node never occurs voltage emergency while the three other identified nodes occur. In other words, the fourth identified node occurring voltage emergency is independent to occurring voltage emergencies of other identified nodes. This scenario proves that our method can effectively cluster the nodes with the activities of patterns.

Table 3: **The miss rate vs. # of placed sensors on the condition of support rate = 0% and support rate = 50%. Our approach can decrease the miss rate to zero by the number of sensors less than half of [15].**

Benchmark	BN1				BN2						BN3				
Support Rate	0%		50%		0%			50%			0%				50%
$\#Node_{L1}$	2		2		3			3			4				1
$\#Node_{Placed}$	1	2	1	2	1	2	3	1	2	3	1	2	3	4	1
Miss Rate	2.5%	0%	2.5%	0%	34.25%	2.5%	0%	34.25%	2.5%	0%	51.75%	34.75%	17.25%	0%	51.75%

• Support Rate: The lower bound of frequent pattern. • $\#Node_{L1}$: # of vertices at first level in the FP-Tree. • $\#Node_{Placed}$: # of sensors can be placed.

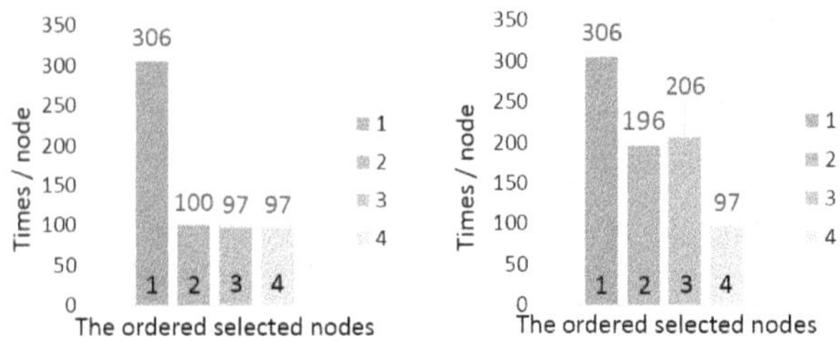

(a) (b)

Figure 8: The times of occurring emergency of the nodes in (a) a subtree. (b) complete FP-Tree.

We also observe the support (support rate × # of transactions), which is the lower bound of frequency. In general FP-Growth algorithm [7], the infrequent items whose occurrences are lower than the support should be pruned out before constructing the FP-Tree. That is, we can find the frequent patterns whose occurrences are larger than the support. However, we do not apply this since we can not predict which nodes will be pruned out. To optimize miss rate and the number of sensors, we need full information including the nodes with fewer occurrences of voltage emergency. As shown in Table 3, the miss rate will be limited at 51.75% since the number of vertices at first level in the FP-Tree is only one. The other significant nodes in other subtree have be pruned out due to their lower occurrence. As a result, we can omit the step while constructing the FP-Tree.

5. CONCLUSION

In this paper, we have proposed a new formulation with considering both the miss rate and the number of sensors for noise sensor placement problem. Besides, we model this problem to the frequent pattern mining problem owing to the inherent feature of FP-Tree. The experimental results show that the miss rate would be convergent quickly even decreased to zero. The number of sensors identified by our work can also be reduced by half in benchmarks while the miss rate is comparable or even smaller than the state-of-the-art.

6. REFERENCES

[1] Itrs report, http://www.itrs.net/.

[2] R. Agrawal and R. Srikant. Fast algorithms for mining association rules in large databases. In *Proceedings of the 20th International Conference on Very Large Data Bases*, pages 487–499, 1994.

[3] S. H. Chen, K. C. Chu, J. Y. Lin, and C. H. Tsai. Dfm/dfy practices during physical designs for timing, signal integrity, and power. In *Asia and South Pacific Design Automation Conference*, pages 232–237, January 2007.

[4] E. Frochowski, D. Ayers, and V. Tiwari. Microarchitectural simulation and control of di/dt-induced power supply voltage variation. In *High Performance Computer Architecture*, pages 7–16, February 2002.

[5] M. S. Gupta, V. J. Reddi, G. Holloway, G.-Y. Wei, and D. M. Brooks. An event-guided approach to reducing voltage noise in processors. In *Design, Automation and Test in Europe*, pages 160–165, April 2009.

[6] M. S. Gutpa, K. K. Rangan, M. D. Smith, G.-Y. Wei, and D. Brooks. Decor: A delayed commit and rollback mechanism for handling inductive noise in processors. In *High Performance Computer Architecture*, pages 381–392, February 2008.

[7] J. Han, J. Pei, and Y. Yin. Mining frequent patterns without candidate generation. In *Proceedings of the ACM SIGMOD International Conference on Management of Data*, pages 1–12, May 2000.

[8] R. Joseph, D. Brooks, and M. Martonosi. Control techniques to eliminate voltage emergencies in high performance processors. In *High Performance Computer Architecture*, pages 79–90, February 2003.

[9] R. Joseph, D. Brooks, and M. Martonosi. Pipeline damping: a microarchitectural technique to reduce inductive noise in supply voltage. In *International Symposium on Computer Architecture*, pages 72–83, June 2003.

[10] X. Liu, S. Sun, P. Zhou, X. Li, and H. Qian. A statistical methodology for noise sensor placement and full-chip voltage map generation. In *Design Automation Conference*, pages 1–6, June 2015.

[11] A. Muhtaroglu, G. Taylor, and T. Rahal-Arabi. On-die droop detector for analog sensing of power supply noise. In *IEEE Journal of Solid-State Circuits*, volume 39, pages 651–660, April 2004.

[12] S. K. Nithin, G. Shanmugam, and S. Chandrasekar. Dynamic voltage (ir) drop analysis and design closure: Issues and challenges. In *International Symposium on Quality Electronic Design*, pages 611–617, March 2010.

[13] M. D. Powell and T. Vijaykumar. Pipeline muffling and a priori current ramping: architectural techniques to reduce high-frequency inductive noise. In *International Symposium on Low Power Electronics and Design*, pages 25–27, August 2003.

[14] V. J. Reddi, M. S. Gupta, G. Holloway, G.-Y. Wei, M. D. Smith, and D. Brooks. Voltage emergency prediction: Using signatures to reduce operating margins. In *High Performance Computer Architecture*, pages 18–29, Fabruary 2009.

[15] T. Wang, C. Zhang, J. Xiong, and Y. Shi. Eagle-eye: A near-optimal statistical framework for noise sensor placement. In *International Conference on Computer-Aided Design*, pages 437–443, June 2013.

MCFRoute 2.0 : A Redundant Via Insertion Enhanced Concurrent Detailed Router

Xiaotao Jia†, Yici Cai†, Qiang Zhou†, Bei Yu‡
†Tsinghua National Laboratory for Information Science & Technology
†Department of Computer Science & Technology, Tsinghua University, Beijing, China
‡CSE Department, The Chinese University of Hong Kong, NT, Hong Kong
jxt11@mails.tsinghua.edu.cn,{caiyc,zhouqiang}@tsinghua.edu.cn,byu@cse.cuhk.edu.hk

ABSTRACT

In modern VLSI design, manufacturing yield and chip performance are seriously affected by via failure. Redundant via insertion is an effective technique recommended by foundries to deal with the via failure. However, due to the extreme scaling of feature size, it is more and more difficult to resolve redundant via insertion (RVI) with limited routing resource while obeying complicated design rules. In this paper, we propose an RVI enhanced concurrent detailed router, MCFRoute 2.0, which effectively avoids design rule violations through a compact integer linear programming (ILP) model. The proposed router can not only route all nets simultaneously but also search for redundant via positions for all via simultaneously during routing stage. In addition, it proposes an RVI aware pin access allocation to further improve the routing performance. Experimental results show that our detailed router outperforms an industry EDA tool that it improves the redundant via insertion rate by 21%, while reducing design rule checking violation count, total wire length and via count by 47%, 4% and 14%, respectively.

Keywords

Detailed Routing, ILP, Redundant Via Insertion, Design Rule

1. INTRODUCTION

In modern very large scale integrated (VLSI) circuit design, due to the extreme scaling of transistor feature size and the complicated design rules, ensuring manufacturing yield and chip reliability is facing more and more issues. Among all the issues, the via failure has a critical impact on chip performance, functionality, and manufacturing yield [1]. In circuits, a via is used to connect two components on two adjacent metal layers. A via may fail due to various reasons such as random defects, electromigration, cut misalignment, or thermal stress included voiding. A partial via failure may cause timing problem due to the increasing resistance of the via; while a complete via failure may lead to net open (unconnected) that will cause severe function error.

Redundant via (also known as double via) insertion is one of the most effective techniques recommended by foundries to provide via reliability. Through the redundant via insertion (RVI), a chip can not only reduce the via failure probability but also improve timing, especially for those critical nets [1]. In this paper, the initial single via is called *main via*.

GLSVLSI '16, May 18-20, 2016, Boston, MA, USA
© 2016 ACM. ISBN 978-1-4503-4274-2/16/05...$15.00
DOI: http://dx.doi.org/10.1145/2902961.2902966

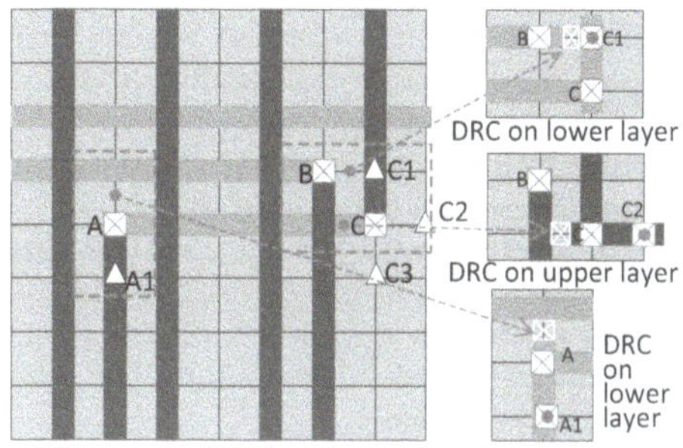

Figure 1: DRC violation by via enclosure.

The RVI problem has been well-studied in post-routing stage with the objective function to insert as many redundant vias as possible [2–7]. To further improve the via insertion rate, the RVI is also considered in early physical design stages [8–11]. Xu et al. [8] propose the first study on the RVI aware maze routing problem, which is transformed to a multi-constrained shortest path problem and solved by Lagrangian relaxation technique. Both [9] and [10] develop unified RVI aware routing frameworks consisting of global routing, detailed routing, and post-layout optimization. Lin et al. [11] propose an RVI aware track assignment and a dead-via aware detailed router.

However, very few of previous RVI aware routers consider practical via rule violations, thus they are divorced from reality. A *via enclosure* measures the distance from the cut array edge to the metal edge that encloses the cut array [12]. A conventional routing example with three vias is given in Fig. 1, where the white triangles represent the redundant via candidates. Different from [8], via A has no redundant via candidate if advanced design rules of via enclosure are considered. Meanwhile, via C only has one candidate. Take via C for example. If $C1$ is redundant via of C, there is a spacing violation between it and via B on bottom layer; if $C2$ is used, spacing violation is introduced on top layer. Therefore, only $C3$ is a legal candidate. The white rectangles with cross line in the right figures represent design rule checking (DRC) violation markers. Although in this paper we assume each via has at most one redundant via candidate, the proposed techniques are generic enough that they can be naturally extended to the cases with multiple redundant vias.

Moreover, many existing detailed routing works are designed on a sequential manner, thus they suffer from the net-order problem that may affect the performance of final via insertion rate. By contrast, some routing works are implemented through a concurrent manner (e.g. [13,14]), which

Table 1: Notions of MCF Model

notion	meaning
$E/V/N$	edge/vertex/net set (indexed by $i/j/k$)
E_{v_j}	adjacent edges set of vertex v_j
$E_{v_j,out}$	edges set whose start point is vertex v_j
$E_{v_j,in}$	edges set whose end point is vertex v_j
$E^{\eta}_{v_j}$	via edges set of vertex v_j
$dg(v_j, d)$	the vertex degree of redundant via on direction d
$u(e_i)$	binary variable, the capacity of edge e_i
$c(e_i)$	positive variable, the cost of edge e_i
$d(n_k, v_j)$	the flow command of vertex v_j with value of -1, 0, or 1 that commodity n_k demands
$f(n_k, e_i)$	binary variable, flow of commodity n_k by edge e_i

overcomes the net-order problem and can get a global optimal solution in theory. In detailed routing area, Jia et al. [15] propose a concurrent methodology based on multi-commodity flow model and achieve good results. However, how to seamlessly integrate practical via design rules into the concurrent framework is still unclear.

In this paper, we present an RVI enhanced detailed router, which is following the concurrent method. To the best of our knowledge, this is the first work where complex via rules are considered in concurrent detailed router. The main contributions of this paper include:

- The proposed router is able to search for redundant via position for every via, while all the nets are routed simultaneously.
- We propose a comprehensive analysis on the effect of via enclosure, which is rarely discussed by previous academic works. It makes the proposed algorithm practical.
- We propose a routing resource aware heuristic technique, where an RVI aware pin access allocation algorithm is proposed to improve the via insertion rate on layer Via12.
- Our detailed router outperforms an industry tool, in terms of redundant via insertion rate, wirelength, via number, and DRC violation count.

The rest of this paper is organized as follows. Section 2 introduces some preliminaries and provides the problem formulation. Section 3 gives the overview of our proposed detailed routing framework. Section 4 further describes the details of RVI enhanced detailed router, and presents RVI aware pin access allocation algorithm. Section 5 shows the experimental results, followed by conclusion in Section 6.

2. PRELIMINARIES

In this section, we briefly introduce some preliminaries on detailed routing, and then provide the problem formulation.

2.1 Graph Model

A detailed routing problem usually consists of several routing layers and each layer has a prefer direction of vertical or horizontal. Graph model is used to simplify the detailed routing problem. Given a multi-layer detailed routing problem, usually a 3-D routing graph $G = (V, E)$ representing the routing resources is constructed. On each layer, the intersection points of current layer routing grids and neighbor layers routing grids are called as *vertices*. *Edges* are routing grid segments divided by vertices. Through the routing graph, the detailed routing problem is formulated as a path finding problem. Based on the requirement of routing algorithm, the routing model could be directed or undirected. As illustrated in Fig. 2, in this paper we label the routing graph as a directed graph, and divide the whole routing problem into many subproblems.

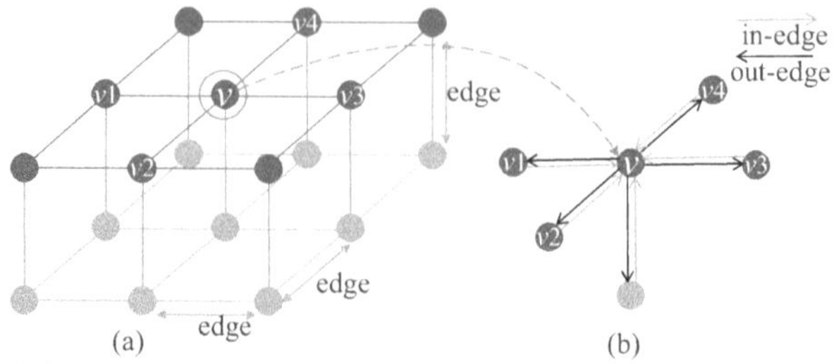

Figure 2: Graph model for detailed routing problem [15].

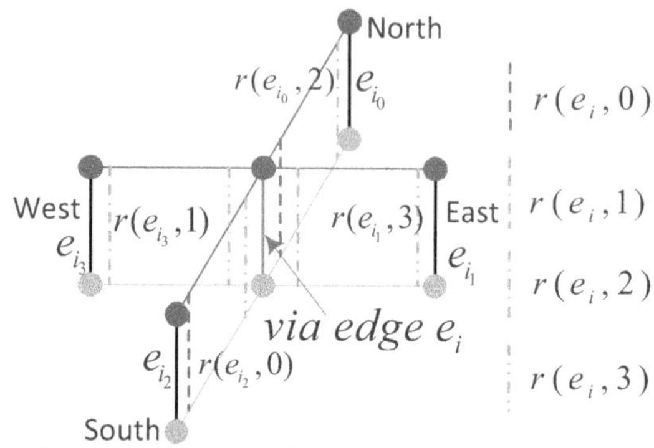

Figure 3: Direction-based redundant via variable.

2.2 Notions and Variables

The variables and sets used in this paper are presented in Table 1. The meanings and value ranges of them are also given.

Here we further introduce some new variables since the conventional variables defined in Table 1 are unable to build an effective model under the practical redundant via design rules. The position of redundant via is next to an existing via. Therefore, whether a redundant via is necessary to be inserted depends on the existence of single via. However, before a routing window is routed, the position of single via is unknown. So if we only use the existing decision variable $f(n_k, e)$ in Table 1 to control the insertion of redundant via, lots of logic constraints will be introduced to the ILP model. These logic constraints will make the problem nonlinear and more complex to solve. In order to maintain a good nature of linearity, redundant via variables related to via edges are introduced to the model.

In this work, direction-based redundant via variables are proposed as shown in Fig. 3. e_i is a via edge (without direction). Four binary variables $r(e_i, d)$ $(d = 0 \sim 3)$ related to e_i are added to ILP model. $r(e_i, 0)$, $r(e_i, 1)$, $r(e_i, 2)$ and $r(e_i, 3)$ represent the north, east, south and west redundant via variable of e_i, respectively. e_i is called as the *father edge* of these redundant via variables. If e_i is used as a redundant via, one of the four variables should be 1. Furthermore, the position of main via is also indicated by redundant via variable. For example, e_i and the neighbor via edge which is to its east compose a double via if and only if $r(e_i, 1)$ is equal to 1. At the same time, via enclosure direction is also determined.

For convenience, 0, 1, 2 and 3 represent north, east, south and west respectively when directions are represented by numbers. $opp(d)$ indicates the opposite direction of d. $opp(1) = 3$, $opp(0) = 2$, $opp(3) = 1$ and $opp(2) = 0$. In our model we introduce a variable to represent the degree of each vertex.

Definition 1 (Vertex Degree). *$dg(v_j, d)$ indicates the vertex degree of redundant via on direction d. It can be calculated by the sum of redundant via variables on direction d whose father edge terminates at v_j $(v_j \in V,\ d = (0, 1, 2, 3))$.*

2.3 Problem Formulation

Based on the notations in preceding section, we define the RVI enhanced detailed routing problem as follows:

Problem 1 (RVI enhanced detailed routing). *Given global routing (GR) and track assignment (TA) results, as well as routing region, RVI enhanced detailed routing is to route all nets in given region simultaneously. The objective is to insert as many redundant vias as possible without introducing DRC violations.*

3. OVERALL FLOW

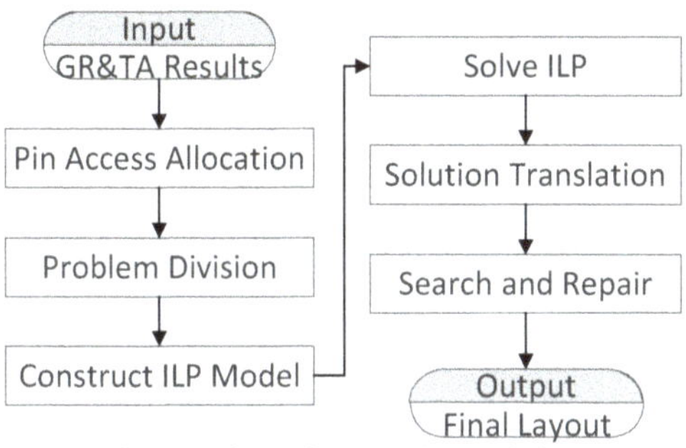

Figure 4: Overall flow of RVI enhanced detailed router

The overall flow of the proposed detailed router is illustrated in Fig. 4. The inputs of the proposed router consist of global routing results and track assignment results. Pin access allocation is the first step that will be detailed discussed in Section 4.5. Then the whole routing region will be divided into many subregions with smaller scale by global routing cell. For each subregion, detailed routing problem is formulated into an ILP problem. After solving a set of ILP problems, the 0-1 solutions will be translated into routing solution. Finally, a search and repair stage is implemented to handle the DRC violations between different regions. The output is a final detailed routing result.

4. RVI ENHANCED DETAILED ROUTER

In this section, we formulate the RVI enhanced detailed routing problem as an ILP problem based on the multi-commodity flow model. The objective function as in Eqn. (1) aims to select an optimal detailed routing and redundant via solution, while the costs are minimized. Our costs consist of via edge cost, metal edge cost, and some penalty terms about DRC violations and redundant via insertion:

$$Cost = \sum_{k=1}^{|N|} \sum_{e \in E} (f(n_k, e) \cdot c(e)). \tag{1}$$

4.1 Connectivity Constraints

The basic goal of detailed routing is that all components of each net are connected. This is guaranteed by connectivity constraints in ILP model. Connectivity constraints can be formulated as Eqn. (2), which is based on flow conservation theory.

$$\sum_{e \in E_{v_j,out}} f(n_k, e) - \sum_{e \in E_{v_j,in}} f(n_k, e) = d(n_k, v_j), \tag{2}$$

where $v_j \in V$ and $n_k \in N$.

4.2 Direction-based Capacity Constraints

In detailed routing, a *short* violation means the crossover of different nets. No short violation is the primary task of a detailed router. In routing graph, the crossover may occur on graph edges or vertices. The ILP model needs to build edge and vertex capacity constraints to remove short violation from the solution space. The work of [15] has proven that edge capacity constraints are redundant. It can be guaranteed by connectivity constraint (2) and vertex capacity constraint (3):

$$\sum_{k=1}^{|N|} \sum_{e_i \in E_{v_j}} f(n_k, e_i) \leq 2. \tag{3}$$

Constraint (3) is not suitable in this work because it dose not consider redundant via variables. However, it can make help when we construct new constraints. For convenience, vertex v_j is taken as an example to present the vertex capacity constraints.

A vertex v_j is used by the routing path and it could be indicated by $\sum_{k=1}^{|N|} \sum_{e_i \in v_j} f(n_k, e_i) = 2$. If it is also served as a redundant via, there must be $dg(v_j, 1) = 1$. And we can find that if $dg(v_j, 1) = 1$, there must be a segment between vertex v_j and one of its neighbor vertex. Based on this observation and the introduction method of redundant via variable, in this paper we construct four direction-based capacity constraints for each vertex as Eqn. (4).

$$dg(v_j, d) + \sum_{k=1}^{|N|} \sum_{e_i \in E_{v_j}^d} f(n_k, e_i) \leq 2 \quad (d = 0 \sim 3), \tag{4}$$

where for each d, $E_{v_j}^d = E_{v_j} \backslash \{(v_j, v_{j_d}), (v_{j_d}, v_j)\}$.

The new constraint of given direction has two differences compared with Eqn. (3). The first one is that the adjacent net edges of given direction are removed from Eqn. (3). The second one is redundant via variables related to given direction are added to Eqn. (3). The correctness of this constraint can be proven by enumeration method. Due to the page limit it is omitted here.

4.3 Redundant Via Insertion Method

The constraints formulated in this section aim to insert as many redundant vias as possible without introducing DRC violations.

Normally, each via edge has four neighbor via edges on via layer. As shown in Fig. 3, variables $r(e_{i_d}, opp(d))$ $(d = 0, 1, 2, 3)$ are related with edge e_i.

A. Ideal Solution. The ideal solution of redundant via insertion is achieving a 100% insertion rate. Each via has its own redundant via. In our model, the usage of via edge e_i is expressed by $\sum_{k=1}^{|N|} f(n_k, e_i)$. The capacity constraint restricts the sum to be either 0 or 1. The sum is 0 means edge e_i is unused, otherwise it is used. The generation of redundant via is expressed by $\sum_{d=0}^{3} r(e_{i_d}, opp(d))$. So constraint (5) could achieve the ideal redundant via insertion solution:

$$\sum_{k=1}^{|N|} f(n_k, e_i) = \sum_{d=0}^{3} r(e_{i_d}, opp(d)). \tag{5}$$

B. Realistic Solution. However, not all the solutions are ideal. If the insertion of a redundant via violates with around geometries, the redundant via should be given up to avoid DRC violations generation. Under this circumstance, the right item of Eqn. (5) should be 0 even the left one is 1. And Eqn. (5) is no longer suitable.

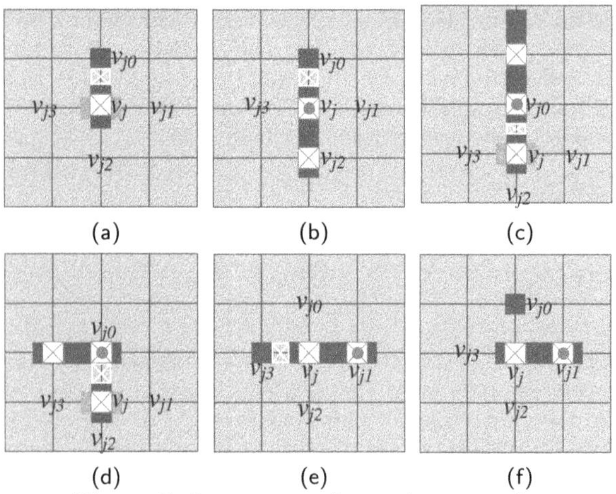

Figure 5: Layout cases for spacing constraint.

In this work, a penalty variable is added into Eqn. (5) to make the redundant via insertion realistic as Eqn. (6) shows.

$$\sum_{k=1}^{|N|} f(n_k, e_i) = \sum_{d=0}^{3} r(e_{i_d}, opp(d)) + \lambda, \quad (6)$$

where λ is a penalty variable whose value range is 0 or 1. Constraint (6) allows abandon redundant via insertion for e_i by assigning λ as 1. λ multiplied with a penalty factor μ is added to the objective function Eqn. (1) to penalize the abandon of redundant via. In our experiments, the penalty factor μ is smaller than via cost.

4.4 Via Enclosure aware Spacing Constraints

Spacing constraints considering redundant via variables and via enclosure are constructed in this subsection. Spacing rule is very important in technology file which specifies the distance between two geometries. Inequation (7) is a spacing constraint formulated in [15] for vertex pair (v_{j1}, v_{j2}) whose distance satisfies Eqn. (8):

$$\sum_{k=1}^{|N|} \Big(\sum_{e_i \in E^{\eta}_{v_{j1}}} f(n_k, e_i) + \sum_{e_i \in E'_{v_{j2}}} f(n_k, e_i) \Big) \leq 2, \quad (7)$$

$$\alpha_m + \gamma_m \leq \Gamma(v_{j1}, v_{j2}) < \alpha_m + \beta + \gamma_m. \quad (8)$$

Here, $\Gamma(v_{j1}, v_{j2})$ represents the distance of vertex v_{j1} and vertex v_{j2}. α_m, β and γ_m are the metal wire width, the via enclosure length, and the metal layer spacing, respectively. $E^{\eta}_{v_{j1}}$ denotes the set of via edges of vertex v_{j1}. $E'_{v_{j2}}$ is the adjacent edges set of vertex v_{j2} excluding inner edges of vertex pair (v_{j1}, v_{j2}), *i.e.* $E'_{v_{j2}} = E_{v_{j2}} \backslash \{(v_{j1}, v_{j2}), (v_{j2}, v_{j1})\}$.

Constraint (7) indicates that if the via edges of v_{j1} is occupied by net n_k, all adjacent edges of vertex v_{j2} can not be used by other nets again except for net n_k. However, constraint (7) is no longer capable to avoid spacing violations in this work, because it does not take redundant vias into consideration. Actually the enclosure of double via makes the spacing violation avoidance much difficult.

Without loss of generality, vertex pair (v_j, v_{j_d}) whose distance satisfies Eqn. (8) is taken as an example. New constraints are constructed by discussing the usage of via edges on vertex v_j and all edges on neighbor vertex $v_{j_d} (d = 0, 1, 2, 3)$.

Taking a vertical layer for example, the discussion is made from the following aspects.

Case 1: Vertex v_j is occupied by a single via.

In this case, Fig. 5(a) shows the geometry shape of vertex v_j on metal layer. This is the same as the problem discussed in [15]. So constraint (7) still works.

Case 2: Vertex v_j is a redundant via for neighbor vertex on vertical direction.

Here, we assume that double via consists of v_j and the south neighbor vertex, *i.e.* v_{j_2}. As shown in Fig. 5(b), v_{j_2} is a main via and v_j is a redundant via. It is obviously that $dg(v_j, 2) = 1$ represents the usage of via edge on vertex v_j. In this case, the usage of vertex v_{j_0} should be restricted. Constraint (7) is unable to avoid the spacing violation in this case. So new constraint (9) is needed to prohibit the concurrently usage of vertex v_j and vertex v_{j_0}:

$$dg(v_j, 2) + \sum_{k=1}^{|N|} \sum_{e_i \in E'_{v_{j_0}}} f(n_k, e_i) \leq 2. \quad (9)$$

In detailed routing problem, if a via edge is occupied by one net, it can be on longer used as a redundant via for neighbor vias, *i.e.* it is not possible that $\sum_{k=1}^{|N|} \sum_{e_i \in E^{\eta}_{v_j}} f(n_k, e_i) \geq 1$, meanwhile $dg(v_j, 2) = 1$. So Eqn. (7) and Eqn. (9) can be merged together.

Case 3: Vertex v_{j_0} is a redundant via, but not for vertex v_j.

In this case, we can get the following two conclusions. The first one is that $dg(v_{j_0}, 2)$ must be 0, and the second one is $dg(v_{j_0}, 0) + dg(v_{j_0}, 1) + dg(v_{j_0}, 3) = 1$ as illustrated in Fig. 5(c) ($dg(v_{j_0}, 0) = 1$) and Fig. 5(d) ($dg(v_{j_0}, 3) = 1$). From the layout in Fig. 5(c)(d), It can be found that if the usage of vertex v_j belongs to *case 1* or *case 2*, spacing violation is introduced to the routing solution. In our model, constraint (10) is formulated to eliminate this routing solution.

$$dg(v_j, 2) + \sum_{k=1}^{|N|} \sum_{e_i \in E^{\eta}_{v_j}} f(n_k, e_i) + \sum_{d=0, d!=2}^{3} dg(v_{j_0}, d) \leq 1. \quad (10)$$

Case 4: Vertex v_j and one of its neighbor vertex on horizontal direction construct a double via.

Without loss of generality, we take the east vertex v_{j_1} for example as shown in Fig. 5(e)(f). When only single via is considered, almost all the enclosure direction is preferred. But there are plenty of non-preferred direction enclosures when double via is considered. So it is necessary to build special constraints for them.

When referring to non-preferred direction via enclosures, two differences must be emphasized.

(I) The usage of edges adjacent to vertex v_{j_3} is restricted by via enclosure. As illustrated in Fig. 5(e), the via enclosure extends to the west. It is the same as *case* 1 described above but in a horizontal layer. A constraint similar to Eqn. (7) is needed to avoid spacing between vertex v_j and vertex v_{j_3}. No matter the redundant via locates at v_j or v_{j_1}, a layout like Fig. 5(e) is generated, so the new constraint is formulated as Eqn. (11):

$$dg(v_j, 1) + dg(v_{j_1}, 3) + \sum_{k=1}^{|N|} \sum_{e_i \in E'_{v_{j_3}}} f(n_k, e_i) \leq 2. \quad (11)$$

(II) The usage of adjacent vertical vertices *i.e.* v_{j_0} and v_{j_2} is no longer limited by via edges on vertex v_j. As we can see from Fig. 5(f), the extension on vertical direction of vertex v_j is half of wire width, and the enclosure influence on vertices v_{j_0} and v_{j_2} no longer exists. In other words, v_{j_1} serves as redundant via of v_j counteracts the effects of via enclosure on preferred direction neighbor vertices. Based on

Algorithm 1 RVI aware Pin Access Allocation Algorithm

Input: Pins and blockages;
Output: Via candidates;

```
1: C ← searchCandidates();
2: for each candidate in C do
3:     SgVias ← createSingleVias();
4:     for each via in SgVias do
5:         valid ← checkDRCAndAssignCost();
6:         if valid = true then
7:             RdntVias ← createRdntVias();
8:             for each redundant via in RdntVias do
9:                 checkDRCAndUpdateCost();
10:            end for
11:        end if
12:    end for
13: end for
```

this observation, item $-dg(v_{j_1}, 3)$ is added to the left hand expression of Eqn. (7) and Eqn. (9).

If vertex v_{j_3} is served as a redundant via, the layout is similar to Fig. 5(e). Moreover, it can easily prove that east redundant via variables of v_{j_3} and west redundant via variables of v_{j_1} are impossible to be 1 at the same time. So item $-dg(v_{j_3}, 1)$ should be further added to the left hand expression of Eqn. (7) and Eqn. (9). As discussed above, Eqn. (7) and Eqn. (9) can be merged together, so we can get the constraint (12).

$$dg(v_j, 2) + \sum_{k=1}^{|N|} \sum_{e_i \in E^{\eta}_{v_j}} f(n_k, e_i) + \sum_{e_i \in E'_{v_{j_0}}} f(n_k, e_i) - dg(v_{j_1}, 3) - dg(v_{j_3}, 1) \leq 2. \tag{12}$$

Likewise, Eqn. (10) also needs to be modified as in Eqn. (13) to deal with non-preferred direction via enclosure.

$$dg(v_j, 2) + \sum_{k=1}^{|N|} \sum_{e_i \in E^{\eta}_{v_j}} f(n_k, e_i) + \sum_{d=0, d!=2}^{3} dg(v_{j_0}, d) - dg(v_{j_1}, 3) - dg(v_{j_3}, 1) \leq 1. \tag{13}$$

As a result, three types of spacing constraints similar to constraints (11), (12) and (13) are added to ILP model to avoid spacing violations.

4.5 RVI Aware Pin Access Allocation

By now, we have described the ILP model in details that processes all nets concurrently, meanwhile considers redundant via insertion properly.

We make a survey on the via count on each via layer, and the statistic data shows that about 50% vias are generated on the Via12 which locates between Metal1 and Metal2. The high percent is as expected because most of the pins on Metal1 need to be lead to Metal2 by Via12. Points which are covered by pin and can be served as the candidates for via creation are called *pin accesses*. Pin access allocation is standard cell-based and proceeded pin by pin before routing stage. In this work, an RVI aware pin access allocation algorithm is proposed to increase the number of via candidates on Via12.

The details of our pin access allocation are in Algorithm 1. The inputs of pin access allocation are pins and blockages in the design, while the output is the candidate via position with creation cost. The first step is searching for candidate points which is the intersection points of routing grid covered by this pin (line 1). Taking each candidate point as center, two virtual vias with different via enclosure (preferred and non-preferred direction on Metal1) will be created (line 3). Then via creation cost is assigned to each via based on the DRC result (line 5) by the following principle: If virtual via is violated with existing geometries, *valid* in line 5 is set to false, *i.e.* the candidate point is given up; otherwise the cost is less than or equal to via cost.

For each valid virtual via, two redundant vias are inserted in turn based on enclosure direction (line 7). For example, if enclosure direction is horizontal, redundant vias are inserted on the east and west point. Then DRC procedure is executed to determine whether the redundant via is valid (line 9). If yes, the candidate cost will be further reduced.

5. EXPERIMENTAL RESULTS

The proposed algorithm is implemented with C++ language on Linux server with 2.4GHz Intel Xeon CPU and 24GB memory. It has been integrated into an industrial routing flow. In the experiments, a multi-thread algorithm is implemented utilizing the dependence between any two routing regions. It has been tested that the multi-thread algorithm can achieve a linear speedup ratio. By default, MCFRoute 2.0 utilizes 16 threads. `GUROBI` [16] is applied as our ILP solver.

Our experiments are executed on two benchmark suites. The first one includes eight benchmarks mapped to a 65*nm* design library. The second one includes five benchmarks mapped to a 45*nm* design library. All the benchmarks are in OpenAccess (OA) format. All engines work on and exchange data through the OA database.

Even though there are many previous published works, few of them consider design rule and report DRC results. To better demonstrate the effectiveness of our router, three RVI aware routing engines are implemented in our experiments. 1) 'MCFRoute 2.0' which is proposed in this paper has a concurrent manner both of routing and redundant via insertion. 2) 'MCFRoute + RVI' routes all net concurrently by `MCFRoute` [15] first and then inserts redundant via in post-routing stage by `Encounter v10.10` [17]. 3) 'Encounter' processes RVI aware detailed routing by `Encounter v10.10` [17], which is executed in NanoRoute mode and RVI is considered during routing stage rather than post-routing stage. In the experiments, we try to let Encounter run longer until the improvement is negligible.

The results for comparison in the experiments are wirelength ('WL') measured by *millimeter*, total via count ('#Via', $\times 10^3$), redundant via count ('#Rt', $\times 10^3$), redundant via insertion rate ('Rate'), DRC violation count ('#DRC') and runtime ('Time'). The runtime is measured by *second*.

Table 2 shows the experimental results on eight 65*nm* benchmarks. All of the three routing engines can achieve a DRC-clean results, so DRC violation count column is omitted. In Table 2, the first two columns are the name and net count ('#Net') of each benchmark. Firstly, a comparison is made between 'MCFRoute + RVI' (columns 3-7) and 'MCFRoute 2.0' (columns 13-17). Experiments of these benchmarks show that MCFRoute 2.0 can improve the redundant via insertion rate by 25.9% compared with MCFRoute with post-routing redundant via insertion by Encounter. It demonstrates that although both routing engines route nets in concurrent manner, inserting redundant via during routing stage could achieve higher insertion rate than in post-routing stage. At the same time, the wirelength is increased by 1%, but via count is reduced by 3.4%, respectively. Runtime is 1.33× of 'MCFRoute + RVI'. The experimental data is as expected because our router prefers to make detours rather than use single via if redundant via insertion is

Table 2: Results on Academic Benchmarks

benchmark		MCFRoute [15] + RVI					Encounter					MCFRoute 2.0				
Name	#Net	WL	#Via	#Rt	Rate	Time	WL	#Via	#Rt	Rate	Time	WL	#Via	#Rt	Rate	Time
b20	9309	120	61	34	55.7%	160	126	61	37	61.5%	60	121	59	41	70.7%	215
b21	9575	129	63	34	53.8%	213	133	63	38	61.2%	62	129	61	43	70.3%	282
b22	10046	177	68	42	61.8%	174	186	67	47	68.9%	65	179	65	46	70.8%	235
dma	12475	303	102	52	50.7%	301	314	102	59	57.3%	99	304	97	62	64.4%	406
frisc	15869	292	117	57	48.7%	332	304	117	69	58.8%	112	294	112	72	63.7%	429
dsp	24129	550	196	93	47.2%	735	572	198	106	53.5%	191	550	187	115	61.5%	926
pci	30835	328	158	96	61.1%	345	339	159	115	72.8%	152	329	158	125	79.3%	481
eth	43169	1006	332	183	55.2%	1025	1049	332	207	62.2%	380	1009	319	211	66.1%	1395
ratio		0.99	1.04	0.82	0.79	0.75	1.04	1.04	0.95	0.91	0.25	1	1	1	1	1

Table 3: Results on Industry Benchmarks

benchmark		Encounter						MCFRoute 2.0					
Name	#Net	WL	#Via	#Rdnt	Rate	DRC	Time	WL	#Via	#Rdnt	Rate	DRC	Time
chip1	37584	684	400311	162436	40.6%	115	1534	628	369980	221666	59.9%	72	2392
chip2	53400	832	462701	250055	54.0%	159	1478	808	401074	260785	65.0%	33	2003
chip3	101817	1696	908599	514129	56.6%	101	1849	1639	779529	506149	64.9%	54	3660
chip4	92046	1550	828688	464708	56.8%	81	1592	1504	703770	457310	65.0%	46	3357
chip5	101729	1731	907323	510295	56.2%	93	1865	1674	778938	505296	64.9%	79	3732
ratio		1.04	1.15	0.98	0.83	1.89	0.55	1	1	1	1	1	1

not valid. Secondly, we compare 'MCFRoute 2.0' with 'Encounter' (columns 8-12). Experimental results show that the proposed router improves the redundant via insertion rate by 10% compared with Encounter. It indicates that although both routing engines consider redundant via insertion during routing stage, concurrent manner could achieve higher insertion rate than sequential manner. Benefiting from concurrent routing manner of the proposed router, the wirelength, via count are also reduced by 3.6% and 3.6%, respectively. Running time is 4.06× of 'Encounter'.

'MCFRoute + RVI', 'Encounter' and 'MCFRoute 2.0' can achieve DRC-clean results on these 65*nm* benchmarks. In order to further verify the advantages of our concurrent router in DRC violation handling, we derive some difficult industry benchmarks. Because proceeding redundant via insertion in post-routing stage by Encounter requires a DRC-clean layout, the comparison is only made between 'Encounter' and 'MCFRoute 2.0' as shown in Table 3. The first two columns are benchmark information including name and net count. Columns 3-8 are results of 'Encounter' and columns 9-14 are results of 'MCFRoute 2.0'. From the experimental results, it can be found that the proposed router improves the insertion rate by 21% and reduces the wirelength and via count by 4% and 14% respectively compared with Encounter. Moreover, it is worth to emphasize that the router can reduce the DRC violation count by 47% for these complex industry benchmarks. The runtime is 1.82× of 'Encounter'. Both two engines use the same netlists and design rules. The better results of our router mainly profit from the concurrent manner of routing and redundant via insertion that overcomes net-order problem. The experimental results demonstrate that the proposed algorithm is capable to improve redundant via insertion rate and handle difficult routing problems while maintaining a good quality in wirelength and via count.

6. CONCLUSION

In this paper, we present an RVI enhanced concurrent detailed router based on multi-commodity flow method. The router can route all nets simultaneously, at the same time trying to insert as many redundant vias as possible. The effects of via enclosure are taken into consideration thoroughly in this paper that makes the algorithm much practical. An RVI aware pin access allocation flow is proposed to improve the redundant via insertion rate on Via12. Experimental results show the effectiveness of the proposed method. The further work of this article will focus on improving the capability of handle design rule violations in difficult benchmarks and saving our algorithm with the more challenging constraints in 22*nm* and beyond.

Acknowledgment

This work is supported in part by NSFC No.61274031 and CUHK Direct Grant for Research.

7. REFERENCES

[1] S.-H. Chen, K.-C. Chu, J.-Y. Lin, and C.-H. Tsai, "DFM/DFY practices during physical designs for timing, signal integrity, and power," in *ASPDAC*, 2007, pp. 232–237.

[2] K.-Y. Lee and T.-C. Wang, "Post-routing redundant via insertion for yield/reliability improvement," in *ASPDAC*, 2006, pp. 303–308.

[3] K.-Y. Lee, T.-C. Wang, and K.-Y. Chao, "Post-routing redundant via insertion and line end extension with via density consideration," in *ICCAD*, 2006, pp. 633–640.

[4] K.-Y. Lee, C.-K. Koh, T.-C. Wang, and K.-Y. Chao, "Optimal post-routing redundant via insertion," in *ISPD*, 2008, pp. 111–117.

[5] C.-K. Lei, P.-Y. Chiang, and Y.-M. Lee, "Post-routing redundant via insertion with wire spreading capability," in *ASPDAC*, 2009, pp. 468–473.

[6] S.-T. Lin, K.-Y. Lee, T.-C. Wang, C.-K. Koh, and K.-Y. Chao, "Simultaneous redundant via insertion and line end extension for yield optimization," in *ASPDAC*, 2011, pp. 633–638.

[7] J. Pak, B. Yu, and D. Z. Pan, "Electromigration-aware redundant via insertion," in *ASPDAC*, 2015, pp. 544–549.

[8] G. Xu, L.-D. Huang, D. Z. Pan, and M. D. Wong, "Redundant-via enhanced maze routing for yield improvement," in *ASPDAC*, 2005, pp. 1148–1151.

[9] H. Yao, Y. Cai, X. Hong, and Q. Zhou, "Improved multilevel routing with redundant via placement for yield and reliability," in *GLSVLSI*, 2005, pp. 143–146.

[10] H.-Y. Chen, M.-F. Chiang, Y.-W. Chang, L. Chen, and B. Han, "Full-chip routing considering double-via insertion," *IEEE Transactions on CAD*, vol. 27, no. 5, pp. 844–857, 2008.

[11] C.-T. Lin, Y.-H. Lin, G.-C. Su, and Y.-L. Li, "Dead via minimization by simultaneous routing and redundant via insertion," in *ASPDAC*, 2010, pp. 657–662.

[12] "LEF/DEF language reference," http://www.ispd.cc/contests/14/web/doc/lefdefref.pdf.

[13] C. Albrecht, "Provably good global routing by a new approximation algorithm for multicommodity flow," in *ISPD*, 2000, pp. 19–25.

[14] T.-H. Wu, A. Davoodi, and J. T. Linderoth, "GRIP: scalable 3D global routing using integer programming," in *DAC*, 2009, pp. 320–325.

[15] X. Jia, Y. Cai, Q. Zhou, G. Chen, Z. Li, and Z. Li, "MCFRoute: a detailed router based on multi-commodity flow method," in *ICCAD*, 2014, pp. 397–404.

[16] Gurobi Optimization Inc., "Gurobi optimizer reference manual," http://www.gurobi.com, 2014.

[17] "Cadence SOC Encounter," http://www.cadence.com.

Modular Placement for Interposer based Multi-FPGA Systems

Fubing Mao[1], Wei Zhang[2], Bo Feng[3], Bingsheng He[1], Yuchun Ma[3]
[1]School of Computer Engineering, Nanyang Technological University, Singapore
[2]Department of Electronic and Computer Engineering, HKUST, Hong Kong
[3]Department of Computer Science and Technology, Tsinghua University, Beijing 100084, China
{fmao001, bshe}@ntu.edu.sg, wei.zhang@ust.hk, {fengb15, myc}@tsinghua.edu.cn

ABSTRACT

Novel device with multiple FPGAs on-chip based on interposer interconnection has emerged to resolve the IOs limit and improve the inter-FPGA communication delay. However, new challenges arise for the placement on such architecture. Firstly, existing work does not consider the detailed models for the path wirelength and delay estimation for interposer, which may significantly affect the placement quality. Secondly, previous work is mostly based on traditional tile-based placement which is slow for the placement of large design on multiple FPGAs.

In this paper, we propose a new fast two-stage modular placement flow for interposer based multiple FPGAs aiming for delay optimization with the incorporation of a detailed interposer routing model for wirelength and delay estimation. Firstly, we adopt the force-directed method for its global property to get an efficient solution as a start point of the placement. Secondly, we adopt the simulated annealing (SA) for its efficiency and effectiveness in searching the refinement solution. In order to speed up the refinement, the hierarchical B*-tree (HB*-tree) is employed to enable a fast search and convergence. The experiments demonstrate that our flow can achieve an efficient solution in a comparable time. The proposed approach is scalable to different design size.

Keywords

Silicon Interposer; Modular Placement; Hierarchical B*-tree

1. INTRODUCTION AND MOTIVATION

Recently, interposer-based FPGAs are proposed to significantly improve the logic capacity, interconnection bandwidth and performance [9]. For instance, Xilinx Inc., a major FPGA vendor, firstly develops the largest interposer-based FPGA, the Virtex-7 XC7V2000T, which has 4 dies and 1.95 million logic elements [9]. A general two-and-a-half-dimensional (2.5D) FPGA with interposer is shown in the Fig. 1 [9], where four FPGA dies are placed vertically and are connected by the interposer. The interposer is an electric interface routing for connecting different components and can be used to spread connections, e.g., providing alternative routes for a connection [9]. In order to connect between different dies, the signal needs to go through the internal track of the current die, microbump, and super long line (SLL) of interposer, and then into the other die.

GLSVLSI '16, May 18-20, 2016, Boston, MA, USA

DOI: http://dx.doi.org/10.1145/2902961.2903025

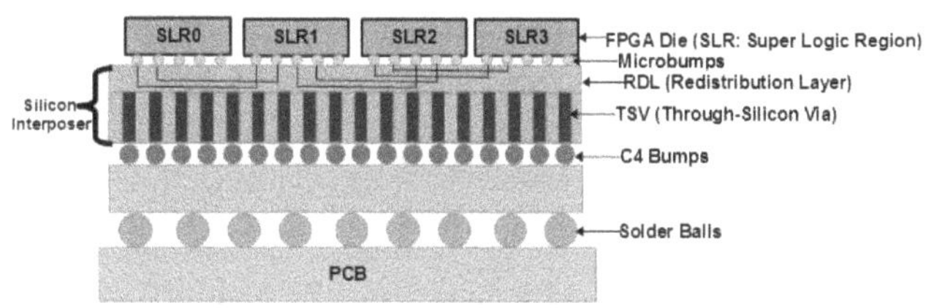

Figure 1: A general 2.5D FPGA with interposer.

FPGA placement is a very important step for synthesis in the modern FPGA [13] which significantly affects the implementation delay and the optimal placement is a NP-complete problem [7]. The increasing design complexity and logic capacity of the FPGA system, especially the multi-FPGA system, have further complicated the problem. In traditional design flow, fine-grained tile-based (CLB level) placement is performed to achieve the efficient solution. However, it usually requires a prohibitively long searching time from hours to days, especially for a large-scale design [16]. To accelerate the placement of large-scale design, module based placement has been employed for single FPGAs [2]. Here, module represents a rectangle region containing some logic resources and each module can be a reconfigurable region [26]. To our best knowledge, there is no existing flow to support the module based placement for multiple FPGAs, especially taking into consideration the new interconnect architecture through interposer.

In this work, we propose a new flow to address the placement for multi-FPGA system with interposer targeting delay optimization. Our approach consists of two steps. Firstly a force-directed placement is performed to obtain an efficiently initial solution. Secondly, the initial solution is represented by the Hierarchical B*-tree (HB*-tree) [5] and based on it, simulated annealing is performed to obtain the refined solution. A detailed routing model for interposer is built and integrated in the flow for addressing the interposer impact on the placement. The B*-tree representation is introduced to speed up the search and convergence of the solution [5]. The HB*-tree matches the multi-FPGA system well where the multi-FPGA can correspond to a B*-tree and each chip can correspond to a sub B*-tree to enable the swap of modules in different chips. In addition, we also exploited the impact of different width-height ratios of the modules for delay optimization.

Our results demonstrate that 1) Interposer impacts the placement result significantly and compared with the traditional model, our proposed model can reduce the wirelength, total delay, delay from nets crossing the interposer by 8%, 7%, 19%, respectively; 2) The ratios of the module impact the placement results. When considering the different ratios of modules, the wirelength, total delay and delay from nets crossing interposer are improved by 8%, 4%, 9% compared to the results considering modules with only one ratio; 3) Our proposed flow can speed up the placement and achieve higher quality compared to the state-of-the-art min-cut based flow derived from [11].

2. RELATED WORK

2.1 Modular Placement for 2D single FPGA

There was a large amount of tile-based placement for a single 2D FPGA. They could be based on heuristic approach [19] or analytical approach [6] [30]. However, as we discussed in the previous section, tile-based placement faced great challenge for placement of large-scale design. Thus module based placement and hierarchical placement have been proposed to address the challenge as well as support the partial reconfiguration [2] [3]. However, placement in multiple FPGAs is fundamentally different from placement in a single FPGA due to the impact of inter-chip delay and assignment of modules into different chips.

2.2 Placement for 2D Multi-chip and 3D FPGA

Traditional multiple FPGAs had a limited number of IOs for passing signals between different dies. Hence, cut-size optimization was the common goal to reduce the number of signals crossing chips as well as the long inter-chip delay. [22] proposed an algorithm to minimize net crossings for addressing system partitioning and considered the block assignment of multi-chip modules during the high level design of an application-specific IC. [12] developed a new performance driven partitioning algorithm to implement a large circuit in multiple FPGAs to minimize the cut size. [25] developed a method named MP2 to minimize the total number of terminals of all blocks during network partitioning. [20] presented a rectilinear partitioning algorithm to minimize the cut sizes of the partitions and handle timing specifications for traditional multiple FPGAs.

Recently, 3D chip emerged for achieving higher integration density and better performance. The 3D FPGA has multiple dies stacked vertically which utilized through-silicon vias (TSVs) as vertical connections [14]. The TSV density was closely related to the cost and hence, most of 3D FPGA placements target the minimization of TSVs which was similar to the cut-size optimization. [1] adopted the updated popular partitioner hMetis derived from [11] to divide the circuit into several parts and minimize the connections between dies. [23] adopted a TSV-aware partitioning algorithm for 3D FPGA to achieve higher performance for applications. [14] proposed a reconvergence-aware layer partition (RALP) algorithm for 3D FPGA design targeting performance optimization. However, they were targeting different routing models and all were tile-based flow rather than module-based flow.

2.3 Placement for 2.5D IC and FPGA with Interposer

Little work has addressed the interposer-based FPGA placement, although there was some work proposed for ASIC floorplanning using the 2.5D integration with interposer. In [10], the authors proposed the first work of chip-interposer codesign to place multiple chips on an interposer-based IC to reduce the inter-chip wirelength. They also proposed a hierarchical B*-tree to simultaneously place multiple chips and IO buffers. The work in [15] presented an enumeration-based algorithm and a network-flow-based algorithm to solve the multi-die floorplanning and signal assignment problem for 2.5D IC respectively. [21] adopted simulated annealing for die placement and I/O assignment in 2.5D IC. However, all the approaches have been focusing on the ASIC flow instead of the FPGA flow. Since FPGA had a different architecture, placement methods targeting FPGA were needed to be developed and the approaches used in specific IC design were not directly applicable to the FPGA architecture.

The work in [9] was the first work to consider the tile based placement in the multi-FPGA system with interposer. In comparison, our work employs a much more detailed interposer routing model and mainly focuses on the development of module based placement flow for delay optimization.

3. PROBLEM FORMULATION

In this work, we aim to develop the modular placement flow for the interposer-based 2.5D FPGAs. A wirelength estimation model for the interposer routing is developed for the placement flow. We describe the notations used in the placement problem below. $E = \{e_1, e_2, ..., e_m\}$ is the set of dies in the 2.5D FPGAs. $IO = \{io_1, io_2, ..., io_k\}$ is the set of available IOs in the 2.5D FPGAs. $B = \{m_1, m_2, ..., m_n\}$ is the set of modules to be placed in the 2.5D FPGAs.

We define the problem of interposer based multi-FPGA placement as follows. Given a set of B with n rectangular modules $B = \{m_1, m_2, ..., m_n\}$, where each module has a width and height denoted by w_i, h_i, $1 \leq i \leq n$ respectively. The aspect ratio of module b_i is defined by w_i/h_i. Given a set of E with m dies $E = \{e_1, e_2, ..., e_m\}$, where each die has the same width and height denoted by EW, EH. Given a set of IO with k IOs $IO = \{io_1, io_2, ..., io_k\}$. A placement $p = \{(x_i, y_i)\}(1 \leq i \leq n)$ with modules (m_i) is an assignment of the rectangular modules such that the bottom-left corner coordinate of module m_i is assigned to (x_i, y_i), no two rectangular modules are overlapped, and the different dies are connected by interposer. A routing model described in 4.1 is used to estimate the wirelength and delay through interposer. We consider each function in the overall design as a rectangle module in this work, and the objective is to optimize the total delay of the mapped circuit as well as meet the IO and area constraints.

4. PROPOSED MODULAR PLACEMENT FLOW

The complexity of the placement for a multi-FPGA system is much larger than that of a single FPGA. An efficient approach should consider both the runtime and placement quality. In order to optimize the placement as well as speed up the convergence, we take two stages to achieve the placement for the interposer based multi-FPGA system. Firstly, we adopt the force-directed method [30] for its global property to obtain a high-quality initial placement and then partition modules into different dies. Secondly, we adopt the simulated annealing (SA) [19] for its efficiency and effectiveness in finding the approximately optimal solution. In order to accelerate the refinement, we introduce the hierarchical B*-tree (HB*-tree) [10] to enable a fast search [5] and convergence. Moreover, a wirelength estimation model for the interposer is developed to allow a more accurate evaluation of the interposer impact on the placement flow.

4.1 Routing Model for Interposer

Based on the study of Xilinx commercial FPGA with interposer, e.g., Virtex-7 XC7V2000T [9], we know that the logic

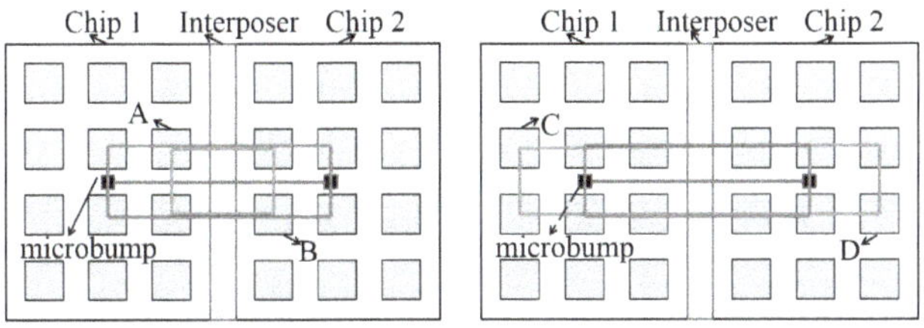

(a) Original bounding box smaller than SLL length. (b) Original bounding box larger than SLL length.

Figure 2: Difference of wirelength estimation when using interposer compared traditional bounding box calculation.

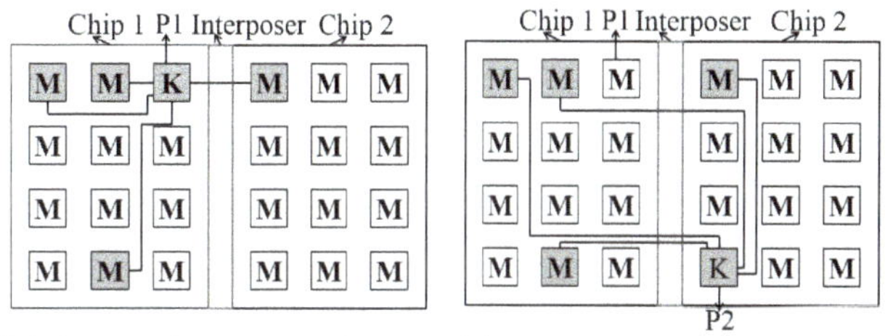

(a) Original position of Module K. (b) New position of Module K.

Figure 3: Example for attraction force considering interposer.

block in one FPGA die connects to another logic block in a different FPGA die in the following way. Firstly, the logic block in one FPGA die connects to the track (length-12) and the track connects to the corresponding microbump. Next, the microbump links to another microbump of the different FPGA die through the super long line (SLL) in the interposer [27]. Then, the signal goes through microbump and corresponding track and finally connects to the logic block in a different FPGA die. The SLL wires for connecting the adjacent FPGA dies through interposer have the same length as the chip length according to the Xilinx interposer-based FPGA, Virtex-7 XC7V2000T [9] [28]. To extend the model for general multiple FPGAs with interposer interconnection, we assume that any two adjacent chips can connect to each other directly through interposer and the SLL wire for connecting the adjacent FPGA dies through interposer have the same length as the die length, and the non-adjacent chips are connected by the intermediate chips.

We use an example as shown in Fig. 2 to illustrate the difference of wirelength estimation when considering the interposer compared to traditional bounding box calculation. We assume that the CLB A in the FPGA die one is connected to the CLB B in FPGA die two. For the case in Fig. 2(a), we can not use the green bounding box for wirelength estimation as in the traditional model, since there is routing restriction that SLL only connects to the local tracks at its ending points. Instead, we consider the SLL length and use the red bounding box for wirelength estimation which is more accurate to model the interposer. For the case in Fig. 2(b) where the bounding box is larger than the SLL length, the traditional way of bounding box calculation can be applied.

4.2 Force-directed Placement

We adopt the force-directed approach [30] since it is a scalable approach for large designs and able to avoid being trapped in local minimum solution. It is also suitable for optimizing average delay of the mapped circuit. We adopt the force-directed algorithm which is similar to the [30]. However, we consider the interposer in the following two forces used in the force equation [30]. The basic definition can be found in [30] and we do not describe it due to the page limitation.

4.2.1 Force Computing

We define two types of force for balancing the placement result: Filling Force and Attraction Force [30]. The two forces are combined together using linear weighted function to form the d_x and d_y which is described in [30]. We adopt the approach (Barnes-Hut quad-tree for n-body force calculation) described in [4] to compute the filling force due to its accuracy, $O(nlog^n)$ complexity and high-quality of force calculation. To tradeoff the computation time and accuracy, in our work we model a quad-tree with at most ten levels for the placement region and recursively divide the placement region into grids with the termination condition that the bin size is not less than $(w_{min} + h_{min})/4$ [17], where w_{min}, h_{min} are the minimum width and height of all the modules.

Filling Force (f_x^F, f_y^F): it is used to remove overlap between modules and distribute the modules evenly over the 2D placement area. It pushes modules away from the regions with high density and pull the modules towards regions with low density in the 2D space (filling force direction). We define the density as the total module area that covers the bin. The filling force of each bin is equal to the bin density of each bin. The filling force of each module is equal to the sum of the filling force of all the bins that the module covers. We add an additional force for the modules which lie on the partition boundary to prohibit them from crossing the interposer and ease the final partition stage, since if modules are placed in a partition boundary, it is difficult to choose which die they belongs to.

Attraction Force (f_x^A, f_y^A): it is used to reflect the relation between the old coordinate (start point of the force) and new coordinate (end point of the force) of the module. The two different positions of the module form an attraction force. Since the delay in the interposer is larger than the wire delay with the same length in the single die, we consider the interposer in the attraction force in the following way. If the two positions of the module cross the interposer, we add an additional force where the force can be positive or negative. If the number of nets crossing interposer increases after moving the module to a new position, we will add a negative force, e.g., decrease the attraction force to avoid delay increase and vice versa. Fig. 3 shows an example for considering the interposer in the attraction force. We assume that Chip (die) 1 and Chip (die) 2 are two FPGA dies connected by interposer and 'M' represents a module. Currently we consider a module labelled with 'K' and the modules with color represent that they are used. P1 and P2 are the original position and new position for the module K, respectively. Fig. 3(a) shows one net crossing the interposer and Fig. 3(b) shows three nets crossing the interposer. Hence, we decrease the attraction force for moving K from P1 to P2 which may reduce the delay. Considering interposer in the force and cost function Eq. 1 of Section 4.3.4 can help to reduce the number of wires crossing the interposer.

4.2.2 Partition and Legalization

In each iteration of force-directed placement, we consider the interposer in the filling force and attraction force described above since the delay in the interposer is larger than the wire delay with the same length in a single die. Through considering interposer in the filling force it eases the partition stage. We divide the force-directed result into several parts according to their coordinates and chip boundary and each part represents a chip (die). After we assign the modules to

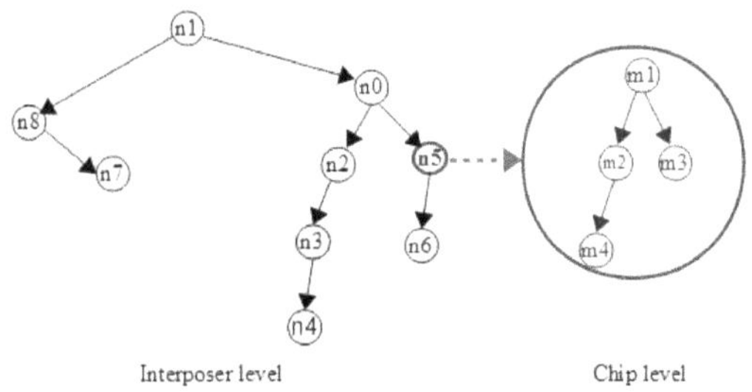

Figure 4: An Hierarchical B*-tree. In the interposer level, it has 9 chips. Chip n5 has 4 modules in the chip level.

the chips, we legalize (remove overlap) them using sequence pair [18] which is a floorplan representation and powerful for maintaining the relative relation of modules.

4.2.3 Aspect Ratio Selection of Modules

Since ratio impacts the circuit delay, we consider it in our flow. For each iteration of force calculation, we pick one of the ratio from the ratio list of the module and update its width and height. Thus it may impact the density of the bin that the modules cover. Through this way the filling force may change and finally it impacts the placement results.

4.3 Hierarchical B*-tree Based Module Placement

4.3.1 Hierarchical B-tree*

B*-tree is an ordered binary tree structure proposed in modern floorplanning of ASIC designs [5]. Compared to other data structures, B*-Tree provides faster search and area estimation, convenient handling of constraints, linear time transformation between the tree and placement [5]. B*-tree representation has used for the single FPGA placement [5]. To support the multi-FPGA placement, we adopt the hierarchical B*-tree (HB*-tree) since it matches the multi-FPGA system well in which the multi-FPGA corresponds to a B*-tree and each chip corresponds to a sub B*-tree. Moreover, HB*-tree based placement can enable a fast search [5] and convergence of the solution.

The hierarchical B*-tree consists of two levels: interposer level and chip level. At interposer level, each chip is a node of a B*-tree and the nodes determine the relative position of each chip. At chip level, each module is a node of sub B*-tree and the nodes in this level determine the placement of modules in each chip. Fig. 4 shows a structure of HB*-tree for illustration. At the interposer level, it has 9 chips and each chip is a node represented by n_i, $0 \leq i \leq 8$ respectively. At chip level, chip n_5 (one of the nodes in interposer level), contains 4 modules, and each module is a node represented by m_j, $1 \leq j \leq 4$ respectively.

4.3.2 Hierarchical B-tree Operations*

To explore the solution space, we apply the following operations.

At the interposer level, each chip is a node of the B*-tree and the following operations are performed on the nodes. **OP1:** Swap chips. **OP2:** Move a chip to another places.

At the chip level, each module is a node of the sub B*-tree and the following operations are performed on the nodes. **OP3:** Load module with shape of 1/(aspect ratio). **OP4:** Move module to an empty space. **OP5:** Swap two modules. **OP6:** Load a different aspect ratio of the module.

The following operations at the interposer level and chip level are performed at the same time. **OP7:** Move a module in a chip to another chip. **OP8:** Swap two modules that are in different chips.

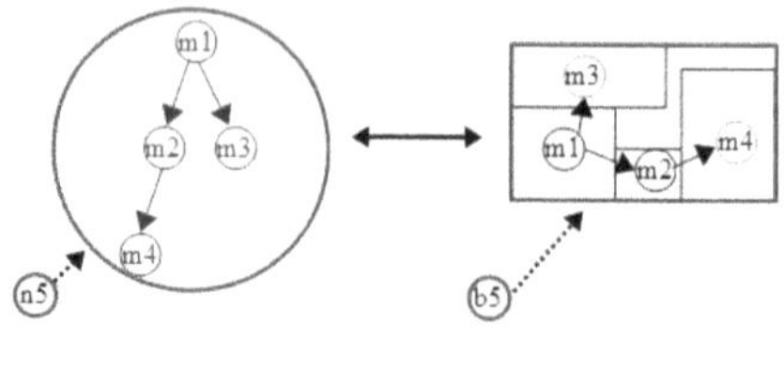

Figure 5: Chip-level packing: a sub-B*-tree of the chip n5 and its corresponding placement.

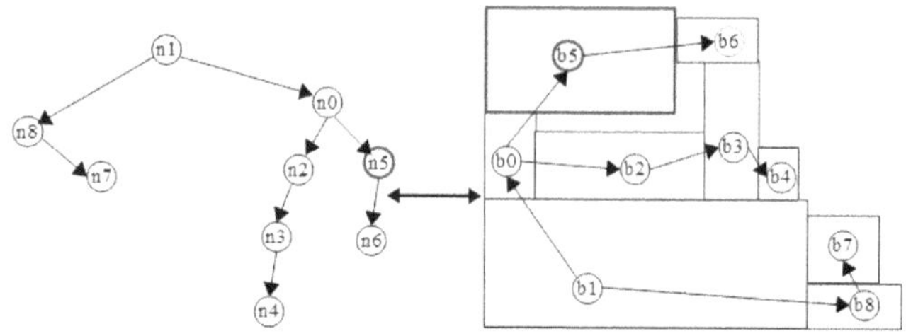

Figure 6: Interposer-level packing: a sub-B*-tree for chips and its corresponding placement

Here we use 'swap chips' (OP1) since all chips are the same and each node represent a chip in a tree of the interposer level. Swapping nodes in the tree is similar to swap chips.

4.3.3 The Packing of the Hierarchical B-tree*

We use two steps to pack the HB*-tree to a placement. Initially, we pack all the sub-B*-tree of the chip level one by one and get all the placement results for all the chips. Next, we pack the chip of interposer-level B*-tree to get a placement of the whole design. Finally, we map the placement of whole design using our proposed approach to the corresponding architecture.

A general example of a chip-level and interposer-level packing is shown in Fig. 5 and Fig. 6. Fig. 5 shows the sub-B*-tree of the chip $n5$ and its corresponding placement result. Fig. 6 shows that after packing the sub-B*-tree of each chip, we can pack the B*-tree at the interposer level, and each node of the B*-tree at the interposer level corresponds to the placement result of the chip. In our work, the dies are the same (same size: width and height).

4.3.4 Cost Metric in HB-tree based Module Placement*

To simplify the operation, we combine OP.3 and OP.6 together. We use τ which is area $\times$ delay of a shape of a module to evaluate the module generated by running VPR on the corresponding verilog file. The internal block information has already predefined, since VPR can achieve an efficient placement for the module. Simulated annealing is performed together with HB*-Tree operation to explore the solution space and the approach for choosing the temperature is the same as the [5]. In each iteration, the operations are randomly selected. Different weights are given to the operations to control the probability of choosing each operation. After each operation, the cost function [24] is calculated as shown in Eq. 1. Here Wirelength and Delay represent the current total wirelength and total delay containing all nets of the design respectively. $Wirelength^*$ and $Delay^*$ represent the average wirelength and delay of the design respectively.

$$Cost_{system} = \alpha(\frac{Wirelength}{Wirelength^*}) + (1 - \alpha)\frac{Delay}{Delay^*} \quad (1)$$

Table 1: Benchmarks From VPR Suite

Casename	Modules	Tiles	Casename	Modules	Tiles
bgm128	128	33160	bgm224	224	58030
bgm320	320	82900	spree121	121	2453
spree209	209	4237	spree308	308	6244
stereovision2112	112	60944	stereovision2210	210	40010
stereovision2308	308	180488	stereovision1105	105	20005
stereovision1210	210	40010	stereovision1315	315	60015

We divide the result by the average wirelength and delay to normalize the results. The α is a parameter to bias the cost function to wirelength or delay. If the net crosses the interposer, we will use our wirelength estimation model to calculate the wirelength and also consider the delay in the interposer described in detail in the Section 4.1. Thus the delay of each net includes the module delay and wirelength delay generated by Elmore delay [29]. We use the popular linear weighted function which is similar to [8] to bias the wirelength and total delay.

5. EXPERIMENTAL RESULTS

To evaluate the performance of our proposed flow, we first create benchmarks based on the VPR benchmark suite [19] by decomposing each of the verilog file into multiple verilog files according to subfunctions, which are known as modules. Each module with one aspect ratio is obtained by running VPR on each verilog file. Information of the cases are shown in Table 1. The number of modules ranges from 110 to 320 for the current case set. We also show the number of tiles contained to compare the difference in the size among these cases. The absolute tile values are for reference only since it varies in different architectures. In the experiment, each module has 9 ratios 0.2, 0.4, 0.6, 0.8, 1.0, 1.2, 1.6, 2.5, 5.0 based on our evaluating and we set α to be 0.4. The multi-FPGA system is assumed to contain 6 chips (3 columns $\times$ 2 rows). All the experiments were performed on a IBM server x3650 with Intel Xeon(R) CPU and 42 GB DDR2 RAM.

5.1 Impact of Interposer

In the first experiment, we evaluate the interposer impact using proposed routing model to the force-directed placement for the initial placement and to the whole flow for the finally refined placement. In previous work, the constant delay, e.g., $1ns$ has been used for interposer [9]. Here we compare our results with the constant delay model used in [9] for interposer in our flow to show the impact of the detailed routing model. The results are listed in Table 2 and Table 3, respectively. In the table, **WL**, **Delay**, **CrossD**, **Time** denote the **total wirelength (tile)**, **total delay (ns)**, **the delay generated by the nets crossing the interposer (ns)** and the **runtime (s)**, respectively. The results in Table 2 show that our proposed model does not impact the force-directed placement much. The wirelength, total delay and delay from nets crossing the interposer are reduced by **1%**, **1%**, **5%** respectively, for the initial placement step. The time increases by 4%. However, the proposed model shows great impact on the final placement results for our flow. Table 3 shows that our proposed model reduces the wirelength, total delay, delay from nets crossing the interposer and runtime by **8%**, **7%**, **19%**, **2%** respectively. Hence these results demonstrate that a detailed routing model for interposer can help to improve the placement quality.

5.2 Impact of Different Module Ratios

We compare the results between modules with only one ratio and the modules with different ratios in the placement flow to show the impact of module ratios. Similarly, we evaluate the impact of different module ratios on the force-directed placement and the whole flow which usually uses one ratio in the previous work. The corresponding results are listed in Table 4 and Table 5. Table 4 shows that when considering different ratios of modules in force-directed placement, the wirelength, total delay and delay from nets crossing interposer are significantly improved by **18%**, **11%**, **12%** respectively with an extra 7% runtime. The results in Table 5 indicate that when considering different ratios of modules in the whole flow, the wirelength, total delay and delay from nets crossing interposer are improved by **8%**, **4%**, **9%** respectively and the runtime increase 46%. We can see that considering different module ratios in the force-directed placement can significantly optimize the total delay of the circuits and improve the placement quality. However, in the HB*-tree based solution refinement, the benefits from module ratios is reduced. It is because that when considering multiple module ratios in the SA, the design space is enlarged significantly and within a comparable time, only suboptimal placement can be reached by SA. While since force-directed placement is based on analytical solution, considering multiple module ratios will not increase its running time much.

Table 2: Comparison between Constant Delay Model used in [9] and Our Proposed Model in Enhanced Force-Directed Placement

Casename	Traditional Model used in [9]				Our Proposed Model			
	WL	Delay	CrossD	Time	WL	Delay	CrossD	Time
bgm128	22624	2140.28	145	9.49	21118	2052.59	104	10.63
bgm224	60676.5	4409.36	264	14.87	66748	4618.57	285	15.96
bgm320	110199.5	7072.01	421	45.26	105856.5	6936.38	420	48.67
spree121	10554.5	835	239	8.33	10416.5	827.73	236	8.57
spree209	23372	1575.85	387	39.15	24506.5	1617.02	393	39.74
spree308	48270	2810.62	630	132.3	48110	2775.66	600	135.97
stereovision1105	19941.5	1096.39	176	3.63	20353.5	1085.16	152	3.86
stereovision1210	59339	2892.92	449	16.09	54163	2672.46	389	16.7
stereovision1315	121681	5198.73	520	50.96	120186.5	5177.4	545	51.49
stereovision2112	61572	3035.49	296	4.86	62939	3042.87	261	4.83
stereovision2210	193964	8148.55	578	22.02	173945.5	7494.98	545	22.68
stereovision2308	330379.5	13498.35	972	68.55	342486.5	13877.66	976	69.94
Average	**1**	**1**	**1**	**1**	**0.99**	**0.99**	**0.95**	**1.04**

5.3 Speed Up of the Placement Flow

We compare our flow with the traditional flow (min-cut + SA) (module-level) [14] [11]. We use hmetis [11] for partitioning for its high quality and fast speed. Hmetis [11] is a software package for partitioning large hypergraphs and is based on min-cut. Its goal is to minimize the total cut weight. The weights of hyperedges and vertices are two parameters in Hmetis. Here the hyperedges and vertices are set to the same weight. The results are shown in the Table 6 and it shows that our approach improves the wirelength, total delay and the delay from nets crossing interposer by **21%**, **14%**, **17%** respectively in a shorter time (improve by **15%**). The benefits are achieved from the following two parts. On one hand, min-cut is optimized to minimize the cut size. Although it also helps on reduction of the delay, our force-directed placement can achieve similar or better initial placement due to its optimization for delay and consideration of the detailed interposer model. On the other hand, HB*-tree based SA can search and converge much faster than SA which enables our flow to find a more efficient solution than SA within the same time.

6. CONCLUSIONS

Our work proposes a module based mapping flow to address the placement for multi-FPGA systems with interposer. A routing model is developed to more accurately model the wirelength and delay of the interposer. The proposed mapping flow contains two stages. Firstly, we adopt the force-directed method to get a good-quality initial solution as a start point of the refinement step. Secondly, we adopt the

Table 3: Comparison between Constant Delay Model used in [9] and Our Proposed Model in Our Proposed Flow

Casename	Traditional Model used in [9]				Our Proposed Model			
	WL	Delay	CrossD	Time	WL	Delay	CrossD	Time
bgm128	14493	1849.22	106	26.24	11962	1722.75	58	28.27
bgm224	48274	4025.88	265	62.17	41004	3752.51	217	63.64
bgm320	77255	6028.74	399	144.58	77292	6022.88	392	126.04
spree121	11605	945.57	317	52.46	9706	775.7	206	53.4
spree209	28582	1935.36	585	152.58	25840	1702.35	437	158.78
spree308	57323	3391.27	930	344.77	52813	3083.46	762	331.17
stereovision1105	16639	990.01	172	64.93	16051	945.79	146	62.73
stereovision1210	63454	3116.48	545	207.44	56506	2772.1	416	204.56
stereovision1315	151125	6390.49	799	379.34	136079	5819.06	694	362.14
stereovision2112	37709	2215.74	216	58.3	33657	2017.12	143	58.59
stereovision2210	133026	6239.48	558	196.85	140514	6458.6	545	189.62
stereovision2308	236712	10409.65	787	351.94	247117	10784.21	839	313.57
Average	1	1	1	1	**0.92**	**0.93**	**0.81**	**0.98**

Table 4: Comparison between Modules with only one ratio and different ratios in Enhanced Force-directed Placement

Casename	Modules with Only One Ratio				Modules with Multiple Ratios			
	WL	Delay	CrossD	Time	WL	Delay	CrossD	Time
bgm128	21118	2052.59	104	10.63	17143.5	1933.66	97	12.41
bgm224	66748	4618.57	285	15.96	43157	3798.16	174	27.21
bgm320	105856.5	6936.38	420	48.67	72906.5	5847.29	324	74.55
spree121	10416.5	827.73	236	8.57	10399.5	832.27	233	8.67
spree209	24506.5	1617.02	393	39.74	24960	1662.51	413	40.07
spree308	48110	2775.66	600	135.97	48810	2852.7	640	134.77
stereovision1105	20353.5	1085.16	152	3.86	17306.5	991.03	141	4.05
stereovision1210	54163	2672.46	389	16.7	52014	2594.46	359	16.74
stereovision1315	120186.5	5177.4	545	51.49	111136	4841.78	460	52.42
stereovision2112	62939	3042.87	261	4.83	42946	2419.61	241	3.06
stereovision2210	173945.5	7494.98	545	22.68	116621.5	5649.92	446	16.04
stereovision2308	342486.5	13877.66	976	69.94	216465.5	9700.96	658	73.41
Average	1	1	1	1	**0.82**	**0.89**	**0.88**	**1.07**

simulated annealing (SA) to efficiently search the solution space and find the approximately optimal placement solution. In order to speed up the refinement of placement in SA, we employ the HB*-tree representation to enable a fast search and convergence. The mapping flow supports the modules with different ratios which impact the total delay of the circuit to achieve the delay optimization. Our proposed approach gets efficient result in comparable time and is able to scale for large design.

7. ACKNOWLEDGEMENT

This work is partly supported by a MoE AcRF Tier 2 grant (MOE2012-T2-1-126) in Singapore and by Grant R9336 from Hong Kong SAR.

8. REFERENCES

[1] C. Ababei. Tpr: Three-d place and route for fpgas. In *FPL*. 2004.

[2] S. Areibi and etc. Hierarchical fpga placement. *CJECE*, 2007.

[3] P. Banerjee and etc. Floorplanning for Partially Reconfigurable FPGAs. *TCAD*, 2011.

[4] J. Barnes. and P. Hut. A hierarchical $o(nlog^n)$ force calculattion algorithm. *Nature*, 1986.

Table 5: Comparison between Modules with only one ratio and different ratios in Our Proposed Flow

Casename	Modules with Only One Ratio				Modules with Multiple Ratios			
	WL	Delay	CrossD	Time	WL	Delay	CrossD	Time
bgm128	13015	1773.4	76	32.1	11205	1713.57	61	42.35
bgm224	47655	3994.69	253	69.22	39079	3686.74	189	101.59
bgm320	80676	6092.79	357	126.96	70302	5792.55	350	216.36
spree121	9112	739.29	188	56.87	8368	704.29	168	79.49
spree209	26101	1724.45	451	160.23	27454	1788.82	462	252.81
spree308	57054	3286.93	834	368.82	52148	3022.18	706	555.97
stereovision1105	14872	891.24	128	61.38	14386	892.49	133	98.11
stereovision1210	59430	2893.74	447	225.12	47977	2421.32	311	342.94
stereovision1315	130223	5576.53	633	440.75	122744	5379.63	638	581.6
stereovision2112	39531	2265.22	209	65.54	30941	1965.45	159	86.8
stereovision2210	121576	5806.53	480	212.96	134006	6292.84	550	292.07
stereovision2308	238414	10487.42	812	377.91	229232	10208.72	770	548.46
Average	1	1	1	1	**0.92**	**0.96**	**0.91**	**1.46**

Table 6: Comparison between Min-cut + SA and Our Proposed approach

Casename	Min-cut + SA				Our Approach			
	WL	Delay	CrossD	Time	WL	Delay	CrossD	Time
bgm128	15599	1871.5	94	33.84	11962	1722.75	58	28.27
bgm224	58225	4360.36	291	75.12	41004	3752.51	217	63.64
bgm320	93559	6610.16	475	132.66	77292	6022.88	392	126.04
spree121	12794	960.43	295	64.8	9706	775.7	206	53.4
spree209	33301	2069.65	573	195.18	25840	1702.35	437	158.78
spree308	66616	3601.35	852	386.76	52813	3083.46	762	331.17
stereovision1105	23122	1234.99	216	78.96	16051	945.79	146	62.73
stereovision1210	90325	3970.49	566	236.1	56506	2772.1	416	204.56
stereovision1315	214682	8442.76	881	465.18	136079	5819.06	694	362.14
stereovision2112	38384	2221.66	201	67.2	33657	2017.12	143	58.59
stereovision2210	151469	6793.21	540	215.94	140514	6458.6	545	189.62
stereovision2308	215396	9542.86	581	345.54	247117	10784.21	839	313.57
Average	1	1	1	1	**0.79**	**0.86**	**0.83**	**0.85**

[5] T. Chen and Y. Chang. Modern Floorplanning Based on B*-Tree and Fast Simulated Annealing. *TCAD*, 2006.

[6] J. Cong and G. Luo. An analytical placer for mixed-size 3d placement. In *ISPD*, 2010.

[7] W. Donath. Complexity theory and design automation. In *DAC*, 1980.

[8] K. Eguro and S. Hauck. Enhancing timing-driven fpga placement for pipelined netlists. In *DAC*, 2008.

[9] A. Hahn Pereira and V. Betz. Cad and routing architecture for interposer-based multi-fpga systems. In *FPGA*, 2014.

[10] Y.-K. Ho and Y.-W. Chang. Multiple chip planning for chip-interposer codesign. In *DAC*, 2013.

[11] G. Karypis and etc. Multilevel hypergraph partitioning: Application in vlsi domain. In *DAC*, 1997.

[12] C. Kim and etc. Performance-driven circuit partitioning for prototyping by using multiple fpga chips. In *ASP-DAC*, 1995.

[13] S.-J. Lee and K. Raahemifar. Fpga placement optimization methodology survey. In *CCECE*, 2008.

[14] Q. Liu and etc. Ralp: Reconvergence-aware layer partitioning for 3d fpgas. In *ReConFig*, 2013.

[15] W.-H. Liu, M.-S. Chang, and T.-C. Wang. Floorplanning and signal assignment for silicon interposer-based 3d ics. In *DAC*, 2014.

[16] G. Marcel and A. Jason. Design Re-use for Compile Time Reduction in FPGA High-level Synthesis Flows. In *FPT*, 2014.

[17] F. Mo, A. Tabbara, and R. Brayton. A force-directed macro-cell placer. In *ICCAD*, 2000.

[18] H. Murata and etc. Rectangle-packing-based module placement. In *ICCAD*, 1995.

[19] J. Rose and et al. The VTR Project: Architecture and CAD for FPGAs from Verilog to Routing. In *FPGA*, 2012.

[20] K. Roy-Neogi and C. Sechen. Multiple fpga partitioning with performance optimization. In *FPGA*, 1995.

[21] D. Seemuth and etc. Automatic die placement and flexible i/o assignment in 2.5d ic design. In *ISQED*, 2015.

[22] M. Shih and etc. Performance-driven system partitioning on multi-chip modules. In *DAC*, 1992.

[23] K. Siozios and D. Soudris. A tabu-based partitioning and layer assignment algorithm for 3-d fpgas. *Embedded Systems Letters, IEEE*, 2011.

[24] T.-C. Wang and D. Wong. An Optimal Algorithm for Floorplan Area Optimization. In *DAC*, 1991.

[25] N.-S. Woo and J. Kim. An efficient method of partitioning circuits for multiple-fpga implementation. In *DAC*, 1993.

[26] Xilinx. Partial Reconfiguration of Xilinx FPGAs Using ISE Design Suite, 2012.

[27] Xilinx. White Paper: Vivado Design Suite, 2012.

[28] Xilinx. 7 Series FPGA Overview, 2013.

[29] M. Xu and etc. Near-linear wirelength estimation for fpga placement. In *CCECE*, 2009.

[30] P. Zhou and etc. 3d-staf: scalable temperature and leakage aware floorplanning for three-dimensional integrated circuits. In *ICCAD*, 2007.

A Parallel Random Walk Solver for the Capacitance Calculation Problem in Touchscreen Design

Zhezhao Xu[1], Wenjian Yu[1,2], Chao Zhang[1], Bolong Zhang[1,3], Meijuan Lu[1], Michael Mascagni[3]
[1]Department of Computer Science and Technology, [2]Tsinghua National Laboratory for Information Science and Technology, Tsinghua University, Beijing 100084, China. [3]Departments of Computer Science, Mathematics, and Scientific Computing, Florida State University, Tallahassee, FL 32306, USA.
Email: zhezhaoxu@gmail.com, yu-wj@tsinghua.edu.cn, eric.3zc@gmail.com, blzhang.m@gmail.com, 857815138@qq.com, mascagni@fsu.edu.

ABSTRACT
In this paper, a random walk based solver is presented which calculates capacitances for verifying a touchscreen design. To suit the complicated conductor geometries in touchscreen structures, we extend the floating random walk (FRW) method for handling non-Manhattan conductors. A unified dielectric pre-characterization scheme is proposed to suit arbitrary dielectric profiles while keeping high accuracy. The algorithm is finally implemented on a computer cluster, which enables massively parallel computing. Numerical experiments validate the accuracy of the proposed techniques and the up to 67X parallel speedup. Compared with other schemes, the unified dielectric pre-characterization scheme exhibits the highest accuracy while costing the least in terms of memory usage.

Keywords
Capacitance calculation; Floating random walk; Massively parallel computing; Multi-dielectric pre-characterization; Non-Manhattan geometry; Touchscreen.

1. INTRODUCTION
The flat panel display (FPD) has been a widespread and important human-computer interaction device in our daily life. In recent years, touch panel technology has been combined with FPD to largely enhance the interactivity and user experience of various customer electronics. This kind of touchscreen device includes both the display components, like those based on the thin-film transistor (TFT) active matrix [1, 2], and touch sensor components. This makes the internal structure of the touchscreen even more complicated. Most touchscreens utilize the capacitive touch sensor (see Fig. 1), because of its advantages in durability, reliability and capability [5]. To validate the functionality (like Multi-Touch, Force-Touch) and sensitivity of the touchscreen, calculating the relevant capacitances becomes an important and frequent task during the design of high-quality touchscreens.

The capacitance calculation problem in touchscreen design involves simulating the electrostatic field within the whole structure including touch sensor, surrounding FPD wires, and even the finger stylus. It calls for an accurate and efficient field-solver based solution. This problem is similar to the capacitance extraction problem in the design of vary large scale integrated

GLSVLSI '16, May 18 - 20, 2016, Boston, MA, USA

ACM 978-1-4503-4274-2/16/05...$15.00
DOI: http://dx.doi.org/10.1145/2902961.2903011

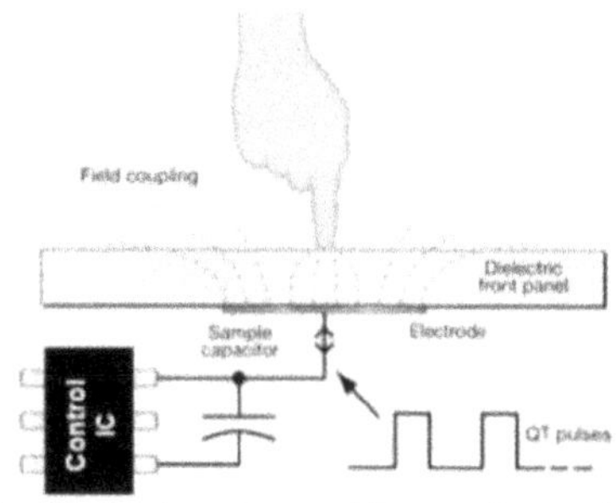

Fig. 1. The illustration of capacitive touch panel.

(VLSI) circuits. However, there are distinct differences between them, as listed in Table 1.

Table 1. The differences between capacitance extraction for VLSI circuit and capacitance calculation for touchscreen design.

	VLSI circuit capacitance extraction	Touchscreen capacitance calculation
Conductor geometry	Mostly Manhattan shape, with moderate aspect ratio	Generally non-Manhattan shape, with very large aspect ratio
Dielectric environment	On-chip dielectric insulators; relatively fixed dielectric profile	In-device dielectrics and out-device air; arbitrary dielectric configuration
Accuracy demand	Mainly on self-capacitance for accurate delay calculation	Need accurate coupling capacitances

A lot of field-solver techniques have been proposed for accurate capacitance extraction for VLSI design. They include the domain discretization method (finite difference method [6] and finite element method), the boundary element method (BEM) [7, 8], and the floating random walk (FRW) method [9-12]. The first two classes of methods involve volume or surface discretization and result in a system of linear equations. On the contrary, the FRW method is based on the Monte Carlo method, and has the advantages of more scalability for very large structures, tunable accuracy, better parallelism, and much smaller memory usage. Recent work on structures with large cylindrical through-silicon vias [13] also revealed that, the FRW method is more reliable on accuracy than the BEM capacitance solvers. However, the efficiency of FRW based techniques mainly depends on the assumption that the considered geometries are all of Manhattan shape, which is only true for VLSI circuits.

As for the capacitance calculation problem in the touchscreen design, the assumption of Manhattan shapes is not hold (see Table 1). Furthermore, the aspect ratio (lateral dimension over thickness) of metal in touchscreen structures can be larger than 1000, which causes difficulty for the discretization based methods like BEM. Secondly, the manufacturers of touchscreens are very diverse, which means a good capacitance solver for touchscreen verification should suit various configurations of dielectric material. Therefore, the strategies that pre-characterize the FRW transition probabilities for certain multi-dielectric profiles (process technology) in [10, 14] are unfavorable. And, a larger range of dielectric permittivity should be considered due to the inclusion of air. Lastly, since the touch sensor acquires the touch location by detecting the difference of coupling capacitances, more accuracy in capacitance calculation is needed for simulating the touchscreen structures. This makes the FRW method with more reliable accuracy the best choice. The remaining problem is how to reduce its runtime while pursuing high accuracy.

There is some work on capacitance extraction for the liquid crystal display (LCD) based FPD design [3, 4]. However, they did not consider the touchscreen structure and related problems. The methods were based on pattern matching or an unknown field solver technique, and do not have sufficient accuracy or runtime efficiency for our purpose.

In this work, we aim to extend and apply the state-of-the-art FRW capacitance extraction techniques to the problem of touchscreen design. By proposing a technique to handle arbitrary conductor shape and a unified dielectric pre-characterization scheme, we are able to perform FRW based simulation for the touchscreen structures. The experiments on several touchscreen structures validate the accuracy and efficiency of the proposed techniques. To further reduce the runtime for accurate simulation, we implemented the algorithm on a large-scale computer cluster. The results of massively parallel computing reveals good scalability of the FRW based capacitance solver.

2. BACKGROUND

2.1 Floating Random Walk Algorithm for Capacitance Extraction in VLSI Design

The FRW method for calculating electrostatic capacitance originated from expressing the electric potential of a point $\boldsymbol{r}$ as an integral of the potential on surface S enclosing $\boldsymbol{r}$ [9], [10]:

$$\phi(\boldsymbol{r}) = \oint_S P(\boldsymbol{r}, \boldsymbol{r}^{(1)})\phi(\boldsymbol{r}^{(1)})\mathrm{d}\boldsymbol{r}^{(1)}, \quad (1)$$

where $P(\boldsymbol{r}, \boldsymbol{r}^{(1)})$ is called surface Green's function and can be regarded as a probability density function with non-negative values. Therefore, $\phi(\boldsymbol{r})$ is the statistical mean of $\phi(\boldsymbol{r}^{(1)})$, and can be calculated with a Monte Carlo (MC) procedure sampling S. The domain enclosed by S is called the transition domain, and usually $\boldsymbol{r}$ is the center of the transition domain.

The problem of capacitance extraction is to calculate the capacitances related to a specified conductor (called *the master conductor*). For master conductor i, a Gaussian surface G_i is constructed to enclose it (see Fig. 2). According to Gauss's theorem, the charge of conductor i is given by

$$Q_i = \oint_{G_i} F(\boldsymbol{r}) g \int_{S^{(1)}} \omega(\boldsymbol{r}, \boldsymbol{r}^{(1)}) q(\boldsymbol{r}, \boldsymbol{r}^{(1)}) \phi(\boldsymbol{r}^{(1)}) \mathrm{d}\boldsymbol{r}^{(1)} \mathrm{d}\boldsymbol{r}, \quad (2)$$

where $F(\boldsymbol{r})$ is the dielectric permittivity at point $\boldsymbol{r}$, $q(\boldsymbol{r}, \boldsymbol{r}^{(1)})$ is the probability density function for sampling on $S^{(1)}$, the surface of a transition domain. g is a constant, which satisfies $\oint_{G_i} F(\boldsymbol{r}) g \mathrm{d}\boldsymbol{r} = 1$. $q(\boldsymbol{r}, \boldsymbol{r}^{(1)})$ may be different from $P(\boldsymbol{r}, \boldsymbol{r}^{(1)})$, and $\omega(\boldsymbol{r}, \boldsymbol{r}^{(1)})$ is the weight value [10]. Thus, Q_i can be estimated as the statistical mean of sampled values on G_i, which is also the mean of sampled potentials on $S^{(1)}$ multiplying the weight value. If the sampled potential is unknown, the construction of the transition domain and the spatial sampling procedure will repeat until a point with known potential is obtained (e.g. on a conductor surface). This forms a floating random walk (FRW) including a sequence of hops. Each hop is from the center of a transition domain to its boundary. With a number of such walks, the statistical mean of the weight values for the walks terminating at conductor j approximates the capacitance C_{ij} between conductors i and j (if $j \neq i$), or the self-capacitance C_{ii} of master conductor i.

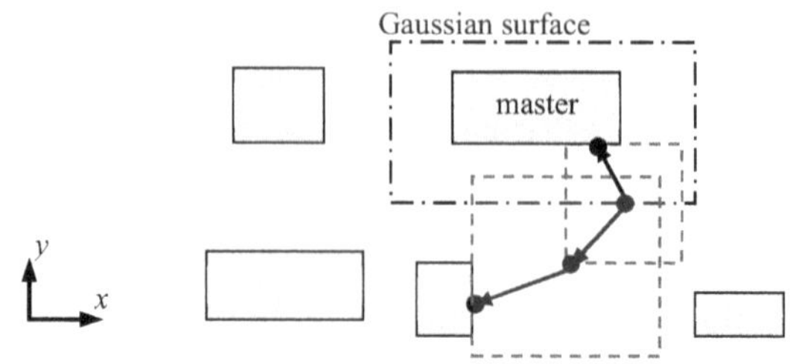

Fig. 2. Two examples of random walk in the FRW method for capacitance extraction (a 2-D top view).

Although the surface Green's function for a spherical transition domain has simple analytical expression, the cubic transition domain is widely adopted because it fits well with the VLSI layout including mostly Manhattan shapes [9-12]. This yields larger probability for terminating a walk quickly. The sampling probability and weight value for a cubic domain can be pre-calculated and tabulated, so as to accelerate the sampling operation.

The runtime of the FRW method is proportional to the number of random walks. Several variance reduction techniques has been proposed to reduce the number of walks [10], [13], i.e. accelerate the convergence of MC procedure. A walk consists of a couple of hops. For a structure including many conductors, employing an efficient space management technique [12] is crucial for reducing the time for performing a hop.

2.2 Characteristics of the Touchscreen Structure and Its Capacitance Calculation

With Table 1, we have already summarize the differences between the capacitance calculation problems in VLSI design and touchscreen design. In Fig. 3, we show a typical dielectric profile and example conductor layouts (in top view) of the touchscreen structure. In Fig. 3(a) we see that the top dielectric layer is air, i.e. the relative permittivity ε_5=1. And, the lateral dimension of a metal is usually much larger than its thickness. Fig. 3(b)~(c) show arbitrary-angle polygons and conductor with slits (holes). They include the geometries of a touch sensor and the wiring structures around it. It is obvious that the FRW method should be extended to handle these general non-Manhattan geometries.

The non-Manhattan conductor considered in this work can be regarded as a straight prism with an arbitrary polygon as the bottom. It has top and bottom faces parallel to the *xoy* axis plane.

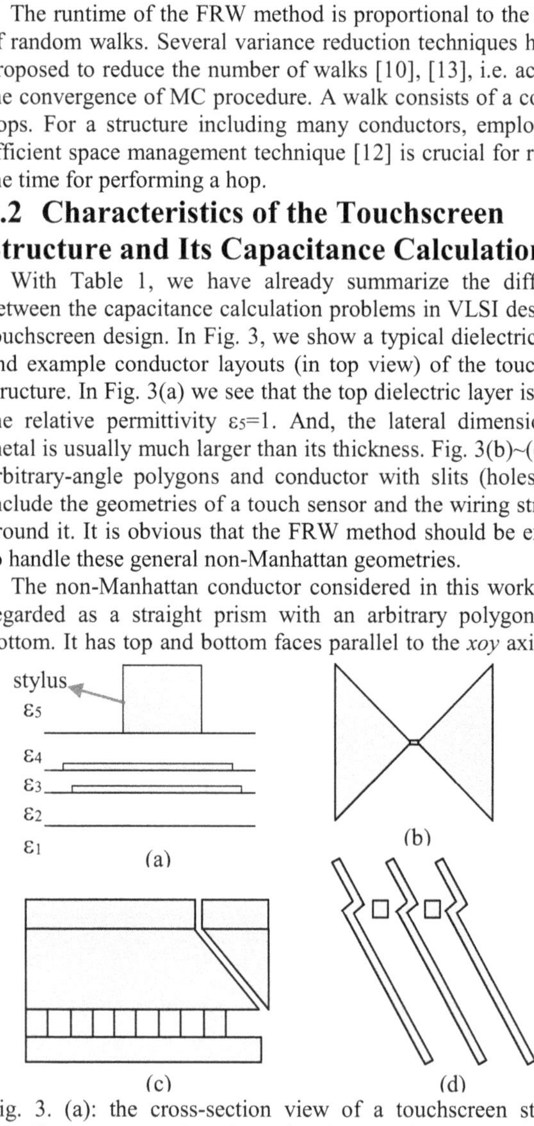

Fig. 3. (a): the cross-section view of a touchscreen structure. (b)~(d): some examples of top-view layout of the structure.

However, its projection on the *xoy* plane (i.e. the top view) is an arbitrary 2-D polygon, instead of an axis-aligned rectangle.

Now, the problem includes a number of 3-D conductor blocks. Each block is either a Manhattan cuboid or a convex straight prism with side faces perpendicular to the *xoy* plane. Note that a concave polygon can be easily decomposed into several convex ones. The master conductor may include a couple of connected conductor blocks. While running the FRW algorithm for a capacitance calculation, the cubic transition domain is only considered, since it nicely touches the surface of the conductor and leads to a faster termination of the random walk.

In the FRW method, the distance calculation between a point and a block or between two blocks is required. Because of the non-Manhattan conductors, the calculation becomes complicated, creating difficulty for the following parts of FRW method:

1) The generation of the Gaussian surface, which must enclose the master conductor and not intersect any conductor.

2) The construction of the transition cube for each hop, which requires finding the nearest conductor for a point.

Finally, because we are facing divergent process technology recipes for the touchscreen, it is desirable to have a unified dielectric pre-characterization scheme instead of pre-calculating the FRW transition tables for each process technology [10, 14]. Also note that the inclusion of air leads to a large range of dielectric permittivities. This prevents us from building a unified set of pre-characterization tables for VLSI capacitance extraction [11] and applying them to the touchscreen structure.

3. TECHNIQUES FOR CALCULATING THE TOUCHSCREEN CAPACITANCES

In this section, we first extend the FRW method for handling non-Manhattan conductor geometry. Then, a technique for building and using unified dielectric pre-characterization tables is proposed. Lastly, the FRW method is implemented on a large computer cluster to achieve considerable computational speedup.

3.1 Handling Arbitrary Conductor Geometry

To tackle the two difficulties caused by the non-Manhattan conductors, we first extend the aligned-box distance for Manhattan geometry to the non-Manhattan situation.

Definition 1: The 2-D aligned-box distance between a 2-D point P and a convex polygon A: $dist_a$(P, A), is the half size of the axis-aligned square which is centered at P and touches A.

In Fig. 4(a), we show some typical positions of points around polygon, A. The Manhattan transition squares centered at the point and the corresponding aligned-box distance are illustrated. In Fig. 4(b), we show the basic idea for calculating $dist_a$(P, A). We first find the visible edges of A in relation to point P. If the Manhattan square centered at P touches A's edge, the edge must be a visible edge. For each edge A_iA_{i+1}, we calculate the cross product of $\overrightarrow{A_iP}$ and $\overrightarrow{A_iA_{i+1}}$. If the result is a positive value, the edge A_iA_{i+1} is visible, and we get the area of triangle PA_iA_{i+1}. As shown in Fig. 4(b), the area is useful for calculating the size of the transition square. Triangle PA_iA_{i+1} can be regarded as the combination of four triangles: PA_iR, PRA_{i+1}, RA_iS, and RSA_{i+1}, where S is the contact point and R is the midpoint of a transition square's edge. The four triangles all have half the size of the transition square as a bottom edge, while the corresponding heights form the *x*-distance and *y*-distance between points A_i and A_{i+1}. So, the cross product of $\overrightarrow{A_iP}$ and $\overrightarrow{A_iA_{i+1}}$ over the sum of the *x*-distance and *y*-distance equals the half edge length. $dist_a$(P, A) is the maximum of such half edge length got from all visible edges, or corresponds to the situation where the Manhattan square touches A's vertex [see P_3's square in Fig. 4(a)]. The latter can be obtained with the Manhattan bounding box of A, using an existing technique. This analysis gives as Theorem 1.

Theorem 1: Suppose polygon A has vertices $A_1, A_2, \ldots, A_n$, in the anti-clockwise order. A_i has coordinates (x_i, y_i), $i=1, 2, \ldots, n$. Suppose the point P has coordinates (x, y). Then,

$$dist_a(\mathrm{P},\mathrm{A}) = \max\{\max_{1\le i\le n}\frac{(x-x_i)(y_{i+1}-y_i)-(y-y_i)(x_{i+1}-x_i)}{|x_{i+1}-x_i|+|y_{i+1}-y_i|},\ dist_a(\mathrm{P},\mathrm{B_A})\} \quad (3)$$

where B_A is the Manhattan bounding box of polygon A. ■

The vertical distance between a point and a conductor block is defined as follows.

Definition 2: The vertical distance between a point P (x, y, z) and a non-Manhattan conductor block A is:

$$dist_v(\mathrm{P, A}) = \max\{z - z_{max}(\mathrm{A}), z_{min}(\mathrm{A}) - z\}, \quad (4)$$

where z_{min}(A) and z_{max}(A) are the minimum and maximum z coordinates of A, respectively. So, the 3-D aligned-box distance is:

$$dist_a(\mathrm{P, A}) = \max\{dist_v(\mathrm{P, A}), dist_a(\mathrm{P, P_A})\}, \quad (5)$$

where P_A stands for the *xoy* projection of A. The minimum distance between current position of random walk and its surrounding conductors is used to construct the Manhattan transition cube.

Based on the above definitions, we can further define the aligned-box distance between two convex polygons, and the 3-D distance between two non-Manhattan conductor blocks. They can be used to generate a valid Gaussian surface. We first calculate the minimum distance d_{min} between a master conductor A and its neighboring conductors. Then, we place the Gaussian surface G_A about $d_{min}/2$ distance away from A. It is guaranteed that such a Gaussian surface will not intersect any conductor. Based on the considered conductor geometry, the Gaussian surface surrounding the master conductor also forms a convex straight prism. In Fig. 5, the *xoy* projection of the Gaussian surface is shown. Each edge of A's projection is inflated outward to obtain an edge where every point's aligned-box distance to A is $d_{min}/2$. Then, the edges obtained by inflation are connected by adding edges, resulting in the *xoy* projection of G_A. If A's projection has *n* edges, the number of edges of G_A's projection is between *n* and 2*n*. The whole Gaussian surface is finally obtained by raising the *xoy* projection along the *z* axis.

In our approach, we still use Manhattan (axis-aligned) transition cubes in the FRW algorithm. During the random walk procedure, the 2-D aligned-box distance can be used to determine

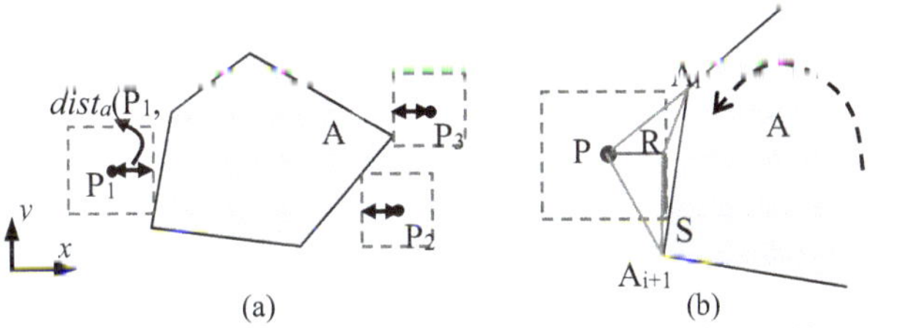

Fig. 4. (a) A convex polygon A and the aligned-box distances between it and nearby points. (b) The illustration for calculating the aligned-box distance.

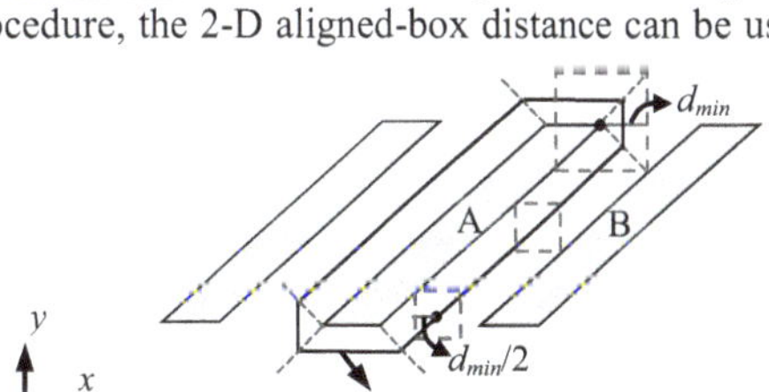

Fig. 5. The top view of a non-Manhattan conductor structure, and a valid generation of the Gaussian surface.

the Manhattan transition cube touching the side face of a non-Manhattan conductor. An idea is to allow the transition cube to rotate so as to help the transition cube touch the conductor surface better [13]. However, for touchscreen structures this is unnecessary because the walker seldom appears near the side walls of those thin-slice-alike conductors.

3.2 A Unified and Accurate Dielectric Pre-Characterization Method

In order to make the FRW method using transition cubes workable for multi-dielectric structures, the sampling probabilities and weight values for transition cubes containing multiple dielectrics must be pre-calculated. We call this the procedure of dielectric pre-characterization. In this subsection, we first outline the dielectric pre-characterization approaches used for extracting VLSI structures [11, 14]. We explain why they are not suitable for touchscreen structures. Then, an idea of building a unified set of dielectric pre-characterization tables is proposed. We also discuss how to balance the memory cost and the runtime benefit.

3.2.1 Two existing approaches

Based on a technique numerically characterizing the surface Green's function for two-dielectric-layer transition cubes, an approach was proposed in [10] for handling structures with multiple dielectric layers. For a given dielectric profile, the sampling probabilities and weight values for various two-dielectric-layer cubes are calculated and tabulated offline, and then used during the random walks. It is less efficient for actual VLSI process technology with 10 or more dielectric layers, because each FRW hop crosses one dielectric interface at most. An improvement was recently presented in [14], which pre-characterizes cubic transition domains with three or four dielectric layers so as to reduce the runtime of FRW. However, this greatly increased the number of dielectric configurations of the transition cube, and therefore the memory cost. A distinct drawback of this approach [10, 14] is that we must re-calculate the dielectric pre-characterization if the process technology changes.

Another pre-characterization approach is called the dielectric homogenization method [11]. Its main idea is assuming that any cubic transition domain with multiple dielectric layers can be approximated by a cube with four equal-thickness dielectric layers, no matter how many dielectric layers it actually contains. In Fig. 6, we show a structure with five dielectric layers to illustrate different transition cubes and pre-characterization strategies. When employing the dielectric homogenization method, one can use the blue transition cube, whereas one has to choose the red one if the approach of [10] is used. So, the dielectric homogenization method brings better runtime efficiency to FRW.

Now, we explain how to pre-characterize the cube with four equal-thickness dielectric layers. Suppose the four dielectrics have relative permittivities: $\bar{\varepsilon}_1$, $\bar{\varepsilon}_2$, $\bar{\varepsilon}_3$, $\bar{\varepsilon}_4$, their ratios determine the sampling probabilities and weight values for the cube. This means the cube with permittivities $(\bar{\varepsilon}_1, \bar{\varepsilon}_2, \bar{\varepsilon}_3, \bar{\varepsilon}_4)$ is equivalent to that with $(\bar{\varepsilon}_1/\bar{\varepsilon}_{max}, \bar{\varepsilon}_2/\bar{\varepsilon}_{max}, \bar{\varepsilon}_3/\bar{\varepsilon}_{max}, \bar{\varepsilon}_4/\bar{\varepsilon}_{max})$, where $\bar{\varepsilon}_{max} = \max\{\bar{\varepsilon}_1, \bar{\varepsilon}_2, \bar{\varepsilon}_3, \bar{\varepsilon}_4\}$. So, we need only consider situations where one permittivity is 1, and the other three have values in the interval (0, 1], for the pre-characterization. Suppose the value of three permittivities is sampled with step size t, and the value range is [s, 0.1] instead of (0, 1]. For the VLSI capacitance extraction, s equals 0.5 is a reasonable setting, which means the adjacent dielectrics always have permittivities with ratio no more than 2. So, the number of sampling dielectric configurations is about $4\times[(1-s)/t+1]^3$, the constant 4 means that any one of $(\bar{\varepsilon}_1, \bar{\varepsilon}_2, \bar{\varepsilon}_3, \bar{\varepsilon}_4)$ can be 1. By symmetry, which means dielectric configuration $(1, a, b, c)$ is equivalent to $(c, b, a, 1)$, the number of sampling dielectric configurations can be reduced to $2\times[(1-s)/t+1]^3-[(1-s)/t+1]^2$. The reason for subtracting $[(1-s)/t+1]^2$ is that the dielectric configurations for the form $(1, 1, b, c)$ are counted twice.

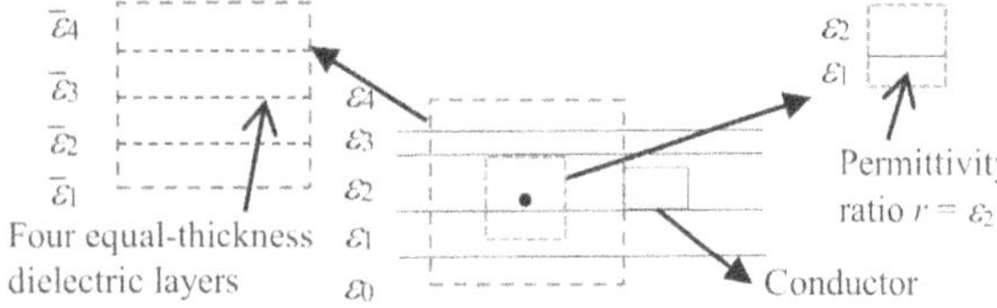

Fig. 6. An example for illustrating the transition cubes in the dielectric homogenization method and the proposed method.

We further count the data size for the dielectric homogenization method. According to [10], $4\times 6N^2$ real numbers are needed to store the sampling probabilities and weight values (i.e. GFT and WVT tables) for a single configuration, where N is the segment number along transition cube edge. So, the dielectric homogenization method pre-calculates:

$$Size_{DHM} = 48N^2[(1-s)/t+1]^3-24N^2[(1-s)/t+1]^2 \quad (6)$$

real numbers. If $N = 32$, $s = 0.5$, $t = 0.05$, and single-precision numbers are used, the size of the pre-calculated data is about 238 MB. This is also the memory cost for running the FRW procedure.

Besides the runtime efficiency, another advantage of this approach is that the pre-characterization does not depend on the process technology. It is unified for arbitrary dielectric profiles. However, it has two drawbacks. The first one is on the error related to this four equal-thickness dielectric approximation. As pointed out in [14], this may induce significant error while handling the structures with more dielectric layers. The second one is the large memory cost for handling touchscreen structures. Since air, with ε=1.0, is usually involved, the adjacent dielectrics may have permittivity ratio larger than 2. This means we set a smaller value for s, for example $s = 0.1$. With (6), we can calculate that the total memory cost for the pre-characterization increases to about 1.22 GB. This is a large number, and will limit the usage of the capacitance calculation.

3.2.2 The proposed method

To meet the requirements for simulating the touchscreen structures, we wish to combine the high accuracy and low memory cost of the approach in [10] and the unified aspect of the dielectric homogenization method. The idea is to compute pre-characterization for arbitrary two-dielectric cube configurations and then employ two-dielectric transition cubes during random walks. As shown in Fig. 6, we need to consider different choices of permittivities (ε_1, ε_2) and the position of dielectric interface. Due to the equivalence of different in-cube dielectric configurations and symmetry, we need only consider the situation where the two permittivities are $(1, r)$, $0<r\leq 1$. We may use r, denoting the two-dielectric configuration $(1, r)$ when there is no ambiguity. Let s denote the smallest value of r, and N_{TDC} denote the number of sampling two-dielectric configurations. If we use equal-sized sampling of the r value, the number of samples is n= (1-s)/t+1, where t is the step size. Because there are N-1 positions for dielectric interface, we finally get:

$$N_{TDC} = n(N-1) = (N-1)[(1-s)/t+1]. \quad (7)$$

This approach pre-calculates:

$$Size_{OUR} = 24N^2 \cdot N_{TDC} = 24N^2(N-1)[(1-s)/t+1]. \quad (8)$$

real numbers. It corresponds to about 177 MB, if $N = 31$, $s = 0.1$, t= 0.015. Note that we have considered that the ratio of dielectric permittivity can increase to 10 in touchscreen structures. And, t is set to a smaller value to achieve higher accuracy.

This is a unified dielectric pre-characterization method, which means that the generated sampling probabilities and weight values suit any dielectric configuration. If the actual permittivity ratio r of two adjacent dielectrics is between two sampled values: r_i and r_{i+1}, linear interpolation is employed. For example, let V_r denote the sampling probabilities of a two-dielectric configuration r. Then,

$$V_r = V_{r_i}\frac{r-r_i}{r_{i+1}-r_i} + V_{r_{i+1}}\frac{r_{i+1}-r}{r_{i+1}-r_i} \quad . \tag{9}$$

This approach overcomes the shortage of the approaches in [10, 14], and avoids the large error caused by dielectric homogenization [11]. Although there are over 100 MB of pre-characterized data, not all of this is loaded to the memory while calculating a given structure. For example, if the structure includes dielectrics with permittivities (4, 3.2, 4, 1), corresponding to the permittivity ratios 0.8 and 0.25, we only need load data corresponding to dielectric configurations (1.0, 0.790), (1.0, 0.805), (1.0, 0.235) and (1.0, 0.250), which is only about 11 MB. This is an advantage over the dielectric homogenization method.

The only drawback of the proposed method is the computational speed, which is essentially the same as the FRW method in [10]. To reduce the runtime, an idea is to combine the dielectric homogenization method (with s=0.5) and our proposed idea to trade off running speed, memory and accuracy. We generate the data for both pre-characterization methods. While performing FRW, we use the homogenization method to allow making the large hop as long as possible. Otherwise, there is a permittivity ratio exceeding 2 within the four equal-thickness dielectrics, and we use the two-dielectric transition cube pre-characterized by the proposed method. This mixed approach improves memory/runtime tradeoff. However, it may still induce significant error because dielectric homogenization is employed. We will show this in the section on numerical experiments.

3.3 Massively Parallel Simulation on a Computer Cluster

The computational time of the FRW algorithm is inversely propositional to the square root of number of walks. This means its runtime increases substantially with greater accuracy. For calculating capacitances during the touchscreen design, highly accurate coupling capacitances are required. But, there is not an efficient way to accelerate the calculation of coupling capacitances [13]. So, a feasible way may be leveraging its potential for straightforward parallelization. To this aim, we implement the parallel FRW algorithm on a Cluster Environment with MPI. Fig. 7 shows the flowchart of this algorithm. Each process executes the random walk procedure independently and

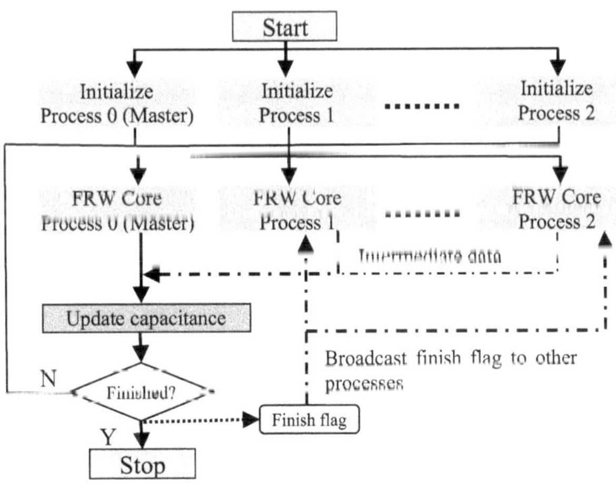

Fig. 7. Flowchart of the parallel FRW on a computer cluster.

all processes except the master process will send intermediate data to the master every m walks (m=1000). Then, the master process updates the capacitance value, we check the program termination criteria via total number of walks or estimated error. If it is satisfied, the master process broadcasts the finish flag to all other processes to terminate the computation. This is the classic master/worker parallel paradigm.

4. EXPERIMENTAL RESULTS

We have implemented the FRW method and the proposed techniques in C++. With the TechGFT program in [10], we have pre-calculated the sampling probabilities and weight values (i.e. GFTs and WVTs) for handling multi-dielectric structures. Three multi-dielectric touchscreen structures are tested. They include non-Manhattan conductor blocks. Some details are as follows.

Case 1: This case contains 1423 conductor blocks in two metal layers. The dielectric layers have relative permittivity of 4.0, 3.2, 4.0, 1.0. The metal heights in the two layers are 70nm and 220nm.

Case 2: This case is a small structure with 11 conductor blocks in two metal layers. The dielectric layers have relative permittivity of 4.0, 3.5, 7.0. The heights of the two metal layer are both 100nm. The top-view of one layer is similar to that shown in Fig. 3(b).

Case 3: This case contains 808 conductor blocks in four metal layers. The dielectric layers have relative permittivity of 3.9, 6.5, 3.5, 6.5, 4.2, 3.2, 4.0, 1.0. The heights of the four metal layers are 340nm, 220nm, 400nm and 70nm, respectively. The metal layout include the geometry patterns shown in Fig. 3(c)(d).

We first validate the accuracy of the proposed techniques with Raphael [6], which employs FDM with dense discretization. Then, we compare different approaches of dielectric pre-characterization. The experiments in Section 4.1 are carried out on a Linux server with Intel Xeon E5-2650 2.0GHz CPU with the termination criterion set to 0.5% $1-\sigma$ error on the self-capacitance. In Section 4.2, we carry out the parallel-computing experiment on a High-Performance Computing Cluster which consists 740 nodes with Intel Xeon X5670 2.93GHz CPU and InfiniBand QDR network.

4.1 Accuracy Validation and Comparisons

Because RWCap in [10] is not able to handle non-Manhattan shapes, we cannot compare our algorithms with it. Instead, following the strategy treating multiple dielectrics in [10], we obtain an algorithm called **FRW-2** for our non-Manhattan touchscreen structures. The FRW algorithms including the proposed unified dielectric pre-characterization method in Section 3.2 are denoted by **FRW-2unify** and **FRW-mixed**, corresponding to the strategy only using two-dielectric transition cubes and the strategy combining it and the dielectric homogenization approach, respectively. The results of FRW-2 with Raphael are listed in Table 2. Note that the results for Case 3 are not listed, because Raphael runs out of memory for it. We see that the results of FRW-2 are well correlated with those of Raphael even though they employ different methods and boundary assumptions. The results of coupling capacitances are also compared, which show similar correlation. This validate the accuracy of the techniques proposed in Section 3.1.

Table 2. The computational results of FRW-2 and Raphael (Capacitance in unit of 10^{-12}F, Memory in unit of MB)

Case	C_{self} (Raphael)	C_{self} (FRW-2)	Mem. (FRW-2)	Error (%)
1	621.0	600.1	96.0	+3.4
2	78.4	78.7	56.9	+0.4

Now, regarding FRW-2 as the standard, we evaluate the approaches in FRW-2unify and FRW-mixed for handling multiple dielectrics. We run the both for 3000 times for each case and use the mean value as the capacitance value extracted. For Case 1 and

Case 2, the both methods produce negligible error, i.e. 0.03%. For Case 3, we plot the distributions of C_{tot} in Fig. 8. From it, we see that they both approximate the normal distribution, with Std about 0.5% of the means value as prescribed. The relative errors of FRW-2unify and FRW-mixed are 0.01% and −13.13%, respectively. This reveals a significant error caused by the mixed method, which includes the dielectric homogenization procedure.

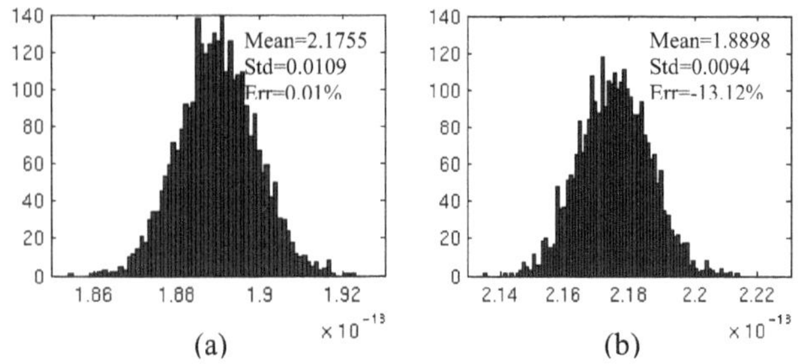

Fig. 8. Distribution of C_{self} calculated with (a) FRW-2unify and (b) FRW-mixed running 3000 times, respectively.

The runtime (for single run) and memory usage of the three FRW programs are listed in Table 3. From it, we see that FRW-2unify has almost the same runtime as FRW-2, which is shorter than FRW-mixed for Case 1 and 2. For Case 3, FRW-mixed is the fastest, because the dielectric homogenization takes effect for the case with more dielectric layers. However, FRW-mixed consumes over 10X more memory, and has significant error as shown in Fig. 8. The pre-calculated data sizes of FRW-2uinify and FRW-mixed are about 177MB and 415MB, respectively. Obviously, FRW-2unify is superior to FRW-mixed, and more adaptable to the technology change in touchscreen design problems than FRW-2.

Table 3. The CPU time and memory usage of FRW-2, FRW-2unify and FRW-mixed (Memory in unit of MB).

	FRW-2		FRW-2unify		FRW-mixed	
Case	Time (s)	Mem.	Time (s)	Mem.	Time (s)	Mem.
1	2.3	9.6	2.4	12.4	2.8	250.9
2	538.9	5.7	530.2	11.2	629.0	249.6
3	221.5	21.0	227.1	34.7	40.3	273.2

4.2 Performance of Parallel Computing

To obtain more accurate coupling capacitances, the FRW-2unify is run with 0.1% 1–σ error criterion on the self-capacitance. The parallel speedup for the three cases is shown in Fig. 9, with different number of processes. Because of the divergence among random walks, and the communication and synchronization costs among different computing nodes, the speedup cannot reach the ideal situation. With 120 processes, the runtime for simulating Case 3 is reduced from 7452 seconds in serial computing to 111 seconds. This means a 67× speedup.

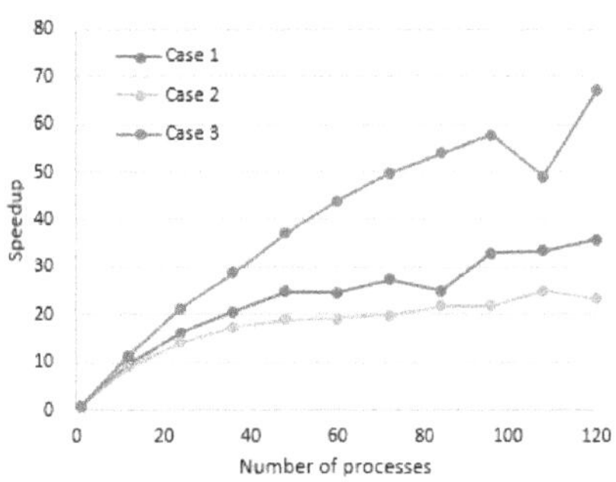

Fig. 9. The parallel speedup vs. the number of processes.

5. CONCLUSIONS

A floating random walk based solver (i.e. FRW-2unify) is presented for the capacitance-calculating problem in touchscreen design. It includes the technique handling non-Manhattan geometries and a unified and accurate dielectric pre-characterization scheme. Experiments validate their effectiveness and advantages, and show the speedup brought by parallel computing on a large computer cluster as well.

6. ACKNOWLEDGMENTS

This work is supported by National Natural Science Foundation of China under Grant No. 61422402.

7. REFERENCES

[1] Park H., Kim S., Kim S., Jo Y., Kim S. and McCartney R. I. 2008. Electrical models of TFT-LCD panels for circuit simulations. *Journal of the Society for Information Display*, 16 (2008), 509-515.

[2] Son Y. S. and Cho G. H. 2008. Design considerations of channel buffer amplifiers for low-power area-efficient column drivers in active-matrix LCDs. *IEEE Trans. Consumer Electronics*, 54 (Feb. 2008), 648-656.

[3] Takagi M., Yamaguchi K., Chida H. et. al. 2012. Layout and reticle verification for FPD. In *Proc. SPIE* 84410M (2012), 1-4.

[4] Uchida Y., Tani S., Hashimoto M., et. al 2005. Interconnect capacitance extraction for system LCD circuits. In *Proc. the 15th ACM Great Lakes Symposium on VLSI (GLSVLSI)*, (2005). 160-164.

[5] Egan J. 2014. Resistive vs. Capacitive Touchscreens. Available: http://blog.junipersys.com/resistive-vs-capacitive-touchscreens/

[6] Synopsys Inc.. Raphael: 2D, 3D resistance, capacitance and inductance extraction tool. Available: http://www.synopsys.com/Tools/TCAD/InterconnectSimulation/Pages/Raphael.aspx

[7] Nabors K. and White J. 1991. FastCap: A multipole accelerated 3-D capacitance extraction program. *IEEE Trans. Computer-Aided Design*, 10 (Nov. 1991), 1447–1459.

[8] Yu W. and Wang Z. 2004. Enhanced QMM-BEM solver for three-dimensional multiple-dielectric capacitance extraction within the finite domain. *IEEE Trans. Microwave Theory Tech.*, 52 (Feb. 2004), 560–566.

[9] Le Coz Y. and Iverson R. B. 1992. A stochastic algorithm for high speed capacitance extraction in integrated circuits. *Solid-State Electronics*, 35 (Jul. 1992), 1005–1012.

[10] Yu W., Zhuang H., Zhang C., Hu G. and Liu Z. 2013. RWCap: A floating random walk solver for 3-D capacitance extraction of very-large-scale integration interconnects. *IEEE Trans. Computer-Aided Design*, 32 (Mar. 2013), 353–366. Available: http://learn.tsinghua.edu.cn:8080/2003990088/rwcap.htm

[11] Rollins G. 2010, Rapid3D 20X performance improvement. Available: http://www.synopsys.com/Community/UniversityProgram/Pages/Presentations.aspx

[12] Zhang C. and Yu W. 2013. Efficient space management techniques for largescale interconnect capacitance extraction with floating random walks. *IEEE Trans. Computer-Aided Design*, 32 (Oct. 2013), 1633–1637.

[13] Zhang C., Yu W., Wang Q. and Shi Y. 2015. Fast random walk based capacitance extraction for the 3-D IC structures with cylindrical inter-tier-vias. *IEEE Trans. Computer-Aided Design*, 34(Dec. 2015), 1977-1990.

[14] Zhang B., Yu W. and Zhang C. 2015. Improved pre-characterization method for the random walk based capacitance extraction of multi-dielectric VLSI interconnects. *International Journal of Numerical Modelling: Electronic Networks, Devices and Fields*, DOI: 10.1002/jnm.20

Real-Time Hardware Stereo Matching Using Guided Image Filter

Chen Yang, Yan Li, Wei Zhong, Song Chen
University of Science and Technology of China
cyang906@mail.ustc.edu.cn, songch@ustc.edu.cn

ABSTRACT

Stereo matching is a key step in stereo vision systems that require high accurate depth information and real-time processing of high definition image streams. This work presents a high-accuracy hardware implementation for the stereo matching based on the guided image filter, which is an edge-preserving filter and simplifies the adaptive support window algorithm. The coefficients in the guided image filter are calculated by the proposed mean filter tree structure, which saves hardware resources by sharing large amounts of additions among filter operations. The reference image is enhanced using Laplacian Filter, which improves the accuracy for the discontinuous disparity regions. Moreover, an 8×8 matching window and customized ping-pong caches are used to improve the whole throughputs. The proposed hardware architecture is implemented on a Cyclone IV FPGA resulting in a throughput of 1080p resolution images at 80fps with high accuracy of disparity.

Keywords

stereo matching; guided image filter; mean filter tree;

1. INTRODUCTION

Stereo matching is widely adopted in a great amount of embedded vision systems, e.g., automatic navigation of robots, where real-time processing and high accurate depth information are required.

Stereo matching infers the depth of scene from a pair of images with large overlapping and is generally solved in four stages [1]: 1) pixel-wise matching cost computation, 2) cost aggregation, 3) disparity computation, and 4) disparity refinement. Moreover, stereo matching can be done globally or locally according to the method used in the cost aggregation (stage 2).

Global matching algorithms typically use graph cuts, dynamic programming and belief propagation based approximate methods for optimizing Markov random field based energy functions, which are in general NP-hard. Global algorithms produce high accurate disparity information, but it is hardware-unfriendly due to huge memory consuming, and large volumes of irregular data accessing. The semi-global matching method minimizes the energy function using a dynamic programming based method to aggregate costs along multiple paths in different directions. However, the result depends on the number of aggregation paths, which directly determine the hardware complexity [2]. It is still unaffordable for resource-limit high-speed system, especially, with the increasing image resolution.

GLSVLSI '16, May 18-20, 2016, Boston, MA, USA
© 2016 ACM. ISBN 978-1-4503-4274-2/16/05...$15.00
DOI: http://dx.doi.org/10.1145/2902961.2902995

Local matching algorithms aggregate cost over a single or multiple small size windows rather than full image, and, generally lead to low accuracy, especially, in low-texture, repetitive texture, occluded regions, or discontinuous disparity regions. But they are easy to be implemented on hardware [3-5] with high parallelism to realize high frame rate image processing. The adaptive support window (ADSW) algorithm becomes a milestone in local algorithms. The algorithm assigns weights to costs over a fixed window according to the distance/intensity differences between the central pixel and surrounding pixels in the reference image, and shows excellent performance competitive with global algorithms, especially in discontinuous disparity regions. However, the calculation of pixel weights includes large amounts of exponential operations, which requires complicated arithmetic architecture, control signals and massive memory resources. Some dedicated hardware implementations have been proposed for accelerating the computations. However, some modification and simplification have been made compared with the original algorithm and lead to a reduction of the disparity quality.

Hosni et al proposed a guided image filter (GIF), where the reference image is used to guide the space of cost volume and greatly reduces the complexity of the cost aggregation in the ADSW algorithm by avoiding exponential operations. The GIF is also implemented in Hardware [6]. But, the mean value of two coefficients in GIF is calculated over horizontal direction and the reference image is not enhanced by high pass filter. Moreover the throughputs of whole system can be improved.

Consequently, this paper proposes a hardware implementation of stereo matching based on the guided image filter and our contributions are as follows.

1) Processing 1920x1080 image streams at 80fps thanks to the customized ping-pong cache and the 8x8 matching window.

2) Laplacian filter is used to enhance the edge information of the reference image, which is used as the guided image and improves the accuracy in discontinuous disparity region.

3) Memory free mean filter tree is used to calculate more accurate coefficients of the GIF, which result in better disparity.

In the remainder of this paper, Section 2 provides basic flow of the GIF-based algorithm and Section 3 presents the proposed hardware. Section 4 gives the experimental results. Finally, Section 5 concludes the paper.

2. THE GIF-based ALGORITHM

The GIF-based algorithm is followed by the four stages above and roughly divided into three parts: pre-processing, initial map generating and post-processing. The remains of this part will discuss flows in detail.

2.1 Pre-processing

In the pre-processing stage, the input RGB image stream is transformed into 8-bit intensity image stream for the following processing. Then, a Gaussian Filter (GF) is used for denoising as the Gaussian noise is widely existed in the image acquisition process, and a Laplacian Filter (LF) is used for edge enhancement.

2.2 Initial map generating

2.2.1 Pixel-wise matching cost computation

In this paper, a truncated absolute difference of intensity and divergence of gradient are used as an operator. Due to epipolar constraint and pre-rectified assumption, the search direction is horizontal along the scan-line.

Let C(x,y,d) be the cost of matching two pixels, (x, y) in the reference image and $(x \pm d, y)$ in the target image. The C(p,d) (= C(x,y,d)) is calculated as follows.

$$C(p,d) = \alpha \cdot \min(|I_{left}(p) - I_{right}(p-d)|, Ti) + \beta \cdot \min(|\nabla^2 I_{left}(p) - \nabla^2 I_{right}(p-d)|, Tg), \quad (1)$$

where α, β is used to control the weight of two terms. Ti and Tg are truncated threshold. Given d_{max}, all possible C(x,y,d) form a space of cost volume (SCV), where each *d* corresponds to a slice.

2.2.2 Cost aggregation

In GIF, the costs values over a fixed window with radius r, centered at p, are fitted into a linear function of intensities in the reference image, defined as follows:

$$q'(p', d) = a_{(p,d)} I_{ref}(p') + b_{(p,d)} \quad (p' \in w_r), \quad (3)$$

where w_r is the window with radius r, centered at p. $I_{ref}(p')$ is the intensity in w_r. And $a_{(p,d)}$ and $b_{(p,d)}$ corresponding to p is calculated using the least square method:

$$a_{p,d} = \frac{\overline{I_g(p,r) \cdot I_f(p,r)} - \overline{I_g(p,r)} \cdot \overline{I_f(p,r)}}{\overline{I_g(p,r)^2} - \overline{I_g(p,r)}^2},$$

$$b_{p,d} = \overline{I_f(p,r)} - a_{p,d} \overline{I_g(p,r)} \quad (4)$$

Where $I_g(p,r)$ is the set of intensities within a fixed window with radius r, centered at *p* in the reference image, and $I_f(p,r)$ is the costs within a fixed window with radius r, centered at *p* in the slice corresponding *d.* Considering a given *p* can be covered by at most $(2r+1)^2$ fixed windows, the aggregated cost over a fixed window w_r with radius r, centered at *p,* is calculated as follows.

$$q(p,d) = \frac{1}{(2r+1)^2} \left(\sum_{p' \in w_r} (a_{(p',d)} I_{ref}(p) + b_{(p',d)}) \right)$$

$$= \overline{a_{(p,d)}}\, I_{ref}(p) + \overline{b_{(p,d)}} \quad (5)$$

where w_r is the window with radius r, centered at *p*.

2.2.3 Disparity computation

The Winner-Take-All (WTA) strategy is applied as following:

$$q(p, d_p) = \min_{0 \le d \le d_{max}} q(p,d) \quad (6)$$

2.3 Post-processing

The reliability threshold is firstly used to reduce the error disparity in weak texture regions. Let d_p' is the disparity that make q(p, d_p') be the second minimum of q(p, d), $0 \le d \le d_{max}$.

$$d_p = \begin{cases} 0, & \text{condition1} \\ d_p, & \text{otherwise} \end{cases} \quad (7)$$

Condition 1 is as follows:

$|dp - dp'| > 2 \&\& ((q(p,d_p) \cdot c1 > q(p,dp') \cdot c2) \| (q(p,d_p) + c3 > q(p,dp')))$. The c1, c2, and c3 are 386, 256, and 16 respectively, which are empirical values. Secondly, the gray saturated filter is used to smooth disparity map:

$$d_p = \begin{cases} 0 & I_{ref}(p) > 250 \text{ or } I_{ref} < 5 \\ d_p & \text{otherwise} \end{cases} \quad (8)$$

Thirdly, the disparities, which are set to zero above, are interpolated. Then the L-R check and mean filtering are applied.

3. THE PROPOSED HARDWARE

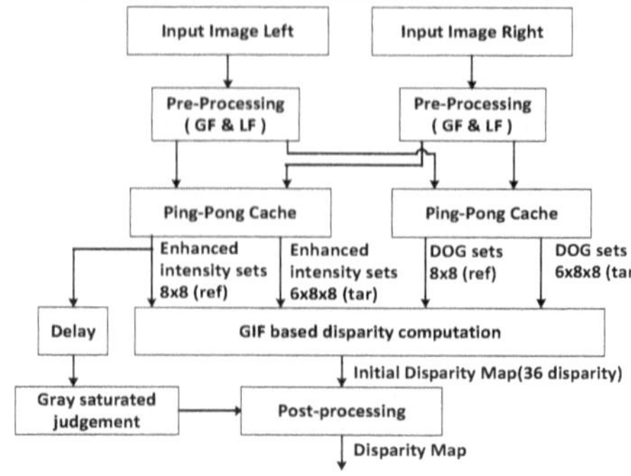

Figure 1. Brief architecture of proposed hardware

The architecture is shown in Figure 1. Firstly, the image streams are sent into the pre-processing unit. Secondly, the enhanced intensities and the divergence of gradient (DOG) are both read into two customized ping-pong caches. Thirdly, 36 initial disparities are generated every 8 cycles by the GIF based disparity computation unit. Finally, post-processing unit refines the initial disparity map using several filters, pixel interpolation and L-R check.

3.1 Pre-processing unit

The architecture of the pre-processing unit is shown in Figure 2. The GF performs convolution over 3x3 window (fetched from the Liner Buffer, where N=1920), in the component CONV. As the sum of the coefficients in the Gaussian kernel is 16, a shifter (shifting right for 4) is used instead of a divider for normalizing the convolution result. The LF is used to calculate the DOG and the enhanced intensity. It consists of one normalizer, which keeps the enhanced value in the range [0,255], 4 adders, 1 subtractor and 1 shifter. The difference between two kernels is only center coefficient. So the intermediate value can be reused.

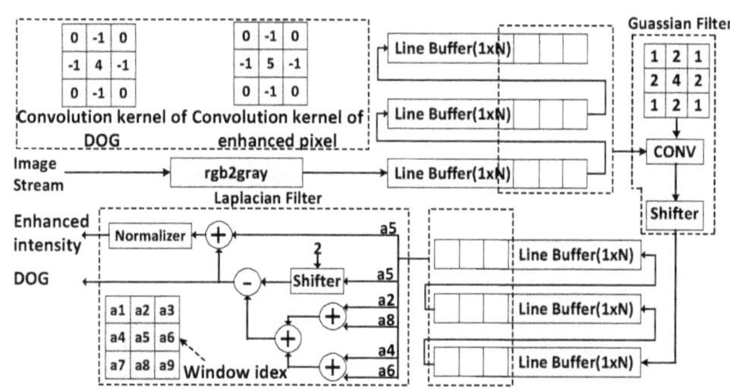

Figure 2. The architecture of pre-processing unit

3.2 Ping-pong cache

Two ping-pong caches, shown in figure 3, are respectively used to buffer the enhanced intensity and DOG to improve the throughputs. The data should be buffered 8xN row (where N=1920) for the 8x8 matching window. The reference/target cache consists of two groups, which have mutually exclusive working manner, that is, one group works for matching and the other group prepares data for next 8xN rows concurrently.

The reference cache is shown in Figure 3(a). Due to the aggregation costs computed over 3x3 window, only 36 pixels are handled in an 8x8 window. Every adjacent matching blocks on the 8xN rows has 2 overlapped columns, so the initial column for every matching block is 6i (i =0, 1, 2 ...319), assuming that the index of column is from 0. Each group contains two 8xN line buffers which contain same content. However for the sake of the pipeline architecture, they do not work concurrently. For example, when the 8x8 matching block in upper line buffer with initial column 0 is computing disparity, the lower line buffer must shift right to prepare the next matching block. The target cache is shown in Figure 3(b). Due to the limitation of hardware resource, the disparity range is divided into 8 sets and 6 disparities are done in one cycle. For a certain working group, the working line buffer must shift to get 6 matching blocks belonging to new disparity in one cycle. The value of parameter i is looping between 0 to 7 and the value increase 1 in the new cycle. Meanwhile, another line buffer shifts to prepare data for the next 8x8 matching block. Mux1/Mux array1 or Mux2/Mux array2 chooses the line buffer for matching and Mux3/Mux array3 selects the group for matching. Every Mux array consists of six multiplexers. Demux chooses the group for preparing. The cycle for computing a whole 8xN row needs (N/6) x 8 cycles, while the cycle for preparing data is 8N. It means that the data preparing must be 6 times faster than the processing.

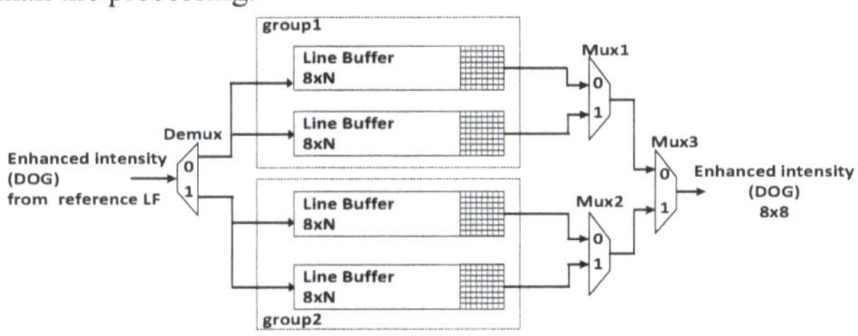

(a) The reference cache

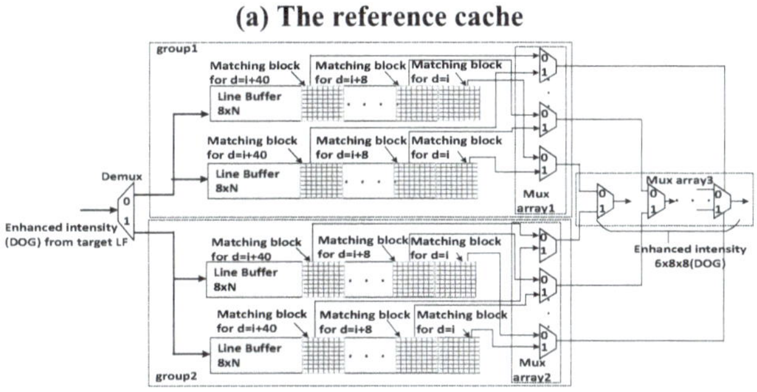

(b) The target cache

Figure 3. The architecture of ping-pong cache

3.3 GIF based disparity computation unit

The GIF based disparity computation unit, shown in Figure 4, includes 6 Cost Computation Units, 6 GIF Filter Units, 6 WTA Units, and 1 Delay Unit. These hardware units are fully pipelined. 36 disparities are calculated every 8 clock cycle.

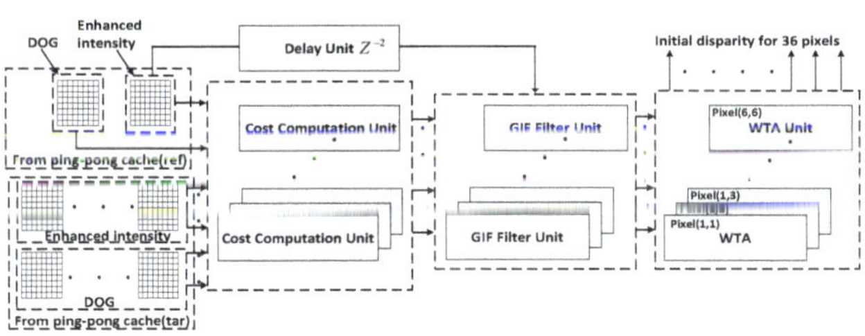

Figure 4. GIF based disparity computation unit

3.3.1 Cost computation unit

The cost computation unit (CCU) is illustrated in Figure 5(b). It consists of 64 pixel-wise cost computation unit (PWCCU) shown in Figure 5(a). The function of PWCCU is to calculate the cost value for a certain d of one pixel using Formula (1). The PWCCU unit includes two absolute difference units, two comparators, two shifters and one adder. For reducing the complexity of calculation, the shifter replaces the multiplier as $\{\alpha,\beta\}=\{1,8\}$. The architecture of PWCCU adopts two-stage pipeline. To synchronize the GIF unit, the 8x8 enhanced intensities of reference image are store in Delay Unit with 2x8x8 byte. The disparities 0, 8, ..., 40 are processed in one cycle. With shifting of the target cache, 6 matching block for next 6 disparities 1,9, ..., 41 that are processed in next cycle can be fetched.

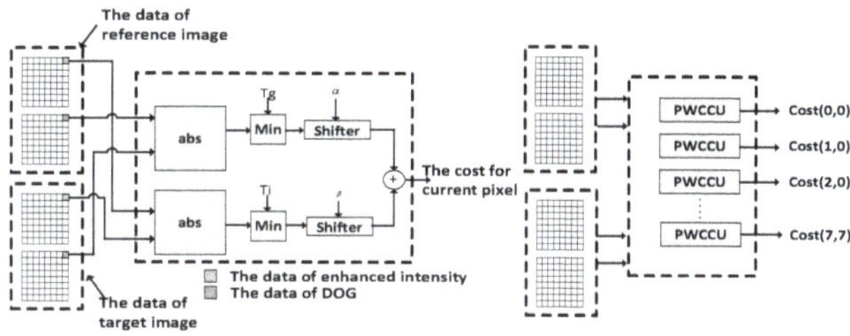

(a)Pixel-wise cost computation unit (b) Cost computation unit

Figure 5. The architecture of cost computation unit

3.3.2 GIF filter unit for cost aggregation

The GIF Filter Unit, shown in Figure 6, includes 4 mean filter tree for cost aggregation (MFTCA), 2 mean filter tree for coefficient (MFTC), arithmetic processing units, 36 shifters, and 36 approximators. The 4 MFTCAs compute $\overline{I_g(p,r)\cdot I_f(p,r)}$, $\overline{I_g(p,r)}$,$\overline{I_f(p,r)}$ and $\overline{I_g^{\,2}(p,r)}$ corresponding to 36 $c_{p,d}$. The results of $\overline{I_g(p,r)^2}-\overline{I_g(p,r)}^2$ are approximated by the power of 2 using the approximators. Two MFTCs are respectively used to calculate $\overline{a_{(p,d)}}$ and $\overline{b_{(p,d)}}$ corresponding to 36 $c_{p,d}$.

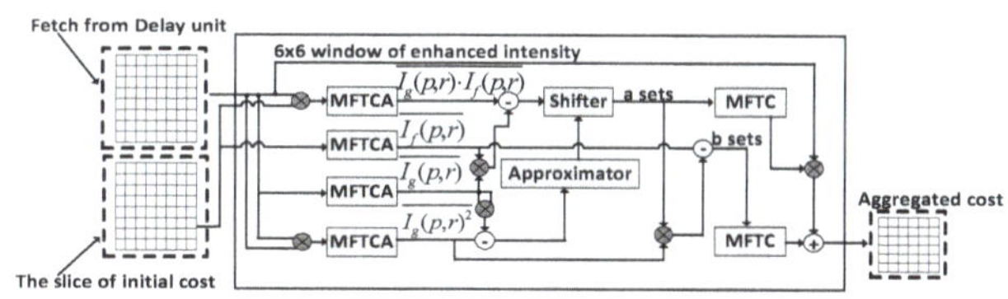

Figure 6. The architecture of GIF filter unit

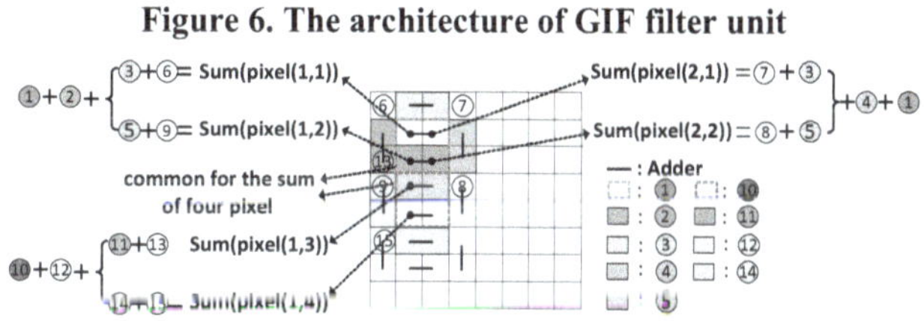

(a) The sharing relationship in MTFCA

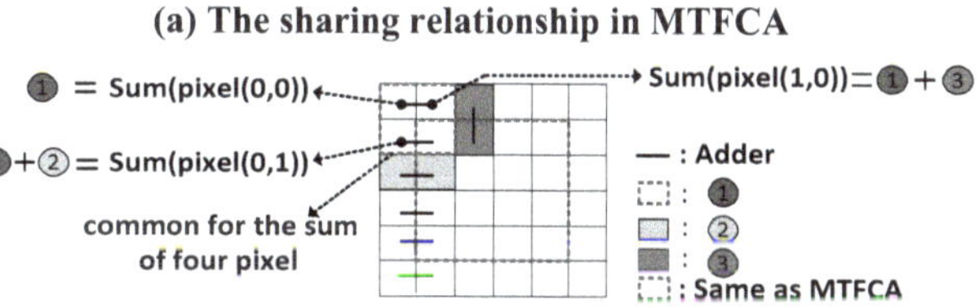

(b) The sharing relationship in MTFC

Figure 7. The relationship of mean filter tree

The proposed mean filter has high throughputs and less memory-consuming compared with Ttofis [6]. [6] uses a customized mean filter similar to boxing filtering technique. And memory is used to store the sum for each column. In this work, as 8x8 matching window are used, the intermediate result can be shared directly without storing these values in memory. And the sharing tree architecture similar to [7] is used to calculate the mean operation in GIF. As shown in Figure 7(a), window sum of pixel (1, 1) and window sum of pixel (2, 1) differ from each other for only three pixels, so do the window sum of pixel (1, 1) and pixel (1, 2) and the rest of pixels. The common part of different sums can be calculated only once and shared. Considering the MTFC shown in Figure 7(b), the sharing relationship in the inner 4x4 window is same as the MTFCA. However, the coefficients on the outmost window boundaries also have to be calculated. As a sequence, the 2x2 window or the 2x3 window are used for the boundary coefficients. The hardware architecture of MFTCA consists of adders and fix-point multipliers. There are 392 additions in an 8x8 window in normal situation. However, 139 additions are in the proposed MFTCA. The hardware of MFTC is similar to MFTCA. The 108 additions exist in the proposed architecture.

3.3.3 *Disparity computation and post-processing*

WTA is composed of a parity exchange network to get d_p for minimum aggregated cost and d_p' for the second-minimum aggregated cost in every 8 cycles. Then d_p and d_p' are sent to the module of reliability threshold. The module of gray saturated judgment is used to generate a set of mux control signals, which determine whether the disparity for a pixel is set to zero. Then, the zero disparities are interpolated. Meanwhile L-R check and mean filtering over 3x3 windows are done sequentially.

4. EXPERIMENTAL RESULTS

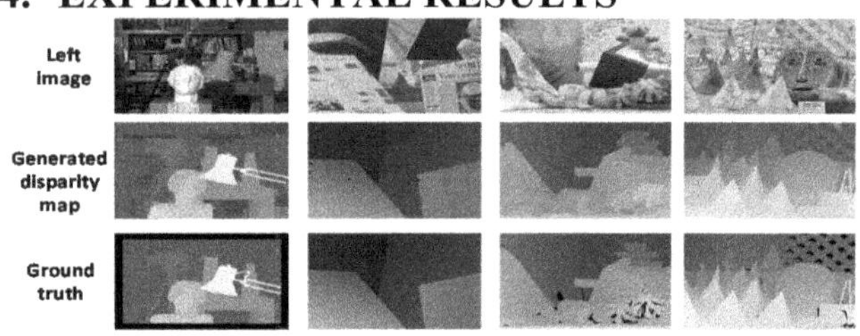

Figure 8. Evaluation results on Middlebury benchmark

The proposed architecture is implemented in Verilog HDL and simulated by Modelsim-Altera 10.1d. The RTL code is synthesized with Quartus II 13.0SP1 on device EP4C115F29C7, and the maximum allowed frequency is 108.5 MHz after place-and-route. The Middlebury benchmark datasets [1] including "Tsukuba", "Venus", "Teddy", "Cones" are used to evaluate the accuracy. For the parameters $\{\alpha, \beta, Ti, Tg\}$, in Formula (1) are set at {1, 8, 15, 7}. The evaluation results are shown in Figure 8.

Table 1 lists the quality and the throughputs for proposed hardware. Considering the accuracies in 2-9 columns, the proposed architecture shows the best average error rates, especially in disc condition. The proposed hardware shows the competitive results with the best ones in nonocc condition. The accuracies is higher than [6], because more accurate coefficients and the enhanced edge information in the reference image could improve the accuracy. Considering the throughputs, MDES (millions of disparities estimated/second, a widely-used index) of the proposed architecture is the highest, 7962M. And the system can process a pair of 1080p images at the frame rate of 108.5Mhz/(1920/6) *8*(1080/6) = 235 fps if the speed of original image stream is 6 times faster than the clock frequency of whole system, which means the frequency of external image stream is nearly 651Mhz when the stereo matching hardware works at the highest frequency. However, the external data stream cannot satisfy the speed sometimes. In our experiments, the frequency of external image streams is set at 250 Mhz, so the system throughputs is 80fps. The resource utilization is as follows: 91.6% logic elements, 81.4% registers, and 100% 9-bit embedded multiplier elements.

5. CONCLUSION

This work presented a high-accuracy hardware implementation for the GIF based stereo matching. The coefficients in the guided image filter were calculated by the proposed mean filter tree structure. Laplacian Filter was used to enhance the reference image for improving the accuracy of discontinuous disparity regions. Moreover, 8×8 matching window and customized ping-pong caches are used to improve the whole throughputs. The proposed hardware architecture is implemented on a Cyclone IV FPGA resulting in a throughput of 1080p resolution images at 80fps with improved disparity accuracy.

6. ACKNOWLEDGMENTS

This work was partially supported by the National Natural Science Foundation of China (NSFC) under grant No.61404123and Anhui Provincial Natural Science Foundation (1508085MF134, China). The authors would like to thank Information Science Laboratory Center of USTC for the hardware & software services.

Reference

[1] D. Scharstein, & R. Szeliski, (2002). A taxonomy and evaluation of dense two-frame stereo correspondence algorithms. *International journal of computer vision*, 47(1-3), 7-42.

[2] W. Wang, J. Yan, N. Xu, Y. Wang, & F. H. Hsu (2015). Real-time high-quality stereo vision system in FPGA. *IEEE Trans. on Circuits and Systems for Video Technology*, 25(10), 1696-1708.

[3] S. Perri, P. Corsonello, & G. Cocorullo, (2013). Adaptive Census Transform: A novel hardware-oriented stereo vision algorithm. *Computer Vision and Image Understanding*, 117(1), 29-41.

[4] Jin, S., Cho, J., Pham, X. D., Lee, K. M., Park, S. K., Kim, M., & Jeon, J. W. (2010). FPGA design and implementation of a real-time stereo vision system. *IEEE Trans. on Circuits and Systems for Video Technology*, 20(1), 15-26.

[5] Zhang, L., Zhang, K., Chang, T. S., Lafruit, G., Kuzmanov, G. K., & Verkest, D. (2011, February). Real-time high-definition stereo matching on FPGA. In *Proc. of the 19th ACM/SIGDA International symposium on FPGA*, (pp. 55-64). ACM.

[6] Ttofis, C., & Theocharides, T. (2014, March). High-quality real-time hardware stereo matching based on guided image filtering. In *Design, Automation and Test in Europe Conference and Exhibition (DATE)*, 2014 (pp. 1-6). IEEE.

[7] S. Perri, D. Colonna, P. Zicari, & P. Corsonello, (2006). SAD-based stereo matching circuit for FPGAs. In *IEEE International Conference on Electronics, Circuits and Systems.*

Table 1. Quality and throughputs comparison (error rate of non-occluded pixels at error threshold=1.0)

Work	Tsukuba	Venus	Teddy	Cones	Average Error Rates				Image Size	Speed (fps)	Disparity	MDE/s (10^6)	Platform
	Nonocc				nonocc	all	disc	Overall					
Perri[3]	5.92	1.17	5.5	5	4.39	10.1	19.6	11.4	640x480	45	60	829	FPGA
Jin[4]	9.79	3.59	12.5	7.34	8.31	14.0	27.1	16.5	640x480	230	64	4522	FPGA
Zhang[5]	3.84	1.20	7.17	5.41	4.41	7.41	12.8	8.2	1024x768	60	64	3019	FPGA
Ttofis[6]	4.04	1.55	7.52	2.77	3.97	6.80	9.30	6.69	1280x720	60	64	3538	FPGA
proposed	3.65	1.43	7.21	2.32	3.65	6.56	9.08	6.43	1920x1080	80	48	7962	FPGA

Computing Complex Functions using Factorization in Unipolar Stochastic Logic

Yin Liu and Keshab K. Parhi
University of Minnesota, Twin Cities
200 Union Street SE, Minneapolis, MN, 55455
Email: {liux1394, parhi}@umn.edu

ABSTRACT

This paper addresses computing complex functions using unipolar stochastic logic. Stochastic computing requires simple logic gates and is inherently fault-tolerant. Thus, these structures are well suited for nanoscale CMOS technologies. Implementations of complex functions cost extremely low hardware complexity compared to traditional two's complement implementation. In this paper an approach based on polynomial factorization is proposed to compute functions in unipolar stochastic logic. In this approach, functions are expressed using polynomials, which are derived from Taylor expansion or Lagrange interpolation. Polynomials are implemented in stochastic logic by using *factorization*. Experimental results in terms of accuracy and hardware complexity are presented to compare the proposed designs of complex functions with previous implementations using Bernstein polynomials.

Categories and Subject Descriptors

B.2 [**Arithmetic and logic structures**]; B.4.5 [**Reliability, Testing, and Fault-Tolerance**]; B.6 [**Logic design**]

Keywords

Stochastic logic, unipolar representation, stochastic subtraction, stochastic division, complex functions, polynomial factorization.

1. INTRODUCTION

Stochastic computing (SC), first proposed in 1960s [1], has recently regained significant attention due to its fault-tolerance and extremely low-cost of arithmetic units [2]. Despite these advantages, stochastic circuits suffer from long processing latency and degradation of accuracy. Stochastic computing has been exploited in the fields of neural networks, control, image processing, data mining and error control coding applications. SC has also been applied to the design of digital FIR filter, IIR filter and Gabor filter.

GLSVLSI '16, May 18-20, 2016, Boston, MA, USA
© 2016 ACM. ISBN 978-1-4503-4274-2/16/05...$15.00
DOI: http://dx.doi.org/10.1145/2902961.2902999

One advantage of stochastic computing is that complex computations on stochastic bit streams can be realized using extremely low-cost designs. It has been illustrated in [3] that complex functions can be approximated in stochastic logic by using Bernstein polynomials. However, for some functions, high-degree Bernstein polynomials are required for a precise approximation, and this requires higher hardware complexity. Recently, a linear transformation method has been proposed to reduce computational error of complex function implementation using Bernstein polynomials [4].

This paper makes two main contributions towards stochastic implementations of arithmetic functions using the unipolar representation. First, an approach to implementing unipolar subtractor based on stochastic division is presented. An accurate implementation of subtraction is required for computing arithmetic functions in unipolar stochastic logic. Second, we propose a method based on polynomial factorization to compute complex functions, such as trigonometric, exponential and logarithmic functions. In this method, complex functions are first described with polynomials by using Taylor expansion or Lagrange interpolation.

This paper is organized as follows. In Section II the stochastic implementation of subtraction based on stochastic division is proposed. Section III presents implementations of complex functions using polynomial factorization. Simulation and synthesis results are described in Section IV. Finally, some conclusions are given in Section V.

2. SUBTRACTION USING STOCHASTIC LOGIC

In this section, we describe the approach to subtraction in unipolar logic based on stochastic division. The stochastic division is implemented using a counter and an LFSR as shown in Fig. 1. Details of stochastic unipolar division can be found in Section 4 of [1].

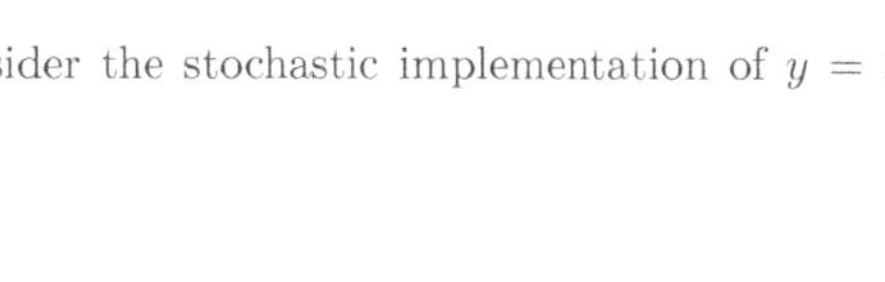

Figure 1: Stochastic divider in unipolar format where $p_1 < p_2$.

Consider the stochastic implementation of $y = x_1 - x_2$,

where $0 < x_2 < x_1 < 1$. Fig. 2 shows the overall circuit diagram of subtraction using stochastic unipolar divider, which can be implemented using the divider proposed by Gaines [1]. The division module is used to generate the stochastic bit stream representing x_2/x_1. The final result is given by

$$y = x_1(1 - x_2/x_1) = x_1 - x_2, \tag{1}$$

which corresponds to the Boolean expression

$$y = x_1 \wedge (\overline{x_2/x_1}). \tag{2}$$

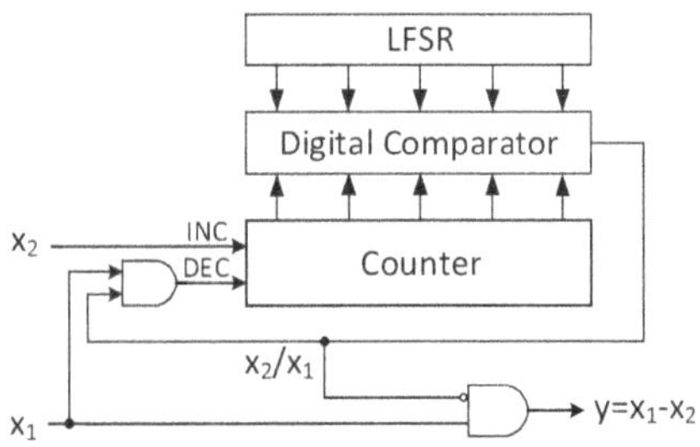

Figure 2: Stochastic subtractor after simplification.

3. COMPUTING COMPLEX FUNCTIONS

Stochastic implementations of complex functions are presented in this section. The general procedure of the implementation includes two steps. Consider an objective function $f(x)$. First, $f(x)$ is approximated using a polynomial with a finite order as follows:

$$f(x) \approx p(x) = a_0 + a_1 x + a_2 x^2 + \cdots + a_n x^n. \tag{3}$$

The polynomial is derived based on Lagrange interpolation or Taylor expansion. The method used to derive $p(x)$ is determined by the objective function. In the second step, the polynomial $p(x)$ is factorized as follows:

$$\begin{aligned} p(x) &= a_0 + a_1 x + a_2 x^2 + \cdots + a_n x^n \\ &= d \cdot \prod_{i=0}^{n_1} (1 - c_i x) \cdot \prod_{j=0}^{n_2} (1 - a_j x + b_j x^2), \end{aligned} \tag{4}$$

where d denotes the scaling of stochastic implementation. Since all coefficients are real, roots of $p(x) = 0$ are either real or complex conjugates. Therefore, $p(x)$ can be represented by a product of first-order and second-order factors. Assume that the number of first-order and second-order factors are n_1+1 and n_2+1, respectively. In stochastic unipolar representation, $p(x)$ can be implemented by multiplying all factors using AND gates. The approach to computing complex functions using unipolar stochastic logic is illustrated by four examples presented in [4].

3.1 Case-I: $0.5\sin(8x) + 0.5$

Consider the function $f_1(x) = 0.5\sin(8x) + 0.5$. The function can be described by a polynomial $p_1(x)$ derived by using Lagrange interpolation. Data points for polynomial interpolation include $(0, 0.5)$, $(\frac{\pi}{16}, 1)$, $(\frac{\pi}{8}, 0.5)$, $(\frac{3\pi}{16}, 0)$, $(\frac{\pi}{4}, 0.5)$ and $(\frac{5\pi}{16}, 1)$ as shown in Fig. 3. The Lagrange polynomial is given by:

$$\begin{aligned} p_1(x) = 0.5 &+ 4.7525x - 4.3153x^2 - 55.0652x^3 \\ &+ 112.1590x^4 - 57.1202x^5, \end{aligned} \tag{5}$$

which is also shown Fig. 3. Then $p_1(x)$ is factorized as follows:

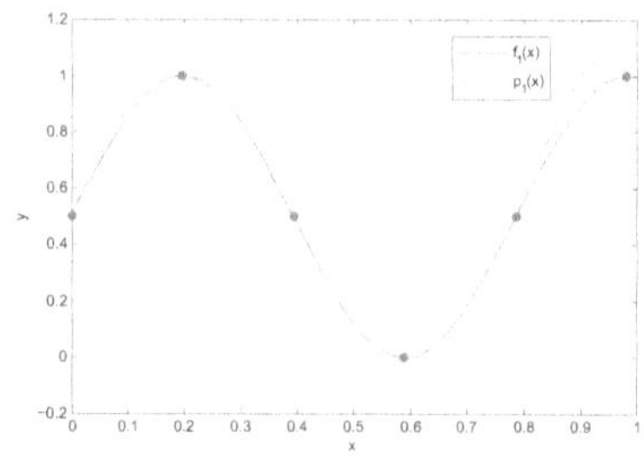

Figure 3: The $f_1(x)$ is described by Lagrange polynomial $p_1(x)$.

$$\begin{aligned} p_1(x) &= 0.5 \cdot (1 + 5.0978x)(1 + 8.6714x)(1 - 1.6981x) \\ &\quad (1 - 1.6357x)(1 - 0.9304x) \qquad (6) \\ &\approx 0.5 \cdot (1 + 5.0978x)(1 + 8.6714x)(1 - 1.6667x)^2 \\ &\quad (1 - 0.9304x) \qquad (7) \end{aligned}$$

Notice that from equation (6) to (7), $(1 - 1.6981x)(1 - 1.6357x)$ is approximated by $(1-1.6667x)^2$ since $(1-1.6981x)$ and $(1 - 1.6357x)$ can not be implemented using unipolar stochastic logic, where these two factors violate the required range of $[0, 1]$ for unipolar representation. The stochastic implementation of $f_1(x)$ using equation (7) is shown in Fig. 4. In this implementation, one-bit delay elements

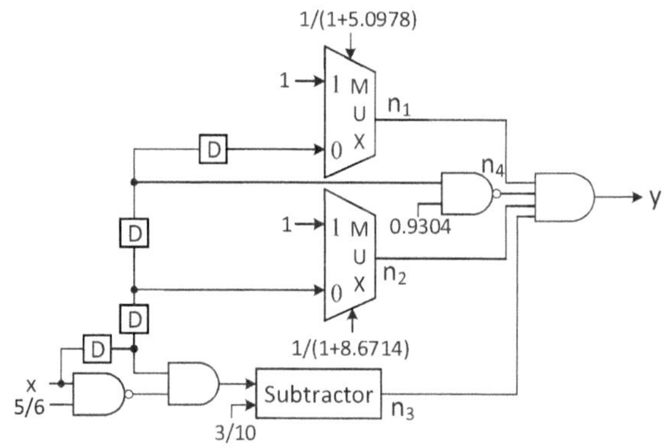

Figure 4: Stochastic implementation of $f_1(x)$.

are used to decorrelate input signals [1]. Scaled factors $(1 + 5.0978x)/6.0978$ and $(1 + 8.6714x)/9.6714$ are computed by n_1 and n_2 using multiplexers. Node n_3 computes $\frac{(1-1.6667x)^2}{10/3} = 3/10 - x(1 - 5x/6)$, where a subtractor based on stochastic division is required. The factor $(1 - 0.9304x)$ is computed by a NAND gate. The final result y is given by multiplying all factors using an AND gate, where y is scaled by:

$$\frac{1}{6.0978 \times 9.6714 \times (10/3) \times 0.5} = 0.0102 \tag{8}$$

3.2 Case-II: $1 - 4(x - 0.5)^2$

The second example is given by $f_2(x) = 1 - 4(x - 0.5)^2$. The function is expanded as follows:

$$f_2(x) = 1 - 4(x^2 - x + 0.25) = 4x(1 - x). \tag{9}$$

The stochastic implementation of $f_2(x)$ using unipolar representations is shown in Fig. 5. This implementation com-

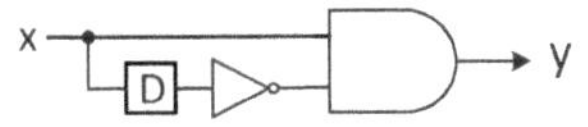

Figure 5: Stochastic implementation of $f_2(x)$.

putes scaled version of $f_2(x)$, where $y = f_2(x)/4 = x(1-x)$. The one-bit delay element is used for decorrelation.

3.3 Case-III: $4x^2\log(x+0.1)+0.53$

Consider the function $f_3(x) = 4x^2\log(x+0.1)+0.53$. The function is approximated by a polynomial $p_3(x)$ derived from Taylor expansion. The 5th-order Taylor polynomial expanded at $x = 0.5$ is given by:

$$\begin{aligned} p_3(x) &= 0.0192 - 0.3766(x-0.5) + 3.2345(x-0.5)^2 \\ &\quad + 2.6543(x-0.5)^3 - 1.3117(x-0.5)^4 \\ &\quad + 1.0288(x-0.5)^5 \\ &= 0.5701 - 0.6430x - 4.0006x^2 + 7.8498x^3 \\ &\quad - 3.8838x^4 + 1.0288x^5 \end{aligned} \tag{10}$$

The factorized $p_3(x)$ is described as follows:

$$\begin{aligned} p_3(x) &= 0.5701(1+3x)(1-0.5594x+0.1867x^2) \\ &\quad (1-3.5736x+3.2172x^2). \end{aligned} \tag{11}$$

Polynomial Roots are given by $r_1 = -0.3328$, $r_{2,3} = 1.4984 \pm 1.7640i$ and $r_{4,5} = 0.5554 \pm 0.0486i$. The stochastic implementation of $f_3(x)$ using equation (11) is shown in Fig. 6. In this implementation, $(1+3x)/4$ is computed at node n_1

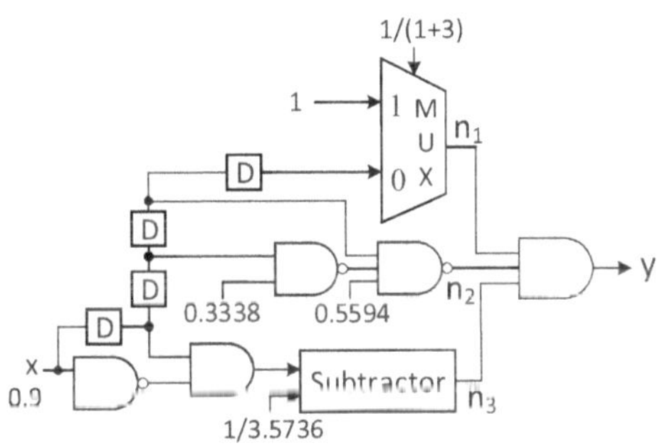

Figure 6: Stochastic implementation of $f_3(x)$.

using a multiplexer. The node n_2 computes $(1-0.5594x+0.1867x^2)$ as follows:

$$1 - 0.5594x + 0.1867x^2 = 1 - 0.5594x(1-0.3338x) \tag{12}$$

Scaled version of $(1-3.5736x+3.2172x^2)$ is computed at node n_3 as follows:

$$\frac{1}{3.5736}(1-3.5736x+3.2172x^2) = \frac{1}{3.5736} - x(1-0.9x). \tag{13}$$

The final result y is given by multiplying all factors using an AND gate, where y is scaled by

$$\frac{1}{4 \times 3.5736 \times 0.5701} = 0.1227. \tag{14}$$

3.4 Case-IV: $59.2x^4 - 118.7x^3 + 74.9x^2 - 15.4x + 1$

Consider the function $f_4(x) = 59.2x^4 - 118.7x^3 + 74.9x^2 - 15.4x + 1$. The function is factorized as follows:

$$f_4(x) = 59.2(x^2 - 0.3044x + 0.0233)(x^2 - 1.7x + 0.7236) \tag{15}$$

Fig. 7 shows the circuit diagram used for the implementation of second order factors in $f_4(x)$. The output of the module is given by $y = sx^2 + (1-s)(1-x^2) = x^2 - 2(1-s)x + (1-s)$. The stochastic implementation of $f_4(x)$ using the equation

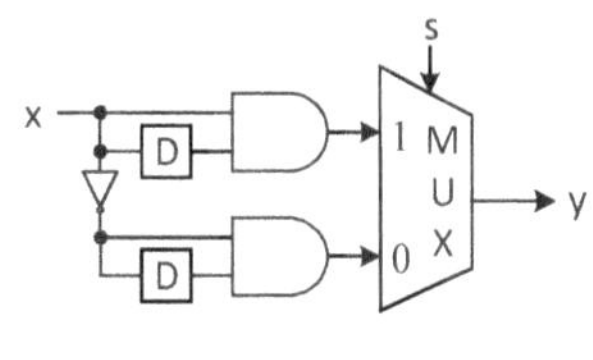

Figure 7: The module used to implement the second order factor in $f_4(x)$.

above is shown in Fig. 8. In this implementation, the factor

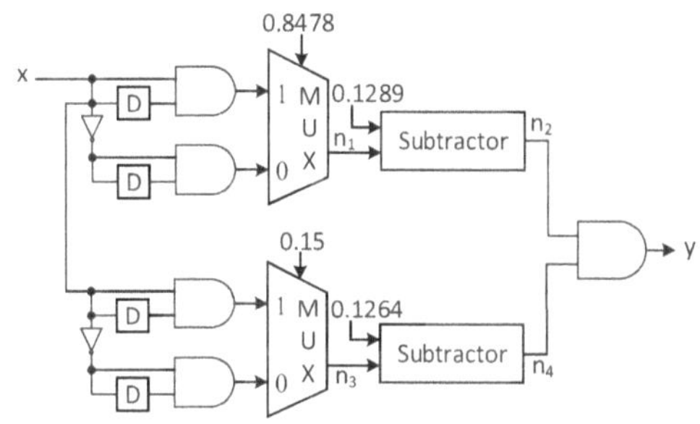

Figure 8: Stochastic implementation of $f_4(x)$.

$x^2 - 0.3044x + 0.0233$ is computed at node n_2 as follows:

$$\begin{aligned} n_2 &= n_1 - 0.1289 \\ &= [0.8478x^2 + (1-0.8478)(1-x^2)] - 0.1289 \\ &= (x^2 - 0.3044x + 0.1522) - 0.1289 \\ &= x^2 - 0.3044x + 0.0233 \end{aligned} \tag{16}$$

The factor $x^2 - 1.7x + 0.7236$ is computed at node n_4 as follows:

$$\begin{aligned} n_4 &= n_3 - 0.1264 \\ &= [0.15x^2 + (1-0.15)(1-x^2)] - 0.1264 \\ &= (x^2 - 1.7x + 0.85) - 0.1264 \\ &= x^2 - 1.7x + 0.7236 \end{aligned} \tag{17}$$

The final output is computed using an AND gate to perform the multiplication of n_2n_4. The computational result is scaled by $1/59.2$.

4. EXPERIMENTAL RESULTS

We performed experiments to test performance and generate synthesis results for proposed complex function computations using unipolar stochastic logic. Comparisons of accuracy and hardware complexity for proposed designs and implementations using Bernstein polynomials are presented.

Table 1: Functions used in our experiment.

Test1	$0.5\sin(8x) + 0.5$
Test2	$1 - 4(x - 0.5)^2$
Test3	$4x^2\log(x + 0.1) + 0.53$
Test4	$59.2x^4 - 118.7x^3 + 74.9x^2 - 15.4x + 1$

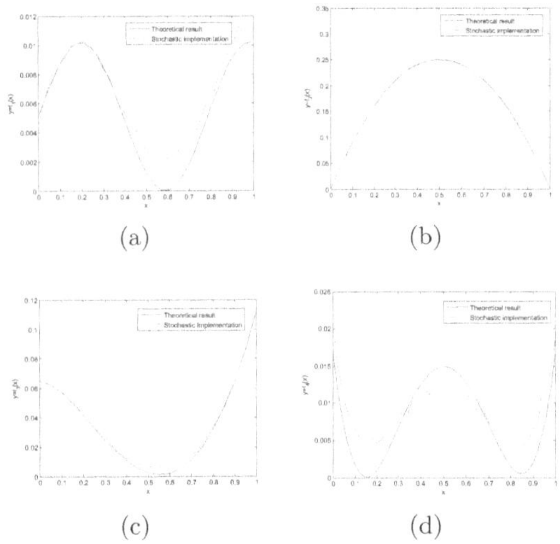

Figure 9: Simulation results for (a) $f_1'(x) = 0.0102 f_1(x) = 0.0102(0.5\sin(8x) + 0.5)$, (b) $f_2'(x) = f_2(x)/4 = (1 - 4(x - 0.5)^2)/4$, (c) $f_3'(x) = 0.1227 f_3(x) = 0.1227(4x^2\log(x+0.1) + 0.53)$ and (d) $f_4'(x) = f_4(x)/59.2 = (59.2x^4 - 118.7x^3 + 74.9x^2 - 15.4x + 1)/59.2$.

4.1 Accuracy

In our simulation, the length of the stochastic sequence is 1024. The proposed implementations of four functions in Section III are considered [4]. Four functions are listed in Table 1.

Fig. 9 shows simulation results of the proposed designs for four tests. Same as [4], input signal x is given by 0:0.01:1. 100 Monte Carlo runs were performed for each data point. Simulation results of the proposed implementations and previous designs using Bernstein polynomials are shown in Table 2. Compared to the Bernstein polynomial-I implementation [3], computational error of proposed design is reduced by more than 50%. For test1 and test4, the Bernstein implementation-II [4] outperforms the proposed design. For test2 and test3, better performance is obtained by the proposed design, compared to Bernstein implementation-II.

4.2 Hardware Complexity

The area consumption of stochastic implementations of complex functions are evaluated using 65nm technology. The architectures are synthesized using Synopsys Design Compiler. We also compare hardware complexity between proposed designs and implementations using Bernstein polynomials. In stochastic implementations, the length of stochastic sequences is 1024. Table 3 shows hardware complexity of the proposed designs and implementations using Bernstein polynomials.

Table 2: Mean error of the proposed designs and previous implementations using Bernstein polynomials.

	Test1	Test2	Test3	Test4
Proposed	0.0715	0.0022	0.0101	0.0759
Bernstein-I [3]	0.1539	0.0354	0.0251	0.1959
Bernstein-II [4]	0.0396	0.0128	0.0103	0.0422

Table 3: Hardware complexity (μm^2) of complex functions using the proposed implementations and Bernstein implementations.

		Test1	Test2	Test3	Test4
Proposed	Area	1635	204	1627	1746
Bernstein-I [3]	Degree	17	14	12	17
	Area	3164	2693	2370	3164
Bernstein-II [4]	Degree	6			
	Area	1655			

The implementation of Bernstein polynomial can be found in [3]. In our synthesis, all coefficients are represented using stochastic bit streams. The area results of Bernstein implementations from our synthesis are consistent with results given in [4] after the scaling of $(65nm/45nm)^2$. Synthesis results of the proposed designs include all SNGs required to generate input signals and coefficients. For the Bernstein polynomial implementation, input signals are generated from one SNG and one-bit delay elements are used for decorrelation.

The hardware complexity of Bernstein implementations is determined by degrees of Bernstein polynomials. From results listed in Table 3, we observe that for test1 and test3, hardware complexity of the proposed design is slightly reduced compared to the Bernstein implementation-II. Area consumption of the proposed design for test2 is 88% less than the Bernstein implementation-II since only one SNG is required to generate the input signal.

5. CONCLUSION

Stochastic logic based subtraction and complex function computation in unipolar format have been presented in this paper. A stochastic subtractor using unipolar division is described. The computation of complex functions based on polynomial factorization and stochastic subtractors is also considered. Future work will be directed towards generation of more accurate polynomials for different functions.

6. REFERENCES

[1] B. Gaines, "Stochastic computing systems," in *Advances in information systems science*, pp. 37–172, Springer, 1969.

[2] A. Alaghi and J. P. Hayes, "Survey of stochastic computing," *ACM Transactions on Embedded computing systems (TECS)*, vol. 12, no. 2s, p. 92, 2013.

[3] W. Qian, X. Li, M. D. Riedel, K. Bazargan, and D. J. Lilja, "An architecture for fault-tolerant computation with stochastic logic," *IEEE Transactions on Computers*, vol. 60, no. 1, pp. 93–105, 2011.

[4] Y. Wu, C. Wang, and W. Qian, "Minimizing error of stochastic computation through linear transformation," in *Proceedings of the 25th edition on Great Lakes Symposium on VLSI*, pp. 349–354, ACM, 2015.

DCC: Double Capacity Cache Architecture for Narrow-Width Values

Mohsen Imani, Shruti Patil, Tajana Rosing
CSE Department, University of California San Diego, La Jolla, CA 92093, USA
{moimani, patil, Tajana}@ucsd.edu

ABSTRACT

Modern caches are designed to hold 64-bits wide data, however a proportion of data in the caches continues to be narrow width. In this paper, we propose a new cache architecture which increases the effective cache capacity up to 2X for the systems with narrow-width values, while also improving its power efficiency, bandwidth, and reliability. The proposed double capacity cache (DCC) architecture uses a fast and efficient peripheral circuitry to store two narrow-width values in a single wordline. In order to minimize the latency overhead in workloads without narrow-width data, the flag bits are added to tag store. The proposed DCC architecture decreases cache miss-rate by 50%, which results in 27% performance improvement and 30% higher dynamic energy efficiency. To improve reliability, DCC modifies the data distribution on individual bits, which results in 20% and 25% average static-noise margin (SNM) improvement in L1 and L2 caches respectively.

Keywords

Cache, SRAM; NBTI; SNM; Low power design

1. INTRODUCTION

Scaling the CMOS technology creates two new challenges: static power and device reliability. This has been a major concern for the design of integrated circuits. Due to the exponential dependency of sub-threshold current to the threshold voltage, the static power increases significantly as technology nodes shrink [1, 2]. In addition, increasing temperatures and current density of devices degrades lifetime and performance of CMOS technology due to the aging mechanisms such as bias temperature instability (BTI) and hot carrier injection (HCI) [3]. The negative bias temperature instability (NBTI) is an important factor that causes aging and reliability degradation of PMOS devices. This phenomenon increases the absolute threshold voltage of PMOS transistors and slows down circuits by up to 20% slower [4]. In memories, NBTI increases the probability of failure during the expected lifetime due to the soft-errors [5, 6]. Since embedded SRAM comprises a large portion of chip area and holds critical data for processing, it is crucial to improve performance, power, bandwidth and reliability in the face of such scaling challenges [7].

In modern microprocessors, the word length has increased to 64-bits to enable higher memory addressability, however much of the data continues to be 32-bits wide or less [8-11]. This is due to availability of the high number of small and zero values on the processor computation. Such narrow width values waste valuable memory capacity when represented as 64-bits values. Further, non-uniform data distribution of narrow-width values on upper 32-bits of the wordline decreases memory/register file lifetime due to negative bias temperature instability (NBTI) degradation [3].

In this paper, we introduce double capacity cache (DCC) architecture which stores two narrow-width data on a single wordline in order to increase the effective cache capacity up to **2X**. We define four modes that determine the data placement in cache line, and allow the system to write/read in half or full wordline schemes. The DCC design incurs low overheads even for workloads without narrow-width values. To meet the cache deadlines, we use different DCC implementations on L1 and L2 caches. Our evaluations on SPEC CPU 2006 benchmarks shows higher effective cache capacity in DCC decreases cache miss-rate and improves the system performance by 27% on average. Half write/read operation and lower cache miss-rate decrease the dynamic power of system by 30% and 35% on L1 and L2 caches. Further, DCC improves the average static-noise margin (SNM) degradation by 20% and 25% in L1 and L2 caches respectively.

GLSVLSI '16, May 18-20, 2016, Boston, MA, USA
 ISBN 978-1-4503-4274-2/16/05$15.00
DOI: http://dx.doi.org/10.1145/2902961.2902990

2. RELATED WORK

Several previous efforts improve soft-error protection or power/performance efficiency of the narrow-width values in register files and caches [8-11]. Brooks *et al.* [8] implemented clock gating technique to turn off non-active part of narrow-width values in register file. Using register file with different sizes is another method to decrease the power and area overhead in narrow-width values [12]. However, finding the exact size of narrow-width data and assigning it to an appropriate register file consumes significant power. Hu *et al*, in [13] used narrow-width characteristics to make a duplicate of the value within the same data item. This in-register duplication (IRD) eliminates the requirement for additional copy registers and improves the architectural vulnerability factor of register files. The work in [9] introduced a thermal behavior of a low-power value-aware register file (VARF) which relates to internal hotspots on register file. They proposed three thermal control techniques and added two flag bits to balance the access activity across partitions of VRAF by shifting the narrow-width data between the upper and lower 32-bits halves of register file. Kong *et al*, [14] designed a process tolerant last level cache in 3D microprocessors. They divide data values into four groups with 16-bits, 32-bits, 48-bits and 64-bits narrow-width granularity which allows them to store more data in cache with the same storage capacity. Wang et al, in [10] utilized an extra flag bit to keep track of the register file lines with narrow-widths. They considered values of lower 34-bits as narrow-width data implement power gating method for the other 30-bits to reduce register file power consumption.

Although power/clock gating of non-active part of narrow-width data improves power efficiency, it is not an efficient solution since it generally wastes about half of register file capacity or cache area. In addition the aging-aware techniques used extra flag bits to balance the data distribution. An efficient method should be able to use the inactive part of narrow-width data to increase the cache utilization or balance the data with no performance overhead.

3. DOUBLE CACHE CAPACITY

In this paper we leverage the narrow-width value observation to improve the power efficiency for caches with narrow-width values. Our proposed architecture, double capacity cache (DCC), adds two flag bits to cache architecture to detect the narrow-width values and stores their valuable lower 32 bits. We use the upper 32-bit memory available to store another narrow-width value. Modifying data placement in such a way improves power, performance, bandwidth and lifetime of caches in systems with narrow-width values. In the best case, this technique improves the effective cache capacity and memory bandwidth by up to 1.78**X** depending on the percentage of narrow-width values used by the workload.

To implement DCC, we add flag bits (*HalfW* & *UpW*) to the tag store. This increases the effective cache size (cache associativity) by making the tag store larger. Flag *HalfW* indicates whether the data read/write should be performed with half or full length. *HalfW*=1 shows that only one of the data entry is valid, and only half of the wordline is necessary for the read or write. We therefore activate partial read/write circuitry as required. This significantly improves the power efficiency of the memory access. In contrast, *HalfW*=0 indicates that valid data uses full cache line length (64-bits mode). In this case, the data can be either 64-bits wide or a combination of two 32-bits values. The second flag bit (*UpW*) provides information about the data placement or width based on the first flag bit. When the system is in half mode (*HalfW*=1), *UpW* indicates whether data is placed on upper (*UpW*=1) or lower 32-bits (*UpW*=0) of cache line. In full-length mode, this flag determines whether the value in cache line is wide-width data (*UpW*=0) or the combination of two narrow-width data (*UpW*=1). Using the two flag bit values, the proposed cache has four different modes as follows (see Figure 1):

(i) HalfW=0, UpW=0:

In read mode, this bit combination shows that the value in this wordline is wide-width. The system puts the original data {upper half, lower half} on the output bus. In write mode if input data is not narrow-width, we reset both flags to zero.

(ii) HalfW=1, UpW=0:

This combination shows that one value in cache line is narrow-width and it saved on the lower 32-bits of cache line. In read mode the peripheral circuitry puts *{32'b 0, Lower 32-bits}* on output bus. In write mode, the system writes the lower 32-bits of this data on the least significant 32-bits of cache line.

(iii)HalfW=1, UpW=1:

This mode indicates that the data stored data on cache is narrow-width and it is saved in the upper 32-bits of cache entry. In read mode, the upper 32-bits of cache line are written on the lower 32-bits of the output bus as *{32'b 0, Upper 32-bits}*. During write operation, the system writes the first 32-bits of data in upper half of cache line.

(iv) HalfW=0, UpW=1:

Both lower and upper halves of wordline cache contain narrow-width data and in read mode, the peripheral circuitry reads the entire 64-bits wordline *{Upper 32-bits, lower 32-bits}*. If the read is from processor, only the desired word is put on the output bus, while if it is from a lower level cache, both words are put on the bus for higher bandwidth. In write mode, the system writes the whole wordline on cache in full length to increase the cache bandwidth utilization (double narrow-width write).

The flag bits can be accessed in parallel with address decoding, without adding extra latency to the system. In L1, tag store and data store are also often accessed together to reduce latency, while in L2, tag store and data store are typically accessed in serial order. Thus, in case of narrow-width data in L2, the system only needs to read half of the data line once tag is read.

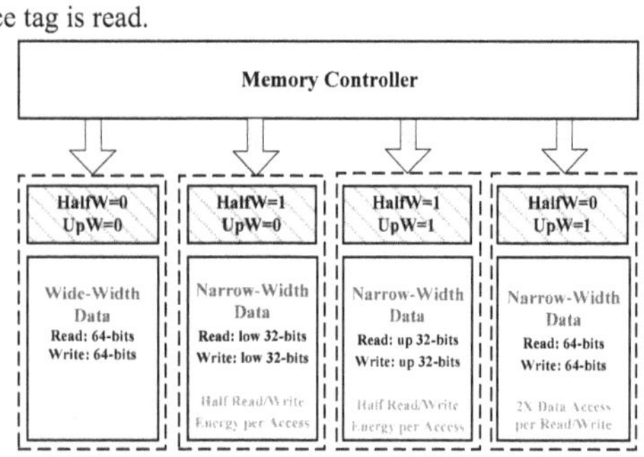

Figure 1. Different modes of proposed DCC based on flag bits.

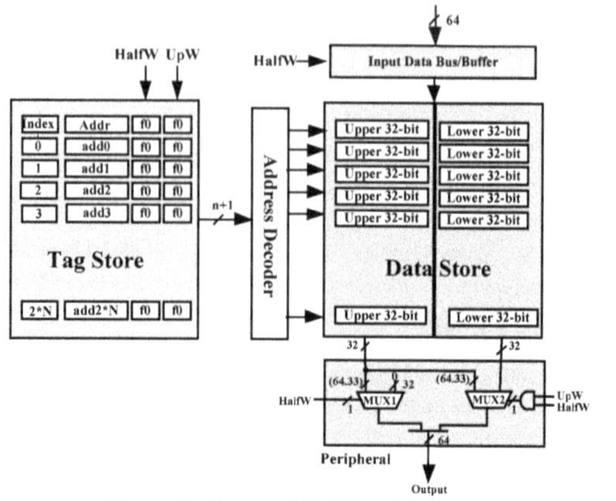

Figure 2. Proposed DCC architecture.

4. CACHE RELAIBILITY

Our simulation results show that non-uniform data activity (0% or 100%) has the most effect on SNM degradation of cell. We use NBTI model in [15] to calculate the shift in threshold voltage of PMOS transistor. In order to find the SNM degradation after three years, we used HSPICE to simulate a conventional 6T-SRAM cell with 45nm predictive technology model. For pull-up PMOS transistors we changed the threshold voltage of transistor based on different data activity (see Table 1). Our evaluation shows that after three years with zero data activity (one PMOS always biased with zero) the threshold voltage of transistor deceases by 43mV. This shift in threshold voltage decreases the SNM stability by 14.9% with respect to baseline 6T cell. Having ones and zeros 50% of the time on SRAM storage nodes results in lowest SNM degradation. In this case, the SNM degradation is 2.9%. Table 1 shows the SNM degradation in SRAM cells for a range of data activity.

Table 1. SNM degradation on SRAM at different data activity.

Data activity	0%	10%	20%	30%	40%	50%
SNM degradation	14.9%	11.3%	8.6%	6.3%	4.1%	2.9%

5. EXPERIMENTAL SETUP

We use GEM5 simulator [16] to extract data traces from L1 and L2 caches when executing SPEC 2006 benchmarks. We fast-forward 500 million instructions and then simulate the next 1 billion instructions in detail. The processor configuration is shown in Table 2. Our evaluation with SPEC CPU 2006 benchmarks shows that more than 87% and 85% of data in L1 and L2 caches respectively can be represented by using only the lower 32-bits. We use *Synopsys Design Compiler* tool in 45nm TSMC technology to evaluate the effect of power, delay and area of peripheral circuitry. The extracted data is added to the number of cycles in L2 cache in GEM5 simulator.

Table 2. Baseline processor configuration.

Frequency	2 GHz
L1 Cache	32KB, 2-way association, 64B cache line
L2 Cache	512KB, 8-way association, 64B cache line
Memory	DRAM, DDR3, 4GB

5.1. Dynamic energy

Based on cache traces from the conventional cache and the DCC cache, and using hit/miss access energy from *NVSIM* tool, the normalized energy consumption of L1 and L2 caches is depicted on

Figure 3. The first bar in every axis represents the normalized read, write and miss energy of the conventional cache. Total dynamic energy of proposed L1 and L2 cache improves by 30% and 35% on average.

This improvement is due to:

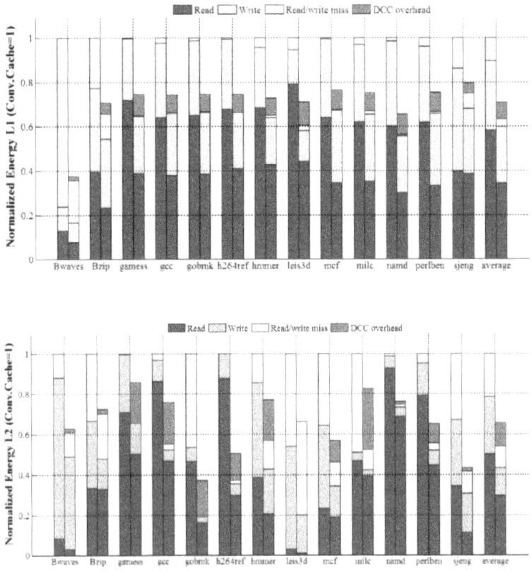

Figure 3. Dynamic energy consumption in conventional and DCC caches.

Effective cache capacity (Miss rate): Higher effective cache capacity on DCC decreases the average miss rate in L1 and L2 caches. This reduction directly improves the energy consumption of the system.

Half read/write of narrow-width data: In DCC, the number of narrow-width reads/writes is high. Each consumes approximately half the energy of a full read/write in L2. This is because we activate only half of the cache wordline for read/write on half values. However merging the data after a read operation adds energy overheads. In L2 cache this overhead is the energy of multiplexers, while in L1 cache, this comes from input/output buffer circuitry that is controlled by *HalfW* and *UpW* signals. This energy overhead is shown as a red bar in Figure **3**.

Write back bandwidth: When the data misses in L1 cache, the system sends a request to L2 cache to find that address. In case of a hit, a part of L2 data is transferred to L1 to improve data locality. In DCC, this operation can be performed at up to **2X** higher rate with lower energy consumption. The average time that the system is in 2X bandwidth mode is directly proportional to the percentage of narrow-width values, since each wordline now carries two data values and handles two write operations in the lower level of cache. In addition, in a write-back operation that updates the cache data in higher memory levels, we have a similar advantage in terms of energy improvement.

5.2. Performance

The second DCC opportunity is using the higher cache capacity to improve the system performance. The effect of this capacity increase is significant, especially for data-intensive workloads with higher data availability/locality and reduced number of cache misses. When both L1 and L2 caches are implemented as DCC, the system also benefits from double rates of data transfer between caches, or cache to register file. This advantage is lost when only L1 or L2 is implemented as DCC. Figure 4 compares the performance of the proposed architecture with a conventional cache for SPEC CPU2006 benchmarks. For single L1 and L2 DCC architectures, performance improves by 19% and 16% respectively. There are two reasons why implementing DCC in L2 cache has higher overhead than DCC in L1; first, the system performance is mostly sensitive to L1 effective size rather than L2 cache size. Second, the access to data and tag stores is done in parallel in L1 cache to decrease the system latency while in L2 cache these accesses are serial. As Figure 4 shows, implementing both L1 and L2 as DCC architectures enhances the system performance by 27% on average compared to baseline.

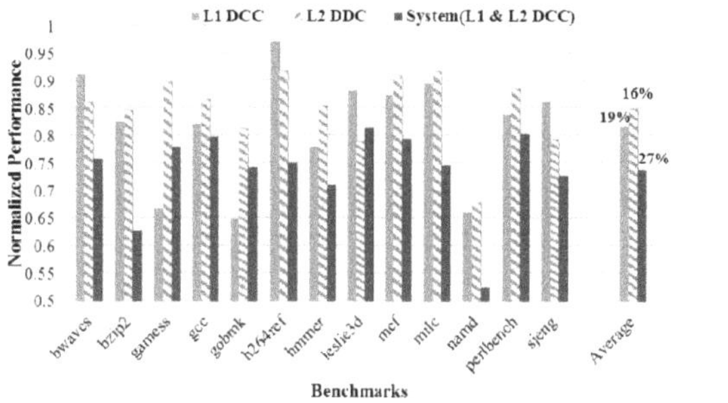

Figure 4. Normalized performance of implementing DCC technique on L1, L2 and both L1 & L2 caches.

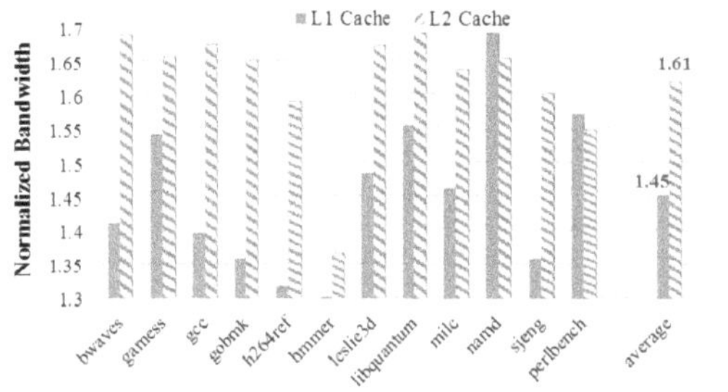

Figure 5. Normalized L1 and L2 cache bandwidths in different benchmarks.

5.3. Bandwidth

The ability of DCC to read and write double narrow-width data (on same line) can increase the data cache bandwidth up to **2X** during transfer of narrow-width values between caches. When flag bits are {0, 1}, both upper and lower halves of wordline store narrow-width data. In this case, both data values are read simultaneously. This increases the cache bandwidth up to 1.78**X** for narrow data. This maximum cache bandwidth improvement is less than double rate since during the miss or write back operation the tag store uses 12-bits as tag values. For workloads with high data locality this increment has major impact on system performance. This advantage is available only when both levels of cache are implemented as DCC. Figure 5 shows normalized total bandwidth to/from the caches for different benchmarks when both L1 and L2 are utilized DCC architecture. The results show that the DCC L1 and DCC L2 architecture can achieve 1.45**X** and 1.61**X** higher bandwidth (# of bits per second) with respect to conventional L1 and L2 caches respectively. This reflects the number of dense transfers that are accomplished during execution of the benchmarks. Note that the additional bandwidth may also be used to transfer up to cache blocks per read (instead of a single cache block as is done typically) if narrow-width values are present. However, in this paper, we instead experiment with transferring 64-bit sets of data stored in the cache lines.

5.4. Area and Static Power

Figure 6 shows the leakage power and area of L1 and L2 cache in conventional and DCC implementations. We estimate area and power of caches with the NV*sim* [17] tool in 45nm technology. We consider the impact of the peripherals on power and area of both L1 and L2 caches. The area overhead of DCC L2 cache due to the added multiplexers and flag bits is less than 14% of conventional L2 cache area. As Figure 6 shows, double tag size in L1 cache increases the area and leakage power, but this increment is less than 16% and 9% total cache overhead respectively.

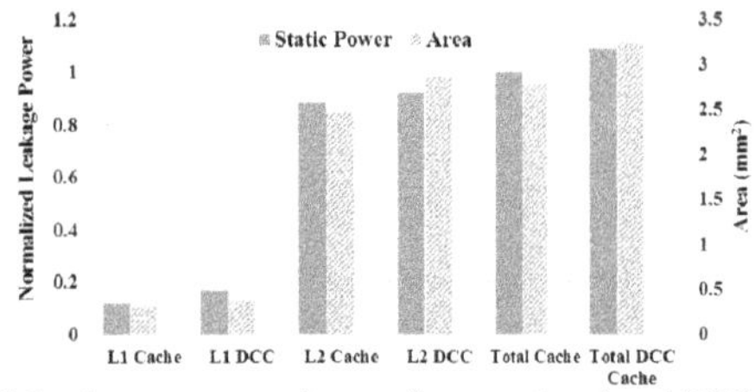

Figure 6. Leakage power and area of conventional and DCC caches.

As we noted before, DCC incurs very low overhead for workloads without narrow-width values. Our evaluations show that the power overhead of proposed system (due to extra flag bits in tag store) is close to zero when the caches must store 12% or more narrow-width values during execution in the benchmark. These proportions are observed in most CPU/GPU workloads since they work with many zeros and small values. The other advantage of DCC is that power gating can be applied to a larger area of cache. Compressing narrow-width data and saving two of them in single word line, increases the effective cache capacity by up to 2X. This provides more idle space in the cache to implement power gating. This is true especially in large memory units such as L2/LLC, where the leakage power is critical. In theory, if all data were narrow-width, this technique could achieve up to 2X power saving. However, this is difficult to achieve in L1 cache since the L1 cache has higher activity and is typically nearly full with data cached from higher level caches/memory.

5.5. NBTI improvement

DCC cache not only improves the effective cache capacity, power, performance and bandwidth but also has significant effect on NBTI degradation of cache structure. As Figure 2 shows, our DCC architecture does not change the data distribution of critical bits. For example the bit indices 1 to 4, 30 to 36 and 62 to 64 have still high percentage of zeroes in proposed architecture. Thus, in the worst case SNM does not change with respect to conventional cache. However, improving the average SNM in cache structures results in lower cell soft-error rate. This is because the soft-error rate in a cache is a function of the average SNM degradation. We analyze the impact of BTI on average SNM degradation. Figure 7 shows the average SNM improvement of the proposed architecture for L1 and L2 cache after three years. The modified data distribution in DCC L1 and L2 caches improves the average SNM degradation by 25% and 29% with respect to conventional L1 and L2 caches.

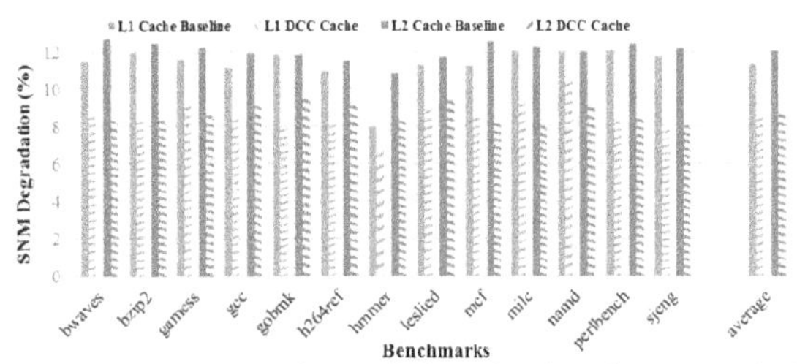

Figure 7. SNM degradation on different benchmarks on L1 and L2 conventional caches and DCC.

6. CONCLUSION

This paper introduces a new double capacity cache (DCC) architecture which can store up to **2X** data by exploiting the presence of narrow-width values. The proposed cache has four modes of operation for each cache line defined using two added flag bits. These determine data placement and allow the system to save two narrow-width values on a single wordline in order to increase the effective cache capacity. Implementing DCC architecture for all levels of cache allows us to have double cache bandwidth for data transfers between caches. This, along with larger effective cache capacity, improves cache miss rate and cache performance. In addition, storing narrow data on upper and lower 32-bits of a cache entry modifies the cache data distribution and improves the average SNM degradation.

7. ACKNOWLEDGMENTS

This work was sponsored by NSF grant #1527034 and UC San Diego Jacobs School Focht-Powell Fellowship.

8. REFERENCES

[1] N. S. Kim, et al., "Leakage current: Moore's law meets static power," *IEEE computer*, vol. 36, pp. 68-75, 2003.

[2] M. Jafari, et al., "Design of an ultra-low power 32-bit adder operating at subthreshold voltages in 45-nm FinFET," *IEEE DTIS*, pp. 167-168, 2013.

[3] S. Borkar, "Electronics beyond nano-scale CMOS," IEE/ACM DAC, pp. 807-808, 2006.

[4] M. A. Alam, et al., "A comprehensive model of PMOS NBTI degradation," *Microelectronics Reliability Elsevier*, vol. 45, pp. 71-81, 2005.

[5] M. Imani, et al, "Low Power Data-Aware STT-RAM based Hybrid Cache Architecture," *IEEE ISQED,* 2016.

[6] M. Imani, et al., "Hierarchical design of robust and low data dependent FinFET based SRAM array," *IEEE/ACM NANOARCH*, pp. 63-68, 2015.

[7] M. Ansari, et al., "Estimation of joint probability density function of delay and leakage power with variable skewness," IEEE ICECCO, pp. 251-254, 2013.

[8] D. Brooks, et al., "Dynamically exploiting narrow width operands to improve processor power and performance," *IEEE HPCA*, pp. 13-22, 1999.

[9] S. Wang, et al., "Exploiting narrow-width values for thermal-aware register file designs," *IEEE/ACM DATE,* pp. 1422-1427, 2009.

[10] S. Wang, et al., "Low power aging-aware register file design by duty cycle balancing," *IEEE/ACM DATE*, pp. 546-549, 2012.

[11] G. Duan, et al., "Exploiting narrow-width values for improving non-volatile cache lifetime," *IEEE/ACM DATE,* 2014.

[12] A. Aggarwal, et al., "Energy efficient asymmetrically ported register files," *IEEE ICCD*, pp. 2-7, 2003.

[13] J. Hu, et al., "On the exploitation of narrow-width values for improving register file reliability," *IEEE TVLSI*, vol. 17, pp. 953-963, 2009.

[14] J. Kong, et al., "Exploiting narrow-width values for process variation-tolerant 3-D microprocessors," *IEEE/ACM DAC*, 2012, pp. 1197-1206.

[15] T. Grasser, et al., "The paradigm shift in understanding the bias temperature instability: from reaction–diffusion to switching oxide traps," *IEEE Electron Devices*, vol. 58, pp. 3652-3666, 2011.

[16] N. Binkert, et al., "The gem5 simulator," *ACM SIGARCH Computer Architecture News*, vol. 39, pp. 1-7, 2011.

[17] X. Dong, et al., "Nvsim: A circuit-level performance, energy, and area model for emerging nonvolatile memory," IEEE ICCAD, vol. 31, pp. 994-1007, 2012.

Static Noise Margin based Yield Modelling of 6T SRAM for Area and Minimum Operating Voltage Improvement using Recovery Techniques

Nidhi Batra[#1], Pawan Sehgal[#2], Shashwat Kaushik[#3], Mohammad S. Hashmi[#4], Sudesh Bhalla[$5], Anuj Grover[$6]
[#]Indraprastha Institute of Information Technology, Delhi
[$]STMicroelectronics, Greater Noida, India
{[1]nidhi1462, [2]pawan1463, [3]shashwat1473, [4]mshashmi}@iiitd.ac.in,
[5]sudeshbhalla@gmail.com, [6]anuj.grover@st.com

ABSTRACT

In advanced technology nodes, the process variations deteriorate SRAM performance and greatly affect yield. It is necessary to formulate yield estimation models to optimize SRAMs and effectively trade-off area, performance and robustness. We propose models that in addition to enabling yield estimates also enable evaluation of lowering minimum operational voltage (VDD_{MIN}). We present a quantitative analysis for SNM limited SRAM yield using Design of Experiments (DOE) method. The proposed framework for yield based design can also utilize recovery techniques like Error Correcting Codes (ECC) and redundancy and quantifies yield, area, and VDD_{MIN} improvements. We also present a case study that trades-off ECC recovery budget, VDD_{MIN} and area gain. We show 25% improvement in area and VDD_{MIN} lowering by 300mV at constant yield levels by using 50% of ECC recovery budget.

Keywords

Static Noise Margin (SNM); Design of Experiments (DOE); SRAM; yield; regression; redundancy.

1. INTRODUCTION

In advanced technology, SRAMs occupy up to 70% area of SoCs [1]. The continuing trend of technology scaling has led to the design of highly dense SRAMs. At such advanced technology nodes, the device parameters such as the threshold voltage, V_t, and the effective channel length can be highly deviated from the expected value due to random process variations. These process variations substantially degrade SRAM cell performance [2]-[4], and this essentially limits the yield of the scaled SRAMs.

The yield estimation approaches, such as Monte Carlo and importance sampling, although primarily are parametric in nature, but for analog/mixed signal circuits, they are extremely useful for yield based design and to minimize the number of memory chips failing on silicon [5]. Alternatively, failure probabilities of SRAM due to process variations can also be modeled using Monte Carlo analysis, albeit with a large number of simulations, and through this it can be deduced that the yield can be improved by increasing device size [6]. However such design schemes will be usually limited due to the area constraints. An analytical formulation for SNM is reported in [7]; however it assumes the threshold voltage of all the six devices in the SRAM cell to be same which is not practically logical. In order to expedite the estimation of SRAM yield, a statistical technique based on Design of Experiments (DOE) can thus be employed [8]. The DOE technique requires less number of simulations and exhibits comparable accuracy when compared to Monte Carlo approach. Further, it is possible to have high-end tail σ coverage for each transistor under consideration. Owing to the said benefits, DOE is utilized in our work.

In this paper, models for SNM based yield estimation that takes into account the effect of independent Vt variations on SRAM transistors are proposed. Subsequently, effort has been made to quantify the SNM specifications for different targeted yields. In addition, yield recovery techniques have been incorporated in the proposed models and this clearly demonstrates the benefits in terms of cell area and VDDMIN improvements.

GLSVLSI '16, May 18-20, 2016, Boston, MA, USA

DOI: http://dx.doi.org/10.1145/2902961.2903005

2. DEPENDE NCE OF SNM ON THRESHOLD VOLTAGE V_T

2.1 Read SNM and V_t Variations

The SRAM cell stores binary data ('1' or '0') at its internal nodes, denoted as BLTI and BLFI in Figure 1. The read operation in this cell is facilitated with the help of access transistors M5 and M6. During the cell read operation, both the bit lines are initially precharged high. When the WL is asserted, BLF (near side storing '0') discharges through M5 and M1 and in turn creates a bump voltage at node BLFI. If this bump voltage is greater than the trip voltage of inverter, consisting of devices M3 and M4, the cell contents get flipped resulting in read failure. The maximum bump voltage which prevents the cell flip is defined as SNM. Random variations affecting the V_t also have a direct impact on SNM as verified in regression analysis models in subsequent section.

2.2 Sensitivity analysis using DOE

In DOE evaluation, V_t of the devices (M1-M6) is varied individually in the range of ± 6σ (total of 13 V_t observations), one at a time and the impact on SNM is observed. The corresponding deviation is shown in Figure 2. The device with the higher slope in the plot indicates higher sensitivity.

It is evident that SNM is most sensitive on M1, M3 and M5. This is in line with our expectation because at the side storing '1', the V_t of M3 will control how fast it may turn on at a particular bump voltage, consequently flipping the cell state. If V_t reduces due to variations, then even a smaller voltage bump on BLFI node will switch on M3 thereby flipping the bit.

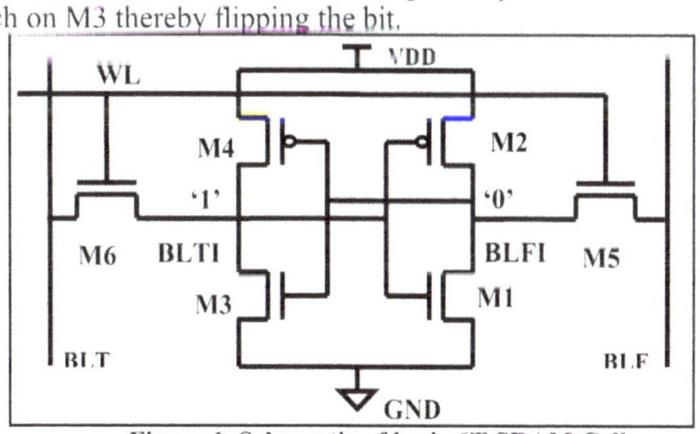

Figure 1. Schematic of basic 6T SRAM Cell

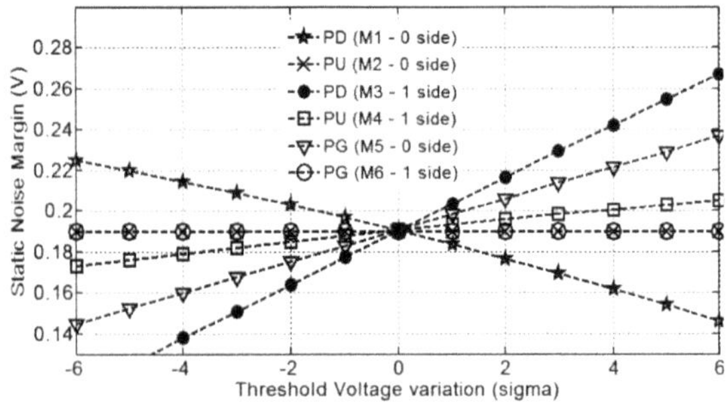

Figure 2. Sensitivity Plot for SNM

Also, M1 and M5 constitute a potential divider; hence their individual strengths will affect the bump voltage at BLFI which can cause the bit flip.

After identifying critical devices, the V_t of those devices is varied together in accordance with DOE method. A total of 2197 samples (13 samples for each of M1, M3 and M5) are observed to ascertain the relationship between SNM and V_t variations in the devices.

3. STATISTICAL MODELING OF SNM

3.1 Regression Analysis

We have employed regression technique to model the dependence of SNM on the V_t variations of the devices and their inherent noise. Expressions (1) and (2) models Tri-variate linear (TL) fit and Tri-variate non-linear quadratic (TNLQ) dependence. Here x, y and z represents the effective V_t of devices M1, M3, M5 with variation respectively.

$$SNM = px + qy + rz + s \quad (1)$$

$$SNM = ax + by + cz + dx^2 + ey^2 + fz^2 + g \quad (2)$$

Regression analysis is performed to arrive at the correct values of coefficients. To validate the accuracy of the model, analysis is done for various cell ratios (CRs). Similar samples are generated for different V_{DD} and temperature values. Tables 1 (a) and (b) depict the regression data for TL and TNLQ models respectively at 1.2 V and 27°C. Based upon the R^2 and error estimate values one can infer that TNLQ is more accurate model for predicting the yield.

It can also be noticed that at a particular operating voltage, the increase in CR leads to increased SNM sensitivity on corresponding devices (the coefficient representing the sensitivity slope for each device is increasing). From the TL model, it is evident that SNM is more sensitive to the variations in M1 and M5 when CR is low. Sensitivity to M3 increases at higher CR. This is intuitively valid since when large CR is used, then the voltage bump generated during read operation is low. However, reduced V_t of M3 triggers a bit flip more easily.

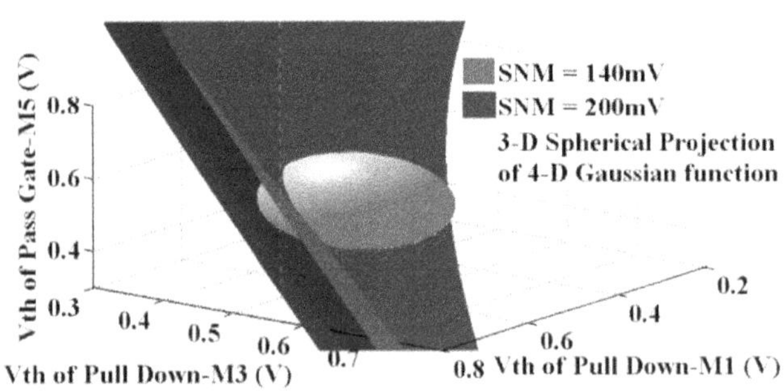

Figure 3. SNM contours for TNLQ model on 3D projection

3.2 Yield Prediction

For yield estimation, Satisfying Boundary-Statistical Integration (SB-SI) approach [9] is adopted. In this work, the expressions obtained by the SNM model in (2) define the separating boundaries. It is important to note that Gaussian distribution is considered for the V_t variations. In Figure 3, the 3-Dimensional spherical projection of the joint probability 4-D function for TNLQ SNM model is depicted. As an illustration, the contours for CR=2 are shown in Figure 3 for different target SNM values, resulting in different yield values. The sphere covers $\pm 6\sigma$ range to estimate the yield. The failure probability is computed by integrating the failure region over the depicted contours. Similarly, the yield is computed at different CR values without any loss in generality, for which the results are compared and reported in Section 5.

4. YIELD RECOVERY TECHNIQUES

ECC and redundancy are frequently used to compensate for the SRAM cell failures. ECC employs redundant bits within each word to provide robustness and error detection as well as correction capabilities. The redundancy utilizes the spare column (or row) of bit-cells, to replace a bit-cell column (or row) containing any defective SRAM bit-cell.

Considering the memory capacity of 'M' bits, the overall yield of the SRAM with single cell failure probability 'P' is given by (3).

$$Yield_{WITHOUT\_RECOVERY} = (1 - P)^M \quad (3)$$

This modifies to (4) when ECC based SECDED technique is deployed. Here, P represents the probability of error of a single cell derived from our TNLQ models, M is the memory size in bits, W is the word length.

$$Yield_{ECC} = ((1 - P)^W + WP(1 - P)^{W-1})^{\frac{M}{W}} \quad (4)$$

On the other hand, the yield with redundancy can be determined using (5) – (8), as per formulations in [10].

$$P_{col} = 1 - (1 - P)^i \quad (5)$$

$$P_{seg} = 1 - (1 - P_{col})^m - m.P_{col}(1 - P_{col})^{m-1} \quad (6)$$

$$P_{array} = 1 - \left(1 - P_{seg}\right)^k \quad (7)$$

$$Yield_{Redn} = (1 - P_{array})^l \quad (8)$$

In the expressions (5)-(8), the terms i, m, k, l denote number of cells in a column, number of sections, number of redundant rows, and number of arrays respectively. Whereas the terms P_{col}, P_{seg} and P_{array} represent the probability that a column, a segment (made up of columns) and an array (made up of segments) will fail.

TABLE 1(a) Regression data for Trivariate Linear (TL) model

Cell Ratio (CR)		1.25	1.50	1.75	2.0
Coefficients	p	-0.33112	-0.32282	-0.31498	-0.30472
	q	0.64639	0.65543	0.66287	0.67158
	r	0.38123	0.33891	0.31142	0.28282
	s	-0.11513	-0.08653	-0.06985	-0.05416
R^2 (%)		99.65	99.61	99.58	99.57
Error in Estimate		0.36	0.37	0.38	0.38

TABLE 1(b) Regression data for Trivariate Non Linear Quadratic (TNLQ) model

Cell Ratio (CR)		1.25	1.50	1.75	2.0
Coefficients	a	0.029791	0.056309	0.072831	0.090059
	b	0.732067	0.744678	0.753928	0.758784
	c	0.356278	0.318323	0.289039	0.260422
	d	-0.39045	-0.41241	-0.42062	-0.42817
	e	-0.09598	-0.0979	-0.09875	-0.09457
	f	0.02834	0.027431	0.024277	0.024298
	g	-0.20834	-0.20657	-0.18885	-0.17338
R^2 (%)		99.76	99.73	99.71	99.72
Error in Estimate		0.29	0.31	0.32	0.32

5. CASE STUDY

5.1 Experimental Setup

A memory of size 4Mb is analyzed, having 8 banks (arrays) of 512Kb each. Each bank has 512 rows and 1K columns. Word size is taken to be 32 bits. For yield calculations, the operating voltage is varied in the range of 0.9 V to 1.2 V and CR is varied from 1 to 2.5. For ECC analysis, word size of 39 bits is considered which involves 7 redundant bits. Similarly, for row redundancy analysis, 8 local redundant rows for each array of 512Kb are utilized (with each pair of redundant rows having ability to correct one defect). Column redundancy involved 8 local redundant columns for each of the arrays (with bit repair on each side assuming replacing chunks of 4 columns together).

5.2 Impact of CR on Cell Yield

The SNM values obtained using (1) and (2) are deployed as contours for the yield estimation. For SNM based yield, the probability of single cell passing is depicted in Figure 4 for a range of CR. It can be clearly observed that the yield improves with the increase in CR. This is owing to the fact that the voltage bump reduces as the strength of pull down devices increase. This indicates that for a particular target yield, the use of higher CR enables us to benchmark higher SNM value for yield qualification.

5.3 Cell Area and Operating Voltage Tradeoff

Figure 5 depicts the tradeoff between the operating voltage and the CR required to achieve a target SNM. We observed that to achieve a target yield of 95%, a cell with higher CR (CR = 2) can be used to operate on voltage as low as 0.88V in comparison to a cell with CR = 1.25 operating at 1.05 V; a clear saving of 170 mV. However, there is a definite trade-off in a way that a compromise must be made of either operating voltage or net memory area in lieu of another. This compromise can be waived off if recovery techniques like ECC and redundancy are utilized.

Apart from correcting the soft errors, some margin of the benefits provided by ECC can be utilized to save upon area as well as on the operating voltage. This is so because the errors induced by operating a cell on low voltage with less CR value (in addition to the aforementioned soft errors) can be more than compensated by the correction capability provided by these recovery techniques. The next subsection quantifies the said benefits in much clear format.

5.4 Benefits derived out of ECC

Figure 6 clearly depicts the impact of ECC on yield improvement and area reduction. It must be mentioned that the piecewise linear nature of the plots is because of the less number of sample points that were present in the 6σ range (99.999999 %).

The following observations are deduced from Figure 6:

- ***Yield Improvement**:* It is observed that for a particular target SNM, ECC boosts the yield of the memory. Dashed marking on the plot indicate the yield improvement. Table 3 clearly quantifies the same.
- ***Area Improvement**:* Since CR directly contributes to cell area, it can be considered as a metric for area estimation. We infer that using recovery techniques, a denser bit-cell can be used thereby saving area. This fact can be appreciated by the following example: A memory word of CR=1.25 with ECC (39 bits) roughly covers the same area as a non-ECC 32-bit word of CR=1.5. But it can be observed from Table 4 that taking yield into account, CR=1.25 with ECC can more than compensate for CR=2 without ECC thereby contributing to 25% area improvement. The oval band in Figure 7 similarly relates the area improvement between CR=1 and 1.25.
- ***Operating Voltage Improvement**:* Apart from extracting benefits out of ECC in terms of soft error removal, yield and area improvement, the ECC budget can also be utilized to save VDD_{MIN} i.e. operate the cell on lesser V_{DD}. Table 4 clearly depicts that target yield can be more than compensated by operating a memory with CR = 1.25 on 0.9 V than that of memory with CR = 2 on 1.2 V thereby saving up to 300mV in VDD_{MIN}.

All the above mentioned scenarios can be generalized for different operating voltages and CRs.

5.5 Redundancy and its Impact

Redundancy (both row and column) is a static recovery technique in which the random cell failures are compensated by replacing row/column with their redundant counterpart. However, error correction capability is limited to a few defects. It does not provide the kind of dynamic robustness and benefits in terms of area and VDD_{MIN} reduction that one extracts from ECC. But in order to generalize the recovery techniques as whole, yield recovery by utilizing extra repair resources is estimated and compared with ECC in Table 3.

Figure 7 depicts the benefit of utilizing redundancy to recover memory yield. It is evident that row redundancy outperforms column redundancy, but both offer lesser recovery than ECC. In the case of Hybrid redundancy, in Table 3, both redundant rows and columns local to each bank are used. We note that though area penalty is slightly higher, but the yield improvement is much higher than the individual cases.

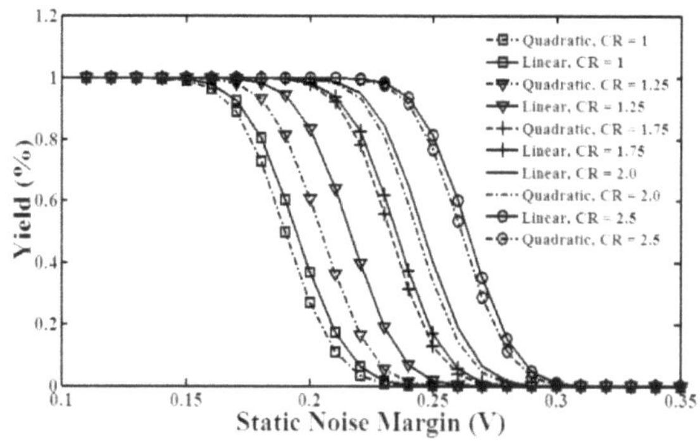

Figure 4. Impact of CR on Cell Yield

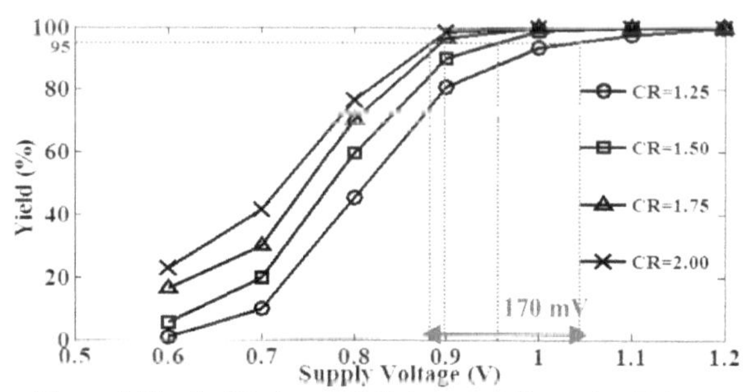

Figure 5. Tradeoff between Cell Area and Operating Voltage

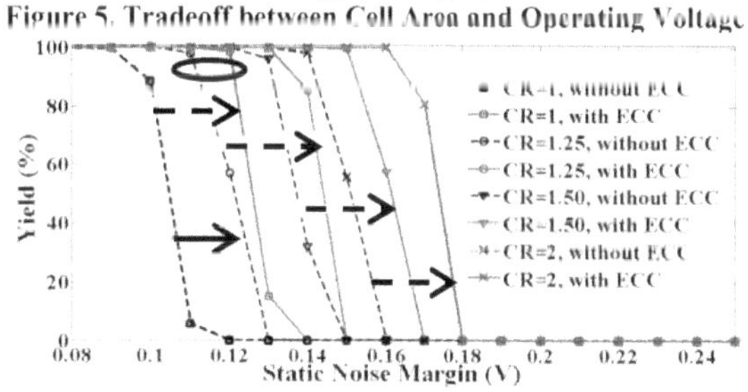

Figure 6. Benefit of ECC on SNM yield with different CR

TABLE 3 SNM yield and Area Penalty analysis (for CR = 2)

Target SNM	Yield w/o recovery (%)	With 8-Column Redundancy		With 8 - Row Redundancy		With Hybrid Redundancy		With ECC (SECDED)	
		Yield (%)	Area Penalty (%)	Yield (%)	Area Penalty (%)	Yield (%)	Area Penalty (%)	Yield (%)	Area Penalty (%)
185mV	0.015	00.23	0.78	00.68	1.56	00.76	2.35	41.32	21.87
175mV	00.25	33.65		52.09		68.21		99.71	
170mV	00.64	50.09		94.98		97.49		99.95	
165mV	43.66	81.63		97.99		99.63		99.99	
Worst Case Correction Capability		2 defects in entire bank		4 defects in entire bank		6 defects in entire bank		1 defect for each word	

TABLE 4 Cell Ratio (CR) and Operating Voltage Tradeoff w.r.t memory yield (SNM = 150mV)

Operating Voltage (V)	Cell Ratio (C.R.)							
	1.25		1.50		1.75		2.0	
	Without ECC (%)	With ECC (%)	Without ECC (%)	With ECC (%)	Without ECC (%)	With ECC (%)	Without ECC (%)	With ECC (%)
0.9	80.10	99.98	90.03	99.98	96.31	99.99	98.53	99.99
1.0	93.42	99.98	98.77	99.98	99.78	99.99	99.96	99.99
1.1	97.47	99.98	99.77	99.99	99.98	99.99	99.99	99.99
1.2	99.93	99.98	99.95	99.99	99.98	99.99	99.99	99.99

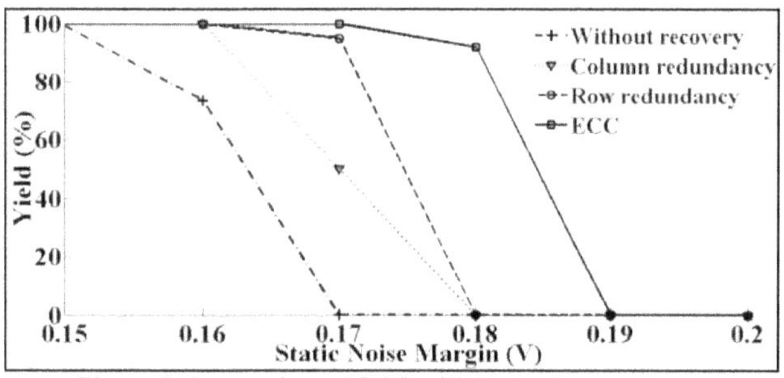

Figure 7. Comparison of ECC with Redundancy scheme

5.6 ECC and Redundancy Trade-off Summary

A quick comparison between ECC and redundancy in terms of yield and area penalty (with respect to memory having no recovery technique) can be done. Following observations can be made from Table 3 and 4:

- Although ECC has higher area penalty (up to 20%) than redundancy, yield improvement is significantly higher (99.7% for a target SNM of 175mV). This is expected because row redundancy has a correction capability of only one defect per two consecutive redundant rows or for every set of redundant columns. Whereas, with ECC (SECDED), one defect in each word can be corrected. This is a huge advantage over redundancy as nearly 16K defects (one for each word in a memory bank) can be corrected effectively.
- From Table-4, it is evident that even if half of the total recovery budget provided by ECC can be utilized for yield recovery, then a cell with smaller CR (= 1.25) can replace a cell with higher CR (=2) thereby leading to a final area gain of about 25% (even though extra ECC bits are used with 1.25 cell). This gain can be a little higher/ lower depending on design rules of the technology. The results are based upon the design rules of 28-FDSOI.

6. CONCLUSION

In this paper, we used DoE method to create linear and non-linear models to estimate SNM of a 6T SRAM cell. Trivariate non-linear quadratic model is found to be more accurate than the linear model. The model is then used to estimate capacity linked yield of SRAM instances. We extend the framework to include benefit of repair resources and also Error Correction Codes (SEC-DED) to recover SNM soft-fails. We show that for a 4Mb SRAM, use of ECC allows a denser SRAM to be used for same reliability, with a 25% improvement in area. Alternately, this framework also shows that for the 4Mb capacity and SRAM cell with CR of 2.0, can be operated at 300mV lower, at same reliability, and thus conserve power. The framework allows designers to optimize Power/ Area/ Yield of embedded memories.

7. REFERENCES

[1] International Technology Roadmap for Semiconductors, International technology roadmap for semiconductors 2004.

[2] R.Venkatraman, R.Castagnetti and S.Ramesh, "The Statistics of Device Variations and its Impact on SRAM Bitcell Performance, Leakage and Stability," in *7th International Symposium on Quality Electronic Design (ISQED)*, 2006.

[3] D. Burnett, K. Erington, C. Subramanian and K. Baker, "Implications of Fundamental Threshold Voltage Variations for High-Density SRAM and Logic Circuits," *Symposium on VLSI Technology Digest of Technical Papers*, pp. 15-16, 1994.

[4] A. J. Bhavnagarwala, X. Tang and J. D. Meindl, "The Impact of Intrinsic Device Fluctuations on CMOS SRAM Cell Stability," in *IEEE Journal of Solid-State Circuits*, April 2001.

[5] F. Gong, H. Yu, Y. Shi and L. He, "Variability-Aware Parametric Yield Estimation for Analog/Mixed-Signal Circuits: Concepts, Algorithm, and Challenges," *IEEE Design and Test, Vol. 31, Issue 4, pp. 6-15, Aug 2014.*

[6] S. Mukhopadhyay, H. Mahmoodi and K. Roy, "Modeling of Failure Probability and Statistical Design of SRAM Array for Yield Enhancement in Nanoscaled CMOS," in *IEEE Transactions on Computer-Aided Design of Integrated Circuits and Systems*, 2005.

[7] E. Seevinck, F. J. List and J. Lohstroh, "Static-Noise Margin Analysis of MOS SRAM Cells," *IEEE Journal of Solid-State Circuits*, vol. 22, pp. 748-754, 1987.

[8] E. Rémond, E. Nercessian, C. Bernicot and R. Mina, "Mathematical approach based on a "Design of Experiment" to simulate process variation," in *Design, Automation & Test in Europe Conference & Exhibition*, 2011.

[9] E. I. Vatajelu and J. Figueras, "Statistical Analysis of 6T SRAM Data Retention Voltage under Process Variation," in *IEEE 14th International Symposium on Design and Diagnostics of Electronic Circuits & Systems (DDECS)*, 2011.

[10] G. Shamanna, R. Gaurav, Raghavendra, Y. K, P. Marfatia and B. Kshatri, "Using ECC and Redundancy to minimize VMIN induced Yield Loss in 6T SRAM Arrays," in *IEEE International Conference on IC Design & Technology (ICICDT)*, 2012.

Asynchronous High Speed Serial Links Analysis using Integrated Charge for Event Detection

Aditya Dalakoti*
aditya@ece.ucsb.edu

Carrie Segal*
chsegal@ece.ucsb.edu

Merritt Miller*
merrittmiller@ece.ucsb.edu

Forrest Brewer*
forrest@ece.ucsb.edu

ABSTRACT

We present a metric for event detection, targeted for the analysis of CMOS asynchronous serial data links. Our metric is used to analyze signaling strategies that allow for coincident or nearly coincident detection of both data and event timing. The metric predicts that the CMOS link signaling mechanism has substantial implicit dispersion and inter-symbol interference [ISI] tolerance when compared to conventionally timed links. In fact, it predicts correct link operation in situations where eye-diagram techniques predict link failure. Practical operation margins and metrics are described and evaluated for PCB and cabling solutions suggesting 10+ Gb/s low-power asynchronous links could be implemented in CMOS 130nm technology.

1. INTRODUCTION

High speed serial links are commonly used in digital systems to move data between physically separated functional units. Serial links are attractive, because a single bit stream is easy to route and synchronize. High bit-rate links require low-jitter clocks and accurate clock-data recovery. Inevitably, the time base (clock) used to transmit the serial signal and the natural time base of the receiving circuit drift relative to each other. The circuits that compensate for this can be synchronous to, at most, one of the two time domains, giving rise to the use of asynchronous state-machines to handle the transition (phase alligners, FIFOs, bus arbiters, etc). Effectively, asynchronous machines are used in transmission regardless of whether the data is synchronous to a local clock. Thus, signaling methods that are naturally compatible with asynchronous logic become a promising subject of investigation. Asynchronous link design has been the subject of a number of recent studies [1], [2], [3]. Traditional asynchronous protocols are limited in speed due to the need to acknowledge data [2], [4]. In [5] asynchronous protocols share data lines, but performance depends on wire delays. In this work, we target (impolite) asynchronous links that do not use handshaking such as [6]. This subset of links lacks the feed-back bottle-neck allowing link time-of-flight to be longer than a bit transfer. The critical point of this model is that timing (arrival) of each bit must be unambiguous despite the unknown arrival time and the guarantee of this feature is designed into the system with margins. Signal integrity analysis is thus critical to determining if such a link has sufficient margins to meet the standards of unambiguous reception.

We introduce an integral charge model as a detection and analysis metric. The metric has the advantage that it mimics the behavior of CMOS transistors, which by nature accumulate charge and act when a threshold is reached. This metric is used to examine a variety of link signaling strategies and compare the suitability of the strategies in terms of noise, bandwidth, and practicality on realistic media models such as inexpensive coaxial cable and PCB transmission lines. For a signaling pulse, the critical measure becomes the integral of the pulse shape, rather than its amplitude or duration. Detection of edges, by contrast, is achieved by integrating a voltage level and subsequently integrating a new level leading to both *setup* and *hold* specifications for edge-detection. In that case, the integral is analogous to a slew measurement or RC delay model.

In Section 2 an integrated charge ($Q_\int$) metric is described. Section 3 presents an example application based on the integrated charge ($Q_\int$) metric. Section 4 defines metrics to analyze integrated charge ($Q_\int$) in a transmission media and describes transmission line effects on integrated Charge ($Q_\int$). Section 5 evaluates how to determine the data transfer rate of a practical link implementation. Section 6 presents results of datarate (Gb/s) for two different transmission media simulated over a range of lengths for edge and pulse based encoding.

2. INTEGRATED CHARGE METRIC

CMOS circuits, in general, have capacitive, voltage-sensitive, inputs. Digital logic, by design, provides well-defined, stable outputs between transitions. With a well-defined starting voltage, and a capacitive input one can define the amount of charge required to reach a given voltage as $Q_\int$, the integrated input charge. When $Q_\int$ reaches some value (Q_{crit}) the decision voltage (V_{trig}) is reached on the front-end, and the gate, from an event-driven perspective, is triggered. Timing critical asynchronous machines, such as synchronizers and phase detectors, have made use of integrated charge as early as some of the first CMOS based sawtooth phase de-

*The authors are affiliated with UC Santa Barbara

GLSVLSI'16, May 18-20, 2016, Boston, MA, USA.

DOI: http://dx.doi.org/10.1145/2902961.2902998

tectors [7]. Equation 1 formalizes a $Q_\int$ metric which models a gate triggering condition.

$$\int g_m \cdot min(0, V_{in}(t) - V_{Imin}) \geq Q_{crit} = V_{trig} \cdot C_{eff} \quad (1)$$

This triggering condition signifies the minimum charge (Q_{crit}) to successfully recieve information. V_{Imin} represents the minimum voltage required to start integrating charge at the critical node (the noise rejection threshold). g_m represents the transconductance of the circuit averaged over the decision region. C_{eff} is the effective capacitance at the detection node. The validity of the $Q_\int$ measure is dependent on g_m being a valid representation of transconductance over a range of inputs between V_{Imin} and V_{trig}. Note that if the $Q_\int$ is below the V_{Imin} it should not affect the critical node at all. If the $Q_\int$ above V_{Imin} is less than $V_{DD}C_{crit}$ then the critical node should not be affected and no event must be detected. Lastly, two equal $Q_\int$ above V_{Imin} should have similar effects on the event detection.

3. EXAMPLE APPLICATION

To demonstrate the use of the $Q_\int$ concept we examine a circuit designed for data transmission, using self-resetting logic [6]. A receiver/pulse-shaper circuit from this family is shown in Figure 1. The critical values for Equation 1 are derived from the behavior of this pulse shaper: $Q_\int \geq Q_{crit}$ will cause a pulse on the output, while V_{Imin} is established by the noise suppressing keeper, the 10k resistor, and V_{trig} is set by the decision voltage of the inverter driving the output.

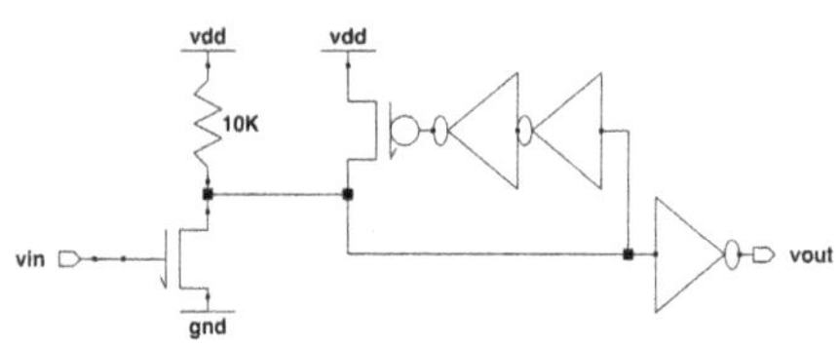

Figure 1: Logic circuit for detection of Integrated Charge ($Q_\int$) encoded as a pulse.

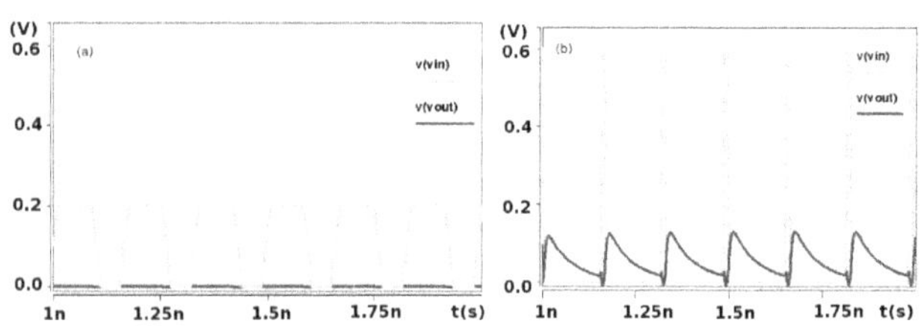

Figure 2: (a) Incoming pulse amplitude below V_{Imin} at critical node. (b) Incoming pulse amplitude above V_{Imin} at the critical node but $Q_\int$ is below Q_{crit}

Figure 2 shows circuit critical node behavior for two cases where $Q_\int < Q_{crit}$. In the first case (Figure 2(a)), Pulses don't cross above V_{Imin}, and no charge is accumulated. In the second case, (Figure 2(b)) Pulses cross V_{Imin} but V_{trig} is not reached and no pules result on the output. By contrast, Figure 3 demonstrates two cases of $Q_\int > Q_{crit}$. Here two pulse trains (dashed lines) at input both result as pulse trains a the output (solid lines). The relative difference in pulse shapes does not alter the one-pulse-in-one-pulse-out function. Thus, this simple model can be used to validate detection in this and similar signaling strategies.

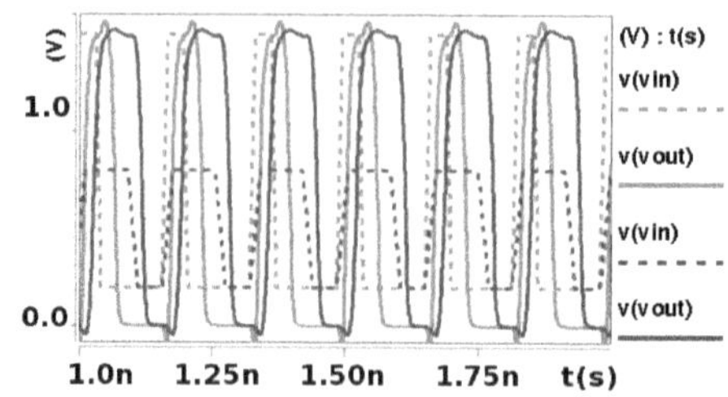

Figure 3: Different input pulses (dotted line) with same $Q_\int$ result in equivalent output.

4. INTEGRATED CHARGE AND SIGNAL INTEGRITY

$Q_\int$ has promise as an evaluation tool for signal integrity for asynchronous links, because it can describe the triggering conditions of asynchronous circuits. Classic measures of signal integrity for synchronous links, such as eye diagrams, focus on amplitude and timing uncertainty, while $Q_\int$ can better describe circuits where there is a trade-off between the two.

4.1 Timing variance & voltage noise

Variance in signal timing can be induced by loss in transmission media or from coupled noise. For example, Figure 4 shows strong loss applied to both edge, and pulse encoded signals. A lossy line induces a delay in the signal that is dependent on the previous, incomplete transmission.

To first order, $Q_\int$ can be viewed as the area in the signal above the defined threshold V_{Imin}. If this area is above Q_{crit} then the signal is successfully transmitted. $Q_\int$ here matches the human intuition that the signals in Figure 4 are interpretable if one were to set the levels correctly, even though neither of these curves would have an open eye. Hence $Q_\int - Q_{crit}$ serves as a noise margin allowing the selection of both V_{Imin} and Q_{crit}.

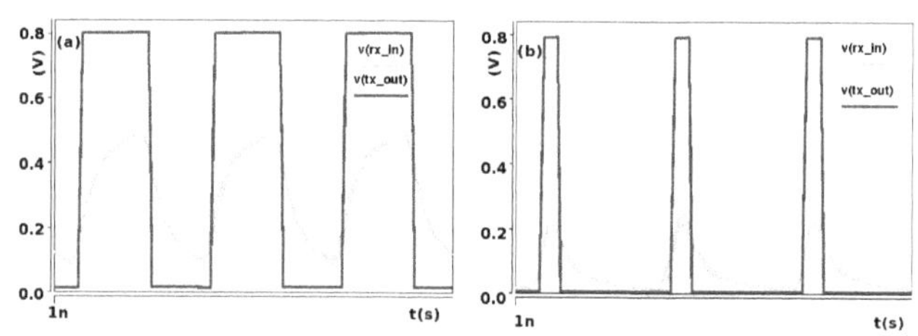

Figure 4: Jitter & attenuation for (a) Edge (b) Pulse

4.2 Inter Symbol Interference (ISI)

ISI, mainly caused by reflections, is a significant potential source of noise in a link. Such reflections are often due to impedance mismatches in the transmission media. Reflections can cause two effects, either interfere with the detection of an intended signal or inject a detectable unintended signal.

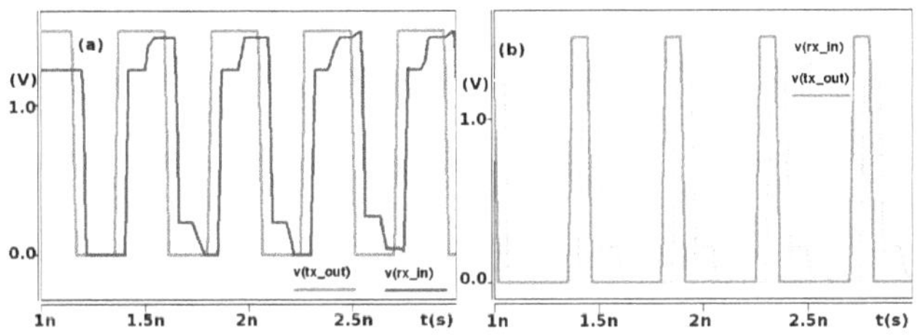

Figure 5: (a) Positive edge reflections have potential for double edge detection (b) Positive pulse reflections adding the charge where is does not exist and decreasing noise margin

Figure 5 shows the effect of positive reflections, due to under-termination, on both pulse and edge coded links. It can be seen that if the $Q_{\int}$ added because of positive reflection between the encoded information remains below noise margin, the information will be transmitted reliably. In case of negative reflections, if the $Q_{\int}$ remains above the noise margin the signal would be detected and the information will be successfully transmitted. It can be seen that it is advantageous to have positive reflections in the receiver as it adds to the signal, but it needs to be ensured that the noise created because of it remains below the noise margin.

4.3 Attenuation, Jitter and Dispersion

Attenuation is the result of losses in the transmission media, which are frequency dependent as higher frequencies are more susceptible to skin-effect, dielectric loss, and radiative loss. Attenuation is given by Equation 2 according to [8], where frequency dependent resistance and inductance are given by Equation 3 and Equation 4. If the information is represented as $Q_{\int}$, the effect of attenuation is decreased in the $Q_{\int}$ value as the signal passes through the transmission media.

$$atten = 20\ log_{10}[\exp(Re\sqrt{(R+j\omega L)(G+j\omega C)})] \tag{2}$$

$$R(f) = \omega\frac{\delta}{2}\frac{\partial L}{\partial n}; \delta = \sqrt{\frac{\rho}{\pi f \mu}} \tag{3}$$

$$L(f) = L_{external} + L_{internal} = L_{external} + \frac{\delta}{2}\frac{\partial L}{\partial n} \tag{4}$$

Dispersion is a spreading of signal energy in time. Dispersion is given by Equation 5 according to [8], where Equation 3 and Equation 4 are its frequency dependent resistance and inductance. Dispersion leads to phase variance in the transmitted information. Dispersion has a major effect in setting the data rate through the transmission media. The pulse encoding suffers from pulse widening and edge encoding from increase in rise and fall times. Jitter is the phase shift of the symbol resulting in external and internal noise in the system.

$$\beta(f) = Im[\sqrt{(R+j\omega L)(G+j\omega C)}] \tag{5}$$

Figure 4 shows the effect of attenuation, jitter and dispersion on the $Q_{\int}$ encoded as a pulse and an edge. Channel jitter also shows up as phase variance and can be similarly accounted for. Dispersion and jitter both result in phase variance and have been taken into account collectively as phase variance in this paper for analysis in the later sections. Successful reception requires that the $Q_{\int}$ after the attenuation and phase variance in the media remain above the noise margin.

4.4 Baseline Shift

For 2-wire transmission schemes, common mode (both wires changing in the same direction) content in the information sent over the transmission line shifts the reception baseline at the receiver. This results in a shift in the V_{Imin} value at the receiver as compared to that at the transmitter. For example baseline shift at the receiver event detector when constant pulses are sent down a meter of 50 ohms trace in a FR4 PCB can be about 300 mV. The offset is proportional to media length and can be mitigated by differential transmission or by chosing line codes with minimal common mode content.

5. DATA TRANSFER RATE

The maximum data rate of a link can be limited by the transmission media due to frequency dependent loss. Since loss and noise grow with distance, there is a trade off between data rate and link length. Data transmission over longer distances require that the $Q_{\int}$ remains above the noise margin after ISI, attenuation and jitter effects. Additionally, two adjacent symbols need to be kept from colliding due to jitter. A working link needs to maintain sufficient signal strength and temporal separation such that $Q_{\int}$ over the noise threshold represents an achievable Q_{crit} at the receiver.

For RZ pulse encoding, there is a minimum separation between pulses at the transmitter output to allow reliable detection at the end of the transmission line. The attenuation provides with different charge loss at different lengths of transmission media. Thus, the minimum charge needed by the detector to work reliably puts the limit on transmission line lengths. Phase variance allows determination of the minimum separation of pulses for different lengths of transmission media. This result is highly dependent on the jitter in the transmitter. The separation of effects determine the data rate depending on how many pulses can be accommodated in a given clock cycle. Hence if:

$$Q_{initial} - Q_{loss} \geq Q_{min\ detectable} \tag{6}$$

where $Q_{initial}$ is the charge in the minimum sized pulse. The minimum sized pulse generation is technology dependent. Then:

$$data\ rate = \left\lfloor \frac{T_{clock}/2}{T_{min\ pulse}} \right\rfloor \times \frac{2}{T_{clock}} \tag{7}$$

Else increase $Q_{initial}$ and calculate date rate according to new $T_{min\ pulse}$.

For edge based encoding, the minimum charge needed at the receiver directly helps in determining the minimum separation between the edges. T_{min} is the value of time it takes to reach the minimum detectable charge at the event detector. The value increases with length as the edge slope decreases with length. It is ensured that transmitter can transmit this minimum separation reliably. Thus, the data rate is determined by how many edges can be accommodated in a single clock cycle. Hence if:

$$T_{min\ edge} \geq T_{min}\ and\ T_{detector\ edge} \geq T_{min} \tag{8}$$

where $T_{min\ edge}$ is the minimum possible separation between the edges from the transmitter and $T_{detector\ edge}$ is the separation between the edges at the receiver or detector measured from V_{Imin}. then:

$$data\ rate = \left\lfloor \frac{T_{clock}/2}{T_{min\ edge}} \right\rfloor \times \frac{2}{T_{clock}} \quad (9)$$

Else increase $T_{min\ edge}$ and calculate the data rate again. Hence data rate in general is given by:

$$data\ rate = \left\lfloor \frac{T_{clock}/2}{T_{min\ symbol}} \right\rfloor \times \frac{2}{T_{clock}} \times N_{transition} \quad (10)$$

where $T_{min\ symbol}$ is the minimum possible separation between the symbols (edges or pulses) and $N_{transition}$ is the number of valid transitions possible after each transition.

6. RESULTS

The minimum detectable charge for the receiver based on circuit topology in Figure 1 is shown in Figure 6. The plots are done for 75ps pulse width at the transmitter and hence an initial charge of $44.25 V.ps$. The minimum detectable

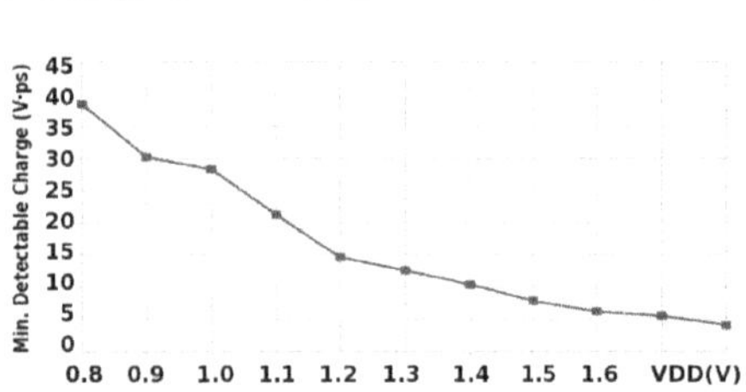

Figure 6: Minimum Detectable Charge

charge from Figure 6 has the value of 7.8 V.ps for 1.5V VDD. The minimum separation between the 75 ps pulses taking phase variance into account is 185ps. This value is highly dependent on jitter due to transmitter. This results in a 5.12 Gb/s data rate in the RZ encoded pulse link using Equation 10. The minimum time difference between the edges to take phase variance in the link and transmitter design constraints into account is 185ps, which is greater than T_{min}. This results in a data rate of 5.12 Gb/s using Equation 10 for 2 level edge based encoding. Figure 7 shows the increasing loss with length in the edge and pulse based links. This results in data rate as shown in Figure 8, which can be seen to be above 5Gb/s for about 5 feet in FR4 stripline. Data rates remain above 5Gb/s for RG-178 in lengths up to 6 feet.

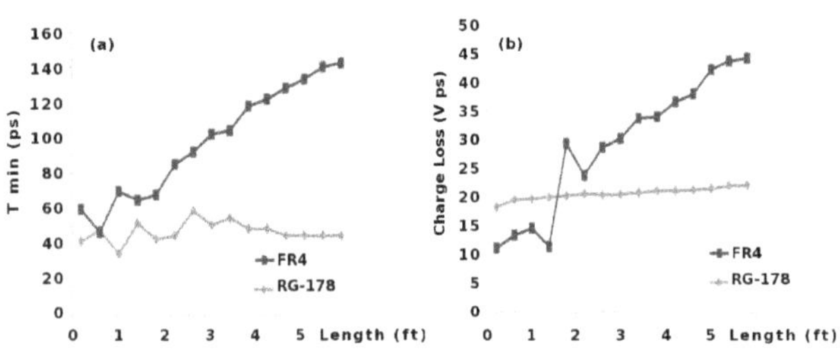

Figure 7: Loss vs Length in (a) Edge and (b) Pulse

The constraints on minimum separation of edges in two and three level encoding does not change but $N_{transition}$ has a value of two in three level encoding. Hence, data rate of the order of 10.24 Gb/s in the lengths in order of

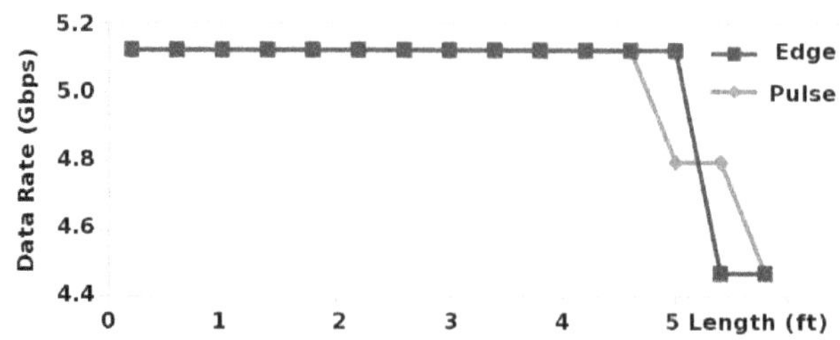

Figure 8: Data Rate vs Length

5 feet in PCB and coaxial cables is achievable with 130nm technology using Equation 10. The implementation must be fully differential to alleviate the baseline shift or line coding schemes must be used to reduce the integral common mode content in all these implementations. $Q_{\int}$ metric used in the presented results has an advantage over conventional eye diagram based metric as the effects mentioned in section 4 only become apparent at lengths greater than 5 ft in the analyzed media. Hence a substantially higher data rate is achievable at a given length with the use of $Q_{\int}$ metric.

7. CONCLUSIONS

A new methodology to alleviate the problems associated with conventional serial link designs was proposed. The proposed $Q_{\int}$ metric can help us make a jitter tolerant link, which can be self timed to get away from time of flight issues in handshaking and not have additional circuitry for synchronization and maintaining signal integrity. The link also has negligible idle state power consumption and can be used with conventional asynchronous techniques alongside the link. The margins for proper utilization of the metric were described and a design was proposed for implementation of a 10+ Gb/s link in 130nm.

8. REFERENCES

[1] R. Dobkin, M. Moyal, A. Kolodny, and R. Ginosar, "Asynchronous Current Mode Serial Communication," *(VLSI) Systems, IEEE Trans*, 2010.

[2] J. Teifel and R. Manohar, "A high-speed clockless serial link transceiver," *ASYNC*, 2003.

[3] M. Singh, S. M. Nowick, S. N, and N. Stage, "MOUSETRAP : Ultra-High-speed Transition-Signaling Asynchronous Pipelines *," in *ICCD*, 2001, pp. 9–17.

[4] W. Bainbridge and S. Furber, "Delay insensitive system-on-chip interconnect using 1-of-4 data encoding," in *ASYNC*, 2001, pp. 118–126.

[5] R. Ho, J. Gainsley, and R. Drost, "Long wires and asynchronous control," *ASYNC 2004. Proceedings.*, pp. 240–249, 2004.

[6] M. Miller, G. Hoover, and F. Brewer, "Pulse-mode link for robust, high speed communications," *ISCS*, 2008.

[7] C. By, "Properties and Design of the Phase- Sawtooth Comparator," 1961.

[8] A. Deutsch, "Electrical characteristics of interconnections for high-performance systems," *Proceedings of the IEEE*, vol. 86, no. 2, pp. 315–357, 1998.

Design and Comparative Evaluation of a Hybrid Cache Memory at Architectural Level

Wei Wei
ECE Dept, Northeastern University
Boston, MA 02115, USA
+1-617-373-7780
wei.w@husky.neu.edu

Kazuteru Namba
A.I.S, Chiba University
Chiba, Japan
+81-43-290-3255
namba@ieee.org

Fabrizio Lombardi
ECE Dept, Northeastern University
Boston, MA 02115, USA
+1-617-373-4854
lombardi@ece.neu.edu

ABSTRACT

A hybrid memory cell usually consists of a Static Random Access Memory (SRAM) and an embedded Dynamic Random Access Memory (eDRAM) cell; hybrid cells are particularly suitable for cache design. A novel hybrid cache memory scheme (that has also non-volatile elements) is initially proposed; this scheme is assessed through extensive simulation to show significant improvements in performance. Different design implementations of the hybrid cache are then proposed at architectural level and different features (such as the memory hit rate, the Instruction Per Cycle (IPC) access pattern and the memory cell access time) are also simulated at this level using benchmarks to show the advantages of the proposed scheme for use as an hybrid cache.

General Terms: Design

Keywords

Memory Design; Static and Dynamic random-access-memory; Low power; Hybrid cache memory; Non-volatile memory

1. INTRODUCTION

With the rapid development of technology, the highest level (Level 1, or L1) in the memory hierarchy consists of cache and accounts for a substantial proportion of the power dissipation for an embedded microprocessor. A L1 memory consists of many modules, such as the Memory Management Unit (MMU), the cache tag and the data memory arrays [1]. Moreover, periphery circuits (such as wordline (WL), bitline (BL), sensing and decoding) must be also considered for proper power management as well as performance [1].

On-chip memory occupies a significant portion of the overall die area and is very important in power management and high performance computing [2]. Static Random-Access-Memory (SRAM) is still largely used as on-chip memory cache due to its high performance; however, SRAMs are highly vulnerable to transient errors, so necessitating schemes for reliability enhancement. Moreover, other concerns (such as leakage power) are still present in the operation of a SRAM. At nanoscales to supersede the limitations of a SRAM, different types of memory have been proposed. [2] reduces leakage by utilizing dynamic memories (DRAM); for example, the IBM logic-based embedded DRAM (eDRAM) technology [3] integrates a trench DRAM storage cell into a logic-circuit technology and achieves a significant density improvement compared with a SRAM (i.e. a factor of 16 to 20 in DRAM versus SRAM capacity per unit area [3, 4]). This type of memory is usually referred to as hybrid.

Emerging non-volatile memory devices, such as ferroelectric random access memory (FRAM), magnetic random access memory (MRAM), phase-change memory (PRAM), and resistive RAM (RRAM) have also been proposed for future computing and mobile systems [5, 6]. Among them, the RRAM is extensively used for on-chip cache due to its high density, good scalability and low power dissipation [7]. [8] has proposed a novel energy efficient memory architecture based on PRAM and DRAM; it incorporates PRAM into the main memory hierarchy and adopts a low overhead hardware/software solution for management [8].

In this manuscript, issues related to hybrid cache memory designs are discussed and evaluated at an architectural level by utilizing the memory cell circuits of [2]. Different schemes and features (such as address decoding, access pattern and refresh requirements) are considered and assessed; compared to a conventional cache memory, the proposed schemes based on non-volatile hybrid memory circuits can be used to save power dissipation and decrease circuit complexity, thus further mitigating process variability and providing non-volatile storage.

2. PROPOSED HYBRID CACHE MEMORY

2.1 Improved Macrocell

In the macrocell (MCT) of [2], a NMOS transistor stores the data using the gate capacitance and replaces the capacitor. Similar to MCC [10], the dynamic part of the MCT has n-1 eDRAM cells; each eDRAM is connected to the SRAM by an NMOS pass transistor (acting as a *"bridge"* and controlled by the corresponding Selection Decoder (SD) signal). Using SD, the stored data in the SRAM cell is initially bidirectionally moved (through the Storage Node (SN)) to/from the selected eDRAM; as no Bitline (BL) is involved, this data transfer is referred to as internal. The "Write" operation is controlled by the signal on the Wordline (WL) and the data is stored at the storage node D. For the "Read" operation, the Wordline Read (WLD) is used to pass the stored data to the BL Read (BLD). By utilizing this circuit, the "Read" process for the data stored in the eDRAM is non-destructive, while attaining multiple read-outs.

GLSVLSI'16, May 18–20, 2016, Boston, MA, USA.
 ISBN 978-1-4503-4274-2/16/05…$15.00.
DOI: http://dx.doi.org/10.1145/2902961.2903002

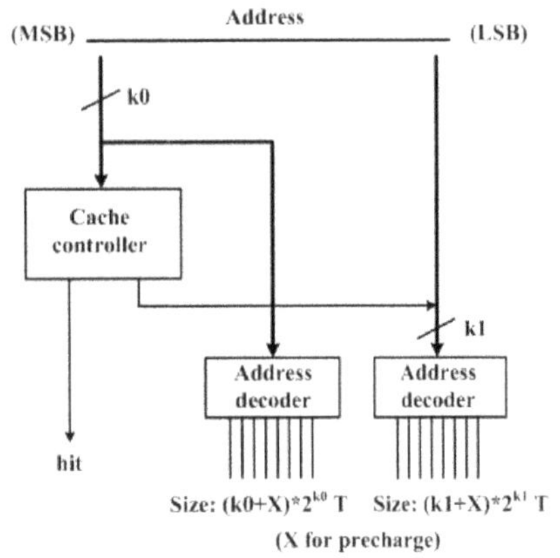

Figure 1. Scheme for cache memory address decoding

2.2 Non-volatile hybrid memory

Different from the MCT cell circuit, a novel non-volatile hybrid memory has also been proposed for memory cache implementation. Within this circuit, an embedded RRAM (eRRAM) is added to the corresponding eDRAM for non-volatile storage. This circuit also takes advantages of the bridge, so the stored data is also used to control whether the RRAM is programmed (such as when the data transfer from the SRAM to the respective eDRAM is required). To achieve non-volatile storage, the cell requires to perform a "Reset" for implementing the RESET process of the RRAM. Thus, a full operational cycle of this memory cell utilizes the following sequence: "Reset", "Write", "Transfer" and "Read" operations (as discussed in more detail in [2]).

2.3 Hybrid Cache Access

At architectural level, address decoding and control of data transfer for the different memory types must be performed in the cache itself; this process consists of different steps. The first step requires the access of the eDRAM cells only for a hit in the corresponding tag. In the second step, the percentage of hits in the SRAM blocks is increased to reduce the number of data transfers between the SRAM and eDRAM cells. A memory cache is faster than main memory, so data is transferred from main memory to cache in fixed blocks, known as cache "lines" [11]. Consider the address decoding scheme in Figure 1; it consists of a cache controller and two address decoders for the SRAM and the corresponding eDRAM cells. The cache controller is shown in Figure 2, it consists of an address decoder, a Content-Addressable Memory (CAM) and comparators.

High performance processors overlap data access and tag arrays, such that the target data is already available during a successful tag comparison. For example, consider the 4-way cache of Figure

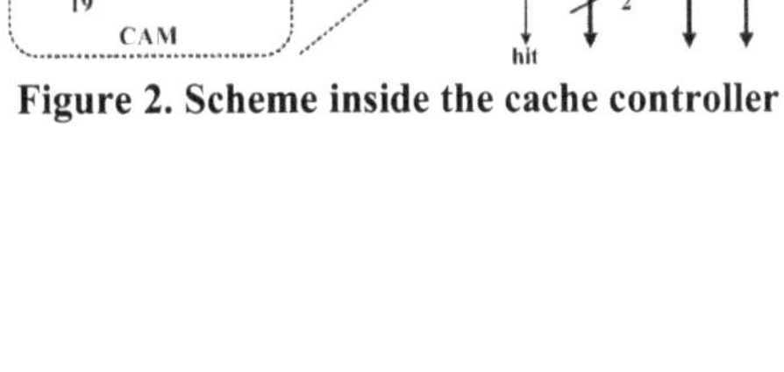

Figure 2. Scheme inside the cache controller

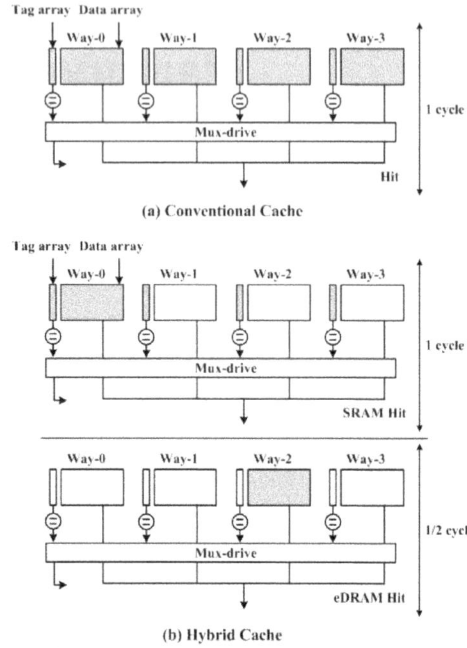

Figure 3. Access scheme for conventional and hybrid caches [10]

3(a); the small box represents the tag array, while the corresponding large box represents the data array of the cache. The hybrid cache consists of hybrid memory cells, so a different scheme is utilized (Figure 3(b)). A hybrid cache requires a different scheme, because the read operation of the eDRAM cells is destructive and previous designs do not include the refresh logic [10] (Figure 3(b)). In this scheme, the number of state losses from the read operation must be reduced, so the tags of the all-way set are accessed in parallel with the data array in the block located in the way-0. If there is a hit in the way-0 (SRAM hit), the connected eDRAM will not be read. If there is a miss for the data, but a hit in the other tag associated with the eDRAM block, the corresponding data array is subsequently accessed (Figure 3(b)). This scheme requires an additional cycle when a miss happens in the SRAM for tag comparison; this has been adopted for the hybrid cache design made of MCC cells and the proposed types due the destructive reading process of the eDRAMs.

Moreover, MCC [10] must utilize a write-through policy, because the read is destructive when a hit occurs in an eDRAM. Although this solution is capable of addressing this event, it needs to read the data from the L2 cache and so incurring in a large power consumption (as well as a deterioration of performance). The proposed non-volatile hybrid memory can efficiently mitigate the above drawback and the data can be transferred back to the eDRAM from the corresponding eRRAM. Data is "exchanged" between the SRAM, eDRAMs and eRRAMs; so, compared with the previous MCC circuit, the proposed hybrid memory can attain substantial power savings by utilizing the eRRAMs for data storage and transfer.

2.4 Refresh Scheme

Although data can be transferred between the SRAM and the eDRAM through a "swap" operation (as detailed previously), the access scheme is capable of effectively mitigating the state loss after the read access. Moreover, the data stored in the eDRAM

Table 1. Cache Memory Configuration

Parameter	Value
Data Cache Block Size	64 B
Data Cache Capacity	16 KB, 32 KB, 64 KB, 128 KB
Set Associative	2 Way, 4 Way
Replacement Policy	Least-Recently Used (LRU)
Write Policy	Write-Through

may also be lost after a long time access; this results in a performance penalty for the cache.

Several approaches address the limitation of the retention time in a hybrid memory; these approaches include periodic data refreshing, replacement policies, allowing data to expire without refresh and/or a combination of these approaches [12]. Similar to the 6T SRAM cache, the proposed memory scheme suffers from the disadvantage that the operational frequency is determined by the slowest cells for clock generation and synchronization. The retention time of the eDRAM cells internal to a hybrid cache memory has also been investigated at circuit-level [2]; larger is the retention time of the eDRAM circuits, the lower is the refresh frequency, so it can achieve a reduction in power dissipation.

3. ARCHITECTURAL EVALUATION

This section presents the architectural evaluation of a hybrid memory cache using the proposed cells. The cache memory is modeled by a modified version of the Hotleakage simulation framework [13] running the SPEC2000 benchmark suites [14]. The simulated results are presented and analyzed for different cache organizations at the 45nm technology node using different configurations (Table I).

3.1 SRAM and eDRAM Hit Rate

As discussed previously, the "Read" operation in the eDRAM may lead to data loss in the MCC and the proposed hybrid memory cells due to the storage capacitance, so further resulting in a cache miss. Therefore, to efficiently mitigate unnecessary refresh operations, the eDRAMs are only accessed after checking the tags; this access process is analyzed in more detail next.

The hit rates of the SRAM and eDRAM cells are used to find the percentages of cache accesses for the static and dynamic memories. The simulation results are obtained by running the SPEC2000 benchmark suite [14] for different cache sizes (16KB, 32KB and 64KB) and are presented in Figures 4 and 5; the number of ways are shown in Table I. The frequency to access the

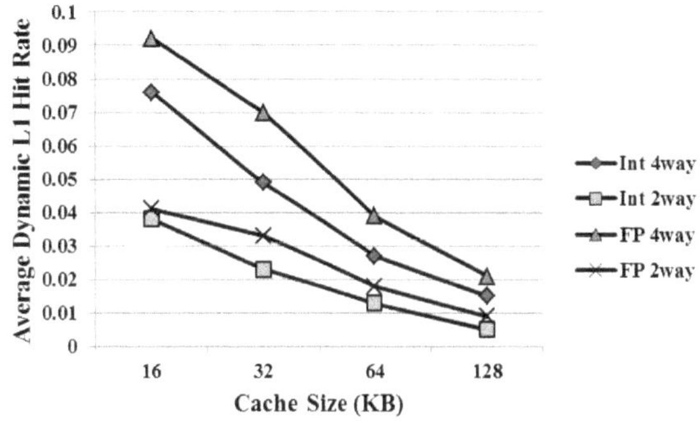

Figure 5. Average dynamic L1 hit rate for integer and floating-point benchmarks vs cache size

static memory is significantly larger than the dynamic memory for both cases. The access frequencies of the static memory for the integer (Int) benchmark simulations are higher than for the floating-point (FP) cases; so, the hybrid cache has a larger percentage of tag hits for the integer programs. A further important observation is that the number of hits significantly depends on the storage capacity, because the Most Recent Used (MRU) block is used in the SRAMs. Moreover, for a given associative degree, a larger cache size leads to a lower eDRAM hit rate, but also a higher overall L1 hit rate. Finally, the associative degree results in an increase of the total L1 hit rate, so inclusive of a smaller (larger) contribution for the static (dynamic) memory.

The results of the L1 hit rate are presented in Figures 4 and 5 for the static and dynamic memories (as average values when simulating various benchmarks); as expected, a larger cache capacity results in a higher hit rate. Although for dynamic memory, there is a decrease, the sum of the hit rates (so including both static and dynamic memories) increases, because a larger cache size provides a high probability for hits to occur. Moreover it shows the same static hit rate value for all memory schemes in the 16KB-2way and 32KB-4way cases (as also applicable to 32KB-2way, 64KB-4way, 64KB-2way and 128KB-4way) because both cache schemes have the same static size. Both memories have the same number of misses; however, the difference is that the incoming block may be fetched from a different memory (e.g., eDRAM cells or at a different level of the memory hierarchy). The 4way cache has a higher overall hit rate, although the SRAM hit rate decreases with an increase of the eDRAM hit rate. The lower eDRAM hit rate has two causes. The overall access time of the eDRAM cells requires an additional

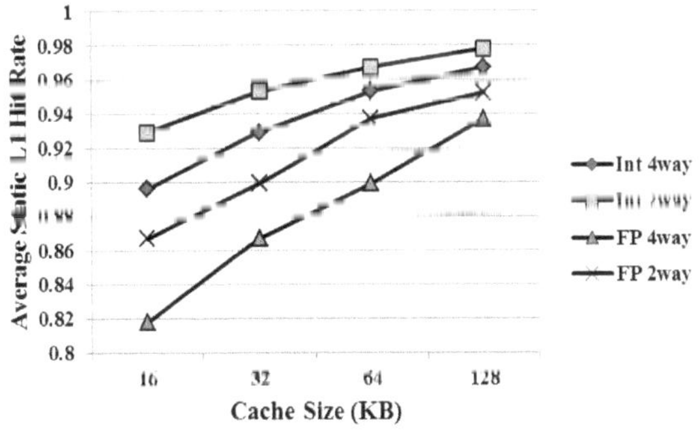

Figure 4. Average static L1 hit rate for integer and floating-point benchmarks vs cache size

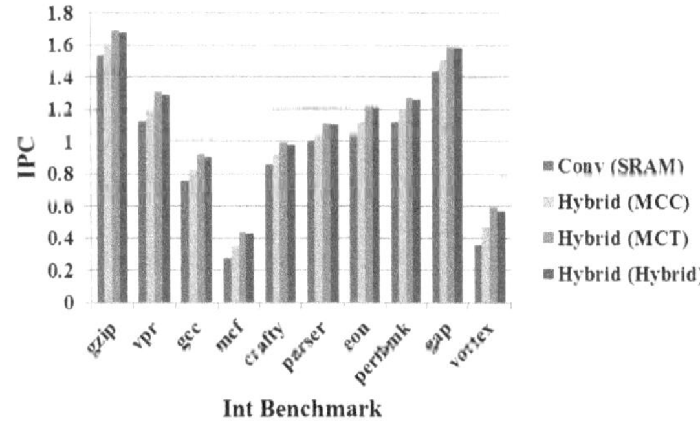

Figure 6. IPC performance with respect to the integer benchmarks for 16KB-4way memory cache

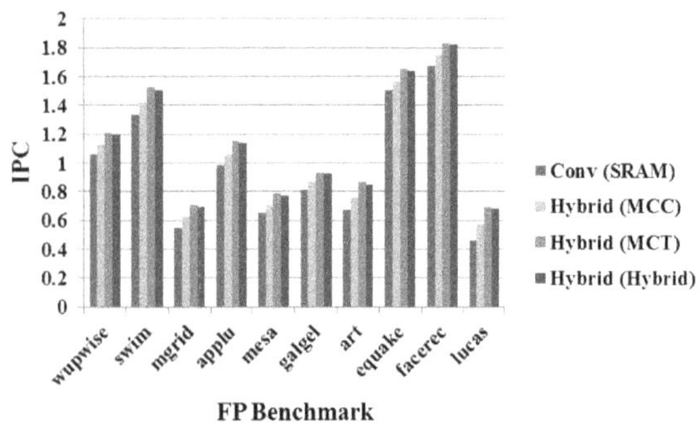

Figure 7. IPC performance with respect to the floating-point benchmarks for 16KB-4way memory cache

cycle for tag comparison; also for a hit in the eDRAM, a swap occurs between the SRAM and eDRAM cells. As shown in the simulation results, the access frequencies of the SRAM and eDRAM are rather different. Therefore, this is the fundamental difference between the proposed hybrid cache memory and a conventional cache implemented by utilizing SRAM only.

3.2 Instruction Per Cycle (IPC)

The performance of the proposed hybrid circuits is further evaluated by using the Instruction Per Cycle (IPC) for the benchmark executions in different memories (the 16KB-4way cache is considered). The simulation results of the integer and floating-point benchmarks are presented in Figures 6 and 7, respectively. Although the various benchmarks show differences in IPC values, the variations of the different memory circuits for each program are consistent; the proposed scheme (for all three hybrid memory cells) shows its advantages when compared with a conventional cache. Among the three hybrid types, the proposed MCT cache achieves significant improvements compared with the MCC of [10]. The proposed non-volatile hybrid memory incurs in a very small penalty compared to MCT; however, it still achieves better performance than a conventional cache and MCC with the data restored from the eRRAM (for cases when there is a hit in the respective eDRAM and a possible state loss).

4. CONCLUSION

Recently, novel designs of hybrid cells have been proposed in the technical literature [2, 9, 10]. The hybrid memory scheme proposed in this manuscript brings a great potential also at the architectural level design and operation. Extensive evaluation results show that for IPC performance the MCT hybrid memory is significantly better than previous cache schemes. The cache implemented by the proposed non-volatile hybrid memory cell takes advantage of non-volatile storage and IPC penalties.

In conclusion, this paper has proposed hybrid cache memory schemes with custom access pattern for low power and non-volatile storage. Their operational correctness and performance have been demonstrated through an extensive analysis and simulation assessment; the proposed hybrid memory types are applicable to cache design and operation while offering significant performance improvements for implementation in the nanoscaled CMOS ranges.

5. REFERENCES

[1] J. R. Haigh, M. W. Wilkerson, J. B. Miller et al., "A low-power 2.5-GHz 90-nm level 1 cache and memory management unit," *IEEE Journal of Solid-State Circuits*, vol. 40, no. 5, pp. 1190-1199, 2005.

[2] W. Wei, K. Namba and F. Lombardi, "Novel Designs of Embedded Hybrid Cells for High Performance Memory Circuits," *Proceedings of IEEE/ACM Great Lakes Symposium on VLSI 2015*, pp. 91-94, 2015.

[3] R.E. Matick and S.E. Schuster, "Logic-Based eDRAM: Origins andRationale for Use," *IBM J. Research and Development*, vol. 49, no. 1, pp. 145-165, 2005.

[4] X. Liang, R. Cannal, G.-Y. Wei et at., "Process Variation Tolerant 3T1D-Based Cache Architectures," *40th IEEE/ACM International Symposium on Microarchitecture 2007 (MICRO 2007)*, pp. 15- 26, 2007.

[5] B. M. Lee and G. H . Park, "Performance and energy-efficiency analysis of hybrid cache memory based on SRAM-MRAM," *2012 International SoC Design Conference*, pp. 247-250, 2012.

[6] H. Noguchi, K. Nomura, K. Abe et al., "D-MRAM cache: Enhancing energy efficiency with 3T-1MTJ DRAM/MRAM hybrid memory," *2013 Design, Automation & Test in Europe Conference & Exhibition (DATE)*, pp. 1813-1818, 2013.

[7] H. Akinaga, H. Shima, "Resistive Random Access Memory (ReRAM) Based on Metal Oxides," *Proceedings of the IEEE*, pp. 2237-2251, 2010.

[8] G. Dhiman, R. Ayoub and T. Rosing, "Pdram: A hybrid pram and dram main memory system," *ACM/IEEE 46th Design Automation Conference (DAC)*, pp. 664-669, 2009.

[9] W. S. Yu, R. Huang, S. Xu et al., "SRAM-DRAM hybrid memory with applications to efficient register files in fine-grained multi-threading," *in Proc. ISCA*, pp. 247-258, 2011.

[10] A. Valero, S. Petit, J. Sahuquillo et al., "Design, performance, and energy consumption of eDRAM/SRAM macrocells for L1 data caches," *IEEE Transactions on Computers*, vol. 61, no. 9, 2012.

[11] J. L. Hennessy, D. Patterson, "Computer architecture: a quantitative approach (Fourth Edition)," *Morgan Kaufmann*, ISBN: 0123704901, 2006.

[12] X. Y. Liang, R. Canal, G. Y. Wei et al., "Replacing 6T SRAMs with 3T1D DRAMs in the L1 data cache to combat process variability," *IEEE Micro*, Vol. 28, no. 1, pp. 60-68, 2008.

[13] Y. Zhang, D. Parikh, K. Sankaranarayanan et al., "Hotleakage: A Temperature-Aware Model of Subthreshold and Gate Leakage for Architects," *technical report*, Dept. of Computer Science, Uni. of Virginia, 2003.

[14] Standard Performance Evaluation Corporation, http://www.spec.org/cpu2000.

A Sampling Clock Skew Correction Technique for Time-Interleaved SAR ADCs

Daniel Prashanth
Massachusetts Institute of Technology
Cambridge, MA 02140
dpik@alum.mit.edu

Hae-Seung Lee
Massachusetts Institute of Technology
Cambridge, MA 02140
hslee@mit.edu

ABSTRACT

A technique for sampling clock skew correction by adjusting the delay in the input signal to each channel in a time-interleaved (TI) ADC is proposed. A proof-of-concept TI ADC employing this technique was implemented in a 65 nm CMOS process. The four-way TI ADC operates at an effective sampling rate of 150 MS/s, and achieves 60.2 dB and 58.2 dB SNDR for an input signal frequency of 2.1 MHz and 74.1 MHz, respectively. The ADC consumes 12.4 mW from a 1.2 V supply and occupies an area of 0.9 mm^2.

Keywords

ADC; time-interleaving; correction

1. INTRODUCTION

As more signal processing is moved to the digital domain, there is an ever-increasing demand for high-resolution and high-speed ADCs that operate in an energy efficient manner. One effective method to increase the input signal bandwidth of an ADC is to utilize a TI architecture. In a TI ADC, N channels each operating at a sampling rate of f_s are used to achieve an effective sampling rate of $N{\cdot}f_s$. However, in TI ADCs, gain mismatch, offset mismatch, and sampling clock skew between channels can degrade the overall performance of the ADC [1]. The effects of gain and offset mismatch can be easily removed by digital calibration. However, sampling clock skew results in errors that increase with increasing input signal frequencies, and can be the limiting error source in TI ADCs. In this paper, we propose a new sampling clock skew correction technique for SAR ADCs.

The calibration of sampling clock skew can be broken into two phases: the skew detection and skew correction phases. In the detection phase, the sampling clock skew between channels is estimated using background [2, 3] or foreground [4] techniques. After the sampling clock skew between channels has been estimated, correction can be performed in the analog or digital domains. The analog skew correction typically includes adding a controllable delay in the clock path, which can lead to increased sampling jitter [2]. On the other hand, digital correction of the output data [5] is power hungry especially at the high sampling rates that TI ADCs operate at. In this paper, we propose a simple sampling clock skew correction technique that adjusts the inherent delay in the input signal sampling network rather than the sampling clock, which allows the mitigation of the effects of sampling clock skew without increasing the jitter of the sampling clock.

A block diagram of such a system for sampling clock skew correction is illustrated in Fig. 1. The control bits for the i-th channel, $CalBits_i$ are chosen appropriately such that the input signal delay is adjusted to match the skew on its sampling clock, Clk_i, thus removing the sampling clock skew for the i-th sub-channel. By repeating this process for all channels in a TI ADC, the effect of sampling clock skew on the TI system can be mitigated.

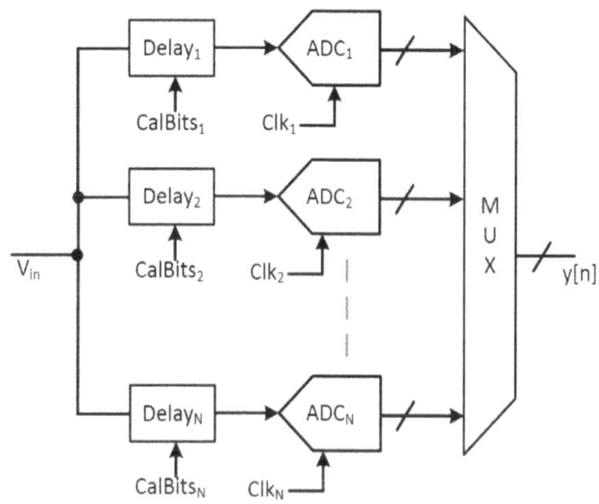

Figure 1. Block diagram of a TI ADC with input signal delay control.

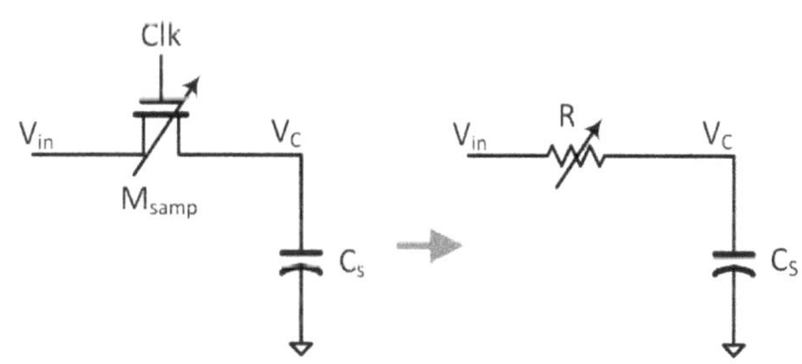

Figure 2. Sampling network during the tracking phase.

The input signal delay can be controlled by varying the input sampling switch resistance. During the track phase of the SAR ADC, the input network can be modeled as a low-pass RC circuit as shown in Fig. 2, where R is the resistance of MOS switches and C is the DAC capacitance. Typically, the RC time constant is designed to be short enough to track the input accurately, thus requiring that the input signal frequency, $f_{in} \ll 1/(2\pi RC)$. Therefore, for an input signal of the form,

GLSVLSI '16, May 18 - 20, 2016, Boston, MA, USA

ACM 978-1-4503-4274-2/16/05$15.00
DOI: http://dx.doi.org/10.1145/2902961.2903008

$$v_l = \sin(2\pi f_{in} t),$$

the voltage across the capacitor v_C can be approximated as,

$$v_C \approx \sin(2\pi f_{in}(t - T_D)),$$

where $T_D = RC$ is the effective delay of the input signal by the RC network. Thus, in typical ADCs, where the input signal frequency is much lower than the corner frequency of the sampling network, the sampled voltage has a group delay corresponding to RC. Hence, by varying the sampling switch resistance, the delay in the input signal can be adjusted.

Varying the corner frequency of the input sampling network also introduces a small magnitude mismatch. However, if the corner frequency of the sampling network is sufficiently high, the magnitude error introduced is negligible within the accuracy requirement of the overall TI ADC. Fig. 3 shows the plot of gain mismatch induced error $\sigma^2_{g,cal}$ [2] normalized by the quantization noise σ^2_q at 12 bits for different minimum corner frequencies f_L of the sampling circuit. If $\sigma^2_{g,cal}/\sigma^2_q < 1$, the gain mismatch is not a limiting factor. It can be seen that for input signal frequencies up to 100 MHz, f_L of only 3.5 GHz, is enough to ensure that the residual gain mismatch does not limit the ADC performance at 12 bits. At higher input frequencies, for example 400 MHz, f_L of 17.5 GHz is required. Although higher f_L reduces the skew correction range, 6 ps timing skew correction range is still achievable at this f_L, which is adequate to correct typical timing skew in time-interleaved ADCs [2].

It should be noted that the proposed technique only corrects the timing skew once the skew between channels has been estimated. Existing techniques presented in [2, 3, 4] can be used for sampling clock skew estimation.

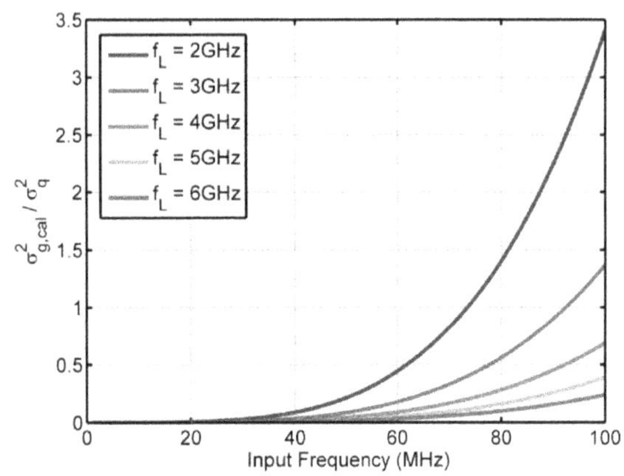

Figure 3. Simulation results of the maximum error due to variance in gain mismatch normalized by the quantization noise for a 12-bit TI ADC

2. CHIP ARCHITECTURE

2.1 Block Diagram

The block diagram of the prototype TI ADC is shown in Fig. 4. The TI ADC is composed of four interleaved channels. The SAR DAC is implemented using a hybrid capacitive-resistive (C-R) DAC design instead of the popular split DAC [6] to avoid sub-DAC calibration due to the parasitics introduced by the bridge capacitor. The drawback of the hybrid structure is higher power consumption due to the DC current through the resistor sub-DAC. In this proof-of-concept chip, the focus was the sampling clock skew correction, thus common power saving measures such as merged capacitor switching (MCS) were not employed. Asynchronous SAR logic, similar to that presented in [7] is used to avoid the need for a high-frequency bit-cycling clock and to enable high conversion rates. The DAC settling time of the MSB and LSB sections are also programmable to allow for longer settling of the MSB bits.

2.2 Input Signal Delay Control

In order to implement the signal delay control method, we need to be able to control the tracking switch resistance of the input tracking circuit. The circuit implementation of the tracking switch resistance control is shown in Fig. 5. The actual implementation is differential, but only one half of the circuit is shown in this figure for simplicity.

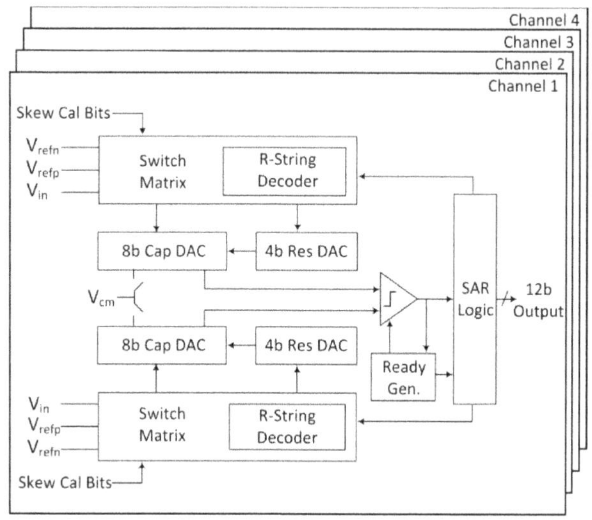

Figure 4. Block digram of the prototype TI ADC.

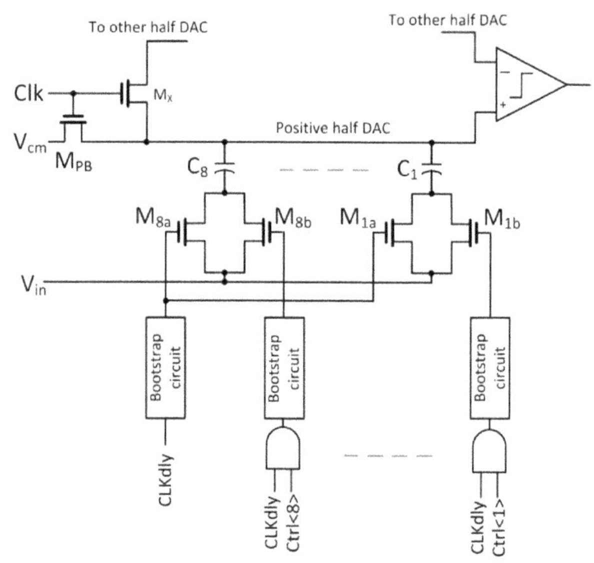

Figure 5. Schematic of the input sampling network implementing the input signal delay control method for sampling clock skew calibration.

The SAR ADC architecture provides a natural means for binary-weighted delay adjustment via the capacitor array. Two tracking switches, the main switch M_{ia}, and a second calibration switch M_{ib}, are connected to each capacitor C_i as shown in Fig. 5. If the control bit, *Ctrl<i>*, is high, the calibration switch operates in parallel with the main switch, lowering the ON-resistance, thus reducing the effective delay. By choosing which of the calibration control bits, *Ctrl<i>*, are turned on during sampling, the input signal delay can be adjusted with the resolution of the capacitor array. In the prototype, the sampling switches were designed to provide a 15 ps delay adjustment range, with an 8-bit resolution corresponding to <100 fs LSB.

Switches M_{pb} and M_x are used to implement bottom plate sampling. The switch M_x is used shuffle charge between the two half DACs rather than drawn from the common mode reference (V_{cm}) to improve settling speed. The logic delay of the AND gate only affects when the track switches are turned on and do not set the sampling instant. Consequently, the control logic in the track switch selection does not affect the sampling operation of the ADC.

2.3 Comparator

A dynamic latch-based comparator based on [8] is used in this design. The schematic of the comparator is shown in Fig. 6. Compared to the StrongArm comparator [9], this comparator provides further isolation between the latch outputs and the inputs, thus reducing the effect of kickback noise. Furthermore, this comparator requires only a single clock phase as compared to the comparator presented in [10]. The latch is turned on automatically by the output of the first stage (D_{i+} and D_{i-}).

Offset calibration was included in the comparator via a capacitor bank at the output of D_{i+} and D_{i-}. The offset calibration capacitor banks consist of five binary-scaled capacitors made up of 31 switches. The parasitic capacitances of the switches were sufficient to obtain fine enough calibration steps over the required offset calibration range. The offset can be calibrated between -8 mV and +8 mV with a step size of 250 μV, which corresponds to about 0.4 LSB.

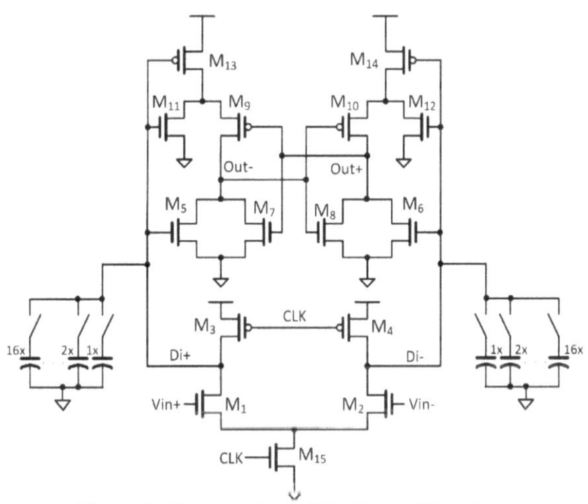

Figure 6. Comparator with offset calibration.

3. MEASUREMENT RESULTS

A prototype IC implementing the input signal delay control method was designed and fabricated in a 65 nm CMOS LP process. The TI ADC consists of four interleaved channels with an effective sampling rate of 150 MS/s. The prototype chip was wire-bonded directly to the test PCB to minimize the parasitics associated with IC packages. Before sampling clock skew calibration is performed, offset calibration is carried out to calibrate the offsets between channels. The output spectra of the prototype ADC for high input frequencies (74.1 MHz) close to the Nyquist rate of the converter is shown in Fig. 7(a). At high input signal frequencies, spurs due to sampling clock skew between channels are clearly visible in the time-interleaved spectrum and degrades the SNDR and SFDR performance of the time-interleaved output. In the presence of sampling clock skew, the SNDR of the TI ADC is limited to 53.1 dB while the SFDR is limited to 56.9 dB.

For sampling clock skew detection, we used the zero-crossing counting method described in [4]. The detection algorithm is carried out off-chip and was implemented in MATLAB using 500k samples/cycle. All sampling clock skew correction was done with an input signal frequency of 74.1 MHz. The sampling clock skew correction bits obtained were then frozen for all other tests at other input frequencies. The calibration process begins by choosing two channels separated by 180° in phase to calibrate first (e.g. Channel 3 and Channel 1). Once the sampling clock skew calibration between these two channels is complete, a third channel is calibrated against Channel 1 and Channel 3 (eg. Channel 2). Finally, Channel 4 is calibrated against Channel 2.

The time-interleaved output spectra of the prototype ADC after sampling clock skew correction for high input frequencies (74.1 MHz), close to the Nyquist rate of the converter is shown in Fig. 7(b). The tones due to sampling clock skew between channels have been reduced significantly. After calibration, the time-interleaved output achieves 58.2 dB SNDR and 68.0 dB SFDR. The SNDR and SFDR improved by 5.1 dB and 11dB, respectively.

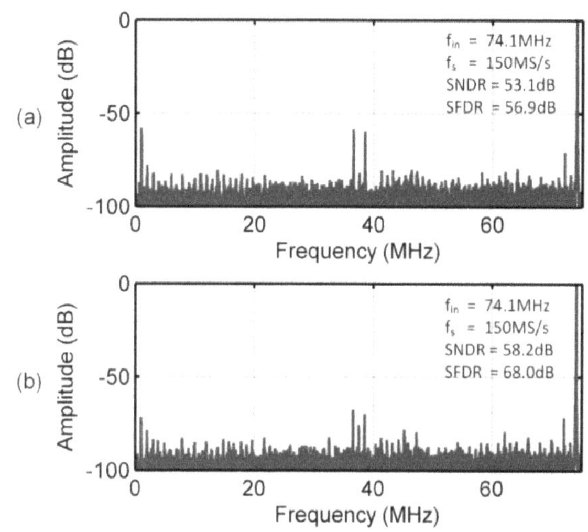

Figure 7. Output spectra of the TI ADC before and after sampling clock skew calibration.

The SNDR for the time-interleaved output for various input signal frequencies is plotted in Fig. 8. From this plot, it can be seen that without sampling clock skew calibration, the SNDR of the time-interleaved converter keeps decreasing with increasing input signal frequency due to the effects of sampling clock skew. With sampling clock skew calibration enabled, the SNDR curve "flattens out" with increasing input signal frequency and maintains less than 2 dB degradation throughout the entire Nyquist bandwidth.

The INL and DNL performance of the prototype ADC is shown in Fig. 9. The INL and DNL for a typical single channel are shown in the left column, while the INL and DNL of the time-interleaved ADC are shown in the right column. The maximum INL and DNL for a single channel are +1.37/-1.34 LSBs and +0.85/-0.91 LSBs respectively. For the time-interleaved converter, the INL and DNL are +1.07/-1.17 LSBs and +0.60/-0.69 LSBs respectively. The main sources of INL and DNL are parasitic capacitances from layout between the bottom and top plates of the capacitive DAC.

The ADC dissipates 12.4 mW from a 1.2 V supply, which corresponds to a Walden FoM of 98 and 124 fJ/step at low input frequencies and at Nyquist, respectively, and a Schreier FOM of 156 dB at Nyquist. Fig. 10 summarizes the performance of this work and shows the power breakdown for this ADC. Fig. 11 shows a die photo of the ADC and Fig. 12 compares its performance to other recently reported TI ADCs. This proof-of-concept TI ADC describes a technique whereby sampling clock skew can be mitigated without clock delay adjustment methods that introduces additional sampling clock jitter. This ADC was not optimized for power efficiency. The static power consumption of the resistor string dominates the power dissipated by the references. If a split capacitor DAC with calibration is employed in conjunction with power efficient switching methods such as MCS [11], the power consumption of the ADC can be reduced by approximately 40%.

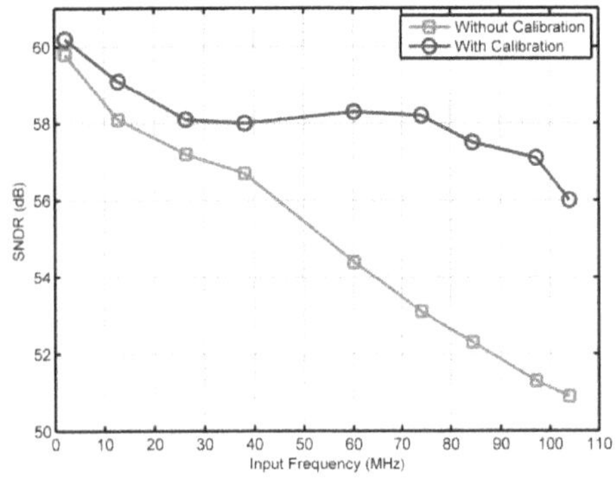

Figure 8. SNDR vs. input signal frequency.

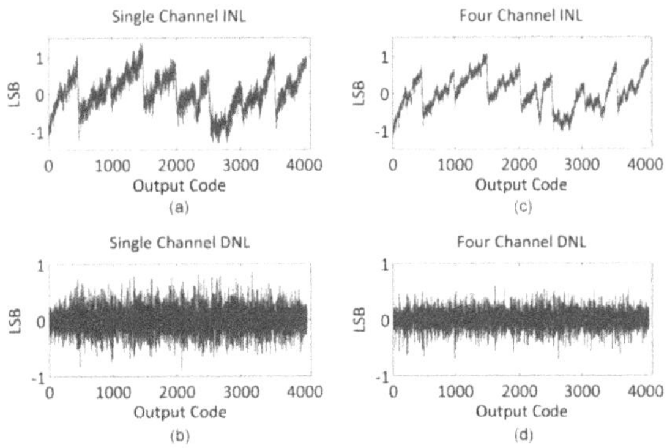

Figure 9. INL/DNL measurements of the TI ADC.

Parameter	Value
Architecture	TI SAR
Technology	65 nm
Supply	1.2 V
Sampling Rate	150 MS/s
Resolution	12 bits
Power	12.4 mW
Area	0.9 mm^2
SNDR @ 2.1 MHz	60.2 dB
FoM Walden	98 fJ/step
SNDR @ 74.1 MHz	58.2 dB
FoM Walden	124 fJ/step

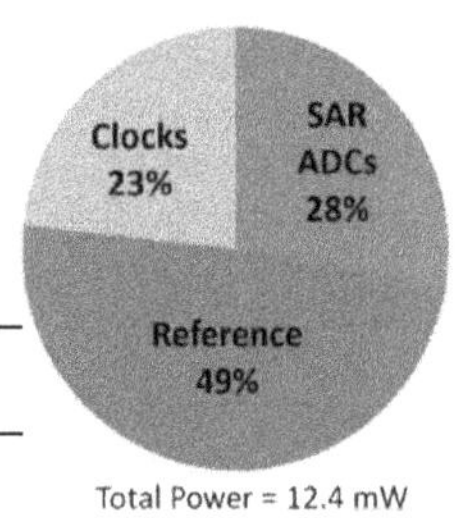

Figure 10. Performance summary and power breakdown of the TI ADC

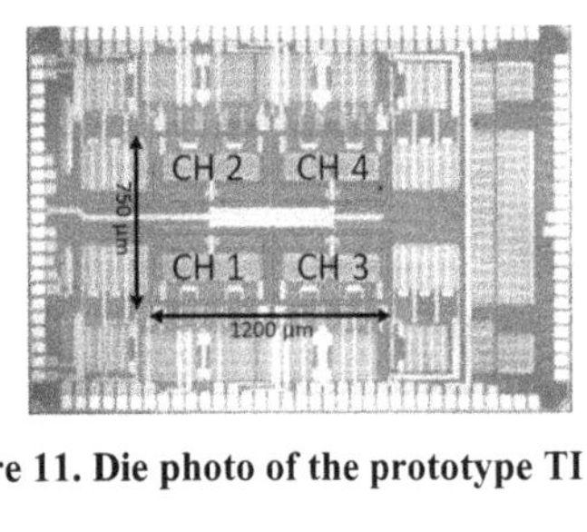

Figure 11. Die photo of the prototype TI ADC.

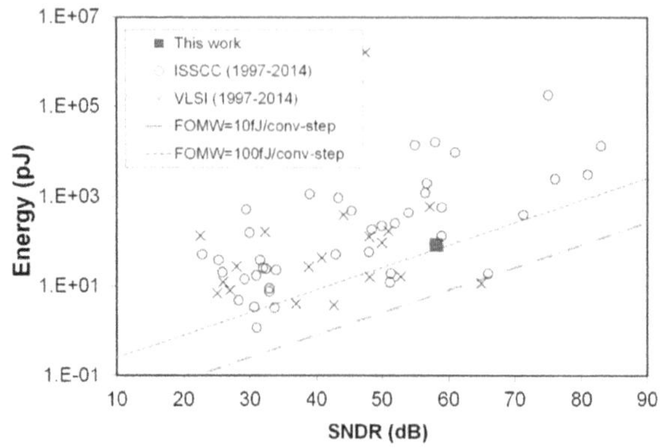

Figure 12. Comparison with other TI ADCs [12].

4. ACKNOWLEDGMENTS

This work is supported by MIT Center for Integrated Circuits and Systems, MIT/Masdar Institute Cooperative Program, and TSMC University Shuttle program.

5. REFERENCES

1. N. Kurosawa, et al., "Explicit analysis of channel mismatch effects in time-interleaved ADC systems," Circuits and Systems I: Fundamental Theory and Applications, IEEE Transactions on, vol.48, no.3, pp.261-271, Mar 2001.
2. M. El-Chammas, B. Murmann, Background Calibration of Time-Interleaved Data Converters, New York, NY: Springer, 2012.
3. S. Lee, et al., "A 1 GS/s 10b 18.9 mW Time-Interleaved SAR ADC With Background Timing Skew Calibration," IEEE J. Solid-State Circuits, vol. 49, no. 12, pp. 2846-2856, Dec. 2014.
4. C.-C. Huang, C.-Y. Wang, and J.-T. Wu, "A CMOS 6-bit 16- GS/s time-interleaved ADC using digital background calibration techniques," IEEE J. Solid-State Circuits, vol. 46, pp. 848-858, April 2011.
5. N. Le Dortz, et al., "A 1.62GS/s time-interleaved SAR ADC with digital background mismatch calibration achieving interleaving spurs below 70dBFS," Digest of Technical Papers - IEEE International Solid-State Circuits Conference, vol. 57, pp. 386-387, 2014.
6. R. J. Baker, "CMOS Circuit Design, Layout, and Simulation," 3rd Ed., New York, NY: Wiley-IEEE Press.
7. J. Yang, T. L. Naing, and R. W. Brodersen, "A 1 GS/s 6 bit 6.7 mW successive approximation ADC using asynchronous processing," IEEE Journal of Solid-State Circuits, vol. 45, no. 8, pp. 1469-1478, 2010.
8. M. Miyahara, Y. Asada, D. Paik, and A. Matsuzawa, "A low-noise self-calibrating dynamic comparator for high-speed ADCs," Proceedings of 2008 IEEE Asian Solid-State Circuits Conference, A-SSCC 2008, pp. 269-272, 2008.
9. J. Montanaro, et al., "A 160-MHz, 32-b, 0.5-W CMOS RISC microprocessor," IEEE Journal of Solid-State Circuits, vol. 31, no. November, pp. 1703-1714, 1996.
10. D. Schinkel, et al., "A double-tail latch-type voltage sense amplifier with 18ps setup-hold time," Digest of Technical Papers - IEEE International Solid-State Circuits Conference, pp. 314-316, 2007.
11. A. H. Chang, H.-S Lee, D. Boning, "A 12b 50MS/s 2.1mW SAR ADC with redundancy and digital background calibration," ESSCIRC 2013, Proceedings of the, vol., no., pp.109-112, 2013.
12. Murmann, "ADC Performance Survey 1997-2014," 2014.[Online]. Available: http://web.stanford.edu/~murmann/adcsurvey.html

Secure and Low-Overhead Circuit Obfuscation Technique with Multiplexers

Xueyan Wang, Xiaotao Jia, Qiang Zhou, and Yici Cai
CST Department, Tsinghua University
Beijing, China
{wangxueyan13, jxt11}@mails.tsinghua.edu.cn

Jianlei Yang
ECE Department, University of Pittsburgh
Pittsburgh, PA, USA
jiy64@pitt.edu, {zhouqiang, caiyc}@tsinghua.edu.cn

Mingze Gao, Gang Qu
ECE Department, University of Maryland
College Park, MD, USA
{mgao1, gangqu}@umd.edu

ABSTRACT

Circuit obfuscation techniques have been proposed to conceal circuit's functionality in order to thwart reverse engineering (RE) attacks to integrated circuits (IC). We believe that a good obfuscation method should have low design complexity and low performance overhead, yet, causing high RE attack complexity. However, existing obfuscation techniques do not meet all these requirements. In this paper, we propose a polynomial obfuscation scheme which leverages special designed multiplexers (MUXs) to replace judiciously selected logic gates. Candidate to-be-obfuscated logic gates are selected based on a novel gate classification method which utilizes IC topological structure information. We show that this scheme is resilient to all the known attacks, hence it is secure. Experiments are conducted on ISCAS 85/89 and MCNC benchmark suites to evaluate the performance overhead due to obfuscation.

1. INTRODUCTION

With the rapid development of embedded systems and the Internet of Things, application specific integrated circuits (IC) are playing a more and more important role in electronic products market. However, the hardware design intellectual-property (IP)[1, 2] in these circuits is facing severe threats from reverse engineering (RE) attacks, where an attacker analyzes a design and reproduces it with no or much less investment in research and development[3]. These low cost illegitimate products can bring security vulnerabilities to critical commercial and military systems, also, they can be sold at a much lower price, giving them an unfair competitive edge against the authenticated products.

Circuit obfuscation techniques have emerged as an effective countermeasure for RE attacks. These techniques seek to modify the design and implementation of a circuit in order to make it hard to interpret and hence increase the cost and complexity of RE attacks[4–12]. For an obfuscation technique to be effective, we argue that it must satisfy the following two requirements: First, the obfuscated circuit should be resilient to any potential attack and ideally make RE attack complexity exponential. Second, the obfuscation method should require a low design complexity (polynomial to the size of the circuit) and incur little overhead to circuit's performance. Clearly, when the first requirement violated, the obfuscated circuit can be reverse engineered with ease thus fail to achieve its goal of IP protection. When the second requirement violated, the design cost increases and/or the performance of the IP decreases, causing the IP to lose its value.

However, current representative circuit obfuscation methods, K_Based[9, 10] and R_Based[11, 12], do not meet one or both of the requirements. For example, [9–12] are vulnerable to at least one of the known attacks (ITA, CPA, SCA, BFA, which will be elaborated in Section 2.) thus being weak to thwart RE; [10] and [11] require exponential design time to select gates for obfuscation; [12] makes the obfuscated module 2.75x slower. Therefore, it is an urgent need to design a both secure and low-overhead obfuscation approach to thwart RE attacks. Our work in this paper is an attempt towards such an ideal obfuscation scheme with the following innovations:

- Leverage multiplexers (MUXs) and programmable camouflage connectors to replace certain conventional logic gates without changing the function of IC[1].
- Locate candidate to-be-obfuscated gates based on a novel gate classification method, which classifies logic gates to non-intersecting classes utilizing IC topological structure information.

The rest of paper is organized as follows: in Section 2, we survey the known attacks to obfuscated circuits. Section 3 elaborates the proposed multiplexer replacement based circuit obfuscation technique. Experimental results are presented in Section 4 and Section 5 concludes the paper.

[1]We are not the first to obfuscate circuits with MUXs, but we are the first to use programmable camouflage connectors to configure MUXs, and we judiciously guarantee the high-security of obfuscation.

GLSVLSI '16, May 18-20, 2016, Boston, MA, USA
© 2016 ACM. ISBN 978-1-4503-4274-2/16/05...$15.00
DOI: http://dx.doi.org/10.1145/2902961.2903000

2. PRELIMINARY

2.1 Known Attacks to Obfuscated Circuits

Given an obfuscated circuit, a tricky attacker may apply the following attacks to resolve the original netlist of IC[2].

IC Testing based Attack (ITA). An attacker can leverage justification and sensitization principles in IC testing techniques to get the input-output pairs of an obfuscated gate to resolve its functionality[10, 11]. Justification is the process of justifying the inputs of a gate to a known value by controlling one or more of the IC's primary inputs (PIs), and sensitization is the process of sensitizing the value of a net to a primary output (PO) so that one can observe the value by setting all side inputs of gates in between to non-controlling values.

Circuit Partition Attack (CPA). An attacker can leverage the *'divide and conquer'* methodology to partition obfuscated gates into multiple subcircuits, then target each subcircuit individually. To ensure effectiveness, each subcircuit's function should be ensured not affected by other parts of the circuit, thus can be tested separately from an unpackaged functional IC.

Side Channel Attack (SCA). This indicates a group of attacks that utilize side channel information, such as power and timing, to break security primitives. For gate replacement based obfuscation, an attacker may resolve functionalities of obfuscated gates if such side channels are varied and observable by the attacker when they are configured to perform different functionalities[11].

Brute Force Attack (BFA). An attacker may directly brute force search possible functionality combinations of obfuscated gates[10, 11]. For each possible combination, the attacker will simulate to get the corresponding function of the IC, then compare it with a functional IC bought from the market. If they are the same, the attacker has found out the right combination and thus these obfuscated gates are resolved.

3. CIRCUIT OBFUSCATION WITH MULTIPLEXERS

3.1 Attack Model and Necessary Assumptions

Our discussions in this paper are based on the following assumptions:

1. The attacker seeks to identify the functionality of each obfuscated gate to reverse engineer the obfuscated IC.

2. The attacker is able to extract an obfuscated netlist with regular gates and obfuscated gates by state-of-art reverse engineering tools and techniques.

3. For an unpackaged functional IC bought from the market, the attacker only has access to the IC's PIs and POs.

To resolve the original circuit of an obfuscated one, a tricky attacker may first try to perform SCA and ITA considering their cost is relatively low. Once SCA and ITA infeasible, the attacker has to brute force search possible functionality combinations of obfuscated gates. In this case, he will try to minimize the needed brute force efforts by performing CPA. Thus only when an obfuscation approach resilient to SCA, ITA, and CPA, the BFA/RE complexity can be truly exponential to the number of gates obfuscated.

[2]We elaborate the attacks with the cases for R_Based obfuscation approaches, things are similar for the K_Based ones.

3.2 Configuring Multiplexers to Logic Gates

In our approach, multiplexers and camouflage connectors are combined as 'configurable logic units' to replace certain conventional logic gates. Any 2^m-by-1 multiplexer can be configured with $2 \cdot 2^m$ camouflage connectors to perform 2^{2^m} possible m-input 1-output boolean functions. Specifically, each input line of the MUX is connected to Vdd and Vss by two camouflage connectors, but only one is programmed to be a connection, the other one is programmed to be an isolation. For example in Fig.1, when input lines X1 X2 X3 X4 configured to be 1110, the MUX will perform the functionality of a NAND gate.

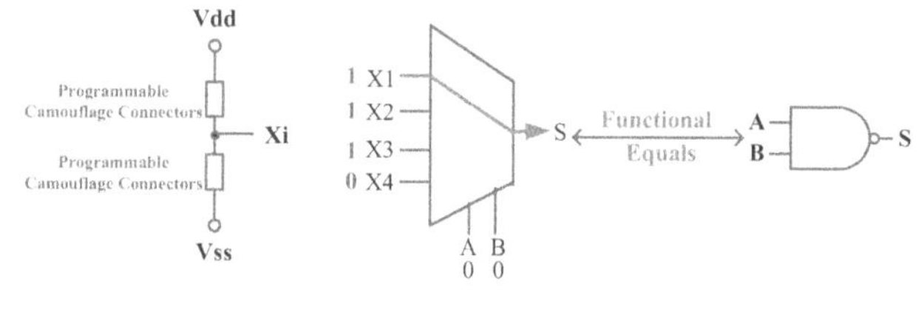

Figure 1: Configure MUX4x1 with programmable camouflage connectors to perform 16 possible 2-input 1-output boolean functions.

We adopt such a structure for two reasons. First, it will be more difficult to attack with more possible functionalities a configurable logic unit could perform. The MUX4x1 can be configured by our scheme to perform 16 possible 2-input 1-output boolean functions, while the configurable CMOS cells in [11] can only perform 3 possible functionalities which are those of {NAND, NOR, XOR}. Second, we only need to configure a MUX to perform certain boolean function one time and the overheads brought by configurable memory cells[12] can be non-trivial, thus we adopt the lightweight 'programmable camouflage connectors'[5, 13–16] instead.

3.3 Locating Candidate Gates based on IC Topological Information

We obfuscate circuits by replacing some conventional logic gates with MUXs that configured with programmable camouflage connectors. Considering the additional performance overhead, it is not realistic to replace all logic gates with MUXs. Thus the first step will be locating candidate gates, following the principle of maximizing attack complexity with minimum logic gates obfuscated.

3.3.1 A novel gate classification method

We first have the following definitions:

Definition 1. A gate is defined to be an *outGate* if its output signal is a PO of the circuit, otherwise, the gate is defined to be an *innerGate*.

Definition 2. The **M**aximum **F**anIn-**C**one rooted at a primary output PO_i, $MFIC_{PO_i}$, is the set of gates whose outputs will directly or indirectly feed into PO_i. Formally, $MFIC_{PO_i}$=$\{G|\exists path, G \rightarrow PO_i\}$[3].

Definition 3. For a gate G, $MFICS_G$ is the set of $MFIC_{PO}$ that G belongs to.

Formally, $MFICS_G$=$\{MFIC_{PO_i}|G \in MFIC_{PO_i}\}$.

Definition 4. Gates with exactly the same $MFICS$ are classified to the same class. Formally, gates $G1$, $G2$,

[3]We will also refer $MFIC_{PO}$ as the corresponding subcircuit, which can be easily differentiated according to contexts.

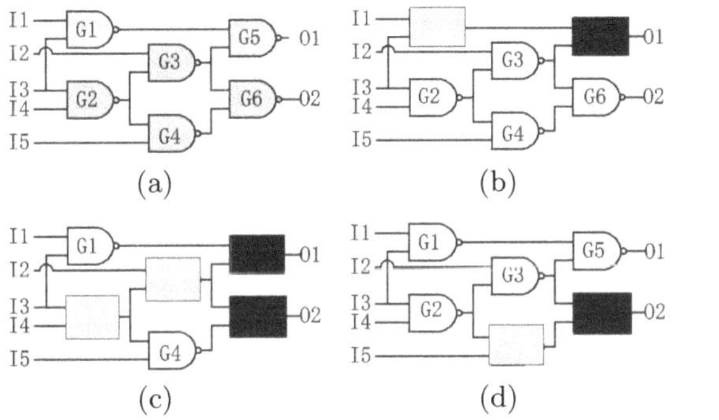

Figure 2: (a) Gates that classified to the same class are marked with the same color. (b) Select gates to obfuscate from class $C1$. The black rectangles indicate securely obfuscated gates which appear as black boxes to the attacker, and the green rectangles indicate candidates to be obfuscated in the selected class. (c) Select gates to obfuscate from class $C2$. (d) Select gates to obfuscate from class $C3$.

$\cdots$, Gn are partitioned to the same class C if and only if $MFICS_{G1} = MFICS_{G2} = \cdots = MFICS_{Gn}$. Class C's $MFICS$ is defined as the $MFICS$ of gates in C.

For example in Fig.2(a), gates $\{G1, G5\}$, $\{G2, G3\}$, and $\{G4, G6\}$ are classified to class $C1$, $C2$, and $C3$, respectively.

3.3.2 Locating candidate gates

Our approach is based on the proposed gate classification method to select gates to obfuscate from the same gate class. Specially, once a certain class selected, the *outGates* of the class's $MFICS$ are obfuscated to appear as black boxes to the attacker, blocking sensitizations of outputs of gates in the class to any PO. Then the designer can select the desired number of gates he(she) wants to obfuscate from the class. To minimize performance overhead, some principles can be applied when selecting gates to obfuscate (such as avoiding too many obfuscated gates congested in one single path). Fig.2(b), Fig.2(c) and Fig.2(d) show examples of selecting candidate gates to obfuscate from class $C1$, $C2$ and $C3$, respectively.

3.4 Obfuscation Analysis

Programmable camouflage connectors are leveraged to configure MUXs in our approach. It is infeasible to differentiate between connection and isolation of a camouflage connector for real-world RE attackers. On one hand, the camouflage connectors are carefully designed to be physically identical from the top view under optical or electron microscopy[13–10]. On the other hand, for chemical erosion and imaging based top-down reverse engineering, the camouflage connectors which are placed in bottom layers are almost eroded by the time the attacker reaches the layer. The attacker will not know whether a broken/isolated connector is because of chemical erosion or camouflaging[5, 11]. As an alternative, a tricky attacker may try to resolve the functionalities of obfuscated gates by indirect attacks such as ITA, CPA, SCA, BFA that elaborated in Section 2.1. We now consider the resilience of our obfuscation approach to these possible attacks.

IC Testing Based Attack (ITA). In our gate selection scheme, for each MUX that replaces an *innerGate*, its output cannot be sensitized to any PO of the circuit, because for any $MFIC_{PO_i}$ it belongs to, the *outGate* that directly feeds PO_i is obfuscated. And for each MUX that replaces an *outGate*, its inputs cannot be justified from PIs because the MUX's at least one input blocked.

Circuit partition based attack (CPA). We select gates to obfuscate from the same gate class in which gates belong to exactly the same set of $MFIC_{PO}$. As a result, for any $MFIC_{PO_i}$ of the circuit, either none of the obfuscated gates belong to it, or all the obfuscated gates belong to it. Thus the attacker will not be able to partition the obfuscated gates into multiple subcircuits to perform attacks individually.

Side channel attack (SCA). The differences of power and timing between differently configured MUX4x1 are trivial. Moreover, considering that the attacker do not have access to individual logic gate of unpackaged functional IC, such trivial difference in single logic gate is unobservable when placed in the entire circuit. As a result, the attacker will not be able to get configuration information of MUXs by side channel information.

Brute force attack (BFA). The functionality of each camouflaged MUX appears 16 possibilities to the attacker, and as analyzed above, our approach is resilient to ITA, SCA and CPA, thus the brute force efforts needed by the attacker will be no less than $16^M = 2^{4M}$, where M is the number of *innerGates* obfuscated. Such exponential brute force complexity actually means infeasible for the attacker to perform, especially when M is large.

4. EXPERIMENTAL RESULTS

4.1 Experimental Setup

We investigate the impact of our proposed obfuscation approach to design quality (area and delay) on standard ISCAS 85/89 and MCNC benchmark suites. To accomplish this, a program was written in JAVA to do gate classification and identify candidate gates to replace with MUXs. Synthesis tool ABC program[17] and Oklahoma State University (OSU) standard cell library based on the TSMC 0.35μm PDK are used for performance overhead measurement.

4.2 Performance Overheads of MUX Replacement based Obfuscation

To study the performance overhead of the proposed obfuscation scheme, we consider different number of *innerGates* in the circuit obfuscated. In Table 1, column 2-6 demonstrate the detailed information of each benchmark circuit, and columns 7-8 show the largest gate class information of the circuit. Columns 9-12 indicate an average overhead of 47.7% in delay and 14.8% in area when 5% of the logic gates in the circuit are obfuscated. Although the delay overhead varies from 9.1% to 85.9%, the area overhead is more stable due to the fact that a fixed portion (5% in this case) of the gates are obfuscated. The benefit of such high overhead is the high security against RE attackers. In the smallest 142-gate circuit s713, the attacking complexity is 16^6 or 2^{24}. For the largest circuit s13207, this complexity is 2^{344}.

To achieve a required level of security, we obfuscate 64 and 16 *innerGates*, which delivers attacking complexity of $2^{256}$and 2^{64}, respectively. As we can see from the rest columns in Table 1, both delay and area overheads drop. The most notable observation is that when we obfuscate 16 *innerGates*, there is no delay overhead on four benchmarks (c3540,

Table 1: Performance Overheads when Obfuscating Different Number of Gates.

Bench	Gates	Nets	Area	Delay	Levels	Largest Class		Obfuscate 5% Gates				Obfuscate 64 *innerGates*			Obfuscate 16 *innerGates*		
						$MFIC_{PO}$	*Gates*	total	inner	delay	area	total	delay	area	total	delay	area
s713	142	290	359.2	2.67	16	1	19	7	6	41.2%	14.5%	-	-	-	-	-	-
c432	180	363	448	3.94	23	5	41	9	8	26.1%	16.4%	-	-	-	-	-	-
i2	222	460	598.4	1.82	10	1	222	11	10	52.7%	13.4%	-	-	-	-	-	-
s1196	398	897	1051.2	2.94	17	6	22	17	16	51.0%	14.0%	-	-	-	17	50.7%	14.0%
s1238	445	999	1178.4	3.03	18	1	25	22	21	50.2%	16.2%	-	-	-	17	35.3%	12.3%
too_large	519	1125	1340	4.17	25	1	149	25	24	9.1%	14.7%	-	-	-	17	9.1%	9.8%
c2670	721	1324	1704.8	2.74	18	1	134	36	34	55.5%	15.6%	-	-	-	17	43.4%	8.0%
c3540	861	1967	2360.8	4.94	31	10	82	43	35	59.5%	15.1%	-	-	-	17	0.0%	5.5%
t481	1098	2596	3324	2.46	15	1	1098	54	53	45.5%	13.5%	-	-	-	17	45.5%	4.4%
s5378	1151	2423	2980.8	2.2	14	2	84	57	55	85.9%	18.1%	-	-	-	18	50.9%	5.5%
c5315	1345	2907	3672.8	5.67	34	5	166	67	57	28.6%	14.4%	-	-	-	19	0.0%	3.5%
s9234	1505	3105	4126.4	4.35	23	1	87	75	74	49.9%	17.3%	65	37.2%	15.3%	17	0.0%	2.9%
c7552	1612	3372	4617.6	4.8	28	1	112	80	77	37.9%	12.2%	69	14.6%	10.3%	19	4.6%	2.1%
i10	1904	4145	5135.2	5.94	36	10	121	95	76	64.8%	14.5%	83	48.5%	12.6%	24	16.2%	3.8%
c6288	2267	5220	6140.8	15.18	89	16	142	113	82	55.3%	13.3%	93	23.4%	10.4%	23	12.4%	2.5%
s13207	2480	4741	6831.2	4.23	26	19	137	124	86	50.1%	14.0%	102	39.7%	11.4%	17	0.0%	1.5%
Average										47.7%	14.8%		32.7%	12.0%		20.6%	5.8%

c5315, s9234 and s13207) because none of the obfuscated gates is on any of the critical paths. For the last five large benchmarks with more than 1500 logic gates, the average delay overheads are 32.7% and 6.6%; while the area overheads are 12.0% and 2.6%, respectively. This trend clearly shows that for large real-life circuits, our approach can achieve both low performance overhead and high security level against RE attacks.

5. CONCLUSIONS

Circuit obfuscation is a promising approach to thwart reverse engineering attacks. In this paper, we propose such a scheme based on replacing carefully selected logic gates with special designed MUXs to make RE complexity exponential. We also report the performance overhead of the obfuscated circuits which is expected to be small for real-life circuits.

Acknowledgment

This work is supported by the National Natural Science Foundation of China under Grant No. 61176035 and 61228204. Mingze Gao and Gang Qu are partially supported by AFOSR MURI under award number FA9550-14-1-0351.

References

[1] Gang Qu and Miodrag Potkonjak. Intellectual property protection in VLSI designs: Theory and practice, kluwer academic publishers, ISBN 1-4020-7320-8. January 2003.

[2] Masoud Rostami, Farinaz Koushanfar, and Ramesh Karri. A primer on hardware security: Models, methods, and metrics. *Proceedings of the IEEE*, 102(8):1283–1295, 2014.

[3] Randy Torrance and Dick James. The state-of-the-art in semiconductor reverse engineering. In *Proc. ACM/IEEE Design Automation Conference (DAC)*, pages 333–338, 2011.

[4] L.W. Chow, J. Baukus, and W. Clark. Integrated circuits protected against reverse engineering and method for fabricating the same using an apparent metal contact line terminating on field oxide, 2002, US Patent 20020096776.

[5] R.P. Cocchi, J.P. Baukus, B.J. Wang, L.W. Chow, and P. Ouyang. Building block for a secure cmos logic cell library, 2012, US Patent 8,111,089.

[6] Alex Baumgarten, Akhilesh Tyagi, and Joseph Zambreno. Preventing IC piracy using reconfigurable logic barriers. *IEEE Design & Test of Computers*, 27(1):66–75, 2010.

[7] Yousra Alkabani and Farinaz Koushanfar. Active hardware metering for intellectual property protection and security. In *Proceedings of the 16th USENIX Security Symposium*, 2007.

[8] Rajat Subhra Chakraborty and Swarup Bhunia. HARPOON: an obfuscation-based soc design methodology for hardware protection. *IEEE Trans. on CAD of Integrated Circuits and Systems (TCAD)*, 28(10):1493–1502, 2009.

[9] Jarrod A. Roy, Farinaz Koushanfar, and Igor L. Markov. EPIC: ending piracy of integrated circuits. In *Proc. IEEE Design, Automation and Test in Europe (DATE)*, pages 1069–1074, 2008.

[10] Jeyavijayan Rajendran, Youngok Pino, Ozgur Sinanoglu, and Ramesh Karri. Security analysis of logic obfuscation. In *Proc. ACM/IEEE Design Automation Conference (DAC)*, pages 83–89, 2012.

[11] Jeyavijayan Rajendran, Michael Sam, Ozgur Sinanoglu, and Ramesh Karri. Security analysis of integrated circuit camouflaging. In *Proc. ACM Conference on Computer and Communications Security (CCS)*, pages 709–720, 2013.

[12] Bao Liu and Brandon Wang. Embedded reconfigurable logic for ASIC design obfuscation against supply chain attacks. In *Proc. IEEE Design, Automation and Test in Europe (DATE)*, pages 1–6, 2014.

[13] W.M. Clark, L.W. Chow, G. Harbison, and P. Ouyang. Programmable connection and isolation of active regions in an integrated circuit using ambiguous features to confuse a reverse engineer, 2008, US Patent 20080079082.

[14] W.M. Clark, J.P. Baukus, and L.W. Chow. Implanted hidden interconnections in a semiconductor device for preventing reverse engineering, 2007, US Patent 7,166,515.

[15] L.W. Chow, W.M. Clark, G.J. Harbison, and J.P. Baukus. Conductive channel pseudo block process and circuit to inhibit reverse engineering, 2006, US Patent 7,049,667.

[16] L.W. Chow, W.M. Clark, and J.P. Baukus. Integrated circuit with reverse engineering protection, 2005, US Patent 6,897,535.

[17] Robert K. Brayton and Alan Mishchenko. ABC: an academic industrial-strength verification tool. In *Proc. CAV Computer Aided Verification, 22nd International Conference*, pages 24–40, 2010.

Task-Resource Co-Allocation for Hotspot Minimization in Heterogeneous Many-Core NoCs

Md Farhadur Reza Dan Zhao Hongyi Wu
The Center for Advanced Computer Studies
University of Louisiana at Lafayette
Lafayette, LA, USA
{mxr7945, dzhao, wu}@louisiana.edu

ABSTRACT

To fully exploit the massive parallelism of many cores, this work tackles the problem of mapping large-scale applications onto heterogeneous on-chip networks (NoCs) to minimize the peak workload for energy hotspot avoidance. A task-resource co-optimization framework is proposed which configures the on-chip communication infrastructure and maps the applications simultaneously and coherently, aiming to minimize the peak load under the constraints of computation power and communication capacity and a total cost budget of on-chip resources. The problem is first formulated into a linear programming model to search for optimal solution. A heuristic algorithm is further developed for fast design space exploration in extremely large-scale many-core NoCs. Extensive simulations are carried out under real-world benchmarks and randomly generated task graphs to demonstrate the effectiveness and efficiency of the proposed schemes.

1. INTRODUCTION

Multicore chip design has been increasingly deployed in embedded computing systems ranging from small mobile devices (e.g., Nvidia Tegra 3 [1]) to large telecommunication servers (such as ARMv8-A [2]) to meet ever-increasing computational demands under a stringent energy budget. Such systems are moving towards the integration of tens or hundreds of heterogeneous cores on a single chip to accomplish emerging applications through low-power highly parallel computing. The heterogeneous many-core architecture offers a feasible approach that embraces high-performance "Big" cores (e.g., CPUs) for computation intensive applications and low-power "Little" cores (e.g., GPUs and DSPs) for majority workloads execution. As the number of cores increases, Network-on-Chips (NoC) has been adopted as a viable solution to manage complex interconnection and provide energy efficient performance. The mapping optimization in heterogeneous NoC faces new challenges of very limited on-chip resource usage including tight energy and area cost budgets.

Various task mapping algorithms has been developed for NoC-based multicore chips, some are based on graph theoretic, some use mathematical programming, and others are heuristic algorithms.

GLSVLSI '16, May 18-20, 2016, Boston, MA, USA

DOI: http://dx.doi.org/10.1145/2902961.2903003

For example, variations of shortest path algorithms [3–6] has been devoted to mapping highly correlated tasks on the task graph to nearby cores, in order to shorten the communication delay, to reduce the routing distance, or to improve locality of data access. In a similar spirit, the work in [7] intends to map the tasks in the same application together by using graph partitioning techniques such as maximal empty rectangle. Some work in [8] concerns about the overlapped traffic over shared communication links, aiming to minimize the traffic contention in the network. This work is formally formulated in Sec. 2. We propose a heuristic algorithm in Sec. 3 for fast design space exploration in large-scale many-core NoCs, and demonstrate extensive simulations in Sec. 4. The uniqueness of this work is outlined below:

i) Explicit Hotspot Minimization: Chip overheating due to workload (distributed computation and communication) asymmetry is a crucial issue in chip design. Although some prior work (e.g., [8]) attempts to avoid energy hotspots due to regional overcrowded communication loads, this is the first work that explicitly tackles the hotspot minimization problem in many-core NoCs, taking into the consideration of both computation and communication workloads.

ii) Task-Resource Co-Allocation: This is the first attempt that task mapping and NoC configuration are co-designed for energy orchestration. A heterogeneous NoC is established accordingly with non-identical routers and varying bandwidth links under the restricted on-chip resource budget.

iii) Extensive Exploration of Solution Space: Most prior work presumes a reduced solution space, e.g., by mapping tasks of an application to nearby cores [3–6] or in an empty rectangle [7]. Such approaches, although intuitively reasonable, cannot guarantee an optimal solution. In this work, we search though the entire solution space for mapping optimization and NoC configuration.

2. PROBLEM FORMULATION AND LP SOLUTION

Given a many-core chip plane with n processor tiles connected into a $\sqrt{n} \times \sqrt{n}$ 2D mesh, each node i (or tile interchangeably) has its maximum computation power of P_i. Two adjacent nodes i and j are connected by a bidirectional link l_{ij} with a maximum communication capacity of W_{ij}. Here we have assumed a 2D mesh architecture that employs XY-routing for data delivery. However it is worth mentioning that our proposed mapping algorithm is generally applicable to any network topology and routing scheme, with only minor modification in the calculation of traffic load.

Given a set of K applications $A = \{A_1, A_2, ..., A_k, ...A_K\}$ to be executed on the many-core chip, and each application consists of a set of tasks to be run on different computing nodes in parallel. For example, application A_k is partitioned into M tasks, i.e., $A_k = \{T_k^1, T_k^2, ..., T_k^m, ..., T_k^M\}$, where T_k^m is the mth task for

Table 1: Link configuration with varying width and cost.

Link Configuration (h)	1	2	3	...	H
Link Width (B_h, bit)	8	16	24	...	256
Link Cost (C_h, μm^2)	1600	3200	4800	...	51200

application A_k. The task computation demands and the communication dependency among the tasks are represented by a task graph $TG(V, E)$, where each vertex v_k^m denotes a task T_k^m with computation demand of $(D_{cmp})_k^m$, and each directed edge e_k^{mn} represents communication from task T_k^m to task T_k^n with a bandwidth demand of $(D_{com})_k^{mn}$.

Let $(X_k^m)^i$ be a binary variable to indicate if a task T_k^m is mapped to node i, i.e.,

$$(X_k^m)^i = \begin{cases} 1, \text{if task } T_k^m \text{ is mapped to Node } i, \\ 0, \text{otherwise.} \end{cases} \tag{1}$$

$(X_k^m)^i$ is to be determined in order to achieve the optimization goal.

Next, based on $(X_k^m)^i$, we first outline the communication and computation constraints and then discuss the optimization objection function.

2.0.1 *Communication Constraints and Link Configuration*

The adjacent tasks (e.g., T_k^n and T_k^m) need to communicate with each other, with a traffic load of $(D_{com})_k^{mn} + (D_{com})_k^{nm}$. When they are mapped to two nodes, e.g., p and q, the traffic is delivered through a path in the NoC, denoted as Ph_{pq} which consists of a set of NoC links. Such a path is determined by the underlying routing algorithm. Note that multiple traffic flows may simultaneously traverse through a communication link l_{ij}, thus the total communication traffic loads via it is:

$$\omega_{ij} = \sum_{\substack{1 \le p,q \le n \\ 1 \le m,n \le M \\ 1 \le k \le K \\ \exists l_{ij} \in Ph_{pq}}} (D_{com})_k^{mn} \cdot (X_k^m)^p \cdot (X_k^n)^q. \tag{2}$$

Since each communication link l_{ij} has a maximum bandwidth capacity of W_{ij}, we arrive at the communication constraint:

$$\omega_{ij} \le W_{ij}, \forall 1 \le i, j \le n. \tag{3}$$

If the link bandwidth capacity (i.e., W_{ij}) is given as a constant, the communication constraint is straightforward. However, W_{ij} is often non-uniform and configurable. For example, a list of typical link width configuration options $B = \{B_h\}$ and their associated cost C_h are given in Table 1 in 22 nm process technology. The cost is measured by the area of chip occupied by the link.

Given the link configuration options, the bandwidth of link l_{ij} can be configured as,

$$W_{ij} = (\sum_{h=1}^{H} Y_{ij}^h \cdot B_h) \cdot f_{NoC}, 1 \le i, j \le n, \tag{4}$$

where f_{NoC} is the uniform frequency of the NoC[1], and Y_{ij}^h is a binary variable to indicate the chosen h^{th} link width configuration for l_{ij}, i.e.,

$$Y_{ij}^h = \begin{cases} 1, \text{if the } h^{th} \text{ link configuration is chosen,} \\ 0, \text{otherwise.} \end{cases} \tag{5}$$

[1]Note that NoC frequency scaling is out of scope of this paper. We assume f_{NoC} is given in this work.

Note that, only one configuration can be chosen for a link, thus we have

$$\sum_{h=1}^{H} Y_{ij}^h = 1. \tag{6}$$

Accordingly, the cost of link l_{ij} can be calculated as,

$$C_{ij} = \sum_{h=1}^{H} Y_{ij}^h \cdot C_h. \tag{7}$$

Obviously, the overall link cost should not exceed the total cost budget of the NoC, denoted as C_{NoC}:

$$\sum_{1 \le i,j \le n} C_{ij} \le C_{NoC}. \tag{8}$$

Combining Eqs. (2)-(8), we have the communication constraints with adaptive link bandwidth configuration.

2.0.2 *Computation Constraints*

The computation constraint is straightforward. Given that each node i has a maximum computation power of P_i, the total computation power of all tasks assigned to node i must not exceed P_i, i.e.,

$$\rho_i = \sum_{\substack{1 \le k \le K \\ 1 \le m \le M}} (D_{cmp})_k^m \cdot (X_k^m)^i \le P_i, \forall 1 \le i \le n. \tag{9}$$

2.0.3 *Optimization Objective Function*

Our objective is to map the application tasks with load balancing and link bandwidth configuration so as to avoid energy hotspots due to excessive computation and overcrowded communication in the NoC. We define the load of node i as the weighted sum of its overall computation and communication workloads, i.e., $\gamma_1 \cdot \rho_i + \gamma_2 \cdot \sum_{\forall j \in l_{ij}} \omega_{ij}$, where ρ_i denotes the total computation load at node i (see Eq. (9)) and ω_{ij} is the total communication traffic load going over link l_{ij} (as shown in Eq. (2)). The parameters γ_1 and γ_2 are the energy coefficient of computation and communication loads at node i, respectively. For instance, under 22 nm process technology, computation and communication energy dissipation are around 45 picojoule/FLOPS and 65 picojoule/bit, respectively. The maximum load among all nodes in the NoC (i.e., the peak load) should be minimized, i.e.,

$$Minimize : max(\gamma_1 \cdot \rho_i + \gamma_2 \cdot \sum_{\forall j \in l_{ij}} \omega_{ij}), 1 \le i \le n, \tag{10}$$

subject to the constraints given in Eqs. (2)-(9).

The above objective function along with the communication, computation and cost constraints form a Linear Programming (LP) model.

3. MINHOTSPOT MAPPING HEURISTIC

The above LP model achieves optimal mapping of the tasks, but its high computation complexity restricts its application in extremely large-scale many-core NoCs. To this end, we further develop a near-optimal heuristic algorithm for fast design space exploration, as outlined below.

3.1 Selection of Applications and Tasks

First, the applications are sorted in a descending order according to their total computation and communication demands, i.e., $TD(A_k) = \gamma_1 \cdot \sum_{m=1}^{M} (D_{cmp})_k^m + \gamma_2 \cdot \sum_{\forall e_k^{mn} \in G} (D_{com})_k^{mn}$, where G is the task graph introduced earlier. It is desirable to first allocate applications that demand more resources, because it is often more difficult to map such applications in later stage when the remaining resources become fragmentary. Thus the application with the highest total demands $max(TD(A_k))$ is mapped first, and the remaining applications are mapped in the sorted order.

Similarly, for a given application, its tasks are sorted according to their total load, which comprises the computation demand of the task and the communication demands with its neighboring tasks. But note that, when we choose the next task to be mapped, we are only concerned about the communication load between a candidate task and the tasks that have already been mapped. Thus, the load of a task is calculated as follows: $TD(T_k^m) = \gamma_1 \cdot (D_{cmp})_k^m + \gamma_2 \cdot \sum_{\forall e_k^{mn} \in G, n \in G'} (D_{com})_k^{mn}$, where G' is the partial task graph that has been mapped so far.

3.2 Selection of Nodes

Once a task is selected, we examine all hypotheses of placing the task onto every possible node. The node with the lowest peak load is chosen to map the task. Note that, we consider a hypothesis only if the computation and communication constraints are satisfied according to Eqs. (9) and (3). Link configuration is also incorporated here. When a hypothesis is considered, we allocate the smallest bandwidths for the involved links that satisfy the following two conditions. First, the bandwidth should be sufficient to meet the communication constraint (i.e., $\omega_{ij} \leq W_{ij}$), and second, the overall link cost should not exceed the total cost budget of the NoC, i.e., $\sum_{1 \leq i,j \leq n} C_{ij} \leq C_{NoC}$.

3.3 Iterative Assignment Procedure

The task-to-node assignment follows a greedy iterative procedure. Briefly, we pick the first unmapped task from the sorted list, and assign it to the node that results in the lowest peak load. If there is a tie in lowest peak load, the total load of the NoC and the capacity utilization are used as tie-breaker. The process repeats until all tasks are mapped, or is aborted if the constraints cannot be satisfied. This greedy procedure aims to achieve the lowest peak load in each iteration. Our research reveals that it can effectively guide the mapping process in general but has a drawback in dealing with the first task in each application. First, if the first task is mapped to a node with insufficient resources around it, the rest tasks have to be mapped to remote nodes, increasing the overall communication load, and accordingly the peak load. The problem is due to the fact that the first task is essentially the anchor point of the application. So, during first-task mapping, we should give the higher priority to a node that has higher number of available neighbors (that have enough capacity to accommodate other tasks in the same application). Second, if the first task is mapped to a heavily loaded node, then the rest tasks can further increase the load (due to communication), and eventually, can become a bottleneck in the network. Because of that, we should give the higher priority to a node that has lower load.

To this end, we introduce a parameter, named node selection factor (f_i), which is the weighted sum of the number of available neighbors (N_i) and the reciprocal of existing computation load (ρ_i) at node i, i.e., $f_i = \delta_1 \cdot N_i + \delta_2 \cdot \frac{1}{\rho_i}$, where δ_1 and δ_2 are the constant weights. The former indicates the likelihood that, after the first task is placed at the node, other tasks of the same application can be accommodated in the nearby region. The latter contributes to minimizing the peak load while providing computation capacity for the incoming (first) task. It is desirable to find a light-loaded node with sufficient resources in its neighborhood to accommodate the first task of a highly demanding application. Thus the node with the highest selection factor, i.e., $max\{f_i | 1 \leq i \leq n\}$ is chosen to map the first task.

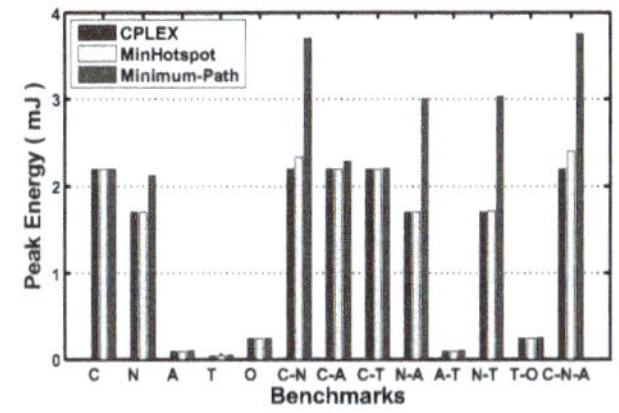

Figure 1: Peak load comparison under E3S Benchmarks.

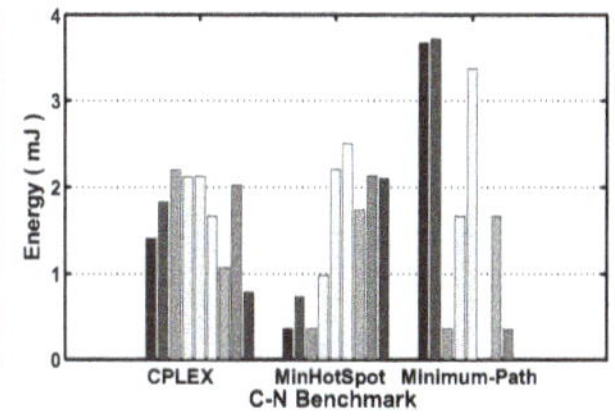

Figure 2: Load distribution under C-N E3S Benchmark.

3.4 Further Refinement

To further reduce the peak load, we refine the mapping result by exploring options to relocate the tasks. More specifically, we randomly choose a task currently assigned to a node, and evaluate its peak load would it be moved to every other node. The task is reassigned to the node that results in the lowest peak load (if it is different from the current node). We repeat the process until the peak load cannot be further reduced. The overall complexity of the proposed *MinHotspot* algorithm is $O(KMn)$ since we must examine n hypotheses for each task in each application.

4. SIMULATION & COMPARISON

We implement the Linear Programming (LP) optimization model using a commercial LP solver IBM CPLEX [9] which searches for the optimal solution for the task-resource co-allocation problem. We also implement the minimum-path approach [3] as the baseline to compare with our proposed solutions. Both the *MinHotSpot* and the minimum-path approaches are implemented in C++. Real system experiments are further carried out using GEM5 [10] platform to evaluate the NoC performance in terms of end-to-end latency and network throughput.

The experiments are carried out based on three platforms: embedded system synthesis benchmark suite (E3S) [11], COSMIC benchmark suite [12], and randomly generated problem settings using task graph generator [13]. We run the algorithms on a host machine with 6-core Intel Xeon E5-2667 2.9GHz processors, 15MB LLC, and 16GB DDR3.

4.1 Comparison under E3S Benchmarks

The applications are mapped in a 3×3 2D-mesh NoC. As shown in Fig. 1, *MinHotSpot* delivers nearly the same peak load performance as CPLEX under all five E3S benchmarks, e.g., Consumer (C), Networking (N). Furthermore, multi-application systems are configured under eight different combinations of applications to evaluate the robustness of the proposed schemes. As can be seen, *MinHotSpot* again produces the same peak load performance as CPLEX except two cases, i.e., C-N and C-N-A, where the peak load of *MinHotSpot* is slightly higher than that of CPLEX by 6% and 9%, respectively. Our proposed approaches achieve significantly better performance than the traditional minimum-path scheme [3] by 10-80%. This is also evidenced by the load distribution shown in Fig. 2, where the load is extremely unevenly distributed among the nine nodes of the NoC under the minimum-path scheme, as it only considers communication distance during mapping. We also notice the long computation time for CPLEX to discover the optimal solution. For example, for an 8-application mapping (such as N-A), it takes about 5 hours for CPLEX to search for the solution while *MinHotSpot* can finish it in only 2 seconds. When the num-

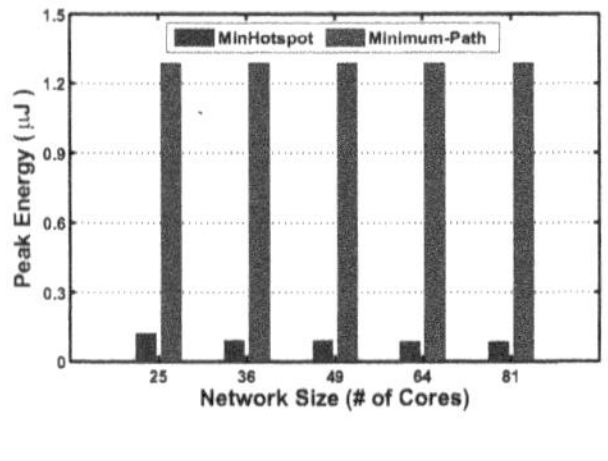

Figure 3: RS-Decoder Application load comparison.

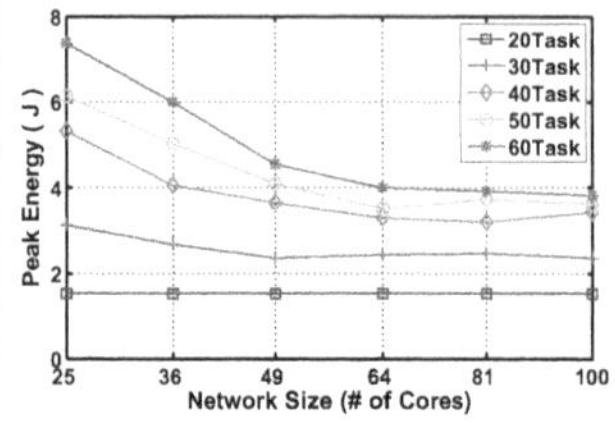

Figure 4: Peak Load under different network scales.

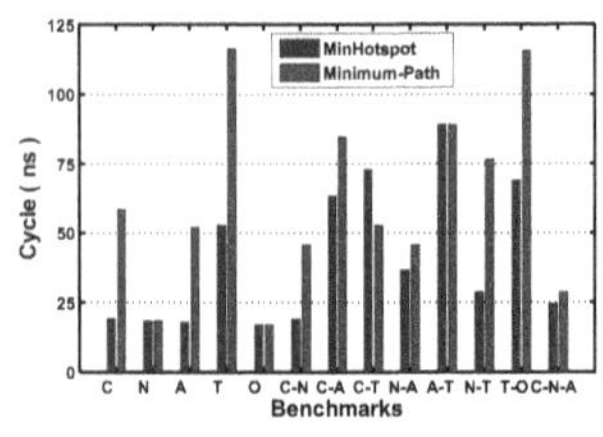

Figure 5: Latency comparison for E3S Benchmarks.

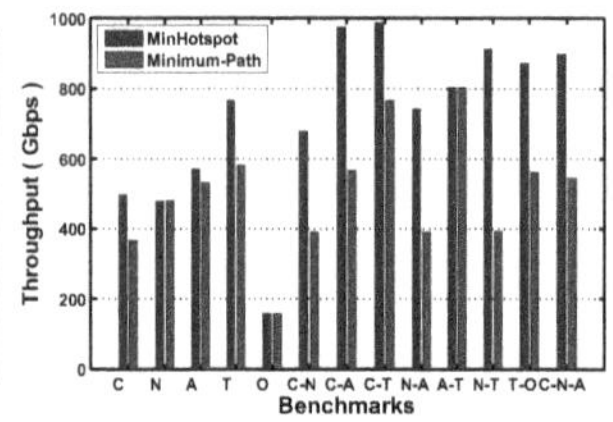

Figure 6: Throughput comparison for E3S Benchmarks.

ber of applications to be mapped increases, CPLEX cannot deliver a solution in a reasonable time period.

4.2 Study Large-Scale Problem Settings

Next we evaluate the performance trend by varying different system parameters under large-scale settings. COSMIC benchmark suite is used here because it is based on real applications with a large number of tasks per application. As shown in Fig. 3, MinHotspot achieves 25%-100% lower peak loads than the baseline approach for RS decoder application. Impact of NoC scaling is observed based on application task graphs generated by the task graph generator [13]. As can be seen in Fig. 4, the peak load generally decreases when the network size scales up.

4.3 NoC Comparison under GEM5

In order to study the impact of different NoC configurations on the overall system performance, we run MinHotSpot and baseline approaches offline and deploy the obtained heterogeneous NoCs on GEM5 platform, respectively. The heterogeneous bandwidth is properly modeled in GARNET by applying different link latencies to support varying communication capacity requirements. The corresponding mapping solutions (of E3S benchmarks) are integrated in GEM5 to generate the computation and communication workloads. The experiments are carried out on 4×4 2D-mesh NoCs. The simulations are run in fixed-pipeline mode in ALPHA architecture for 1,000 cycles and the maximum number of packets to be injected by each node is set at 50,000. Other configuration parameters are default setting in GEM5.As shown in Fig. 5 and Fig. 6, MinHotSpot outperforms the baseline by 30%-200% in terms end-to-end latency and network throughput.

4.4 Power Consumption Evaluation

Power data for several E3S benchmarks running on a 4×4 2D mesh NoC is derived by using DSENT power tool [14]. The power consumption for each individual link is obtained based on heterogeneous link bandwidth configuration from mapping heuristics. We then calculate the overall power consumption by summing up the link powers. As shown in Fig. 7, the NoC system configuration derived from MinHotSpot results in up to 6% lower power consumption than the baseline approach.

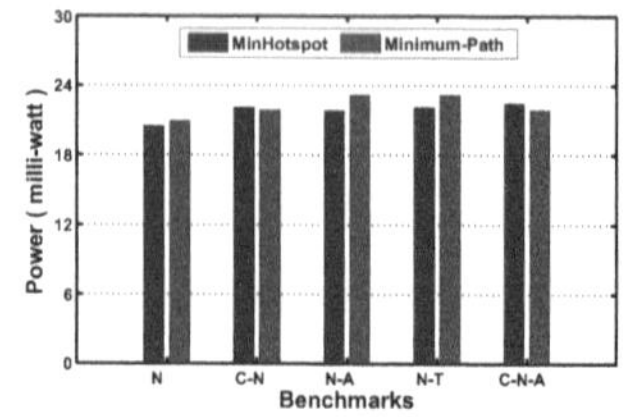

Figure 7: Power comparison under E3S Benchmarks.

5. CONCLUSION

The capacity and cost-constrained application mapping problem in many-core on-chip networks has been addressed in this paper. The optimization of task placement and resource configuration has been modeled and implemented by using an IBM CPLEX optimization solver. A fast and practical heuristic algorithm namely *MinHotspot* has been proposed to provide feasible solutions for large-scale problems. The simulation results obtained for the real world benchmark suites and random generated problem domains have demonstrated the effectiveness and efficiency of the proposed schemes.

6. REFERENCES

[1] "Nvidia tegra," in *http://www.nvidia.com/object/tegra-3-processor.html.*
[2] "Broadcom armv8," in *http://www.broadcom.com/press/release.php?id=s797235.*
[3] S. Murali and G. De Micheli, "Bandwidth-constrained mapping of cores onto noc architectures," in *Proc. DATE*, pp. 896–901, 2004.
[4] J. Hu and R. Marculescu, "Energy- and performance-aware mapping for regular noc architectures," *IEEE Trans. TCAD*, vol. 24, no. 4, pp. 551–562, 2005.
[5] C.-L. Chou and R. Marculescu, "Incremental run-time application mapping for homogeneous nocs with multiple voltage levels," in *Proc. CODES+ISSS*, pp. 161–166, 2007.
[6] M. Fattah, M. Daneshtalab, P. Liljeberg, and J. Plosila, "Smart hill climbing for agile dynamic mapping in many-core systems," in *Proc. DAC*, pp. 1–6, 2013.
[7] B. Y. et. al, "Multi-application multi-step mapping method for many-core network-on-chips," in *Proc. NORCHIP*, pp. 1–6, 2010.
[8] C.-L. Chou and R. Marculescu, "Contention-aware application mapping for network-on-chip communication architectures," in *Proc. ICCD*, pp. 164–169, 2008.
[9] "Cplex optimization studio," in *http://www-01.ibm.com/software/commerce/optimization/cplex-optimizer/.*
[10] N. B. et. al, "The gem5 simulator," *SIGARCH Comput. Archit. News*, vol. 39, no. 2, pp. 1–7,2011.
[11] R. Dick, "Embedded system synthesis benchmarks suites (e3s)," in *http://www.ece.northwestern.edu/ dickrp/e3s/.*
[12] Z. W. et. al, "A case study on the communication and computation behaviors of real applications in noc-based mpsocs," in *Proc. ISVLSI*, pp. 480–485, 2014.
[13] H. Topcuoglu, S. Hariri, and M.-Y. Wu, "Performance-effective and low-complexity task scheduling for heterogeneous computing," *IEEE Trans. Parallel and Distributed Syst.*, vol. 13, no. 3, pp. 260–274, 2002.
[14] C. S. et. al, "Dsent - a tool connecting emerging photonics with electronics for opto-electronic networks-on-chip modeling," in *Proc. NOCS*, pp. 201–210,2012.

Guiding Power/Quality Exploration for Communication-Intense Stream Processing

Hamed Tabkhi, Majid Sabbagh and Gunar Schirner
Department of Electrical and Computer Engineering
Northeastern University, Boston (MA), USA
{tabkhi,msabbagh,schirner}@ece.neu.edu

ABSTRACT

In this paper, we explore the power/quality trade-off for streaming applications with a shift from the computation to the communication aspects of the design. The paper proposes a systematic exploration methodology to formulate and traverse power/quality trade-off for the class of adaptive streaming applications. The formalization enables to procedurally transition from a set of design requirements to architecture goals. The architecture goals can then be realized through design choices yielding system designs that meet the initial requirements. The reported results are based on an actual implementation of Mixture of Gaussian (MoG) background subtraction on Xilinx Zynq platform.

Keywords

Streaming Applications; Operational Data; Power/Quality Trade-off

1. INTRODUCTION

Streaming applications make up a large portion of the embedded high-performance market. Examples include multimedia and vision computing, software defined radio, radars and cryptography [3][7]. For the high-performance power-efficient execution of streaming applications, the general trend is to move the computation-intense kernel into hardware accelerators (either on FPGAs, or as an ASIC), and more intelligent/control processing into software. While the computation aspect of accelerators has been fairly optimized, the communication aspect has been left as a challenge; particularly the memory wall is an increasing hurtle. This shifts attention toward communication-centric design principles.

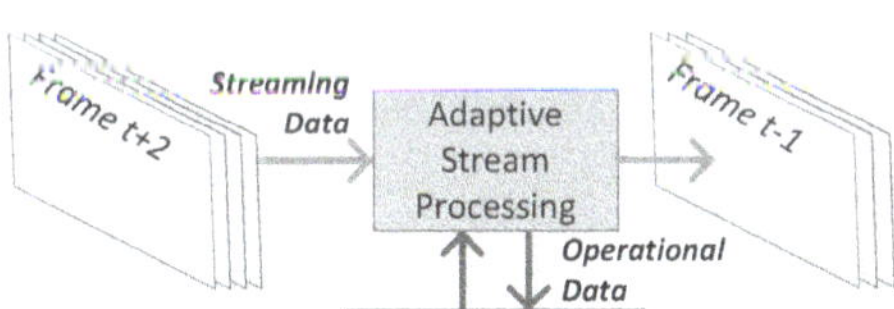

Figure 1: Streaming and operational data in adaptive vision kernels

The communication/memory access overhead is more pronounced in streaming applications; in particular, adaptive stream processing [4]. A good class of applications are vision algorithms. Fig. 1 outlines a typical data access flow for adaptive vision algorithms with a separation between streaming data and operational data paths. Streaming data is data under processing (pixels in the case of vision) and is typically read from input ports and written to output ports (each bypassing the memory hierarchy) or system memory. Conversely, operational data is data used for realizing the computation (e.g. kernel density histogram or Gaussian parameters).

The operational data is accessed and updated per individual frame and directly hits system memory. The volume of operational data often exceeds any on-chip cache, thus driving up the system power consumption. As an example, Mixture of Gaussian (MoG) background subtraction [4] uses about 8GB of memory access while processing 128 MPixels/s. This imposes significant bandwidth limitations as well as significant power overhead. Our power analysis demonstrates that for the case of MoG around 90% of overall power is consumed by operational data access.

Much research focuses on analyzing the power / quality trade-off in the context of video coding [2][1]. However, the trade-offs mainly focus on adjusting computational complexity (as a matter of power) and the quality of video compression. New generation of algorithms (e.g. MoG, KLT, optical flow) have an adaptive nature with lots of data interaction between frames and thus far more demands for operational data. These algorithms are still implemented at a much lower resolution (300*200) [7] while market demand is already there for HD resolution.

In this paper, we focus on power/quality trade-off with respect to communication aspects of the design. We primarily zoom into the operational data access demand for adaptoive streaming applications. To simplify future designs and for exploration, we use our previously introduced communication-centric architecture template [5]. The template offers configurable knobs for exploring the quality/power trade-off. Through a methodological exploration, we formulate the trade-off and propose a tool to automate the process. The reported power numbers are based on an actual implementation of our proposed architecture template on Xilinx Zynq platform [6] with a running MoG kernel. We quantify our result for Mixture of Gaussian (MoG) background subtraction [4].

The remainder of this paper is organized as follows. Section 2 further explains the background and motivation of our work. Section 3 describes our approach and formulation in detail. Section 4 presents the experimental results on power/ quality exploration. Finally, Section 5 concludes the paper and touches on future work.

2. BACKGROUND

In this paper, we selected Mixture of Gaussian (MoG) [4] to explore and quantify our trade-off. Fig. 2 includes the MoG coarse-grain mathematical formulation. MoG uses multiple Gaussian distributions, to model a pixel's background. Each Gaussian has its own

GLSVLSI '16, May 18-20, 2016, Boston, MA, USA

DOI: http://dx.doi.org/10.1145/2902961.2903004

set of parameters: weight, intensity mean and standard deviation. With a new pixel coming in, all Gaussian parameters are updated at frame basis to track BG changes of the pixel. For an individual pixel, while the streaming traffic is only 17-bits (16-bit for input pixel and 1-bit for foreground mask), the operational traffic hit on the memory access is 960-bits combining both memory read and write-back access (assuming 32 bit per Gaussian parameter with 5 Gaussian distributions).

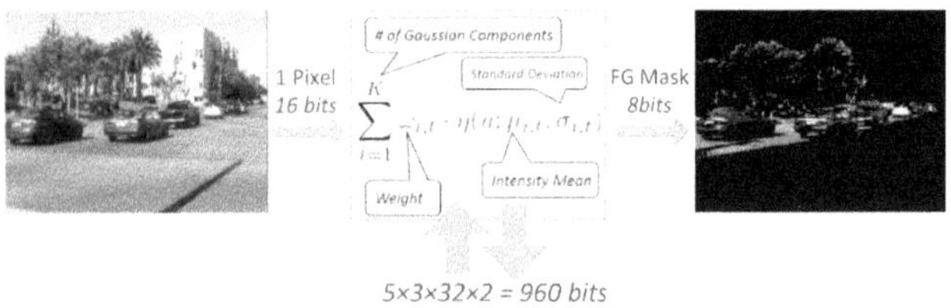

Figure 2: Memory access per pixel in MoG algorithm

To reduce the memory bandwidth for accessing operational data, we proposed adding a support block to compress / de-compress parameters in data memory read/write access [5]. The compression module is interfacing the running kernel and system memory and is configurable to compress/de-compress operational data at different bit width, while the internal processing is still being performed at the highest accuracy (e.g. 32 bits). Fig. 3a demonstrates the result of quality exploration as a trade-off between bandwidth per frame (1080*1920 resolution) on the x-axis and quality on y-axis. Fig. 3b presents the maximum quality over the increasing size of bits per pixel, derived from Pareto curve. We define bit per pixel as an indicator of quality metric. As an example, for 70-bits per pixel the quality would be only 0.64, or 244-bits per pixel for the maximum possible quality.

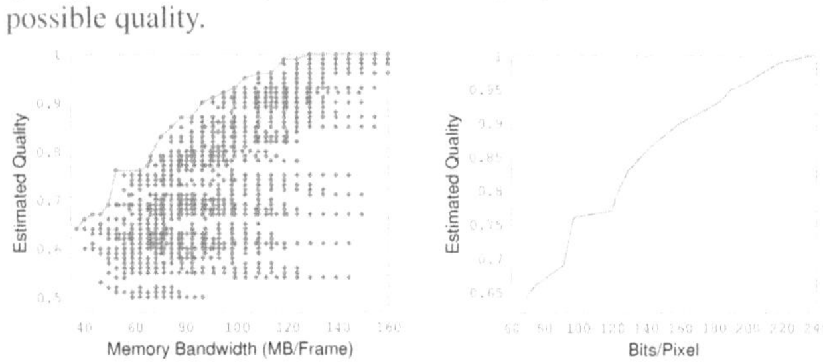

(a) Quality / Bandwidth trade-off (b) Quality over bits per Pixel

Figure 3: Quality exploration for 1080*1920 resolution

We also use our previously introduced communication-centric architecture template [5] (highlighted in Fig. 4). It consists of two clock domains: the computation clock domain driven by streaming data (pixels), and the communication clock domain set by the bus/interconnect frequency. The two clock domains are connected via *Async. FIFOs*. The compression/de-compression blocks provides run-time mechanism to reduce the bandwidth demand for operational data. Our architecture template offers a set of configurable knobs (design choices) including operational bits per pixel (as a quality indicator), Async. FIFO depth, DMA inline buffers as well as DMA channels and communication bus/interconnect width and frequency.

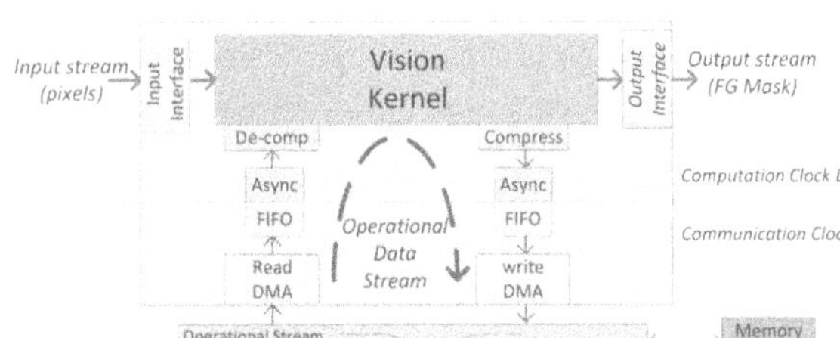

Figure 4: Architecture template for adaptive streaming kernels

3. APPROACH

In this section, we deploy a procedural method to traverse the axes of a design space. We consider the axes of exploration to be (a) requirements (e.g. quality), (b) architecture goals (e.g. operational bit width per pixel) (c) design options (e.g. bus bandwidth) and (d) metrics (e.g. power). After defining the axes of exploration, we need a procedural flow for step-by-step exploration and formulating of the problem.

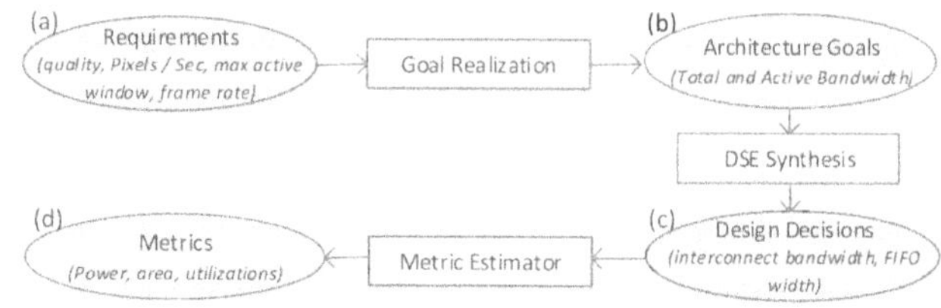

Figure 5: Requirement, design, metric exploration flow

Fig. 5 outlines the major steps of exploration. In a general view, the flow proposes three step exploration: (1) from requirements to architecture goals ((a)->(b)), (2) from architecture goals to design decisions ((b)->(c)), (3) from design decisions to metrics ((c)->)(d)). The goal is transferring the requirements to realizable architecture goals understandable in terms of architecture.

For MoG, $Quality$, $Frame\_Rate$, $Frame\_resolution$ and $Active\_resolution$ define the requirement set (highlighted by (1)). For simplicity, we did not define the concept of an active window until now. $Active\_resolution$ defines the window of interest under actual MoG processing. Although video can be processed full-frame, many developers in practice will focus on a part of the frame rather than the whole. The active window is a subset of original frame resolution representing the pixels under MoG processing. For high definition resolution (1080*1920), not all pixels are part of active window, but instead only a subset (window of interest) is processed at each period of time, which we call active window. Active window location and resolution can be changed over time.

$$Requirements = \{Quality, Frame\_Rate, Frame\_resolution, Active\_resolution\} \tag{1}$$

Similarly (2) defines the architecture goals as $Bits_{Pixel}$, BW_{active}, BW_{active_width}. $Bits_{Pixel}$ defines the bits per pixel as a quality indicator, BW_{active} defines the overall active bandwidth required for processing the active window of a frame. It can be derived from the requirements (highlighted in (2)). BW_{active_width} also demonstrates the bandwidth requirement for processing one row of the active_window (highlighted in (4)). BW_{active_width} is an architecture goal to make sure that the operational data are available during the processing of each active_window row.

$$Architecture\_Goal = \{Bits_{Pixel}, BW_{active}, BW_{active\_width}\} \tag{2}$$

$$BW_{active} = Frame\_Rate \times Width_{active} \times Height_{active} \times Bits_{pixel} \tag{3}$$

$$BW_{active\_width} = Width_{active} \times Bits_{Pixel} \tag{4}$$

As we highlighted in Fig. 5, after defining the requirements and deriving the architecture goals, it is time for DSE synthesis. The goal of DSE synthesis is identifying a set of design decisions that can satisfy the architecture goals. With respect to our architecture template, the design options are f_{Bus} (bus frequency), W_{Bus} (bus width)as well as Async. FIFOs depth D_{FIFO}. The architecture knobs should be set in such a way as to satisfy the architecture goals. For that, two pre-conditions have to be verified: (a) total active bandwidth (BW_{active}) validation and (b) BW_{active_width} validation. The first step is validating that the communication bandwidth can supply the volume of bits demanded by the quality requirement. (5) describes the sustainable bus bandwidth. U_{bus} is bus utilization. The bus utilization is an indicator of how many bus cycles are transferring actual data. The architecture goal is satisfied only if the condition ($BW_{bus} > BW_{active}$) is true.

$$BW_{bus} = f_{bus} \times Width_{bus} \times U_{bus} \tag{5}$$

To meet condition B(BW_{active_width}), the communication system has to offer enough operational data per active row. (6) formulates the volume of data that can be supported by the bus per active row executed in computation domain which we name $\frac{f_{Bus}}{f_{comp}}$. It is an indicator of clock mismatch between the computation and communication clock domains; f_{Bus} represents communication clock frequency and f_{comp} is computation clock frequency. In practice, f_{Bus} appears to be lower than f_{comp}. Due to this the communication sub-system should guarantee that it can provide enough data per active row execution; otherwise, the application kernel is starved of data and does not operate correctly.

$$BW_{bus\_active} = width_{frame} \times width_{Bus} \times Util_{Bus} \times \frac{f_{Bus}}{f_{comp}} \tag{6}$$

The Async. FIFOs are utilized for both bridging the two clock frequencies as well as compensating for the shortcoming of bus in supplying operational data. Satisfying ($BW_{Bus\_width} > BW_{active\_width}$) means that communication bandwidth can provide enough pixels per active row, resulting in smaller FIFO depth. In this case, FIFOs are just utilized for bridging between two clock domain. (7) formulates the FIFO size for condition of ($BW_{comm\_width} > BW_{active\_width}$). As $Width_{active}$ increases, a larger FIFO is required. Conversely, by increasing bus clock frequency f_{Bus} lower FIFO size is required.

$$if(BW_{Bus\_width} > BW_{active\_width}) \quad D_{FIFO} = Width_{active} \times U_{comm} \times \frac{f_{comp}}{f_{Bus}} \tag{7}$$

If the bus cannot satisfy ($BW_{comm\_width} > BW_{active\_width}$),a much larger FIFO would be required. In this case, FIFOs significantly contribue to compensating for the data supply shortcoming. Computation is halted while out of the active window so the communication bus can keep fetching data and fill the Async FIFOs to make sure that enough data are available during active window processing. (8) formulates the FIFO depth for these conditions. In this case, the maximum size of the active window $Height_{active}$ also contributes to the FIFO size; larger compensation is required maximum window size increases.

$$if(BW_{comm\_width} < BW_{active\_width}) \quad Depth_{FIFO} = \frac{(BW_{active\_width} - BW_{Bus\_width})}{Width_{Bus}} \times Height_{active} \tag{8}$$

Note that, the purpose of (7) and (8) is not just for identifying the FIFO sizes. These equations can be used determine the minimum bus frequency or bus width for a predetermined FIFO sizes as well. Fig. 6b demonstrates the minimum required bus frequency over different bus widths with different FIFO sizes. In Fig. 6b, we assume a fixed active_frame size of 512*512 pixels with a fixed quality of 128-bits per pixel. Overall, what we observe is that the larger depth of FIFO size allows lower frequency and can potentially result in lower power usage. Furthermore, there is a trade-off between bus width and frequency while delivering identical bandwidth. The architecture knob sizing of Fig. 6b allows identical bandwidth but potentially different power costs. The architecture design knobs can

(a) FIFO depth over active width (b) Bus frequency over bus width

Figure 6: Design dimensions

be tweaked to achieve minimum power usage while maintaining a given quality requirement.

We have now defined the design space exploration and narrowed down the exploration space to only design choices can satisfy the architecture goals. Based on our architecture template, each design choice can be described by (9) including f_{Bus}, $Width_{Bus}$ and $Depth_{FIFO}$.

$$Choice_i = (Depth_{FIFO}, freq_{Bus}, Width_{Bus}) \tag{9}$$

4. RESULTS

To quantify the trade-off, we have prototyped our proposed architecture template on the ZedBoard with Zynq. Overall, the system power can be divided into off-chip and on-chip portions. Off-chip memory accesses for operational data impose a significant power overhead to the system (around 65% of entire system power in our implementation). By parameter compression and thus cutting access volume in half, the off-chip power halved as well. After optimizing off-chip accesses, on-chip communication elements need to be explored further for optimum power point per quality. We have analyzed the on-chip power by using Xilinx X-Power Analyzer tool after post synthesis and mapping of the entire design on Zynq platform.

Fig. 7a describes the quality / bandwidth trade-off. With respect to formulation, we configure and synthesize our architecture templates to reflect the targeted bandwidth. Clearly, power demand increases with increasing communication bandwidth. However, we observe identical bandwidths with yet different power consumptions. This is due to the fact that different template configurations can result in identical bandwidth but differing power. Fig. 7b illustrates the trade-off between power and quality. Again based on the formulation, we calculated the design choices that can satisfy the quality point and change the architecture template to reflect this decision. We observe that some design choices lead to a lower power consumption while achieving same quality.

Fig. 8a demonstrates the bus width and power over increasing bus frequency. All these configurations can provide exactly enough bandwidth to satisfy the requirements for quality point of 0,8 (mean-

(a) Power over memory bandwidth (b) Achieved quality over power

Figure 7: Power / Quality exploration

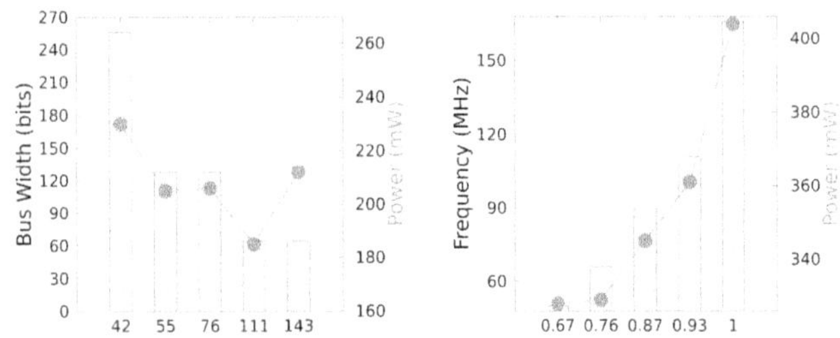

(a) Frequency (b) Quality

Figure 8: Power / Quality trade-off

ing 128 operational bit width per pixel). Different configurations lead to different power consumptions. For example, the configuration with a 64-bit wide 111 MHz bus, has a lower power consumption than a 128-bit bus with 76 MHz. However, these two differ in quality (bit width per pixel). Fig. 8b presents the frequency and power for different quality points for a fixed bus width of 128-bits. Clearly, higher quality means larger bit-width per pixel and results in higher power demand.

Defining the step-by-step exploration (highlighted in Fig. 5) and formulation of problem for case of MoG set the stage for automating the exploration. Our proposed Design Space Synthesizer (DSS) takes as an input the application requirements (quality, active resolution) and converts them into architecture goals. Then, it identifies design candidates that can satisfy architecture goals based on the formulations. We implemented a prototype in Matlab, realizing the exact formulations.

The proposed DSS is a significant step toward reducing the exploration space complexity. The output of DSS is a set of design decisions which satisfy the architecture goals. Fig. 9 highlights all 150 considered design candidates for realizing MoG on the Zynq platform. Out of these design candidates, only four satisfy the requirement for a quality of 0.99, which leads to 244-bit operational data per pixel. The identified designs points satisfying the constraints are highlighted in red.

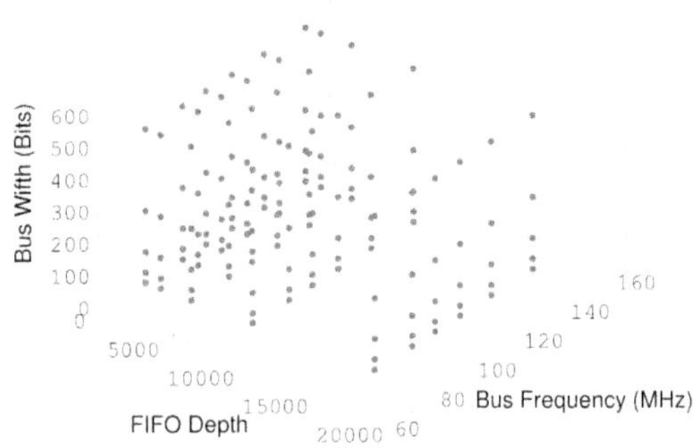

Figure 9: Identified design choices by the DSE tool

After identifying valid design configurations, their design metrics have to estimated (e.g. power, area ...) in order to achieve an optimization goal. In our example, the goal is to reduce power. Obtaining design metrics can be achieved by either an actual implementation (which is too time consuming), or by a metric estimation tools.

Many complex power estimators exist. For the purpose of initial estimation, we focus on first order rapid estimation that provide some boundaries for decision making. For this we develop a linear model. Our linear model is calibrated with a measured base power consumption and with incremental costs for each design choice dimension. For example, we assume a linear increase in power with FIFO size. We also assume linear relation with bus width. An increase in bus frequency has a multiplicative effect. The power model is driven by the actual sample points. The developed model, allows interpolation and estimation of new combinations.

Fig. 10 plots quality over power consumption for both estimated and real powers. The tool-estimated numbers are optimized for powers per quality point, while the actual powers (highlighted by red stars) are varies depending on their design decisions. The colors define the optimal design decisions (FIFO depth, bus frequency, bus width) made by tool for minimizing power consumption per quality. We observe that the estimated tool power numbers are very close to the actual powers (10 mW on average). Furthermore, the identified design decisions guide the user to the optimum power per quality point without need to exhaustive experimentation. Even the proposed first order estimation driven by the proposed DSS is a utility to quickly identify and evaluate design choices. We see a tremendous research potential in elaborating and refining automation of design space exploration that takes architecture and application knowledge into account.

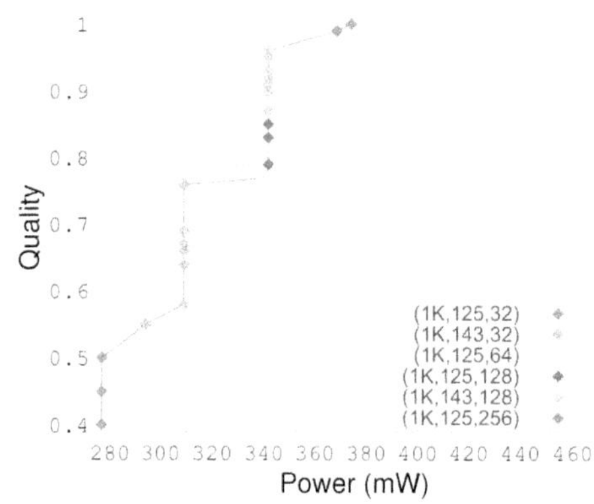

Figure 10: Quality over power for estimated and real execution

5. CONCLUSIONS

This paper explores the power/quality trade-off for communication-intense designs with a focus communication design aspect. The paper proposes a systematic exploration, which follows a procedural model to resolve design decisions in a step-by-step manner. We offer a formalization the exploration challenges for a case study of mixture of Gaussian (MoG) background subtraction. Our trade-off analysis, architecture template, and formalization example guide system designs realizing high-performance communication-intense streaming applications.

6. REFERENCES

[1] G. Chen, M. Kandemir, N. Vijaykrishnan, M. J. Irwin, and W. Wolf. Energy savings through compression in embedded java environments. In *Proceedings of the Tenth International Symposium on Hardware/Software Codesign*, CODES '02, pages 163–168, 2002.

[2] T. Lv, I. Ozer, S. Chakradhar, J. Xu, W. Wolf, and J. Henkel. A methodology for architectural design of multimedia multiprocessor socs. *Design Test of Computers, IEEE*, 22(1):18–26, 2005.

[3] H. Nikolov, M. Thompson, T. Stefanov, A. Pimentel, S. Polstra, R. Bose, C. Zissulescu, and E. Deprettere. Daedalus: toward composable multimedia mp-soc design. In *Proceedings of the 45th annual Design Automation Conference (DAC)*, pages 574–579, 2008.

[4] C. Stauffer and W. E. L. Grimson. Adaptive background mixture models for real-time tracking. In *Computer Vision and Pattern Recognition, 1999. IEEE Computer Society Conference on.*, volume 2, pages -252 Vol. 2, 1999.

[5] H. Tabkhi, M. Sabbagh, and G. Schirner. Power-efficient real-time solution for adaptive vision algorithms. *IET Computers Digital Techniques*, 9(1):16–26, 2015.

[6] Xilinx. Zynq-7000 all programmable soc. In *Technical Reference Manual*, 2013.

[7] J. Xu, W. Wolf, J. Henkel, S. Chakradhar, and T. Lv. A case study in networks-on-chip design for embedded video. In *Design, Automation and Test in Europe Conference and Exhibition, 2004. Proceedings*, volume 2, pages 770–775 Vol.2, 2004.

Graphene-PLA (GPLA): a Compact and Ultra-Low Power Logic Array Architecture

Valerio Tenace, Andrea Calimera, Enrico Macii, Massimo Poncino
Politecnico di Torino, 10129, Torino, Italy
andrea.calimera@polito.it

ABSTRACT

The key characteristics of the next generation of ICs for wearable applications include high integration density, small area, low power consumption, high energy-efficiency, reliability and enhanced mechanical properties like stretchability and transparency. The proper mix of new materials and novel integration strategies is the enabling factor to achieve those design specifications.

Moving toward this goal, we introduce a graphene-based regular logic-array structure for energy efficient digital computing. It consists of graphene p-n junctions arranged into a regular mesh. The obtained structure resembles that of Programmable Logic Arrays (PLAs), hence the name Graphene-PLAs (GPLAs); the high expressive power of graphene p-n junctions and their resistive nature enables the implementation of ultra-low power adiabatic logic circuits.

Categories and Subject Descriptors

B.6.1 [**Logic Design**]: Design Styles

Keywords

Graphene; Low-Power; Adiabatic; Logic Synthesis; Logic Array

1. INTRODUCTION

During the last decade, graphene, a two-dimensional allotrope of carbon, has emerged as one of the most appealing option for silicon replacement in the consumer electronics industry [1]. Mechanical strength and flexibility, combined with higher carrier mobility w.r.t. silicon, make graphene a perfect material for the implementation of wearable devices and sensing applications [2]. Nevertheless, pristine graphene is a zero band-gap material, i.e., valence and conductance bands touch each other near the Dirac points; this avoids graphene to efficiently implement the OFF-state.

Most of the worldwide research projects are pushing efforts to find practical, low-cost methods to open a band-gap in the material equal, or at least close, to that of silicon. Unfortunately, today's available solutions, e.g., patterning [3], chemical doping [4] and/or combination with other materials [5], increase the level of disorder of graphene with rather huge impact on the resulting electrical characteristics. Hence, the need of alternative techniques to adapt graphene for digital applications. Other solutions face the problem from a different perspective, that is, identify alternative techniques that better exploit the intrinsic properties of graphene rather than trying to modify them.

Electrostatic doping [6] falls in the latter category. External electrical fields applied through metal split gates allow a fine-tuning of the Fermi Energy level across the graphene sheet resulting into an equivalent p-type or n-type doping. Face to face regions with opposite doping profiles form an equivalent p-n junction [7], the key component behind any electronic circuit.

A p-n junction is a four-terminal device with two *control* pins, implementing the electrostatic doping, one *input* pin to which the input evaluation signal is fed, and one *output* pin, that eventually collects the input evaluation signal. When control signals have same polarity, the junction is in the ON-state, i.e., a low-resistive state which allows the input evaluation signal to propagate through the junction and reach the output pin. With opposite polarities, the junction is in the OFF-state, i.e., high impedance state which avoids the input signal to propagate.

This behavior resembles that of a MOS transmission gate with an enhanced logic XNOR functionality; hence the name of *Pass-XNOR* gate. Such devices can be used as a new logic primitive to compactly implement logic circuits that are potentially faster and more power-efficient than silicon counterparts. Since graphene p-n junctions behave as voltage-controlled resistors, rather than ideal switches, when integrated in a CMOS-like strategy, they imply excessive static power consumption. This gave the basis for the introduction of new dynamic design styles that can fruitfully exploit the higher expressive power of graphene p-n junctions, e.g., the PXL style proposed in [8]. How to place and organize this new class of circuits has not been addressed yet.

Recent advances in wearable technologies, especially for medical applications [9, 10], have shown that circuit built upon a regular and programmable structure represent a more suited integration strategy. Our intuition is that the physical geometries and the layout topology of a graphene p-n junction well fit the regular organization of standard logic arrays and, in particular, *Programmable Logic Arrays (PLAs)* used for MOS technologies. We therefore introduce the *Graphene PLA* (GPLA), a PLA-like architecture which

GLSVLSI '16, May 18-20, 2016, Boston, MA, USA

DOI: http://dx.doi.org/10.1145/2902961.2902970

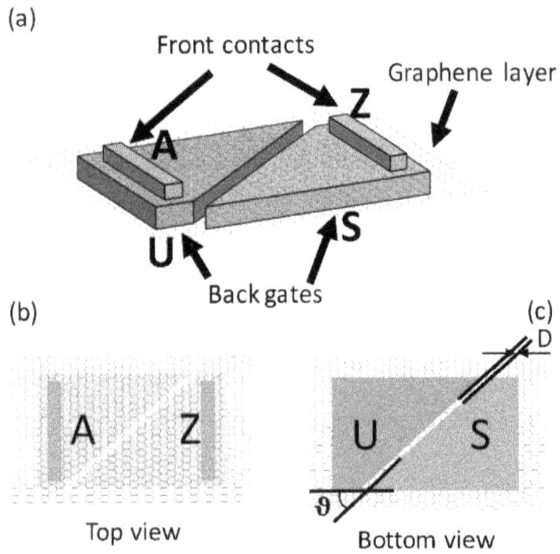

Figure 1: Graphene p-n junction, (a) 3-D view, (b) top view, and (c) bottom view.

integrates graphene p-n junctions for combinational Boolean logic functions.
The main contributions of this paper can be summarized as follows: *(i)* we describe a design methodology aimed at the representation of generic Boolean functions by means of Pass-XNOR gates arranged in a GPLA structure, *(ii)* an algorithmic approach that allows to reduce area occupation (52% less devices) and improve performance/power figures (3.5X lower power-dealy product) over traditional silicon-based PLA structures.

2. BACKGROUND

2.1 Graphene p-n junction

Figure 1-(a) shows an abstract 3-D view of a graphene p-n junction. It consists of a graphene sheet on top of which two metal-to-graphene contacts, A and Z, serve as signal input and output respectively, and a thick layer of oxide that isolates the two back-gates, S and U, from the graphene itself. Exploiting the principle of the electrostatic doping, voltage potentials on terminals S and U work as a control knob to tune the Fermi Energy (E_F) of the overlapping graphene regions [11]; a negative voltage shifts down E_F in the valence band leading to p-type doping, whereas a positive voltage shifts E_F up in the conductance band leading to n-type doping. When symmetric voltages are concurrently applied on S and U terminals, i.e., $V(S) = +V$ and $V(U) = -V$, the device implements the p-n junction. As described in [11], under such configuration, carriers transmission from the p-region towards the n-region is subject to the transmission probability $T(\theta)$:

$$T(\theta) = \cos^2(\theta)e^{-\pi kD\sin^2(\theta)} \quad (1)$$

where θ is the angle between the electron's wave vector $\vec{k}$ and the normal of the junction (45° as imposed by the triangular shape of the back-gates), and D is the width of the metal gap between the back-gates, assumed to be $18nm$, as described in Figure 1-c. It is worth noticing that $T(\theta) = 1$, i.e., 100% of carrier transmitted, when voltages applied at the back-gates are concordant (n-n or p-p doping configurations). Concerning physical dimensions, the equivalent area occupation of a graphene p-n junction is $0.191\mu m^2$ [7].

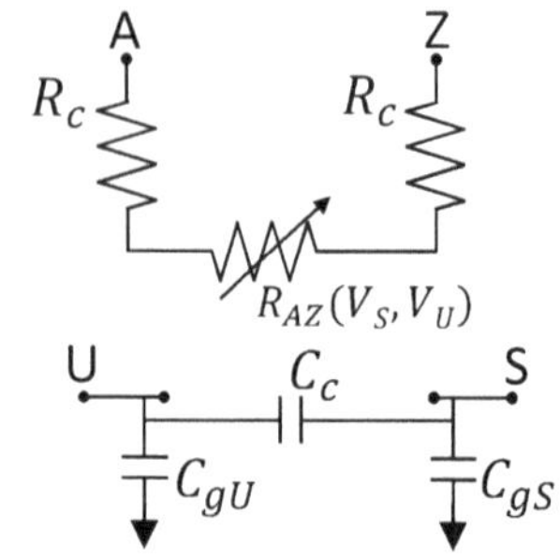

Figure 2: Electrical model of a graphene p-n junction.

2.2 p-n junction electrical model

Figure 2 shows the electrical model of the p-n junction. There are two R_C resistors connected to pins A and Z representing the parasitic resistance of metal-to-graphene contacts. The resistor R_{AZ} models the resistive path across the graphene layer between the input A and the output Z; its analytical expression is given as $R_{AZ} = \frac{R_0}{N_{ch}T(\theta)}$, where $R_0 = \frac{h}{4q^2}$ is the quantum resistance per propagation mode, N_{ch} is the number of excited propagation modes, and $T(\theta)$ is the transmission probability described by (1). As reported in [7], values of R_{AZ} ranges from $R_{ON} = 300\Omega$, (under n-n or p-p configurations), to $R_{OFF} = 10^7\Omega$ (p-n or n-p configurations). The model also integrates the coupling capacitance C_C between the two metal split gates, and two lumped capacitances connected to the back-gates S and U, namely, C_{gS} and C_{gU} respectively, which consist of the series of the oxide capacitance and the quantum capacitance of the graphene sheet[1].

2.3 Pass-XNOR Gate

A Pass-XNOR gate (PXG), depicted in the leftmost picture of Figure 3, simply consists of a p-n junction where the back-gates U and S are fed with digital control signals, while the front contacts A and Z work as source and drain of a stimulus ramp pulse (the *evaluation signal*) used to evaluate the logic function.
As shown in the table of Figure 3, when U and S have same logic value, the equivalent in-to-out front resistance R_{AZ} is set to R_{ON} allowing the input pulse on A to pass through the junction reaching Z; this represents the '1'-logic at the output. Opposite logic values, on the contrary, set the in-to-out front resistance R_{AZ} to R_{OFF} ($\gg R_{ON}$), forcing Z in a high-impedance state; this represents the '0'-logic at the output.

3. GRAPHENE LOGIC ARRAYS

3.1 Logic computation through PXGs

Pass-XNOR gates show a higher expressive power if compared to CMOS counterparts, i.e., they require a smaller number of devices to implement XNOR/XOR-dominated logic functions [8]. Unfortunately, the XNOR operator ($\neg\oplus$)

[1]For a more detailed discussion on the p-n junction and its electrical model, interested readers can refer to [7].

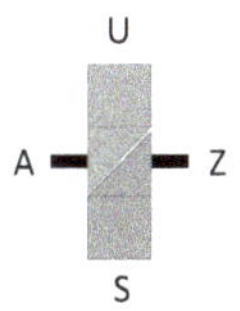

A	U	S	R_{AZ}	Z
Pulse	0	0	R_{ON}	A
V_{dd}	0	1	R_{OFF}	Hi-Z
	1	0	R_{OFF}	Hi-Z
0 V	1	1	R_{ON}	A

Figure 3: Logic symbol and functional behavior of the Pass-XNOR logic gate.

per sé is not functional complete, therefore other logic connectives are needed. It is possible to pattern multiple PXGs in series in order to obtain a product-of-XNOR, i.e., an AND operation ($\wedge$) between XNOR terms. In other words, since information is propagated by means of the input evaluation signal, the latter is allowed to propagate throughout all the PXG gates *iff* all PXG devices are in the ON-state. On the other hand, multiple PXGs in parallel implement a sum-of-XNOR, i.e., an OR operation ($\vee$) between XNOR terms. This means that the XNOR is the primitive logic function, whereas AND and OR connectives are implemented by means of different circuit topologies, series and parallel connections, respectively. Such a simple, yet effective, circuit organization allows to fruitfully exploit the expressive power of PXGs to implement any complex Boolean function. As an example, let us assume a Boolean function defined by:

$$f = ((x_1 \neg\oplus x_2) \wedge x_3) \vee ((x_3 \neg\oplus x_4) \wedge (\neg x_5)) \qquad (2)$$

Figure 4 depicts the equivalent PXG-based implementation. Each product term is defined over a single physical row of PXG devices (*AND-connections*); the overall function f is achieved by parallel connections of those product terms (*OR-connections*). The regularity of the structure is guaranteed by a particular property of PXG devices, that is, the possibility to easily implement *identity* and *complement* ($\neg$) functions by means of proper control-signal patterns. For our example, variable x_3 is paired with 1-logic to implement the corresponding identity operation, whereas x_5 is paired to a 0-logic signal as to obtain its complement $\neg x_5$.

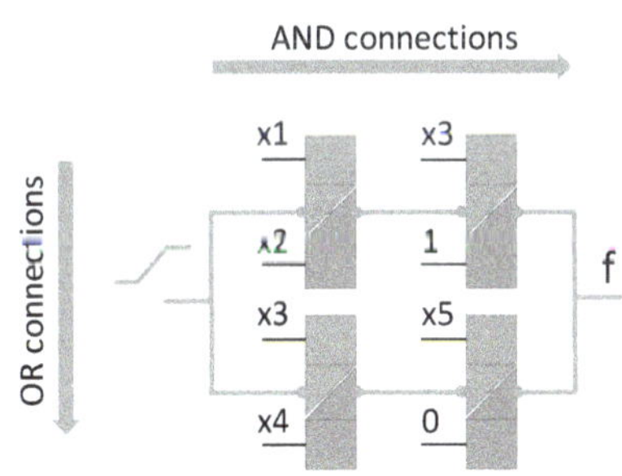

Figure 4: Graphene-based regular strcuture

As one can intuitively understand, graphene PXG gates can be efficiently packed as to form regular, two-dimensional meshes very similar to MOS Programmable-Logic-Arrays. Logic computing through the proposed Graphene-PLA (GPLA) consists of two distinct phases: the *configuration phase* and the *evaluation phase*. In the configuration phase the primary logic inputs, i.e., the literals composing the logic function, are fed to the back-gates of the p-n junctions. At the end of this phase the doping profile of each and every PXG device is fixed and the resistive paths of the network set up. In the evaluation phase, the input ramp pulse is injected in the network through the front input, i.e., the root of the network, and eventually propagated to the front output. A pulse detected at the front output evaluates the implemented function as TRUE.

3.2 From PLAs to GPLAs

The Programmable Logic Array (PLA) is a well-known implementation style for Boolean logic functions described in the form of Sum-of-Products (SOP). A PLA is made up of two main components: the *AND plane*, where primary inputs are properly connected in order to generate the product terms of the function, and an *OR plane* that collects the product terms for their sum.
Let us consider the single output Boolean function $f(x_1, x_2, x_3)$ described by the equation (3):

$$\begin{aligned} f(x_1, x_2, x_3) &= \neg x_1 \neg x_2 \neg x_3 \\ &\vee \neg x_1 x_2 x_3 \\ &\vee x_1 \neg x_2 x_3 \\ &\vee x_1 x_2 \neg x_3 \\ &= \pi_1 \vee \pi_2 \vee \pi_3 \vee \pi_4 \end{aligned} \qquad (3)$$

The resulting PLA is depicted in Figure 5. As can be seen, the AND plane (left side) implements all the four product terms π_k by means of physical connections between primary inputs. The latter can be obtained by connecting a MOSFET transistor, typically an n-type MOSFET, through a fuse/anti-fuse mechanism as to create/drop connections. The same happens in the OR plane (right side), where selected product terms are fused/anti-fused to the primary output they belong to. Neglecting the pre-charge transistors, the total number of devices employed for AND/OR connections counts of 16 transistors (black dots in Figure 5).

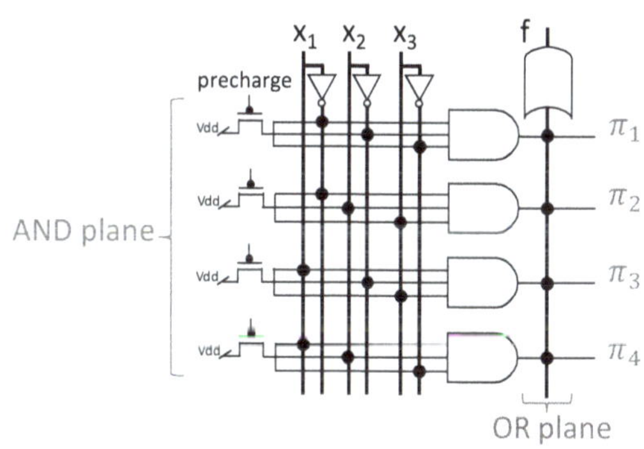

Figure 5: PLA structure of function (3)

The PLA structure is well suited for the binding of graphene PXG-based circuits. It is straightforward to map AND/OR connections among PXGs using a PLA-like style. Moreover, while for standard silicon PLAs the physical primitives are simple switch transistors, with GPLAs those primitives work as XNOR operators thereby enabling more compact circuit implementations.
It is worth noticing that, while for PLAs standard SOP-based synthesis methodologies do apply, GPLAs require a different decomposition method for representing Boolean logic functions in terms of Sum-of-XNOR-Products. To this extent, we resort to the PXL-expansion paradigm described in [12].

Let us consider the same example described in (3); the function f can be XNOR-decomposed as described in (4), where each π_k^{gpla} represent the k-th product term:

$$\begin{aligned} f(x_1,x_2,x_3) &= (x_1 \neg\oplus x_2) \wedge (x_2 \neg\oplus x_3) \wedge (\neg x_3 \neg\oplus 1) \\ &\vee (\neg x_1 \neg\oplus x_2) \wedge (x_2 \neg\oplus x_3) \wedge (x_3 \neg\oplus 1) \\ &\vee (\neg x_1 \neg\oplus x_2) \wedge (\neg x_2 \neg\oplus x_3) \wedge (x_3 \neg\oplus 1) \\ &\vee (x_1 \neg\oplus x_2) \wedge (\neg x_2 \neg\oplus x_3) \wedge (\neg x_3 \neg\oplus 1) \\ &= \pi_1^{gpla} \vee \pi_2^{gpla} \vee \pi_3^{gpla} \vee \pi_4^{gpla} \end{aligned} \quad (4)$$

The equivalent GPLA structure is depicted in Figure 6-(a). The AND plane is composed of a chain of graphene PXG devices with control signals connected to the primary inputs; the OR plane is obtained by connecting the product terms to the output rail. Notice that logic signals `1-logic` and `0-logic` are needed for the implementation of identity and complement operators. The resulting GPLA counts of 12 PXG devices, achieving a 25% device reduction w.r.t. the classical PLA structure. It is also worth noticing that PXGs are smaller than MOS devices.
Moreover, due to the resistive nature of PXGs, the *adiabatic charging principle* [8] holds for GPLAs, that is, given a slow-rising ramp as the input evaluation signal, the network switches adiabatically, i.e., at zero power consumption (at least ideally).

3.3 GPLA optimization

Though GPLAs, by themselves, are more compact that standard SOP-based MOS implementations, it is still possible to apply optimization rules that sensible reduce their complexity.
Let us first explain this by the same example given in (4). The terms π_1^{gpla} and π_4^{gpla} can be grouped together, with an equivalent expression described as:

$$((x_1 \neg\oplus x_2) \wedge (\neg x_3 \neg\oplus 1)) \wedge ((x_2 \neg\oplus x_3) \vee (\neg x_2 \neg\oplus x_3)) \quad (5)$$

Since the term $(x_2 \neg\oplus x_3) \vee (\neg x_2 \neg\oplus x_3)$ results in a tautology, we can say that both π_1^{gpla} and π_4^{gpla} can be represented with a single product term:

$$\pi_1^{gpla} = \pi_4^{gpla} = (x_1 \neg\oplus x_2) \wedge (\neg x_3 \neg\oplus 1) \quad (6)$$

The same rule holds between π_2^{gpla} and π_3^{gpla}.
The original Boolean function (4) can be therefore represented as:

$$\begin{aligned} f(x_1,x_2,x_3) &= (x_1 \neg\oplus x_2) \wedge (\neg x_3 \neg\oplus 1) \\ &\vee (\neg x_1 \neg\oplus x_2) \wedge (x_3 \neg\oplus 1) \end{aligned} \quad (7)$$

Equation (7) demonstrates that, with few Boolean optimizations, the total number of product terms can be reduced by 50%. The optimized GPLA structure is depicted in Figure 6-(b).
As a rule of thumb, we can state that this *Tautology-based elimination* is feasible only between product terms with overlapping support set. Using a more formal description: *given a Boolean function F, defined over a support set S, there exist at least two generic product terms $\pi_p^{gpla}(S_s)$ and $\pi_q^{gpla}(S_s)$, where $\pi_p^{gpla}, \pi_q^{gpla} \in F$ and $S_s \subset S$, such that grouped factors $\phi_p \in \pi_p^{gpla}(S_s)$ and $\phi_q \in \pi_q^{gpla}(S_s)$ are subject to the $\phi_p \vee \phi_q = 1$ equality.*
Algorithm 1 reports the pseudo-code of the *Tautology-based elimination* routine we implemented in C language. As main

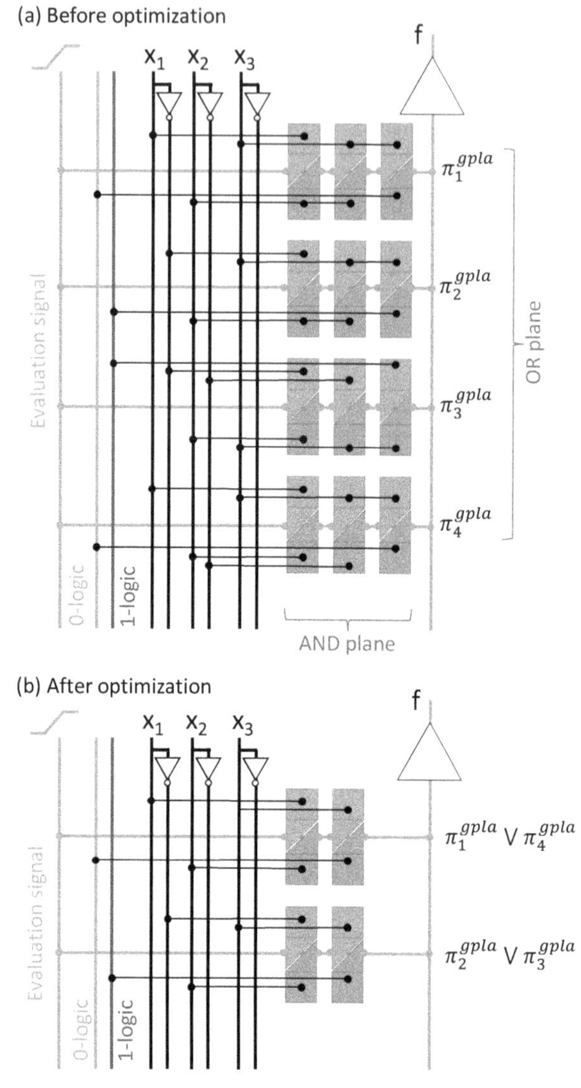

Figure 6: GPLA structure of function (4) w/o optimization (a) and w/ optimization (b)

input parameter, it takes an XNOR-decomposed function obtained through the synthesis procedure described in [12]. The algorithm compares each product term $\pi_j \in F$ with any other product term $\pi_h \in F$ that belongs to the same output cone. As soon as two product terms can be grouped, the algorithm checks whether they result in a tautology. If so, the reduction rule applies; both product terms are removed from the original function F and the reduced term is appended to the optimized function OF. Otherwise, product term π_j cannot be optimized, and hence it is included in the final solution as it is.

4. EXPERIMENTAL RESULTS

4.1 GPLA simulation models

4.1.1 Delay Modeling

The total delay D_p of a GPLA logic circuit is estimated as the sum of delays due to the configuration phase D_{conf} and the evaluation phase D_{eval}, namely, $D_p = D_{conf} + D_{eval}$;

Algorithm 1: Tautology-based elimination routine

Input: PXL-expanded function F
Output: Optimized function OF

$OF = \emptyset$
foreach $\pi_j \in F$ **do**
  foreach $\pi_h \in F$, *where* $\pi_j \neq \pi_h$ **do**
    if *Group*(π_j, π_h) *returns a tautology* **then**
      $\pi_t \leftarrow$ new $\Pi(\pi_j, \pi_h)$
      OF.append(π_t)
      F.remove(π_j) *F.remove*(π_h)
    else
      OF.append(π_j)
    end
  end
end

D_{conf} is the time primary logic inputs take to charge the parasitic capacitances at the back-gates of the graphene PXG device, whereas D_{eval} is the propagation delay of the input pulse through the front resistive paths of the network.
In this work, we make use of SPICE simulations for accurate delay estimation, but more compact analytical models based on an Elmore delay approximation are currently under development.

4.1.2 Dynamic Power Modeling

Also the total dynamic power consumption is estimated as the sum of the two contributions during the configuration and the evaluation phase, i.e., $P_{dynamic} = P_{conf} + P_{eval}$, where P_{conf} is due to charging/discharging the input gate capacitance at the back-gates (similar to the input power consumed by CMOS gates) and P_{eval} is the power consumed when charging/discharging the capacitive load at the front output.
A more accurate analysis, however, reveals that a GPLA network simply reduces to an equivalent resistor R_{eq} (calculated as series/parallel connections of R_{ON} and R_{OFF} depending on the back-gates configurations) in series with the load capacitance C_l. Hence the power consumed across the resistor mesh can be calculated as $P_{eval}(t) = R_{eq} i^2_{C_l}(t)$, with i_{C_l} the current finally injected into C_l. The average value can be therefore obtained as:

$$P_{eval} = \frac{1}{T_{rf}} \int_0^{T_{rf}} R_{eq} i^2_{C_l}(t) dt = \frac{R_{eq}}{T^2_{rf}} C_l^2 V_{dd}^2 \qquad (8)$$

where T_{rf} is the rise/fall output transition time, and $i_{C_l}(t)$ is the current charging C_l. As one can observe, the slower the ramp signal, i.e., larger T_{rf}, the smaller the amount of power consumed across the resistors. When T_{rf} is large enough, the entire charging phase completes at zero-power, namely, adiabatically [13]. As for delay estimation, in this work we use accurate SPICE simulations to estimate R_{eq} and $i_{C_l}(t)$.

4.1.3 Static Power Modeling

Concerning the static power consumption, it is worth emphasizing that during the configuration phase and the idle periods, the front input ramp signal is quiescent, i.e., frozen at 0V. This implies a zero potential difference between front input and front output, and thus, *zero static power consumption*, which is the key strength of the proposed logic style.

	PLA		GPLA			
	PT	**T**	**PT**	**P-N**	**Savings (%)**	**Time (s)**
xnor3	4	12	2	4	66.67	4.6e-5
4gt4	11	44	8	29	34.09	6e-5
alu	16	80	12	56	30.00	7e-5
xor5	16	80	8	32	60.00	6.2e-5
sym6	50	300	29	153	49.00	2.97e-3
max64	46	395	42	355	10.13	1.85e-4
9sym	87	522	81	480	8.05	3.31e-4
apex4_z03	72	568	69	541	4.75	2.78e-4
apex4_z01	81	592	78	566	4.39	2.88e-4
life	84	672	63	483	28.13	6.67e-4
table5_z01	74	823	72	805	2.19	3.64e-4
alu4_z07	290	2934	276	2766	5.73	2.83e-3
sym10	837	8370	456	4179	50.07	6.83e-2
parity	32768	524288	16384	245760	53.13	52.35
Total	-	**539680**	-	**256209**	**52.53**	-
Average	**2459.71**	-	**1255.71**	-	-	**3.74**

Table 1: PLA vs. GPLA synthesis results

The only contribution to static power is given by the tunneling current at the back-gates, similar to the gate current of MOSFETs. An intuitive model is given as follows:

$$P_{static} = \sum_{i}^{2N} I_g \qquad (9)$$

where N is the number of PXG devices, each of them with two back-gates, and I_g is the tunneling current through a single back-gate.

4.2 Results

This section has a twofold objective: *(i)* demonstrate that the proposed GPLA architecture compactly implements a wide variety of Boolean functions; and *(ii)* prove that GPLAs can reach ultra-low power regimes thanks to the adiabatic charging principle. In order to give a comparison between GPLAs and traditional silicon PLA architectures we implemented two different design flows, described as follows.
GPLA architecture: the subject of this work. Each benchmark is first processed with the ABC synthesis tool [14] in order to guarantee the optimum SOP representation for each Boolean function. The resulting implicant table is firstly used to obtain the equivalent XNOR-decomposed function [8]. The optimized GPLA description is obtained by applying the *Tautology-based elimination* algorithm. The resulting circuit is then mapped using PXGs devices, as described in Section 3.
PLA architecture: each benchmark is processed with the ABC synthesis tool and mapped into a standard silicon PLA structure, i.e., AND/OR connection done through n-MOS transistors.
The selected benchmarks represent a set of heterogeneous (i.e., not just XOR/XNOR-rich) open-source logic circuits. Simulation results are obtained through accurate SPICE simulations. For graphene PXGs we used the Verilog-A model discussed in Section 2.2.
Table 1 summarizes the collected results. It reports the total number of product terms describing the logic circuits (columns **PT**), as well as the total number of devices deployed, n-type MOSFET transistors for PLA (column **T**) and PXGs (graphene p-n junctions) for the GPLA (column **P-N**). For GPLA the table also shows the total area sav-

ings w.r.t. PLA (column **Savings**), and the execution time (column **Time**) of the synthesis procedure.
As first comment, one can note that the proposed GPLA architecture has, on the average, 52% less devices. Best results are obtained for those circuits where *Tautology-based elimination* does apply, namely, circuits whose internal Boolean functions contain a large number of product terms with overlapping support set, e.g., `sym10` and `parity`. This characteristic is more frequent for well-specified circuits (implicant tables with fewer don't cares). By contrast, benchmarks `table5_z01` and `apex4_z01`, the circuits with smallest savings, just have a handful of product terms with overlapping support set.
Similar conclusions can be obtained by looking at the total number of product terms (columns **PT**). On the average, with the proposed GPLA flow, PT is reduced by a roughly 49% w.r.t. the original minimum-sized SOP representation (from 2460 to 1256). This is due to the higher expressive power of the XNOR-operator, but, above all, thanks to the efficiency of the proposed elimination rule.
Also notice that the GPLA synthesis and optimization flow is quite efficient in terms of CPU usage (below 1 second for most of the benchmarks, just 52.35 seconds for the largest one with more than 32k implicant rows)[2].

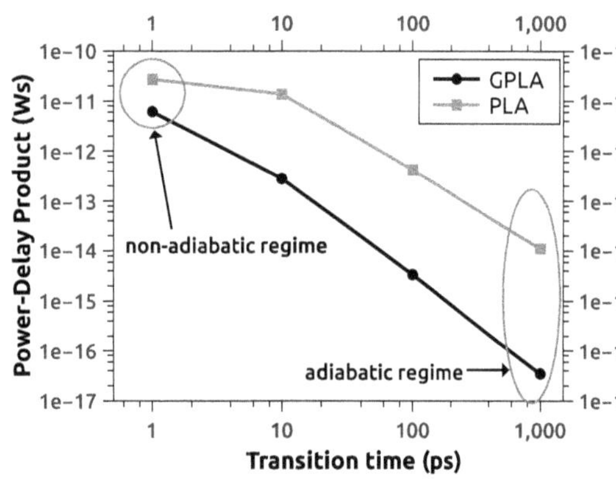

Figure 7: Power-Delay Product (averaged over benchmarks)

Last, but not for importance, Figure 7 depicts the power-delay product (PDP), averaged over all the benchmarks, as function of the transition time T_r of the input evaluation signal.
The internal structure of regular arrays combined with their dynamic nature (pre-charge of the evaluation signal) enable the adiabatic charging principle. PDP reduces by more than 5 orders of magnitude (for GPLA) and 3 orders of magnitude (for PLA) when moving from fast T_r (non-adiabatic regime) to slower T_r (adiabatic regime). This reflects into larger energy-per-operation efficiency, particularly suited for wearable applications.
Moreover, and this is the most important aspect, GPLAs (circle mark) show better PDPs than PLAs (square mark) along the entire range, from a minimum of 0.5X less PDP at $T_r = 1ps$, namely when circuits are outside the adiabatic region, up to a maximum of 3.5X when $T_r = 1ns$, i.e., in the deep-adiabatic region. This result is motivated by the fact that: *(i)* MOSFET-based PLAs show a higher power consumption due to the large amount of simultaneous active/switching devices; *(ii)* MOSFET transistors are active devices, namely, they behave as resistors only in the triode, while p-n junction are pure resistors, more suited for adiabatic operation.

[2]For larger benchmarks we collected CPU times in the order of 10 seconds.

5. CONCLUSIONS

In this work we introduced a graphene-based regular array, the GPLA, that efficiently implements a wide class of Boolean logic functions. We demonstrated that, through XNOR-decomposition and Tautology-based elimination, the proposed architecture outperforms classical PLA structure by means of area occupation (52% improvement). Finally, exploiting the adiabatic charging principle, we also proved that GPLAs have remarkable ultra-low power features.

6. REFERENCES

[1] A. K. Geim and K. S. Novoselov, "The rise of graphene," *Nature materials*, vol. 6, no. 3, pp. 183–191, 2007.
[2] J. A. Rogers, T. Someya, and Y. Huang, "Materials and mechanics for stretchable electronics," *Science*, vol. 327, no. 5973, pp. 1603–1607, 2010.
[3] P. Sessi, J. R. Guest, M. Bode, and N. P. Guisinger, "Patterning graphene at the nanometer scale via hydrogen desorption," *Nano letters*, vol. 9, no. 12, pp. 4343–4347, 2009.
[4] H. Liu, Y. Liu, and D. Zhu, "Chemical doping of graphene," *Journal of materials chemistry*, vol. 21, no. 10, pp. 3335–3345, 2011.
[5] H. Wang, L.-F. Cui, Y. Yang, H. Sanchez Casalongue, J. T. Robinson, Y. Liang, Y. Cui, and H. Dai, "Mn3o4- graphene hybrid as a high-capacity anode material for lithium ion batteries," *Journal of the American Chemical Society*, vol. 132, no. 40, pp. 13 978–13 980, 2010.
[6] C. Ahn, A. Bhattacharya, M. Di Ventra, J. Eckstein, C. D. Frisbie, M. Gershenson, A. Goldman, I. Inoue, J. Mannhart, A. J. Millis *et al.*, "Electrostatic modification of novel materials," *Reviews of Modern Physics*, vol. 78, no. 4, p. 1185, 2006.
[7] S. Tanachutiwat, J. U. Lee, W. Wang, and C. Y. Sung, "Reconfigurable multi-function logic based on graphene pn junctions," in *DAC'10: Design Automation Conference*. ACM/IEEE, 2010, pp. 883–888.
[8] V. Tenace, A. Calimera, E. Macii, and M. Poncino, "Pass-xnor logic: A new logic style for pn junction based graphene circuits," in *DATE'14: Design, Automation and Test in Europe Conference and Exhibition*. IEEE, 2014, pp. 1–4.
[9] T. Ahola, P. Korpinen, J. Rakkola, T. Ramo, J. Salminen, and J. Savolainen, "Wearable fpga based wireless sensor platform," in *EMBS'07: International Conference of Engineering in Medicine and Biology Society*. IEEE, 2007, pp. 2288–2291.
[10] A. Armato, E. Nardini, A. Lanata, G. Valenza, C. Mancuso, E. P. Scilingo, and D. De Rossi, "An fpga based arrhythmia recognition system for wearable applications," in *ISDA'09: International Conference on Intelligent Systems Design and Applications*. IEEE, 2009, pp. 660–664.
[11] V. V. Cheianov and V. I. FalâĂŹko, "Selective transmission of dirac electrons and ballistic magnetoresistance of n- p junctions in graphene," *Physical Review B*, vol. 74, no. 4, p. 041403, 2006.
[12] V. Tenace, A. Calimera, E. Macii, and M. Poncino, "One-pass logic synthesis for graphene-based pass-xnor logic circuits," in *DAC'15: Design Automation Conference*. ACM/IEEE, 2015, pp. 1–6.
[13] S. Miryala, A. Calimera, E. Macii, and M. Poncino, "Ultra low-power computation via graphene-based adiabatic logic gates," in *DSD'14: Euromicro Conference on Digital System Design*. IEEE, 2014, pp. 365–371.
[14] B. L. Synthesis and V. Group, "ABC: A System for Sequential Synthesis and Verification," http://www.eecs.berkeley.edu/~alanmi/abc/, 2014.

A Metastability Immune Timing Error Masking Flip-Flop for Dynamic Variation Tolerance

Govinda Sannena[1] and Bishnu Prasad Das[2]
Department of Electronics and Communication Engineering
Indian Institute of Technology, Roorkee, India
E-mail: [1]govinda.sannena@gmail.com and [2]bpdasfec@iitr.ac.in

ABSTRACT

In this paper, two timing error masking flip-flops have been proposed, which are immune to metastability. The proposed flip-flops exploit the concept of either delayed data or pulse based approach to detect timing errors. The timing violations are masked by passing direct data instead of master latch output to slave latch. Simulation results show that the proposed flip-flops such as type-A and type-B reduce the error masking latency up to 23% and 42% respectively in typical process corners and increase the effective timing error monitoring window compared to state of the art metastable immune flip-flops [14]. The proposed flip-flops can be used in dynamic voltage and frequency scaling (DVFS) applications. A 16-bit adder is implemented to evaluate the functionality of the proposed flip-flops in DVFS frame work and the simulation results show that the adder using the proposed flip-flop can reduce up to 48% power consumption or improve the performance up to 50% in typical process corners compared to conventional worst case design.

Keywords

DVFS; Metastability; Timing error detection; Timing error masking.

1. INTRODUCTION

The scaling of CMOS devices is the primary reason for improved performance of digital integrated circuits. However, meeting the performance specifications of energy and power efficient designs is a critical challenge with increased process, voltage and temperature (PVT) variations in deep submicron (DSM) technologies. Moreover, aging mechanism in DSM technologies severely limits the reliability of CMOS devices. The standard way of addressing the worst case PVT variations in circuit design is by providing safety margins [1]-[3]. However, the probability of occurrence of these worst case conditions is very less. So adding safety margins to tolerate the variations leads to overdesign which operates correctly under worst case conditions but either limit the performance or increase the power overhead.

An attractive approach to reduce the safety margins is to use DVFS with timing error detection and correction or error prediction techniques. In these techniques, the supply voltage of the design is reduced until the timing error detection circuits flag an error signal. These circuit techniques are mainly classified into three categories (1) error detectors, (2) error predictors, and (3) error masking techniques. The error detection techniques detect the timing violations after their occurrence and correct timing violations in successive clock cycles and can completely eliminate safety margins. Error prediction techniques predict possible occurrence of timing errors and can reduce safety margins due to slow changing variations. Error masking techniques either detect or predict timing errors and mask errors within the same clock cycle and can reduce margins due to all variations.

Error detection and correction techniques proposed in [1]-[4] detect timing violations by using double sampling or transition detection approaches. Clock gating or instruction relay mechanisms are used for timing error correction. These techniques do not allow the forward error correction and requires pipeline stalling for error correction. Correction overhead increases with probability of timing error. These techniques are suitable for processor architectures where instruction replay mechanism is available for error correction.

Error prediction techniques proposed in [5], [6] do not require any correction overhead as the output of flip-flop is always correct and can only detect slow changing variations. Moreover, the error prediction techniques reduce the time available for logic by the amount equal to timing margin provided for error prediction. Any data transitions after timing margin are not flagged as errors and leads to malfunctioning of system.

In error masking techniques, timing violations has been detected by using error detection techniques and timing errors are masked in the same clock cycle. The timing error masking techniques can be classified into two categories (1) logical and (2) temporal. In logical error masking techniques, timing errors are masked by using redundant logic which incurs large area overhead [8]. In temporal timing error masking techniques, the timing errors are masked by using time borrowing. As the time is borrowed from next pipeline stage, the time available for next stage logic evaluation is reduced. The clock stretching technique [9] can be used for providing enough time for next stage logic evaluation. In [7], a metastability immune timing error detection technique has been proposed which uses positive latch in data path instead of flip-flop (FF). In [9], timing error masking techniques have been proposed which uses pulsed latches. These latch based timing error masking techniques use the time borrowing property of latch to mask timing errors.

In [10], TIMBER flip-flop has been proposed which uses double sampling architecture. The shadow latch is driven by delayed clock and the amount of delay is determined by using error relay logic and clock control unit. As delay elements used for clock control are fixed at the design time, the design becomes a function of operating frequency. Moreover, a metastable detector is required to detect the metastable condition of master latch output. Metastable detector, clock control unit and error relay logic require large area and power.

GLSVLSI '16, May 18-20, 2016, Boston, MA, USA
© 2016 ACM. ISBN 978-1-4503-4274-2/16/05 $15.00
DOI: http://dx.doi.org/10.1145/2902961.2902976

In [11], the timing error is detected at half way point and the clock of the master latch is changed dynamically to mask timing errors. As the error is predicted at half way point, it may result in false error prediction because the data transition at half way point does not guarantee data transition at the end of critical path. The output of the flip-flop is erroneous if data arrives early at half way point but delayed at the end of critical path. Moreover, the timing violation predictor requires a metastable detector as the output of timing violation prediction flip-flop may enter into metastable state. This can be resolved by using a transition detector for timing violation prediction instead of a flip-flop.

An error masking technique based on a bit flipping concept has been proposed in [12]. It uses an XOR gate to detect timing error by comparing the input and output of the flip-flop. The output of XOR gate is stored using a pulsed latch. The output of pulsed latch is used to flip the output of flip-flop by using an XOR gate. As the error is detected by comparing the input and output of flip-flop, a metastability detector is required at the output of flip-flop. Even if the metastable state at the output of flip-flop is flagged as error, the output of bit flipping XOR may not be the correct data as the metastable output of flip-flop may resolve to either 0 or 1. The bit flipping flip-flop incurs large area overhead because of pulsed latch and metastable detector.

In [13], an error resilient flip flop has been proposed which monitors late data arrivals at the input of flip-flop to detect possible timing errors. A multiplexer is used to select one out of master output and direct data based on error signal. If there is no timing error, the master output is passed to slave latch whereas in case of timing error the direct data is passed to slave latch. The error detector uses the internal nodes of master latch to detect late data arrivals which increases the delay and setup time of the flip-flop. Moreover, the intermediate nodes are at metastable state if the data transition happens during setup time window. The intermediate nodes can resolve to either 1 or 0. The late arrival detector might not detect data transition as error if it happens during setup time window.

Error masking flip-flops proposed in [14], monitor delayed data to avoid metastable detector and mask the timing error by using asynchronous preset and clear or modifying the master latch. A flip-flop with preset and clear inputs requires large area compared to conventional master slave D flip-flop. The setup time and the clock to Q delay of the flip-flop are increased because of extra elements in feedback path of master latch and extra loading at the input of flip-flop respectively. Even in case of timing error, the data is supplied to slave latch by using master latch which significantly reduces the timing error monitoring window and increases error masking latency.

In this paper, two timing error masking flip-flops have been proposed. The major contributions of this paper are:

(1) The proposed error masking flip-flops exploit the concept of either delayed data or pulse generator to detect timing errors
(2) The proposed flip-flops are metastable immune
(3) The use of proposed error masking flip-flops in dynamic voltage and frequency scaling framework has been studied using a 16-bit adder.

This paper is organized as follows. Section 2 introduces the concept of timing error masking. Section 3 describes the timing analysis of the design with error masking flip-flops. The operation of proposed designs is described in Section 4. The simulation results are presented in Section 5. Finally, the conclusions are drawn in Section 6.

2. CONCEPT OF ERROR MASKING

In timing error masking, the possible timing errors are detected by using timing error detectors and the correct data is maintained at the output of flip-flop within the same cycle while reducing the time available for next stage logic evaluation. The conceptual timing diagram of error masking is shown in Figure 1. If the data arrives early i.e. before the setup time window of the flip-flop, the flip-flop samples the data correctly and error signal is at logic low state. As the data is sampled correctly, no masking is required. If the data arrives late because of the PVT variations, the flip-flop still samples correct data with a delay equal to error masking latency with the error signal at logic high state.

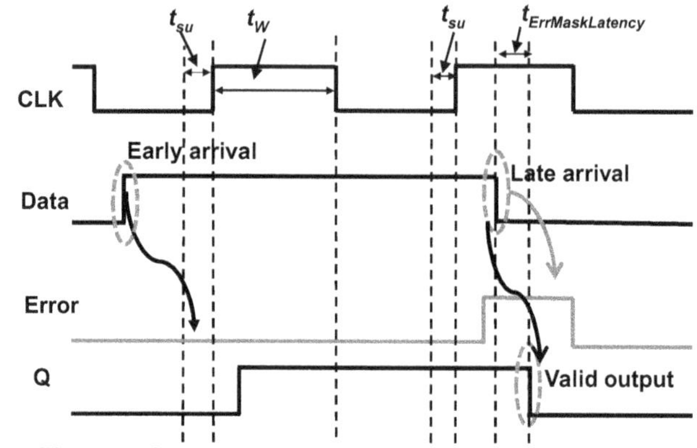

Figure 1. Conceptual timing diagram of error masking

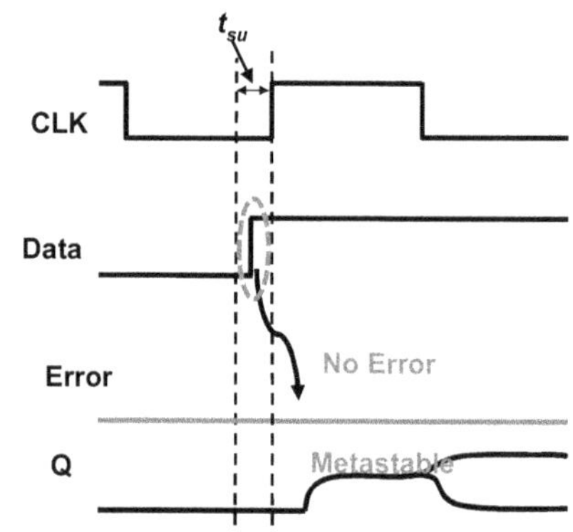

Figure 2. Conceptual timing diagram of error masking for metastability

The major disadvantage of conventional error masking techniques is that the timing error is not masked if the data transition happens during the setup time window. Moreover, the error signal does not indicate any error if the data transition happens during setup time window as shown in Figure 2. Even a metastable detector is not useful for masking timing error if the metastable nodes take more than half clock cycle to resolve to a stable value. This interesting problem is addressed in this work.

3. TIMING ANALYSIS WITH ERROR MASKING FLIP-FLOPS

The timing error masking flip-flops monitor delayed data transitions after the rising edge of clock to detect timing violations. If any data transitions happen at the input of flip-flop after rising edge of the clock, the error signal is flagged and the output of flip-flop needs to be corrected with a valid data. The time interval during which error masking flip-flop observes timing violations is called timing error monitoring window (T_W). As the timing error masking flip-flops monitor timing violations during the window T_W, any input data transitions after this window are not flagged as errors. So the worst case maximum path delay constraint for error masking techniques is given by

$$T_{max} \leq T_{CLK} + T_W - t_{ErrMaskLatency} \quad (1)$$

T_{max} is the maximum path delay under dynamic variations, clock skew and clock jitter, T_{CLK} is the clock period of the design and $t_{ErrMaskLatency}$ is error masking latency which comprise of error detection delay and time required to have a valid data at the output of flip-flop. As the error masking flip-flop treats any data transition during the monitoring window T_W as late arrival data transitions, the data transitions because of short paths should come after this window. So the minimum path delay constraint for error masking techniques with a monitoring window T_W is given by

$$T_{min} \geq T_W - t_{ClktoQ} \quad (2)$$

T_{min} is the minimum path delay and t_{ClktoQ} is the clock to Q delay of the previous stage flip-flop. In order to satisfy minimum path constraint, buffers need to be inserted in all the short paths which increases the area and power. The number of paths which violate the minimum path delay constraint increase with increase in error monitoring window which in turn requires large area for short path padding. Use of small error monitoring window will reduce the area and power overhead due to short path padding but limits the amount of variations that can be tolerable which in turn reduces energy savings. So there is a tradeoff between error monitoring window and energy savings.

4. PROPOSED ERROR MASKING FLIP-FLOPS

4.1 Proposed Flip-Flop (type-A)

The proposed timing error masking flip-flop is based on the concept of delayed data transition detection. It consists of conventional master slave flip-flop, edge detector and an error detector. The delayed data is monitored to detect the possible timing errors. The edge detector generates a pulse if the data transition occurs. If the edge detector output pulse is generated during high phase of the clock, the error detector asserts error signal. If there is no timing error, the error signal is at low state and the output of master latch is passed to slave latch whereas in case of timing error, the error signal is asserted and the direct data is passed to slave latch. The data transitions during setup time window can be monitored if the delay of the delay buffer and edge detector is greater than the worst case setup time. As the delayed data is monitored, any data transitions during the setup time window will be flagged as errors making the flip-flop metastable immune. The conceptual diagram of timing error masking flip-flop is shown in Figure 3.

The conceptual timing diagram of the proposed timing error masking flip-flop is shown in Figure 4. In clock cycle I, the input data transition occurs early, so the data transition at output of delay buffer happens during the low phase of clock. A pulse is generated by the edge detector for both rising and falling transitions of delay buffer output. The pulse generated by edge detector does not cover high phase of the clock and error signal is not activated, so the output of master latch drives slave latch. In clock cycle II, the input data arrives during setup time window (t_{su}) and the output of flip-flop is at metastable state but the error generator asserts the error signal as it is monitoring delayed data. As the error signal is asserted, the slave latch is driven by direct data instead of master latch output. When timing violations occur, the direct data is passed to slave latch instead of changing the clock of master latch as in case of [14], with an error masking latency which is approximately equal to sum of error detection delay, delay of multiplexer and the delay of slave latch.

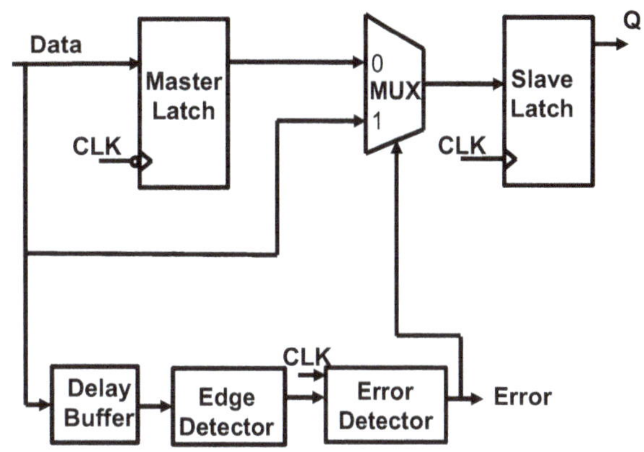

Figure 3. Conceptual diagram of proposed flip-flop (type- A)

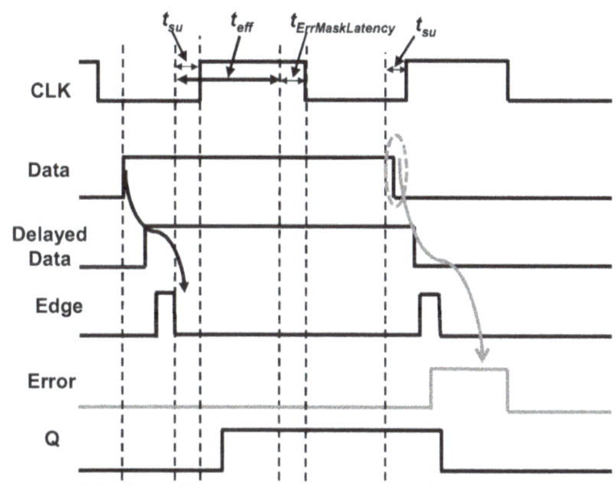

Figure 4. Timing diagram of proposed flip-flop (type- A)

The transistor level implementation of proposed flip-flop is shown in Figure 5. The edge detector is implemented by using a pass transistor based XOR gate proposed in [6]. The error generator uses a dynamic AND gate. The multiplexer is implemented using a transmission gates. To detect timing violations in all operating conditions, the worst case setup time of flip-flop should be less than the data to error detection delay which comprises combined delay of buffer, edge detector and error detector. As the error detector lies very near to the master latch, the mismatch in delay occurs because of local process variations. So the delay buffer should include margin for mismatch between worst case setup time and error detection delay which may lead to false error detection i.e. error signal may be flagged as high even when the data transition happens just before the setup time, if the actual setup time is less than the worst case setup time. The effective timing error masking window of the proposed flip-flops is given by

$$t_{eff} = T_{CLK/2} - t_{ErrMaskLatency} + t_{Wsu} \quad (3)$$

Where t_{eff} is the effective error masking window and t_{Wsu} is the worst case setup time.

The critical issue of the timing error masking flip-flops is susceptibility to metastability. If the data transition at the input of flip-flop happens just before the rising edge of the clock, the output of the flip-flop enters into metastable state. In the proposed design, as the delayed data is used to monitor the timing violations, any input data transitions at input of flip-flop just before the rising edge of the clock are treated as timing violations and the error generator flags an error signal. As the error signal is high, the slave latch is driven by the direct data. Monitoring delayed data prevents the output of flip-flop from entering into metastable state.

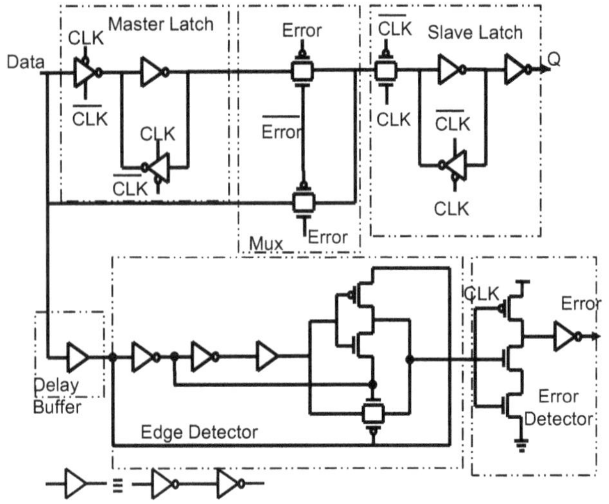

Figure 5. Transistor level implementation of proposed flip-flop (type- A)

4.2 Proposed Flip-Flop (type-B)

As the delayed data is monitored to avoid the metastable state in proposed flip-flop (type-A), the error masking latency increased by the amount of buffer delay which reduces the effective error monitoring window. This problem has been solved by using a pulse generator to generate a pulse for both rising and falling transitions with a pulse width equal to worst case setup time as shown in Figure 6. If the pulse generated by the pulse generator covers the high phase of the clock, an error signal will be generated. As the rising edge of the pulse is generated after data transition instead of delayed data transition, the data to error detection delay will be reduced, which in turn reduces the error masking latency of flip-flop.

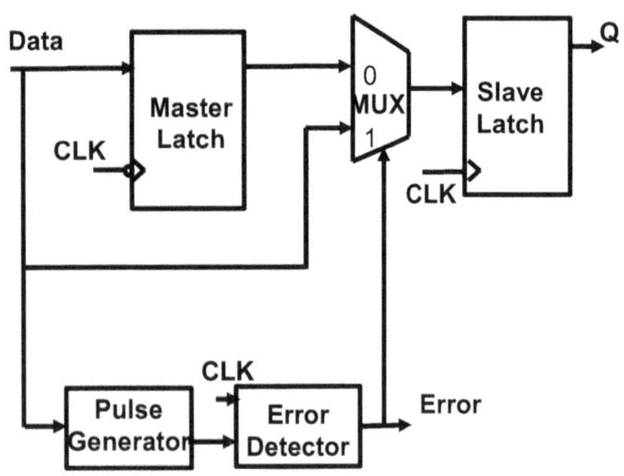

Figure 6. Conceptual diagram of proposed flip-flop (type- B)

The conceptual timing diagram of pulse based timing error masking flip-flop is shown in Figure 7. In clock cycle I, the input data transition occurs early. A pulse is generated by the pulse generator for both rising and falling transitions of data input. As the generated pulse does not cover high phase of the clock, error signal is not activated so the output of master latch drives slave latch. In cycle II, the input data arrives during setup time window (t_{su}) and the pulse generator output is high during positive clock cycle so the error detector asserts the error signal.

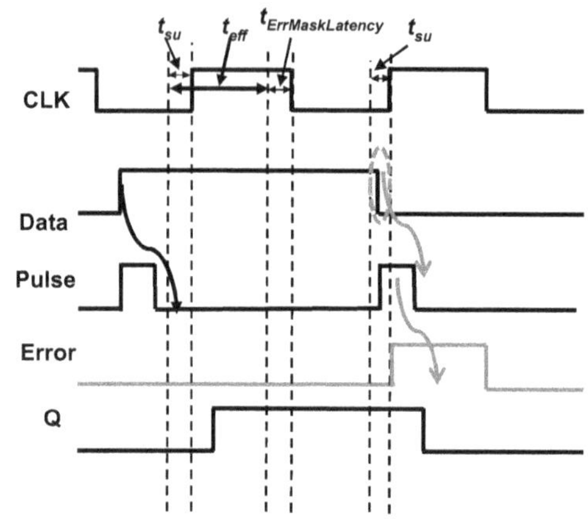

Figure 7. Timing diagram of proposed flip-flop (type- B)

The transistor level implementation of the pulse generator is shown in Figure 8. The rising edge of pulse is controlled by the direct data whereas the falling edge is controlled by delayed data. The pulse generator uses same delay buffers which are used for delaying data and edge detection in proposed flip-flop (type –A).

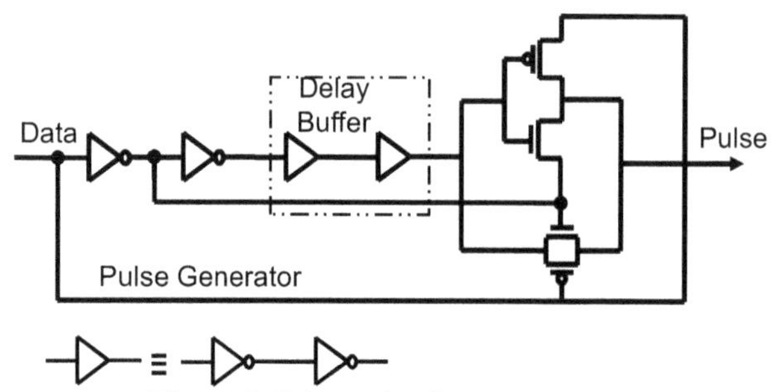

Figure 8. Schematic of pulse generator

5. SIMULATION RESULTS

5.1 Flip-flop Level Evaluation

The proposed timing error masking flip-flops are implemented using industrial 130nm CMOS technology. Parasitic extracted layout simulations are carried out to verify the functionality of the proposed error masking flip-flops using HSPICE. The extra loading on data input of flip-flop because of error detection circuit and mux between master latch and slave latch increases the clock to Q delay of the flip-flop. The normalized clock to Q delay of the proposed flip-flops and conventional transmission gate flip-flop (TGFF) for different process corners is shown in Figure 9. All delays mentioned in this paper are normalized with respect to FO4 delay of inverter.

5.1.1 Data to Error Detection Delay

The data to error detection delay of proposed flip-flop (type –A) and error masking flip-flop in [14] includes buffer delay as they monitor delayed data whereas the data to error detection delay of proposed flip-flop (type –B) does not include the buffer delay as it monitors direct data which significantly increases the effective timing error masking window. Schematic level simulations are carried out to verify the improvement in data to error detection delay. The data to error detection delay of the proposed flip-flops for different process corners at a nominal supply voltage of 1.2 V using same delay buffer is shown in Figure 10. It is evident from simulation results that the data to error detection delay of the proposed flip-flop (type-B) is less than that of proposed flip-flop (type-A).

5.1.2 Error Masking Latency

The error masking latency of the timing error masking flip-flops should be as small as possible as the error masking flip-flops borrow time from next pipeline stage logic. The error masking latency of the proposed flip-flops and error tolerant flip-flop in [14] are simulated for different process conditions. The error masking latency of proposed flip-flop (type-A) is 23% less than that of flip-flop in [14] at typical operating conditions whereas the error masking latency of proposed flip-flop (type-B) is 42% less than that of flip-flop in [14]. The small error masking latency is because of the mux which is used to select either direct data or master data depending on error signal rather than changing master latch clock[14]. The average error masking latency of both the flip-flops are shown in Figure 11 for different process corners at nominal supply voltage of 1.2V. The proposed flip-flop (type-B) error masking latency is less than that of proposed flip-flop (type-A) because data to error detection delay of the former is less.

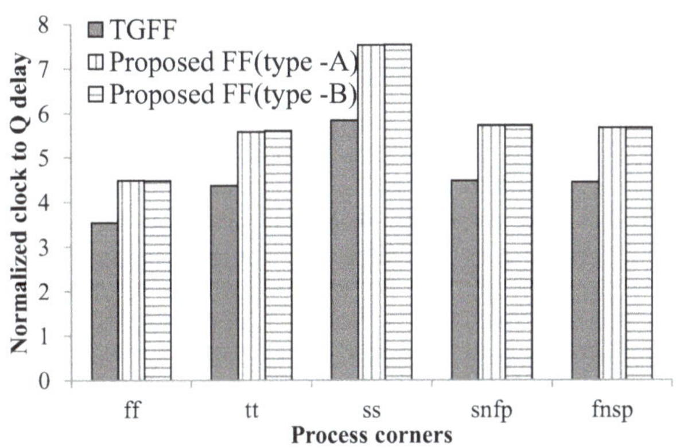

Figure 9. Comparison of normalized clock to Q delay

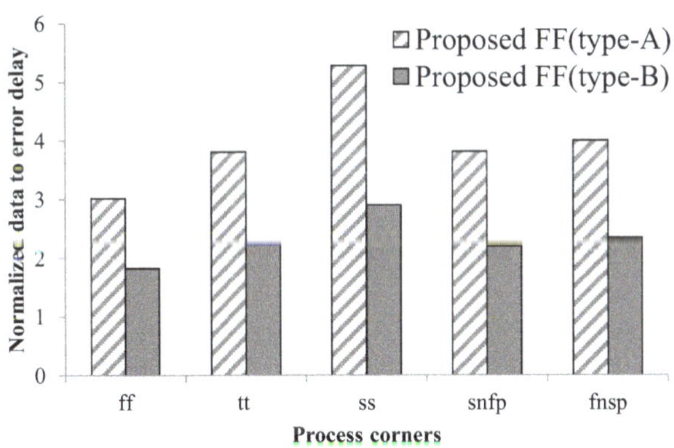

Figure 10. Data to error detection delay for different process corners

5.2 Block Level Evaluation

The functionality of the proposed flip-flops in dynamic voltage and frequency scaling framework is verified by implementing a 16-bit adder. The 16-bit adder is synthesized to operate at a clock frequency of 500 MHz under worst case conditions with slow process corners, supply voltage of 1.08 V and temperature of 125 °C. The conventional adder is made synchronous by adding 33 conventional flip-flops at the input and 17 flip-flops at the output. The conventional adder without dynamic voltage and frequency scaling is simulated for different process corners and temperatures. The flip-flop at the end of the critical path is replaced with proposed timing error masking flip-flop (type-B) so that the design can be used in dynamic voltage and frequency scaling framework.

5.2.1 Dynamic Voltage Scaling (DVS)

The conventional adder with transmission gate based flip-flop (TGFF) is simulated for different temperature and process corners without dynamic voltage scaling. The adder with proposed error masking flip-flops at the end of critical path is simulated for different process corners and temperatures with dynamic voltage scaling. The supply voltage of the design is reduced until the error signal is high. The simulation results show that the proposed design consumes 62%, 48% and 22% less power compared to the conventional design without dynamic voltage and frequency scaling in best, typical and worst process conditions respectively. The power savings are higher in best case corners as the adder is synthesized for worst case conditions. The comparison of conventional adder with proposed adder using error masking flip-flops is shown in Table 1.

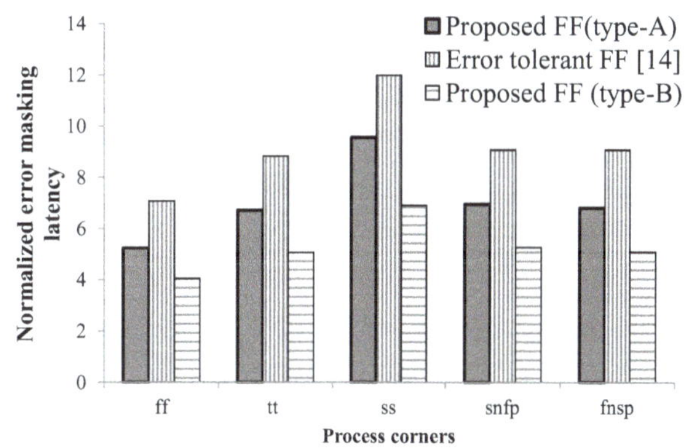

Figure 11. Error masking latency for different process corners

The normalized power consumption of the conventional design and the proposed design with error masking flip-flop (type-B) at an operating frequency of 500 MHz is shown in Figure 12. The power consumption of designs is normalized with respect to power consumption of TGFF based adder with slow process corners at a temperature of 25°C. The conventional design at typical and fast corners consumes more power compared to slow corners which shows the power overhead of the design when it is synthesized for worst case conditions.

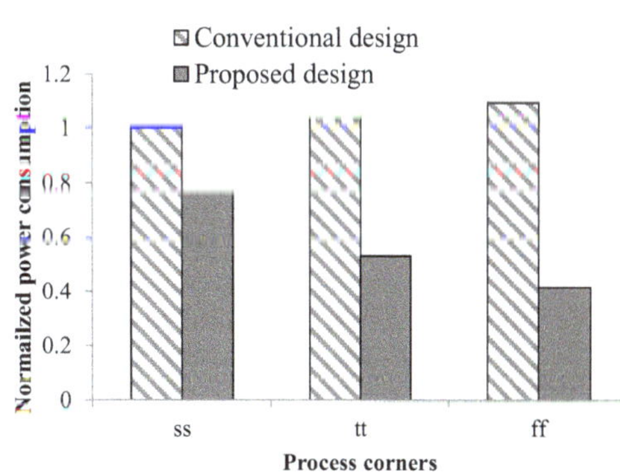

Figure 12. Comparison of normalized power consumption

Table 1. Comparison of proposed design with conventional design at different process corners and temperatures

Process	Temperature (°C)	Conventional Design		Proposed Design		% Saving in Power dissipation
		Supply Voltage (v)	Power dissipation (μW) P_{DC}	Supply Voltage (v)	Power dissipation (μW) P_{DP}	$[(P_{DC} - P_{DP})/P_{DC}] * 100\%$
Worst	-40	1.08	676	0.92	501.3	25.84
Worst	25	1.08	702.2	0.94	540.4	23.04
Worst	125	1.08	740.2	0.98	617.6	16.56
Typical	-40	1.08	701.9	0.75	340.6	51.47
Typical	25	1.08	728	0.77	372.4	48.84
Best	25	1.08	769	0.67	290.9	62.17

5.2.2 Dynamic Frequency Scaling (DFS)

The conventional 16-bit adder with TGFF is synthesized to operate at 500 MHz. The adder with error masking flip-flop is simulated for different process and temperature conditions with frequency scaling. The clock frequency of the adder with TGFF at a constant supply voltage of 1.08V is selected as the minimum operating frequency of the design. The frequency of the proposed design with error masking is increased until the error signal is high. The performance improvement of proposed adder with error masking flip-flops is shown in Table 2. It is evident from the simulation results that the performance of the adder is improved up to 50% in typical operating conditions with a supply voltage of 1.08V compared to performance at worst case conditions.

Table 2. Performance of proposed design at different process corners and temperatures with fixed V_{DD}= 1.08V

Process	Temperature (°C)	Proposed design		% Improvement in performance
		Supply voltage (V)	Frequency (MHz)	
Worst	125	1.08	588	0
Worst	25	1.08	649	10.37
Worst	-40	1.08	709	20.57
Typical	25	1.08	885	50.5
Typical	-40	1.08	972	65.3
Best	25	1.08	1098	86.7
Best	-40	1.08	1219	107.3

6. CONCLUSIONS

We proposed two metastability immune timing error masking flip-flops based on the concept of data transition detection during high phase of the clock. Delayed data concept or pulse generator with large width is responsible for making the flip-flops immune to metastability. The proposed flip-flops significantly reduce the error masking latency and increase the effective error masking window compared to designs in [14]. The proposed flip-flops have been used for dynamic voltage and frequency scaling of a 16-bit adder and it is found that the proposed designs reduce either the power consumption up to 48% or performance improvement up to 50% in typical corner compared to a conventional design without dynamic voltage and frequency scaling.

7. REFERENCES

[1] D. Ernst, N. S. Kim, S. Das, S. Pant, R. Rao, T. Pham, C. Ziesler, D. Blaauw, T. Austin, K. Flautner, T. Mudge, B. Ave, and A. Arbor, "Razor: a low-power pipeline based on circuit-level timing speculation," in *International Symposium on Microarchitecture, MICRO-36.*, 2003, pp. 7–18.

[2] S. Das, D. Roberts, Seokwoo Lee, S. Pant, D. Blaauw, T. Austin, T. Mudge, and K. Flautner, "A self-tuning DVS processor using delay-error detection and correction," *IEEE J. Solid-State Circuits*, vol. 41, no. 4, pp. 792–804, Apr. 2006.

[3] S. Das, C. Tokunaga, S. Pant, W. Ma, S. Kalaiselvan, K. Lai, D. M. Bull, and D. T. Blaauw, "RazorII : in situ error detection and correction for PVT and SER tolerance," *IEEE J. Solid-State Circuits*, vol. 44, no. 1, pp. 32–48, Jan. 2009.

[4] I. Kwon, S. Kim, D. Fick, M. Kim, Y. Chen, and D. Sylvester, "Razor-lite : a light-weight register for error detection by observing virtual supply rails," *IEEE J. Solid-State Circuits*, vol. 49, no. 9, pp. 2054–2066, Sept. 2014.

[5] H. Fuketa, M. Hashimoto, Y. Mitsuyama, and T. Onoye, "Adaptive performance compensation with in-situ timing error predictive sensors for subthreshold circuits," *IEEE Trans. Very Large Scale Integr. Syst.*, vol. 20, no. 2, pp. 333–343, Feb. 2012.

[6] B. P. Das and H. Onodera, "Frequency independent warning detection sequential for dynamic voltage and frequency scaling in ASICs," *IEEE Trans. Very Large Scale Integr. Syst.*, vol. 22, no. 12, pp. 2535–2548, Dec. 2014.

[7] K. A. Bowman, J. W. Tschanz, N. S. Kim, J. C. Lee, C. B. Wilkerson, Lu S. L., T. Karnik, and V. K. De, "Energy-efficient and metastability-immune resilient circuits for dynamic variation tolerance," *IEEE J. Solid-State Circuits*, vol. 44, no. 1, pp. 49-63, Jan. 2009.

[8] M. R. Choudhury and K. Mohanram, "Masking timing errors on speed-paths in logic circuits," in *Proc. Design, Automation & Test in Europe Conference & Exhibition*, 2009, pp. 87-92.

[9] K .Chae and S. Mukhopadhyay, "A dynamic timing error prevention technique in pipelines with time borrowing and clock stretching," *IEEE Trans. Circuits Syst. I Regul. Pap.*, vol. 61, no. 1, pp. 74–83, Jan. 2014.

[10] M. R. Choudhury, V. Chandra, R. C. Aitken, and K. Mohanram, "Time-borrowing circuit designs and hardware prototyping for timing error resilience," *IEEE Trans. Comput.*, vol. 63, no. 2, pp. 497–509, Feb. 2014.

[11] Nejat, M. , Alizadeh, B. , and Afzali-Kusha, A., "Dynamic flip-flop conversion: a time-borrowing method for performance improvement of low-power digital circuits prone to variations," *IEEE Trans. Very Large Scale Integr. Syst.*, vol. 23, no. 11, pp. 2724–2727, Nov. 2015.

[12] Stefanos Valadimas, Yiorgos Tsiatouhas, and Angela Arapoyanni, "Timing error tolerance in small core designs for SoC applications", *IEEE Trans. Comput.*, vol. PP, no. 99 *(Early access).*

[13] Che-Min Huang, Tsung-Te Liu , and Tzi-Dar Chiueh, "An energy-efficient resilient flip-flop circuit with built-in timing-error detection and correction," in *Proc. VLSI Design, Automation and Test (VLSI-DAT)*, 2015, pp.1-4.

[14] Stefanos Valadimas,Yiorgos Tsiatouhas, A. Arapoyanni, and Petros Xarchakos, "Effective timing error tolerance in flip-flop based core designs," *J. electronic testing,* vol. 29, no. 6, pp. 795–804, Dec. 2013.

Exploring Configurable Non-Volatile Memory-based Caches for Energy-Efficient Embedded Systems

Tosiron Adegbija
Department of Electrical and Computer Engineering
University of Arizona
Tucson, Arizona
tosiron@email.arizona.edu

ABSTRACT

Non-volatile memory (NVM) technologies have recently emerged as alternatives to traditional SRAM-based cache memories, since NVMs offer advantages such as non-volatility, low leakage power, fast read speed, and high density. However, NVMs also have disadvantages, such as high write latency and energy, which necessitate further research into robust optimization techniques. In this paper, we propose and evaluate *configurable non-volatile memories (configNVM)* as a viable NVM optimization technique, and show that configNVMs can reduce the cache's energy consumption by up to 60%, with minimal performance degradation. We describe the knowledge gaps that must be filled to enable configNVMs, and show that configNVMs offer new opportunities for energy efficient caching in embedded systems.

CCS Concepts

•Computer systems organization → Embedded systems; Processors and memory architectures; •Hardware → Non-volatile memory;

Keywords

Configurable memory, non-volatile memory, cache memories, low-power design, low-power embedded systems, adaptable hardware.

1. INTRODUCTION AND MOTIVATION

Caches have been the focus of much optimization research, since they significantly impact performance and account for a large percentage of a microprocessor's total system power and energy consumption, especially in embedded systems. A commonly researched cache optimization involves using highly configurable caches [10, 24] whose configurations (cache size, associativity, and line size) can be dynamically adapted to varying runtime application execution requirements. Previous work has shown that such configurable caches can reduce cache energy consumption by up to 62% [11].

GLSVLSI '16, May 18 - 20, 2016, Boston, MA, USA

ISBN 978-1-4503-4274-2/16/05...$15.00
DOI: http://dx.doi.org/10.1145/2902961.2903009

More recently, non-volatile memories (NVMs), such as spin-torque-transfer random access memory (STTRAM) and resistive RAM (ReRAM) have emerged as promising alternatives to the traditional volatile, SRAM-based memories [13]. While NVM-based memories are still nascent, studies have shown that they offer advantages over traditional memories, such as low leakage power, non-volatility, and high density [20]. These advantages make NVM-based technologies especially attractive for caches in resource constrained embedded systems. However, NVMs also result in overheads, such as high write latency, dynamic energy, that necessitate much ongoing research into NVM optimization techniques [14]. For example, previous works [19, 22, 25] have explored architectural-level and circuit-level techniques for masking the effects of high write latencies and write energy. Alternatively, a recent work [13] explored the tuning of data retention time in order to reduce write latencies and write energy.

In this paper, our overarching goal is to design an NVM-based cache that is energy efficient, low-overhead (in terms of performance and area), adaptable to varying application requirements, and easy to implement. Therefore, we propose and draw attention to *configurable NVMs (configNVMs)* as a viable low-overhead optimization technique for energy efficient caches in low-power embedded systems. ConfigNVMs dynamically adapt the cache's configurations to varying application cache requirements, in order to minimize the energy consumption without incurring significant performance overheads. Due to the optimization potential that configurability affords, we motivate research focus on robust and efficient techniques for designing configNVMs, and propose that configurability/adaptability should be an intrinsic design characteristic of NVM technologies, and not an afterthought. We explore the energy benefits of configNVMs and show that by adapting NVM-based caches' configurations to different applications' characteristics, significant energy savings are achievable as compared to non-configurable NVM-based caches. We show that augmenting an NVM-based cache for configurability incurs little design time overhead, and suggest techniques for achieving configNVMs.

The main contributions of this paper are summarized as follows:

• Focusing on embedded systems benchmarks, and using the ReRAM and STTRAM as case studies of promising NVM technologies, we empirically show that configNVMs can reduce average energy consumption by up to 60%, as compared to non-configurable NVMs, without degrading the performance.

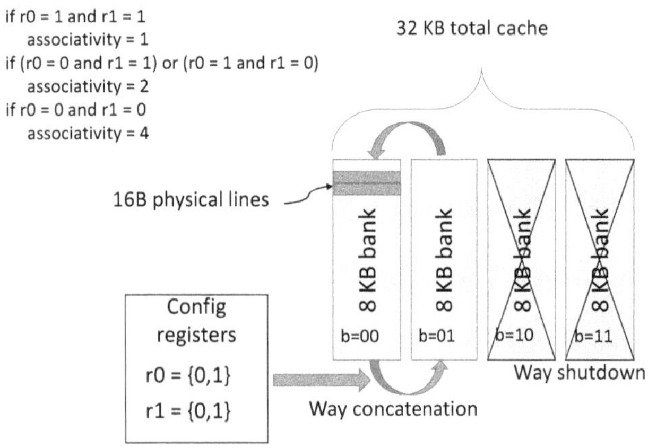

Figure 1: Illustration of configNVM architecture

• We analyze the tradeoffs of STTRAM- and ReRAM-based configNVMs for different applications, and show that the different technologies perform differently for different applications. Therefore, we give insight into which of the two technologies designers should focus on when researching and designing configNVM techniques.
• Drawing from previous work on configurable SRAM-based caches, we describe the knowledge gaps that must be filled in order to enable configNVMs.

2. RELATED WORK

Different circuit-level and architecture-level techniques have been proposed for reducing the high write latency and energy consumption imposed by NVMs. Smullen et al. [18] proposed to reduce the high energy and write latency by lowering the STTRAM's retention time, thereby relaxing the non-volatility. The authors used a combination of SRAM-based L1 caches and reduced-retention STTRAM L2 and L3 caches to eliminate performance loss and reduce the energy-delay product. Rasquinha et al. [15] proposed a microarchitectural optimization that reduced the STTRAM's write energy by preventing the premature eviction of cache lines to lower cache levels. They used a replacement algorithm that increased the residency of dirty lines in the L1 cache in order to accommodate all the stores to those lines, at the expense of higher miss rates.

Xu et al. [23] quantitatively studied the impact of the STTRAM's memory cell sizing on overall computing system performance and showed that different applications have different memory sizing expectations. The authors used the STTRAM for the L2 cache in their studies. Xu et al. [21] studied the memristor-based ReRAM design and provided insight on the different design choices for the best tradeoffs in performance, energy, and area. In this paper we focus on low-power, resource constrained embedded systems, and propose configNVMs as a complementary low-overhead microarchitectural optimization to previous optimization techniques. ConfigNVMs reduce non-volatile memories' energy consumption, while incurring minimal performance degradation. Our major design goals are high energy savings, adaptability to application resource requirements, low performance and area overheads, and ease of design and implementation.

3. ARCHITECTING CONFIGNVMS

Configurable non-volatile memory-based caches (ConfigNVMs) allow the cache configurations to be dynamically adapted to varying runtime application resource requirements. To architect configNVMs, three key design challenges must be addressed: *augmenting NVM caches for configurability, cache tuning heuristics/algorithms*, and *low-overhead cache tuners*. Since configurable caches have been well researched in traditional SRAM-based caches, several previous techniques can be reused and/or modified for configNVMs, allowing previous design efforts to be amortized. Furthermore, NVMs generally have similar electrical interfaces to SRAMs [8], thus, configNVMs can also be organized similarly to traditional configurable SRAM-based caches. The most important criterion for techniques used to architect configNVMs is that they most impose minimal area and performance overhead on the system. In this section, we describe our approaches to addressing the configNVM design challenges.

3.1 Augmenting NVM Caches for Configurability

To augment NVM caches for configurability, we use way shutdown, way concatenation, and line concatenation [24] to configure the cache size, associativity, and line size, respectively. In the following discussions, we assume a cache with a maximum of four ways, however, the techniques described herein can be extended to any n-way system.

Figure 1 illustrates the configNVM's architecture. Each configNVM comprises of four banks, with each bank composed of the memory cells (e.g., STTRAM or ReRAM cells). The banks act as ways, and are organized such that different ways can be concatenated and/or shutdown (using power-gating) to configure the configNVM cache configurations. Using two single-bit configuration registers (r0 and r1), way concatenation allows the cache to be configured as one-way/direct-mapped (when r0 = 0 and r1 = 0), two-way (when r0 = 0 and r1 = 1 or r0 = 1 and r1 = 0), or four-way set associative (when r0 = 1 and r1 = 1). Each bank also has a bank ID, b, which specifies the bank that should be gated for way shutdown (Section 3.2). For example, given a 32 KB configNVM as shown in Figure 1, the configNVM comprises of four 8 KB banks, each of which serves as a way, and can be gated to configure the cache size into 8 KB (shutdown three banks), 16 KB (shutdown two banks) or 32 KB (no bank shutdown). When the banks are shut down for 8 KB and 16 KB caches, the value of b determines which specific banks are shutdown, based on the cache tuning heuristic (Section 3.2). Finally, the cache's physical line size is 16 B, and multiple contiguous lines can be fetched to logically configure the line size to 32 B or 64 B.

3.2 Cache Tuning Heuristics/Algorithms

Given a configNVM with several possible configurations, the design space exploration method is critical to mitigating runtime overheads, and necessitates efficient tuning heuristics/algorithms. To enable our experiments and analysis, we developed a simple cache tuning heuristic. Since the goal of this work is to show the benefits of configNVM, we decided to use a simple heuristic for our evaluations, however, we intend to develop more elaborate and robust heuristics/algorithms for future work. Figure 2 depicts our tuning heuristic, which explores different cache configurations and determines the best cache configurations for the different

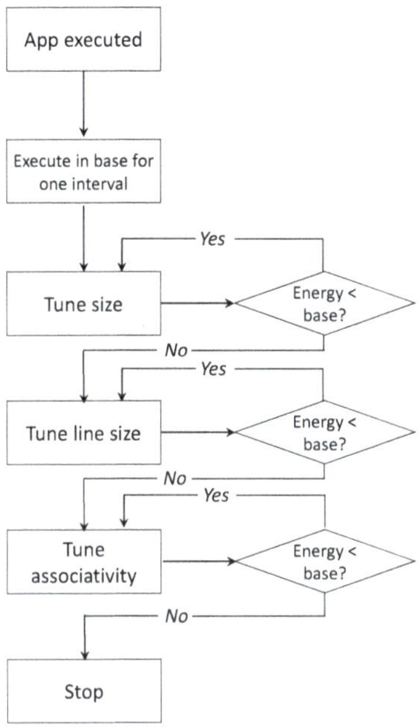

Figure 2: Tuning heuristic

applications based on the energy consumption. Each potential configuration is explored for one tuning interval, which could be measured by the number of executed instruction or in time [17]. For our experiments, we used a tuning interval of 10ms, during which we empirically determined that stable execution statistics can be gathered. Some modern operating systems (e.g., Linux) also use sampling intervals (OS scheduler ticks) of 10ms.

When an application is executed for the first time, the heuristic first executes the application in the largest/base cache configurations for one tuning interval. The heuristic then decreases the cache size as long as decreasing the cache size reduces the energy consumption as compared to the base configuration. Thereafter, the heuristic decreases the line size as long as decreasing the line size reduces the energy consumption, followed by similar adjustments to the associativity. The final configuration is then stored in a configuration table for subsequent executions of that application. Figure 3 depicts the basic structure of the configuration table. The configuration table is a small hardware structure that consists of three fields: *appID*, *config*, and *bankID* fields. The *appID* field stores the application's identification, *config* stores the application's best configuration as determined by our tuning heuristic, and *bankID* stores the identification of the application's most recently used cache bank. In order to potentially reduce the number of compulsory cache misses, when the application is subsequently executed, the application's most recently used banks are reused. Since

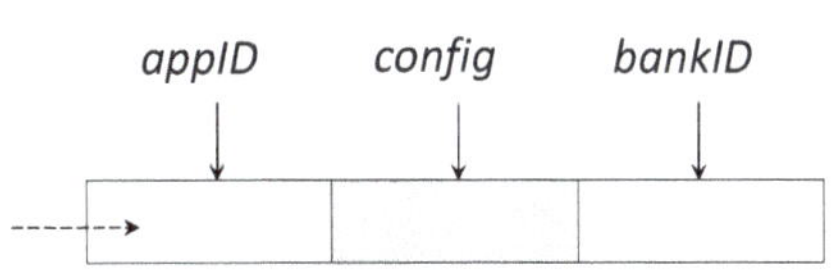

Figure 3: Basic structure of the configuration table

NVM caches retain their data after the banks are shutdown, reusing the banks may allow some of that application's previously fetched memory blocks to be used without having to fetch the blocks from lower levels of the memory hierarchy. However, if the banks are occupied, then alternate banks can be used.

3.3 Cache Tuners

In order to orchestrate the tuning process and implement the tuning heuristics, low-overhead software or hardware cache tuners are required. Software tuners use the system's processor to execute the tuning heuristics, which enables easy system integration. However, software tuners can also affect the cache and runtime behavior due to context switching. These effects can cause the heuristic to choose inferior configurations. Alternatively, hardware tuners alleviate these effects by incorporating custom hardware that execute the heuristics [4]. For our work, we designed a custom hardware tuner using synthesizable VHDL, and quantified the area and power overheads using Synopsys Design Compiler [7]. Relative to an ARM Cortex A9 microprocessor [1], which we used to represent current embedded systems, our tuner imposes 1.2% and 1% area and power overheads, respectively. We omit low level details of the tuner designs for brevity, since that is not the focus of this paper.

4. EXPERIMENTS

In this section, we compare the proposed configNVM with a base NVM cache with fixed configurations for both the STTRAM and ReRAM technologies.

4.1 Experimental Setup

We evaluated the proposed configNVM by comparing a system that switches to the best cache configuration for each executing application to a base system with fixed cache configurations. The base system had 32 KB, 4-way private level one (L1) instruction and data caches with 64 B line sizes, similar to several state-of-the-art embedded systems microprocessors' cache configurations [1]. Thus, the configNVM offered 8 KB, 16 KB, and 32KB cache sizes, 1, 2, and 4-way set associativity, and 16 B, 32 B, and 64 B line sizes. We simulated our work using a combination of the GEM5 simulator [6], to gather cache execution statistics, and NVSim [9] to calculate the energy and latency statistics for the STT-RAM and ReRAM technologies. GEM5 is a widely used simulator for computer architecture research, while NVSim is a circuit-level model for NVM performance, energy, and area estimation, which has been validated against industrial NVM prototypes.

To model a variety of embedded systems applications, we used a total of seventeen embedded systems benchmarks, comprising of twelve EEMBC Automotive benchmarks [2] and five Mibench benchmarks [12] that were selected to represent different application domains. We used a tuning interval of 10 ms, and assumed a system with persistent applications that execute several times throughout the system's lifetime. For all the benchmarks, the tuning process completed during a few executions, thus, the tuning overhead amortized very rapidly over subsequent executions (details in Section 4.4).

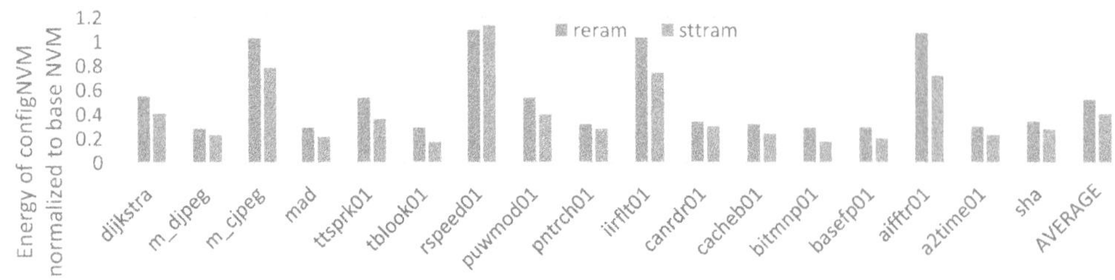

Figure 4: Energy consumption of configNVM normalized to the base NVM

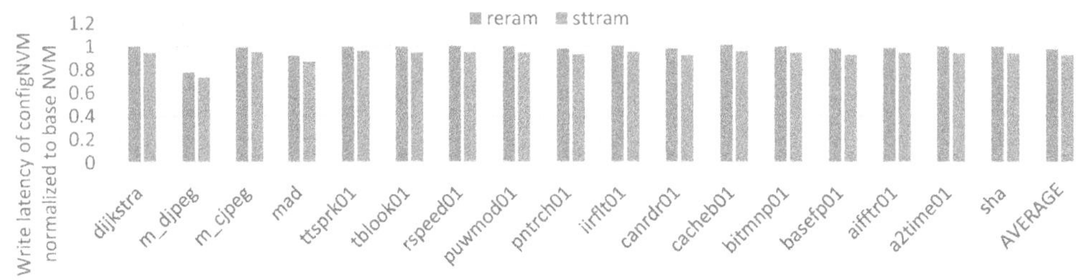

Figure 5: Write latency of configNVM normalized to the base NVM

4.2 Energy Savings

Figure 4 depicts the ReRAM and STTRAM configNVMs' energy consumption normalized to the base NVM cache for a single execution of each of the benchmarks. To consider a worst case scenario, we used a variation of our heuristic (Section 3) in which the configuration did not revert to the base configuration when the heuristic could not find a better configuration than the base. Rather than reverting to the base configuration, the heuristic used the best configuration other than the base, i.e., the best among all the other explored configurations.

On average over all the benchmarks, compared to the base ReRAM cache, ReRAM configNVM cache achieved 48% energy savings, with savings ranging from 45% for *dijkstra* to 72% for *m_djpeg*. The energy was reduced mainly because of the significant reduction in leakage power when the cache banks were shut down as determined by our tuning heuristic. In addition, the dynamic energy was also reduced when the set associativities were adapted to the access requirements of the executing applications. However, for four out of the fifteen benchmarks (*m_cjpeg, rspeed01, iirflt01,* and *aifftr01*), the ReRAM configNVM increased the energy by an average of 6%, with an increase of up to 10% for *rspeed01*. This energy degradation can be prevented (or amortized over multiple executions) by reverting to the base configuration for applications for which configNVM degraded the energy, as is the case with our original heuristic.

On the other hand, compared to the base cache, the STTRAM configNVM achieved 60% energy savings on average over all the benchmarks, with savings ranging from 22% for *m_cjpeg* to 82% for *bitmnp01*. Unlike in the case of ReRAM, the STTRAM configNVM increased the energy for only *rspeed01* by 13%. We observed some significant differences in the configNVM's impact on the energy consumption when using ReRAM versus STTRAM. For example, even though ReRAM configNVM degraded *aifftr01's* and *iirflt01's* energy consumption by 7% and 4%, respectively, STTRAM improved the energy consumption for both benchmarks by 28% and 26%, respectively.

In general, STTRAM configNVM outperformed ReRAM configNVM in energy savings for all the benchmarks, except for *rspeed01*, for which STTRAM's energy increase was higher than that of ReRAM. These results illustrate the optimization potential achievable by configNVM, even with a naive tuning heuristic. We expect the energy savings to be even higher with a more robust and intelligent tuning heuristic, which we intend to explore in future work. The results also show that while configNVM achieves significant energy savings on average, the choice of the specific NVM technology used for implementing the configNVM may differ for different applications and use-cases. Other design tradeoffs that must be considered include design cost, endurance, scalability, etc. For example, even though STTRAM outperforms ReRAM in energy savings, STTRAM is also known to be more expensive and less scalable than ReRAM [5]. Thus, use-case-specific design tradeoffs and goals must be carefully considered when deciding which technologies to use for implementing configNVMs.

4.3 Write Latency

Our goal in exploring configNVM was to optimize the cache's energy consumption without significant latency degradation. However, we also found that configNVM nominally improved the write latency as compared to the base NVM. Figure 5 depicts the ReRAM and STTRAM configNVMs' write latency normalized to the base NVM. On average over all the benchmarks, ReRAM configNVM reduced the write latency by 2%, and by up to 23% for *m_djpeg*. ReRAM configNVM degraded *cacheb01's* latency by 1%, but the latency for all the other applications either improved or remained the same. Similarly, STTRAM configNVM reduced the average write latency by 7.5%, and by up to 27% for *m_djpeg*. STT-RAM configNVM did not degrade any benchmark's write latency.

4.4 Tuning Overheads

We measured the tuning overheads imposed by configNVM with respect to an application's tuning performance and energy overheads. We calculated the tuning performance overhead as the number of tuning stall cycles incurred while determining an application's best configuration, given as *(number of configurations explored - 1) * tuning stall cycles* [4, 16]. We calculated the tuning energy overhead as the energy consumed during the tuning process, when inferior configurations are executed while determining an application's best configuration. Table 1 depicts the benchmarks, number of configurations explored, number of tuning intervals in a single execution, and number of tuning stall cycles. The number of tuning stall cycles on average over all the applications was 3176 cycles, which imposed a maximum of 0.02% performance overhead relative to the tuning interval of 10 ms (20 million cycles). Since the tuning stall cycles were so few relative to the tuning interval, the tuning energy overheads were also infinitesimal and imposed minimal dent on the overall energy savings. These overheads were negligible because of our relatively large tuning interval, and are likely to increase with a smaller tuning interval or a higher tuning frequency, such as in phase-based tuning [3], where configurations are adapted to application phase changes rather than application changes.

Furthermore, we also observed that the tuning overheads imposed by configNVM amortized rapidly during application execution iterations. Figure 6 depicts the number of iterations required to determine the best configurations for each application. On average over all the application, two iterations were required to determine the best configuration, with as many as 3.3 iterations required for *mad*, and as few as 0.7 iterations for *m_cjpeg*. Some applications required more than one iteration to determine the best configuration because there were more configurations explored by our heuristic than tuning intervals in a single execution of the applications (Table 1). The number of iterations required can be reduced even further by using a tuning heuristic/algorithm that explores fewer configurations per application.

5. CONCLUSIONS

In this paper, we proposed configNVMs as a viable optimization for non-volatile memory-based caches in low-power embedded systems, in order to reduce the energy consumption. ConfigNVMs significantly reduce the energy consumption by adapting NVM-based caches' configurations to varying application execution requirements, without imposing significant performance overheads. We discussed potential approaches for implementing configNVMs and empirically showed that configNVMs reduce the average energy consumption by up to 60% as compared to an NVM cache with fixed configurations. We also showed that different NVM technologies perform differently for different applications, thus careful analysis must be performed to determine the appropriate technology for specific use-cases.

Table 1: Benchmarks, number of configurations explored, number of tuning intervals, and tuning stall cycles

Benchmark	Configs explored	# of intervals	stall cycles
dijkstra	14	8	3458
m_djpeg	13	5	3192
c_djpeg	10	14	2394
mad	13	4	3192
ttsprk01	11	6	2660
tblook01	13	5	3192
rspeed01	11	4	2660
puwmod01	12	6	2926
pntrch01	11	8	2660
iirflt01	12	4	2926
canrdr01	15	6	3724
cacheb01	13	5	3192
bitmnp01	13	17	3192
basefp01	18	12	4522
aifftr01	11	10	2660
a2time01	16	9	3990
sha	14	9	3458

For future work, we intend to develop additional robust and low-overhead cache tuning heuristic/algorithms that take into account the different NVM technologies' characteristics and application behaviors. We also intend to explore the benefits of phase-based tuning for configNVMs where configurations are adapted to different application phases to achieve finer-grained optimization. Finally, we intend to explore other novel techniques complementary to configNVMs for minimizing the write latency and energy consumption.

6. REFERENCES

[1] Arm. http://www.arm.com. Accessed: January 2016.

[2] The embedded microprocessor benchmark consortium. http://www.eembc.org/. Accessed: January 2016.

[3] T. Adegbija, A. Gordon-Ross, and A. Munir. Phase distance mapping: a phase-based cache tuning methodology for embedded systems. *Design Automation for Embedded Systems*, 18(3-4):251–278, 2014.

[4] T. Adegbija, A. Gordon-Ross, and M. Rawlins. Analysis of cache tuner architectural layouts for multicore embedded systems. In *Performance Computing and Communications Conference (IPCCC), 2014 IEEE International*, pages 1–8. IEEE, 2014.

[5] R. Aitken, V. Chandra, J. Myers, B. Sandhu, L. Shifren, and G. Yeric. Device and technology implications of the internet of things. In *VLSI Technology (VLSI-Technology): Digest of Technical Papers, 2014 Symposium on*, pages 1–4. IEEE, 2014.

[6] N. Binkert, B. Beckmann, G. Black, S. K. Reinhardt, A. Saidi, A. Basu, J. Hestness, D. R. Hower, T. Krishna, S. Sardashti, et al. The gem5 simulator. *Computer Architecture News*, 40(2):1, 2012.

[7] D. Compiler. Synopsys inc, 2000.

[8] X. Dong, X. Wu, G. Sun, Y. Xie, H. Li, and Y. Chen. Circuit and microarchitecture evaluation of 3d stacking magnetic ram (mram) as a universal memory replacement. In *Design Automation Conference, 2008.*

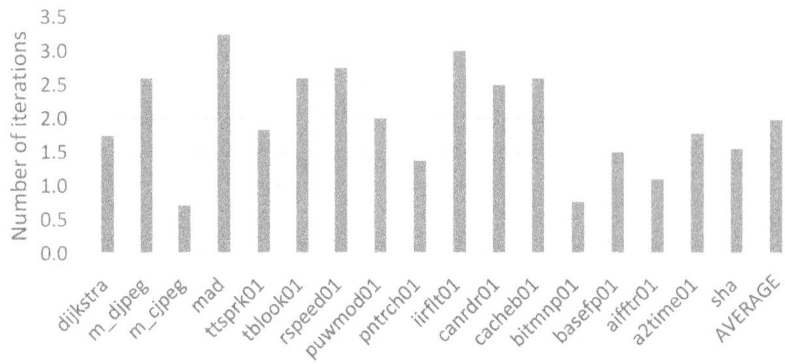

Figure 6: Number of iterations required to determine the best configuration

DAC 2008. 45th ACM/IEEE, pages 554–559. IEEE, 2008.

[9] X. Dong, C. Xu, Y. Xie, and N. P. Jouppi. Nvsim: A circuit-level performance, energy, and area model for emerging nonvolatile memory. *Computer-Aided Design of Integrated Circuits and Systems, IEEE Transactions on*, 31(7):994–1007, 2012.

[10] A. Gordon-Ross and F. Vahid. A self-tuning configurable cache. In *Proceedings of the 44th annual Design Automation Conference*, pages 234–237. ACM, 2007.

[11] A. Gordon-Ross, F. Vahid, and N. D. Dutt. Fast configurable-cache tuning with a unified second-level cache. *Very Large Scale Integration (VLSI) Systems, IEEE Transactions on*, 17(1):80–91, 2009.

[12] M. R. Guthaus, J. S. Ringenberg, D. Ernst, T. M. Austin, T. Mudge, and R. B. Brown. Mibench: A free, commercially representative embedded benchmark suite. In *Workload Characterization, 2001. WWC-4. 2001 IEEE International Workshop on*, pages 3–14. IEEE, 2001.

[13] A. Jog, A. K. Mishra, C. Xu, Y. Xie, V. Narayanan, R. Iyer, and C. R. Das. Cache revive: architecting volatile stt-ram caches for enhanced performance in cmps. In *Proceedings of the 49th Annual Design Automation Conference*, pages 243–252. ACM, 2012.

[14] O. Mutlu and L. Subramanian. Research problems and opportunities in memory systems. *Supercomputing Frontiers and Innovations*, 1(3), 2014.

[15] M. Rasquinha, D. Choudhary, S. Chatterjee, S. Mukhopadhyay, and S. Yalamanchili. An energy efficient cache design using spin torque transfer (stt) ram. In *Proceedings of the 16th ACM/IEEE international symposium on Low power electronics and design*, pages 389–394. ACM, 2010.

[16] M. Rawlins and A. Gordon-Ross. An application classification guided cache tuning heuristic for multi-core architectures. In *Design Automation Conference (ASP-DAC), 2012 17th Asia and South Pacific*, pages 23–28. IEEE, 2012.

[17] S. Sharifi, A. K. Coskun, and T. S. Rosing. Hybrid dynamic energy and thermal management in heterogeneous embedded multiprocessor socs. In *Proceedings of the 2010 Asia and South Pacific Design Automation Conference*, pages 873–878. IEEE Press, 2010.

[18] C. W. Smullen, V. Mohan, A. Nigam, S. Gurumurthi, and M. R. Stan. Relaxing non-volatility for fast and energy-efficient stt-ram caches. In *High Performance Computer Architecture (HPCA), 2011 IEEE 17th International Symposium on*, pages 50–61. IEEE, 2011.

[19] G. Sun, X. Dong, Y. Xie, J. Li, and Y. Chen. A novel architecture of the 3d stacked mram l2 cache for cmps. In *High Performance Computer Architecture, 2009. HPCA 2009. IEEE 15th International Symposium on*, pages 239–249. IEEE, 2009.

[20] X. Wu, J. Li, L. Zhang, E. Speight, and Y. Xie. Power and performance of read-write aware hybrid caches with non-volatile memories. In *Design, Automation & Test in Europe Conference & Exhibition, 2009. DATE'09.*, pages 737–742. IEEE, 2009.

[21] C. Xu, X. Dong, N. P. Jouppi, and Y. Xie. Design implications of memristor-based rram cross-point structures. In *Design, Automation & Test in Europe Conference & Exhibition (DATE), 2011*, pages 1–6. IEEE, 2011.

[22] C. Xu, D. Niu, X. Zhu, S. H. Kang, M. Nowak, and Y. Xie. Device-architecture co-optimization of stt-ram based memory for low power embedded systems. In *Proceedings of the International Conference on Computer-Aided Design*, pages 463–470. IEEE Press, 2011.

[23] W. Xu, H. Sun, X. Wang, Y. Chen, and T. Zhang. Design of last-level on-chip cache using spin-torque transfer ram (stt ram). *Very Large Scale Integration (VLSI) Systems, IEEE Transactions on*, 19(3):483–493, 2011.

[24] C. Zhang, F. Vahid, and W. Najjar. A highly configurable cache for low energy embedded systems. *ACM Transactions on Embedded Computing Systems (TECS)*, 4(2):363–387, 2005.

[25] P. Zhou, B. Zhao, J. Yang, and Y. Zhang. Energy reduction for stt-ram using early write termination. In *Proceedings of the 2009 International Conference on Computer-Aided Design*, pages 264–268. ACM, 2009.

Multiple Attempt Write Strategy for Low Energy STT-RAM

Jaeyoung Park and Michael Orshansky
Dept. of Electrical and Computer Engineering
The University of Texas at Austin
{jypark22, orshansky}@utexas.edu

ABSTRACT

In this paper, we demonstrate an energy-reduction strategy that exploits the stochastic switching characteristics of STT-RAM write operation and propose a multiple-attempt write technique needed for it. In contrast to the traditional approach which uses the pulse that guarantees writes for all cells, the proposed technique uses multiple short pulses. Individually, these pulses result in high probability of write error therefore multiple attempts are made until a successful write for all bits. Average write energy is significantly reduced because the average write duration is far shorter than the worst-case duration. We developed a self-validation write circuit that allows bit-wise validation and current deactivation without adding energy and area overhead. We evaluated the proposed circuit using a compact STT-RAM model targeting an implementation in a 10nm technology node. Results indicate that the proposed architecture reduces write energy by 94.6% compared to the conventional design. Compared to the best previously known architectures that rely on write-read-verify strategy we reduce write energy by 2.1× without area overhead.

CCS Concepts

•**Hardware → Non-volatile memory;** Circuits power issues;

Keywords

STT-RAM, Memory design, Multiple attempt

1. INTRODUCTION

Spin-transfer torque magnetic RAM (STT-RAM) is an emerging non-volatile memory technology that has the potential to become the next-generation universal memory device [1, 2]. Yet there are significant challenges that stem from the fundamental physics of the magnetic tunnel junction (MTJ). The unique physics of the spin-transfer torque action of the MTJ results in significant stochasticity of the MTJ write process [3, 4]. This creates serious challenges in terms of reliable and high yielding commercial manufacturing of large systems utilizing STT-RAM technology. The

GLSVLSI '16, May 18-20, 2016, Boston, MA, USA

DOI: http://dx.doi.org/10.1145/2902961.2903015

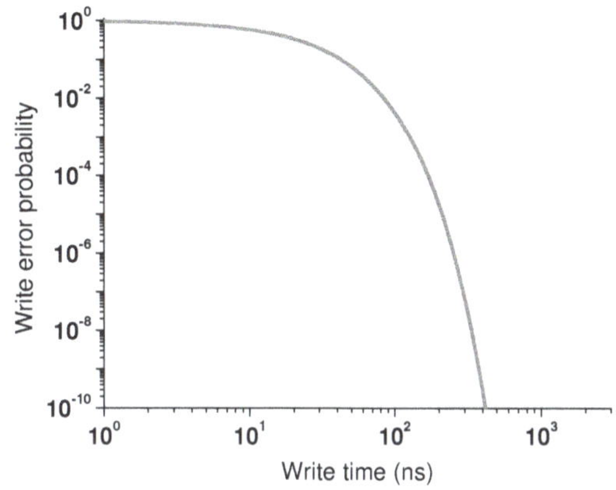

Figure 1: Stochastic distribution of write times

worst-case approach, which uses the longest pulse duration, guarantees a successful write with high probability; however, it introduces a significant energy penalty since the average write duration is far shorter than the worst case duration. The ratio of the high-quantile write duration to the mean write duration can easily be 20× (Fig. 1).

In order to move away from the deterministic worst-case approach, several stochastic write strategies have been explored [5–9]. Early-write termination (EWT) [5], verify-on-write (VOW) [6], and variation-tolerant variable energy write (VT-VEW) [7,8] exploit the wide distribution of write time to greatly reduce energy via a mechanism that continuously checks the instantaneous state of the MTJ and deactivates the write current once the correct value has registered. Because the distribution is quite wide, the potential gain of variable energy writes is a 3-10× in write-energy efficiency. However, the energy overhead of the monitoring operation is non-negligible since it is used continuously until the switching occurs. In addition, circuits for state change detection and bit-line termination introduce area overhead.

A different approach is based on a hypothesis that an MTJ can be written by a current pulse of some magnitude and duration over multiple attempts even when the likelihood of a successful write on each attempt is low. Write-verify-rewrite with adaptive period (WRAP) [6] and low-current probabilistic writes (LCPW) [9] exploit an iterative write algorithm for reducing write energy by lowering individual write currents. Lowering write current leads to a high error rate; however, the writing ultimately succeeds on the following trials.

In this paper, we propose a technique that is also built on the principle of applying multiple write attempts to realize low-energy writes. We refer to our technique as the multiple

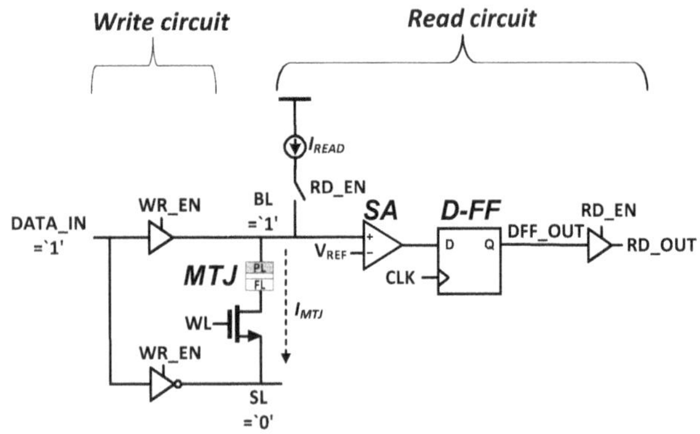

Figure 2: A 1-bit STT-RAM cell with conventional write and read circuits [10–12].

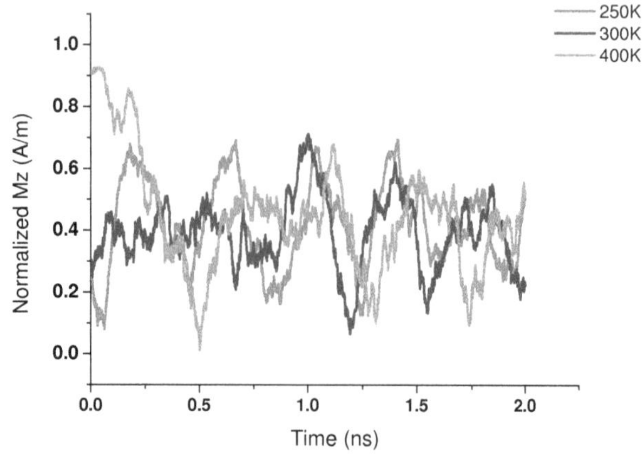

Figure 3: Magnetization on Z-direction (Mz) over time obtained via numerical simulations.

attempt write (MAW) architecture. Our work makes several contributions. Our first contribution is a self-validating write circuit that allows bit-wise validation and deactivation with near-zero energy and area overhead. In contrast, WRAP and LCPW require a comparator for bit-wise validation and sizable amount control logic for deactivation. Because they are needed on every column of a memory array, a significant overhead is introduced. Our second contribution is the formalization of the notion of re-randomization time as the interval needed for sufficient randomness to develop such that subsequent write attempts become stochastically independent. We quantify the value of re-randomization time via accurate numerical simulation.

We evaluate the proposed architecture using a compact STT-RAM cell model targeting an implementation in a 10nm technology node. Our evaluation indicates that the overall write energy is reduced by 95.3% compared to the conventional worst-case write. Compared to WRAP and LCPW we reduce write energy by 2.1× without area overhead because the proposed architecture does not introduce energy overheads by the validation and the deactivation.

2. MODELING STOCHASTIC STT-RAM WRITES

In this section, we describe the STT-RAM write process, explain the opportunity for reducing energy, and discuss the stochastic model and the re-randomization process.

The core component in an STT-RAM cell is its magnetic tunnel junction (MTJ) and an access transistor which is connected to the MTJ to control its operation as shown in Fig. 2 [10–12]. The MTJ consists of two layers of magnetic material separated by a dielectric layer. The two magnetic layers have their own spin directions, with one layer pinned to a fixed polarization and the second layer being free. The spin of the free layer (FL) can be switched from one orientation to its opposite by applying a current pulse through the MTJ. The MTJ as a unit can be in one of two states, *anti-parallel* (AP) and *parallel* (P). In the AP state the free and pinned layers have opposite spin directions and in the P state both have the same spin direction. Each of these two states exhibits a distinct resistance corresponding to storing a binary '0' or '1' (e.g., P and AP).

An access transistor is connected with the MTJ to control its operation. Write '0' and write '1' operations proceed by turning on the access transistor and injecting a high write current in one of two directions. Consider a write '1' operation. If an incoming data is '1', the voltage is raised on the bitline (BL) and lowered on the source line (SL). The access transistor turns on, and the current flows through the MTJ and the access transistor. If the current supplied by the access transistor is sufficiently large, the MTJ undergoes a state change to the AP.

As seen in Fig. 1, the time needed for the MTJ to switch is stochastic and the distribution is quite wide [3, 4]. The wider part of the distribution is dominated by the so-called thermally activated switching [13]. A probability model for the thermally activated switching duration has been proposed [3]. The model describes the switching probability $p_{sw}(t, I)$, which is the probability of switching occurring for a pulse duration t at current I:

$$p_{sw}(t, I) = 1 - \exp\left\{-\frac{t}{\tau_0}\exp\left[-\Delta\left(1 - \frac{I}{I_{C0}}\right)\right]\right\} \quad (1)$$

where Δ is the thermal stability factor, τ_0 is the inverse of the thermal attempt frequency, and I_{C0} is the critical current at zero Kelvin. Because of a wide distribution, the traditional approach which uses the pulse that guarantees writes for all cells wastes energy since the average write time is far shorter than the worst-case pulse duration. The critical observation that we exploit is that the stochastic behavior of writes of the same cell occurs when write events are interleaved with sufficient thermal re-randomization processes [13–15]. This means that a certain time is required for the MTJ to develop sufficient randomness to ensure that writes are stochastically independent and are charcterized by different switching durations. We call this time the re-randomization time (τ_r) and define it as the time needed to de-correlate the switching times of subsequent write events. At non-zero temperatures, thermal energy leads to spontaneous agitation of magnetization, producing randomization of the initial angle (θ_0), which is the angle between the magnetic moment and easy anisotropy axis [13]. Differences in the initial magnetization angle lead to differences in switching time. Therefore, at above-zero temperature, the switching time of each write attempt is changed.

To evaluate re-randomization time, we use the detailed magnetics numerical simulator OOMMF [16]. OOMMF is a solver of the Landau-Lifshitz-Gilbert equation [17] describ-

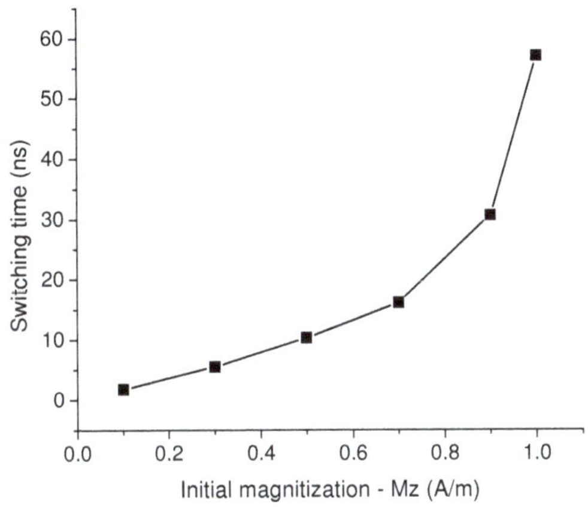

Figure 4: The simulated switching time as a function of initial magnetization.

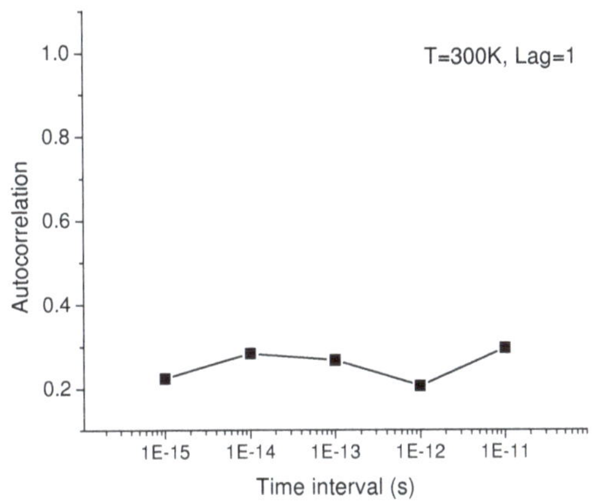

Figure 5: The autocorrelation function of Mz.

ing the magnetization dynamics in a solid. It is commonly used to model the time-domain behavior of a magnetic field in ferromagnetic materials. We use OOMMF to simulate the dynamics of magnetization of an MTJ device and the evolution of the magnetic field due to temperature. The simulation experiment is as follows. We use a common device design that has a CoFeB-MgO interface [18]. We simulate the normalized magnetization on the Z-direction (Mz), which represents the macro-spin angle in a free layer, over time and at various temperatures. The simulations are conducted without any applied current to only study the dependence of spins on temperature. When all spins in a free layer are up, the value of Mz is 1. If all spins are down, the value of Mz is -1. At 250-400K, which is the temperature range used in commercial electronic devices, Mz shows significant fluctuation over time as shown in Fig. 3. The modified angle becomes an initial angle for a subsequent write attempt, leading to different switching times. In Fig. 4, we observe that depending on the initial Mz, the switching time varies significantly.

To find the re-randomization time, we plot the autocorrelation function for Mz(t) simulated at 300K at various time intervals (Fig. 5). We find that autocorrelation remains low down to the limit of OOMMF's time resolution (0.2fs). This indicates that at sub-fs scale the subsequent values of Mz are random. We observe that sub-fs is, for current technologies,

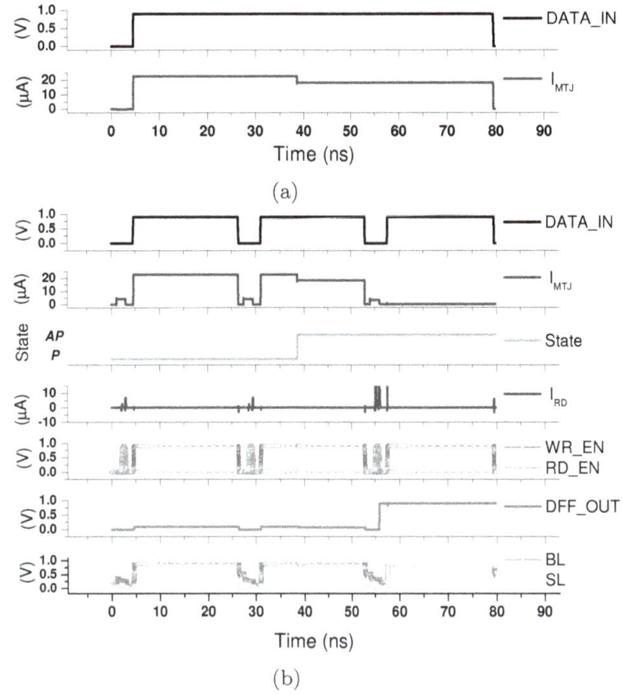

Figure 6: Waveforms of (a) the conventional worst-case approach and (b) MAW for the write '1' operation.

significantly below the typical gate delay and is easily accrued within MAW during a validation step without any effort.

3. MULTIPLE ATTEMPT WRITE

In this section, we introduce a multiple attempt write (MAW) algorithm to overcome the wide distribution of write time by exploiting the re-randomization process. We describe both the MAW algorithm and its implementation.

MAW utilizes a multiple-iteration mechanism that (1) writes to a cell and (2) validates that the correct value has registered. If the cell is not written correctly, the MAW algorithm attempts to write the cell again until the cell is written successfully. Once the correct value has registered, the write current is deactivated, eliminating unnecessary energy consumption. Even though the probability of a write-fail on any individual attempt is high, the writing ultimately succeeds on the following attempts. That allows MAW to achieve high overall write success rate while reducing the needed energy.

Fig. 6 shows the waveforms for the incoming data (DATA_IN), the current through an MTJ (the write current pulse) for both (a) the conventional worst-case approach and (b) the MAW approach. The applied pulse duration (DATA_IN) is fixed at 80ns for the conventional strategy and at 20ns for MAW. We assume that in both cases switching occurs at 38ns: at that time a cell is written successfully and the write current is no longer necessary. Despite that, in the conventional approach, the write current (I_{MTJ}) continues to be drawn until 80ns. MAW deactivates the write current after the second attempt because MAW reads out the cell content and validates the state of the MTJ before each write attempt. In this example, a higher than 40% energy reduc-

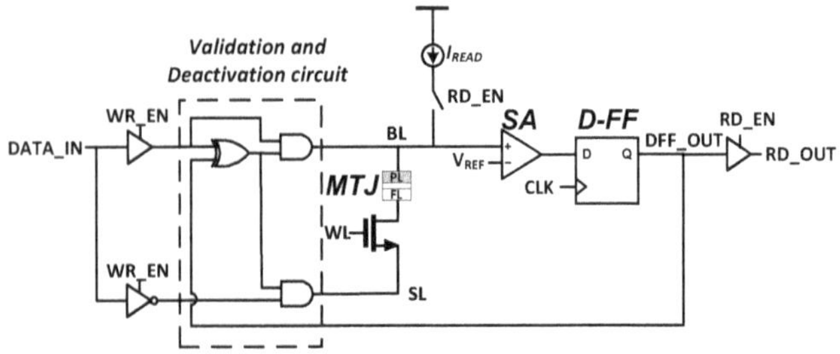

Figure 7: The validation and deactivation circuits of WRAP and LCPW. LCPW additionally requires a write buffer.

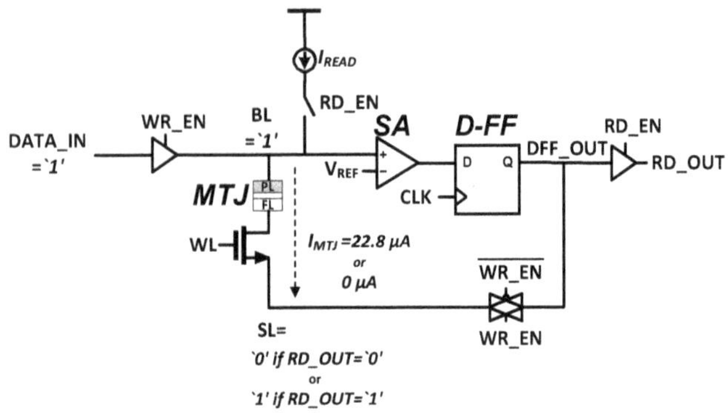

Figure 8: The self-validation write circuit (write '1' operation).

tion is achieved by cutting the unnecessary write current assuming the validation energy overhead is negligible.

To maximize the advantages of MAW, we need to minimize the energy cost of validation. What is the best way to realize the strategy of writing, validation, and current-deactivation? One possibility is to use a digital comparator (e.g., XOR gate). This is a strategy of WRAP and LCPW. The comparator output could then disable the write as shown in Fig. 7. However, as our results show, the additional circuits for validation consume non-negligible area and energy. The area overhead can be significant as the additional circuits need to be placed on every column for bit-wise validation. As we show below, the area cost of WRAP and LCPW is 8.2% and 13.5%, respectively. In contrast, our solution requires no extra area.

To minimize the overhead, we propose to modify the MTJ cell directly to allow a self-validation/deactivation process. This is accomplished if the value stored on the cell (i.e., DFF_OUT) is delivered to SL by a read before a write. The cell content available on SL is compared with the incoming data on BL during a write. Fig. 8 shows a schematic view of the proposed circuit. SL is connected to DFF_OUT via a switch. DFF_OUT becomes equal to the cell content after a cell is read out via the sense amplifier and D-FF. Note that this utilizes the standard read infrastructure. Now, the write current is determined by SL's value. Consider a write '1' operation. If SL is 0, the write current is passed through the cell from BL to SL. If SL is 1, the write current is deactivated since both BL and SL are 1.

We obtain the waveforms at each node of the proposed circuit using SPICE simulation [19] as shown in Fig. 6. The waveforms show the change of the current across an MTJ, and the voltage on DFF_OUT and SL as the state of the

Table 1: Key parameters of the perpendicular MTJ [15, 18, 22].

Parameter	Value	Unit
Interface Material	CoFeB-MgO	
Intrinsic critical current	24	μA
Thermal stability factor	58	
Tunnel Magnetoresistance ratio (TMR)	~100	%
Diameter of MTJ	20	nm
Out-of-plane magnetic field	0.4	T
Product of resistance and area (RA)	12	$\Omega\mu m^2$

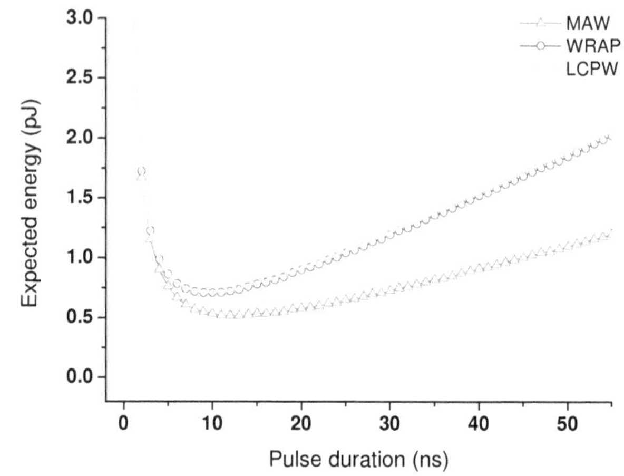

Figure 9: Expected write energy of MAW, WRAP, and LCPW at various write pulse durations.

MTJ changes. Note that the MTJ is set to P state at the beginning. As the MAW sequence is read/validate/write, the proposed sequence starts with a read operation. At the start of the first read operation, the voltages on DFF_OUT and SL are lowered since the MTJ is in P state. The voltage on BL is raised by DATA_IN. During the first write operation, the write current (I_{MTJ}) is passed through the cell. Switching does not occur in the first write attempt; therefore, DFF_OUT remains low during the second read operation. The state transition occurs in the middle of the second write attempt. The state change is captured in the third read operation and modifies the voltage on DFF_OUT. The voltage on SL is raised in the third write attempt. Therefore, the write current is deactivated in the third write attempt because both BL and SL are high.

4. EVALUATION

In this section, we evaluate energy savings achieved by applying MAW. We first calculate the average bitcell write energy and then evaluate the savings on SPEC benchmarks [20, 21].

4.1 Write energy for a bitcell

We designed a 1-bit cell with the proposed MAW write circuit using the 10nm Predictive Technology Model (PTM) MOSFET model and a compact MTJ model [14, 15, 22] to verify functionality and extract single bit write energy using SPICE simulation. MTJ parameters are derived from a perpendicular MTJ manufactured by Tohoku University [18], as detailed in Table 1. We also implemented WRAP and LCPW to extract their area and energy overheads.

We first extract the 1-bit write energy of MAW, WRAP,

and LCPW. We use the MTJ parameters of Table 1 and the same basic components, such as a write driver. The power supply voltage is 0.9V and the write current across an MTJ (I_{MTJ}) is $22.8\mu A$. The single attempt write energy is 0.27pJ at the 13ns pulse duration. To compute the *expected (average)* write energy of MAW, we derive a simple probabilistic model. The average write energy is the expected value of the cost of performing Bernoulli trials with error probability, p, until the first success [23]. The single-attempt error probability can be found from Eq. 1 as $p = 1 - p_{sw}(t, I)$. If X is the number of trials until the first success, $p(X = k) = p^{k-1}(1 - p)$. The expected energy is found by summing up the geometric series when e is the cost of an individual write attempt including the contribution from read energy:

$$E(energy) = e \sum_{k=1}^{n} kp^{k-1}(1-p) = e(\frac{1-p^n}{1-p} - np^n) \quad (2)$$

We plot the expected energy to find the optimal pulse duration and the minimum total energy. Fig. 9 shows the expected energy of WRAP, LCPW, and MAW at different write pulse durations. For short pulses, the number of attempts needs to be increased, leading to higher energy. The minimum expected energy of MAW is 0.52pJ. It occurs at the pulse of 13ns and requires 1.9 write attempts on average and 22 write attempts in the worst case.

The average power of additional circuits of WRAP and LCPW is $14.4\mu W$ and $15.3\mu W$, respectively. The minimum expected energy of WRAP and LCPW are 0.70pJ and 0.72pJ, respectively. The write energy of the conventional approach is 5.86pJ, where the pulse duration is set to 286ns to achieve the typically required error rate (1.5×10^{-7}) [24]. Note that the worst-case latencies of WRAP, LCPW, and MAW are increased by additional read latency since a read operation is inserted between each write attempt. The read circuitry is designed to enable 1ns read time at 0.01pJ energy. The total read energy overhead is 3.8% (0.22pJ/5.86pJ) and the latency overhead is 7.7% (22ns/286ns). We observe the longer latency does not impact performance under a write scheme utilizing a write buffer. Write buffers are typically used to mitigate the impact of long latency [9, 25, 26].

We now estimate the area costs of WARP, LCPW and MAW. The area cost of WARP is one XOR gate and two AND gates per column. The area cost of LCPW is one XOR gate, two AND gates, two inverters, and one flip-flop. We estimate the area overheads of WRAP and LCPW to be $840F^2$ and $1380F^2$, respectively. If the area of a 1-bit cell is $20F^2$ and a sub-array is comprised of 512 rows, the area overhead of WRAP and LCPW is 8.2% and 13.5%, respectively. The area cost of MAW is one CMOS switch that connects DFF_OUT to SL (Fig. 8). However, one inverter, which is originally connected to SL in the conventional write driver (Fig. 2), is removed. Because the area of a CMOS switch is generally similar to the area of an inverter, our solution requires no extra silicon area.

4.2 Program-level energy evaluation

We now evaluate energy savings of MAW in a memory system using SPEC benchmarks [20, 21]. We use the expected write energy for a bit for $P \rightarrow AP$ and $AP \rightarrow P$ write cases. In cases when a cell already stores the desired values ($P \rightarrow P$ and $AP \rightarrow AP$), only the read energy is required because of MAW's read-first sequence. In contrast, WRAP and LCPW use write energy for the first write attempt even for $P \rightarrow P$ and $AP \rightarrow AP$ cases because of their write-read-verify sequence.

We use memory traces from eight integer and eight floating point applications with the largest number of memory accesses with PIN application programming interface [27], assuming an on-chip memory hierarchy with a single X86 core, 32KB L1, 256KB L2 and 1MB 16-way set-associative last-level cache. Fig. 10 shows the relative energy consumption of MAW and earlier techniques. Write energy is normalized to the conventional write. MAW reduces energy by more than 95% in 7 applications. On average, MAW reduces write energy by 94.6%. WRAP and LCPW only achieve 88.6% and 86.5% reduction, respectively. Thus, compared to the best previously known architecture, MAW achieves a 2.1× larger energy reduction. This improvement is due to two factors. The first is that MAW does not introduce any energy overhead for validation in contrast to other tech-

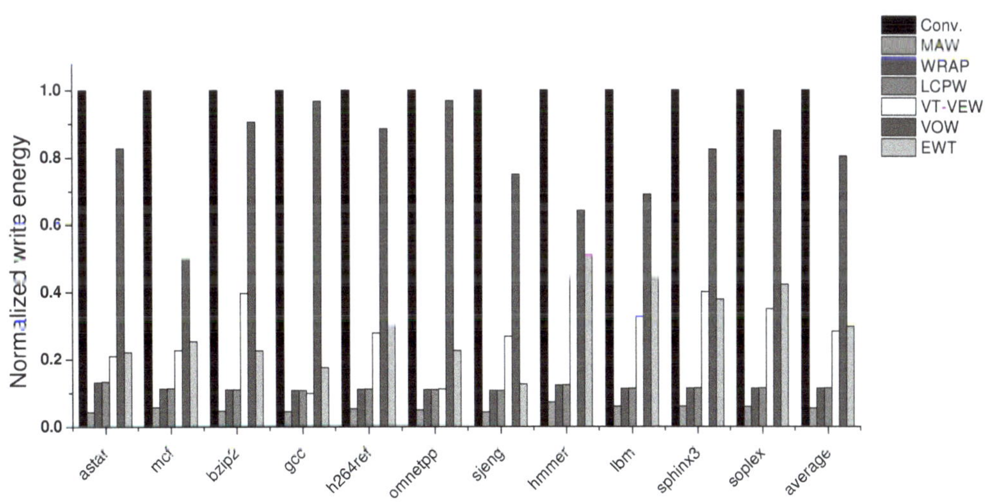

Figure 10: Write energy of the conventional worst-case, MAW, WRAP, LCPW, VT-VEW, VOW, and EWT approach (normalized to the conventional worst-case write) by SPEC 2006 benchmarks.

Table 2: Performance summary and comparison with the related techniques.

	MAW	WRAP [6]	LCPW [9]	VT-VEW [8]	VOW [6]	EWT [5]
Technology	10nm	45nm	-[a)]	16nm	45nm	45nm
Addi. circuit	**No**	Comparator Comb. circuits	Comparator Comb. circuits, Buffer	S/H, Diff. Amp, D-FFs Comb. circuits	Sense Amp. Comb. circuits	Diff. Amp., Sense Amp. Comb. circuits
Area overhead	**0**	$840F^2$	$1380F^2$	$990F^2$	$860F^2$	$2025F^2$
Latency overhead	7.7%	7.7%	7.7%	0	0	0
Energy saving	94.6%	88.6%	88.5%	71.6%	19.6%	70.2%

[a)] Not described in references.

niques. The second is that MAW's read-first sequence allows energy reduction in the cases when cells already store desired values. All performances are summarized in Table 2.

5. CONCLUSION

This paper proposes a multiple attempt write architecture to reduce average write energy. In the proposed architecture, a cell is validated before each write attempt and the write operation is deactivated once the correct value has registered. We developed a novel circuit for the write operation based on self-validation. Our analysis indicates that at the required write-error rate the proposed architecture reduces write energy by 94.6%.

6. ACKNOWLEDGMENTS

This work was partially funded by Samsung Global Outreach Research Program.

7. REFERENCES

[1] A. Nigam *et al.*, "Delivering on the promise of universal memory for spin-transfer torque ram," in *ISLPED*, 2011.

[2] R. F. Freitas *et al.*, "Storage-class memory: The next storage system technology," *IBM Journal of Research and Development*, 2008.

[3] Z. Diao *et al.*, "Spin-transfer torque switching in magnetic tunnel junctions and spin-transfer torque random access memory," *Journal of Physics: Condensed Matter*, 2007.

[4] X. Wang *et al.*, "Thermal fluctuation effects on spin torque induced switching: Mean and variations," *Journal of Applied Physics*, 2008.

[5] P. Zhou, *et al.*, "Energy reduction for stt-ram using early write termination," in *ICCAD*, 2009.

[6] X. Bi *et al.*, "Probabilistic design methodology to improve run-time stability and performance of stt-ram caches," in *ICCAD*, 2012.

[7] T. Zheng *et al.*, "Variable-energy write stt-ram architecture with bit-wise write-completion monitoring," in *ISLPED*, 2013.

[8] J. Park *et al.*, "Variation-tolerant write completion circuit for variable-energy write stt-ram architecture," *IEEE Trans. of VLSI*, 2015.

[9] N. Strikos *et al.*, "Low-current probabilistic writes for power-efficient stt-ram caches," in *ICCD*, 2013.

[10] M. Hosomi *et al.*, "A novel nonvolatile memory with spin torque transfer magnetization switching: Spin-ram," in *IEDM*, 2005.

[11] H. Li *et al.*, "An overview of non-volatile memory technology and the implication for tools and architectures," in *DATE*, 2009.

[12] Y. Chen *et al.*, "A 130 nm 1.2 v/3.3 v 16 kb spin-transfer torque random access memory with nondestructive self-reference sensing scheme," *IEEE J. of Solid-State Circuits*, 2012.

[13] A. Khvalkovskiy *et al.*, "Basic principles of stt-mram cell operation in memory arrays," *Journal of Physics D: Applied Physics*, 2013.

[14] W. Kim *et al.*, "Extended scalability of perpendicular stt-mram towards sub-20nm mtj node," in *IEDM*, 2011.

[15] Y. Zhang *et al.*, "Compact modeling of perpendicular-anisotropy cofeb/mgo magnetic tunnel junctions," *IEEE Trans. Electron Devices*, 2012.

[16] "Oommf user guide, version 1.0, interagency report nistir 6376, national institute of standard and technology, gaithersburg, md, 1999," *URL: http://math. nist. gov/oommf*, 1999.

[17] T. Gilbert *et al.*, "Anomalous rotational damping in ferromagnetic sheets," in *Conference on Magnetism and Magnetic Materials*, 1955.

[18] H. Sato *et al.*, "Comprehensive study of cofeb-mgo magnetic tunnel junction characteristics with single-and double-interface scaling down to 1x nm," *IEDM Tech. Digest*, 2013.

[19] L. Meares *et al.*, *Simulating with SPICE.* Intusoft, 1988.

[20] K. M. Dixit, "The spec benchmarks," *Parallel computing*, vol. 17, no. 10, pp. 1195–1209, 1991.

[21] J. L. Henning, "Spec cpu2006 benchmark descriptions," *ACM SIGARCH Computer Architecture News*, vol. 34, no. 4, pp. 1–17, 2006.

[22] W. Zhao *et al.*, "Predictive technology model for nano-cmos design exploration," 2010.

[23] A. Papoulis *et al.*, *Probability, random variables, and stochastic processes.* McGraw-Hill Education, 2002.

[24] D. Worledge *et al.*, "Switching distributions and write reliability of perpendicular spin torque mram," in *IEDM*, 2010.

[25] B. Govindarajalu, *Computer Architecture and Organization: Design Principles and Applications.* McGraw-Hill, 2004.

[26] G. Sun *et al.*, "A novel architecture of the 3d stacked mram l2 cache for cmps," in *HPCA*, 2009.

[27] C. Luk *et al.*, "Pin: building customized program analysis tools with dynamic instrumentation," in *PLDI*, 2005.

Secret Sharing and Multi-user Authentication: From Visual Cryptography to RRAM Circuits

Md Tanvir Arafin
Department of Electrical and Computer Engineering
University of Maryland, College Park, USA
marafin@umd.edu

Gang Qu
Department of Electrical and Computer Engineering
University of Maryland, College Park, USA
gangqu@umd.edu

ABSTRACT

In this era of Internet of Things (IoT), connectivity exists everywhere, among everything (including people) at all times. Therefore, security, trust, and privacy become crucial to the design and implementation of IoT devices [12]. However, it is challenging to build security into IoT devices because most of them are constrained by extremely limited resources such as the battery, memory, and computation power *etc*. Inspired by the concept of visual cryptography [4] that requires the least amount of computation and a recent work on pure hardware-based single-user authentication [6], we present a novel solution to the secret sharing and multi-user authentication problem. Our solution is built on the observation that non-volatile resistive memories display nice monotonic and additive properties during resistive state transitions. We demonstrate how to design a hardware dependent multi-user authentication protocol using resistive random access memory (RRAM)-based hardware and provide the necessary circuits for the application. Finally, we simulate the proposed circuit to understand the nature of the operation and practical problems that these designs encounter during operation.

CCS Concepts

• **Security and Privacy → Security in Hardware → Hardware Security Implementation → Hardware-based security protocol.**

Keywords

Secret Sharing; Visual Cryptography; Multi-User Authentication; Resistive Memory.

1. INTRODUCTION

With the advent of the Internet of Things (IoT), where more and more devices are connected by the Internet infrastructure, there is an increased demand for ultra-low power for computing and communication. Meanwhile, the pervasive nature of the IoT devices in modern life ranges from medical devices to critical infrastructures, and the fact that these devices often need to collaborate to accomplish the desired mission, make security, trust, and privacy new important design objectives for the IoT devices [12]. However, solutions based on modern cryptography are computationally expensive and not suitable for the extremely resource constrained IoT devices. As a result, security and privacy are becoming the *Achilles' heel* for IoT system design and implementation. For example, most of the wearable and implantable medical devices (such as pacemaker and insulin pump) communicate without any encryption or protection. Therefore, research on novel low-power security primitive is imperative for a safe and secure realization of IoT applications.

GLSVLSI '16, May 18-20, 2016, Boston, MA, USA

DOI: http://dx.doi.org/10.1145/2902961.2903039

In [6], we have proposed a couple of resistive random access memory (RRAM) based lightweight user authentication protocols. In this work, we consider the problem of how to design and implement simple and lightweight secret sharing and multi-user authentication scheme for IoT devices. Secret sharing is a well-studied problem, which seeks to distribute pieces of information (or called the secret) to multiple parties in a way such that the information (the secret) can be revealed when all or a sufficiently large subset of the parties contribute their shares. Shamir's secret sharing algorithm [1] defined the concept of *threshold scheme* for secret sharing. This so-called *(k,n) threshold scheme* (where $k \leq n$) can be described as follows:

> Assume that a secret S needs to be shared by n parties. The secret is divided into n pieces such that, the knowledge of k or more pieces would be sufficient to reconstruct S. However, if the knowledge of any $k-1$ pieces or less is available, it would be impossible to reconstruct S.

A direct application of this problem is the multi-user authentication problem, where at least k authentic users must present to gain the access to a system. One example of this is the "*two person rule*" originally designed to prevent the accidental or malicious launch of nuclear weapons by a single individual [13] and later on enforced by NSA for the access to sensitive operation and information after the infamous Snowden case [14]. One may argue that authenticating each individual user and counting the authenticated users can trivially solve the multi-user authentication problem. This does solve the problem but has two significant drawbacks in scalability and user privacy. First, the expensive authentication protocol has to be applied at least k times and some mechanism to check duplicate users must be implemented. Second, unlike the traditional secret share-based approaches [1-4], this method will reveal the identity of each authenticated user, creating user privacy concerns.

Our goal is to perform multi-user authentication without using any computation intensive cryptographic operations so it can be applied to IoT applications. Our approach is inspired by the *Visual Cryptography scheme* proposed by Naor and Shamir [4], which also completely avoids cryptographic calculations but is limited to secret image information. We design resistive random access memory (RRAM) based circuits to demonstrate the concept of hardware-based multi-user authentication.

The rest of this paper is organized as follows. In the next section, we survey the classic solutions, which unfortunately are computationally expensive, and review the fundamentals of RRAM as well as the RRAM based authentication protocols proposed in [6]. In Section 3, we discuss the basic ideas of secret sharing, then elaborate our multi-user authentication protocol, and describe the proposed RRAM circuit. We report simulation results in Section 4 before concluding in Section 5.

2. RELATED WORK

In this section, we provide the background on classical secret sharing schemes, RRAMs and recently proposed RRAM-based single user authentication protocols.

2.1 Classical Secret Sharing Schemes

Shamir [1] and Blakley [2] independently proposed solutions for the aforementioned problem of *(k,n)-threshold scheme*. More specifically, Blakley used techniques from finite geometry to provide a solution for safeguarding and sharing cryptographic keys. Shamir's solution is based on the polynomial interpolation over a finite field. It has since become a widely acceptable solution for secure secret sharing and distribution of cryptographic keys. A detailed explanation of the scheme and the impact of subsequent works can be found in [3].

One of the drawbacks of these early solutions is their high computational cost. For example, Shamir's secret sharing algorithm requires calculations over the finite field during both secret share generation phase and secret reconstruction phase. This, in turn, requires complex digital circuitry for hardware implementation, which is known to be more efficient than the software implementation. The *Visual Cryptography scheme* proposed by Naor and Shamir [4] is an alternative lightweight scheme for secret sharing to Shamir's original scheme. In visual cryptography, the secret shared among multiple parties is simply an image. The secret image is broken into *n* pieces and each piece is printed on a transparency. When *k* or more pieces of these transparencies are placed as a stack, the secret image is revealed and can be comprehended by human eyes. In this scheme, the secret share generation needs only very simple calculations and the revelation of the secret image does not involve any mathematical computation. In essence, this is an example of how inherent physical properties of hardware can be used in designing lightweight security primitives to avoid complex mathematical computation and formal cryptography protocols.

One of the many interesting applications of secret sharing is the *simultaneous multi-user authentication* problem. Naor and Pinkas first discussed the application of visual cryptography for authentication and identification [11]. When an entity (say Alice) tries to simultaneously authenticate *k-out-of-n*-other entities (B_1, … B_k), the problem turns into simultaneous verification of *k-out-of-n* cryptographic keys (*i.e.,* passwords). If these keys are generated from a secret that Alice knows or possesses, then, instead of checking *n*-keys separately, Alice can use the keys provided by B_1, … B_k to regenerate her secret and authenticate all entities at once. Note that, as Alice uses a *k-out-of-n* secret sharing scheme, Alice can reconstruct the secret from any of the k-users shares. To avoid collusion among the users, this procedure requires Alice to have some interference in key/password generation process during the registration of the users.

2.2 Hardware Dependent Secret Sharing and Properties of RRAM

In this work, we discuss hardware dependent secret sharing and multi-user authentication ideas that require minimum computational effort during authentication. We explore on how to create hardware-dependent or hardware-biased secrets that can only be revealed by that hardware used during authentication. Physical variations in electronic devices due to fabrication variations can be exploited to create hardware specific secret-sharing process. Therefore, computational hardware would not only be the engine for computation, but also an active party in the secret sharing and authentication purposes. We have demonstrated our ideas using multivalued RRAM-based circuits.

Resistive random access memory (RRAM) is a promising candidate for non-volatile solid-state memory. RRAM devices have a very simple geometry- in most cases, a metal-insulator-metal (MIM) structure. In this work, we are focusing on HfO_x-based RRAMs. These devices have high packing density, multibit storage capacity, large ON/OFF ratio, and good switching endurance (>10^6 cycles) [10]. Device properties of RRAMs are dependent on the dynamics of the conductive thin-film formation in the HfO_x layer. This is a highly non-linear process, which leads to non-linear properties of these devices. Recent works have shown that unique properties of resistive non-volatile memories can be useful in designing security primitives. A survey of these works can be found in [5].

For this work, we have considered the 1T1R-configuration of RRAM devices, where an access transistor is used for controlling the voltage (and current) across the RRAM device as shown in Figure 1.

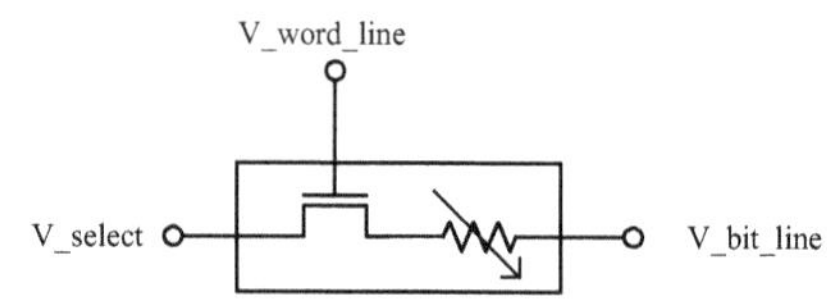

Figure 1. One-transistor-one-resistor (1T1R) configuration of an RRAM cell.

Non-volatile memory elements such as RRAMs can be used to remember different resistive states. By applying voltage/current pulses through the memory elements these resistive states can be changed. We define ON pulse as a small duration voltage pulse (applied to the gate of the 1T1R configuration) that can reduce the resistance of a given RRAM. The duration of an ON pulse is a magnitude lower than the write-time of the device, therefore, a single ON pulse cannot produce a noticeable change in the resistance of a device that is in a high resistive state. However, with proper V_select and grounded V_bit_line, a collection of ON pulses can put an RRAM from a higher resistive state (HRS) to a lower resistive state (LRS). It has been demonstrated that using pulse train- a sequence of ON pulses, one can control the HRS to LRS transition [6]. This pulse-controlled transition of the RRAM's resistive state has two interesting properties:

P1. Changes due ON pulses are "*additive*" in nature. For example, two consecutive ON pulses would put the device in a lower resistive state than a single ON pulse.

P2. The memory elements are *monotonic*, *i.e.,* applying an ON pulse will always decrease the resistance and its effect cannot be undone without resetting the device.

After applying input pulses, logical decisions can be made based on whether an element's resistance is above or below a given threshold. This is the key idea of the threshold detector circuit described in later sections. The "*additive*" property along with the *monotonicity* can be useful for designing cryptographic primitives. Since the properties described above are also common for memristive devices, this work can be extended to other designs of resistive memories.

2.3 RRAM-based Authentication

Recently, we have demonstrated the application of RRAM-based circuits and protocols for single user authentication in [6]. For RRAM-based single user authentication, an entity Alice tries to authenticate Bob by using a voltage profile that Bob possess. Bob's voltage profile (*i.e.*, password) consists of a random sequence of ON pulses. A straightforward way for authenticating Bob is to digitize his voltage profile and save it the RRAM-based memory. Each time Alice wants to authenticate, she will read the provided voltage profile, digitize it and match it with the one she stored in the RRAM-based memory. However, this approach suffers when an adversary tries attacks such as password stealing from the database. To address such issues, we have developed device dependent authentication protocols in [6].

In hardware dependent single user authentication, Alice can only authenticate Bob using the exact device she used for registering him. Physical properties of the given hardware play the role of non-linear function that "*encrypts*" Bob's password. To design such protocols, we notice that along with the "*additive*" and *monotonic* properties, RRAM-based circuits also show unobservability property of the intermediate resistance during resistive state transition. The state-transition of an RRAM is dependent on the initial conditions, applied voltage profile or the physical construction of the device. Therefore, without knowing the device, the required initial conditions, and the correct voltage profile to apply, it is difficult to put a given RRAM in a certain intermediate state. Based on this key concept, we have designed simple authentication protocols in [6].

For RRAM-based authentication, during the registration phase, Alice preconditions the device to a certain state using her key. Then, Bob applies a segment of his voltage profile to the RRAM. This would put the RRAM in a certain intermediate state. Alice then *reads out* the intermediate state and stores it for later authentication. During authentication, Alice preconditions the corresponding device and let a user apply his voltage profile. If the user can successfully put the RRAM in the correct intermediate state, Alice recognizes the user as Bob. This scheme is secure from password stealing and guessing attacks since it requires exact hardware to be present, and the data stored (*hashed* value of Bob's password) in Alice's memory is dependent on the RRAM used.

This RRAM-based single-user authentication protocol is the basis for our solution to the multi-user authentication problem. However, one cannot apply this multiple times to authenticate each user for the following reasons: (1) scalability: For the *k-out-of-n* user authentication problem, this will require running the single-user authentication, at least, *k* times and additional circuit or memory to check for duplicate users. So it will not scale well for large *k* and n. (2) privacy: The *k-out-of-n* user authentication problems demand *k* authentic users, but it does not need the identification of each user. Simply applying the single-user authentication protocol *k* times will reveal the identity of the users and create privacy concerns.

3. MULTI-USER AUTHENTICATION PROTOCOL

3.1 Motivational Example

To address the problems regarding multi-user authentication (as discussed in the previous section), we have designed a *Visual Cryptography* inspired RRAM-based multi-user authentication scheme. A small motivational example for a 2-out-of-3-user authentication using RRAM-based threshold detector circuit is given below to illustrate the key concepts.

Assume that an entity Alice wants to authenticate three users B_1, B_2, and B_3. Alice chose a random key *K*, and for each bit of the key, for each user, Alice randomly choose a row from the following matrix C0 and C1 using the given rules and gives the corresponding 3-bits to the users. The matrices are given as:

C0 = all the matrices obtained by permuting the columns of
$$\begin{pmatrix} 0 & 1 & 1 \\ 0 & 1 & 1 \\ 0 & 1 & 1 \end{pmatrix};$$

C1 = all the matrices obtained by permuting the columns of
$$\begin{pmatrix} 1 & 0 & 1 \\ 0 & 1 & 1 \\ 1 & 1 & 0 \end{pmatrix};$$

and the distribution rules are:

- If the *i'th*-bit of the key is 0, distribute the rows of C0 to B_1, B_2, and B_3.
- If the *i'th*-bit of the key is 1 distribute the rows of C1 to B_1, B_2, and B_3.

Note that for a single user, it would be impossible to guess the key bit. For authentication, Alice let any 2 or more users to access the RRAM for the duration of three pulses. The users apply their keys in each pulse. The keys are taken through an OR gate. An ON pulse is applied at a cycle if the result of the OR gate is 1 otherwise no pulse is applied. If the *i'th* bit of the key is zero, then for only two of the cycles the users will give an ON pulse but there will be no ON pulse for one cycle. However if the *i'th* bit is 1, there will be three ON pulses. As a result, after the duration of three pulses, the device's resistance should be lower if the key was 1 and higher if the key was 0. A threshold detector can easily detect this and reconstruct the key. This scheme can easily be modified to an *n-out-n* or a *k-out of-n* authentication scheme.

One weakness with the above example is that to reconstruct a bit of the key, the users do not necessarily need Alice. If any two of the valid users come together, they can reconstruct the bits. If we want a hardware dependent authentication, where the participating hardware should also be a factor during authentication, this might cause a collusion problem. However, this problem does not exist if Alice has some interference in key generation. We have elaborated on this in later sections.

3.2 Authentication Protocol

In this section, we will discuss an RRAM-based multi-user authentication protocol. This hardware dependent protocol uses the core ideas of *Visual Cryptography* to ensure its security and completeness.

3.2.1 Key Generation and Registration

For generating and distributing hardware dependent keys, Alice first chose a random key X and a global bit-line voltage V_{BL}. For each bit of X (x_i), Alice uses distinct an RRAM R_i. Since Alice owns the hardware and controls the V_{BL}, Alice knows the number of ON pulses (NP_i) required for pushing the resistance of the

RRAM R_i from a fixed HRS state to the reference resistance (R_{in}). Therefore, R_i would be perceived to be in an LRS iff the number of applied pulses is greater than NP_i. Due to the fabrication variations, each RRAM would have different write-time, which will lead to different (but of same order) values of NP for different devices. Since Alice owns the device, Alice knows the value of NP_i for any given R_i at a given V_{BL}.

To generate keys for each user, Alice needs to construct the matrices C0 and C1 similar to the ones presented in the motivational example. For a *k-out-of-n* visual secret sharing these two collections of $n \times m$ Boolean matrices (*i.e.,* C0 and C1) is required. These two metrics can be constructed by the construction rules given in [4,7]. Here we have provided a rule from [4] for completeness of the discussion:

For a *k-out-of-k* scheme, let us consider a ground set $W=\{e_1,e_2,...,e_k\}$ consisting of k elements. All subsets of W with even cardinality is denoted by $p_1, p_2, ..., p_{2^{k-1}}$ and all the subsets of W of odd cardinality is denoted by $q_1, q_2, ..., q_{2^{k-1}}$. To design a *k-out-of-k* scheme, Boolean metrics S0 and S1 of dimensions $k \times 2^{k-1}$ are required. From the constructions given in [4], we define, S0[i,j]=1iff $e_i \in p_j$ and S1[i,j]=1iff $e_i \in q_j$, where $1 \leq i \leq k$ and $1 \leq j \leq 2^{k-1}$. Then, by permuting all the column of S0 and S1 metrics we can derive collections of C0 and C1 respectively [4]. This *k out-of-k* scheme can easily be expanded into a k-out-of-n scheme as discussed in [4] and [7].

Since different RRAM needs different numbers of ON pulses, additional 1s need to be padded in each row of C0 and C1. A simpler solution is to *precondition* each RRAM with this additional 1s. Since Alice knows the value of NP_i for any given R_i at a given V_{BL}, Alice can precondition each RRAM so that each requires the same number of additional ON pulses to reach LRS. Another way is to use the block-length defined constructs presented at [7]. Block-length is the number of ones resulted by *or*-ing all the columns of C1. Therefore, Alice can easily design block length adjusted matrices C0' and C1' depending on the number of ON pulses required for a state transition.

To share a bit (x_i) of the key X, Alice would follow the rules R1 and R2 which are given below:

R1. If the *i'th*-bit of the key is 0, distribute the rows of C0' to the users

R2. If the *i'th*-bit of the key is 1 distribute the rows of C1' to the users.

To make a hardware dependent authentication scheme, Alice can choose smaller block length or to pad less number of 1s at the end of C1' for some of the random bits of the key X. Since the users do not own the hardware, they do not know the exact value of NP_i's for a given R_i. Therefore, Alice can share a 0 by sharing contents of C1' for cases where C1' is not properly generated from C1. Thus, it would be impossible for *k*-users (or even all the users) to collude and guess the secret key (X).

To complete the registration phase, Alice would provide each user distinct rows of either C0' or C1' (based on R1 and R2) for every corresponding bit of X along with the respective id of the RRAM used.

3.2.2 Authentication

The authentication process is trivial. Alice would simultaneously accommodate *k* or more users to apply their keys in the circuit shown in Figure 2. For each x_i, Alice will first RESET the corresponding R_i and then accommodate the users to apply their keys. If the total number of ON pulses applied by the users is correct, corresponding device's resistance should be lower than the reference resistance if the key was 1 or higher if the key was 0 (as designed in the registration phase). Alice can check the generated bit with her secret and simultaneously authenticate *k*-users.

3.3 Authentication Hardware

The user keys consist of voltage pulses (ON pulses), which are applied simultaneously to the gate of the respective 1T1R cell as shown in circuit presented in Figure 2. During authentication, Alice keeps V_BL_ALICE to the bit-line voltage used at registration.

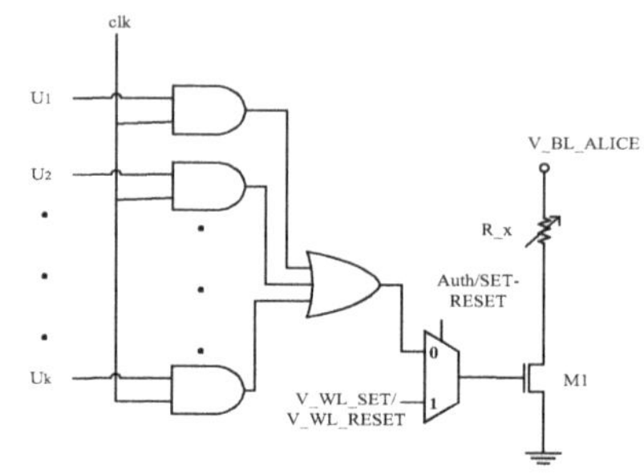

Figure 2. Circuit for applying the pulsed input from k-users.

To reconstruct a key, after the entire user input is received, the authenticator (*e.g,* Alice) applies another ON pulse to V_WL and activates V_BL_REF. We define it as the READ pulse. If R_x is sufficiently lower, then the drain voltage of M1 falls below a certain threshold. This can be sensed using the voltage-mode sense-amplifier-buffer circuitry as shown in Figure 3. Alice can examine the output at V_out during the READ pulse and reconstruct the key bit.

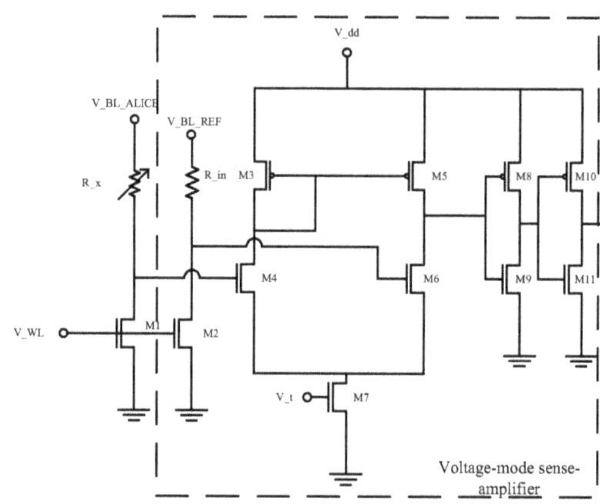

Figure 3. Voltage-mode sense amplifier-buffer circuit for reconstructing the secret.

4. EXPERIMENTS

We have simulated the proposed circuits to understand the effect of physical variations and hardware dependence of the scheme. For these simulations, we have used PTM's 65nm MOSFET models [8] and RRAM models proposed by Guan *et al.* [9]. We have used HSPICE platform for the simulations and MATLAB for calculation and post-processing. Common parameters used for the experiments are presented in table 1.

Table 1. Common parameters used for the experiments presented in this work.

Parameter Name	Value
Clock frequency (f_{clk})	50MHz
V_BL_SET	1.8V
V_WL_SET	1.0V
V_WL_RESET	2.7V
V_BL_RESET	1.9V
R_in	250kΩ
Gap_ini	1.367nm
ΔGap_0	0.05nm

For the given parameters, we find that it requires eight ON pulses (*i.e.,* SET operation) to move the device in question from a high resistive state to the low resistive state. Therefore, after 8 consecutive ON pulse to R_x, one would observe logic 1 at V_out. Since we want Alice to reveal the secret by applying the final ON pulse, a system with block-length of 7 would be required for multi-user authentication. If we consider a 3-out-of-3 user authentication system, then using the constructions provided in [7], we have C0' and C1' respectively as:

$$C0' = \begin{pmatrix} 0001111 \\ 0110011 \\ 0111100 \end{pmatrix}; \quad C1' = \begin{pmatrix} 0001111 \\ 0110011 \\ 1010101 \end{pmatrix}$$

In Figure 4, we have shown how Alice verifies a 1 and a subsequent 0 shared to the participating entities.

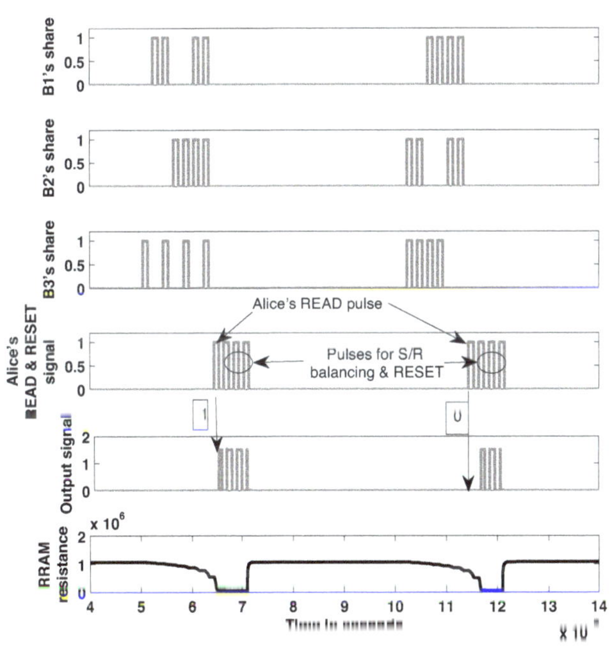

Figure 4. Simultaneous multi-user authentication using RRAM based hardware. Alice verifies a 1 and a 0 shared to the participating entities. The first pulse from Alice is the READ pulse and the three subsequent pulses are for ensuring balanced SET/RESET operation.

Note that, after authentication Alice still needs to apply two consecutive SET pulses for overcoming the SET-RESET balancing problem. SET/RESET unbalancing is a common problem for resistive memory-based circuits and properly balanced operations are required to mitigate this effect. Also, consecutive authentication cycles without properly resetting the device can aggravate the SET/RESET balancing problem as shown in Figure 5. Furthermore, a longer pattern of zeros or ones in the secret can also cause SET/RESET balancing problem.

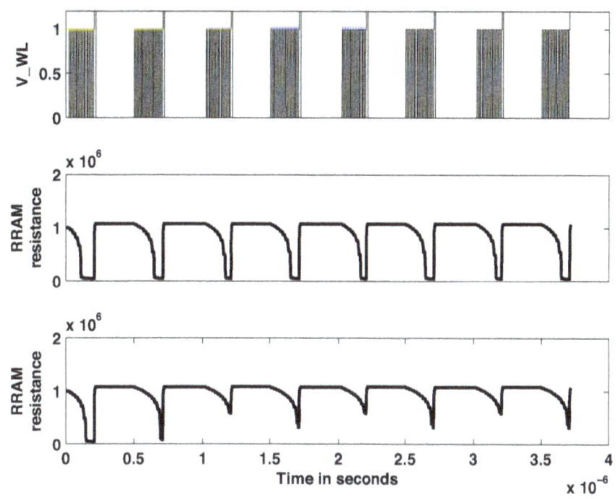

Figure 5. SET/RESET unbalance problem after consecutive authentication cycles. Here, the effect of unbalanced SET voltage in V_BL_SET line is presented. The top plot represents the word line voltage for consecutive authentication cycles. The plot in the middle shows the changes in the RRAM resistance for balanced condition (V_BL_SET=1.8V). The bottom plot shows the effect of unbalanced biasing where the V_BL_SET voltage is lowered by 12mV.

Another weakness of this authentication protocol comes from the adverse effects of noise on the RRAM-based circuits. As noticed in Figure 5, small deviations from SET/RESET voltages can produce significant errors in the reconstructed output. Therefore, the voltage sources that dictate SET and RESET operations should be carefully designed.

As discussed in [6], random filament formation and spatial variations in filament formation can create reliability issues during authentication. Since random fluctuation in the resistive values will void any reliable operation of the device, careful fabrication and testing are required before deploying these devices in a security application. Furthermore, experimental evidence suggests that RESET operations in RRAM devices are more stable and reliable than the SET operations. Therefore, one can choose either HRS-LRS transition or HRS-LRS transition based on the device to ensure more reliable performance. RRAMs with lower endurance values should be eligible for the authentication protocol discussed since each authentication process with [illegible] only corresponds to one read-write cycle. Finally, common factors such as temperature, aging *etc.* that threaten the reliability of RRAMs should be taken into consideration before deploying such hardware.

5. CONCLUSIONS

Non-volatile memory based devices and circuits are monotonic in nature. Exploiting this monotonicity can be useful in designing secure circuits and security protocols. In this work, we have connected the "*additive*" and *monotonic* nature of RRAM devices with secret sharing and simultaneous multi-user authentication ideas. We have reported the designed protocol and the necessary circuits required for multi-user authentication using RRAM based hardware. This robust, hardware dependent multi-user authentication scheme can be useful in designing security primitives in the extremely resource constrained IoT applications.

ACKNOWLEDGMENT

The authors would like to thank Dr. Swarup Bhunia and Dr. Ajay Joshi for their helpful comments. This work was supported by AFOSR MURI under award number FA9550-14-1-0351.

6. REFERENCES

[1] Shamir, Adi. "How to share a secret." *Communications of the ACM* 22.11 (1979): 612-613.

[2] Blakley, George Robert. "Safeguarding cryptographic keys." *AFIPS*. IEEE, 1979.

[3] Stinson, Douglas R. "An explication of secret sharing schemes." *Designs, Codes and Cryptography* 2.4 (1992): 357-390.

[4] Naor, Moni, et al. "Visual cryptography." *Advances in Cryptology—EUROCRYPT'94*. Springer Berlin/Heidelberg, 1995.

[5] Arafin, M. T., et al. "A survey on memristor modeling and security applications." *Quality Electronic Design (ISQED), 2015 16th International Symposium on*. IEEE, 2015.

[6] Arafin, Md Tanvir, and Gang Qu. "RRAM based lightweight user authentication." *Computer-Aided Design (ICCAD), 2015 IEEE/ACM International Conference on*. IEEE, 2015.

[7] Verheul, Eric R., and Henk CA Van Tilborg. "Constructions and properties of k out of n visual secret sharing schemes." *Designs, Codes and Cryptography* 11.2 (1997): 179-196.

[8] Predictive technology model (PTM), http://ptm.asu.edu/

[9] Guan, Ximeng, et al. "A SPICE compact model of metal oxide resistive switching memory with variations." *IEEE electron device letters* 33.10 (2012): 1405-1407.

[10] Wong, H-S. Philip, et al. "Metal–oxide RRAM." *Proceedings of the IEEE* 100.6 (2012): 1951-1970.

[11] Naor, Moni, and Benny Pinkas. "Visual authentication and identification." *Advances in Cryptology—CRYPTO'97*. Springer Berlin Heidelberg, 1997. 322-336.

[12] Qu, Gang, and Lin Yuan. "Design THINGS for the Internet of Things—An EDA perspective." *Computer-Aided Design (ICCAD), 2014 IEEE/ACM International Conference on*. IEEE, 2014.

[13] "Two-person integrity" available online at http://informationtechniciantraining.tpub.com/14222/css/14222_85.htm, pp. 3-9 & 3-10

[14] "How the NSA is preventing another Snowden (and why you should do the same) ", Computer World, Jan. 7, 2014. Available online at http://www.computerworld.com/article/2474270/cybercrime-hacking/how-the-nsa-is-preventing-another-snowden--and-why-you-should-do-the-same-.html

Defense Systems and IoT: Security Issues in an Era of Distributed Command and Control

Doug Palmer
Booz Allen Hamilton
Arlington, Virginia
770-355-5204
palmer_doug@bah.com

Saverio Fazzari
Booz Allen Hamilton
Arlington, Virginia
703-526-1476
fazzari_saverio@bah.com

Scott Wartenberg
Wartenberg Consulting LLC
Vienna, Virginia
703-526-1436
scott.wartenberg.ctr@darpa.mil

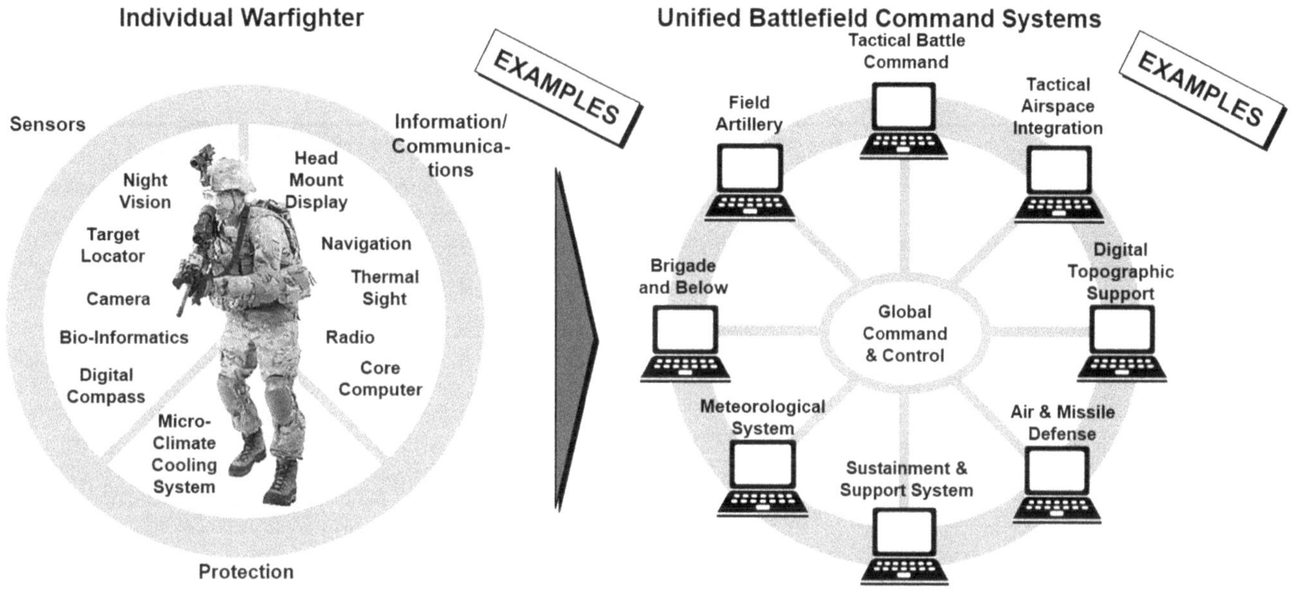

Figure 1. The IoT as It Relates to Integrated Defense Systems

1. INTRODUCTION

Just as the Internet of Things (IoT) stands to revolutionize the way we sense, analyze, and apply data in civilian life, defense systems are also working to enhance future mission capabilities with IoT logic and devices. Recently, Gen. James Cartwright, former vice chairman of the Joint Chiefs of Staff, stated: "The ability to move from number of men per machine to the number of machines per man is the ultimate objective here in a command and control construct." In defense systems, IoT stands to dramatically affect cost, data, and response time advantages through distributed sensing, analysis, and action. This summarizes a key need of the defense community as it relates to IoT: the creation of an organizational construct that allows effective man-machine partnering and action that conforms to the command and culture of the US military (see Figure 1).

The creation and implementation of such a command and control construct presents many security issues. Rather than simply executing direct commands, future swarms of connected devices and machines will receive objectives and interpret at a system level how the devices, sensors, and capabilities work as a team to accomplish the commanded objective. While the individual units have become more attritable, command objectives are increasingly interpreted at the unit level rather than by the warfighter. Greater unit-level interpretation leaves many aspects of the system vulnerable to exploitation.

Counterfeit electronic parts present a key exploitable vulnerability in modern defense systems. While the Department of Defense (DoD) spends billions of dollars each year building new electronic weapon systems, these systems depend on semiconductor parts purchased on the commercial market. In addition, future IoT systems will contain many more semiconductors than before, particularly wireless networking, sensing, and programmable logic devices. Some propose that a solution to ensure security of components is to acquire parts from trusted sources where the foundries are qualified by the US Government. This may work for specialized semiconductor chips but is not practical for every part in the system, particularly in a future where many IoT devices will exponentially expand the number of parts. Testing is required to protect against counterfeit chips but can be expensive to perform in the face of every threat. While the threat of counterfeit semiconductors has been recognized to be real, it's not obvious how much money defense organizations should spend on addressing the problem.

GLSVLSI '16, May 18 - 20, 2016, Boston, MA, USA

ACM 978-1-4503-4274-2/16/05…$15.00
DOI: http://dx.doi.org/10.1145/2902961.2903038

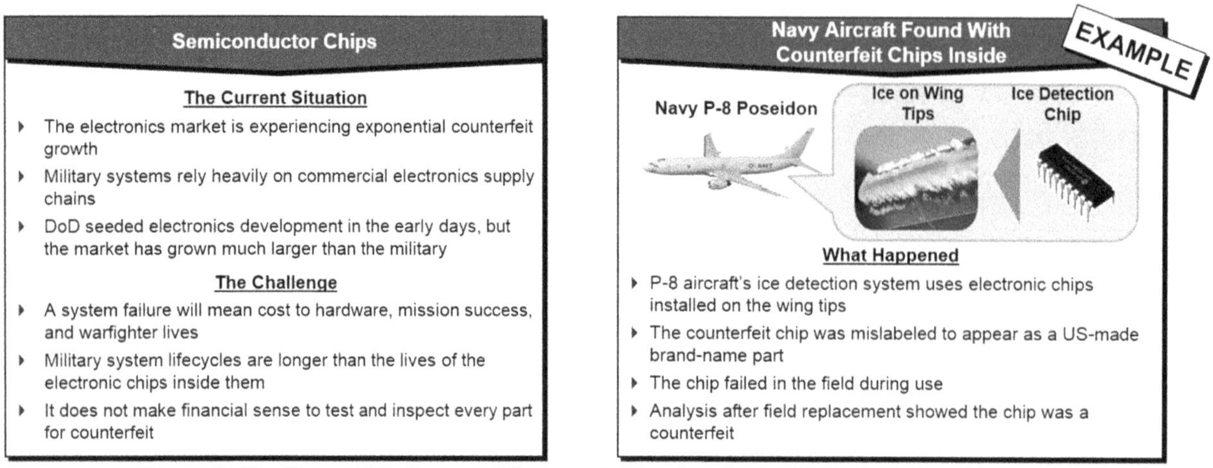

Figure 2. The Use and Challenges of Commercial Semiconductor Chips in Defense Electronics

Program managers struggling with this issue ask: "How do I make acquisition choices that prevent or lessen the chance of a counterfeit electronic chip getting into my system with the information on hand?" To answer this, we need to know two things. First, we need to know the security of the supply chain that provided the part. For instance, who was the vendor the chip was bought from? What is the vendor's reputation and history? Is there travel documentation associated with the part (i.e., any weak links in the supply chain)? How many semiconductor foundries build the same or similar parts (i.e., any threat of substitution)? What is the value of the part (i.e., will counterfeiting be attractive for expensive parts)? The second thing to know is how important the part is to the function of the weapon system. For instance, a decoupling capacitor on a power supply line with many capacitors is less likely to result in a noticeable failure. However, encountering a counterfeit microprocessor that controls critical functions of the system is alarming.

To quantify the problem of counterfeits, it is important to use a statistical method to calculate the risk of encountering a counterfeit semiconductor part in a weapon system. The method should use two sets of data—one covering logistics and another covering technology. The logistics data involves knowing the supply chain for the semiconductor part. For instance, how rigorous was the purchasing department in examining where the part came from? The technical data involves analyzing the part's technical function within the weapon system: the performance of the semiconductor part in relation to the weapon system, the circuit it serves, and how the weapon system relies on the part. By bringing together two major sets of information—supply chain and technical—an actual risk number comes into focus. This risk number is the percentage chance of encountering a counterfeit semiconductor chip in a weapon system. This paper outlines how to quantify the risk of finding a counterfeit semiconductor chip in a weapon system.

2. THE VULNERABILITY TO COUNTERFEIT ELECTRONIC CHIPS

In 2011, an ice detection system on board a new P-8 Poseidon failed (see Figure 2) [1]. The ice detection system serves to alert the pilot of ice forming on the wings. After troubleshooting by Navy and Boeing technicians and engineers, the problem was tracked down to a new semiconductor chip installed in the system. Closer examination of the bad chip revealed the chip wasn't new after all. Rather, the chip was used. It had been plucked from an old, discarded printed circuit board. Unknown to the defense system integrator who had purchased it, the chip had been cleaned up and sold as new via an established supply chain. Further investigation of the supply chain revealed the chip originated in China.

Vulnerabilities like this exist in weapon systems today. This is because modern weapon systems rely on many commercial off-the-shelf electronic chips. Given the complexity of electronic systems, it's simply not practical for defense integrators to custom-make every semiconductor chip in every system. There are specific areas where we can expect threats to increase (see Figure 3). In this environment, how do you protect against the threat of counterfeit chips?

The obvious solution is to test and inspect every chip in the system. However, electrically testing and inspecting for every part is expensive; costs would quickly add up considering the number of chips in every weapon system. Instead, it would make sense to

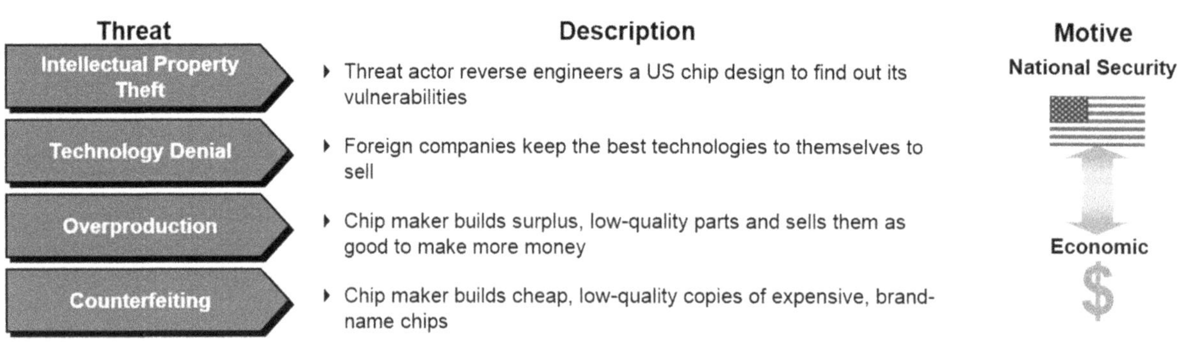

Figure 3. Current and Emerging Threats to Semiconductor Chips

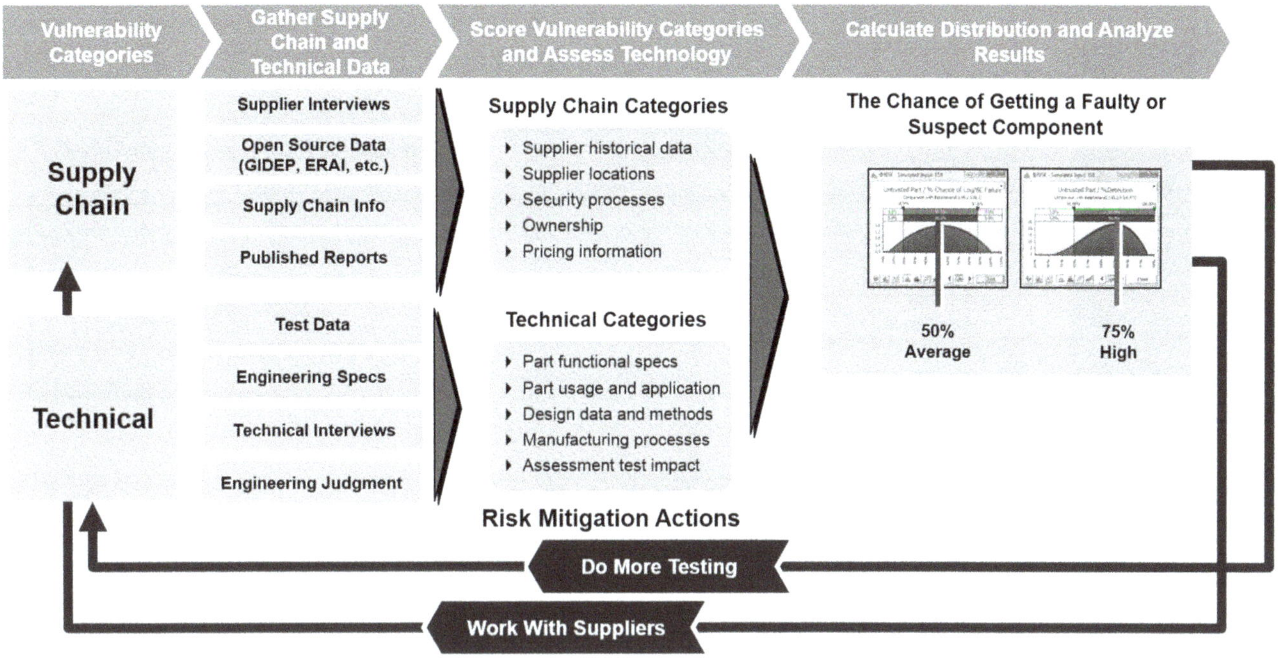

Figure 4. Counterfeit Risk Assessment Methodology

narrow the list of chips to test to those that are critical to the operation of the system. Depending on what the system is designed to do, the system's most important functions typically rely on the performance of a few critical chips. Many of the other chips are not nearly as impactful and would not necessarily lead to catastrophic failure if they go bad. For instance, a decoupling capacitor on a power supply line can fail and go unnoticed, yet its failure when feeding a microprocessor power supply line can bring down the entire system. The importance of the chip depends on the chips involved. It also depends on how the system was designed. Determining the importance of each chip and the system design requires analysis by a circuit designer who can interpret the technical documents (the chip's specification sheets, schematics, etc.) and understand the chip in the context of how the system was designed.

3. USING SUPPLY CHAIN AND TECHNICAL INFORMATION TO QUANTIFY THE RISK OF A COUNTERFEIT CHIP

The risk of a weapon system having a counterfeit chip inside depends on two major factors. The first major factor is *supply chain*—how much the defense integrator knows about the part's past. The second major area is *technical importance* of the chip—what will happen to the defense system if the chip fails. These two major areas can be fully explored by using a rigorous methodology (see Figure 4). Within the methodology, each category of analysis addresses its own set of issues. For instance, supply chain categories include supplier historical data, the locations of the suppliers, their security processes, ownership of each distributor/shipper/manufacturer, and how much the part sells for. Technical categories include the chip's specifications,

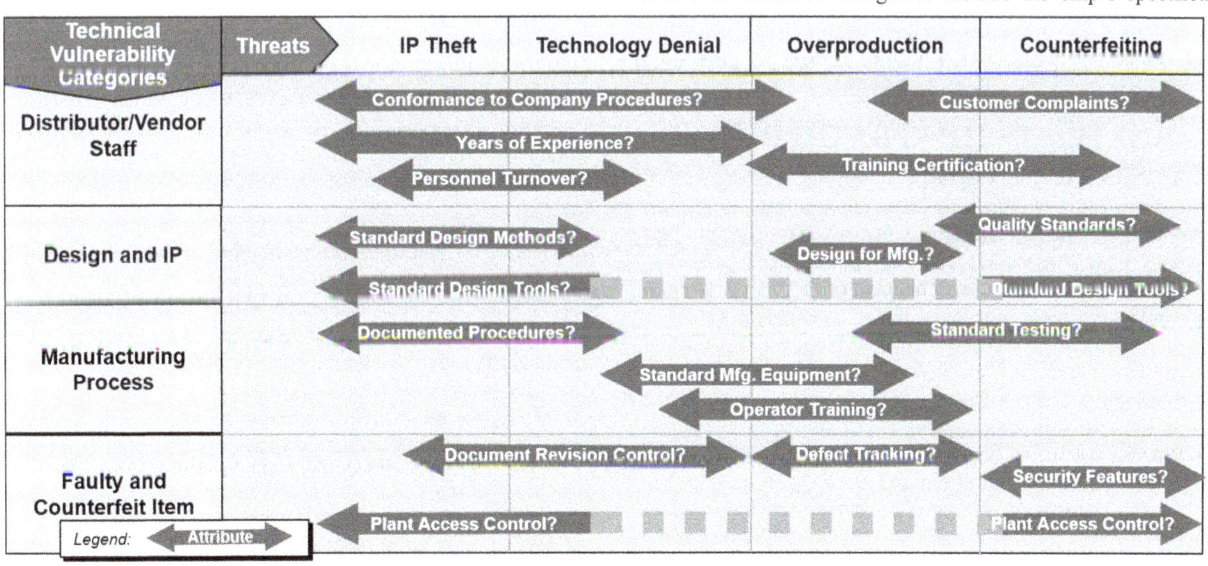

Figure 5. Counterfeit Risk Assessment Methodology: Technical Category and Questions to Uncover Specific Vulnerabilities

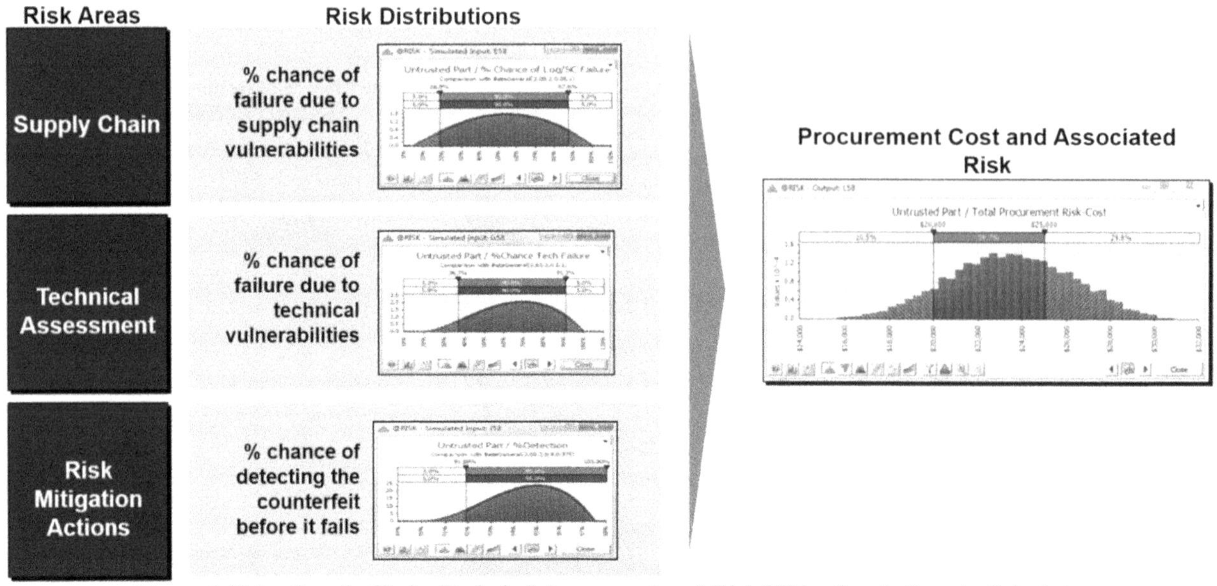

Figure 6. Using Supply Chain, Technical Assessment, and Risk Mitigation Actions to Calculate Counterfeit Risk vs. Procurement Cost

how important the chip is to the system's function, how important the chip is to the function of the circuit board designed around the chip, the complexity of the semiconductor manufacturing process used to make the chip, and the tests used to validate the chip both by the chip maker and by the distributors and shippers handling the chip along the way (see Figure 5). All this information can be brought together within a single framework, scored, and grouped into vulnerability categories. In this way, the objectivity of the approach becomes clear because it's easy to see what information is known and unknown about the chip. This approach also makes it easy to see how the categories and questions are weighted in terms of importance, which maximizes the effectiveness of the methodology.

Most buyers think that purchasing electronic chips from authorized resellers who buy directly from the foundry that manufactured the chip eliminates any need to question the supply chain. Only distributors, resellers, and aftermarket sellers (i.e., brokers) are suspect. In truth, vulnerabilities in the supply chain start at the manufacturer and accumulate as the part is transported from place to place. Even when chips are purchased from the original component manufacturer via an authorized distributor chain, questions should be asked of the supplier.

4. TARGETED TESTING RATHER THAN EXHAUSTIVE TESTING

Specific electrical tests can be done to exercise important functions of the chip. The idea is that testing a few critical chips with a few, targeted electrical tests may be all that's needed to know if the system has a counterfeit. To do this without having to perform every electrical test possible, a technology expert is needed to identify which electrical tests are the most impactful to the system. In general, the impact of an electrical test depends on the functions the system designer expects from the chip and the mission of the chip within the system. A technology expert would also narrow the number of chips to test and reduce the number of electrical tests. This ultimately reduces the cost of testing and maximizes the chances of uncovering a counterfeit chip. While this approach won't guarantee there is no counterfeit chip in the system, knowing the important chips work dramatically lowers the chances of a catastrophic system failure. Passing a few electrical tests does not guarantee that a chip is genuine and not a counterfeit, but passing a targeted set of tests gives the buyer a sense of confidence that the system will work in the ways that are mission critical. If the buyer—a defense system integrator—would like to increase the level of confidence, then additional targeted electrical tests can be done, further increasing the measure of confidence that the chip is real and reliable. Some tests are more expensive than others; however, a expensive more expensive test does not necessarily increase the level of confidence that the chip is not counterfeit.

5. HOW MUCH DOES IT COST TO DEFEND AGAINST A COUNTERFEIT CHIP? WHAT IS THE RETURN ON INVESTMENT?

The cost of testing each and every chip and gathering supply chain information on every one goes up dramatically as we approach 100-percent certification. Given that 100-percent protection against all counterfeits is prohibitively expensive, it would be useful to know how much protection you actually receive for each dollar spent on anti-counterfeit protection. The question becomes how to maximize the money spent on counterfeit protection. The methodology shown in Figure 4 is based on both supply chain and technical information.

Testing electronic parts is expensive and may not buy as much protection as you think. For one thing, it depends on whether or not the test is important to the system. For another, it costs to protect against each and every possible risk. Certain types of counterfeits are rare, yet testing to protect against them costs a lot and may not give much return on investment (ROI). In such cases, the risk versus ROI falls off rapidly. In Figure 6, this ROI is shown as the tail of the distribution represented by red-and-white striped regions.

Shown in Figure 7 is the procurement cost. This is the upfront cost of buying and testing a chip from different suppliers. For instance, a program manager may choose not to test a chip rigorously from a particular supplier, meaning the system is taking

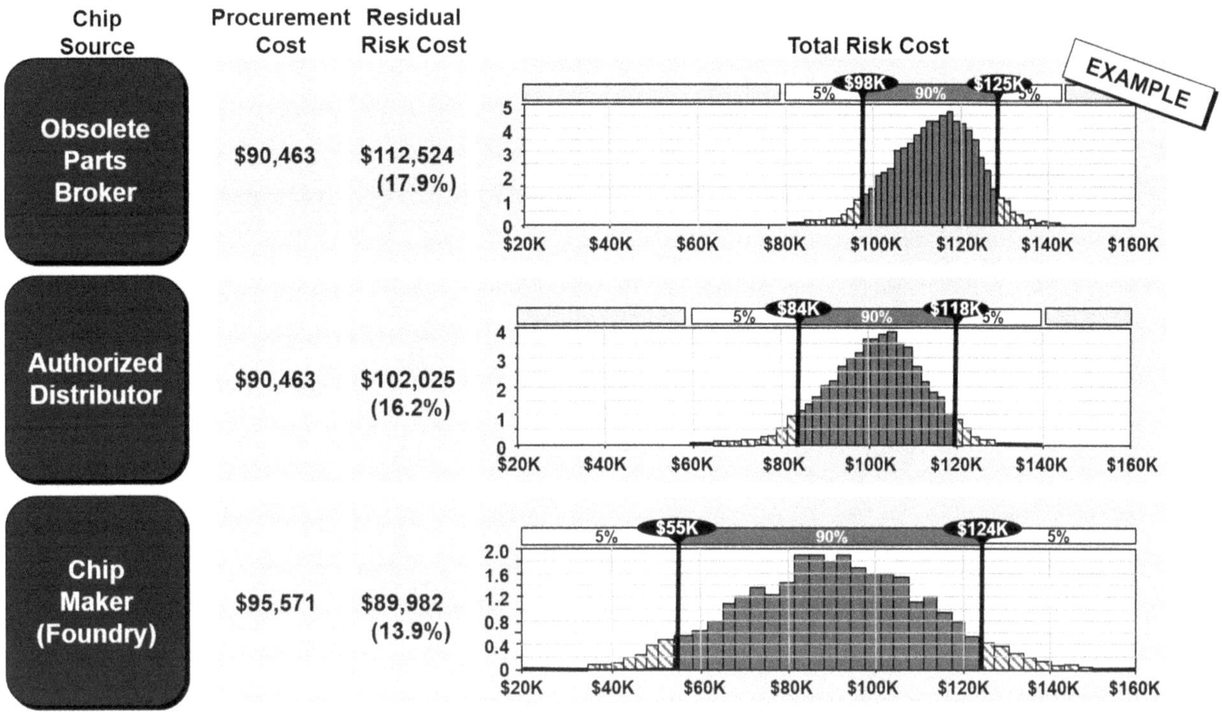

Figure 7. Comparing Procurement Costs, Residual Risks, and Resulting Distribution of Cost Versus Risk for Various Chip Sources

on more risk. This means some inherent risk is being accepted by the program. If it turns out the part is counterfeit, there will be costs associated with replacing the part in the field. This replacement cost is captured as the residual risk cost. Replacing a part in the field is expensive because it requires maintenance personnel to take down the system, troubleshoot the problem, and replace the part. Compared to this, testing a chip upfront is cheaper than replacing a part in the field. Hence, there's a tradeoff between the supplier selected, the testing performed, the chance of encountering a counterfeit chip, and the cost of replacing a part in the field. Statistical methods can be brought to bear to calculate the total risk cost. The total risk cost is a statistical distribution around a mean value. In Figure 7, all three statistical distributions capture 90% of the counterfeits for a defined scenario of tests performed, supplier information that is known, and estimated replacement costs. The distribution will shift if different tests are selected. Furthermore, the distribution narrows as more information becomes available. This method can also show the cost and risk impact when alternative tests are chosen.

6. SUMMARY

Hardware assurance will become even more crucial in future connected defense systems, particularly when the systems are interpreting a limited set of objective-based instructions from a small number of controllers. New segments of the system functionality will be susceptible to exploitation, including increased wireless communications, sensor data, and programmable logic. To prevent counterfeit electronic chips from turning up in weapon systems, the easiest solution is to do more testing. However, a little spending on few, specific tests may protect just as well. Using statistical methods with technical and supply chain analysis will quantify decisions on counterfeit risk so the program manager has some idea of the cost-versus-risk tradeoffs.

An efficient approach combines supplier input with technical analysis to statistically forecast the risk of counterfeits, including testing strategies to mitigate the risk. Two areas are important: supply chain and technical analysis. First, incorporating the latest supply chain information is important to clarify gaps in global supply chain information. This information should also be updated as supply chains evolve and new tracking capabilities become available. Second, technical analysis leverages an understanding of the electronics industry, the importance of the chip, and the importance of choosing the right tests. Taken together, this information can be put into a statistical framework to give a quantitative measure of the risk of encountering a counterfeit chip and the effectiveness of testing strategies to mitigate this risk.

7. REFERENCES (HEADING 1)

[1] Reed J. "Counterfeit Parts Found on P-8 Poseidons." *Defense Tech.* (Accessed Nov 8, 2011). DOI: http://www.defensetech.org/2011/11/08/counterfeit-parts-found-on-new-p-8-poseidons/

Security Meets Nanoelectronics for Internet of Things Applications

Garrett S. Rose
The University of Tennessee
Department of Electrical Engineering and Computer Science
Knoxville, Tennessee 37996 USA
garose@utk.edu

ABSTRACT

The internet of things (IoT) is quickly emerging as the next major domain for embedded computer systems. Although the term IoT could be defined in a variety of different ways, IoT always encompasses typically ordinary devices (e.g., thermostats and kitchen appliances) augmented with computational power that allows regular communication via the internet. Given the simplicity of typical IoT devices, their on-board computer systems must also be simple in the sense that they be small and consume minimal power. However, the IoT itself presents new privacy and security concerns that must be considered when designing IoT devices. In order to provide robust security with minimal area and power overhead, it is the premise of this paper that IoT security be implemented using nanoelectronic security primitives and nano-enabled security protocols. Such nanoscale security primitives are expected to utilize a very small amount of area and consume a negligible amount of power, all while providing the required levels of security. This paper presents some examples of nanoelectronic security primitives and discusses how such circuits and systems can be of use for inclusion in emerging IoT devices.

CCS Concepts

•**Security and privacy** → *Embedded systems security; Hardware security implementation;* •**Hardware** → *Emerging architectures;*

Keywords

Hardware security; Nanoelectronics; Internet of Things

1. INTRODUCTION

The ever growing "internet of things" (IoT) presents many exciting possibilities in terms of simplifying the way we live. At the same time, allowing everyday devices, some with intimate access to our personal lives, access to the internet

GLSVLSI '16, May 18-20, 2016, Boston, MA, USA

DOI: http://dx.doi.org/10.1145/2902961.2903045

presents profound security and privacy concerns. For example, many of us now use fitness devices that track our daily activity, heart rate and other vital statistics. Such devices have proven useful for many who want to lose weight or simply lead healthier lifestyles. However, these benefits come at the cost of personal information being shared over public channels, in this case the internet. Certainly, security features for such applications are important and security must be a first class design consideration when implementing IoT devices. Even hardware security concerns, such as counterfeiting and piracy, are important in that end users need the ability to trust the authenticity of their IoT devices.

It is also important to note that most IoT devices (e.g., a fitness wristband) are small, wireless and operate using limited battery supply. The resource limits of the IoT devices themselves leads to the need for security mechanisms that consume as little power as possible and rely on area-efficient hardware security primitives. The emergence of novel nanoscale electronic technologies (e.g., memristors, carbon nanotubes, graphene) offers the potential for constructing such small-scale, energy-efficient security primitives. Thus, it is the premise of this paper that IoT security be implemented using nanoelectronic security primitives as a way of managing the overall overhead required.

As technology scales further into the nanometer regime, several research groups have started to consider the implementation of security primitives using nanoelectronic technologies, such as metal-oxide memristors (a conjunction of "memory resistors") [7, 1, 3]. A common example that has been explored extensively in the last 2-3 years is the idea of memristor based physical unclonable functions (PUFs). For example, a PUF based on the write-time of a memristor was first proposed by Rose *et al.* [6]. An experimental realization of this design was later presented by Mazady *et al.* [4], substantiating the concept of memristor-based security primitives. As another example, Kavehei *et al.* presented a combination of memristors and ring-oscillator (RO) PUFs named mrPUF[3]. Rose *et al.* later extended the idea of the write-time memristive PUF by proposing a PUF constructed from a dense crossbar array of memristive devices, the memristive crossbar PUF (XbarPUF)[5]. Because the XbarPUF depends on the relative write-time of pairs of memristive circuits, it does not require exact knowledge or control of the minimum write-time of the device. The XbarPUF is discussed in some detail in this work as an example of a low-overhead security primitive that could be useful for IoT devices.

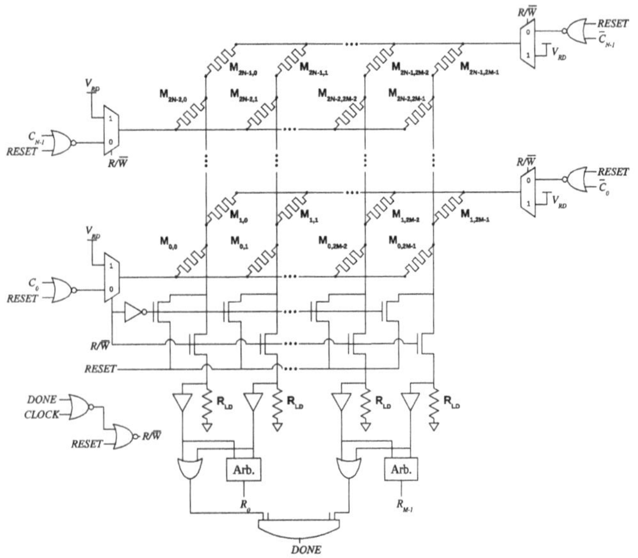

Figure 1: Schematic of the proposed crossbar-memristive PUF design for N configuration and M response bits. The design as proposed requires a memristive crossbar of size $2N \times 2M$ including $4NM$ total memristors [5].

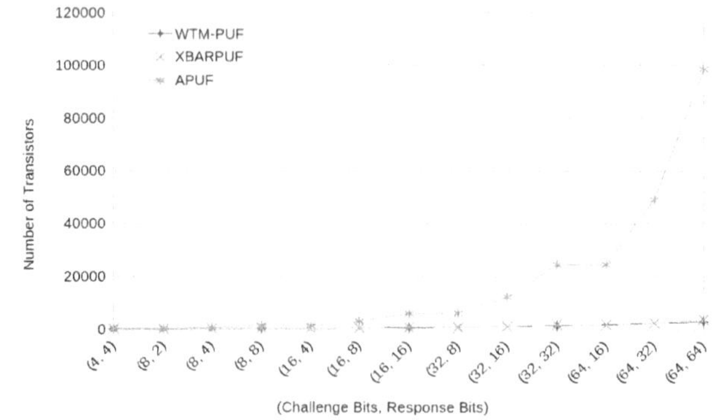

Figure 2: Plot of area (transistor count) vs. number of challenge and response bits for three different PUF designs. CMOS APUF area increases quadratically in area while the memristive PUF designs only require a linear increase in the number of transistors [5].

2. A CASE EXAMPLE: THE MEMRISTIVE CROSSBAR PUF

The memristive crossbar PUF (shown in Fig. 1 and described in [5]) is based on the write-time memristive PUF (WTMPUF) first described in [6]. As with the WTMPUF, the XbarPUF's primary entropy source is the minimum time it takes for memristors to SET during a write operation. Additionally, the XbarPUF is somewhat a reimagining of the arbiter PUF (APUF) [2] in the sense that the "racing" when writing to pairs of memristive circuits is analogous to racing delay paths. More specifically, for each challenge bit, there are two corresponding rows of memristors: one written based on the challenge bit and another by the inverted challenge bit. If the challenge bit is high, then memristors driven by the true challenge bit are incrementally SET while those driven by the inverted challenge bit remain in the HRS. Likewise, a low or '0' challenge bit causes the memristors driven by the inverted challenge bit to SET while the others remain in the HRS. This ensures one row will be actively written to while the other remains inactive (remains at HRS) during the write operation. To generate each response bit, two columns are compared during a write. The current from both colums, dependent on all memristors connected to the columns, are pulled down over identical loads. Once the output of one column reaches a certain threshold the arbiter selects a "winner" which determines the corresponding response bit. More detail on the operation of the XbarPUF is provided in [5].

The performance of the XbarPUF is similar to that of the WTMPUF, while removing the dependency on a precise write-time. Additionally, the XbarPUF has comparable performance to that of the APUF, while decreasing the transistor count (Fig. 2). For the transistor count of the APUF, we make the assumption that we want all response bits simultaneously, as opposed to computing them over multiple cycles, due to the difference in nature of the different PUF designs. A comparison of the three PUF designs (CMOS APUF, WTMPUF, XbarPUF) in terms of transistor count can be seen in Fig. 2. Due to the constraint of single-cycle response generation, the APUF transistor count is quadratic with the number of challenge-response bits while that of the two memristive PUF designs is linear. This is an expected result as the entropy source for the memristive PUFs is the memristor itself which isn't being counted toward the area even though the XbarPUF does include a quadratic number of memristors as a function of number of challenge-response bits.

In the context of the internet of things, a PUF has the potential to provide security enhancements in the form of robust authentication or secret key generation. It is worth mentioning that challenges do exist. For example, PUF responses are not 100% consistent/reliable in the sense that some response bits could flip over time. This less than perfect reliability is particularly undesirable for applications such as secret key generation for encryption engines since cryptographic algorithms are not typically tolerant to imperfect keys, by design. That said, solutions utilizing error correction [8] have been proposed that can deal with this particular issue, thus making PUFs viable options as emerging hardware security primitives.

For IoT devices, it is important to note that area utilization and power consumption for any security mechanism must be minimal. As can be seen from Fig. 2, the XbarPUF utilizes a very small amount of area relative to similar circuits implemented using CMOS, in this case the arbiter PUF. This is an expected result since the entropy source in the case of the XbarPUF is based on memristive devices that are integrated into the crosspoints of a dense array of nanowires that exist in the back-end-of-line (BEOL) metal layers of a typical CMOS process. In addition to area improvements, the XbarPUF was shown to consume a small amount of power and this power consumption is expected to be further reduced as memristor technology scales [5].

The area and power advantages of security primitives, specifically PUFs, such as the XbarPUF are not as convincing when considering the need for mechanisms such as error correction. Certainly, any error correction code implemented in hardware could be expensive in terms of area and even software solutions will consume more power than desired. One solution that has been proposed recently is the idea of a weak memristive PUF where error correction is not needed [1]. Of course, the potential advantages gained depend on the required security applications.

3. CONCLUSIONS

This paper makes the argument that nanoelectronic hardware should be considered for the implementation of security primitives and protocols in emerging IoT devices. The rationale being that IoT devices are resource limited and nanoelectronic technologies can be leveraged as a way of implementing small, energy-efficient security mechanisms. As an example, the crossbar memristive PUF is described, primarily from the perspective of the area saved relative to CMOS-based counterparts. Since memristors are dense, two-terminal devices, the area and power savings can be quite considerable. However, many of the same challenges remain for nanoscale PUFs as exist for CMOS-based PUF implementations. Specifically, reliability and the need for error correction could offset the area and power savings when using nanoscale PUF circuits. Thus, future work should include the development of more resource efficient techniques for improving the reliability of nanoelectronic security primitives.

4. ACKNOWLEDGMENTS

The author would like to thank Mesbah Uddin and Md. Badruddoja Majumder, both of the University of Tennessee, Knoxville, for stimulating discussions and related contributions.

5. REFERENCES

[1] W. Che, J. Plusquellic, and S. Bhunia. A non-volatile memory based physically unclonable function without helper data. In *Proceedings of the 2014 IEEE/ACM International Conference on Computer-Aided Design*, pages 148–153, 2014.

[2] B. Gassend, D. Clarke, M. van Dijk, and S. Devadas. Silicon physical random functions. In *Proceedings of the 9th ACM Conference on Computer and Communications Security*, pages 148–160, 2002.

[3] O. Kavehei, C. Hosung, D. Ranasinghe, and S. Skafidas. mrPUF: A Memristive Device based Physical Unclonable Function. *Phys. Lett.*

[4] A. Mazady, H. Manem, M. Rahman, D. Forte, and M. Anwar. Memristor puf - a security primitive: Theory and experiment. *IEEE Journal on Emerging and Selected Topics in Circuits and Systems*, 5(8):222–229, June 2015.

[5] G. Rose and C. Meade. Performance analysis of a memristive crossbar puf design. In *52nd ACM/EDAC/IEEE Design Automation Conference (DAC)*, pages 1–6, June 2015.

[6] G. S. Rose, N. McDonald, L. Yan, and B. Wysocki. A write-time based memristive puf for hardware security applications. In *Proceedings of the IEEE/ACM International Conference on Computer-Aided Design (ICCAD)*, pages 830–833, November 2013.

[7] G. S. Rose, N. McDonald, L. Yan, B. Wysocki, and K. Xu. Foundations of memristor based puf architectures. In *Proceedings of the IEEE/ACM International Symposium on Nanoscale Architectures (NANOARCH)*, pages 52–57, July 2013.

[8] G. Suh and S. Devadas. Physical unclonable functions for device authentication and secret key generation. In *44th ACM/EDAC/IEEE Design Automation Conference (DAC)*, pages 9–14, June 2007.

Tracking Data Flow at Gate-Level through Structural Checking

Thao Le, Jia Di
University of Arkansas
{tpl001, jdi}@uark.edu

Mark Tehranipoor, Domenic Forte
University of Florida
{tehranipoor, dforte}@ece.ufl.edu

Lei Wang
University of Connecticut
leiwang@engr.uconn.edu

ABSTRACT

The rapid growth of Internet-of-things and other electronic devices make a huge impact on how and where data travel. The confidential data (e.g., personal data, financial information) that travel through unreliable channels can be exposed to attackers. In hardware, the confidential data such as secret cipher keys are facing the same issue. This problem is even more serious when the IP is from a 3rd party and contains scan-chains. Thus, data flow tracking is important to analyze possible leakage channels in fighting against such hardware security threats. This paper introduces a method for tracking data flow and detecting potential hardware Trojans in gate-level soft IPs using assets and *Structural Checking* tool.

Keywords

Data Flow Tracking; Hardware Security; Structural Checking; Asset; Trojan Detection.

1. INTRODUCTION

Billions of devices are expected to connect to the Internet as Internet-of-things (IoT) in the near future. The advanced integrated circuit (IC) manufacturing processes allow for a highly complex computing system to be packed on a single chip for such IoT devices. At the same time, systems designed from 3rd party IPs and the mass production of ICs reduce the cost of System-on-Chips (SoCs). However, this lowered cost brings security threats such as 3rd party IP trust. Since hardware is the foundation for other system components to be built on, not only must these systems have their own defense against software and network attacks, but the hardware itself must also possess additional defense against hardware-specific threats. Hardware Trojans have been considered a major threat to the IC industry. Trojans can cause information leakage, data tampering, and denial-of-service without the end user's knowledge. Hardware Trojans can be categorized by traits such as physical, activation and action [1]. There are many methods to detect hardware Trojans in ASIC design flow. In [2]-[4], a Trojan is detected in an abstract level. At the physical level, [5]-[8]

GLSVLSI '16, May 18-20, 2016, Boston, MA, USA
 ISBN 978-1-4503-4274-2/16/05...$15.00
DOI: http://dx.doi.org/10.1145/2902961.2903040

proposed techniques to detect Trojans using thermal, power measurement, and switching activities.

A part of fighting against hardware Trojan threats is protecting the integrity of data. The spurious data attack performed in [14] and [15] can compromise the entire critical system such as smart power grid. Therefore, it is important to check the integrity of the sensitive data at many levels. Recent works include tracking data flow in abstract programming language [9] and the gate-level information flow tracking (GIFT) [10]. SHIFT in [11] and DIFT in [12] are two other information flow tracking approaches that mitigate real time buffer-overflow vulnerability. GIFT provides multiple security lattices for analysis and logic verification using taint method. Different from GIFT, the *Structural Checking* tool uses assets to analyze the flow of an untrusted gate-level netlist and detect the possible data leakage. This paper includes a brief overview of assets, the *Structural Checking* tool and explains how the *Structural Checking* tool tracks the flow of information in the netlist of an unknown soft IP.

2. BACKGROUND

2.1 Asset Concept Overview

The term "asset" refers to a signal's property. A signal of a circuitry may have one or more properties. Thus, one or more assets are given to a signal of a gate-level netlist. This concept of assets was first introduced in [3].

2.1.1 External Assets

A primary I/O port signal of a netlist has one or more external assets. External assets are manually assigned by a user. The user can select multiple signals that have the same property and give them an appropriate asset. Currently, external assets are differentiated by 4 categories: data, system control, timing and miscellaneous assets.

2.1.1.1 Data Assets

The data asset category is devoted to data signals. In this category there are five specific assets and one general data asset. Five specific data assets are *DATA_COMPUTATIONAL*, *DATA_COMMUNICATION*, *DATA_ENCRYPTION*, *DATA_MEMORY*, *DATA_PERIPHERAL*, and the general data asset is *DATA_SENSISTIVE*. For example, based on the analyzed IP's description, the user should assign *DATA_SENSITIVE* asset to the plain text primary input signals and the *DATA_ENCRYPTION* asset to the primary cipher output signals of an encryption netlist.

2.1.1.2 System Control Assets

The system control asset is devoted to signals that operate a system. There are 13 specific and one general system control asset. However, in this paper the *MODE*, *RESET*, *SHIFT*, *SCAN_ENABLE* assets are the main focus. For example, a reset signal has the *RESET* asset. Since this signal does not contribute other properties to the overall circuitry, it should not have any other asset.

2.1.1.3 Timing Assets

This category covers the timing signals of a system. The timing category include assets such as *SYSTEM_TIMING*, *READY* and *COUNT*. For example, the *clk* signal has *SYSTEM_TIMING* asset, and the *data_valid_in* signal has *READY* asset.

2.1.1.4 Miscellaneous Assets

This category includes any asset that does not belong to other categories such as *ENCRYPTION_KEY*, *CRITICAL* and *STATE*. For example, for any system that contains an encryption unit, it is important for users to assign *ENCRYPTION_KEY* asset to cipher key signals.

2.1.2 Internal Assets

Internal assets are classified into 2 types. One is used for register-transfer level (RTL) structures and is automatically assigned to internal signals and port signals. The other type is used for gate-level netlist and requires users to assign manually. In this paper, the second type of the internal asset is the main focus, and it consists of *CONTROLLABLE*, *OBSERVABLE* and *PROTECTED* assets.

- *CONTROLLABLE* asset – the signal is controllable during test mode
- *OBSERVABLE* asset – the signal is observable during test mode
- *PROTECTED* asset – the signal is trusted

For example, users are able to choose a scan flip flop cell to assign *CONTROLLABLE* and *OBSERVABLE* assets; the assets are then automatically assigned to other instances of this standard scan flip flop cell.

2.2 Structural Checking Overview

The *Structural Checking* software analyzes RTL code to detect hardware Trojans [2]. *Structural Checking* is developed with the ability to analyze scan chain inserted soft IPs. The tool operates in 4 steps as shown in Figure 1 – VHDL parsing, asset assignment, asset filtering, and data flow tracking analysis. The VHDL parsing process first compiles an unknown VHDL gate-level code (denoted as *X*) in order to build *X*'s primary signals, internal signal nets, and logic gates. After the parsing process, users are able to assign assets to primary port signals and internal signals. The graphical interface of the tool helps navigate users through each of these processes. A set of rules for external and internal assets built into the *Structural Checking* tool determines what asset(s) can or cannot be passed from one signal to another. During the asset filtering process, the tool applies the built-in set of rules to filter asset(s) from inputs to outputs and vice versa. Finally, the *Structural Checking* tool uses scenarios to track information flow for potential data leakage. *Structural Checking* can be useful to track data flow of a soft IP in a short amount of time since it does not simulate the IP's functionality. Through the nets between primary inputs and outputs (I/O) of a soft IP, an asset from an input can be filtered throughout the circuit and reveals the outputs that it affects. Because of this nature of the tool, several data flow analysis methods have been developed to detect information leakage in soft IPs.

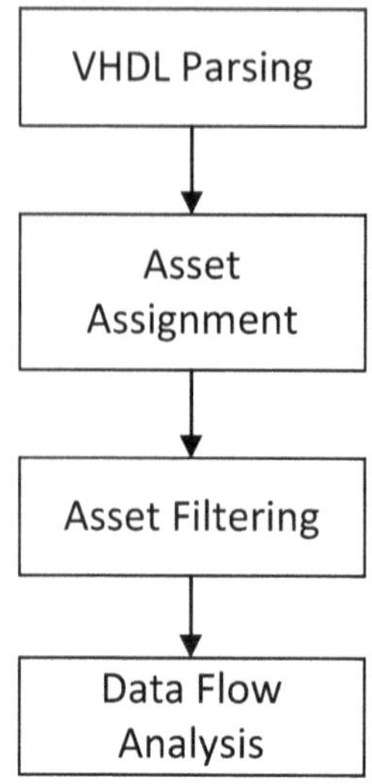

Figure 1. Structural Checking tool flow chart.

For further demonstration of how the *Structural Checking* tool analyzes *X*, a sample *X* design is shown in Figure 2. After the parsing process, the tool has a detailed port map of gates consisting of primary signals and internal signal connections. The *DATA_COMMUNICATION* asset is assigned to input signal *A*. The *DATA_MEMORY* asset is assigned to input signal *B*, and the *CONSTANT* asset is assigned to signal *CIN*. During the filtering process, *Structural Checking* tool starts at the input signal *A*, it then checks what signal that signal A is driving. In this case, signal *A* and signal *B* is driving internal signal *n4*. Hence, the tool gives signal *n4* the *DATA_COMMUNICATION* asset and marks the asset as a filtered asset. It then continues to check what signals *n4* is driving. In this example, the signal *n4* is driving signal *COUT*, and thus the signal COUT receives a *DATA_ COMMUNICATION* asset. The same filtering process applies to signal *B* and *CIN*. Table 1 shows assets that assigned and filtered to all signals of this example.

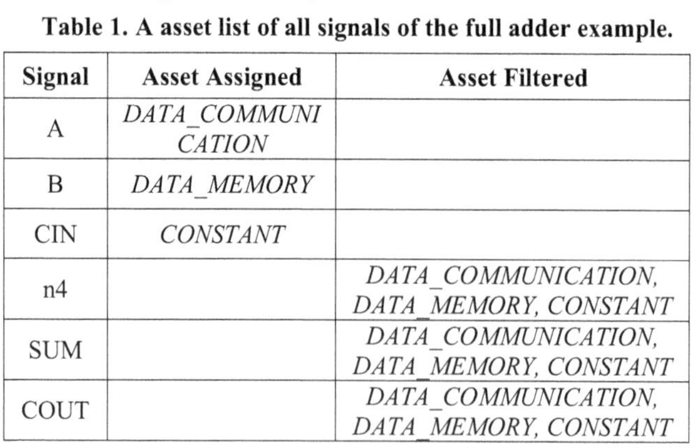

Figure 2. A sample *X* circuit – full adder.

Table 1. A asset list of all signals of the full adder example.

Signal	Asset Assigned	Asset Filtered
A	*DATA_COMMUNICATION*	
B	*DATA_MEMORY*	
CIN	*CONSTANT*	
n4		*DATA_COMMUNICATION, DATA_MEMORY, CONSTANT*
SUM		*DATA_COMMUNICATION, DATA_MEMORY, CONSTANT*
COUT		*DATA_COMMUNICATION, DATA_MEMORY, CONSTANT*

3. DATA FLOW TRACKING ANALYSIS

Currently there are three application scenarios developed for the *Structural Checking* tool. These application scenarios were created under the assumption that scan chain IP *X* may contain malicious internal signals and/or logic which lead to information leakage.

3.1 Scenario 1 Flow

The key concept of scenario 1 is to raise awareness to the user about malicious internal signals which can affect the critical signals that operate the system. The flow of scenario 1 (see Figure 3) starts with checking if the *scan_enable* signal is assigned by an internal signal. If this occurs, the *Structural Checking* tool continues to check if the signal contains any asset in the system control category. For example, the *scan_enable* signal is assigned to an AND gate with another internal signal *n500*, and *n500* is assigned by '1'. Logically, *n500* does not affect *scan_enable*'s function but the presence of an extra logic gate and a signal is unusual and needs to be examined by the user. Thus, a report of suspicious internal signals is generated. In a similar case, the signal *n500* is assigned by a *reset* signal which has a *RESET* asset through an inverter, hence the *n500* signal is not suspicious. An example of the scenario 1 report is indicated in a frame in Figure 5.

3.2 Scenario 2 Flow

The concept of scenario 2 is to track the confidential data flow and raises awareness to the end user. Cipher key signals are considered as confidential data, and they are given the *ENCRYPTION_KEY* asset by the end user. The *Structural Checking* tool then checks if the nets that the *ENCRYPTION_KEY* asset is filtered to also have the *OBSERVABLE* asset. If the nets have the *OBSERVABLE* asset, the tool continues to check if those nets also have *PROTECTED* assets. If the conditions above are not met, the tool reports those as suspicious observable nets.

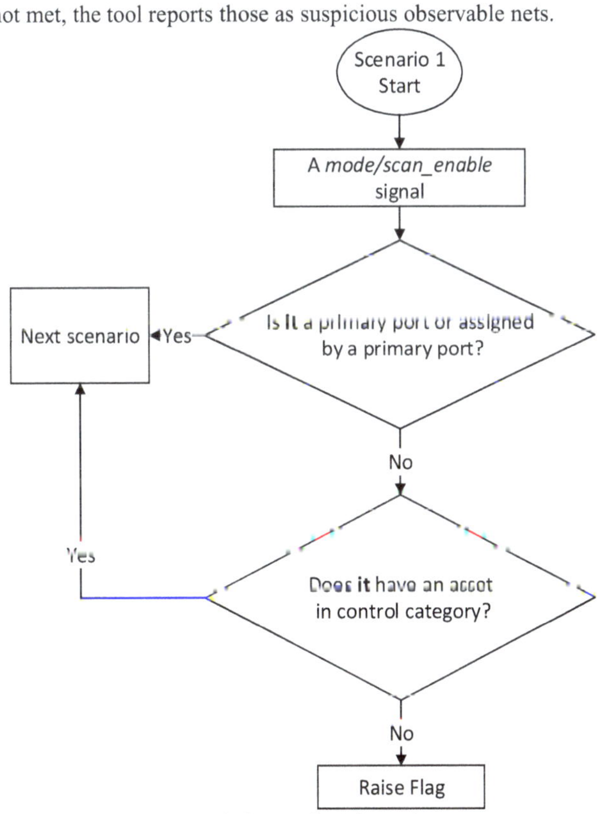

Figure 3. Scenario 1 flow chart.

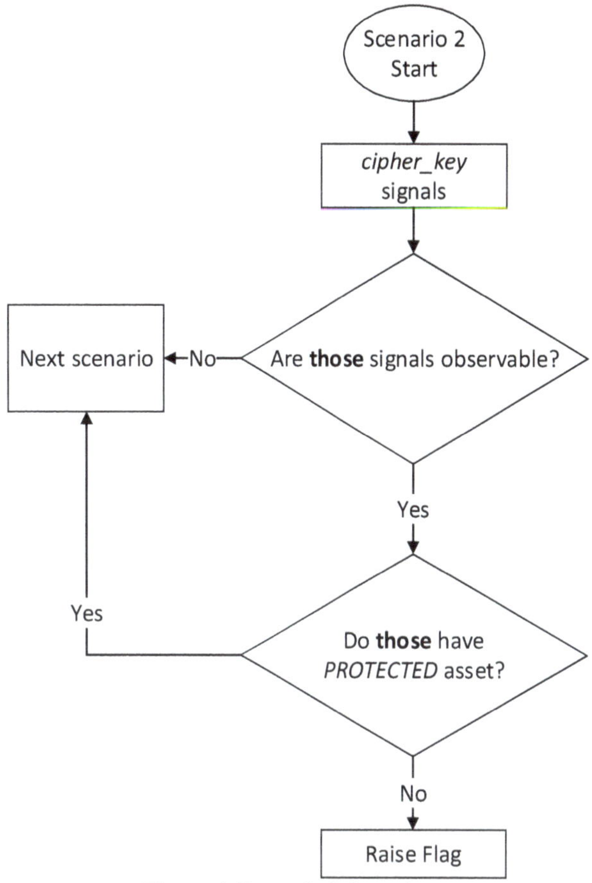

Figure 4. Scenario 2 flow chart.

A suspicious signal with M/SE asset: n500
The instance has observable net: valid_out_reg
The observable signal leaks a KEY is: Q
The instance has observable net: valid_out_reg
The observable signal leaks a KEY is: QN
The instance has observable net: data_out_reg_3_inst
The observable signal leaks a KEY is: Q
The instance has observable net: data_out_reg_3_inst
The observable signal leaks a KEY is: QN
The instance has observable net: data_out_reg_2_inst
The observable signal leaks a KEY is: Q
The instance has observable net: data_out_reg_2_inst
The observable signal leaks a KEY is: QN
The instance has observable net: data_out_reg_1_inst
The observable signal leaks a KEY is: Q
The instance has observable net: data_out_reg_0_inst
The observable signal leaks a KEY is: QN
The instance has observable net: data_out_reg_0_inst
The observable signal leaks a KEY is: QN

Figure 5. An example report of Scenario 1 and Scenario 2.

3.3 Scenario 3 Flow

The purpose of scenario 3 is to detect possible critical data being bypassed. The scenario 3 concept assumes the end user integrates his/her own IPs with another 3rd party IP. The user's IPs are considered trustable. Hence, signals from those trustable IPs have the *PROTECTED* asset. It is important to record all the possible data paths that connect to *PROTECTED* assets signals because suspicious data could potentially disable the trusted entity. For example, system X has an encryption unit integrated. The user knows that this encryption entity is trusted, thus assigns the *PROTECTED* asset to port signals of this entity. The *Structural Checking* tool records all possible data paths from primary inputs to primary outputs of X. It then reports to the user if the signals with the *PROTECTED* asset are on any of these data paths.

A second assumption of scenario 3 is that the end user wants to track data flow from a 3rd party IP only. Thus, the user does not assign the *PROTECTED* asset to any signal. In this case, the *Structural Checking* tool reveals all possible data paths that contain observable nets within the system.

4. A COMPREHENSIVE EXAMPLE

Consider a small gate-level netlist as shown in Figure 6. This netlist is a small section of a 128-bit pipeline AES from [13]. This netlist also has a scan chain inserted. An AND gate is inserted to illustrate Scenario 1 (refer to Section 3.1). After the VHDL parsing process is complete, all signals of X should be given appropriate external and internal assets.

For Scenario 1, the *test_se* signal is given the *SCAN_ENABLE* asset. Since *test_se* and *n500* signal are both assigned to the inputs of AND gate U11, the *Structural Checking* tool filters the *SCAN_ENABLE* asset to the signal *n500*. It then checks if the *n500* signal is a port signal. The result is shown in Figure 5. The flow in Scenario 2 is similar to the flow of scenario 1 because the *ENCRYPTION_KEY* asset is given to all *round_key* signals, and the *OBSERVABLE* asset is given to the Q and QN signal of the gate SDFFAR. The *PROTECTED* asset is not given to signal *round_key* in order to activate Scenario 2. The report of the Scenario 2 is also shown in Figure 5. Lastly, the *data_in*, *data_out* and *test_si* signals are given a *DATA_SENSITIVE* asset. The *PROTECTED* asset is not given to any signal so the tool shows all possible data paths in Figure 7. Moreover, signals' names quoted with "<" and ">" are observable signals. In Figure 7, the first 10 rows show the direct data path from input *data_in* to output *data_out,* and from input *test_si* to *data_out(0)*. The last 8 rows in Figure 7 show that the unknown design X has a chain of register. Signals *n_8540 – n_8543* also appear because they are internal signals assigned to each unused port QN of the scan flip flop SDFFAR.

5. CONCLUSION

In conclusion, this paper presents the concept of data flow tracking and malicious signal detection in a scan-enabled gate-level netlist using *Structural Checking* with assets. The three scenarios' implementations are proof of concept models, and they have been tested on a relatively small gate-level netlist. Scenario 3 can be improved by reporting unused signals that connect to data paths of the system. More scenarios can be added to the tool such as revealing data paths that do not have direct correlation to the primary output.

6. ACKNOWLEDGEMENTS

This research is sponsored by Semiconductor Research Corporation.

7. REFERENCES

[1] M. Tehranipoor and F. Koushanfar. A Survey of Hardware Trojan Taxonomy and Detection. In *Design & Test*. IEEE, vol. PP, pp. 1-1, 2013

[2] J. Yust, M. Hinds and J. Di. Structural Checking: Detecting Malicious Logic without a Golden Reference. *In Journal of Computational Intelligence and Electronic Systems*, vol. 1, no. 2, p. 169177, 2012.

[3] M. Hinds, J. Brady and J. Di. Signal Assets - a Useful Concept for Abstracting Circuit Functionality. In *2013 Government Microcircuit Applications & Critical Technology Conference (GOMACTech)*, 2013.

[4] Salmani, H. and Tehranipoor, M. Analyzing circuit vulnerability to hardware Trojan insertion at the behavioral level. In *Defect and Fault Tolerance in VLSI and Nanotechnology Systems (DFT)*, 2013 IEEE International Symposium on. (). , 2013, 190-195.

[5] A. N. Nowroz, K. Hu, F. Koushanfar and S. Reda. Novel Techniques for High-Sensitivity Hardware Trojan Detection Using Thermal and Power Maps. IEEE Transactions on Computer-Aided Design of Integrated Circuits and Systems, 33, 12 (2014), 1792-1805. DOI=10.1109/TCAD.2014.2354293.

[6] D. Forte, Chongxi Bao and A. Srivastava. Temperature tracking: An innovative run-time approach for hardware Trojan detection. In *Computer-Aided Design (ICCAD), 2013 IEEE/ACM International Conference on.* , 2013, 532-539.

[7] H. Salmani and M. Tehranipoor. Layout-Aware Switching Activity Localization to Enhance Hardware Trojan Detection. IEEE Transactions on Information Forensics and Security, 7, 1 (2012), 76-87. DOI=10.1109/TIFS.2011.2164908.

[8] Saqib, F., Ismari, D., Lamech, C. and Plusquellic, J. Within-Die Delay Variation Measurement and Power Transient Analysis Using REBEL. In *Very Large Scale Integration (VLSI) Systems*, IEEE Transactions on, 23, 4 (2015), 776-780. DOI=10.1109/TVLSI.2014.2318307.

[9] Xun Li, Mohit Tiwari, Ben Hardekopf, Timothy Sherwood, and Frederic T. Chong. 2010. Secure information flow analysis for hardware design: using the right abstraction for the job. In *Proceedings of the 5th ACM SIGPLAN Workshop on Programming Languages and Analysis for Security (PLAS '10)*. ACM, New York, NY, USA, Article 8, 7 pages. DOI=http://dx.doi.org/10.1145/1814217.1814225.

[10] Wei Hu, Dejun Mu, Jason Oberg, Baolei Mao, Mohit Tiwari, Timothy Sherwood, and Ryan Kastner. 2014. Gate-Level Information Flow Tracking for Security Lattices. *ACM Trans. Des. Autom. Electron. Syst.* 20, 1, Article 2 (November 2014), 25 pages. DOI=http://dx.doi.org/10.1145/2676548

[11] Haibo Chen, Xi Wu, Liwei Yuan, Binyu Zang, Pen-chung Yew, and Frederic T. Chong. 2008. From Speculation to Security: Practical and Efficient Information Flow Tracking Using Speculative Hardware. *SIGARCH Comput. Archit. News* 36, 3 (June 2008), 401-412. DOI=http://dx.doi.org/10.1145/1394608.1382156

[12] Olatunji Ruwase, Phillip B. Gibbons, Todd C. Mowry, Vijaya Ramachandran, Shimin Chen, Michael Kozuch, and Michael Ryan. 2008. Parallelizing dynamic information flow tracking. In *Proceedings of the twentieth annual symposium on Parallelism in algorithms and architectures* (SPAA '08). ACM, New York, NY, USA, 35-45. DOI=http://dx.doi.org/10.1145/1378533.1378538

[13] http://opencores.org

[14] M. A. Rahman and H. Mohsenian-Rad. False data injection attacks with incomplete information against smart power grids. In *Global Communications Conference (GLOBECOM), 2012 IEEE*, Anaheim, CA, 2012, pp. 3153-3158. DOI=10.1109/GLOCOM.2012.6503599

[15] A. Giani, E. Bitar, M. Garcia, M. McQueen, P. Khargonekar and K. Poolla. Smart Grid Data Integrity Attacks. In *IEEE Transactions on Smart Grid*, vol. 4, no. 3, pp. 1244-1253, Sept. 2013. DOI=10.1109/TSG.2013.2245155

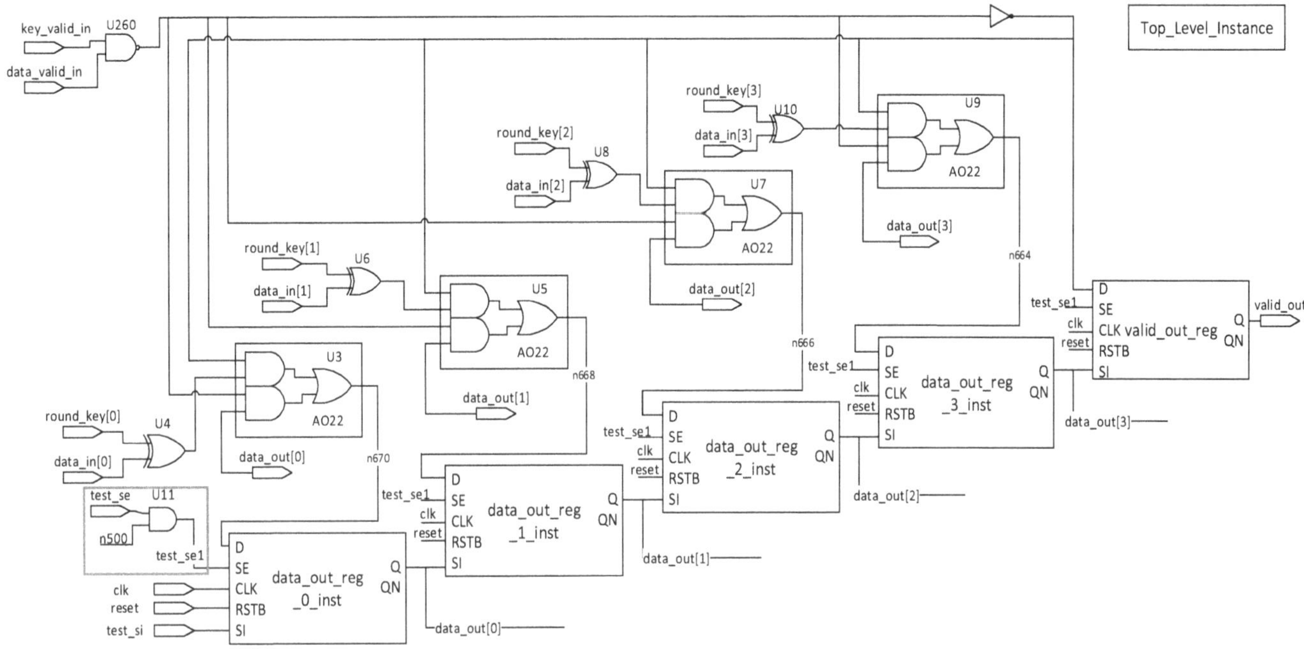

Figure 6. Scan chain inserted gate-level netlist with a malicious internal signal.

A data path of instances: [Top_Level_Instance, U4, U3, data_out_reg_0_inst]
The data signals path: [data_in(0), IN2, Q, n800, IN4, n670, D, <data_out_0_port>]
A data path of instances: [Top_Level_Instance, U6, U5, data_out_reg_1_inst]
The data signals path: [data_in(1), IN2, Q, n799, IN4, n668, D, <data_out_1_port>]
A data path of instances: [Top_Level_Instance, U8, U7, data_out_reg_2_inst]
The data signals path: [data_in(2), Q, n798, IN4, n666, D, <data_out_2_port>]
A data path of instances: [Top_Level_Instance, U10, U9, data_out_reg_3_inst]
The data signals path: [data_in(3), IN2, Q, n797, IN4, n664, D, <data_out_3_port>]
A data path of instances: [Top_Level_Instance, data_out_reg_0_inst]
The data signals path: [test_si, SI, <Q>, <data_out_0_port>]
A data path of instances: [U3, Top_Level_Instance, data_out_reg_0_inst, data_out_reg_1_inst]
The data signals path: [IN2, Q, n670, D, <QN>, <n_8543>, data_out_0_port, SI, <data_out_1_port>]
A data path of instances: [U5, Top_Level_Instance, data_out_reg_1_inst, data_out_reg_2_inst]
The data signals path: [IN2, Q, n668, D, <QN>, <n_8542>, data_out_1_port, SI, <data_out_2_port>]
A data path of instances: [U7, Top_Level_Instance, data_out_reg_2_inst, data_out_reg_3_inst]
The data signals path: [IN2, Q, n666, D, <QN>, <n_8541>, data_out_2_port, SI, <data_out_3_port>]
A data path of instances: [U9, Top_Level_Instance, data_out_reg_3_inst, valid_out_reg]
The data signals path: [IN2, Q, n664, D, <QN>, <n_8540>, data_out_3_port, SI]

Figure 7. An example of Scenario 3 report.

Design of Error-Resilient Logic Gates with Reinforcement Using Implications

Xijing Han, Marco Donato, R.Iris Bahar, Alexander Zaslavsky, William Patterson
School of Engineering
Brown University
Providence, RI 02906

ABSTRACT

Operating circuits in the sub-threshold region can save power, but at the cost of higher susceptibility to noise. This paper analyzes various gate-level error-mitigation designs appropriate for sub-threshold circuits. Previous works have proposed a modified version of the Schmitt trigger gate that uses logic implications to reinforce correct functional behavior. However, the increased error resilience requires increased area, delay, and power overhead. To address these shortcomings, we introduce two alternative and less costly approaches to reinforcing correct logic behavior via implications. In addition, to provide more flexibility in implication selection, we consider not just simple implications that reinforce relationships between two signals, but also more complex 3-signal implications within the circuit. Our simulation results demonstrate that these alternative gate structures can outperform the Schmitt trigger version as long as the noise on the reinforcement signals themselves is sufficiently low.

Keywords

sub-threshold circuit; noise immunity; logic implication

1. INTRODUCTION

Operating circuits in the sub-threshold region minimizes energy consumption, but also causes the circuit to be much more susceptible to noise. Past approaches for error mitigation in combinational circuits used techniques such as triple modular redundancy [4] or duplicating only a portion of the circuit [10], but required significant area and power overhead. Other approaches, such as [17], selectively target nodes that are most susceptible to noise and increase the transistor sizes of the gates driving these nodes in order to achieve higher noise immunity. While the approach of [17] is reported to achieve 90% coverage for soft errors, average overhead is 38%, 27%, and 4% respectively in area, power, and delay. Finally, approaches based on probabilistic methods such as Markov Random Field gates [13] or Turtle Logic [9] have been proposed for mitigating the effects of noise. While there are many potential sources of noise, from current noise due to charge trapping in transistors to crosstalk voltage noise, in this paper we will focus on thermal noise as a fundamental, technology-independent noise source that has a clear statistical description. Thermal noise is expected have a significant impact in determining the fault rate in future low-power [11] and especially sub-threshold circuits, so new solutions that provide error mitigation at lower cost are needed.

Logic implications have been effectively used for online error detection [2], [3], [12], as well as error correction [1], [8]. As was shown in [8], the correction can be implemented by translating the logic relationship described by an implication using a modified version of a Schmitt trigger gate [5]. While the modified Schmitt gate was shown to have some useful error correction properties, it can only mitigate errors caused by noise on the inputs of the gate. That is, if there is a noise spike on the output of the gate, the Schmitt gate cannot mitigate this error. In addition, the extra series transistors in the Schmitt gate can lead to increased switching delays.

The method proposed in [1] adds redundant source wires as inputs to gates to correct erroneous values on a target wire. While this approach has modest area overhead, the usage of implications between source and target wires to mitigate errors is constrained: the value on the source wire may be masked by other input signals on the gate, so even when the implication is active, the error on the target wire may not be corrected.

To extend implication-based error correction beyond prior work, in this paper we investigate two alternative gate structures to reinforce correct behavior in the presence of thermal noise. Our two new gate designs provide more flexible use of implications than either [1] or [8] by considering both single-node and 2-node implications. That is, the implication can consist of a single source signal (also called the *control* signal) or two sources. Our new gates also require less transistor overhead than the modified Schmitt gate [8].

We compare these reinforcement gates in terms of area, power, delay, and noise immunity. Our simulation results show improved noise immunity with 2-node implications. In addition, we show that our gates can provide better error correction than the Schmitt gate when noise appears at the output of the gate. However, the Schmitt gate remains an attractive choice when the controlling signals for the implication are themselves susceptible to significant noise.

The remainder of this paper is organized as follows. Sec-

GLSVLSI '16, May 18 - 20, 2016, Boston, MA, USA

ISBN 978-1-4503-4274-2/16/05...$15.00

DOI: http://dx.doi.org/10.1145/2902961.2902983

tion 2 provides the background on logic implications and how they may be used for error mitigation in combinational circuits. In Section 3, we propose three versions of logic gates with reinforcement implemented to mitigate errors and analyze their advantages and disadvantages. In Section 4, we discuss the optimal selection of implications. Experimental results in terms of delay, power and noise resiliency are provided in Section 5, where we also discuss the impact on performance of sizing the control transistors. Concluding remarks and future directions are given in Section 6.

2. BACKGROUND

The proposed method is based on the existence of logic implications, or invariant relationships, between signal nodes in a circuit. In this paper, we propose two types of implications: 1-node-implications and 2-node-implications.

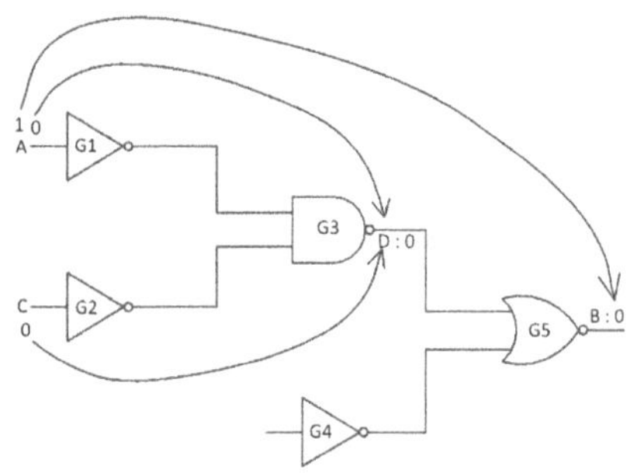

Figure 1: Illustrative circuit for defining 1-node and 2-node implications. Implications shown are $[A : 1 \rightarrow B : 0]$ and $[A : 0, C : 0 \rightarrow D : 0]$

2.1 1-node-implications

The 1-node-implication between nodes A and B is illustrated in Figure 1 and can be expressed in the form of [A: 1] →[B: 0], where A is the *source*, or *control* signal and B is the *target*. There exist four types of logic value implications: [0→0], [0→1], [1→0] and [1→1]. As will be clarified in Section 4, based on the error-mitigation performance of our reinforcement gates, we prefer to use [0→1] and [1→0]. If we want to reinforce implications [1→1] and [0→0] we have to add an inverter to transform the implication to the desired form; this requires additional area and delay overhead, so we try to avoid these implications as much as possible.

2.2 2-node-implications

The 2-node-implication uses a combination of two nodes as the controlling signals to reinforce the output of a gate. The 2-node-implication is similar to the multi-site implication proposed in [3], but in our case is used for error correction. In Figure 1, the implication between nodes A, C and D is an example of a 2-node-implication. In this case, we can express this implication is in the form of [A: 0], [C: 0] → [D: 0], where A and C are the control signals and D is the target. For the same reason given for 1-node-implications, we prefer using [1,1→0] and [0,0→1] implications for reinforcement. However, we can use [0,0→0] and [1,1→1] implications by adding a NAND gate or NOR gate to transform the 2-node-implication to a 1-node-implication. For example, by adding a NOR gate with inputs A and C from Figure 1, the output of the NOR gate can be used to realize the implication $[NOR : 1 \rightarrow D : 0]$.

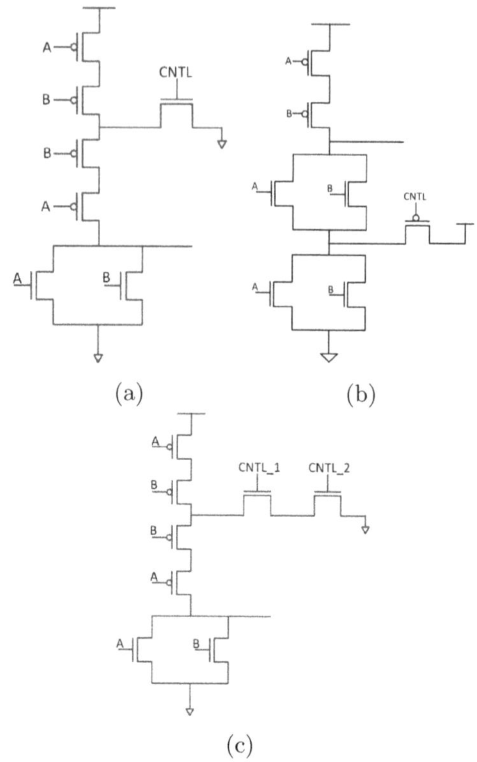

Figure 2: Modified Schmitt gates using: (a) 1-node-implications $(CNTL : 1 \rightarrow Out : 0)$ (a) and $(CNTL : 0 \rightarrow Out : 1)$ (b); (c) 2-node-implication $(CNTL1 : 1, CNTL2 : 1 \rightarrow Out : 0)$.

The 2-node-implication provides more flexibility to choose reinforcement options. For example, when implication sets [0→1] or [1→0] cannot be found, we can use [0,0→1] or [1,1→0] instead. The 2-node-implication also has higher reliability than the 1-node-implication due to error-masking, since noise on either control signal alone is less likely to incorrectly alter the output of the gate.

3. LOGIC GATES WITH REINFORCEMENT

Logic gate reinforcement with implications uses a controlling signal to bias or force the value of the output. In this section, we propose three versions of reinforcement gates: Schmitt trigger, Direct Control (DC) and Complementary Direct Control (CDC).

3.1 Schmitt gate

The version of Schmitt gate considered in this work was originally presented in [8]. Figure 2(a) shows the architecture of a 2-input NOR Schmitt gate with implication $CNTL : 1 \rightarrow Out : 0$. Figure 2(b) shows the architecture of a 2-input NOR Schmitt gate with implication $CNTL : 0 \rightarrow Out : 1$. This specific implication type allows us to highlight some important aspects of the noise response of this gate. Applying the reinforcement on the pull-up network of a NOR gate requires having four transistors in series to the output, causing a significant increase in delay. While this solution has a negative impact on the circuit performance, it mitigates the effects of noise at the input. Applying the reinforcement on the pull-down network of a NOR gate, as

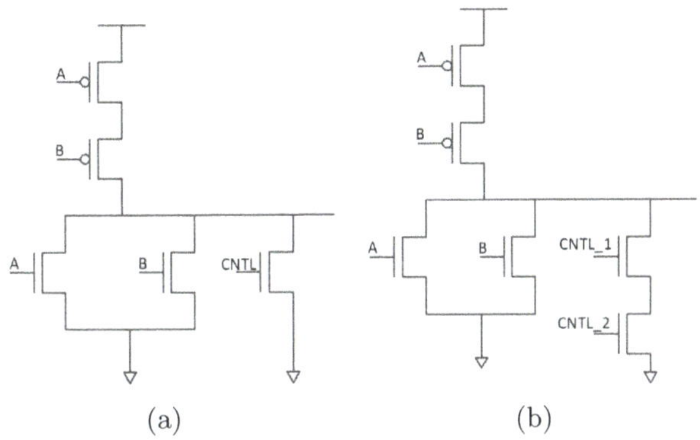

Figure 3: The Direct Control gate using (a) 1-node-implication and (b) 2-node-implication.

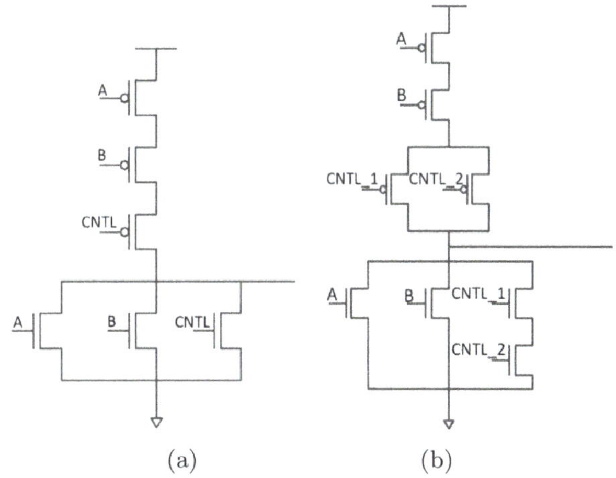

Figure 4: The Complementary Direct Control gate using (a) 1-node-implication and (b) 2-node-implication.

shown in Figure 2(b), requires having two transistors in series which has a smaller delay. However, the area overhead for this gate does not scale well with the number of inputs. Another critical aspect of the Schmitt gate circuit is that the control branch is not directly tied to the gate's output. As a consequence, the Schmitt gate can attenuate the input noise but cannot prevent noise at the output from impacting the gate's logic behavior. Figure 2(c) shows the architecture of the Schmitt gate implementing a 2-node-implication, which faces the same drawbacks as the 1-node versions.

3.2 Direct Control (DC) gate

To address the relatively high area overhead of the Schmitt gate and its inability to mask noise at the output, we investigated an alternative method for adding implication reinforcement to logic gates. The DC gate uses transistors to connect the output and the control branch directly. The additional transistors are controlled by the source signals of the implication. Figure 3(a) shows the DC implementation for a 2-input NOR gate with implication $CNTL : 1 \rightarrow Out : 0$. In this case, we are forcing rather than biasing the value at the output based on the implication values. The DC gate has advantages in terms of size and speed; in particular, the transistor overhead is independent of the number of inputs. However, it is sensitive to the noise on the control signal (i.e., the implication source node) since this signal affects the output directly. Figure 3(b) shows the architecture of a Direct Control gate implementing a 2-node-implication.

3.3 Complementary Direct Control (CDC) gate

The DC gate in Section 3.2 uses the implication in either the pull-up or the pull-down network. Therefore, when the implication is actively correcting an error on one polarity (*i.e.*, either V_{DD} or ground), the network connected to the opposite polarity could introduce contention at the output node. To make sure that only one network can determine the value of the output, we propose a CDC gate that was previously used in [1]. Figure 4(a) shows the architecture of the CDC gate. When the implication is active, the control signal will reinforce one polarity while cutting off the connection to the other polarity. The drawback is that this implementation is even more sensitive to noise on the control signal, with the risk of reinforcing the wrong value at the output. Figure 4(b) shows the architecture of the CDC gate implementing a 2-node-implication.

4. IMPLICATION SELECTION

Once a full list of implications in a circuit is determined (e.g., by using the implication discovery procedure proposed in [2]), it is not necessary or feasible to use all of them to reinforce the circuit. Instead, we follow a set of rules to select an optimized set of implications. As mentioned in Section 2, there exist four types of 1-node-implications: [0→0], [1→0], [0→1],[1→1]. Note that for MOSFET transistors, an NMOS passes a weak V_{DD} signal and a PMOS passes a weak zero voltage, so using an NMOS on the pull-up path to reduce the noise in a V_{DD} signal results in a poorer error-mitigation performance, compared to using a PMOS. Therefore, for the four types of implications, [0→1] and [1→0] are our first choice. For the same reason, for 2-node-implications, [1,1→0] and [0,0→1] are preferred.

An implication consists of source (i.e., control) node and target node. The target node can be of 2 different types:

- An "essential node" such as a primary output.
- A node that is easily affected by noise, such as the output of an inverter (i.e., errors on the input cannot be masked)

Once the target node is decided, the next step is choosing its corresponding control node. This control node should be reliable, have a high probability of being active, and be at a distance of more than one gate from the target node. The steps to select the control node are as follows:

1. For all implications involving the target node, calculate the probability of the implication being active (i.e., the probability the control node is at the appropriate logic value) and pick the implications with the highest activation probability.
2. Among the high-activation implications chose the one with the most reliable control node. As a simple initial metric, in this paper we assume that nodes closer to the primary inputs have higher reliability.

1-node-implication				
	implication 1→0		implication 0→1	
	Active	Inactive	Active	Inactive
Schmitt gate	7.43ns	6.78ns	5.29 ns	5.38ns
DC gate	2.98ns	4.57ns	2.69ns	4.69ns
CDC gate	4.09ns	5.05ns	3.62ns	5.04ns
2-node-implication				
	implication 11→0		implication 00→1	
	Active	Inactive	Active	Inactive
Schmitt gate	8.37ns	6.36ns	4.88ns	5.57ns
DC gate	4.60ns	5.10ns	4.55ns	5.40ns
CDC gate	5.53ns	6.19ns	6.54ns	5.48ns

Table 1: Delays of three versions of 2-input NOR gate with reinforcement

1-node-implication				
	implication 1→0		implication 0→1	
	Active	Inactive	Active	Inactive
Schmitt gate	3.01nW	2.51nW	2.60nW	1.74nW
DC gate	2.24nW	2.12nW	2.17nW	1.57nW
CDC gate	2.18nW	2.02nW	2.15nW	1.53nW
2-node-implication				
	implication 11→0		implication 00→1	
	Active	Inactive	Active	Inactive
Schmitt gate	3.08nW	2.36nW	2.74nW	1.48nW
DC gate	2.39nW	1.35nW	2.37nW	1.38nW
CDC gate	2.48nW	2.00nW	2.42nW	1.56nW

Table 2: Power of three versions of 2-input NOR gate with reinforcement

5. EXPERIMENTAL RESULTS

5.1 Simulation set-up

The proposed circuits were simulated in SPICE using a 7nm FinFET Predictive Technology Model [15]. The supply voltage was set to $V_{DD} = 180mV$, which is below the threshold voltage of $\sim 500mV$ for both PMOS and NMOS transistors. Thermal noise was modeled using current pulse time series generated using the method presented in [6]. We used this approach as it allows to generate accurate noise samples for sub-threshold circuits at a reasonable computational cost. The RMS noise voltages of minimum-size inverters and two-input gates in the 7nm technology operated at $V_{DD} = 180mV$ are $\sim 5.88mV$ and $\sim 5mV$, respectively [6]. In order to emphasize the characteristic noise response of each of the circuits under analysis, we applied a 12× gain to all noise traces. This leads to highly exaggerated noise, but permits the evaluation of noise resilience and error mitigation within a reasonable computation time in SPICE. More realistic thermal noise transients with unamplified noise were presented in [6] and a custom simulator of rare errors due to unamplified noise in [7], but standard SPICE simulation requires noise amplification. The amplified uncorrelated thermal noise sources were connected to the output node of each gate. All primary inputs were sent through buffers to apply the same noise to those signals as well.

5.2 Delays and power

The delays and power results were calculated for a 2-input NOR gate using three versions of logic gate with reinforcement. A minimum-sized inverter was connected at the output of the NOR gate. Tables 1 and 2 summarize the performance of the three versions of gates in terms of delays and power. The Schmitt gate has larger delay and power dissipation than the other two gates for both the 1-node or the 2-node implications. There is no significant difference between the DC gate and CDC gate in terms of delay and power. In most cases, delays and power dissipation of the 2-node-implication method are both slightly higher than the 1-node-implication method.

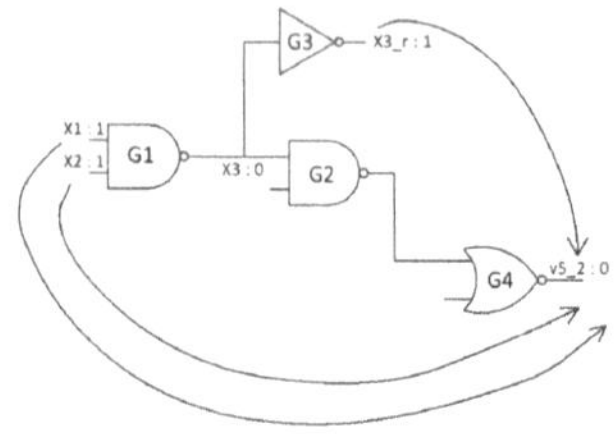

Figure 5: A portion of the *rd53* circuit.

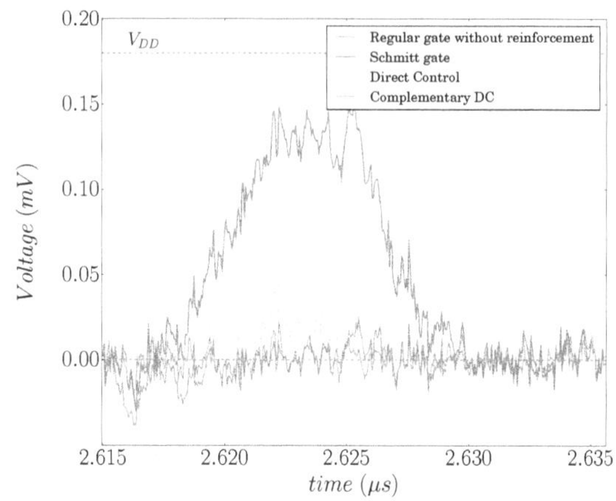

Figure 6: Simulation of v5_2 with active implication using different versions of gates (error caused by noise in the input of gate G4).

5.3 Error-correcting behavior

The experimental results come from *rd53*, a circuit from MCNC benchmark suite [16]. To illustrate the performance of three versions of gates using different kinds of implications, we use implications to reinforce the node v5_2, which is the final output, when the output is low. The relevant portion of the *rd53* circuit is shown in Figure 5.

Figures 6 and 7 show a period of a transient simulation for v5_2 using three versions of gates with the active implication [x3_r:1→v5_2:0]. The ideal output should stay at zero, but the output occasionally drifts to a high voltage because of noise. The error in Figure 6 is caused by the noise in the inputs of G4. If there is no implication reinforcement for v5_2, the maximum value of the error is around 148mV. All of the three versions of reinforcement gates mitigate the error. However, the DC gate has the worst error-mitigation performance when the error is caused by the input, with the nominally low output reaching a maximum value of 48mV. The Schmitt gate has a better error-mitigation performance because it can bias the input-output transfer function towards the correct output value. The CDC gate also has

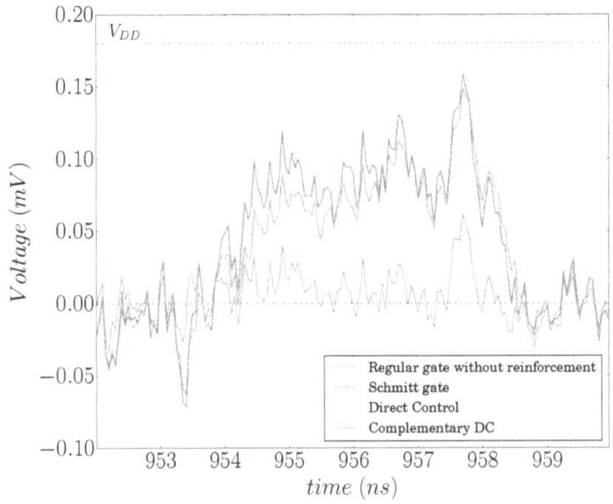

Figure 7: Simulation of v5_2 with active implication using different versions of gates (error caused by noise added at v5_2).

a better error-mitigation performance because it eliminates the contention between the two paths.

The error in Figure 7 is caused by the noise added at v5_2. If there is no implication reinforcement for v5_2, the maximum value of the error is around 158mV. The maximum value of the Schmitt gate, DC gate and CDC gates are 148mV, 66mV and 61mV respectively. Note that the control signal of the Schmitt gate does not directly create a path to the output of the gate, and since the noise is added directly at the output, the Schmitt gate is ineffective at attenuating the error. The other two versions still work to mitigate the error since both of them force the value at the output directly. By adjusting the size of control transistor, the 2-node-implication method can achieve the same error-correcting performance as the 1-node-implication method, which is demonstrated by Figure 8.

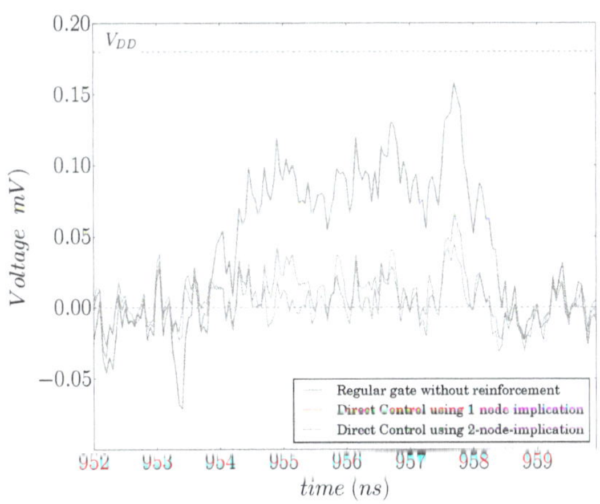

Figure 8: Simulation of v5_2 comparing 1-node and 2-node implications for the DC gate. Implications are active in both cases, with error caused by noise on the output node.

Figure 9 shows a period of transient simulation for v5_2 using three versions of gates with the inactive 1-node-implication [x3_r:1→v5_2:0] and the DC gate with inactive 2-node-implication [x0:1,x1:1→v5_2:0]. In this simulation, the ideal output should stay at 180 mV but the output jumps to low voltage values at times because of noise in the control node. The implication [x3_r:1→v5_2:0] should not be active when the control node x3_r has a value of zero. However, the noise in the control node sometimes makes it jump to a high enough voltage such that the implication becomes erroneously active, forcing the value of v5_2 to an error. In Figure 9, the output of the DC and CDC gates using the 1-node-implication can be less reliable than the output of a normal gate, whereas the error is mitigated by a Schmitt gate due to its biasing behavior. The CDC gate has more noise-immunity than the DC gate because the control signal is connected to two transistors, which will attenuate the noise due to larger gate capacitances. The DC gate using a 2-node-implication has an even higher immunity to the noise in the source node, which is due to large capacitances and logic masking effect.

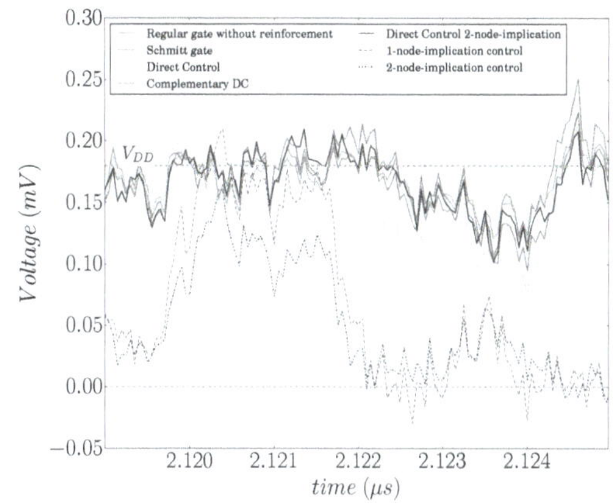

Figure 9: Simulation of v5_2 with inactive implication using different versions of gates.

5.4 Transistor sizing for noise immunity

It is worth noting that increasing the size of a noise-susceptible node is a known technique for improving noise immunity [14], [17]. In our error-correcting gates, the size of the control transistor is critical, since it affects the delay and error-mitigation performance, as well as immunity from noise on the implication control signals. The error-correcting behavior improves as the size of the control transistor increases. However, the output becomes more sensitive to noise on the control signal. That is, while the larger sized transistor can dampen noise due to larger gate capacitance, it will also switch on more easily when there are high levels of noise on the control signal. Sizes of transistors implementing 2-node-implications are larger than 1-node-implications in order to compensate for the series resistance across the 2 control transistors.

As in [17], gate-upsizing can achieve error-mitigation at the cost of area, delay and power. We compared the gate-upsizing method and our implication-based approach in terms of area, delay, power and error mitigation performance. We simulated a double-sized 2-input NOR gate and found the delay to be approximately 4.78ns and the average power dissipation to be around 1.60nW. Compared to the results in Tables 1 and 2, there are no significant differences between a double-sized NOR gate and the DC and CDC gates.

Figure 10 shows a simulation comparing error-mitigation performance between our implication-based approaches and gate up-sizing. Shown is the voltage trace of signal v5_2

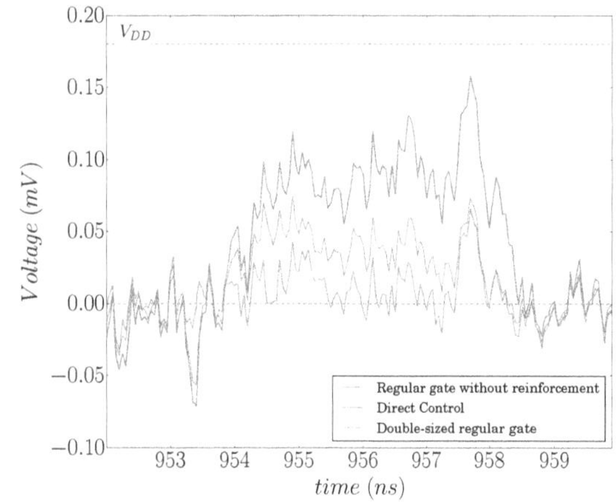

Figure 10: Comparison of error-mitigation behavior between the DC gate and gate-upsizing approach.

from Figure 5. The red trace shows v5_2 when the transistor sizes of gate G4 are doubled, whereas the green trace shows v5_2 when gate G4 is replaced with a DC reinforcement gate implementing the implication [x3_r: 1 → v5_2:0]. Visually, the error-mitigation performance of the DC is better than a regular double-sized NOR gate. An explanation for this behavior is that while gate sizing helps filtering out the noise at the input of the gate by increasing the input capacitance, our reinforcement approach forces the output to the correct logic value. Also, our method is more cost-effective in terms of area for reinforcing a single node.

6. CONCLUSIONS

As circuit operating voltages move to increasingly lower levels, new techniques will be required to provide immunity from various sources of noise. In this work, we propose and analyze two types of logic implications and three version of reinforced logic gates. The 2-node-implication method gives more choices of implications and more tolerance to noise due to error-masking effect and large capacitances. However, this method causes larger delays and power consumption than the 1-node-implication method. The Direct Control (DC) and Complementary Direct Control (CDC) gates are more efficient than the previously proposed Schmitt gate in terms of area, power and delay. Also, the Schmitt gate can only mitigate the error caused by the inputs while the other two versions can also mitigate the error caused by the noise added at the output. However, the DC and CDC gates are more sensitive to the noise in the control signal than the Schmitt gate. Future work will focus on increasing the reliability of the control signal and implication selection. In addition, we will investigate whether our reinforcement technique is useful for mitigating the effects of other types of errors, such as timing errors due to aging effects. We plan to investigate a broader range of signal failures as we continue to analyze the benefits of our approach.

7. ACKNOWLEDGMENTS

This work is supported by NSF under Grant CCF-1525486.

8. REFERENCES

[1] S. Almukhaizim and Y. Makris. Soft error mitigation through selective addition of functionally redundant wires. *IEEE Trans. Rel.*, 57(1):23–31, 2008.

[2] N. Alves, A. Buben, K. Nepal, J. Dworak, and R. I. Bahar. A cost effective approach for online error detection using invariant relationships. *Trans. Comp.-Aided Des. Integ. Cir. Sys.*, 29(5):788–801, 2010.

[3] N. Alves, Y. Shi, J. Dworak, R. I. Bahar, and K. Nepal. Enhancing online error detection through area-efficient multi-site implications. In *VTS*, pages 241–246, 2011.

[4] M. Baze, S. Buchner, and D. McMorrow. A digital CMOS design technique for SEU hardening. *IEEE Trans. Nucl. Sci.*, 47(6):2603–2608, 2000.

[5] B. L. Dokic. CMOS NAND and NOR schmitt circuits. *Microelectronics J.*, 27(8):757 – 765, 1996.

[6] M. Donato, R. I. Bahar, W. Patterson, and A. Zaslavsky. A simulation framework for analyzing transient effects due to thermal noise in sub-threshold circuits. In *GLSVLSI*, pages 45–50, 2015.

[7] M. Donato, R. I. Bahar, W. Patterson, and A. Zaslavsky. A fast simulator for the analysis of sub-threshold thermal noise transients. In *DAC*, 2016.

[8] M. Donato, F. Cremona, W. Jin, R. I. Bahar, W. Patterson, A. Zaslavsky, and J. Mundy. A noise-immune sub-threshold circuit design based on selective use of Schmitt-trigger logic. In *GLSVLSI*, pages 39–44, 2012.

[9] L. Garcia-Leyva, A. Calomarde, F. Moll, and A. Rubio. Novel redundant logic design for noisy low voltage scenarios. In *LASCAS*, pages 1–4, 2013.

[10] K. Mohanram and N. Touba. Cost-effective approach for reducing soft error failure rate in logic circuits. In *ITC*, volume 1, pages 893–901, 2003.

[11] G. Moore. Cramming more components onto integrated circuits. *Proc. IEEE*, 86(1):82–85, 1998.

[12] K. Nepal, N. Alves, J. Dworak, and R. I. Bahar. Using implications for online error detection. In *ITC*, pages 1–10, 2008.

[13] K. Nepal, R. I. Bahar, J. Mundy, W. Patterson, and A. Zaslavsky. Designing nanoscale logic circuits based on markov random fields. *J. Electron. Test.*, 23(2):255–266, 2007.

[14] R. Rao, D. Blaauw, and D. Sylvester. Soft error reduction in combinational logic using gate resizing and flipflop selection. In *ICCAD*, pages 502–509, 2006.

[15] S. Sinha, G. Yeric, V. Chandra, B. Cline, and Y. Cao. Exploring sub-20nm FinFET design with Predictive Technology Models. In *DAC*, pages 283–288, 2012.

[16] S. Yang. Logic synthesis and optimization benchmarks user guide: Version 3.0. Technical report, MCNC Technical Report, 1991.

[17] Q. Zhou and K. Mohanram. Gate sizing to radiation harden combinational logic. *IEEE Trans. Comput.-Aided Design Integr. Circuits Syst.*, 25(1):155–166, 2006.

Reducing Soft-error Vulnerability of Caches using Data Compression

Sparsh Mittal and Jeffrey S. Vetter
Oak Ridge National Laboratory
Oak Ridge, Tennessee, USA 37830
{mittals,vetter}@ornl.gov

ABSTRACT

With ongoing chip miniaturization and voltage scaling, particle strike-induced soft errors present increasingly severe threat to the reliability of on-chip caches. In this paper, we present a technique to reduce the vulnerability of caches to soft-errors. Our technique uses data compression to reduce the number of vulnerable data bits in the cache and performs selective duplication of more critical data-bits to provide extra protection to them. Microarchitectural simulations have shown that our technique is effective in reducing cache vulnerability and outperforms another technique. For single and dual-core system configuration, the average reduction in cache vulnerability is 5.59× and 8.44×, respectively. Also, the implementation and performance overheads of our technique are minimal and it is useful for a broad range of workloads.

Keywords

Reliability; resilience; fault-tolerance; soft/transient error; cache; vulnerability; data compression.

1. INTRODUCTION

Recent trends of feature size scaling have exacerbated the impact of faults on modern processors, for instance, the soft-error failure rate at 16nm node is expected to be 100 times that at 180nm node [1]. With ongoing voltage scaling, the critical charge required for flipping a stored bit has been decreasing. Due to this, even lower-energy particles, which outnumber higher-energy particles in the atmosphere, can also cause soft-errors [2, 3]. In extreme cases, the social and financial impact of soft-errors can be very high, e.g., it has been reported that a single soft-error had disastrous impact on a billion-dollar automotive factory [4]. Due to these, reliability has now become the primary optimization target in processor design [3].

Further, the ongoing quest for performance has led the researchers to integrate increasingly larger last level caches (LLCs) in both CPUs and GPUs. However, with rising cache size, the overhead of error correction/detection techniques such as scrubbing or flushing also increases since a progressively larger number of blocks need to be accessed within the same time period (e.g. within one retention period of embedded DRAM cache) to maintain low error rates [3, 5]. Also, critical data stay in large caches for longer time due to reduced eviction and due to this, an increase in cache size can cause superlinear increase in its vulnerability to soft errors [6]. These factors and trends necessitate novel techniques to reduce soft-error vulnerability of processor caches.

In this paper, we present a technique for improving the soft-error resilience of last level caches (SERC) using data compression. While previous works have utilized cache compression primarily for achieving capacity benefits [7], in this paper, we use compression for improving cache reliability. Specifically, SERC uses compression to reduce the number of bits required for storing a cache line. This also reduces the number of data bits which are vulnerable to soft-errors. SERC does not store more than one cache line in a block and thus, it forgoes the capacity benefits of compression. By virtue of this, SERC does not incur the overheads generally associated with compression techniques such as extra tags, compaction, fragmentation, etc.

As for compression algorithm, we use Base Delta Immediate (BDI) algorithm [8]. BDI algorithm represents a cache line using a base value and a set of deltas; the decompression step involves addition of base with delta values. Due to this, the base value becomes most critical since an error in it during compressed state can propagate to other elements at the time of decompression. Thus, a naive application of BDI algorithm can compromise reliability and fail to exploit reliability-specific optimization opportunities. To address these, we adapt BDI algorithm and store two copies of the base to detect and correct (if parity bits are also used) any error in the base. Also, for 'zero' compression state, we do not store any byte (versus 1 byte in [8]), since it can be easily reconstructed from the compression encoding (refer §3.4 for more details). We show that our reliability-optimizations achieve higher reduction in vulnerability than that achieved using original BDI algorithm (§5.1).

SERC has several salient features. Unlike duplication-based techniques (e.g., [9, 10, 11]), SERC does not degrade cache capacity for improving reliability. Also, unlike early writeback-based techniques (e.g., [12, 13, 14]) which protect blocks *by writing them back to memory*, SERC protects the blocks *in the cache itself* using compression and selective duplication. Thus, SERC does not increase off-chip traffic or cause latency/energy overheads. The implementation

GLSVLSI'16, May 18–20, 2016, Boston, MA, USA.

ACM ISBN 978-1-4503-4274-2/16/05. . . $15.00.
DOI: http://dx.doi.org/10.1145/2902961.2902977

and performance overheads of SERC are minimal (§3.5) and hence, it can be easily integrated in commercial processors.

We perform microarchitectural simulations of single and dual-core configurations using an X86-64 simulator and benchmarks from SPEC2006 suite and HPC field (§4). Also, we compare SERC with a 'narrow value detection' (NVD) technique which works by using additional flags to signal narrow value for avoiding soft-errors in high-order bits (refer §4.3 for details). For single and dual-core configurations, SERC provides 5.59× and 8.44× reduction in vulnerability, respectively and these values for NVD are only 3.56× and 5.44×, respectively (§5.1). Clearly, data compression approach used in SERC is more effective than the narrow-value detection technique. Also, the reduction in vulnerability provided by SERC grows with increasing cache size and thus, SERC is especially effective for future systems with large LLCs (§5.2).

2. BACKGROUND AND MOTIVATION

A background on soft errors: Soft errors are logical faults which lead to change in data values [3]. For example, if a charged particle from atmosphere strikes an SRAM cell, the data may flip from 0 to 1 or vice versa. Modern processors feature increasingly larger sized LLCs. However, for writeback caches, increasing the cache size reduces the eviction of modified (dirty) blocks which increases their residency time in the cache. Thus, ACE (i.e. required for architecturally correct execution) data blocks stay in cache for longer time which can increase the vulnerability in superlinear manner. For example, Biswas et al. [6] observe that for *art* benchmark of the SPEC2000 suite, increasing the L2 cache size from 1MB to 2MB increases the DUE (detected unrecoverable error) rate by 4.25×, which implies an increase of 2.125× (=4.25/2) in architectural vulnerability factor (AVF) since the number of bits increase by 2X from 1MB to 2MB cache. This highlights the need of reducing soft-error vulnerability for reliable operation of caches.

Duplication-based techniques for cache reliability: The duplication-based techniques seek to improve cache reliability by increasing the storage redundancy. Zhang et al. [9] present a technique which uses the space of dead blocks (those not used for a certain period) to store replicas of hot cache blocks. Chakraborty et al. [10] present a technique which maintains two copies of clean cache lines and three copies of dirty lines in the same set. Yalcin et al. [11] present a technique which keeps a single copy of every line at nominal voltage, two copies at medium-low voltages and three copies at near-threshold voltages to tolerate increasingly higher error-rates at reduced voltages.

A limitation of these techniques is that duplication of cache lines leads to severe degradation in cache capacity (i.e. number of distinct blocks stored by the cache) which harms performance, for example, keeping three copies of a block reduces cache capacity to only 33%. By comparison, SERC performs selective duplication within compressed lines only, and hence, the final size always remains less than the uncompressed size (64B). Thus, SERC does not degrade cache capacity. Also, while these techniques duplicate an entire cache block (64B), SERC duplicates only a sub-block (e.g. 2B, 4B or 8B).

Zhang [15] proposes keeping a replica of every write to the cache in a small fully associative cache. This technique is useful for L1 cache due to its high temporal locality, however, due to reduced locality in L2 cache, the required size of additional cache becomes large which incurs high overhead. By comparison, SERC does not require an additional cache for storing the replicas. While from reliability perspective, SERC is useful for both first-level and last-level cache, in this paper, we use SERC for the last-level cache only. This is because the first-level cache is optimized for low latency [16] and an increase in its latency due to (de)compression has large impact on performance.

Early writeback-based techniques for cache reliability: On a change in working set, several cache blocks become 'dead' [16] and will not be read in the future. A soft-error in these blocks can propagate to memory on a write-back. To address this, early writeback-based techniques have been proposed. Asadi et al. [12] writeback dirty data of cache after a fixed period (e.g., every 1M cycles) and Li et al. [13] writeback dirty data after a fixed time (e.g., 10K cycles) has passed from the last write to a block. The technique of Gold et al. [14] predicts last write to a block and then initiates its early write-back. The limitation of these techniques, however, is that they greatly increase the off-chip traffic and main memory energy consumption. Also, when the flushed blocks are later accessed (e.g., due to premature flushing or incorrect dead-block prediction), they need to be fetched from memory, which incurs latency/energy overheads. Once in cache, these blocks are again vulnerable to soft-errors. By comparison, SERC does not generate additional writebacks or incur latency/energy costs, and hence, it is very effective for protecting last level caches.

3. METHODOLOGY

We first discuss the approach for quantifying soft-error vulnerability and then explain the working of SERC.

3.1 Measuring soft-error vulnerability

To measure the vulnerability of the cache to soft-errors, we use the cache vulnerability metric [17, 12] which allows studying the soft-error behavior irrespective of the actual raw error rate. Architectural vulnerability factor (AVF) measures the fraction of time the cache is vulnerable to soft errors, or in other words, the average time when a soft-error occurring at circuit level in the cache does not get masked (e.g., due to write or eviction), but rather gets propagated to other processor components. A block which propagates to other levels in the cache hierarchy is termed as 'critical block' [12]. Critical time is defined as the time period in which the context of critical block is important. Then, AVF of the cache is the average critical time of all the critical blocks. Let M = total critical blocks in cache, CT_i = critical time of a critical block i, TT = total execution time, B = total blocks in cache and bpB = bits per block. Then,

$$AVF = \frac{\sum_{i=1}^{M} CT_i}{TT \cdot B} \quad (1)$$

Assuming failure rates of all bits are linearly uncorrelated, cache vulnerability ($Vulnerability$) is defined as [12]

$$Vulnerability = B \cdot bpB \cdot AVF = \frac{bpB \cdot \sum_{i=1}^{M} CT_i}{TT} \quad (2)$$

Based on this, $Vulnerability_{baseline}/Vulnerability_{technique}$ shows the relative reduction in cache vulnerability due to a technique. A higher value of this is better from the reliability perspective. The baseline does not use any policy for mitigating soft-errors. Due to the small size of tag bits, we ignore their contribution in vulnerability, since they can be easily designed with radiation-hardened circuits (e.g. [18]).

3.2 Key Idea

From Eq. 2, it is clear that cache vulnerability depends on the number of bits in a critical block and its critical time in the cache. Thus, vulnerability can be reduced by decreasing either or both of them. The early writeback-based techniques (e.g. [12, 13, 14]) reduce the residency time of dirty data in cache and thus, they reduce the critical time of vulnerable blocks. By comparison, SERC technique reduces cache vulnerability by using compression to lower the number of bits used for storing a data block. For example, assuming a hypothetical case where every 64B critical block is compressed to 24B, the vulnerability can be reduced to 0.375× (=24/64) of its original value, since only 37.5% bits remain vulnerable to soft-errors. SERC performs compression at the time of cache write and decompression at the time of cache read or writeback to memory.

3.3 Compression algorithm

In this paper, we use BDI compression algorithm [8] due to its low decompression latency and reasonable compression ratio. However, most of the ideas presented here will apply equally well to other compression techniques.

BDI compression algorithm works on the intuition that for many cache blocks, the difference between the values stored in the blocks are small (e.g., see Figure 1(a)). Thus, the block can be represented by storing a base along with an array of delta (difference) such that their total size is much smaller than the original size (refer Figure 1(b)). BDI algorithm uses two bases, where one base is always zero and the second base is chosen from actual contents of the line [8]. This allows BDI to compress cache blocks having two different dynamic ranges.

A BDI-compressed block has $Base_p\Delta_q$ pattern, where p and q represent the size of base and *Delta* (difference), respectively. Of the multiple possible patterns, BDI uses 6 patterns, viz. $Base_8\Delta_1$, $Base_8\Delta_2$, $Base_8\Delta_4$, $Base_4\Delta_1$, $Base_4\Delta_2$ and $Base_2\Delta_1$. In addition, BDI also checks if the block is all zero or has repeated 8 byte values. BDI algorithm attempts to compress a cache line using these 8 compression states, and the state which provides the smallest compressed size is finally chosen.

BDI algorithm works in two steps. In first step, it tries to compress all elements using an implicit base of zero. In second step, compression is attempted for those elements which could not be compressed in the first step (if any), by taking the first uncompressed element as the base. The size of delta is kept same in both the steps. With each element, a 1-bit mask is stored to signify whether the corresponding base is zero.

3.4 Optimizations performed

Data compression for vulnerability reduction also presents some unique challenges. For decompression in BDI algorithm, the original value of the block is reconstructed by adding the base with the delta values. Due to this, the base value becomes very critical from reliability perspective, since an error in it during compressed state can propagate to multiple elements in the decompressed data. Hence, even a single-bit error in the base can lead to multi-bit error in the final value. Clearly, a naive application of BDI algorithm may not strike a right balance between compression ratio[1] and reliability optimization. Further, the compression-state encoding also need to be protected from soft-errors since an error in them can lead to wrong decompression.

To address these issues, we propose the following optimizations.

1. For achieving higher reliability, we slightly sacrifice the compression ratio by storing two copies of the base (refer Figure 1(c)). Similarly, in the 'repeated value' compression-state, we keep two copies of the repeated value. Despite this duplication, the total size of the compressed block remains smaller than the uncompressed size (refer Table 1).

2. In the compressed block, the first delta is computed as the difference between the non-zero base with itself and thus, it is always zero. Hence, we do not store this delta (refer Figure 1(c)). The decompression logic implicitly assumes this and generates the element corresponding to it.

3. For zero-compression state, no bit needs to be stored in the cache block since the original (i.e. decompressed) data can simply be reconstructed based on compression state encoding bits.

4. The compression-state encoding requires 4 bit storage. Since it is a negligible fraction of the block size (64B, i.e. 512 bits), we assume that these bits are stored in radiation-hardened circuits (e.g. [18]) which are immune to soft-errors.

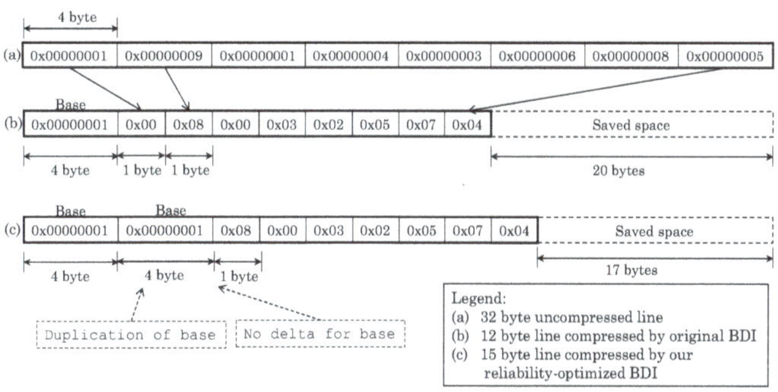

Figure 1: An illustration of original and reliability-optimized BDI (for illustration, this figure uses 32B block size. All our experiments use 64B block size).

Since the probability of multi-bit error in a block is negligible [10], we assume that maintaining a parity bit at byte granularity is sufficient to detect any (single-bit) error. For the base value, presence of two copies can be used to also correct the error, as follows. At the time of decompression, the error in a copy is detected by checking the parity bit. Since multi-bit errors are rare, the probability of having error in the same bit position of both copies of the base is negligible. Thus, if an error is found in a copy, another copy can be taken as the correct base value. Thus, the correct value can be immediately recovered instead of signaling an error or issuing an exception.

[1] In this paper, we use 'compression ratio' to denote the ratio of bytes occupied by uncompressed blocks to those occupied by compressed blocks. Other works have used compression ratio to denote the ratio of number of cache lines stored in cache without and with compression, and this ratio is always 1 for SERC since it stores only one line in a block.

Table 1: Encoding and compressed sizes for original and reliability-optimized BDI algorithm design, all sizes are in bytes (Enc. = encoding, Opt. = optimized, Uncomp. = uncompressed)

Enc.	State	Original Size	Reliability Opt. Size	Enc.	State	Original Size	Reliability Opt. Size
0000	Zeros	1	0	0101	$Base_4\Delta_1$	20 (=4+16×1)	23 (=2×4+(16-1)×1)
0001	Repeated	8	16 (=2×8)	0110	$Base_4\Delta_2$	36 (=4 +16×2)	38 (=2×4 +(16-1)×2)
0010	$Base_8\Delta_1$	16 (=8+ 8×1)	23 (=2×8+ (8-1)×1)	0111	$Base_2\Delta_1$	34 (=2+32×1)	35 (=2×2+(32-1)×1)
0011	$Base_8\Delta_2$	24 (=8+ 8×2)	30 (=2×8+ (8-1)×2)	1111	Uncomp.	64	64
0100	$Base_8\Delta_4$	40 (=8 +8×4)	44 (=2×8 +(8-1)×4)				

Due to the above mentioned optimizations, the compressed size of a block becomes different from that shown in original BDI paper [8]. For this reason, Table 1 shows the compressed size of each state with original BDI [8] and reliability-optimized BDI (this paper) algorithm. From Table 1, we note that on optimizing for reliability, the compressed size of $Base_4\Delta_1$ and $Base_8\Delta_1$ become equal (23). For sake of ease, we use both the patterns and if a line can be compressed using both these, we select the $Base_8\Delta_1$ pattern.

Unless otherwise mentioned, the experiments performed in this paper use the reliability optimized size for different compression states. In Section 5, we also show the results on using original sizes as used by [8] and found that our optimizations achieves *larger reduction in cache vulnerability*. Thus, the optimizations (2) and (3) more than offset the loss in compression ratio due to optimization (1), i.e., duplication of base and repeated value.

3.5 Overhead assessment

SERC does not store more than one cache line in a block. Due to this, SERC does not require additional tags and also does not affect set decoding or cache replacement policy. Clearly, implementation of SERC is straightforward. The latency overhead of BDI compression and decompression is 2 and 1 cycles, respectively [8]. Since BDI algorithm has low (de)compression latency, and a small increase in the latency of LLC can be easily hidden by modern processors, SERC does not harm the performance of the processor.

Some researchers propose radiation-hardened circuits which reduce soft-error rate by increasing the critical charge required to flip a value [18]. However, these circuit designs incur high overheads, e.g., Zhou et al. [18] show that on using their circuit-design, achieving 90% coverage for soft-error failure rate reduction in 70nm node incurs area and power overheads of *56%* and *44%*, respectively. Clearly, using radiation-hardened circuits for entire cache is infeasible. Hence, SERC only keeps compression state bits (4 bits for every 64B block) in radiation-hardened circuits which incurs negligible overhead.

4. EXPERIMENTATION DETAILS

4.1 Simulation platform

We perform microarchitectural simulations using detailed timing model in Gem5 simulator [19]. L1 data/instruction caches have 32KB size with 4-way associativity. The L1 caches are private to core and the L2 cache (which is LLC in this paper) is shared between cores. The size of L2 cache in single and dual-core configurations is 4MB and 8MB, respectively. All caches are write-back and use LRU replacement policy. The L2 cache parameters are obtained using DESTINY [20] for 32nm feature size for SRAM memory. We assume that the cache is optimized for write EDP (energy-delay-product) and uses sequential tag-data access. The values obtained are shown in Table 2.

Table 2: L2 cache latency values (in ns)

	4 MB	8 MB	16 MB
Hit latency	2.13	3.38	6.57
Miss latency	0.44	0.52	0.76
Write latency	1.08	1.67	3.49

4.2 Workloads

We use all the 29 benchmarks from SPEC2006 suite with *reference* inputs and 3 benchmarks from HPC field (shown as italics in Table 3) as single-core workloads. Using these, we randomly create 16 dual-core multiprogrammed workloads, such that a benchmark is used exactly once. Table 3 shows the workloads.

Table 3: Workloads used in the paper

Single-core workloads and their acronyms
As(astar), Bw(bwaves), Bz(bzip2),Cd(cactusADM) Ca(calculix), Dl(dealII), Ga(gamess), Gc(gcc) Gm(gemsFDTD), Gk(gobmk), Gr(gromacs), H2(h264ref) Hm(hmmer), Lb(lbm), Ls(leslie3d), Lq(libquantum) Mc(mcf), Mi(milc), Nd(namd), Om(omnetpp) Pe(perlbench), Po(povray), Sj(sjeng), So(soplex) Sp(sphinx), To(tonto), Wr(wrf), Xa(xalancbmk) Ze(zeusmp), *Co(comd)*, *Lu(lulesh)*, *Xb(xsbench)*
Dual-core workloads (using acronyms shown above)
AsDl, GcBw, GmGr, SoXa, BzMc, OmLb, NdCd, CaTo SpCo, LqMi, SjWr, LsZe, HmGa, GkH2, PePo, LuXb

Simulation is performed for 500M cycles for single-core applications and 250M cycles for dual-core applications. This helps in keeping simulation time manageable since we simulate a large number of workloads and techniques (baseline, SERC and NVD) using detailed timing model.

4.3 Comparison with other technique

We compare SERC with a narrow-value detection (NVD) technique based on Ergin et al.'s work [21]. NVD works by identifying narrow values and using extra flags to signal that, so that the particle-strike induced soft-errors in these higher order bits can be avoided. At the time of a cache write, NVD first checks whether a block has all the bits as zero and if so, the block is flagged as 'all zero'. Otherwise, it checks whether only the lower k-bytes have non-zero bits and if so, the block is flagged as 'narrow', thus, for these narrow blocks, only k lower bytes are vulnerable. Otherwise, the block is considered as normal and entire 64B data are considered vulnerable to errors. We assume that flag

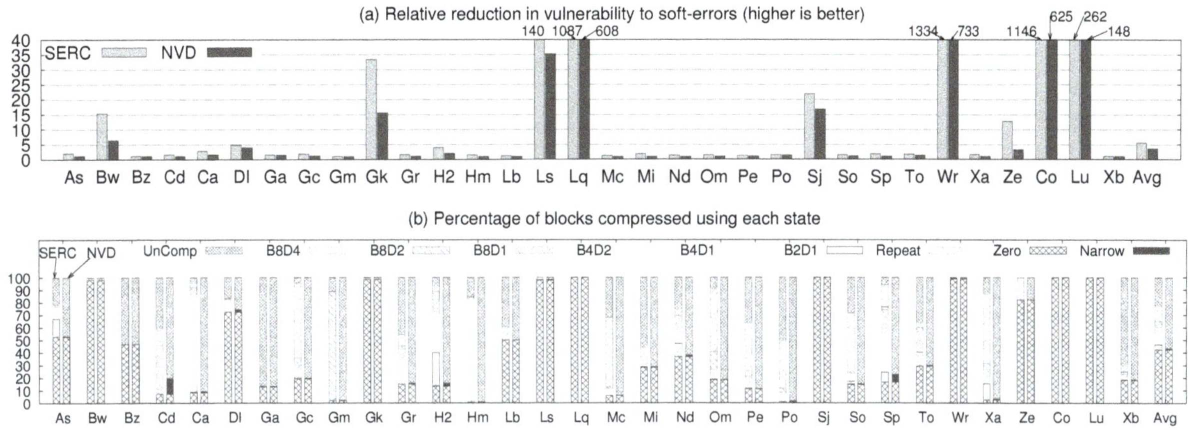

Figure 2: Results for single-core system (Here, $\text{Base}_p\Delta_q$ is shown as BpDq)

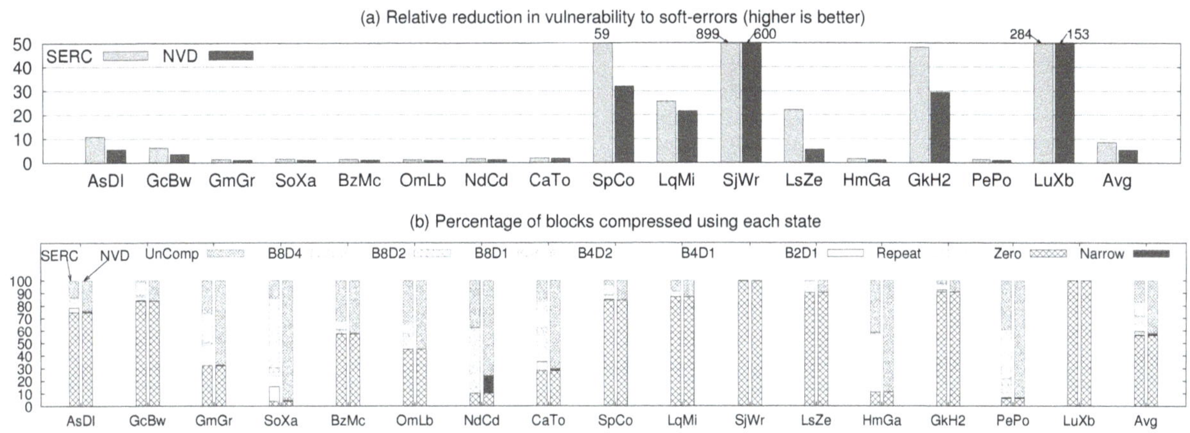

Figure 3: Results for dual-core system

bits themselves are stored in radiation-hardened storage and hence, they are immune to soft-errors.

The choice of k allows a tradeoff since a larger value of k allows flagging higher number of blocks as narrow, although it also increases the number of bits considered vulnerable in those blocks and vice versa. Since the size of in-built data types in most programming languages is generally 2, 4 or 8 bytes, we experimented with $k = 2$, 4 and 8 bytes. We observed that $k = 8$ provides largest reduction in vulnerability for both single and dual-core systems and hence, we chose $k = 8$ for experiments with NVD in this paper.

5. RESULTS AND ANALYSIS

5.1 Results with default cache size

Since SERC does not harm performance, in this section, we evaluate the impact of SERC on soft-error resilience. Figures 2(a) and 3(a) present the relative reduction in cache vulnerability on using different techniques for single and dual-core systems. To get insights, in Figure 2(b) and 3(b), we show the fraction of times a block was compressed into each compression state or remained uncompressed. For example, in Figure 2(b), for SERC, on average (see the bar 'Avg'), 42.5%, 2.1%, 1.9%, 3.0%, 5.5%, 5.6%, 4.4% and 12.7% blocks were compressed into all-zeros, repeated value, $\text{Base}_2\Delta_1$, $\text{Base}_4\Delta_1$, $\text{Base}_4\Delta_2$, $\text{Base}_8\Delta_1$, $\text{Base}_8\Delta_2$ and $\text{Base}_8\Delta_4$ states, respectively. Remaining 22.2% blocks remain uncompressed. We now analyze the results.

For single and dual-core system, SERC reduces cache vulnerability by 5.59× and 8.44×, respectively and on average, 77.79% and 82.99% data blocks can be compressed, respectively. The amount of reduction in vulnerability depends on the compressibility of data. For applications with highly compressible data, number of vulnerable bits and hence vulnerability are greatly reduced. For several workloads, more than 99% of blocks can be compressed, and hence, SERC brings large reduction in their vulnerability, e.g., Bw (15.4×), Gk (33.4×), Ls (140.2×), Lq (1086.7×), Sj (21.9×), Wr (1334.0×), Ze (12.8×), Co (1145.8×), Lu (261.8×), SjWr (898.6×), LsZe (22.2×), LuXb (283.9×), etc. Jung et al. [22] have also observed that a large fraction of data-blocks in Gk(gobmk), Sj(sjeng), Lq(libquantum), Ze(zeusmp), etc. are zero.

Results on using original sizes in BDI algorithm: We have also computed the reduction in vulnerability on using original sizes of compression states (as used by [8]), instead of reliability-optimized sizes (refer Table 1). On using original sizes, the reduction in vulnerability for single and dual-core systems was found to be 4.05× and 6.15×, respectively. Clearly, our reliability-optimizations provide much larger reduction in vulnerability than the original BDI algorithm. This can be understood as follows. From Figures 2(b) and 3(b), we observe that for single and dual-core systems, 42.5% and 56.5% (respectively) of the total blocks have been compressed using 'zero compression' state. Hence, allocating 'zero' byte (optimization proposed in §3.4) instead of 'one' byte (used in [8]) for this state increases the compression ratio significantly. Also, the original BDI algorithm is optimized for performance and hence, it does not provide extra protection to the base. By comparison, our optimizations allow detecting and correcting any error in the base.

Comparison with NVD technique: For single and dual-core systems, NVD reduces the vulnerability by 3.56× and 5.44×, respectively and compresses 43.44% and 57.68% of the blocks, respectively. Clearly, SERC is more effective in compressing the data blocks and reducing cache vulnerability than NVD. For several applications, data of different types may be stored in the same cache block, for example, a C `struct` of pointers and 2-byte integers. NVD fails to reduce number of vulnerable bits for such cases, since it works only for narrow data values. By comparison, SERC works by compressing data and hence, it can reduce vulnerability for wide data values also. The advantage of NVD is that its implementation is simpler than that of SERC, for example, (de)compression operations in NVD do not require addition/subtraction or selection of bases. However, SERC also provides larger reduction in vulnerability and hence, its slightly higher overhead is easily justified. Also, SERC is applicable to much broader range of workloads than NVD.

5.2 Cache size sensitivity study

We now focus exclusively on SERC. To study the impact of cache size, we experiment with half and double of default L2 cache size (4MB for single-core and 8MB for dual-core) and show the results in Table 4. For comparison purpose, the results with default cache size are also shown.

Table 4: Relative reduction in vulnerability (Vuln.) with SERC for different cache sizes

	Single-core		Dual-core	
	Cache size	⇓ Vuln.	Cache size	⇓ Vuln.
Half	2MB	4.89×	4MB	7.57×
Default	4MB	5.59×	8MB	8.44×
Double	8MB	6.17×	16MB	9.10×

Clearly, with increasing cache size, the relative reduction in cache vulnerability provided by SERC also increases. In general, on decreasing the cache size, cache contention is increased and the residency time of data blocks in cache is reduced. Thus, blocks are evicted more often which has same effect as early write-back mechanisms. Due to this, smaller caches have smaller vulnerability and hence, the scope of reducing vulnerability is also smaller in them. Opposite trend is seen on increasing the cache size. It is clear that SERC is effective in reducing vulnerability at different cache sizes. Since future systems will have larger sized LLCs [16], the utility of techniques such as SERC will grow even further.

6. CONCLUSION

In this paper, we presented a technique to reduce soft-error vulnerability of caches. Our technique uses data compression to reduce the number of bits used for storing data. This reduces the number of critical bits in the cache. Duplication is used to ensure higher protection of more important bits. Experimental results over single and dual-core systems confirm that our technique is effective in reducing architectural vulnerability factor. Our future work will focus on integrating our technique with early write-back scheme for proactively writing back dead blocks to further reduce the amount of vulnerable data in the cache.

Acknowledgments

Support for this work was provided by U.S. DoE, Office of Science, Advanced Scientific Computing Research.

7. REFERENCES

[1] S. Borkar, "Designing reliable systems from unreliable components: the challenges of transistor variability and degradation," *Micro, IEEE*, pp. 10–16, 2005.
[2] E. Normand, "Single-event effects in avionics," *IEEE Trans. Nucl. Sci.*, vol. 43, no. 2, pp. 461–474, 1996.
[3] S. Mittal *et al.*, "A Survey of Techniques for Modeling and Improving Reliability of Computing Systems," *IEEE TPDS*, 2015.
[4] J. F. Ziegler *et al.*, *SER–history, Trends and Challenges: A Guide for Designing with Memory ICs.* Cypress, 2004.
[5] S. S. Mukherjee *et al.*, "Cache scrubbing in microprocessors: Myth or necessity?" *PRDC*, 2004.
[6] A. Biswas *et al.*, "Explaining cache SER anomaly using DUE AVF measurement," in *HPCA*, 2010, pp. 1–12.
[7] S. Mittal *et al.*, "A Survey Of Architectural Approaches for Data Compression in Cache and Main Memory Systems," *IEEE TPDS*, 2015.
[8] G. Pekhimenko *et al.*, "Base-delta-immediate compression: practical data compression for on-chip caches," in *PACT*, 2012, pp. 377–388.
[9] W. Zhang *et al.*, "ICR: In-Cache Replication for Enhancing Data Cache Reliability," in *DSN*, 2003.
[10] A. Chakraborty *et al.*, "E < MC2: less energy through multi-copy cache," in *CASES*, 2010, pp. 237–246.
[11] G. Yalcin *et al.*, "Flexicache: Highly reliable and low power cache under supply voltage scaling," in *High Performance Computing*, 2014, pp. 173–190.
[12] G.-H. Asadi *et al.*, "Balancing performance and reliability in the memory hierarchy," in *ISPASS*, 2005.
[13] L. Li *et al.*, "Soft error and energy consumption interactions: a data cache perspective," *ISLPED*, 2004.
[14] B. T. Gold *et al.*, "Mitigating multi-bit soft errors in L1 caches using last-store prediction," in *ASGI*, 2007.
[15] W. Zhang, "Replication cache: a small fully associative cache to improve data cache reliability," *IEEE TC*, vol. 54, no. 12, pp. 1547–1555, 2005.
[16] S. Mittal, "A survey of architectural techniques for improving cache power efficiency," *SUSCOM*, 2014.
[17] S. S. Mukherjee *et al.*, "A systematic methodology to compute the architectural vulnerability factors for a high-performance microprocessor," in *MICRO*, 2003.
[18] Q. Zhou *et al.*, "Gate sizing to radiation harden combinational logic," *IEEE TCAD*, pp. 155–166, 2006.
[19] N. Binkert *et al.*, "The Gem5 simulator," *Computer Architecture News*, 2011.
[20] M. Poremba *et al.*, "DESTINY: A Tool for Modeling Emerging 3D NVM and eDRAM caches," *DATE*, 2015.
[21] O. Ergin *et al.*, "Exploiting narrow values for soft error tolerance," *CAL*, vol. 5, no. 2, pp. 12–12, 2006.
[22] J. Jung *et al.*, "Energy-efficient Spin-Transfer Torque RAM cache exploiting additional all-zero-data flags," in *ISQED*, 2013, pp. 216–222.

Workload-Aware Worst Path Analysis of Processor-Scale NBTI Degradation

Song Bian, Michihiro Shintani, Shumpei Morita
Hiromitsu Awano, Masayuki Hiromoto, Takashi Sato
Department of Communications and Computer Engineering, Kyoto University
Yoshida-hon-machi, Sakyo, Kyoto 606-8501, Japan
paper@easter.kuee.kyoto-u.ac.jp

ABSTRACT

As technology further scales semiconductor devices, aging-induced device degradation has become one of the major threats to device reliability. In addition, aging mechanisms like the negative bias temperature instability (NBTI) is known to be sensitive to workload (i.e., signal probability) that is hard to be assumed at design phase. In this work, we analyze the workload dependence of NBTI degradation using a processor, and propose a novel technique to estimate the worst-case paths. In our approach, with careful examination, we exploit the fact that the deterministic nature of circuit structure limits the amount of NBTI degradation on different paths, and proposes a two-stage path extraction algorithm to identify the invariable critical paths in the processor. Through numerical experiment on a MIPS32 processor, we performed a detailed signal probability analysis, and successfully extracted 85 invariable critical paths out of the 24,978 path candidates, achieving nearly 300x reduction in the sheer number of paths.

1. INTRODUCTION

In a time where semiconductor devices are scaling near the limit of physical laws, they become more and more unpredictable and uncontrollable. Nano-scale transistor devices vary their characteristics greatly even within a single chip, and one of the major factors for the variations is the fact of aging-induced device degradation. These variations have great impact on design decisions, since that without knowing how the device age, designers could potentially waste time optimizing paths that become non-critical in less than a year.

Among various aging mechanisms, negative bias temperature instability (NBTI) is considered to be one of the most crucial factors that shorten the lifespan of VLSI circuits. NBTI causes a gradual increase in threshold voltage ($V_{\rm th}$) while a negative bias is applied to a pMOS transistor, which causes the increase of the delay of combinational paths, eventually violating the design timing constraint. The state-of-art NBTI mitigation techniques include internal node control (INC) [8], input vector control (IVC) [2], and aging-aware logic synthesis [10]. Obviously, these methods require path delays in the circuit to be predicted correctly, such that the NBTI-induced stresses along those paths can be reduced. Unfortunately, accurate design-time NBTI prediction is known to be hard, since the amount of degradation varies greatly depending on the type of workload [6, 14, 16]. Thus, more recent research tried to focus on predicting NBTI degradation at runtime [5, 13]. Nonetheless, these techniques generally require excessive computational time that has not been systematically characterized, or regular scan-chain-based register dump that is both expensive and unrealistic for real-time systems or for constantly running processors. Existing workload-aware design-phase approaches for predicting NBTI degradation includes [15]. This work essentially analyzes and converts the verilog source code into a somewhat gate-like netlist, and determines which part of the circuit is susceptible to NBTI degradation. However, this technique only provides high-level indication of possible parts of circuit that *could* be under high NBTI stress, and cannot be used as a worst-case timing analyzer.

In this paper, we propose a novel approach to the problem of estimating worst-case path delay when NBTI degradation is considered. By observing the fact that certain paths in a design are much more likely to become critical when the workload is varied, a two-stage path extraction technique is proposed to find the group of paths that have a chance to become the most critical path under NBTI degradation. Theoretically, the number of elements in this critical-path group is indefinite. However, by conducting an experiment on a processor, we argue that *practically*, a small number of paths can be selected to represent the delay of all of the critical paths. In other words, when the workload applied to the design changes drastically, the delay for each path may change significantly, but the relative path delay between paths stays still. By exploiting this property, we can identify the critical paths under NBTI degradation, regardless of the workload being applied to the design.

In this paper, we use the term *invariable critical paths* to refer to this small subset of paths that, independent from workload, are the most timing critical in the design after a particular time of use. Note that, the invariable critical paths extracted in our analysis mostly do not match with the critical paths of a fresh chip in a regular sense. *Workload* here refers to the probabilities of the *primary inputs* of the processor, and is also sometimes referred to as the *primary-input vector*. *Signal probability* is mainly used to indicate the probability of a signal being in stress bias for the connecting

GLSVLSI '16, May 18 - 20, 2016, Boston, MA, USA

ISBN 978-1-4503-4274-2/16/05...$15.00
DOI: http://dx.doi.org/10.1145/2902961.2903013

gates, and is annotated for each signal. The signal probabilities are determined by the primary-input probabilities through probability propagation, and the NBTI degradation for each gate along paths is then determined by the signal probabilities annotated on this gate.

The key contribution of this work is summarized as follows:

- Observation of the relative invariability of critical paths under NBTI stress in practical designs when different workloads are applied.
- A systematic approach to extract the *invariable* critical paths under NBTI stress regardless of the workload being applied.

The following chapters of the paper are organized as follows. First, the NBTI model and our preliminary research is presented in Sec. 2. Second, the invariable critical path analysis along with our proposed two-stage path extraction algorithm is described in Sec. 3. An experiment is conducted on a MIPS processor, and the details will be discussed in Sec. 4.

2. BACKGROUND AND MOTIVATION

In this section, the NBTI model used in this paper and the main motivation are presented, in Subs. 2.1 and 2.2, respectively. It is noted that although we have chosen a particular NBTI model as the subject of study, the proposed path-extraction methodology is independent from the NBTI model being used and can be applied using any models that define long-term NBTI degradation in terms of signal probability.

2.1 NBTI Model

To predict NBTI-induced V_{th} degradation, NBTI measurements and mathematical models are studied in [6, 4]. Our degradation calculation is based on an analytical model in [6]. This model is based on the reaction-diffusion mechanism, and the long-term degradation is defined as the function of the signal probability α. The V_{th} degradation at a given time t can be approximated as

$$|\Delta V_{\text{th}}(t)| \approx \left(\frac{0.001 n^2 K^2 \alpha C t}{0.81 t_{\text{ox}}^2 (1-\alpha)} \right)^n, \quad (1)$$

where, K is a function of gate-source voltage, V_{th}, and temperature. t_{ox} is the oxide thickness, n is the time exponent which holds the value 1/6, α expresses the signal probability of a pMOS transistor, and C is a function of temperature. When $\alpha = 100\%$, $|\Delta V_{\text{th}}|$ becomes infinite and the model becomes incorrect. In a similar manner to what has been shown in [14], an upper limit is thus defined by

$$|\Delta V_{\text{th}}(t)| = (K^2 t)^n. \quad (2)$$

2.2 Motivation

A preliminary experiment is conducted to capture the signal switching characteristics in a typical five-stage pipelined processor [1] implementing the MIPS instruction set architecture. A subset of application programs in the MiBench [11] and high-level C sources from GAUT [9] is selected to be simulated on the target processor using a commercially-available simulator [17]. The processor is stressed under the condition of 400 K temperature for 10 years. A more detailed description on the experimental setup can be found in Sec. 4, and is cut out here for the sake of simplicity.

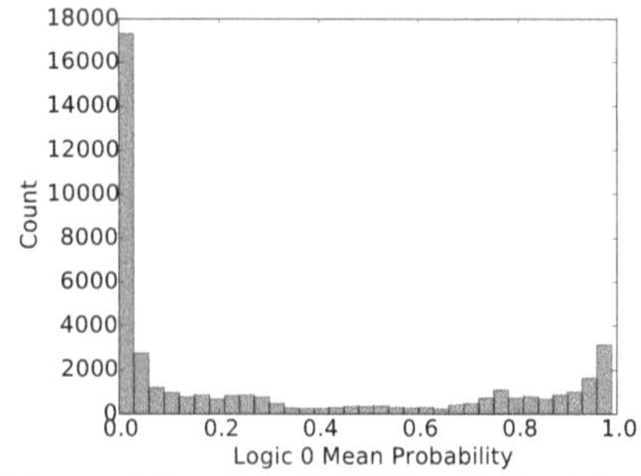

Figure 1: Mean of signal probability obtained from application program simulation.

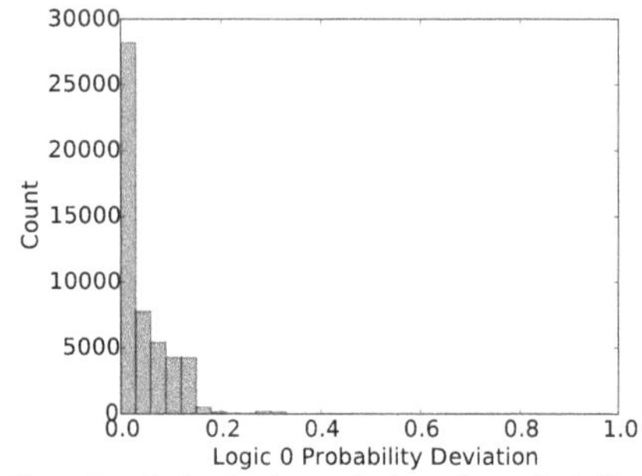

Figure 2: Standard deviation of signal probability obtained from application program simulation.

Table 1: Worst-case path delay and worst-case path ID when different application programs are applied to the processor.

Program	Worst-path ID	Worst-path delay (ns)
lms	3042	5.8651
aes	2929	6.0152
sobel	2929	6.0152
qsort	3042	6.0158
cordic	417	6.0399
sieve	441	6.3299
fft	417	6.4929
conv3x3	2929	6.6932

Figs. 1 and 2 show the distribution of probabilities of all signals in the processor across application programs. As shown, the majority of signal probabilities are static (i.e., standard deviation close to 0). Moreover, a certain number of gates are completely static with their means equal to either 0 or 1 with a 0 standard deviation. Despite the small standard deviation for most cells, Table 1 demonstrates that the worst-case delay varies significantly. More importantly, the worst-path ID column shown in Table 1 suggests that, although the worst-path delay varies greatly (from 5.8 ns to 6.8 ns), the worst-path ID is somewhat invariant (path 3042 becomes the worst path multiple times with distinctive delays). This motivated us to explore the relationship between NBTI-induced path delay and workload, especially the relationship between primary-input probabilities and critical paths.

In sections that follow, it is eventually discovered that, although path delays change significantly as primary-input probabilities change, the paths that degrade the most under NBTI is not changing. We define this behavior to be the *invariability* of critical paths under different workloads.

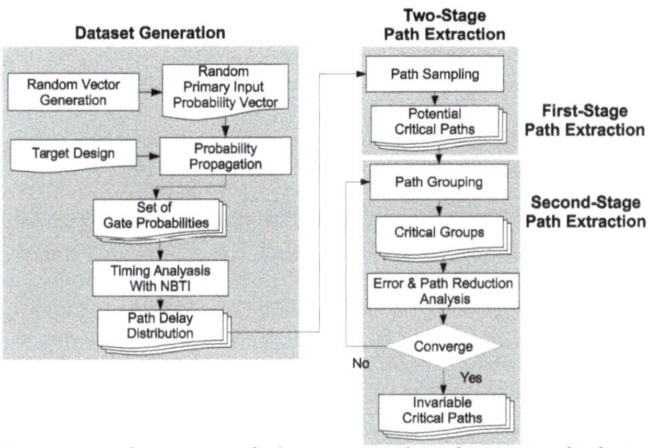

Figure 3: Overview of the proposed technique, which includes a dataset generation process and a two-stage path extraction algorithm.

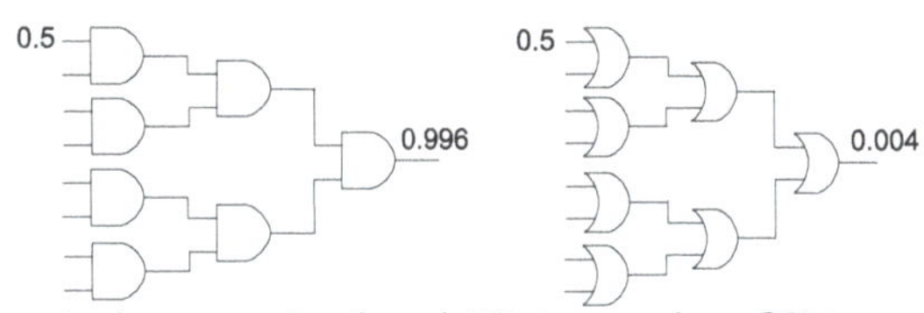

Figure 4: An example of an AND tree and an OR tree where the inputs are set to have a probability of 0.5 of being at logic 0. It can be observed that the AND tree amplifies the probability of logic 0, and the OR tree decreases the probability of logic 0.

3. INVARIABLE CRITICAL PATH ANALYSIS

In this section, the proposed two-stage path extraction process is introduced. Fig. 3 presents an overview of the proposed technique. In the beginning, a dataset is generated. One piece of data refers to a set of signal probabilities for all signals in the target design, and is generated from propagating one particular random primary-input vector through the design. A *dataset* then is defined as a set of such data. After generating the dataset, each signal in the target design will obtain a set of probabilities. A timing analysis is then applied to the dataset to obtain a set of timing distributions for paths in the target design. Next, a two-stage path extraction is performed to extract the invariable critical paths in the design. Last but not least, after the path extraction, an error analysis is performed to ensure that the extracted paths correctly captures the worst-case path delay generated in the dataset. When the error converges, the extracted paths are thus the invariable critical paths in this design.

3.1 Path Extractability

Before getting into the discussion of the path-extraction algorithm, an important assumption needs to be explained; that is, if the design is extractable. Here, an extractable design is defined as a design where a *small proportion* of its critical paths are *invariable* under workload-induced NBTI degradation. This definition coincide with the definition of *invariable critical paths* in Sec. 1. Thus, an extractable design always contains invariable critical paths, and vice versa.

Under some special design decision, as NBTI degrades the circuit, all paths have nearly equal chances to become the most critical path. This design is not extractable. However, it is also *special* since this condition requires all paths to be virtually the same, such that the amount of degradation in a particular path solely depends on the workload being applied to it. NBTI degradation in such design is trivial to estimate in such case (e.g., clock tree, multiple ALU units), where one path/unit can represent all other paths/units in the design. On the other hand, *general* designs tend to have distinct paths, and here, distinct paths are defined as paths that share very little gates in common. In such case, even if the paths have the same depth (i.e., same number of stages of gates), as Fig. 4 demonstrates, they may have extremely different NBTI degradation pattern, and is thus extractable. From hereon in this paper, the target design is assumed to be extractable.

3.2 Dataset and Empirical Variables

Signal probability propagation has been studied extensively in the field of power analysis [18] and NBTI-related probability propagation [20]. In this paper, a similar approach is taken in calculating the propagation of signal probabilities from the primary inputs. The generated dataset then acts as a series of independent Monte-Carlo samples for determining parameters for the proposed path extraction algorithm. These samples are then analyzed using an NBTI-aware timing analysis tool. Through timing analysis, gate delays will be calculated, and if we add up the gate delays for each path, a collection of path delay distributions can be obtained. This set of path delay distributions, denoted as $\mathcal{D}_{\mathcal{P}_{\text{all}}}$, works as a training dataset for the path extraction algorithm, and helps to determine the empirical variables T^{em} . The threshold delay T^{em} is used in the first-stage path extraction and will be explained in Subs. 3.3.1.

3.3 Extraction Algorithm

After calculating the timing distribution of the target design under different workloads using the previously mentioned timing analysis, path extraction can finally be performed. The two-stage path extraction algorithm is summarized in Alg. 1. The algorithm can be better understood through Fig. 3. In Alg. 1, line 1~5 corresponds to the first-stage path extraction, and line 6~15 completes the second stage of the path extraction. Line 16~22 is the error analysis step, and the algorithm repeats until error converges or $k = N$. The inputs to the algorithm include the predetermined T^{em} , the delay distribution of all paths in the design $\mathcal{D}_{\mathcal{P}_{\text{all}}}$, the path list that contains all paths in the design $\mathcal{P}_{\text{all}}$, as described in the previous Subs. 3.2. An additional term ϵ is added for error analysis, which will be discussed in Subs. 3.3.2.

3.3.1 First-Stage Path Extraction and T^{em}

The value of T^{em} is chosen based on $\mathcal{D}_{\mathcal{P}_{\text{all}}}$, the path timing distribution of the generated dataset as (a) in Fig. 5. At first, the choice of T^{em} can be made arbitrarily. A simple path sampling is carried out once T^{em} is determined. The main purpose of this stage is to reduce the large number of paths, such that later stages of the algorithm run faster and more efficient. The sampling process basically extracts paths that, according to the result of timing analysis, have ever crossed the barrier determined by T^{em} . Larger T^{em} reduces the number of paths to be considered significant, but increases the chance of missing paths that *could* have a chance to become the most critical path under some primary-input patterns that have not been applied (e.g.,

Algorithm 1 Two-Stage Path Extraction Algorithm.

```
Require: T^em , D_{P_all}, P_all, ε
1: for each path ∈ P_all do
2:     for each D ∈ D_{P_all} do
3:         if D(path) has value > T^em then
4:             add path to path_list
5: initialize k (0 or 1)
6: while (max_error < ε) && (k < N) do
7:     increment k
8:     initialize Rep_List
9:     G_all = partition path_list into k groups
10:    for each G ∈ G_all do
11:        for each D ∈ D_{P_all} do
12:            order paths in G according to their delays in D
13:            increment the count for the most critical path in G according to D
14:        P_REP = path with the maximum count in G
15:        Rep_List.append(P_REP)
16:    max_error = −1
17:    for each D ∈ D_{P_all} do
18:        worst = Worst path delay in D
19:        worst_rep = Worst path delay in D only considering paths in Rep_List
20:        error = worst - worst_rep
21:        if error > max_error then
22:            max_error = error
23: return Rep_List, k
```

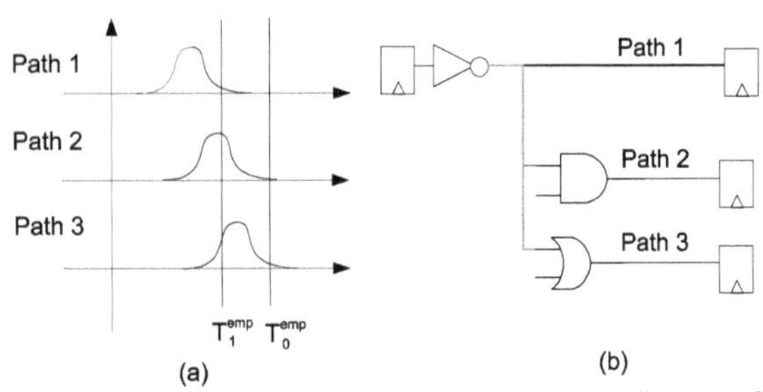

Figure 5: An example of three paths with two different T^{em} choices. (a) is an example of path delay distribution where the x-axis is delay. Depending on T^{em} , path 1 will or will not be extracted in the first stage. (b) is an example circuit that could have a delay distribution in (a).

path 1 is left out with T_0^{em} , but it could become the most critical path under some primary-input vector). However, it is also likely that path 1 can never obtain a longer path delay than path 2 and path 3, if the real circuit looks like the one in Fig. 5 (b). Hence, by the assumption of extractable design, if the selected T^{em} correctly captures all possible critical-path candidates (path 2 and path 3), further deduction in T^{em} will result in no change in the result of the two-stage path extraction (this will be further elaborated in Subs. 3.3.2. Thus, by performing the proposed path extraction algorithm on several T^{em} steps, the true empirical delay boundary T_{true}^{em} can be found and verified.

3.3.2 *Second-Stage Path Extraction*

Although the first stage of the proposed path-extraction algorithm already reduces the number of paths to be considered significant, it fails to take into account the correlation between paths. That is, suppose two paths P and P can both have their delays to be greater than T^{em} , both of them are assumed to be paths that have a chance to become the most critical paths in the design. However, if P and P are mostly the same, with only a slight difference at some stages along the path, the delays of these two paths are going to be extremely close. In addition, if, in stages when P and P have different gates and the delays for the different gates in P are always greater than P (e.g., and gate versus inverter), then P essentially has no chance to become the most critical path in the deign, regardless of the primary-input pattern (i.e., workload). Thus, to further reduce the number of paths needed to be considered, the second stage of the path-extraction algorithm is performed.

The main procedure in the second-stage path extraction is to partition the paths selected in the first stage into groups, and select a representative path for each group. This grouping process can be modeled as a classic multiclass classification problem and potentially be solved by some advanced machine learning algorithm. In this paper, we used the simple yet effective k-means++ clustering algorithm for path partitioning [3]. The k-means++ algorithm is a popular algorithm mainly used in data mining [3] that partitions n observations into k sets, where each observation is a d-dimensional vector. The vector used here is path similarity measured in Jaccard similarity coefficient [12]. Each path has its Jaccard coefficient calculated with respect to every other path and forms an N-dimensional vector, where N is the number of paths after the first-stage of path extraction algorithm.

Since the k-means++ algorithm works only as a classifier, it is necessary to elect a "real" representative path from each group, instead of the centroid point. This representative election actually determines the maximum error. For example, if P in the previous example is selected as a representative instead of P , the delays of this path group is going to be constantly underestimated. In this work, we used a simple majority approach for representative election, as line 11∼15 indicates. The result of timing analysis is again used, and the path in the group that has the highest number of times being the worst-delay path in the group is selected to be the representative.

After the group representatives are elected, the maximum error is calculated in line 16∼22 in Alg. 1, where the difference between the true worst-case path delay of all paths in one piece of data D is compared to the worst-case path delay of the paths in the representative list. This error needs to be small, and a constraint ϵ is added to make sure that the maximum error is below this value. If the error is larger than ϵ, we consider the number of groups for the k-means++ algorithm to be insufficient, such increment the number of groups by 1 and repeat the grouping process. Due to the stochastic nature of the dataset generation, for extremely small number of datasets, this approach may result in more groups being used than necessary. However, with a reasonable amount of datasets, as will be described in Sec. 4.2, representative paths quickly converge.

4. EXPERIMENT

Numerical experiments are conducted using a five-stage pipelined processor [1] that implements the full MIPS32 instruction set with a co-processor handling exceptions. In the experiment, Nangate 45 nm Open Cell Library [19] is used for circuit synthesis. The tools used in our analysis flow are all commercial quality — the processor is synthesized

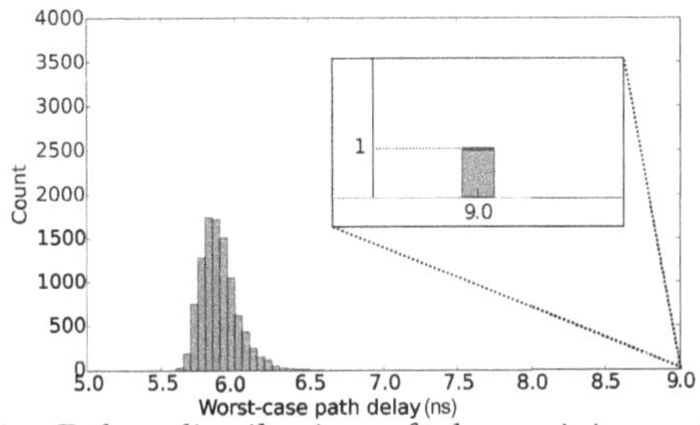

Figure 6: Delay distribution of the training set + test dataset (10,000 samples).

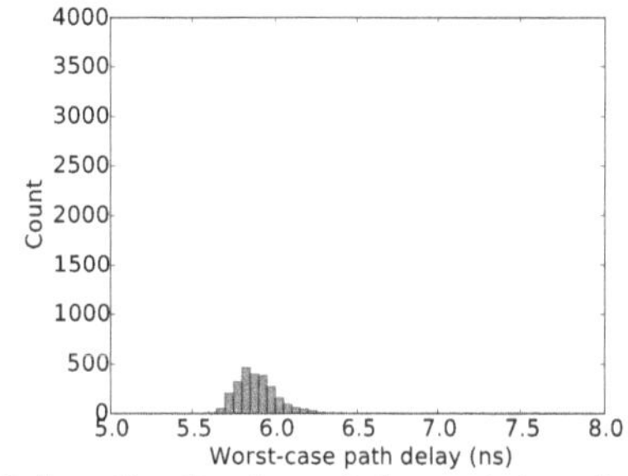

Figure 7: Delay distribution of the training dataset (2,500 samples).

using a logic-synthesis tool [21]. Gate-level probability is calculated using [23], and post-synthesis simulation is conducted using [17]. A static timing analysis (STA) tool [22] is used to extract paths from the processor. We have extracted the top 24,978 paths, ordered by worst-case slack, from the processor design. As later explained in Subs. 4.2, further increasing the number of paths extracted by the STA tool becomes irrelevant. For timing analysis with NBTI, as fast method described in [7] is implemented using the Python language, where the traditional STA library is replaced with a three-dimensional Look-Up Table (LUT) that returns the gate delay with NBTI degradation when the input signal probabilities are given. The degradation condition, as also described in Sec. 2, is 400 K for 10 years. The technology library used in this experiment is Nangate 45 nm Open Cell Library [19].

4.1 Experimental Setup

To carefully evaluate the quality of the extracted invariable critical paths, we used a training-test approach, where a training set is used for path extraction, and a test set is used for invariable critical path evaluation. In this experiment, a training dataset of size 2,500 samples is generated, and the proposed two-stage path extraction process is applied. The extracted invariable critical paths are then evaluated on both the training set and a test dataset of size 7,500 samples (total of 10,000 samples). We also show that the result of random input vector applies to real-world application programs as well. The error bound ϵ is taken to be 1 %.

Figs. 6 and 7 are the results of timing analysis on the set of test+training (10,000) and training only (2,500) samples where only the delay of the worst-slack path is shown. The two figures share a similar shape of distribution. However, the largest delay recorded is drastically different. The largest delay observed in training dataset is 6.7 ns, while it is an astonishing 9.025 ns for the test dataset. Comparing to the fresh-time worst-case delay without NBTI degradation (4.74 ns), depending on the workload variation, the delay can be as much as 1.9x times longer than the fresh-time delay. Thus, the training dataset we used cannot capture the full degraded delay range. Nevertheless, due to the relative order property described in Sec. 1, by calculating the path delays of the selected paths, it is demonstrated in Subs. 4.2 that this value can be captured without considering a large amount of paths in the design.

4.2 Experimental Result

To determine the T^{em}, we assumed a normal distribution on the worst-case delay on the small dataset, and set T^{em} according to the μ and σ of the normal distribution. It is noted that the worst-case delay does not necessarily obey a normal distribution, and the T^{em} selection can be

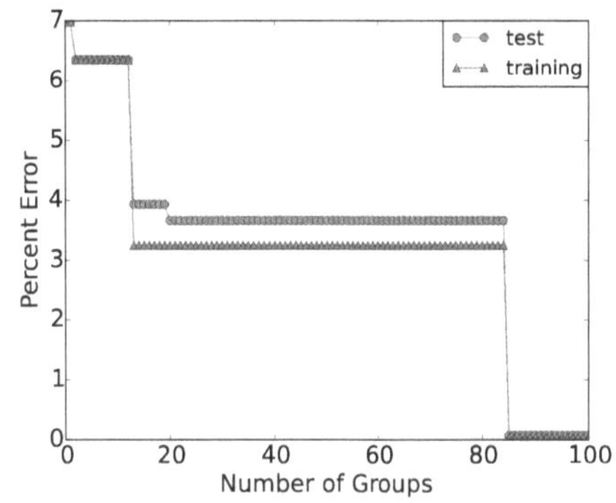

Figure 8: Maximum percent error calculated using training and test datasets as the number of groups used for k-means++ algorithm increases.

Table 2: T^{em} selection and the corresponding number of paths extracted when T^{em} is set to the particular delay.

T^{em} Selection	Delay (ns)	Path 1st Stage	Path 2nd Stage	% Error
$\mu+3\sigma$	6.321	98	98	6.77
$\mu+2\sigma$	6.180	142	142	6.15
$\mu+\sigma$	6.039	225	85	0.07
μ	5.898	405	85	0.07
$\mu-\sigma$	5.757	595	85	0.07
$\mu-2\sigma$	5.616	890	85	0.07
$\mu-3\sigma$	5.475	1510	85	0.07

made using any approach. Our T^{em} choices, their corresponding delays and the number extracted in the first stage as well as in the second stage are summarized in Table 2. It can be observed that the number of paths extracted in the first stage increases in a log-like manner as we decrease the boundary delay. However, as the result from the second stage shows, only an extremely limited number of paths are actually important. Other paths are generally considered to be paths that can obtain a large path delay, but always less than the delay of the invariable critical path. On the other hand, if T^{em} is too large, as in the case of $\mu+3\sigma$ and $\mu+2\sigma$, the error never converges, and the path extraction algorithm actually fails at these T^{em} choices. Overall, it can be observed that the training phase of the invariable critical path selection correctly captured the relative path orders between paths, resulting in negligible errors when evaluated on the full dataset (10,000 samples).

Fig. 8 gives the result of second-stage path extraction for a single T^{em} choice. The horizontal axis denotes the number of groups initially given for k-means++ classification, and

Table 3: Worst-case delay evaluated on the extracted invariable critical paths and its ID, compared to the True delay, which is the same as specified in Table 1.

Program	Extracted Worst ID	Extracted delay (ns)	True delay (ns)	% Error
lms	2929	5.8602	5.8651	0.08
aes	2929	6.0152	6.0152	0
sobel	2929	6.0152	6.0152	0
qsort	2929	6.1524	6.0158	0.008
cordic	417	6.0399	6.0399	0
sieve	417	6.3255	6.3299	0.07
fft	417	6.5584	6.4929	0
conv3x3	2929	6.8651	6.6932	0

the vertical axis shows delay error. The figure reveals that when distinctive paths are not separated, both training set and test set retain large errors. Once the necessary paths are separated, the errors drop significantly below ϵ, which is 1 %. The same result is obtained evaluating application programs.

To echo with the preliminary research in Sec. 2, the extracted 85 paths are evaluated against all paths using different signal probabilities determined by each application programs. Table 3 summarizes the result for each application. It is clear from the table that worst-path delays are completely captured by the extracted invariable critical path with a 1 % ϵ (actually ϵ can be as small as 0.1 %, since all errors are around 0.08 % at 85 groups). Note that these errors are all results evaluated on the full dataset with 10,000 samples.

5. CONCLUSION

In this paper, we proposed a novel approach for the extraction of design-time workload-independent critical paths, named *invariable* critical paths in this paper, with NBTI-induced delay degradation. Motivated by the fact that the number of invariable critical paths may be extremely small, we utilized a systematical approach of dataset generation and two-stage path extraction to carefully classify and extract the invariable critical paths from a design, ensuring these extracted paths really represent the whole group. By conducting a numerical experiment, we extracted the invariable critical paths in an example five-stage pipelined processor, and verified the extracted paths on a test dataset. We have shown that with a tiny error bound (< 1 %), worst-case path delay can be successfully obtained by only calculating the delays of 85 paths in a large processor design.

6. ACKNOWLEDGMENT

This work was partially supported by JSPS KAKENHI Grant No. 26280014 and 15K15960. The authors also acknowledge support from VLSI Design and Education Center (VDEC), the University of Tokyo in collaboration with Synopsys, Inc.

7. REFERENCES

[1] OpenCores. http://www.opencores.org.

[2] A. Abdollahi, F. Fallah, and M. Pedram. Leakage current reduction in CMOS VLSI circuits by input vector control. *IEEE Trans. VLSI Systems*, 12(2):140–154, 2004.

[3] D. Arthur and S. Vassilvitskii. k-means++: The advantages of careful seeding. In *Proc. ACM-SIAM Symp. Discrete Algorithms*, pages 1027–1035, 2007.

[4] H. Awano, M. Hiromoto, and T. Sato. BTIarray: a time-overlapping transistor array for efficient statistical characterization of bias temperature instability. *IEEE Trans. Dev. Mater. Rel.*, 14(3):833–843, 2014.

[5] R. Baranowski et al. On-line prediction of NBTI-induced aging rates. In *Proc. DATE*, pages 589–592, 2015.

[6] S. Bhardwaj, W. Wang, R. Vattikonda, Y. Cao, and S. Vrudhula. Predictive modeling of the NBTI effect for reliable design. In *Proc. CICC*, pages 189–192, 2006.

[7] S. Bian, M. Shintani, S. Morita, M. Hiromoto, and T. Sato. Nonlinear delay-table approach for full-chip NBTI degradation prediction. In *Proc. ISQED*, pages 307–312, 2016.

[8] D. R. Bild, R. P. Dick, and G. E. Bok. Static NBTI reduction using internal node control. *ACM TODAES*, 17(4):45–75, 2012.

[9] C. Chavet et al. A design flow dedicated to multi-mode architectures for DSP applications. In *Proc. ICCAD*, pages 604–611, 2007.

[10] M. Ebrahimi, F. Oboril, S. Kiamehr, and M. B. Tahoori. Aging-aware logic synthesis. In *Proc. ICCAD*, pages 61–68, 2013.

[11] M. Guthaus et al. MiBench: A free, commercially representative embedded benchmark suite. In *Proc. WWC*, pages 3–14, 2001.

[12] L. Hamers et al. Similarity measures in scientometric research: the Jaccard index versus Salton's cosine formula. *Information Processing & Management*, 25(3):315–318, 1989.

[13] A. Koneru, A. Vijayan, K. Chakrabarty, and M. B. Tahoori. Fine-grained aging prediction based on the monitoring of run-time stress using DfT infrastructure. In *Proc. ICCAD*, pages 51–58, 2015.

[14] H. Konoura, Y. Mitsuyama, M. Hashimoto, and T. Onoye. Comparative study on delay degrading estimation due to NBTI with circuit/instance/transistor-level stress probability consideration. In *Proc. ISQED*, pages 646–651, 2010.

[15] J. A. Kumar, K. M. Butler, H. Kim, and S. Vasudevan. Early prediction of NBTI effects using RTL source code analysis. In *Proc. DAC*, pages 808–813, 2012.

[16] D. Lorenz, G. Georgakos, and U. Schlichtmann. Aging analysis of circuit timing considering NBTI and HCI. In *Proc. IOLTS*, pages 3–8, 2009.

[17] Mentor Graphics, Inc. *ModelSim SE 10.2c.*

[18] F. N. Najm. A survey of power estimation techniques in VLSI circuits. *IEEE Trans. VLSI Systems*, 2:446–455, 1994.

[19] Si2.org. Nangate 45nm open cell library. http://www.si2.org.

[20] A. Stempkovsky, A. Glebov, and S. Gavrilov. Calculation of stress probability for NBTI-aware timing analysis. In *Proc. ISQED*, pages 714–718, 2009.

[21] Synopsys, Inc. *Design Compiler I-2013.06.*

[22] Synopsys, Inc. *PrimeTime Fundamental H-2013.06.*

[23] Synopsys, Inc. *PrimeTime PX H-2013.06.*

Enhancing Fault Emulation of Transient Faults by Separating Combinational and Sequential Fault Propagation

Ralph Nyberg
Fraunhofer AISEC
ralph.nyberg@aisec.fraunhofer.de

Johann Heyszl
Fraunhofer AISEC
johann.heyszl@aisec.fraunhofer.de

Dietmar Heinz
Infineon Technologies AG
dietmar.heinz@infineon.com

Georg Sigl
Fraunhofer AISEC
georg.sigl@aisec.fraunhofer.de
Technische Universität München
sigl@tum.de

ABSTRACT

We present a fault emulation environment capable of injecting single and multiple transient faults in sequential as well as combinational logic. It is used to perform fault injection campaigns during design verification of security circuits such as smart cards. In order to reduce the unacceptable hardware overhead of fault emulation for combinational faults, we split the problem of combinational fault modeling into two steps: 1) Fault injection in combinational cells and propagation into sequential cells, processed by a software approach, and 2) fast FPGA-based fault emulation of faults in sequential logic. We used the presented tool to emulate single and multiple faults in two different designs used for security applications. We analyzed how faults propagate from combinational to sequential logic, discuss the resulting consequences for developers of security circuits and fault analysis environments and derive performance optimizations. We demonstrate the performance of our method with varying tests and varying fault multiplicities. Interestingly, we found that the presented method outperforms conventional standalone FPGA-based approaches, while it requires 45% less logic elements on the FPGA.

1. INTRODUCTION

Transient faults in digital circuits may occur infrequently and temporarily at runtime and are caused by high-energetic particle strikes or other radiation sources. Moreover, faults are deliberately injected by attackers to compromise security devices, so-called fault attacks, which also result in transient faults that ranges from single faults to multiple faults with a very large multiplicity (number of simultaneously present faults) [1, 2]. Decreasing feature sizes [3] and multi beam laser attacks increase the probability of multiple fault occurrences even further. In the worst case, a secret such as a cryptographic key could be extracted because of a fault attack, which is the major concern for designers of security circuits.

GLSVLSI '16, May 18 - 20, 2016, Boston, MA, USA

ISBN 978-1-4503-4274-2/16/05...$15.00

DOI: http://dx.doi.org/10.1145/2902961.2903021

In order to check proper circuit behavior in the presence of faults and to hinder attackers from gaining advantages out of fault attacks, security devices such as security controllers and smart cards deploy fault countermeasures. To reduce design costs and time-to-market, the effectiveness of fault countermeasures has to be verified through performing fault injection campaigns during a limited time frame for verification early in the development cycle of the circuit [1]. For this purpose, a huge amount of transient faults (varying locations and timings) need to be injected into the Device Under Test (DUT).

Unfortunately, the fault space for multiple faults is so large that it renders the analysis of all faults impossible. Even if only single points of attacks in real-world designs are considered, millions of fault experiments already have to be performed. Analyzing faults is therefore usually prioritized as follows: 1) all single faults in sequential and combinational cells and 2) relevant multiple faults. Furthermore, fault analysis environments have to provide high performance and relevant multiple faults are selected using either layout [4] or structural information [1, 5, 2], or statistical fault injection is performed [6]. However, multiple faults in combinational cells have only been tackled with slow software-based approaches, e.g. [7, 8]. Fault analysis environments are also required to handle both circuit and test complexity of security controllers. These are typically synchronous sequential circuits, which are usually composed of a microprocessor, crypto co-processors and some other peripheral devices. The software executed by a security controller has to use security relevant hardware properly, following a programming guidance, and may implement additional software-based fault countermeasures. Because of this and also because of very limited top level interfaces, security controllers are stimulated with functional tests as a representative of relevant situations during fault analysis. For these complex designs software-based approaches struggle, especially when functional tests lasting thousands or ten-thousands of clock cycles or multiple faults are considered, whereas FPGA-based fault emulation offers high speed even for large designs.

FPGA-based fault emulation is the fasted method to perform extensive fault analysis. It is three to six orders of magnitude faster [9, 10, 11] than simulation and software-based approaches. This high performance provided by fault emulation allows to benefit as much as possible from limited verification times during design. To allow fault emulation, the DUT is altered so that it provides fault injection capability based on a fault model, e.g. using the circuit instrumentation technique [11, 9, 12]. An FPGA is then configured with the instrumented DUT. For fault injection into combinational or sequential cells, at least one additional flip-flop (FF) for controlling the fault injection, some combinational cells for implementing the fault model and additional routing on the FPGA are required for each instrumented cell. Digital designs usually comprise about five to ten times more combinational cells than sequential cells. The hardware overhead for fault emulation can be kept in check by only considering fault injection in sequential cells. However, these setups do not allow to analyze the combinational logic's vulnerability to faults. Fault emulation environments that support fault injection in combinational cells, e.g. [12], [9] and [10], demand a lot of hardware resources on FPGAs. Additional logic is inserted into the data path, not only once per register but for each combinational cell. This causes two issues: 1) The hardware overhead for fault injection increases, which limits fault emulation to smaller circuits because of limited hardware resources on FPGAs. 2) The critical timing path gets longer. We experienced a 68% reduced maximum operating frequency when the combinational logic of an 8051-like micro-controller is instrumented for fault injection. Therefore, existing emulation-based approaches restrict fault injection in combinational logic to few locations. As a consequence, these approaches can not be used for multiple fault selection based on layout or structural information, for which it is mandatory to be able to select any multiple fault.

This work overcomes the discussed issues w.r.t. combinational fault modeling of FPGA-based fault emulation and is suitable as an accelerator for extensive multiple fault injection in combinational logic (e.g. based on layout information). We achieve this with a new combined approach that utilizes a software-based method to propagate faults from combinational logic into sequential cells and then proceeds with fast FPGA-based fault emulation for faults in sequential cells. In this way, we remove the hardware overhead for instrumenting combinational cells completely. As a result, our method can be applied to much bigger circuits. Furthermore, it is able to inject any multiple transient fault into combinational and sequential cells. Interestingly, our method is also faster compared to existing work, as we will demonstrate in the result section.

The rest of this work is structured as follows: Our method for efficient fault emulation is proposed in Section 2. The implementation is outlined in Section 3. Hardware requirements and performance results for single and multiple faults, carried out for two DUTs and varying functional tests, are discussed and compared to existing work in Section 4. Finally, Section 5 concludes this work.

2. PROPOSED METHOD

The proposed method is applicable to inject *Single* and *Multiple Event Transients (SET, MET)*, which correspond to single and multiple faults in combinational logic. Basically, in the very first cycle of fault propagation, SETs and METs are mapped to equivalent faults at inputs of sequential cells by utilizing Boolean constraint propagation provided by a SAT-solver. *Single* and *Multiple Event Upset (SEU, MEU)*, which correspond to single and multiple faults in sequential logic, can be modeled with the used fault emulator by default and without any software-based preprocessing. A high-level transient fault model similar to the one presented in [13] is used. The fault duration in combinational and sequential logic is modeled for one clock cycle. This fault model considers only logical fault masking, which is one of three different masking effects that can prevent fault propagation into sequential cells. Therefore, high-level fault models pose a more pessimistic approach, compared to low-level fault models that consider electrical and latching-window masking in addition. However, high-level fault models allow to focus on cases where faults actually lead to errors and are already applicable early in the development cycle when low-level information such as timings are not available [13]. This is of importance for validating fault countermeasures [13] and for identifying security flaws early during circuit design [1].

2.1 Combinational Fault Propagation

Again, only in case of fault injection into combinational cells, we split the problem of fault modeling into two steps, as depicted in Figure 1. First (depicted left), the assumption[1] function of a SAT-solver is used to inject SETs or METs F_k into the combinational logic *comb'* and to apply stimuli $x_C[t]$ (composed of top level stimuli $x[t]$ and states $s[t]$) at combinational inputs. In the very first cycle t of fault propagation, i.e. the fault injection time, the propagate function of a SAT-solver is used to map these SETs and METs to equivalent transient faults at inputs of sequential cells (SEUs, MEUs). As depicted in Figure 1, equivalent sequential faults are determined by XORing the fault-free next-state $s[t+1]$, generated by a fault-free instance of the combinational logic *comb*, and the faulty next-state $s'[t+1]$, generated by the faulty combinational logic *comb'*.

2.2 Sequential Fault Propagation

In the second step (depicted right in Figure 1), the determined transient faults at inputs of sequential cells (SEUs, MEUs) are captured and mapped onto the fault emulator by means of XORing it with the fault-free next-state $s[t+1]$. The fault emulator performs fault-free state transitions in advance until the fault injection cycle t is reached, in which the fault effects determined in the first step are mapped onto the fault emulator by means of XORing it with the fault-free next-state $s[t+1]$. The result is the faulty next-state $s'[t+1]$, which is latched by DFFs. That is, an equivalent sequential fault (SEU or MEU) is injected, which is present at outputs of DFFs in the next clock cycle. Now, the fault injection is deactivated and the sequential fault emulation is continued until the end of the test.

2.3 Optimizations

To increase performance, only distinguishable faults, which are faults that differ in timing and affected sequential cells from any other determined fault, are mapped onto the fault emulator. Furthermore, we propose to analyze all SEUs in advance to performing fault injection campaigns for METs. In this way, all SETs and METs that result in SEUs are

[1]Assumption functions can be used to constrain input variables by assuming values of Boolean variables.

already covered for subsequent fault injection campaigns, i.e. only distinguishable METs (dMETs) need to be further considered for fault emulation. These optimizations were derived from the following fault propagation results.

Among other experiments, we analyzed 22.4 million SETs in an 8051-like microcontroller. In total, 46.9% of these SETs are propagated and latched by sequential logic (37.6% SEUs and 9.3% MEUs). Only 3.8% of analyzed SETs result in distinguishable MEUs (dMEUs), which provides a very good optimization. We performed similar fault injection campaigns for randomly generated 2bit-METs, 3bit-METs and 10bit-METs. When increasing the fault multiplicity of METs, it is more likely that MEUs are latched, while the number of SEUs decreases and distinguishable faults in sequential logic are generated less frequently. Therefore, the fault emulator is optimized to handle single as well as multiple transient faults in sequential cells without performance loss compared to fault free test runs. We noticed that a random MET with fault multiplicity m_{MET} is latched with a probability expressed by $1-(1-P_{latched}(SET))^{m_{MET}}$, where $P_{latched}(SET)$ is the probability that a SET is latched. This is useful to approximate fault effects of METs when results for SETs are available. Note, this relationship is based on randomly generated multiple faults, which are not locally constraint by layout or structural information.

2.4 Discussion

From these results we conclude several points: Considering only SEUs and dMEUs for fault emulation reduces the effort spent during fault emulation drastically. Furthermore, fault analysis environments that are able to handle multiple faults efficiently (such as the presented one) and new selection strategies for relevant multiple faults are required to evaluate fault countermeasures against these kind of faults efficiently. Moreover, because of the high probability of a laser shot to inject multiple faults into a circuit [1, 2], security concepts are required to deal with single faults as well as multiple faults with varying fault multiplicities. Papadimitriou et al. [1], who use structural and layout information to select faults without considering actual stimuli, report fault multiplicities in the thousands. In our experiments, which consider actual stimuli, we experienced that SETs result in MEUs with fault multiplicities of several hundreds. The proposed method therefore already poses a less pessimistic, but stimuli-dependent, selection strategy for multiple faults in sequential logic.

The proposed method enables us to inject any single and multiple fault. Hence, it is perfectly suitable for accelerating complex fault injection campaigns based on layout or structural information. It allows to profit from the high performance that FPGA-based fault emulation provides without limiting fault injection to few locations and does not generate hardware overhead for combinational fault injection. This makes the proposed method applicable to larger DUTs and, as shown by the results in Section 4, results in a higher overall performance because of both the proposed optimizations and a higher operating frequency.

3. IMPLEMENTATION

This section presents the tool flow implementing the fault analysis environment. Implementation details about combinational fault injection and propagation with a SAT-solver and sequential fault propagation utilizing FPGA-based fault emulation are outlined as well. Our previous work [14] provides a detailed description of the utilized fault emulator. The proposed method is suitable for fault emulators that are able to inject SEUs and MEUs into sequential cells.

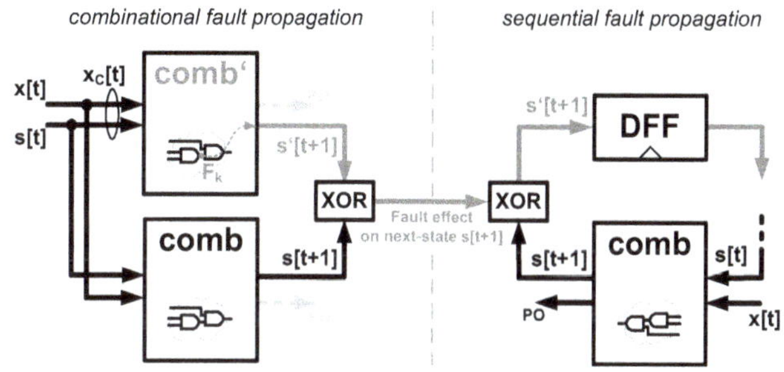

Figure 1: Combined approach of a) combinational fault injection and propagation of fault F_k at fault injection time t, processed in software (left), and b) sequential fault propagation, processed by FPGA-based fault emulation, depicted for the first faulty state transition $s[t] \rightarrow s'[t+1]$ (right)

3.1 Tool Flow

The fault analysis environment is depicted in Figure 2. The red-colored items highlight the implementation of the fault propagation depicted in Figure 1. The tool flow utilizes two EDA tools, a customized version of MiniSAT 2.2.0, an FPGA-based fault emulator and custom scripts written in Perl and TCL. First, a *pre-processing* is performed to generate the input of our methodology. A synthesis tool (Synopsys Design Compiler) divides the DUT into sequential and combinational logic, writes a complete netlist and writes the pure combinational part of the circuit into a second netlist. The synthesis tool also generates a fault list composed of SETs, based on which fault lists composed of METs are generated. Input stimuli for the combinational logic are generated through gate level simulation of the complete netlist. These input stimuli are then used together with the other pure combinational netlist, which is translated into DIMACS[2] CNF[3] format, for combinational fault propagation with MiniSAT. MiniSAT performs a *combinational fault propagation* flow, which is outlined in Section 3.2. The result is a list of fault effects captured at inputs of sequential cells, i.e. a sequential fault list, which covers all determined SEUs and MEUs. The sequential fault list is collapsed to distinguishable faults (only dMEUs if all SEUs are analyzed in advance), with which the fault emulator is fed for *sequential fault propagation*, as outlined in Section 3.3. Synthesis and logic simulation are automated using TCL scripts. Several custom scripts, written in Perl, combine all tools and subscripts into a completely automated flow, handle file format conversion and perform result analysis.

3.2 Combinational Fault Propagation

The fault injection and propagation flow presented in this section has been implemented using Boolean constraint propagation, provided by the open source SAT-solver MiniSAT [15]. We use MiniSAT instead of fault simulation because fault simulators supporting METs were not available, neither from academia nor industry. Furthermore, fault simulators drop a fault from simulation as soon as it is detected at observation points, whereas we require to extract

[2]Center for Discrete Mathematics and Theoretical Computer Science

[3]Conjunctive Normal Form, excepted by MiniSAT as input

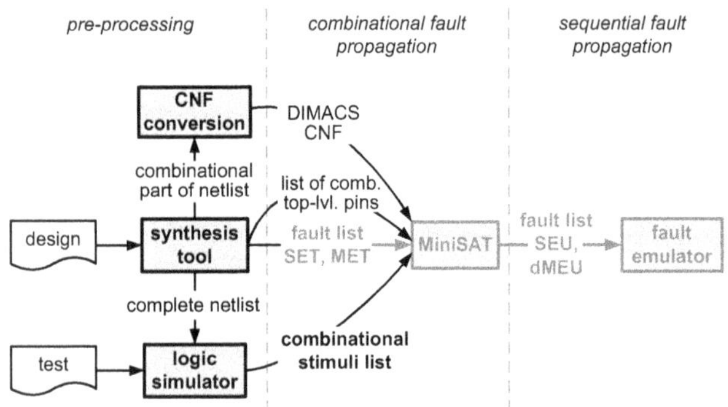

Figure 2: Automated tool flow utilizing a synthesis tool and a logic simulator to generate the input for our methodology processed by MiniSAT and an FPGA-based fault emulator.

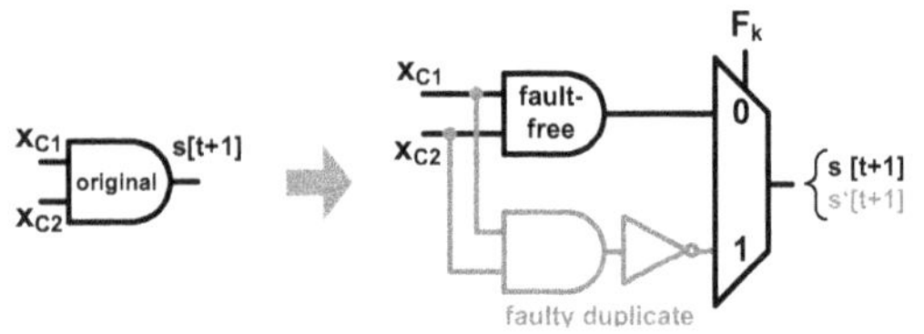

Figure 3: Adding fault injection capability to an AND-gate

the exact output levels of the combinational logic part for each fault. Propagate functions of SAT-solvers are highly optimized (linear complexity). As long as the circuit input is completely constraint, which is the case in the presented application, conflicts do not occur, and MiniSAT is able to solve the problem with unit clause propagation. Additionally, using multiple instances of MiniSAT, the effort spent is well scalable without generating license costs. However, a fault simulator that is optimized for the problem tackled in this contribution could provide a further performance enhancement.

We enabled MiniSAT to automatically add fault injection capability for each output of combinational gates in its internal CNF representation of the circuit, as depicted for an example AND-gate in Figure 3. The original gate is duplicated with an inverted output. An additional multiplexer is used to chose between the original fault-free gate and the duplicated, faulty gate. This can be represented in CNF in a very efficient and easy to generate way. A similar modification is performed for each combinational gate in the circuit. Each gate output is assigned to a consecutive number $k \in \{1, ..., n_F\}$, where n_F is the number of combinational fault locations F_k. Fault locations are gathered in a fault vector $F := (F_1, F_2, ..., F_{n_F})$ with $F_k \in \{0, 1\}$. Each component of the fault vector defines whether the corresponding gate pin is faulty ($F_k = 1$) or fault-free ($F_k = 0$) by applying it to the corresponding multiplexers, using MiniSAT's assumption function. This way, SETs as well as METs are configured in a very generic way. The described approach is effective for single-output gates only. If a gate has multiple outputs, e.g. adders, the gate will be instantiated multiple times. For example, the gate will be instantiated twice for gates with two outputs. For each instance, only one output is connected in the netlist, i.e. the first output of the first instance and the second output of the second instance and so on. Corresponding inputs of all instances are connected in parallel. In this way, the concept of adding fault injection capability to single-output gates is still valid.

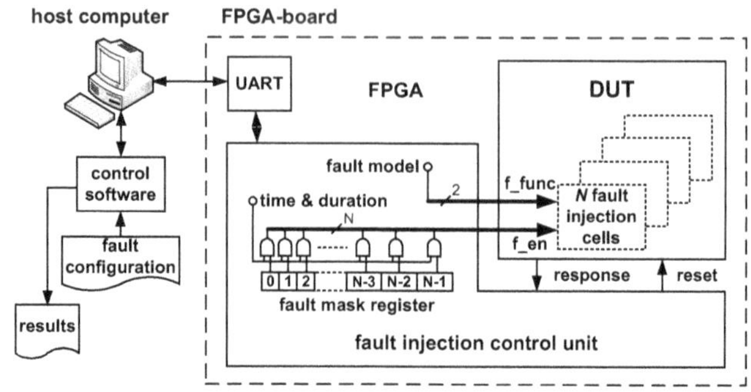

Figure 4: The FPGA-based fault emulator for SEUs and MEUs

Our modified version of MiniSAT iterates a combinational fault list (SETs and METs) and a list of combinational stimuli, consisting of one stimulus $x_c[t]$ for each fault injection time t. A fault-free propagation for each stimulus is performed in advance in order to determine a fault-free reference for all next-states $s[t+1]$. Then, MiniSAT iterates both the list of combinational stimuli and the fault list in a double nested loop. For each iteration, MiniSAT determines the fault effect on the next-state ($s[t+1]$ xor $s'[t+1]$) according to Figure 1, as outlined in Section 2, resulting in a sequential fault list composed of SEUs and MEUs. Two lists of CNF variables specify the appropriate top-level inputs and outputs where stimuli are applied and the result is captured. As already mentioned and further discussed in Section 4, the resulting fault list is optimized by collapsing it to distinguishable representatives before it is then used as input for sequential fault emulation. In order to increase the tool performance, multiple (20 in our experiments) MiniSAT instances are executed in parallel for independent fault sets.

3.3 Sequential Fault Propagation

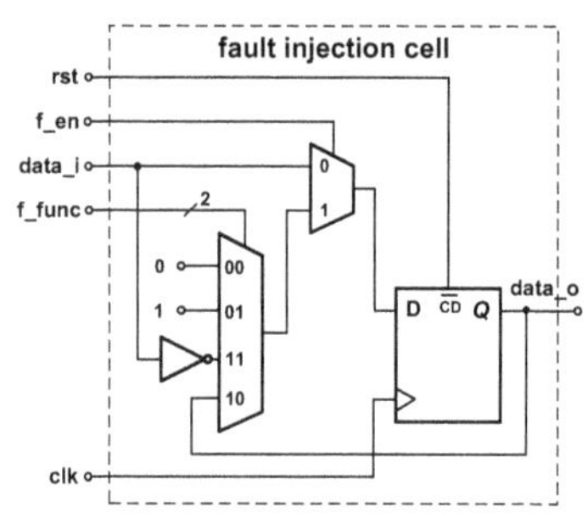

Figure 5: Instrumented flip flop

The fault emulator utilized for sequential fault propagation is illustrated in Figure 4. The software (depicted on the left) is executed by a host computer, which uses a UART communication interface to initiate and control the fault emulation. The Device Under Test (DUT), e.g. a security controller, and a *fault injection control unit* are configured into an FPGA (depicted as a dashed rectangle). Faults, configured by the *fault injection control unit* according to fault lists received over the UART interface, can be injected in FFs of the DUT. A *fault mask register* in which each bit can be set separately for multiple fault selection is used. Bits of the *fault mask register* are addressed by their index $n_{FF} \in \{0, ..., N-1\}$ and, if set to '1', select corresponding fault locations in the DUT to be faulty. Selecting multiple fault locations results in a multiple fault. FFs in the DUT are replaced by *fault injection cells* (depicted in Figure 5) in order to provide fault injection capability. *Fault injection cells* can be configured to either represent a bit-flip, stuck-at-0 or stuck-at-1 fault. The fault duration and injection time are also configurable. This allows to emulate, e.g., temporary stuck-at faults (also known as Set and Reset faults [3, 2]), which is useful to model fault effects at asynchronous pins. The signal *f_en* of each *fault injection cell* is connected to an individual bit of the *fault mask register* and selects either a fault-free or a faulty behavior of the particular *fault injection cell.* An additional AND gate per *fault injection cell* (depicted in Figure 4) activates the fault injection when the fault injection time t is reached. The control signals *f_func* select one of the four possible functions stuck-at-0, stuck-at-1, flip and hold (realizes the fault duration). For instance, forcing the data input to zero and then holding the faulty value for additional x clock cycles realizes a Reset fault for the duration of $x + 1$ clock cycles. A configurable fault duration is useful to model long duration laser-induced faults at RTL, which were recently investigated at transistor level [16].

4. EXPERIMENTAL RESULTS

The following subsections discuss the hardware requirements on the FPGA and the tool performance with varying test lengths and varying fault multiplicities.

4.1 Test Setup and Hardware Requirements

We applied the presented fault injection environment to two different micro-controller designs[4] (*80251-mc, 8051-mc*) used for security applications. *80251-mc* is an 80251-like microcontroller with a co-processor for AES (Advanced Encryption Standard) and DES (Data Encryption Standard) acceleration. In order to analyze all single points of attack in combinational cells and FFs, we performed three fault injection campaigns covering SETs and SEUs, as outlined in the columns *#MET*[5] and *#SEU* in Table 1. Faults are injected in either the CPU (5726 FFs, 39,038 comb. gates) or the co-processor (2775 FFs, 17,603 comb. gates).

To stimulate the relevant circuit parts, one out of three different functional tests *cpu*, *des* and *aes*, which lasts 79,000, 6800 and 5553 cycles respectively, are executed. Fault injection was concentrated to cycles in which cryptographic operations, security operations or the actual operations under test were executed by the DUT. That is, the initialization of the circuit, which is steady for all tests and sets the circuit into an initial state, as well as the test result evaluation, which compares the internal states versus an expected state after executing the instructions under test, were excluded from fault injection. This prevents unrealistic fault emulation results caused by corrupted initialization or, even worse, corrupted test result evaluation. Potential vulnerabilities during initialization can be discovered by performing a dedicated fault injection campaign that executes a test dedicated for this purpose.

Using our method, the instrumented circuit *80251-mc* including 8501 instrumented FFs and additional controlling hardware for fault injection fits into 55,520 adaptive logic modules (ALMs) on a Stratix II FPGA, which is clocked with 26.5 MHz.

[4]Combinational fault propagation for circuit 80251 is executed by Intel(R) Xeon(R) X5667 CPUs clocked with 3.06 GHz, located in a server farm with an average workload, and for circuit 8051 it is executed by a single Intel(R) Xeon(R) X5660 CPU clocked with 2.80 GHz.

[5]For simplification, SETs are assumed to be METs with multiplicity of one.

For comparison to previous FPGA-based approaches, we also implemented a conventional standalone emulation-based approach for circuit *80251-mc*. We have chosen a circuit instrumentation technique similar to the one presented by Kundu et al. [12], which we expected to require the least hardware overhead. Still, we could not fit it into the FPGA. For this reason, we performed fault analysis in a second smaller DUT (*8051-mc*), which is composed of 1911 FFs and 19,029 combinational gates. For this smaller circuit the conventional approach does not fail. This allows us to compare our method to existing work with 1) varying test lengths and 2) increasing fault multiplicities.

Using our method, the instrumented circuit *8051-mc* including 1911 instrumented FFs and additional hardware for controlling fault injection fits into 16,906 logic elements on an Altera Cyclone IV FPGA, which is clocked with 20 MHz (F_{max} = 22 MHz). Using the conventional setup [12], where all combinational cells are instrumented instead, 30,232 LEs are required on the FPGA, i.e. about 79% more LEs compared to the proposed method. Furthermore, because of additional logic in combinational paths, the maximum operating frequency of the conventional setup is limited to F_{max} =7 MHz, which is a reduction of 69%. Note, the conventional approach only allows fault injection in combinational logic, compared to our method, which is able to inject faults into FFs as well.

Eight fault injection campaigns were performed for circuit *8051-mc*. Either SETs or randomly generated 2bit-, 3bit- or 10bit-METs are injected (22.4 million each) and either one of two functional tests (*isax1*, *isax2*) is executed. Note, METs are generated randomly only for benchmark purposes. We suggest to use layout or structural circuit information for multiple fault selection, as presented in [1, 5, 2].

4.2 Performance for 80251-mc

In our experiments we wanted to emulate all single faults in combinational and sequential logic for all relevant cycles. Therefore, we used the fault emulator to inject all SEUs and additionally we injected all dMEUs that were generated by SETs. The runtimes of three fault injection campaigns for circuit *80251-mc* are listed in column *time* in Table 1. Column *speed-up* indicates with an ∞ sign that the conventional approach (instrumenting all combinational gates) fails for this circuit since the instrumented circuit does not fit into the FPGA. In contrast, our approach fits into the FPGA and executes all three fault injection campaigns for circuit *80251-mc* in about 19 hours, during which about 49.5 million SETs and 13.2 million SEUs are injected.

Table 1: Setup of performed fault injection campaigns covering all possible SEUs and all determined dMEUs caused by SETs or METs. The runtime is given in hour:minute.

circuit	test	$\#MET \cdot 10^6$	$\#SEU \cdot 10^6$	multi.	time	speed-up
80251	cpu	35.95	5.27	1	**13:40**	∞
80251	aes	15.88	2.50	1	**3:48**	∞
80251	des	8.43	1.33	1	**1:45**	∞
8051	isax1	22.40	4.27	1	3:05	**3.64**
8051	"	"	"	2	3:36	**3.12**
8051	"	"	"	3	4:21	**2.58**
8051	"	"	"	10	6:01	**1.87**
8051	isax2	"	"	1	3:51	**5.87**
8051	"	"	"	2	5:01	**4.50**
8051	"	"	"	3	6:59	**3.23**
8051	"	"	"	10	8:00	**2.82**

4.3 Performance for 8051-mc

Fault injection campaigns for *8051-mc* are constructed in such a way that these allow to analyze the impact of the test length and the multiplicity of METs on the performance. Both tests *isax1* and *isax2* cover the instruction set architecture. Test *isax1* lasts 11,851 clock cycles and *isax2* lasts 23,811 clock cycles. During each fault injection campaign, 22.4 million METs and 4.3 million SEUs are injected. The conventional emulation-based approach [12] takes about 11 minutes and 23 minutes for fault injection campaigns that execute tests *isax1* and *isax2*, respectively. As can be seen in Table 1, our method performs noticeably better (*speed-up* 1.9 to 5.9) compared to conventional emulation-based approaches. We noticed that our method performs the best for test *isax2*, which lasts two times longer than test *isax1*, whereas the performance is decreased with increasing fault multiplicities. However, the runtime for combinational fault propagation with MiniSAT (about 2 hours and 30 minutes) is almost not affected by varying fault multiplicities. This is reasonable since the same number of iterations (22.4 million) with MiniSAT is required for each fault injection campaign, and the number of MiniSAT's assumption function calls increases just slightly with the multiplicity of METs. Instead, the increased runtime for higher fault multiplicities of METs is caused by generating more distinguishable faults. As a consequence, the efficiency of the proposed performance optimizations decreases since less emulations can be skipped. However, since the runtime per fault for combinational fault propagation with MiniSAT is almost constant, skipping longer emulations results in a better overall performance. This is the reason why our method performs better for longer tests. Note, the complexity of MiniSAT's propagate function (Boolean constraint propagation without conflicts) is linear with the circuit size and the runtime of sequential fault propagation increases linearly with the test length. Hence, the proposed fault injection environment is also suitable for even more complex circuits and tests.

5. CONCLUSION

We presented a new method, which uses a software-based method to inject SETs and METs and to propagate these into sequential cells. Equivalent faults in sequential cells (SEU, MEU) are then determined and mapped onto an FPGA-based fault emulator for sequential fault propagation. Extensive fault injection campaigns covering SETs, METs and SEUs with varying tests and fault multiplicities for two designs used in security applications have been performed. In contrast to existing work, the proposed method provides designers with one tool to perform extensive fault emulations for SETs, METs, SEUs and MEUs in feasible time. Faults can be injected into any cell without limiting fault injection to just few locations. Therefore, the presented method is suitable as accelerator for multiple fault injection campaigns based on layout and structural information. It reduces hardware overhead for circuit instrumentation on FPGAs by 45% and is, hence, still applicable for larger circuits for which conventional approaches already fail. Moreover, it performs up to 6x better for performed fault injection campaigns. The increased performance can be used to analyze more faults in given time for design verification, which is required to further improve security designs.

6. REFERENCES

[1] A. Papadimitriou, M. Tampas, D. Hély, V. Beroulle, P. Maistri, and R. Leveugle, "Validation of RTL laser fault injection model with respect to layout information," in *HOST*, 2015.

[2] P. Vanhauwaert, P. Maistri, R. Leveugle, A. Papadimitriou, D. Hély, and V. Beroulle, "On error models for RTL security evaluations," in *DTIS*, 2014.

[3] B. Selmke, S. Brummer, J. Heyszl, and G. Sigl, "Precise laser fault injections into 90 nm and 45 nm SRAM-cells," in *CARDIS*, 2015.

[4] M. Ebrahimi, H. Asadi, and M. B. Tahoori, "A layout-based approach for multiple event transient analysis," in *DAC*, 2013.

[5] A. Papadimitriou, D. Hély, V. Beroulle, P. Maistri, and R. Leveugle, "A multiple fault injection methodology based on cone partitioning towards RTL modeling of laser attacks," in *DATE*, 2014.

[6] R. Leveugle, A. Calvez, P. Maistri, and P. Vanhauwaert, "Statistical fault injection: Quantified error and confidence," in *DATE*, 2009.

[7] H. Abbasitabar, H. R. Zarandi, and R. Salamat, "Susceptibility analysis of LEON3 embedded processor against multiple event transients and upsets," in *CSE*, 2012.

[8] N. Miskov-Zivanov and D. Marculescu, "Multiple transient faults in combinational and sequential circuits: A systematic approach.," *IEEE Trans. on CAD of Integrated Circuits and Systems*, vol. 29, no. 10, 2010.

[9] L. Entrena, M. G. Valderas, R. F. Cardenal, M. P. Garcia, and C. L. Ongil, "Set emulation considering electrical masking effects," *IEEE Transactions on Nuclear Science*, vol. 56, no. 4, 2009.

[10] A. Pellegrini, R. Smolinski, L. Chen, X. Fu, S. K. S. Hari, J. Jiang, S. V. Adve, T. M. Austin, and V. Bertacco, "Crashtest'ing swat: Accurate, gate-level evaluation of symptom-based resiliency solutions.," in *DATE*, 2012.

[11] M. Ebrahimi, A. Mohammadi, A. Ejlali, and S. G. Miremadi, "A fast, flexible, and easy-to-develop FPGA-based fault injection technique," *Microelectronics Reliability*, 2014.

[12] S. Kundu, M. D. Lewis, I. Polian, and B. Becker, "A soft error emulation system for logic circuits," in *DCIS*, 2005.

[13] I. Polian, J. P. Hayes, S. M. Reddy, and B. Becker, "Modeling and mitigating transient errors in logic circuits.," *IEEE Trans. Dependable Sec. Comput.*, vol. 8, 2011.

[14] R. Nyberg, J. Heyszl, D. Rabe, and G. Sigl, "Closing the gap between speed and configurability of multi-bit fault emulation environments for security and safety–critical designs," *Microprocessors and Microsystems*, May 2015.

[15] N. Eén and N. Sörensson, "The MiniSAT Page (online)." http://www.minisat.se/.

[16] F. Lu, S. De Castro, G. Di Natale, M.-L. Flottes, and B. Rouzeyre, "Dynamic fault model for long duration laser-induced fault simulation," in *TRUDEVICE*, 2015.

A Novel On-Chip Impedance Calibration Method for LPDDR4 Interface between DRAM and AP/SoC

Yongsuk Choi
Electrical and Computer Engineering
Northeastern University
Boston, MA, United States
ychoi@ece.neu.edu

Yong-Bin Kim
Electrical and Computer Engineering
Northeastern University
Boston, MA, United States
ybk@ece.neu.edu

ABSTRACT

In this paper, a novel on-chip impedance calibration methodology for a LPDDR4 (low power double data rate) application is proposed. The background calibration operates to compensate mismatches and variations of the output NMOS drivers from process and temperature variations. The impedance matching concept uses process sensor and temperature monitoring sensors closely located to DQ pins as a means to detect output driver transistor mismatches due to process and temperature variations. In addition, digitized sensor outputs from ADCs are used as inputs of look-up tables, which control calibration codes of the transmitter driver. The proposed circuitry is designed with DRAM bidirectional transceiver and implemented using a standard 180nm CMOS technology, and the impedance calibration technique is demonstrated with external termination resistance of 40/48/60/80/120/240 ohm, respectively. In the receiver end, a PMOS input sense amplifier is designed considering the required common mode range for the LVSTL (low voltage swing termination logic) signal interface, and an adaptive gain control scheme is also applied on the receiver design. The process sensor is utilized to control the gain factor of the receiver. The active area including power-ring of the transmitter is $14.4mm^2$ with only $0.48mm^2$ of the proposed calibration circuit overhead.

General Terms

Design, Performance, Reliability

Keywords

DRAM interface; high-speed data transmission; LPDDR4; high-speed transmitter; impedance calibration

1. INTRODUCTION

Due to rapidly increasing graphics technology with high-resolution display as well as wireless communication speed, the amount of data transmission is increased along with the processing contents. In the meantime, the growth of mobile device demand makes not only performance but also battery lifetime even more important. To extend data bandwidth, it is inevitable to increase the number of I/O pins, which increases I/O power consumption. To satisfy fast memory operating speed and low power consumption, the low power double data rate (LPDDR4) standard is applied with low voltage swing termination logic (LVSTL) interface in the recent mobile applications. The LVSTL interface has advantages of low C_{io} (input/output capacitance) and low power consumption with lowered V_{OH} level and no static power consumption while driving logic low.

With the low voltage signal swing, the signal integrity in transmitting and receiving the signal becomes more important along with the data transmitting speed. Since the serial interface between two different digital systems with communication channel is limited by the bandwidth, not only those problems caused by switching noise or crosstalk but also signal attenuation or reflection problems caused by high frequency become a challenging issue. The problems are exacerbated at the low power application, where the V_{OH} is scaled down to one-third of supply voltage in the new low power DDR standard.

Several I/O training operations have been used. CA, ZQ, and VREF training are such I/O training operations for proper signal transmission. Moreover, the training sequences have to be placed between data transmitting sequences due to V_{OH} drift. In addition, most of conventional on-die termination (ODT) schemes have to use the ZQ pin to compensate the impedance mismatches [1]-[2]. Moreover, thermal issue becomes more important not only in the currently used LPDDR4 standard but also beyond the LPDDR4 including wide I/O signal transmission. As an efficient solution, in this paper, we proposed a novel on-chip impedance calibration

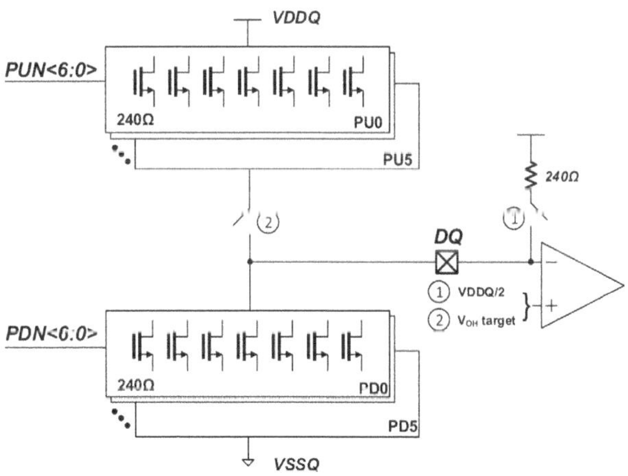

Figure 1. Conventional ZQ calibration scheme.

GLSVLSI'16, May 18–20, 2016, Boston, MA, USA.
Copyright 2016 ACM. ISBN 978-1-4503-4274-2/16/05…$15.00.
DOI: http://dx.doi.org/10.1145/2902961.2902982

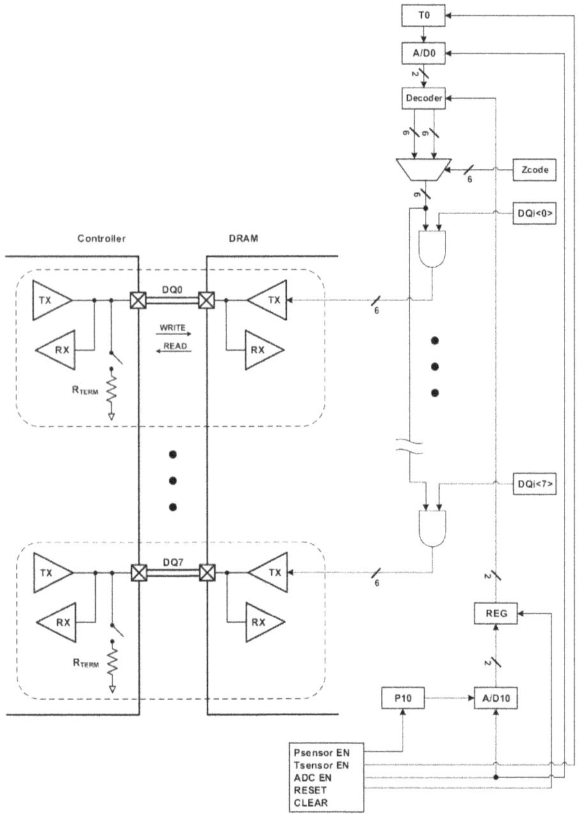

Figure 2. Impedance calibration algorithm.

method to run the background calibration method to improve the conventional calibration technique. In addition, a low common mode voltage in receiver is inevitable due to the lower signaling. Therefore, PMOS input sense amplifier is also designed for the receiver end, and the input MOSFETs are design with a set of array to provide an adaptive gain control feature to compensate process and temperature variation, which enables to accomplish performance optimization and low power consumption.

2. IMPEDANCE CALIBRATION

A conventional ZQ calibration scheme for an output driver of DRAM transmitter is shown in Figure 1. One pull-up slice is composed of an n-bit pull-up transistor array to set 240Ω pull-up driver. There are 6 slices connected in parallel for different termination impedances, and pull-down driver is constructed in the same manner. When a ZQ calibration command is enabled, pull-down driver is calibrated firstly. The pull-down transistors are all turned off and the DQ node connects 240Ω resistor to VDDQ, and the DQ node voltage is compared to VDDQ/2 value. The calibration continues by turning on the pull-down transistors from LSB until the comparator detects that DQ node is low. The next step is to set V_{OH} level from pull-up driver calibration. The comparator inputs are reference voltage of V_{OH} level and the DQ node. The drive strength of pull-up driver is adjusted in the same manner as the pull-down driver. The main drawback of the conventional ZQ calibration technique is that the calibration has to be performed sequentially for each of the slices and each of DQ pins due to voltage and temperature drift.

Figure 2 illustrates the proposed on-line impedance calibration method to compensate impedance mismatches from process corner and local temperature variations, which is improved from our previous work [3]. In this technique, ZQ pin and external termination resistance are not required. Instead of that, calibration codes are stored in a look-up table for each of the process corner profiles and a wide temperature range of operation. Once the impedance calibration process is enabled, process sensor is activated and produces voltage output. The sensor output put voltage range represents one of slow/typical/fast process corners. The analog output value is quantized using a simple flash ADC that generate 2-bit digital signals and the resulted digital bits are stored in a register and the process sensor is disabled for power efficiency. On the other hand, the temperature-monitoring sensor operates in real-time mode in background to adjust V_{OH} level variation due to temperature drift. The analog output of the temperature-monitoring sensor is digitized as well. The two digital codes representing process corner and temperature are sent to the inputs of look-up table to find an optimized calibration code for the driver transistor array of the transmitters.

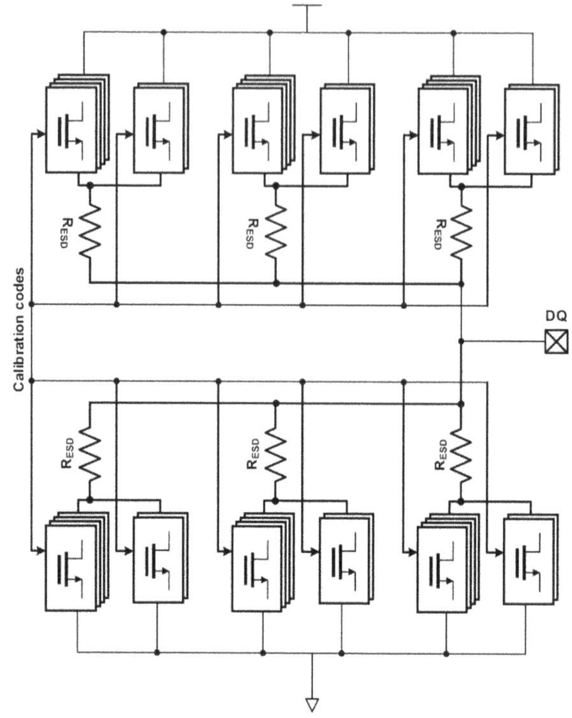

Figure 3. Proposed transmitter impedance calibration.

Different from a conventional transmitter where the same 6 slices connected in parallel, the proposed transmitter is designed with 3 slices as shown in Figure 3. Each of the slice includes series resistor to protect from ESD damage, and also improve linearity. Moreover, the resistors are connected to two different transistor arrays, the first array can be tuned to 440 Ω and the latter array is used to tune to 366 Ω in the pull-up network. Likewise, the pull-down network is designed to set 200 Ω and 133 Ω for each of the array.

The on-chip process sensor utilized in the calibration architecture is shown in Figure 4. In Figure 4(a), the NM1 and NM3 are operated in linear region, and the DC voltage applied to gates of NM1 and NM3 are V_B and V_B+dV, respectively. Each of the drain currents is noted in (1).

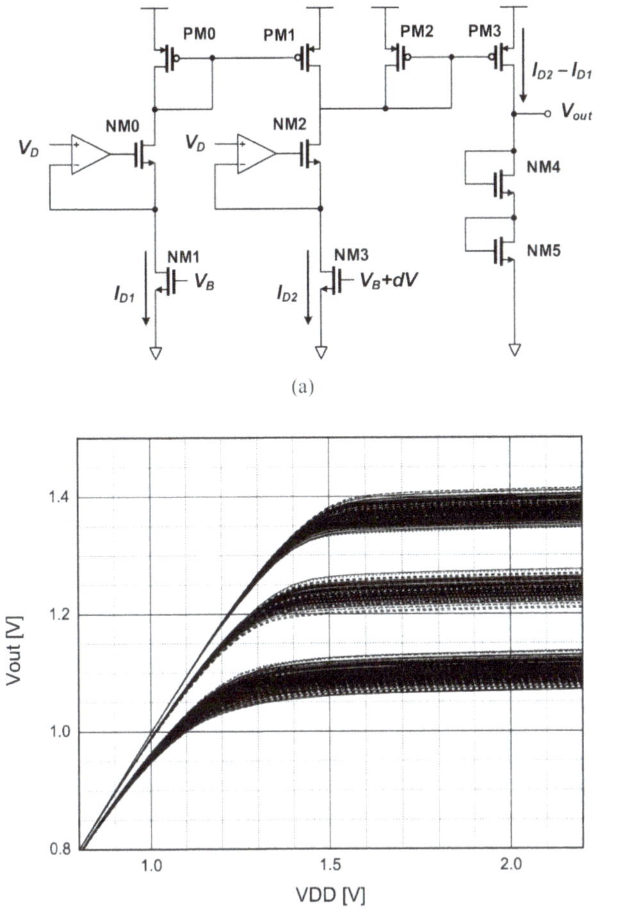

Figure 4. On-chip process sensor circuit (a) schematic of process sensor (b) simulation results with local and global variations.

$$I_{D1} = \mu_n C_{ox} W/L \left(V_B - V_{th} - \frac{V_D}{2}\right) V_D$$

$$I_{D2} = \mu_n C_{ox} W/L \left(V_B + dV - V_{th} - \frac{V_D}{2}\right) V_D \qquad (1)$$

$$I_{REF} = I_{D2} - I_{D1} = \mu_n C_{ox} W/L \cdot dV \cdot V_D \qquad (2)$$

As can be seen in equation (2), the threshold voltage term in the current equation is canceled out, and the threshold voltage independent current in PM2 mirrors the I_{REF} to PM3. Therefore, the output voltage of the process sensor is dependent only on NMOS threshold voltages of NM4 and NM5 (independent of temperature), which detects the process variation of NMOS transistor. The output voltages of the process sensor are displayed in Figure 4(b) for different process corners. The voltage gap among NMOS slow/typical/fast corners is more than 70mV from the simulation data with global, local mismatch variations, and supply voltage variation, which makes it possible to detect process corner even with measurement errors.

In addition, the temperature-monitoring sensor utilized in the calibration technique is shown in Figure 5. The temperature sensor is composed of startup circuit, proportional to absolute temperature

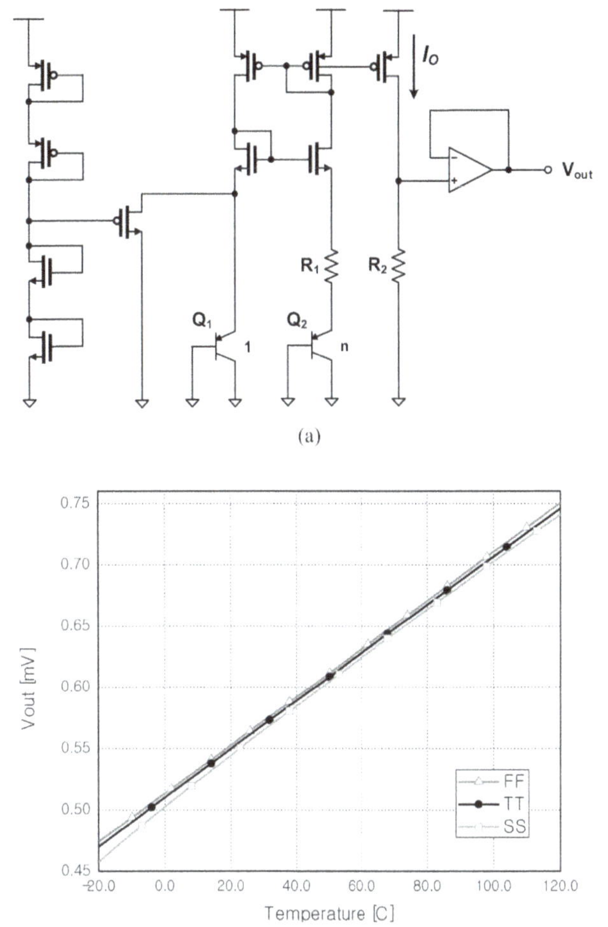

Figure 5. On-chip temperature monitoring sensor circuit (a) schematic of temperature monitoring sensor [4] (b) simulation results with process variations.

(PTAT) current generation circuit, and temperature dependent voltage output. The output voltage is obtained as following:

$$V_{R1} = V_{BE1} - V_{BE2} = V_T \ln n,$$

$$V_{out} = \frac{R_2}{R_1} V_T \ln n. \qquad (3)$$

The output voltage of the temperature-monitoring sensor is displayed in Figure 5(b) under all process corners and temperature range of -20C to 120C. The result shows that the output has a good linearity on temperature in the operation range and it is insensitive to process variations.

3. RECEIVER DESIGN FOR LVSTL

3.1 Low Common Mode Receiver Circuit

According to the convention of the LVSTL signaling, the input common mode on receiver is significantly decreased to one sixth of the supply voltage. Therefore, it is more efficient to design PMOS input sense amplifier considering the input common mode range to equalize and detect incoming signal through transmission line as shown in Figure 6(a). In this design, one of the output nodes is charged during the evaluation phase. Also, the reference voltage (V_{REF}) is lowered than the conventional NMOS input sense

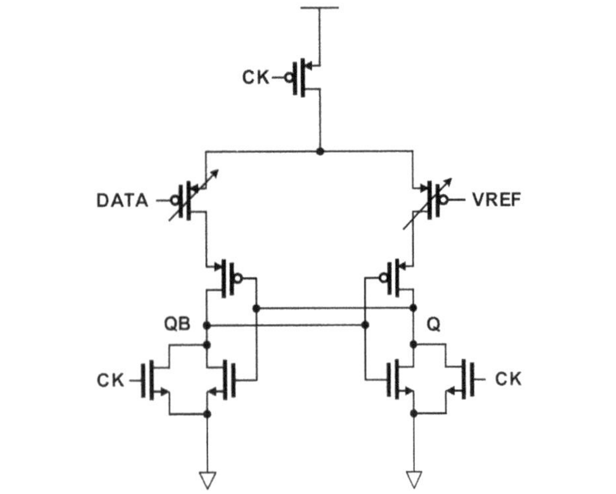

(a)

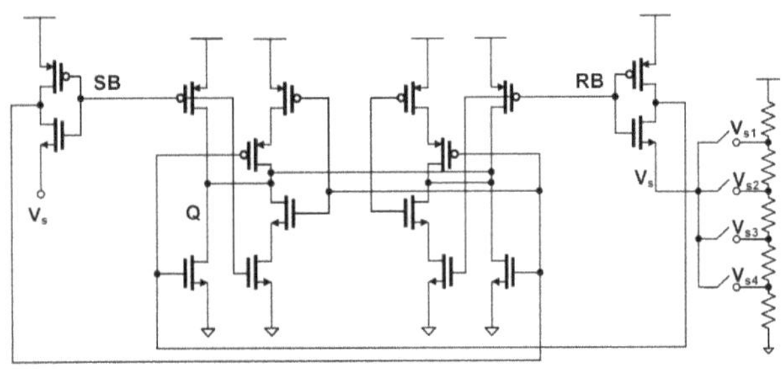

(b)

Figure 6. Sense-amplifier flip-flop on receiver (a) low common mode input sense-amplifier with adaptive gain control (b) modified slave latch with voltage control.

amplifiers. Therefore, the gain of the input transistor is more important. In addition to that, the input transistor is designed as digitally controlled 3-bit array to control the gain adaptively to optimize the performance for PVT variations and to achieve low power consumption as well. The input signal to the adaptive loop is provided from process sensor utilized in transmitter impedance calibration circuit.

3.2 Modified SR-latch

The slave latch followed by sense-amplifier is shown in Figure 6(b), where the SR latch is modified from [5] because the input transistors of the sense amplifier should be PMOS due to the low common mode input voltage and SR latch truth table needs to be corrected. To improve the performance of the slave latch, the source node voltage of NMOS transistor is adjusted to increase the threshold voltage of the inverter by applying the control voltage. The voltage is connected from resistor ladder, and the connection switches are controlled by ADC output followed by process sensor. The increased threshold voltage improves clock-to-Q time from fast pull-down of inverter and reduces decision time.

4. SIMULATION RESULTS

The proposed design is implemented and demonstrated using an 180nm standard CMOS process technology. The circuit simulation setup is shown in Figure 3, and the channel between DRAM and controller is modeled as a 3-inch RLGC model and pad/package parasites are also modeled. The clock frequency is 800MHz, which

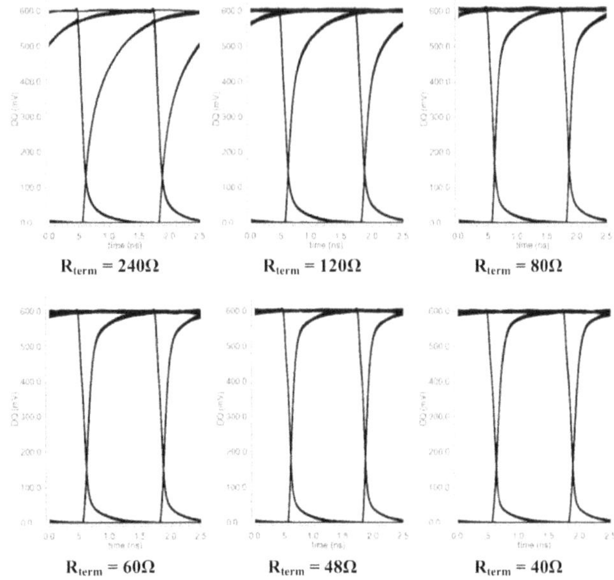

Figure 7. Eye-diagrams of the calibrated transmitter output with the proposed impedance calibration method.

corresponds to technology scaling from standard LPDDR4 speed. The results of the impedance calibration are evaluated as V_{OH} level measurements. Figure 7 shows eye-diagrams of the transmitter outputs after the proposed impedance calibration process. The supply voltage is 1.8V, and the target voltage level of output logic high is 600mV. For the six different termination cases (40/48/60/80/120/240Ω), the deviation from the specifications is less than 20mV. The layout of the proposed transmitter calibration circuit (including process sensor, temperature sensor, ADCs, decoders, and current source) and DRAM output driver is shown in Figure 8.

5. CONCLUSION

In this paper, we proposed a novel on-chip impedance calibration method for LPDDR4 standard memory interface. The proposed circuit detects impedance mismatch due to process and temperature variations using analog sensors and it turns out that the proposed calibration method is a viable solution for background calibration

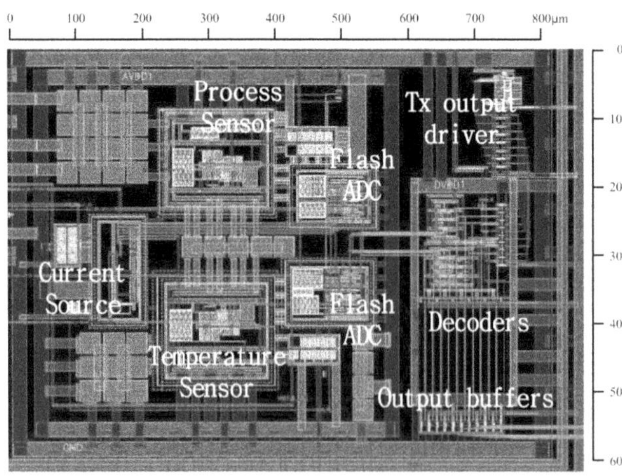

Figure 8. Layout of the proposed transmitter calibration circuit and DRAM output driver.

for each of termination resistances. In addition, PMOS input sense amplifier is designed for low common mode voltage of the LVSTL signaling. The proposed circuit is implemented and demonstrated using an 180nm standard CMOS process technology. The calibration circuits takes only 3% of the transmitter circuits. However, the overall area is reduced by more than 20% since the transmitter circuit area is significantly reduced by using the proposed calibration method. The conventional transmitter circuits for LPDDR4 use more and larger transistors for calibration and its control after fabrication.

6. ACKNOWLEDGMENTS

This research has been supported by SK Hynix, and the authors want to appreciate Dr. Hae-Kang Jung in SK Hynix for his insightful comments and discussions.

7. REFERENCES

[1] Kalyan, G. and Srinivas, M.B., 2010. An efficient ODT calibration scheme for improved signal integrity in memory interface. In *2010 IEEE Asia Pacific Conference on Circuits and Systems*.

[2] Jung, H.K., Yang, J., Lee, J., Ko, H., Lee, H., Song, T., Shim, J., Lee, S.K., Song, K., Kim, D.K. and Kim, H., 2015, June. A 4.35 Gb/s/pin LPDDR4 I/O interface with multi-VOH level, equalization scheme, and duty-training circuit for mobile applications. In *VLSI Circuits (VLSI Circuits), 2015 Symposium on* (pp. C184-C185). IEEE.

[3] Lee, H.J. and Kim, Y.B., A Process Tolerant Semi-Self Impedance Calibration Method for LPDDR4 Memory Controller. In *Circuits and Systems (MWSCAS), 2015 IEEE 58th International Midwest Symposium on , vol., no., pp.1-4, 2-5 Aug. 2015*

[4] Kronmueller, F. and Knoedgen, H., Dialog Semiconductor GmbH, 2003. *Threshold voltage-independent MOS current reference*. U.S. Patent 6,570,436.

[5] Nikolic, B., Oklobdžija, V.G., Stojanovic, V., Jia, W., Chiu, J.K.S. and Leung, M.M.T., 2000. Improved sense-amplifier-based flip-flop: Design and measurements. *Solid-State Circuits, IEEE Journal of*, *35*(6), pp.876-884.

A General Sign Bit Error Correction Scheme for Approximate Adders

Rui Zhou and Weikang Qian
University of Michigan-Shanghai Jiao Tong University Joint Institute
Shanghai Jiao Tong University, Shanghai, China
Email: {zhouruisjtu, qianwk}@sjtu.edu.cn

ABSTRACT

Approximate computing is an emerging design technique for error-tolerant applications. As adders are the key building blocks in many applications, approximate adders have been widely studied recently. However, existing approximate adders may introduce sign bit error when doing two's complement signed addition, which is not tolerable for some applications. In this work, we propose a scheme that can correct sign bit error with low area and delay overhead. It is a general design applicable to many block-based approximate adders. This design not only can correct the sign bit error when it occurs, but also can fix some errors in the most significant bits even if there is no sign bit error. Experimental results on a real application, namely edge detection, showed that the approximate adders with our sign bit error correction module were up to 5.5 times better in peak signal-to-noise ratio than the original approximate adders, while the area and delay overhead is small.

Keywords

Approximate computing, approximate adder, sign bit error correction

1. INTRODUCTION

With the continuous scaling down of CMOS transistors, energy consumption has become a major concern in designing VLSI chips. Approximate computing, an emerging technology that improves circuit performance and energy efficiency by allowing a little amount of inaccuracy in the computation result, attracts many research efforts recently, due to its applicability to many error-tolerant applications, such as image processing, machine learning, multimedia, and data mining [1].

As adders are key building blocks for many error-tolerant applications, a number of approximate adders were proposed recently [2-9]. Most of them fall into the category of *block-based approximate adder*. It splits the entire adder into several blocks of sub-adders in order to reduce computation delay. Each sub-adder takes a speculated carry-in, which is produced based on some previous input bits. The computation of each sub-adder is correct. Due to the popularity of the block-based approximate adder, it is the focus of this work.

GLSVLSI'16, May 18-20, 2016, Boston, MA, USA.

DOI: http://dx.doi.org/10.1145/2902961.2903012

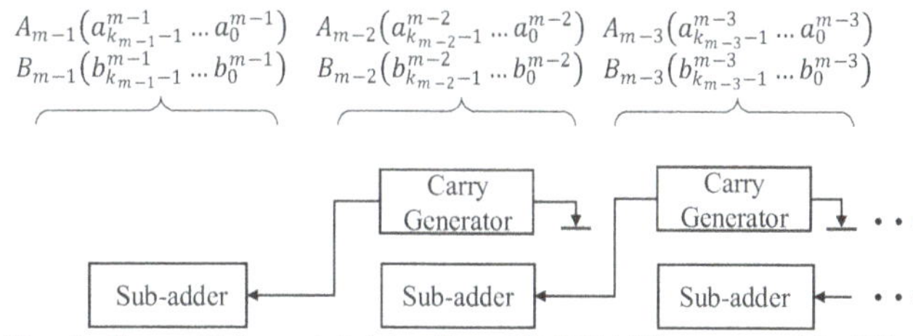

Fig. 1: Error Tolerant Adder Type II (ETAII) proposed in [2].

A representative of the block-based approximate adder is the Error Tolerant Adder II (ETAII) proposed in [2], which is shown in Fig. 1. In ETAII, it segments the whole adder into m blocks, and the carry-in signal of each sub-adder is produced by a carry generator operating on the input bits in the previous block. The carry-in signal of each carry generator is set as 0. There are many other examples of block-based approximate adder. The Carry Skip Approximate Adder (CSA) proposed in [3] also has m blocks, but the carry-in signal of the i-th sub-adder depends on input bits of the $(i-1)$-th block and the $(i-2)$-th block. The Low Relative Error Approximate Adder (LREA) proposed in [4] and the Speculative Carry Select Adder (SCSA) proposed in [5] have similar design styles.

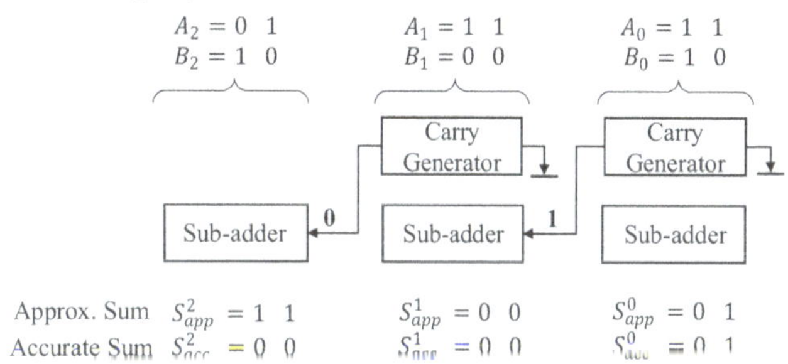

Fig. 2: An example of sign bit error in ETAII.

However, all these typical approximate adders mentioned above may generate an error in the sign bit when doing two's complement signed addition. For example, in a 6-bit 3-block ETAII adder, the sign bit is wrong when the two inputs are 011111 (base 2) and 100010 (base 2), as shown in Fig. 2. The approximate sum is 110001 (base 2), but the accurate sum is 000001 (base 2). The error is caused by the wrong carry-in signal fed into the leftmost sub-adder, which is produced by the carry generator in the previous block.

Having a sign bit error in approximate addition may cause a catastrophic failure for many applications and may not be tolerable. There are only few existing approximate adders which can correct the sign bit error, and their designs all have some limitations. For example, the Variable Latency Speculative Adder (VLSA) proposed in [6] combines a proposed approximate adder with an accurate adder for error recovery. However, it requires a large circuit area. To ensure correct sign bit calculation, it takes two clock cycles. Furthermore, when the correction module is enabled, its result is always correct, which is not necessary for error-tolerant applications. In the LREA, the authors proposed a sign bit error correction module, but it is only applicable to LREA itself [4].

In this paper, we proposed a low-overhead module to correct sign bit error for block-based approximate adders. Compared to the previous approaches used in [4] and [6], our module is a general design which is applicable to many existing approximate adders regardless how the speculated carry-in to the sub-adder is generated. The only requirement is that all sub-adders are correct.

In summary, the main contributions of our work are as follows:

1) We give a general and comprehensive analysis on when sign bit error occurs.
2) Based on the error analysis, we propose an efficient design to correct the sign bit error.
3) We apply the proposed design to several existing approximate adders and experimentally demonstrate its good performance.

The remainder of this paper is organized as follows. In Section 2, we give an analysis on when sign bit error occurs. In Section 3, we propose a method to correct sign bit error. In Section 4, we show our optimized circuit design. In Section 5, we show the experimental results. Finally, in Section 6, we draw the conclusion.

2. ERROR ANALYSIS

In this section, we will analyze all kinds of situations where a sign bit error might occur in the computation of approximate adder and provide the correction mechanism for each situation. In our analysis, we assume that the inputs do not cause an overflow.

The only pre-requisite of our analysis is that the sub-adder of each block is correct. This requirement is satisfied for all the existing block-based approximate adders. Before the formal analysis, we define the following notations.

- $A = (a_{n-1}a_{n-2} \dots a_0)$ and $B = (b_{n-1}b_{n-2} \dots b_0)$ are the two inputs of the adder, where a_i and b_i represent the i-th bits of A and B, respectively
- We assume the approximate adder has m blocks and the i-th $(0 \le i \le m-1)$ block has k_i bits. Therefore, we have $n = \sum_{i=0}^{m-1} k_i$.
- s_i, c_i, p_i, and g_i represent the i-th $(0 \le i \le n-1)$ sum bit, carry-out bit, propagation bit, and generation bit of the accurate adder, respectively. c_{in} represents the carry-in of the entire adder. For the ease of discussion, we define $c_{-1} = c_{in}$. By the behavior of the adder, we have
$$s_i = a_i \oplus b_i \oplus c_{i-1},\ \ c_i = a_i b_i + (a_i + b_i)c_{i-1}$$
$$p_i = a_i \oplus b_i,\ \ g_i = a_i b_i.$$
Note that the sum bit and the carry-out bit can be calculated by the propagate bit and the generate bit as follows:
$$s_i = p_i \oplus c_{i-1},\ \ c_i = g_i + p_i c_{i-1}.$$

For analysis purpose, we also split the accurate adder into m blocks. For each block of approximate adder and accurate adder, we define the following signals.

- $C_{app\_sum\_in}^{i}$: the carry-in signal of the i-th sub-adder of the approximate adder. This signal varies for different approximate adders.
- $C_{acc\_sum\_in}^{i}$: the carry-in signal of the i-th block of the accurate adder.
- S_{app}^{i}: the k_i-bit sum of the i-th sub-adder of the approximate adder.
- S_{acc}^{i}: the k_i-bit sum of the i-th block of the accurate adder.
- $s_{app,j}^{i}$ $(0 \le j \le k_i - 1)$: the sum bit at position j in block i of the approximate adder.
- $s_{acc,j}^{i}$ $(0 \le j \le k_i - 1)$: the sum bit at position j in block i of the accurate adder.
- $c_{app,j}^{i}$ $(0 \le j \le k_i - 2)$: the carry-out bit at position j in the i-th sub-adder of the approximate adder.
- $c_{acc,j}^{i}$ $(0 \le j \le k_i - 2)$: the carry-out bit at position j in block i of the accurate adder.
- A_i and B_i: the 2 k_i-bit inputs of block i.
- a_j^i and b_j^i $(0 \le j \le k_i - 1)$: the 2 input bits at position j in block i.
- p_j^i $(0 \le j \le k_i - 1)$: the propagate bit at position j in block i.
- g_j^i $(0 \le j \le k_i - 1)$: the generate bit at position j in block i.

Some of the above signals for approximate adder and accurate adder are shown in Fig. 3(a) and 3(b), respectively.

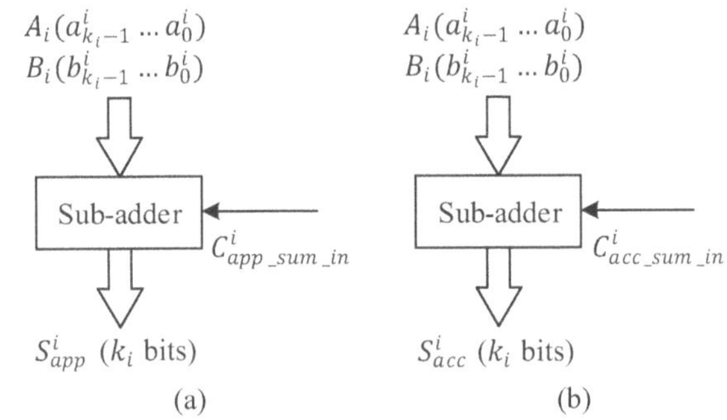

Fig. 3: Signal definitions for (a) an approximate adder and (b) an accurate adder.

The necessary condition for a sign bit error to occur is that for block $m-1$, $C_{app\_sum\_in}^{m-1} \ne C_{acc\_sum\_in}^{m-1}$. This condition can be further divided into two cases:

- Case 2.1: $C_{app\_sum\_in}^{m-1} = 0$ and $C_{acc\_sum\_in}^{m-1} = 1$;
- Case 2.2: $C_{app\_sum\_in}^{m-1} = 1$ and $C_{acc\_sum\_in}^{m-1} = 0$.

We will discuss them separately in the following sections.

2.1 $C_{app\_sum\_in}^{m-1} = 0$ and $C_{acc\_sum\_in}^{m-1} = 1$

Without loss of generality, we assume that the input $A \ge B$. Then, there are four cases where a sign bit error occurs:

1. $A \ge 0, B \ge 0, S_{app}^{m-1} < 0$;
2. $A < 0, B < 0, S_{app}^{m-1} \ge 0$;
3. $A \ge 0, B < 0, S_{acc}^{m-1} \ge 0, S_{app}^{m-1} < 0$;
4. $A \ge 0, B < 0, S_{acc}^{m-1} < 0, S_{app}^{m-1} \ge 0$.

We consider these four cases in the following subsections.

2.1.1 The Case where $A \ge 0, B \ge 0, S_{app}^{m-1} < 0$

This case is shown in Fig. 4(a). In this case, we must have $S_{app}^{m-1} = 11 \dots 11$ and $S_{acc}^{m-1} = 00 \dots 00$. However, since $C_{app\_sum\_in}^{m-1} = 0$ and $s_{app,j}^{m-1} = 1$ for $j = 0, 1, \dots, k_{m-1} - 2$, we must have $a_j^{m-1} \oplus b_j^{m-1} = 1$ for $j = 0, 1, \dots, k_{m-1} - 2$. Thus, the speculated carry-in to the sign bit is $c_{app,k_{m-1}-2}^{m-1} = 0$. Given that the sign bits of the inputs A and B are both 0, we must have $S_{app}^{m-1} = 01 \dots 11$, which contradicts with the claim that $S_{app}^{m-1} = 11 \dots 11$. Therefore, this situation cannot happen.

2.1.2 The Case where $A < 0, B < 0, S_{app}^{m-1} \ge 0$

This case is shown in Fig. 4(b). In this case, we must have $S_{app}^{m-1} = 01 \dots 11$ and $S_{acc}^{m-1} = 10 \dots 00$. This situation is possible. For example, when $A_{m-1} = 1010$ and $B_{m-1} = 1101$, then we have $S_{app}^{m-1} = 0111$ and $S_{acc}^{m-1} = 1000$. To correct the error in this case, we need to invert the sign bit and set the other sum bits in block $(m-1)$ to 0.

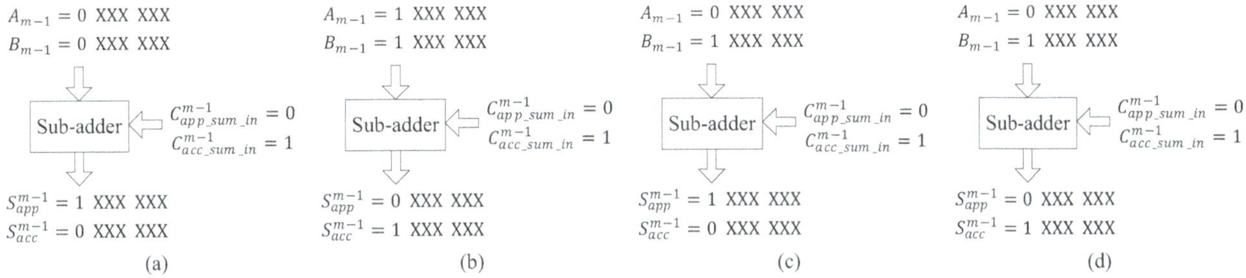

Fig. 4: Illustration of (a) Case 2.1.1, (b) Case 2.1.2, (c) Case 2.1.3, and (d) Case 2.1.4.

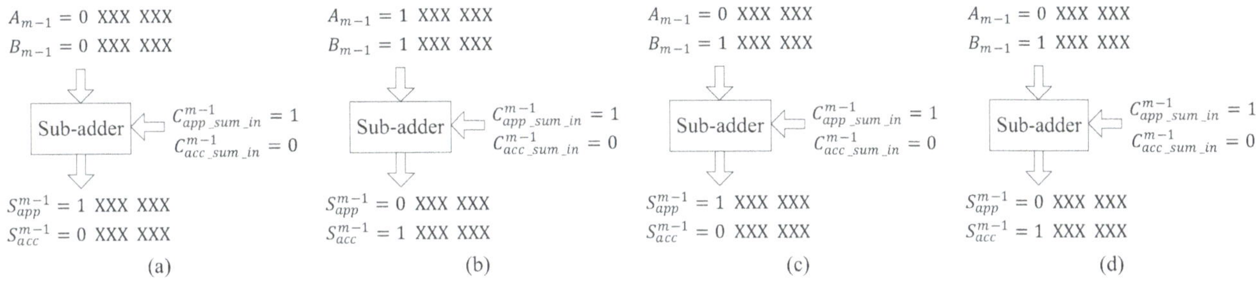

Fig. 5: Illustration of (a) Case 2.2.1, (b) Case 2.2.2, (c) Case 2.2.3, and (d) Case 2.2.4.

2.1.3 The Case where $A \geq 0, B < 0, S^{m-1}_{acc} \geq 0, S^{m-1}_{app} < 0$

This case is shown in Fig. 4(c). In this case, we must have $S^{m-1}_{app} = 11 \ldots 11$ and $S^{m-1}_{acc} = 00 \ldots 00$. This situation is possible. For example, when $A_{m-1} = 0010$ and $B_{m-1} = 1101$, then we have $S^{m-1}_{app} = 1111$ and $S^{m-1}_{acc} = 0000$. To correct the error in this case, we need to invert the sign bit and set the other sum bits in block $(m-1)$ to 0.

2.1.4 The Case where $A \geq 0, B < 0, S^{m-1}_{acc} < 0, S^{m-1}_{app} \geq 0$

This case is shown in Fig. 4(d). In this case, we must have $S^{m-1}_{app} = 01 \ldots 11$ and $S^{m-1}_{acc} = 10 \ldots 00$. However, applying the same argument used for Case 2.1.1, we can show that S^{m-1}_{app} should be $11 \ldots 11$. Therefore, this situation cannot happen.

2.2 $C^{m-1}_{app\_sum\_in} = 1$ and $C^{m-1}_{acc\_sum\_in} = 0$

We consider the same four cases as shown in Section 2.1.

2.2.1 The Case where $A \geq 0, B \geq 0, S^{m-1}_{app} < 0$

This case is shown in Fig. 5(a). In this case, we must have $S^{m-1}_{app} = 10 \ldots 00$ and $S^{m-1}_{acc} = 01 \ldots 11$. This situation is possible. For example, when $A_{m-1} = 0010$ and $B_{m-1} = 0101$, then we have $S^{m-1}_{app} = 1000$ and $S^{m-1}_{acc} = 0111$. To correct the error in this case, we need to invert the sign bit and set the other sum bits in block $(m-1)$ to 1.

2.2.2 The Case where $A < 0, B < 0, S^{m-1}_{app} \geq 0$

This case is shown in Fig. 5(b). In this case, we must have $S^{m-1}_{app} = 00 \ldots 00$ and $S^{m-1}_{acc} = 11 \ldots 11$. However, since $C^{m-1}_{acc\_sum\_in} = 0$ and $s^{m-1}_{acc,j} = 1$ for $j = 0,1,\ldots,k_{m-1}-2$, we must have $a^{m-1}_j \oplus b^{m-1}_j = 1$ for $j = 0,1,\ldots,k_{m-1}-2$. Thus, the correct carry-in to the sign bit is $c^{m-1}_{acc,k_{m-1}-2} = 0$. Given that the sign bits of the inputs A and B are both 1, we must have $S^{m-1}_{acc} = 01 \ldots 11$, which contradicts with the claim that $S^{m-1}_{acc} = 11 \ldots 11$. Therefore, this situation cannot happen.

2.2.3 The Case where $A \geq 0, B < 0, S^{m-1}_{acc} \geq 0, S^{m-1}_{app} < 0$

This case is shown in Fig. 5(c). In this case, we must have $S^{m-1}_{app} = 10 \ldots 00$ and $S^{m-1}_{acc} = 01 \ldots 11$. However, applying the same argument used for Case 2.2.2, we can show that S^{m-1}_{acc} should be $11 \ldots 11$. Therefore, this situation cannot happen.

2.2.4 The Case where $A \geq 0, B < 0, S^{m-1}_{acc} < 0, S^{m-1}_{app} \geq 0$

This case is shown in Fig. 5(d). In this case, we must have $S^{m-1}_{app} = 00 \ldots 00$ and $S^{m-1}_{acc} = 11 \ldots 11$. This situation is possible. For example, when $A_{m-1} = 0010$ and $B_{m-1} = 1101$, then we have $S^{m-1}_{app} = 0000$ and $S^{m-1}_{acc} = 1111$. To correct the error in this case, we need to invert the sign bit and set the other sum bits in block $(m-1)$ to 1.

2.3 Summary

The above discussion considers all cases where a sign bit error might occur when we do two's complement addition. To sum up, if a sign bit error happens, we need to identify whether the case is Case 2.1 or Case 2.2. To correct a sign bit error for Case 2.1, we invert the sign bit and set all the other sum bits in block $(m-1)$ to 0. To correct a sign bit error for Case 2.2, we invert the sign bit and set all the other sum bits in block $(m-1)$ to 1.

3. METHODOLOGY FOR CORRECTING SIGN BIT ERROR

In this section, we show a general methodology for correcting sign bit error.

First, we define the group propagate signal pp_i for each block. For any block $0 \leq i \leq m-2$, $pp_i = \prod_{j=0}^{k_i-1} p^i_j$. If $pp_i = 1$, then all the propagate signals of block i are 1. Thus, in the accurate adder, the carry-in of block i propagates to the carry-out of block i, which is just the carry-in of block $(i+1)$. Therefore, we have $C^{i+1}_{acc\_sum\_in} = C^i_{acc\_sum\_in}$ when $pp_i = 1$.

The group propagate signal for block $(m-1)$ is defined slightly different from the other blocks in that it does not include

$p^{m-1}_{k_{m-1}-1}$. Specifically, $pp_{m-1} = \prod_{j=0}^{k_{m-1}-2} p^{m-1}_j$. For the ease of discussion, we also define $pp_{-1} = 0$.

When $pp_{m-1} = 0$, the carry-out signal $c^{m-1}_{app,k_{m-1}-2}$ in the $(m-1)$-th sub-adder of the approximate adder does not depend on the speculated carry-in signal of the sub-adder. Therefore, it is equal to the correct carry-out signal $c^{m-1}_{acc,k_{m-1}-2}$. As a result, the sign bit produced by the approximate adder is correct. Thus, in the following, we assume that $pp_{m-1} = 1$.

From the analysis shown in Section 2, we can see that to check whether there is a sign bit error, we need to know $C^{m-1}_{acc\_sum\_in}$.

To obtain $C^{m-1}_{acc\_sum\_in}$, we first modify each sub-adder in the approximate adder by adding some extra logic to produce a carry-out. The carry-out of the i-th sub-adder, denoted as $C^i_{app\_out}$, can be calculated by the existing signals in the sub-adder as

$$C^i_{app\_out} = g^i_{k_i-1} + p^i_{k_i-1} \cdot c^i_{app,k_i-2}.$$

The circuit is shown in Fig. 6. For the ease of discussion, we define $C^{-1}_{app\_out} = c_{in}$.

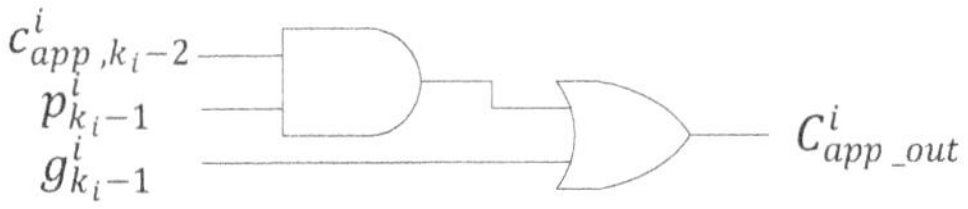

Fig. 6: Circuits for generating the carry-out signal of a sub-adder.

It is easy to see that when $pp_i = 0$, the carry-out $C^i_{app\_out}$ is equal to the correct carry-out in the accurate adder. Indeed, in our proposed design, the modification to each sub-adder is not necessary, as long as when $pp_i = 0$, there is a signal equal to the correct carry-out of block i. This is true for many existing approximate adders in which for any block $0 \le i \le m-2$, there is a carry generator that produces a speculated carry-out signal based on at least all the input bits in that block. For example, the ETAII shown in Fig. 1, the CSA proposed in [3], and the LREA proposed in [4] all satisfy this condition. For this type of approximate adder, when $pp_i = 0$, the speculated carry-out produced by the carry generator is equal to the correct carry-out of block i. We can just use the speculated carry-out as the signal $C^i_{app\_out}$, which takes no extra circuitry.

Since we assume $pp_{m-1} = 1$ and $pp_{-1} = 0$, there must exist a $0 \le t \le m-1$ such that $pp_{m-1} = pp_{m-2} = \cdots = pp_t = 1$ and $pp_{t-1} = 0$. This value t plays an important role in our correction scheme. Since $pp_{t-1} = 0$, by the above discussion, the signal $C^{t-1}_{app\_out}$ in the approximate adder gives the correct carry-out of block $t-1$, which is just the correct carry-in of block t, $C^t_{acc\_sum\_in}$. Because $pp_{m-2} = pp_{m-3} = \cdots = pp_t = 1$, the accurate carry-in of block $m-1$, $C^{m-1}_{acc\_sum\_in}$ is equal to $C^t_{acc\_sum\_in}$, which in turn is equal to $C^{t-1}_{app\_out}$. This gives us a way to obtain $C^{m-1}_{acc\_sum\_in}$. Note that the speculated carry-in $C^{m-1}_{app\_sum\_in}$ is also available in the given approximate adder. Then we can compare these two signals to check for sign bit error. If $C^{m-1}_{acc\_sum\_in} = C^{m-1}_{app\_sum\_in}$, there is no sign bit error. Otherwise, the computation might have a sign bit error and we can fix the error based on the different correction strategies discussed in Section 2.

However, in our actual implementation, we use a better strategy that not only can fix sign bit error when it occurs, but also can fix some errors in the most significant bits even if there is no sign bit error.

Our idea utilizes the signal $C^{t-1}_{app\_out}$ and the fact that $pp_{m-1} = \cdots = pp_t = 1$. When $C^{t-1}_{app\_out} = 0$, for the accurate adder, we have $s^i_{acc,j} = 1$ for $t \le i \le m-2$ and $0 \le j \le k_i - 1$, $s^{m-1}_{acc,j} = 1$ for $0 \le j \le k_{m-1} - 2$, and $c^{m-1}_{acc,k_{m-1}-2} = 0$. When $C^{t-1}_{app\_out} = 1$, for the accurate adder, we have $s^i_{acc,j} = 0$ for $t \le i \le m-2$ and $0 \le j \le k_i - 1$, $s^{m-1}_{acc,j} = 0$ for $0 \le j \le k_{m-1} - 2$, and $c^{m-1}_{acc,k_{m-1}-2} = 1$.

Summarizing the above patterns, we can conclude that no matter whether $C^{t-1}_{app\_out}$ is 0 or 1, for the accurate adder, we have $s^i_{acc,j} = \overline{C^{t-1}_{app\_out}}$ for $t \le i \le m-2$ and $0 \le j \le k_i - 1$, $s^{m-1}_{acc,j} = \overline{C^{t-1}_{app\_out}}$ for $0 \le j \le k_{m-1} - 2$, and $c^{m-1}_{acc,k_{m-1}-2} = C^{t-1}_{app\_out}$. Thus, no matter whether the above output bits in the approximate adder have error or not, we can simply set them to their correct values shown above. Once we get the correct carry-out $c^{m-1}_{acc,k_{m-1}-2}$, the correct sign bit can be easily obtained as

$$s^{m-1}_{acc,k_{m-1}-1} = p^{m-1}_{k_{m-1}-1} \oplus c^{m-1}_{acc,k_{m-1}-2}.$$

For the remaining sum bits in blocks $t-1, \ldots, 0$, we just keep them unchanged.

4. CIRCUIT DESIGN

In this section, we show the circuit design for correcting the sign bit error, which implements the methodology discussed in Section 3.

The implementation needs to address two key questions: (1) how to identify the specific value t for any input vector? (2) how to obtain the value $C^{t-1}_{app\_out}$?

To address the above questions, we define the following signals.

- $pc_i = pp_{m-1} \cdot pp_{m-2} \cdot \cdots \cdot pp_i$, for $0 \le i \le m-1$. By the definition of the value t, for $t \le i \le m-1$, we have $pc_i = 1$. For $0 \le i < t$, since $pp_{t-1} = 0$, we have $pc_i = 0$. This gives us a way to test whether $i \ge t$ or $i < t$.
- $pt_i = pc_i \cdot \overline{pp_{i-1}}$, for $0 \le i \le m-1$. By the definition of the value t, we have $pt_t = 1$. For any $t < i \le m-1$, since $pp_{i-1} = 1$, we have $pt_i = 0$. For any $0 \le i < t$, since $pc_i = 0$, we have $pt_i = 0$. In summary, among all pt_i's, only $pt_t = 1$. This gives us a way to identify t.
- $cv = \sum_{i=0}^{m-1} pt_i \cdot C^{i-1}_{app\_out}$. Since among all pt_i's, only $pt_t = 1$, we have $cv = C^{t-1}_{app\_out}$. This gives us a way to obtain $C^{t-1}_{app\_out}$.

The circuits for the signals pc_i, pt_i, and cv are shown in Fig. 7.

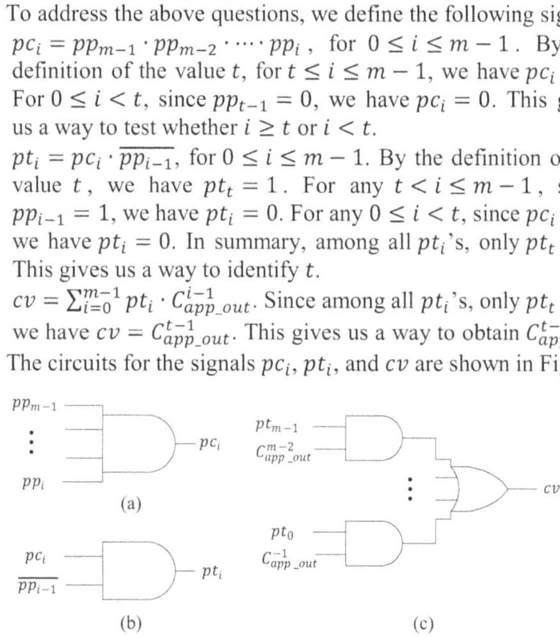

Fig. 7: Circuits for (a) the signal pc_i, (b) the signal pt_i, and (c) the signal cv.

For any $0 \le i \le m-2$, if $pc_i = 1$, then by the property of signal pc_i, we must have $i \ge t$. Based on the correction methodology discussed in Section 3, for any $0 \le j \le k_i - 1$, we set $s^i_{new,j} = \overline{cv}$, where $s^i_{new,j}$ is the new sum bit at position j in block i of the approximate adder. For any $0 \le i \le m-2$, if $pc_i = 0$, then we must have $i < t$. Based on the correction methodology, we keep $s^i_{new,j}$ as the old approximate value $s^i_{app,j}$. If $pc_{m-1} = 1$, then we set $s^{m-1}_{new,j} = \overline{cv}$, for any $0 \le j \le k_{m-1} - 2$, and set $c_{new,k_{m-1}-2}^{m-1} = cv$, where $c_{new,k_{m-1}-2}^{m-1}$ is the new carry-out bit at position $k_{m-1} - 2$ in block $m - 1$ of the approximate adder. If $pc_{m-1} = 0$, the old sum bits $s_{app,j}^{m-1}$ $(0 \le j \le k_{m-1} - 2)$ and the old carry-out bit $c_{app,k_{m-1}-2}^{m-1}$ are kept.

Based on the above discussion, we can realize $s_{new,j}^{i}$ by a MUX, as shown in Fig. 8(a). The new sign bit $s_{new,k_{m-1}-1}^{m-1}$ is realized by the circuit shown in Fig. 8(b).

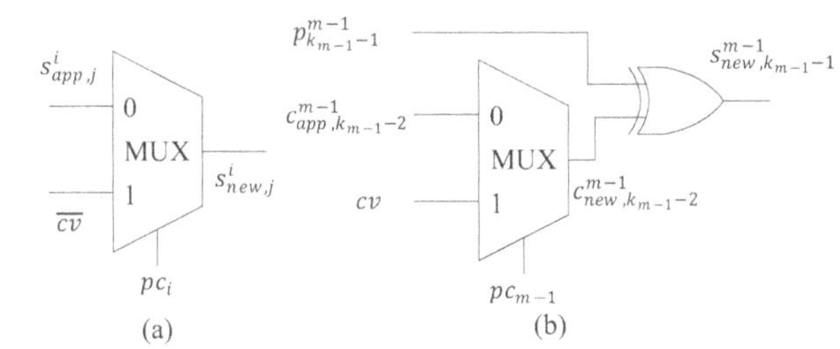

Fig. 8: Circuits for (a) the new sum bits and (b) the new sign bit of the approximate adder.

5. EXPERIMENTAL RESULTS

In this section, we present the experimental results on our proposed sign bit error correction module. The circuits were synthesized using Synopsys Design Compiler [10] and mapped to a 45nm Nangate cell library [11].

5.1 Overhead for Different Approximate Adders

We applied the proposed sign bit error correction module to three existing approximate adders, ETAII [2], CSA [3], and LREA [4]. Table 1 shows the area, delay, power consumption, and power-delay product (PDP) of the three approximate adders with (denoted by "sign") and without (denoted by "basic") the sign bit error correction module. For comparison purpose, we also list the four metrics of the conventional ripple carry adder (RCA) and carry look-ahead adder (CLA). All the adders are 16-bit adders. The three approximate adders are divided into 4 blocks of equal size of 4. For each approximate adder with the sign bit error correction module, the percentage increase of each metric due to the sign bit error correction module is shown inside the parentheses after the absolute value.

Table 1. Area, delay, power consumption, and power-delay product (PDP) of different 16-bit adders.

	Area (μm^2)	Delay (ns)	Power (mW)	PDP (fJ)
ETAII(basic)	99.5	0.97	22.3	21.6
ETAII (sign)	129.1 (30)	1.12 (15)	22.8 (2.2)	25.5 (18)
CSA (basic)	114.6	1.16	23.0	26.7
CSA (sign)	138.1 (21)	1.31 (13)	23.9 (3.9)	31.3 (17)
LREA(basic)	121.0	1.24	25.8	31.9
LREA (sign)	139.6 (15)	1.28 (3.2)	26.2 (1.6)	33.5 (5.0)
RCA	109.8	2.32	23.9	55.4
CLA	145.3	1.78	29.9	53.2

From the table, we can see that by adding the sign bit error correction module, the area increases 15%~30%, the delay increases 3.2%~15%, the power consumption increases 1.6%~3.9% and the PDP increases 5.0%~18%. The overhead for ETAII is the largest, since ETAII design is the simplest among the three. Overall, the overhead of the sign bit error correction module is small. Compared with RCA, although the approximate adders with the sign bit error correction module have slightly larger power consumption, they have much smaller delay and PDP. Compared with CLA, all of the four metrics of the approximate adders with the sign bit error correction module are smaller.

5.2 Overhead for Same Approximate Adder of Different Sizes

In this experiment, we applied the proposed sign bit error correction module to ETAIIs of different design parameters. We considered 5 different ETAIIs, which are listed in Table 2. The pair (n, k) indicates the adder is an n-bit adder with n/k blocks of equal size k. For example, the pair (32, 4) indicates a 32-bit ETAII with 8 blocks of equal size 4. Table 2 shows the area, delay, and power consumption of them with (column "sign") and without (column "basic") the sign bit error correction module. The values in the parentheses are the percentage increases.

Table 2. Area, delay, and power consumption of different ETAIIs with and without the sign bit error correction module.

ETAII parameters	Area (μm^2)		Delay (ns)		Power (mW)	
	basic	sign	basic	sign	basic	sign
(16, 2)	91.0	112.4 (24)	0.68	1.05 (54)	22.3	22.4 (0.4)
(16, 4)	99.5	129.1 (30)	0.97	1.12 (15)	22.3	22.8 (2.2)
(32, 2)	178.8	255.3 (43)	0.57	1.76 (209)	23.2	23.8 (2.6)
(32, 4)	208.5	261.8 (26)	0.97	1.42 (46)	23.6	23.8 (0.8)
(32, 8)	223.4	257.8 (15)	1.64	1.76 (7.3)	25.9	26.3 (1.5)

From the table, we can see that when the number of blocks increases, the overhead in area and delay due to the sign bit error correction module also increases. The reason is that some sub-modules in the sign bit error correction module, such as the circuits for the signals pc_i and cv, have area and delay complexity proportional to the number of blocks.

5.3 Performance Study on Edge Detection Application

To evaluate the effect of our sign bit error correction module in real applications, we applied several approximate adders with and without the sign bit error correction module to an image processing application, namely Roberts cross-based edge detection [12]. We used peak signal-to-noise ratio (PSNR) of the image as the performance metric. It is defined as

$$PSNR = 10 \cdot \log_{10}\left(\frac{MAX_I^2}{MSE}\right),$$

where MAX_I is the maximum possible pixel value of the image. MSE is the mean square error (MSE), which is defined as

$$MSE = \frac{1}{WH}\sum_{i=0}^{W-1}\sum_{j=0}^{H-1}[I(i,j) - K(i,j)]^2,$$

where W and H are the width and the height of an image, respectively. The values $I(i,j)$ and $K(i,j)$ are the results calculated by the accurate adder and the approximate adder, respectively, at location (i,j) in the image. For an accurate adder, its $MSE = 0$ and hence, its $PSNR = +\infty$. The higher the PSNR is, the better the performance of the adder is.

We used three existing approximate adders, ETAII, CSA, and LREA in our experiment. We applied these adders with and without the sign bit error correction module to perform edge detection on 10 sample images chosen from an online library [13].

Table 3 shows the average PSNR over the 10 images in our simulation. The adder parameter pairs (10, 2) and (10, 5) in the table have the same meaning as before. The pair (10, 3) refers to an adder with 4 blocks, of which the leftmost three are of size 3 and the rightmost one is of size 1. Note that some entries in the table is $+\infty$ because the MSE is either zero or very small. From the table, we can see that the approximate adders with the error correction module are up to 5.5 × better in PSNR than the original ones.

Table 3. PSNRs of different approximate adders with and without the sign bit error correction module.

Adder parameter	ETAII		CSA		LREA	
	basic	sign	basic	sign	basic	sign
(10, 2)	9.34	28.2	7.95	33.8	9.88	42.7
(10, 3)	11.0	31.7	13.3	42.6	9.83	54.5
(10, 5)	$+\infty$	$+\infty$	$+\infty$	$+\infty$	17.8	$+\infty$

To visually demonstrate the effectiveness of our proposed module, we show one sample image processed by the accurate adder and the LREAs with and without the sign bit error correction module for $n = 10$ and $k = 2,3,5$ in Fig. 9.

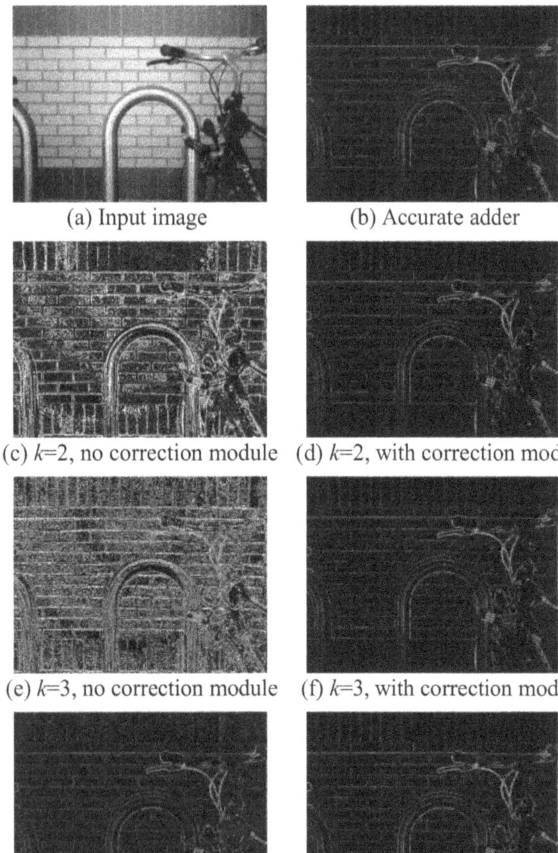

(a) Input image (b) Accurate adder

(c) k=2, no correction module (d) k=2, with correction module

(e) k=3, no correction module (f) k=3, with correction module

(g) k=5, no correction module (h) k=5, with correction module

Fig. 9: Roberts cross-based edge detection using different adders.

From Fig. 9, we can clearly see that the approximate adders with our sign bit error correction module have much better performance than those adders without the correction module.

Finally, we did another comparison between two approximate adders. One is an LREA with $(n, k) = (10,5)$ and no sign bit error correction module. The other is an LREA with $(n, k) = (10,2)$ and the sign bit error correction module. The comparison of their PSNRs, areas, delays, and power consumptions is shown in Table 4.

Table 4. Comparison of two approximate adders.

	PSNR	Area (μm^2)	Delay (ns)	Power (mW)
LREA (10, 5), basic	17.8	76.3	1.40	19.0
LREA (10, 2), sign	42.7	85.3	1.01	18.2

From the table, we can see that the LREA with $(n, k) = (10,2)$ and the sign bit error correction module is 12% larger in area than the LREA with $(n, k) = (10,5)$ and no sign bit error correction module. However, the delay and the power consumption of the former are 28% and 4.2% smaller than those of the latter, respectively. Furthermore, the PSNR of the former is 140% better than that of the latter. This result shows that in the case where the circuit area, delay, and power consumption are comparable, an approximate adder with the proposed sign bit error correction module is much better in PSNR than an approximate adder without the correction module.

6. CONCLUSION

In this paper, we proposed a general sign bit error correction scheme, which is applicable to many block-based approximate adders. The only requirement our scheme relies on is that each sub-adder in the approximate adder is correct, which is usually held. Our design is very efficient with low area, delay, and energy overhead. According to the properties of each specific approximate adder, the proposed design may be further simplified. The proposed module not only can correct the sign bit error when it occurs, but also can fix some errors in the most significant bits even if there is no sign bit error. Thus, it can further reduce the relative error and error rate of the original approximate adder. We applied our proposed module to an edge detection application and demonstrated the good performance of it.

ACKNOWLEDGEMENTS

This work is supported by National Natural Science Foundation of China (NSFC) under Grant No. 61574089.

7. REFERENCES

[1] J. Han and M. Orshansky, "Approximate computing: An emerging paradigm for energy-efficient design," in ETS, 2013, pp. 1–6.

[2] N. Zhu, W. L. Goh, and K. S. Yeo, "An enhanced low-power high speed adder for error-tolerant application," in ISIC, 2009, pp. 69–72.

[3] Y. Kim, Y. Zhang, and P. Li, "An energy efficient approximate adder with carry skip for error resilient neuromorphic VLSI systems," in ICCAD, 2013, pp. 130–137.

[4] J. Hu and W. Qian, "A new approximate adder with low relative error and correct sign calculation," in DATE, 2015, pp. 1449–1454.

[5] K. Du, P. Varman, and K. Mohanram, "High performance reliable variable latency carry select addition," in DATE, 2012, pp. 1257–1262.

[6] A. K. Verma, P. Brisk, and P. Ienne, "Variable latency speculative addition: A new paradigm for arithmetic circuit design," in DATE, 2008, pp. 1250–1255.

[7] A. B. Kahng and S. Kang, "Accuracy-configurable adder for approximate arithmetic designs," in DAC, 2012, pp. 820–825.

[8] R. Ye, T. Wang, F. Yuan, R. Kumar, and Q. Xu, "On reconfiguration-oriented approximate adder design and its application," in ICCAD, 2013, pp. 48–54.

[9] H. R. Mahdiani, A. Ahmadi, S. M. Fakhraie, and C. Lucas, "Bio-inspired imprecise computational blocks for efficient VLSI implementation of softcomputing applications," IEEE Transactions on Circuits and Systems I, vol. 57, no. 4, pp. 850–862, 2010.

[10] Design Compiler, Synopsys Inc., http://www.synopsys.com

[11] Nangate 45nm Library, Nangate Inc., http://www.nangate.com

[12] L. G. Roberts, "Machine perception of three-dimensional soups," Ph.D. dissertation, Massachusetts Institute of Technology, 1963.

[13] Image databases: standard test images, http://www.imageprocessingplace.com/root_files_V3/image_databases.htm

RRAM Refresh Circuit: A Proposed Solution To Resolve The Soft-Error Failures For HfO_2/Hf 1T1R RRAM Memory Cell

Amr M.S.Tosson
University of Waterloo
atosson@uwaterloo.ca

Mohab Anis
American University at Cairo
manis@aucegypt.edu

Lan Wei
University of Waterloo
lan.wei@uwaterloo.ca

ABSTRACT

RRAM-based memory is a promising emerging technology for both on-chip and stand-alone non-volatile data storage in advanced technologies. In addition to its small dimensions, the RRAM device has many technological advantages including its low-programming voltages, high speed, low power, CMOS-compatible fabrication process, and potentially monolithic 3D integration. However, one of the critical challenges for RRAM technology is the reliability concerns due to retention and endurance failures. In this paper, we propose a novel Refresh circuit for 1T1R RRAM array which detects and distinguishes soft and hard errors from retention and endurance failures, as well as corrects the soft errors through refreshing. Using the HfO_2/Hf RRAM array, our simulation results show that the proposed solution increases the resilience to soft-error of an 8Gb RRAM-based memory by 80% with a small penalty on the energy and delay of the Read operations (6% and 0.4% respectively). The proposed methodology can be used for other RRAM arrays with minor modifications to the design parameters depending on the characteristics of RRAM cell.

1. INTRODUCTION

Due to the ability to retain data in the absence of power supply, Non-Volatile Memories (NVMs) were first used as a mean to protect important system data from being erased when the power supply is cut-off (e.g FPGA configuration bits [1] and the boot-code of the processor [2]). With the rapid development of portable electronic devices in the past decades, the NVMs have been widely adopted as a fast (compared to magnetic disks), low power, and low cost solution (compared to DRAM) for data storage either on-chip or stand-alone. Flash memory is the dominant NVM technology in today's market. However, the geometrical and voltage scaling requirements in sub-20nm technologies make the advancement of flash memory quite challenging due to its charge based floating gate structure [3]. New structures are actively explored in seek of the next generation of low-cost, low-power, high speed, and high capacity NVM technologies. Examples of emerging NVM technologies include Spin Torque Transfer Magnetic Random Access Memory (STT-MRAM) [4], Phase Change Random Access Memory (PCRAM) [5], and Resistive Random Access Memory (RRAM) cells. Due to its compact size (as small as 10 nm x 10nm [6]), fast switching speed (in order of 10ns [7]), low programming voltage (as low as 1V [8]), and easy integration with the CMOS fabrication process, the Resistive Random Access Memory (RRAM) device is one of the most promising NVM technologies nowadays. In comparison to other NVM devices, RRAM has smaller cell area than STT-MRAM and consumes less energy than PCRAM [9]. The RRAM device has a simple sandwich structure with oxide materials (e.g. HfO_x, AlO_x, etc) in between two metal electrodes which can be easily integrated between the metal layers or within the contact vias to the source and/or drain of a metal-oxide-semiconductor field effect transistor (MOSFET) [10] to form the 1T1R memory cell. The RRAM device has two resistive states: the High Resistance State (HRS) (typical resistance around 1M - 10M Ω) and the Low Resistance State (LRS) (typical resistance around 10 - 100k Ω). The LRS and HRS are caused by the creation/rupture of conductive filaments made of oxygen vacancies within the oxide material, depending on the polarity of the voltage applied to the device electrodes.

The 1T1R cell suffers, however, from endurance and retention failures. Other than its own endurance limit, using unbalanced programming conditions can reduce the device lifetime from 10^{10} to 10^6 cycles [11, 12]. The retention failures cause the data saved in the memory cell to be lost over time due to the drift in the RRAM resistive state either from LRS to HRS or from HRS to LRS. In this paper, we propose a novel Refresh circuit which resolves the soft errors (recoverable errors) coming from retention and endurance failures. Our resolution is based on analyzing the physical origins of the drift of the RRAM resistive state to determine whether it can be recovered or not. In case of soft-errors, re-programming the device restores its correct state. Our proposed Refresh circuit has little impact on the memory design since it is not attached to each cell individually, instead it is integrated into the sense-amplifier (SA) of each Bitline (BL). Moreover, the Refresh operation in our suggested methodology is triggered either a) after the read-operation if the cell data indicates that a Refresh operation is required or b) after a pre-defined period of time. The Refresh period for the RRAM is on the order of days to months [13] instead a few μ secs as in DRAM. This preserves the

GLSVLSI '16, May 18-20, 2016, Boston, MA, USA

DOI: http://dx.doi.org/10.1145/2902961.2903017

advantage of using the RRAM-based array as a low-power memory technology. Our system level simulations with an 8Gb memory show that the overhead of the newly added structure on the read energy and delay is marginal (6% and 0.4% respectively).

The rest of this paper is organized as follows: In section 2, we describe the concept of our suggested Refresh methodology. Then, in section 3, we discuss in details the architecture of the Refresh circuit. Following that, we summarize the results from our SPICE and system level simulation in sections 4.1 and 4.2. Finally, we conclude the different discussions of this article in section 5

2. THE CONCEPT OF THE PROPOSED REFRESH METHODOLOGY

The failure mechanisms of the RRAM devices are extensively studied [11,13–16] and they can be classified into two categories:

- **Hard-Error**: This is mainly caused by the fact that the RRAM device, like all other NVM devices, has an endurance limit (on the order of 10^{10} cycles for HfO_2/Hf RRAM). If the device reaches this limit, its state can not be recovered due to the depletion of oxygen vacancies in the oxide material and the device can not be used further.
- **Soft-Error**: The RRAM state drift due to such an error can be recovered by re-programming the device to its original state. There are several reasons that can cause soft-error:
  - **Diffusion of the oxygen vacancies out of the conductive filament constriction**: This is coming from uneven heat generation and dissipation due to frequent programming operation.
  - **Unbalanced programming pulses**: This causes the oxygen vacancies inside the oxide to be either more dispersed or more dense depending on the programming pulses amplitude and polarity. It weakens the effect of the pulses to form/rupture the conductive filaments and shorten the device lifetime.
  - **Manufacture defects**: The free oxygen atoms, created when patterning the layers of the device, can easily recombine with the oxygen vacancies of the filament and hence contributes to the degradation of the LRS of the RRAM

In this work, to reduce the power consumption of the memory array, we focus on the case of using low-programming conditions to alter the state of the RRAM device ($\leq 40\mu A$). Under this circumstance, the soft-error failures in these arrays mainly cause the drift of the RRAM state from LRS to HRS due the reduced number of oxygen vacancies which leads to lack of the conductive filaments and increase of the resistance [14] because any of the soft-error failure mechanisms mentioned above tends to rupture the "weakly" created conductive filaments. The process of LRS drifting to HRS is gradual and, if detected early enough, it can fixed by refreshing the device to its LRS. Accordingly, the operation of the proposed Refresh circuit is based on the concept of dividing the resistance range defined by the HRS and LRS of the RRAM device into four regions as shown in Fig.1

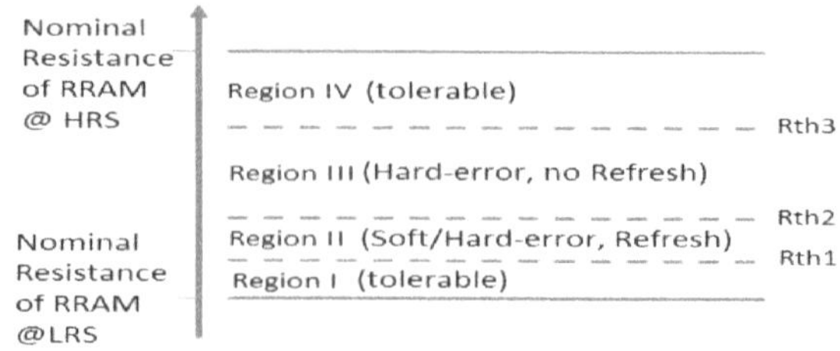

Figure 1: Regions of operation of the Refresh circuit

Region I defines the zone where the resistance of a RRAM device is within the tolerance of the LRS and hence it does not trigger a Refresh operation. The purpose of this region is to:

- Allow for minor changes in the resistance of RRAM devices coming from the variation in the fabrication process and the write/Read operation conditions
- Limit the amount of Refresh needed in order to save energy and to reduce the impact of the Refresh operation on the device endurance since it is basically a Write operation

This region is bounded by the threshold resistance value Rth_1. We show how Rth_1 is selected after explaining how the threshold value Rth_2 is computed later in the section.

Region II defines the zone where the Refresh operation is triggered to restore the LRS of the RRAM device. This region is bounded by the two threshold resistance values: Rth_1 and Rth_2. Rth_2 is the resistance value that maps to the RRAM state above which it is no longer considered as LRS. Since the resistance change due to soft-error is gradual, as long as the cell is refreshed frequently enough, the RRAM resistance does not drift beyond Rth_2 unless severe hard-error failures occur. Based on [13–15], Rth_2 is chosen to be 10 times of the resistance value of the RRAM device at its nominal LRS.

To determine the value of Rth_1, there are two contradicting requirements to consider. On one hand, Rth_1 needs to be as close as possible to Rth_2 in order to reduce the frequency of the Refresh operation. On the other hand, the larger the difference between Rth_2 and Rth_1, the better is the performance of the sense amplifier of the Refresh circuit due to the larger difference between the reference voltages of the RRAM cell corresponding to Rth_1 and Rth_2 (V(Rth_1) and V(Rth_2) respectively) . Using the SPICE models built based on the data in [13–15], we create the graph in Fig.2. This graph shows that, as we move away from the Rth_2 (value of $|R - Rth2|$ increases), the difference between $V(Rth_1)$ and $V(Rth_2)$ increases but the Refresh cycle duration decreases. The Rth_1 represents the optimal threshold value after which any change in the resistance increases the power of Refresh operation due to the exponential reduction in its cycle duration.

Region III defines the zone where the Read operation is unable to differentiate whether the original state of the RRAM was LRS or HRS. When the RRAM resistance is in this region, it indicates that the device has encountered a permanent failure which can not be recovered (hard-error). Since the drift of the RRAM state is a gradual process, if the Rth_1 and Rth_2 are properly selected, soft-errors are fixed

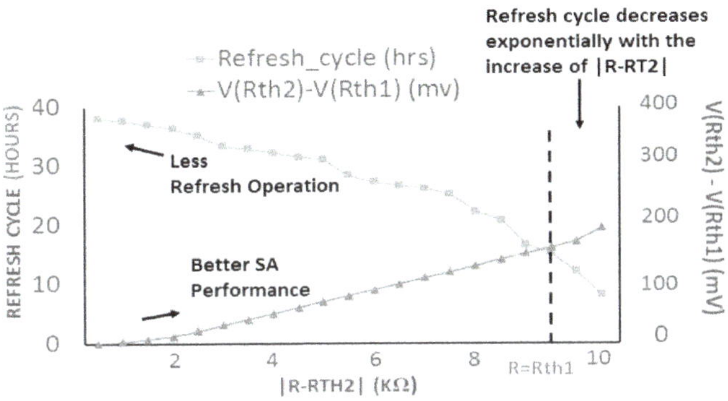

Figure 2: Rth_1 threshold value selection

before the RRAM resistance reaches this region. The upper bound of this domain is Rth_3 which is defined as 3 times Rth_2 according to [14].

Region IV defines the zone where the state of the RRAM device is considered as HRS. In this region, we do not initiate the Refresh operation since the soft-errors in low-programming conditions mainly cause the drift of the RRAM state from LRS to HRS (i.e the device in HRS tends rarely to drift to LRS).

Based on the type of the RRAM cell, the region boundaries might require re-evaluation based on the device characteristics

3. REFRESH CIRCUIT SCHEMATIC AND OPERATION

The block diagram of the Refresh circuit is shown in Fig.3

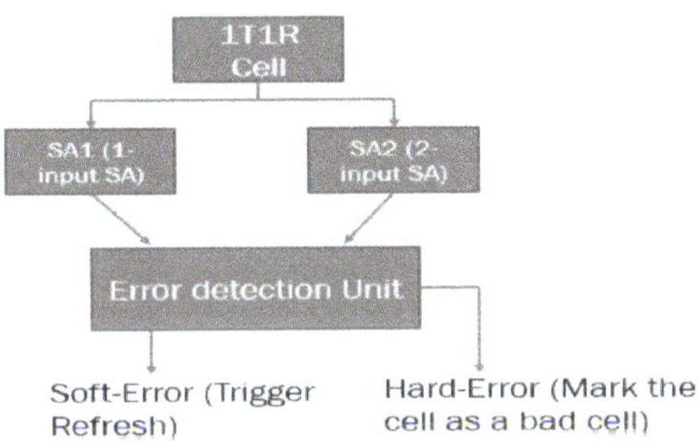

Figure 3: Block diagram of Refresh circuit.

The Refresh circuit consists of:

- **SA1 (1-input) and SA2 (2-input)**: These are the voltage-sense amplifiers used to detect the RRAM state of the 1T1R cell. At the beginning of the Read operation, the Bitline (BL) is precharged to VDD. Then, a pulse is applied to the wordline (WL) to enable the transistor of the 1T1R cell for a certain period of time (3ns in our experiments as explained in section 4.1). During the WL pulse, the voltage of the BL changes depending on the state of the RRAM device. At the end of the WL pulse, the voltage of the BL (V_{sense}) is sensed and compared to reference voltages ($V(Rth_1)$, $V(Rth_2)$, $V(Rth_3)$) corresponding to the different threshold resistance values discussed in section 2. The SA1 (1-input) compares the V_{sense} to $V(Rth_3)$ in order to detect whether the RRAM state is at HRS (Region IV of Fig.1) or not. The SA2 (2-input) is used for checking whether the RRAM resistance is in Region I/II or not. If the RRAM resistance is not in any of those regions, this means that the RRAM device is in Region III (hard-error region). The schematic and operation of SA1 and SA2 are discussed in section 3.1.
- **Error detection unit**: This is a logic circuit which combines the results from SA1 and SA2 to decide a) whether a Refresh operation is needed or not and b) whether the RRAM device has reached its endurance limit (by checking if its resistance is in the Hard Error zone (Region III in Fig.1)) or not. The circuit operation is explained in section 3.2. In case if Refresh is needed, the unit sends a signal (Soft-Error signal in Fig.3) to the memory controller to initiate a Write operation on the currently selected cell in order to restore its LRS. In case if the RRAM device of the selected 1T1R cell has encountered a non-recoverable error, the error detection circuit sends another signal (Hard-Error signal in Fig.3) to the memory controller to mask the address to this erroneous cell by mapping it to another 1T1R cell which is still functional [17].

3.1 Sense Amplifier of the Refresh circuit

The SA1 (1-input) and SA2 (2-input) circuits in Fig.3 uses two-tail sense-amplifier design similar to that in [18]. These two sense amplifier designs are basically the same with the difference that SA2 has two input reference voltages while SA1 has only one. Fig.4 shows the circuit schematic for SA2. The SA1 has the same design as that of SA2 without the

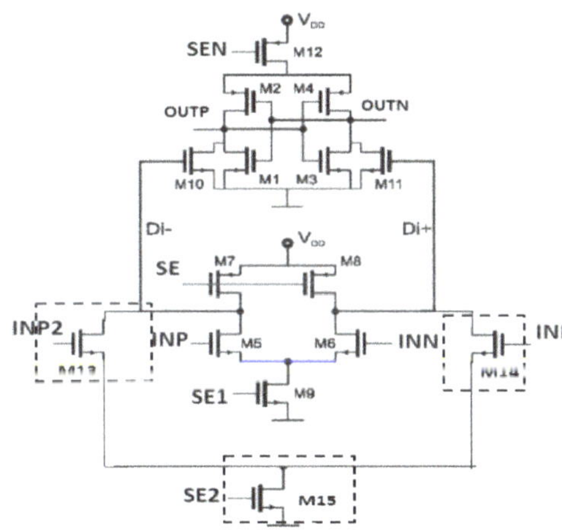

Figure 4: Circuit schematic for the SA2 block

marked transistors (M13,M14,M15) in Fig.4. These MOS devices are added to the SA2 circuit in order to have four input voltages (two input nodes connected to reference voltages and the other two are connected to the voltage that needs to be sensed) instead of two. This is basically because SA2 needs to compare the BL voltage (V_{sense}) versus two independent reference voltages ($V(Rth_1)$ and $V(Rth_2)$) in two separate sub-operations. The voltages $V(Rth_1)$ and $V(Rth_2)$ are connected to the nodes INN and INN2 in Fig.4 while the V_{sense} is connected to both of nodes INP and INP2. All the control signals in Fig.4 (SE1,SE2,SE,SEN) are generated by the Error detection unit as explained in section 3.2. The SA2 works in the following sequence:

1. Signals SE,SE1,SE2 are first disabled (connected to ground) in order to discharge the output nodes OUTN and OUTP to ground (logic "0")

2. Only the signals SE and SE1 are raised to VDD (logic "1") to compare V_{sense} versus $V(Rth_1)$. If $V_{sense} < V(Rth_1)$, the signal OUTN goes to VDD while OUTP remains at logic "0". This indicates that RRAM device of the selected 1T1R cell is at LRS (Region I) and hence no Refresh operation is needed. Oppositely, if $V_{sense} > V(Rth_1)$, the node OUTP goes to logic "1" while node OUTN remains at logic "0" which means that a second comparison cycle between V_{sense} and $V(Rth_2)$ is needed (Steps 3 and 4 below).

3. All the control signals are disabled again (SE,SE1,SE2 are connected to ground while SEN, which is the inverted version of SE, is set to logic "1") to discharge both of the output nodes OUTN and OUTP to ground.

4. Only the signals SE and SE2 are set to logic "1" to compare V_{sense} with $V(Rth_2)$. If $V_{sense} < V(Rth_2)$, the output node OUTN charges to VDD while OUTP remains at logic "0". This indicates that the RRAM resistance is in Region II and hence a Refresh operation is needed. If $V_{sense} > V(Rth_2)$, this means that RRAM resistance is either in Region III or Region IV. The output nodes of SA1 are hence used to indicate whether the device is in HRS or not as described in section 3.2.

Fig.5 shows the waveforms of the operation of SA2 circuit for the case if $V_{sense} > V(Rth_1)$ and $V_{sense} < V(Rth_2)$.

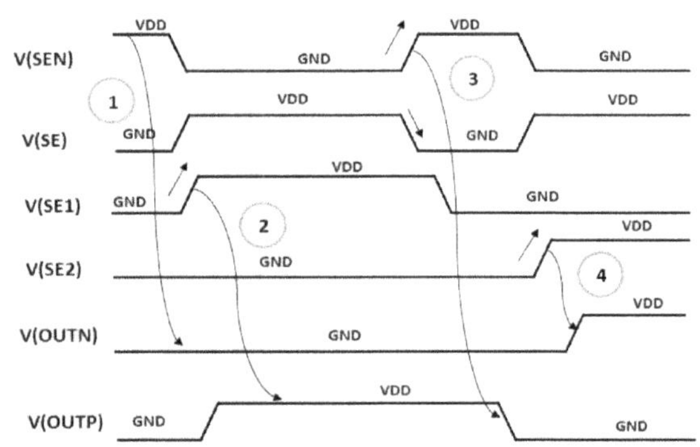

Figure 5: Waveforms for the operation of SA2 circuit for the case if $V(Rth_1) < V_{sense} < V(Rth_2)$

The SA1 design works exactly as SA2 with the exception that it uses only one reference voltage to compare the V_{sense} with $V(Rth_3)$ discussed in section 3. Hence, only the steps 1 and 2 of the SA2 operation are applicable for SA1 circuit.

3.2 Error Detection Unit

The Error Detection has two main functions:

- Control the generation of the enable signals (SE1,SE2,SE,SEN in Fig.4) for SA1 and SA2 circuits
- Decide whether to raise the Hard-Error or the Soft-error signals (shown in Fig.3) based on the output from the SA1 and SA2 designs

The logic circuit of this unit is shown in Fig.6. The signal

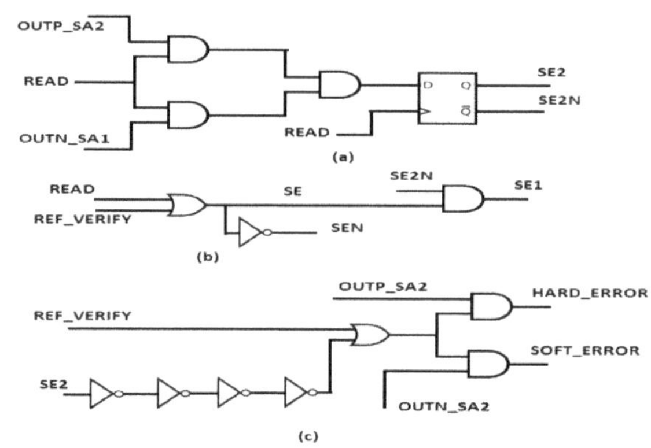

Figure 6: Circuit schematic of the error detection unit. Part a) The SE2 generation circuit, Part b) The SE/SE1 generation circuit, Part c) Refresh detection unit

READ is generated by the memory controller to initiate the Read operation. The *REF_VERIFY* signal is set by the memory controller at the end of Refresh cycle duration to check the RRAM state in the array independent of whether there is a Read operation or not. The *REF_VERIFY* pulse is also used to verify that RRAM state has successfully been restored to its LRS (Region I in Fig.1) after the Refresh operation. This is done by starting a Read operation using a *REF_VERIFY* pulse after the Refresh is completed. If the RRAM state is not at its LRS (Region I) after Refresh, the *HARD_ERROR* pulse is generated to the memory controller to prevent any future access to this cell.
There are three subcircuits in the Error detection unit:

- The **SE2 generation circuit** in Fig.6a creates the SE2 pulses needed for comparing the V_{sense} versus $V(Rth_2)$ as explained in section 3.1. If $V_{sense} > V(Rth_1)$ (the node OUTP of the SA2 circuit (*OUTP_SA2* in Fig.6) goes to logic "1") and $V_{sense} < V(Rth_3)$ (the node OUTN of SA1 (*OUTN_SA1* in Fig.6) goes to logic "1"), this means that the resistance of the RRAM is either in Region II or III of Fig.1. In this case, we need to generate the SE2 pulse in order to compare the V_{sense} versus $V(Rth_2)$.

- The **SE/SE1 generation circuit** in Fig.6b creates the SE/SEN/SE1 pulses needed to enable reading the RRAM state through the SA1 and SA2 circuits as described in section 3.1. Those signals are generated in response to the *READ* or the *REF_VERIFY* signals.

- The **Refresh detection circuit** in Fig.6c determines whether the RRAM needs a Refresh operation or not based on the output from SA2 design. In response to SE2 pulse, if $V_{sense} < V(Rth_2)$, the output node OUTN of SA2 (*OUTN_SA2* in Fig.6) rises to VDD. This means that the resistance of the RRAM device is in region II and a Refresh operation is needed. Hence, the signal *Soft_Error* is raised. Oppositely, if $V_{sense} >$

$V(Rth_2)$, the output node OUTP of SA2 ($OUTP\_SA2$ in fig.6) goes to logic "1" in response to having the resistance of the RRAM is region III. In this case, the signal $Hard\_Error$ is raised and the cell is marked by the memory controller as a bad cell and hence the address to this memory cell is masked.

4. EXPERIMENTAL RESULTS

4.1 SPICE-level Simulation Results

In this subsection, we mainly focus on the performance of the sensing circuit during the Read operation since the suggested Refresh circuit is integrated to it. Table 1 shows the SPICE simulation results of the sensing circuit in section 3 incorporated with a 128x128 1T1R macro designed with a 65nm technology. We use the RRAM device model described in [7] after updating it based on the studies in [11–15] to add the soft-error failure effects to the device characteristics. The reference voltages of the sense amplifier ($V(Rth_1), V(Rth_2), V(Rth_3)$) discussed in sections 2 and 3 are chosen assuming that the WL pulse used to discharge the bitline is 3 ns. This discharging time is chosen in order to create a minimum 0.15V change in the SA output for every 0.1nm drift in the gap between the top of the filament and the electrode.

Table 1: Sensing circuit performance for a 128x128 1T1R macro

Metric	Reference SA	SA1 + SA2 + Error detection unit	
		Region I/IV	Region II/III
Delay (ps)	56.2	61.1	143.7
Energy (pJ)	18.2	47.4	72.5

The column **Reference SA** in Table 1 describes the case when only the regular two-tail sense amplifier is attached to BL while the other column refers to the proposed Refresh design integrated to the sensing circuit as in Fig.3. The sub-column **Region I/IV** lists the simulation results for the case when the resistance of the RRAM is in Region I or IV (i.e no need to check for Hard/soft-errors) while the sub-column **Region II/III** describes the case when the RRAM resistance is in Region II or III (i.e need to check for Hard/soft-errors). Due to the overhead from the Refresh circuit, the delay and energy consumption of the sensing design has increased. The results listed in column **Region II/III** are higher than those in column **Region I/II** because of the need to trigger a second cycle of comparison in order to determine whether the resistance of the RRAM is in Region II or III as detailed in section 3. When integrated with the other modules used to form a 8Gb memory, the impact of the Refresh circuit on the system performance is much less prominent as discussed in section 4.2.

4.2 System-level Simulation Results

4.2.1 Effect on read delay and energy

Using the SPICE simulation results in section 4.1, the C++ files of CACTI program [19] are updated (basically modifying the delay and the the energy consumption of the sense amplifier module as specified in Table 1) to calculate the estimated impact of the proposed Refresh circuit on the Read operation for a 65nm technology of a 8Gb memory (capacity of the 1T1R array is consistent with the current NVM capacities which is in the range of Gb). Table 2 summarizes the comparison results of the Read operation before and after adding the Refresh circuit.

Table 2: Read operation in 8Gbit RRAM array

Metric	1T1R Array	1T1R Array + Refresh Circuit	
		Region I/IV	Region II/III
Delay (ns)	5.37	5.39	5.47
Energy (nJ)	4.16	4.4	4.61
ΔDelay (%)	-	0.4	1.8
ΔEnergy (%)	-	5.74	10.68

Table 2 shows that the other memory modules (such as address decoders, repeaters, etc.) have more impact on the energy and delay of the Read operation than the Refresh circuit. The impact on the read delay from the Refresh circuit is very marginal. As for the read energy increase, in most cases where no Refresh is needed (Region I/IV), the penalty for a 8Gb memory is about 6%. In case when a second cycle of comparison is needed (Region II/III), an 10.68% increase in the read energy happens. However, it is worth mentioning that the Refresh rate of the RRAM array is in the range of days to months as explained in [13]. Hence, the increase in the memory power consumption due the Refresh circuit is ≈ 6% on average for a 8Gb memory array. To prove the small overhead of our proposed Refresh methodology, the circuit is integrated to other various memory capacities. The percentage of change in the read delay and energy is plotted in Fig.7.

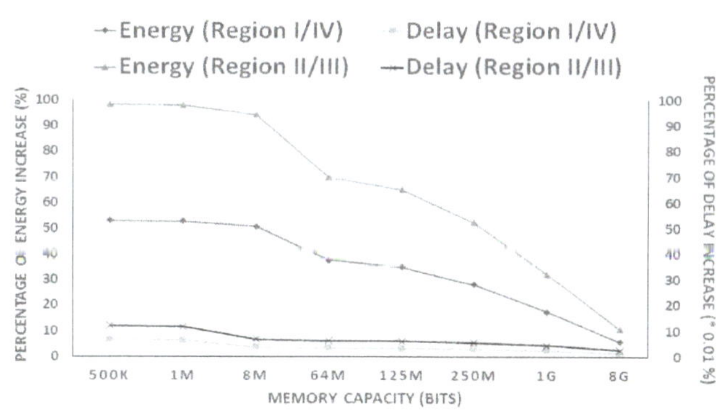

Figure 7: Refresh circuit impact on read energy and delay for different array sizes

Fig.7 shows that decreasing the memory capacity increases the impact of the Refresh circuit on the energy consumption of the system. This is because the weight of the other components in the memory system, such as address decoders, decreases with smaller memory capacity. Accordingly, the increased energy consumption of the sensing circuit becomes more dominant. The change in the read delay in Fig.7 and Table 2 is negligible since the latency of the read operation is mostly determined by the other sub-operations like the time required to precharge and discharge the bitlines (3ns as in section 4.1) rather than the extra delay added to the Refresh operation (in the order of picosecond as in Table 1).

4.2.2 *Effect on the resilience of the RRAM array to soft-errors*

Using the data in [13], where RRAM cells were programmed for failure tests taking into account the different sources of soft-error discussed in section 2, Fig.8 shows the percentage of the cells which retained their LRS state ("Good devices" in Fig.8) before and after adding the Refresh circuit. The proposed Refresh methodology can improve the immunity of the RRAM-based array to the soft-errors by about 80%.

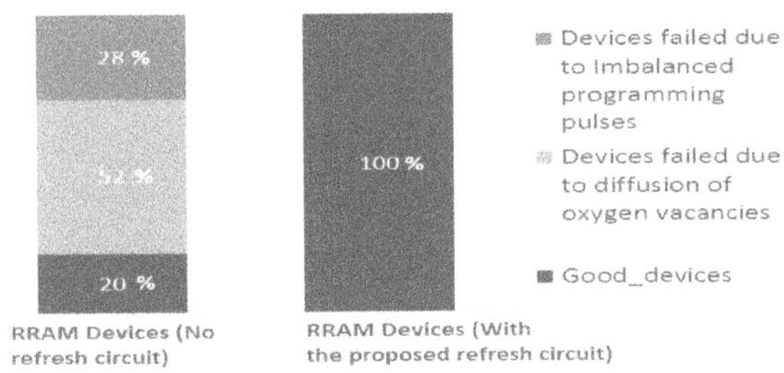

Figure 8: Refresh circuit effect on the tolerance of the RRAM-based memory to soft-errors

5. CONCLUSION

In this article, we have proposed a new Refresh circuit that can efficiently resolve the soft-error issues encountered in the 1T1R RRAM-based memories. We have discussed the circuit structure and its different modes of operation. Simulation data shows that, for a 8Gb 1T1R RRAM memory, the Refresh circuit has a small impact on the energy and delay of the read (6% and 0.4% respectively) yet it improves the memory resilience to soft-errors by 80%. The proposed methodology can be used for other RRAM arrays but the region of operations of the Refresh circuit might need to change depending on the characteristics of the device used in the array.

Acknowledgments

The authors would like to acknowledge Prof. S. Yu (ASU) for helpful discussion and compact model support, and Prof. Y. Xie and Dr. C. Xu (UCSB) for useful discussion.

6. REFERENCES

[1] M. Pasotti *et al.*, "An application specific embeddable flash memory system for non-volatile storage of code, data and bit-streams for embedded FPGA configurations," in *Symposium on VLSI circuits Digest of Technical Papers*, pp. 213 – 216, June 2003.

[2] J.Jex, "Flash memory BIOS for PC and notebook computers," in *IEEE Pacific Rim Conference on Communications, Computers and Signal Processing*, pp. 692 – 695, May 1991.

[3] M.A.A.Sanvido *et al.*, "NAND Flash Memory and Its Role in Storage Architectures," *Proceedings of IEEE , Vol. 96, No. 11*, pp. 1864 – 1874, Dec. 2008.

[4] X.Dong *et al.*, "Circuit and Microarchitecture Evaluation of 3D Stacking Magnetic RAM (MRAM) as a Universal Memory Replacement," in *Design Automation Conference (DAC)*, pp. 554 – 559, June 2008.

[5] A.Toffoli *et al.*, "Phase Change Memory advanced electrical characterization for conventional and alternative applications," in *IEEE International Conference on Microelectronic Test Structures (ICMTS)*, pp. 114 – 118, Mar. 2012.

[6] J. Yang *et al.*, "Memristive devices for computing," *Nature Nanotechnology, Vol. 8*, pp. 13 – 24, Jan. 2013.

[7] P.-Y. Chen and S. Yu, "Compact modeling of RRAM devices and its applications in 1T1R and 1S1R array design," *IEEE Transaction on Electron Devices, Vol. 62, No. 12,*, pp. 4022 – 4028, Dec. 2015.

[8] J. Strachan *et al.*, "State Dynamics and Modeling of Tantalum Oxide Memristors," *IEEE Transactions on Electron Devices, Vol. 60, No. 7,*, pp. 2194 – 2202, Jul. 2013.

[9] C. Xu *et al.*, "Design Implications of Memristor-Based RRAM Cross-Point Structures," in *Design, Automation and Test in Europe (DATE) Conference*, pp. 1 – 6, Mar. 2011.

[10] Y.-W. Chin *et al.*, "Point Twin-bit RRAM in 3D Interweaved Cross-point Array by Cu BEOL Process," in *Proc. IEEE Int. Electron Devices Meeting (IEDM)*, pp. 6.4.1 – 6.4.4, Dec. 2014.

[11] Y.Chen *et al.*, "Balancing SET/RESET Pulse for > 1010 Endurance in HfO2/Hf 1T1R Bipolar RRAM," *IEEE Transactions on Electron devices , Vol. 59, No. 12*, pp. 3243 – 3249, Dec. 2012.

[12] M.Mao *et al.*, "Programming strategies to improve energy efficiency and reliability of ReRAM Memory Systems," in *IEEE Workshop on Signal Processing Systems (SiPS)*, pp. 1 – 6, Oct. 2015.

[13] Y.Y.Chen *et al.*, "Postcycling LRS Retention Analysis in HfO2/Hf RRAM 1T1R Device," *IEEE Electron Device Letters, Vol. 34, No. 5*, pp. 626 – 628, May 2013.

[14] Y.Y.Chen *et al.*, "Understanding of the Endurance Failure in Scaled $HfO2$-based 1T1R RRAM through Vacancy Mobility Degradation," in *IEEE International Electron Devices Meeting (IEDM)*, pp. 20.3.1 – 20.3.4, Dec. 2012.

[15] Y.Y.Chen *et al.*, "Improvement of data retention in HfO2 / Hf 1T1R RRAM cell under low operating current," in *IEEE International Electron Devices Meeting (IEDM)*, pp. 10.1.1 – 10.1.4, Dec. 2013.

[16] S.Ambrogio *et al.*, "Data retention statistics and modeling in HfO2 resistive switching memories," in *IEEE International Reliability Physics Symposium (IRPS)*, pp. M.Y.1 – M.Y.6, Apr. 2015.

[17] S. Schechter *et al.*, "Use ECP, not ECC, for Hard Failures in resistive memories," in *International Symposium on Computer architecture (ISCA)*, pp. 141 – 152, June 2010.

[18] D. Shinkel *et al.*, "A Double-Tail Latch-Type Voltage Sense Amplifier with 18ps Setup+Hold Time," in *IEEE International Solid-State Circuits Conference (ISSCC)*, pp. 314 – 315, Feb. 2007.

[19] S. Thoziyoor *et al.*, "CACTI 5.3 technical report," in *HP Labs, Palo Alto, CA, Tech. Rep. HPL-2008-20*, 2008.

Exploratory Power Noise Models of Standard Cell 14, 10, and 7 nm FinFET ICs

Ravi Patel, Kan Xu, and Eby G. Friedman
University of Rochester, Rochester, NY, USA
rapatel, kxu8, friedman@ece.rochester.edu

Praveen Raghavan
IMEC Research, 3001 Leuven, Belgium
Praveen.Raghavan@imec.be

ABSTRACT

The physical dimensions of standard cells constrain the dimensions of power networks, affecting the on-chip power noise. An exploratory modeling methodology is presented for estimating power noise in advanced technology nodes. The models are evaluated for 14, 10, and 7 nm technologies to assess the impact on performance. Scaled technologies are shown to be more sensitive to power noise, resulting in potential loss of performance enhancements achieved by scaling. Stripes between local track rails is evaluated as a means to reduce power noise, exhibiting up to 56.5% improvement in power noise for the 7 nm technology node. A strong dependence on the width of a stripe is observed, indicating that fewer wide stripes are more favorable then many thin stripes. As a promising alternative material for power network interconnects, graphene is shown to exhibit good potential in reducing power noise. The effects of different scaling scenarios of local power rails on power noise are also discussed.

Keywords

Power noise model; advanced technology nodes; on-chip power networks; on-chip interconnect resistance

1. INTRODUCTION

Technology development for modern integrated circuits is a complex process that balances speed and power consumption with circuit density, manufacturability, and process yield [11]. Classical scaling theory predicts that the global interconnects are the dominant limitation to performance as compared to local interconnects, which scales with lithographic improvements [1, 2, 11, 13]. Local interconnect scaling, however, is unlikely to significantly lower RC delay. The resistivity of individual metal lines increases superlinearly as the minimum feature size shrinks [3].

Physical design information is typically unavailable during technology development. Lithographic constraints, device parameters, and standard cells are typically developed without a clear understanding of post-manufactured IC behavior. As a result, the resistance of a local power network is often constrained early in the design process. To maintain system performance under these constraints, aggressive global power grid design methodologies are required to reduce power noise [5]. To assess the impact of technology development, a procedure is described here for analyzing current distribution in standard cell CMOS circuits with little initial information of the process technology, enabling early projections of power noise and current distribution.

The paper is organized as follows. Background information is presented in Section 2. The modeling approach is discussed in Section 3. Power noise for different technology nodes, stripe conditions, interconnect materials, and power rail scaling scenarios are discussed in Section 4, followed by some conclusions in Section 5 and acknowledgments in Section 6.

GLSVLSI '16, May 18-20, 2016, Boston, MA, USA

DOI: http://dx.doi.org/10.1145/2902961.2903035

2. BACKGROUND

The trend of resistivity changes in on-chip interconnects as technology is scaled is discussed in Section 2.1. The structure and impedance characteristics of power networks are presented in Section 2.2. The topology of a standard cell circuit influences the design and switching activity of the power network, and, therefore, an overview of the structure is provided in Section 2.3.

2.1 On-chip interconnect resistance

As interconnects scale to more advanced technology nodes, highly resistive interconnects degrade performance improvements due to faster devices and greater integration. The resistivity of copper, used in traditional on-chip interconnects, sharply increases as the metal line pitch decreases [14]. Local power and ground rails therefore become significantly more resistive due to the "resistivity wall" phenomenon resulting in a more challenging power network design process.

Replacing copper with low resistivity materials in power grids is one way to reduce the effect of the "resistivity wall." Due to the excellent conductivity of both heat and electricity, graphene has been considered for different applications [8, 10]. Silver is another material whose bulk level resistivity is lower than copper. The thin film resistivity of two materials, silver and graphene, has been investigated, respectively, in [6, 9]. A comparison of the resistivity of different material with interconnect width scaling is illustrated in Figure 1. The thin film resistivity of silver increases significantly at 50 nm, and eventually becomes larger than copper as the metal line pitch is scaled to 10 nm. Graphene exhibits

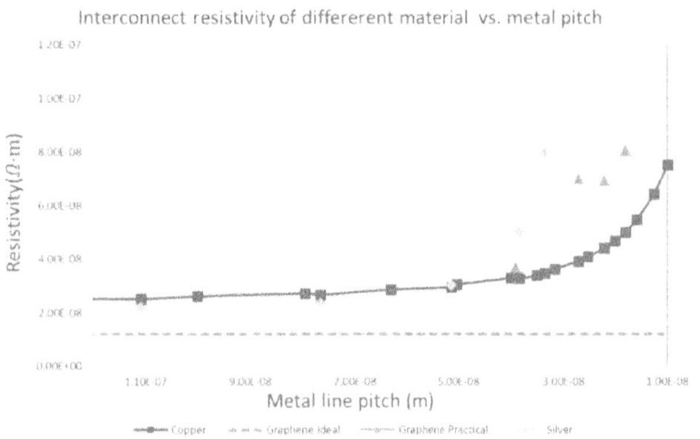

Figure 1: Interconnect resistivity of different materials versus line width.

higher resistivity than copper when the metal line pitch is small (from 40 nm to 10 nm).

2.2 Power grids

The resistance of power metal lines is also affected by the structure of the power grids. A power grid is a hierarchical structure consisting of power (V_{DD}) and ground (V_{SS}) backmetal pads, a global interdigitated mesh, and local power and ground rails, as illustrated in Figure 2. Four backmetal pads produce an effective global V_{DD} or V_{SS} mesh, as illustrated in Figure 2(a). Each pad is connected to several pairs of power and ground pairs (P/G pair) within a global power mesh. Each metal layer in the mesh consists of parallel P/G pairs separated from adjacent pairs by tens of micrometers. Metal layers are oriented orthogonal to the adjacent layers to create a mesh structure. The impedance of the global mesh, therefore, typically exhibits low resistance and significant inductance.

Standard cell tracks are patterned beneath the grid with local power and ground rails *(track rails)* placed horizontally between each P/G pair, as illustrated in Figure 2(b). The track rail impedances are dominated by the metal resistance and decoupling capacitance. On-chip power noise is due to switching on the track rails with the largest contribution arising from the clocked gates and buffers placed throughout the IC [7].

2.3 Standard cell design

An individual standard cell track is structured as a row with a substrate region patterned between the power and ground rails, as illustrated in Figure 2. Gates within a technology library are structured to fit within a track with transistors patterned within the substrate. Standard cells exhibit several characteristics that affect the power network. Most notably, the size and material of the power and ground rails within the standard cells affect the resistance of the metal line. The height of a standard cell is typically controlled by lithographic limits introduced by double and quadruple patterning processes [15]. Standard cell gates are mirrored to ensure that two tracks share a common power rail, doubling the effective current load on the line. After the gates are placed, interconnections are routed among the internal gates, constraining the available metal resources.

3. CIRCUIT MODELS

The overall grid model consists of a global mesh model, a local rail model, and a load model, as illustrated in Figure 3. The global grid is modeled by an interdigitated mesh with the parameters described in [4]. The mesh size is determined by an effective mesh based on the space between the pads, as illustrated in Figure 2(a). The model considers the physical area, supply current, and stage delay for each process technology (14 nm, 10 nm, and 7 nm). The global mesh, track rail, and load models are discussed in the following sections.

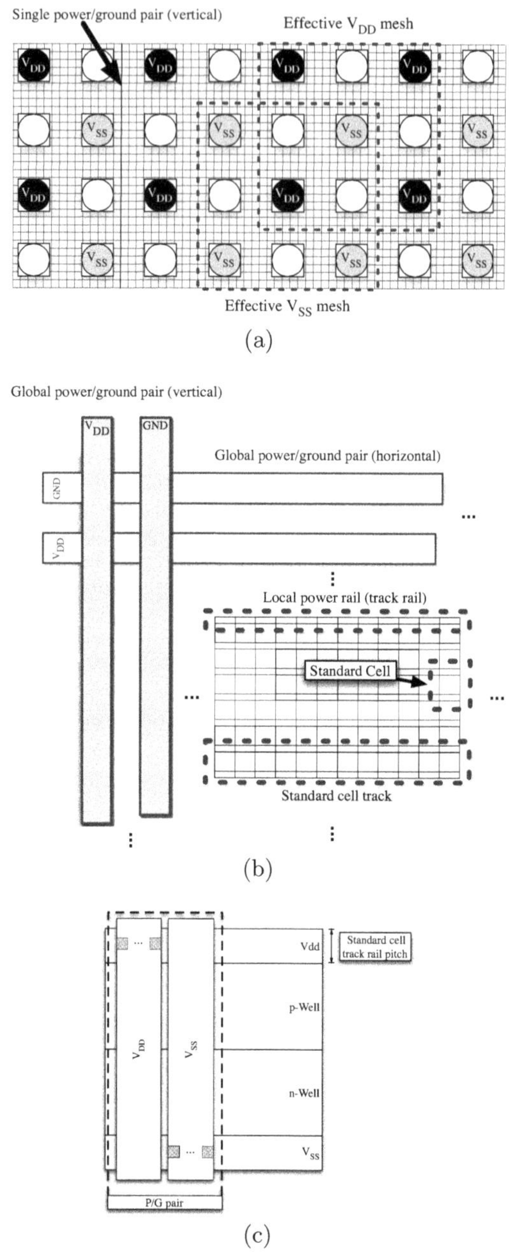

Figure 2: Topology of a standard cell power network with a) pad to global mesh, b) local rails attached to the tracks, and c) an individual standard cell connected to a global power/ground pair.

3.1 Load model

The peak power noise is dependent on the clock network The load model is based on the current demands of a register and the adjacent gates within a standard cell track. An individual load on a track rail is modeled as a current source with a triangular load characteristic [12], as illustrated in

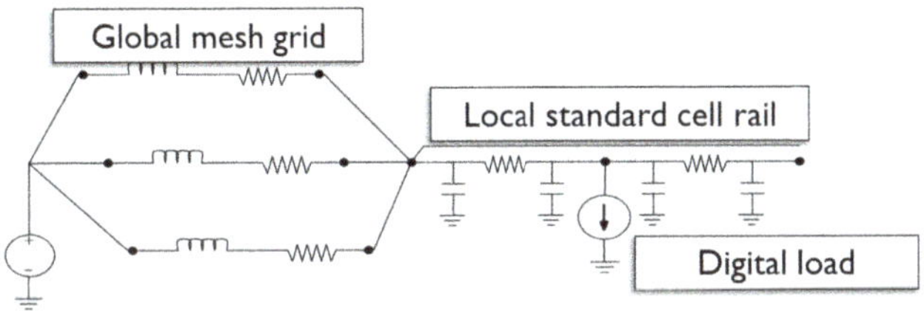

Figure 3: Model of power network

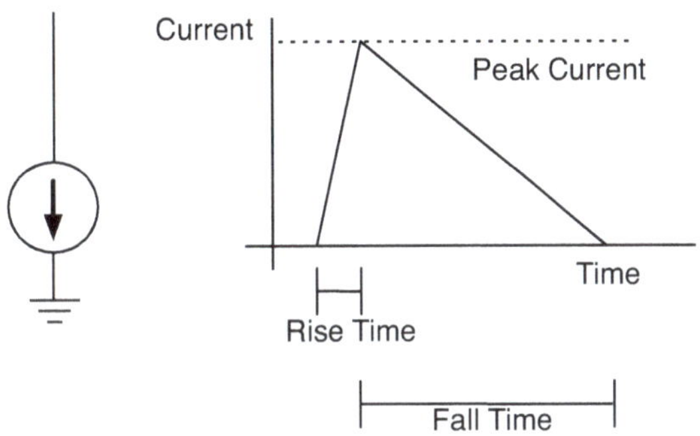

Figure 4: Model of an individual load on the power network. The rise and fall times are extracted from a loaded inverter and peak current, as described by (2).

Figure 4. The timing parameters of the model are extracted from a fan-out 4 (FO4) loaded inverter.

Those gates spatially adjacent to the register are also likely to switch at approximately the same time as the register and contribute to the local current draw. If an adjacent gate at the load switches before the track rail is recharged to the supply voltage, the magnitude of the noise increases. If the gate does not switch before the voltage is restored to V_{DD}, the gate does not contribute to the peak noise. Recharging determines the noise window (t_{window}) during which the loads that switch within the window are summed and the gates that switch outside of the window are ignored. The noise window, which determines the recharge time of a track rail, is approximated by three RC time constants,

$$t_{window} \approx 3\frac{N_{cell}^2}{4}R_{cell}(C_{cell} + C_{decap}), \quad (1)$$

where N_{cell} is the number of cells between each P/G pair, R_{cell} and C_{cell} are, respectively, the resistance and capacitance of the track rail within a standard cell, and C_{decap} is the decoupling capacitance per cell.

An adjacent logic gate only switches if the gate delay is within the noise window of the load. The delay of the adjacent gates is approximated by the delay of an inverter. The load current is

$$I_{Load} = \frac{\alpha 2 t_{window}}{t_{inv1}} I_{inv1} + 2I_{invd4}, \quad (2)$$

where t_{window} is the noise window, t_{inv1} and I_{inv1} are, respectively, the delay and peak current of a 1x inverter, I_{inv4} is the peak current of a 4x inverter, and α is the switching factor of the circuit.

3.2 Rail model

Each local rail is modeled as a distributed resistor-capacitor with multiple loads, with the length of the rail determined by the space between two P/G pairs in the global power network. At least one load is placed at the center of the rail to model a single register in the worst case position. The number of loads and the space between loads are determined by the target clock frequency of the circuit. An individual logic gate is modeled with an inverter delay (t_{inv}) where the logic depth (D) at a given frequency (f_{clock}) is

$$D = \frac{1}{f_{clock}t_{inv}(1+U)}, \quad (3)$$

where D is the delay uncertainty. The logic depth is the number of gates between adjacent loads on a rail. The width of an inverter is used to estimate the size of a standard cell. The physical distance between loads on a local rail is therefore known. Based on this assumption, the total number of active loads and the impedance between each active load can be estimated. The logic depth is also used to determine the decoupling capacitance,

$$C_{decap} = C_{gate}(1-\beta)D, \quad (4)$$

where C_{gate} is the gate capacitance of an inverter, and β is the fill factor of the standard cell layout. The fill factor is a common metric which is the fraction of silicon area occupied by the standard cells.

3.3 Striping of the power rail

Each track rail is typically distinct. Recently, however, connections between adjacent track rails have been used to reduce the local rail resistance and any associated power noise, as illustrated in Figure 5(a). These connections between power ground rails, called stripes, ensure that loads on the adjacent rails interact. For any interaction, however, the

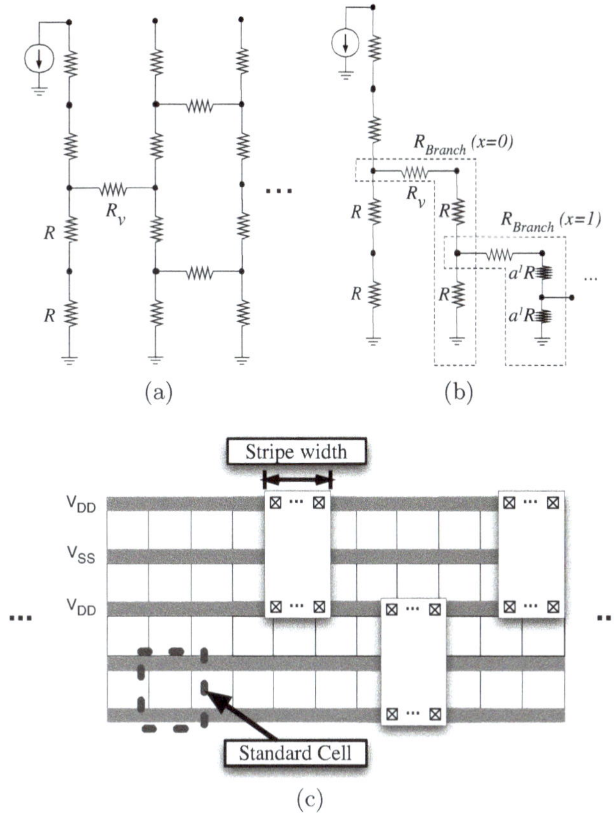

Figure 5: Impedance of a) striped power rails, b) R_{branch} approximation of impedance, and c) physical structure of a stripe.

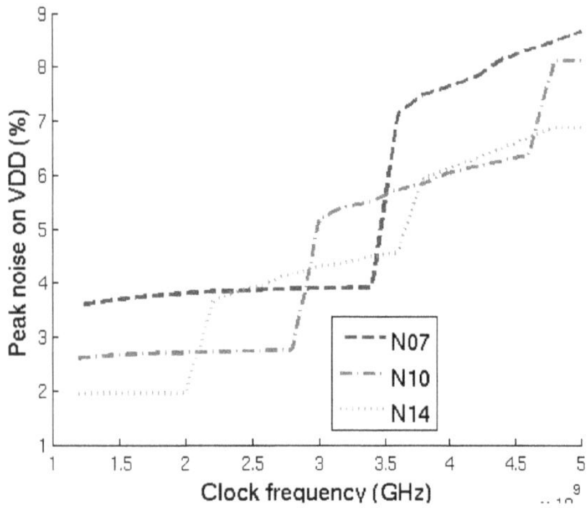

Figure 6: Local peak power noise in 14 nm, 10 nm, and 7 nm technologies with increasing clock frequency.

worst case noise is equivalent to the case of a single track rail without striping. The maximum reduction in power noise from striping occurs when the adjacent rails do not have loads that switch at the same time. These two conditions, therefore, bound the potential noise generated by a circuit. The number of interacting rails is determined by approximating a set of rails as a resistive tree, as illustrated in Figure 5(b). The resistance from the center load to the edge of the track rail is

$$R_{branch} = R_v + a^x * R + \left(\frac{1}{a^x * R} \frac{1}{R_{branch}(x+1)} \right)^{-1}, \quad (5)$$

where R_v is the resistance of a stripe, x is the number of additional branches, and a is the scaling factor of the resistance. As x increases, the error decreases. Note that (5) is used to estimate the maximum number of rails that minimizes the error. A distributed resistance across the rail is included in the model.

4. EVALUATION OF POWER NOISE

The model has been evaluated for power networks in 14 nm, 10 nm, and 7 nm CMOS FinFET technologies. The global power grid dimensions are determined from a 14 nm circuit. The global grid pitch is scaled to 10 nm and 7 nm. Model generation and simulation are based on MATLAB and Cadence Spectre. A power noise analysis with different technology nodes, stripes conditions, interconnect materials, and interconnect scaling scenarios is presented in the following sections.

4.1 Different technology nodes

The local V_{DD} rails exhibit a peak power noise that ranges from 3% to 10% of V_{DD} with a trend of increasing power noise with technology scaling. As the clock frequency supported by the track increases, the power noise increases in discrete steps, as illustrated in Figure 6. Each step is due to an increase in the number of loads that simultaneously switch on a track rail, which corresponds to a relative decrease in logic depth. Local noise levels also increase with each technology node, although the magnitude of the noise is strongly dependent on the clock frequency and number of loads per rail. At lower frequencies with only a single load switching per rail, N10 and N07 exhibit, respectively, power noise increases of 0.7% and 1.8% as compared to N14. With higher frequencies with two loads per rail, the power noise increases by, respectively, 1.8% and 4.1%. This behavior is expected as the width of a standard cell gate is proportionally larger with scaled technologies, producing a larger track rail resistance per cell.

To measure the effects of power noise on circuit performance, a five stage ring oscillator (RO) is driven with power noise injected into both the power and ground rails. The per cent reduction in ring oscillator frequency is depicted in Figure 7. As the power noise increases with frequency, the performance of the ring oscillator decreases. As expected, the RO performance increases with each technology generation and drops in discrete amounts with increasing clock frequency. Notably, the magnitude of the decrease in oscillator frequency is much higher in N07 than in N10 and N14, indicative of the increasing sensitivity to power noise with device scaling. At frequencies above 3 GHz, the performance of the N07 ring oscillator drops below the performance of the N10 ring oscillator operating at a lower clock frequency. Intuitively, the delay of an N07 circuit degrades, losing the advantages of scaling. Maintaining performance requires a proportionally smaller P/G pitch that is more aggressive than a linearly scaled grid.

4.2 Stripes across power rails

To reduce local power noise, an individual track rail can use multiple stripes to adjacent rails, each with a variable width. The noise exhibited by a 3.6 GHz circuit with striping for variable width and count is illustrated in Figure 8. For reference, the peak noise of a 3.6 GHz circuit without striping for the N14, N10, N07 technology nodes are, respectively, 4.6%, 5.7%, 7.1%. The stripe count is the number of stripes per track rail, and the stripe width is the pitch of a stripe with additional via contacts. Both the stripe count and stripe width are normalized to the minimum metal pitch of the technology node.

Introducing striping reduces power noise by almost a factor of two for each technology, with a slight increase in noise reduction with each technology generation. The maximum stripe width and count, with nine stripes at a stripe width of ten, is impractical in conventional circuits for any technology node. In these cases, ten cells are between each stripe, and each stripe is approximately the size of four inverter cells. These additional interconnects cause significant routing congestion and area overhead.

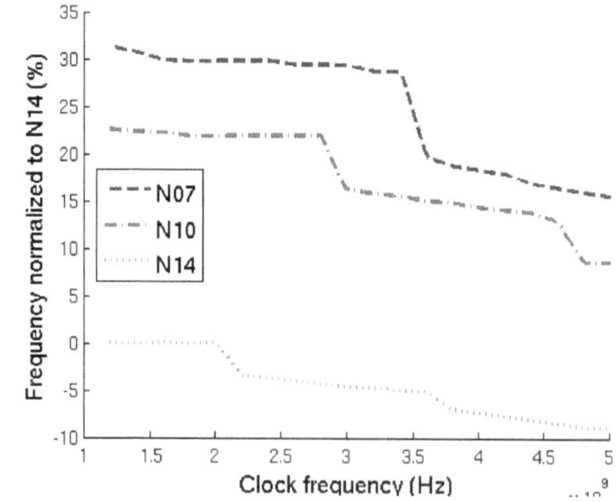

Figure 7: Per cent performance decrease of average power noise on five stage ring oscillator in 14 nm, 10 nm, and 7 nm technologies normalized to an N14 ring oscillator.

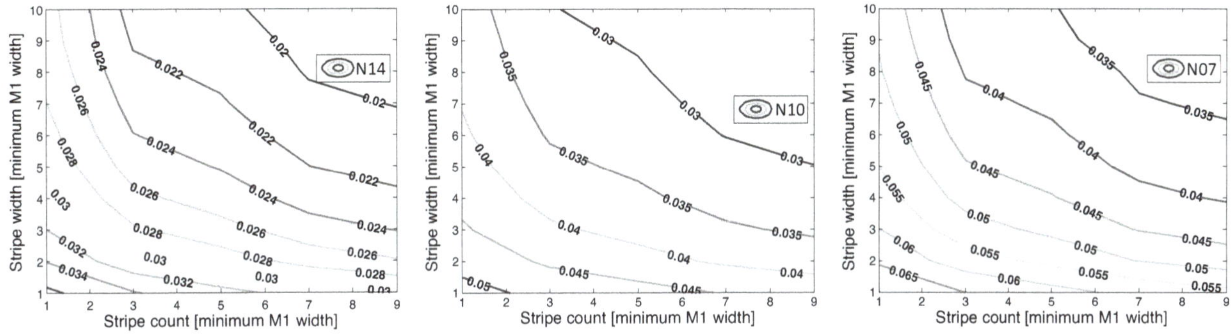

(a) (b) (c)

Figure 8: Effect of track stripe count and stripe width on noise for 3.6 GHz track rails in a) 14 nm, b) 10 nm, and c) 7 nm technologies.

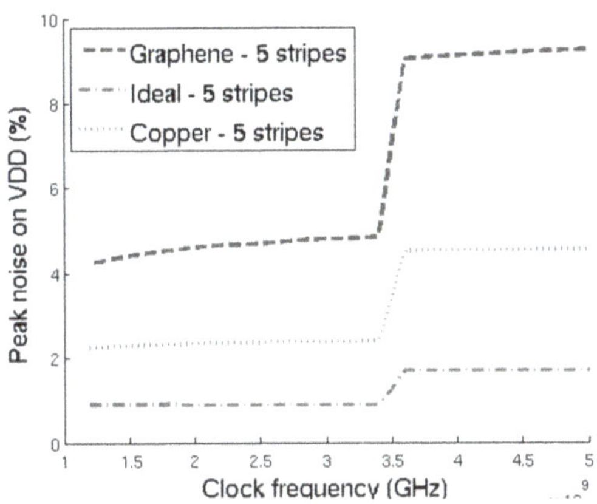

Figure 9: Peak power noise in graphene, ideal graphene, and copper power grids with increasing clock frequencies in 7 nm technology.

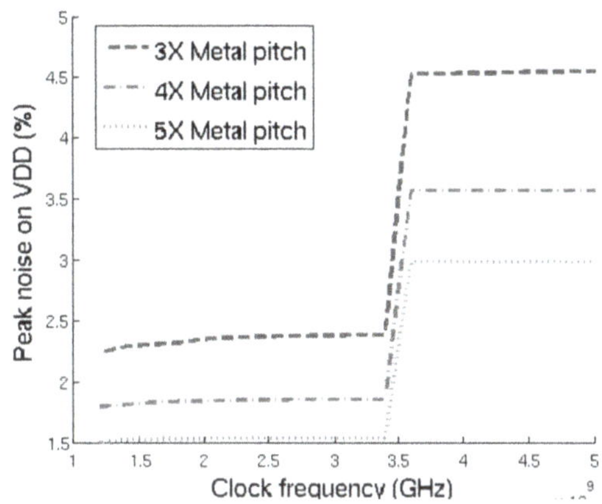

Figure 10: Peak noise in 3X, 4X, and 5X minimum metal pitch interconnect scaling scenarios with increasing clock frequencies in 7 nm technology.

Much of the benefit, however, can be achieved by utilizing wide stripes. A single stripe with a stripe width of ten can reduce the power noise by almost a third for N14, N10, and N07. This reduction in noise is due to the relatively large resistance of the via contacts for each stripe. As the stripe width increases, additional via contacts can be added, reducing the effective resistance of the stripe, thereby lowering the resistance of the path to the power supply. At stripe counts greater than five, there are diminishing returns on the reduction in power noise. In this case, a stripe width above six reduces much of the power noise without incurring excessive overhead.

4.3 New material interconnects

Another way to reduce power noise is exploiting lower resistivity material in power grids. As illustrated in Figure 1, the resistivity of graphene is comparable to copper in deeply scaled metal lines. Although integrating graphene with CMOS technology is not yet practical, graphene as an interconnect replacement would provide significant improvement in reducing power noise.

Power noise is evaluated for the 7 nm technology with five stripes across the power ground rails for three different materials. The resistivity of graphene is extracted from experimental data based on the local interconnect width used in 7 nm technology [9]. The theoretically lowest resistivity achievable by graphene is described here as ideal graphene and is used for comparative purposes. The third material is copper. As illustrated in Figure 9, a large difference in power noise between graphene and copper is exhibited since the difference in resistivity is large in the 7 nm interconnect technology. A 59.1% reduction of peak noise is achieved with ideal graphene as compared with copper. The bottleneck is the vias between two adjacent metal layers, which is highly resistive in advanced technology nodes as compared to the resistance of the metal lines.

4.4 Power rail scaling

For a mesh global power grid, the pitch of each power/ground pair is decreased with technology scaling. The width of global power/ground interconnect is however fixed in advanced technology nodes to prevent an increase in impedance within the global power grid. Enlarging the width of the global power grid significantly increases on-chip area while also introducing larger parasitic capacitances between adjacent metal layers. For interdigitated local power rails, the pitch of the adjacent power and ground rail is proportional to the gate pitch to match the standard cell height for each technology node. The width of the local power rail is proportional to the minimum metal pitch of each technology. This scaling process is a primary source of power noise due to IR drops.

In evaluating power noise, the local power rail width is set to three times the minimum metal pitch of each technology. With technology scaling, a tradeoff should be considered between the footprint of the local power rails and the impedance characteristics of the power rails to satisfy power noise budgets in advanced technology nodes. A smaller standard cell height makes it possible to increase the on-chip area of the local power rails while maintaining performance improvements over previous technology nodes. As illustrated in Figure 10, a 32.4% reduction in peak noise is exhibited after increasing the power rail width from three times to five times the minimum metal pitch in 7 nm technology. As compared with Figure 9, the reduction in power noise with larger power rail widths is lower than exploiting new interconnect materials. Changing the metal width is however more practical since it does not require novel fabrication and integration technologies. Increasing the width of the local power rail degrades the performance due to the large area overhead of the local metal layer.

5. CONCLUSIONS

An exploratory modeling methodology is proposed for assessing power network noise in standard cell digital circuits. Models are evaluated for 14, 10, and 7 nm technologies to evaluate noise trends. It is shown that local resistive noise increases with technology scaling. The effects of the local stripes are evaluated on power grids, exhibiting a 2x reduction in local power noise. Trends evaluating the effects of noise on performance are also discussed. The sensitivity to power noise is shown to increase with clock frequency and scaling, potentially reducing performance gains achievable in deeply scaled technology nodes. Performance degradation in 7 nm is sufficiently severe that no delay advantage to linear scaling is exhibited. Below 10 nm, more aggressive power networks with a shorter distance between adjacent P/G pairs are required to compensate for the increase in noise. Exploiting new materials in on-chip interconnect exhibits good potential to lower power noise in advanced technology nodes. Tradeoffs between power noise and performance need to be carefully considered when scaling local power rails.

6. ACKNOWLEDGMENTS

This research is supported in part by the Binational Science Foundation under Grant No. 2012139, the National Science Foundation under Grant Nos. CCF-1329374, CCF-1526466, and CNS-1548078, the IARPA under Grant No. W911NF-14-C-0089, and by grants from Cisco Systems and Intel.

7. REFERENCES

[1] H. B. Bakoglu and J. D. Meindl. Optimal interconnection circuits for vlsi. *IEEE Transactions on Electron Devices*, 32(5):903–909, May 1985.

[2] M. T. Bohr et al. Interconnect scaling-the real limiter to high performance ulsi. In *Proceedings of the IEEE International Electron Devices Meeting*, pages 241–244, December 1995.

[3] J. A. Davis et al. Interconnect limits on gigascale integration (gsi) in the 21st century. *Proceedings of the IEEE*, 89(3):305–324, March 2001.

[4] R. Jakushokas and E. G. Friedman. Multi-layer interdigitated power distribution networks. *IEEE Transactions on Very Large Scale Integration (VLSI) Systems*, 19(5):774–786, May 2011.

[5] R. Jakushokas, M. Popovich, A. V. Mezhiba, S. Köse, and E. G. Friedman. *Power Distribution Networks with On-Chip Decoupling Capacitors, Second Edition.* Springer Science & Business Media, 2011.

[6] F. Lacy. Developing a theoretical relationship between electrical resistivity, temperature, and film thickness for conductors. *Nanoscale Research Letters*, (1), December 2011.

[7] S. Lin and N. Chang. Challenges in power-ground integrity. In *Proceedings of the IEEE/ACM International Conference on Computer-Aided Design*, pages 651–654, November 2001.

[8] J. S. Moon and D. K. Gaskill. Graphene: Its fundamentals to future applications. *IEEE Transactions on Microwave Theory and Techniques*, 59(10):2702–2708, October 2011.

[9] R. Murali, K. Brenner, Y. Yang, T. Beck, and J. D. Meindl. Resistivity of graphene nanoribbon interconnects. *IEEE Electron Device Letters*, 30(6):611–613, June 2009.

[10] P. Pasanen, M. Voutilainen, M. Helle, X. Song, and P. J. Hakonen. Graphene for future electronics. *Physica Scripta*, 2012(T146):014025, January 2012.

[11] E. Salman and E. G. Friedman. *High Performance Integrated Circuit Design.* McGraw Hill Professional, 2012.

[12] E. Salman, E. G. Friedman, R. M. Secareanu, and O. L. Hartin. Worst case power/ground noise estimation using an equivalent transition time for resonance. *IEEE Transactions on Circuits and Systems I: Regular Papers*, 56(5):997–1004, May 2009.

[13] K. C. Saraswat and F. Mohammadi. Effect of scaling of interconnections on the time delay of vlsi circuits. *IEEE Journal of Solid-State Circuits*, 17(2):275–280, April 1982.

[14] W. Steinhögl, G. Schindler, G. Steinlesberger, M. Traving, and M. Engelhardt. Comprehensive study of the resistivity of copper wires with lateral dimensions of 100 nm and smaller. *Journal of Applied Physics*, 97(2):023706-1— 023706-7, January 2005.

[15] K. Vaidyanathan, S. H. Ng, D. Morris, N. Lafferty, L. Liebmann, M. Bender, W. Huang, K. Lai, L. Pileggi, and A. Strojwas. Design and manufacturability tradeoffs in unidirectional and bidirectional standard cell layouts in 14 nm node. *Proceedings of SPIE*, 8327:83270K–83270K–12, March 2012.

8T1R: A Novel Low-power High-speed RRAM-based Non-volatile SRAM Design

Amr M.S.Tosson, Adam Neale
University of Waterloo
atosson/ajneale@uwaterloo.ca

Mohab Anis
American University at Cairo
manis@aucegypt.edu

Lan Wei
University of Waterloo
lan.wei@uwaterloo.ca

ABSTRACT

With continuous and aggressive technology scaling, suppressing the stand-by power is among the top priorities for SRAM design. Switching off the less-frequently accessed blocks is an efficient way to reduce the stand-by power, provided that the information stored in these blocks can be restored. Non-volatile memories (NVMs) are integrated into SRAM cells to perform the required store and restore functions. Among various types of NVMs, memristors (a.k.a. RRAM) have several advantages including their small device size, low voltage operation, high speed, and CMOS-compatible fabrication process. In this article, we propose a new 8T1R RRAM-based non-volatile SRAM (NV-SRAM) which adds non-volatility to the SRAM with minimum impact on the Write and Read operations. Simulation at cell-level and array-level have confirmed that the new design performs Read and Write operations at a compatible delay, energy and noise margin as the conventional 6T SRAM, and it is among the best of all reported RRAM-based NV-SRAM designs to our knowledge. In addition, since our 8T1R design uses only one RRAM device per cell, the energy required for storing/restoring the SRAM data to/from the RRAM is significantly reduced by 60%/70% compared to the lowest storing/restoring energy of the previously proposed RRAM-based NV-SRAM designs.

1. INTRODUCTION

With the mobile chips and many other power constrained integrated circuits applications, the demand for reducing the chip power becomes a major challenge in VLSI design. On one hand, the device leakage has increased significantly due to continuous technology scaling. On the other hand, practical requirements such as extending battery life are prioritized in recent years. Static Random Access Memories (SRAM) cells are used extensively in VLSI systems to provide on-chip storage. Despite their high-speed Read/Write operations and their various low-supply voltage (V_{DD}) designs (e.g 7T [1], 8T [2], and 10T [3] cells), the SRAM cells suffer from high leakage power. The dynamic voltage scaling (DVS) [4–6] has been a popular approach to reduce the leakage power by adjusting the transistor gate-source and substrate-source voltages depending on whether the SRAM cell is in active or stand-by mode. Power gating [7, 8] is another widely used approach to reduce the cell leakage by adjusting the supply voltage level during the inactive periods. Yet, the power saving from these techniques is diminishing in the latest technology nodes due to non-scalable leakage and threshold voltage.

Nonvolatile memory (NVM) devices are suggested to further suppress the stand-by power by switching off the power supply of the less-frequently used SRAM blocks without losing their data. The SRAM data are first stored into the NVM device before switching off the power of SRAM cell. This configuration consumes much less power, area compared to using high threshold voltage (High Vth) retention latches which rely on having "always on" flip-flops to save the data of the SRAM blocks before switching off their power supply[9]. When access to SRAM is required later on, the data saved in the NVM devices are written back to the storage nodes of the SRAM through a Restore operation. Such SRAM cells are often referred to in literature as Non-Volatile SRAM (NV-SRAM). Several types of NVM devices (e.g Magnetic Random Access Memory (MRAM), Phase change Memory (PCM), etc.) have been proposed to be used with variations of CMOS SRAM cells

Compared to other NVM devices, the memristor (also known as Resistive Random Access Memory (RRAM) device) has various advantages including: a) compact sizes (as small as 10nm x 10nm as reported in [10]), b) fast switching operation (in the order of 10 ns [11, 12]), c) low programming voltage requirements (around 1V programming voltage as reported in [13]), and d) CMOS compatible fabrication process with potential monolithic 3D integration. In previous works, such as [14–17], the RRAM has been integrated with the SRAM cell but each of those designs either introduces significant degradation to the basic Read-Write operations of SRAM or consumes a large amount of energy to store/restore data to/from the RRAM device as discussed in more details in section 4. In this paper, we propose a new 8T1R NV-SRAM cell which has a comparable energy, delay, and noise immunity for the read and Write operations as those of the conventional 6T SRAM design. Also, since only one RRAM cell is used to save the SRAM data during the off-time, the energy required for storing the information on RRAM device is reduced by more than 60 % compared to the lowest energy value reported by the previously pro-

GLSVLSI '16, May 18-20, 2016, Boston, MA, USA

DOI: http://dx.doi.org/10.1145/2902961.2903016

posed RRAM-based NV-SRAM designs. Moreover, the energy consumption for the Restore operation is decreased by more than 70% as discussed in more details in section 4.2.

The rest of this paper is organized as follows: In section 2, a brief introduction about the RRAM device is presented. Then, in section 3, the new 8T1R SRAM cell architecture and its different modes of operations are explained. Following that, we summarize the SPICE simulation results for a 128x128 array of the newly suggested SRAM cell in section 4 and compare them with other previously proposed RRAM-based NV-SRAM arrays. Finally, we conclude our discussions in section 5

2. RRAM DEVICE PHYSICS AND IV CHARACTERISTICS

Basically, the RRAM device has a simple sandwich structure with oxide materials (e.g. HfO_x, AlO_x, etc) in between two metal electrodes. The device nowadays can be manufactured with only a few steps using the standard CMOS fabrication process. The CMOS back-end-of-the-line (BEOL) process allows the RRAM device to be integrated between the metal layers or within the contact vias of the source and drain of a metal-oxide semiconductor field effect transistor (MOSFET) [18–20] for 3D integration [21].

According to the widely accepted filamentary theory explaining the switching mechanism of the device, conductive oxide vacancies are created in the oxide materials after a one-time initial electroforming process involving high voltage. These oxide vacancies form conductive filaments reaching from the bottom electrode to the top electrode. The filaments form or rupture at the interface with top electrode, controlled by the voltage applied across the terminals of the device. Hence, the RRAM cell can be switched between a high resistance state (HRS) (typical resistance around 1M - 10M Ω) and a low resistance state (LRS) (typical resistance around 10 - 100k Ω) by applying proper voltage (in the range of ± 1.5V) to the top and bottom electrode as illustrated in the I-V characteristics curve of Fig.1. In HRS, a gap filled with high resistive oxide materials exists between the filaments and the top electrode while in LRS, the conductive filaments practically touch the top electrode.

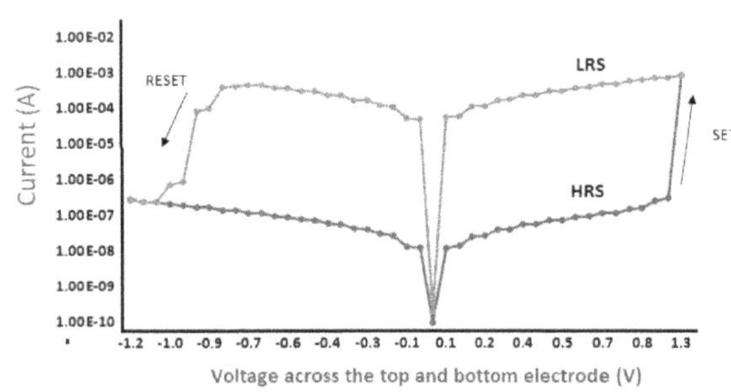

Figure 1: I-V characteristics of Memristor.

In the bipolar RRAM device, which is more commonly used and which is incorporated in our 8T1R SRAM cell, the SET operation (i.e the process of switching from its HRS to its LRS) occurs by applying a positive voltage above a certain threshold between the top and bottom electrodes as shown in Fig.1. Oppositely, the RESET operation (i.e the switching process from LRS to HRS) happens when a negative voltage less than a certain threshold is applied. Altering the dielectric and the electrode materials change the I-V characteristics of the RRAM device. In this work, we integrate the $TiN/HfO_x/TiN$ RRAM cell, whose switching dynamics are described in [22], to our 8T1R NV-SRAM design which is discussed in the next sections. A RRAM compact model [11, 12] calibrated to the experimental data of the $TiN/HfO_x/TiN$ device [22] is used for circuit design and simulation.

3. THE PROPOSED 8T1R CELL

Fig. 2 shows the schematic of the proposed 8T1R SRAM cell. The nodes named "P" and "N" in Fig.2 denote the anode

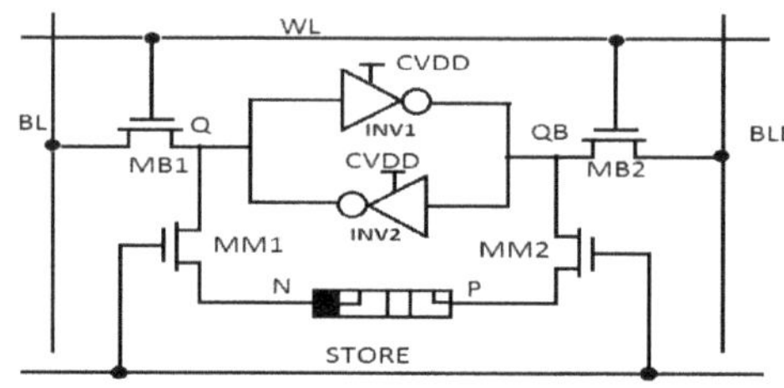

Figure 2: The 8T1R NV-SRAM Cell

(top) and the cathode (bottom) electrodes of the RRAM device respectively. In comparison to the previously proposed RRAM-based NV-SRAM designs, the 8T1R cell uses only one RRAM device to save the state of the SRAM which simplifies the Store operation. Moreover, the 8T1R cell does not add extra capacitances to the BL/BLB lines, unlike some other RRAM-based NV-SRAM designs (e.g the Rnv8T cell [16]), which improves the speed and noise immunity of the Read operation. In the subsequent subsections, we explain each of the operations of the 8T1R cell.

3.1 Read/Write Operation

During the Read/Write operation, the "STORE" signal is grounded disconnecting the RRAM cell and its access transistors (MM1 and MM2) from the storage nodes (Q,QB). Accordingly, the 8T1R NV-SRAM works similarly to the conventional 6T SRAM design in this mode of operation. The only difference is the additional source/drain capacitances at the storage nodes (Q, QB) coming from the access transistors of the RRAM device. This causes a slight increase in the read and write energy and delay of the 8T1R cell compared to the 6T SRAM design as discussed in section 4.1.

3.2 Store Operation

To save the data on the RRAM device before cutting off the SRAM power, a sequence of steps is required:

1. The WL is grounded and the access transistors (MB1 and MB2) disconnect the SRAM cell from the BL/BLB lines

2. Raise the cell supply signal (CVDD) to VDDH which is determined by the SET/RESET voltages of the RRAM device and usually higher than VDD

3. Connect the STORE signal to VDDH to allow the RRAM cell to change its state depending on the SRAM data.

For example, let us assume that the storage nodes "Q" and "QB" are at the logical "1" (VDD) and "0" (GND) respectively before starting the Store operation. Raising the CVDD to VDDH, causes the voltage of the node "Q" to be at VDDH while the node "QB" is still grounded. Hence, after subtracting the voltage drop across the RRAM access transistors (MM1 and MM2), the net voltage applied on the device is negative enough to program it to its HRS state. Oppositely, if the nodes "Q" and "QB" are initially at logic "0" and "1" respectively, the net voltage drop across the RRAM is positive enough to push its resistance to LRS. Fig. 3 shows the waveforms explaining the Store operation of the 8T1R SRAM cell when the nodes Q and QB are at logic "1" and logic "0" (changing the state of the RRAM cell to HRS).

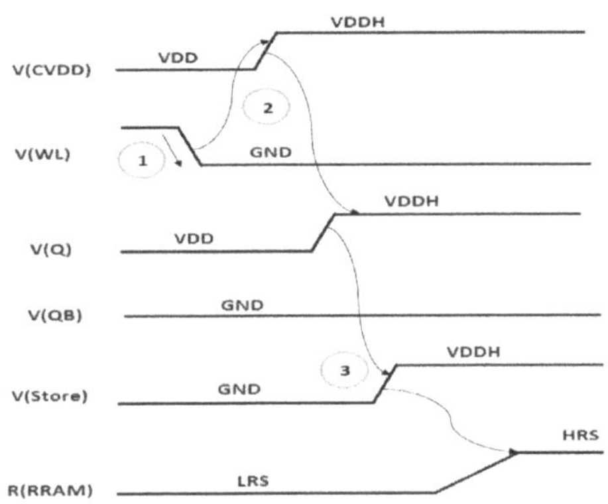

Figure 3: The Store operation waveform (Q at logic "1" and QB at logic "0"). The numbers in circles correspond to the step numbers mentioned in the text. In our experiments, VDD=1.1V and our VDDH=2.0V

In comparison to the other RRAM-based NV-SRAM cells, the 8T1R Store operation is simpler and faster as summarized in section 4.2.

3.3 Restore Operation

The Restore operation retrieves the data stored in the RRAM cell to the storage nodes of the SRAM when it is reconnected to the power supply signals. To complete the Restore operation, it is required to:

1. Precharge the BL to VDD while BLB is connected to ground
2. Activate the access transistors (MM1, MM2, MB1, MB2) by applying a pulse on the WL and STORE lines
3. Reconnecting the CVDD signals of the SRAM block to VDD with the CVDD signal of the feed-forward inverter (INV1 in Fig.2) being slightly reactivated before that of the feedback inverter (INV2 in Fig.2)

The basic concept behind this sequence of operation is to precharge the storage node Q to a certain voltage depending on the state of the RRAM device. If the RRAM device is at its HRS, then voltage of the node Q is higher than the threshold voltage of the NMOS transistor ($V_{th,NMOS}$) in the inverters. Accordingly, when the power signal of INV1 is reactivated, the current coming from the supply through the PMOS device of the inverter, tries to charge the node QB to VDD. Yet, since the NMOS device of INV1 is ON, the charges previously built up on the QB node by PMOS discharge to ground keeping the voltage of node QB close to ground. Oppositely, if the RRAM cell is at its LRS, the voltage of the node Q is less than $V_{th,NMOS}$ and the current coming from the power signal of INV1 charges the node QB to a high voltage (higher than $V_{th,NMOS}$ of the feedback inverter INV2). Hence, when the INV2 is reconnected to the power supply in step 3, based on the charge collected on the node QB by INV1, the state of the SRAM is restored through the positive feedback loop of the back-back inverters. Fig. 4 shows the waveforms describing the Restore operation when the RRAM cell is at its LRS.

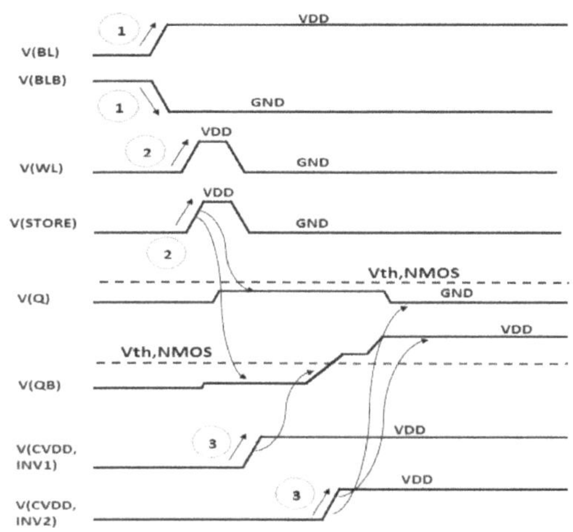

Figure 4: The Restore operation waveforms when RRAM cell is at its LRS

In order to guarantee the delay between the reactivation of the power supply signals of the feed-forward (CVDD, INV1) and the feedback (CVDD, INV2) inverters as indicated in Fig.4, we add a delay chain between a pair of PMOS transistors connecting the power supply to the inverter storage elements of each cell as shown in Fig.5. This circuit can be shared across all cells within a column.

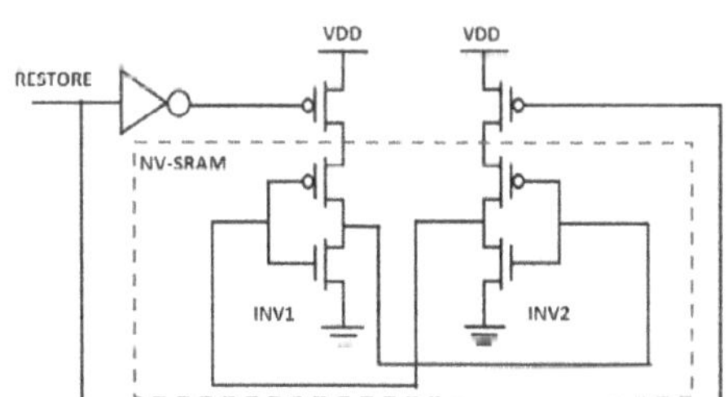

Figure 5: The power supply Restore circuit

The "RESTORE" signal in Fig.5 is the control pulse issued by the memory controller to initiate the Restore operation.

4. EXPERIMENTAL RESULTS

We simulate an 128x128 array for the different RRAM-based NV-SRAM cells using the SPICE models of a 40nm technology. Table 1 lists the sizes of the transistors used in the 8T1R SRAM cell. The names of the transistors listed in Table 1 are the same as those shown in Fig.2. MN_{inv} and MP_{inv} are the transistors used in the cross-coupled inverters of the SRAM cell. The same transistor sizes and RRAM device model (based on [11,12]) of the 8T1R NV-SRAM are used to compare its performance versus the other RRAM-based NV-SRAM cells discussed in literature. In the next subsections, we describe the simulation results for each of our experimental studies. The 128x128 array is a typical size of the SRAM bank as described in [23]

Table 1: Transistor sizes of the 8T1R nv-SRAM cell

Transistor Name	W/L value
MN_{inv}	315n/40n
MP_{inv}	173n/40n
$MB1$, $MB2$	275n/40n
$MM1$, $MM2$	275n/40n

4.1 Read and Write Operations

Table 2 summarizes the simulation results for the Read and Write operations for the various types of the RRAM-based SRAM arrays reported in the literature.

In order to calculate the noise immunity of the different NV-SRAM designs in Table 2, we use the dynamic noise margins (DNM) which accounts for the noise effect on the SRAM storage nodes (Q/QB) for the pulse duration of the Read/Write operation. We can divide the listed results in Table 2 into three categories:

Comparison with the conventional 6T SRAM design: Comparing the results listed in the column **Conventional 6T** with those in the column **8T1R** in Table 2, it shows that the performance of the 8T1R array is comparable to that of the conventional 6T array. The slight change in the delay and energy consumption of the Write operation of the 8T1R cell is due to a) the existence of low-leakage current passing between the nodes Q and QB through the transistors MM1 and MM2 in Fig.2 and b) The small extra capacitances at the storage nodes (Q, QB) coming from the source/drain junction capacitances of the MM1 and MM2 transistors.

Comparison with low-power NV-SRAM designs: In this part, we focus on discussing the results of our newly proposed 8T1R design versus those of the 8T2R[15], Rnv8T[16], and 9T2R[17] designs. We consider those designs as low-power NV-SRAM designs, since they do not have the high-leakage currents found in the 6T2R [14] and 7T2R [24] designs. **The Rnv8T cell** improves the performance of the Write operation (in terms of delay (4.5%) and WDNM (3%)) compared to the conventional 6T cell, as listed in Table 2, at the expense of slight increase in the energy consumption (4%). This is coming from using the RRAM devices and their access transistors to create a parallel path to write the data to the storage nodes Q and QB. Yet, due to increasing the capacitance of the BL and BLB, the read delay and noise margin are worsened (delay is almost doubled and RDNM is lowered by 10%).

The 9T2R cell uses the same structure as that of the Rnv8T cell but with the addition of isolating the Read and Write operations by having an extra transistor which acts as a dedicated read-port for the cell. This comes at the expense of increasing the write delay by 23% compared to the results of the Rnv8T cell due to the imbalance between the capacitances at the storage nodes Q/QB. Despite the fact that the 9T2R improves the performance of the Read operation (lowering the delay and increasing the RDNM by 50%), the cell has a few disadvantages:

- The Read operation becomes single-ended which introduces challenges such as a) increasing the sensing range which limits the number of cells per bitline or b) reducing the sense-amplifier immunity to supply noise as in [23].
- The SRAM cell area increases by about 30% compared to the Rnv8T cell. Figures 6a and 6b show the layout of the Rnv8T and the 9T2R NV-SRAM cell. For simplicity, the routing metal layers are omitted from the figures. The RRAM device in figures 6a and 6b is vertically stacked in the BEOL connectivity layers above the access transistors MM1 and MM2. Hence, its area does not affect that of the NV-SRAM cell.

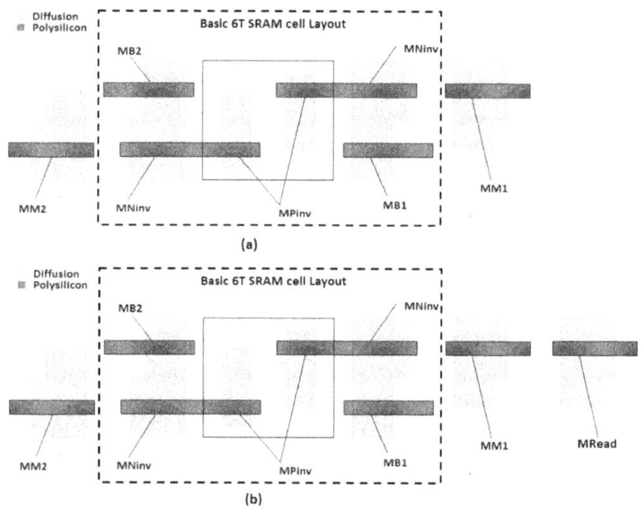

Figure 6: The Layout of (a) the Rnv8T cell and (b) 9T2R cell. The names of the transistor are aligned with those in Fig.2. MRead is the transistor connected to the dedicated read port as in [17]

As for **the 8T2R cell** [15], it has almost the same performance as that of our proposed 8T1R cell. The results are quite similar since the effect of the extra access transistor of the RRAM device is the same except the 8T1R has slightly higher leakage current between the storage nodes. This causes more energy consumption for the write and Read operations as in Table 2. The extra control line in the 8T2R cell adds an overhead to the peripheral circuits in terms of area and power consumptions in order to generate the required pulse widths and amplitudes for this extra control signal. The 8T2R design also adds overhead to the Restore operation as in discussed section 4.2.

Comparison with dense NV-SRAM designs: In this part, we discuss the results of the 8T1R in Table 2 with those of the 6T2R and 7T2R designs which add less transistors to the conventional 6T SRAM cell. The 6T2R and 7T2R NV-SRAM arrays suffer from high-leakage currents due to

Table 2: **Comparison results for the Read and Write operations of the different RRAM-based SRAM arrays**

Parameter Name	6T2R [14]	8T2R [15]	Rnv8T [16]	9T2R [17]	7T2R [24]	8T1R (this work)	Conventional 6T
Write Energy (fJ)	850	74.7	76.5	76.7	139	74.8	74
Write latency (ps)	27.6	26.4	24.7	30.3	33.8	26.3	25.6
Read Energy (fJ)	1190	1.14	1.20	0.356	55.3	1.16	1.1
Read latency (ps)	35	50.6	93.1	26.9	72.9	50.6	50
RDNM (V)	0.0038	0.224	0.204	0.411	0.193	0.224	0.224
WDNM (V)	0.258	0.337	0.35	0.349	0.338	0.337	0.34
Leakage currents (μA)	18.1	0.0364	0.0383	0.0934	1.22	0.0365	0.036

the existence of direct paths through the RRAM devices to GND. This degrades the performance of both the Read and Write operations specially in terms of RDNM and WDNM. **The 7T2R cell** has a better performance than the 6T2R cell since the path, which connects the RRAM devices together with the storage nodes, has always one RRAM device in HRS state. This actually decreases the leakage current by almost 90% compared to that in the 6T2R design. However, the energy is still significantly higher than that of the low-power NV-SRAM designs which makes the 7T2R cell less-attractive. As suggested in [24], keeping both of the RRAM devices in HRS could further decrease the leakage current but this comes at the expense of increasing both the delay and energy consumption of the Restore operation as discussed in section 4.2

In summary, the 8T1R design provides the best trade-off among all the previously proposed RRAM-based NV-SRAM designs in terms of having a good write and read energy and delay while keeping the cell area as small as possible without significantly increasing its leakage currents.

Table 3: **Comparison of Store and Restore operations of the RRAM-based NV-SRAM designs**

Parameter Name	6T2R	8T2R	Rnv8T	7T2R	8T1R
Store Energy (pJ)	1.17	1.04	2.08	0.954	0.387
Store Speed (ns)	9	9	18	9	9
Restore Energy (fJ)	18 + 1170*	13.6 +1040 *	13.6	13.6 + 954 *	4.1
Restore Speed (ps)	63.4 + 9x10^{3*}	63.8 + 9x10^{3*}	63.8	63.8 + 9x10^{3*}	170

* The second number refers to the RESET operation energy and delay requirements which is needed after each Restore operation. The Rnv8T and 8T1R designs do not require a RESET operation

4.2 Store and Restore Operations

In comparison with the other RRAM-based NV-SRAM designs, the most significant improvement of the proposed 8T1R cell is that it greatly reduces the energy consumptions for the Store/Restore operations. Table 3 summarizes the simulation results for the store and Restore operations of the various RRAM-based NV-SRAM designs. The 9T2R and the Rnv8T designs are using the same store and restore methodology [16,17]. Hence, the listed results for the Rnv8T design in Table 3 are also applicable for the 9T2R array. **For the Store operation**, the time to change the state of the RRAM device is about 9 nsec. The reason why the Rnv8T design needs double this time is because the Store operation in this NV-SRAM cell consists of two distinct operations as explained in [16]: a) increase the voltage of the BL and BLB to VDDH and then b) increase the CVDD to VDDH and grounding the BL and BLB lines. This is mainly to write the SRAM data on both of the RRAM devices connected to the storage nodes which is a unique behavior for this design. In 6T2R [14], 8T2R [15], and 7T2R [24] arrays, the RRAM devices connected to the storage nodes of the SRAM are required to be at HRS at normal operation mode. Accordingly, the Store operation for those designs changes only the state of the RRAM device connected to the storage node at logical state '0' to LRS. Hence, the Store operation for the 6T2R, 7T2R, and 8T2R arrays is achieved in only one step. The 8T1R reduces the store energy by at least 60 % (compared to the store energy of the 7T2R design which is the lowest value in Table 3 other than that of our circuit) since the programming conditions are only applicable to one RRAM device instead of two. For instance, in the 8T2R design [15], the voltage of the control line connected to both of the RRAM devices is raised to VDDH. Hence, although only one RRAM device is expected to be programmed, the current passing through the other RRAM cell, causes more energy dissipation.

For the Restore operation, as explained in section 3.3, our 8T1R requires more time (2.6x compared to the Rnv8T design) to retrieve the value saved on the RRAM device due to the multiple steps involved in this operation. However, for the 6T2R,7T2R, and 8T2R designs, there is an extra "RESET" operation which is needed after the data saved on the RRAM is retrieved as indicated in Table 3. The "RESET" operation re-programs the two RRAM devices to their HRS and it requires the same delay ($\approx$ 9ns) and energy as that of the Store operation. Accordingly, the total delay results of the Restore operation for those designs in Table 3 are higher by order of 2. Compared to the Rnv8T design, the 8T1R consumes almost 70% less energy for the same pulse width of the Restore operation. This is because the RRAM access transistors (MM1, MM2 in Fig.2) are only activated for a portion of the duration of the restore pulse. In the Rnv8T design, the RRAM access transistors, which connect both the RRAM devices and the storage nodes of the SRAM to ground, are turned ON throughout the Restore operation and hence increases their energy consumption in comparison to the 8T1R.

5. CONCLUSIONS

In this article, we present a new RRAM-based NV-SRAM cell. The different modes of operations are explained, and simulation results for the new 8T1R cell are demonstrated. Compared to the previously proposed RRAM-based NV-SRAM designs, our 8T1R cell adds non-volatility to the conventional 6T SRAM with marginal impact on the write and Read operations, and provides one of the best all-around performance among all proposed RRAM NV-SRAM so far. Moreover, since our proposed cell uses only one RRAM device to save the SRAM data, it also reduces the energy of Store operation by more than 60% compared with previously proposed designs. We have also showed that, despite the extra steps added to the Restore operation, the 8T1R design saves at least 70% of the energy consumption for the same restore pulse width.

Acknowledgments

The authors would like to thank Prof. S. Yu from Arizona State University for compact model support and discussion and Prof. K.Salama (KAUST) for the useful discussions about the NV-SRAM designs

6. REFERENCES

[1] L. Chang *et al.*, "Stable SRAM cell design for the 32 nm node and beyond," in *Symp. on Digest of Technical Papers in VLSI Technology*, Jun. 2005, pp. 128 – 129.

[2] K. Takeda *et al.*, "A read-static-noise-margin-free SRAM cell for low-vdd and high-speed applications," *IEEE Journal of Solid-State Circuits, Vol. 41, No. 1,*, pp. 113 – 121, Jan. 2006.

[3] I. Chang *et al.*, "A 32 kb 10T sub-threshold SRAM array with bit-interleaving and differential read scheme in 90 nm CMOS," *IEEE Journal of Solid-State Circuits, Vol. 44, No. 2,*, pp. 650 – 658, Feb. 2009.

[4] T.D.Burd *et al.*, "A dynamic voltage scaled microprocessor system," *IEEE Journal of Solid-State Circuits , Vol. 35, No. 11*, pp. 1571 – 1580, Nov. 2000.

[5] K.J.Nowka *et al.*, "A 32-bit PowerPC system-on-a-chip with support for dynamic voltage scaling and dynamic frequency scaling," *IEEE Journal of Solid-State Circuits , Vol. 37, No. 11*, pp. 1441 – 1447, Nov. 2002.

[6] M.-F.Chang *et al.*, "Wide VDD embedded asynchronous SRAM with dual-mode self-timed technique for dynamic voltage systems," *IEEE Trans.Circuits Syst. I, Reg.Papers, Vol. 56, No. 8*, pp. 1657 – 1667, Aug. 2009.

[7] K. Zhang *et al.*, "SRAM design on 65-nm CMOS technology with dynamic sleep transistor for leakage reduction," *IEEE Journal of Solid-State Circuits, Vol. 40, No. 4,*, pp. 895 – 901, Apr. 2005.

[8] C. H. Kim *et al.*, "PVT-Aware leakage reduction for on-die caches with improved read stability," *IEEE Journal of Solid-State Circuits, Vol. 41, No. 1,*, pp. 170 – 178, Jan. 2006.

[9] Y.Kanno *et al.*, "Hierarchical Power Distribution With Power Tree in Dozens of Power Domains for 90-nm Low-Power Multi-CPU SoCs ," *IEEE Journal on Solid-State Circuits, Vol. 42, No. 1,*, pp. 528 – 535, Jan. 2007.

[10] J. Yang *et al.*, "Memristive devices for computing," *Nature Nanotechnology, Vol. 8*, pp. 13 – 24, Jan. 2013.

[11] Z.Jiang *et al.*, "Verilog-A compact model for oxide-based resistive random access memory (RRAM)," in *Proc. of Int. Conference on Simulation of Semiconductor Processes and Devices (SISPAD)*, Sept. 2014, pp. 41 – 44.

[12] P.-Y. Chen and S. Yu, "Compact modeling of RRAM devices and its applications in 1T1R and 1S1R array design," *IEEE Transaction on Electron Devices, Vol. 62, No. 12,*, pp. 4022 – 4028, Dec. 2015.

[13] J. Strachan *et al.*, "State dynamics and modeling of tantalum oxide memristors," *IEEE Transactions on Electron Devices, Vol. 60, No. 7,*, pp. 2194 – 2202, Jul. 2013.

[14] W. Wang *et al.*, "Nonvolatile SRAM cell," in *Int. Electron Devices Meeting (IEDM)*, Dec. 2006, pp. 27 – 30.

[15] S.Yamamoto *et al.*, "NonvolatileSRAM (NV-SRAM) using functional MOSFET merged with resistive switching devices," in *IEEE Custom Integrated Circuits Conf. (CICC) Tech. Dig. Papers*, Sep. 2009, pp. 531 – 534.

[16] P.-F. Chiu *et al.*, "Low Store Energy, Low VDDmin, 8T2R Nonvolatile Latch and SRAM With Vertical-Stacked Resistive Memory (Memristor) Devices for Low Power Mobile Applications," *IEEE Journal of Solid-State Circuits, Vol. 47, No. 6,*, pp. 1483 – 1496, Jun. 2012.

[17] M.-F. Chang *et al.*, "Endurance-aware circuit designs of nonvolatile logic and nonvolatile SRAM using resistive memory (memristor) device," in *Proc. Asia and South Pacific Design Automation Conference (ASP-DAC)*, Feb. 2012, pp. 329 – 334.

[18] Y.-W. Chin *et al.*, "Point Twin-bit RRAM in 3D Interweaved Cross-point Array by Cu BEOL Process," in *Proc. IEEE Int. Electron Devices Meeting (IEDM)*, Dec. 2014, pp. 6.4.1 – 6.4.4.

[19] Liaw *et al.*, "Nonvolatile 3D-FPGA with monolithically stacked RRAM-based configuration memory," in *Proc. IEEE Int. Solid-State Circuits Conference (ISSCC)*, 2012, pp. 406 – 408.

[20] Wong *et al.*, "Metal oxide RRAM," *Proceedings of the IEEE, vol.100, No. 6,*, pp. 1951 – 1970, June 2012.

[21] S.H.Jo, "Nanoscale memristive devices for memory and logic applications," *PhD thesis, University of Michigan*, 2010.

[22] Y.S.Chen *et al.*, "Challenges and opportunities for HfOx based resistive random access memory," in *Proc. of IEEE Int. Electron Devices Meeting (IEDM)*, Dec. 2011, pp. 31.3.1 – 31.3.4.

[23] M. H. Abu-Rahma and M. Anis, *Nanometer Variation-Tolerant SRAM: Circuits and Statistical Design for Yield.* Springer, 2012.

[24] S.-S.Sheu *et al.*, "A ReRAM integrated 7T2R non-volatile SRAM for normally-off computing application," in *Proceedings of IEEE Asian Solid-State Circuits Conference (A-SSCC)*, Nov. 2013, pp. 245 – 248.

Polynomial Arithmetic Using Sequential Stochastic Logic

Naman Saraf and Kia Bazargan
Department of Electrical and Computer Engineering
University of Minnesota Twin Cities
200 Union St SE, Minneapolis, Minnesota, USA 55455
{saraf012,kia}@umn.edu

ABSTRACT

We present the design of stochastic computing systems based on sequential logic to implement arbitrary polynomial functions. Stochastic computing is an emerging alternative computing paradigm that performs arithmetic operations on real-valued data represented as random bitstreams using digital logic gates. Stochastic computing systems are capable of realizing complex mathematical operations using a small number of hardware resources by expressing the computation in terms of probabilities. Moreover, the stochastic representation of data using random bitstreams is extremely robust against bit errors. We present a systematic approach to implement arbitrary polynomial functions in stochastic computing using sequential logic, and compare our approach against prior conventional and stochastic implementations.

1. INTRODUCTION

CMOS technology has been instrumental in the proliferation of digital computing with submicron CMOS transistors realizing complex computing systems operating at GHz clock frequencies. However, concerns about increasing power dissipation and declining reliability in recent nanometer scale CMOS technologies have prompted research into unconventional computing paradigms. Stochastic computing [2] is an emerging alternative to conventional computing that represents data as random bitstreams, and performs arithmetic operations using digital logic gates by expressing the computation in terms of probabilities. Stochastic computing systems, in general, have lower hardware requirements than conventional systems, and the random bitstream representation improves the fault tolerance of the computation. We present the design of stochastic computing systems based on sequential logic to implement arbitrary polynomial functions, and compare our proposed approach against prior conventional and stochastic implementations.

As previously mentioned, stochastic computing relies on random bitstreams to represent data. In particular, a real number x $(0 \leq x \leq 1)$ is represented in a stochastic computing system as a sequence of random bits, where each bit in the sequence is logic '1' with a probability x. The random bitstream representation of numbers enables us to express a computation in terms of probabilities. As an example, consider a two-input AND gate driven by `independent` random bitstreams A and B representing real numbers a and b.

GLSVLSI'16, May 18-20, 2016, Boston, MA, USA

DOI: http://dx.doi.org/10.1145/2902961.2902981

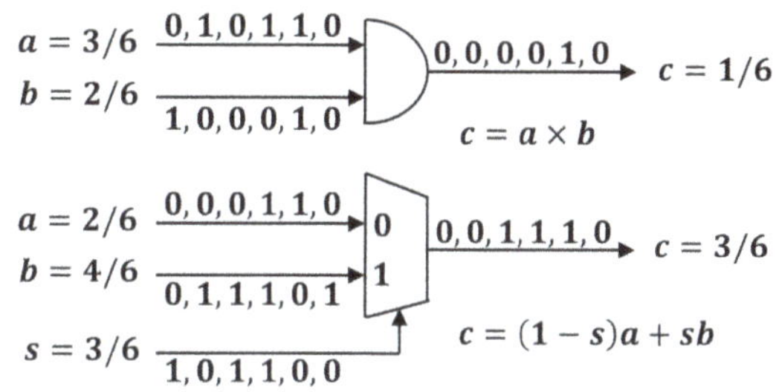

Figure 1: Addition and multiplication operations in stochastic computing.

$$Prob(A = 1) = a,\ Prob(B = 1) = b \tag{1}$$

The real number c represented by the output random bitstream of the AND gate is given by,

$$Prob(C = 1) = c = Prob(A = 1, B = 1) \tag{2}$$

$$\implies Prob(A = 1)Prob(B = 1) = ab \tag{3}$$

A two-input AND gate, therefore, performs multiplication in stochastic computing. Similarly, a $2:1$ multiplexer performs scaled addition, as depicted in Figure 1. The stochastic implementations of addition and multiplication, therefore, require far fewer hardware resources than a conventional implementation. The simple illustrations likewise extend to more complex arithmetic operations in image processing [8, 5] and digital communications [11].

The random bitstream representation of numbers, moreover, is extremely robust against bit errors. Consider an M-bit weighted binary number system, representing 2^M fixed-point numbers, $0.b_1\ b_2\ \ldots\ b_M$. An error of magnitude $|1/2|$ results when the most significant bit b_1 of a fixed-point number is corrupted by noise. In contrast, the random bitstream representation is unweighted. Specifically, a random bitstream of length L, $[b_1\ b_2\ \ldots\ b_L]$, represents the number $p = \sum_{i=1}^{L} b_i/L$. Therefore, a smaller error of magnitude $1/L$ results if a bit in the random bitstream is erroneous.

The high fault tolerance and low hardware overhead have fueled a growing interest in stochastic computing with an increasing number of successful stochastic implementations of artificial neural networks [4], digital filters [6], and image processing systems [8, 5]. We present the design of stochastic computing systems based on sequential logic to realize arbitrary polynomial functions.

2. PRIOR RESEARCH

Polynomials are an important class of functions that frequently arise in numerous scientific disciplines, and are often employed to approximate other complicated functions such as the trigonometric functions. Specifically, a polynomial function $f(x)$ of degree n is an expression of the form,

$$f(x) = \sum_{i=0}^{n} a_i x^i \tag{4}$$

where x is the known as the input variable and a_i are the $(n+1)$ polynomial coefficients.

A previous stochastic implementation of polynomial functions was presented in [9], where the authors described a method to realize arbitrary polynomial functions using purely combinational logic circuits. However, a serious drawback of their proposed architecture (Figure 2) is the requirement of `multiple independent` random bitstreams for the input variable x. Concretely, their architecture requires at least n independent random bitstreams representing the input variable x, in order to implement a polynomial function of degree n. The linear dependence of the input interface complexity on the polynomial degree presents a significant hardware overhead as multiple independent random bitstreams ought to be generated corresponding to the input variable x, thereby restricting the practical applicability of the approach to low degree polynomials.

In contrast, we propose sequential logic circuits to implement polynomial functions in stochastic computing. Specifically, we present finite state machines (FSMs) in the form of binary counters that realize arbitrary polynomial functions. Our proposed approach requires an FSM containing at least $(n+1)$ states, and a `single` random bitstream for the input variable x, in order to implement a polynomial function of degree n. Using a binary encoding for the FSM states, we notice that the apparent linear dependence of the FSM complexity on the polynomial degree only translates into a logarithmic dependence in hardware area. As an example, a 7th degree polynomial function is realized by an 8-state FSM in our approach that only requires 3 flip flops. However, of greater significance is the massive simplification in the input interface, and the corresponding reduction in the auxiliary circuitry that is required to generate the multiple independent input random bitstreams in the purely combinational solution. To summarize, our proposed approach realizes an arbitrary polynomial function of degree n using a single random bitstream for the input variable x that drives an FSM containing at least $(n+1)$ states.

3. BERNSTEIN POLYNOMIALS

The theory of Bernstein polynomials [7] forms the bedrock of the stochastic implementations of polynomial functions. In particular, the Bernstein `basis` polynomials of degree n are a family of $(n+1)$ polynomials given by,

$$B_{i,n}(x) = \binom{n}{i} x^i (1-x)^{n-i}, \ i = 0, 1, \ldots, n \tag{5}$$

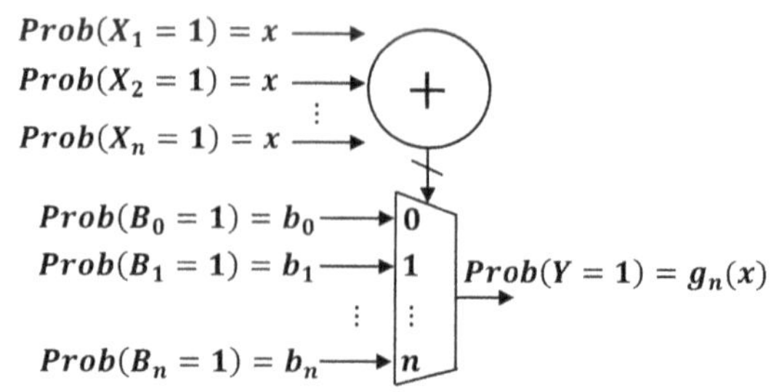

Figure 2: A stochastic implementation of a degree n polynomial using combinational logic [9].

and a linear combination of the Bernstein basis polynomials, $g_n(x)$, is called a Bernstein polynomial of degree n.

$$g_n(x) = \sum_{i=0}^{n} b_i B_{i,n}(x) \tag{6}$$

where b_i are known as the $(n+1)$ Bernstein coefficients.

In general, a `power-form` polynomial of degree n, as depicted in Equation (4), has an equivalent representation as a Bernstein polynomial of degree n, where the polynomial coefficients a_i are related to the Bernstein coefficients b_i as,

$$b_i = \sum_{j=0}^{i} \frac{\binom{i}{j}}{\binom{n}{j}} a_j, \quad 0 \leq i \leq n \tag{7}$$

The Bernstein coefficients for an arbitrary polynomial, however, seldom lie inside the unit interval $[0, 1]$ as required for a stochastic implementation. Fortunately, by elevating the degree of the Bernstein polynomial representation, we can express a power-form polynomial of degree n as a Bernstein polynomial of degree q ($q \geq n$) with the Bernstein coefficients $b_i \in [0, 1]$. In fact, due to a theorem [10], a power-form polynomial $f(x)$ of degree n can be converted into a Bernstein polynomial of degree q ($q \geq n$) with the Bernstein coefficients inside the unit interval $[0, 1]$ if,

1. $f(x) = 0$ or $f(x) = 1 \ \forall x \in [0, 1]$, or
2. $f(x) \in (0, 1) \ \forall x \in (0, 1)$ and $0 \leq f(0), f(1) \leq 1$

The details of the conversion method are provided in [9]. Following a successful conversion of a power-form polynomial to a Bernstein polynomial, we proceed with the stochastic implementation of the Bernstein representation by,

1. generating the Bernstein basis polynomials (Equation 5),
2. forming a linear combination of the Bernstein basis polynomials with the Bernstein coefficients (Equation 6)

4. MARKOV CHAINS

Before describing our stochastic implementation of polynomial functions, we present a brief review of Markov chains. Markov chains are crucial to the understanding of sequential logic based stochastic computing systems because an FSM with random bitstream inputs is mathematically equivalent to a Markov chain.

A Markov chain is a random process that models probabilistic transitions between states on a `state space`. We restrict our attention to `finite-state` Markov chains since only finite memory systems are physically realizable.

Consider a finite-state Markov chain with a state space S containing $(n+1)$ states,

$$S = \{0, 1, \ldots, n\} \quad (8)$$

Let X_t denote the state of the Markov chain at time instant t. The next state of the Markov chain, X_{t+1}, depends only on X_t, and is independent of the past system history.

$$Pr(X_{t+1} = j | X_t = i, \ldots, X_0 = s_0) \quad (9)$$
$$= Pr(X_{t+1} = j | X_t = i) = p_{i,j}, \; \forall t, \; \forall i, j \in S \quad (10)$$

The probability that a Markov chain transitions from a state i to another state j in the state space is known as the **transition probability**, and is denoted as $p_{i,j}$.

$$p_{i,j} \geq 0, \; \forall i, j \in S; \; \sum_{j=0}^{n} p_{i,j} = 1, \; \forall i \in S \quad (11)$$

Contrary to the transition probabilities $p_{i,j}$, $\forall i, j \in S$ that capture the probabilistic transitions between the states, the **stationary probabilities** π_i, $\forall i \in S$ of a Markov chain determine the probability of observing the states at equilibrium. Concretely, starting from a random initial state, a Markov chain reaches equilibrium after making a number of state transitions, at which point the probability of observing the Markov chain in a particular state i becomes a constant π_i, independent of the initial state.

$$\pi_i \geq 0, \; \forall i \in S; \; \sum_{i=0}^{n} \pi_i = 1 \quad (12)$$

The relationship between the stationary probabilities π_i and the transition probabilities $p_{i,j}$ of a Markov chain, in general, is complicated. However, by restricting a Markov chain to a **linear** arrangement of states with only nearest neighbor transitions, as illustrated in Figure 3, a powerful set of **detailed balance conditions** become available. The detailed balance conditions relate the stationary probabilities of neighboring states to the transition probabilities between the states. Specifically,

$$\pi_i p_{i,i+1} = \pi_{i+1} p_{i+1,i}, \; i = \{0, 1, \ldots, n-1\} \quad (13)$$

$$\implies \frac{\pi_{i+1}}{\pi_i} = \frac{p_{i,i+1}}{p_{i+1,i}} = r_{i+1,i} \quad (14)$$

We notice that the stationary probabilities of neighboring states in a **Reversible** Markov chain only depend on the ratio of the transition probabilities between the states.

To summarize, the stationary probabilities of a Reversible Markov chain are conveniently obtained by applying Equation 12 and the detailed balance conditions listed in Equation 14. We next describe a specific Reversible Markov chain construct where the stationary probabilities equal the Bernstein basis polynomials.

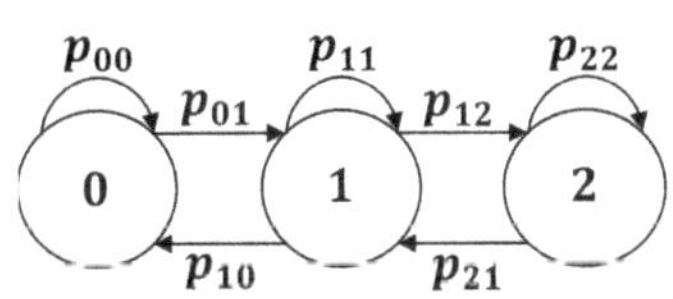

Figure 3: A 3-state Reversible Markov chain. The vertex labels denote the state while the edge annotations depict the transition probabilities.

5. THE STOCHASTIC INTEGRATOR

Consider the $(n+1)$-state Reversible Markov chain depicted in Figure 4. Using Equation 14, the stationary probabilities of the Reversible Markov chain are related to the transition probabilities as,

$$\frac{\pi_{i+1}}{\pi_i} = \frac{x}{1-x}\frac{n-i}{i+1}$$
$$\implies \pi_{i+1} = \pi_i \frac{x}{1-x}\frac{n-i}{i+1}, \; 0 \leq i \leq n-1 \quad (15)$$

Let us select π_0 as the reference stationary probability.

$$\pi_0 = \binom{n}{0}[\frac{x}{1-x}]^0 \pi_0 \quad (16)$$

$$\pi_1 = \pi_0 \frac{x}{1-x} n = \binom{n}{1}[\frac{x}{1-x}]^1 \pi_0 \quad (17)$$

$$\pi_2 = \pi_1 \frac{x}{1-x}\frac{n-1}{2} = \pi_0 [\frac{x}{1-x}]^2 \frac{n(n-1)}{2}$$
$$= \binom{n}{2}[\frac{x}{1-x}]^2 \pi_0 \quad (18)$$

$$\ldots$$

$$\pi_i = \binom{n}{i}[\frac{x}{1-x}]^i \pi_0 \quad (19)$$

$$\ldots$$

$$\pi_n = \binom{n}{n}[\frac{x}{1-x}]^n \pi_0 \quad (20)$$

Invoking Equation 12,

$$\sum_{i=0}^{n} \pi_i = \pi_0 \sum_{i=0}^{n} \binom{n}{i}[\frac{x}{1-x}]^i = 1 \quad (21)$$

and solving for the reference stationary probability π_0,

$$\pi_0 = \frac{1}{\sum_{i=0}^{n} \binom{n}{i}[\frac{x}{1-x}]^i} = \frac{1}{[1 + \frac{x}{1-x}]^n} = [1-x]^n \quad (22)$$

Therefore, the stationary probabilities of the Reversible

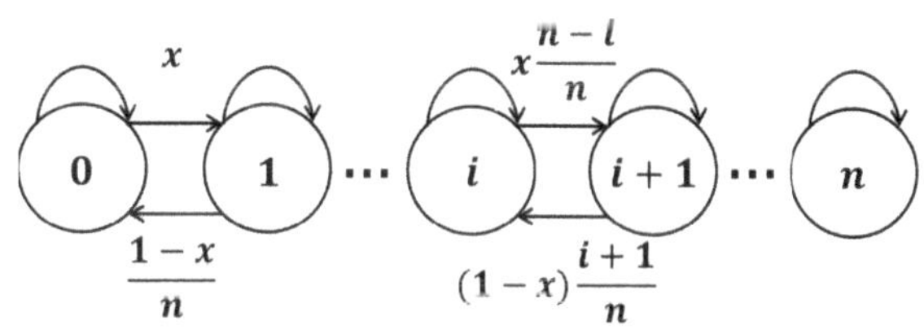

Figure 4: Reversible Markov chain representation of the stochastic integrator. The transition probabilities on the self-loops are omitted for clarity.

Markov chain in Figure 4 are given as,

$$\pi_0 = [1-x]^n = \binom{n}{0} x^0 (1-x)^n \quad (23)$$

$$\pi_1 = \binom{n}{1} [\frac{x}{1-x}]^1 [1-x]^n = \binom{n}{1} x^1 (1-x)^{n-1} \quad (24)$$

...

$$\pi_i = \binom{n}{i} x^i (1-x)^{n-i} \quad (25)$$

...

$$\pi_n = \binom{n}{n} x^n (1-x)^0 \quad (26)$$

Comparing with Equation 5, we conclude that the stationary probabilities of the Reversible Markov chain in Figure 4 form the Bernstein basis polynomials of degree n.

A hardware realization of the Reversible Markov chain in Figure 4 is a **stochastic integrator** [3] with parameter n. As illustrated in Figure 5, a stochastic integrator consists of an up/down counter, a binary comparator, and source of random numbers. The input to the stochastic integrator is a random bitstream X representing the input variable x.

The up/down counter of a stochastic integrator with parameter n stores binary numbers from 0 through n in unit integer increments, and saturates at the maximum or minimum count. A summary of the up/down counter operation is presented in Table 1.

The binary comparator compares the present counter state with a random number sampled from a uniform distribution on the integers $\{1, 2, \ldots, n\}$, and produces a logic '1' bit if the counter state equals or exceeds the random number. Thus, if the present counter state is i, $0 \leq i \leq n$, the probability of the comparator output to be logic '1' is given by,

$$Prob(Z=1) = \frac{i}{n} \implies Prob(Z=0) = \frac{n-i}{n} \quad (27)$$

Consequently, the probability that the up/down counter increments to $i+1$ at the next clock becomes,

$$\begin{aligned} p_{i,i+1} &= Prob(X=1, Z=0) \\ &= Prob(X=1)Prob(Z=0) = x\frac{n-i}{n} \end{aligned} \quad (28)$$

Similarly, the probability of the counter state to decrement to $i-1$ is given by,

$$\begin{aligned} p_{i,i-1} &= Prob(X=0, Z=1) \\ &= Prob(X=0)Prob(Z=1) = (1-x)\frac{i}{n} \end{aligned} \quad (29)$$

where we assume that the random bitstreams X and Z are independent.

Table 1: Operation of the up/down counter.

up	down	present state	next state	probability
1	0	i	$i+1$	$x(n-i)/n$
0	1	i	$i-1$	$(1-x)i/n$
1	1	i	i	xi/n
0	0	i	i	$(1-x)(n-i)/n$

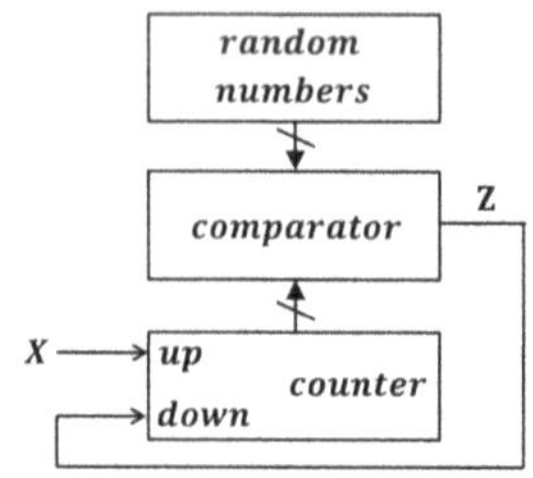

Figure 5: A hardware realization of the stochastic integrator.

Comparing the probabilities of the up/down counter to increment (Equation 28) and decrement (Equation 29) with the transition probabilities of the Reversible Markov chain in Figure 4, we ascertain that a stochastic integrator with parameter n implements the Bernstein basis polynomials of degree n. Specifically, the probability of observing counter state i at equilibrium equals the Bernstein basis polynomial $B_{i,n}(x)$ (Equation 5).

6. HARDWARE ARCHITECTURE

As previously mentioned, a stochastic implementation of a Bernstein polynomial representation consists of,

1. generating the Bernstein basis polynomials (Equation 5),
2. forming a linear combination of the Bernstein basis polynomials with the Bernstein coefficients (Equation 6)

We have demonstrated in the previous section that a stochastic integrator with parameter n generates the Bernstein basis polynomials of degree n. The remaining task of forming the linear combination is performed by an $(n+1):1$ multiplexer. The inputs to the multiplexer are random bitstreams B_i, $0 \leq i \leq n$ representing the $(n+1)$ Bernstein coefficients b_i, while the multiplexer select input is driven by the count, cnt, of the up/down counter of the stochastic integrator. As the counter states are mutually exclusive and exhaustive, the probability of the output random bitstream of the multiplexer to be logic '1' is obtained by invoking the law of total probability as,

$$Prob(Y=1) = \sum_{i=0}^{n} Prob(Y=1|cnt=i)Prob(cnt=i)$$

$$\sum_{i=0}^{n} Prob(B_i=1)Prob(cnt=i) = \sum_{i=0}^{n} b_i B_{i,n}(x) \quad (30)$$

Comparing with Equation 6, we conclude that our proposed architecture, depicted in Figure 6, realizes an arbitrary polynomial of degree n expressed as a Bernstein polynomial.

Furthermore, our stochastic implementation of polynomial functions (Figure 6) using sequential logic requires a single random bitstream for the input variable x, compared to the combinational implementation (Figure 2) that relies on multiple independent random bitstreams.

7. EXPERIMENTAL RESULTS

Finally, we compare the fault tolerance and the hardware costs of our proposed stochastic implementation of polynomial functions using sequential logic with the combinational implementation proposed in [9], and a conventional architecture based on the weighted binary number system.

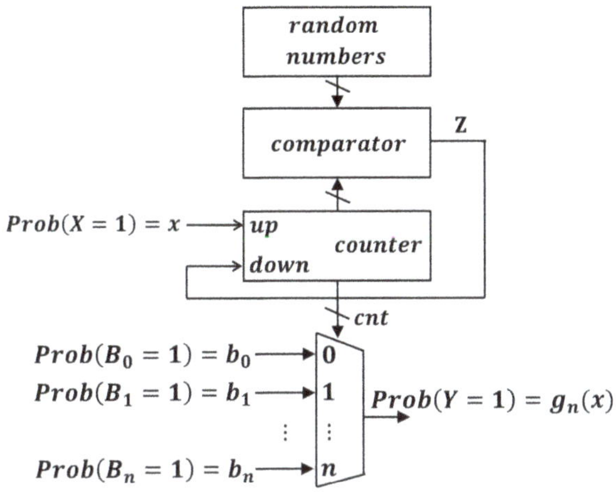

Figure 6: The proposed stochastic implementation of a degree n polynomial using sequential logic.

7.1 Fault Tolerance

In order to compare the fault tolerance of the different polynomial implementations, we consider the gamma correction function. Gamma correction is a non linear operation used to efficiently encode image luminance as,

$$f(x) = x^{\gamma} \tag{31}$$

Selecting $\gamma = 0.45$, the non linear gamma correction function is approximated by a degree 6 Bernstein polynomial with the following Bernstein coefficients [8],

$$b_0 = 0.0955,\ b_1 = 0.7207,\ b_2 = 0.3476,\ b_3 = 0.9988$$
$$b_4 = 0.7017,\ b_5 = 0.9695,\ b_6 = 0.9939 \tag{32}$$

We construct a conventional implementation of the gamma correction function using binary multipliers and adders performing arithmetic on 8-bit data, and generating 8-bit results. The stochastic implementations, on the contrary, were realized using random bitstreams of length 256, as the 8-bit weighted binary representation is equivalent to a random bitstream representation of length 256. We performed simulations on a test image by adding random noise to the input data and measuring the average output error. Specifically, we randomly corrupted ϵ% of the input data bits, computed the gamma correction function using the conventional and the stochastic implementations, and measured the average percent error between the result and the correct output in the absence of noise. Figure 7 presents the results of the simulation experiments. The results clearly indicate that the stochastic implementations outperform the conventional implementation in terms of fault tolerance. The stochastic implementations do produce small errors in the absence of noise ($\epsilon = 0$) as a result of the random nature of the computation. However, unlike the conventional implementation, the average output error of the stochastic implementations grows gradually as the input error increases, confirming the robustness of the unweighted random bitstream representation over the weighted binary number system.

The simulation results also reveal that between the two stochastic implementations, the combinational implementation [9] is slightly better at tolerating random noise than our proposed sequential implementation. The lower fault tolerance of the sequential implementation is a result of the correlation between successive counter states of the stochastic integrator. Specifically, the counter state at time t is not independent of the state at time $t-1$. Consequently, unlike the combinational implementation (Figure 2), successive bits in the output random bitstream Y of the sequential implementation (Figure 6) exhibit correlation. The correlation in the random bitstream Y leads to a higher variance in the real-valued output $g_n(x)$. However, the multiplexer and the Bernstein coefficient random bitstreams B_i mitigate the impact of correlation in the counter states, as evidenced by the small difference in the fault tolerance of the combinational and the sequential implementations. The average output error of the sequential implementation is within 1% of the combinational implementation (Figure 7). Moreover, the gamma correction results at input error $\epsilon = 15\%$ in Figure 8 reinforce our assertion as the output images of the combinational and sequential implementations are virtually indistinguishable, whereas the output image of the conventional implementation is barely recognizable.

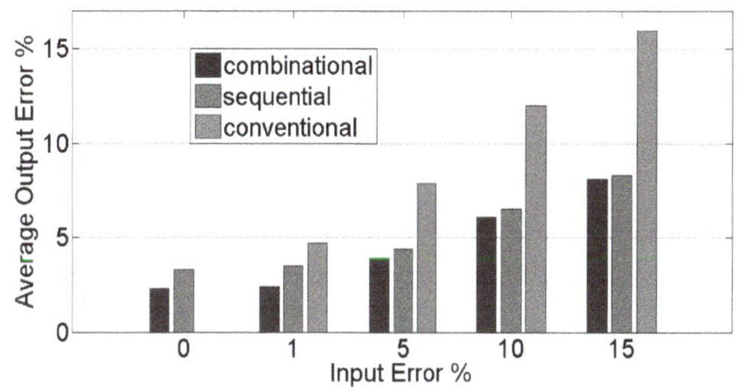

Figure 7: A comparison of the fault tolerance of the different polynomial implementations of the gamma correction function.

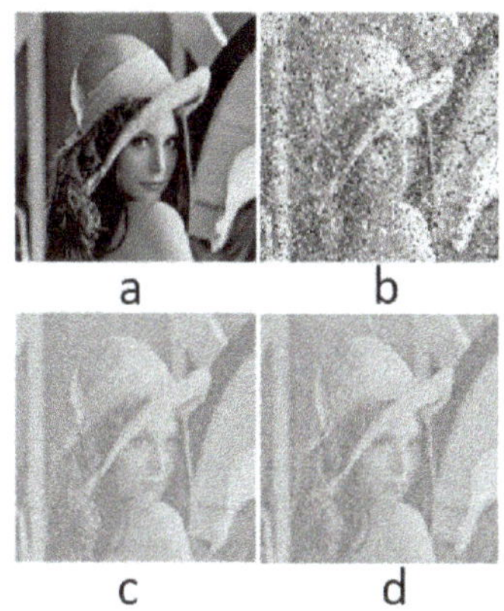

Figure 8: Gamma correction results at input error $\epsilon = 15\%$ a) Original image b) Conventional implementation c) Combinational implementation d) Sequential implementation.

7.2 Hardware Costs

To compare the hardware costs of the different polynomial implementations, we follow the approach outlined in [9]. We synthesize and optimize our proposed architecture in Figure 6 using *ABC* [1], and map the optimized implementation to a circuit consisting of only inverters, and 2-input

Table 2: A comparison of the area and delay of the stochastic polynomial implementations.

n	combinational implementation [9]			proposed sequential implementation		
	area	delay	product	area	delay	product
3	22	10	220	45	7	315
4	40	17	680	75	10	750
5	49	20	980	79	9	711
6	58	20	1160	85	9	765

NAND, NOR, AND, OR, XOR, and XNOR logic gates. We assume that each logic gate requires a unit area and contributes a unit delay to the circuit. Moreover, each memory element is composed of 6 2-input NAND logic gates. Table 2 compares the area and delay of our proposed sequential implementation with the combinational implementation [9]. The presence of memory elements does increase the area of our sequential implementations, but reduces the critical path delay, resulting in a better `area-delay` product as the Bernstein polynomial degree n increases.

Finally, we compare the different polynomial implementations using the `area-delay-latency` product metric. The latency of a stochastic implementation corresponding to an M-bit weighted conventional implementation is 2^M, since a random bitstream of length 2^M is equivalent to an M-bit binary number. Table 3 presents the area-delay-latency products (q_{xx}) of the different polynomial implementations. The ratios of the area-delay-latency products in the final two columns of Table 3 indicate that our proposed sequential implementation better competes with the conventional implementation as the Bernstein polynomial degree n and the data resolution M increase.

To conclude, we have presented a stochastic implementation of polynomial functions using sequential logic. Our proposed approach is able to realize arbitrary polynomials with a better area-delay-latency product than the previously described combinational implementation [9]. Moreover, our architecture requires a single random bitstream for the input variable, unlike the combinational implementation that relies on multiple independent random bitstreams. The fault tolerance of our sequential implementation, albeit slightly lower than the combinational implementation, is still better than the conventional implementation. Overall, our proposed sequential stochastic computing system is a competitive solution to realize arbitrary polynomial functions.

8. ACKNOWLEDGMENTS

This material is based on work supported by the National Science Foundation under grant CCF-1408123.

9. REFERENCES

[1] Berkeley logic synthesis and verification group, ABC: A system for sequential synthesis and verification, release 10216. http://www.eecs.berkeley.edu/ alanmi/abc/.

[2] A. Alaghi and J. P. Hayes. Survey of stochastic computing. *ACM Trans. Embed. Comput. Syst.*, 12(2s):1–19, May 2013.

[3] B. Gaines. Stochastic computing systems. *Advances in information systems science*, pages 37–172, 1969.

Table 3: A comparison of the area-delay-latency products of the polynomial implementations. The bold entries indicate the points of equal performance between the conventional and the stochastic implementations.

n	M	q_{conv} [9]	q_{comb} [9]	q_{seq}	$\frac{q_{comb}}{q_{conv}}$	$\frac{q_{seq}}{q_{conv}}$
3	7	99207	28160	40320	0.284	0.406
3	8	152745	56320	80640	0.369	0.528
3	9	222615	112640	161280	0.506	**0.724**
3	10	310977	225280	322560	**0.724**	1.037
3	11	419991	450560	645120	1.073	1.536
4	7	132276	87040	96000	0.658	0.726
4	8	203660	174080	192000	**0.855**	**0.943**
4	9	296820	348160	384000	1.173	1.294
4	10	414636	696320	768000	1.679	1.852
4	11	559988	1392640	1536000	2.487	2.743
5	7	165345	125440	91008	0.759	0.550
5	8	254575	250880	182016	**0.986**	0.715
5	9	371025	501760	364032	1.352	**0.981**
5	10	518295	1003520	728064	1.936	1.405
5	11	699985	2007040	1456128	2.867	2.080
6	7	198414	148480	97920	0.748	0.494
6	8	305490	296960	195840	**0.972**	0.641
6	9	445230	593920	391680	1.334	**0.880**
6	10	621954	1187840	783360	1.910	1.260
6	11	839982	2375680	1566720	2.828	1.865

[4] Y. Ji, F. Ran, C. Ma, and D. J. Lilja. A hardware implementation of a radial basis function neural network using stochastic logic. In *Proc. Design, Automation & Test in Europe Conf. (DATE)*, pages 880–883, 2015.

[5] P. Li, D. Lilja, W. Qian, K. Bazargan, and M. Riedel. Computation on stochastic bit streams digital image processing case studies. *IEEE Trans. Very Large Scale Integr. (VLSI) Syst.*, 22(3):449–462, Mar. 2014.

[6] Y. Liu and K. Parhi. Lattice FIR digital filter architectures using stochastic computing. In *IEEE Int. Conf. Acoustics, Speech and Signal Processing (ICASSP)*, pages 1027–1031, 2015.

[7] G. Lorentz. *Bernstein polynomials.* University of Toronto Press, 1953.

[8] W. Qian, X. Li, M. D. Riedel, K. Bazargan, and D. J. Lilja. An architecture for fault-tolerant computation with stochastic logic. *IEEE Trans. Comput.*, 60(1):93–105, Jan. 2011.

[9] W. Qian and M. D. Riedel. The synthesis of robust polynomial arithmetic with stochastic logic. In *Proc. Annu. Design Automation Conf. (DAC)*, pages 648–653, 2008.

[10] W. Qian, M. D. Riedel, and I. Rosenberg. Uniform approximation and bernstein polynomials with coefficients in the unit interval. *European Journal of Combinatorics*, 32(3):448–463, 2011.

[11] S. Sharifi Tehrani, S. Mannor, and W. J. Gross. Fully parallel stochastic LDPC decoders. *IEEE Trans. Signal Process.*, 56(11):5692–5703, Nov. 2008.

Ultra-Robust Null Convention Logic Circuit with Emerging Domain Wall Devices

Yu Bai
University of Central Florida
4000 Central Florida Blvd.
Orlando, FL, 32817
ybai@knights.ucf.edu

Bo Hu
University of Central Florida
4000 Central Florida Blvd.
Orlando, FL, 32817
bo.hu@knights.ucf.edu

Weidong Kuang
The University of Texas Rio Grande Valley
1201 W University Drive
Edinburg, TX 78539
kuangw@utrgv.edu

Mingjie Lin
University of Central Florida
4000 Central Florida Blvd.
Orlando, FL, 32817
mingjie@eecs.ucf.edu

ABSTRACT

Despite many attractive advantages, Null Convention Logic (NCL) remains to be a niche largely due to its high implementation costs. Using emerging spintronic devices, this paper proposes a Domain-Wall-Motion-based NCL circuit design methodology that achieves approximately 30x and 8x improvements in energy efficiency and chip layout area, respectively, over its equivalent CMOS design, while maintaining similar delay performance for a 32-bit full adder. These advantages are made possible mostly by exploiting the domain wall motion physics to natively realize the hysteresis critically needed in NCL. More Interestingly, this design choice achieves ultra-high robustness by allowing spintronic device parameters to vary within a predetermined range while still achieving correct operations.

CCS Concepts

•Hardware → Asynchronous circuits; Reconfigurable logic applications; Spintronics and magnetic technologies;

Keywords

Spintronics and magnetic technologies; NULL Convention Logic; Asynchronous circuit

1 Introduction

Delay-insensitive asynchronous circuit possesses many attractive properties, such as low PVT device susceptibility, high energy efficiency, high robustness, great module reusability due to its clockless nature, and the much-coveted correct-by-construction property, i.e., timing analysis is not required for its correct operation [1]. Among many architectural variations of asynchronous circuits, NULL Convention Logic (NCL) is one of the most promising candidates. In fact, many prior studies, including real chip fabrications, have shown that NCL can be effectively designed and implemented with standard-cell based methodology [9, 7, 10].

GLSVLSI '16, May 18-20, 2016, Boston, MA, USA
© 2016 ACM. ISBN 978-1-4503-4274-2/16/05. . . $15.00
DOI: http://dx.doi.org/10.1145/2902961.2903019

Unfortunately, NCL circuits have some notable shortcomings despite many significant advantages. First, the correct operation of a NCL circuit critically depends on the use of *hysteresis*, which requires the support of complicated control mechanism. Second, its use of dual-rail logic signalling based on 1-hot delay-insensitive code needs two wires per bit in NCL, thus approximately doubling its transistor usage relative to traditional CMOS circuits. Finally, the NCL circuit design is largely incompatible with the existing commercial EDA tools. As a result, fewer people are trained in this style compared to synchronous design.

Clearly, given its high hardware overhead, NCL is justifiably hard to adopt without innovations in circuit design. Fortunately, emerging spintronic device technology may offer at least two precious opportunities to revive the NCL circuit design.

- One essential requirement of NCL's correct operation is to keep delay insensitivity with hysteresis, which is significantly expensive to implement with conventional CMOS circuits. Interestingly, some emerging spintronic-based devices naturally exhibits certain physics property similar to the hysteresis in nature. Therefore, it is quite plausible to devise innovative circuit design to natively exploit these physics behavior without complicated control mechanism.

- Spintronic devices, such as magnetic tunnel junctions (MTJ's), spin-valves, and domain-wall magnets (DWM), use spin transfer torque, instead of charge, as the medium of information processing, therefore offering not only ultra-low critical current (e.g., $\leq 100\ \mu$ A at 65 nm), simple switching scheme, and ultra-fast-speed, but also many fascinating probabilistic-related physical properties. All these can potentially enable new NCL design methodologies in order to circumvent the reliability issues caused by the large device variations widely found in spintronic devices.

In this paper we propose a new asynchronous NCL circuit topology based on magnetic domain wall logic. Our major contributions include:

1. In conventional CMOS-based circuit design, complicated and costly control modules have to be added in order to support the hysteresis critically needed for the correct NCL operations. In this study, we instead exploit the inherent hysteresis switching property possessed by the domain-wall-motion devices. This significantly reduces the circuit design complexity of our spintronic-based NCL circuits.

2. Leveraging emerging device technology for high performance, even for NCL circuit design, is not a new idea. However, most existing studies focus on using spintronic devices as high-performance switching devices, therefore following almost identical circuit design methodologies as with CMOS. We instead deviate from this common approach. As a result, the correct operation of our spintronic-based NCL circuits only requires the device parameters to be in a predetermined range, thus being ultra-tolerant to the high spintronic device variations.

The rest of this paper is organized as follows. First, Section 5 introduces the basic concept and circuit design of NCL. Next, Section 3 briefly describes the basic physics and the operational physics of a DWM device. In particular, we attempts to make a connection between the physics of spintronic devices and the NCL mechanism. In Section 4 and 5, we present the implementation details of a typical $\mathrm{TH}_{m,n}$ gate and a spintronic-based dual-rail NCL circuit, respectively. Subsequently, Section 6 presents the performance comparison results between our spintronic-based dual-rail NCL circuit and its CMOS counterpart for a full adder with variable bit width. Finally, we conclude our study in Section 7.

2 NCL Concept and Circuit Design

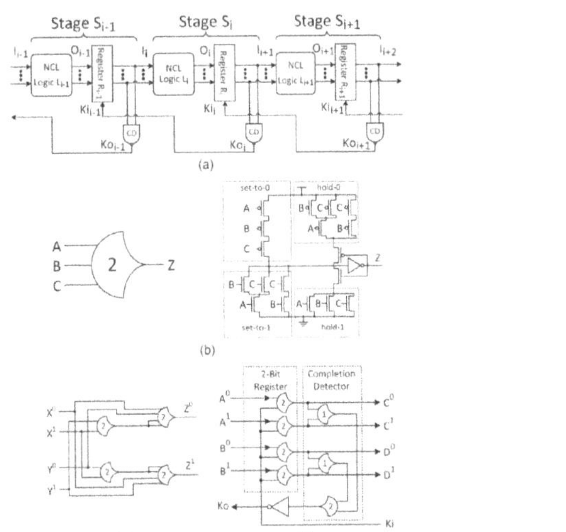

Figure 1: NCL overall scheme: input wavefronts are controlled by local handshaking and completion detection signals. (a) Traditional NCL pipeline. (b) Symbol and structure of threshold gate TH23. (c) Implementation of logic function $Z = X \oplus Y$. (d) Two-bit register and completion detector [2].

NCL circuit typically consists of multiple stages, each of which contains at least two registers, one at the input and one at the output, and can be finely pipelined by inserting additional registers. As shown in Figure. 1(a), two adjacent register stages interact through their request and acknowledge signals, K_i and K_o, respectively. To prevent the current DATA wavefront from overwriting the previous DATA wavefront, these two DATA wavefronts are always separated by a NULL wavefront. The acknowledge signals are combined in the Completion Detection circuitry to produce the request signal(s) to the previous register stage, utilizing either the full-word or bit-wise completion strategy. Specifically, NCL circuit methodology exploits two core ideas, dual-rail signaling and NULL signal propagation, to achieve delay-insensitivity. In NCL, each dual-rail signal, D, transported by two wires, (D_0,D_1), can assume one of three possible values, logic 0, logic 1, NULL state, encoded as (1,0), (0,1), and (0,0), respectively. The unique Null state has special meaning that the value of D is not yet available. Note that D_0 and D_1 are mutually exclusive, such that both rails can never be asserted simultaneously, therefore (1,1) is defined as an illegal state.

NCL commonly uses threshold gates with hysteresis for its basic circuit elements. The primitive type of threshold gate is the $\mathrm{TH}_{m,n}$ gate with n inputs $(1 \leq m \leq n)$, where at least m of n inputs must be asserted before the output will become asserted. The typical gate symbol denoting a TH23 is shown in Figure. 1(b). Threshold gates can be composted to construct NCL combinational logic blocks, NCL registers, and completion detectors. Figure. 1(c) illustrates the implementation of an NCL combinational logic block $Z = X \oplus Y$ using threshold gates. Figure. 1(d) depicts the implementation of a 2-bit NCL register and a 2-bit completion detector using threshold gates. Generally, the implementation of an n-bit NCL register needs $2n$ TH22 gates, and the implementation of an n-bit completion detector requires n 2-input OR (i.e., TH12) gates and an n-input C-element (i.e., THnn). One important result in designing NCL circuits is that a set of only 27 fundamental NCL gates can implement any logic function with four or fewer variables, i.e., logically complete.

3 Spin-Hall-Effect Device Physics

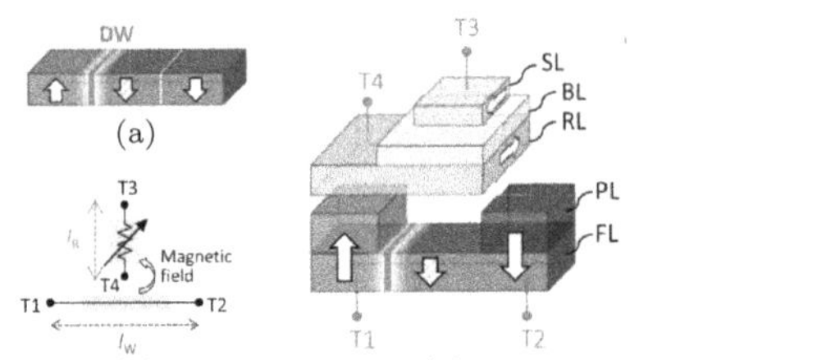

Figure 2: Schematic illustration of domain wall motion device. (a) Simplistic conceptual view. (b) and (c) More realistic four-terminal DWM cell structure. PL: Pinning layer. RL: Reference layer with fixed magnetization. FL: Free layer.

The basic concept of the DW-motion device is that the stored information is associated with the DW position in a magnetic wire. As shown in Figure. 2(a), through controlling the position of the domain wall (DW), a current-induced magnetic domain wall (DW)-motion device with a three- or four-terminal structure can potentially enable interesting memory and logic functions. Both ends of the magnetic wire have their magnetization fixed in the antiparallel direction relative to each other. The bidirectional current applied into the wire drags the DW back and forth, thus switching the stored information. As such, many recent studies have explored to implement novel integrated circuits with DWM devices, although mainly focused on Boolean-based logic circuits and used DWM devices as high-performance logic switches. For example, the DW motion depicted in Figure. 2(a) has been proposed to replace high-speed working memories in integrated circuits such as static random access memories (SRAMs), which are now facing the scaling limit. Furthermore, since the DW-motion devices, like other spintronics devices, require no power supply to retain information and can be integrated in the back-end-of-line process, their implementation into integrated circuits with logic-in-memory architecture and power gating techniques allows drastic reduction of data transfer delay and power consumption originating from charge-discharge in the interconnection and leakage current in standby mode, which are also urgent issues concerning recent electronics development.

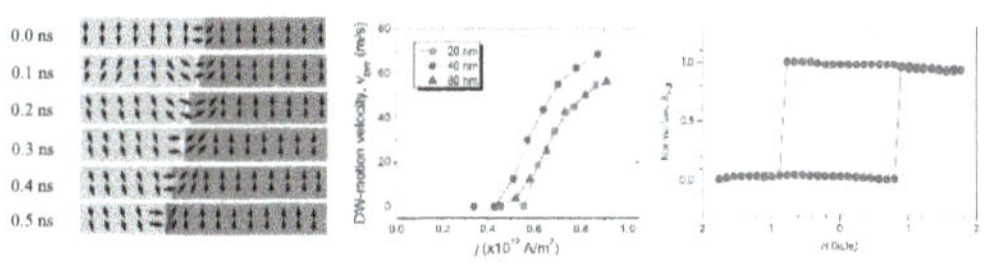

(a) (b) (c)

Figure 3: (a) Simulation of domain wall moving by current injection in terminal T1, the domain wall is moving to right by the spin polarized electrons. (b) Compact model presents good agreement with micromagnetic simulation for DW motion speed V as a function of current density j_p [12]. (c). A non-zero current inject to DW motion and obtains results in a hysteresis in the DW switching characteristics [3, 8].

More practically, as shown in Figure. 2(b), a MTJ device is laid on the top of DW with a fixed polarity magnetic used to read the resistance. The moving of domain wall is effected by magnitude, direction and duration of injection current. To illustrate and validate such behavior, we have conducted a domain wall moving simulation with the standard mumax^3 software. Our obtained results, presented in Figure. 3(a), clearly show the domain wall moving with different velocity by injecting different magnitudes of current (1.5×10^{13}A/m^2) into the terminal T1. This simulation utilizes the device parameters: damping coefficient $\alpha = 0.02$, uniaxial anisotropy constant $Ku = 5.9 \times 10^5$J/m^3, saturation magnetization $\text{Ms} = 6 \times 10^5$A/m, exchange stiffness $\text{A}_{\text{ex}} = 1 \times 10^{11}$, and polarization P = 1 [6]. The terminal T3 is used to read the position of domain wall according to MTJ resistant. The resistant model of MTJ is based on supplied voltage, tunnelling oxide thickness(t_{ox}), and angle of magnetization between free layer and pinned layer. The resistant model of proposed domain wall device is described in [4, 5] with $R = \frac{A}{B \cdot x + C}$, where $A = RA_{AP} \cdot RA_P \cdot RA_{DW}$, $B = (RA_{AP} - RA_P)RA_{DW} \cdot W$, and $C = RA_P \cdot RA_{DW} \cdot W \cdot L + (RA_{AP} \cdot RA_P - 0.5RA_P \cdot RA_{DW} - 0.5RA_{AP} \cdot RA_{DW})W \cdot L_{DW}$. According to these modelling equations, given the length of free layer (100nm), width of free layer W, DW position x (middle point), all MTJ resistances, RA_{AP}, RA_{DW}, and RA_P can be readily computed. Therefore, the output voltage can be computed as a rational function of DW positions ($0 < x < 100$ nm). Finally, Figure. 3(c) exhibits a hysteresis phenomenon found in the DW switching characteristics. The Figure. 2 (c) shows the critical current simulation for DW motion speed V as a function of current density j. The domain wall velocity is equal to 0, when input current density is equal and less than current density j. This critical current can be adjusted either by changing memristor memristances or by changing device width to. In this paper, we employ different combination of input and NULL module memristor to achieve hysteresis of NCL gate.

4 Spin-Based TTL Gate Implementation

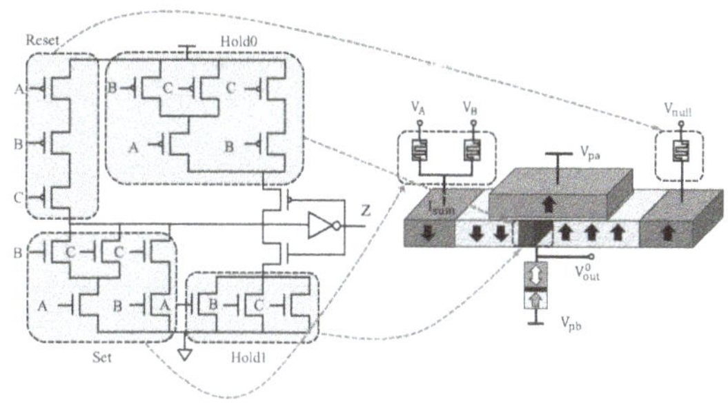

(a) (b)

Figure 4: (a) TH23 static NCL gates. (b) TH23 DWL NCL gate.

A conventional NCL gate typically consists of *four* transistor sub-networks: SET, RESET, HOLD0, and HOLD1, each of which incurs significant hardware usage. Furthermore, conventional NCL gates rely on parasitic capacitors to keep state information and logic inverters to implement feedback mechanisms. Unfortunately, these practices render NCL gates quite vulnerable to leakage, noise, and charge sharing problem. Finally, these feedback inverters can slow down the gates due to the intrinsic switching contention involved. Specifically, as shown in Figure. 4(a), the extra transistors to build $HOLD0$ and $HOLD1$ make NCL gates quite expensive to build. It is obviously to see that large numbers of transistor are used to keep delay-insensitive performance, rather than "doing the real work", in a conventional static NCL gate.

In contrast, our spintronic-based NCL TH gate consumes much less hardware to implement. To compare, in Figure. 4(c), we have drawn a side-by-side circuit diagram of a CMOS-based and a spintronic-based TH23 gate, with their component correspondence in red dashed lines. In our method, domain wall NCL gate employs both memristors, whose conductance can be precisely modulated by a charge or flux through it, and domain wall motion devices to implement. Specifically, the weighted currents can be generated through programming different memristors by constants V_{dd}, $\frac{V_{dd}}{m_{i,j}d}$. The sum of analog current is obtained through connecting in parallel of inputs based on Kirchhoff's Current Law with I-V resistor, which is implemented by a domain wall device. Figure. 4 (a) shows architecture of proposed DWL NCL gate. The inputs binary are represented by $V_1, \cdots V_n$ with V_{dd} is 1 and GND is 0, receptively. The sum of input current is depend on number of inputs is equal to 1. So that, the more number of input is 1, the bigger sum of input current is obtained to inject to domain wall logic device. The hysteresis of NCL logic can be also implemented by domain wall device through critical current and NULL module memristor.

However, transforming the standard Boolean-based NCL circuit into a spintronic-based NCL circuit is not straightforward. On the contrary, different inputs memristances and NULL module memristance have to be carefully computed to ensure the correct NCL operation. Before diving into algorithm details, we first introduce some default definitions and values shown in step $1-8$ in Algorithm 1. The given Boolean NCL netlist G is input to the algorithm. The index i, j indicates different NCL gates and different inputs of an individual NCL gate. Moreover, a given value of V_{dd} is used to generate different weighted current through memristor. T_i and $w_{i,j}$ are written by function of $Thres(G)$ and $Weigh(G)$, which is used to read the logic threshold and weight of individual NCL gate from given Boolean NCL netlist. The calculated memristance of input $m_{i,j}$ and NULL module M_i are the outputs of Algorithm 1, which is constrained in range of m_{min} and m_{max} obtained from memristor device parameters. In our case, this range is between 100Ω to $< 38000\Omega$. Finally, two domain wall device critical current densities, Jc, i^1 and $J_{c,i}^2$, are used to achieve hysteresis of NCL based on the measurements of a DW device [6]. The domain wall device critical current density $J_{c,i}^2 = 6.2 \times 10^{12} A/m^2$ will cause domain wall moving with $20m/s$ velocity. On another side, current density $J_{c,i}^1 = 5.2 \times 10^{12} A/m^2$ will cause domain wall moving with $0m/s$ velocity. The critical current $I_{c,i}^1$ and $I_{c,i}^2$ can be calculated by the injection area and critical current density. In order to explain the algorithm clearly, we consider two Boolean NCL gates TH23W2 and TH44 with function of $f = A+BC$ and $f = ABCD$, respectively. For boolean NCL function $f = A + BC$, three inputs weights are (2,1,1) with threshold is 2. Since the weights of each input are different with each other, therefore, the algorithm from step $19 - 27$ are used. By given those conditions, the three input and NULL module memristance values are calculated for function $f = A + BC$ as follows, the sequence of memristance A, B, C is $m_{1,1}, m_{1,2}, m_{1,3}$. In general, four cases need to be considered. In Case 1: Hysteresis-set 1, the sum of input current needs to be smaller than the threshold, therefore, both $\frac{V_{dd}}{m_{1,2}} - \frac{V_{dd}}{M_1} < I_{c,1}^1$ and $\frac{V_{dd}}{m_{1,3}} - \frac{V_{dd}}{M_1} < I_{c,1}^1$ have to be true. In Case 2: Set 1, the sum of all input currents has to be larger than the threshold value in order to move the domain wall, therefore, both $2 \cdot \frac{V_{dd}}{m_{1,2}} - \frac{V_{dd}}{M_1} > I_{c,1}^2$ and $\frac{V_{dd}}{m_{1,1}} - \frac{V_{dd}}{M_1} > I_{c,1}^2$ have to be true. In Case 3: Hysteresis-set NULL, the sum of input currents needs to be larger than the negative threshold in order to not make domain wall moving back, therefore, both $\frac{V_{dd}}{m_{1,2}} - \frac{V_{dd}}{M_1} > -I_{c,1}^1$ and $\frac{V_{dd}}{m_{1,1}} - \frac{V_{dd}}{M_1} > -I_{c,1}^1$ hold. Finally in Case 4: NULL, the sum of input currents needs to be reset to be zero, thus making the domain wall moving back to initial position, thus $-\frac{V_{dd}}{M_1} < -I_{c,1}^2$ is true.

The possible memristance of 3 different inputs and Null module are given by equation above. with V_{dd} is equal to $0.3V$ The memristance of input A is $m_{i,A} = 608\Omega$, memristance of input B is $m_{i,B} = 1209$, memristance of input C is $m_{1,C} = 1209\Omega$, memristance of Null module is $M_i = 1209\Omega$, receptively. For the TH44 gate $f = ABCD$, the method is similar with above, the memristance of input A is $m_{i,A} = 2418\Omega$, memristance of input B is $m_{i,B} = 2418\Omega$, memristance of input C is $m_{i,C} = 2418\Omega$, memristance of input D is $m_{i,D} = 2418\Omega$, memristance of Null module is $M_i = 1209\Omega$.

The algorithm is applying to 27 typical TH gate truth tables, in order to verify results. This algorithm shows that the TH gate can be classified to 5 different groups according to its threshold. The parameter of domain wall device is based on paper [6]. According to the configuration of this DW device, current density $6.2 \times 10^{12} A/m^2$ will cause domain wall moving with $20m/s$ velocity, on the contract, current density $5.2 \times 10^{12} A/m^2$ will cause domain wall moving with $0m/s$ velocity. The results of mapping Algorithm1 is shown in Figure. 1. There are 3 special NCL function, which are not threshold gates. In order to use our method, we decompose these gates to sub NCL gate.

Algorithm 1: Calculating Stochastic weight and threshold algorithm

Input : G-Boolean NCL netlist
Output: N-DWL NCL netlist

1 $V_{dd} \leftarrow 0.3V$
2 $S \leftarrow 40nm^2$ // injection area of domain wall
3 $T_i \leftarrow \text{Thres(G)}$ // read threshold of each node
4 $w_{i,j} \leftarrow \text{Weigh(G)}$ // read weight of each node
5 $m_{min} \leftarrow 100\Omega$ // set minimal memristance
6 $m_{max} \leftarrow 38000\Omega$ // set minimal memristance
7 $Ic_i^1 \leftarrow S \cdot 5.2 \times 10^{12} A/m^2$ // set critical current density for DW velocity=0
8 $Ic_i^2 \leftarrow S \cdot 6.2 \times 10^{12} A/m^2$ // set critical current density for DW velocity=20m/s
9 **for** $i = 1 : N$ **do**
10 **if** $w_{i,j} = w_{i,1}, \cdots, = w_{i,n_i}$ **then**
11 $\text{minimize}(\mathrm{m_{i,j=1:n}})$ // find the minimal memristance of input j=1:n
12 subject to :
13 $T_i \cdot \frac{V_{dd}}{m_{i,j}} - \frac{V_{dd}}{M_i} > Ic_i^2$ // set 1
14 $(T_i - w_{i,j}) \cdot \frac{V_{dd}}{m_{i,j}} - \frac{V_{dd}}{M_i} < Ic_i^1$ // hysteresis
15 $-\frac{V_{dd}}{M_i} < -Ic_i^2$ // null
16 $\frac{V_{dd}}{m_{i,j}} - \frac{V_{dd}}{M_i} > -Ic_i^1$ // hysteresis
17 $m_{min} < m_{i,j}, M_i < m_{max}$ // device constraint
18 **else**
19 $w_{min} \leftarrow findmin(w_{i,j})$ // find the minimal boolean weight of input j=1:n
20 $m_{i,j=1:n} \leftarrow m_{w_{min}} \cdot \frac{w_{i,j}}{w_{min}}$ // calculate memristance of each input
21 $\text{minimize}(\mathrm{m_{w_{min}}})$ // find the minimal memristance of input j=1:n
22 subject to :
23 $T_i \cdot \frac{V_{dd}}{m_{w_{min}}} - \frac{V_{dd}}{M_i} > Ic_i^2$ // set 1
24 $(T_i - w_{min}) \cdot \frac{V_{dd}}{m_{w_{min}}} - \frac{V_{dd}}{M_i} < Ic_i^1$ // hysteresis
25 $-\frac{V_{dd}}{M_i} < -Ic_i^2$ // null
26 $\frac{V_{dd}}{m_{w_{min}}} - \frac{V_{dd}}{M_i} > -Ic_i^1$ // hysteresis
27 $m_{min} < m_{i,j}, M_i < m_{max}$ // device constraint

NCL gate	Boolean function	Weight:Threshold	Memristance Range(Ω)
TH12	A+B	(1,1:1)	$m_{i,A}, m_{i,B} \in [100, M_i/2]; M_i \in [100, 1209]$
TH13	A+B+C	(1,1,1:1)	$m_{i,A}, m_{i,B}, m_{i,C} \in [100, M_i/2]; M_i \in [100, 1209]$
TH14	A+B+C+D	(1,1,1:1)	$m_{i,A}, m_{i,B}, m_{i,C}, m_{i,D} \in [100, M_i/2]; M_i \in [100, 1209]$
TH22	AB	(1,1:2)	$m_{i,A}, m_{i,B}, M_i \in [100, 1209]$
TH23	AB+AC+BC	(1,1,1:2)	$m_{i,A}, m_{i,B}, m_{i,C}, M_i \in [100, 1209]$
TH23W2	A+BC	(2,1,1:2)	$m_{i,A} \in [100, M_i/2]; m_{i,B}, m_{i,C}, M_i \in [100, 1209]$
TH24	AB+AC+AD+BC+BD+CD	(1,1,1,1:2)	$m_{i,A}, m_{i,B}, m_{i,C}, m_{i,D}, M_i \in [100, 1209]$
TH24W2	A+BC+BD+CD	(2,1,1,1:2)	$m_{i,A} \in [100, M_i/2]; m_{i,B}, m_{i,C}, m_{i,D}, M_i \in [100, 1209]$
TH24W22	A+B+CD	(2,2,1,1:2)	$m_{i,A}, m_{i,B} \in [100, M_i/2]; m_{i,C}, m_{i,D}, M_i \in [100, 1209]$
TH33	ABC	(1,1,1:3)	$m_{i,A}, m_{i,B}, m_{i,C} \in [100, (2/3) \cdot M_i]; M_i \in [100, 1209]$
TH33W2	AB+AC	(2,1,1:3)	$m_{i,A} \in [100, (3/4) \cdot M_i]; m_{i,B}, m_{i,C} \in [100, (3/2) \cdot M_i]; M_i \in [100, 1209]$
TH34	ABC+ABD+ACD+BCD	(1,1,1,1:3)	$m_{i,A}, m_{i,B}, m_{i,C}, m_{i,D} \in [100, (3/2) \cdot M_i]; M_i \in [100, 1209]$
TH34W2	AB+AC+AD+BCD	(2,1,1,1:3)	$m_{i,A} \in [100, (3/4) \cdot M_i]; m_{i,B}, m_{i,C}, m_{i,D} \in [100, (3/2) \cdot M_i]; M_i \in [100, 1209]$
TH34W3	A+BCD	(3,1,1,1:3)	$m_{i,A} \in [100, M_i/2]; m_{i,B}, m_{i,C}, m_{i,D} \in [100, (3/2) \cdot M_i]; M_i \in [100, 1209]$
TH34W22	AB+AC+AD+BC+BD	(2,2,1,1:3)	$m_{i,A}, m_{i,B} \in [100, (2/3) \cdot M_i]; m_{i,C}, m_{i,D} \in [100, (3/2) \cdot M_i]; M_i \in [100, 1209]$
TH34W32	A+BC+BD	(3,2,1,1:3)	$m_{i,A} \in [100, M_i/2]; m_{i,B} \in [100, (2/3) \cdot M_i]$ $m_{i,C}, m_{i,D} \in [100, (3/2) \cdot M_i]; M_i \in [100, 1209]$
TH44	ABCD	(1,1,1,1:4)	$m_{i,A}, m_{i,B}, m_{i,C}, m_{i,D} =\in [100, 2 \cdot M_i]; M_i \in [100, 1209]$
TH44W2	ABC+ABD+ACD	(2,1,1,1:4)	$m_{i,A}, M_i \in [100, 1209]; m_{i,B}, m_{i,C}, m_{i,D} \in [100, 2 \cdot M_i]$
TH44W3	AB+AC+AD	(3,1,1,1,4)	$m_{i,A} \in [100, (2/3) \cdot M_i]; m_{i,B}, m_{i,C}, m_{i,D} \in [100, 2 \cdot M_i]; M_i \in [100, 1209]$
TH44W22	AB+ACD+BCD	(2,2,1,1:4)	$m_{i,A}, m_{i,B}, M_i \in [100, 1209]; m_{i,C}, m_{i,D} \in [100, 2 \cdot M_i]$
TH44W322	AB+AC+AD+BC	(3,2,2,1:4)	$m_{i,A} \in [100, (2/3) \cdot M_i]; m_{i,B}, m_{i,C}, M_i \in [100, 1209]; m_{i,D} \in [100, 2 \cdot M_i]$
TH54W22	ABC+ABD	(2,2,1,1:5)	$m_{i,A}, m_{i,B} \in [100, (5/4) \cdot M_i]; m_{i,C}, m_{i,D} \in [100, (5/2) \cdot M_i]; M_i \in [100, 1209]$
TH54W32	AB+ACD	(3,2,1,1:5)	$m_{i,A} \in [100, (5/4) \cdot M_i], m_{i,B} \in [100, (5/4) \cdot M_i]$ $m_{i,C}, m_{i,D} \in [100, (5/2) \cdot M_i]; M_i \in [100, 1209]$
TH54W322	AB+AC+BCD	(3,2,2,1:5)	$m_{i,A} \in [100, (5/6) \cdot M_i]; m_{i,B}, m_{i,C} \in [100, (5/4) \cdot M_i]$ $m_{i,D} \in [100, (5/2)\text{cdot} M_i]; M_i \in [100, 1209]$

Table 1: Mapping results of proposed Algorithm1 for 27 foundational NCL functions.

Symbol	Description	Value
α	damping coefficient	0.02
Ku	uniaxial anisotropy constant	$0.59 \times 10^6 \mathrm{J/m^3}$
Xi	Non-adiabaticity of spin-transfer -torque anisotropy constant	0.2
Ms	saturation magnetization	$6 \times 10^5 \mathrm{A/m}$
P	polarization	0.6
A_{ex}	exchanges stiffness	$1.1 \times 10^{11} \mathrm{J/m}$

Table 2: Device simulation used in simulation of TH44 gate.

To validate our NCL scheme, we have simulated our proposed DWL architecture for a single TH44 gate with the software mumax^3 with its parameters determined by Algorithm 1 and shown in Figure. 2. When the sum of input current which is less or equal to critical current may not cause any movement of domain. At the time of 4 inputs are high, the sum of current is larger than critical current and move domain move to right terminal. Therefore, the different combinations of inputs can make domain wall moving or stepping. The simulation of TH44 gate is shown

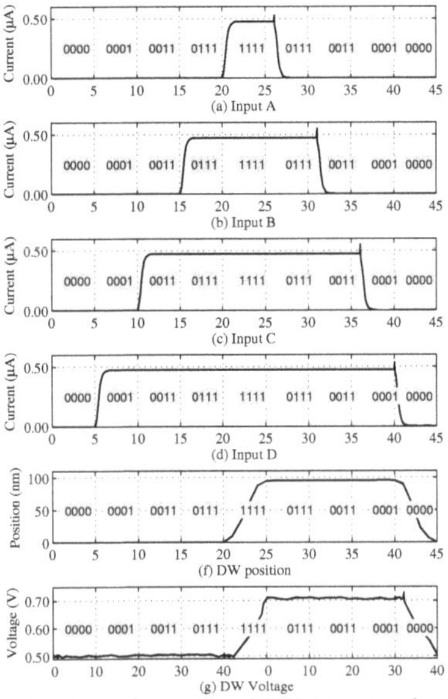

Figure 5: Simulation of proposed TH44 gate through domain wall logic device.

in Figure. 5. The number of inputs is increasing sequentially to test hysteresis. Before the four inputs are all ones, the different combinations of input are shown in Figure. 5, $A = 0, B = 0, C = 0, D = 0$, $A = 0, B = 0, C = 0, D = 1$, $A = 0, B = 0, C = 1, D = 1$, , $A = 0, B = 1, C = 1, D = 1$. At those cases, domain wall is stepped since the sum of input current and NULL module current are not larger than critical current. While the four inputs are all active, the sum of input current and NULL module current is larger than critical current and making domain wall moving. After the domain wall is moving to specific position at time duration of all input currents are ones, the number of inputs current is decreasing. At those cases, the domain wall is not moving back to initial position, since inverse current is not larger than resetting critical current, domain wall is still stepped at its current position. At the time of all inputs are zeros, the sum of input currents and Null module current is larger than resetting critical current, and pushing domain wall back to its original position. The simulation is shown in Figure. 5. From the simulation, hysteresis of NCL logic is implemented through domain wall hysteresis by using different memristance.

5 Spin-Based Dual-Rail NCL Circuits

Figure. 6(1.a) illustrates our architecture of a DWL-based dual-rail NCL. The two adjacent domain wall devices with same resistance are connected with a shared terminal injected by a NULL module current. The two other terminals are injected by different current sums of inputs combinations. Usually, one side is injected by current sum of D^0, another side is injected by current sum of D^1. The resistance of vertical write-current path for left R_l and R_r right side domain wall are same and given by the device measurements. To clearly explain its operation, we also depicted its equivalent analog circuit model as shown in Figure. 6 (1.b), (1.c), (1.d). In Figure. 6(1.b), the NULL case happens with two input combinations: the inputs are all zero, $V^0_{sum} = 0$ and $V^1_{sum} = 0$, V_{null} is larger, thus, the two currents with opposite direction are created. If we set current direction from NULL to input terminal in positive direction, the combinations of sum of input currents and the NULL

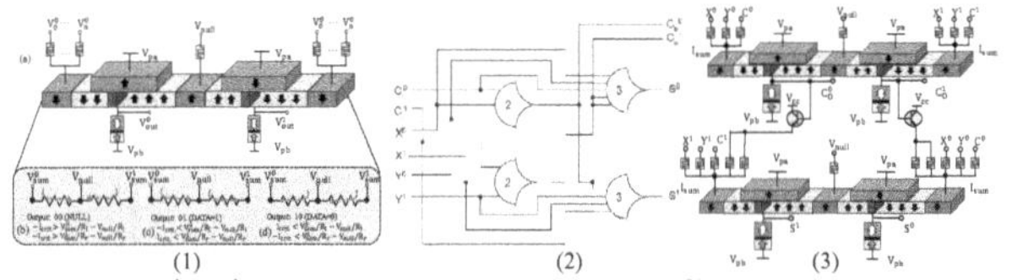

Figure 6: (1.a) DWL-based dual-rail NCL implementation, the two dual rail bits can be implemented through two domain wall device which is separated by a shared terminal. (1.b) The equivalence analog circuit of proposed DWL duail rail architecture in NULL case. (1.c) The equivalence analog circuit of proposed DWL duail rail architecture in DATA 1 case. (1.d) The equivalence analog circuit of proposed DWL duail rail architecture in DATA0 case. (2) CMOS duail rail NCL architecture of one bit full adder. (3) DWL duail rail NCL architecture of one bit full adder, the NPN amplifier is used to increase output current of DW device.

module current will be smaller than the negative critical current, therefore, the domain wall will move back to its initial positions. In Figure. 6(1.c), the input vector $V^0_0 \cdots V^0_n$ has smaller voltages than the NULL module supplied voltage V_{null}, therefore, the domain wall device for input $V_{sum}0$ is not moving. On the other side, the input vector $V^1_0 \cdot V^1_n$ has higher voltages than the NULL module supplied voltage V_{null}, therefore, the domain wall device for input $V_{sum}1$ will move. Finally in Figure. 6(1.d), the input vector $V^0_0 \cdots V^0_n$ has a higher voltage than the NULL module supplied voltage V_{null}, therefore, the domain wall device for input $V_{sum}0$ will move. On the other side, the input vector $V^1_0 \cdots V^1_n$ has a smaller voltage than the NULL module supplied voltage V_{null}, therefore, the domain wall device for input $V_{sum}1$ will not move.

To further exam our proposed DWL-based dual-rail logic, one-bit NCL full adder is implemented. In Figure. 6 (2), this one-bit full adder employs double TH23 and TH34W2 gate to implement DATA0 and DATA1. The schematic of one bit full adder is shown in Figure. 6 (2), where X and Y are input addends and C is carry input. The optimized circuit is obtained through TCR method 2 [11], and the carry out is given by $C^0_o = X^0Y^0 + C^0X^0 + C^0Y^0$, $C^1_o = X^1Y^1 + C^1X^1 + C^1Y^1$, $S^0 = X^0C^0_1 + C^1_oY^0 + C^1_oC^0 + X^0Y^0C^0$, and $S^1 = X^1C^0_0 + C^0_oY^1 + C^0_oC^1 + X^1Y^1C^1$. Therefore, the one bit full adder can be implemented through four TH NCL gates, TH34W2 and TH23 gates. Although, the paper [11] try to reduce transistor size by TCR optimization, the area and power consumption are still significant. In contrast, Figure. 6(3) shows our proposed DWL-based NCL implementation. The two TH23 NCL gates are implemented by two domain wall devices connected through a shared terminal and similarly to TH34W2 gate. The operation of DWL for dual rail architecture is as same as previous proposed single static DWL NCL gate.

6 Performance Comparison and Analysis

In this section, we compare the performance between the conventional and our proposed DWL NCL circuit for 1-bit, 4-bit, 8-bit, 16-bit, 32-bit full adders. The conventional NCL full adder follows the previous architecture presented. The circuit is implemented and simulated using IBM SOI1250 45nm CMOS process standard cell library. The simulation is using nominal power supply voltage of 0.92V , temperature 27C, and capacitive load of 10fF. The proposed DWL is using the parameter in Figure. 2. In Figure. 7(a), we compare their delay performance. Our proposed DWL-based

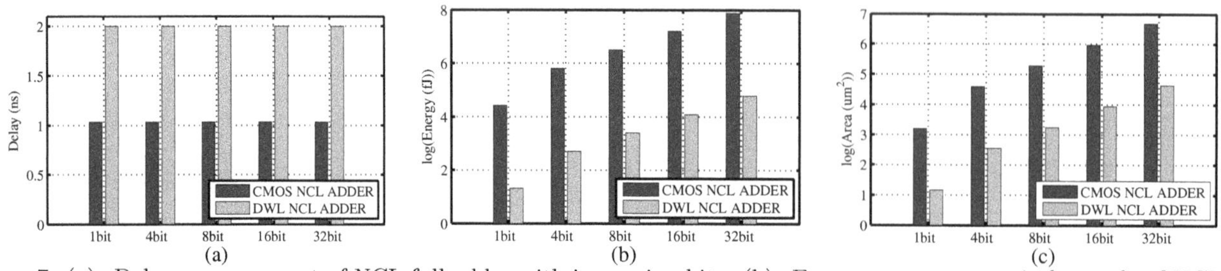

Figure 7: (a). Delay measurement of NCL full adder with increasing bits. (b). Energy measurement in log scale of NCL full adder with increasing bits.(c). Area measurement in log scale of NCL full adder with increasing bits.

adder has a slightly higher delay than its CMOS counterpart, mainly because the velocity of its DW moving is only around 20m/s. This limitation can be mitigated by adjusting device thresholds to create larger writing current. In our case, we use only $Jc_i^2 = 6.2 \times 10^{12}\mathrm{A/m^2}$ in order to achieve higher energy efficiency. Since the full adder is fully pipelined, its delay does not increase with bit width. In Figure. 7(b), we also compared the energy consumption of these two different implementations. Our proposed NCL circuit is running under very low operation current, only few μW for memristors, 0.15μW for sensing unit and a few μW fro DW device. The Figure. 7(b) shows its power saving in log scale. On average, our proposed DWL full adder can achieve about 20 times energy saving for a 32bit full adder. Finally in Figure. 7(c), we compare the chip layout area between the CMOS-based NCL and DWL-based NCL full adders. By using 3D structure for our proposed dual-rail DWL-based NCL full adder, the area of our proposed full adder is only about 1/8 of the size of CMOS version.

7 Conclusion

Implemented with the CMOS device technology, many innovative logic circuit design methodologies, such as threshold logic and NCL, prove to be difficult for wide adoption due to their high costs. Fortunately, emerging spintronic devices present ample opportunities to innovate in logic circuit design. This work a first step towards this direction. One valuable lessor we learned from this study is that the key to the success in using emerging devices for logic circuits is how to natively exploit the inherent physical property of these emerging devices, instead merely treating them simply as some "super" switches to replace CMOS transistors.

8 References

[1] P. A. Beerel, R. O. Ozdag, and M. Ferretti. *A Designer's Guide to Asynchronous VLSI*. Cambridge University Press, New York, NY, USA, 1st edition, 2010.

[2] M.-C. Chang, M.-H. Hsieh, and P.-H. Yang. Low-power asynchronous ncl pipelines with fine-grain power gating and early sleep. *Circuits and Systems II: Express Briefs, IEEE Transactions on*, 61(12):957–961, Dec 2014.

[3] D. Fan, M. Sharad, A. Sengupta, and K. Roy. Hierarchical temporal memory based on spin-neurons and resistive memory for energy-efficient brain-inspired computing. *arXiv preprint arXiv:1402.2902*, 2014.

[4] D. Fan, Y. Shim, A. Raghunathan, and K. Roy. STT-SNN: A spin-transfer-torque based soft-limiting non-linear neuron for low-power artificial neural networks. *CoRR*, abs/1412.8648, 2014.

[5] X. Fong, S. Gupta, N. Mojumder, S. Choday, C. Augustine, and K. Roy. Knack: A hybrid spin-charge mixed-mode simulator for evaluating different genres of spin-transfer torque mram bit-cells. In *Simulation of Semiconductor Processes and Devices (SISPAD), 2011 International Conference on*, pages 51–54, Sept 2011.

[6] S. Fukami, M. Yamanouchi, K.-J. Kim, T. Suzuki, N. Sakimura, D. Chiba, S. Ikeda, T. Sugibayashi, N. Kasai, T. Ono, and H. Ohno. 20-nm magnetic domain wall motion memory with ultralow-power operation. In *Electron Devices Meeting (IEDM), 2013 IEEE International*, pages 3.5.1–3.5.4, Dec 2013.

[7] C. Jeong and S. Nowick. Optimal technology mapping and cell merger for asynchronous threshold networks. In *Asynchronous Circuits and Systems, 2006. 12th IEEE International Symposium on*, pages 10 pp.–137, March 2006.

[8] T. Koyama, K. Ueda, K.-J. Kim, Y. Yoshimura, D. Chiba, K. Yamada, J.-P. Jamet, A. Mougin, A. Thiaville, S. Mizukami, et al. Current-induced magnetic domain wall motion below intrinsic threshold triggered by walker breakdown. *Nature nanotechnology*, 7(10):635–639, 2012.

[9] M. Ligthart, K. Fant, R. Smith, A. Taubin, and A. Kondratyev. Asynchronous design using commercial hdl synthesis tools. In *Proceedings of the 6th International Symposium on Advanced Research in Asynchronous Circuits and Systems*, ASYNC '00, pages 114–, Washington, DC, USA, 2000. IEEE Computer Society.

[10] F. Parsan, W. Al-Assadi, and S. Smith. Gate mapping automation for asynchronous null convention logic circuits. *Very Large Scale Integration (VLSI) Systems, IEEE Transactions on*, 22(1):99–112, Jan 2014.

[11] S. Smith, R. DeMara, J. Yuan, D. Ferguson, and D. Lamb. Optimization of {NULL} convention self-timed circuits. *Integration, the {VLSI} Journal*, 37(3):135 – 165, 2004.

[12] Y. Zhang, W. S. Zhao, D. Ravelosona, J.-O. Klein, J. V. Kim, and C. Chappert. Perpendicular-magnetic-anisotropy cofeb racetrack memory. *Journal of Applied Physics*, 111(9):–, 2012.

Inter-Tier Crosstalk Noise on Power Delivery Networks for 3-D ICs with Inductively-Coupled Interconnects

Ioannis A. Papistas and Vasilis F. Pavlidis
Advanced Processor Technologies Group
School of Computer Science, The University of Manchester
{papistai, pavlidis}@cs.man.ac.uk

ABSTRACT

Inductive links have been proposed as an inter-tier interconnect solution for three-dimensional (3-D) integrated systems. Combined with signal multiplexing, inductive links achieve high communication bandwidth comparable to that of through silicon vias. However, being a wireless medium, electromagnetic coupling between the inductive link and near-by on-chip interconnects can cause voltage fluctuations affecting interconnect performance. Although the interference of interconnects on the operation of inductive links has been investigated, the inverse problem has yet to be explored. Consequently, this paper performs an investigation on the effect of electromagnetic coupling on different topologies of power delivery networks (PDNs) in the vicinity of on-chip inductors. Results indicate that the interdigitated PDN topology suffers from the induced noise due to the inductive links of the neighbouring tiers exhibiting a minimum aggregate noise of 131.3 mV. Alternatively, the paired topologies exhibit a superior noise behaviour, achieving a 39.4% and 35.4% decrease in noise level for paired type I and paired type II topologies, respectively, compared to the interdigitated topology.

Keywords

Inductive Links; Crosstalk Noise; Power Delivery Networks; Wireless 3-D Systems

1. INTRODUCTION

Heterogeneous three-dimensional integration is an emerging technology that provides a platform for multifunctional, high performance, and low power electronics [1], by vertically stacking ICs of disparate technologies. Through silicon vias (TSVs) and inductive links provide low latency and low power interconnections [2] for inter-tier communication, exhibiting comparable performance, when signal multiplexing is employed for inductive links [3].

This work was supported in part by EPSRC UK under Grant EP/M009238/1 and scholarships from the School of Computer Science and the Doctoral Training Centre at the University of Manchester.

GLSVLSI '16, May 18-20, 2016, Boston, MA, USA

DOI: http://dx.doi.org/10.1145/2902961.2903020

TSVs, however, can be an expensive means due to manufacturing complexity and possibly low yield [4]. Alternatively, inductive links comply with standard (2-D) CMOS processes. Furthermore, inductive links provide unique advantages to heterogeneous integration, such as die detachability [5], and although the transceiver can be designed with different nominal voltage supplies there is no need for level shifters [6].

High performance inductive links have been developed recently [7, 8]. In addition to design methods, the crosstalk between inductive links [5, 9] and the interference of interconnects on inductive links have both been explored [10]. Nevertheless, the effect of inductive links on global interconnects has yet to be investigated. Due to the magnetic flux, on-chip wireless communication leads to parasitic coupling with nearby conductors, such as power delivery interconnects, which operate as accidental antennas [11]. Consequently, undesirable voltage fluctuations are induced on the power delivery network, that can limit the performance of the system and increase power consumption.

This work focuses on the noise caused by electromagnetic coupling between the inductive link interface and different topologies of power delivery networks (PDN). This crosstalk noise is added to the other components of noise experienced by a power delivery network topology. Power/ground (P/G) wires suffer from static IR-drop noise due to the wire resistance and transient, high frequency voltage drop, $L\frac{di}{d}$ due to device switching [12]. In 3-D systems with inductive links, voltage fluctuations are induced on the P/G wires adjacent to the inductive link array, deteriorating system robustness.

Standard design methodologies provision for the static and dynamic noise on PDNs. However, traditional PDN design can not cope with the additional noise, originating from the on-chip inductors in contactless 3-D systems. Consequently, the combined effect of noise onto PDNs is addressed in this paper, including the induced noise by multiple inductors and the resistive IR-drop noise[1]. Interconnect structures are simulated, considering the spatial alignment of power and ground loops to the inductive link and the area of the PDN topology that couples with the inductor.

An expression to determine the impact of an inductive link array onto a P/G grid is also provided. Analysis indicates that crosstalk coupling between inductors and P/G wires can lead to harmful levels of power supply noise. The susceptibility of a PDN to this type of noise is shown to

[1]The spatial behaviour of power supply noise is considered in this work, while the temporal component is left as future work and is therefore beyond the scope of this paper.

strongly depend on the inductance and placement of the P/G wires with respect to the inductive links. Considering these important dependencies, measures to diminish the induced noise are proposed.

The remainder of this paper is organised as follows. In Section 2, physical models are utilised to describe crosstalk noise between an inductive link and various topologies of power delivery networks. Moreover, the behaviour of the induced noise is presented for each topology, as a function of the area and spatial position of the PDN with respect to the inductive link. A practical scenario is investigated in Section 3 where an array of inductive links couples with a portion of the power network and the location of P/G wires is adapted to satisfy both the induced noise and IR-drop constraints. Some conclusions are drawn in the last section.

2. INDUCTIVE LINK - PDN CROSSTALK ANALYSIS

The coupling between an inductive link and different PDN topologies is presented in this section. This coupling is analysed as a function of the area of a PDN loop and as a function of the spatial position with respect to the inductive link in subsections 2.1 and 2.2, respectively. The combined effect of these (physical) parameters is investigated in Section 2.3.

The investigated PDN topologies are depicted in Fig. 1. The chosen PDN topologies include the interdigitated P/G, shown in Fig. 1(a), and paired P/G type I and II illustrated in Figs. 1(b) and 1(c), respectively [12]. The power and ground wires are denoted with grey and white colours, respectively. Those topologies are chosen for being commonly used, while also presenting different physical traits. An analysis of the non-interdigitated topology is omitted, as it can be devised from the interdigitated topology.

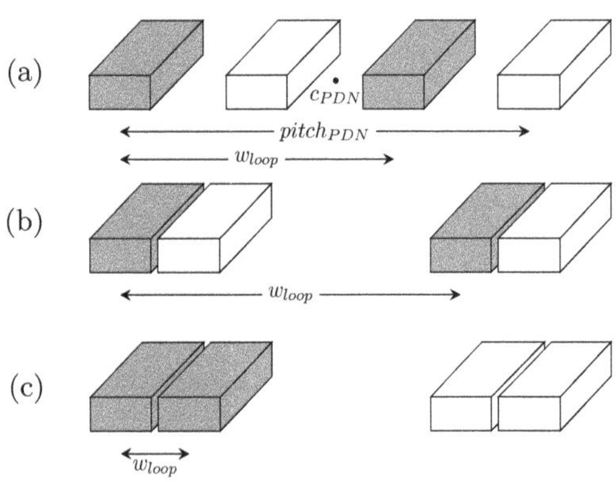

Figure 1: PDN topologies, where (a) is an interdigitated P/G-P/G topology, (b) is a paired type I P/G-P/G topology, and (c) is a type II P/P-G/G topology.

The centre and pitch of an elemental PDN segment, c_{PDN} and $pitch_{PDN}$, respectively, are depicted in Fig. 1. As the width of the loop, w_l , between the power or ground wires is different for each topology, $pitch_{PDN}$ is used for all topologies to provide a fair comparison. The centre of the PDN segment, c_{PDN} is used to define the relative spatial position of the PDN with respect to the inductive link.

The simulated structure is based on a flip-chip and face-to-back 3-D integration approach consisting of an inductive link and one interconnection loop. The cross-section of the structure is depicted in Fig. 2(a), showing the communication distance X between the inductors of the link. The top view of this structure is seen in Fig. 2(b). Distance δ denotes the spatial separation between the geometric centre of the inductor, c and the geometric centre of the interconnect loop, c_{PDN}.

Each closed path formed within the PDN is susceptible to eddy currents and, consequently, voltage fluctuations induced by the inductor. Closed paths are formed between two or more power or ground wires. The amplitude of the induced voltage on the PDN depends on the geometric and electrical characteristics of the closed path that alter the coupling between the inductor and the PDN loop. Furthermore, the induced voltage depends upon the magnetic flux density, that changes according to the spatial position of the PDN with respect to the inductor. As shown in Section 2.2 this spatial dependency is the primary factor that contributes to the induced noise for all of the investigated topologies.

Voltage fluctuations $V_{n\ ise,P}$ induced by the inductor to the power loop are extracted by the S-parameters of the simulated structure. As the transmission coefficient S_{ij} describes the transmitted voltage ratio between the respective structures [13], $V_{n\ ise,P}$ is given by

$$V_{n\ ise,P} = (S_{31} + S_{21}S_{32})V_{dd}, \tag{1}$$

where S_{31} is the transmission coefficient from the transmitter inductor to the PDN wire. S_{21} describes the transmission coefficient from the transmitter inductor to the receiver inductor and S_{32} the transmission coefficient from the receiver inductor to the PDN wire, modelling the impact of both inductors. Note that both inductors induce some voltage on the power wire, yet the level of noise from the receiver is significantly lower. A similar analysis also applies to ground wires. The accumulated noise induced by the inductive link on the PDN is given by

$$V_{n\ ise,} \quad = V_{n\ ise,P} + V_{n\ ise,G}, \tag{2}$$

where $V_{n\ ise,P}$ is the noise induced on power loops and $V_{n\ ise,G}$ is the noise induced on ground loops, respectively.

To quantify this noise, the structure in Fig. 2 is simulated for a 65 nm technology [14]. A width and spacing of 0.45 μm are used for the windings of the inductive link, while a width of 4.5 μm is used for the power loop. The structure is assumed to occupy the three topmost interconnect layers, with a thickness of 1.2 μm each and the inductor is laid out on the uppermost metal layer. The inductive link model is based on [6], where an inductor with an outer diameter of $d \quad = 79\ \mu m$ and $n = 8$ turns is implemented. Due to the symmetry of the structure, each inductor can transmit or receive data, and therefore, there is no need to add another wire beneath the inductor in the lower tier (see Fig. 2(a)). With this approach the electromagnetic simulation is simplified, without sacrificing accuracy.

2.1 Effect of the Pitch of the PDN Topology on the Induced Noise

The results concerning the pitch of the PDN topology and the respective accumulated induced noise are presented in this subsection. To investigate the effect of the PDN pitch, the PDN loop and the inductive link are considered centred, $\delta \ = 0\ \mu m$, while the pitch of the PDN is swept across a range of typical values, $pitch_{PDN} = [45\ \mu m, 105\ \mu m]$ [12].

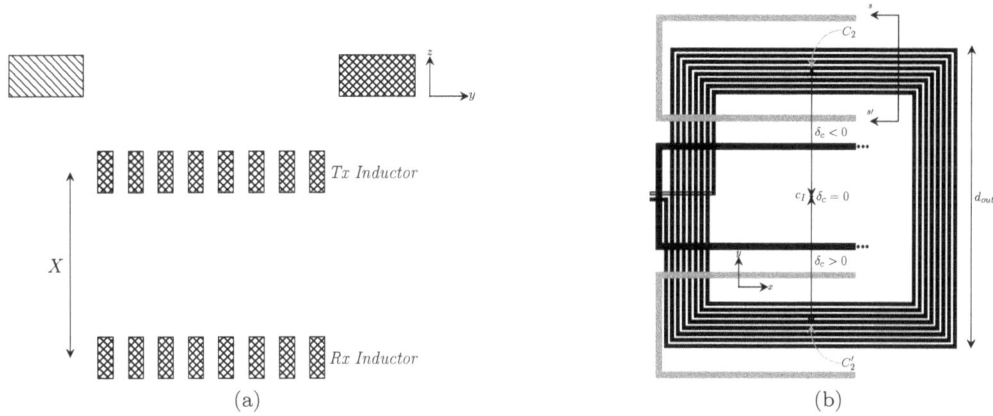

Figure 2: Inductive link with adjacent P/G loop, (a) cross-section of the structure along $s - s\prime$ in Fig 2(b) and (b) top view of the structure with the loop placed in different locations.

The susceptibility of the PDN topologies to the induced noise with respect to the PDN pitch is illustrated in Fig. 3. Solid lines denote the noise induced on the interdigitated PDN topology, while dotted and dashdotted lines indicate the noise on the paired type I and type II topologies, respectively. As the PDN is symmetric and centred to the inductive link, noise induced on the power loop can be considered equal to the noise induced on the ground loop with negligible error.

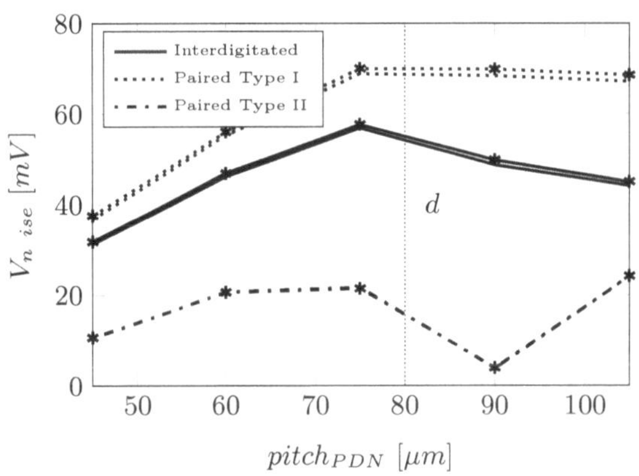

Figure 3: Induced noise by the inductive link depending on the pitch $pitch_{PDN}$ of the PDN topology. Lines marked with asterisks indicate ground loops, whereas unmarked lines label the power loops.

For pitches $pitch_{PDN} \leq d$, the induced noise worsens with increasing pitch for all three topologies. This outcome can be attributed to two factors. An increasing PDN pitch leads to higher inductance for the PDN loop and consequently increased coupling. Moreover, by increasing the PDN pitch, the conductors of the PDN shift closer to the windings of the inductor. The shortened horizontal distance between the PDN segments and the inductor windings leads to increased coupling, resulting in higher levels of induced noise. Nevertheless, the behaviour is different for $pitch_{PDN} > d$. For the interdigitated and paired type I topologies, increasing the pitch of the PDN more than the outer diameter of the inductor leads to a slight decrease in the induced noise, since the PDN conductors are shifted away from the inductor windings. Between these two topologies, the interdigitated topology exhibits a larger drop in the induced noise, as the curve in Fig. 3 suggests, implying a lower susceptibility to induced noise.

Alternatively, the paired type II topology exhibits a significant decrease in induced noise, before increasing again for larger pitches. For $pitch_{PDN} = 90\ \mu m$, the topology resembles the structure shown in Fig. 2, with C_2 the geometric centre of the power loop and C_2' the geometric centre of the ground loop, respectively. This placement results in a minimum induced noise, due to the opposite polarity of the accrued magnetic flux that couples with the conductors of the PDN loops. The magnetic flux coupled with the conductor of the wire loop lying on the inner side of the inductor ($y_{C_2'} - w_l\ \ /2$) presents an opposite polarity compared to the conductor lying on the outer side of the inductor ($y_{C_2'} + w_l\ \ /2$). Thus, induced currents flow in opposite directions, effectively minimising the induced noise. Nevertheless, increasing the pitch further, the power and ground loops lie completely outside the inductor and the currents induced by the magnetic flux present the same polarity, leading to higher levels of noise. Beyond this point nevertheless, the noise amplitude steadily decreases, due to the reduced magnetic flux for those distances.

2.2 Effect of Spatial Position of the PDN Topology on the Induced Noise

In this subsection, the induced noise due to the spatial position of the PDN with respect to the inductive link is presented. To this end, the pitch of the PDN is kept constant to $pitch_{PDN} = 60\ \mu m$. Alternatively, the distance δ between the geometric centres of the PDN and the inductive link is swept across a range of values, $\delta\ = [0, d\ \ ]$.

Results relating to the spatial position of the PDN are shown in Fig. 4. The depicted accumulated noise includes the impact of both the power and ground loops according to (2). The solid line denotes the induced noise on the interdigitated topology, while the dotted and dashdotted lines the noise on the paired type I and paired type II topologies, respectively.

Since the pitch of the PDN is constant in this analysis, the loop inductance for each topology remains constant throughout the experiment. Due to the smaller loop size (see w_l in Fig. 1) of the paired type II compared to the other topologies, the coupling between the PDN and the in-

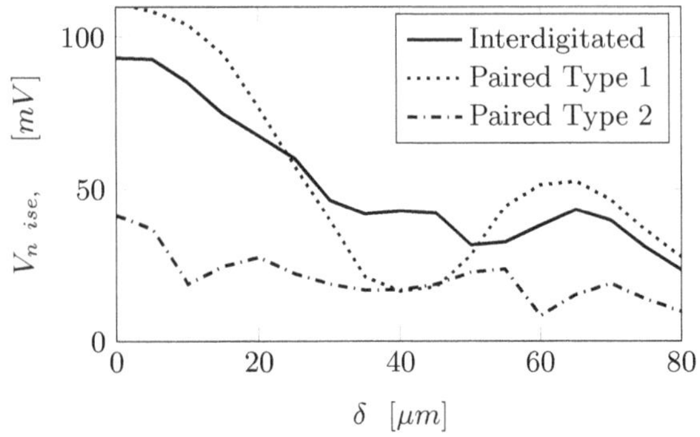

Figure 4: Noise induced by the inductive link for increasing distance δ .

ductive link is weaker, thus being less susceptible to noise. Differently, the interdigitated and paired type I topologies exhibit stronger coupling with the inductor, due to their higher inductances caused by the increased distance between the power (or ground) wires forming a power (ground) loop. Consequently, these topologies exhibit a stronger coupling with the inductive link and, therefore, higher levels of noise are induced.

Nevertheless, as the noise is also a funtion of the magnetic flux density, all of the PDN topologies exhibit positions where the induced noise is reduced, exploiting the opposite polarity of the magnetic flux, as mentioned in subsection 2.1. The density of the magnetic flux is spatially dependent, thus, placing the PDN in different positions leads to a different amount of magnetic flux coupled with the PDN. As a result, even the paired type I topology, which due to the wider P/G loops (see Fig. 1) exhibits increased noise susceptibility, presents a minimum noise level for $\delta\ = 40\ \mu m$. This behaviour indicates that proper placement of the PDN is more important than the pitch of the PDN, when aiming to mitigate the effect of induced noise.

2.3 PDN Susceptibility to Induced Noise

The results relating to both the PDN pitch and the spatial positioning with respect to the inductive link are collectively compiled in this subsection. The pitch, $pitch_{PDN}$ and spatial distance, δ vary as in subsections 2.1 and 2.2, respectively.

A 3-D plot is produced for each topology, illustrating the induced noise behaviour against both the pitch and spatial position. The 3-D surface plots are illustrated in Fig. 5, where results relating to the interdigitated topology are presented in Fig. 5(a). The outcome for the paired type I and paired type II topologies are depicted in Figs. 5(b) and 5(c), respectively. The results are symmetric for negative values of the spatial distance, $\delta\ = [-d\ \ , 0]$.

For the interdigitated PDN topology, the induced noise amplitude significantly increases as the structure shifts closer to the centre of the inductor. For a distance of $\delta\ < 50\ \mu m$, the amplitude of the induced noise becomes prohibitive for typical power supply noise constraints. As the pitch of the PDN, $pitch_{PDN}$ increases, the spatial distance where a minimum induced noise is observed also increases.

Similar results are produced for the paired type I PDN topology. The induced noise levels for $\delta\ < 50\ \mu m$ render this topology unusable for typical power supply noise constraints, even for small widths, that lower the inductance of the PDN loop. Minimum noise can be observed for the full range of $pitch_{PDN}$, when the PDN is placed in such a position that the magnetic flux that couples with each PDN conductor has opposite polarities.

For the paired type II PDN topology, the overall noise behaviour is improved as the accumulated noise is below $V_{n\ ise,}\ \ = 40\ mV$ for most of the simulated range of δ . As the pitch of the PDN increases, a rise in the induced noise amplitude is incurred, due to the increased inductance of the PDN loops. Nevertheless, there exist positions that minimise the induced noise, independently of the pitch size, such as for $pitch_{PDN} = 30\ \mu m$ and $\delta\ = 0\ \mu m$.

3. CASE STUDY: INDUCTIVE LINK ARRAY

Although the structure implemented so far is sufficient to demonstrate the harmful effects that an inductive link can have on P/G lines, a 3-D system that employs wireless inter-tier communication will utilise an array of inductors as in [7, 8] to support sufficient inter-tier bandwidth. Consequently, more than one inductor can couple with the long P/G wires, further aggravating the crosstalk noise.

3.1 Simulation Setup for Inductive Links

In the case of a high performance communication link, N inductors are assumed to be placed along the length of the power (or ground) loop and are simulated with HFSS [15] to model the induced noise. However, this approach significantly increases the simulation time particularly as noise for varying frequencies and δ or $pitch_{PDN}$ must be determined. To address this problem, the noise from a single inductor is determined where this inductor is placed successively at the location of N inductors. Using superposition, the noise from N inductors along the length of the loop can be described as

$$V_{n,\ \ \ y} = 2V_{n\ ise,l} + (N-2)V_{n\ ise,m}, \tag{3}$$

where $V_{n\ ise,l}$ is the noise due to the inductors placed at the edges of the loop and $V_{n\ ise,m}$ is the noise produced by the remaining $N-2$ inductors coupled to the loop.

To verify the accuracy and simulation time gains of this approximation using (3), four inductors ($N = 4$) are assumed to couple to a power loop along the x-axis. The distance between subsequent inductors is given by $pitch = d\ \ \ + 30\ \mu m$, with the added space used to reduce crosstalk between the inductors during simultaneous operation. The noise due to a single inductor placed at specific locations along the x-axis is listed in column 2 of Table 1. This noise is compared with the noise reported in column 3 resulting by each of the four inductors where all four inductors are simulated. The low error of ~2% and the reduced simulation time reported in the last row of Table 1 show that superposing the noise due to a single inductor which is successively placed along the power loop is a computationally effective approach.

Table 1: Noise Induced by Four Inductive Links

x-distance, 6 GHz	$V_{n\ ise}$ $[mV]$ Single	$V_{n\ ise}$ $[mV]$ Multiple	Error [%]
$x = 0$	17.7	17.4	1.6
$x = pitch$	15.1	15.1	0
$x = 2 \times pitch$	15.0	15.0	0
$x = 3 \times pitch$	18.0	17.9	0.5
Simulation Time	$4 \times 1'\ 37''$	$16'$	—

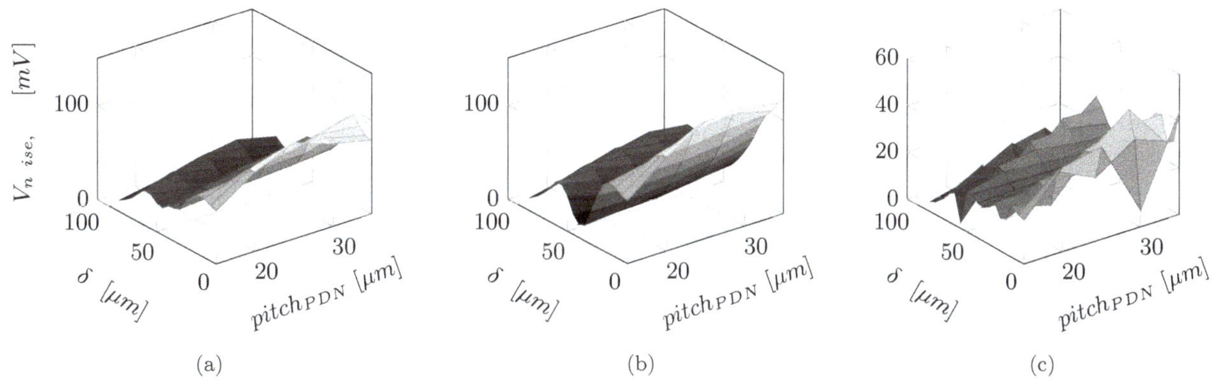

Figure 5: Noise induced by the inductive link for varying PDN physical parameters ($pitch_{PDN}$, δ), (a) interdigitated topology, (b) paired type I, and (c) type II topology, respectively.

3.2 Induced Noise by Inductive Link Arrays

The induced voltage due to the presence of inductive links on the power grid in the neighbouring tier appears as another component of power supply noise for contactless 3-D systems. To limit this noise a ground shield between the inductor and the PDN could be a valid approach, which would also improve the quality factor of the inductor and reduce the coupling with the substrate for the implemented frequency [16]. Nevertheless, a ground shield between the inductors of the inductive link would be detrimental for inter-tier coupling, as it would absorb the magnetic flux that forms the inter-tier link. Consequently, this approach is only applicable to face-to-face bonding. Alternatively, relocation of the P/G wires in a great distance from the inductors is another straightforward approach to avoid coupling. However, an increase in the IR-drop is inevitable. The tradeoff between these two different noise components (i.e., the crosstalk noise and IR-drop) is considered in this section to determine suitable locations for the P/G lines so that the overall power supply noise is restricted within acceptable limits.

An array of 4×4 inductive links is assumed, with a spacing of 30 μm between each link to reduce crosstalk during simultaneous transmission. The area of the array is 436 $\mu m \times$ 436 μm. Each inductive link consists of the transceiver and multiplexing circuits consuming a current of $I = 7.1\ mA$ [7], and are modelled as uniformly distributed current sources across the area of each inductor. The array is supplied by a power grid that utilizes the global and intermediate metal layers of a 65 nm technology node. The power loops on the topmost global layer are illustrated in Fig. 6 as solid lines. The power loops span the entire array connecting to $C4$ bumps placed symmetrically at the periphery of the array. A spacing of $s_{C4} = 150\ \mu m$ and diameter of $d_{C4} = 75\ \mu m$ are assumed for the bumps, satisfying the minimum size requirements for $C4$ pad placement [17]. The surrounding C4 bumps are assumed to supply the total current drawn by the array of inductors at nominal $V_{dd} = 1.1\ V$. The design of the grid results in a worst case IR-drop of 20 mV to 39 mV, depending on the PDN topology and geometry, which satisfies a 10% V_{dd} power supply noise constraint assumed in this case study.

The power loops are connected to each of the supply pads through a global wire, modelled by the resistance R_{dis} . This resistance is used to capture the added IR-drop as the power lines are shifted away from the pads, also changing the overall magnetic flux that couples with the PDN. To

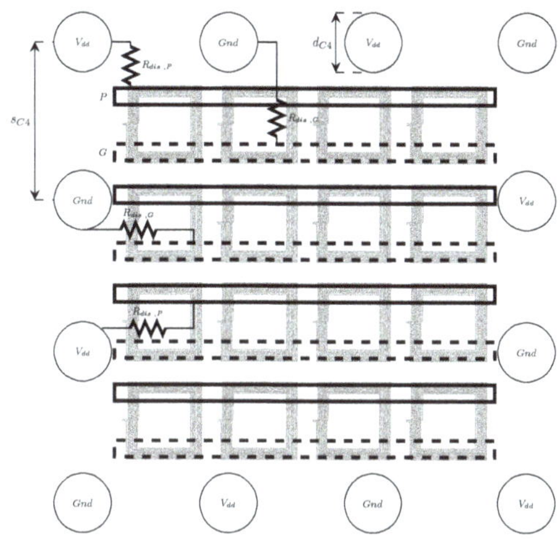

Figure 6: Inductive link array and P/G loops connected to $C4$ supply and ground pads. Power and ground wires are depicted by solid and dashed lines, respectively. Not all of the metal layers are shown for the sake of clarity.

include both the inductive link noise from (3) and the additional IR-drop due to relocation of the P/G wires, R_{dis} is also described as a function of δ , yielding a sheet resistance of $R_{dis\ ,\ m}$ $= 23.7\ m\Omega/\mu m$. For δ $= -77\ \mu m$ (or -($d\ \ /2 + d_{C4}/2$)) the power lines are aligned with the pads at the top of the array and there is no added resistance (R_{dis} $= 0$). As the wires are shifted away from the pads, R_{dis} increases, reaching a maximum of 3.8 Ω for δ $= d\ \ /2 + d_{C4}/2$. Note that increasing the fineness of the grid to mitigate the added IR-drop due to R_{dis} results in a grid with prohibitively high induced noise levels due to the inappropriate positions of specific P/G wires.

Results for an array of the 4×4 grid of inductive links are reported in Table 2. Several cases are listed for each PDN topology, for pairs of ($pitch_{PDN}$, δ) that can provide acceptable noise levels for a constraint of 10%. The induced noise $V_{n,\ \ y}$ is given by (3), considering the induced noise both on the power and ground loops.

Concerning the interdigitated PDN topology, results indicate a higher sensitivity to induced noise compared to the paired topologies. Even in the spatial positions where the induced noise is minimum, the added IR-drop noise due to R_{dis} for the power and ground loops increases the total noise to prohibitive amplitudes. Overall, a minimum noise of 13.9% V_{dd} is noted, surpassing the 10% noise constraint.

Table 2: Total Accumulated Noise for Different PDN Geometries

Topology	Geometry		V_{noise}, $[mV]$	IR-Drop $[mV]$		Total $[mV]$	Overall Noise
	$pitch_{PDN}$ $[\mu m]$	δ $[\mu m]$		Power Loop	Ground Loop		
Interdigitated	45	-45	108	5.25	18.1	131.3	13.9% (Fail)
	45	70	92	52.8	61.3	153.8	18.1% (Fail)
Paired Type I	45	-40	56.1	11.1	14.1	81.3	*7.3% (Pass)*
	60	-40	59.2	14.2	6.1	79.5	*7.2% (Pass)*
	105	-50	69.2	35.2	27.7	132.1	12% (Fail)
	105	50	69.2	56.2	63.7	189.1	17.1% (Fail)
Paired Type II	45	-35	58.1	9.7	27.2	95	*8.6% (Pass)*
	75	-45	65.3	16.7	26.3	108.3	*9.8% (Pass)*
	90	0	28.5	10.8	45.5	84.8	*7.7% (Pass)*

Alternatively, both paired topologies present pairs of ($pitch_{PDN}$, δ), where the overall noise is below the specified limit. For the type I topology, a noise level of 7.1% is achieved, well below the specified limit. The overall noise mainly occurs due to the induced noise, while the added IR-drop is relatively small for the accepted spatial positions. For the type II topology, the ground loop IR-drop significantly increases the overall noise, due to the larger distance from the pads. Nevertheless, locations exist where the overall noise level is tolerable, such as the positions shown in Fig. 6, with an overall noise of 7.7%.

4. CONCLUSION

The impact of inductive link interfaces on different power delivery networks is investigated. Noise induced by the inductive link and the IR-drop on the P/G wires, for interdigitated, paired type I and paired type II PDN topologies is explored based on the area that couples with the inductor and the spatial position. Results indicate that the increased inductance of specific topologies leads to higher levels of noise, due to the increased coupling. However, the spatial position is the primary factor affecting the induced noise amplitude. Analysis suggests that the interdigitated topology is the most susceptible to induced noise, as the lowest induced noise amplitude is 92 mV. Alternatively, paired topologies exhibit placement locations where the induced noise is considerably lower, and consequently are better candidates for power delivery in 3-D systems that employ inductive links.

5. REFERENCES

[1] J.-Q. Lu, "3-D Hyperintegration and Packaging Technologies for Micro-Nano Systems," *Proceedings of the IEEE*, Vol. 97, No. 1, pp. 18–30, January 2009.

[2] J. Ouyang *et al.*, "Evaluation of Using Inductive/Capacitive-Coupling Vertical Interconnects in 3D Network-on-Chip," *Proceedings of the IEEE International Conference on Computer-Aided Design*, pp. 477–482, November 2010.

[3] I. A. Papistas and V. F. Pavlidis, "Bandwidth-to-Area Comparison of Through Silicon Vias and Inductive Links for 3-D ICs," *Proceedings of the IEEE European Conference on Circuit Theory and Design*, pp. 1–4, August 2015.

[4] J. Lau, "TSV Manufacturing Yield and Hidden Costs for 3D IC Integration," *Proceedings of the IEEE Electronic Components and Technology Conference*, pp. 1031–1042, June 2010.

[5] N. Miura *et al.*, "Cross Talk Countermeasures in Inductive Inter-Chip Wireless Superconnect," *Proceedings of the IEEE Custom Integrated Circuits Conference*, pp. 99–102, October 2004.

[6] N. Miura *et al.*, "Inductive Coupled Communications," in *Coupled Data Communication Techniques for High-Performance and Low-Power Computing*, pp. 79–125, ISBN: 978–1–4419–6587–5. Springer, 2010.

[7] N. Miura *et al.*, "A 1 TB/s 1 pJ/b 6.4 QDR Inductive-Coupling Interface Between 65-nm CMOS Logic and Emulated 100-nm DRAM," *IEEE Journal on Emerging and Selected Topics in Circuits and Systems*, Vol. 2, No. 2, pp. 249–256, May 2012.

[8] N. Miura and T. Kuroda, "A 1 Tb/s 3 W Inductive-Coupling Transceiver Chip," *IEEE Asia and South Pacific Design Automation Conference*, pp. 92–93, January 2007.

[9] N. Miura *et al.*, "Crosstalk Countermeasures for High-Density Inductive-Coupling Channel Array," *IEEE Journal of Solid-State Circuits*, Vol. 42, No. 2, pp. 410–421, February 2007.

[10] K. Niitsu *et al.*, "Interference From Power/Signal Lines and To SRAM Circuits in 65 nm CMOS Inductive-Coupling Link," *IEEE Asian Solid-State Circuits Conference*, pp. 131–134, November 2007.

[11] E. K. Armstrong, *The Physical Basis of EMC*. ISBN: 978-0955511837. Nutwood UK, 2010.

[12] M. Popovich *et al.*, *Power Distribution Networks with On-Chip Decoupling Capacitors*. ISBN: 978-1-4419-7870-7. Springer Science & Business Media, 2007.

[13] D. M. Pozar, *Microwave Engineering*. ISBN: 978-81-265-4190-5. Wiley, 4 Edition, 2010.

[14] Predictive Technology Models (PTM). [Online]. Available: http://ptm.asu.edu/

[15] *Ansys Electronics Desktop, v16*, Ansys, December 2014. [Online]. Available: http://www.ansys.com/.

[16] C. P. Yue and S. S. Wong, "On-Chip Spiral Inductors with Patterned Ground Shields for Si-Based RF ICs," *IEEE Journal of Solid-State Circuits*, Vol. 33, No. 5, pp. 743–752, May 1998.

[17] W. Koh *et al.*, "Copper Pillar Bump Technology Progress Overview," *Proceedings of the International Conference on Electronic Packaging Technology and High Density Packaging*, pp. 1–5, August 2011.

Delay Estimates for Graphene Nanoribbons: A Novel Measure of Fidelity and Experiments with Global Routing Trees

Subrata Das
Dept. of CSE
Jadavpur University, India
dsubrata.mt@gmail.com

Soma Das
University of Calcutta, India
soma.das11@gmail.com

Adrija Majumder
MIS Group , Indian Institute of Management Calcutta, India
adrijam13@iimcal.ac.in

Parthasarathi Dasgupta
MIS Group , Indian Institute of Management Calcutta, India
partha@iimcal.ac.in

Debesh Kumar Das
Dept of CSE
Jadavpur University, India
debeshd@hotmail.com

ABSTRACT

With extreme miniaturization of traditional CMOS devices in deep sub-micron design levels, the delay of a circuit, as well as power dissipation and area are dominated by interconnections between logic blocks. In an attempt to search for alternative materials, Graphene nanoribbons (GNRs) have been found to be potential for both transistors and interconnects due to its outstanding electrical and thermal properties. GNRs provide better options as materials used for global routing trees in VLSI circuits. However, certain special characteristics of GNRs prohibit direct application of existing VLSI routing tree construction methods for the GNR-based interconnection trees. In this paper, we address this issue possibly for the first time, and propose a heuristic method for construction of GNR-based minimum-delay Steiner trees based on linear-cum-bending hybrid delay model. Experimental results demonstrate the effectiveness of our proposed methods. We propose a novel technique for analyzing the relative accuracy of the delay estimates using rank correlation and statistical significance test. We also compute the delays for the trees generated by hybrid delay heuristic using Elmore delay approximation and use them for determining the relative accuracy of the hybrid delay estimate.

Keywords

Carbon nanomaterial; Garphene Nanoribbon; Global Routing; Hexagonal Steiner tree; Fidelity.

1. INTRODUCTION

As suggested by Moore's law, the number of transistors per integrated circuit grows exponentially. Increased wire resistivity due to surface and grain-boundary scattering, significant mobility degradation, increased leakage power and large dopant fluctuation are the major problems of conventional CMOS devices with decreasing feature sizes [20]. Distribution of signal to circuit components and the interconnection of a circuit to power and ground is done in chips through interconnects. With increased scaling, the interconnects have to meet the high-bandwidth low-power signalling needs without introducing performance bottlenecks [8]. According to ITRS report, interconnect performance is at the forefront as a key challenge to achieve overall chip performance [8]. Graphene nanoribbon and carbon nanotube-based devices and interconnects are observed to be better replacements for conventional devices and interconnects.

Low dimensional allotropes of carbon, are known as carbon nano-materials. The structure of carbon nano-material is similar to the hexagonal benzene rings. Each edge of the hexagonal ring is a sp^2 carbon-carbon bond with a bond length approximately $0.14nm$ [20]. Graphene nanoribbons are a kind of such materials. Based on the experiments with graphene samples on band gap and edge chirality, it is observed that Graphene nanoribbon with predominantly zigzag edges are metallic and those with armchair edges are semiconductor [6], [20]. Figure 1 shows the structure of zigzag and armchair Graphene nanoribbon. Metallic GNR are oriented at 30°, 90° and 150° angles and semiconducting GNR are oriented at 0°, 60° and 120° angles. But the bending of GNR at 0°, 60° and 120° angles maintain the chirality i.e. for bending in these angles metallic GNR remains metallic and semiconducting GNR remains semiconducting. A change in the chirality from predominantly zigzag (metallic) to predominantly armchair (semiconducting) will form a metal-semiconductor junction [20].

GNR has been proposed to be potential candidate material for both transistors [11] and interconnects [14], [18] owing to its excellent thermal and electrical conductivities. Interestingly, compared to copper wire, the power consumption and interconnect delays in GNR can be reduced by up to 50% and 60% respectively for global interconnect [12]. In this paper, we attempt to exploit the outstanding properties of $GNRs$ for the construction of global routing trees in VLSI chips. We also propose a novel measure of relative accuracy.

GLSVLSI '16, May 18-20, 2016, Boston, MA, USA

DOI: http://dx.doi.org/10.1145/2902961.2903036

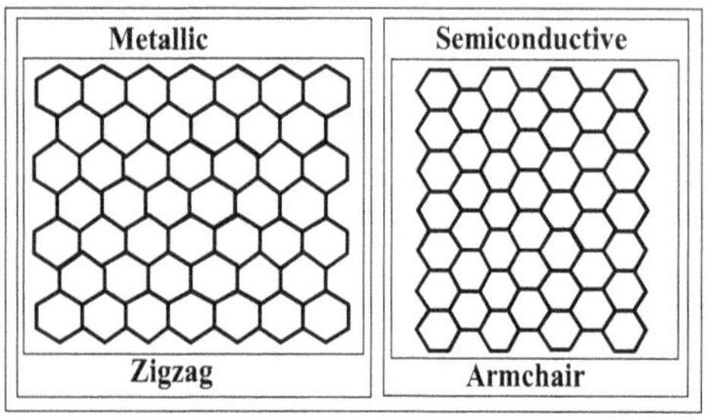

Figure 1: Structure of Zigzag and Armchair Graphene Nanoribbon

2. LITERATURE REVIEW

Traditional interconnect tree construction methods are usually based on Manhattan routing architecture [3], [9]. However, construction of routing trees of non-Manhattan geometric patterns (hexagonal, octagonal, etc.) have also been reported in literature [16], [17]. Most of these tree construction methods rely on the construction of Steiner Minimal Trees [2], [7]. A theoretical framework for constructing Steiner routing trees with minimum Elmore delay was reported in [2]. Y-routing only consider $0°$, $60°$, $120°$ oriented global or semi global wiring [16]. A comprehensive model for the resistance in Graphene nanoribbon (GNR) interconnects appears in [15]. The analysis of fundamental physics, conductance and delay calculation and hence industrial prospect as VLSI interconnects of GNR is discussed in [19].

In connection with the construction of efficient routing trees, the accuracy of delay estimators is of prime importance. In spite of the availability of several such estimators, none of them can guarantee accuracy and convenience of use at the same time. As such, relative performances of the delay estimators is often considered to be a standard figure of merit [5]. The notion of fidelity has been discussed in [17] in terms of rank correlation coefficients.

3. GNR ROUTING PROBLEM

The GNR routing problem for a pair of source and target terminals have been discussed in [20]. For a given pair of locations of terminals, the objective is to interconnect them with metallic GNR wires so that the delay of the path is minimized. Since $0°$, $60°$ and $120°$ bending maintains chirality, hence routing are possible along these degrees. The delay of metallic GNR wires is a function of length of the wire, the number of bending of the wires and the angle of the bending of the wires. If the length of the GNR wires is less than the mean free path length then the interconnection resistance is constant. Interconnect resistance increases with the extra length beyond the mean free path length and is proportional to the interconnect wire length. Bending in different angles results in different resistances [20]. The cost of a $120°$ bending is 3 times the cost of a $60°$ bending [20]. In this paper, we propose an algorithm for GNR routing with single source and multiple sink terminals to construct the corresponding routing tree.

4. MOTIVATION OF THE WORK

To the best of our knowledge, none of the existing works on GNR interconnects consider the construction of routing trees. In this paper, we address this problem considering the hybrid cost model of [20]. Since $GNRs$ are new kind of materials to be used as interconnects, and the hybrid cost model is also introduced very recently based on some simulation experiments [1], there is a need to test the accuracy of this cost estimate with respect to certain well-known interconnect delay estimate. In an attempt to address this issue, we propose a new way to measure the relative accuracy of the hybrid cost estimate with respect to Elmore delay estimate in line with the existing definition of fidelity of delay estimators [17]. We compare the costs obtained from these two estimates using Spearman's rank correlation and statistical significance test [13].

5. PROBLEM FORMULATION

In global routing, a signal net consisting of a set of fixed terminals $N = n_0, n_1, \ldots, n_k$ is connected by a routing tree $T(N)$. The cost of the tree $T(N)$ is the sum of costs of its constituent edges. The tree may be constructed by choosing a terminal n_0 ($\in N$) as the source and connecting the remaining terminals as sinks to this source [17]. As in [4], positions of the potential Steiner points are obtained recursively through a generalization of Hanan grid [7], [10] with axes in three directions, generating a triangular grid. A straight line segment between any pair of points (Steiner or terminal) along any of the valid directions is an edge. A path is a collection of the edges connecting two points. Figure 2 shows a triangular grid. The hybrid cost (edge cost + bending cost) model used in [20] is considered for computation of path costs.

To define Elmore delay for the routing tree $T(N)$ rooted at n_0, e_i denotes the edge between n_i and its parents. Let r_{ei} and c_{ei} respectively represent the resistance and the capacitance for edge e_i. Let T_i denotes the subtree of $T(N)$ rooted at n_i, and c_i denotes the sink capacitance for n_i. Then, C_i, denoting the tree capacitance of T_i, is given by the sum of the capacitances of the sink terminal and edges of T_i. The Elmore delay along edge e_i is given by $r_{ei} \times (\frac{c_{ei}}{2} + C_i)$. The Elmore delay $\delta_{ED}(n_i)$ between source n_0 and sink n_i is given by

$$\delta_{ED}(n_i) = r_d \times C_0 + \sum_{e_j \in path(n_0, n_i)} r_{ej} \times (\frac{c_{ej}}{2} + C_j) \quad (1)$$

Here r_d denotes the output driver resistance at the source n_0 of the net. Both r_{ej} and c_{ej} are proportional to the length of the edge e_j . Thus, $\delta_{ED}(n_i)$ contains the lengths of the individual edges between n_0 and n_i appearing as quadratic terms. Total Elmore delay of a routing tree is the sum of the Elmore delays of all the sink terminals from the source terminal [17].

6. PROPOSED METHOD

We now state a few results and observations to be used in the proposed methods.

DEFINITION 1. *In a triangular grid, the intersecting point between two straight lines passing through the source and the sink at an angle* $60°$ *or* $120°$ *is known as bending point.*

DEFINITION 2. *A straight line passing through the bending point and the sink point is known to be a bending line.*

Definition 3. *A path from the source to the sink through the bending point is known to be a bending path.*

Figure 2 shows bending point, bending line and bending path in a triangular grid.

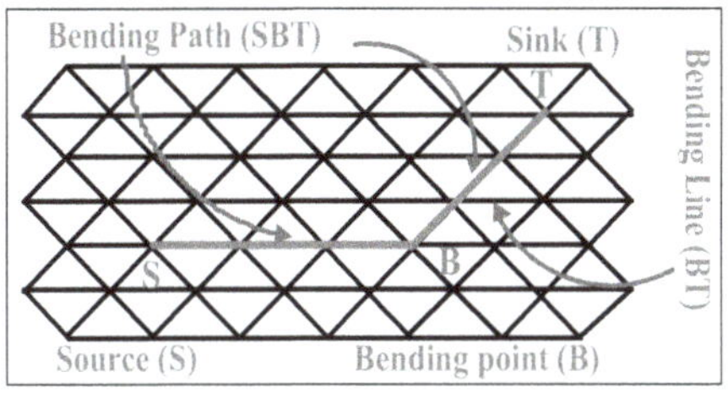

Figure 2: Bending point, bending line and bending path in a triangular grid

Lemma 1. *In absence of any obstacle, any pair of the source and the sink terminals may be connected using at most one bend of the bending angle of either* 60° *or* 120°*.*

Proof. Clear by construction. □

Observation 1. *In any routing path between two terminals on a triangular grid, a* 120° *bending can be replaced by a* 60° *bending with an additional detour path.*

Consider Figure 3(a), a direct path $S \rightarrow B \rightarrow T$ using 120° bending has a length of 5. The distance between B and T is 3. Extending edge SB to D results in an extra detour length of 3 in edge BD. Thus, the routing path $S \rightarrow B \rightarrow D \rightarrow T$ has a routing length of 8 with a bending angle of 60°. Figure 3 (b), shows reduction of two 120° bending by a 60° bending with extra detour path cost of 3.

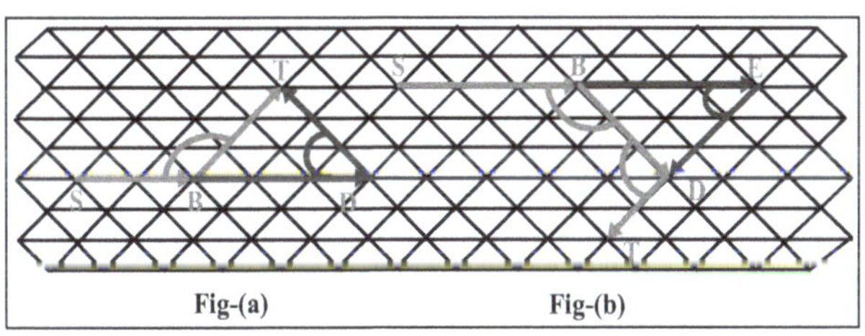

Figure 3: Triangular routing grid for GNR routing path:reduction of 120° bending by 60° bending with extra detour path

Observation 2. *In absence of any obstacle, the number of possible paths between any pair of source and sink with only one* 60° *bending is 4 (see Figure 4).*

Lemma 2 proposes a condition under which a detour may be introduced in a path.

Lemma 2. *We can rearrange the routing path as shown in Figure 5 if the distance of the sink from the* 120° *bending point times resistance per unit length of interconnect is less than or equal to the twice cost due to* 60° *bending.*

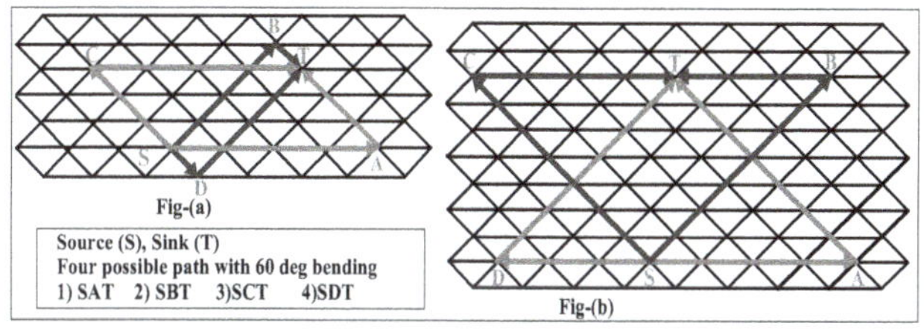

Figure 4: Four possible routing paths between source and sink with 60° bending

Proof. If p be the cost due to 60° bending then cost due to 120° bending is $3p$. r is the cost of resistance per unit length. If x be the distance of the sink from 120° bending point, then from figure 5 it is clear that resistance in the 60° path is smaller than or equal to that of the 120° path if, $2xr + p \leq xr + 3p \Rightarrow xr \leq 2p$ □

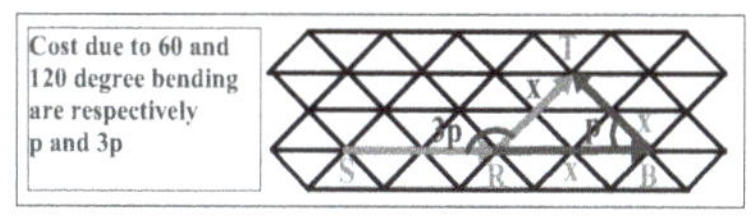

Figure 5: Figure for Lemma 2

Lemma 3. *For a pair of the source and the sink terminals, there exists two paths of equal length each having exactly one 60* $^\circ$ *bending.*

Proof. The proof is omitted for paucity of space. □

In Figure 4, the paths SDT and SBT are of equal length. Similarly SAT and SCT are of equal length.

6.1 Delay Calculation using Elmore Delay Model

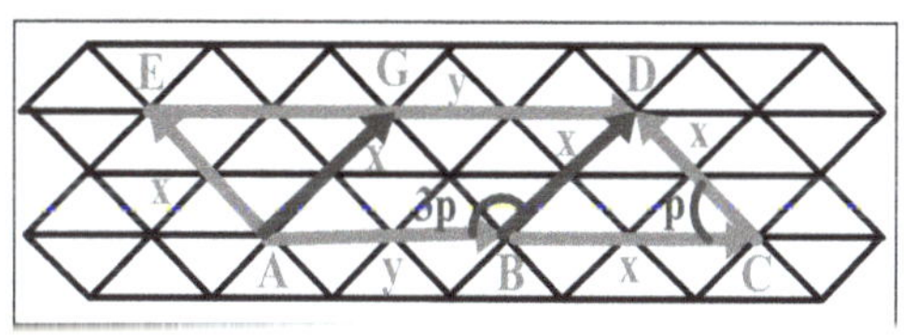

Figure 6: Routing of GNR interconnect by reducing angle of bending.

In Figure 6, for GNR interconnects, resistance*(R=rl)* is insignificant and constant up to mean free path length, beyond which it increases with increasing length of the wire. The capacitance*(C=cl)* also increases with the length of the wire. Moreover, the resistance of GNR interconnect depends on the bending of the wires [20]. Consider the two routing paths (ABD and ACD) as shown in Figure 6. In the path ABD there is a 120° bending between source and terminal. In the path ACD there is a 60° bending. The length of ABD path is $(x + y)$ where x and y respectively denote the lengths of the segments BD and AB. Total resistance of the path is $R_{1^{st}} = r(x + y) + 3p$, since the bending in this path is 120°. Capacitance of the path is $C_{1st} = c(x + y)$. Hence the Elmore delay expression for this path is $D_{1^{st}}$=$\{r(x+y)+3p\}.c(x+y)/2 + C_{load}$, where

C_{load} is the load capacitance. Similarly Elmore delay along other paths can also be computed. Total Elmore delay of the routing tree is the sum of these path delay expressions.

6.2 Algorithm for GNR Routing

Suppose on a triangular grid, $S(x_s, y_s)$, $T(x_t, y_t)$ and $B(x_b, y_b)$ represent the coordinates of the source, the sink and the bending points respectively. Let m is the slope of the line joining BT. Since we are only considering the triangular grid hence the bending angle is $0°$ or $60°$ or $120°$. Hence the value of m is only one of 0, $\sqrt{3}$, $-\sqrt{3}$.

LEMMA 4. *If $y_t > y_s$ and $x_t + (y_s - y_t)/\sqrt{3} \leq x_s \leq x_t - (y_s - y_t)/\sqrt{3}$, then $B_1(x_t + (y_s - y_t)/\sqrt{3}, y_s)$ and $B_2(x_t - (y_s - y_t)/\sqrt{3}, y_s)$ respectively represent the two routing(bending) points with $60°$ bending. The coordinates of other two routing(bending) points with $60°$ bending are respectively $(B_3(x_s + (y_t - y_s)/\sqrt{3}), y_t)$ and $B_4((x_s - (y_t - y_s)/\sqrt{3}), y_t)$*

PROOF. The proof is omitted for paucity of space. □

In a similar way, we can obtain four bending points with bending angle $60°$ for any values of (x_t, y_t) and (x_s, y_s).
The *GNR* routing problem is described for routing between the single source and the multiple sinks in a triangular grid. The algorithm first finds the sink at maximum distance from the source.
The function *find_bending*() finds four bending points with bending angle $60°$ between a pair of source and sink terminal. The function *dist_source_sink_bendpoint*() finds the distance between the source and the sink terminals via a specified bending point. Among the four possible paths between a pair of source and sink terminal, there exists a pair of paths of equal length. In our proposed algorithm, at first the sink terminal farthest from the source terminal is determined. For this purpose, for all the sinks, all the bending points are determined. For a particular sink, those pair of bending points are selected for which the distance from the source to the sink is minimum. Then the sink with maximum of these minimum distances is selected.
Now for this maximum distant sink terminal, *hybrid cost* for both $60°$ and $120°$ bending paths are calculated. The bending angle with minimum *hybrid cost* is selected. In either case two routing paths are possible. It is clear to see that the two bending points lie diagonally opposite corners of a parallelogram (as shown in Figure 4). To select the appropriate bending point for the maximum distant sink, at first a decision line is selected as a straight line passing through the mid point between the source and the first bending point. The function *find_decision_line*() is used for this purpose. The average distances of the remaining sinks on each side of the decision line is calculated. The bending point of that side of decision line is selected for which the average distance is minimum.

The functions *min_dsitance*() and *max_dsitance*() finds minimum distant path and maximum distant path respectively. The remaining sinks are divided into two clusters depending on the side of the 1st routing line. Here 1st routing line means the line from source to furthest sink via appropriate bending point.

The function *selection_of_cluster*() (Figure 7) decide whether a sink terminal is in cluster 1 or in cluster 2.

We need to construct a hexagonal Steiner tree so that the total *hybrid cost* is minimum. The Steiner point of the remaining sinks are selected in such a way for which the *hybrid cost* is minimum.

selection_of_cluster()

Input: Equation of a 1st routing line and Coordinate of a sink terminal
Output: Selection of a cluster from the cluster 1 or cluster2 for a sink.

1. If the slope of the decision line is negative then
2. sinks right to the decision line will be in cluster 1 and left to the decision line will be in cluster 2.
3. else
4. sinks left to the decision line will be in cluster 1 and right to the decision line will be in cluster 2

Figure 7: Selection of Cluster

The functions *find_first_steiner_point_cluster*1() (Figure 8) finds the first Steiner point for cluster 1 so that the hybrid cost is minimum. And *find_steiner_point_cluster*1() (Figure 9) finds the Steiner points for the remaining sinks of cluster-1.

*find_first_steiner_point_cluster*1()

Input: Equation of a straight line and Coordinate of a point
Output: Steiner point on the straight line.

1. Take the maximum distant sink from bending line.
2. Find the intersection of the sink with the bending line and source bending point (extended) line making angle $60°$ or $120°$.
3. Find the *hybrid cost* for all such intersection points.
4. Intersection point with minimum *hybrid cost* is chosen for first steiner point.

Figure 8: Find first Steiner point of Cluster1

*find_steiner_point_cluster*1()

Input: Equation of a straight line, previous Steiner points and Coordinate of a sink point.
Output: Steiner point.

1. Find the intersection of the line passing through the sink making $60°$ or $120°$ angles to the bending line, all previous Steiner points, source bending point extended line and destination bending point extended line.
2. if *hybrid cost* for $60°$ bending is minimum then
3. the point with $60°$ bending is selected as Steiner point.
4. else
5. the point with $120°$ bending is selected as Steiner point.

Figure 9: Find Steiner point for any sink point of Cluster1

Similar functions (*find_first_steiner_point_cluster*2() and *find_steiner_point_cluster*2()) can be used for cluster 2. Here minimum distance sink is selected first.
A formal description of the Algorithm is given in Figure 10. Here we assume that the source and all the sink terminals are within the routing region of the triangular grid.

6.3 Effectiveness of the Algorithm

If the sinks are in cluster 1, then sink can be easily connected to bending line with $60°$ bending keeping y coordinate constant. Hence maximum distant sink is consider first,

GNR Routing ()

Data structures: Array dist[]: store the distances between each pair of source and sink, min_dist[]:store the minimum of these four distances,
Input: Single source and multiple sink terminals on triangular grid
Output: Minimum cost Hybrid hexagonal steiner tree

```
For each sink begin loop
    find_bending()
    For each bending points for a sink begin loop
        dist[]= dist_source_sink_bendpoint().
    End for loop
    min_dist[]=find_minimum_dist(dist[])
End for loop
max_dist=find_maximum_dist(min_dist[])
Consider the sink for which the distance from source is maximum (max_dist)
if(hybrid cost is minimum in 60° routing path ) then
        60° routing path is selected
else
        120° routing path is selected
for routing path
        find_decission_line()
Find average distances ave_dist1, ave_dist2 of sinks for each side of the decision line
if(ave_dist1 < ave_dist2) then
        that side of bending point is selected for which this condition is satisfied
else
        second bending point is selected for routing
selection_of_cluster()
for cluster 1 begin loop
       find the maximum distance sink for cluster 1
       find_first_steiner_point_cluster1()
Take the remaining sinks of cluster 1 with decreasing distance
       find_steiner_point_cluster1()
End for
for cluster 2 begin loop
       find the minimum distance sink for cluster 2
       find_first_steiner_point_cluster2()
Take the remaining sinks of cluster 2 with increasing distance
       find_steiner_point_cluster2()
End for
End of algo.
```

Figure 10: Algorithm for GNR routing

in this case, and if more than one sinks have same y coordinate, then the total *hybrid cost* for these sinks will be the same. Sinks with lower distance are considered successively and *hybrid cost* is increased minimally. But to connect the sinks in cluster 2 with the bending line or the source bending point connecting line with 60° bending, both x and y-coordinate are changed hence minimum distance sink from bending line is considered first and sinks with successive increased distance are considered successively. This will increase minimum *hybrid cost.*

LEMMA 5. *The complexity of the algorithm is* $\mathcal{O}(n^2)$.

6.3.1 *Parameters Affecting the Performance*

Parasitic effects may degrade the performance. In our proposed method, we consider *hybrid cost* as design parameter. In addition to the *hybrid cost* if parasitic effects such as parasitic capacitance, inductance are considered, then it will be a good cost function.

Thermal noise may affect on signal to noise ratio. But as the resistance in GNR interconnect is much less than that of copper interconnect, it does not much affect on signal to noise ratio. Hence signal to noise ratio is not considered in our proposed method.

7. COMPARISON OF DELAY ESTIMATORS

In order to compare the relative accuracies of two delay estimators ϵ_1 and ϵ_2, we consider one of them, say ϵ_1 as the standard, and find the rank correlation coefficient of the two estimators. Here Spearman's rank correlation coefficient is used for this purpose. For any sample data, this coefficient is denoted by r_s and signifies a linear correlation coefficient between the ranks of a pair of data points, say X and Y. No assumption on the type of distribution of the two variables $x \in X$ and $y \in Y$ is made. The Spearman's rho rank correlation [5], [13] is computed as follows,

$$r_s = 1 - \frac{6\sum d_i^2}{n(n^2-1)} \tag{2}$$

where n is the total number of data points, and d_i is the difference of x_i and y_i. In our delay-related experiments, for the same routing tree T_i generated using heuristic based on ϵ_i, say, x_i and y_i represent respectively the ranks given by ϵ_1 and ϵ_2 respectively. For instance, ϵ_1 might represent the hybrid cost estimate, and ϵ_2 might represent the Elmore estimate. Subsequently, statistical hypothesis testing is done on the range of correlation coefficients to find the statistical significance. We consider the following:
H_o (Null Hypotheses): There is no correlation between the total costs obtained from our proposed algorithm and Elmore's existing algorithm.
H_1 (Alternative Hypotheses): There is a correlation between the total costs obtained from our proposed algorithm and Elmore's existing algorithm.

For a given set of data points, the corresponding upper bound and lower bound critical values are obtained from Spearman's rho rank correlation significance table. Depending on the correlation coefficient value obtained by the experiments, either of the above these is proved, and the other is disproved. Thus, considering Elmore delay estimate as more precise, the correlation of the hybrid-cost model with it may be confirmed or rejected.

8. EXPERIMENTAL RESULT

As in [20] we assume the cost of unit wire length as 1, where as the cost due to 60° and 120° bending are respectively 10 and 30 and we set the cost of unit capacitance as 1. The experimental results are summarized in Figure 11. For studying relative accuracy (fidelity) of hybrid cost (refereed to as *our*) estimate with respect to Elmore delay estimate, the total cost computed by our proposed algorithm and Elmore's algorithm represents the two variables. The data points under each set are ranked. Next, pair-wise differences of ranks are obtained to calculate the rho rank correlation coefficient.

In our sample we have 12 data points. The corresponding upper bound and lower bound critical values obtained from Spearman's rho rank correlation significance table at 1% are +.727 and −.727 respectively (Figure 12). Since the correlation coefficient obtained in this study is greater than

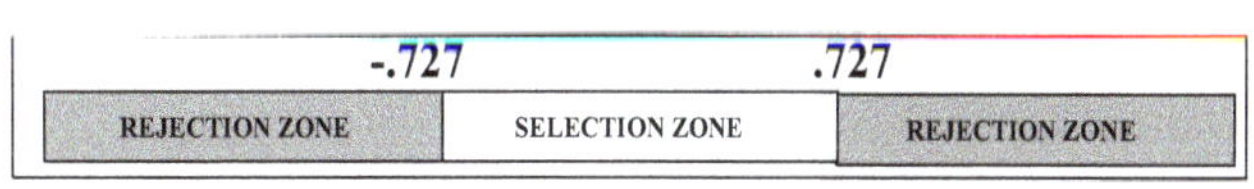

Figure 12: Selection and rejection zone.

Test case	# Sink terminals	Wire length		# 60 deg bending		# 120 bending		Total cost		Rank(u)	Rank(v)	Diff
		Our	Elmore	Our	Elmore	Our	Elmore	Our	Elmore			
ex1	16	67	67	11	11	0	0	177	117	1	1	0
ex2	23	80	61	21	12	0	6	290	361	8	9	-1
ex3	29	78	104	18	7	0	5	258	324	6	6	0
ex4	28	70	64	24	19	0	2	310	314	9	5	4
ex5	20	86	75	15	14	0	2	236	275	3	3	0
ex6	26	86	84	18	16	0	3	266	334	7	8	-1
ex7	24	97	88	15	15	0	0	247	238	5	2	3
ex8	35	118	117	21	13	1	5	358	397	11	11	0
ex9	28	127	121	25	21	0	3	377	421	12	12	0
ex10	18	89	72	15	11	0	5	239	332	4	7	-3
ex11	28	91	86	14	17	0	1	231	286	2	4	-2
ex12	24	137	132	18	20	0	1	317	362	10	10	0

r_s=0.86014

Figure 11: Comparison of wire length, bending and delay & rank calculation.

the upper bound critical value (.86014 is greater than .727), we can conclude that at 1% (and higher) significance level we can reject the null hypothesis. Thus, there exists sufficient correlation between the total costs of our model and Elmore's model.

9. CONCLUSION

In this paper, we attempt to construct a global routing tree for a given source terminal and multiple sink terminals using the hybrid cost model of *GNRs*. We also propose a new technique for computation of relative accuracy of the delay estimates. Our results indicate high relative accuracy of the hybrid cost model vis-a-vis the Elmore delay model. Future work could involve the construction of routing trees based on required arrival times, and computation of relative accuracies of the hybrid cost model based on some practical simulation tool.

10. REFERENCES

[1] D. A. Areshkin and C. T. White. Building blocks for integrated graphene circuits. *Nano Letters*, 7(11):3253–3259, 2007.

[2] K. D. Boese, A. B. Kahng, B. A. McCoy, and G. Robins. Rectilnear steiner trees with minimum elmore delay. In 31st *ACM/IEEE Design Automation Conference*, pages 381–386, 1994.

[3] K. D. Boese, A. B. Kahng, B. A. McCoy, and G. Robins. Near-optimal critical sink routing tree constructions. *IEEE Transactions on Computer-Aided Design of Integrated Circuits and Systems*, 14(12):1417–1436, December 1995.

[4] C. S. Coulston. Constructing exact octagonal steiner minimal trees. In *13th ACM Great Lakes symposium on VLSI(GLSVLSI 03)*, pages 1–6, April 2003.

[5] P. Dasgupta. Revisiting vlsi interconnects in deep sub-micron: Some open questions. In 18th *International Conference on VLSI Design*, pages 615–620, 2005.

[6] M. Y. Han, B. Ozyilmaz, Y. Zhang, , and P. Kim. Energy band-gap engineering of graphene nanoribbons. *Physical Review Letters*, 98:206805, 2007.

[7] M. Hanan. On steiner's problem with rectilinear distance. *SIAM Journal on Applied Mathematics*, 14(2):255–265, March 1966.

[8] http://www.itrs.net/reports.html.

[9] A. B. Kahng and B. Liu. Q-tree: A new iterative improvement approach for buffered interconnect optimization. In *IEEE Comp. Society Annual Symp. on VLSI(ISVLSI)*, pages 183–188, February 2003.

[10] D. T. Lee and C. F. Shen. The steiner minimal tree problem in λ-geometry plane. In *In International Symposium on Algorithms and Computation*, pages 247–255, 1996.

[11] M. C. Lemme, T. J. Echtermeyer, M. Baus, and H. Kurz. A graphene field-effect device. *IEEE Electron Device Letters*, 28(4):282–284, April 2007.

[12] H. Li, C. Xu, and K. Banerjee. Carbon nanomaterials: The ideal interconnect technology for next-generation ics. In *IEEE Design & Test of Computers*, pages 20–31, 2010.

[13] P. S. Mann. *Introductory Statics*. John Wiely & Sons, 2007.

[14] A. Naeemi and J. D. Meindl. Performance benchmarking for graphene nano-ribbon, carbon nanotube, and cu interconnects. In *IEEE Int. Interconnect Technology Conference*, pages 183–185, June 2008.

[15] T. Ragheb and Y. Massoud. On the modeling of resistance in graphene nanoribbon (gnr) for future interconnect applications. In *Proceedings of the IEEE/ACM International Conference on Computer-Aided Design*, pages 593–597, 2008.

[16] T. Samanta, P. Ghosal, H. Rahaman, and P. Dasguptata. A heuristic method for constructing hexagonal steiner minimal trees for routing in vlsi. In *IEEE International Symposium on Circuits and Systems (ISCAS 2006)*, pages 1788–1791, 2006.

[17] T. Samanta, P. Ghosal, H. Rahaman, and P. Dasguptata. Revisiting fidelity: A case of elmore-based y-routing trees. In *International Workshop on System Level Interconnect Prediction (SLIP08)*, pages 27–34, 2008.

[18] Q. Shao, G. Liu, D. Teweldebrhan, and A. A. Balandin. High temperature quenching of electrical resistance in graphene interconnects. *Applied Physics Letters*, 92(20):202108, May 2008.

[19] C. Xu, H. Li, and K. Banerjee. Modeling, analysis, and design of graphene nano-ribbon interconnects. *IEEE Transactions on Electron Devices*, 56(8):1567–1578, August 2009.

[20] T. Yan, Q. Ma, S. Chilstedt, M. D. F. Wong, and D. Chen. A routing algorithm for graphene nanoribbon circuit. *ACM Transactions on Design Automation on Electronic Systems*, 18(4):61:1–61:18, October 2013.

VarDroid: Online Variability Emulation in Android/Linux Platforms

Pietro Mercati
SEELAB
UC San Diego
pimercat@eng.ucsd.edu

Francesco Paterna
Strategic CAD Labs
Intel Corporation
francesco.paterna@intel.com

Andrea Bartolini
Integrated System Laboratory
ETH Zurich
DEI, University of Bologna
barandre@iis.ee.ethz.ch

Mohsen Imani
SEELAB
UC San Diego
moimani@eng.ucsd.edu

Luca Benini
Integrated System Laboratory
ETH Zurich
DEI, University of Bologna
luca.benini@iis.ee.ethz.ch

Tajana Šimunić Rosing
SEELAB
UC San Diego
tajana@ucsd.edu

ABSTRACT

Variability is the real big challenge for integrated circuits. Today, simulators help to estimate the effect of variability, but fail to capture real workload dynamics and user interactions, which are fundamental to mobile devices. This paper presents VarDroid, a low-overhead tool to emulate power and performance variability on real platforms, running on top of the Android operating system. VarDroid enables analyzing the effect of variability in power and performance while capturing the complex interactions characteristic of mobile workloads, thus relating to user's quality of experience. The paper presents use cases to show the utility of VarDroid to test applications, device and OS robustness under the effects of variability. Our results show that a variability-agnostic OS can incur in a performance penalty of up to 60% and a power penalty of up to 20%.

1. INTRODUCTION

Variability in integrated circuits refers to the deviation of the actual value of a design parameter from its nominal value, such as transistor channel length and threshold voltage. Sources of variation are static and dynamic. Static variations are due to the intrinsic inaccuracy of the fabrication process. Dynamic sources, such as ambient temperature and system workload, change their impact over time.

In multicore processors, transistor-level static variability determines power and performance distributions across cores of the same model. Consequently, computing units have a power consumption and operating voltage/frequency which is different from nominal right after fabrication [7]. As the scaling of CMOS technology progresses and dimensions of transistors shrink, the impact of variations is more dramatic, up to the point in which counteracting with higher design margins is extremely costly [5].

Simulators have been developed to help designers make chips more robust to variations [21, 20]. These tools can be integrated into the design flow to estimate the resulting impact of variability. However, they cannot account for dynamic variations and cannot capture real workloads behavior. Moreover, they require a highly detailed architectural description, which may not be always available.

Given that dynamic variations play an important role, a key idea is to leverage sensors to expose variability to higher levels of the software stack (e.g. the operating system) to manage it at runtime. This strategy is referred to as Dynamic Variability Management (DVM). DVM can leverage common hardware sensors such as performance counters and temperature sensors, or more sophisticated ones, such as degradation sensors and frequency sensors (which are devices capable of monitoring path delays) [14]. The latter, however, are only available on prototypes and research platforms. The community needs a tool to evaluate the impact of variability and to test DVM strategies on real commercial devices.

This is particularly urgent for mobile devices, as they are growing in popularity and work in a variety of environments, from mountains to deserts. Mobiles are characterized by interactive workloads, which are hard to simulate and predict, as they strongly depend on users [8]. Moreover, the goal of mobiles is to provide quality user experience, rather than high performance. Therefore, it is crucial to be able to estimate the impact of variability on user experience, which is not possible with simulators.

Most of mobile devices today adopt the Android operating system. Android builds on top of the Linux kernel, which offers access to hardware resources through drivers. It also offers the possibility to switch operating conditions dynamically to implement DVM policies. Finally, Android implements interfaces between user and kernel space that enable cross-layer synchronization. Flexibility and open-source make Android a perfect candidate for our purpose.

In this work, we develop and implement VarDroid, a low-overhead framework to emulate the effect of performance and power variability on Android devices. The emulation on real devices enables capturing the effects of environmental changes and interaction with users, which is not possible with simulators. Thanks to this, VarDroid can estimate the impact of variability on power and quality of user experience. Also, the Variability-induced Power Breakdown (VIP) allows estimating the ratio of dynamic and leakage power under variability. We present the assumptions of our work, the details of the implementation, and use-cases to demonstrate the feasibility and ease of use of our framework. We also make VarDroid available online for download [3]. Figure 1 better explains the motivation and goal of VarDroid. At

GLSVLSI '16, May 18-20, 2016, Boston, MA, USA

DOI: http://dx.doi.org/10.1145/2902961.2902971

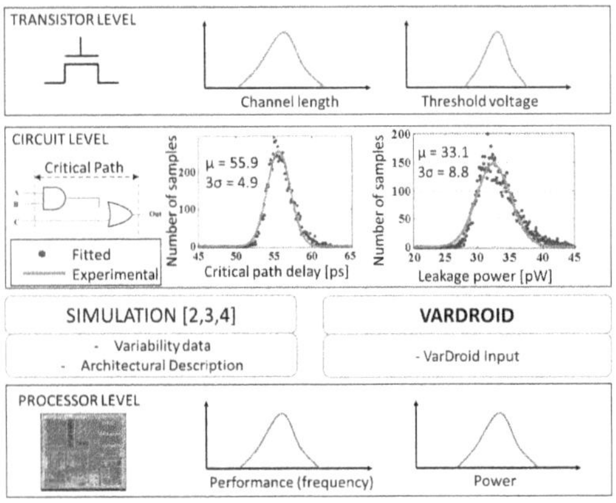

Figure 1: VarDroid context and motivation

the transistor level, variability mainly affects channel length and threshold voltage. At the circuit level, this has an impact on path delay and power consumption. As a preliminary study, we implement a circuit consisting of AND and OR gates using 32-nm technology with HSPICE simulator. For each transistor, we consider a variation in both channel length and threshold voltage which follows a Gaussian distribution with 3σ equal to 10% of the original value, similarly as in [6]. A Monte Carlo simulation with 5000 iteration produces the distributions of path delay (which affects operating frequency) and leakage power. The figure shows that such distributions are also well fitted by Gaussian curves. Finally, at the processor level, previous work [7, 24, 20] (on the left) focuses on simulating the effect of variability on a multiprocessor starting form detailed data on transistor parameters and propagates it to the processor level. In the end, it achieves Gaussian distributions for power and performance (i.e. operating frequency) for a large number of processors. In our work, instead, we emulate variability on a real device, by injecting perturbations in the Operating System (denoted as *VarDroid input*). Thanks to this, we do not require detailed low-level information about transistor variability. Nevertheless, we will show that we still obtain Gaussian distributions for power and performance, thus matching the results of state-of-the-art simulator and low level models. To clarify this, in the paper we describe models for power and frequency as a reference.

In our experiments, we use VarDroid to investigate the robustness of applications with respect to variability, the impact of variability on user experience and the tolerance of current OS migration policy. Our results show that performance of applications may drop by up to 35% in presence of variability and that a variability-agnostic OS can incur in a performance penalty of up to 60% and a power penalty of up to 20%.

The rest of the paper is organized as follows: Section 2 presents the related work, Section 3 describes the variability models, Section 4 describes the framework implementation and Section 5 presents experimental results. Finally, Section 6 concludes this paper.

2. RELATED WORK

In the last decade, variability has been the subject of numerous publications, from device-level simulation up to approximate computing for applications.

Architectural-level variability simulators have been developed, such as VARIUS [24], VAM [20], and VARIUS-NTV [11]. These tools can be integrated with simulators such as GEM5, but they require detailed architectural description. Garg et al. [9] propose a framework to analyze the impact of variability at the system level to help designers determining the tradeoff between performance and clock domain granularity. These techniques extract random values for architectural parameters and inject variability in the configuration of the simulator. The main drawback of such an approach is that simulations are very slow, as a few seconds of clock time for a real device could take hours.

An alternative approach in represented by variability emulation, which consists in injecting variations on a real device. In ERSA [15], errors are injected in architecturally visible registers. Similarly, in [23] a large fault injection campaign is conducted in the openSPARC T1 core logic. In [16], a combined hardware and software solution aims at identifying anomalous software behavior in presence of hardware faults. However, solutions based on hardware prototypes and FPGAs present low flexibility and portability. Work in reference [13] proposes VESPA, a variability emulation framework for SoC performance analysis. The proposed solution addresses the challenge of translating component-level characteristics into system-level performance distribution. The approach is evaluated for a 802.11 MAC processor and an MPEG encoder. Moreover, VESPA is used to assess the performance distribution of processors design prior to fabrication, given the design synthesis. Therefore is not effective in capturing real workload and the effects of real environment. Work in [25] proposes VarEmu. Implemented as an extension of the QEMU operating system, this can be used to evaluate variability-aware software techniques. VarEmu extracts timing and cycle count from the emulated code. This information is fed into a variability model with configurable parameters that determines energy consumption and fault variations in the virtual machine. VarEmu relies on models for power estimation, which have to be adapted to different platforms and may present accuracy problems. None of the previous work on variability emulation addresses mobiles and the crucial need of capturing interactive workload on variability-affected devices. Our approach is different in that we inject faults directly in the native OS of real mobiles in the form of a VarDroid input.

Recent publications on Dynamic Variability Management (DVM) propose scheduling and DVFS algorithms for embedded platforms [21] and for Android-based devices [19]. However, these solutions do not account for real workload and real user interaction.

Emulation in Android has been addressed before for reliability [18, 17]. Work in [18] implements a kernel module to virtualize the presence of degradation sensors to emulate the effect of degradation mechanisms. Our work is orthogonal to [18], in that we focus on performance and power variability, while the technique in [18] aims at emulating degradation. At this time, no publication presents power and performance variability emulation capable of running on real mobiles.

In this work, we develop and implement a framework for emulating the effects of performance and power variability on real Android devices, while capturing real mobile workloads. Finally, we show how to use it to test system robustness against variability.

3. VARIABILITY MODELS

Variability in integrated circuits manufacturing has two components: D2D (die-to-die) and WID (within-die) [24]. WID variations can be further separated into systematic and random variations. At the microarchitectural level, the elements of key importance for variability are the transistor threshold voltage V_{th} and the effective channel length L_{eff} of transistors. More recently, C2C (core-to-core) variations have been considered [7]. Following this model, low-level variations in V_{th} and L_{eff} result in operating frequencies and power consumption which are distributed among cores. Since V_{th} and L_{eff} can be considered normally distributed with good approximation, power consumption and critical path delay (thus, operating frequency) can be considered normally distributed among cores as well [24]. Power is the sum of dynamic and leakage contributions. Dynamic power has a well-known dependency on frequency and voltage [12]. Leakage power, instead, depends on leakage current, which can be modeled as in Equation 1.

$$I_{leak} = b\left(\frac{kT}{q}\right)^2 \exp\left(\frac{q(V_{off} - V_{th})}{\eta kT}\right) \quad (1)$$

Where q is the electron charge and k is the Boltzmann constant. The terms b, η and V_{off} are empirically determined parameters. As shown in [24], the knowledge of V_{th} variance can be exploited to assess the impact on chipÂĄ leakage power. As a result, the value of the ratio between perturbed and nominal leakage can be expressed as in Equation 2.

$$\frac{P_{leak}}{P_{leak_0}} = \frac{V_{leak}}{V_{leak_0}} = \exp\left(\frac{1}{2}\left(\frac{q\sigma}{\eta kT}\right)^2\right) \quad (2)$$

Where P_{leak_0} and I_{leak_0} are the nominal values of leakage power and current. This indicates that the variation in leakage depends on the standard deviation σ of V_{th}. As for critical path delay, this is related to the switching delay of an inverter gate, which is expressed by Equation 3.

$$T_g = a\frac{L_{eff}V}{\mu^*(V - V_{th})^\alpha} \quad (3)$$

Where a is an empirically determined parameter, α is typically 1.3 and μ^* is the mobility of carriers. Given the critical path delay T_g, which depends on gate switching delays, the maximum frequency at which a processor can be clocked is given by its inverse $f_{MAX} = 1/T_g$.

In this work, we refer to Equations 1, 2 and 3 to characterize VarDroid configurations of the target platform. This is done assuming a diverse impact of variability in L_{eff} and V_{th}, expressed as the ratio μ/σ of the underlying Gaussian distribution. Finally, at the processor level, variability results in Gaussian distributions of maximum frequency (e.g. performance) and power. VarDroid naturally captures dynamic variations, such as workload and environmental conditions (such as SoC and ambient temperature), given that it is implemented on real devices.

4. VARDROID ARCHITECTURE

Figure 2 shows the block diagram of the proposed implementation. It has two main components: the **VarDroid Engine** and the **VarDroid Monitor**. The **VarDroid Engine** is the software element which perturbs the system to emulate the effect of variability and has four components: the input configurations PERT, SCHED and INJ, and the Variability-Induced Power breakdown emulator (VIP). The components are described into details in the following.

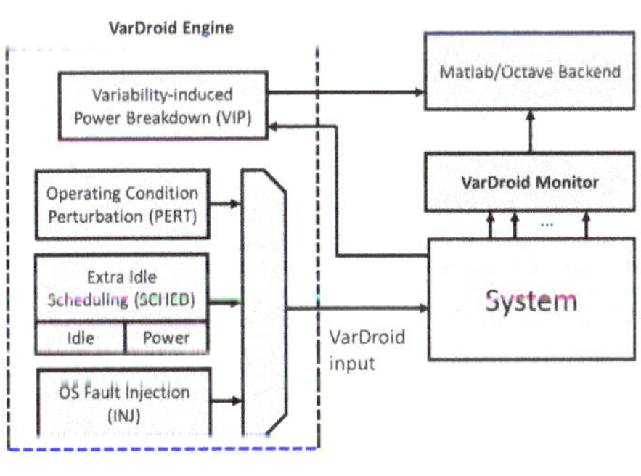

Figure 2: VarDroid block diagram

Operating conditions perturbation (PERT): The operating frequencies of cores are limited by PERT to mimic the effect of performance variability. We generate a Gaussian distribution for f_{MAX}, extract and assign randomly one value to each core. In this way, operating conditions are limited as if the multicore was affected by variations on performance. This emulates a scenario in which L_{eff} and V_{th} of transistors have variability, which reflects in f_{MAX} variability (i.e. performance), as described by Equation 3. The operating condition perturbation is implemented at the userspace level, and exploits the *sysfs* fields exposed by the *cpufreq* driver that allows to set an upper bound on operating frequency. The selected f_{MAX} represents the input of PERT to the system. Figure 3 shows that PERT perturbs the behavior at a high level (i.e. system level), by selecting an upper bound for operating conditions.

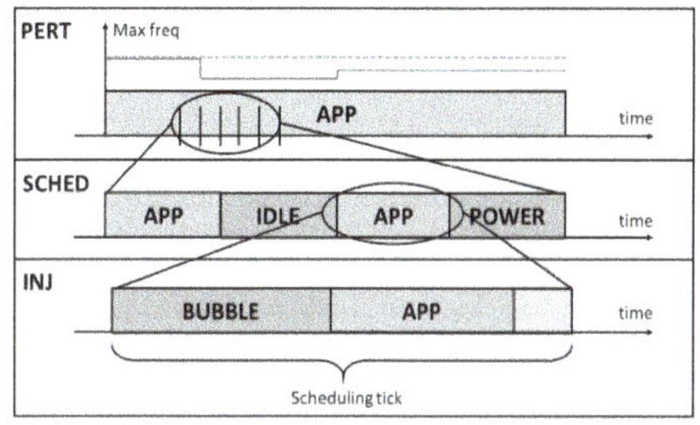

Figure 3: VarDroid input configuration

Extra scheduling (SCHED): SCHED forces the scheduling of extra periods to interleave the normal execution of applications. It is implemented as a program that alternates periods of execution and sleep (implemented with *nanosleep*). The effect of SCHED is varied by tuning the *nanosleep* duration, which affects the SCHED duty cycle. SCHED can be configured with an *Idle* application for performance variation (a program executing a long sequence of NOPs) and a *Power* application for power consumption variation (a sequence of cpu-intensive operations). In the first case, the emulated scenario is similar to the one achieved with PERT, in which L_{eff} and V_th variations result in frequency variations. In the second case, the scenario includes power variability, both dynamic and leakage. Figure 3 shows that SCHED occupies some scheduling intervals with spurious applications. Both PERT and SCHED are implemented as C programs and cross-compiled with Android NDK toolchain to run on the target platform.

OS fault injection (INJ): INJ is implemented by inserting in the OS kernel source code execution *bubbles* that perturb performance. The *bubble* is a fixed sequence of instruction which is inlined in the kernel source code. A single bubble executes a sequence of 20 NOPs (for the current design of VarDroid) at the beginning of each scheduling tick. The impact of variability can be tuned by choosing the number of bubbles (referred to as *bubble length*). INJ also emulates the scenario in which variability in L_{eff} and V_{th} results in performance variability. The fault injector is implemented as an inlined function which is invoked in the *scheduling_tick()* function in the scheduler source code (*core.c*). Figure 3 shows that INJ occupies part of the scheduling interval itself with spurious instructions.

We denote the VarDroid input ν in the three configurations respectively as the percentage of frequency degradation over f_{MAX} for PERT, the nanosleep duration for SCHED and the bubble length for INJ.

The three input configurations have complementary benefits. PERT and INJ can emulate performance variations, but are not effective in emulating power variations. INJ emulates performance variations at a finer granularity compared to PERT, but requires recompiling the Linux kernel. PERT and SCHED, instead, can be more easily ported, as they are userspace programs. Note that the three input configurations inject variability at different layers of the software stack, and consequently at different time granularity, as Figure 3 shows.

Variability-induced Power Breakdown (VIP): Beside the three input configurations, VarDroid features VIP, a framework to estimate the proportion of dynamic to leakage power depending on input variation on performance. The main motivation for the design of VIP is that on a real platform, we can only measure the total power consumption, but we cannot distinguish the dynamic and leakage contributions. This is important, because the variation on parameters L_{eff} and V_th determines a variation in the ratio between dynamic and leakage power. It is well known that dynamic power P_{dyn} is directly proportional to frequency, and VarDroid establishes a relation between the input variability ν and f_{MAX}. Since f_{MAX} depends on V_{th}, this can be derived from ν as well. The leakage power P_{leak} depends exponentially on V_{th}. Overall, this allows deriving the ratio P_{dyn}/P_{leak} as ν varies, as expressed by Equation 4.

$$\frac{P_{dyn}}{P_{leak}} \approx \sigma \frac{f(\nu)}{\exp(g^{-1}(\beta f(\nu)))} \tag{4}$$

Where σ, β are fitting parameters. The function g can be derived from Equation 3, and it is so that $g(V_{th}) = f(\nu)$, while $f(\nu)$ can be fitted experimentally. As ν increases, the ratio should also increase, as this reflects a scenario in which V_{th} is higher than nominal. VIP computes a ratio, thus it does not depend on which power is actually consumed and measured. We will better characterize VIP in the results section.

The **VarDroid Monitor** infrastructure has been implemented by modifying the one described in [18]. It has a kernel sampling function, a monitor driver to transfer data to the user space and a monitor daemon to regulate the data transfer. The monitor infrastructure is able to get one sample per each scheduling tick (10ms in our setup) and transfers data to the userspace with low overhead. Finally, the Matlab backend allows parsing and plotting results.

5. EXPERIMENTAL EVALUATION

We implemented VarDroid on the Odroid XU3 board. This board has a Samsung Exynos 5422 Octa core based on ARM big.LITTLE architecture, with a Cortex^{TM}-A15 2.0Ghz quad core cluster and Cortex^{TM}-A7 quad core cluster [1]. The platform has a 2MB L2 cache and a 2GB RAM. The OS is Android 4.4.4 with Linux kernel 3.10.9.

5.1 VarDroid Validation

The key idea for validating Android is to show that when varying the VarDroid input (for each one of the three configuration) we obtain a Gaussian distribution of frequency and power consumption, similar as in [7]. This proves that a variation of the VarDroid input reflects a scenario in which transistor parameters L_{eff} and V_{th} are subject to variability.

For validating VarDroid, we conduct a series of experiments using single-threaded microbenchmarks. The *cpu-bound* executes a series of ALU operations without accessing memory, the *L2-bound* executes a series of loads from the L2 memory and the *mem-bound* similarly executes a series of loads from the main memory. To avoid the effect of migrations, microbenchmarks exploit the *set affinity* mechanism to run on a specific core.

Performance Variability: In the following experiments, we keep only one LITTLE core active, running at fixed maximum frequency. Analogous results can be obtained for big cores. Figure 4 shows the normalized execution time of the three microbenchmarks for the three VarDroid configurations. The execution time of the benchmarks increases as the VarDroid input increases. This means that VarDroid effectively makes the processor behave as if it had a maximum frequency lower than the nominal. To further validate

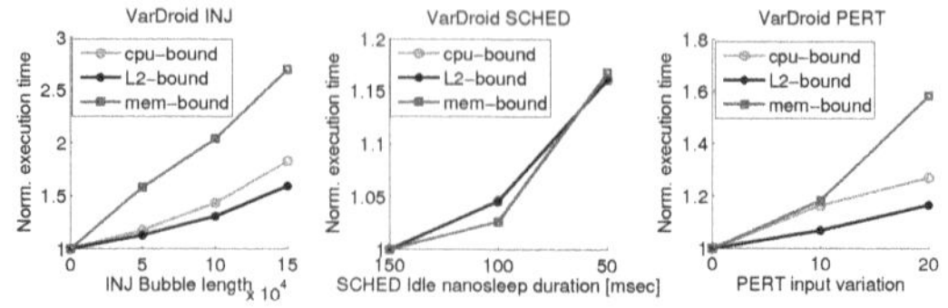

Figure 4: Microbenchmarks execution times

this behavior, we run the *cpu-bound* benchmark with random VarDroid input extracted from a normal distribution, in the three configurations. In Figure 5, the plots on the left show the histogram of VarDroid input. Then we collect the execution times and build a histogram, shown in the plots on the right. In the case of SCHED, we employed a smaller number of samples and a version of the *cpu-bound* benchmark of longer duration. The resulting shape match with the low-level models discussed from Section 3 and the example of Figure 1. In this way VarDroid emulation shows results as if the benchmarks were executed by different instances of the same processor, affected by performance variability. No variation in execution time is present when VarDroid is disabled. **Power Variability**: Next, we verified the effect of VarDroid on power variability. In Figure 6 we show the histogram of random input for the SCHED Power configuration (e.g. *nanosleep* duration) and the corresponding histogram of average power consumption. In this experiment, we are measuring only the power consumption of the LITTLE cluster, but a similar result can be obtained for the big cluster. One sample of power consumption is computed by averaging the power over a period of 120 seconds, with a given SCHED power input. Also in this case, the histograms match the behavior expected from low-level models of Section 3. In Figure 7, we perform the same measurement while executing a sequence of *cpu-bound* benchmarks. The second plot shows the power variability, while the third plot shows the execution time variability. The variation in the execution times is very low (in the 2% of the mean value). This means that the SCHED power setting can be effectively used to decouple power and performance variability effects. Finally, Figure 8 shows the qualitative behavior of the VIP ratio. For simplicity, the relations involved in Equation 4 are assumed linear. Dynamic and leakage power are scaled in the [0,1] interval and the final ratio is normalized with respect to the minimum. The final behavior is that of a log-normal distribution. As reported in [12] the log-normal shape is generated by the exponential increase in leakage current, thus matching with the model described by Equations 2 and 3. Note that the distribution of the VarDroid

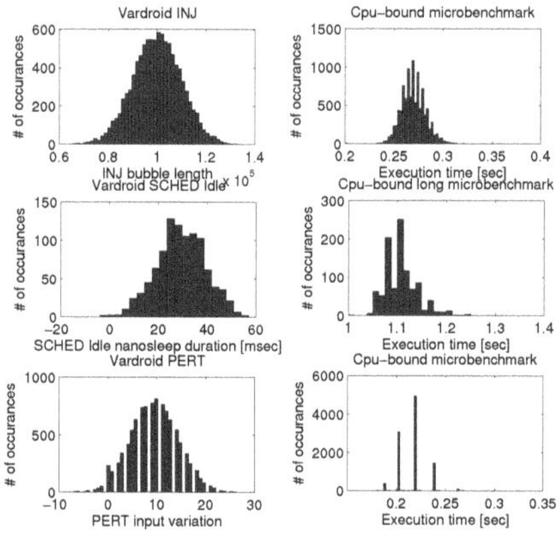

Figure 5: VarDroid performance distribution

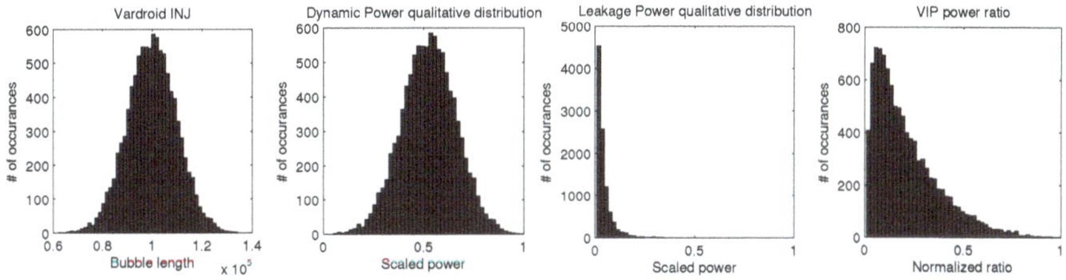

Figure 8: Variability-induced Power breakdown distribution

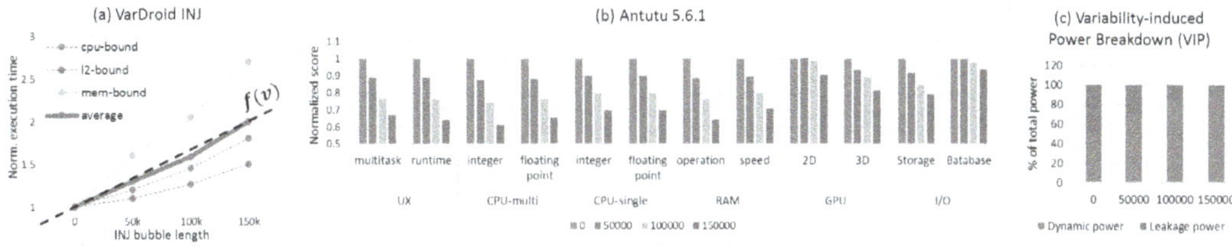

Figure 9: Performance degradation and VIP in Antutu benchmark

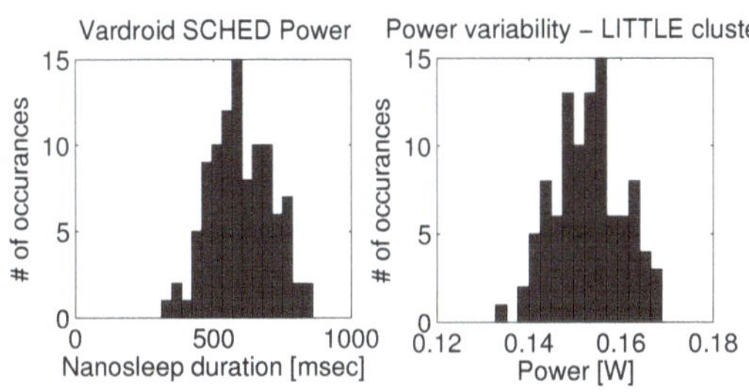

Figure 6: SCHED power variability of little cluster

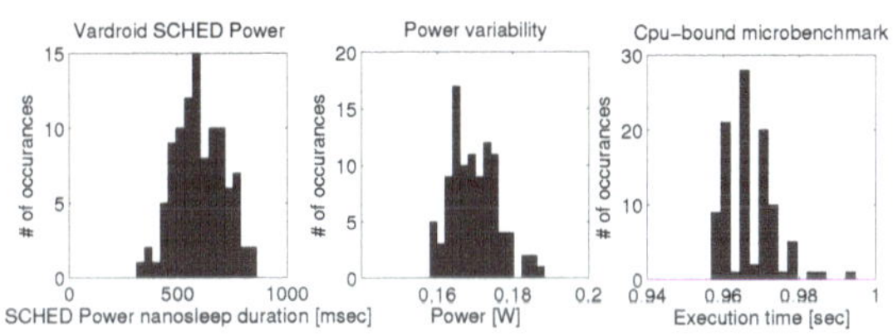

Figure 7: Power variability with cpu-bound benchmark

input can be tuned to achieve a desired power and performance variation.

5.2 Use Cases

In the following experiments, we present use cases in which we can exploit VarDroid.

Application Robustness: VarDroid can be used to investigate the impact of variability on real application performance and power consumption. In Figure 9b, we present the scores obtained with the mobile benchmark Antutu v5.6.1 [4] with increasing impact of INJ. Scores of mobile benchmarks are a common metric to compare the quality of execution of different devices. As expected, all the scores decrease as the INJ input increases, by up to 35%, also in accordance with the results obtained on microbenchmarks. Therefore, VarDroid can be used by application developers to test the performance of their apps in a real device affected by variability. Figure 9c shows the ratio between dynamic and leakage power obtained with VIP. The base case is assumed to have 50% of dynamic and 50% of leakage power, in accordance with ITRS [5]. In this case, the function f is derived from the results in Figure 3 from INJ microbenchmarking, also shown in Figure 9a. As expected, the ratio P_{dyn}/P_{leak} increases with the VarDroid input.

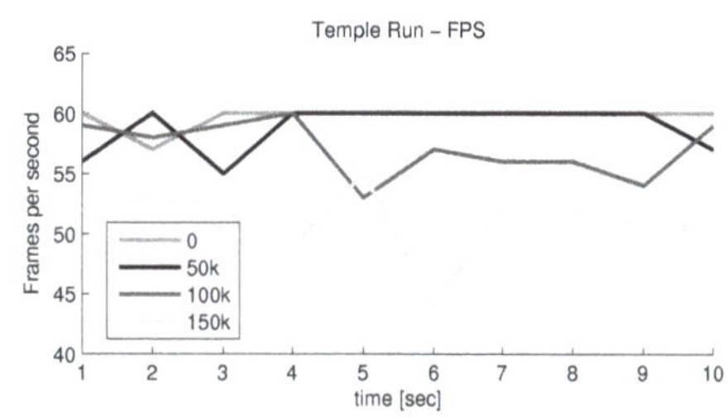

Figure 10: VarDroid impact on FPS

User Experience: Since VarDroid is implemented on a real device, it can capture real workload dynamics and user interaction, therefore it can be used to assess the impact of variability on user experience. For this experiment, we record and replay a 10 seconds-long touch event trace of a popular Android 3D game (Temple Run [2]), in order to reproduce the same workload [10]. Then, we execute the trace with different INJ configurations, and measure Frame per Seconds (FPS) by monitoring the SurfaceLinger service. Indeed, it is well recognized that FPS in 3D gaming is a good metric for quality of experience [22]. In particular, the closer to 60fps (which is the maximum allowed by Android), the better. The results in Figure 10 show the different FPS traces. As expected, the FPS lowers as the INJ input increases. In particular, in a scenario of severe variability impact (bubble length of 150k), user experience is heavily affected, as FPS drops below 50.

Variability Tolerance of the OS: VarDroid can be used to detect limitations and bugs of existing OS design. In this experiment, we focus on the workload migration policy employed in ARM big.LITTLE architectures [1]. In such architecture, a hysteresis mechanism regulates the task migration between LITTLE and big cores, with a high a and a low utilization threshold. When the high threshold is exceeded, the task is migrated to the big core, and is returned to the

LITTLE core if utilization decreases below the low threshold. The limitation of such mechanisms is that migration thresholds are fixed. Because of this, the execution can incur significant performance penalties. To show this, we im-

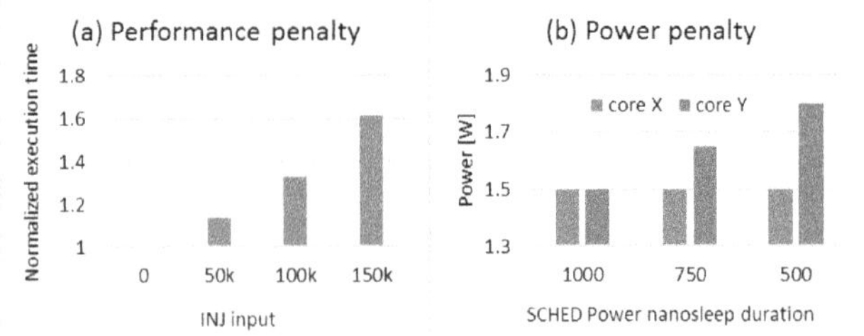

Figure 11: Migration (a) performance and (b) power penalty

plemented a single threaded cpu-bound synthetic workload that periodically alternates between three execution phases, respectively with low, medium and high utilization. Then, we execute it with only one LITTLE core and one big core active. The workload is initially allocated on the LITTLE core and execute low and medium phases. The high phase instead triggers the migration to the big core. We execute the program with increasing INJ input, and measure execution times. Figure 11a shows the normalized execution times of the medium phase. Results show a penalty of up to 60%. A lower migration threshold in this case would have avoided such penalty. The variability tolerance of the migration policy in this case could be improved by changing the migration threshold dynamically. In a scenario in which platforms can actually detect the variability at runtime thanks to dedicated sensors [14], thresholds should be adapted dynamically.

As a final example, we make the case in which the LITTLE core can choose to migrate the workload between two big cores, a core X of the big cluster with nominal power consumption (which is 1.5W from our measurements) and a core Y with higher power consumption due to variability. Results in Figure 11b show that a variation-agnostic migration policy can incur in a power penalty of up to 20%.

6. CONCLUSION

This paper presents VarDroid, the first tool for power and performance emulation for mobiles, implemented on top of the Android operating system. VarDroid is validated with microbenchmarks for performance and power variability. We presented use cases to show how VarDroid can be used to analyze the robustness of existing applications against variability, evaluate the impact of variability on user experience and highlight the limitations of current OS design on heterogeneous architectures.

7. ACKNOWLEDGMENTS

This work was supported in part by NSF grant 1527034.

8. REFERENCES

[1] Arm white paper. 2014. big.little technology: The future of mobile.

[2] https://en.wikipedia.org/wiki/temple_run.

[3] https://github.com/pietromercati/vardroid.

[4] http://www.antutu.com/en/ranking.shtml.

[5] Itrs reports, december 2014 [online] http://www.itrs.net. 2014.

[6] A. Agarwal, D. Blaauw, and V. Zolotov. Statistical timing analysis for intra-die process variations with spatial correlations. In *Computer Aided Design, 2003. ICCAD-2003. International Conference on*, pages 900–907, Nov 2003.

[7] K. A. Bowman, A. R. Alameldeen, S. T. Srinivasan, and C. B. Wilkerson. Impact of die-to-die and within-die parameter variations on the clock frequency and throughput of multi-core processors. *IEEE Transactions on Very Large Scale Integration (VLSI) Systems*, 17(12):1679–1690, Dec 2009.

[8] H. Falaki, R. Mahajan, S. Kandula, D. Lymberopoulos, R. Govindan, and D. Estrin. Diversity in smartphone usage. In *Proceedings of the 8th International Conference on Mobile Systems, Applications, and Services*, MobiSys '10, pages 179–194, New York, NY, USA, 2010. ACM.

[9] S. Garg and D. Marculescu. System-level throughput analysis for process variation aware multiple voltage-frequency island designs. *ACM Trans. Des. Autom. Electron. Syst.*, 13(4):59:1–59:25, Oct. 2008.

[10] L. Gomez, I. Neamtiu, T. Azim, and T. Millstein. Reran: Timing- and touch-sensitive record and replay for android. In *Proceedings of the 2013 International Conference on Software Engineering*, ICSE '13, pages 72–81, Piscataway, NJ, USA, 2013. IEEE Press.

[11] U. R. Karpuzcu, K. B. Kolluru, N. S. Kim, and J. Torrellas. Varius-ntv: A microarchitectural model to capture the increased sensitivity of manycores to process variations at near-threshold voltages. In *Dependable Systems and Networks (DSN), 2012 42nd Annual IEEE/IFIP International Conference on*, pages 1–11, June 2012.

[12] N. S. Kim, T. Austin, D. Baauw, T. Mudge, K. Flautner, J. S. Hu, M. J. Irwin, M. Kandemir, and V. Narayanan. Leakage current: Moore's law meets static power. *Computer*, 36(12):68–75, Dec 2003.

[13] V. J. Kozhikkottu, R. Venkatesan, A. Raghunathan, and S. Dey. Vespa: Variability emulation for system-on-chip performance analysis. In *Design, Automation Test in Europe Conference Exhibition (DATE), 2011*, pages 1–6, March 2011.

[14] L. Lai, V. Chandra, R. C. Aitken, and P. Gupta. Slackprobe: A flexible and efficient in situ timing slack monitoring methodology. *IEEE Transactions on Computer-Aided Design of Integrated Circuits and Systems*, 33(8):1168–1179, Aug 2014.

[15] L. Leem, H. Cho, J. Bau, Q. A. Jacobson, and S. Mitra. Ersa: Error resilient system architecture for probabilistic applications. In *Design, Automation Test in Europe Conference Exhibition (DATE), 2010*, pages 1560–1565, March 2010.

[16] M.-L. Li, P. Ramachandran, S. K. Sahoo, S. V. Adve, V. S. Adve, and Y. Zhou. Understanding the propagation of hard errors to software and implications for resilient system design. In *Proceedings of the 13th International Conference on Architectural Support for Programming Languages and Operating Systems*, ASPLOS XIII, pages 265–276, New York, NY, USA, 2008. ACM.

[17] P. Mercati, A. Bartolini, F. Paterna, L. Benini, and T. S. Rosing. An on-line reliability emulation framework. In *Proceedings of the 2014 12th IEEE International Conference on Embedded and Ubiquitous Computing*, EUC '14, pages 334–339, Washington, DC, USA, 2014. IEEE Computer Society.

[18] P. Mercati, A. Bartolini, F. Paterna, T. S. Rosing, and L. Benini. A linux-governor based dynamic reliability manager for android mobile devices. In *Design, Automation and Test in Europe Conference and Exhibition (DATE), 2014*, pages 1–4, March 2014.

[19] P. Mercati, F. Paterna, A. Bartolini, L. Benini, and T. S. Rosing. Dynamic variability management in mobile multicore processors under lifetime constraints. In *Computer Design (ICCD), 2014 32nd IEEE International Conference on*, pages 448–455, Oct 2014.

[20] M. Miranda, B. Dierickx, P. Zuber, P. Dobrovoln, F. Kutscherauer, P. Roussel, and P. Poliakov. Variability aware modeling of socs: From device variations to manufactured system yield. In *Quality of Electronic Design, 2009. ISQED 2009. Quality Electronic Design*, pages 547–553, March 2009.

[21] F. Paterna, A. Acquaviva, and L. Benini. Aging-aware energy-efficient workload allocation for mobile multimedia platforms. *IEEE Transactions on Parallel and Distributed Systems*, 24(8):1489–1499, Aug 2013.

[22] A. Pathania, Q. Jiao, A. Prakash, and T. Mitra. Integrated cpu-gpu power management for 3d mobile games. In *Proceedings of the 51st Annual Design Automation Conference*, DAC '14, pages 40:1–40:6, New York, NY, USA, 2014. ACM.

[23] A. Pellegrini, R. Smolinski, L. Chen, X. Fu, S. K. S. Hari, J. Jiang, S. V. Adve, T. Austin, and V. Bertacco. Crashtest'ing swat: Accurate, gate-level evaluation of symptom-based resiliency solutions. In *Design, Automation Test in Europe Conference Exhibition (DATE), 2012*, pages 1106–1109, March 2012.

[24] S. R. Sarangi, B. Greskamp, R. Teodorescu, J. Nakano, A. Tiwari, and J. Torrellas. Varius: A model of process variation and resulting timing errors for microarchitects. *IEEE Transactions on Semiconductor Manufacturing*, 21(1):3–13, Feb 2008.

[25] L. Wanner, S. Elmalaki, L. Lai, P. Gupta, and M. Srivastava. Varemu: An emulation testbed for variability-aware software. In *Hardware/Software Codesign and System Synthesis (CODES+ISSS), 2013 International Conference on*, pages 1–10, Sept 2013.

Neural Network-based Prediction Algorithms for In-Door Multi-Source Energy Harvesting System for Non-Volatile Processors

Ning Liu[1]*, Caiwen Ding[1]*, Yanzhi Wang[1], and Jingtong Hu[2]
[1]Dept. of Electrical Engineering and Computer Science, Syracuse University, Syracuse, NY
[2]School of Electrical and Computer Engineering, Oklahoma State University, Stillwater, OK
{nliu03, cading, ywang393}@syr.edu, jthu@okstate.edu

ABSTRACT

Due to size, longevity, safety, and recharging concerns, energy harvesting is becoming a better choice for many wearable embedded systems than batteries. However, harvested energy is intrinsically unstable. In order to overcome this drawback, non-volatile processors (NVPs) have been proposed to bridge intermittent program execution. However, even with NVPs, frequent power interruptions will severely degrade system performance. Hence, in this paper we adopt a multi-source in-door energy harvesting architecture to compensate the shortcoming of single energy source. We further investigate power harvesting prediction techniques, which are critical for NVP systems since they can coordinate with task scheduler in the NVP system to compensate the intermittent ambient energy harvesting. We investigate prediction methods both for single energy harvesting source and for multiple energy harvesting sources, the total output power of which is more stable compared with the single source case. A comprehensive evaluation framework has been developed using actually measured harvesting traces on the proposed neural network-based power harvesting prediction methods. It turns out that the most favorable prediction methods are directly predicting the total output power of DC-DC converters (connecting between energy sources and NVP), or predicting the total input power of DC-DC converters first and then inferring the total output power using a learned mapping function, for multi-source power harvesting predictions.

Keywords

Non-volatile processors; neural network; energy harvesting; multiple energy source

*Ning Liu and Caiwen Ding contributed equally to this work.

GLSVLSI '16, May 18-20, 2016, Boston, MA, USA
© 2016 ACM. ISBN 978-1-4503-4274-2/16/05...$15.00
DOI: http://dx.doi.org/10.1145/2902961.2903037

1. INTRODUCTION

Wearable technologies and Internet of Things (IoT) are increasingly attracting attention in personal and commercial applications, which are changing our daily life to some extent. Many of such devices are equipped by interweaving embedded system technologies into our daily routine, such as smart bands and smart watches. However, there are still several challenges that need to be tackled in improving the limited performance of the existing wearable devices. One of the primary challenges is how to constantly power these wearable devices since the traditional battery is not a suitable way due to its size, recharging, longevity, and safety concerns. To improve the performance of wearable devices, researches are diligently pursuing alternative power supplies. Energy harvesting is one of the most promising techniques to meet both the characteristics and power requirements of wearable devices.

Energy harvesting technologies convert harvestable energy from ambient environment using energy conversion techniques. Harvesting energy sources include solar power, motion, body heat, etc. They are environmentally friendly due to the characteristic of battery-less by nature. However, none of these harvestable energy sources are relatively stable. Also, most of these energy sources operate at relatively low conversion efficiency since only a small portion of total system input power can be transmitted. Meanwhile, the execution of processors will be interrupted frequently with an unstable power supply. These unreliable energy sources will cause frequent disruption and then degrade the performance of the whole embedded system. Non-volatile processors (NVPs) have been proposed in order to operate under unstable power supply condition. Theoretically, NVPs' state will be stored to the nonvolatile Ferroelectric Random Access Memory (FRAM) every time when the power goes off. NVPs can be fast recovered when the power resumes with several cycles from the interrupted point.

However, frequent power failures may cause severe performance degradation such as computation errors and excessive energy consumption even with NVPs. In energy harvesting systems, NVPs primarily operate under in-door environment and strongly rely on in-door energy harvesting techniques due to the fact that in-door energy sources are relatively difficult to be harvested. A single in-door source energy harvesting is sporadic and variable due to its dependency on energy flow fluctuation and ambient conditions. To make it worse, the available harvestable power is usually limited within few milliwatts. In this paper, we combine multiple in-door energy sources, e.g., Photovoltaics (PV), Thermo-electric Generator (TEG), and piezoelectric (PZ), in order to compensate the limitation of single energy source and increase the total output power of (buck and boost) DC-DC converters, thereby realizing a stable and sufficient power source for the NVP system.

Accurate power harvesting prediction is critical for the ambient energy harvesting-based NVPs because it can coordinate with the task scheduler in the operating system (OS) of NVP for scheduling tasks and performing checkpointing once a power failure is predicted. In this paper we propose artificial neural network-based power harvesting prediction methods which are responsible for predicting the time of the next power failure and compensating the power failure through triggering the OS scheduler. We perform comprehensive comparison works regarding mean square error (MSE) of the multiple proposed prediction mechanisms. More specifically, the major contributions of this paper include:

- We adopt the feed-forward back propagation neural network-based prediction algorithm for power harvesting predictions. More specifically, we use the power harvesting results in previous time slots as features in neural network to predict the power harvesting result in the next second. Afterward, the gradient descent algorithm with momentum weight and bias learning is adopted to train the neural network to find the best neural network configuration and parameters to match the measured data. Extensive evaluations are performed on the performance of prediction algorithms with respect to MSE.

- We begin with single-source power harvesting predictions using neural networks. Two methods are presented. The first method predicts the output power of DC-DC converter (connecting to PV or TEG) directly, whereas the second method predicts the input power of DC-DC converter and then estimates the output power based on accurate converter modeling. We evaluate the prediction accuracies of these two methods on PV and TEG power harvesting traces.

- Next we present neural network-based prediction algorithms for multi-source power harvestings, which exhibit more stable power output compared with single-source cases. We introduce three prediction methods. Method I directly predicts the summation of output powers of DC-DC converters (connecting to PV, TEG, etc.), which is the input power of NVP. Method II predicts input powers of converters separately and then estimates and combines their output power values using accurate converter modeling. Finally, Method III predicts the total input power of converters, and then infers the total output power by utilizing a learned mapping function. We evaluate the performances of these three methods using PV and TEG power harvesting traces.

The rest of this paper is organized as follows: Section 2 briefly discusses the related works. The proposed multi-source energy harvesting architecture is introduced in Section 3. Neural network-based single-source power harvesting prediction and multi-source power harvesting prediction algorithms are presented in Section 4 and Section 5, respectively. Finally, Section 6 concludes this paper.

2. RELATED WORKS

In order to make computing systems power failure-proof, NVPs were developed [1, 2]. Research has shown that by saving the computation state onto an on-chip NVM quickly when the power fails and restoring the state when the power resumes, system can work accumulatively under unstable power supply. Energy harvesters scavenge ambient power from surrounding environment through energy conversion techniques. Energy harvesters thus can be applied to develop battery-less wearable devices. Thermal, solar [3], vibration, radio frequency and body movements [4, 5, 6] are all potential available energy sources. These energy sources are different in controllability, magnitude, stability, and predictability. However, for ultra-low power devices such as NVPs and wearable devices, solar energy, breathing ($0.42W$), and body heat ($2.4\sim4.8W$) are capable of providing sufficient power to power them at a low duty cycle [7, 8].

3. MULTI-SOURCE ENERGY HARVESTING SYSTEM

To overcome the limitation of a single energy harvesting source, we combine multiple in-door energy sources (e.g., PV, TEG, and PZ) to build a relatively stable and adequate energy source that efficiently drives the NVPs. The overall power conversion efficiency can be increased due to the lower variation of harvested energy.

Fig. 1 demonstrates the multi-source energy harvesting system architecture for NVPs with three input energy sources: in-door PV, TEG, and PZ devices. Instead of cascading two stages of DC-DC converters in traditional energy harvesting systems with battery, single DC-DC converter is used between in-door PV (or TEG) and the NVP with approximately 1V operating voltage. Consequently, parameters of the single-stage converter need to be optimized for maximizing energy efficiency with fixed output voltage determined by NVPs. On the other hand, a cascade connection of AC-DC rectifier and DC-DC converter is required between PZ energy source and NVP due to the inherent AC characteristic of PZ devices. Given the required output voltage of the harvesting system, buck converters are required for PV and PZ devices because of their relatively higher output voltage. Boost converter is required for TEG device due to its relatively lower output voltage [9].

The DC-DC converters in the energy harvesting system share a single filter capacitor at output in order to simplify the multi-source energy harvesting system structure. Our structure simplifies the system control methodology and also provides separate maximum power extraction methods for different input energy harvesting sources compared with [10], which used complex circuity in order to control the maximum extractable power from energy sources. Thus, the overall efficiency is improved through the flexible structure.

Multi-input Energy Harvesting Traces

A single in-door energy source is variable and sporadic such that it cannot serve as a reliable energy supply for the NVPs due to its high dependency on ambient conditions. On the other hand, employing multiply energy sources (PV, TEG, and PZ) can compensate the limitation of single energy

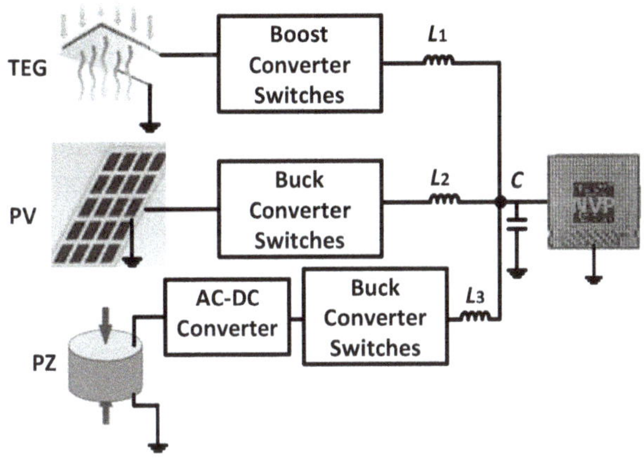

Figure 1: System architecture of multi-input energy harvesting for NVPs.

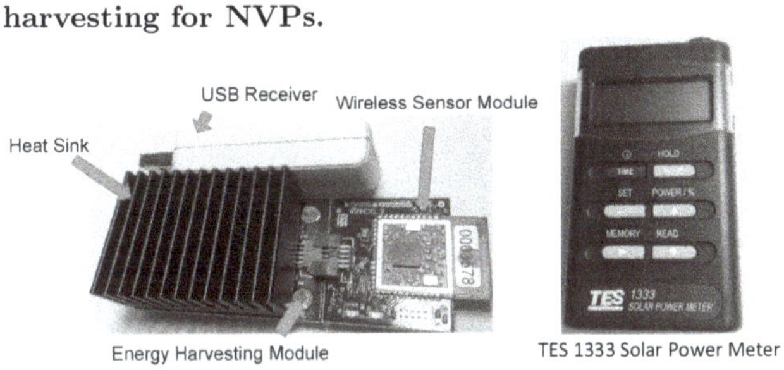

Figure 2: TEG harvester and solar power meter for the energy harvesting traces measurement

source harvesting system and improve the reliability of energy harvesting, which provides a more stable and adequate power source for NVPs.

We select TES 1333 Solar Power Meter [11] to measure different indoor PV irradiance intensity traces as shown in Fig. 2, which can be translated into power harvesting traces based on accurate PV models [12]. We measure different indoor PV power traces under different in-door lights: filament lamps and daylight lamps. For TEG, we adopt a thermal energy harvesting module [13] as shown in Fig. 2 attached on different heat sources to obtain different TEG power traces, at ambient temperature of 25°C with a heat sink attached on the TEG devices.

4. NEURAL NETWORK-BASED SINGLE SOURCE POWER HARVESTING PREDICTION

This section presents neural network-based prediction algorithms for single-source power harvesting. Once a power failure is predicted, i.e., the input harvesting power is predicted to drop below a predefined threshold value P_{th}, the prediction algorithm will trigger the scheduler with the predicted power failure time, and coordinates with the task scheduler in the OS of NVP for scheduling tasks and performing checkpointing. In the coming clock cycles, the scheduler will work with the harvesting system to compensate the power failure caused by unstable ambient energy sources.

We adopt the feed-forward back propagation neural network, which is one of the most prevailing neural algorithms, for prediction of the future power harvesting. We use the power harvesting results in previous time slots to predict the power harvesting in the next time slot (with duration of one second). The input feature vector $[P_{t-n}, ..., P_{t-1}, P_t]$ includes the previous and current power harvesting values (assuming current time t), while the output is the prediction $\hat{P}^{t+1}$ of the harvesting power in the next second (time $t+1$). In this network, we use 35 as the number of features in the input feature vector based on numerical optimizations. As shown in Fig. 3, the neural network has 4 layers. The input layer has 35 neuron and the two hidden layers have 12 and 4 neurons, respectively. The output layer has one dimension ($\hat{P}^{t+1}$). Each neuron uses the sigmoid function to regularize the inner product of the input and weight vectors of the neuron, and then propagates to the next layer.

When training the neural network, we need to update the weights of neurons. More specifically, we adopt the *gradient descent algorithm with momentum weight and bias learning function* [14], which calculates the weight change ΔW for a given neuron. The weight updating equation is given as follows:

$$\Delta W = C_m \Delta W_{prev} + (1 - C_m) R_l G_w \tag{1}$$

where ΔW_{prev} is the previous weight change, R_l is the learning rate, C_m is the momentum constant, and G_w is gradient with respect to performance.

The back propagation and gradient descent are implemented to minimize the cost function (average error) of the neural network. For each iteration, the weight vector of neurons in each layer will be updated backward, and the training algorithm will find the optimal point, which is the best neural network configuration and parameters to match the measured data of harvesting power. The computation complexity is low due to (i) the limited number of features and nodes in the hidden layer of neural network and (ii) the relatively low frequency (once every 1s) of the execution of prediction algorithm. The proposed prediction algorithms are adaptive, i.e., the weight updating procedure is implemented in every time slot and new weights are used for future predictions. As we shall see later, the neural network can yield effective prediction results of future power harvesting.

The multi-source energy harvesting system adopts buck converters (for PV and PZ) and boost converter (for TEG) to connect the energy harvesting devices and NVPs. These power converters will cause additional variations on their output powers. More specifically, the conversion efficiency will degrade when its input power is low, thereby further reducing the output power and causing larger variations. Consequently, the additional variation decreases the predictability of the converter output power. Thus, in this section we aim to investigate the most suitable single-source power harvesting prediction for the NVP. We propose and evaluate two prediction methods based on artificial neural network (ANN). The first method directly predicts the output power of DC-DC converter, as presented in Section 4.1. The second prediction method, as presented in Section 4.2, first predicts the input power of (buck or boost) DC-DC converter, and then estimates the output power using accurate DC-DC converter modeling [15, 16] from actual measurements.

4.1 Method I: Directly Predict Output Power of DC-DC Converter

The first method directly predicts the output power of DC-DC converter (connecting to in-door PV or TEG) using a back propagation-based neural network [14]. The in-

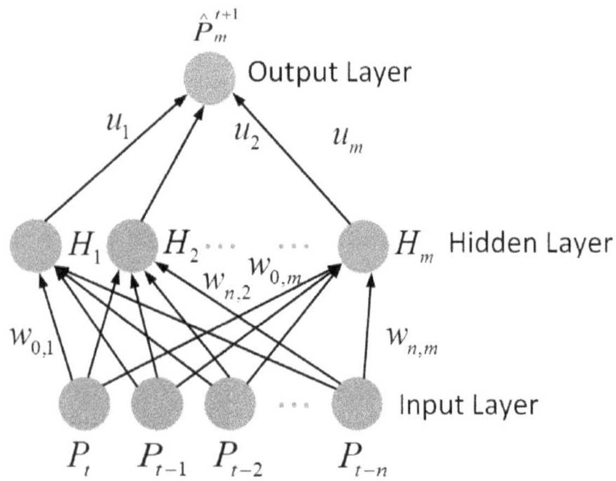

Figure 3: Artificial neural network for harvesting power prediction

put feature vector includes the previous and current output power values of DC-DC converter. The output of neural network is the prediction of the output power of DC-DC converter in the next second as shown in Fig. 4. We use *mean squared error* (MSE) to evaluate the performance of the prediction algorithm. MSE is utilized to measure how close the predictions are to the final outcomes. The prediction MSE for output power of the buck converter connecting to indoor PV is 33.0%, while the prediction MSE for output power of the boost converter connecting to TEG is 1.38%. A reasonable explanation of the MSE difference between PV and TEG power harvesting is that the temperature change is relatively slow, while the in-door PV irradiance exhibits dramatic temporal variations.

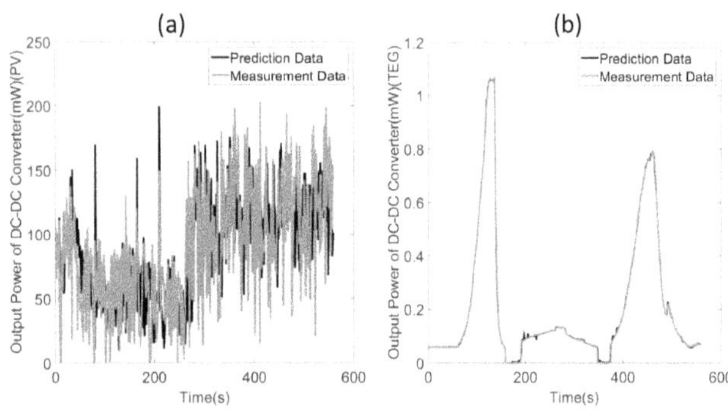

Figure 4: Prediction versus actual output power of DC-DC converters for in-door PV (a) and TEG (b)

4.2 Method II: Predict Input Power of DC-DC Converter, and then Estimate Output Power

The second prediction method first predicts the input power of (buck or boost) DC-DC converter, which exhibits lower temporal variations and higher predictability, and then estimates its output power using accurate DC-DC converter modeling [15, 16]. The input feature vector of ANN algorithm includes the previous and current input power values of DC-DC converter (collected by energy harvesters as shown in Fig. 2) connecting to in-door PV or TEG. The prediction versus actual input power results of DC-DC converter connecting to PV and TEG are shown in Fig. 5.

For in-door PV harvesting, the prediction MSE for input power of buck converter reduces to 26.6%. However, the MSE of output power of buck converter even slightly increases to 33.9% comparing to the first method. This is because as shown in Fig. 5, the prediction results of input power of buck converter exhibits less variations compared with actual results, which implies that it is difficult to predict the time when the converter actually exhibits low conversion efficiency (i.e., when its input power is extremely low). For TEG harvesting, the prediction MSE for output power of boost converter decreases to 1.18% comparing to the first method. In summary, the second method (predicting the input power of DC-DC converter and then estimating its output power using electrical model) may be suitable when the harvesting power variation is less significant (e.g., for the TEG case).

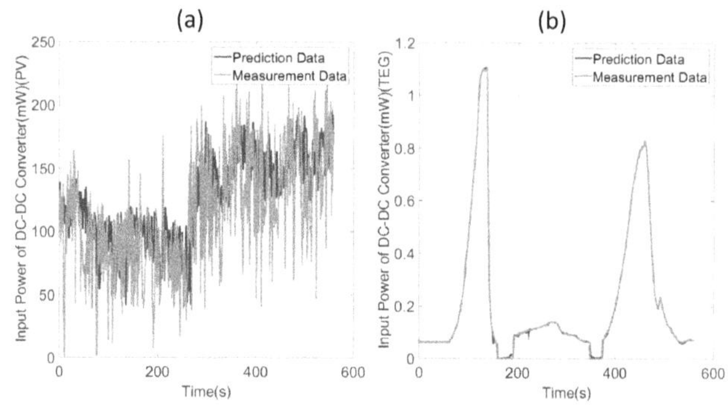

Figure 5: Prediction versus actual input power of DC-DC converters for in-door PV (a) and TEG (b)

5. NEURAL NETWORK-BASED MULTIPLE SOURCE POWER HARVESTING PREDICTION

The prediction algorithm of single-source power harvesting has a major limitation due to the high variation of output power of the DC-DC converter. To overcome the shortage of single energy source which is sporadic and variable, we propose and evaluate the more favorite prediction method for multiple-source power harvesting traces, since the total output power of multiple energy harvesting sources is more stable. For multi-source power harvesting predictions, we aim to investigate (i) whether it is more desirable to predict the total output power or output power of each harvesting source separately, and (ii) whether it is more desirable to predict the total output power of DC-DC converters directly or predict the input power first and then infer/estimate the total output power.

In order for thorough investigations, we introduce in this section three prediction methods for multi-source power harvesting, as shown in Fig. 6. Method I directly predicts the summation of output powers of DC-DC converters, which is the input power of the NVP. Method II predicts the input power of DC-DC converters *separately*, estimates the output power of each DC-DC converter using electrical models, and finally calculates the summation of estimated output power values. Method III predicts the total input power of DC-DC converters, and then infers the total output power by utilizing a learned mapping function. We evaluate the performances of these three methods using the measured PV and TEG power harvesting traces. In order to appropriately combine PV power traces and TEG power traces (which is in different orders of magnitudes), we normalize the collected data to the same order of magnitude.

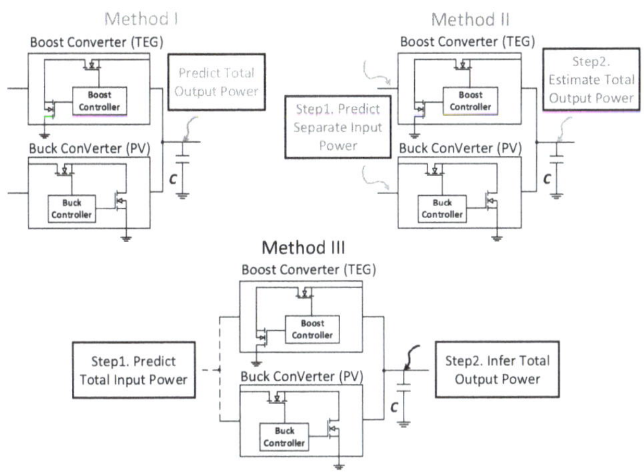

Figure 6: Three Prediction Methods for Neural Network-based Multi-Source Power Harvesting Prediction

5.1 Method I: Directly Predict the Total Output Power

This method predicts the total output power of DC-DC converters using the similar back propagation-based neural network [14] as discussed in Section 4.1. The input feature vector includes the previous and current total output power data of two DC-DC converters (buck converter and boost converter). While the output of neural network is the prediction of the total output power of the two DC-DC converters in the next second. The prediction versus actual total output power of DC-DC converters connecting to PV and TEG are shown in Fig. 7. The prediction MSE for the total output power of converters is 19.3%. Comparing to the single-source power harvesting prediction, predicting the total output power of DC-DC converters can significantly improve the prediction accuracy and mitigate the MSE. We verify that employing multiple energy sources can compensate the limitation of single renewable energy source and improve the reliability of energy harvesting, and provide a more stable and adequate energy source for NVPs.

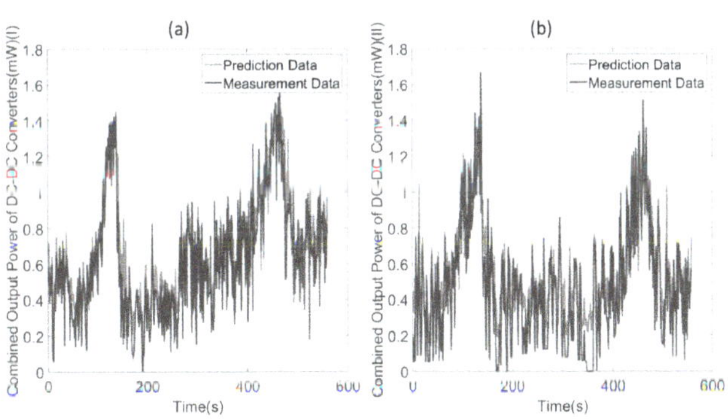

Figure 7: Prediction (using Method I) versus actual total (PV and TEG) output power of DC-DC converters for different traces

5.2 Method II: Predict Separate Input Powers of DC-DC Converters, then Estimate the Total Output Power

In this method, we first predict the input power values of buck and boost DC-DC converters separately, and then estimate their output power values using accurate DC-DC converter modelings as discussed in Section 4.2. We finally combine the estimated output power values of DC-DC converters as shown in Fig. 8. At last, the prediction MSE of the inferred total output power can be obtained. In this case, the MSE of total inferred output power of DC-DC converters is 27.19%, which is notably higher than directly predicting the total output power values (Method I). It confirms that predicting the total output power of DC-DC converters directly is a better method due to less variations compared with predicting input powers of DC-DC converters separately and then estimating the total output power.

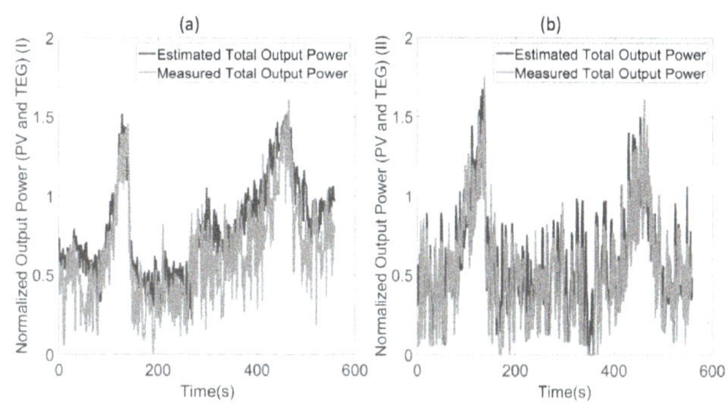

Figure 8: Estimated (using Method II) versus actual total (PV and TEG) output power of DC-DC converters for different traces

5.3 Method III: Predict Total Input Power, then Infer Total Output Power Using a Learned Mapping Function

This method is different from the previous two methods, in that it first predicts the total input power of DC-DC converters (connecting to PV, TEG, etc.) and then infers the total output power. In this prediction procedure, we use the previous 35 slots of total input power values as input feature vector in order to predict the total input power of next time slot. However, because the converters are different and the input powers are also different, we cannot directly estimate the total output power of DC-DC converters in a straightforward way. To solve this issue, we adopt a machine learning-based method which uses a trained mapping function to map the total input power to the total output power of DC-DC converters without using detailed converter modeling. Prediction results versus actual results are depicted in Fig. 9. In this case, the MSE is 19.6%, which is about the same compared with Method I that directly predicts the total output power of DC-DC converters.

6. CONCLUSION AND FUTURE WORKS

In this work, we adopt a multi-source in-door energy harvesting architecture to compensate the shortcoming of single energy source. Meanwhile, we adopt artificial neural network-based power harvesting prediction methods which are responsible for predicting the time of the next power failure and compensating the power failure through triggering

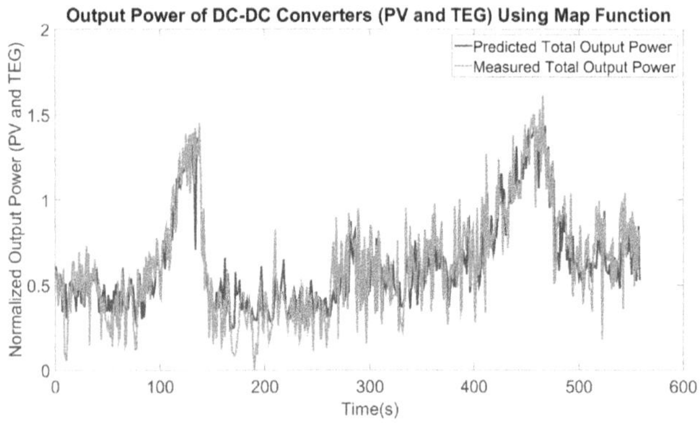

Figure 9: Inferred (using Method III) versus actual total (PV and TEG) output power of DC-DC converters using map function

the OS scheduler. We further investigate prediction methods both for single energy harvesting source and for multiple energy harvesting sources. We perform comprehensive comparison works regarding mean square error (MSE) of the proposed prediction mechanisms by evaluating the prediction accuracies of different methods. The comprehensive evaluation framework has been developed using actually measured harvesting traces on the proposed neural network-based power harvesting prediction methods. We verify that the multiple energy harvesting sources are more stable compared with the single source case and can effectively compensate the shortcoming of single energy source. Experimental results demonstrate that the most favorable prediction methods are directly predicting the total output power of DC-DC converters (connecting between energy sources and NVP), or predicting the total input power of DC-DC converters first and then inferring the total output power using a learned mapping function, for multi-source power harvesting predictions. There are several lines of research arising from this work which could be pursued. PZ devices could be applied into the proposed algorithms and more elaborate comparative research could be conducted in the future. Additionally, near-threshold computing (NTC) could be adopted into the algorithms.

7. ACKNOWLEDGMENTS

This work was supported in part by the National Science Foundation under grants CNS-1464429 and CCF-1527506.

8. REFERENCES

[1] B. Ransford, J. Sorber, and K. Fu, "Mementos: system support for long-running computation on rfid-scale devices," *ACM SIGPLAN Notices*, vol. 47, no. 4, pp. 159–170, 2012.

[2] M. Zwerg, A. Baumann, R. Kuhn, M. Arnold, R. Nerlich, M. Herzog, R. Ledwa, C. Sichert, V. Rzehak, P. Thanigai, and B. Eversmann, "An 82ua/mhz microcontroller with embedded feram for energy-harvesting applications," in *ISSCC,*, Feb 2011, pp. 334–336.

[3] C. Park and P. H. Chou, "Ambimax: Autonomous energy harvesting platform for multi-supply wireless sensor nodes," in *SECON*, vol. 1, 2006, pp. 168–177.

[4] T. Starner, "Human-powered wearable computing," *IBM systems Journal*, vol. 35, no. 3.4, pp. 618–629, 1996.

[5] J. Kymissis, C. Kendall, J. Paradiso, and N. Gershenfeld, "Parasitic power harvesting in shoes," *Digest of Papers. Second International Symposium on Wearable Computers, 1998.*, pp. 132–139, 1998.

[6] Q. A. Khan and S. J. Bang, "Energy harvesting for self powered wearable health monitoring system," *Health*, pp. 1–5, 2009.

[7] P. Mitcheson, "Energy harvesting for human wearable and implantable bio-sensors," in *EMBC*, 2010, pp. 3432–3436.

[8] C. Wang, N. Chang, Y. Kim, S. Park, Y. Liu, and H. Lee, "Storage-less and converter-less maximum power point tracking of photovoltaic cells for a nonvolatile microprocessor." *ASP-DAC*, pp. 379–384, 2014.

[9] S. Carreon-Bautista, A. Eladawy, A. Mohieldin, and E. Sanchez-Sinencio, "Boost converter with dynamic input impedance matching for energy harvesting with multi-array thermoelectric generators," *IEEE Trans. on Industrial Electronics*, vol. 61, no. 10, pp. 5345–5353, Oct 2014.

[10] S. Bandyopadhyay and A. Chandrakasan, "Platform architecture for solar, thermal, and vibration energy combining with mppt and single inductor," in *IEEE Journal of Solid-State Circuits*, 2012.

[11] "Tes-1333 solar power meter," http://www.btmco.ir/images/EditorUpload/tes1333.pdf, TES Electrical Electronic, 2006.

[12] Y. Kim, N. Chang, Y. Wang, and M. Pedram, "Maximum power transfer tracking for a photovoltaic-supercapacitor energy system," in *ISLPED*, Aug 2010, pp. 307–312.

[13] "Te-core /rf thermoharvesting wireless sensor system," http://www.micropelt.com/down/datasheet_te_core_rf.pdf, Micropelt GmbH, 05 2015, ver. 1.9.

[14] C. M. Bishop, *Pattern Recognition and Machine Learning (Information Science and Statistics).* Secaucus, NJ, USA: Springer-Verlag New York, Inc., 2006.

[15] X. Lin, Y. Wang, S. Yue, D. Shin, N. Chang, and M. Pedram, "Near-optimal, dynamic module reconfiguration in a photovoltaic system to combat partial shading effects," in *DAC*, June 2012, pp. 516–521.

[16] Y. Choi, N. Chang, and T. Kim, "Dc-dc converter-aware power management for low-power embedded systems," *IEEE Trans. on Computer-Aided Design of Integrated Circuits and Systems*, vol. 26, no. 8, pp. 1367–1381, Aug 2007.

A Unified Model of Power Sources for the Simulation of Electrical Energy Systems*

Sara Vinco, Yukai Chen, Enrico Macii and Massimo Poncino
Department of Control and Computer Engineering, Politecnico di Torino, Torino, Italy
name.surname@polito.it

ABSTRACT

Models of power sources are essential elements in the simulation of systems that generate, store and manage energy. In spite of the huge difference in power scale, they perform a common function: converting a primary environmental quantity into power. This paper proposes a unified model of a power source that is applicable to any power scale, and that can be derived solely from data contained in the specification or the datasheet of a device. The key feature of our model is the normalization of the energy generation characteristic of the power source by means of a reduction to a function expressing extracted power *vs.* the "scavenged" quantity. The proposed model proved to apply to two kinds of power sources, *i.e.*, a wind turbine and a photovoltaic panel, and to provide a good level of accuracy and simulation performance *w.r.t.* widely adopted models.

Keywords

Electrical Energy Systems; Power simulation; Power source modeling; Datasheet; Electronic design automation

1. INTRODUCTION

Simulation is an essential step in the design of Electrical Energy Systems (EES) for the assessment or the sizing of both the system and its components, as experimenting with EESs or their components is not only time consuming, but sometimes even dangerous due to high voltages or currents.

Among the various components of EESs, the most diverse of all are power sources, *i.e.*, elements that generate power by transforming some environmental quantity in electrical energy. The variety of their characteristics tends in fact to follow the scale of the relative EES: they range from the μW/mW scale of MEMS-based energy micro-scavengers to the MW scale of large wind turbines, and the very scavenging mechanism can be quite different. This variety in their typologies makes their modeling poorly scalable and marginally re-usable, thus complicating the objective of using an as much as possible unified modeling approach. Another difficulty towards a possibly unified view of the models lies in the fact that most works focus on a specific application context (*e.g.*, smart electronic systems, micro-grids, large-scale power grids). Therefore, from their perspective, there is no need of deriving models able to cover multiple energy scales.

The context of our work is the *system-level simulation of an EES* for its early validation and fast assessment through a model-based design scenario [10, 16, 23]. Modeling approaches comparable to ours include functional models suitable for system-level simulation and adopted for early prototyping of large scale systems [10, 30].

Our approach is similar in scope and in the abstraction level to the works of [14] and [19]. Besides some basic differences in the abstract semantics of the models and the languages used for their description, the fundamental distinction between those solutions and ours lies in the *identification of the model parameters*: these works do not describe how the model parameters can be derived for a generic device; the models are described and built for one specific example device and how to extend them to a different instance is not specified. The lack of an identification method implies that the input/output characteristic of the device can be obtained only by resorting to empirical measures of some physical parameters. Needless to say, this is costly and it requires instrumentation that may not always be available in-house. Furthermore, this would restrict exploration of the possible alternatives, as the designer would have to acquire a number of components to estimate the most suitable one. The alternative is to use data provided by the manufacturer together with the power source. However, the latter rarely provides the required information for populating the models, thus preventing the mapping of an abstract model to the specific power source.

The goal of this paper is to derive a *unified model for power sources* that is *applicable to any power scale and to any kind of power source*. Thanks to this unified approach, the model can be derived solely from data available from a specification of the device. The approach is based on a "normalization" of the energy generation characteristic of the power source in terms of a function expressing extracted power *vs.* the environmental scavenged quantity. The model is then used to generate the simulation traces of voltage and current corresponding to the generated harvested power, to allow simulation of the power source in the context of the overall EES. Experimental results have shown a high level of accuracy *w.r.t.* state-of-the art models and a significant simulation speed up, up to 7x.

2. RELATED WORK

The large variety of types of power sources is reflected by the many available options for their modeling. A general classification is outside the scope of this work, and in any case the landscape of

*This work was supported by the EC co-funded CONTREX (Design of embedded mixed-criticality CONTRol systems under consideration of EXtra-functional properties) project Grant Agreement FP7-ICT- 611146

GLSVLSI '16, May 18-20, 2016, Boston, MA, USA
© 2016 ACM. ISBN 978-1-4503-4274-2/16/05...$15.00
DOI: http://dx.doi.org/10.1145/2902961.2903024

options is so wide that an exhaustive coverage of models for all types of power sources is virtually impossible. A possible generic classification concerns their abstraction level, which typically maps onto a well-defined simulation semantics [23]:

- *multiphysics-based mechanical models* generally focus on the description of the mechanical or fluidic characteristics of the power source, *e.g.*, tools like COMSOL or CoventorWare [7,8];
- *equation-based models* analytically express the physical phenomena that govern the energy generation process [11];
- *electrical circuit equivalent models*, in which the dynamic behavior of electrical components is used to emulate the operation of the device [5,24];
- *functional (continuous or discrete-time) macro-models* suitable for system-level simulation, often specified using hardware description languages [9,29].

Given our system-level, model-based perspective, methods somehow comparable to ours both in scope and in the abstraction level are proposed in [19] and [14]. The models resulting from [19] have an abstraction level similar to ours and are usable in a system-level simulation scenario. However, their derivation is based on the characteristic equations of the specific power sources (*e.g.*, the diode-based equation for a PV cell). [14] provides a more abstract model, in which a power source is modeled as a charge reservoir in which the environment adds and a load draws charge. Although this method goes in the direction of a generalization of the models, the usage in a real scenario (*e.g.*, different load conditions, tracking of maximum power point) is not immediate.

Besides some differences in the abstract semantics of the models, the fundamental distinction between those solutions and ours lies thus in the *identification of the model parameters*: these works do not describe how the model parameters can be derived for a generic device. Conversely, our approach determines a "meta-modeling" procedure that is applicable to any type of power source and relies only on information provided as devices specifications.

3. A UNIFIED MODEL FOR POWER SOURCES

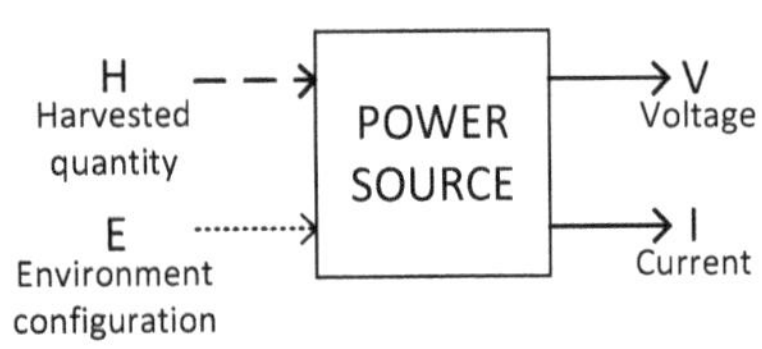

Figure 1: Unified model for power sources.

Any power source can be considered as a system component that generates *voltage and current waveforms over time*, as shown in Figure 1 (signals **V** and **I**). The power produced by the power source strictly depends on the harvested quantity, modeled as an input waveform over time (signal **H**). The power source may be further affected by other environment characteristics, such as temperature (signal **E**). The proposed model is clearly agnostic both of the type of power source (*e.g.*, photovoltaic panel or wind turbine) and of the scale of managed energy (*i.e.*, micro or macro). Our model currently supports power sources that harvest a single environmental quantity (*e.g.*, wind, solar radiation, ambient noise or vibrations). Dependency from other environmental quantities, such as temperature, will be part of future work. The abstraction resulting from the model interface shown in Figure 1 is essential to guarantee the generality and flexibility of the model. In particular, it allows to identify the parameters of the models without requiring any knowledge of instance-specific characteristics of the device, such as the physics of the underlying energy generation process or technological parameters.

Conversely, as mentioned in Section 1, our model can be derived solely from available data contained in specification of the device such as a datasheet. As many types of data can be found, the energy generation characteristic of the power source is *normalized to a canonical form*, in terms of a function expressing *extracted power* vs. *the harvested quantity*. This allows to automate the construction of the power source model and to generate the simulation traces of voltage and current *vs.* the harvested quantity.

4. PROPOSED METHODOLOGY

4.1 Methodology Overview

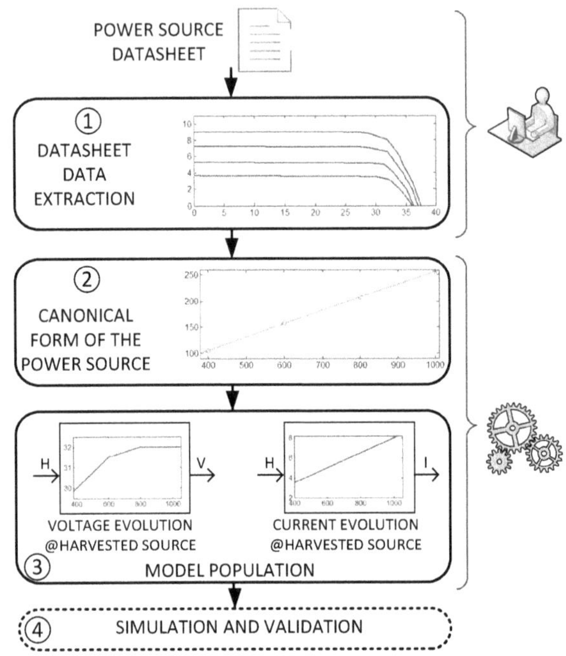

Figure 2: Proposed Modeling Methodology.

Figure 2 shows an overview of the proposed methodology. The starting point is the datasheet of the power source. The designer extracts and translates the required information into appropriate data files (step **1**). This is the only step that requires manual intervention, and it only consists of image digitation, that can be achieved almost instantaneously through automatic tools [1]. Once that the data files are filled, the canonical model of the power source is automatically constructed by casting the information in the datasheet into a function of generated power *vs.* the harvested quantity (step **2**). This step allows us to unify power source modeling and to automate the construction of model, independently of the variety of information provided by datasheets.

The canonical model is then used to automatically determine the behavior of the power source in terms of the evolution of voltage and current *vs.* time (step **3**). Finally, the model for the power source model is then inserted in an EES system for simulation and validation (step **4**).

4.2 Datasheet Data Extraction

The proposed methodology relies solely on information provided by datasheets. It was thus necessary to determine (i) how the required information are presented in typical datasheets, and (ii) how

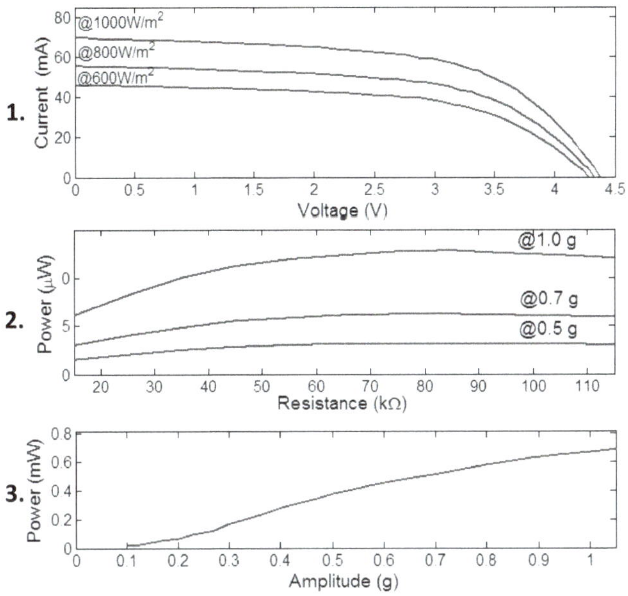

Figure 3: Examples of datasheets graphs: (1) a Class 1 graph for the photovoltaic cell in [6] (each curve is associated to a value for irradiance); (b) a Class 2 graph for the piezo-electric harvester in [4] (parameterized w.r.t. the corresponding acceleration value); (c) a Class 3 graph for the piezoelectric harvester in [3].

to represent them in a standardized file format for the automation of the methodology.

4.2.1 Analysis of Power Source Datasheets

The analysis of more than 50 datasheets for different types of power sources, including photovoltaic panels and piezoelectric harvesters, lead to the definition of three main templates.

Class 1: Current vs. *Voltage or Power* vs. *Voltage.* The most popular type of datasheets describes the characteristic behavior in terms of output current (or power) *vs.* the voltage of the power source [6,20,25]. An example of current *vs.* voltage graph for the photovoltaic panel in [6] is depicted in Figure 3.1. In this type of datasheets, the dependency *w.r.t.* the harvested quantity is reproduced by a number of current/voltage (power/voltage) curves, each one associated with a specific value for the harvested quantity. As an example, the curves in Figure 3.1 show the relationship between panel current and voltage for different values of solar irradiance (measured in $\frac{W}{m^2}$). Power/voltage plots are similar, since they are straightforwardly derived from current/voltage ones by multiplying voltage and current values.

Class 2: Power vs. *Resistance.* Power/resistance graphs model the power source as a family of power/resistance curves, each associated with a specific value of the harvested quantity. An example for the piezo-electric power source in [4] is shown in Figure 3.2, where power curves are parameterized *w.r.t.* the corresponding acceleration value of the oscillating mass (expressed as a multiplicative factor of g).

Class 3: Power vs. *Harvested Quantity.* Power vs. harvested quantity graphs directly explicit the dependency of power *w.r.t.* the environmental parameter. They are popular as specifications of wind power sources that operate at a fixed voltage output level, but also for some piezo-electric harvesters [2,3,20]. Voltage is defined in the datasheet as one or more pre-defined voltage levels, while current must be derived from the voltage and the power behavior. An example for the wind turbine in [3] is provided in Figure 3.3.

4.2.2 Definition of Data File Format

Definition of data format is an essential step for the automation of the overall methodology. Each power source is modeled with one file. The first line contains two strings representing the physical quantity associated with the x-axis and the y-axis, respectively. The strings can be any of the following: *"P"* for power, *"V"* for voltage, *"C"* for current, *"R"* for resistance and *"H"* for harvested quantity. The second line reports the number n of parametric values associated with the family of curves. If the graph contains one curve, n is set to 1. Else, the number n is followed by the zero-dimensional values associated to the curves. The next lines describe the curves as a list of quantized values. Each line contains *n+1* values, the first of which being the considered sampled value for the x-axis. This is followed by a number of y-axis values, describing the value assumed in correspondence to x in each curve. *E.g.*, the data file for modelling the curve in Figure 3.2 is:

R	P		
3	0.5	0.7	1.0
20,000	$19.0E-6$	$34.1E-6$	$71.3E-6$
30,000	$22.0E-6$	$44.9E-6$	$92.2E-6$
...			

4.3 Canonical Form of Power Sources

Power vs. *harvested quantity* graphs are used as the canonical form to represent power source behavior, since they conceptually represent the actual "behavior" of a power source, *i.e.*, a device that generates power according to some environmental quantity. The other two classes of graphs must thus be re-cast to the canonical form.

4.3.1 Class 1: Current/Voltage or Power/Voltage

Current *vs.* voltage and power *vs.* voltage graphs associate *a curve* to each value of the harvested quantity, thus not univocally identifying a single value of output power and voltage. Some transformations are thus necessary to reduce the current *vs.* voltage and power *vs.* voltage graphs to the canonical form. In particular, the transformation entails determining a load condition for the device.

The most typical load condition consists of trying to match the internal device resistance with that of the load, in order to extract the *maximum power point* (MPP) of the device *w.r.t.* the harvested quantity [17]. The MPP is determined by the voltage and current values that yield the maximum power for a given environmental condition. In the power *vs.* voltage graphs, the MPP for each value of the harvested quantity can be easily determined by finding the maximum of the corresponding curve. In the current *vs.* voltage graphs, the MPP is determined by reducing the graph to a power *vs.* voltage graph (*i.e.*, by multiplying voltage values per the corresponding current values). As an example, Figure 4 highlights with red circles the MPP for each irradiance value on the current *vs.* voltage graph in Figure 3.1. The canonic form can then be easily constructed by plotting the MPPs for the known values of the harvested quantity, which can be interpolated to define a continuous curve. The line with round markers on the right-hand side of Figure 4 shows the resulting canonical form for the current *vs.* voltage graph in Figure 3.1.

The values of voltage and current can be easily derived from the original current/voltage or power/voltage plot: the voltage for each value of the harvested quantity is the x-coordinate of the MPP, and the current is determined either by dividing power by voltage or by looking at the current *vs.* voltage graph.

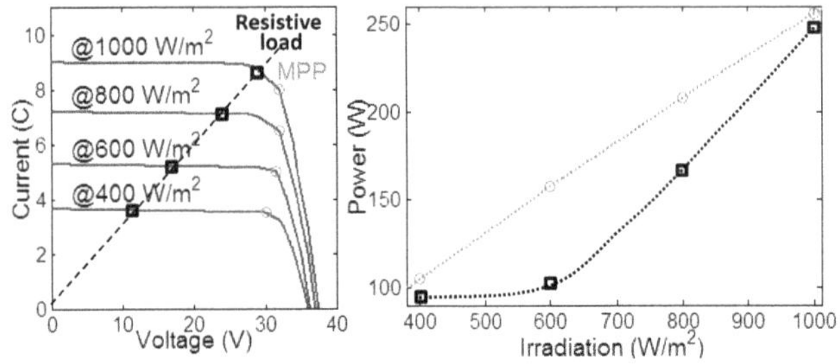

Figure 4: Canonical form of the panel in Figure 3.1, built through MPP identification (round markers) or by applying a resistive load (squared markers).

Another typical load condition would be assuming a *fixed resistive load*. This case corresponds to a line in the current/voltage graph (with slope $1/R$) or a quadratic curve ($P = V^2/R$) in the power/voltage graph. An example of linear resistive load is provided by the line with square markers on the left-hand side of Figure 4. Despite of the kind of resistive load, the curve intersects each current/voltage or power/voltage curve in exactly one point, thus determining a value for voltage (given by the x-coordinate) and a corresponding value for current. The power *vs.* harvested quantity graph is then constructed by plotting the intersection points for the known values of the harvested quantity, similarly to the case of the MPP, thus obtaining the line with squared markers on the right-hand side of Figure 4. This second case can also be used if one wants to model MPP tracking separately from the power source.

4.3.2 Class 2: Power/Resistance Characteristic

The reduction of power *vs.* resistance graphs to the canonical form follows a process similar to that of Class 1. Again, since this type of graphs associates a curve to each value of the harvested quantity rather than a single point, an identification of the load conditions is necessary. Therefore, either the MPPs of the various curves are identified in the case of matched loads, or the points intersecting a fixed resistive load (in this case a vertical line) are transposed onto the power *vs.* harvested quantity graph. Figure 5 shows the result of applying this approach to the graph in Figure 3.2, by using both the MPP approach (round markers) and a resistive load (squared markers). The corresponding voltage and current values are determined by using the voltage-current relationship $V = RI$, which allows to derive voltage and current given the power and the resistance values.

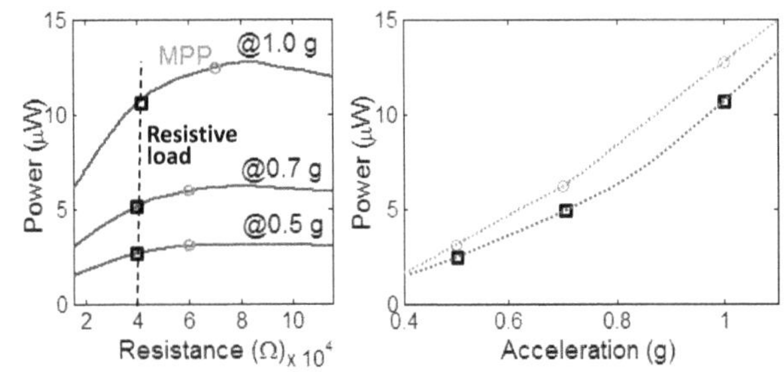

Figure 5: Canonical form of the piezo-electric harvester in Figure 3.2, built through MPP identification (round markers) or by applying a resistive load (squared markers).

4.4 Model Population

The reduction of different typologies of power sources to the canonical form allows to consider each power source as a power *vs.* harvested quantity graph that is used to automatically populate the power source model in an EES simulator. The behavior of the power source is described as a pair of curves, modeling voltage and power *vs.* the harvested quantity. The former relation is easily determined from the points used in the derivation of the latter curve (*i.e.*, the MPPs or points for a resistive load). The points are then interpolated to obtain a continuous line. Current can then be easily estimated as the ratio between power and voltage. The extraction of such information is agnostic both of the type of power source and of the scale of managed energy, and it allows to include the power source models in a wide range of simulation infrastructures, and to match requirements both on the model interface and on the system information flows [28, 29].

5. EXPERIMENTAL RESULTS

The following of this Section validates the proposed unified model for power sources, and then applies it in the context of the design of an EES system. Methodology application is automated through Matlab/Simulink R2015b.

5.1 Validation of the Proposed Unified Model

This section validates the proposed approach on power sources belonging to class **1** and class **3**, respectively. We do not show an example of class **2** power sources as they can be easily reduced to class **1** power sources. No experimental data were available for both of the power sources, and comparing the proposed model *w.r.t.* the respective datasheets would give zero error, as the models are derived from the datasheets. The methodology is thus validated against previously published and widely accepted accurate models.

5.1.1 Modeling of a Photovoltaic Panel

The power source of class **1** adopted for validation is the SunPower A300 photovoltaic panel in [26]. The datasheet models the panel through a current *vs.* voltage graph, with 4 different curves corresponding to different irradiance levels, as depicted on the left-hand side of Figure 6. We derived the corresponding canonical form by selecting the MPPs. The result is the power *vs.* irradiance graph on the right-hand side of Figure 6.

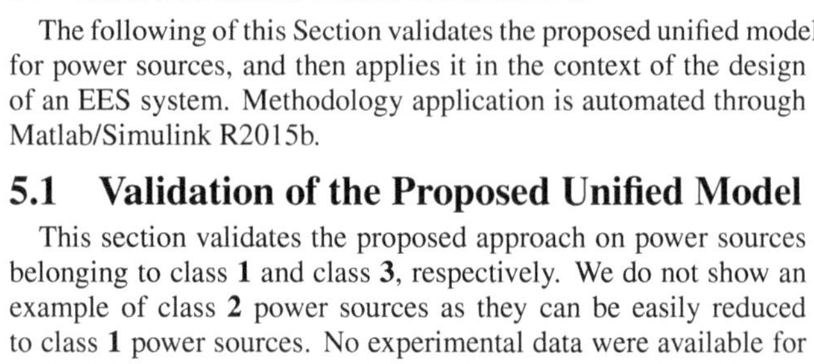

Figure 6: Datasheet specification and canonical form for the photovoltaic panel in [26].

The generated model is validated against the electrical circuit equivalent model proposed in [13], characterized for the same photovoltaic panel. Validation is performed by comparing the output power when applying the same irradiance trace, *i.e.* the irradiance in San Francisco on June 20th 2010 from 8a.m. up to 6p.m. [22].

Figure 7 depicts the evolution of the system in terms of irradiance and of correspondingly produced power. The figure shows that the produced power (middle) is directly proportional to the received irradiance (top). The center figure compares also the power resulting from our model (dashed lines) against the values provided by the circuit model of [13] (solid lines). The two curves are almost totally overlapped. For a better quantification of error, the bottom plot

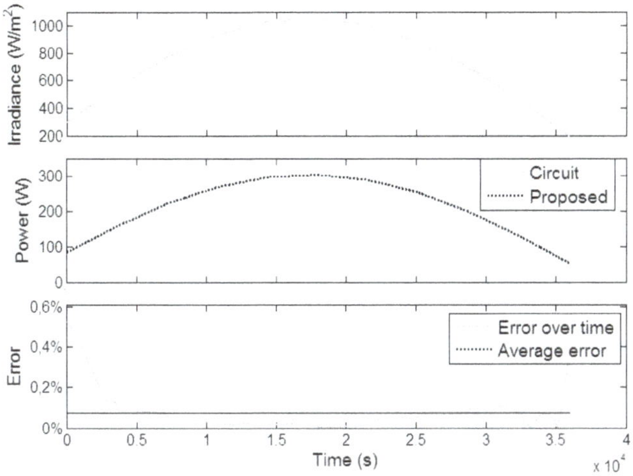

Figure 7: Model Validation of the A300 Panel: irradiance over time (top), power over time with the two models, (center), and error committed by the proposed approach *w.r.t.* the circuit model (bottom).

of Figure 7 reports the sample-by-sample error between our model and the one of [13]; average error is extremely low, *i.e.* 0.075% (dashed line). Overall, error is always below 1% (solid line), with maximum error 0.52%. This confirms that the proposed approach allows to accurately model power sources. The bottom plot of Figure 7 also highlights that error tends to be larger at the beginning and at the end of simulation time, where irradiance is about $200\frac{}{m^2}$. This is due to the almost linear growth (reduction) of irradiance in the corresponding time slots. Furthermore, the datasheet does not provide any trace for irradiance values lower than $200\frac{}{m^2}$ (as in Figure 6). This may induce errors in the interpolation process, and thus the estimation of the produced power becomes less accurate.

It is worth emphasizing that the model in [13] must be populated with detailed characteristics of the panel, *e.g.*, open-circuit and short-circuit characteristics and technology specific coefficients. On the contrary, a major advantage of the proposed approach is that panel behavior is inferred only from the available datasheet information. A further advantage is that our model took only 1.363s to compute the whole simulation, with a 7.707x speedup *w.r.t.* the circuit model, whose simulation lasted 10.505s.

5.1.2 Modeling of a Wind Turbine

Multiphysics based mechanical models are amongst the most accurate models for power sources. For this reason, we decided to validate the proposed approach against the wind turbine model described in [27], based on a stator-flux-oriented electromechanical model of a doubly fed induction machine.

We first implemented the approach in [27] in Matlab/Simulink and we configured it for simulating the WT2000 wind turbine [3]. It is important to note that this configuration step was challenging, as it required to acquire very detailed information about the wind turbine, both by analysing the specifications and through physical measurements. As a next step, we reproduced the same wind turbine by adopting the approach proposed in this work. The datasheet provides a power *vs.* wind curve (depicted in Figure 3.3), that was extracted and used as canonical form for our power source.

Figure 8 shows the evolution of output power given the same wind trace for both models, *i.e.*, the wind traced at Long Island on February 03rd 2005 [22]. The figure shows that the produced power (bottom) reflects the observed wind (top). The middle figure also compares the approach proposed in this work (dashed lines) with the mechanical model (solid lines).

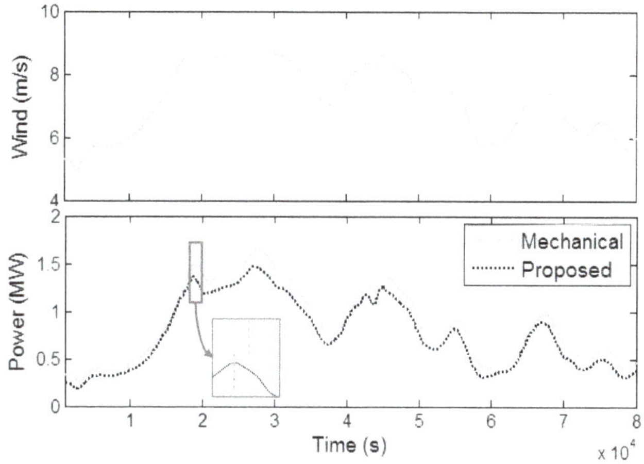

Figure 8: Validation of the modeling of a wind turbine *w.r.t.* the multiphysics-based model in [27].

It can be noted that this case study exposes a lower level of accuracy *w.r.t.* the previous one. The proposed approach underestimates the mechanical model, with *avg.* error of 11.09% and maximum error 21.88%. On the other hand, [15] showed that the mechanical model, hereby used as reference, tends to overestimate the actual generated power, even if no accurate statistics were provided. Thus, the error is not entirely caused by the proposed approach, as it is compared *w.r.t.* an inherently approximate model, rather than with experimental results.

The accuracy of the model proposed in this work is also granted by the fact that datasheet plots, used for the construction of the model, are built based on experimental measurements. As a result, the model adheres to the actual behavior of the wind turbine. On the contrary, mechanical models tend to deepen mechanical aspects and to lose accuracy on complex physical mechanisms, such as practical mechanical losses, or factors impacting on the energy conversion. Thus, the error can not be ascribed only to the model proposed in this work, but it is generated by the adjunct approximations of both the proposed model and the mechanical one.

A limitation of the proposed approach is that the generated model does not keep into account delays caused by the inherent mechanical inertia of the turbine. This is highlighted by the zoom-in in Figure 8: our model reacts instantaneously to changes in the wind speed, while the mechanical model delays the response of power generation. This could be easily avoided by determining the delay timing constant, *e.g.*, by extracting it from the mechanical model, and by adding a moving-average filter just after the canonical model. This analysis will be part of future work.

5.2 Using the Unified Model for System Level Simulation

This section demonstrates that the proposed system-level abstract model for power sources allows one to implement an explorative analysis using in-the-loop simulation of different configurations for realistic time durations in the order of a few weeks. Running such an experiment using detailed mechanical or circuit models of the power sources would be prohibitive, as a day-long simulation would be too costly in terms of memory and time.

Specifically, we model an EES featuring a SunPower A300 PV panel [26] (as in Section 5.1.1) and a Dolphinz Z-300w wind turbine, with a rated power of 300W [12]. The energy storage consists of a pack of Li-ion batteries built from a cell by Qinetiq with capacity of 5.8Ah. The system includes also the necessary DC-DC converters and a CTI bus.

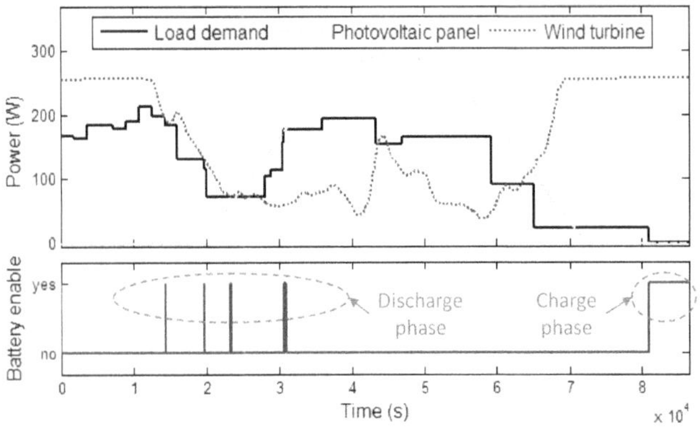

Figure 9: Adoption of the canonical models of a photovoltaic panel and a wind turbine in an example EES: evolution of load demand and power sources production over time (top), and corresponding activation of the battery pack (bottom).

The system is managed by a charge allocation policy that operates as follows: As long as the the power drawn from the power sources satisfies the loads power demand, loads are supplied directly by the power sources. Otherwise, loads are supplied by the battery pack, until the state-of-charge (SOC) is below 10%. Finally, the battery is charged whenever load power demand is 0. Although this policy is sort of naive, the focus here is not to develop sophisticated policies but rather to show the effectiveness of the proposed canonical model for power sources.

To estimate the correct sizing of the battery pack, we evaluated the EES with three different capacities (*i.e.*, 200Ah, 320Ah and 440Ah). Each simulation reproduces one month of simulated time, with variable irradiance and wind values. To emulate the variance in irradiance we assumed about 1/3 of cloudy days and 2/3 of sunny days. For wind speed, we used a typical daily profile taken from published data [14, 15], with small perturbations at random time points in the different days.

Figure 9 depicts the typical trace over one (sunny) day, in terms of load demand and power produced over time by the PV panel and the wind turbine (top). The Figure shows also the activation of the battery pack *w.r.t.* the policy (bottom), either to provide power to the loads when power sources production is insufficient (activations 1–4) or to charge the battery (activation 5).

Each simulation (three 1-week runs) lasted in average 767.04s. Table 1 reports minimum and average SOC and average residual SOC at midnight (after the charge phase) of the three configurations. The best configuration is obviously achieved with largest capacity (440Ah), which guarantees an almost complete recovery of battery SOC during the day. However, the designer may use this analysis to determine a cost-benefit tradeoff, *e.g.*, to choose a target minimum or average daily SOC level and choose the capacity configuration that satisfies that constraint.

Battery Capacity (Ah)	Min. SOC (%)	Avg. SOC (%)	Avg. SOC at midnight
200	60.22	91.05	86.18
320	76.65	94.66	91.82
440	83.52	96.21	94.21

Table 1: Effect of variation of the battery pack capacity over the evolution of SOC over time.

6. CONCLUSIONS

This work proposed a unified model for power sources, built solely from the information available in their datasheet specifications, with the goal of providing designers with a system level model and of easing EES simulation and validation. The proposed methodology is entirely automatic, despite of data extraction from the provided datasheet. The proposed approach allows thus early simulation of power sources and EES without empirical measurements, still guaranteeing a good approximation of the power source behavior. Experimental results showed that the proposed approach reaches a high level of accuracy *w.r.t.* widely accepted accurate models, together with a simulation speed up of up to 7x. Furthermore, the proposed model proved to enhance EES design with instantaneous system modeling and simulation. Future work will support dependency from other environment characteristics, such as temperature and humidity.

7. REFERENCES

[1] S. A. van der Wulp. *Graph Digitzer.* www.mathworks.com/matlabcentral/fileexchange/23317-graph-digitzer.

[2] AMSC. *SeaTitan 10 MW Wind Turbine.* www.amsc.com.

[3] AMSC. *WindTec wt2000df and wt2000fc.* www.amsc.com.

[4] R. Andoscaa, T. McDonald, et al. Experimental and theoretical studies on MEMS piezoelectric vibrational energy harvesters with mass loading. In *Sensors and Actuators A: Physical*, volume 178, pages 76–87. Elsevier, 2012.

[5] A. Bauer, J. Hanisch, and E. Ahlswede. An Effective Single Solar Cell Equivalent Circuit Model for Two or More Solar Cells Connected in Series. *IEEE PHOT*, 4(1):340–347, Jan 2014.

[6] Canadian Solar. *CS6P-250 255 260P Datasheet.* www.mitsubishielectric.com.

[7] COMSOL. *COMSOL Multiphysics.* www.comsol.com.

[8] Coventor. *CoventorWare MEMS Design.* www.coventor.com.

[9] J. Eker, J. Janneck, E. Lee, et al. Taming heterogeneity - the Ptolemy approach. *Proc. of the IEEE*, 91(1):127–144, Jan 2003.

[10] M. A. Faruque and F. Ahourai. A Model-Based Design of Cyber-Physical Energy Systems. In *Proc. of IEEE ASPDAC*, pages 97–105, 2014.

[11] P. Fritzson. *Introduction to Modeling and Simulation of Technical and Physical Systems With Modelica.* Wiley-IEEE Press, 2011.

[12] GoGreenSystems. *Doplphinz 300 Z-300w wind turbine.* gogreensystems.se.

[13] F. Gonzalez-Longatt. Model of Photovoltaic Module in Matlab. In *Proc. of CIBELEC*, pages 1–5, 2005.

[14] K. Heussen, S. Koch, A. Ulbig, and G. Andersson. Unified system-level modeling of intermittent renewable energy sources and energy storage for power system operation. *IEEE SJ*, 6(1):140–151, March 2012.

[15] M. Hurajt. Simulation of a wind energy conversion system utilizing a vector controlled doubly fed induction generator. Technical report, University of Windsor, 2013. scholar.uwindsor.ca/etd/4979.

[16] M. Ilic, L. Xie, U. Khan, and J. Moura. Modeling future cyber-physical energy systems. In *IEEE PES General Meeting*, pages 1–9, July 2008.

[17] D. Karanjkar, S. Chatterji, et al. An improved current feedback based maximum power point tracking controller for solar photo-voltaic system. In *Proc. of IEEE AICERA/ICMiCR*, pages 1–6, 2013.

[18] Y. Kim, D. Shin, et al. Computer-aided design of electrical energy systems. In *Proc. of IEEE ICCAD*, pages 194–201, 2013.

[19] C. Lu, V. Raghunathan, and K. Roy. Efficient design of micro-scale energy harvesting systems. *IEEE ETCAS*, 1(3):254–266, Sept 2011.

[20] MIDE. *Volture EHE004 Datasheet.* www.mide.com.

[21] J. M. Morales et al. Integrating renewables in electricity markets. In *International Series in Operations Research & Management Science*, 205. Springer, 2014.

[22] National Renewable Energy Laboratory. *Leading Clean Energy Innovation.* www.nrel.gov.

[23] P. Palensky, E. Widl, and A. Elsheikh. Simulating cyber-physical energy systems: Challenges, tools and methods. *In Proc. of IEEE SMC*, 44(3):318–326, 2014.

[24] M. Singh and S. Santoso. Dynamic Models for Wind Turbines and Wind Power Plants. Technical report, National Reneawable Energy Laboratory, May 2011. www.osti.gov/bridge.

[25] SpectroLab. *GaAs/Ge Single Junction Solar Cells Datasheet.* www.spectrolab.com.

[26] SunPower. *300 Solar Panel.* www.energymatters.com.au.

[27] G. Tapia, A. Tapia, and J. Ostolaza. Two alternative modeling approaches for the evaluation of wind farm active and reactive power performances. *IEEE EC*, 21(4):909–920, Dec 2006.

[28] The MathWorks, Inc. *SimPowerSystems - Model and simulate electrical power systems.* mathworks.com.

[29] S. Vinco, A. Sassone, et al. An open-source framework for formal specification and simulation of electrical energy systems. In *Proc. of IEEE/ACM ISLPED*, pages 287–290, 2014.

[30] S. Yue, D. Zhu, et al. SIMES: A Simulator for Hybrid Electrical Energy Storage Systems. In *Proc. of ACM/IEEE ISLPED*, pages 33–38, 2013.

Hardware-Accelerated Software Library Drivers Generation for IP-Centric SoC Designs

Munish Jassi, Uzair Sharif, Daniel Müller-Gritschneder, Ulf Schlichtmann
Institute for Electronic Design Automation
Technische Universität München
München-80333, Germany
munish.jassi@tum.de, uzair.sharif@tum.de, daniel.mueller@tum.de, ulf.schlichtmann@tum.de

ABSTRACT

In recent years, the semiconductor industry has been witnessing an increasing reuse of hardware IPs for System-on-Chip (SoC) designs and embedded computing systems on FPGA platforms with hard-core processors. The IP-reuse comes with an increasing complexity at the hardware-software (HW-SW) interface. The efforts required to access the HW through the increasingly complex HW-SW interface diminishes the potential IP-reuse productivity gain. In our work, we are proposing hierarchical drivers for accessing IP-subsystems and its generation for enabling easier SW application adaptation to HW-changes and faster design space exploration (DSE) on a targeted HW-accelerated SW libraries. At the lowest level, closest to the HW, is the hardware abstraction layer (HAL), these are the platform-specific register-access drivers. At the next layer are the drivers to access the registers and bit-fields of each IP component of the IP-library. Next are the IP-subsystems drivers. At the top-layer, closest to the SW, is the simple scheduler with SW interface library that provides access functions to the SW application. The drivers generator uses the HW knowledge of IPs and IP-subsystems encoded in IP-XACT for generating the drivers for both operating system (OS) and non-OS based applications. For the OS-based applications, user-space drivers are generated, as well as device tree source (DTS) and drivers mapping in the kernel-space. In a case study, we have validated our methodology while performing DSE for a video processing application targeted to an IP-library, both as non-OS and with OS on Xilinx Zynq-based FPGA.

Keywords

SoC; Xilinx Zynq; IP-centric SoCs; Software-defined SoCs

1. INTRODUCTION

In an IP-centric SoC design approach, multiple independently implemented sub-modules (IPs) or IP-subsystems are integrated together to design a complete SoC. Conventionally, the IP components or IP-subsystems are not implemented by SoC design teams, but are supplied by some third-party IP-suppliers. These IP-subsystems are also finding usage in the recent SoC prototyping FPGA chips that have powerful CPUs with programmable fabric [1]. Hardware acceleration using these FPGA chips is helpful for the applications that carry-out repetitive data processing, e.g. computer vision applications. Some suppliers also provide HW-accelerated SW libraries, that have SW functions with functionally equivalent HW IPs, e.g. Xilinx OpenCV [2]. For performing DSE over provided HW-accelerated library, developers have to perform multiple iterations to reach optimal HW-SW allocation for application tasks. Integrating an IP-subsystem is itself a cumbersome task, on top, adapting a SW application to seamlessly transfer the processing control from a CPU to a dedicated HW-subsystem and appropriately handle the data communication can add a significant overhead for a SW developer. It becomes more difficult if an operating system (OS) is considered, which requires developing kernel-space and user-space drivers.

Our work tries to ease this HW-SW interface handling overhead for IP-integration by concealing the HW details from a SW developer with the generated hierarchical HW-access drivers for the targeted IP-library. We also propose generalization of the HW-SW interface, which manages the data and control handling among HW-based or SW-based processing. Using IP-XACT descriptions [3] of IPs, IP-subsystems and SoC design, our tool generates drivers and the generic HW-SW interface for a targeted SoC and environment (OS or non-OS). From the SW perspective, we establish HW-SW interface generation in two steps. First, we add an additional layer on the existing SW library functions to make them aware of the underlying HW. Second, we generalize the SW tasks scheduling according to the available HW resources. An IP-supplier can generate and package the drivers with IP-library, as IP-supplier has the most knowledge about HW IPs. The IP-package so prepared contains HW information as well as drivers for SW development. Using the available IPs drivers, an SoC architect can generate IP-subsystems drivers for SoCs. It is difficult to completely automate the optimal drivers generation because of the required intricate HW behavioral details. Rather, the objective is to utilize maximum available structural information from IP-XACT for generating drivers that enable functional HW-SW interface to be employed for SoC optimizations.

The main contributions of our work are the hierarchical generation of drivers for both OS and non-OS environments from IP-XACT and the proposed generic HW-SW interface in compliance with the generated drivers for HW-accelrated

GLSVLSI '16, May 18-20, 2016, Boston, MA, USA

DOI: http://dx.doi.org/10.1145/2902961.2903026

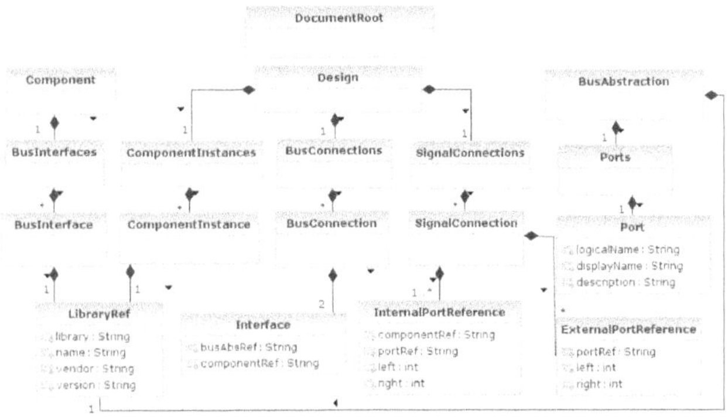

Figure 1: Simplified UML model diagram for IP-XACT showing design and components hierarchies

SW libraries enabling IP-centric SoC design. This enables SW applications to get automatically adapted to an underlying SoC architecture, especially during DSE. The rest of this paper is organized as follows: Sec. II discusses the related work, Sec. III describes the generic HW-SW interface and drivers generation, Sec. IV describes implementation details for drivers and HW-SW interface. Sec. V describes a DSE case study for an SoC, and Sec. V concludes.

2. RELATED WORK

The idea of generation of the HW-SW interface has been already proposed, with multiple proposed solutions [4] [5]. The work from [5] proposed the Chinook tool for HW/SW co-synthesis, in which specifications in a single specification language captures design behavior and requirements. I/O resource allocation and device driver generation is managed from these specifications. More recent work from [6] handles the problem of HW-SW interface details in the early design stages by using the Bluespec Codesign Language that permits HW-SW partitioning in the source code. In our work, we have looked into this problem from the perspective of HW-SW interface generalization and hierarchical drivers generation in an IP-centric SoC design environment. We have utilized widely accepted IP-XACT standard for the required HW descriptions while generating drivers for both OS and non-OS based systems. Some other works from [7–10] proposed the HW-SW interface generation for Unix-like OS using custom driver specification languages.

Recent initiative from Xilinx on Software-defined SoC (SDSoC) development platform [11] enables access to HW acceleration IPs by generalizing communication flags within an IP's interface registers and generating drivers accordingly. In this approach, IP implementation (or high-level synthesis) must follow strict register-map guideline, and its extension for integrating custom IPs from external suppliers is limited. The usage of generated drivers is limited to fundamental tasks of starting, stopping and checking busy status of an IP, with no known support for interrupts, multiple functional modes, and IP-subsystem drivers.

Work from [12] comes closest to ours. It proposes extensions of IP-XACT to contain additional information on the SW by introducing 13 new XML-tags. Any SW change w.r.t. a HW change needs to be accounted for by adapting SW-tags accordingly. Another work from [13] proposes extensions to IP-XACT to integrate HW dependent SW (HdS) for fast performance models, which provides the SW mapping on the HW. The IP-XACT models are extracted from UML/-MARTE [14] and executable performance models are generated targeted to SCoPE [15] for performance estimations. In our case, we conceal the HW specific information for SW development via generic HW-SW interface which gets aligned to HW changes by the generated drivers stack. This enables to perform prototyping on target platforms (e.g. FPGAs), rather generating executable models.

3. GENERIC HW-SW INTERFACE AND HW DRIVERS GENERATION

One proposed idea in this work is to use the IP-XACT descriptions to generate generic HW-SW interface and drivers.

3.1 Generic Hardware-Software Interface

Separating generic HW-SW interface and IP-subsystem/IP drivers maximizes automation, and concealing HW details while providing access to HWs as simple function calls. IP-XACT is the IEEE 1685-2009 standard [16], which was established for describing electronic components and systems in a hierarchical way. Fig. 1 describes the simplified IP-XACT design and component modeling hierarchy as UML. IP-XACT design description contains instantiated components, bus and signal interconnections among these components, top-level design IO ports, and design parameters. The instantiated components are described by their respective IP-XACT component descriptions. This hierarchical system description makes it suitable to accumulate design knowledge at multiple usage level and realize reuse at different design abstractions. Using the proposed tool, an IP-supplier can use the IP-XACT component descriptions to generate drivers and include them in the IP-package. We extract the registers memory-map and bit-fields from IP-XACT component descriptions, and SoC memory-map, IP-blocks interfaces and HW architecture information from IP-XACT design to generate drivers. Previously, a tool has been presented [17] that uses IP-XACT to automate IP-integration for SoC implementation in IP-centric design. The limitation of the tool is that even though it automates tedious IP-integration, but SW application needs to be adapted manually for each modification. This limitation becomes more apparent when performing DSE over HW IP-library.

Fig. 2(a) shows, in the traditional SW development, a SW is adapted when the underlying SoC architecture changes. Using the proposed generic HW-SW interface, SoC architectural changes are accounted by automatically adapting the generic HW-SW interface and drivers (Fig. 2(b)). In our approach, a function call from a SW goes to the generic HW-SW interface, and the task scheduler performs the HW checks to process the tasks as SW on a CPU or HW processing on an IP-subsystem (Fig. 3). It checks for the existence of targeted IPs/IP-subsystem in an SoC, and if an IP-subsystem is "not busy" for allocating a SW task. If multiple IP-subsystems exist in an SoC for a SW task, the scheduler does round-robin-based SW task allocation. The generic interface provides an identical function call access to the SW as by the SW methods. For the target SoC, the HW-SW interface functions use generic configs (IPs base-address, interrupt-IDs, register maps and drivers mapping for OS) obtained from an IP-XACT designs.

3.2 Hardware-Access Drivers from IP-XACT

In this work, the HW drivers are generated from the available IP-XACT descriptions. The registers and bit-fields

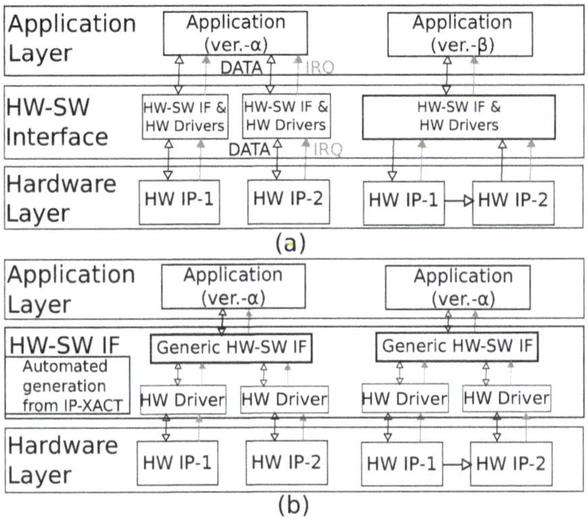

Figure 2: a) SW adapting for the traditional HW-SW interface, b) proposed generic HW-SW interface, interface accommodates the HW changes,

mapping of IPs are extracted from IP-XACT component descriptions. In our work, we have considered only memory-mapped HW IPs. But, the used principles are generic and compliant to the IP-XACT standard, hence are extendible.

For a non-OS SW application, the most typical HW-access tasks include IP or IP-subsystem initialization (_INIT), availability check (IS_busy), start HW processing (_START), stop HW processing (_STOP), control handling among CPU and HW IP, and interrupt handling. These are basically the different operational modes of an IP, and are configured by setting appropriate IP control registers values. The tool provides the first level of automation by recognizing all the registers declared in IP-XACT component description, and generating *C header file* with *C registers structs*. These generated *registers structs* abstract the IP-XACT IP registers properties of register names, offsets, bit-fields, etc.. These register structs are associated with read-write (RW) functions to access the registers and bit-fields as declared in IP-XACT. These functions use HW-platform API RW functions, (*READ_REG(u32* address, u32* offset), WRITE_REG(u32* address, u32* offset, u32* value)*) to access the physical memory-map. These platform RW functions form the hardware abstraction layer (HAL) (Fig. 3). In Fig. 3, the HAL contains the functions to access registers and bit-fields for an IP. This uses the registers, bit-fields types and offsets available in IP-XACT component description. At IP drivers layer, drivers are generated for setting operational modes of an IP. A mode of an IP is defined by *C mode struct*, which is the set of register values for the corresponding mode. By default, the *modes struct* for HW initialization, start and stop modes (_INIT, _START, _STOP) are generated, which can be extended further by any other custom modes. Respective functions for setting the IP to desired modes are generated. The mode set-up is executed by utilizing generated function, *setHWMode(struct mode)*. Drivers for IP-subsystem are generated on similar hierarchical structure as for IPs. The values for different *C mode structs* are set in the *registers struct* by the IP-designer as customization.

In the SW interface library, the generated drivers are made available for accessing HW IP-subsystems from SW applications. SW methods in the IP-library are extended with a HW-SW interface layer to provide a generic interface for a SW application. If the corresponding HW IP is available in the considered SoC, a processing task is assigned for HW processing by calling available HW drivers, else the processing is done in SW. The required *flags and configs* extracted from the considered IP-XACT designs for the generated drivers and the HW-SW interface.

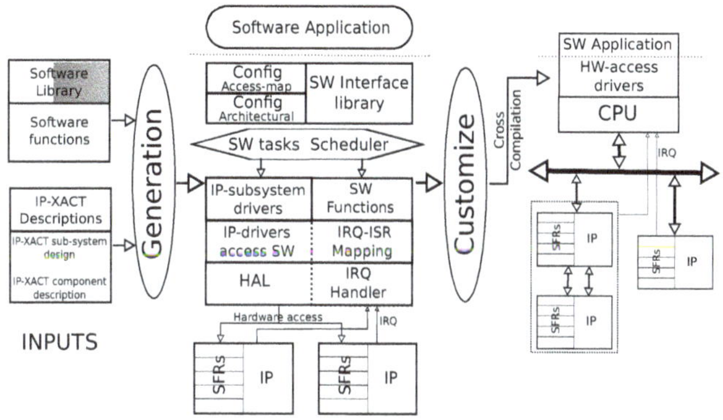

Figure 3: Generic HW-SW interface and drivers generation at different hardware abstraction layers.

For data flow control, commonly used approaches are either acknowledging an issued interrupt or polling of the completion *status bit* within an IP. Interrupt handling requires the initialization of interrupt within an application and the execution of the corresponding interrupt service routine (ISR) by an application. The generated drivers also contains interrupt initialization routines. The interrupt initialization drivers expect a handle of system's general interrupt controller (GIC) instance, interrupt port ID extracted from IP-XACT, and a pointer to a default ISR. With this interrupt handing, the method registers the IP's ISR with the processing system. For polling based communication, IS_Busy method is generated for IP-subsystems which has functions to poll for IP's busy flag.

3.3 Linux Device-Tree and Drivers Generation

For complex SW applications, it is a common practice to use an OS on high-performance processor cores. With the Linux OS, there are two things that make it aware of the underlying system HW architecture, the device drivers and device tree source (DTS) (Fig. 4). Device drivers are a set of functions in the kernel space that can access the HW for its operations. These device drivers in kernel space provide an interface to the user-space drivers to access the system hardware from a software application. The user-space drivers contain the functions to execute the desired functionality from a HW device. This is equivalent to setting the *struct mode* for a non-OS application. Device drivers can be dynamic or static, depending on whether a HW can be attached to the system at run-time or not. For embedded systems in this work we have dealt with static device drivers.

The device tree source (DTS) makes the Linux kernel aware of the system memory map, registers, interrupt lines, and associated driver functions. The custom hardware accelerator IPs or IP-subsystems in the DTS file are mapped to *char* device drivers via *.compatibility* string parameter. Once a DTS is compiled to form a device tree blob (DTB) and loaded into the Linux kernel, the kernel recognizes all the devices declared in that DTS and associate them to corresponding device drivers. The utility binaries for the HW devices are compiled and stored under system direc-

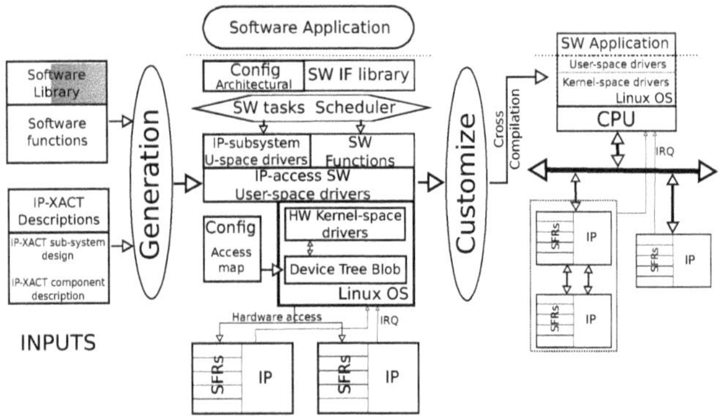

Figure 4: Generic HW-SW interface for Linux OS and associated OS building steps

tory, */sys/**. The recognized HW devices appear under the device directory, */dev/**. The tool provides generation of the user-space drivers and the generic HW-SW interface by using the recognized devices under */dev/**, and corresponding _INIT, _START and _STOP functions just as for non-OS drivers. Drivers also include the functions to recognize HW devices from the Linux HAL. The Fig. 4 shows IP-XACT SoC descriptions are used to generate required platform-specific files, which are taken forward to build Linux kernel.

4. CODE GENERATION FOR THE HW-SW INTERFACE USING IP-XACT

According to [18], the HW-SW interface at the lowest level is about data transfer between different storage elements. These storage elements are registers, or memory resources in the hardware components of an SoC design. This is where a SW application interacts with the HW to do the desired processing. Code 1 shows a sample IP-XACT register element for describing the HW-SW interface. With the complexity of current designs, registers count can go even to hundreds in number, with numerous access possibilities.

```
<spirit:register>
    <spirit:name>myRegister</spirit:name>
    <spirit:addressOffset>0x04</spirit:
      addressOffset>
    <spirit:size>32</spirit:size>
    <spirit:field>
        <spirit:name>mySliceA</spirit:name>
        <spirit:bitOffset>0</spirit:bitOffset>
        <spirit:bitWidth>24</spirit:bitWidth>
        <spirit:access>read-only</spirit:access>
    </spirit:field>
    ...
</spirit:register>
```

Code 1: Sample IP-XACT description for *register*

In our code generation, we generate *C register structs* and corresponding read-write (RW) access functions for each register and bit-fields. Code 2 gives a sample register struct for a VDMA (video direct memory access) device. For OS-based systems, similar *struct* and user-space driver functions are generated. The offset values for the registers in *register map struct* are extracted from IP-XACT, and masking field *mask* can be used to access register bit-fields. Additionally, drivers can superimpose the RW access to HW registers, just by not providing the handle of register RW functions to a SW.

This is the first level of automation for generating functions and structs. Next, in order to set the mode of a HW IP or IP-subsystem, the tool generates *C mode struct* that defines various modes for an IP and sets the register values accordingly. Code 3 is a sample *mode struct* for a VDMA IP. We used Java-based Freemarker template engine [19] and the eclipse modeling framework (EMF) for automating the drivers generation from IP-XACT. The drivers for IP-subsystem are generated by concatenating the *C structs* of the used IPs, which form the IP-subsystem registers map.

```
typedef struct {
    unsigned int offset;
    unsigned int value;
    unsigned int mask;
} VDMARegType;

typedef struct {
  VDMARegType MM2S_DMACR;
  VDMARegType S2MM_VSIZE;
  VDMARegType S2MM_HSIZE;
  VDMARegType S2MM_START_ADDRESS1;
    //... 55 regs not shown here for simplicity
    //
} VDMARegMap;
```

Code 2: Sample VDMA *registers struct* generated from IP-XACT component description.

```
VDMARegMap _VDMAInitMode = {
  .MM2S_DMACR = {.offset = 0x00, .mask = 0
    x00000004, .value = 0x00000004},
  .S2MM_VSIZE = {.offset = 0xa0, .mask = 0
    x00000000, .value = 0xffffffff},
  .S2MM_HSIZE = {.offset = 0xa4, .mask = 0
    x00000000, .value = 0xffffffff},
  .S2MM_START_ADDRESS1 = {.offset = 0xac, .mask
     = 0x00000000, .value = 0xffffffff},
      //... 55 regs not shown here for
    simplicity//
};
VDMARegMap _VDMAStartMode = {...};
VDMARegMap _VDMAStopMode = {...};

void __VDMA_Driver_initialize(<args>);
void __VDMA_Driver_start(<args>);
void __VDMA_Driver_stop(<args>);
bool __VDMA_Driver_isBusy(<args>);
void __VDMA_Driver_ISR(<args>);
```

Code 3: *mode struct* for setting IP operation mode

5. CASE-STUDY

In this section, as a validation of our methodologies, we will discuss a case-study of DSE targeted on a HW-accelerated SW library for a video-processing (VP) application as non-OS and on Linux OS. The application was targeted for Xilinx Zynq FPGA chip and was prototyped on a ZedBoard prototyping board [20]. The Zynq chip supports dual core ARM CPUs (each clocked up to 667 MHz), 512 DDR memory, USB2.0 and HDMI for video interface, AXI4 bus-system, and hardware accelerating sub-systems clocked at 100/150 MHz clocks. The target application fetches video data from an external camera device using a dedicated interface (custom camera interface module for non-OS and using USB interface with OS), and does three filtering tasks of sobel filtering, frame erosion, and gray-scale conversion sequentially before displaying the outputs on the external display monitor. The application is simple, but the constraints to handle

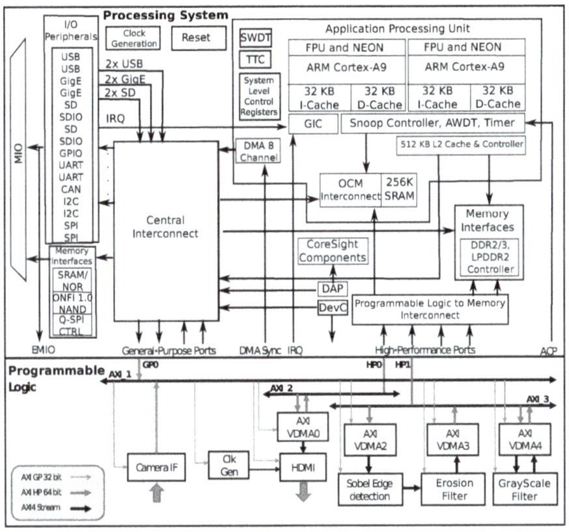

Figure 5: Video processing SoC setup in Zynq chip. In this candidate architecture all three hardware accelerators for SO, ER, and GR can be seen as instantiated in parallel in the PS part.

upto 15fps at 640x480 pixels and scope of HW acceleration with limited FPGA resources makes it a suitable candidate for validation. Fig. 5 illustrates implementation of a target SoC architecture on the Zynq chip with associated components in the Programmable System (PS) and Programmable Logic (PL). In a Zynq chip, PS has fixed HW IPs to interface with ARM CPUs and PL is the FPGA part of the chip. Each of the processing tasks can either be done on a HW accelerator or as a software method. The target of this case study was to obtain the best candidate SoC architectures for the target application by performing a DSE.

For the target application, the IP-library was prepared with three hardware filter IPs (Sobel filter (SO), Erosion filter (ER), and Gray-scale filter (GR)). All three IPs were used with a AXI-VDMA (Video direct memory access) module to form IP-subsystems, which can be integrated either parallel or in pipeline on an AXI bus. If an IP is integrated in parallel, a processing task can be independently allocated. While in pipeline integration, a HW IP is only accessible for a processing task that is done in sequence with other HW processing task. For IP-packaging, using the IP-XACT component descriptions for all three IPs, our tool generated the HW access drivers for non-OS and Linux-OS environments (as described in Sec. 3 and 4). During library preparation, the IP-packages for all three IPs were combined to form HW IP-library for SoC modeling, containing all the drivers, and user-space drivers for Linux for SW development.

The DSE explorers the HW accelerator IPs available in the prepared IP-library. The automation of SoC architectural changes was achieved using an IP-integration tool [17]. DSE starts from the SoC architecture with no hardware acceleration, and progressively the IPs were integrated to obtain twelve SoC architectures. The IP-XACT candidate SoCs were transformed to the HW descriptions to synthesize on ZedBoard FPGA. For each candidate SoC, the tool then generated HW configuration file (*config.h*) for non-OS application and DTS files for Linux OS. DTS was taken forward to be included in the Linux compilation, where the kernel associates the declared SoC hardware IPs in DTS to corre-

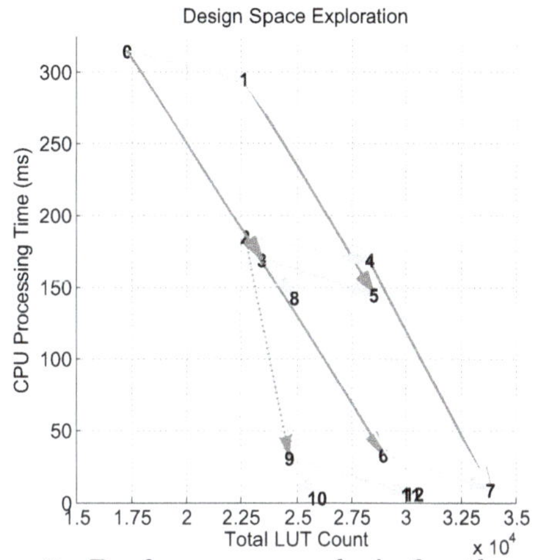

Figure 6: Performance analysis for the application as non-OS.

sponding kernel-space *char drivers*, and further to user-space drivers available in the IP-library. In Fig. 6, DSE starts from non-accelerated SoC Arch. 0, the integration of GrayScale, Erode and Sobel hardware IP is represented respectively by green, red and blue arrows. The figure shows the results of CPU single frame processing time vs. LUTs used for different candidate SoCs obtained during DSE. The solid line represents the integration in parallel and dotted lines for pipelined integration. In this DSE, we obtained Arch. 0, 2, 3, 9, and 10 as the Pareto-optimal SoCs. These results are with non-OS SW and using only single ARM CPU core.

For the DSE with OS, it involved one additional step of compiling the Linux boot image (BOOT.bin) and device tree blob (devicetree.dtb) for each new SoC architecture. We used *linaro-ubuntu-desktop-3.17* Linux kernel compiled for *armv7* architecture. In this case, a performance trade-off was observed between executing filtering tasks using openCV library [21] based software filtering functions, or performed by an equivalent hardware filter if available in the architecture. Fig. 7 shows the performance results for OS. It is interesting to note the performance overhead added because of the OS. From the figure, we obtain the Pareto-optimal SoC architecture as Arch. 0, 2, 9, 10. It can be seen that in the OS-based systems, only the HW IP for the Sobel filter gives the CPU performance improvement, while the overhead of Linux OS limits any performance improvement from GR, and ER HW IPs. One limitation of linux-3.17 is the separate system and non-system memory space. Linux memory management restricts the IP-Subsystems (Master) to access the system-memory space, so the CPU has to transfer the video data from system-memory space to non-system-memory space for IP-subsystems to access and process. This adds an additional OS overhead for data transfers. Comparing OS and non-OS based results, SW processing on OS used openCV functions, which are optimized for performance compared to the custom non-OS SW functions, this resulted in better CPU SW processing with OS than with non-OS. It can be seen from these results that depending on the target platform (w/wo OS) the Pareto front can be different. This justifies the need of choosing a platform independent IP-XACT standard for driver generation. Fig. 8 shows the overhead of hierarchically generated drivers compared to the flat manually written drivers. As compared to HW frame processing of $\sim 6M$ CPU cycles, upto 3.2x overhead over maximum of 16,690 CPU cycles of access latency for manual drivers accounts to less than

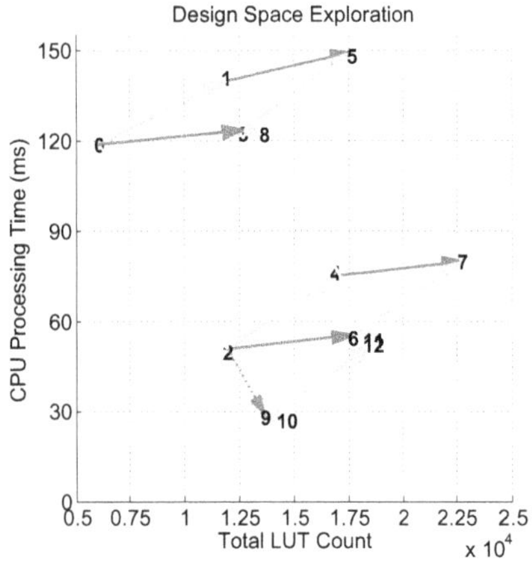

Figure 7: Performance analysis for the application with Linux OS (with data transfer overhead).

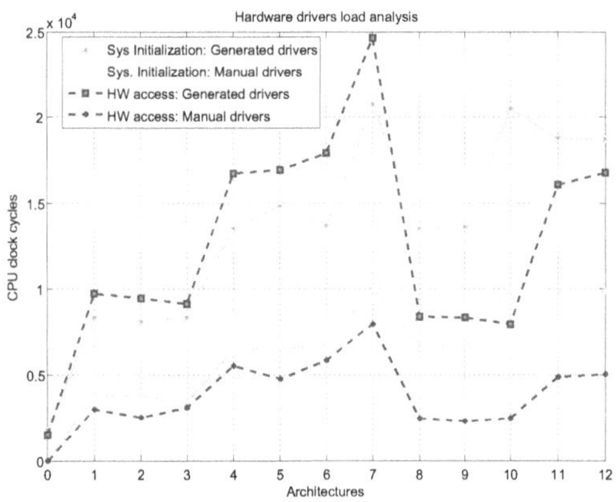

Figure 8: CPU overhead for initializing and accessing IP-subsystems with generated hierarchical drivers and manually written flat drivers.

0.28%. If the HW access frequency is higher, then some level of flattening can to be employed in drivers generation with the loss of generalization.

In this case study, we could able to reduce the DSE iteration cycle-time by utilizing the generic HW-SW interface and HW drivers generation. This approach eliminates the effort to adapt SW according to the HW changes, with additional one-time effort of IP-library preparation.

6. CONCLUSION

In this work, we have proposed a generic HW-SW interface and HW drivers generation to overcome the painstaking effort of manually adapting SW applications and developing drivers for each SoC architectural change. In the proposed approach, we use the IP-XACT standard for electronic system modeling to generate the HW drivers for non-OS as well as device tree source (DTS) and driver mapping for OS-based systems. These generated drivers are packaged with the hardware IP during IP-packaging. The proposed drivers generation can be especially useful for software-defined SoC design targeted on an HW-accelerated SW libraries, by enabling seamless transfer of SW tasks processing to HW processing. HW and SW development for an SoC can go in parallel, with SW automatically getting adapted to the HW changes in the SoC architecture. By adhering to the IP-XACT we have kept the methodology generic for extensions.

Acknowledgment

This research project is sponsored by the German Research Foundation (DFG). We are grateful to Deutsche Forschungsgesellschaft (DFG) for contributing to fund this research. This research is partly funded by the DFG under the research grant SCHL 347/3-1.

7. REFERENCES

[1] A. de la Piedra, An Braeken, and A. Touhafi. Sensor Systems Based on FPGAs and Their Applications: A Survey. *Sensors*, Sept 2012.

[2] Xilinx OpenCV - HLS Video Library. http://www.wiki.xilinx.com/HLS+Video+Library, 2015.

[3] T. Arpinen, T. Koskinen, E. Salminen, T.D. Hamalainen, and M. Hannikainen. Evaluating UML2 modeling of IP-XACT objects for automatic MP-SoC integration onto FPGA. *Design, Automation and Test in Europe Conference (DATE)*, Apr 2009.

[4] L. Ryzhyk, P. Chubb, I. Kuz, E. Le Sueur, and G. Heiser. Automatic device driver synthesis with termite. In *Symposium on Operating Systems Principles*, SOSP '09. ACM, 2009.

[5] P.H. Chou, R.B. Ortega, and G. Borriello. The Chinook Hardware/Software Co-Synthesis System. *International Symposium on System Synthesis*, Sept 1995.

[6] M. King, N. Dave, and Arvind. Automatic generation of hardware/software interfaces. *SIGPLAN Not.*, 47(4), March 2012.

[7] H. Chen, G. Godet-Bar, F. Rousseau, and F. Petrot. Device Driver Generation Targeting Multiple Operating Systems Using a Model-driven Methodology. *Rapid System Prototyping (RSP)*, Oct 2014.

[8] Wang S., S. Malik, and R. Bergamaschi. Modeling and integration of peripheral devices in embedded systems. *Design, Automation and Test in Europe Conference (DATE)*, March 2003.

[9] T. Katayama, K. Saisho, and A. Fukuda. Prototype of the device driver generation system for UNIX-like operating systems. *Proceedings. Intern. Symp. on Principles of Software Evolution*, Nov 2000.

[10] M. King, J. Hicks, and J. Ankcorn. Software-Driven Hardware Development. *ACM/SIGDA International Symposium on FPGA*, Feb 2015.

[11] Software-Defined SoC Development Enviroment. http://www.xilinx.com/products/design-tools/software-zone/sdsoc.html, 2015.

[12] A. Kamppi, L. Matilainen, J.-M. Maatta, and E. Salminen. Extending IP-XACT to Embedded System HW/SW Integration. *System on Chip (SoC)*, Oct 2013.

[13] F. Herrera, H. Posadas, E. Villar, and D. Calvo. Enhanced IP-XACT Platform Descriptions for Automatic Generation from UML-MARTE of Fast Performance Models for DSE. *Digital System Design (DSD)*, Sept 2012.

[14] UML Profile for MARTE: Modeling and Analysis of Real-Time Embedded Systems. OMG, 2009.

[15] P. Botella, P. SÃąnchez, and H. Posadas. Automatic Generation of SystemC SMP Models for HW/SW Co-Simulation". *Conf. on Design of Circuits and Integrated Systems (DCIS)*, 2010.

[16] IEEE 1685-2009 IP-XACT. http://standards.ieee.org, 2009.

[17] Omitted for blind review. Reference will be added later. *Design Automation Conference (DAC)*, June 2015.

[18] W Ecker, W. Müller, and D. Rainer. Hardware-dependent software - principles and practice. 2009.

[19] Freemarker Java-based Template Engine. http://www.freemarker.org/.

[20] ZedBoard. http://www.zedboard.org.

[21] OpenCV: Open Source Computer Vision. http://www.opencv.org/.

Extracting Designs of Secure IPs Using FPGA CAD Tools

Vincent Mirian and Paul Chow
Department of Electrical and Computer Engineering, University of Toronto
Toronto, ON Canada
{mirianvi, pc}@eecg.toronto.edu

ABSTRACT

In today's competitive market, a company's success is strongly dependent on delivering sophisticated and state-of-the-art IPs prior to their competitors. To take a short cut, a company may resort to reverse engineering or pirating their competitor's IP.

In this paper, we examine the feasibility of extracting the design of a secure IP from one technology and using it in another. In particular, we start by extracting the IP from an FPGA vendor tool flow and map the IP blocks to an ASIC technology. We show that there is not a significant degradation in quality compared to starting with the original source, thus showing that taking a pirated IP from an FPGA and using it in another technology is viable, and therefore worth doing. This demonstrates a clear motivation for patching a vulnerability in FPGA CAD tools.

Note that the intent of this work is not to promote the piracy of IPs. Instead, the goal is to demonstrate a mechanism for extracting a design as a means towards understanding what methods of pirating are possible, and whether they can be prevented.

Keywords

Intellectual Property (IP); Protection; Theft; FPGA; ASIC; CAD Tools

1. INTRODUCTION

For technology companies to be successful in today's world, they are required to deliver the next "big thing" prior to their competitors. As a result, these companies invest countless engineering hours, translating into a significant amount of money, in researching and developing sophisticated and state-of-the-art products. For the success to transform into economical gain, it is very important for the company to protect their investment (e.g. product). Therefore, companies also invest in keeping their IPs secure. Typically, a portion of the development cost of IPs is allocated to implementing security for the IP. In the case of IPs for FPGAs, the cost of protecting the IP should range between 5% to 10% of the IP's market value [1].

In hardware design, there are three types of IPs: hard, firm and soft IPs. Hard IPs are physical manifestations of the IP design, such as a circuit layout. Firm IPs typically carry placement data but their final configuration and layout is still flexible so they can fit better with surrounding IPs. Soft IPs are the most flexible of the three types. Typically, soft IPs are written in a hardware description language (HDL) and, the hardware designer implements the IP using a parameterizable module, where the design is configurable and contains hierarchy. In this paper, we focus on soft IPs.

We focus our study on the use of FPGA vendor tools and show how it is possible to extract an encrypted IP from their libraries. The two main vendors are Altera and Xilinx and our approach can work for both vendors. To be able to describe the process in more detail, we focus in this paper on the Xilinx tools, but we could have also done this with the Altera tools.

In this paper, our contributions are:

- present a method for extracting the design of a secure IP using commercial FPGA tools,
- evaluate the impact of using a pirated IP with a different technology, and,
- expose a security hole in FPGA CAD tools to patch.

2. BACKGROUND

In this Section, we define the different types of IP formats used in Xilinx's design flow, ISE Design Suite [2]. We also provide details about the ISE Design Suite as it is the design flow used in this paper. Although the work presented in this paper focuses on the ISE Design Suite, the tools from the ISE Design Suite have a tool or a Tool Command Language (tcl) command equivalent in Xilinx's newer design flow, the Vivado Design Suite. We welcome the reader to reference the Manual [3] for these commands.

2.1 IP Representation in the ISE Design Suite

In the ISE Design Suite, there are three supported formats to represent an IP. The first format is a high-level hardware description language (HDL), such as Verilog or VHDL, used to describe the Register Transfer Level (RTL). When implementing an IP in this format, the designer typically uses a parameterizable module, where the IP can be configured using parameters and the implementation of the IP is coded in reusable design units (e.g. entities in VHDL and modules in Verilog).

To protect IPs written in this format from malicious use, the source code of the IPs can be encrypted. For example,

GLSVLSI '16, May 18-20, 2016, Boston, MA, USA

DOI: http://dx.doi.org/10.1145/2902961.2903033

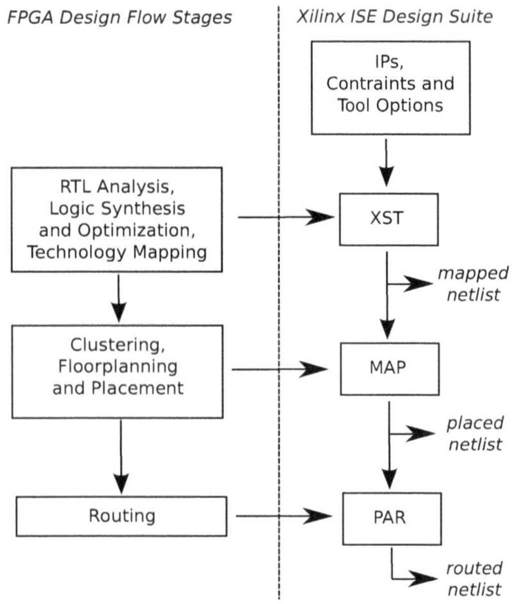

Figure 1: Design flow used in the ISE Design Suite

the tools in the ISE design suite support the IEEE P1735 [4] encryption standard. A few IPs from Xilinx's IP library are encrypted using this standard.

The second format is Electronic Design Interchange Format (EDIF). This format is a vendor-neutral format used by the Electronic Design Automation (EDA) industry. Details on this format are publicly available [5]. And, the third format is a Xilinx proprietary format with an NGC extension. Unlike the EDIF, details on this format are not publicly available. Both these formats describe an IP's implementation using a list of technology's cells and the connection between these cells.

Converting between these three formats can easily be done using FPGA utilities and tools that are described in Section 2.3. Amongst the three formats, non-encrypted HDL and EDIF are the only formats readable by humans.

On a side note, although there has been a trend toward using higher-level abstraction models such as OpenCL and the Vivado HLS tool, the focus of this paper is on designs expressed in HDL.

2.2 The Design Flow Used In ISE Design Suite

An FPGA design flow transforms high-level hardware description language (HDL) to a string of bits, commonly termed a bitstream. Figure 1 shows each stage of this transformation as well as their mapping to the corresponding Xilinx tool from the ISE Design Suite.

The first stage of the flow performs: 1) *Register Transfer Level (RTL) Analysis*, which extracts properties of the design and basic design rules checking, 2) *Logic Synthesis and Optimization*, which transforms the RTL model to logic, and 3) *Technology Mapping*, which maps the logic to the primitives of the target FPGA. These primitives are also known as technology cells.

The input to the first stage is a set of *IPs, Constraints and Tool Options*. The set of IPs describe the design and can be in any of the formats described in Section 2.1. The design Constraints may include timing characteristics for the design. Tool Options enable the designer to change the parameters for processing the design at this stage (e.g optimization

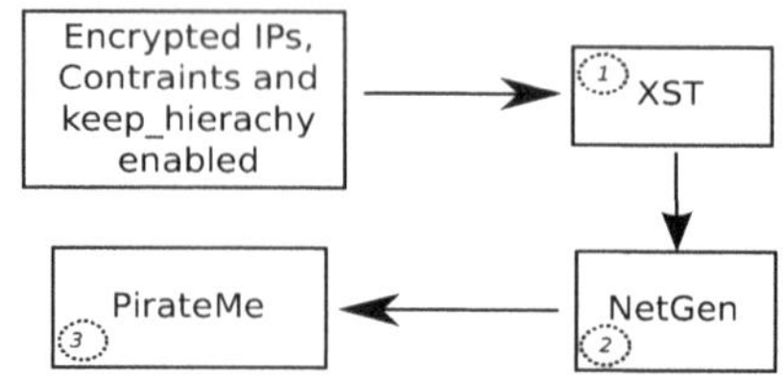

Figure 2: Method for pirating IPs

level). In the ISE Design Suite, this stage is performed by Xilinx Synthesis Tool (*XST*), and the output of this stage is a *mapped netlist* composed of a list of the FPGA primitives and the connections between these primitives. The format of the output file is a Xilinx proprietary format with an NGC extension.

Amongst the various Tool Options for XST, *keep_hierarchy* is an option that enables or disables hierarchical flattening of the design. When enabling the *keep_hierarchy* option, the output of XST groups the primitives and their connections into their respective design unit. When the option is disabled, the primitives and their connections are not grouped.

The second stage of the flow performs *Clustering, Floorplanning* and *Placement*. In the ISE Design Suite, this stage is performed by the *MAP* tool, and the output of this stage is refered to as the *placed netlist*. The third stage of the flow performs *Routing* and is performed by the Place and Route (*PAR*) tool in the ISE Design Suite. The output of this stage is referred to as the *routed netlist*. The forth stage converts the routed netlist into a bitstream. This stage is not shown in Figure 1.

2.3 IP Format Conversion Utilities

The *NetGen* utility [6] generates netlists to be used by third-party tools. NetGen takes the output of any stage from the design flow shown in Figure 1, and outputs a netlist for use by supported third party simulation, equivalence checking, and static timing analysis tools. The output netlist is not secure (e.g. encrypted) as the third party tools may not support this feature.

The *NGC2EDIF* [6] utility is specifically designed to convert a netlist in Xilinx proprietary format with an NGC extension to an EDIF netlist. In the end, the NetGen and NGC2EDIF utilities convert a netlist in Xilinx proprietary format with an NGC extension to a human readable format.

3. METHOD FOR PIRATING IPS

Our objective is to extract a non-proprietary format of a secure IP's implementation (e.g. HDL) so it can be reused in other designs. In this Section, we demonstrate how to extract the HDL source code of a secure IP's implementation. We focus on the HDL format since its syntax is typically preferred and it is a common format for hardware designers to implement their IPs. However, the method is capable of extracting the EDIF format by using the NGC2EDIF utility discussed in Section 2.3 if the user desires.

Figure 2 shows the method for extracting the design of a secure IP, hereafter this method is referred to as *pirating* an IP. The method encapsulates the process of preparing the netlist as well as the process to extract HDL source code from the IP's netlist. The first step is to pass the encrypted IP and design constraints to XST with the keep_hierarchy option enabled. This step produces a mapped netlist with the FPGA primitives grouped with their respective design units. The first step refers to the process of preparing a netlist.

The second step is to take the mapped netlist produced by the first step and feed this netlist to the NetGen utility. The NetGen utility outputs HDL files where each file corresponds to a design unit and the contents of the file is the implementation of the design unit using FPGA primitives.

The output from NetGen is intended for use by simulation, equivalence checking, and static timing analysis tools. As a result, the output from the NetGen utility has directives embedded in the files preventing synthesis tools from processing its content. We developed a tool (*PirateMe*) that modifies the HDL files generated by NetGen so they can be processed by synthesis tools. Our tool removes the directives from the generated HDL files and modifies the libraries preparing the files for synthesis tools.

The third step is to pass the HDL files generated by NetGen to our tool. Steps 2 and 3 extract the HDL source code from the IP's netlist. In the end, the modified HDL files produced by PirateMe are an RTL representation of an IP implemented with FPGA primitives that is ready to be processed by synthesis tools. For completeness, our tool, PirateMe, also removes the directives in the netlist produced by NGC2EDIF making the netlist ready to be processed by synthesis tools. Hereafter, the output of PirateMe is referred to as the *pirated IP*.

On a side note, the keep_hierarchy option is not required for pirating the IP. As mentioned, the benefit of enabling this option is that it preserves the IP's modular implementation. An IP's modular implementation is not required unless the IP is to be modified.

Many IPs have parameters that configure the IP for a particular application or use. These parameters are read at the RTL analysis step of XST and not propagated through the design flow as they are no longer needed. Therefore, the source code of the pirated IP does not contain the parameters nor configurability that would be present in the original version of the source code. If an IP with a different configuration is required, then IP with the required configuration must be obtained before it can be passed through our method and be pirated.

To use an IP from Xilinx's IP library, a license may be necessary. Other than a license, there is no restriction on accessing the IP. Hence, for our method to be functional, a valid license is required. In addition, when using the IP under this license, the user agrees to use the IP within proper legal bounds. When using our method to pirate the IP, these legal bounds are violated. However, the purpose of the paper is to expose the security hole, so FPGA vendors can patch this vulnerability.

In the end, we presented a method for extracting the design of a secure IP.

4. IMPACT OF USING A PIRATED IP WITH A DIFFERENT TECHNOLOGY

In this Section, we will evaluate the the power, performance and cost (PPC) of a pirated IP to assess its quality with a different technology. We do this by generating circuits and then "pirating" them using our methodology. We use LegUp [7], a high-level synthesis tool, as a way to easily generate a large number of benchmark circuits for our study. LegUp outputs Verilog HDL, which we use as the starting point of our analysis. These benchmarks contain several kernels, like *constant division*, *fft*, and *memset*, and some larger applications from the chstone benchmark suite like *blowfish*, *mips* and *mpeg*. Benchmarks with a divider use an IP generated by Coregen, Xilinx's IP generator utility. We perform the evaluation using four ASIC design flows shown in Figure 3 targetting TSMC's 65nm standard cell technology. We will describe the flows as they are introduced throughout this Section.

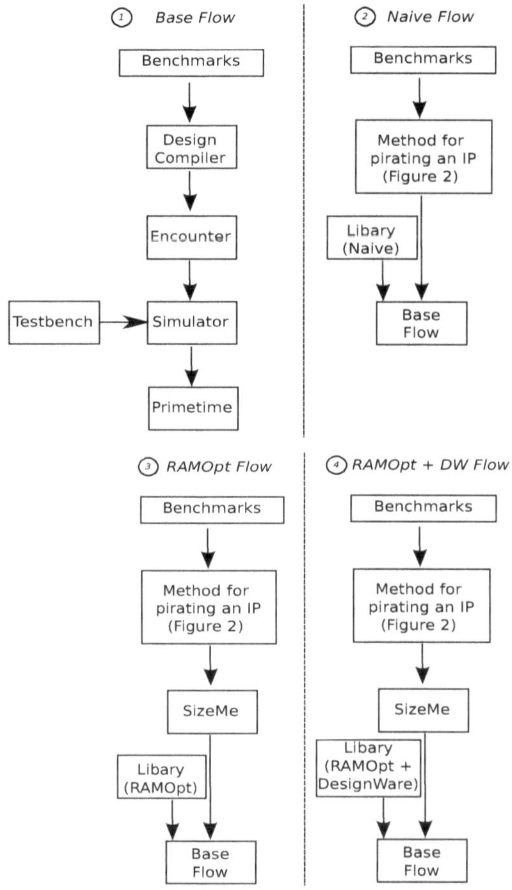

Figure 3: Experimental flows for evaluating the impact of using a pirated IP with a different technology

The first flow is the *Base* flow. In this flow, the Verilog output from LegUp is passed to *Design Compiler* [8], a tool that performs the same steps as XST, but for ASICs. The output of Design Compiler is sent as the input to *Encounter* [9], a tool that performs place and route for ASIC design. We retrieve the area (cost) of the circuit from the report generated by Encounter. Encounter outputs a routed netlist that is passed to the simulator with a testbench that terminates when the benchmark is complete or 10000 cycles have passed. The output of the simulator along with the routed netlist is passed to *Primetime* [10] to compute the maximum frequency (performance) and power usage of the benchmark.

The second flow is identical to the first flow with the exception that the benchmarks are passed through the method for pirating an IP shown in Figure 2. In addition, the Base flow is passed a *library* containing the definitions and implementation of the FPGA primitives using a behavioral model to remove FPGA architectural detail. For example, LUTs are implemented using the sum-of-product function of their inputs, as opposed to its structural implementation where

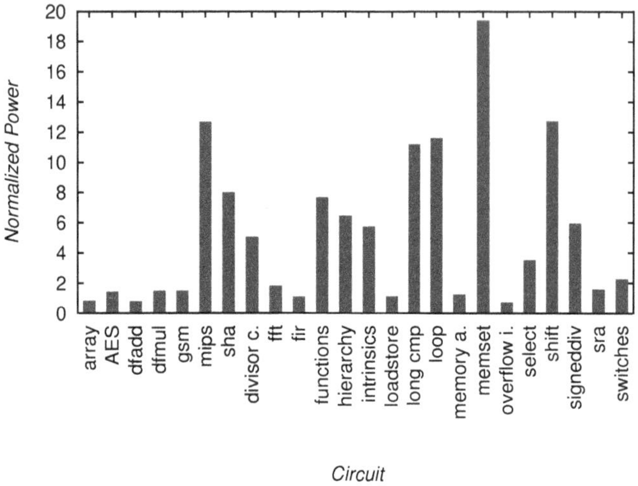

Figure 4: Power Usage of the Naive Flow Normalized to the Base Flow

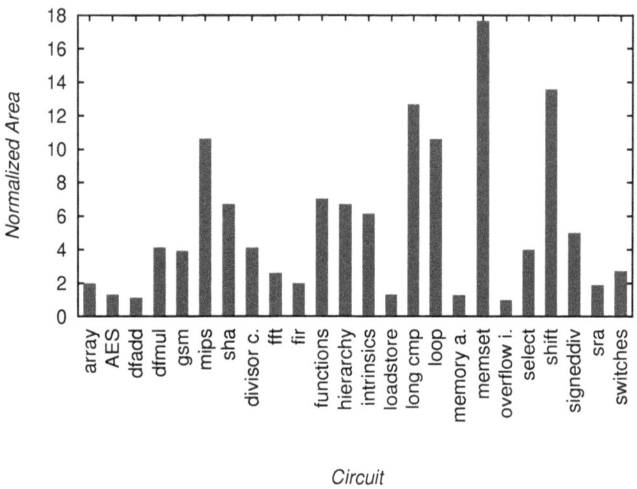

Figure 5: Area of the Naive Flow Normalized to the Base Flow

the inputs select the content of a table. The implementation of the FPGA primitives in the library were developed using Xilinx documentation [11] [12] [13] and their configurations were not influenced by the benchmark implementation. Hereafter, we refer to this flow as the *Naive* flow, since the configuration of the FPGA primitives was not influenced by the benchmark implementation.

For our first experiment, we compare the power usage and area of the Base flow with that of the Naive flow. Figures 4 and 5 show the normalized power usage and area of the Naive flow over the Base flow. Due to space limitations, we only show a smaller set of representative circuits.

In Figure 4, we observe a significant increase in power usage and area with the Naive flow than the Base flow. This increase is a result of poor implementation for the memory primitives (e.g BRAMs) within our library. In the Xilinx architecture, BRAMs have configurable data widths, where the data width dictates the maximum depth of the BRAM. In addition, distributed RAM, memory components built out of LUTs, have fix depth. In our library implementation, the BRAM primitives' depth is set to the maximum allowable depth according to its width configuration as per Xilinx's documentation, and the distributed RAM's depth is

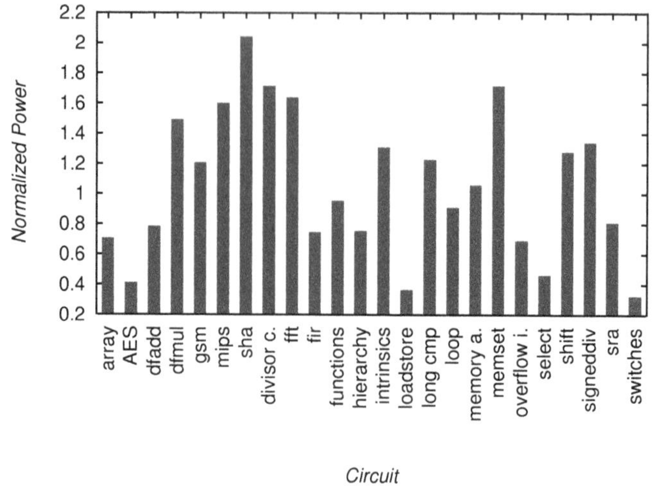

Figure 6: Power Usage of the RAMOpt Flow Normalized to the Base Flow

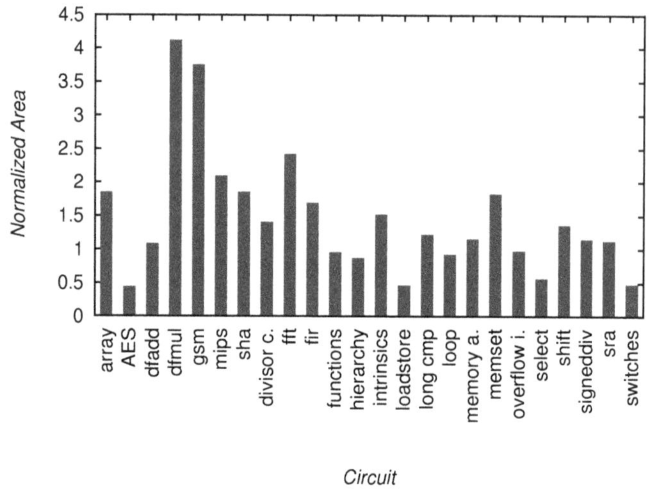

Figure 7: Area of the RAMOpt Flow Normalized to the Base Flow

also set to its fixed depth. As a result, these memory primitives may have unused entries, and thus area is wasted and static power is consumed. Whereas, the Base flow has the depth of their memory components configured accurately since the depth value is retrieved from the original source files that do not use FPGA primitives to represent memory components.

To remove the wasted area and reduce power, we have modified our library implementation by enabling the memory primitives to have configurable depth. In addition, we implemented a tool (*SizeMe*) that analyzes the HDL files to determine the depth of the memory primitives. The tool determines the depth of the memory primitives by analyzing the signals connected to the address port. The tool searches for the largest index of the signal connected to the address port that is active. The index is used to determine the depth of the memory component. The depth is accurate to the highest power of two. The tool takes as input an HDL file, determines the depth of a memory primitive and outputs a modified HDL file with the memory primitive configured to the correct depth.

We use our tool in the third flow, the *RAMOpt* flow. This flow is identical to the Naive flow with the exception that

Table 1: Average Power Usage, Maximum Frequency and Area across all circuits

Flow	Power Usage (Watts)	Maximum Frequency (Mhz)	Area (um^2)
Base	1.84E-002	241	82406
Naive	7.99E-002	290	336367
RAMOpt	2.04E-002	333	132389
RAMOpt + DesignWare	1.39E-002	330	111388

the output from our method of pirating IPs is passed to SizeMe, and the output of SizeMe is passed to the Base flow with a modified version of our library supporting configurable depth for the memory primitives.

For our second experiment, we compare the power usage and area of the Base flow with that of the RAMOpt flow. Figures 6 and 7 show the normalized power usage and area of the RAMOpt flow over the Base flow. For circuits using memory primitives, the average normalized power usage using the Naive flow is 4.69 where the average normalized power usage using the RAMOpt flow is 1.24, a 3.78-fold reduction. And, for circuits using memory primitives, the average normalized area using the Naive flow is 4.55 where the average normalized area using the RAMOpt flow is 0.91, a 5-fold reduction. However, unused memory entries can still occur since the depth calculated by SizeMe is only accurate to a power of two. The *memset* circuit is an example of a circuit with unused memory entries, the results show 70% more power usage and 80% area overhead when using the RAMOpt flow compare to the Base flow.

Circuits using a divider have a higher area overhead with the Naive and RAMOpt flows than the Base flow. The divider implementation extracted from the method for pirating IPs is larger than the divider implementation inferred by Design Compiler. The *fir* circuit is an example that uses a divider and has no unused memory entries. In Figure 7, fir suffers from 74% area overhead. Furthermore, the memory architecture inferred by XST targeting an FPGA is more power and area efficient than the memory architecture inferred by Design Compiler. When using Design Compiler, a memory component is inferred as one large memory structure with complex control logic. Whereas, when a memory component is inferred by XST, the structure is built with a parallel architecture using less control logic. Therefore, circuits with memory components experience a decrease in power and area when using the RAMOpt flow compare to the Base flow.

The signeddiv circuit uses a divider and contains unused memory entries with the RAMOpt flow. It suffers from 34% more power usage and 15% area overhead. The overhead from the divider implementation and unused memory entries dominate the benefit from the inferred memory architecture introduced by XST.

From the results of the previous experiment, we observe that the memory architecture affects the power usage and area of the pirated IP. For our third experiment, we explore memory implementations and their effects on power usage and area. For this experiment, we use the *RAMOpt + DesignWare* flow. This flow is identical to the RAMOpt flow with the exception that the memory primitives in our library are implemented using the components in the DesignWare library [14], which contains efficient memory implementations. By using the DesignWare library, memory implementations are not inferred by Design Compiler. After executing the experiment, we observe that the RAMOpt + DesignWare flow uses less area than the RAMOpt flow.

Table 1 shows the average power usage, Maximum Frequency and Area across all circuits for the four flows. From Table 1, we observe that the RAMOpt + DesignWare flow has a decreased power and area usage compared to the RAMOpt flow. Moreover, compared to the Base flow, the RAMOpt + DesignWare flow has a reduced power usage, an increase in maximum frequency and an increase in area. The latter is due to the divider implementation and unused memory entries in the memory components.

In the end, when using a pirated IP in a different technology, we observe that the memory architecture inferred by XST targeting an FPGA is more power and area efficient than the memory structure inferred by Design Compiler. However, the divider implementation in the FPGA uses more area than the divider implementation inferred by Design Compiler. Furthermore, to achieve an efficient implementation of a pirated IP in a different technology, the depth of the memory components needs to be correctly adjusted for which we provide the SizeMe tool, and an efficient memory implementation needs to be given to the flow for which we use the DesignWare library. By using these techniques, we reduced the average power usage and increased the average maximum frequency of our circuits.

5. RELATED WORK AND DISCUSSION

There is no known related work that presents a method to pirate an encrypted IP. However, there is a significant amount of work that presents mechanisms to prevent IP piracy including digital watermarking [15] and metering [16]. In this Section, we describe these mechanisms as well as others and discuss their impact on preventing piracy when using our method.

Watermarking aims to embed signatures representing the IP's owner without altering the IP's functionality. There is a fair amount of work for demonstrating the feasibility of watermarking in FPGAs. For example, Lach [17] uses the unused LookUp Tables of a design to insert the watermark, and Roy [18] alters non-critical paths in the circuit to embed the keys. If the incorrect key is placed in the circuit, then it will function incorrectly. These works can be implemented as early as the placement step of the design flow. Our method uses the mapped netlist produced at the Technology Mapping step of the design flow, which occurs before the placement step.

Metering is similar to watermarking. It uses a unique *serial number* for every IP instance to identify the IP's owner and the IP instance prior to distributing the IP. Therefore, if an IP with an embedded metering mechanism is pirated, then the unique serial number is used to identify the source of the IP, in turn the culprit. Watermarking nor metering prevent our method from pirating. However, if these methods are applied, then additional measures would need to be taken to remove the tags attached to the IP's.

Copy detection is the method of detecting illegitimate use of the IP and proving the IP's ownership. The method consists of matching the IP to a set of known IPs. For the method to be effective, it would need to function in collaboration with an IP tagging method, such as watermarking or metering mentioned above. If this security method is implemented, then our method would be able to pirate the

IP, however re-using the pirated IP would not be feasible. Nonetheless, given the various input formats to synthesis tools, the various authors of an IP, and the various EDA tools that would need to implement this method, managing copy detection would be very difficult.

Encryption is another effective manner to prevent soft IP theft [19]. As mentioned, Xilinx uses the IEEE P1735 standard [4] to secure selected IPs in their IP library. However, this encryption is ineffective, since the output of NetGen is unencrypted. If the output of NetGen was encrypted, our method would fail to pirate an IP. Furthermore, the EDA vendors would need to agree on a secure system where different tools can read encrypted information from other vendors, which requires collaboration from competing EDA vendors.

In the end, our method leverages a security hole in the FPGA CAD tools, which is the unencrypted output files generated by NetGen. Therefore, amongst the presented methods, encryption is the method that would prevent pirating IPs using our method. The EDA vendors would need to collaborate on a mechanism to enable this, but the key management would not be trivial.

6. CONCLUSION

In today's competitive world, for technology companies to be successful, they need to release sophisticated and state-of-the-art products prior to their competitors. When a company is unable to release its product prior to its competitors, the company may resort to IP theft. To prevent IP theft, companies secure their IPs with a theft-resistant mechanism. For example, Xilinx secures their IPs in their library using source code encryption.

In this paper, we present our method that uses Xilinx's synthesis tool (XST) and NetGen utility as well as our PirateMe tool that modifies the HDL files generated by NetGen so they may be processed by synthesis tools. It is also important to realize that a very similar process can be used for the Altera tools.

When evaluating the impact of using a pirated IP with a different technology, we observed that: in an FPGA architecture, the depth of the memory primitives are fixed, and within a design, these memory primitives may have unused entries. Hence, to use a pirated IP in a different technology efficiently, we developed SizeMe, a tool that analyzes the HDL files to determine the depth of the memory primitives to the closest power of two as its upperbound. When using this tool, we observe a significant reduction in power usage and area overhead. In addition, we observe that the memory structure inferred by XST targeting an FPGA is more power and area efficient than the memory structure inferred by Design Compiler (used for the ASIC flow). However, the divider implementation in the FPGA uses more area than the divider implementation inferred by Design Compiler, because the FPGA implementation is optimized for the FPGA architecture which is inefficient when mapped to a different technology.

Furthermore, we show that there is not a significant degradation in quality when comparing the original source of the IP with the pirated IP's source when using an ASIC flow, thus showing that taking a pirated IP from an FPGA and using it in another technology is viable, and therefore worth doing. This demonstrates a clear motivation for patching a vulnerability in FPGA CAD tools.

7. ACKNOWLEDGMENTS

Vincent Mirian would like to dedicate this paper to his godmother, Bernadette Caradant, for the inspiration to continue his education. Furthermore, we acknowledge Xilinx, CMC/emSYSCAN and NSERC for the funding and material provided for this project.

8. REFERENCES

[1] Austin Lesea. IP Security in FPGAs, 2007.

[2] Xilinx Inc. ISE Design Suite 14: Release Notes, Installation, and Licensing, 2013.

[3] Xilinx Inc. Vivado Design Suite User Guide, 2015.

[4] IEEE Standard. 1735-2014 - IEEE Approved Draft Recommended Practice for Encryption and Management of Electronic Design Intellectual Property (IP). https://standards.ieee.org/findstds/standard/1735-2014.html, 2014.

[5] Government Electronics & Information Technology Association. EIA 682:1996 Edif Version 400 Electronic Design Interchange Format, 1996.

[6] Xilinx Inc. Command Line Tools User Guide, 2012.

[7] Canis, Andrew and Choi, Jongsok and Aldham, Mark and Zhang, Victor and Kammoona, Ahmed and Anderson, Jason H. and Brown, Stephen and Czajkowski, Tomasz. LegUp: High-level Synthesis for FPGA-based Processor/Accelerator Systems. In *Proceedings of the 19th ACM/SIGDA International Symposium on Field Programmable Gate Arrays*, FPGA '11, pages 33–36, 2011.

[8] Synopsys. Design compiler user guide, 2011.

[9] Cadence. Encounter user guide, 2010.

[10] Synopsys. Primetime user guide: Advanced timing analysis, 2007.

[11] Xilinx Inc. Virtex-6 Libraries Guide for HDL Designs, 2009.

[12] Xilinx Inc. Virtex-6 FPGA DSP48E1 Slice, 2011.

[13] Xilinx Inc. Virtex-6 FPGA Memory Resources, 2014.

[14] Synopsys Inc. DesignWare Building Block IP, 2010.

[15] Arlindo Oliveira. Techniques for the creation of digital watermarks in sequential circuit designs, 2001.

[16] Farinaz Koushanfar, Gang Qu, and Miodrag Potkonjak. Intellectual property metering. In *Information Hiding*, volume 2137 of *Lecture Notes in Computer Science*, pages 81–95. Springer Berlin Heidelberg, 2001.

[17] Lach, J. and Mangione-Smith, W.H. and Potkonjak, M. Signature hiding techniques for FPGA intellectual property protection. In *Computer-Aided Design, 1998. ICCAD 98. Digest of Technical Papers. 1998 IEEE/ACM International Conference on*, pages 186–189, Nov 1998.

[18] Roy, J.A. and Koushanfar, F. and Markov, I.L. EPIC: Ending Piracy of Integrated Circuits. In *Design, Automation and Test in Europe, 2008. DATE '08*, pages 1069–1074, March 2008.

[19] Trimberger, S. Trusted Design in FPGAs. In *Design Automation Conference, 2007. DAC '07. 44th ACM/IEEE*, pages 5–8, June 2007.

Security Primitive Design with Nanoscale Devices: A Case Study with Resistive RAM

Robert Karam[1], Rui Liu[2], Pai-Yu Chen[2], Shimeng Yu[2], and Swarup Bhunia[1]
[1] Department of Electrical and Computer Engineering,
University of Florida, Gainesville, FL, 32608
[2] School of Electrical, Computer, Energy Engineering,
Arizona State University, Tempe, AZ 85281
Email: shimengy@asu.edu, swarup@ece.ufl.edu

ABSTRACT

Inherent stochastic physical mechanisms in emerging nonvolatile memories (NVMs), such as resistive random-access-memory (RRAM), have recently been explored for hardware security applications. Unlike the conventional silicon Physical Unclonable Functions (PUFs) that are solely based on manufacturing process variation, RRAM has some intrinsic randomness in its physical mechanisms that can be utilized as entropy sources; for instance, resistance variation, random telegraph noise, and probabilistic switching behaviors. This paper reviews the challenges and opportunities in building security primitives with emerging devices. In particular, it presents research progress of RRAM-based hardware security primitives, including PUF and True Random Number Generator (TRNG).

General Terms

Security

Keywords

Hardware security; RRAM, TRNG; PUF; resistance variation; switching probability; security of nanoscale devices

1. INTRODUCTION

Scaling integrated systems deeper into the nanoscale regime will require unprecedented innovations in device technologies, including structures, materials, and entirely new state variables, such as electron spin or resistance, to represent information. Such fundamental shifts will certainly impact the design of secure systems in profound ways; properties of emerging nanoscale devices, including large variations, accelerated aging, power and timing asymmetry, and non-volatility, could lead to new attack modalities, or potentially render existing defenses unacceptable.

GLSVLSI '16, May 18-20, 2016, Boston, MA, USA © 2016 ACM. ISBN 978-1-4503-4274-2/16/05…$15.00
DOI: http://dx.doi.org/10.1145/2902961.2903042

Still other device properties, such as resistance variation, random telegraph noise (RTN), and probabilistic switching behaviors, can instead be leveraged for drastic improvements in existing hardware-based security primitives. Therefore, there is a critical need to evaluate security properties of integrated systems in the context of nanoscale devices.

In particular, we explore new designs for Physical Unclonable Functions (PUFs) and True Random Number Generators (TRNGs) using nanoscale devices. PUFs and TRNGs are the primitives for security applications such as chip authentication and on-chip cryptographic key generation [1]. Current designs for silicon PUFs, including the delay-based Ring Oscillator and Arbiter PUFs [1], leverage intrinsic process variations as a source of entropy to generate bit vectors that differ between different physical instances of the same design. Similarly, current silicon TRNG designs use variations which manifest as random telegraph noise to generate a truly random sequence of bits. In the deep nanoscale era, however, additional sources of entropy can be leveraged to create more robust security primitives.

As a motivational example, we note that for RO PUFs using deep nanometer FinFET and TFET devices, the intrinsic random variations – including those derived from Oxygen Vacancy (OV) in gate dielectric, Random Dopant Fluctuation (RDF), Metal Gate Granularity (MGG), and Fin (Gate) Edge Roughness (FER / GER) – dominate over the systematic variations. This leads to a higher non-normality and higher spread in the distribution than would be expected for silicon RO PUF. An example is shown in Fig. 1 using 3D-TCAD simulation for FinFET. Using inter-die hamming distance (IHD), it shows that the uniqueness of RO-PUF is significantly affected by the non-Normal nature of these variations. Unlike the case when the distribution is normal, the IHD for FinFET/TFET nanoscale devices is a strong function of the standard deviation of the distribution (Fig. 1). This exemplifies the need for additional analysis of security primitives in the context of nanoscale devices.

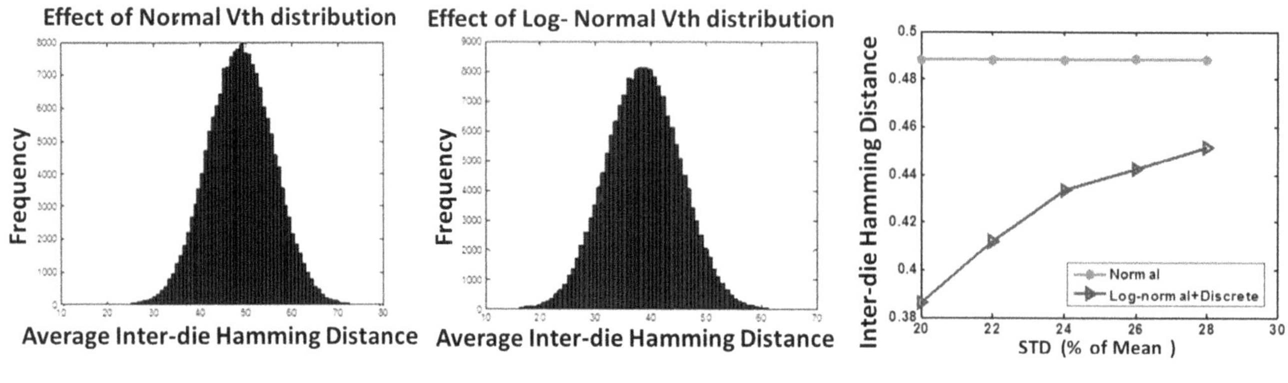

(a) (b) (c)

Fig. 1: Example analysis of security primitives considering nanoscale devices: Analysis of a ring oscillator (RO) PUF considering non-Normal distribution of nanoscale device parameters. Uniqueness of PUF, measured as inter-die hamming distance (a, b) is significantly affected (note the reduction in mean IHD and wider spread) and becomes a strong function of the standard deviation (c).

The rest of the paper is organized as follows: Section 2 gives an overview of resistive random access memory (RRAM) and characteristics which make it attractive for use in security; Section 3 provides sample implementations of PUF and TRNG which leverage the unique properties of RRAM for next generation primitives; finally, in Section 4, we conclude with future directions for the research.

2. RRAM Characteristics for Security Primitives

RRAM is one of the emerging non-volatile memory (NVM) technologies. Other emerging NVMs include phase change memory (PCM) [2] and spin torque transfer magnetic random access memory (STT-MRAM) [3]. The operating principle of an RRAM device is the reversible switching between a high resistance state (HRS, off-state, "0") and a low resistance state (LRS, on-state, "1") by voltage stimulus. The typical RRAM device structure is a metal/oxide/metal stack, which can be integrated in the contact vias between interconnect layers on top of the CMOS circuits. Nominally the oxide is insulating, but when a certain voltage is applied, defects (i.e. oxygen vacancies) are created in the oxide, making it conductive. The physical mechanism of RRAM relies on the formation and rupture of a these conductive filaments that consist of defects in the oxide layer between two metal electrodes [4]. RRAM has shown attractive attributes for NVM applications due to its low programming voltage (<3 V), fast switching speed (<10 ns), excellent scalability (<10 nm), and good programming endurance (>10^6 cycles) and data retention (>10 years at 85 °C by extrapolation), as well as its compatibility with CMOS fabrication [4]. Recently, 4 Mb to 32 Gb RRAM prototype chips have been demonstrated by various companies, including ITRI/TSMC [5], Micron/Sony [6], SanDisk/Toshiba [7]), and embedded RRAM has been adopted for microcontroller commercial products by Panasonic [8]. Therefore, RRAM is a viable technology for practical applications.

Some inherent characteristics of RRAM technology can be leveraged to design hardware security primitives due to the following reasons:

1. RRAM has intrinsic randomness in its physical mechanism – a feature that can be utilized as an entropy source. Examples of randomness include resistance variation, random telegraph noise, and probabilistic switching behaviors [9]. Due to the randomness of the defect generation and annihilation in the oxide, the shape of the conductive filament varies from device to device, and even from cycle to cycle within one device [10]. Since the I-V characteristics of the RRAM device strongly depends on the shape of the conductive filament, any small variations in the atomic change of the filament result in significant variations in the

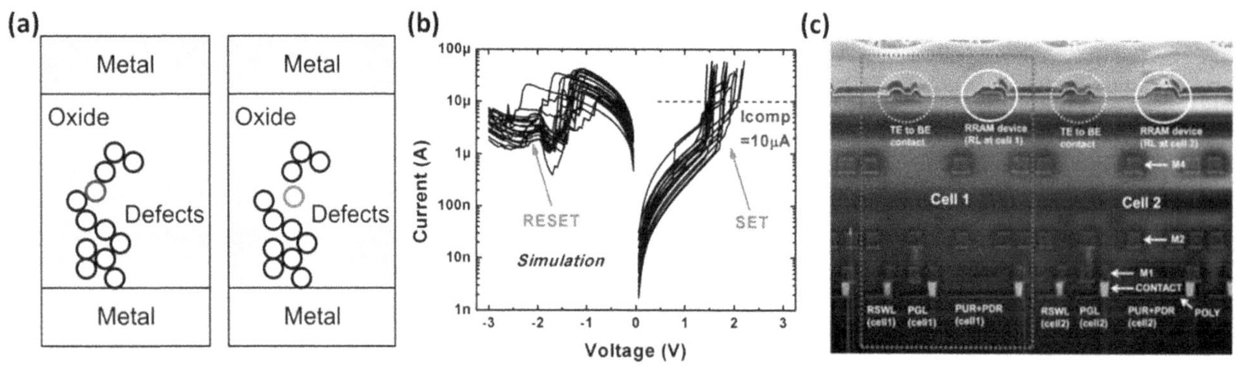

Figure 2. (a) Schematic of one RRAM cell in two programming cycles with atomic change in the defects location. (b) Simulated I-V characteristics of the two RRAM cells by an atomistic Kinetic Montel Carlo simulator [10]. (c) Microscopic cross-section view of the RRAM prototype chip [5]. The RRAM cells integrated on top of CMOS circuits at the interconnect level. The RRAM contact via is similar as the normal contact via. The only difference is that there is very thin (<10 nm) RRAM oxide layer in RRAM contact via.

resistances of the device. Fig. 2 (a) shows the schematic of the filament shape of one RRAM cell in two programming cycles that differ by the atomic displacement of a few defects, Fig. 2 (b) shows the I-V characteristics of the RRAM cell by an atomistic Kinetic-Monte-Carlo physical simulator [10]. It is seen that the current and switching voltage vary from cycle to cycle. This suggests that the RRAM's variability is inherently caused by the stochastic nature of its atomistic dynamics, instead of the purely manufacturing process variation. This cycle-to-cycle programming variation can be used to generate a new set of Challenge Response Pairs (CRPs) for the PUF during, thereby making PUF reconfigurable.

2. Owing to its atomistic nature, RRAM has good immunity to semi-invasive and invasive tampering attacks. The atomic changes in the defect density in the oxide are invisible even under high-resolution transmission electron microscopy (HR-TEM). In addition, RRAM is immune to the photon emission analysis, as trap-assisted-tunneling conduction in oxide RRAM is not expected to emit photons, unlike the hot carriers in the silicon transistors in an SRAM PUF [11].

3. RRAM also has good immunity against environmental variations. If the RRAM is split into on and off states, the RRAM read out noise margin is very large (typically on/off resistance ratio >10X). This is much larger than the STT-MRAM's ~2X on/off resistance ratio.

4. RRAM is also compact and low-power. RRAM's cell area can be as small as $4F^2$ (F is the lithography feature size) for the cross-point (X-point) array architecture, and $6F^2$~$12F^2$ for the 1-transistor-1-resistor (1T1R) array architecture. As compared to PCM, RRAM has >100X less programming energy consumption, featuring small programming energy <1 pJ/bit and read energy <0.1 pJ/bit. RRAM also consumes no standby power owing to its non-volatility.

5. RRAM has very good compatibility with silicon CMOS fabrication. The RRAM cells are integrated in the contact vias between interconnect layers on top of the CMOS circuits using back-end-of-line (BEOL) fabrication processes. Fig. 2 (c) shows the cross-section image of the fabricated RRAM prototype chip [5]. As compared to the normal contact via, the RRAM device adds a very thin oxide layer in the contact via. From the top-view, there is no difference between a normal contact via and RRAM contact via. This opens a new opportunity to employ physical layout obfuscation to further enhance the tamper resistance, because the RRAM contact vias can be mixed with normal contact vias in the design.

3. Example Designs of RRAM-based Hardware Security Primitives

In this section, we describe two different techniques to realize PUF using RRAM, as well as a TRNG that leverages the intrinsic RTN in RRAM.

3.1 Weak PUF without Helper Data Using RRAM Resistance Variability

The weak PUF using RRAM resistance variability was proposed in [12] with the goal of eliminating the helper data (the redundant parity bits) used by error correction code. Fig. 3 shows the enrollment strategy of proposed RRAM PUF without helper data [12]. Recently, the RRAM weak PUF was experimentally implemented in a fabricated 1kb RRAM array with CMOS peripheral circuits [13]. The weak PUF characteristics including uniqueness and reproducibility have been experimentally characterized. Fig. 4(a) shows the microscopic top view image of the fabricated 1kb (128 rows × 8 columns) 1T1R RRAM array with a built-in decoder. The RRAM device structure is TiN/TaOx/HfO_2/TiN stack as shown in the transmission electron microscopic image (inset of Fig. 4 (a)), which is integrated between the interconnect layers on top of the CMOS transistors. Fig. 4(b) shows the proposed circuit diagram of the RRAM PUF macro for the PUF construction phase (red part) and the PUF operation phase (green part).

To implement the RRAM PUF, a pulse forming process is performed row by row to set the devices to on-state in the first cycle. Then the same pulse programming condition is applied to all the cells in an attempt to reset to the off-state. The variation that occurs in the first-time reset process is used as the entropy source for the RRAM PUF. Then, a read voltage is applied across each RRAM cell and the read current is measured. The measured read current distribution of the 1kb array is shown in Fig. 4(c). This variation of the read current can be directly employed to generate the response bit of the PUF, *e.g.* by comparing two read currents from two columns as proposed in [14]. However, due to the RRAM resistance temporal fluctuation and read-out noise, the response bit may not be stable. To address this problem, it is necessary to digitalize the randomness and improve the RRAM PUF's robustness against the read-out noise. This is achieved by choosing a split reference current within the distribution in the array as suggested in [12] and programing the cells with currents

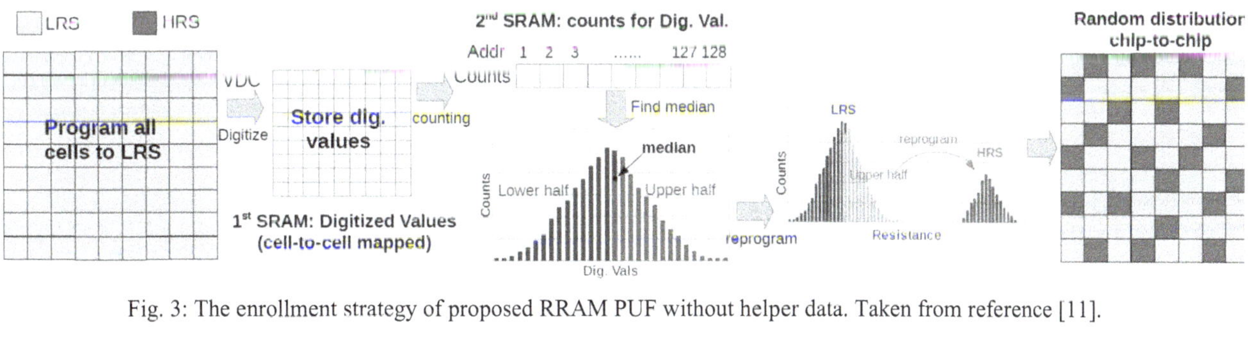

Fig. 3: The enrollment strategy of proposed RRAM PUF without helper data. Taken from reference [11].

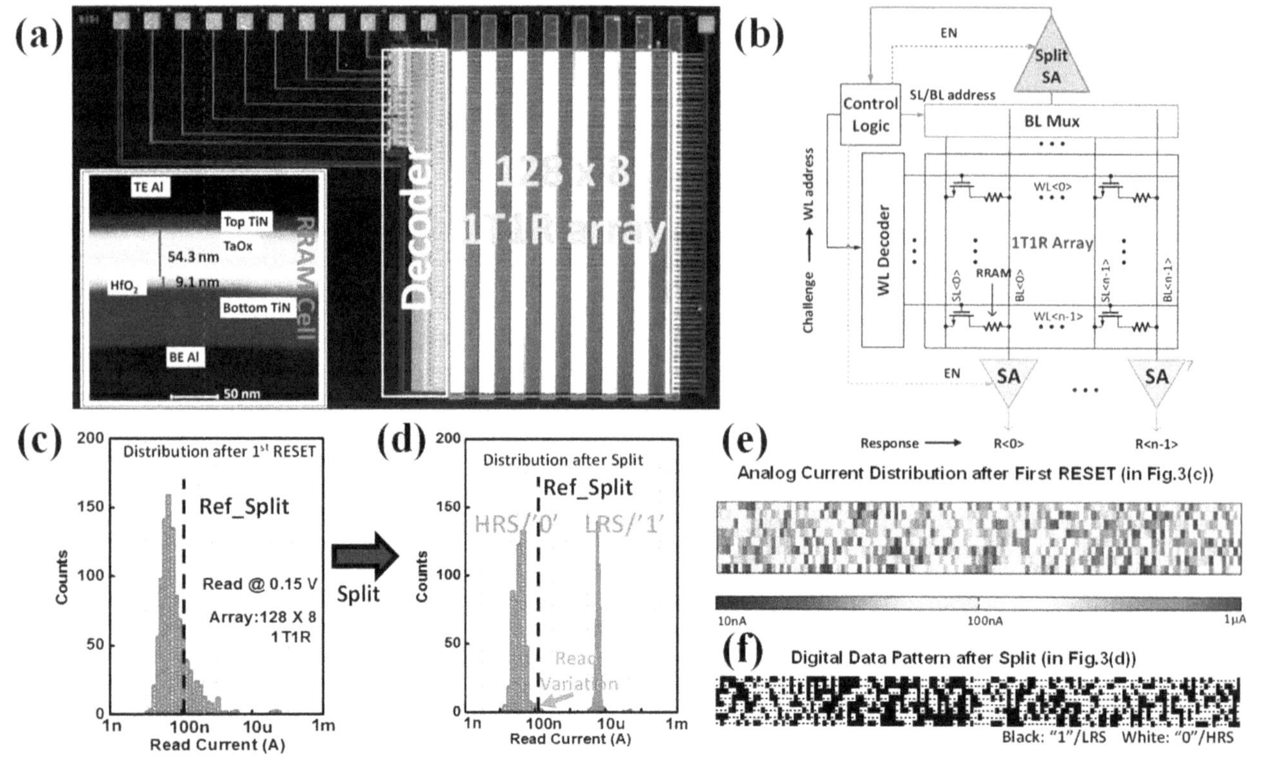

Figure 4. (a) Top view of the fabricated 128×8 1kb 1T1R RRAM array with a built-in decoder under the microscope. The inset is cross-sectional microscopic image of TiN/TaO_x/HfO_2/TiN RRAM device. (b) Proposed RRAM PUF circuit macro for the PUF construction phase (red) and PUF operation phase (green). (c) Distribution of read current after the first reset operation in an RRAM array. (d) Distribution of read current after a part of cells are programmed into "1" state according to the split reference. (e) Analog data pattern before the split process. (f) Digital data pattern after the split process. Taken from reference [13].

above the reference to "1", and the remaining cells to "0". Fig. 4 (d) shows the measured read current distribution in on and off states after the split process. To illustrate the effect of the split process, Fig. 4(e) shows the analog data pattern before the split and Fig. 4(f) shows the digital data pattern after the split. After this split process and the enrollment of CRPs in the database, the RRAM PUF construction is complete. During deployment in the field, only read operations are performed on the PUF: the row address is given as the challenge bit, then the column read-out current through the sense amplifier generates the response bit. As proof of concept, 40 RRAM PUF instances were constructed using this approach. The inter-HD of the 128-bit responses is measured at around 49.8% with a small σ of 4.92%. In addition, a new design where each PUF response bit is represented by multiple RRAM cells is proposed to improve the system's security and reliability without the helper data. The experimental result shows with 8 cells per bit, the retention time is more than 50 hours at 150 °C or equivalently 10 years at 69 °C, ensuring a 0% intra-HD within its lifetime.

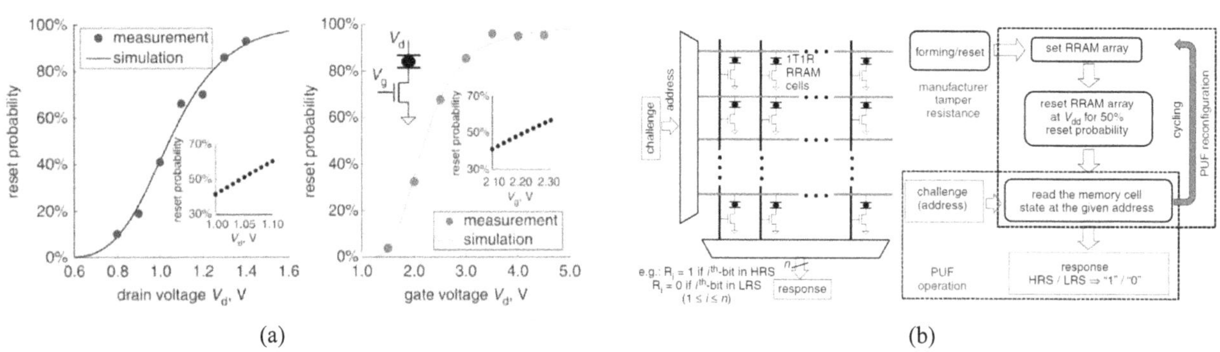

(a) (b)

Figure 5. Reset probability of CuO_x-based RRAM devices. (a) The reset probability as a function of voltage pulse amplitude applied on the drain of the 1T1R cell. (b) The reset probability as a function of voltage pulse amplitude applied on the gate of the 1T1R cell. (c) Proposed design of PUF using RRAM probabilistic switching. Taken from reference [15].

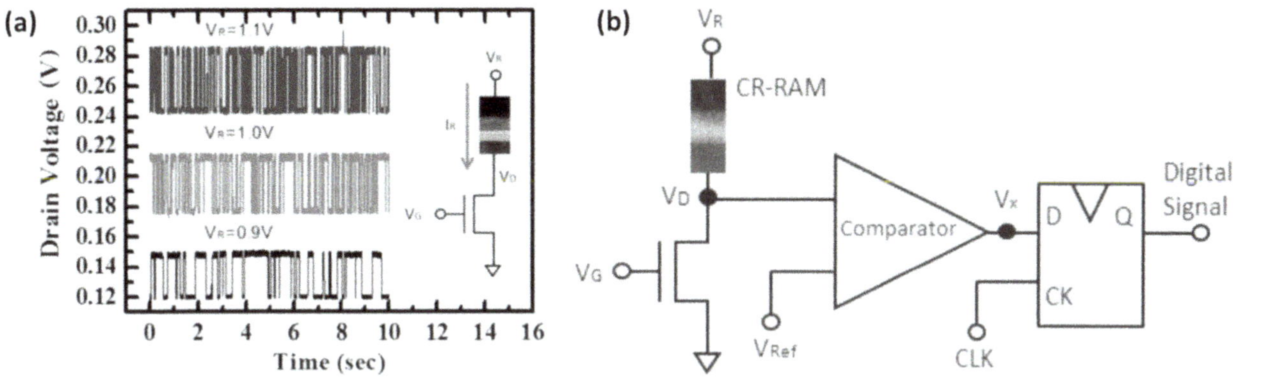

Figure 6. RRAM based TRNG design: (a) Measured RTN of RRAM in a 1T1R structure. (b) A simple comparator circuit to amplify the RTN signal into the random response bit. Taken from reference [22].

3.2 PUF Design Using RRAM Probabilistic Switching

Due to the stochastic nature of the conductive filament formation and rupture, RRAM shows probabilistic switching behaviors. The success rate of switching operation depends on the applied voltage pulse width and amplitude. In a recent study [15], CuOx based RRAM with the 1T1R structure showed probabilistic switching phenomenon during the reset process. Fig. 5(a) and 5(b) show the effects of drain and gate voltages on the reset probability, respectively. Insets of Fig. 5 (a) and 5 (b) show enlarged reset probability in ±10% range around 50%. This voltage-dependent switching probability provides a source of entropy for a PUF design as shown in Fig. 5 (c). Based on a 1T1R RRAM array, all the cells in the array are first set to a LRS. Then, by biasing the memory cells at the voltage for 50% reset probability, each cell has an equal opportunity to reset to HRS or remain in LRS. Ideally, after the reset operation, the RRAM array will have bit "0" and bit "1" with 50% probability randomly distributed in the array. The challenge of this PUF is the address to the memory array and the response is the n-bit data string composed of a random "0" and "1".

3.3 TRNG Design Using RRAM RTN

Previous TRNG designs employed random telegraph noise (RTN) in CMOS transistors as the entropy source [3]. However, it involved the von Neumann extractor to post-process the data and thus is power inefficient. RTN is an intrinsically random phenomenon from the microscopic electron trapping/detrapping process. The RRAM's conduction mechanism is trap-assisted-tunneling in the oxide, which inherently introduces RTN phenomenon [4]. RTN has been widely observed in many RRAM devices [5, 6, 7, 8]. A compact design of TRNG using RRAM's RTN has been proposed in prior work [9]. As shown in Fig. 6(b), the TRNG circuit consists of an RRAM cell, a bias circuit, and a comparator, which are all integrated on a chip using 65 nm CMOS logic process. The RRAM cell is formed on the drain contact via of a transistor, with SiO_2 layer stacked with TiO_xN_y on top. The random numbers are generated based on the RTN of RRAM cell, which are transformed into the corresponding binary signals by the comparator. Fig. 6(a) shows the output signal of the TRNG circuit. The RTN parameters (such as capturing time, emission time, amplitude, etc.) depend on the voltage bias. It is shown that the voltage bias is able to tune the capturing time and emission time, which may further tune the probability of "1" and "0". The TRNG generation speed using RRAM RTN is still limited, typically in the range of kHz. Further design strategies are needed to improve the TRNG generation speed.

4. Conclusion

In this paper, we have provided a brief overview on the use of emerging nanoscale devices for security primitives, namely PUF and TRNG. While we have focused on the use of RRAM, the intrinsic variations in other device structures and materials experience similar intrinsic variations and hold great promise for design of strong security primitives. Going forward, security will continue to be a critical design challenge for diverse computing systems, with many research challenges and opportunities to improve upon existing techniques to meet the needs of next generation devices.

REFERENCES

[1] G. E. Suh, S. Devadas, "Physical unclonable functions for device authentication and secret key generation," in ACM Design Automation Conference, 2007.

[2] H.-S. P. Wong, S. Raoux, S. Kim, J. Liang, J. P. Reifenberg, B. Rajendran, M. Asheghi, and K. E. Goodson, "Phase change memory," *Proceedings of the IEEE,* vol. 98, no. 12, p. 2201–2227, 2010.

[3] B. J. Zhu, "Magnetoresistive random access memory: the path to competitiveness and scalability," *Proceedings of the IEEE,* vol. 96, no. 11, p. 1786–1798, 2008.

[4] H.-S. P. Wong, H.-Y. Lee, S. Yu, Y.-S. Chen, Y. Wu, P.-S. Chen, B. Lee, F. T. Chen, and M.-J. Tsai, "Metal–oxide RRAM," *Proceedings of the IEEE,* vol. 100, no. 6, p. 1951–1970, 2012.

[5] S. S. Sheu, M. F. Chang, K. F. Lin, C. W. Wu, Y. S. Chen, P.-F. Chiu, C.-C. Kuo, Y.-S. Yang, P.-C. Chiang, W.-P. Lin, C.-H. Lin, H.-Y. Lee, P.-Y. Gu, S.-M. Wang, F. T. Chen, K.-L. Su, C.-H. Lien, K.-H. Cheng, H.-T. Wu, T.-K. Ku, M.-J. Kao, and M.-J. Tsai, "A 4Mb embedded SLC resistive-RAM macro with 7.2ns read-write random-access time and 160ns MLC-access capability," in *IEEE International Solid-State Circuits Conference (ISSCC)*, 2011.

[6] R. Fackenthal, M. Kitagawa, W. Otsuka, W. K. Prall, D. Mills, K. Tsutsui, J. Javanifard, K. Tedrow, T. Tsushima, Y. Shibahara, G. Hush, "A 16Gb ReRAM with 200MB/s write

and 1GB/s read in 27nm technology," in *IEEE International Solid-State Circuits Conference (ISSCC)*, 2014.

[7] T.-Y. Liu, T. H. Yan, R. Scheuerlein, Y. Chen, J. K. Lee, G. Balakrishnan, G. Yee, H. Zhang, A. Yap, J. Ouyang, T. Sasaki, S. Addepalli, A. Al-Shamma, C.-Y. Chen, M. Gupta, G. Hilton, S. Joshi, A. Kathuria, V. Lai, D. Masiwal, M. Matsumoto, et al., "A 130.7mm2 2-layer 32Gb ReRAM memory device in 24nm technology," in *IEEE International Solid-State Circuits Conference (ISSCC)*, 2013.

[8] A. Kawahara, R. Azuma, Y. Ikeda, K. Kawai, Y. Katoh, K. Tanabe, T. Nakamura, Y. Sumimoto, N. Yamada, N. Nakai, S. Sakamoto, Y. Hayakawa, K. Tsuji, S. Yoneda, A. Himeno, K. Origasa, K. Shimakawa, T. Takagi, T. Mikawa, and K. Aono, "An 8Mb multi-layered cross-point ReRAM macro with 443MB/s write throughput," in *IEEE International Solid-State Circuits Conference (ISSCC)*, 2012.

[9] A. Chen, "Comprehensive assessment of RRAM-based PUF for hardware security applications," in *IEEE International Electron Devices Meeting (IEDM)*, 2015.

[10] S. Yu, X. Guan, H.-S. P. Wong, "On the stochastic nature of resistive switching in metal oxide RRAM: physical modeling, Monte Carlo simulation, and experimental characterization," in *IEEE International Electron Devices Meeting (IEDM)*, 2011.

[11] C. Helfmeier, C. Boit, D. Nedospasov, J.-P. Seifert, "Cloning physically unclonable functions," in *IEEE International Symposium on Hardware Oriented Security and Trust (HOST)*, 2013.

[12] W. Che, J. Plusquellic, S. Bhunia, "A Non-volatile memory based physically unclonable function without helper data," in *IEEE/ACM International Conference on Computer-Aided Design (ICCAD)*, 2014.

[13] R. Liu, H. Wu, Y. Pang, H. Qian, S. Yu, "Experimental characterization of physical unclonable function based on 1kb resistive random access memory arrays," *IEEE Electron Device Letters,* vol. 36, no. 12, pp. 1380-1383, 2015.

[14] A. Chen, "Utilizing the variability of resistive random access memory to implement reconfigurable physical unclonable functions," *IEEE Electron Device Letters,* vol. 36, no. 2, pp. 138-140, 2015.

[15] A. Chen , "Reconfigurable physical unclonable function based on probabilistic switching of RRAM," *IET Electronics Letters,* vol. 51, no. 8, pp. 615-617, 2015.

[16] R. Brederlow, R. Prakash, C. Paulus, R. Thewes,, "A low-power true random number generator using random telegraph noise of single oxide-traps," in *IEEE International Solid-State Circuits Conference (ISSCC)*, 2006.

[17] J.-K. Lee, J.-W. Lee, J. Park, S.-W. Chung, J. S. Roh, S.-J. Hong, I.-w. Cho, H.-I Kwon, J.-H. Lee, "Extraction of trap location and energy from random telegraph noise in amorphous TiOx resistance random access memories," *Applied Physics Letters,* vol. 98, p. 143502, 2011.

[18] S. Choi, Y. Yang, W. Lu, "Random telegraph noise and resistance switching analysis of oxide based resistive memory," *Nanoscale,* vol. 6, p. 400–404, 2013.

[19] D. Veksler, G. Bersuker, L. Vandelli, A. Padovani, L. Larcher, A. Muraviev, B. Chakrabarti, E. Vogel, "Random telegraph noise (RTN) in scaled RRAM devices," in *IEEE International Reliability Physics Symposium (IRPS)*, 2013.

[20] N. Raghavan, R. Degraeve, A. Fantini, L. Goux, S. Strangio, B. Govoreanu, D.J. Wouters, G. Groeseneken, M. Jurczak, "Microscopic origin of random telegraph noise fluctuations in aggressively scaled RRAM and its impact on read disturb variability," in *IEEE International Reliability Physics Symposium (IRPS)*, 2013.

[21] S. Ambrogio, S. Balatti, A. Cubeta, A. Calderoni, N. Ramaswamy, D. Ielmini, "Statistical Fluctuations in HfOx Resistive-Switching Memory: Part II—Random Telegraph Noise," *IEEE Transactions on Electron Devices,* vol. 61, no. 8, pp. 2920-2927, 2014.

[22] C.-Y. Huang, W. C. Shen, Y.-H. Tseng, Y.-C. King, C.-J. Lin, "A contact-resistive random-access-memory-based true random number generator," *IEEE Electron Device Letters,* vol. 33, no. 8, pp. 1108-1110, 2012.

Enhancing Hardware Security with Emerging Transistor Technologies

Yu Bi
University of Central Florida
Electrical and Computer Engineering Department
Orlando, FL 32816, USA
yubi@knights.ucf.edu

X. Sharon Hu
University of Notre Dame
Computer Science and Engineering
Notre Dame, IN, 46530 USA
shu@nd.edu

Yier Jin
University of Central Florida
Electrical and Computer Engineering Department
Orlando, FL 32816, USA
yier.jin@eecs.ucf.edu

Michael Niemier
University of Notre Dame
Computer Science and Engineering
Notre Dame, IN, 46530 USA
mniemier@nd.edu

Kaveh Shamsi
University of Central Florida
Electrical and Computer Engineering Department
Orlando, FL 32816, USA
kaveh@knights.ucf.edu

Xunzhao Yin
University of Notre Dame
Computer Science and Engineering
Notre Dame, IN, 46530 USA
xyin1@nd.edu

ABSTRACT

We consider how the I-V characteristics of emerging transistors (particularly those sponsored by STARnet) might be employed to enhance hardware security. An emphasis of this work is to move beyond hardware implementations of physically unclonable functions (PUFs) and random number generators (RNGs). We highlight how new devices (i) may enable more sophisticated logic obfuscation for IP protection, (ii) could help to prevent fault injection attacks, (iii) prevent differential power analysis in lightweight cryptographic systems, etc.

CCS Concepts

•Security and privacy → Hardware-based security protocols; •Hardware → *Emerging architectures;*

Keywords

Hardware security, emerging transistors, tunnel transistor, TFET, SymFET, NCFET, IC camouflaging, polymorphic logic

1. INTRODUCTION

Like performance, power, and reliability, security is becoming a critical design consideration. As a representative example, hardware security threats in the integrated circuit (IC) supply chain, including hardware counterfeiting, IP piracy, and reverse engineering cost the US economy more than $200 billion annually [17]. Problems are further exacerbated by the rapid growth in the "Internet of Things" (IoT). This paper will highlight how *emerging transistor technologies* can enhance existing hardware security primitives, and also lead to new hardware security primitives.

GLSVLSI '16, May 18-20, 2016, Boston, MA, USA

DOI: http://dx.doi.org/10.1145/2902961.2903041

More specifically, we highlight how emerging transistor technologies could impact encryption engines. We consider not only how new devices could lead to more sophisticated and robust encryption ciphers in resource constrained environments, but also how new devices may make said ciphers more resilient to attacks such as differential power analysis (DPA). We also include a discussion of how unique I-V characteristics offered by beyond CMOS transistors can enable new hardware security primitives that could facilitate IC supply chain protection, help prevent/stop side-channel attacks, etc.

Presently, most emerging technologies being studied in the context of hardware security are related to designing physically unclonable functions (PUFs) and random number generators (RNGs) [30]. However, most PUF and RNG designs leverage larger device-to-device variations in emerging technologies. Ironically, said variations often represent shortcomings when viewed through the lens of an original device target – i.e., reliable digital logic or memory. In contrast, we will discuss emerging transistor technologies for hardware security related applications that are not RNGs or PUFs, and do not inherently rely on device variations as a means to an end.

2. BACKGROUND

Here, we review hardware security needs and challenges, and the transistor technologies that form the basis of our work.

2.1 Hardware security needs and challenges

To reduce design costs and increase profits, IC manufacturers are continuing to outsource low-profit services (e.g., manufacturing) to offshore facilities. While such outsourcing may reduce total cost, it has exacerbated security concerns. Below, we review ways that emerging technologies may help to alleviate the following threats: **(1) Hardware fingerprinting and authentication** can protect hardware intellectual property (IP) cores against reverse engineering [10]. PUFs have frequently been suggested for the authentication process [33]. However, modeling methods have been devel-

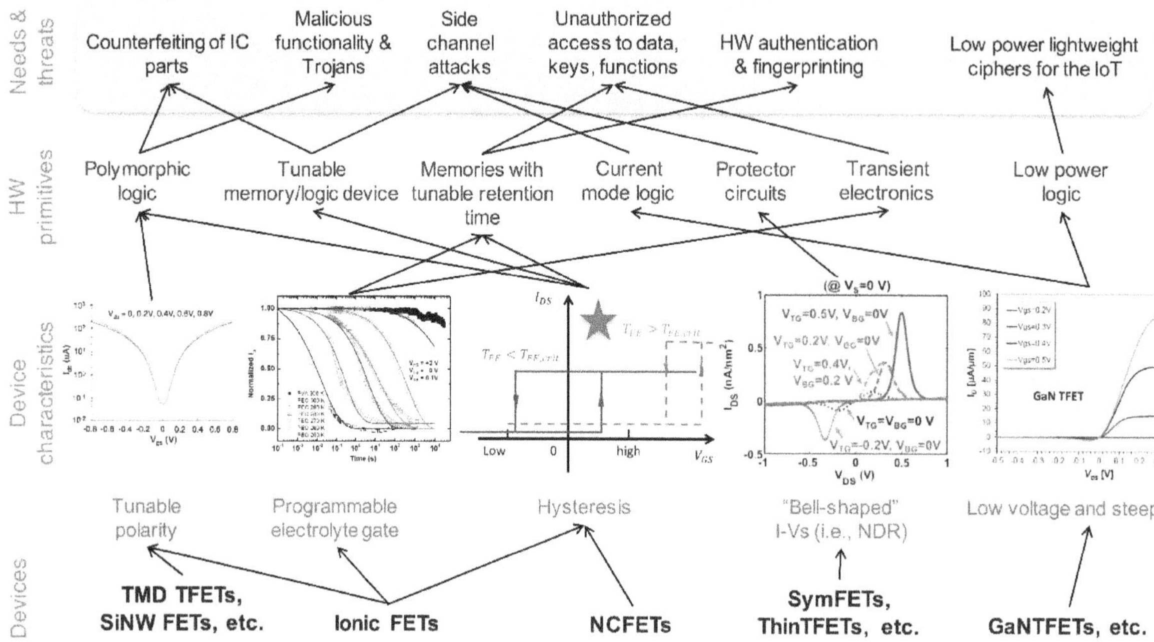

Figure 1: Mapping unique I-V characteristics of emerging transistor technologies to security needs/threats. We particularly note **(a)** the I-V characteristics of a SymFET device for different top, back gate voltage combinations and **(b)** Tunable hysteresis in an NCFET.

oped to predict the PUF responses, which adversely affects this approach [35]. **(2) Camouflaging** [11] relies on layout-level obfuscation that makes it difficult to decipher a circuit's structure via reverse engineering [32]. That said, CMOS camouflaging gates often bring significant performance overhead, area increases, etc – e.g., a XOR+NAND+NOR camouflaging gate has 5.1X-5.5X higher power, 1.1X-1.6X higher delay, and 4X higher area compared to a conventional NAND or NOR gate [32]. Moreover, [27] has suggested that SAT-based techniques could be employed to determine circuit functionality within minutes. **(3) Counterfeit ICs** have recently found their way into safety-critical and military applications [36]. Solutions for detecting counterfeit products are limited. PUFs, aging sensors, etc. [36], often incur high power and area costs. We are also concerned with **(4) side-channel analysis and fault injection attacks** where adversaries can recover internal signals leveraging static/differential analyses on side channels such as timing, power consumption, and electromagnetic emissions – all without any physical intrusion. Again, most countermeasures incur a high performance overhead [7].

2.2 Device characteristics of interest

In Fig. 1 we illustrate how post-CMOS devices could address hardware security needs. **(i)** Security needs/threats are summarized at the top-level, **(ii)** the next level captures what hardware primitives might be employed to address said concerns/needs, **(iii)** the third level illustrates what device I-V characteristics may lead to efficient implementations of said primitives, while **(iv)** the bottom-level indicates what device concepts may lead to desired I-V characteristics. A given device may ultimately address multiple security needs/threats.

New transistor technologies may also offer other "added value." For example, as will be discussed, improved sub-threshold swings can lead to lower power circuits, which could lead to implementations of current mode logic (CML) in resource constrained environments to protect against differential power analysis (DPA). Due to space limitations, in this paper we particularly focus on device technologies that exhibit tunable polarity, hysteresis, and steep slopes.

2.2.1 *Tunable Polarity*

In many nanoscale FETs, the superposition of n-type and p-type carriers is observable under normal bias conditions. The resulting ambipolarity exists in various materials [12], [25], [18]. By controlling ambipolarity, device polarity can be adjusted/tuned post-deployment. Transistors based on carbon nanotubes [22], graphene [19], silicon nanowires (SiNWs) [20], and transition metal dichalcogenides (TMDs) [13] all have configurable polarity.

As representative examples, with SiNW FETs, operation is enabled by the regulation of Schottky barriers at the source/drain junctions. A control gate (CG) turns a device on and off via a gate voltage (i.e., as would be done in a typical MOSFET). A polarity gate (PG) in proximity to the source/drain (S/D) Schottky junctions can then be used to switch device polarity between n- and p-type post-fabrication. Logic gates can still be readily cascaded as input and output voltage levels are compatible [14].

Ambipolarity is also possible with TFETs as different doping types for drain and source are used (i.e., if an n/i/p doping profile is employed [37]). A TFET can function either as an n- or p-type device by properly biasing the n-doped and p-doped regions (as well as the gate). With this approach, no polarity gate is needed in this case.

2.2.2 *Tunable Hysteresis*

The phrase tunable hysteresis implies that (i) a device's I-V curve may contain a hysteresis loop, and (ii) a device's

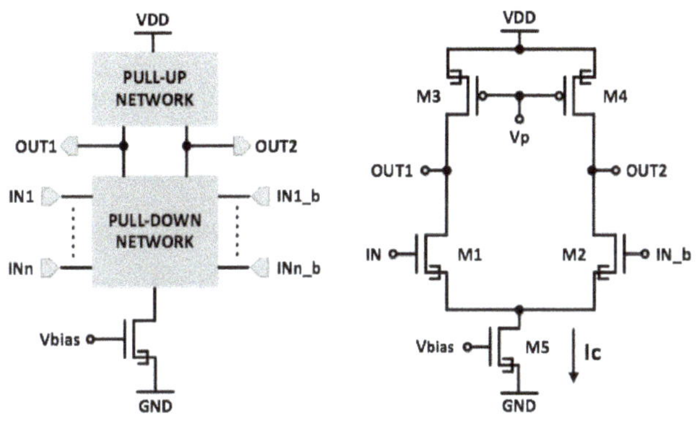

(a) (b)

Figure 2: (a) The universal diagram of CML circuits (b) Schematic of the TFET-based CML inverter.

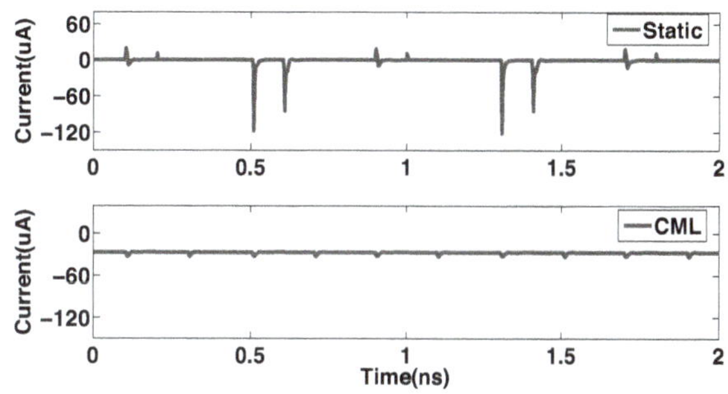

Figure 3: The current traces between static XOR and CML XOR.

hysteresis loop can be moved to different locations along the applied voltage levels, or be made to disappear altogether. In this work, the negative capacitance FET (NCFET) will be considered as a test bench (see starred plot in Fig. 1). To fabricate an NCFET, a ferroelectric (FE) material is added to the gate stack of a MOSFET. The high polarizability of the FE material provides a nonlinear capacitance which becomes negative under certain electric field values. This in turn enables step-up voltage conversion of the applied gate bias to the surface potential leading to switching slope (SS) steeper than 60 mV/decade. By varying the gate stack material composition, NCFETs can be made with or without hysteretic behavior. One can also fabricate an NCFET that has hysteresis or does not have hysteresis by changing the thickness of the FE material.

2.2.3 Bell-Shaped I-Vs

Emerging transistor technologies may also exhibit bell-shaped I-V curves [6, 28, 21]. While useful hardware security primitives may be enabled by such a characteristic (see [3, 4] for further detail), this approach is not considered further in this paper as relative to the other approaches to be discussed, devices are not as mature.

3. TFET CURRENT MODE LOGIC

Current mode logic is a differential digital logic family [38, 7]. A CML gate is essentially comprised of (i) a tail current source, (ii) a current steering core, and (iii) a differential load. The constant current is switched through the differential network of input transistors, and the reduced voltage swing on the two load devices serves as the output. Of particular interest is the fact that the power consumption of a CML circuit is stable, which can serve as a valuable countermeasure when considering a DPA attack [1, 2, 7].

A schematic of a "generic" TFET-based CML circuit – that includes a pull-up network and a pull-down network – is illustrated in Fig. 2a. In more detail, we consider a TFET-based current mode inverter/buffer circuit (Fig. 2b) as a representative example. As first discussed in [5], IN and IN_b are differential inputs.

A constant drive current is provided by transistor M5, which is also tunable by the gate bias voltage V_{bias}. Together with M5, transistors M3 and M4 can be used to charge and discharge the output pair OUT1 and OUT2. If IN is logic 1, (i) M1 is turned on, (ii) the constant current I_C flows through the left-handed path, (iii) OUT1 discharges to a value between VDD and GND, and (iv) OUT2 charges to quasi-VDD. (Again, logic 0 is commonly defined as half VDD, and logic 1 is close to VDD.) If OUT1 is extracted as the output pin and the inverted OUT2 is extracted as complementary output pin, the circuit performs a logical inversion. (Alternatively, the structure can serve as a buffer if pin assignments are switched.)

Turning to hardware security, with static CMOS, differential power analysis is based on the power consumption during circuit transition. Power is consumed when a output undergoes a 0→1 (or 1→0) transition. Because of this symbolic characteristic of static logic, a cryptographic algorithm is vulnerable to DPA attack. Alternatively, a CML circuit is naturally resilient to a DPA attack considering the relatively constant power consumption for almost any transitions.

As an example from our prior work [5], we consider the power traces for TFET-based static XOR gates, and the TFET-based differential style XOR gates (see Fig. 3). The TFET CML XOR gate dissipates almost constant power (in contrast to the significant power overshoot of the static XOR gate). Put another way, the TFET static XOR gate leaks information that an attacker may use to identify the internal activity of a cryptographic system, while the CML gate provides little to no information about logical state transitions. When translated to the application-level, a study in [5] suggests that TFET-based current mode logic (CML) can both improve DPA resilience and preserve low power consumption in lightweight cryptographic ciphers (KATAN32). Compared to the CMOS-based CML designs, the TFET CML circuit consumes 80% less power while achieving a similar level of DPA resistance [5].

4. HARDWARE SECURITY VIA TUNABLE POLARITY

The ability to dynamically change the polarity of a transistor opens the door to defining the functionality of a layout or a netlist post fabrication. While field programmable gate arrays (FPGAs) might also be employed, we believe that the above approach offers a path to ASIC-like performance. We briefly review SiNW FET and TFET-based primitives [3, 4] that could be used to enable IP protection, help to prevent IP piracy, and to counter hardware Trojan attacks.

4.1 Polymorphic logic gates

Polymorphic logic circuits (the terms "logic locking" [34,

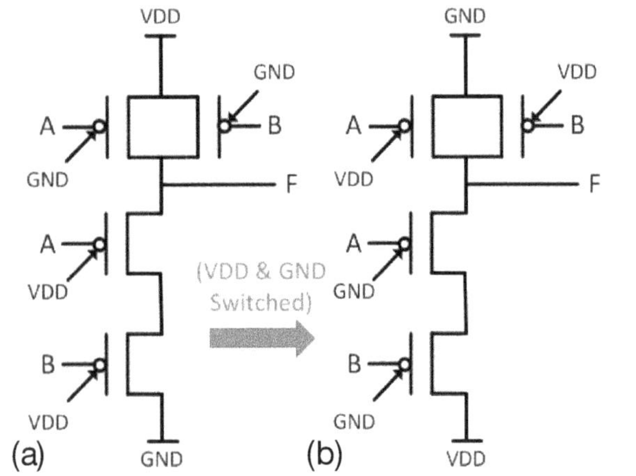

Figure 4: **(a)** SiNW-based NAND [3]; **(b)** SiNW-based NOR [3]

31, 15] or "logic encryption" might also be used) could encrypt logic functionality such that even if an entire netlist were available, an adversary would still not be able to easily decipher a chip's true functionality. With CMOS technology, such circuits have been notoriously difficult to implement efficiently.

To help prevent IP piracy, in [3, 4], we introduced SiNW FET based polymorphic gates. If the control gate (CG) of a SiNW FET is connected to a normal input, while the polarity gate (PG) is treated as the polymorphic control input, we can easily change the circuit functionality (without a performance penalty). For example, per Fig. 4a and Fig. 4b, a SiNW FET based NAND gate can be converted to a NOR gate. However, a CMOS-based NAND cannot be converted to a fully functioning NOR by switching power and ground.

We have recently designed TFET-based polymorphic logic circuits as well [9]. Fig. 5a and Fig. 5b show a 2-input polymorphic NAND/NOR gate. By properly biasing the gate, the n-doped region, and the p-doped region, a TFET device can function either as an n-type or p-type transistor. The circuit behaves like a NAND gate if the n-doped region of the two parallel TFETs is connected to V_{DD}, and the p-doped region of the bottom TFET is connected to *GND*. With opposite connections, the circuit functions as a NOR gate. By using two MUXes (one at the top and the other at the bottom) to select between the two types of connections, the circuit then functions as a polymorphic gate where the control to the MUXes forms a 1-bit key. Simulation results [9] indicate that the circuit functions as intended.

Using low-cost polymorphic logic gates based on SiNW FETs or TFETs, we can design functional modules that only perform a desired computation if properly configured – e.g., if one were to design an ASIC's datapath using said modules, it would only function correctly if a "key" (configuration bits) were supplied. Thus, IP cloning and IP piracy could be prevented with extremely low performance overhead.

4.2 Camouflaging Layout

IC camouflaging is used to secure the CMOS fabrication process. However, with CMOS camouflaging layouts, significant increases to both power and area (in order to achieve useful levels of protection [32]), and adverse effects such

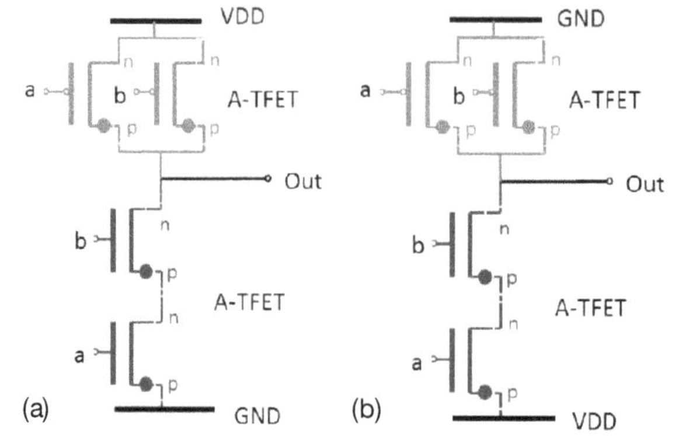

Figure 5: TFET polymorphic **(a)** NAND/ **(b)** NOR gate and simulation result [9]

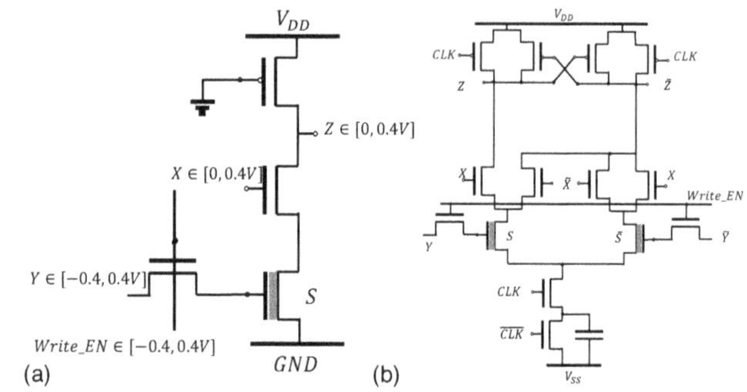

Figure 6: **(a)** NAND-LiM based on pseudo-NMOS logic; **(b)** AND/NAND-LiM based on DyCML.

as decreased circuit reliability are typically incurred. More quantitatively, a CMOS camouflaging layout that can function either as an XOR, NAND or NOR gate requires at least 12 transistors. In our recent work [3, 4], we have shown that by leveraging tunable polarity, just 4 SiNW FETs are required to build a camouflaging layout that can perform NAND, NOR, XOR and XNOR operations.

5. HARDWARE SECURITY LEVERAGING ATYPICAL SWITCHING BEHAVIORS

Post-CMOS devices with tunable hysteresis could enable a device to be dynamically configured as either a switch or a non-volatile storage element. An immediate consequence of such a device is the potential to design simpler and more power efficient logic-in-memory (LiM) cells. From the perspective of security, this could reduce communication between a CPU and memory, which in turn could make a circuit less vulnerable to memory-based attacks during communication [16]. LiM cells can also help to reduce overhead incurred by key access and verification via storing the keys in LiM cells.

We have recently designed several different LiM cells using NCFETs. Fig. 6a shows an example of a LiM cell (performing a NAND function) based on the pseudo-NMOS logic style. The circuit has two modes – update mode and hold mode. In the update mode (i.e., `Write_EN`= 1), the `Y` input is written into the NCFET, and the output realizes the logic function of `Z`= $\overline{X \cdot Y}$. In the hold mode (i.e., `Write_EN`= 0), the circuit outputs `Z`= $\overline{X \cdot S}$, where `S` is the bit value stored in the NCFET which remains unchanged. The pseudo-

NMOS design may lead to relatively large leakage, but similar CMOS-like designs can also be obtained. Fig. 6b shows an AND/NAND-LiM cell design based on the dynamic current mode (DyCML) style. Similar to the circuit in Fig. 6a, this circuit also has an update and hold mode. In the hold mode (i.e., `Write_EN`= 0), the circuit outputs $\mathtt{Z}=\overline{\mathtt{X}\cdot\mathtt{S}}$ and $\overline{\mathtt{Z}}=\mathtt{X}\cdot\mathtt{S}$ where `S` is the bit value stored in the NCFET. In the update mode (i.e., `Write_EN`= 1), `Y` and $\overline{\mathtt{Y}}$ are written into the two NCFETs, respectively, while output does the same evaluation as in the hold mode.

Our preliminary work in exploiting atypical switching behaviors for hardware security reveals exciting opportunities that certain post-CMOS devices can provide to enhance Design for Assurance (DFA). As suggested in [9], devices with tunable hysteresis offer several unique functionalities that are difficult to obtain from MOSFETs. For example, a device can be readily changed from being a non-volatile storage element to a switch. This property could help achieve logic obfuscation. Also, the retention time of such a device as a non-volatile storage element can also be tuned which may be exploited for tamper resistant circuitry.

To exploit the capability of NCFETs being either a storage element or a switch, we will investigate NCFET-based efficient design obfuscation on both combinational logic and sequential logic. In [8, 29, 23], the authors have proposed techniques that use finite state machines (FSMs) together with some combinational logic to help obfuscate an IP design. Thus, one possible approach is to employ NCFETs to implement such FSMs. For example, if we leverage the design concepts of the LiM cells discussed above to construct a FSM, the FSM behavior can be tuned, hence providing another level of obfuscation. The mode control (between being a storage element or a switch) then becomes the encryption key. To ensure that this approach is effective, a thorough study is required to address challenges that include: (i) developing more area and power efficient NCFET based FSMs, and (ii) determining how the placements of these NCFETs impact security levels and other traditional metrics such as power and delay.

The other security need that this work could address is resisting denial-of-service (DoS) attacks and differential power analysis (DPA). DoS attacks can be deployed on energy constrained systems. Sleep deprivation attacks [26] and multilevel authentication methods [24] have been proposed to counter such attacks. LiM cells, if used both to store the security key and for authentication, could provide an extremely energy efficient authentication process through close integration of memory and logic. Also, as noted earlier, DyCML has been widely studied for countering DPA based side channel attacks (e.g., [38, 7]). The DyCML based NCFET LiM cells introduced in our recent work not only achieves balanced power traces but also can be readily integrated with memory components. In future work, we will evaluate these LiM based security primitives in terms of their ability to satisfy the identified security needs as well as energy and performance.

6. CONCLUSIONS

In closing, we have discussed some of our initial work to leverage the unique I-V characteristics of emerging transistor technologies to help enhance/improve hardware security. We emphasize that it is of the utmost importance that any such design space exploration work be done in close conjunction with scientists and engineers working to develop new devices – i.e., to ensure that (i) any circuit design efforts, etc. reflect the true capabilities of the device (e.g,. with respect to reproducible behavior) and (ii) useful and reproducible I-V characteristics (for the purposes of hardware security) are not "optimized away" as a device evolves.

Acknowledgement: This work was supported in part by the Center for Low Energy Systems Technology (LEAST), an SRC STARnet center sponsored by MARCO and DARPA.

7. REFERENCES

[1] K. Baddam and M. Zwolinski. Evaluation of dynamic voltage and frequency scaling as a differential power analysis countermeasure. In *VLSI Design, 2007. Held jointly with 6th International Conference on Embedded Systems., 20th International Conference on*, pages 854–862, Jan 2007.

[2] S. Badel, E. Guleyupoglu, O. Inac, A. Martinez, P. Vietti, F. Gurkaynak, and Y. Leblebici. A generic standard cell design methodology for differential circuit styles. In *Design, Automation and Test in Europe, 2008. DATE '08*, pages 843–848, March 2008.

[3] Y. Bi, P.-E. Gaillardon, X. Hu, M. Niemier, J.-S. Yuan, and Y. Jin. Leveraging emerging technology for hardware security - case study on silicon nanowire fets and graphene symfets. In *Asia Test Symposium (ATS)*, pages 342–347, 2014.

[4] Y. Bi, K. Shamsi, J.-S. Yuan, P.-E. Gaillardon, G. De Micheli, X. Yin, X. Hu, M. Niemier, and Y. Jin. Emerging technology based design of primitives for hardware security. *ACM Journal on Emerging Technologies in Computing Systems (JETC)*. (to appear).

[5] Y. Bi, K. Shamsi, Y.-S. Yuan, Y. Jin, M. Niemier, and X. S. Hu. Tunnel fet current mode logic for dpa-resilient circuit designs. *IEEE Transactions on Smart Grid*, page under review, 2016.

[6] L. Britnell, R. V. Gorbachev, A. K. Geim, L. A. Ponomarenko, A. Mishchenko, M. T. Greenaway, T. M. Fromhold, K. S. Novoselov, and L. Eaves. Resonant tunnelling and negative differential conductance in graphene transistors. *Nature Communications*, 4(1794):1–5, 2013.

[7] A. Cevrero, F. Regazzoni, M. Schwander, S. Badel, P. Ienne, and Y. Leblebici. Power-gated mos current mode logic (pg-mcml): A power aware dpa-resistant standard cell library. In *Proc. of the 48th Design Automation Conference*, DAC '11, pages 1014–1019, 2011.

[8] R. Chakraborty and S. Bhunia. Harpoon: An obfuscation-based soc design methodology for hardware protection. *IEEE Transactions on Computer-Aided Design of Integrated Circuits and Systems*, 28(10):1493–1502, Oct 2009.

[9] A. Chen, X. S. Hu, Y. Jin, M. Niemier, and X. Yin. How emerging devices can address hardware security needs and challenges. In *Design, Automation and Test in Europe, 2016. DATE '16*, page to appear, 2016.

[10] Chipworks. Chipworks: Patent and technology partner, Accessed November 17, 2015. http://www.chipworks.com/.

[11] L.-W. Chow, J. Baukus, and W. Clark. Integrated circuits protected against reverse engineering and method for fabricating the same using an apparent metal contact line terminating on field oxide, 2002.

[12] A. Colli, S. Pisana, A. Fasoli, J. Robertson, and A. C. Ferrari. Electronic transport in ambipolar silicon nanowires. *physica status solidi (b)*, 244(11):4161–4164, 2007.

[13] S. Das and J. Appenzeller. Wse2 field effect transistors with enhanced ambipolar characteristics. *Applied physics letters*, 103(10):103501, 2013.

[14] M. De Marchi, D. Sacchetto, S. Frache, J. Zhang, P. Gaillardon, Y. Leblebici, and G. De Micheli. Polarity control in double-gate, gate-all-around vertically stacked silicon nanowire fets. In *Electron Devices Meeting (IEDM), 2012 IEEE International*, pages 8.4.1–8.4.4, Dec 2012.

[15] S. Dupuis, P. S. Ba, G. D. Natale, M. L. Flottes, and B. Rouzeyre. A novel hardware logic encryption technique for thwarting illegal overproduction and hardware trojans. In *On-Line Testing Symposium (IOLTS), 2014 IEEE 20th International*, pages 49–54, July 2014.

[16] D. G. Elliott, M. Stumm, W. M. Snelgrove, C. Cojocaru, and R. McKenzie. Computational ram: Implementing processors in memory. *Design & Test of Computers, IEEE*, 16(1):32–41, 1999.

[17] Frontier Economics Ltd, London. Estimating the global economic and social impacts of counterfeiting and piracy, 2011.

[18] A. K. Geim and K. S. Novoselov. The rise of graphene. *Nature Materials*, 6:183–191, 2007.

[19] N. Harada, K. Yagi, S. Sato, and N. Yokoyama. A polarity-controllable graphene inverter. *Applied Physics Letters*, 96(1), 2010.

[20] A. Heinzig, S. Slesazeck, F. Kreupl, T. Mikolajick, and W. M. Weber. Reconfigurable silicon nanowire transistors. *Nano Letters*, 12(1):119–124, 2012.

[21] M. Li, D. Esseni, J. Nahas, D. Jena, and H. Xing. Two-dimensional heterojunction interlayer tunneling field effect transistors (thin-tfets). *Electron Devices Society, IEEE Journal of the*, 3(3):200–207, May 2015.

[22] Y.-M. Lin, J. Appenzeller, J. Knoch, and P. Avouris. High-performance carbon nanotube field-effect transistor with tunable polarities. *IEEE Transactions on Nanotechnology*, 4(5):481–489, 2005.

[23] B. Liu and B. Wang. Embedded reconfigurable logic for asic design obfuscation against supply chain attacks. In *Design, Automation and Test in Europe Conference and Exhibition*, pages 1–6, 2014.

[24] D. Liu and P. Ning. Efficient distribution of key chain commitments for broadcast authentication in distributed sensor networks. In *The Network and Distributed System Security Symposium*, 2003.

[25] R. Martel, V. Derycke, C. Lavoie, J. Appenzeller, K. K. Chan, J. Tersoff, and P. Avouris. Ambipolar electrical transport in semiconducting single-wall carbon nanotubes. *Phys. Rev. Lett.*, 87, 2001.

[26] T. Martin, M. Hsiao, D. Ha, and J. Krishnaswami. Denial-of-service attacks on battery-powered mobile computers. In *Proceedings of the Second IEEE Annual Conference on Pervasive Computing and Communications*, pages 309–318. IEEE, 2004.

[27] M. E. Massad, S. Garg, and M. V. Tripunitara. Integrated circuit (ic) decamouflaging: Reverse engineering camouflaged ics within minutes. In *Network and Distributed System Security Symposium (NDSS)*, 2015.

[28] A. Mishchenko, J. Tu, Y. Cao, R. Gorbachev, J. Wallbank, M. Greenaway, V. Morozov, S. Morozov, M. Zhu, S. Wong, F. Withers, C. Woods, Y.-J. Kim, K. Watanabe, T. Taniguchi, E. Vdovin, O. Makarovsky, T. Fromhold, V. Fal'ko, A. Geim, L. Eaves, and K. Novoselov. Twist-controlled resonant tunnelling in graphene/boron nitride/graphene heterostructures. *Nature Nanotechnology*, 9(10):808–13, 2014.

[29] S. Narasimhan, R. Chakraborty, and S. Bhunia. Hardware ip protection during evaluation using embedded sequential trojan. *Design Test, IEEE*, PP(99):1–1, 2013.

[30] J. Rajendran, R. Karri, J. Wendt, M. Potkonjak, N. McDonald, G. Rose, and B. Wysocki. Nano meets security: Exploring nanoelectronic devices for security applications. *Proceedings of the IEEE*, 103(5):829–849, May 2015.

[31] J. Rajendran, Y. Pino, O. Sinanoglu, and R. Karri. Security analysis of logic obfuscation. In *Design Automation Conference (DAC), 2012 49th ACM/EDAC/IEEE*, pages 83–89, June 2012.

[32] J. Rajendran, M. Sam, O. Sinanoglu, and R. Karri. Security analysis of integrated circuit camouflaging. In *Proceedings of the 2013 ACM SIGSAC Conference on Computer & Communications Security*, CCS '13, pages 709–720, 2013.

[33] M. Rostami, M. Majzoobi, F. Koushanfar, D. Wallach, and S. Devadas. Robust and reverse-engineering resilient puf authentication and key-exchange by substring matching. *Emerging Topics in Computing, IEEE Transactions on*, 2(1):37–49, March 2014.

[34] J. A. Roy, F. Koushanfar, and I. L. Markov. Epic: Ending piracy of integrated circuits. In *Design, Automation and Test in Europe, 2008. DATE '08*, pages 1069–1074, March 2008.

[35] U. Rührmair, F. Sehnke, J. Sölter, G. Dror, S. Devadas, and J. Schmidhuber. Modeling attacks on physical unclonable functions. In *Proceedings of the 17th ACM Conference on Computer and Communications Security*, CCS '10, pages 237–249, 2010.

[36] M. M. Tehranipoor, U. Guin, and D. Forte. *Counterfeit Integrated Circuits: Detection and Avoidance*. Springer, 2015.

[37] T. Vasen. Investigation of III-V tunneling field-effect transistors. In *A Dissertation submitted to the University of Notre Dame*, 2014.

[38] M. Yamashina and H. Yamada. Mos current mode logic mcml circuit for low-power ghz processors. *NEC Res. Develop.*, 36:54 – 63, Jan 1995.

The Applications of NVM Technology in Hardware Security

Chaofei Yang, Beiye Liu, Yandan Wang, Yiran Chen, Hai Li
Department of Electrical & Computer Engineering, University of Pittsburgh, Pittsburgh, PA, 15261, USA
{chy61, bel34, yaw46, yic52, hal66}@pitt.edu

Xian Zhang, Guangyu Sun
Center for Energy-Efficient Computing and Applications, Peking University, Beijing, 100871, China
{zhang.xian, gsun}@pku.edu.cn

ABSTRACT
The emerging *nonvolatile memory* (NVM) technologies have demonstrated great potentials in revolutionizing modern memory hierarchy because of their many promising properties: nanosecond read/write time, small cell area, non-volatility, and easy CMOS integration. It is also found that NVM devices can be leveraged to realize some hardware security solutions efficiently, such as *physical unclonable function* (PUF) and *random number generator* (RNG). In this paper, we summarize two of our works about using NVM devices to implement these hardware security features and compare them with conventional designs.

Keywords
Memristor; spin-transfer torque random access memory; hardware security.

1. INTRODUCTION
With significant effort in process and device development, the emerging *nonvolatile memory* (NVM) technologies gradually alleviate their high manufacturing cost and low performance, enabling many promising features like high-density cell structure, nanosecond read/write accesses, CMOS-compatible integration, *etc.* Accordingly, many research studies on NVM technologies have been conducted. In this paper, we will introduce two NVM applications developed by us, aiming at enhancing hardware security.

Physical unclonable functions (PUFs) have been extensively investigated for the purpose of secured and low-cost authentication. There exist various types of PUFs that take advantages of random physical disorders in CMOS process technologies, such as SRAM PUFs based on SRAM power-up states [1], RO PUF based on latency of oscillator [2], Arbiter PUF based on wire connection delay [3], *etc.* Recently, some NVM-based PUFs have also been proposed in order to improve efficiency in energy and area and to enhance the resistance to simulation attack [4] and invasive attack [5]. However, the existing NVM-based PUFs face two major design limitations – the environmental impacts and substantial modification to the peripheral circuitry. Thus, we proposed errPUF design [6], which maximizes the hardware reuse with existing read/write circuits in *spin-transfer torque RAM* (STT-RAM) to enhance the reliability under environmental variations.

Random number generators (RNGs) are widely used in various systems and applications where unpredictable data are required. RNG plays a crucial role in system protection of many applications. There are two types of typical RNG designs: *pseudo random number generator* (PRNG) and *true random number generator* (TRNG). PRNG generates a sequence of pseudo numbers by injecting an initial seed to a given computing algorithm. TRNG usually leverages unpredictable physical phenomenon to generate true random numbers. Memristors are emerging two-terminal nonlinear dynamic devices in which the stochastic processes are well demonstrated [7]. For instance, the distribution of static memristances at *high resistance state/low resistance state* (HRS/LRS) can be approximated by a lognormal probability density function. Previously, we presented a *memristor-based true random number generator* (MTRNG) design by leveraging the stochastic behaviors of memristor [9].

The remainder of the paper is organized as follows: We will start with a brief introduction about memristor and STT-RAM technologies. Then the use of NVM devices in hardware security, including PUF and RNG will be introduced. Finally, we will give our conclusion.

2. RELATED WORK
2.1 NVM-based PUF
NVM-based PUFs include Memristor PUF [4], FPUF [15], PCM PUF [17], DWM PUF [18] and STT-PUF [19], *etc.* They have several advantages over the CMOS-based ones. First, NVM-based PUFs are more energy and area efficient to be used in some resource-constraint scenarios such as sensor nodes [26]. Second, it is more complex to simulate a NVM-based PUF so that it becomes more difficult to launch a simulation attack [4]. Third, NVM-based PUFs are also less vulnerable to invasive attack [5] because the storage units, *e.g.*, GST for PCM, MTJ for STT-RAM, and metal-oxide for RRAM, are stacked atop of the control transistors [27]. Note that all these NVM-based PUFs are CMOS-compatible.

Despite the advantages of NVM-based PUFs, there are two main limitations of current designs. The first limitation is that some designs do not evaluate the environmental impacts which may degrade PUFs' reliability. For example, in FPUF [15], the program cycles before inducing a disturb error for every cell are first evaluated. Then, the correlation coefficient is calculated to distinguish the genuine chip from the faked chips. Besides program cycles, variety of latency and program wear are also measured as a source of randomness. However, when environmental variations are considered, all the measured parameters above may greatly change [20] and FPUF's response may be unreliable. For Memristor-based PUFs, in which node voltage [4] is leveraged to

GLSVLSI'16, May 18–20, 2016, Boston, MA, USA
 ISBN 978-1-4503-4274-2/16/05…$15.00
DOI: http://dx.doi.org/10.1145/2902961.2903043

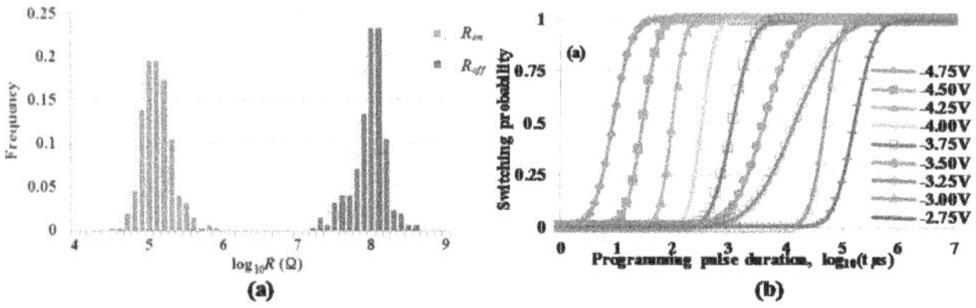

Figure 1: (a) Static stochastic behavior. (b) Probability distribution for ON switching [9].

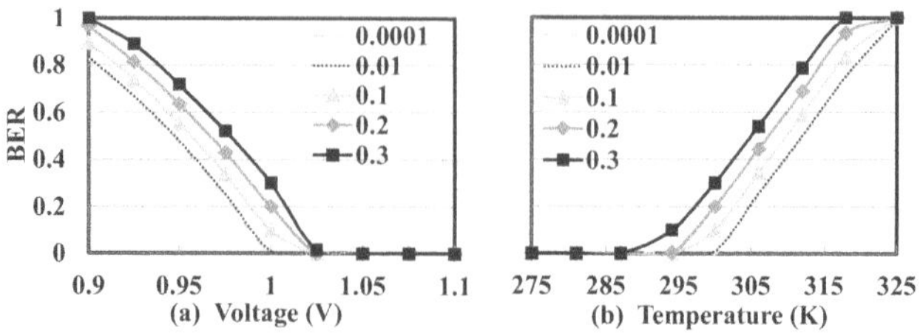

Figure 2: Variation of error rate of STTRAM cells due to change of environments: (a) different voltages (b) different temperatures [6].

generate random and unique fingerprints, the same limitation remains. The second limitation is that some designs require substantial modification to the peripheral circuitry to assist the extraction of device-level parameters, such as voltage sensors in every cell node [4], specified amplifier [17], differential circuit [19] and voltage to digital converter [21]. This will increase the design overhead and may affect normal read and write operations.

2.2 TRNG

TRNG usually leverages unpredictable physical phenomenon, such as thermal noise, random telegraph noise (RTN), atmospheric noise, electromagnetic and quantum [8]. Thermal noise is an intrinsic noise induced by thermal agitation of charge carriers (usually the electrons) inside an electrical conductor at equilibrium, which occurs regardless of applied voltage. RTN refers to a kind of electronic noise in semiconductors: when applying discrete voltage or current levels on semiconductors, sudden step-like RTN signals can be generated. Traditional thermal-noise-based TRNG usually is composed of a stochastic signal source, multi-level amplifiers, A/D converter and post-processing circuits [22]. Recently, a TRNG based on RTN in contact resistive random access memory (CRRAM) was proposed in which the high- and low-resistance states (HRS and LRS) of CRRAM are subject to RTN and therefore the resistance fluctuations can be converted to a stream of random bits [23]. Some TRNG designs leveraging the nanotechnologies have also been investigated. For example, Vivoli *et al.* presented a device-independent quantum TRNGs using a photon pair source based on spontaneous parametric down conversion (SPDC) which can gain both high entropy and high rate of random bit generation [24]. Spin dice is a spintronic-based TRNG that utilizes the stochastic nature of spin-torque switching in a magnetic tunnel junction (MTJ) to generate random numbers [25].

3. PRELIMINARY

3.1 Memristor Technology

3.1.1 Basics of Memristor

As the fourth fundamental component besides resistor, capacitor and inductor, memristor describes the dynamic relationship between charge (q) and flux (φ) [11]. Particularly, it can "remember" the total electric flux flowing through the device and its resistance is determined by the historical profile of the electrical excitations through the device.

3.1.2 Stochastic Behaviors

Stochastic behaviors have been widely observed in metal oxide-based memristor devices, including the variations in static states and dynamic switching processes. Figure 1 shows the static and dynamic stochastic behaviors observed in a TiO_2 device [16].

- ***Static stochastic behavior***: The final resistance value of a memristor during a programming operation is not deterministic but a stochastic variable related to the voltage amplitude and duration of programming pulse. The randomness of R_{on} and R_{off} is denoted as the static stochastic behavior of memristors. The distributions of R_{on} and R_{off} usually follow the lognormal probability density functions [12].
- ***Dynamic stochastic behavior*** is resulted by means of the complicated stochastic oxide electroforming process during ON/OFF switching in which the successful switching probability monotonically increases along with the increase of the amplitude and/or duration of programming pulse. More specific, the cumulative probability function of a successful switching between R_{on} and R_{off} follows a lognormal distribution [13].

3.2 STT-RAM

3.2.1 Basics

The popular STT-RAM cell design contains of one *magnetic tunneling junction* (MTJ) for data storage and one NMOS selective transistor. The logic bit represented by the MTJ is determined by the relative *magnetic direction* (MD) of its free and reference layers. When the MD is at the anti-parallel or parallel state, the MTJ demonstrates high or low resistances, representing logic '1' or '0', respectively. The state of the MTJ can be switched through a polarized current. The larger the write current is, the faster the MTJ switches. The read operation of STT-RAM is similar to those of conventional memories. Errors may happen during both read and write operations but the latter one contributes the most.

3.2.2 Sources of Write Errors

A write error occurs if the write current pulse stops before the MTJ successfully completes the switching. There are two sources of such errors:

Process variations of both the transistor and MTJ can affect the amplitude of write current. For example, the variations of transistor channel size can result in variance of write current driving ability. The variations in MTJ resistance can also influence the bias condition of the transistor and affect the driving current, causing an incomplete MTJ switching.

Thermal fluctuation happens during the MTJ switching. It is an intrinsic character demonstrating a random impact on the MTJ switching time. Thus, the error caused by the thermal fluctuation can only be detected occasionally.

Since both process variations and thermal fluctuation are random effects, the error rates of cells in an STT-RAM array follow a random distribution.

3.2.3 Impact of Environmental Variations

When taking the error rates of STT-RAM cells as a vector, it can be used as a fingerprint [15]. However, environmental variations have a significant impact on the reliability of this fingerprint, *e.g.*, the change of voltage and temperature can vary the amplitude of write currents, which in turns affects the error rates for cells.

Figure 2 shows the impact of different environmental variations on the bit error rates. The legends in the figure represent the error rates when the supply voltage is 1V and the temperature is 300K. It can be observed that the difference of error rates is more stable

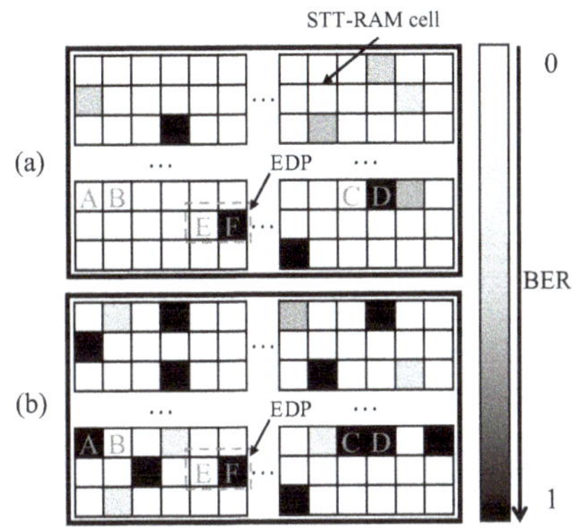

Figure 3: Error rates of a STT-RAM array in (a) Error-Least-State and (b) Error-Most-State. A-B and C-D are not EDPs. E-F is a valid EDP [6].

than the absolute values of error rates. Thus, we introduce a novel concept called *error-rate differential pair* (EDP). It reflects a stable relationship of bit error rates between two cells even with environmental variations.

4. HARDWARE SECURITY SOLUTIONS

4.1 STT-RAM-based PUF

4.1.1 Methodology

In order to simplify the description of EDP, we first introduce several definitions as follows:

Normal Working Environment refers to the working environment under which the PUF authentication works, *e.g.*, the supply voltage and temperature vary in the ranges of 0.9V −1.1V and 275K−325K, respectively.

Error-Most-State means the working environment under which the STT-RAM has the highest error rate, *e.g.*, the supply voltage is 0.9V and the temperature is 325K in Figure 2.

Error-Least-State means the working environment under which the STT-RAM has the lowest error rate, *e.g.*, the supply voltage is 1.1V and the temperature is 275K in Figure 2.

Read-Write-Read (RWR) Test is carried out in three steps: 1) read out the bit value in a cell, 2) write back the compliment bit to the cell, and 3) read the bit out again for comparison.

Having these terminologies, an EDP is defined as a pair of cells, A and B, that satisfy the following condition in both Error-Least-State and Error-Most-State. For N-round RWR tests, we have:

$$|Err_A - Err_B| \geqslant N_{th} \quad (1)$$

Err_A and Err_B represent the total number of errors occur in N rounds of tests for cell A and cell B, respectively.

EDP is the foundation of proposed err-PUF design. An example of valid EDP is shown in Figure 3. One STT-RAM cell is abstracted as one block. The color depth of a block represents the bit error rate (BER). Error rates of the same STT-RAM array under Error-Least-State and Error-Most-State are shown in Figure 3 (a) and (b), respectively. In this case, three pairs of cells are highlighted in the figure: A-B, C-D, and E-F. Only the E-F pair is a valid EDP. Pair A-B and C-D are not EDPs, because the difference is below the threshold under Error-Least-State and Error-Most-State, respectively.

In our err-PUF design, EDPs with a large difference of error rates are preferred. Since the detection of EDP is based on statistical testing results, it is possible that two cells with close error rates

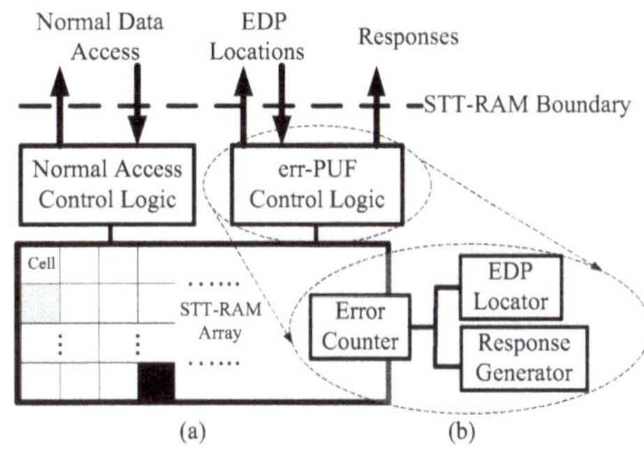

Figure 4: Illustration of err-PUF architecture [6].

are detected as a pair of EDP. We can find that identifying EDPs in a STT-RAM array relies on the setup of N and N_{th}. If we increase N and N_{th}, the probability is decreased for identifying an EDP with low error rate difference. However, increasing N includes more timing overhead in the process of detecting EDPs in a STT-RAM array.

4.1.2 err-PUF Design

Based on EDP, we propose a robust PUF design. The architecture of a STT-RAM with err-PUF is illustrated in Figure 4. As the PUF itself is embedded inside the STT-RAM array naturally, only the memory access control logic needs modification. As shown in the Figure 4, we add a component called "err-PUF control logic". The logic shares the same read/write interfaces for normal data access except for the ECC component. The whole process consists of several components for different phases of the err-PUF work flow, which is described as follows.

Pre-process phase includes two steps:

1) Identify all EDPs by scanning all cells in pair.
2) Store the location information of these EDPs to a database for later PUF verification.

The purpose of this phase is to identify all EDPs in a STT-RAM array after it is fabricated. Then, the location information of these EDPs in the array is stored in a database for later PUF verification. In order to achieve a secured PUF design, there should be enough number of EDPs in the array.

Enrollment phase includes four steps:

1) Randomly select N_{sec} EDP locations from the database as an input (i.e. a challenge).
2) When err PUF receives the input, it will perform R-round RWR tests to the correlated EDPs. For each pair of two cells under test, if the first cell has more errors, a bit '0' is generated. Otherwise, a bit '1' is generated.
3) Add up all N_{sec} bits generated in the last step together and then compare it with $N_{sec}/2$. The comparison result is the final output of PUF circuits.
4) Store the output to a secure database as a reference.

The purpose of enrollment phase is to find challenge-response-pairs (CRPs) for PUF verification. Step-2 is to detect which cell in the EDP has a higher bit error rate. N_{sec} is a parameter that determines the security strength of our design.

Evaluation phase includes five steps:

1) - 3) is the same as Enrollment phase.

4) Compare the output bit with reference output in the database. If two values are different, it means that the response is incorrect.

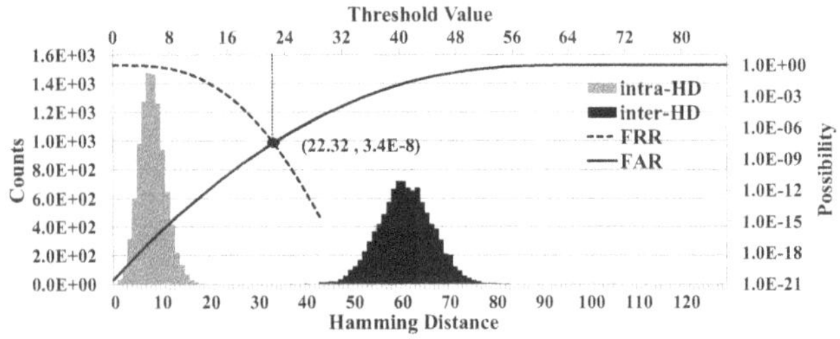

Figure 5: Inter-HD/intra-HD distribution and correlated FAR/FRR curves at 300K, 1.0V [6].

5) Repeat step-1 to step-4 for certain times (*e.g.* 128) and record the total number of incorrect responses, *i.e.*, Hamming Distance of two multi-bit outputs. If it is below a threshold value, the authentication succeeds. Otherwise, the authentication fails.

4.1.3 Experiment

Here we define two evaluation metrics: intra-HD and the inter-HD. **Intra-HD** represents the Hamming Distance between two responses of the same err-PUF design. **Inter-HD** represents the Hamming Distance of two responses from two different err-PUFs.

Reliability without environmental variation: The err-PUF is evaluated in a fixed environment state (V = 1.0V and T = 300K) for both enrollment and evaluation phases. In the Monte Carlo simulation, 10000 sets of challenges are used. The experimental results of intra-HD and inter-HD in our experiments are illustrated in Figure 5. The mean value of intra-HD is 7.76 with a variance of 7.29. For inter-HD, the mean value is 60.56 and the variance is 32.31. Based on these distributions, we can generate results of False Acceptance Rate(FAR) and False Rejection Rate(FRR) with different thresholds, which is also shown in Figure 5. From the results, we have the minimum *max (FAR, FRR)* = 3.4×10^{-8} when the threshold is set to 22.32. If we set the threshold at 23, the FAR and FRR are still less than 1×10^{-7}. Thus, it is acceptable for authentication for a large population of STT-RAM devices.

Reliability with environmental variation: We first set the working state with V = 1.0V and T = 300K for the enrollment phase to get the reference. Then we explore the worst case of evaluation phase when both variations are considered to demonstrate the reliability of errPUF. By exhausted experiments, we find that the worst case (highest FAR and FRR) happens at the state-A (V = 1.1V, T = 275K) for inter-HD and state-B (V = 0.9V, T = 325K) for intra-HD, which is shown in Figure 6. We can see that there is an obvious bias of inter-HD distribution. But even in the worst case, we have FAR=6.2×10^{-8} and FRR=1.3×10^{-7}, when the threshold is selected as 23. In conclusion, we can set the threshold as 23 to ensure FAR and FRR below 1×10^{-7} even with environmental variation.

Randomness of err-PUF: Note that there is nearly no overlap between different STT-RAM arrays' EDP positions, thus the false PUF will always output 0 with the same input of location information. Therefore, the inter-HD can present the randomness of our PUF's outputs which is shown in Figure 5. We can find that

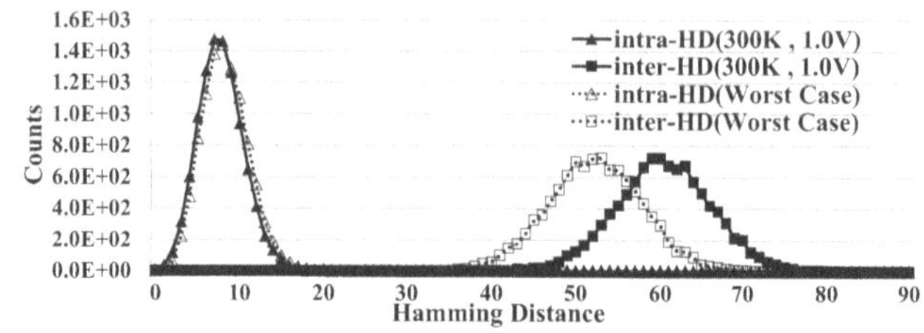

Figure 6: Inter-HD and intra-HD distribution at 300K, 1.0V and the worst case of inter-HD (@1.1V, 275K) and intra-HD (@0.9V, 325K) [6].

there is a slight bias between our result and the ideal one whose mean value should be 64. Despite the slight bias, the guessing probability of err-PUF's 128-bit output is still very low (about 2^{-118}).

Comparison Results with other NVM-based PUFs: In order to compare err-PUF with other typical NVM-based PUFs, we synthesize a prototype of our err-PUF control logic with the 45nm technology. Results of other PUFs are listed in Table 1 from references. Our hardware cost is trivial mainly because we share most hardware with existing structure including the Read/Write control logic and STT-RAM cells. The only cost comes from little extra multiplexors and adders. Also, the test rounds of evaluation phase in our design are substantially fewer than those of SRAM PUF or FPUF. In the evaluation phase, only the cells within EDPs are being read or written, which reduces the dynamic power of our design. Note that we assume that the read/write width of the STT-RAM array is 512-bit. And the energy consumption and latency are calculated when 128-bit response is generated.

4.2 Memristor-based TRNG

4.2.1 Methodology

As aforementioned, the resistance of a memristor in ON or OFF state is not deterministic but random, even for a single identical device. Figure 1(a) presents the real measurement data of a TiO_2 memristor [16]. The distributions of static state resistances R_{on} and R_{off} both can be approximated to the lognormal probability density function such as [13]:

$$f_X(x;\mu,\sigma)=\frac{1}{x\sigma\sqrt{2\pi}}\cdot\exp\left(-\frac{(\ln x/\mu)^2}{2\sigma^2}\right),\quad x>0. \qquad (2)$$

where, μ is the normal mean and σ is the standard deviation of the normal distribution of the initial barrier width of the memristor device. Giving $E[R_{on}]$ and $E[R_{off}]$ as the means of R_{on} and R_{off}, respectively, and their standard deviations are $D[R_{on}]$ and $D[R_{off}]$, respectively. The device demonstrated in Figure 1(a) has $E[R_{on}] \approx 10^5\Omega$ and $E[R_{off}] \approx 10^8\Omega$. Both $D[R_{on}]$ and $D[R_{off}]$, are more than 2 orders smaller than the difference between the means ($E[R_{off}] - E[R_{on}]$). Such a highly isolated binary characteristic in memristors guarantees an ideal physical mechanism for MTRNG design.

The dynamic stochastic behavior refers to the successful switching probability between ON and OFF state. Under an exter-

Table 1. Comparison result between different NVM-based PUFs.

	STT-PUF [19]	PCM PUF [17]	Memristor PUF [4]	FPUF [15]	err-PUF [9]
Technology Node	45nm	45nm	45nm	45nm	45nm
Extra Circuit Area (μm^2)	5.5×10^3	1.7×10^3	9.1×10^3	3.3×10^2	2.9×10^2
Evaluation Phase Latency (μs)	7.18	12.8	10.1	1.5×10^7	2.32
Energy Consumption (pJ)	4.1×10^2	1.1×10^3	9.0×10^4	4.8×10^4	3.1×10^2

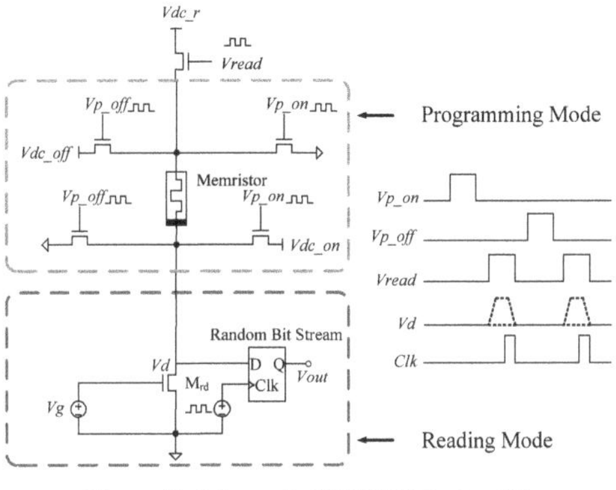

Figure 7: 1-branch MTRNG design [9].

nal programming pulse, the switching probability is determined by the voltage amplitude and the pulse width (duration) t. The cumulative distribution can be approximated by a lognormal distribution [13]:

$$F(t;\tau,\sigma_t)=\int_0^t \frac{1}{\sqrt{2\pi}\sigma_t T} e^{-\left(\frac{\ln T}{\sqrt{2}\tau\sigma_t}\right)^2} dT=\frac{1}{2}erfc\left(-\frac{\ln t}{\sqrt{2}\tau\sigma_t}\right). \quad (3)$$

Where, τ is the mean of the switching time, which has an exponential dependency on the applied voltage amplitude, while its deviation σ_t only has a weak dependence on the voltage [13]. Figure 1(b) shows the cumulative switching probability distributions of ON switching (OFF is similar). Increasing the programming duration of a constant-amplitude pulse can increase the switching probability, and a larger voltage amplitude decreases the required programming duration to reach a given switch probability.

4.2.2 MTRNG Design

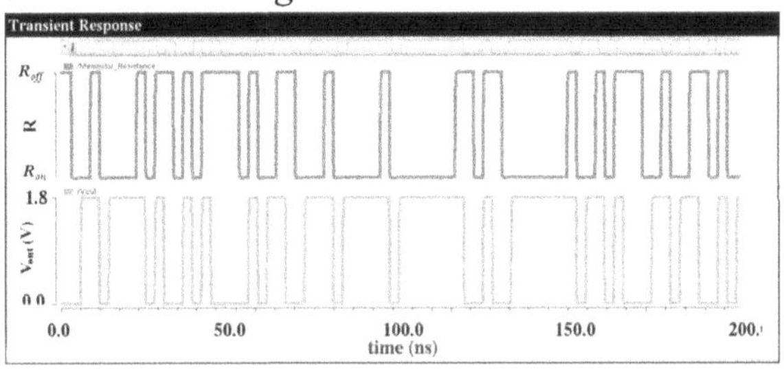

Figure 9. 1-branch MTRNG (R_{on}=10^{5}Ω and R_{off}=10^{8}Ω) [9].

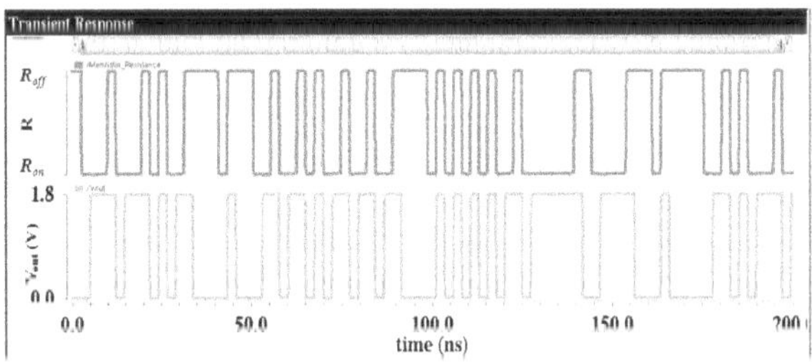

Figure 10. 1-branch MTRNG (R_{on}=10^{6}Ω and R_{off}=10^{7}Ω) [9].

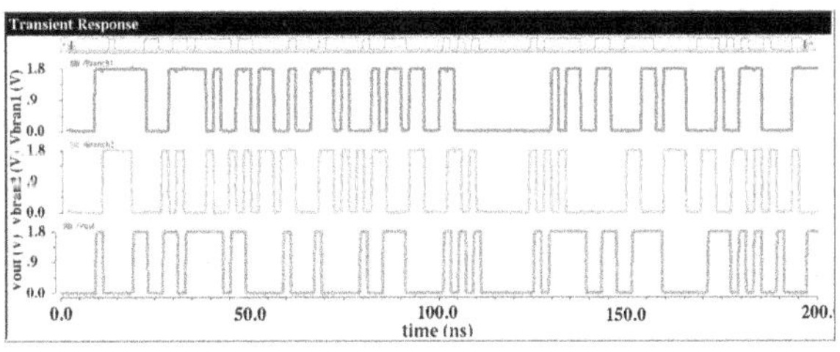

Figure 11. Simulation of 2-branch MTRNG [9].

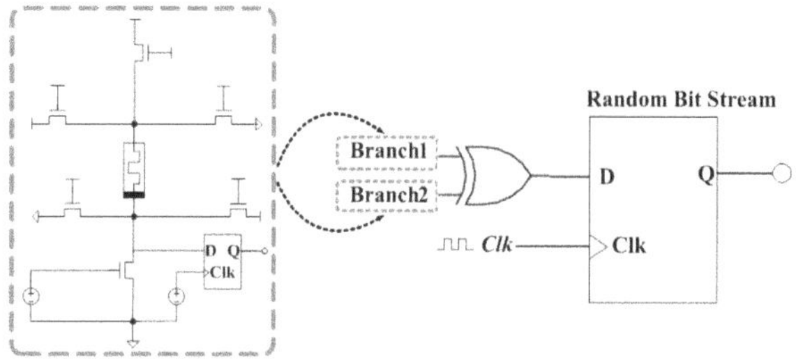

Figure 8: 2-branch MTRNG design [9].

The proposed MTRNG design switches between the programming mode and the reading mode to generate the random bit stream. In the programming mode, a programming pulse is applied on the memristor to trigger a dynamic switching between ON and OFF states. In the reading mode, the programmed resistance is converted to a binary bit. In the design, the selection of the programming pulse amplitude determines the maximal allowable sampling rate of the bit stream. We can control the ratio of the probability of 0's and 1's by modulating the programming duration. Ideally, a uniform distribution of 0/1 bit-stream can be obtained by aligning the pulse width to the switching probability of 0.5 under a given pulse voltage (refer Figure 1(b)).

Figure 7 depicts the proposed MTRNG circuit with the following key control and internal signals:

- V_{dc_r}, V_{dc_on} and V_{dc_off} are the DC voltage sources used in reading mode, the ON switching and the OFF switching programming, respectively.
- V_{read} is the control signal to enable the reading mode to detect the state of the memristor.
- V_{p_on} and V_{p_off} are used for programing the memristor to ON and OFF states, respectively.
- V_d is the bias voltage representing the state of memristor. It determines the generated output bit of the MTRNG.
- V_g is used to modulate V_d for bit generation.
- ***Clk*** is a clock signal to control the data capture at D flip-flop.

The sequence of control signals is also illustrated in Figure 7. V_{p_on} and V_{p_off} are turned on alternatively to enable the ON and OFF switching. Under the ideal condition with the sufficient programming voltage and pulse duration, the memristor can always be programmed, that is, the device switches between ON and OFF states. By properly controlling the programming voltage amplitude together with the pulse duration corresponding to the required bit distribution, the switching of the memristor becomes more random. In our design, following every programming period is a read operation enabled by V_{read}. The ON and OFF states of the memristor will be transferred to 1 or 0, respectively, under appropriate V_g setup. Here, a D flip-flop is used to recover distorted binary signal resulted by stochastic memristance values.

The simple MTRNG in Figure 7 can be used to generate a stream of random bits. However, the scheme cannot obtain the maximal entropy since the memristor will keep at the ON or OFF state if the previous switching fails. Assume the previous state of the memristor is OFF: if an ON switching triggered by V_{p_on} fails so that the memristor remains as OFF, the following OFF switching initialized by V_{p_off} does not affect the state of the memristor. In such a case, this OFF switching is not a stochastic process.

To improve the entropy of the random bit stream, we further enhance the design. As illustrated in Figure 8, it integrates two basic (1-branch) MTRNGs through an XOR gate. Because the

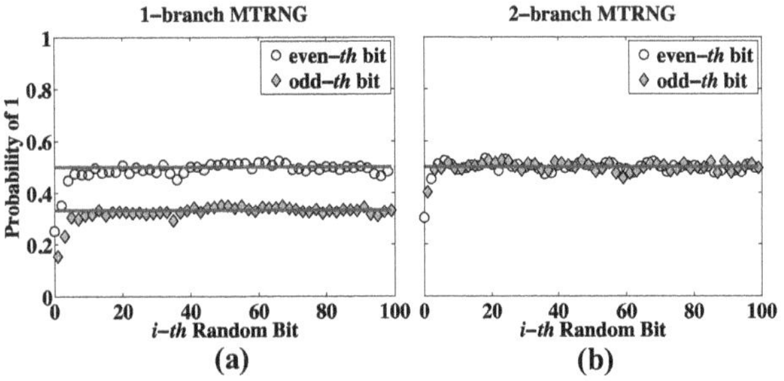

Figure 12: The probability distribution of random bit in the stream generated by 1-branch (a) and 2-branch (b) MTRNG [9].

stochastic switching of one memristor is independent to the other, the entropy of the random bit stream through the XOR function can be maximized under appropriate dynamic switching probability. We name this scheme as 2-branch MTRNG design.

4.2.3 Experiment

Figure 9 and 10 show the simulation results of the basic 1-branch MTRNG at the typical (R_{on}=$10^5\Omega$ and R_{off}=$10^8\Omega$) and the worst-case (R_{on} =$10^6\Omega$ and R_{off} =$10^7\Omega$) conditions, respectively. The simulations show that stochastic binary states of memristor can be successfully converted to random bit stream. Even in the extreme situation when R_{off} is very close to R_{on}, the basic 1-branch MTRNG design still functions properly.

Figure 11 shows the simulation result of the enhanced 2-branch MTRNG, the output random bit stream of which is dependent on the signals of two bit sequences generated by the two 1-branch MTRNGs. The simulations show that stochastic binary states of memristor can be successfully converted to random bit stream.

To analyze the probability distribution of the 1-branch and 2-branch MTRNG designs, the memristor ON switching and OFF switching probabilities are set to P_{on} = 1/4 and P_{off} = 1/3, respectively. To ease the explanation, we show the probability distributions of the first 100 bits generated by 1-branch and 2-branch MTRNG in Figure 12. Here, each point represents the probability of logic 1 at the bit. Simulation shows that both MTRNG schemes rapidly converge towards their stationary distributions in only a few steps.

For the 1-branch MTRNG design, the probability distribution of the odd-*th* bits is non-uniform. The situation can be solved by passing two bit streams of the 1-branch design through an XOR gate. Consistent to the theoretical analysis in Section 3.2.2, a uniformly distributed random bit stream can be generated via the 2-branch MTRNG design.

5. CONCLUSION

In this paper, we summarize two of our hardware security solutions. The proposed STT-RAM-based PUF employed the cell error rates. With the help of EDP, we can overcome the major challenge of PUF – environmental variations. Memristor-based TRNG leverages the stochastic behavior of memristors and converts the programmed resistances to random binary bit stream. 2-branch scheme promises the maximum entropy of random number generation. Both designs exhibit characteristics of simple structure, compact area, low power and show potentiality in hardware security.

Acknowledgement

The presented works were supported by NSF CNS-1253424, ECCS-1202225, and XPS-1337198.

6. REFERENCE

[1] D. E. Holcomb, *et al.*, "Power-Up SRAM State as an Identifying Fingerprint and Source of True Random Numbers," IEEE Transactions on Computers, vol. 58, no. 9, pp. 1198-1210, 2009.

[2] G. E. Suh, *et al.*, "Physical Unclonable Functions for Device Authentication and Secret Key Generation," Design Automation Conference, 2007.

[3] J. W. Lee, *et al.*, "A technique to build a secret key in integrated circuits for identification and authentication applications," VLSI Circuits, 2004.

[4] J. Rajendran, *et al.*, "Nano-ppuf: A memristor-based security primitive," IEEE Computer Society Annual Symposium on VLSI, 2012

[5] D. Nedospasov, *et al.*, "Invasive PUF analysis," Fault Diagnosis and Tolerance in Cryptography, 2013

[6] X. Zhang, *et al.*, "A Novel PUF based on Cell Error Rate Distribution of STT-RAM," in proceeding of Asia and South Pacific Design Automation Conference, 2016

[7] S. Gaba, *et al.*, "Stochastic memristive devices for computing and neuromorphic applications," Nanoscale, vol. 5, pp. 5872-5878, 2013

[8] R. S. DeBellis, *et al.*, "Pseudo random number generator," US Patents US6061703, 2000.

[9] Y. Wang, *et al.*, "A Novel True Random Number Generator Design Leveraging Emerging Memristor Technology," Great Lakes Symposium on VLSI, 2015

[10] F. Pedregosa, "Scikit-learn: Machine Learning in Python," The Journal of Machine Learning Research, 2011.

[11] L. O. Chua, "Memristor-the missing circuit element," IEEE Transactions on Circuit Theory, vol. 18, pp. 507-519, 1971.

[12] M. Hu, *et al.*, "The stochastic modeling of TiO2 memristor and its usage in neuromorphic system de-sign," Asia and South Pacific Design Automation Conference, 2014.

[13] G. Medeiros-Ribeiro, *et al.*, "Lognormal switching times for titanium dioxide bipolar memristors: origin and resolution," Nanotechnology, vol. 22, p. 095702, 2011.

[14] T. Chang, *et al.*, "Short-Term Memory to Long-Term Memory Transition in a Nanoscale Memristor," ACS Nano vol. 5, no. 9, pp. 7669-7676, 2011.

[15] P. Prabhu, *et al.*, "Extracting device fingerprints from flash memory by exploiting physical variations," Trust and Trustworthy Computing, 2011.

[16] W. Yi, *et al.*, "Feedback write scheme for memristive switching devices," Applied Physics A, vol. 102, pp. 973-982, 2011.

[17] L. Zhang, *et al.*, "PCKGen: A Phase Change Memory based cryptographic key generator," International Symposium on Circuits and Systems, 2013.

[18] A. Iyengar, *et al.*, "DWM-PUF: A low-overhead, memory-based security primitive," International Symposium on Hardware-Oriented Security and Trust, 2014.

[19] L. Zhang, *et al.*, "Highly reliable memory-based Physical Unclonable Function using Spin-Transfer Torque MRAM," IEEE International Symposium on Circuits and Systems, 2014.

[20] N. Tega, *et al.*, "Anomalously Large Threshold Voltage Fluctuation by Complex Random Telegraph Signal in Floating Gate Flash Memory," International Electron Devices Meeting, 2006.

[21] W. Che, *et al.*, "A non-volatile memory based physically unclonable function without helper data," International Conference on Computer-Aided Design, 2014.

[22] S. Fujita, *et al.*, "Si nanodevices for random number generating circuits for cryptographic security," International Solid-State Circuits Conference, 2004.

[23] C. Y. Huang, *et al.*, "A Contact-Resistive Random-Access-Memory-Based True Random Number Generator," IEEE Electron Device Letters, vol. 33, no. 8, pp. 1108-1110, Aug. 2012.

[24] V. C. Vivoli, *et al.*, "Device-independent quantum random number generator with a photon pair source," arXiv preprint, 2014.

[25] A. Fukushima, *et al.*, "Spin dice: A scalable truly random number generator based on spintronics," Applied Physics Express, vol. 7, pp. 083001, 2014.

[26] R. Jeyavijayan, *et al.*, "Nano Meets Security: Exploring Nanoelectronic Devices for Security Applications." Proceedings of the IEEE, 2015.

[27] Valamehr, Jonathan, *et al.*, "A qualitative security analysis of a new class of 3-D integrated crypto co-processors." Cryptography and Security: From Theory to Applications, Springer, pp. 364-382, 2012.

Survey of Emerging Technology Based Physical Unclonable Funtions

Ilia A. Bautista Adames
Department of Electrical Engineering, ENB118
University of South Florida
4202 East Fowler Avenue
Tampa, FL 33620
iliabautista@mail.usf.edu

Jayita Das
Department of Electrical Engineering, ENB118
University of South Florida
4202 East Fowler Avenue
Tampa, FL 33620
jayitadas@mail.usf.edu

Sanjukta Bhanja
Department of Electrical Engineering, ENB118
University of South Florida
4202 East Fowler Avenue
Tampa, FL 33620
bhanja@usf.edu

ABSTRACT

Authentication of electronic devices has become critical. Hardware authentication is one way to enhance security of a chip. Along with software, it makes it harder for an intruder to access any computer, smart-phone, or other devices without authorization. One way of authenticating a device through hardware is to use the fabrication anomalies, which are random and unclonable. This mechanism is called a Physical Unclonable Function (PUF). PUFs are easy to evaluate but hard to predict. PUF is a concept that gained popularity since the past decade, when researchers started taking advantage of the randomness of electrical signals in order to build a unique authentication block. This survey will show the state-of-the-art devices that are currently investigated as PUFs. The different technologies are compared by taking into account reproducibility, uniqueness, randomness, area, scalability, and compatibility with CMOS. Emphasis is put on technologies that are emerging and gaining commercial interest. Through comparisons, we will show their applicability to different environments.

Keywords

Physical Unclonable Function (PUF); Spin-Transfer Torque (STT); Magneto-resistive Random Access Memory (MRAM); Memristor; Graphene; Carbon Nanotube Field-Effect Transistors (CNFET); Resonnant Tunnel Diode (RTD)

1. INTRODUCTION

Authentication is a procedure that has been used by societies over the years to identify individuals. Forms of authentication have evolved as per the needs. In this digital age, scope of authentication has increased with complexity of business and the increased number of personal devices with sensitive personal information.

Some of the common methods of authentication available today are: (i) passwords; (ii) PINs; (iii) patterns; (iv) biometrics; (v) smart cards; (vi) perimeter security systems. For authentication, passwords, PINs, patterns, and biometrics are usually compared against a golden copy stored in a database making them susceptible to attacks. For instance, an attacker can succeed in gaining access to the secured information that is stored in a particular location in the database. Similarly, an attacker may gain physical access to smart-cards and personal devices. The next question is how to make it more difficult for them to gain access to the information. One way is to use intrinsic features from its hardware circuitry that are prone to process variations and do not require physical storage. The motivation is to get this random but repeatable (seemingly an oxymoron, which we will describe later in the paper) information to generate an authentication key in real-time. This method is called a Physical Unclonable Function (PUF), and it was termed by Gassend et al. [4] in 2002.

Authentication through PUFs has gained strength in the hardware security domain. PUFs are also used in cryptographic key generation [20] and watermarking of devices [22]. Each of these PUFs applications are not easily tampered while keeping the same challenge response pairs. To achieve these security applications in electronic devices, two main methods are used in CMOS technology. These two methods use anomalies through delay of arriving signals, or bit inclination ('0' or '1') of a cell in power-up. They encompass the groups of delay and memory PUFs, respectively.

Due to the limitations of Moore's Law, new devices are continuously studied. The new devices are required to have a niche application in order to be better in a specific task. Memristors, spin-transfer torque (STT), resonant tunnel diodes (RTDs), and graphene are a few of the novel technologies that we will discuss. We believe that these devices hold more variability due to their complex fabrication methods. In this paper we discuss the performance of these emerging technologies (using the CMOS versions as reference) in order to look ahead into security through PUFs.

While comparing the PUFs we will use two main quantifiers, the inter-distance and intra-distance. In a PUF, these measurements hold the values of reproducibility and uniqueness, respectively. We use these quantities to evaluate which PUFs are more reliable and may be the future device authenticators. Memristors [15, 14], magneto-resistive random access memory (MRAM) [1, 2] and STT-MRAM [24] are implemented as memory PUFs, and we compare them to the different CMOS versions of this kind. We show that MRAM and STT-MRAM PUFs have better reproducibility and uniqueness. MRAM cells have been fabricated in [1], with the intention of studying their geometrical anomalies. Carbon-based PUFs are applied as delay PUFs [9], and we will show how their simulated values outperform conventional arbiter and ring-oscillator PUFs. Quantum PUFs use the anomalies in tunneling, which are used in [16] through RTDs.

Section 2 provides a brief background on PUFs; Section 3 introduces the conventional CMOS PUFs and discusses some state-

GLSVLSI '16, May 18-20, 2016, Boston, MA, USA
 ISBN 978-1-4503-4274-2/16/05...$15.00
DOI: http://dx.doi.org/10.1145/2902961.2903044

of-the-art CMOS PUFs; Section 4 introduces PUF in emerging technologies and is the focus of this survey; Section 5 compares the emerging devices with CMOS technologies and states where the future of this domain is headed.

2. WHAT IS A PUF?

A PUF can be best defined as "an expression of an *inherent* and *unclonable instance-specific* feature of a physical object" [17], which implies: (i) a PUF is inherently created at the time of creation of an instance of an object without any user control over it; (ii) it is unique and specific to every instance; and (iii) creating two instances puf_{i_1} and puf_{i_2}, $i_1 \neq i_2$, that produce the same response is not feasible.

Two terms are closely associated with PUF usage [17]:

(i) *challenge*: which is an input $x_k \in \mathcal{X}_\mathcal{P}$ to the PUF;

(ii) *response*: which is the PUF output y to the challenge.

The process of reading out from a PUF is called "evaluating" the PUF. There are two statistical parameters which determine the usability of a PUF class $\mathcal{P}$, where $puf_i \in \mathcal{P}$.

(i) *Intra-distance* is the hamming distance or the fractional hamming distance between two random evaluations $y_i^{j_1}$ and $y_i^{j_2}$, $j_1 \neq j_2$, of a single PUF instance puf_i with the same challenge $x_k \in \mathcal{X}_\mathcal{P}$.

(ii) *Inter-distance* is the hamming distance or the fractional hamming distance between the evaluations $y_{i_1}^j$ and $y_{i_2}^j$, of two different PUF instances puf_{i_1} and puf_{i_2}, $i_1 \neq i_2$, for the same challenge $x_k \in \mathcal{X}_\mathcal{P}$ [17].

To be considered a PUF, a PUF class $\mathcal{P}$ shall display certain basic properties. Informal quantifiers like easy, hard, high and low are typically used to define the properties.

(i) *Constructibility*: Constructing a random PUF instance puf_i shall be *easy*.

(ii) *Evaluability*: Evaluating the response of any puf_i to a random challenge $x_k \in \mathcal{X}_\mathcal{P}$ shall be *easy*.

(iii) *Reproducibility*: When evaluated multiple times, a PUF shall generate the same response to the same challenge with a *high* probability, i.e. a PUF instance should have a low inter-distance.

(iv) *Uniqueness*: Response of two different PUF instances to the same challenge shall be *highly* dissimilar, i.e. a PUF class should have a high intra-distance.

3. CMOS PUF

CMOS PUFs are very useful due to their application in chip authentication. They were introduced by Gassend et al. [5] in 2002. CMOS PUFs are defined as electronic systems, which use the uncontrollable fabrication anomalies in silicon's CMOS circuits. After being built, each chip holds a different response to every specific challenge. These characteristics shall not be altered without damaging the device. A PUF computes its input in many ways, but this survey will concentrate on two: the delay difference of arriving signals or the final stability (binary '1' or '0') of a cell. These methods define two major classifications of CMOS PUFs: delay and memory.

3.1 Delay PUF

Delay PUFs use the variations in the manufacturing of wires and gates of CMOS circuits in silicon to produce an unpredictable but repeated response to a challenge. Delay can be affected by temperature change causing the circuit to have different responses to the same challenge. This can be fixed by choosing paths with large enough frequency differences [20].

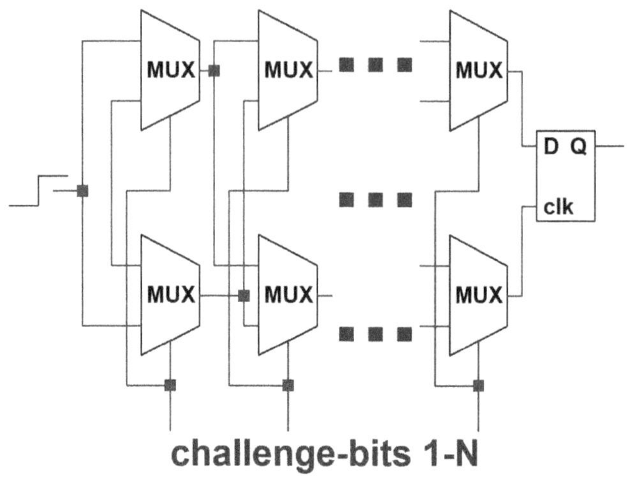

(a) Arbiter

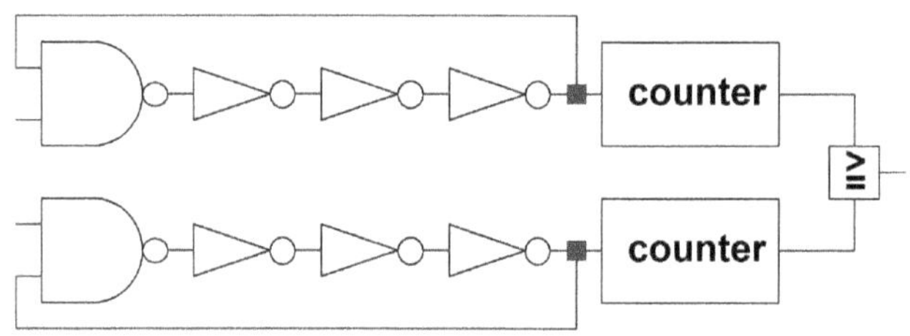

(b) Ring Oscillator

Figure 1: Examples of simple delay PUFS

There are three delay-based PUF families:

(i) *Arbiter PUFs* consist of having a signal race through two different paths, and the decision is made by the slowest or fastest path depending on the scheme utilized [5]. A simple example can be seen in Fig. 1a, where the challenge-bits are used to select the path each signal is going to take [11].

(ii) *Glitch* PUFs use random glitches generated by the process variations during gate's fabrication [21].

(iii) *Ring Oscillator (RO) PUFs* consist of two delay oscillators connected to two different counters that drive the inputs of a comparator as it can be seen in Fig. 1b. This last methodology was introduced in 2007 by Suh and Devadas [20], who explained the advantage of not having to hide the wiring arrangements. This extra process is used in the fabrication of an arbiter-PUF, worrying about an intruder's ability to measure the length of the paths.

Recently Yin et al. have studied RO PUFs using Kendall Syndrome Coding, which shows a 15% improvement from the currently used Compact Syndrome Coding [23]. Also, they introduced a group-based method that outperforms the pair-based method requiring 42% less hardware. Yin and Qu in [13] studied previously different coding schemes coming to the conclusion that their failures to pass the NIST tests are due to poor pairing strategies.

3.2 Memory PUF

There is significant work being done in memory PUFs due to their large utilization in computing. *Memory PUFs* use memory cells inherent properties in a digital circuit. Cells in memory are set in an unstable state (by power up). They are then allowed to settle to their preferred stable state (logic 0 or 1). A concern of this method is that the memory cells may fail to stabilize and remain stuck in an unstable state. There are four different memory PUFs:

(i) *SRAM PUFs* cells are composed of two cross-coupled inverters [7]. The bit and bit complement are set to the same value at power-up (which is an unstable state for the cell). Finally, the cell is released settling to a preferred stable state.

(ii) *Butterfly PUFs* consist of two cross-coupled data latches with a clear/preset input that drives the device to instability. The cell gains stability in a similar way than SRAM cells. It was introduced by Kumar et al. in order to fix the need to restart the memory [10].

(iii) *Latch PUFs* consist of cross-coupled NOR gates. These gates are driven to instability through a reset, then they are released to generate the output relying on the threshold-voltage mismatch [19].

(iv) *Flip-flop PUFs* cells are composed of two cross-coupled flip-flops [12], which use the power up values similar to the procedure in SRAM PUF.

Fig. 2 shows the general flow of authentication through memory PUFs.

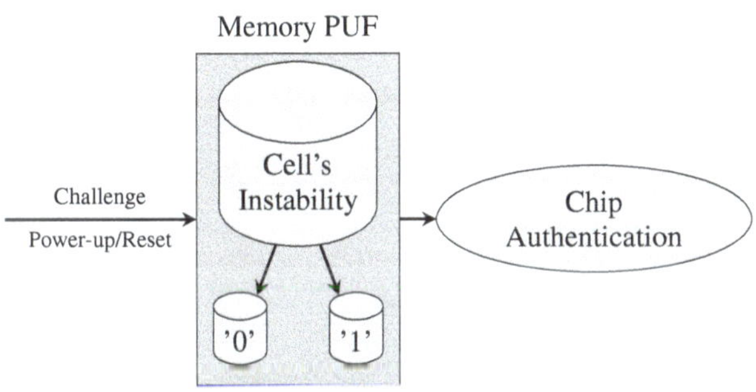

Figure 2: General authentication flow through memory PUFs.

Memory PUFs are currently studied in order to gain reliability and robustness. An 8 transistor-SRAM PUF is proposed in [8], which the authors affirm that is more robust than the 6 transistor-SRAM PUF. The cost of this improvement is some area and leakage overhead. An SR latch PUF is proposed in [6]. This latch PUF is claimed to have high resistance to temperature and voltage fluctuations.

4. PUF WITH EMERGING DEVICES

As transistors dimensions approach the atomic scale, other devices are studied to assist the CMOS transistors. Looking into some of the specific needs of PUF application, the emerging devices require:

(i) *Speed*: to achieve a smooth access with no significant wait by the operator;

(ii) *Size*: to be easily placed inside the chip being protected, with no large area overhead;

(iii) *Reliability*: to guarantee the authentication at any time necessary;

(iv) *Robustness*: to endure environmental changes without any challenge-response pair mismatch.

The novel devices discussed are presented in the following order: spintronics-based, menristive-based, carbon-based, and quantum.

4.1 Spintronics-based PUF

Spin-transfer torque (STT) PUFs used the fabrication anomalies gained by the device in the manufacturing process. The variations may be in geometry, and oxygen vacancy [1, 2, 25]. The geometric parameters of thickness and area are used in [1, 2] in order to create a MRAM PUF. The PUF is evaluated by destabilizing the magnetic cells and letting them relax to a parallel ('0') or antiparallel ('1') state. The two different states of the MRAM cells are shown in Fig. 3. Das et al. research resulted in a PUF with low intra-distance, very high inter-distance, very small footprint, and most importantly a very high entropy.

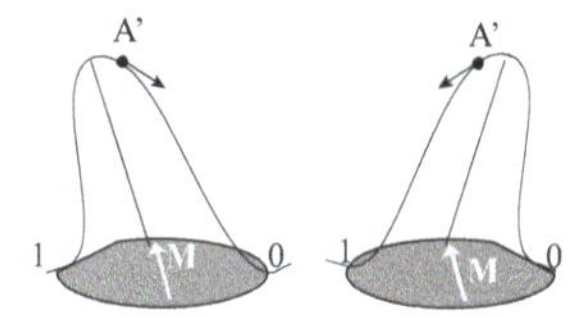

Figure 3: Logic states in MRAM cells [2].

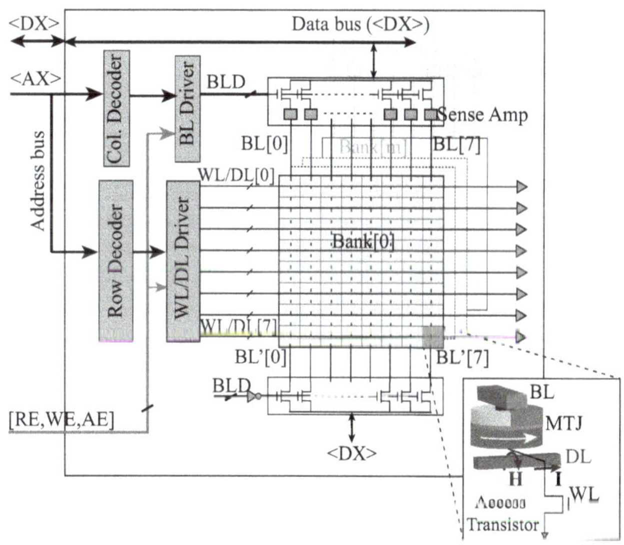

Figure 4: System level architecture of MRAM PUF. Signal descriptions: BL (bit line), BL' (bit line complement), WL (word line), DL (digit line), BLD (bit line driver signal), RE (read enable), WE (write enable), AE (authentication enable) [2].

A more recent study on MRAM PUF is done in [1], by comparing rectangular and elliptical shapes of PUF cells with same aspect ratio. In this investigation, Das et al. found that rectangular shapes are more sensitive to lithography geometric variations. Through choosing to implement rectangular shaped cells in a MRAM PUF, the inter-distance and intra-distance values shown in Table 1 are expected to improve. Pictures of the fabricated samples are in Fig. 5. The response generation steps of their work are: (i) decryption of the input by a decoder; (ii) allocation of the decrypted message in the cell matrix; (iii) creation of a magnetic field by a current sent through the bit line, destabilizing the cells; (iv) stability is reached self-sufficiently; (v) the analog voltage of each cell is converted to digital signals; (vi) the decoder reads the assigned cells from the matrix; (vii) encryption of the information and output. Fig. 4 shows in detail the architecture of the PUF proposed in [1, 2].

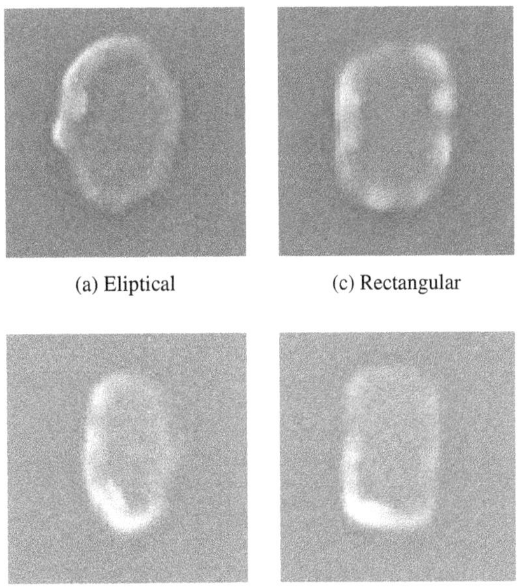

(a) Eliptical (c) Rectangular

(b) Eliptical (d) Rectangular

Figure 5: SEM images of cells with dimensions of 90x60nm^2 and 100x50nm^2 [2], respectively.

In [25], Zhang et al. study the geometry of cells, as well as their oxygen vacancy. They also added an automatic write-back scheme to a STT-MRAM PUF. With this change, Zhang et al. claimed that the bit-error rate of the raw response-bits was reduced by $\sim$5 orders of magnitude. They also included a refresh response-bit map increasing the difficulty of prediction. Zhang et al. claim that the energy and area improvement per bit is at least twice less, and is also eleven times smaller than the conventional memristor-based PUF.

4.2 Memristive-based PUFs

Memristors are devices that relate electric charge and magnetic flux, and are primary devices due to the fact that they cannot be achieved as a system of interconnections between resistors, inductors, and capacitors [18]. Memristive PUFs are used through the irregularities of the write-time in a memristor, which is set at the threshold. In [15], a nano PUF is achieved by interconnecting memristors in a cross-bar pattern recording an inter-distance of 49% which is closed to ideal, but having a very high intra-distance of 49%.

Memristor PUFs are also studied in [18], achieved by reading/ writing cross-bar PUF arrays. In this study, the measured inter-distance of 49.35% was recorded, presenting very small power consumption, with promising scalability. In [3] a cross-bar array of memristors is used, converting their variations from analog to digital. The achieved PUF has close to ideal uniqueness and uniformity. A resistance variation distribution utilized in their work is presented in Fig. 6.

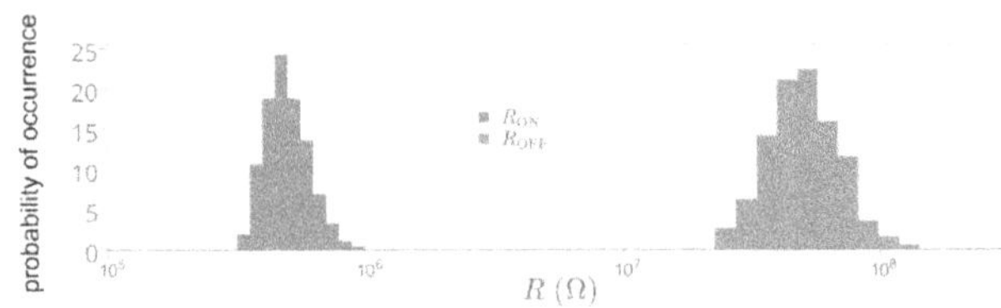

Figure 6: Resistance variation distribution taken from Ref. [3]. Figure by Gao et al. found at http://dx.doi.org/10.1038/srep12785. This work is licensed under the Creative Commons Attribution 4.0 International License.

4.3 Carbon-based PUFs

Carbon-based PUFs are accomplished through carbon nanotube field-effect transistors (CNFETs). Their fabrication variations make them suitable for authentication. The characteristics of these devices are similar to CMOS technology. In [9] a PUF is achieved by having two rows of transistors connected to comparators, as it may be seen in Fig. 7. The variation between each transistor will make each row unique. An advantage of this design is the small foot-print due to the reduction in transistor count. The CNFET PUFs (claim the authors) consume 89.6% less power than the 90nm ultra-low power based PUF, while providing very high reliability.

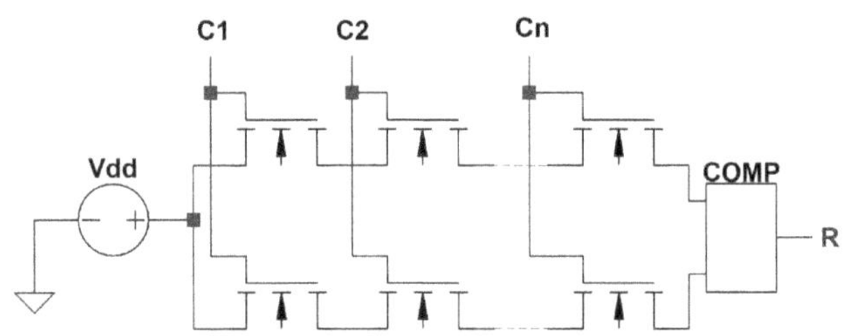

Figure 7: Arbiter-based PUF achieved through carbon nanotubes implemented in [9].

4.4 Quantum PUFs

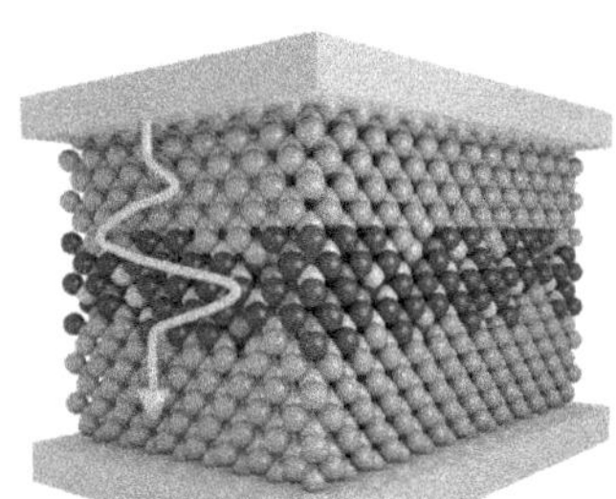

Figure 8: Quantum-mecanical tunneling used on RTDs. The mid-layer is the region with imperfections that is applied as a PUF, taken from Ref. [16]. Figure by Roberts et al. found at http://dx.doi.org/10.1038/srep16456. This work is licensed under the Creative Commons Attribution 4.0 International License.

Recent studies have pushed the boundaries to use the unique particle distribution in quantum confinement. In [16], resonant tunneling diodes (RTDs) are used to measure tunneling fluctuations in order to authenticate (see Fig. 8). Roberts et al. make use of the anomalies at the atomic level, where the layers are very distinctive and impossible to be copied. The authors claim that their RTD-based PUF can achieve $\sim 10^3$ unique particle arrangements. It is suggested that these values will increase when RTD arrays are arranged for practical applications. Their bit density recorded is 2.5bits/μm^2 saving more space than current CMOS technologies, while demanding much less power. In [16] an optical-PUF is also proposed. This achieves a 1D binary key from a 2D speckle, that is reflected by a laser through a 3D token, which can be seen in Fig. 9.

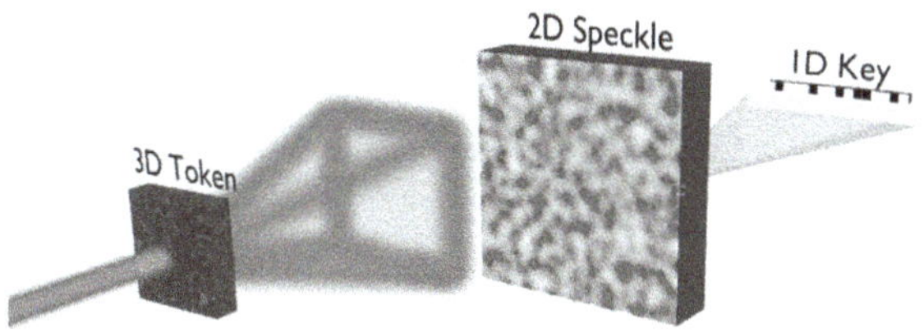

Figure 9: Quantum optical PUF taken from Ref. [16]. Figure by Roberts et al. found at http://dx.doi.org/10.1038/srep16456. This work is licensed under the Creative Commons Attribution 4.0 International License.

5. DISCUSSION

After overviewing CMOS and novel technology based PUFs, we compare them with respect to the measurements of area, reproducibility and uniqueness. As shown in Table 1 size is a factor where some novel devices push the boundaries. MRAM and STT-MRAM area are ~10x smaller than the SRAM PUF. MRAM PUFs size is computed based on the fabrications shown in Fig. 5.

Another measurement where emerging technologies supersede CMOS PUFs is the reproducibility. As seen in Table 1, the CNFET PUF achieved better intra-distance than the arbiter and RO CMOS PUFs. MRAM and STT-MRAM outperformed the other CMOS memory PUFs with reproducibilities of 2.25% and 0.0001%, respectively.

Also from Table 1, we show that most of the emerging technologies have close to ideal uniqueness (i.e. 50%). In general, memristor, MRAM and STT-MRAM PUFs have higher uniqueness than the CMOS memory PUFs. The CNFET PUF also outperforms the CMOS delay PUFs from Table 1. This domination by novel technologies-based PUFs is also reflected in bit-aliasing and uniformity. We consider that uniformity and bit-aliasing relate directly to the uniqueness as they hold the randomness values within a response (i.e. '1' to '0' proportionality, 50/50 ideally) and a single PUF cell, respectively.

In Fig. 10, we see a graphical comparison over the emerging technologies and CMOS PUFs with respect to uniqueness and re-

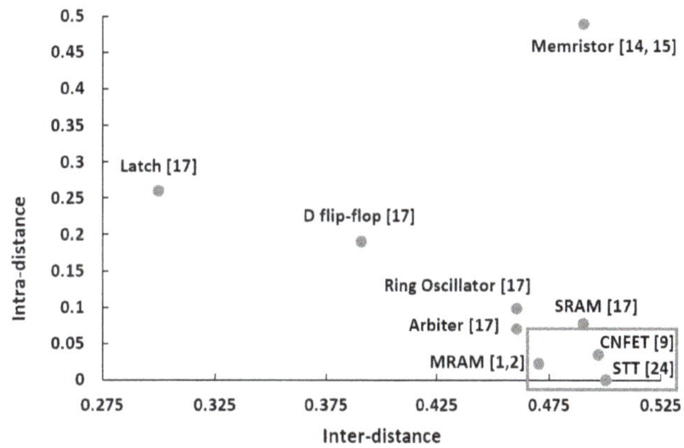

Figure 10: Graphical interpretation of inter-distance and intra-distance values.

producibility. Enclosed in the red square, we illustrate that CNFET, MRAM and STT-MRAM PUFs lead this domain. The memristor PUF has a very low reproducibility, which is a behavior better suited for random number generation.

PUF reconfiguration has awaken interest in researchers. A reconfigurable PUF (rPUF) is able to change its response to the same challenge [3]. In [26], a reconfigurable PUF has been reported to be achieved through the arrangement of phase change memory cells. The novel technologies like memristor, RTD, and STT-MRAM PUFs, possess this innovative quality as well [3, 16, 25].

In general, considerable research and investigation are necessary for PUFs. CMOS compatibility of novel technologies needs confirmation (i.e. taking into account the fabrication constraints, manufacturing cost and overall feasibility). The evaluation complexity needs more attention, as it adds time to the overall process. These factors will add further insights when applied to these state-of-the-art technologies.

6. ACKNOWLEDGMENTS

This work is partially supported by NSF HRD (1400837), and USF Presidential Doctoral Fellowship.

7. REFERENCES

[1] J. Das, K. Scott, and S. Bhanja. Mram puf: A novel geometry based magnetic puf with integrated cmos. *Emerging Technologies in Computing Systems*, Submitted for 2016 publication.

[2] J. Das, K. Scott, S. Rajaram, D. Burgett, and S. Bhanja. Mram puf: Using geometric and resistive variations in mram cells. *Nanotechnology, IEEE Transactions on*, 14(3):436–443, 2015.

Table 1: Performance comparison between the emerging technology based PUFs and CMOS PUFs [17]. The area is for 64-bit length of response.

PUF Types	Area (μm^2)	Reproducibility	Uniqueness	Uniformity	Bit-aliasing	Reconfigurability
SRAM	51.99	7.78%	48.72%	48.72%	48.72%	✓
Latch	531.25	26.33%	30.77%	30.77%	30.77%	✓
D flip-flop	765.63	19.23%	39.50%	39.50%	39.50%	✓
Arbiter	690.56	7.75%	46.43%	46.43%	46.43%	-
Ring Oscillator	7774.2	9.89%	46.45%	46.45%	46.45%	-
STT-MRAM [24]	6.79	0.0001%	~50%	~50%	~50%	✓
MRAM [1, 2]	5.5	2.25%	47%	47%	47%	✓
Memristor [14, 15]	-	49%	49.85%	49.99%	49.99%	✓
CNFET [9]	-	3.5%	49.67%	49.67%	49.67%	-

[3] Y. Gao, D. C. Ranasinghe, S. F. Al-Sarawi, O. Kavehei, and D. Abbott. Memristive crypto primitive for building highly secure physical unclonable functions. *Scientific reports*, 5, 2015.

[4] B. Gassend, D. Clarke, M. Van Dijk, and S. Devadas. Silicon physical random functions. In *Proceedings of the 9th ACM conference on Computer and communications security*, pages 148–160. ACM, 2002.

[5] B. Gassend, D. Clarke, M. Van Dijk, and S. Devadas. Delay-based circuit authentication and applications. In *Proceedings of the 2003 ACM symposium on Applied computing*, pages 294–301. ACM, 2003.

[6] B. Habib, J.-P. Kaps, and K. Gaj. Efficient sr-latch puf. In *Applied Reconfigurable Computing*, pages 205–216. Springer, 2015.

[7] D. E. Holcomb, W. P. Burleson, K. Fu, et al. Initial sram state as a fingerprint and source of true random numbers for rfid tags. In *Proceedings of the Conference on RFID Security*, volume 7, 2007.

[8] J.-W. Jang and S. Ghosh. Design and analysis of novel sram pufs with embedded latch for robustness. In *Quality Electronic Design (ISQED), 2015 16th International Symposium on*, pages 298–302. IEEE, 2015.

[9] S. Konigsmark, L. K. Hwang, D. Chen, and M. D. Wong. Cnpuf: A carbon nanotube-based physically unclonable function for secure low-energy hardware design. In *Design Automation Conference (ASP-DAC), 2014 19th Asia and South Pacific*, pages 73–78. IEEE, 2014.

[10] S. S. Kumar, J. Guajardo, R. Maes, G.-J. Schrijen, and P. Tuyls. The butterfly puf protecting ip on every fpga. In *Hardware-Oriented Security and Trust, 2008. HOST 2008. IEEE International Workshop on*, pages 67–70. IEEE, 2008.

[11] D. Lim, J. W. Lee, B. Gassend, G. E. Suh, M. Van Dijk, and S. Devadas. Extracting secret keys from integrated circuits. *Very Large Scale Integration (VLSI) Systems, IEEE Transactions on*, 13(10):1200–1205, 2005.

[12] R. Maes, P. Tuyls, and I. Verbauwhede. Intrinsic pufs from flip-flops on reconfigurable devices. In *3rd Benelux workshop on information and system security (WISSec 2008)*, volume 17, 2008.

[13] G. Qu and C.-E. Yin. Temperature-aware cooperative ring oscillator puf. In *Hardware-Oriented Security and Trust, 2009. HOST'09. IEEE International Workshop on*, pages 36–42. IEEE, 2009.

[14] J. Rajendran, R. Karri, J. B. Wendt, M. Potkonjak, N. McDonald, G. S. Rose, and B. Wysocki. Nano meets security: Exploring nanoelectronic devices for security applications. *Proceedings of the IEEE*, 103(5):829–849, 2015.

[15] J. Rajendran, G. S. Rose, R. Karri, and M. Potkonjak. Nano-ppuf: A memristor-based security primitive. In *VLSI (ISVLSI), 2012 IEEE Computer Society Annual Symposium on*, pages 84–87. IEEE, 2012.

[16] J. Roberts, I. E. Bagci, M. Zawawi, J. Sexton, N. Hulbert, Y. Noori, M. Young, C. Woodhead, M. Missous, M. Migliorato, et al. Using quantum confinement to uniquely identify devices. *Scientific reports*, 5, 2015.

[17] M. Roel. *Physically Unclonable Functions: Constructions, Properties and Applications*. PhD thesis, University of KU Leuven, 2012.

[18] G. S. Rose and C. A. Meade. Performance analysis of a memristive crossbar puf design. In *Proceedings of the 52nd Annual Design Automation Conference*, page 75. ACM, 2015.

[19] Y. Su, J. Holleman, and B. Otis. A 1.6pj/bit 96variations. In *Solid-State Circuits Conference, 2007. ISSCC 2007. Digest of Technical Papers. IEEE International*, pages 406–611, Feb 2007.

[20] G. E. Suh and S. Devadas. Physical unclonable functions for device authentication and secret key generation. In *Proceedings of the 44th annual Design Automation Conference*, pages 9–14. ACM, 2007.

[21] D. Suzuki and K. Shimizu. The glitch puf: A new delay-puf architecture exploiting glitch shapes. In *Cryptographic Hardware and Embedded Systems, CHES 2010*, pages 366–382. Springer, 2010.

[22] Q. Wu, J. Zhang, Y. Lin, and W. Che. Watermarking fpga bitfile for intellectual property protection. *Radioengineering*, 2012.

[23] C.-E. Yin, G. Qu, and Q. Zhou. Design and implementation of a group-based ro puf. In *Proceedings of the Conference on Design, Automation and Test in Europe*, pages 416–421. EDA Consortium, 2013.

[24] L. Zhang, X. Fong, C.-H. Chang, Z. H. Kong, and K. Roy. Highly reliable memory-based physical unclonable function using spin-transfer torque mram. In *Circuits and Systems (ISCAS), 2014 IEEE International Symposium on*, pages 2169–2172. IEEE, 2014.

[25] L. Zhang, X. Fong, C.-H. Chang, Z. H. Kong, and K. Roy. Highly reliable spin-transfer torque magnetic ram-based physical unclonable function with multi-response-bits per cell. *Information Forensics and Security, IEEE Transactions on*, 10(8):1630–1642, 2015.

[26] L. Zhang, Z. H. Kong, C.-H. Chang, A. Cabrini, and G. Torelli. Exploiting process variations and programming sensitivity of phase change memory for reconfigurable physical unclonable functions. *Information Forensics and Security, IEEE Transactions on*, 9(6):921–932, 2014.

Trellis-search based Dynamic Multi-Path Connection Allocation for TDM-NoCs

Yong Chen, Emil Matus, Gerhard P. Fettweis
Vodafone Chair for Mobile Communications Systems, Dresden University of Technology
yong.chen@ifn.et.tu-dresden.de

ABSTRACT

This paper proposes a centralized approach for connection allocation for TDM-based NoCs by making use of dedicated hardware unit called NoCManager that employs trellis-based search algorithm enabling dynamic parallel multi-path, multi-slot allocation. Be different to the previous unrolled trellis search algorithm, in this paper the folded architecture is employed to achieve efficiency. In comparison with previous TDM connection allocation methods, the proposed design has the following advantages: (1) hardware supported low-latency, high-throughput allocation mechanism, (2) improved success rate due to parallel multi-path search and (3) efficient NoCManager architecture.

Compared to centralized software solutions the proposed design demonstrates two orders of magnitude improvement in allocation speed and ten times higher success rate. It can provide up to several times higher allocation speed and up to 18% higher success rate against recently proposed distributed solution.

Keywords

TDM-NoCs; Guaranteed Services; Connection Allocation

1. INTRODUCTION

In order to guarantee latency, jitter and bandwidth, some NoCs provide Guaranteed Services (GSs). Circuit Switching (CS), which operates by first allocating exclusively channels to form a circuit (connection) from source to destination and then sending data along this connection, is a popular approach to support GS. However, it may lead to considerable system inefficiencies due to the blocking of other traffic. In order to tackle this problem, two extensions have been proposed [1]: i) in Time-Division Multiplexing (TDM) based CS, the NoC resources can be shared by different flows by splitting the available link capacity into time slots, and the resources are allocated exclusively only in specific time slots; ii) in Space-Division-Multiplexing (SDM) [2], only part of a link with its corresponding buffers are exclusively allocated

GLSVLSI '16, May 18–20, 2016, Boston, MA, USA.
© 2016 ACM. ISBN 978-1-4503-4274-2/16/05. . . $15.00
DOI: http://dx.doi.org/10.1145/2902961.2902968

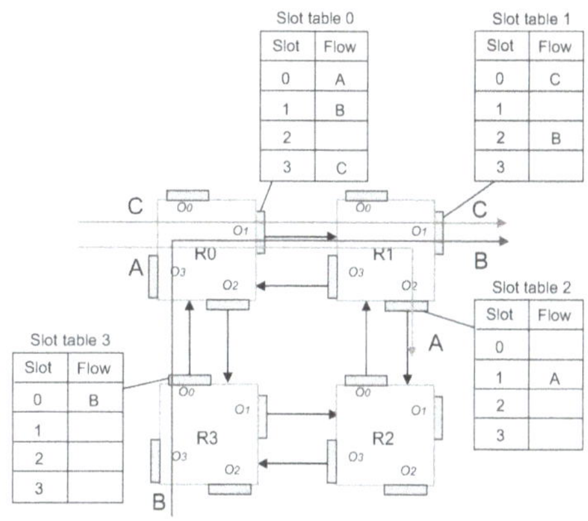

Figure 1: Contention-free TDM routing

to a connection, while the remaining wires of the link can be used by other flows. Since SDM link sharing introduces large crossbars and many physical wires, TDM based CS is more popular and e.g. used in a probe search proposed by Liu et al [1], AEthereal [3,4], an exhaustive path-search proposed by Stefan et al [5,6], etc.

In TDM CS NoCs, the allocation is stored in a slot allocation table of particular router with one table for each shared resource (a link). The allocation tables are synchronized such that a flow, which has slot s in one router, gets slot $(s + 1) \bmod S$ at the next hop, where S is the number of slots in the slot table [7].

Fig. 1 illustrates TDM routing with a router network and its corresponding slot tables. The network contains four routers, R0, R1, R2, and R3. The three arrows labeled A, B and C represent flows. In R0, the slot table 0 of O_1 switches flow A to R1 at slot 0 and flow B to R1 at slot 1, respectively. Flow B travels along path $R3 \rightarrow R0 \rightarrow R1$ with slot sequence $0 \rightarrow 1 \rightarrow 2$.

The major challenge for TDM-based NoCs is the fast, scalable and robust connection allocation that typically comprises i) selection of a contention free path and ii) allocation of the appropriate slots and corresponding resources on the path. In this paper, we propose a dynamic allocation method using dedicated hardware unit called 'NoCManager', solving the connection allocation problem by employing a trellis-search based shortest path algorithm. Be different to the unrolled trellis graph that contains the full length stages [8], in this paper the folded architecture is employed to reuse hardware in order to reduce hardware cost and increase clock frequency. Unlike [9], the in-order selection step is omitted from search algorithm. The algorithm guarantees

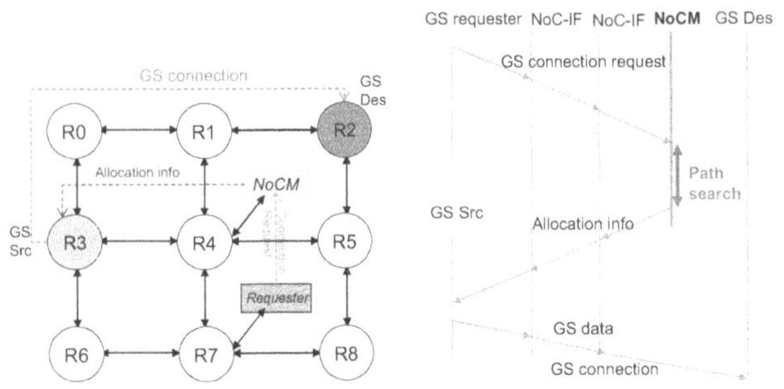

(a) System Model of the MPSoC (b) GS processing procedure diagram

Figure 2: System concept of the MPSoC platform

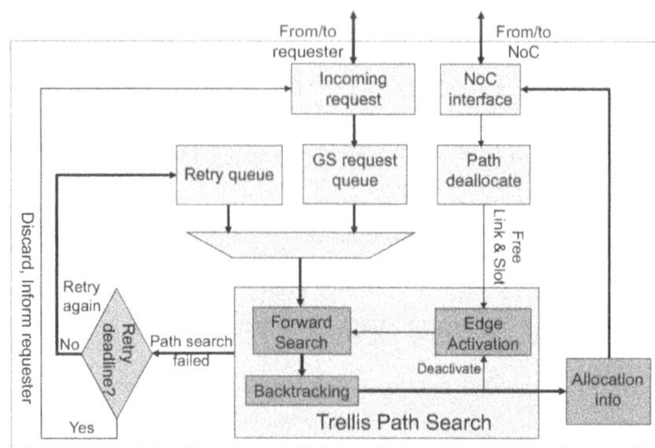

Figure 3: Block diagram of the NoCManager

that if the path is available, it is found in $2 \cdot L$ clock cycles, where L is the path length between source and destination. Moreover, the novel search approach in conjunction with efficient hardware implementation of NoCManager reasonably improves the overall performance against recently proposed methods.

2. BACKGROUND AND RELATED WORK

The allocation techniques can be grouped into two categories: i) static (design-time) [10] allocation and ii) dynamic (run-time) allocation. Since the static allocation is done at the design time and cannot be changed according to the applications' requirements during run time, they are not well suited for dynamic systems.

The dynamic connection allocation techniques can be divided into two categories: i) centralized [5, 11–13] and ii) distributed allocation [1, 3].

The state of the art of distributed allocation is parallel probe search [1], in which the source node sends a setup flit for searching path that traverses through the NoC along minimum paths to try to reach target node. The problem is the failed partial setup path has to be torn down, which might also block other probe search. In this approach, several trials for success might be needed due to the fact that this method investigates single slot at a time. Unfortunately, this approach enables single-slot allocation, and the problem of multi-slot allocation was not addressed in recent work.

The centralized allocation is done by a central module, and are typically based on software solution. The authors in [5, 6] e.g. utilize Microblaze processor while ARM processor is employed in [11, 12]. Software solutions provide excellent flexibility, however, they suffer from relatively long allocation time. For instance, single path exhaustive path-search in [5, 6] tries to add links to the current path if the link provides sufficient slots and is closer to destination. Due to investigation of a single link at a time, and allocation of all required slots on a single path, thousands of processor cycles are required for one allocation. In order to increase the allocation speed, HAGAR approach [13] proposes hardware accelerator allowing to speedup allocation by two orders of magnitude against software methods. However, HAGAR is employed for basic CS, and does not support TDM. This work is motivated by HAGAR algorithm, and proposes a novel trellis-search based allocation algorithm for TDM NoCs, called EHAGAR.

3. SYSTEM ARCHITECTURE

This section presents the system architecture and the concept of a centralized allocation technique based on NoCManager (NoCM) employing the novel EHAGAR approach. The NoCM is the centralized module responsible for processing the incoming GS connection requests and allocating the corresponding connections.

3.1 System Concept

The system model of NoCM based MPSoC architecture employing 3x3 mesh NoC is illustrated in Fig. 2. NoCM attempts to allocate the appropriate GS paths when it receives GS connection requests, and sends the allocated path information to the GS source node.

In our system, the allocated path through the network is determined by source routing. That is, the path is embedded in the packet header by the source node, and the routers follow the path directions in the header. The path is the same for all flits belonging to a specific connection. The packets are inserted into the network only at specific time slots, which is regulated by a TDM slot table in the source node, same as in Aelite [14]. The complete procedure for connection allocation is as follows:

1. The GSs requester, e.g. GS source or centralized system manager, sends the GS connection request to NoCM. These requests are buffered in a queue in NoCM.
2. NoCM attempts to allocate the appropriate path and slots according to the request requirements.
3. NoCM sends the allocation information to source node in the case of success or retries later if it fails. The path from NoCM to source node is selected by NoCM as GS path.
4. After receiving the allocation information, source node starts to transmit data along the GS connection.
5. After the data transfer is finished, the source node informs the NoCM to free the corresponding allocated slots.

Step 2 is the main work of this paper, and is explained in details in the next section.

3.2 NoCManager Architecture

The NoCManager solves the problem of the shortest path search from source to destination node fulfilling the requirement on the minimum number of free slots. A block diagram of the NoCM is shown in Fig. 3 and comprises forward search, backtracking and edge activation/ deactivation

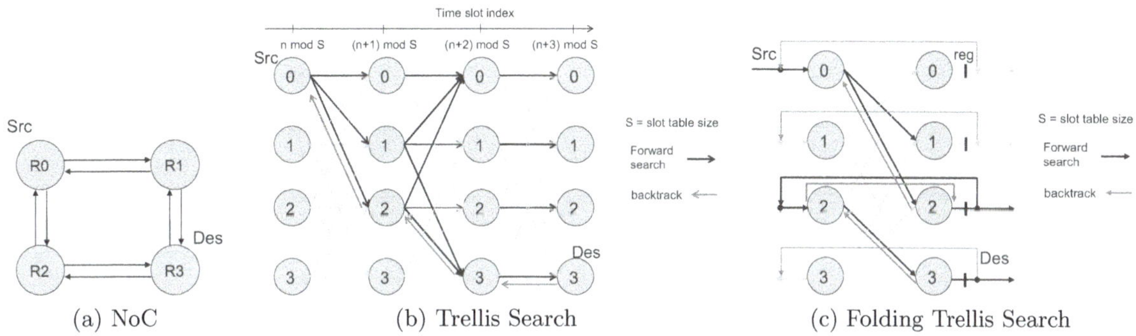

Figure 4: a)2x2 2D-mesh example NoC; b)schematic structure of the trellis Search for the example NoC; c)schematic structure of the folding trellis Search

modules. NoCM collects and processes the connection allocation requests from the requester within the GS queue. The resulting allocation parameters are sent through the NoC interface to respective routers.

3.2.1 *Trellis-Based Path Search*

In general, the connection allocation by the NoCM comprises two steps:

- **Forward search** i.e. traverse the NoC from source to destination node to find the best free path out of all possible survivor paths.
- **Backtracking** i.e. read out the stored survivor path from destination to backtrack the best path and collect the associated path and slot allocation parameters.

The aforementioned path search problem can be considered as a simplification of dynamic programming optimization. Moreover, the successive NoC traversal from source to destination node during the path search can be represented by trellis diagram with i) states, i.e. routers reached on the path, and ii) state transitions acting as the links between two respective routers corresponding to a forward step in the trellis. Time slot is used as a horizontal axis to show the possible paths through the states. Hence, the stage (i.e. the column) of the trellis diagram, is a collection of states with the same partial path length which refers to the same number of hops from the source node. Every slot at the first stage has such a representation of trellis diagram, i.e. if the slot table size is S, there are S representations of trellis diagram. Every slot from the source node searches its own path simultaneously. It is worth to mention that the state transition structure reflects the specific NoC topology. However, the dimension of trellis diagram depends only on the number of NoC routers, and hence, is topology invariant.

Since the NoC topology and size is known at design time the respective trellis diagram can be constructed as e.g. for 2x2 NoC illustrated in Fig. 4a the associated trellis diagram is constructed in Fig. 4b. Assume node 0 is the source (Src) and node 3 is destination (Des). The search signals start from Src at the first stage, traversing through the trellis to try to activate its connected neighbors at next stage. Src activates its connected neighbors node 1 and node 2 at the second stage, and node 1 and node 2 activate their connected neighbors at the third stage. If a node is activated by several nodes at the same stage, only one is remembered as its predecessor. So the Des, node 3, is activated by both node 2 and node 1 at third stage, but only node 2 is remembered as its predecessor. When the Des is activated, backtracking is started from Des to backtrack predecessors. Node 3 backtracks its predecessor node 2 at second stage, and node 2 backtracks node 0 at first stage. Now the path from Src to Des is obtained as $N0 \rightarrow N2 \rightarrow N3$. Assume the beginning slot at Src is 2, and the slot table size is 4, the slot sequence along the path will be $2 \rightarrow 3 \rightarrow 0$.

Proposed path search algorithm exhibits regular structure and, hence, can be efficiently mapped on the folded architecture. In such case, the hardware resources are reused by all partitions of folded algorithm. The folded architecture requires additional output registers in order to hold the values of intermediate results to be used as input values in the next iteration. The folded path search algorithm of example in Fig. 4b is illustrated in Fig. 4c. There is a register for each node to store which predecessor activates it, and it only stores the predecessor that activates it first. When a node is activated, at next cycle it will activate its first stage node, and does the propagation search again. Note now the search consumes several cycles, i.e. one cycle for each iteration. The search of all slots can be stopped in two cases: either the target node has been reached or exceeded deadline. As the search of every slot will be stopped at the same time, the succeed paths established by each slot will be the same length, so the in-order path selection step in [9] can be omitted. Assume node 0 is the source (Src) and node 3 is destination (Des). The search signals started from Src and activated node 2. At the next cycle, node 2 traveled back to the node 2 at first stage and continued activate node 3. The path from Src to Des is obtained as $N0 \rightarrow N2 \rightarrow N3$.

Note that in our method all slots at the source node searches its own path in parallel, which splits the communication bandwidth over multipath [9], which can increase the success rate significantly.

3.2.2 *Path Search Implementation*

The implementation schematic structure of Fig. 4c for the example 2x2 mesh NoC is shown in Fig. 5.

The Detect-Select-Shift (DSS) Unit is the core module, which evaluates the propagated search signals from previous iteration on specific link. The knowledge about the actual link allocation state is stored in the 'Link State' register. When a link is allocated at a specific slot, its corresponding state register is set to '0' excluding it thereby from future search. Correspondingly, state register is set to '1' when the link is released.

The details for an example DSS of node 3 with slot table size of 2 are shown in Fig. 5b. Since the implementation

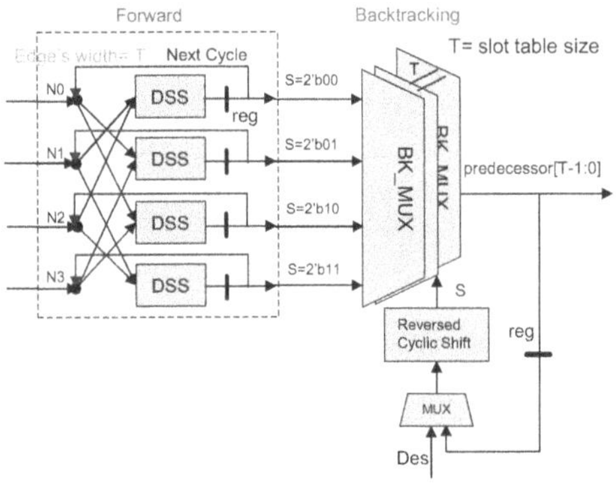

(a) Implementation schematic of the folding trellis

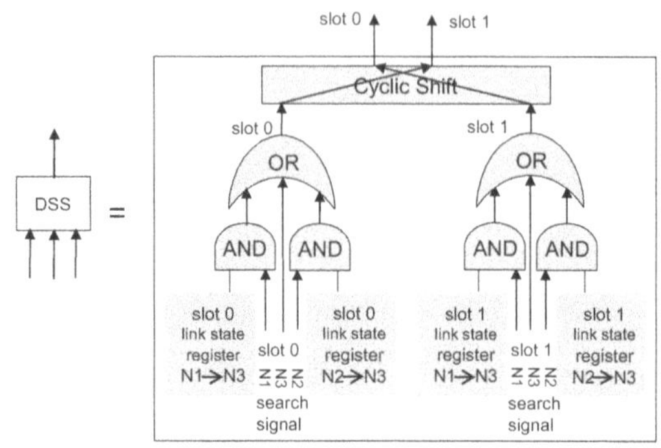

(b) Detect/Select/Shift Unit details of N3

Figure 5: a)implementation schematic of the folding trellis search for the example NoC; b)detailed structure of an example DSS unit

for each slot is the same, we take one slot as example. The work flow for each slot in DSS unit is as follows:

1. **Detect the available slot**: If the search signal from the connected predecessor and its corresponding 'Link State' register are both valid, the current node can be activated at this slot.
2. **Select activated links as path**: If the node can be activated, which predecessor activates it first will be stored in register.
3. **Cyclically shift slot**: Cyclically shift slots to synchronize with next hop. Notice that the cyclic shift now is just wire connection, and thus does not cost any computation resource as consumed in exhaustive path-search [5,6].

The searching begins at the source node by setting its all slots to logic '1', then the search signals propagate forward along the edges to the connected neighbors via DSS Unit that checks the slot's availability. At the next cycle, the still valid signals travel back to the first stage and try to activate its connected neighbors. It continues to propagate in this way until the destination node is activated or exceeds the deadline.

If the destination node is activated with sufficient slots, the backtracking is started with each selected slot backtracking its own path simultaneously. The path is selected by reading the stored predecessors starting at the destination node (Des). The current node that is read out at last cycle will request its predecessor via multiplexer BK_MUX (in Fig. 5a). So predecessors are sorted out in this manner until source node is reached.

We can see (in Fig. 5b) the critical path of DSS unit is only an AND gate and an OR gate, which is quite simple.

4. SYNTHESIS RESULTS

The NoCManager is available in synthesizable VerilogHDL and can be generated out of an XML description for different NoC sizes. Using Synopsys Design Compiler, the NoCM was synthesized with TSMC 65 nm technology, for different mesh networks of size 3x3 to 10x10. The NoCs were synthesized with 1 GHz clock frequency constraints.

From the synthesis results shown in Fig. 6 and Fig. 7, we can see the area of EHAGAR grows with $O(S\cdot N)$ in

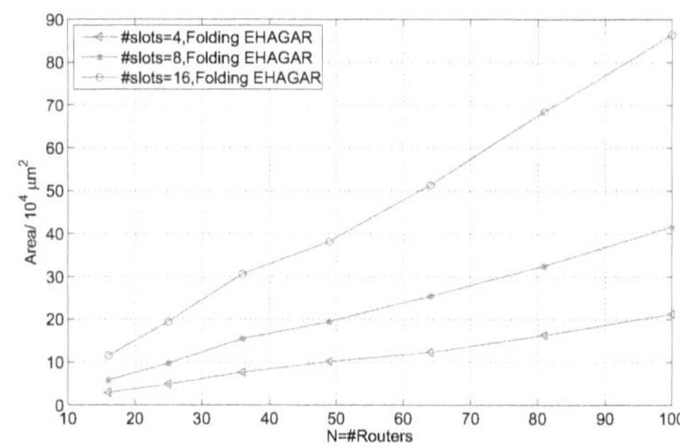

Figure 6: Area of EHAGAR in different size NoC with different slot table size

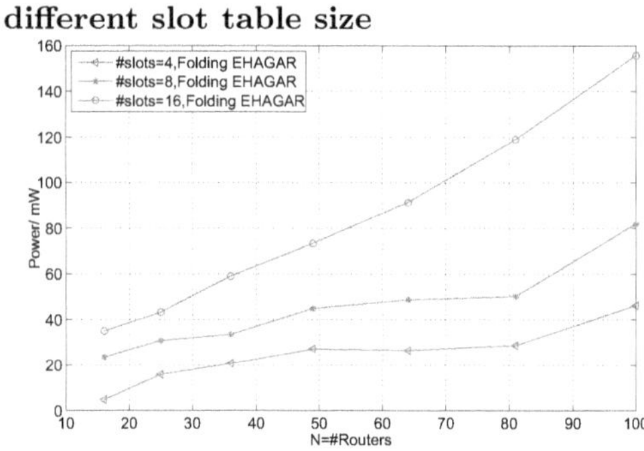

Figure 7: Power consumption of EHAGAR in different NoC

2D-mesh (N= #routers, S=slot table size). The power consumption also grows with $O(S\cdot N)$ in 2D-mesh. Timing analysis after synthesis shows, the EHAGAR can run easily at 1 GHz. A signal processing MPSoC in 65 nm technology typically runs at 500 MHz. In order to make use of the possible high clock frequency, the NoCM can run at higher frequency than the remaining MPSoC.

5. SIMULATION RESULTS

The allocation speed and success rate of EHAGAR NoC-Managers are compared to state of the art TDM centralized and distributed allocation techniques for different NoC sizes with different background traffic and different slot table size. These results are explained in the following sections.

For evaluation several performance metrics are used:

- *success rate* denotes the ratio of successful requests

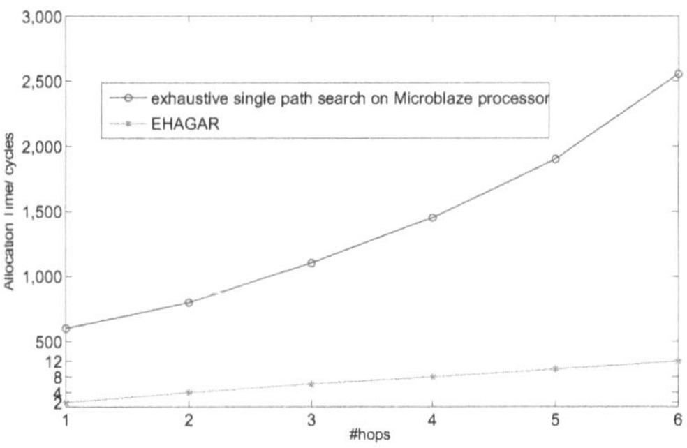

Figure 8: Compared to [5] with 10% background in 4x4 NoC with slot table size of 16. The hops in [5] is adapted to the distance from router to router.

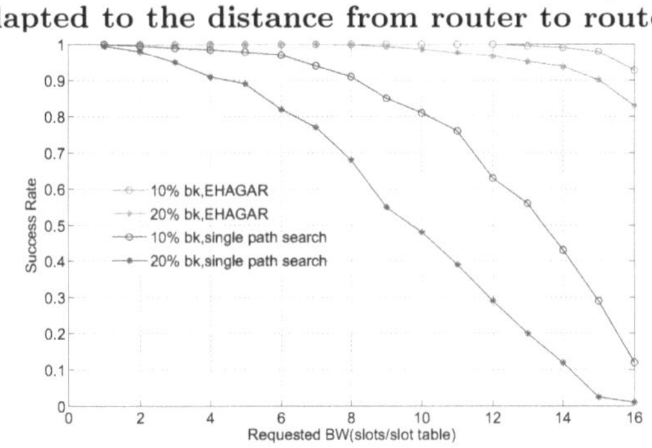

Figure 9: Comparison of Success Rate in 4x4 NoC with different background traffic with Slot Table Size of 16.

that established paths with sufficient bandwidth to the total requests.

- Metrics for comparison with centralized technique:

  background traffic refers to the certain percentage of slots which are already marked as occupied to exclude these slots from path searching. In our experiments for each router, equal number of slots are occupied, but which slots are occupied is randomly selected.

  allocation time denotes the number of clock cycles that the algorithms need to find out a solution or to determine that the allocation is not possible.

- Metrics for comparison with distributed technique:

  master percentage denotes the percentage of nodes which can be GS master. These nodes are uniformly randomly distributed in the system.

  total allocation time denotes the number of clock cycles that the algorithms need to find the solution and plus the time to send the allocation information to source node.

  offered load refers to the required data transfer per connection multiplied by the connection request rate per router. Suppose the request rate per router is 1/2000 cycles, and each connection can deliver 200 flits of data after setup, then the offered load is 200/2000=0.1 flits/cycle.

5.1 Comparison with centralized path-search

5.1.1 Comparison of allocation speed

We do comparison with the exhaustive path-search that runs on Microblaze processor (@288 MHz) [5,6] with 10% random background traffic in 4x4 mesh network.

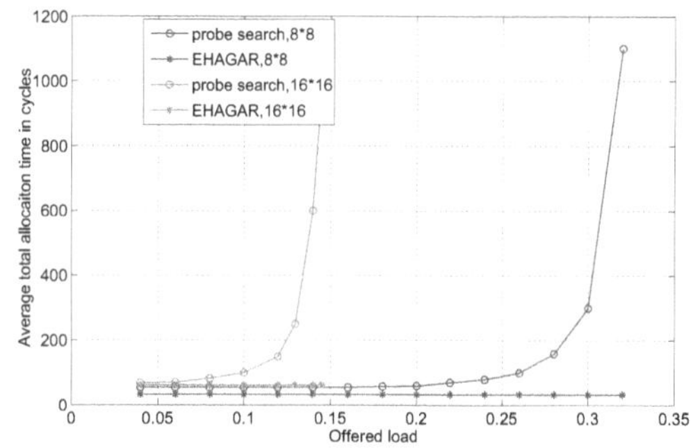

Figure 10: Compared to probe search in different network with different offered load with Slot Table Size of 16.

From the Fig. 8, we can see the speed of EHAGAR is about two hundred times faster than exhaustive path-search. In [5,6], the allocation time increases exponentially with the path length, while the allocation time of EHAGAR increases linearly with the path length. For 6 hops, 12 cycles are needed for EHAGAR, i.e. 6 cycles needed for forward search and 6 cycles for backtracking, while 2550 cycles are needed for exhaustive path-search.

5.1.2 Comparison of Success Rate

The requests sent to NoCM are generated in this way: request to provide an allocation for every feasible source-destination pair combination with certain percentage of background traffic. We produce 1000 samples at each background traffic percentage. We do the simulation for 4x4 meshes with requested slots from 1 to 16 under background traffic (bk) 10% and 20%.

The EHAGAR and single path exhaustive path-search are compared in Fig. 9. Since EHAGAR splits communication over multipath, the success rate is much higher than single path solutions'. Under heavy background traffic with higher requested bandwidth, the EHAGAR becomes much more superior to the single path solution. E.g. in 4x4 mesh under 20% background, the success rate of EHAGAR is 40 times higher when 15 slots requested, and it becomes to 100 times higher than single path solution's when 16 slots requested.

5.2 Comparison with distributed probe search

We simulated 10 millions clock cycles for analysis of the allocation success rate. The requester issues a GS connection request to the NoCM in a POISSON stream meeting the requirements of the offered load and the GS master percentage. The first and last 100,000 simulation cycles were not considered in order to prevent transient effects.

5.2.1 Comparison of allocation speed

In parallel probe search [1] several trials might be needed before success due to investigating single slot at a time. On the contrary, in EHAGAR, all slots are searched in parallel. E.g. in 8x8 mesh with slot table size of 16 at offered load 0.3, the average total allocation time for single slot in probe search is 150 cycles (assume each time slot is one cycle). However, in EHAGAR in average 14 cycles are needed for finding the requested GS path. As NoCM is connected to the center router of the NoC, in average 8 cycles are needed for finding the path from NoCM to source, and 4 cycles are needed for the NoCM to send the allocation information to source. With a slot table size of 16, there is in average 8 time

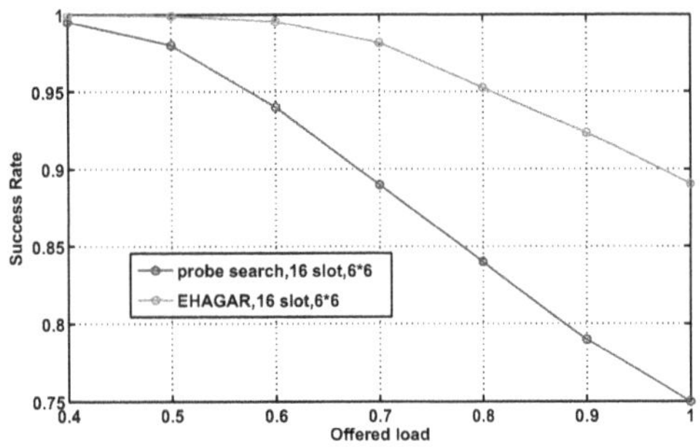

Figure 11: Compared to probe search with master percentage 50% in 6x6 NoC. Each connection delivers 200 flits.

slots waiting time at the NoCM to get its turn in the TDM scheme. So in total in average 34 cycles (= 14+8+4+8) are needed. When n slots are requested, the allocation time for probe search will be n times more, but the allocation time for EHAGAR will be the same as it is independent of the number of requested slots. Fig. 10 shows the average total allocation time when two slots are requested, for different network sizes. In 8x8 mesh at offered load 0.3, the allocation speed of EHAGAR is about 9 times higher than parallel probe; in 16x16 mesh at offered load 0.13, it is 4 times higher than parallel probe. When the offered load becomes higher, the allocation speed of EHAGAR becomes much faster than parallel probe. In parallel probe, after the saturation point of the network (offered load 0.145 in 16x16 mesh and offered load 0.32 in 8x8 mesh), the allocation time will increase dramatically.

5.2.2 *Comparison of Success Rate*

In parallel probe search [1], in which when several connections requested simultaneously, the search flits can block each other. Retry before deadline policy is employed, which can stop the search as failed before all slots are tried even though there may be available path. Fig. 11 shows that the success rate of our method is better than probe search's. For example, in a 6x6 NoC at master percentage 50% and at offered load between 0.6 and 1.0, with slot table size of 16, our solution offers up to 18% higher success rate.

6. CONCLUSION

In this paper we presented a centralized module which does the connection allocation for TDM NoC at run-time. In comparison to other centralized allocations and distributed allocations in terms of allocation speed and success rate, our method demonstrates much better performance.

There are three main reasons for our method being superior to other designs:

- We allocate slots on multipath, which makes success rate much higher than previous methods;
- EHAGAR searches all slots in all directions simultaneously, which makes the search speed quite high;
- The hardware architecture of NoCManager is efficient and scalable since for each iteration the critical path is only an OR gate and AND gate.

Since in EHAGAR all the stages are identical, we can just implement one stage as folding, which can reduce area remarkably and increase frequency significantly though more cycles are needed to do path search. We can also make a compromise that reuses two or more stages based on resource and speed requirement of the system. Moreover, the search can begin at two sides, source and target nodes, simultaneously, and check at the middle stage to see whether signals from two sides meet to determine search succeed or not, which could double the speed but would also double the area.

Acknowledgment

This research work was supported from funding of EuroServer project (FP7-ICT-610456) from the European Union 7th Framework Program and it was partially supported by China Scholarship Council.

7. REFERENCES

[1] Liu S, Jantsch A, Lu Z. Parallel probe based dynamic connection setup in TDM NoCs[C]//Proceedings of the conference on Design, Automation & Test in Europe. European Design and Automation Association, 2014: 239.

[2] Lusala A K, Legat J D. Combining SDM-Based circuit switching with packet switching in a router for on-chip networks[J]. International Journal of Reconfigurable Computing, 2012, 2012.

[3] Goossens K, Dielissen J, Radulescu A. ÃĘthereal network on chip: concepts, architectures, and implementations[J]. Design & Test of Computers, IEEE, 2005, 22(5): 414-421.

[4] Goossens K, Hansson A. The Aethereal network on chip after ten years: Goals, evolution, lessons, and future[C]//Design Automation Conference (DAC), 2010 47th ACM/IEEE. IEEE, 2010: 306-311.

[5] Stefan R, Nejad A B, Goossens K. Online allocation for contention-free-routing NoCs[C]//Proceedings of the 2012 Interconnection Network Architecture: On-Chip, Multi-Chip Workshop. ACM, 2012: 13-16.

[6] Stefan R. Resource Allocation in Time-Division-Multiplexed Networks on Chip[M]. PhD thesis, Delft University of Technology, 2012.

[7] Gebali, Fayez, Haytham Elmiligi, and Mohamed Watheq El-Kharashi, eds. Networks-on-chips: Theory and Practice. CRC Press, 2011.

[8] Y. Chen, E. Matus and G. Fettweis. Centralized Parallel Multi-Path Multi-Slot Allocation Approach for TDM NoCs[C].//IEEE Canadian Conference on Electrical and Computer Engineering. IEEE, 2016, accepted for publication.

[9] Stefan R, Goossens K. A TDM slot allocation flow based on multipath routing in NoCs[J]. Microprocessors and Microsystems, 2011, 35(2): 130-138.

[10] Schoeberl M, Brandner F, SparsÃÿ J, et al. A statically scheduled time-division-multiplexed network-on-chip for real-time systems[C]//Networks on Chip (NoCS), 2012 Sixth IEEE/ACM International Symposium on. IEEE, 2012: 152-160.

[11] Moreira O, Mol J J D, Bekooij M. Online resource management in a multiprocessor with a network-on-chip[C]//Proceedings of the 2007 ACM symposium on Applied computing. ACM, 2007: 1557-1564.

[12] Marescaux T, Bricke B, Debacker P, et al. Dynamic time-slot allocation for QoS enabled networks on chip[C]//Embedded Systems for Real-Time Multimedia, 2005. 3rd Workshop on. IEEE, 2005: 47-52.

[13] Winter M, Fettweis G P. Guaranteed service virtual channel allocation in NoCs for run-time task scheduling[C]//Design, Automation & Test in Europe Conference & Exhibition (DATE), 2011. IEEE, 2011: 1-6.

[14] Hansson A, Goossens K. On-chip Interconnect with Aelite: Composable and Predictable Systems[M]. Springer Science Business Media, 2010.

Prolonging Lifetime of Non-volatile Last Level Caches with Cluster Mapping

Morteza Soltani
Department of Electrical and Computer Engineering
School of Engineering Colleges, University of Tehran
Tehran, Iran
Morteza.soltani@ut.ac.ir

Mohammad Ebrahimi
Department of Electrical and Computer Engineering
School of Engineering Colleges, University of Tehran
Tehran, Iran
Ebrahimi.mo@ut.ac.ir

Zainalabedin Navabi
Department of Electrical and Computer Engineering
School of Engineering Colleges, University of Tehran
Tehran, Iran
Navabi@ece.wpi.edu

ABSTRACT

Recently, work has been done on using nonvolatile cells, such as Spin Transfer Torque RAM (STT-RAM) or Magnetic RAM (M-RAM), to construct last level caches (LLC). These structures mitigate the leakage power and density problem found in traditional SRAM cells. However, the low endurance of nonvolatile caches decreases the lifetime of the LLC. Therefore, an effective wear-leveling technique is required to tackle this issue. In this paper, we propose the inter-set algorithm that distributes the write traffic to all portions of the cache. Our method is based on cluster mapping that dynamically replaces two clusters during the operation of system. Since the inter-set algorithm is based on data movement, a large amount of data must transfer in each replacement. For an efficient data movement with a minimum effect on performance, we develop the novel scheduling technique that utilizes the idle time of the LLC in the computation phase of the processors. Our approach effectively improves the lifetime of LLC with negligible performance and area overhead. Using these methods in a quad core system with 2MB LLC, we can improve the lifetime of non-volatile LLC by 30% on average.

Keywords

Write traffic; cold cluster; data movement; wear leveling technique.

1. INTRODUCTION

For high performance efficiency, designers increase the number of system cores in modern technologies. Therefore, these systems need a large amount of cache capacity for memory intensive applications. For example, Intel's V3 processor has 45MB LLC [1], which consumes high power budget and chip area. Traditional SRAM cells consume about 30% of total power in Intel's Tusla processor [2]. Due to the high leakage power and density problem of SRAM cells, researchers propose to use nonvolatile caches (NV-Caches) that have low leakage power and low density in the LLC. The STT-RAM, Re-RAM, and PCM (Phase Change Memory) are the most popular NV memories used for the LLC and main memory architectures. Although NV memories have near zero leakage power and low density in comparison with SRAM and DRAM, they suffer from low cell endurance. Cell endurance means the maximum number of write operations that can be done on a cell before it gets faulty. Cell endurance of STT-RAM, ReRAM, and PCM are in the order of 4×10^{12}, 10^{11}, and 10^{8} respectively [3-5]

GLSVLSI '16, May 18-20, 2016, Boston, MA, USA © 2016 ACM.
ISBN:978-1-4503-4274-2/16/05…$15.00
DOI: http://dx.doi.org/10.1145/2902961.2902980

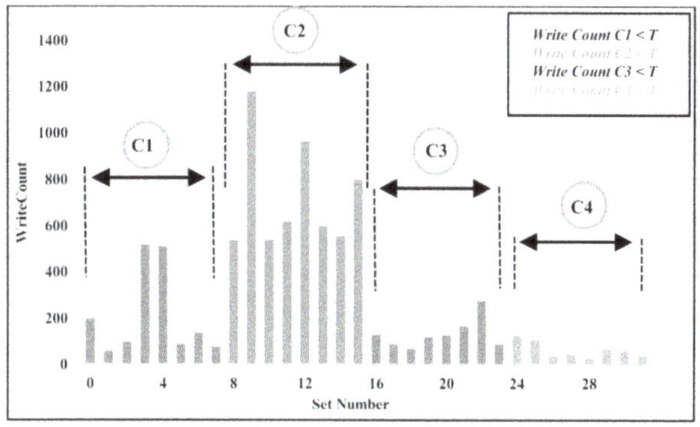

Figure 1. Snapshot of a four-clustered cache

but the cell endurance of SRAM and DRAM are greater than 10^{16}. According to low endurance property after a few years of operation, the correct operation of the cache memory (especially in memory intensive workloads) will be affected if there is no wear-leveling technique to cope with the endurance problem. For example, the lifetime of a 2MB Re-RAM cache runs a mixture of SPEC CPU2006 benchmarks, like $2 \times leslie3d + 2 \times lbm$, is about 3.5 years [6]. The problem happens because of the non-uniform cache traffic distribution which means that there are high write traffic on some portions and low write traffic on the others. Cache sets with high write traffics, called hot sets, have a higher failure rate than low write traffic sets mentioned as cold sets. Distributing write operations over all cache sets is the general solution to overcome the problem [3, 6-8].

Sequoia [6] is the most related work proposing a dynamic indexing technique to improve the LLC lifetime. Sequoia uses on access interset-swapping (OAS) that selects the sets among all cache sets and places them into some groups in the design time. The technique is based on dynamic exchanging of cold and hot set virtual addresses to distribute write traffic uniformly in each group. A counter counting write access for each set specifies whether the set is cold or hot. Exceeding the counter value from a predefined threshold value marks the set as a hot set. Once a set counter reaches the threshold value, the set is replaced by the coldest one in the same group. Some groups may have significant write traffic differences leading to replace hot sets with the other hot sets in the same group while there are cold sets in the other groups. Therefore the hot sets have a lower chance to be replaced by a cold set. Moreover, dedicating a counter to each set imposes a significant power overhead. On the other hand, the state of the cold set (valid, invalid, clean or dirty) is not considered in the replacement phase. Selecting valid, invalid, clean or dirty set is a trade-off between lifetime and performance. Selecting low threshold value results in performance loss because Sequoia requires replacement of two sets on each access demand leading to transferring large amount of data in the access phase of CPU.

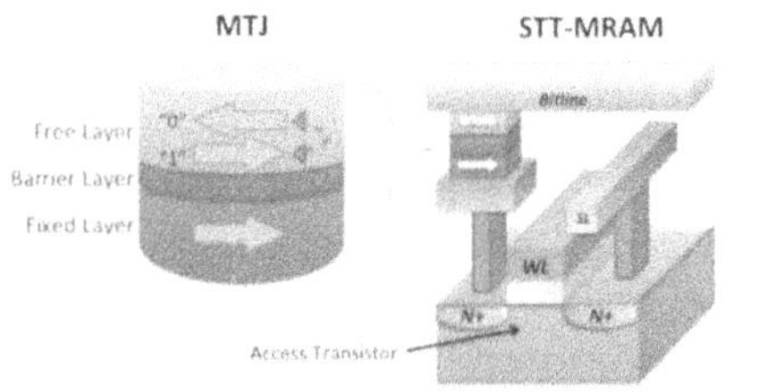

Figure 2. Overall structure of STT-RAMs [9]

In this paper, we propose a method that distributes write traffic to all regions of the cache dynamically. Due to locality property of the cache, only one region of cache will be accessed in each period of time. We call this region as a cluster containing neighbor sets. Unlike Sequoia which replaces sets in each groups, our method is based on replacing hot and cold clusters. A counter counts write operations on each cluster. Running the "$2 \times herf264 + 2 \times povray$" benchmarks, Figure 1 shows a snapshot of four clusters of a 2MB cache where each cluster consists of some sets. As can be seen, because of spatial locality of set access, cluster sets have a similar write traffic behavior which means that sets inside a hot and cold cluster are hot and cold on average, respectively. Dedicating a counter to each cluster instead of each set leads to a lower area and power overhead. Once the counter value reaches a predefined threshold, the cluster must be replaced by one of the cold clusters. To overcome performance issues mentioned in Sequoia method, we propose the following methods:

1- In addition to the counter value, we consider the number of invalid and clean lines in each set of cluster. This method decreases the number of write-backs and data movements. Actually, it is a tradeoff between lifetime and performance.

2- Utilizing idle times to move data between two clusters. By proposing an efficient replacement scheduling. Note that replacing set data immediately after on each access imposes more memory stalls affecting performance. Using idle times can minimize the performance loss significantly.

Rest of this paper is organized in four sections. Section 2 explains the background of nonvolatile memory structure and wear leveling techniques. Section 3 describes our proposed method followed by Section 4 discussing our evaluation results that comprise our algorithm with the baseline and the most related work. Finally, Section 5 concludes the paper.

2. BACKGROUND AND RELATED WORK

2.1 Background of STT-RAM Structure

In this section we briefly explain the structural model of STT-RAM. STT-RAM is a type of nonvolatile memory utilized for cache designs in computer architectures in recent years.

Figure 2 shows the overall structure of STT-RAM formed of two components. One of them is an NMOS transistor that is called access transistor and another component is a magnetic tunnel junction (MTJ). MTJ consists of two ferromagnetic layers called free and fixed layers. Fixed (free) layer has a fixed (variable) magnetic direction. Magnetic direction of the free layer changes based on the direction of the current that passes through these layers. The MTJ resistance can be high or low based on the free layer direction. The relative direction of these layers determines the value stored in each cell. Same (opposite) magnetic directions of layers leads to low (high) resistance of MTJ that causes value of cell to become '1' ('0'). STT-RAM has some advantages and drawbacks. High density and low leakage power of STT-RAMs make them suitable candidates to be replaced by current SRAM

Table 1. NvSim and CACTI results

PROPERTY	STT-RAM	SRAM	DIFFERENCE
READ LATENCY (NS)	4.35	4.84	0.89
WRITE LATENCY (NS)	17.9	4.84	3.69
READ ENERGY (NJ)	0.31	0.35	0.86
WRITE ENERGY (NJ)	2.86	0.35	7.90
CELL AREA (MM2)	1.03	4.04	0.25
LEAKAGE POWER	0.04	0.26	0.15
ENDURANCE (ITRS 2013[10])	4×10^{12}	$>10^{16}$	$< 10^{-4}$

cells, especially in LLC. However, high write energy, latency, and low cell endurance are their main challenging issues. Table 1 shows the results of comparing a 2MB SRAM with an STT-RAM in NVSim [11] and CACTI5.1 [12]. As can be seen, using STT-RAM instead of SRAM can reduce area and leakage power significantly while achieving higher density, but the write energy, latency and cell endurance of STT-RAMs are the main problems. Therefore, we focus on the low endurance issue of STT-RAMs used in LLCs. To read structure of STT-RAM cell in detail, we suggest to see [13].

2.2 Overview of Wear-Leveling Techniques

The main goal of cache wear-leveling techniques is mitigating write traffics in the entire cache for lifetime improvement. Due to low endurance property of STT-RAM, researchers propose some algorithms that can be categorized into three groups. The common aim of these methods is balancing the write traffic or reducing write operations over all cache lines. The first group of algorithms focuses on interset wear-leveling techniques implemented with dynamic indexing [3, 6, 14]. This group, to which our proposed method belongs, attempts to distribute write traffic among all sets of the cache. In other word, their granularity is the set level. An example of this group is i2wap [3] which replaces neighbor sets dynamically. The second group are intraset algorithms that balance the write traffic in the ways inside each set [6-8]. For example, in AYUSH [15], Mittal et. al propose a hybrid cache architecture where some ways fabricate with SRAM and the others fabricate with STT-RAM. They suggest way movement between SRAM and STT-RAM based on write count and age bits of the ways. The third group of algorithms consists of write termination algorithms trying to bypass the write to the cache [3, 8]. For example, i2wap also proposes PoLF (Probabilistic Line Flush). In PoLF, after the write count to a set reaches to a flush threshold, the next write to this set is bypassed and PoLF writes to the main memory directly.

The following considerations should be taken into account to implement an efficient algorithm. 1) The algorithm should not impose significant performance overhead. For example, because of ignoring the state of LLC cache blocks and presence of LLC blocks on upper level caches, all of the previous works force the system to move data among cache sets massively or invalid upper level blocks to maintain consistency of cache levels [3, 6]. 2) The algorithm should not impose significant hardware and energy overhead.

3. CLUSTER MAPPING TECHNIQUE FOR WEAR-LEVELING

Distributing the write traffic over cache sets leads to mitigating the endurance problem of STT-RAM and increasing the lifetime of the LLC. Figure 3 shows the architecture of our proposed method. As shown, the cache composes of a number of clusters each consisting of several sets. Our proposed method is based on dynamic cluster virtual address mapping that changes cluster virtual addresses dynamically in order to distribute the write traffic to all cache sets. As mentioned in Section 1, write traffic on neighbor sets is similar because of the locality property of cache.

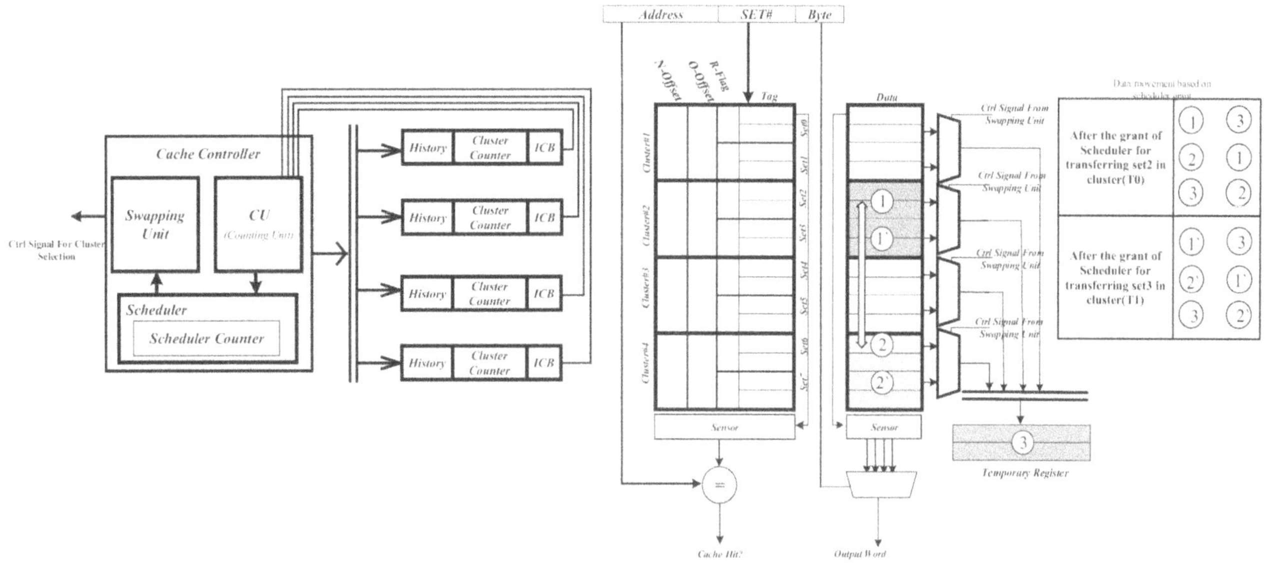

Figure 3. Overall Architecture of our work

Therefore, deciding based on set write traffics imposes unnecessary power and area overhead due to dedicating a counter per set. For example, write traffics on sets of cluster 1 are most likely similar. Therefore, a cluster based policy is chosen to replace hot and cold regions. Deciding based on clusters reduces the number of counters significantly in comparison with dedicating a counter per each set. Hot clusters known with high counter values should be replaced with cold cluster. Choosing a cold cluster is a crucial issue and significantly affects performance. In our policy, in addition to counter value, other factors are considered to select the best cold cluster with the lowest negative impact on performance. On the other side, data movement between the hot and cold clusters are performed during idle times results in fewer CPU cache waiting clocks.

3.1 Lifetime Improvement

3.1.1 Selecting the best candidates for replacing

As shown in Figure 3 a register including three fields --a write counts value, history vector, and a number of invalid-clean blocks (ICB)--, corresponds to each cluster. As mentioned before, the write counts stores the number of write operations of the corresponding cluster. The 2-bit history field preserves the number of times that the cluster has been known as a hot cluster. In the other word, once the write counter value reaches to the threshold value, the history counter increases by one. The ICB field stores the number of invalid-clean blocks of each cluster. To find the best choice among cold clusters, first of all, the write count values of their register are considered. At the next step, a subset of clusters will be selected based on their history vector and ICB fields. In other words, while the write count field is given higher priority to identify the cold cluster, the history vector and IBC play a secondary role in selecting the cold cluster. After selection of a cold cluster, hot cluster sets should be moved to the cold cluster sets and vice versa, but unnecessary movements can be avoided using a state-aware movement algorithm that exchange sets of clusters based on their states. To data movements, an ideal cold cluster is known by a higher value on its IBC field of its register. On the other hand, clusters with lower history vector value are better replacing candidates because they have been known lower times as a hot cluster in comparison with the others. Therefore, selection among cold clusters is a trade-off between performance and lifetime. The comparator unit handles the selection of cold cluster among all clusters.

3.2 Performance Enhancement

After finding hot and cold clusters, virtual addresses of the hot and cold cluster are replaced. In addition to address exchanging, data of the clusters must be exchanged too. Data movement and data invalidation are two mechanisms for mapping each set [5]. Both mechanisms impose area and performance overhead. In the data movement, some temporary storages and extra time are needed to transfer data. In the data invalidation, first, each cache line data is written back to the main memory and then invalided. Then new data are loaded to it. Therefore, it occupies bandwidth of the main memory and decreases the performance. To avoid such performance loss, we propose a hybrid solution using data movement and invalidation mechanism based on the block states.

3.2.1 Decision on data movement or data invalidation

Our proposed mechanism considers block states to exchange data. Block states on upper level caches and LLC determine to choose among data invalidation, movement, or both. Each block associates with a coherency state in the LLC. In the cache-centric architecture, the state of a block in the LLC is an aggregation of the states of this block in each private caches. For example, if a block in all caches is in the *Invalid* state, then the LLC state for this block is *Invalid*. If a block is in *Shared* state in one or more caches, then the LLC state is *Shared [16]*. Table 2 shows different scenarios with which we face. If the block is not present in the upper level cache which specifying with cache coherency states, there would be two possible decisions. 1) If the block is at clean state in the LLC, there is no need to write-back or invalidate the block. 2) If the LLC block is at dirty state, it should be written back and then invalidated. Now, assume that the block is present in the upper level cache causing data movement between two sets using a temporary register. This is because of frequent accesses to this block at upper level cache. Therefore, invalidating the block results in significant performance loss due to invalidation at the upper level cache. As shown in Figure 3 the swapping unit make decision about these policies.

Table 2. Decision making about invalidation or movement

Presence in the upper level	LLC State	Decision
×	Clean	No action
	Dirty	Write-back, Invalidate
✓	Unimportant	Move with temporary storage

3.2.2 Scheduling for data movement

To minimize performance overhead, exchanging set data does not take place immediately after finding the hot and cold clusters. It is shown that many applications consist of computation and memory phases [17]. In the computation phase, there is low traffic on LLC that we call them idle time. Therefore, utilizing these idle times for moving the set data between clusters, improves performance efficiency of the method. Idle times are predicted based on recent access pattern to cache. Suppose that the scheduler needs k cycles to move a set in the worst case. Figure 4 shows the probability of no access to the cache for the next k cycles if the LLC has no access (Read/Write) in the k recent cycles.

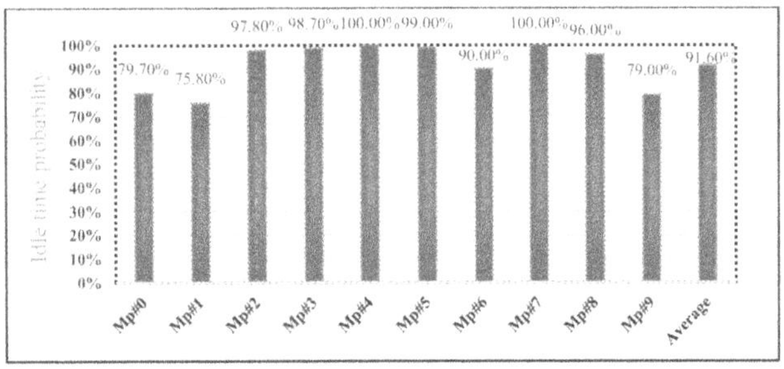

Figure 4. Idle time probability in LCC

We select memory intensive benchmark from SPEC CPU2006 that have a high access rate to the main memory and LLC (the system configuration will be shown in Section 4.1). The value of k is selected based on the worst case scenario in which a set must be transferred (here k=192 cycles). Results shown in Figure. 4, demonstrate that the probability is more than 90% in 70% of the benchmarks. Although the worst case scenario is considered, there are many invalid blocks in clusters, which do not need any data movement.

When the counting unit receives counting values of the clusters, and then finds a hot cluster and a suitable cold cluster is identified as a good replacing candidate, it triggers the scheduler to find a period of time in which the LLC is idle. Now, the scheduler counter starts to count the number of consecutive clocks in which LLC is idle. In the other word, each access to LLC resets the scheduler counter. Once the counter reaches to k (k = 192), it triggers the swapping unit to start data movement between hot and cold clusters. Based on Figure 4, the scheduler assumes there is most likely no access to LLC in the second k consecutive clocks. To save the counter values, SRAM cells which don't have the endurance problem. The scheduler has the request queue that does not permit to service any request before the completion of the present request.

3.3 Access to LLC

As mentioned before, to map two clusters, their virtual addresses must be exchanged. After address mapping, the scheduler exchanges data of cluster sets during idle times. As demonstrated in Figure 5 a new offset (N-Offset), old offset (O-Offset) are added to each cluster while a replacement flag (R-Flag) is dedicated to each set. An example is given for better understanding of cluster mapping. Suppose that the counting unit (CU) identifies cluster#0 (shown in red) as a hot cluster and cluster#2 (shown in green) as a cluster for mapping. At first, N-Offset field of the clusters is updated based on physical address distance between hot and cold clusters. For example, corresponding set distance of the two clusters is 4. Therefore, N Offset field of the cluster#0 is assigned to +4 while the corresponding set in cluster#2 is assigned to -4. Consequently, R-Flag bit of cluster sets is assigned to 1 indicating the sets have not been exchanged yet. After each set's data exchange, the corresponding R-Flag is set to 0 indicating the set data are exchanged. In addition, the O-Offset stores the virtual address offset before the mapping phase. During mapping phase, when the cache controller receives a read/write request to a set, the controller adds N-Offset and O-Offset to the virtual address if the R-Flag is 1 and 0 respectively.

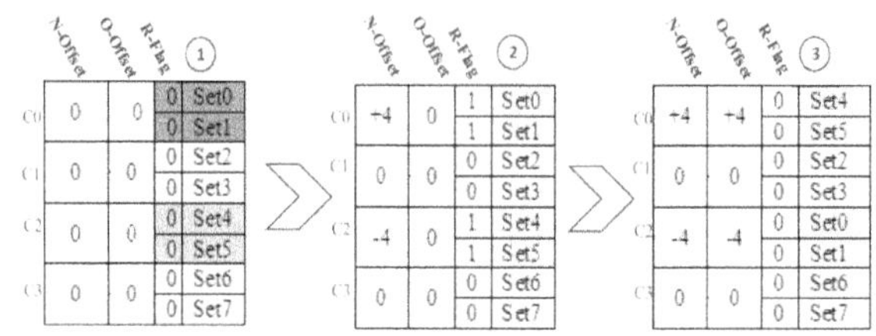

Figure 5. Access to LLC using offset, lookup and dynamic bit

3.4 Hardware Overhead

Table 3 shows overall storage overhead needed for a 2MB 8-way LLC with a block size of 512 bit. The LLC consists of 64 clusters each including 64 sets. The number of clusters is selected based on balancing write traffic variation among clusters and total power optimization analysis (will be explained in 4.2). N-Offset and O-Offset need 12 bits because the maximum distance between physical addresses is 4096. A 12-bit write counter per cluster counts writing operations on each cluster. There are 512 (64 × 8 = 512) blocks per cluster causing to dedicate a 9-bit ICB per cluster. As we need 384 consecutive idle clocks to terminate the movement of set data, a 9-bit scheduler counter is needed. Therefore, the overall storage with overhead is about (including comparator) < 0.1%.

Table 3. Total storage overhead with detail

Module	Storage	Module	Storage
O-Offset	*64 × 12 bits*	ICB	*9 × 64 bits*
N-Offset	*64 × 12 bits*	Scheduling Counter	*9 bits*
R-Flag	*1×4096 bits*	Temporary storage	*4096 bits*
Write Counter	*64 × 12 bits*	History	*64 × 2 bits*

4. EVALUATION RESULTS

4.1 Infrastructure

We evaluate our work with gem5 full system simulator [18]. Table 4 shows the detailed configuration of the system. Each benchmark run in the gem5 simulator is fast-forwarded for 100M instructions, then is simulated for 10B instructions at maximum.

Table 4. Detail system configuration

Detailed infrastructure of our system	
Cores:	4 cores, ISA-Alpha, 3GHz
L1 cache:	32KB, private, 8-way, LRU, 64B, 2 cycles hit latency, SRAM
L2 cache:	2MB, shared, 8-way, LRU, 64B, 10 cycle read latency, 15 cycle write latency, write-back, STT-RAM
Coherency:	MOESI

Table 5. Multiprogram (MP) benchmarks form SPEC CPU2006

Mp	Bench Name	WT	Mp	Bench Name	WT
Mp#0	*2href264+2povray*	*11.8*	Mp#5	*2libquantum+2povray*	*7.5*
Mp#1	*2leslie3d+2lbm*	*10.3*	Mp#6	*2mcf+2sphinx3*	*1.5*
Mp#2	*2bizp2+2milc*	*4.5*	Mp#7	*2perlbench+2gcc*	*3.7*
Mp#3	*2href264+leslie 3d*	*12.3*	Mp#8	*2gcc+2cactulix*	*4.5*
Mp#4	*2hmmer+2astar*	*5.7*	Mp#9	*2omnetpp+gromacs*	*5.3*

4.2 Workloads

We select memory intensive and high write variation benchmarks from SPEC CPU2006 [19] with the *large* input. Table 5 shows the write traffic (WT-Gbps) of selected multiprogram (Mp) benchmarks in each run.

4.3 Determining Write Count Threshold and the Number of Clusters

Figure 6 shows normalized power overhead, the write traffic variation, and instruction per cycle (IPC) degradation for different number of clusters. Such parameters are affected by the number of clusters. Therefore, in order to select the number of clusters, there is a trade-off among these parameters. As can be seen, when the

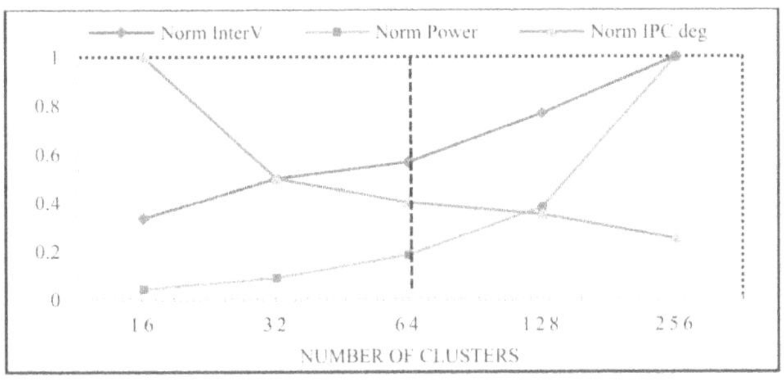

Figure 6. Selection the number of clusters

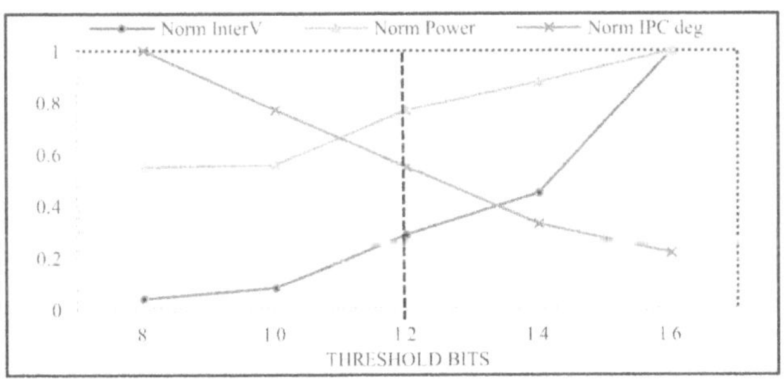

Figure 7. Write count bits width Threshold bits selection

cache consists of 64 clusters (the dotted line), a fairness is achieved among such parameters. After that, the number of clusters is fixed to 64 and the same procedure is used to select the write count threshold. As shown in Figure 7, selecting a 12-bit counter (the dotted line) makes a tradeoff among the parameters.

4.4 Evaluation Metrics

Three parameters are compared to evaluate the proposed method:

- InterV (the coefficient of inter-set variations) [3]
- LLC lifetime
- Performance overhead

All these results are compared with the baseline and the Sequoia method finally.

4.4.1 InterV and lifetime

InterV is the coefficient of interset variation in the wear leveling technique that represents the variation of write traffics in all sets. In addition, according to [6], LLC lifetime is the time that 1% of all cache lines become faulty. Figure 10 shows the comparison between the proposed method and Sequoia (G-OAS). Although the selection of hot and cold clusters is based on clusters instead of sets, our proposed method improves InterV by 63% and 11% in comparison with base line and Sequoia respectively. This values are 31% and 2% for lifetime improvement. Figure 9 shows snapshots captured in three different times: in a random time (t0) before applying our method (Figure 9.a), the time after t0 and before applying the method which C2 becomes hotter in comparison with t0 (Figure 9.b), and t2 in which C2 and C4 are mapped to each other which causes the rising write traffic of C2 is transferred to C4 (Figure 9.c). One may argue that this improvement is slight in comparison with the related work, but the main improvement against that work is performance efficiency explained in the next part.

4.4.2 Performance and power overhead

The main focus of our wear-leveling algorithm is its effectiveness of data movement. comparison with Sequoia.

Table 6 demonstrates IPC degradation, write-back and the miss rate caused by the write-backs. As can be seen, our proposed method imposes IPC degradation, write-back (W-B) and the miss rate (M-R) overhead by 5.38%, 4.8%, and 1.07% respectively. In comparison with Sequoia [6], our method improves IPC degradation, write-back rate and the miss rate by 27.5%, 33.3%, and 23.5% respectively (Figure 8). Because of using a counter per cluster instead of set, the number of counters is reduced significantly causing a considerable power and area saving (89% on average) extracted using a synthesis tool in comparison with Sequoia.

Table 6. Performance overhead of our work

Bench	W-B %	M-R %	IPC %	Bench	W-B %	M-R %	IPC %
Mp#0	*9*	*0.01*	*1.2*	**Mp#5**	*2*	*7.02*	*0.5*
Mp#1	*0.1*	*5.21*	*1.8*	**Mp#6**	*5.15*	*8.11*	*1.7*
Mp#2	*2*	*8.01*	*0.5*	**Mp#7**	*17*	*5.01*	*0.3*
Mp#3	*7.5*	*3.31*	*1.1*	**Mp#8**	*5.12*	*1.12*	*2.4*
Mp#4	*4*	*2.02*	*0.2*	**Mp#9**	*2*	*9.05*	*1*

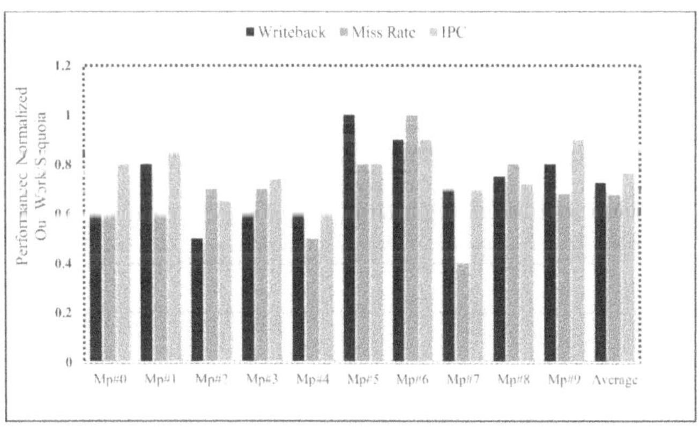

Figure 8. Performance Comparison between our work and Sequoia (G-OAS)

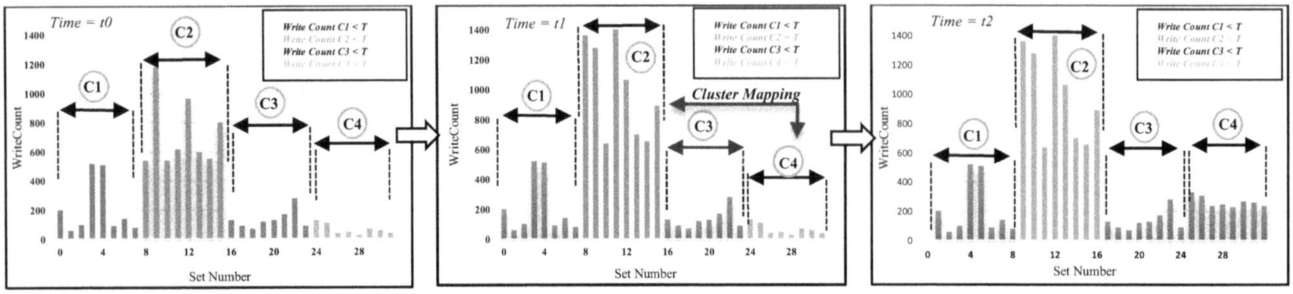

(a) (b) (c)

Figure 9. Write traffic distribution using our method

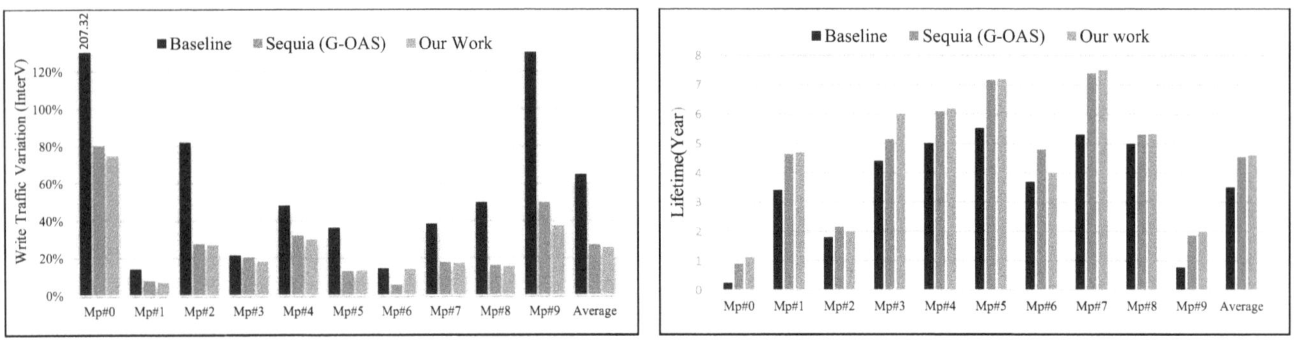

Figure 10. Comparison of lifetime and InterV between the proposed method and Sequoia (G-OAS)

5. CONCLUSION

In this paper, a performance efficient method to improve LLC lifetime is presented. In addition to lifetime, this method imposes low performance overhead in comparison with previous work. To the best of our knowledge, this is the first work which presents a cluster level wear-leveling method causing a significant performance efficiency in comparison with set level techniques. Cluster level wear-leveling comes from the fact that there is a write traffic correlation among near physical sets being on the same cluster. Moreover, to select a cold cluster, the state of its blocks is considered in addition to its write traffic. To minimize CPU stalls caused by data movement among clusters, a heuristic technique is used to utilize idle times for data movement. Experimental results reveal that our method improves life time by 30% and 2% in comparison with baseline and Sequoia. 28.1% and 89% improvement in performance and power proves our claim about performance and power efficiency in comparison with Sequoia.

6. REFRENCES

[1] B. Bowhill *et al.*, "4.5 The Xeon® processor E5-2600 v3: A 22nm 18-core product family." pp. 1-3.

[2] S. Li *et al.*, "CACTI-P: Architecture-level modeling for SRAM-based structures with advanced leakage reduction techniques." pp. 694-701.

[3] J. Wang *et al.*, "i 2 WAP: Improving non-volatile cache lifetime by reducing inter-and intra-set write variations." pp. 234-245.

[4] M. K. Qureshi *et al.*, "Phase change memory: From devices to systems," *Synthesis Lectures on Computer Architecture,* vol. 6, no. 4, pp. 1-134, 2011.

[5] Y.-B. Kim *et al.*, "Bi-layered RRAM with unlimited endurance and extremely uniform switching." pp. 52-53.

[6] M. R. Jokar *et al.*, "Sequoia: A High-Endurance NVM-Based Cache Architecture."

[7] S. Mittal *et al.*, "WriteSmoothing: improving lifetime of non-volatile caches using intra-set wear-leveling." pp. 139-144.

[8] S. Mittal *et al.*, "LastingNVCache: A technique for improving the lifetime of non-volatile caches." pp. 534-540.

[9] http://www.eetimes.com.

[10] http://www.itrs.net.

[11] X. Dong *et al.*, "Nvsim: A circuit-level performance, energy, and area model for emerging nonvolatile memory," *Computer-Aided Design of Integrated Circuits and Systems, IEEE Transactions on,* vol. 31, no. 7, pp. 994-1007, 2012.

[12] S. Thoziyoor *et al.*, "CACTI 5.1," *HP Laboratories, April,* vol. 2, pp. 24, 2008.

[13] H. Li *et al.*, "An overview of non-volatile memory technology and the implication for tools and architectures." pp. 731-736.

[14] S. Mittal, "Using cache-coloring to mitigate inter-set write variation in non-volatile caches," *arXiv preprint arXiv:1310.8494*, 2013.

[15] S. Mittal *et al.*, "AYUSH: A Technique for Extending Lifetime of SRAM-NVM Hybrid Caches," 2014.

[16] D. J. Sorin *et al.*, "A primer on memory consistency and cache coherence," *Synthesis Lectures on Computer Architecture,* vol. 6, no. 3, pp. 1-212, 2011.

[17] Y. Kim *et al.*, "ATLAS: A scalable and high-performance scheduling algorithm for multiple memory controllers." pp. 1-12.

[18] N. Binkert *et al.*, "The gem5 simulator," *ACM SIGARCH Computer Architecture News,* vol. 39, no. 2, pp. 1-7, 2011.

[19] J. L. Henning, "SPEC CPU2006 benchmark descriptions," *ACM SIGARCH Computer Architecture News,* vol. 34, no. 4, pp. 1-17, 2006.

A Low-Power Network-on-Chip Architecture for Tile-based Chip Multi-Processors

Anastasios Psarras
ECE, Democritus University of Thrace, Xanthi, Greece

Junghee Lee
ECE, University of Texas at San Antonio, USA

Pavlos Mattheakis
Mentor Graphics
Grenoble, France

Chrysostomos Nicopoulos
ECE, University of Cyprus, Nicosia, Cyprus

Giorgos Dimitrakopoulos
ECE, Democritus University of Thrace, Xanthi, Greece

ABSTRACT

Technology scaling of tiled-based CMPs reduces the physical size of each tile and increases the number of tiles per die. This trend directly impacts the on-chip interconnect; even though the tile population increases, the inter-tile link distances scale down proportionally to the tile dimensions. The decreasing inter-tile wire lengths can be exploited to enable swift link traversal between neighboring tiles, after appropriate wire engineering. Building on this premise, we propose a technique to rapidly transfer flits between adjacent routers in *half a clock cycle*, by utilizing both edges of the clock during the sending and receiving operations. Half-cycle link traversal enables, for the first time, substantial reductions in (a) link power, *irrespective of the data switching profile*, and (b) buffer power (through buffer-size reduction), without incurring any latency/throughput loss. In fact, the proposed architecture also yields some latency improvements over a baseline NoC. Detailed hardware analysis using placed-and-routed designs, and cycle-accurate full-system simulations corroborate the significant power and latency improvements.

1. INTRODUCTION

Technology scaling and power constraints have led to a fundamental paradigm shift in digital system design: the transition to the multi-core paradigm. Consequently, the role of the on-chip communication fabric has become pivotal to the system's operation. Networks-on-Chip (NoC) have been established as the dominant communication backbone in multi-core environments, primarily due to their innate scalability attributes.

There are two primary variants of multi-core systems: (1) Multi-Processor Systems-on-Chip (MPSoC), and (2) Chip Multi-Processors (CMP). These two multi-core incarnations have distinct attributes, which directly impact their NoC architecture. This work focuses on CMPs and aims to capitalize on one of their key (and differentiating) characteristic: the regularity in their physical layout. Unlike MPSoCs, which typically integrate a variety of IP cores of disparate physical sizes, homogeneous CMPs contain a number of identical CPU cores. This homogeneity in physical size has given rise to tile-based CMPs, whereby the system comprises a number of identically-sized logic blocks, called *tiles*. Each tile contains one, or more, CPU cores, private L1 instruction and data caches, a slice of L2 cache (more cache levels are possible), and a gateway to a NoC connecting the tiles [26, 21]. Tiling facilitates easy integration of multiple cores on the same die, and it enhances the design's scalability to increasing numbers of cores. The prevalent NoC topology in CMP designs is the 2D mesh, which is amenable to tile-based layouts [4].

Since the overall size of a CMP die tends to remain constant across different processor generations (due to yield and cost issues), any increase in the number of on-chip tiles is inevitably accompanied by a corresponding decrease in the size of each tile. This attribute has a profound impact on the system's NoC. The effective network throughput per core decreases (due to elevated cross traffic), while the average source-to-destination hop-count increases (due to increasing network diameter). Thus, both latency and throughput suffer as the NoC mesh size increases to accommodate the extra CMP tiles. At the same time, the escalating numbers of on-chip tiles inevitably affect the NoC's *power* budget. The router buffers and the inter-router links constitute the two major NoC power consumers [4, 11]. To sustain scalability into the many-core realm, it is imperative to curtail the power expended in NoC buffering and link traversal, *without* incurring any latency/throughput penalties.

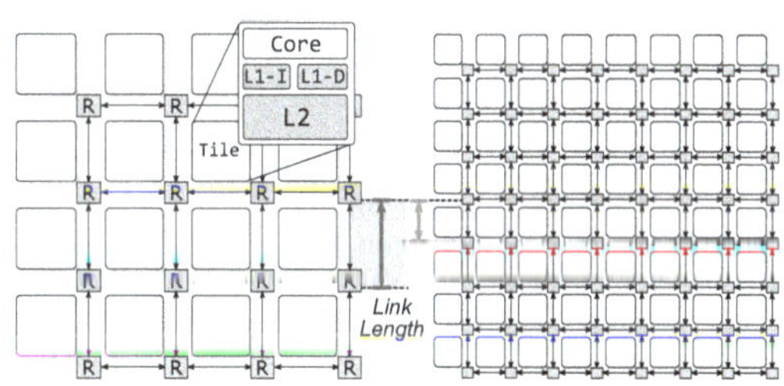

Figure 1: Under equal die size, as the population of tiles increases, the inter-tile link length decreases. This phenomenon is illustrated here by comparing a 16-core CMP (left) to a 64-core CMP (right).

On the other hand, even though the number of tiles increases, the inter-tile link distances scale *down* proportionally to the decreasing tile dimensions. Figure 1 illustrates

GLSVLSI '16, May 18-20, 2016, Boston, MA, USA
© 2016 ACM. ISBN 978-1-4503-4274-2/16/05...$15.00
DOI: http://dx.doi.org/10.1145/2902961.2903010

this effect by comparing the link lengths of two different processor generations, comprising 16 and 64 cores, respectively. For instance, at the 32 nm technology node, the longest side of a typical CMP tile (i.e., CPU core + 32 kB L1 instruction and data caches + 512 kB L2 cache slice) is 3.27 mm, as demonstrated in [23], while this distance is reduced to only 0.9 mm in 15 nm technology [1]. Thus, the inter-tile wire connections of future CMPs will hardly exceed 1 mm.

In this paper, we aim to harness the swift wire traversal made possible by wire engineering to enable low-power NoCs for future CMPs, which are characterized by: (a) scaled inter-tile wire lengths and increasing network sizes (i.e., the tile size decreases due to technology scaling, while the on-chip tile population increases), and (b) constant, or modestly increasing, clock frequencies. Rather than using the wire speed to cover longer distances in a given cycle [23, 1, 13, 14], we propose exploiting said swiftness to *rapidly transfer flits* between adjacent routers in *half a clock cycle*, by *utilizing both edges of the clock* during the sending and receiving of flits. By leveraging half-cycle link traversal we achieve a double-faceted objective:

- **Link-power reduction**, by substantially lowering the effective wire capacitance. The latter is reduced irrespective of the data profile, and by altering only the physical layout of the link wires. The attained wire-capacitance reduction renders, in turn, the half-cycle constraint easier to satisfy.
- **Buffer reduction**, by significantly reducing the credit Round-Trip Time (RTT), which lowers the full-throughput buffering requirements to a size smaller than the current minimum. The decrease in RTT is facilitated by a novel switch allocator micro-architecture.

Both aforementioned achievements translate into **tangible and extensive NoC power savings**, without adversely impacting the latency/throughput performance. On the contrary, the new architecture also yields some latency improvements over a baseline NoC. The proposed design is investigated in detail and quantitatively explored to highlight its potential. Extensive cycle-accurate simulations using both synthetic traffic patterns, and execution-driven full-system simulations with real application workloads, validate the efficiency of the new low-power NoC architecture. Furthermore, detailed hardware analysis using placed-and-routed designs synthesized in a 45 nm standard-cell library corroborates the achieved significant power improvements.

2. BACKGROUND & RELATED WORK

There is a rich body of work related to low-power NoC design, which can be broadly categorized into two main thrusts: (a) *policy-based*, and (b) *structural* approaches. The former category includes such techniques as Dynamic Voltage and Frequency Scaling (DVFS) and power gating, which reap power benefits based on prevailing conditions. Specifically, DVFS techniques have been used to lower the power consumption of the links [24], and/or other components [21, 20, 8]. Power gating has also been employed – at various implementation granularities – to contain the NoC's power envelope [12, 7]. Being policy-driven, all these approaches are complementary to the design proposed here.

The proposed design falls into the second category of *structural* low-power approaches that involve modifications to the NoC topology and architecture, as in [25].As such, the extracted benefits are not traffic- or scenario-dependent; they are inherent to the design and are always present.

Recently, researchers have leveraged ultra-fast wire traversal techniques, enabled by wire engineering, to expedite the traversal of flits across the NoC of tile-based CMPs. The resulting solutions led to either high-radix networks [23, 1, 13] with long connecting links, or to networks that allow flits to traverse multiple network hops of shorter wires in a single clock cycle (through router bypassing) [14]. Both techniques reduce the average hop count, which results in a decrease in the number of buffer read/write operations, and, hence, a decrease in power consumption. Nevertheless, while some power is saved, there is *no impact on buffer sizing*; the buffer size requirements are unaffected, since the credit-notification loop (aka round-trip time) does not change. On the other hand, buffer-less alternatives [9] effectively reduce the total number of buffers, but with significant throughput losses.

The effectiveness of the aforementioned solutions relies on their fundamental property of transferring flits over longer distances in a single clock cycle. This property becomes increasingly difficult to sustain for constant-length wires, since wire delay increases with technology scaling. However, appropriate semi-custom wire engineering, which involves (a) routing in upper metal layers to reduce resistance, (b) increased wire spacing to reduce the wire coupling capacitance, and (c) appropriate repeater placement, can partially alleviate the problem [17]. Several recent NoC designs [1, 14, 17, 15] have achieved single-cycle traversal of medium-to-long links by assuming repeated wire delays of 70–200 ps/mm. Similar wire speeds have been reported by Intel and IBM [21, 10]. Hence, achieving fast wire traversal speeds in *scaled-down* links (i.e., wire lengths that scale *down* as a result of decreasing tile dimensions) is more easily attainable.

The proposed architecture in this paper harnesses: (a) the swift link traversal speed of 70–200 ps/mm facilitated by repeaters and wire spacing in upper metal layers [1, 14, 17, 15], and (b) a fundamental reduction in link-wire capacitance provided by the new design, to reap **benefits in *both* power consumption and network latency**. By deliberately creating an *artificial asymmetry* between the *intra-* and *inter-*router delays of tile-based CMPs, we achieve half-cycle link traversal. Currently, the fastest state-of-the-art NoC routers for 2D meshes exhibit intra-router delays ranging from 600 ps to 1100 ps [21, 23, 14] (measured at voltages of around 0.8 V), i.e., more than 2× longer than the typical inter-tile link delay for scaled tile dimensions. By leveraging this attribute, the proposed NoC architecture can markedly **reduce both the link power and the buffer size**, in addition to improving performance. The designs of [6, 19] also employ both edges of the clock for link traversal. However, their aim is the simplification of clock distribution, without offering any power benefits.

The asymmetry between intra- and inter-router delays is also evident in asynchronous NoCs [3]. However, asynchronous circuits tend to be very complex to design and validate. Thus, the design proposed here infuses some of the benefits of asynchronous NoCs into a synchronous setup.

3. FACILITATING HALF-CYCLE LINKS

In the proposed architecture, adjacent routers (placed at the corners of neighboring tiles, as shown in Figure 2) operate under opposite clock edges. The 2D mesh topology makes the connectivity look like a checkerboard pattern. Flits have a full cycle to execute all router operations, but only half a cycle to get from one router to the next.

Figure 3 illustrates a single-flit packet traversing three network nodes. In the top timing diagram of Figure 3, the network – which employs the proposed architecture – consists of white and gray nodes, which operate on the positive and negative clock edges, respectively. In cycle 0, the flit is injected and written in the input buffer of router A, on the

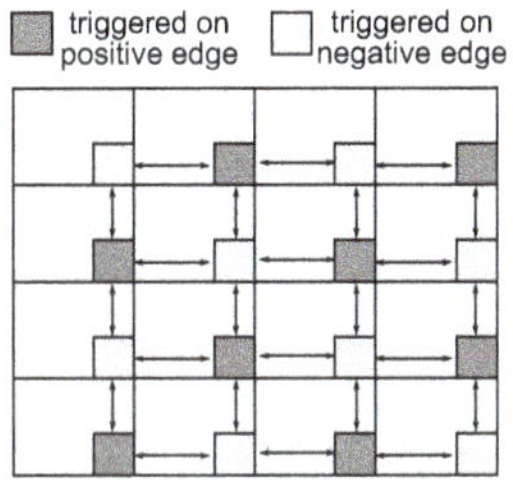

Figure 2: Mesh topology for a tiled CMP employing alternate clock edges for adjacent routers.

positive clock edge. The flit spends a whole cycle executing router operations and is eventually written on the next positive clock edge in the router's output register. Half a cycle later, the flit has crossed the whole link (Link Traversal, LT) and is written in the input buffer of router B, captured on the negative clock edge. A whole cycle is again spent inside the router, until the flit appears at the output link after the negative edge of cycle 2. Router C captures the flit on the positive edge of cycle 3, allowing the flit to eventually appear in the output register, and leave in cycle 4.

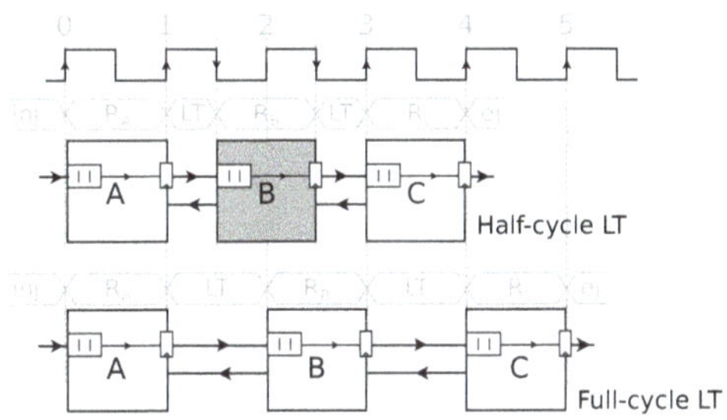

Figure 3: Networks-on-Chip with half-cycle links are built by restricting adjacent routers to operating on opposite clock edges. The small wire delay (for reasonably scaled inter-tile wire lengths) allows wire traversal to be completed in half a cycle.

The same scenario without half-cycle links is depicted in the bottom timing diagram of Figure 3, in which only positive-edge routers are used. The flit spends a full cycle for both link and router traversals, eventually being ejected one cycle later than in the top diagram. Note that, in both cases, the links have the same length; scaling is merely used for illustrative purposes (to depict the timing difference).

Half-cycle links decrease the NoC's zero-load latency, using the same routers, and while working under the same clock frequency, relative to a baseline NoC with full-cycle links. In baseline NoCs with single-cycle routers (i.e., one cycle is spent in the router and one cycle on the link), zero-load latency in absolute time (number of cycles divided by the clock frequency) equals $T = (2H + L - 1)/f_{CLK}$, assuming an L-flit packet that has to traverse H hops to its destination. When the same packet traverses a NoC with half-cycle links, it saves half a cycle in each hop, resulting in a latency of $T_{RL} = (1.5H + L - 1)/f_{CLK}$. This translates to 8% to 25% latency savings, considering a packet length range of 1 to 5 flits, which travel in the NoC from 1 to 8 hops away.

4. LINK CAPACITANCE REDUCTION

Half-cycle links allow for significant effective wire capacitance reduction without any performance overhead. Lower wire capacitance leads to lower power dissipation in the links of the NoC, while it enables faster wire traversal.

The total interconnect capacitance is the sum of ground and coupling capacitances, C_{GND} and C_C. The effective C_C depends on the switching behavior of adjacent wires, which is characterized by the Miller Coupling Factor (MCF) in Equation (1):

$$C_{RE} = C_{GND} + 2 \times MCF \times C_C \qquad (1)$$

The MCF parameter is 0 when all adjacent wires switch in the same direction, and the total wire capacitance is only C_{GND}. On the contrary, MCF is 2 when adjacent wires switch in the opposite direction.

It is possible to reduce coupling capacitance by increasing the wire spacing, or by introducing shielding (interleaving constant VDD/GND wires and data wires), but this comes at the cost of an area penalty. Wire spacing effectively reduces the value of C_C, while shielding decreases MCF. A key challenge in interconnect design is to reduce either C_C, or the worst-case MCF, while maintaining the same physical footprint of the interconnect, thereby reducing the effective wire capacitance, the delay, and energy consumption.

In the new NoC design proposed in this paper, wire capacitance is significantly reduced by exploiting the out-of-phase operation of the two unidirectional links that connect two adjacent routers. Assume, for example, the routers A and B shown in Figure 4. The A→B link is used to transfer data from router A to router B. Data is launched on the positive edge of the clock and captured on the negative edge of the clock by the input buffers of router B. On the contrary, data from B to A is transferred on the other half-period, starting from the negative edge and ending on the next positive edge. In this case, when one direction is activated in one half of the clock cycle, the other one remains idle, waiting for the other half to send its data (the timing diagram of Figure 4 depicts this behavior).

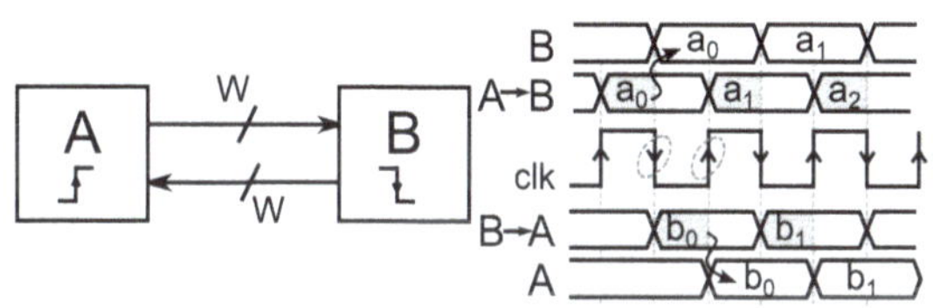

Figure 4: Since flits are launched and captured on alternate clock edges, only one of the two inter-router links is active in each half-cycle.

Based on this property of link activation in different clock phases, we can employ wire interleaving in the physical layout. The wires of the two uni-directional buses connecting adjacent routers are interleaved, as shown in Figure 5. This pattern eliminates the undesired MCF=2 of the coupling capacitances of neighboring wires.

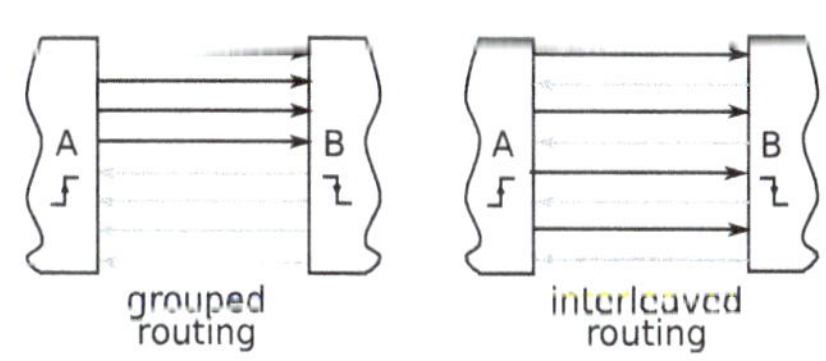

Figure 5: Wire-interleaving of half-cycle links limits the worst-case MCF to 1 (rather than 2), independent of the data-switching activity profile.

Wire-interleaving prohibits adjacent wires from switching in opposite directions, thus **achieving a worst-case MCF of 1 (rather than 2)**, *independent of the switching activity* profile of the transmitted data. Bit i of the link from A to B is routed between bits i and $i-1$ of the link from B to A. Since the two links are **never active in the same half-cycle**, when bit i of the A→B link makes a new transition, it is guaranteed that its adjacent bits – that belong to the B→A link – are "quiet," since they have completed their transitions in the previous half-cycle. The adjacent wires can be considered as active shields for the bit that changes its value. The same situation occurs in the next half-cycle, which drives the wires of the opposite direction. Overall, in any half-cycle, every bit will make a transition with the *guarantee that its neighbors remain constant.* Due to this property, MCF cannot exceed 1, thereby offering a significant reduction in the effective wire capacitance. This guarantee holds for all links of the NoC in either direction, which provides significant overall energy savings. As proven in [22], the energy savings in the links when limiting the largest value of MCF to 1 (as opposed to 2) is equal to

$$E_{s\quad ing} = 1 - \frac{C_{\quad RE(MC\quad =1)} V_{DD}^2}{C_{\quad RE(MC\quad =2)} V_{DD}^2} = 1 - \frac{C_{GND} + 2C_C}{C_{GND} + 4C_C}$$

The energy savings range between 25% and 40%, depending on the value of C_C, relative to C_{GND}, which depends on the metal layer and the wire geometry and spacing [22]. Moreover, note that the lower wire capacitance makes link traversal even faster, thus making the half-cycle requirement easier to achieve for the scaled inter-tile links.

5. ROUTER BUFFER REDUCTION

Half-cycle links change the notification loop of credit-based flow control, since data is sent in the forward direction on one edge of the clock, while credit updates are returned in the reverse direction on the opposite edge of the clock. This effectively *reduces the Round-Trip Time (RTT) by one cycle.* The RTT is the number of elapsed cycles between the time the receiver sends back a credit, and the time a flit using that particular credit arrives at the receiver.

The credit notification loop starts from and ends at flow-controlled storage elements, such as the FIFO buffers. Any pipeline register (without embedded flow control), e.g., the ones used at the outputs of the routers, increase the RTT. The minimum buffering required on the receiver side to achieve full throughput operation is determined by the RTT. A smaller RTT value translates into lower input-buffering requirements to achieve full-throughput operation.

To enjoy the decreased RTT, the credit updates that arrive at the middle of the cycle must be reused immediately. In this way, if credit updates are not handled appropriately, combinational paths launching in the middle of the cycle are created. These could potentially degrade the router's speed. To avoid this negative effect and still enjoy the reduced RTT and its associated buffer-saving properties, we redesign the Switch Allocation (SA) stage of the NoC routers.

In fast VC-based router architectures, such as [16], the SA stage receives only *qualified* requests. A request is qualified to participate in SA, as long as it refers to an output VC that has available credits. If credit-checking is not performed before-hand, then a grant may be given to an input VC that cannot actually use it, thus leaving the selected output port idle. In fast implementations [16], VC allocation occurs through SA: once a head flit is assigned to an output port, it also receives an available output VC for that output port.

In the proposed architecture, we employ two SA units, the

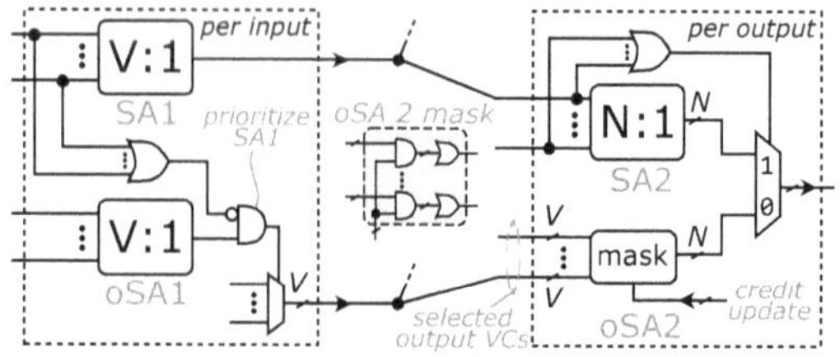

Figure 6: The proposed architecture employs two switch allocation units (one primary and a simplified oblivious one), in order to allow any credit updates arriving at the middle of the cycle to be reused immediately. Parameters N and V represent the number of router input ports and the number of VCs per port, respectively.

Primary SA (*pSA*) and the Oblivious SA (*oSA*) units, placed in parallel, as shown in Figure 6. Being the primary unit, *pSA* performs the normal SA operation, including credit-checking. The *oSA* unit performs, in parallel, the same task (albeit in a simplified manner), but it only accepts the requests of the inputs (or input VCs) that refer to outputs (or output VCs) without any credit available.

When an output VC has available credits and an input VC is requesting it, then this resource will definitely be utilized. In this case, handling the credits returning in the middle of the cycle is not critical. The half-cycle credit updates become critical when the requested resource appears to be unavailable on one edge of the clock, but becomes available on the next opposite edge of the clock (recall that neighboring routers operate on alternate clock edges). For this case, the *oSA* unit allows one request from each input port to qualify for an output request, as long as it refers to an *unavailable* output VC. The request can only eventually be granted if the specific output VC becomes available in the middle of the cycle, through a credit update. In any case, the *pSA* unit's decisions are always prioritized over *oSA*'s.

The operation of *oSA* is split in two stages, as shown in Figure 6. In the first stage (*oSA1*), each input port independently selects one input VC headed to an unavailable output VC. The *oSA1* winners reach their destined output port, where at most one winner is determined in *oSA2*. At this point, half the critical path has been traversed, and, thus, the credit-update signals have arrived. Since only one credit update for a single output VC may arrive for each output port, only the input request that refers to that output VC can be granted. All other requests refer to output VCs that are still unavailable and are discarded through a masking process, without the need for any arbitration. Thus, the *oSA2* stage is a simple masking process, unlike the more complicated second-stage arbitration process typically found in SA units. Note that the only extra logic added by *oSA* can be seen in the lower half of Figure 6; the upper half illustrates the organization of a baseline SA.

In this way, the incoming credit-update signal is used with no delay cost, and this enables immediate credit consumption, which effectively **lowers the credit notification loop by 1 cycle**. One half-cycle is saved in the forward data direction, and one half-cycle is saved in the backward (credit-update) direction. Reducing the RTT by one cycle translates to a saving of one buffer slot per VC. In the case of skewed traffic, each VC (independently of the rest) should have as many buffer slots as the link's RTT, in order to ensure full-throughput of data transfers.

6. EXPERIMENTAL EVALUATION

In this section, we evaluate the performance of the proposed NoC architecture and compare it – in terms of **hardware complexity** and **network performance** – with baseline NoC architectures that assume full-cycle link traversal.

As previously explained, the two fundamental contributions of the new design are: (1) the *link* power reduction, and (2) the *buffer size* reduction (thereby leading to further overall power reduction). We begin our evaluation by assessing the improvements in power consumption obtained when using the proposed architecture.

Figure 7 depicts the normalized power of an 8×8 (2D mesh) baseline NoC with full-cycle links ("Base"), as compared to the proposed design with half-cycle links ("Proposed"). Both designs operate at 1 GHz, support 2, 4, and 6 VCs per port, and the NoC routers (with 5 input/output ports, as needed by the 2D mesh topology) are connected with 2 mm 64-bit links (following the floor-planning sizes of [23]). In each configuration, VC buffers include 3 slots/VC for the baseline case and 2 slots/VC for the proposed architecture, which are enough to cover the RTT in each case. All NoC designs under investigation were implemented in VHDL, synthesized, and placed-and-routed using a 45 nm 0.8 V standard-cell library.

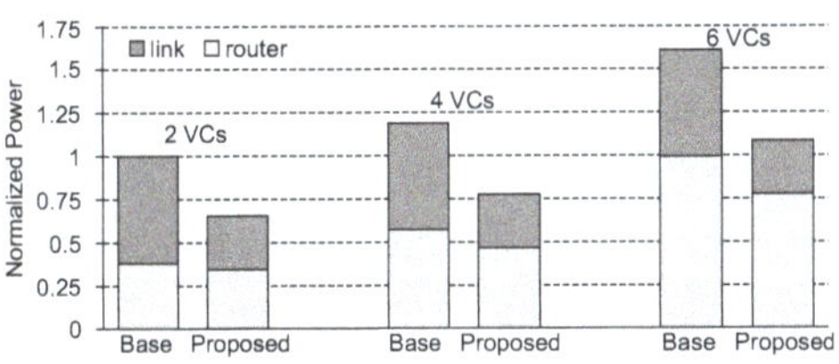

Figure 7: The normalized power consumption of the proposed architecture, as compared to a baseline NoC with full-cycle links. Power savings are due to both link- and buffer-power reductions.

From the obtained results, measured under equal NoC utilization (throughput), we observe that the savings in both the *link* and *buffer* power consumption (due to reduced wire capacitance and smaller buffers, respectively) offered by the new design translate to significant *overall* NoC power savings of 34%, on average. It is evident that the contributions of both the link optimizations and the buffer reduction are significant for all examined VC configurations. Specifically, link power reduction accounts for 75%, on average, of the total power savings, with the remaining 25% being attributed to the buffer power reduction.

Besides power reduction, the proposed router design also achieves small area savings, mostly due to the buffer reduction, which outweighs the small area added by the second SA unit. Recall that the latter is added to handle the credit updates arriving at the middle of the cycle, without any delay penalty.

Note that the results obtained here (i.e., at 45 nm and assuming a 2 mm inter-tile distance) can also scale to smaller technologies, assuming (a) a diminishing tile area, and (b) slowly increasing clock frequencies. As previously mentioned, these two assumptions are already part of the prevailing tendency in current CMP design practices.

Having established the substantial power reduction enabled by the proposed design, it is now imperative to assess its impact on overall system *performance*. Toward this end, we simulate a 64-core tiled CMP system running real application workloads on a commodity operating system.

Table 1: Full-system simulation parameters.

Processor	64 in-order x86 cores in a tiled CMP
OS	Linux Fedora
L1 caches	Private, separate 32 KB I & D, 4-way set associative, 2-cycle latency, 64 B cache-line
L2 cache	Shared NUCA LLC, 4-way set associative, 16 MB total (64 cores×256 KB slice/core), 10-cycle latency, 64 B cache-line
Coherence	MOESI directory-based protocol
Main memory	4 GB, 300-cycle latency
Network	8×8 2D Mesh, 1-cycle routers +1 or +0.5 cycle link delay, XY routing, 128-bit inter-router links (flit width)

The simulation framework employs the Simics simulator, extended with GEMS [18] and the GARNET [2] cycle-accurate NoC simulator. Table 1 shows the full-system simulation parameters.

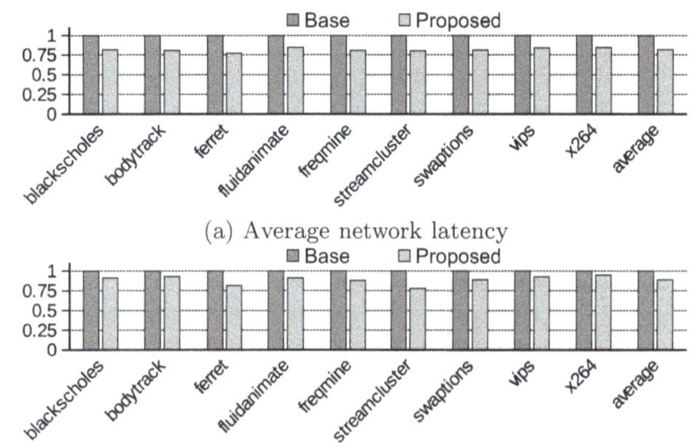

(a) Average network latency

(b) Total execution time

Figure 8: Full-system, execution-driven simulation results: (a) average network latency, and (b) total execution time of various PARSEC applications. The results are normalized to the baseline NoC.

Figure 8 shows the *average network latency* and the *total execution time* of various PARSEC multi-threaded benchmark applications [5], normalized to a baseline NoC with full-cycle links. The proposed architecture offers significant average network latency savings, which range from 16% to 23% (19%, on average). This latency reduction translates to a direct reduction in the total execution time, ranging from 5% to 22% (11%, on average). Most importantly, such savings are achieved while still enjoying significant power reductions.

Despite the authenticity provided by execution-driven, full-system simulations, the flexibility to stress the NoC is somewhat limited, due to the fixed characteristics of the running applications. Hence, we also employ *synthetic* traffic patterns in our evaluation, by operating GARNET in a "network-only" mode, assuming the same NoC configurations. The performance evaluation involves Uniform Random (UR) and Bit-Complement (BC) traffic patterns. Packet lengths follow a bimodal distribution, with half the packets being 1-flit long, and the other half being 5-flit long.

Figure 9 depicts the average network latency versus input load of a baseline NoC with full-cycle links and a NoC using the proposed architecture with half-cycle links. The latter achieves, on average, 18% and 20% lower latency under UR and BC traffic, respectively, as compared to the baseline

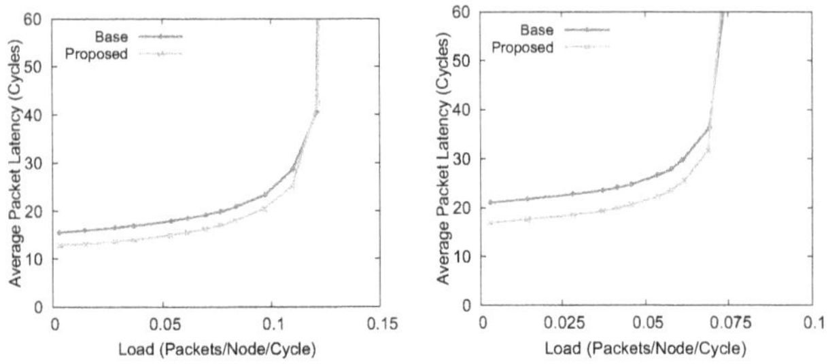

(a) Uniform Random (UR) (c) Bit-Complement (BC)

Figure 9: Latency vs. load curves under UR and BC traffic for a baseline NoC (with full-cycle links) and the proposed NoC (with half-cycle links).

NoC. In terms of throughput, both designs achieve equal performance. The positive effect of half-cycle link traversal is more pronounced under traffic patterns with increased average zero-load latency (i.e., larger average hop count).

Hence, the substantial power savings reaped by the proposed new design come with no negative impact on network performance. On the contrary, our evaluation indicates substantial performance *gains*, in terms of network latency and real-world application performance.

7. CONCLUSIONS

Tile-based homogeneous CMPs are characterized by a regularity in their physical layout. As technology scales, the number of on-chip tiles increases, while the size of each tile decreases. Consequently, the inter-tile distances scale *down* proportionally to the decreasing tile dimensions. In this paper, we exploit decreasing inter-tile wire lengths to facilitate ultra-fast NoC link traversal in half a clock cycle. This feat is achieved using appropriate wire engineering techniques, and by utilizing both edges of the clock during the sending/receiving of flits. The proposed NoC design leverages half-cycle link traversal to reap substantial power savings. The savings are derived by commensurate reductions in (a) link power (irrespective of the data-switching patterns), and (b) buffer power (by reducing the buffer size). Most importantly, the power benefits do not incur any performance penalty; on the contrary, the latency is actually improved. Extensive hardware implementation analysis using placed-and-routed designs validates the efficacy of the proposed architecture, which yields significant power savings of 34%, on average. Additionally, cycle-accurate full-system simulations using real benchmark applications also demonstrate significant performance improvements, i.e., average reductions in network latency and total execution time of 19% and 11%, respectively.

8. REFERENCES

[1] N. Abeyratne and et al. Scaling toward kilo-core processors with asymmetric high-radix topologies. In *HPCA*, 2013.

[2] N. Agarwal and et al. GARNET: A detailed on-chip network model inside a full-system simulator. In *ISPASS*, 2009.

[3] A.Ghiribaldi, D.Bertozzi, and S.Nowick. A transition-signaling bundled data NoC switch architecture for cost-effective GALS multicore systems. In *Proc. of DATE*, pages 332–337, 2013.

[4] J. Balfour and W. J. Dally. Design tradeoffs for tiled CMP on-chip networks. In *ICS*, 2006.

[5] C. Bienia and et al. The parsec benchmark suite: Characterization and architectural implications. In *PACT*, 2008.

[6] T. Bjerregaard and et al. A scalable, timing-safe, noc architecture with an integrated clock distribution method. In *DATE*, 2007.

[7] L. Chen and et al. Power punch: Towards non-blocking power-gating of noc routers. In *Proc. of HPCA*, pages 378–389, 2015.

[8] X. Chen and et al. In-network monitoring and control policy for dvfs of cmp networks-on-chip and last level caches. *ACM TODAES*, (4):47, 2013.

[9] B. Daya, L.-S. Peh, and A. Chandrakasan. Towards high-performance bufferless nocs with scepter. *IEEE Computer Architecture Letters*, 2015.

[10] A. Golander and et al. A cost-efficient L1–L2 multicore interconnect: Performance, power, and area considerations. *IEEE Trans. on Circuits and Systems-I*, (3):529–538, 2011.

[11] S. M. Hassan and S. Yalamanchili. Centralized buffer router: A low latency, low power router for high radix nocs. In *Proc. of NoCS*, 2013.

[12] H.Matsutani and et al. Ultra fine-grained run-time power gating of on-chip routers for cmps. In *Proc. of NoCS*, pages 61–68, 2010.

[13] J. Kim and et al. Flattened butterfly topology for on-chip networks. In *MICRO*, 2007.

[14] T. Krishna, C.-H. O. Chen, W. C. Kwon, and L.-S. Peh. Smart: Single-cycle multi-hop traversals over a shared network-on-chip. *IEEE Micro*, May/June 2014.

[15] P. Lotfi-Kamran and et al. NOC-Out: Microarchitecting a scale-out processor. In *MICRO*, 2012.

[16] Y. Lu and et al. Design of interlock-free combined allocators for networks-on-chip. In *IEEE SOC Conf.*, pages 358–363, 2012.

[17] R. Manevich and et al. Designing single-cycle long links in hierarchical nocs. *Microprocessors and Microsystems*, (8):814–825, 2014.

[18] M. M. K. Martin and et al. Multifacet's general execution-driven multiprocessor simulator (gems) toolset. *SIGARCH Comput. Archit. News*, 33(4):92–99, Nov. 2005.

[19] I. Miro-Panades and et al. Physical implementation of the dspin network-on-chip in the faust architecture. In *Proc of. NoCS*, 2008.

[20] A. Mishra and et al. A case for dynamic frequency tuning in on-chip networks. In *Proc. of MICRO*, pages 292–303, 2009.

[21] P. Salihundam et al. A 2Tb/s 6x4 Mesh Network with DVFS and 2.3Tb/s/W router in 45nm CMOS. In *VLSI Circuits*, 2010.

[22] J. Seo and et al. A robust edge encoding technique for energy-efficient multi-cycle interconnect. *IEEE Trans. VLSI Syst.*, pages 264–273, 2011.

[23] K. Sewell and et al. Swizzle-switch networks for many-core systems. *IEEE Journal on Emerging and Selected Topics in Circuits and Systems*, 2(2):278–294, 2012 2012.

[24] L. Shang, L.-S. Peh, and N. K. Jha. Dynamic voltage scaling with links for power optimization of interconnection networks. In *Proc. of HPCA*, pages 91–102, 2003.

[25] H. Wang, L.-S. Peh, and S. Malik. Power-driven design of router microarchitectures in on-chip networks. In *Proc of. MICRO*, 2003.

[26] D. Wentzlaff and et al. On-Chip Interconnection Architecture of the Tile Processor. *IEEE Micro*, pages 15–31, Sep./Oct. 2007.

Dynamic Real-Time Scheduler for Large-Scale MPSoCs

Marcelo Ruaro, Fernando G. Moraes
PUCRS University, Computer Science Department, Porto Alegre, Brazil
marcelo.ruaro@acad.pucrs.br, fernando.moraes@pucrs.br

ABSTRACT

Large-scale MPSoCs requires a scalable and dynamic real-time (RT) task scheduler, able to handle non-deterministic computational behaviors. Current proposals for MPSoCs have limitations, as lack of scalability, complex static steps, validation with abstract models, or are not flexible to enable changes at runtime of the RT constraints. This work proposes a hierarchical task scheduler with monitoring features. The scheduler is dynamic, supporting changes in RT constraints at runtime. An API enables these features allowing to the application developer to reconfigure the tasks' period, deadline, and execution time by annotating the task code. At runtime, according to the task execution, the scheduler handles the API calls and adjust itself to ensure RT guarantees according to the new constraints. Scalability is ensured by dividing the scheduler into two hierarchical levels: LS (Local Schedulers), and CS (Cluster Schedulers). The LS runs at the processor level, using the LST (Least Slack-Time) algorithm. The CS runs at the cluster level, i.e., a group of processors controlled by a manager processor. The CS receives messages from the LSs, informing the processor slack-time, deadline violations, and RT changes. The CS implements an RT adaptation heuristic, triggering task migrations according to RT reconfiguration or deadline misses. Results show a negligible overhead in the applications' execution time and the fulfillment of the applications' RT constraints even with a high degree of resources sharing, in both processors and NoC.

Keywords

MPSoC; Real-time; Scheduler; Runtime; Slack-time.

1. INTRODUCTION

The increasing number of processing elements (PEs) in modern large-scale multiprocessor systems on chip (MPSoCs) increases the resource sharing among system components [1]. For this reason, scheduling algorithms are essential for managing the processors usage while satisfying the constraints of real-time applications.

A key feature of a complex system, such as an MPSoCs, is the ability to support dynamic workloads. Applications may have moments of heavy computational load and also can have moments of a state close to the idle, waiting, for example, an external input, as a user interaction or a message from another task. For this reason, it is necessary to allow applications to tune the computational workload, avoiding unnecessary resources allocation. Aware of this challenge, this work focuses on a self-adaption technique for MPSoCs, proposing a dynamic RT task scheduler that can support runtime reconfiguration of the tasks' RT constraints. This reconfiguration starts with an API that enables the application developer to characterize the RT workload of each task at different execution points. At runtime, according to the task execution, the API triggers changes in the task RT constraints. The proposed task scheduler handles these changes at runtime to fulfill the new tasks' RT constraints.

Scalability is ensured by dividing the scheduler into two hierarchical levels: LS (*Local Schedulers*), and CS (*Cluster Schedulers*). The LS runs at the processor level, using the LST (Least Slack-Time) algorithm. The CS runs at the cluster level, i.e., a group of processors controlled by a manager processor. The CS receives messages from the LSs, informing the processors' slack-time, deadline violations, and RT changes. The CS implements an RT adaptation heuristic, triggering task migrations according to RT reconfiguration or deadline misses.

The scheduler works as closed-loop control system - Figure 1. The monitoring and notification messages (processor slack-time, deadline miss, RT changes), produced by the LSs, are the inputs for an RT manager executed in the CS, which can trigger an adaptation by generating a task migration action. This process is repeated along the execution of the applications.

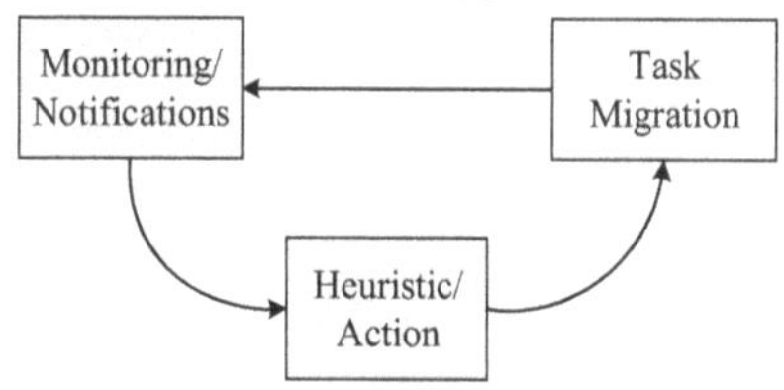

Figure 1. Scheduler support for self-adaptation at runtime.

The *focus of this work* is related to the scheduler ability to support dynamic RT reconfigurations while it satisfies the task RT constraints. Task mapping or schedulability analysis in out of this work scope. Such techniques are broadly explored in the literature [2][3][4] and can be easily combined with the proposed scheduler. Aware of the current state-of-the-art works, this work is the first to support a runtime reconfiguration of the RT task constraints. Besides, the evaluation of the proposed scheduler is executed in a clock cycle accurate description of the MPSoC.

2. RELATED WORK

The literature related to task scheduling contains a large number of proposals focusing on multiprocessor systems [1]. However, most of the works are not suitable for MPSoCs. Most MPSoC schedulers consider design-time steps integrated into frameworks [5][6][7][8]. Such works often employ a MoC (Model of Computation) such as PPN, DAG, and SDGA to model the applications at design-time, making its behavior predictable, and also enabling hard RT scheduling. Static or partial static scheduling is a conservative approach to guarantee hard RT behavior. Those proposals are only effective when the set of applications to execute in the system is fixed at design-time.

Pfair is a state-of-the-art hard RT scheduler for multiprocessor systems [4]. Park et al. [4] propose HPGP, a hybrid scheduler for MPSoCs based on *Pfair*. A partitioned version runs the *Pfair*

GLSVLSI '16, May 18-20, 2016, Boston, MA, USA
© 2016 ACM. ISBN 978-1-4503-4274-2/16/05...$15.00
DOI: http://dx.doi.org/10.1145/2902961.2903027

algorithm together with a global scheduler that makes task mapping and task migrations. The manager selects the ready tasks to be scheduled into a PE. Each PE executes a schedulability analysis. If the task is not schedulable, the core invokes the global scheduler to perform task migration. The task mapping approach is not addressed. The proposal considers only periodic tasks with deadlines equal to their respective periods and constant execution time. Besides, the evaluation is carried out only with four cores, which does not enable validating the algorithm in large MPSoCs. This work also uses a hybrid scheduling organization. Differently from *Pfair*, in this work the scheduler supports variable tasks periods, deadlines and execution times, providing higher flexibility for RT workloads.

The LST (*Least Slack Time*) scheduler was proved to be non-optimal to multiprocessor systems [9]. Hwang et al. [10] propose LSTR, a scheduling algorithm based on LST, with additional features to be optimal for multiprocessor systems. LSTR was designed to support only periodic tasks. Besides a large number of task migrations, the Authors do not consider such overhead.

The design of an RT scheduler for MPSoCs should consider, among other factors, how to inform the RT task constraints to the system, and how to handle interruptions. As the scheduler proposed in this work is a dynamic scheduler, RT task constraints are transferred to the operating system (OS) using task code annotation, a common approach found in the literature. Theodoropoulos et al. [11] use task code annotation (called pragmas) that are used by a runtime manager to perform task mapping. Canella et al. [12] employ task annotation to implement a task migration mechanism based on task replication. The task annotation is used to guarantee inter-task communication synchronization.

The treatment of interruptions may interfere in the execution of RT tasks. Interruptions can be handled immediately using specific system routines, or can be pooled at fixed and predetermined times [13]. Another alternative is to redirect interruptions handling to free cores [4]. However, this option can only be useful when interruptions come from external devices and are not related to inter-task communications.

Concluding, there is a lack of works in the literature addressing dynamic RT schedulers for MPSoCs. To the best of the Authors knowledge, this paper is the first proposal that addresses a scheduling algorithm for MPSoC combining the originalities detailed in the Introduction, combined with an evaluation employing a clock cycle accurate platform model.

3. SYSTEM MODEL

This section describes the system model, detailing important assumption related to this work.

3.1 MPSoC Model

This work adopts the cluster-based architecture, with manager and slave PEs depicted in Figure 2(a). The MPSoC contains a set of PEs, interconnected by a NoC. It is partitioned into n clusters $C=\{c_1, c_2, \ldots, c_n\}$. Each cluster $c_i \in C$ has a set $P(c_i)=\{M, sp_1, sp_2, \ldots, sp_k\}$, where M denotes a CM, k the number of slave processors in the cluster. Only one CM has an interface to input/output devices. Note that the cluster size is not static. At runtime, it can change it size by using a reclustering protocol [14].

The platform uses a distributed memory organization. Inside each PE - Figure 2(b), there is one processor, one dual-port local memory, one NI (Network Interface), NoC router, and one DMA module (Direct Memory Access). The adoption of a DMA module improves the processor performance avoiding stalls to send and receive packets to/from the NoC.

All PEs execute a small operating system (µkernel: ~20KB). The CMs execute a management µkernel, not executing user tasks. One specific CM has access to an *application repository*. This repository contains the applications' tasks object code, and simulates the insertion of new applications into the MPSoC at runtime. SPs execute a µkernel to control the execution of the user tasks. This µkernel also implements a paging mechanism to support multitasking and an inter-task communication protocol based on MPI.

The PEs handle two external interruptions: *NI interruption*, signaling a received packet from the NoC; *scheduler interruptions*, signaling the end of the scheduler timer (only in SPs). In the occurrence of an interruption, the executing task is preempted.

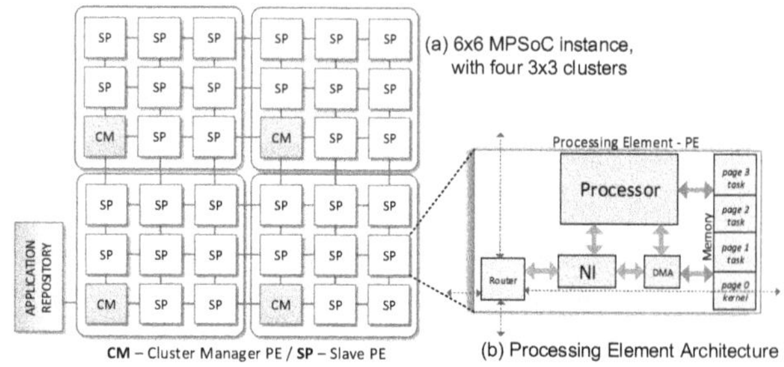

Figure 2. Cluster-based MPSoC example - a 6x6 MPSoC with four 3x3 clusters. CM: cluster manager. SP: slave processor.

3.2 Application and Task Model

An m-task application $A=\{t_1, t_2, \ldots, t_m\}$ is modeled by a task graph G(T, E), with each vertex $t_i \in$ T representing a task and the directed edge (e_i, e_j), denoted as $e_{ij} \in E$, representing the communication between tasks t_i and t_j. Tasks communicate using a non-blocking *Send* and blocking *Receive* MPI-like primitives. A given task t_i can assume four states: *waiting*, *ready*, *running*, and *sleeping*. The *waiting* state implies that the task is blocked, waiting for a producer task to send it a message. The *ready* state means that the task already achieved its release time, and is ready to be scheduled. The *running* state implies that the task is executing on the processor. The *sleeping* state (RT tasks only) means that the task already finished its execution time and its period does not end yet, so the task must be suspended.

The system supports *best-effort* tasks - B_t, and *real-time* tasks - R_t. B_ts do not have time bounds and explore the slack-time of R_ts. R_ts have soft temporal requirements. Figure 3 details the R_t constraints model.

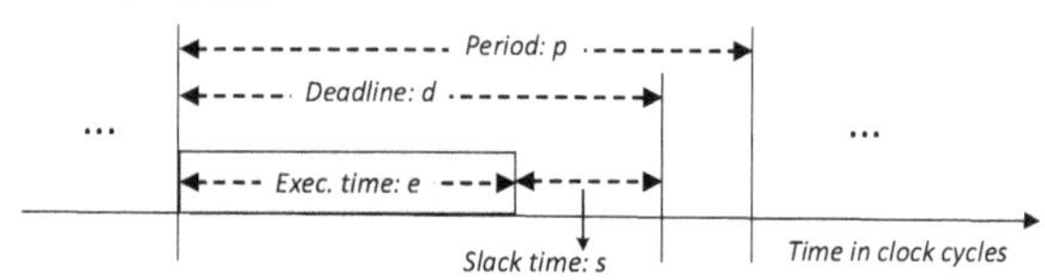

Figure 3. RT constraints model.

***R_t* definition**: R_t is a 6-tuple $\{p, d, e, u, r, s\}$ with a period (p), relative deadline [9] (d), execution time (e), utilization (u), remaining execution time (r), and slack-time (s). Utilization corresponds to u = e * 100 / p. The remaining execution time is the amount of time R_t has to finish it execution time.

To make the system aware of the constraints of a given R_t, the task must execute a system call (*syscall*) named *RealTime*. This *RealTime* syscall is the API provided to the application developer to reconfigure the RT constraints. Figure 4 presents an example of an R_t code that configures the RT constraints dynamically. At line 3, TASK A calls *RealTime*, notifying the µkernel of its RT constraints. Lines 4-8 execute some code. Due to the RT constraints configuration, the scheduler can execute TASK A according to the RT requirements. Next, at line 10 the task calls *RealTime* again to notify the scheduler about its new constraints. The code between lines 11-15 executes according to these new constraints. As can be observed, this system call enables the task to change its RT constraints dynamically.

```
1.  int main(){
2.      int period = 60000, deadline = 8000, execution_time = 2000;
3.      RealTime(period, deadline, execution_time);
4.      for ( i iterations ) {
5.          Receive (msg from producer task);
6.          process1(msg);
7.          Send (msg to consumer task);
8.      }
9.      period = 60000, deadline = 10000, execution_time = 8000;
10.     RealTime(period, deadline, execution_time);
11.     for ( k iterations ) {
12.         Receive (msg from producer task);
13.         process2(msg);
14.         Send (msg to consumer task);
15.     }
16.     return 0;
17. }
```

Figure 4. Example of a task code with runtime RT configuration. It calls the RealTime syscall twice to configure the constraints (in lines 3 and 10).

Note that the RT reconfiguration can be called in any task code point allowing the task can change its period (characterizing an aperiodic behavior), deadline, and/or execution time. Such behavior, where an RT task can change its RT constraints at runtime, is typical in real scenarios. For example, consider a voice recognition application. The application can assume two workloads: the first one is a listening state, where the application is waiting for the user to pronounce some sound, this state requires a moderate RT workload. The second one is the recognition state, where the task uses voice recognition algorithms. In this case, the application tasks can configure two workloads, with different RT requirements.

To handle inter-task dependencies, this work assumes that an iteration of a given application defines a *hyper period*, i.e., an RT application has all its tasks configured with the same *p*. This hyper period can handle with inter-task dependencies because it is composed of the WCET (worst-case execution time) of all tasks and the worst-case of communication between the application's tasks.

This task dependency model does not restrain the application model, accepting sequential, parallel and pipelined applications. The designer can obtain the WCET and communication latencies running the application alone in the system, representing a profiling phase.

4. THE PROPOSED SCHEDULER

Table 1 presents the classification [9][15] of the proposed scheduler.

Table 1 – Proposed scheduler classification.

Criterion	Classification
Organization (Global, Partitioned)	Hybrid (Mixes Global and Partitioned) and clustered
Scheduling decision (Static, Dynamic)	Dynamic
Allocation (Clock, Table, Priority)	Dynamic Priority-driven
Migration (Job level, Task level)	Task-level Migration
Processor Number (Uni.,Multi.)	Multiprocessor (on chip)
Preemption (Yes, No)	Yes
Supported task	Periodic, aperiodic
Real-time (Hard, Firm, Soft)	Soft real-time

Figure 5 presents an overview of the scheduler. It has a hierarchical organization that is divided into two levels:

- *Cluster scheduler* (CS) - runs the high-level part of the scheduler in the CMs. Its job is to perform RT adaptations if a given RT task is missing deadlines or it has changed its RT constraints and its current processor is not able to execute the task;
- *Local scheduler* (LS) - runs the low-level part of the scheduler in the SPs, executing the LST scheduling algorithm.

The LSs send messages to CS. The messages are (*i*) slack-time monitoring; (*ii*) deadline miss; (*iii*) RT change. Messages (*ii*) and (*iii*) are reactive messages, sent when a task misses a deadline, or when a task calls the *RealTime* syscall, respectively. The slack-time messages are generated periodically (slack-time monitoring – STM).

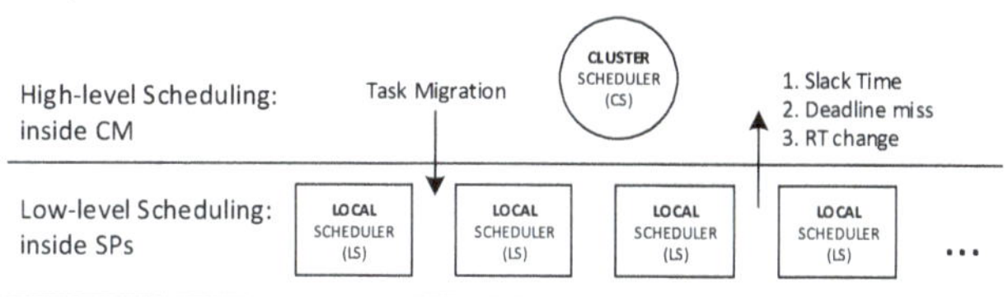

Figure 5. Hierarchical scheduler organization.

The STM provides to the CS the actual slack-time of each SP. The STM has a hardware/software implementation at each SP. The hardware part corresponds to a timer, which generates an interruption to the μkernel according to a monitoring window. This monitoring window is configurable at design time and can be adjusted to provide a tradeoff between NoC communication load and the STM update frequency. The software part corresponds to a slack-time counter and a monitoring interruption handler function, both implemented in the μkernel.

When the STM timer interrupts the μkernel, a message with the current slack-time is sent to the CS and the slack-time counter is reinitialized.

4.1 Cluster Scheduler (CS)

The CS executes into the CMs. The CS have the goal of handling the messages sent by the SPs and execute the RT adaptation if necessary. For the *slack-time* messages, the CS only updates the percentage of the idle state of each processor of its cluster. For *deadline miss* messages the CS executes a heuristic called *RT_adaptation*, which can select a new processor to migrate the penalized task. Finally, for *RT change* messages, the CS verify if the current processor of the task has enough utilization to execute the task, if not, as well as occurs for *deadline miss* message, the CS executes the *RT_adaptation* heuristic.

The *RT_adaptation* heuristic works as a set of decision layers applied to the SPs of the cluster - Figure 6(a). Figure 6(b) presents the heuristic pseudo-code. As input it receives the set $C_{SP} = \{P(c_i) - M\}$ (corresponding to set of SPs in the cluster), and the task *t* to be migrated into a given element of C_{SP}. As output the algorithm returns the selected processor *s*, corresponding to the new processor to receive the task *t*. If all the processors are not available to receive the task, the adaptation process is suspended, the affected task will start to miss deadlines triggering the adaptation process until an available processor can be found.

The decision functions only select the SP(s) which fulfill the function's requirement. The following decision functions are used:

- *utilization*: selects the SP(s) that have a remaining utilization enough to receive the task *t*;
- *max_avg_ST*: selects the SP(s) with the largest average slack-time, information obtained from STM;
- *min_RT task:* selects the SP(s) with the minimum number of RT tasks allocated to it;
- *min_abs_ST:* selects the SP(s) with the largest absolute slack-time measured at the last slack-time monitoring window;
- *min_alloc_tasks:* selects the SP(s) with the minimum number of allocated tasks.

Finally, in line 6, the first SP in C_{SP} is selected to receive task *t*. Using this heuristic, the CS takes advantage of the monitored slack-time of its slave processors (lines 2 and 4), together with traditional RT metrics (line 1 and 3). The information provides a trade-off between the processor RT utilization and load balancing. After the execution of the heuristic, a task migration order in sent to the current SP of task *t* and the task is migrated to the selected processor *s*. The task migration protocol is out of this work scope.

(a)

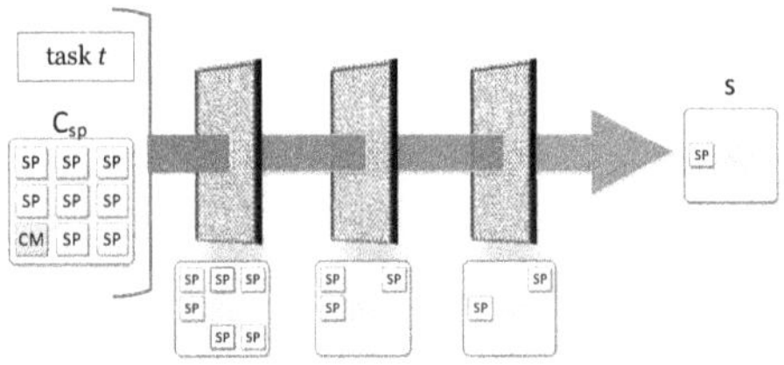

(b) ***RT_Adaptation*** **(C_{sp}, *t*, *s*)**

Input: C_{sp}, t
Output: s
begin
1. C_{sp}= C_{sp} ∩ *utilization*(C_{sp}, t)
2. C_{sp}= C_{sp} ∩ *max_avg_ST*(C_{sp})
3. C_{sp}= C_{sp} ∩ *min_RT_task*(C_{sp})
4. C_{sp}= C_{sp} ∩ *min_abs_ST*(C_{sp})
5. C_{sp}= C_{sp} ∩ *min_alloc_tasks*(C_{sp})
6. s = *first*(C_{sp})
end

Figure 6. (a) layered decision flow. (b) *RT_adaptation* pseudo-code.

4.2 Local Scheduler (LS)

Assuming the task model in 3.2, the LS executes at each SP as a traditional LST scheduler [9]. The LST algorithm was chosen because it has been proved optimal for single cores, and due its support to deadlines different from the period [9], which is not supported in EDF (Earliest Deadline First). Note that in this work the multiprocessor scheduling problem can be reduced to the single core problem, due the presence of the CS, which can migrate a task R_t into an SP with resources to fulfill the task RT constraints.

The RT tasks have scheduling priority over BE tasks. RT tasks are scheduled according to its least slack-time priority. If there are two or more RT tasks with the same slack-time, a round-robin algorithm is used to select the next scheduled task. BE tasks are scheduled only by the round-robin algorithm.

As the system uses an MPI-like communication API, some tasks can be in a waiting state. In this state, BE tasks are simply blocked. However, when an R_t goes to the waiting state, the scheduler handles the R_t as a sleeping task, i.e., the scheduler verifies the end of task period, but do not update its remaining execution time neither schedules the task. When the task receives the requested message, the μkernel changes the state of the task to ready and calls the LS. The scheduler then updates the slack-time and the remaining execution time for all its RT ready tasks, scheduling the task using the LST priority.

Most schedulers use a fixed scheduler timer (S_T), or *quantum*, to schedule the tasks [9][4] (for example, EDF uses fixed time slices). This *quantum* is the interval between the scheduler calls. The proposed LS uses a variable *quantum*. Setting the appropriate S_T is challenging, because it may induce deadline misses caused by excessive scheduler executions. The method to compute S_T is executed after selecting a given task $t_s \in T$ to run. The goal is to let t_s run, minimizing scheduler interruptions, without compromising other RT tasks. Let ψ be the set of R_t allocated into a given SP, minus t_s.

The S_T value is computed applying the following steps:

1. Selection of the *first end of period* for all *sleeping* and *waiting* tasks $s \in \psi$, using Equation 1:

$$S_{tc1} = \begin{cases} C_t - first\_end\_of\_perido(s_1 \dots s_n), & n > 0 \\ t_{s(r)}, & n = 0 \end{cases} \quad (1)$$

where C_t is the current system time, and *n* is the number of tasks $s \in \psi$. The value S_{tc1} ensures that the scheduler will be called at the first end of period of a task $s_i \in \psi$. The S_{tc1} value ensures a scheduler call to awake a sleeping task or to verify if a waiting task missed a deadline. The default value, if n=0, is remaining execution time of t_s: $t_{s(r)}$.

2. Selection of the *minimum slack-time*: *minST()* for all *ready* tasks $r \in \psi$, using Equation 2:

$$S_{tc2} = \begin{cases} \text{minST}(r_1 \dots r_n), & n > 0 \\ t_{s(r)}, & n = 0 \end{cases} \quad (2)$$

where *n* is the number of tasks $r \in \psi$. The S_{tc2} value ensures the execution of t_s up to the expiration of the smallest slack-time of a task $r_i \in \psi$.

3. Selection of the scheduler timer S_T, using the Equation 3:

$$S_T = \min\,(S_{tc1}, S_{tc2}, t_{s(r)}) \quad (3)$$

If $t_{s(r)}$ is smaller than the previously computed values, it is adopted as the *quantum* value. After selecting S_T, tasks t_s start their execution using the S_T value as *quantum*.

5. RESULTS

Results were obtained using a clock-cycle accurate RTL SystemC model of the MPSoC. The μkernel, application code, and the scheduler was implemented in C. Results use two latency metrics:

- *Task iteration latency*, time to execute a task iteration, which can e.g. be a loop (Figure 4).
- *Application iteration latency*, time for an application to execute its hyper period.

5.1 Slack-time Monitoring

The evaluation of the STM includes: *accuracy* and *performance overhead*. The accuracy evaluation employs an 8x8 MPSoC divided into four 4x4 clusters. To estimate the SPs' slack-time, the SPs received only RT tasks. Figure 7(a) presents the annotated utilization for each SP (%). Figure 7(b) presents the monitored slack-time (%). It is possible to note that the monitored slack-time is in practice the remaining utilization of Figure 7(a), with the sum of SPs utilization with the monitored slack-time reaching 99%. In fact, the remaining 1% is related to OS overheads. *Such results demonstrate the accuracy of the monitored slack-time.*

9	11	34	7	81	77	82	10
6	29	15	10	57	5	62	14
21	55	15	44	12	25	80	24
CM	58	86	6	CM	6	12	14
16	47	12	67	69	13	66	9
50	5	10	14	29	15	14	46
9	19	9	74	81	11	12	54
CM	40	79	59	CM	27	15	46

(a) SPs utilization (%)

90	88	65	92	18	22	17	89
93	70	84	89	42	94	37	85
78	44	84	55	87	74	19	75
CM	41	13	93	CM	93	87	85
83	52	87	32	30	86	33	90
49	94	89	85	70	84	85	53
90	80	90	25	18	88	87	45
CM	59	20	40	CM	72	84	53

(b) Monitored SPs slack-time (%)

Figure 7. (a) SPs utilization using RT tasks. (b) Monitored SPs slack-time. Each square represents a PE.

To evaluate the performance overhead due to STM, a 12x12 MPSoC divided into nine 4x4 clusters is used, running a mix of RT and BE applications. The monitoring window is set to 10 ms. Figure 8 presents the STM overhead for each SP. This overhead is related to the time required to handle the STM interruption and to send the slack-time message to the CS. As can be observed, the overhead in most SPs falls between 100 and 150 *clock cycles* (cc), with an average of 132 cc. There are a few large values, which can be explained by NoC congestion, forcing the packet to wait for the router to be released. The overhead in the CM to handle the STM packets was 1620 cc (only software execution). *Such result shows the small penalty to monitor the slack time.*

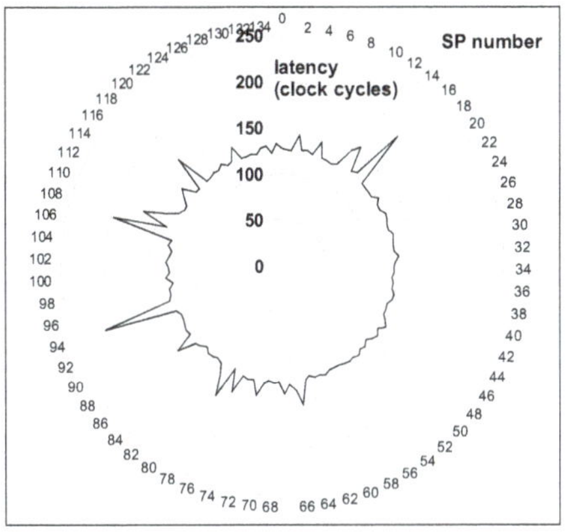

Figure 8. STM overhead for SPs in a 12x12 MPSoC.

Different STM windows were evaluated: 1, 2, 5 and 10 ms. The cost of handling a monitoring message does not change with the STM window. Reducing the monitoring window may reduce the time to adapt the system, at the cost of increased processing in CMs, due to the larger number of packets to deal with. The monitoring window is a design choice, enabling to establish a trade-off between reaction time and performance overhead in the manager processors.

5.2 RT Adaptation Support

This Section evaluates the RT adaptation support, observing the scheduler behavior when a *RealTime* syscall occurs. Figure 9 presents the CPU utilization for a given SP running two RT tasks: *t1* and *t2*. At the beginning of the execution, both tasks configure its RT constraints: $t1_{(u)}$=20%, $t2_{(u)}$=30%. Near 52 ms, *t2* changes its RT constraints, configuring $t2_{(u)}$=65%. It is possible to note that after the second *RealTime*, *t2* executes for a longer period, corresponding to the utilization configured in the second *RealTime* call.

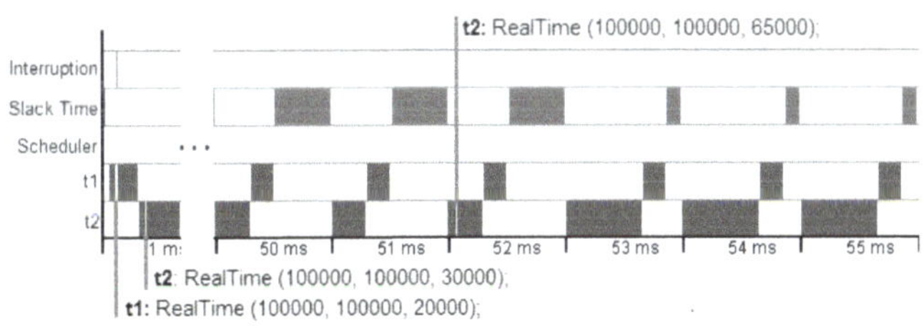

Figure 9. Change in the CPU time utilization during an RT adaptation (rectangles represent the CPU utilization).

Figure 10 presents the *task iteration latency* for *t1* and *t2*, considering the scenario presented in Figure 9. It is possible to note that the *t1* latency is not affected when the *t2* workload increases, demonstrating the capability of the LS to preserve the RT constraints. The small peak near 52 ms observed in the graph occurs due the RT adaptation process. Figure 10(b) shows that after *t2* request more CPU resources, the latency decreases in the same proportion.

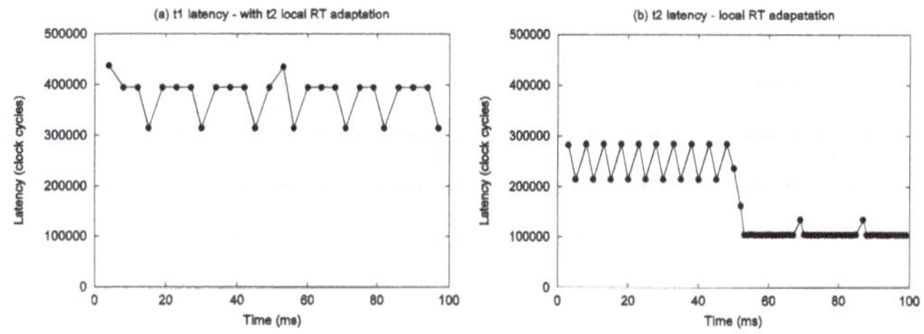

Figure 10. Task iteration latency change during an RT adaptation. (a) *t1* latency. (b) *t2* latency.

5.3 RT Adaptation with Task Migration

This Section presents an RT adaptation, Figure 11, that includes task migration. The same scenario of the previous Section is used. However, the second RT configuration of *t2* exceeds the SP utilization: $t2_{(u)}$=85%. This utilization, with $t1_{(u)}$, would result in an SP utilization equal to 105%. When CS receives the *RT request* message related to the second *t2* RT change, it executes the *RT_adaptation* (Figure 6(b)) to select an SP with enough remaining utilization.

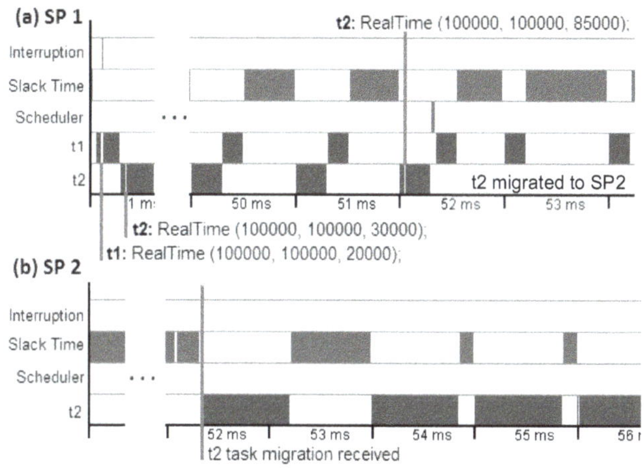

Figure 11. Change of the CPU time occupation during an RT adaptation with task migration. Task t2 start to execute in SP2 when the RT constraint changes.

Observing the chart of Figure 11(a), it is possible to note that near 52 ms *t2* call the second *RealTime*, inducing a task migration from SP 1 to SP 2 (Figure 11(b)). The total time between the start of RT adaptation until the end of task migration was 8906 cc, with 2651 cc (29.7%) required to the RT adaptation process, and 6255 cc (70.3%) required to the task migration protocol.

Figure 12(a) and Figure 12(b) present the *task iteration latency* for *t1* and *t2*, considering the scenario presented in Figure 11. It is possible to observe the negligible impact of RT adaptation even with task migrations taking place.

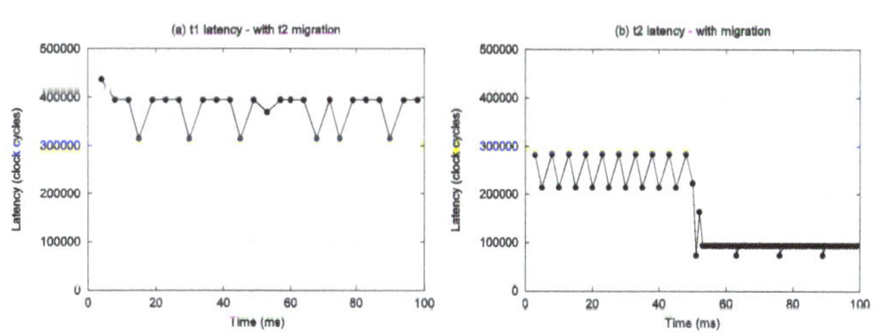

Figure 12 . t1(a) and t2(b) task iteration latency during an RT adaptation with task migration.

5.4 Impact of Disturbing Applications

This Section evaluates two RT applications: DTW (computation intensive, six tasks) and MPEG (communication intensive, five tasks). These applications – named *target applications*, were evaluated in the presence of disturbing applications (RT or BE). The goal is to observe the scheduler behavior with multiple tasks allocated in the same SP, and the impact of the disturbing applications over the target applications.

Initially, target applications execute alone in the system aiming to collect the reference RT constraints for its tasks (profiling step). In sequence, new simulations were performed aiming to insert RT interference over the target applications. According to Figure 3, the available time to execute disturbing tasks, $t_{disturb}$, corresponds to $R_t(p)$- $R_t(e)$. The experiments vary $t_{disturb}$ from 10% (0.1* $t_{disturb}$) to 90% (0.9 * $t_{disturb}$).

Figure 13(a) presents the DTW average *application iteration latency*. The first column presents the *minimal* latency, next columns present the interference of a RT disturbing application varying $t_{disturb}$ from 10% (10% RT) to 90% (90% RT), the column "BE" corresponds to a BE application interference with $t_{disturb}$ equal to 100%. The last column presents the latency when a round-robin scheduler (i.e. without RT support) is used. Is possible to observe that for all RT disturbing scenarios the DTW latency close to the minimal latency (36220.03 cc.), with an average latency increase of 2%, and a standard deviation of 316.4 cc. Such results demonstrate the scheduling ability to preserve the RT application constraints even with high resource sharing. BE disturbing applications do not influence the latency values. Disabling the RT support the latency increase 97.13% compared with the minimal latency, demonstrating that a RT scheduler is required to meet deadline constraints. The deadline miss rate for DTW with RT disturbing was 0.66%, and for the disturbing application was in average 2.7%. Figure 13(b) presents the DTW execution time. The results are similar to the latency results. The additional column "*minimal–no STM*", corresponds to the scenario to obtain the minimal latency, but disabling the STM. Note the negligible impact of STM monitoring, increasing the application execution time by 0.4% (using a 5 ms STM window).

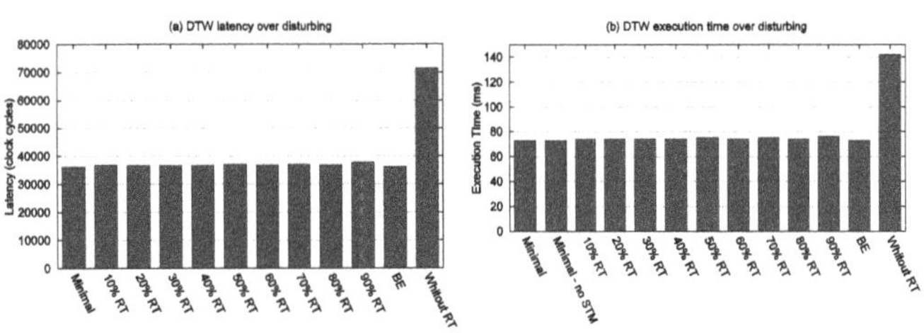

Figure 13. (a) DTW application latency over disturbing. (b) DTW execution time over disturbing.

The *application iteration latency* observed in the MPEG application is similar to the DTW application. All latencies with RT disturbing remain close to the latency of the minimal scenario (55358.5 cc.), with an average latency increase of 0.5% and standard deviation equal to 181.1 cc. The frame rate achieved in the minimal scenario was 178 frames per 100ms. With RT disturbing applications, the frame rate has presented a maximum of 2 frames decrease compared to the minimal scenario. Disabling the RT support, the frame rate drops to 81 frames per 100ms. The impact of STM monitoring in the MPEG application was 0.07% (STM windows of 5 ms). The deadline miss rate for MPEG, with RT disturbing application, was 0.18%, and for the disturbing application was equal to 2.1%.

The deadline miss difference between the disturbing application and the RT application occurs because the disturbing application is computationally intensive, which makes such application more sensitive during RT scheduling. This same observation can be used to explain the difference of deadline misses between DTW and MPEG.

6. CONCLUSIONS

This work presented a hierarchical scheduler for large-scale MPSoCs. The scheduler is completely adaptive, supporting dynamic task RT constraints and slack-time monitoring. The evaluation demonstrated a reliable ability to fulfill RT applications with soft deadlines even for communication or computation intensive applications with the interference of other RT applications. The observed worst-case application latency increase was 2% (DTW), with 90% of RT disturbing over the minimal latency. The STM presented a negligible impact on the execution time of application, with a worst execution time increase of 0.4%.

Large-scale MPSoCs have other issues to achieve QoS. One of these issues is the increasingly NoC unpredictability as the system grows in the number of cores. To cope with this, runtime QoS techniques applied to the NoC can be employed together with the proposed scheduler, to provide a full QoS support. Other future works include to integrate the scheduler with a task mapping and schedulability analysis algorithm and add energy awareness to the heuristic.

ACKNOWLEDGMENTS

The Author Fernando Moraes is supported by CNPq - projects 472126/2013-0 and 302625/2012-7, and FAPERGS - project 2242-2551/14-8.

REFERENCES

[1] Shafique, M.; Garg, S.; Henkel, J.; Marculescu, D. "The EDA challenges in the dark silicon era". In: DAC, 2014, pp.1-6.

[2] Singh, A.K.; Shafique, M.; Kumar, A.; Henkel, J. "Mapping on multi/many-core systems: Survey of current and emerging trends". In: DAC, 2013, pp.1-10.

[3] Jung, H.; et al. "Dynamic Behavior Specification and Dynamic Mapping for Real-Time Embedded Systems: HOPES Approach" ACM Trans. Embed. Comput. Syst., vol 13(4), 2014, 26 p.

[4] Park, S. "Task-I/O Co-scheduling for Pfair Real-Time Scheduler in Embedded Multi-core Systems". In: EUC, 2014, pp.46-51.

[5] Gangadharan, Deepak; Chakraborty, Samarjit; Zimmermann, Roger, "Quality-aware media scheduling on MPSoC platforms". In: DATE, 2013, pp. 976-981.

[6] Rosvall, K.; Sander, I. "A constraint-based design space exploration framework for real-time applications on MPSoCs". In: DATE, 2014, pp.1-6.

[7] Bamakhrama, M.; Stefanov, T. "Hard-real-time scheduling of data-dependent tasks in embedded streaming applications". In: EMSOFT, 2011, pp.195-204.

[8] Tafesse, B.; Raina, A.; Suseela, J.; Muthukumar, V., "Efficient Scheduling Algorithms for MpSoC Systems". In: ITNG, 2011, pp. 683-688.

[9] Liu, J.W.S. "Real-Time System". Printice Hall, New Jersey, 2000.

[10] Hwang, M.; Choi, D.; Kim, P. "Least Slack-time Rate First: New Scheduling Algorithm for Multi-Processor Environment". In: CISIS, 2010, pp.806-811.

[11] Theodoropoulos,D.; Pratikakis,P.; Pnevmatikatos,D. "Efficient runtime support for embedded MPSoCs". In: SAMOS, 2013 pp.164-171.

[12] Cannella, E.; Derin, O.; Meloni, P.; Tuveri, G.; Stefanov, T. "Adaptivity support for MPSoCs based on process migration in polyhedral process networks". VLSI Design, 2012, Article 2.

[13] Hansson, A.; et al. "Design and implementation of an operating system for composable processor sharing". Microprocessors and Microsystems, v. 35 (2), pp. 246-260, March 2011.

[14] Castilhos, G.; Mandelli, M.; Madalozzo, G.; Moraes, F. "Distributed Resource Management in NoC-Based MPSoCs with Dynamic Cluster Sizes". In: ISVLSI, 2013, pp. 153-158.

[15] Davis, R.I.; Burns, A. "A survey of hard real-time scheduling for multiprocessor systems". *ACM Comput. Surv.* Article 35, 2011, 44p.

Leveraging 3D Technologies for Hardware Security: Opportunities and Challenges

Peng Gu, Shuangchen Li, Dylan Stow, Russell Barnes, Liu Liu, and Yuan Xie
University of California, Santa Barbara
Santa Barbara, CA
{peng_gu, yuanxie}@ece.ucsb.edu

Eren Kursun
Columbia University
New York, NY
ek2925@columbia.edu

ABSTRACT

3D die stacking and 2.5D interposer design are promising technologies to improve integration density, performance and cost. Current approaches face serious issues in dealing with emerging security challenges such as side channel attacks, hardware trojans, secure IC manufacturing and IP piracy. By utilizing intrinsic characteristics of 2.5D and 3D technologies, we propose novel opportunities in designing secure systems. We present: (i) a 3D architecture for shielding side-channel information; (ii) split fabrication using active interposers; (iii) circuit camouflage on monolithic 3D IC, and (iv) 3D IC-based security processing-in-memory (PIM). Advantages and challenges of these designs are discussed, showing that the new designs can improve existing countermeasures against security threats and further provide new security features.

1. INTRODUCTION

Three-dimensional Integration (3D) is a promising technology that allows multiple dies to be vertically integrated in a stack [14]. Successful 3D implementations have been demonstrated [44] in a wide range of scenarios from multi-core processor design and high-bandwidth memory design to network-on-chip (NoC) design. Similarly, interposer-based 2.5D integration technology, which interconnects dies by metal routes in the interposer layer, has been explored. Compared with 3D, 2.5D provides benefits of in-package integration with relaxed thermal requirements and design flexibility. An AMD GPU [1] and a Xilinx FPGA [?] have adopted 2.5D integration.

3D and 2.5D integration technologies possess some salient advantages over 2D design [15] such as: (i) providing higher transistor density through die-stacking; (ii) enabling shorter interconnect by partitioning larger dies to smaller ones; (iii) enhancing memory bandwidth by an order of magnitude by eliminating off-chip pin count constraints; (iv) allowing enhanced design flexibility by allowing heterogeneous integration, and (v) offering cost effective alternatives due to improvements in die yield and smaller footprints. While performance, cost and form-factor advantages of 3D integration have been extensively researched in the past, utilizing 3D and 2.5D integration technologies for hardware security enhancement is still an emerging research topic.

In recent years, hardware security has gained significant interest from both industry and academic communities. First of all, various types of attacks aiming at integrated circuits have been increasing rapidly to acquire sensitive information or encrypted keys [45]. Second, there are growing concerns on how to safely manufacture ICs from untrusted manufactories[36]. While a number of security-aware hardware designs and software algorithms have been proposed to address these challenges, they induce considerable overhead and degrade performance by incorporating security components. With technology advancement, 3D and 2.5D integration solutions can improve the existing countermeasures and further add new security features in protection of emerging threats.

In Section 2 of this paper, we review previous efforts on hardware security enhancement based on 3D integration technology, including split fabrication and modular security integration. Then we introduce our major contributions by presenting four new opportunities using 3D design that can promisingly benefit hardware security: (i) A novel 3D architecture is proposed in Section 3.1 to prevent thermal and power side-channel attacks, taking advantage of 3D IC's intrinsic multi-layer structure and heterogeneous integration. (ii) New optimizations to reduce the cost of split manufacturing through 2.5D-based active interposer design are discussed in Section 3.2. (iii) Monolithic 3D IC is shown in Section 3.3 to potentially support a more effective camouflage circuit to hinder reverse engineering by exploiting the multi-layer structure and efficient interconnects. (iv) In Section 3.4, 3D-enabled processing-in-memory architecture is presented to offset the overhead for memory security with its high bandwidth memory. In the end of each section, we also discuss the potential design challenges to implement security mechanisms using 3D and 2.5D integration technologies.

2. RELATED WORK

Pioneering work has already explored leveraging 3D integration technology for hardware security improvement, including 3D IC-based split fabrication [22, 42] and flexible modular security integration with 3D chips [19, 37].

GLSVLSI '16, May 18-20, 2016, Boston, MA, USA
© 2016 ACM. ISBN 978-1-4503-4274-2/16/05...$15.00
DOI: http://dx.doi.org/10.1145/2902961.2903512

2.1 3D IC-based Split Fabrication

As the IC manufacturing industry grew into a global business, security and trustworthiness of the components manufactured or designed by third parties have become a serious concern. Split fabrication is proposed to prevent attacks from untrusted foundries, such as hardware trojans, IC overbuilding, and Intellectual Property (IP) piracy [36]. The key idea is to fabricate different parts of the design in different foundries and assemble those parts with a trusted foundry in the end. Even though the foundries are untrusted, with only part of the design, the risk that the attackers can compromise the entire IP is minimized. Digital IC has already demonstrated feasibility for split-foundry processes [18], and fault analysis-based defense methodologies have been proposed to prevent attackers from bypassing the security afforded by straightforward split manufacturing [30].

3D IC-based split fabrication generally follows the original scheme in 2D design. Compared with 2D IC-based split fabrication that partitions the front-end-of-line processing (FEOL, including transistors and lower level metals) and back-end-of-line processing (BEOL, including higher-level metals) in different foundries, the 3D IC-based method sends layers to different foundries. Imeson *et al.* [22] examined this method and studied the circuit partitioning problem. Using the proposed k-security partition algorithm and layout randomization, they significantly increased the security level at a low cost. A case study on DES circuit was presented to evaluate the proposed method. Considering the challenges of logic-on-logic 3D stacking, recent studies have also investigated interposer-based 2.5D integration technology. Xie *et al.* [42] proposed a physical design flow for limiting the interposer layer that contains inter-chip connections to be fabricated in a trusted foundry. It provided a security-aware design partition and placement method that generated obfuscated chip layout while achieving a significant security improvement with tolerable performance/area overhead.

Although 2D IC-based split fabrication works well in most scenarios, 3D integration offers more benefits. First, 3D integration provides further improvement on system performance and cost efficiency. 3D integration lands itself well to split assembling process. Second, 3D integration provides a much larger design space for security improvement. In 2D IC-based split fabrication, designers can only partition higher metal layers of the chip for security purposes. However, in the 3D scenario, both the transistors and lower metal layers are design knobs. Moreover, in 2D design, the chip can only be split into two parts, but 3D integration provides more flexibility in design with multi-layer die-stacking.

2.2 Modular 3D Integration for Security

Sherwood *et al.* [19, 37] proposed an architecture with an extra control plane stacked on top of the existing computation plane. The control plane provides various security mechanisms, and the computation plane contains processing cores. This approach requires minor modifications in the original design such as providing an interface to the control plane. The computation plane is able to function without the control plane. However, after introducing an extra control plane, the critical signals are detoured to the control plane, where they are either encrypted or monitored [7]. Alternatively, by detouring the important signals, the control plane can also bypass the unsecure circuits in the computation plane and replaces them with secure design.

This idea takes advantage of the flexibility of 3D stacking, and provides modular security design. It benefits from 3D technologies in the following aspects. The control plane can be integrated in a per-need basis for security-sensitive market segments. Second, thanks to the modular design, a variety of different control plane alternatives can be used with the same computation plane. Third, the 3D stacking offers extremely small latency, large bandwidth, and IO connections. Compared with the off-chip co-processor solution, the performance and power overhead of this modular security design is much lower [38]. Also, this idea could be extended to combine split fabrication [39] and data compression [28].

There are also other techniques combining 3D stacking with hardware security improvements. For example, Bao *et al.* [6] proposed a dual cache design that prevents cache side-channel attacks. Since the proposed cache design causes performance degradation, 3D cache stacking was introduced to mitigate the performance loss along with other advantages such as the larger bandwidth and shorter access latency.

3. NEW OPPORTUNITIES

After re-examining the 3D/2.5D-based security design, we propose four opportunities utilizing these technologies to improve the existing hardware security schemes and show that more security features can be added. We further discuss the potential design challenges for these opportunities. As the attacking techniques become more aggressive, thermal side channel attack emerge, which are difficult for conventional 2D design to prevent. In Section 3.1, we show the 3D technology's potential to tackle various security challenges. Recently, with advancements in processing technology, monolithic 3D integration and active interposers in 2.5D integration technologies are possible, providing more choices for security designs. In Section 3.2 and 3.3, we explain how those techniques benefit security design. Finally in Section 3.4, we show new opportunities in the 3D-supported processing-in-memory architecture.

3.1 Shielding Side Channels with 3D Stacking

Side-channel attacks [45] are important security challenges, as they reveal sensitive information about on-chip activities. In cryptographic modules, the cipher hardware is represented as a black box whose internal operations are not observable in theory. However, attackers can bypass the mathematical complexity of the encryption algorithms by extracting and analyzing physical side-channel data such as power dissipation, thermal profiles, electromagnetic radiation, and acoustic traces to determine the secret keys.

Among such attacks, Thermal Side-channel (TSC) attacks have been shown to disclose the activities of key functional blocks and even encryption keys. Built-in thermal sensor data has been used to analyze the task scheduling sequence of encryption algorithms [5]. Nefarious programs have been shown to use the TSC as a covert communication channel for transferring sensitive information in FPGAs [21] and multi-core platforms [27]. By decapsulating an embedded micro-controller and attaching a low-cost thermal sensor, recent studies showed that encryption parameters can be acquired

proposed tech.	3D technology's advantage	benefit for security
Sec. 3.1: shielding side-channel	the die stacking structure	security enhancement
Sec. 3.2: split fabrication on active interposers	cost-efficient integration	cost reduction
Sec. 3.3: camouflage on monolithic 3D IC	flexible and efficient interconnections	perf./power overhead migration
Sec. 3.4: 3D IC-based security PIM	large bandwidth and power efficiency	perf./power overhead migration

Table 1: Overview of the proposed methods and how they benefit from 3D technology.

from the temperature profile [20]. The availability of highly sensitive on-chip and off-chip thermal sensors, infrared cameras, and techniques to calculate power consumption from temperature distribution [11] has enhanced the effectiveness of TSC attacks. As a result, side-channel attacks can be performed by using temperature data without measuring power pins of the chip. This improves the accuracy of other attack types such as Differential Power Analysis [25], which relies on power readings.

While a large range of countermeasures has been explored [45], none of these techniques can fully prevent side-channel attacks. In most cases, they aim to make the process more difficult to deter attackers. Even state-of-the-art hardware solutions such as read-proof static coating layers [35] have been shown to be ineffective in preventing such TSC attacks.

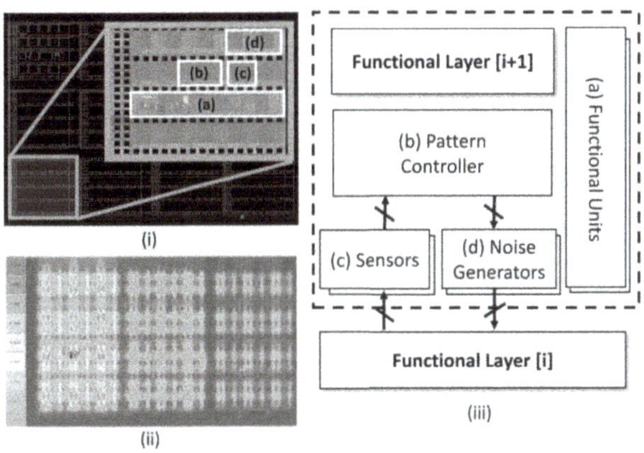

Figure 1: (i) Layout of a Functional Layer. (ii) Patterns Generated by the Pattern Generator Macros. (iii) 3D Side-channel Shielding Hardware Architecture.

The key idea is to protect ICs from thermal side-channel attacks by utilizing intrinsic characteristics of 3D chip integration, as well as proactively using dynamic shielding patterns to conceal critical activities on chip. The proposed technique incorporates targeted strategies to protect from the three attack modes: (i) *Built-in Sensors*: Instead of associating built in thermal sensors with individual functional blocks, sensors are placed to read out a composite thermal profile of the device and layer blocks. Therefore, the attackers cannot directly associate temperature readings with specific functional blocks while the overall system thresholds are implemented to avoid thermal damage or run-away conditions [17]. (ii) *External Sensors*: Since external thermal sensors can be placed flexibly at various locations by attackers, the effectiveness of the thermal readings can vary. The proposed architecture covers all thermal sensor placement options such that noise injected by security layers will decrement the side-channel leakage of any critical areas. (iii) *Infrared Thermal Imaging*: The noise generation in the proposed approach conceals the activity patterns of the functional units from infrared cameras and other imaging devices.

We assume the same 3D manufacturing specification as [41]. As demonstrated in Figure 1, this solution includes: (i) A micro-controller unit that dynamically generates complementary activity patterns to prevent side-channel data leakage. Thermal patterns are generated in a randomized, non-repeating manner such that side-channel attackers cannot extract meaningful information by observing any pattern sequence. (ii) 3D noise generators that run dynamic patterns.

In addition to targeting the individual attack modes separately, the proposed technique works with on-chip power budget and thermal management policies. The power overhead is minimized by intelligently controlling the activity in layers. In side-channel secure mode, the pattern generator macros produce noise according to the security level set by the pattern controllers through the power and thermal constraints. This approach works with on-chip thermal management policies, which will activate appropriate actions in the rare cases where the thermal thresholds are exceeded, causing the whole chip to cool down, without leaking any TSC information.

3D integration provides a number of inherent advantages in side-channel attacks:

Invasive Attacks: Historically, removing packaging to reveal device layers has been an effective step in invasive attacks. However, due to the bonding process, 3D layers cannot be removed without harming the normal functionality of the ICs. This protection becomes even more prominent in advanced 3D technologies due to the increased number of thinned device layers [24].

Semi-Invasive Attacks: Simple photonic analysis [16]-based attacks require wafer thinning. 3D integration provides protection from such attacks due to the multi-layer stacking that shields the device layers.

Non-Invasive Attacks: 3D stacking provides additional protection from non-invasive attacks as device layers and inter-layer bonding materials inherently complicate the radiated side-channel information out of the chip. Thermal profiles of the intermediate layers experience an inherent shielding effect of the layers on top.

The proposed 3D architecture could effectively shield the activity patterns in the critical area by the dynamic patterns produced in the noise generators. As the activity level in the functional layer grows, the power consumed by the noise generators will increase accordingly. The challenges are how to minimize the side-channel information leakage under limited power budget, and how to design power-efficient algorithms to maximally reduce side-channel vulnerability while maintaining acceptable power and thermal overhead. Studies on tradeoff between power consumption and side-channel vulnerability and the relationship between thermal patterns and side-channel information are necessary to optimize runtime management of the proposed 3D architecture.

3.2 Cost-aware Hardware Security Using Active Interposers

The interposer in 2.5D integration technology connects multiple dies with micro-bumps (μbumps) through interconnecting them with higher-level metal wires. It provides higher degree of integration with less power and smaller latency than PCB or in-package integration, since the μbumps are much smaller than the IO C4 bumps, and the interconnects are basically on-chip metal wires. The interposer technique has already been applied in various products, such as FPGA [?] and GPU [1]. So far, studies mainly focus on passive interposers, where only high-level metal layers exist. However, 2.5D integration also enables active interposers, which contain both transistors and low-level metal layers. The degree of integration is significantly improved in this approach, while extra costs are incurred due to interposer yield reduction and additional masks. As previous work pointed out [23] in Table 2, as the portion of the active region increases, the yield goes down. For example, a fully-active solution can degrade the yield from 94.1% to 61.5%. Therefore, the number of transistors on the active interposer are typically kept to a minimum.

D_0 :	500	1000	1500	2000
Passive	98.5%	97.0%	95.5%	94.1%
Active 1%	98.4%	96.9%	95.4%	93.9%
Active 10%	98.0%	96.1%	94.2%	92.4%
Fully-Active	87.2%	76.9%	68.5%	61.5%

Table 2: Interposer yield rates with various active regions calculated by Kannan *et al.* [23] (D_0 is in defects per m^2).

In this context, split manufacturing techniques (as discussed in Section 2) can be re-examined. With an active interposer, which is already utilized for performance purposes (e.g., high bandwidth memory, HBM [1] integration), an extra 3D layer is not required to split the target die for security purposes. Instead, the die could simply be split into an active interposer and the original die. Now, a cost-aware split fabrication on the active interposer is needed. Previous work developed partition methods either in 3D or passive interposer conditions, where the original designs are equally partitioned into different dies, as shown in Figure 2 (a). However, in split fabrication with an active interposer, the original design is split into both the stacked dies and the active interposer.

The challenge is how to minimize the number of transistors placed in the active interposer while meeting the security requirement, as shown in Figure 2 (b). If the number of transistors that are partitioned in the active interposer increases, the yield will decrease, and the cost will rise. In summary, the problem is formulated as minimizing the cost while meeting the security constraints by exploring different partitioning solutions.

3.3 Efficient Camouflage IC with Monolithic 3D Technologies

Monolithic three-dimensional (M3D) integration enables revolutionary digital system architectures. Based on metal pitch-scale inter-layer vias (ILV) instead of the large through-silicon via (TSV), it provides massive connectivity, leading to ultra-high bandwidth with power consumption reduction. We propose leveraging M3D to enhance security, i.e., as protection from reverse engineering.

The goal of this approach is to provide a camouflage IC design using M3D technology with smaller overhead but better security. The camouflage IC scheme attempts to make the design uniform. Inside a standard cell, the camouflage IC design ensures the layouts of different logic gates to show indistinguishable patterns. Among standard cells, the method tries to fill in the whitespace around macros so that the boundary of the standard cells cannot be recognized. The challenge for conventional camouflage IC design is the performance/area/power overhead. As a result, most chips can only afford partial camouflage of the critical parts. We envision that M3D will improve both of inter/intra-standard cell camouflage while reducing lower overhead.

Unlike the current 2.5D and 3D integration using TSVs to connect multiple circuit layers, M3D integration can fabricate a circuit layer directly on top of a previous layer with ILVs, which provides significantly high integration density [40]. Fine-grained M3D integration with CMOS-compatible carbon nanotube FETs or ReRAM [33, 13] at gate-level and circuit-level is also demonstrated.

Reverse Engineering [26] uses imaging recognition techniques to analyze ICs. The images can be obtained by destructive de-layering or nondestructive forms of imaging, after which the schematic can be extracted and analyzed, with the help of pattern recognition and pattern matching [34]. The goal of camouflage IC is to obfuscate the layout (active devices, poly layers, and lower-level metal layers) in order to prevent the reverse engineering. The camouflage IC can be classified into two categories: intra- and inter-standard cell camouflage. The intra-standard cell method [31, 9, 8] redesigns the original standard cell. The camouflage standard cell layouts for various gates look identical. It adds a hidden contact layer for each via, which is hard to detect with reverse engineering. The contact layer determines whether the via is connected or just a dummy via. Therefore, with different interconnections, the identical gates provide different functionalities (NAND, NOR, etc.). For the inter-standard cell camouflage, the scheme fills dummy circuits in the empty space among standard cells [10, 12] such that the attackers can not figure out standard cell parts. In M3D context, both the intra- and inter- standard cell camouflage can be improved, as described below.

Intra-Standard Cell Camouflage with M3D. The camouflage standard cell leads to area (4X), delay (1.5X), and power (5X) overhead [31, 32]. Therefore, it is not affordable to replace and camouflage all standard cells. A tradeoff has to be made between the security and the cost. The overhead of camouflaged standard cells, especially for the delay and power, is mainly caused by the extra wiring inside of the standard cell. However, in the M3D, this could be easily solved by fine-grained ILV. Therefore, the overhead is reduced. A series of 3D camouflage IC libraries is required, along with the M3D design flow. M3D also offers a larger

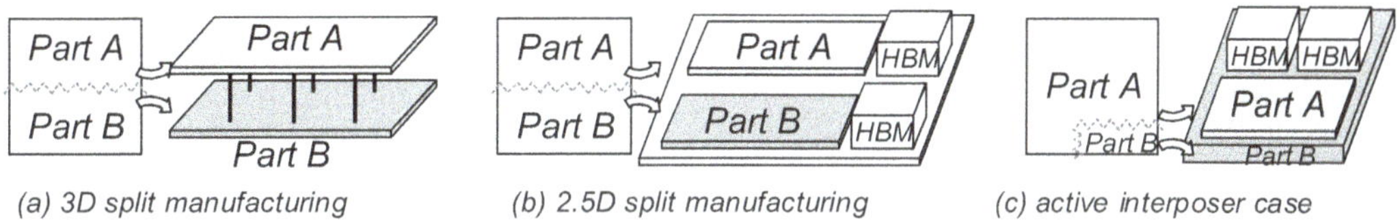

Figure 2: Previous split fabrication on 3D (a) or passive interposer (b). Cost-aware split fabrication on active interposer (c).

design space, which provides more potential for minimizing performance/area/power overhead, and more flexibility to tune the tradeoff between overhead and trust level.

Inter-Standard Cell Camouflage in M3D. The boundary of standard cells which makes reverse engineering more difficult [10] also needs to be blurred. Previous studies proposed filling in the whitespace with dummy cells. In order to hinder the dummy cells, this approach also needs to randomly connect dummy cells to the working cells, which leads to performance degradation. For the M3D structure, it provides higher security with the same overhead. This is because in the 2D design, the rectangle cell has four edges to merge with the dummy cell. For attackers, they only need to recognize 4 edges. However, for 3D monolithic cells, it has 6 faces to merge with dummy cells, which leads to extra difficulties for reverse engineering. Moreover, the 3D partition also makes the attacking challenging, as shown in Figure 3. Multiple partition options increase the search space for reverse engineering.

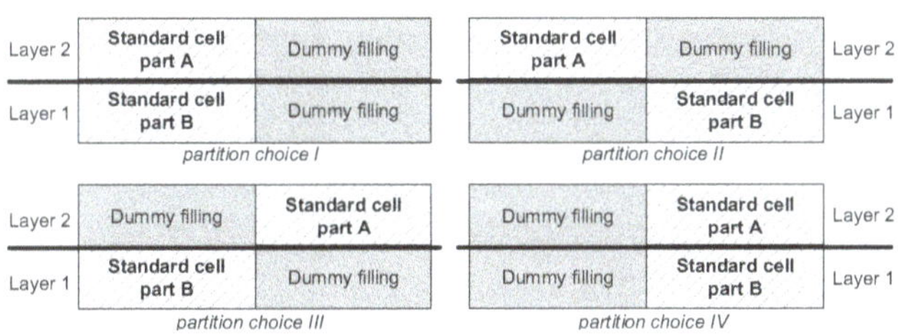

Figure 3: Inter-Standard Cell Camouflage in M3D.

3.4 Mitigating Security Overhead with 3D PIM Architecture

In order to mitigate the "memory wall", recent studies have focused on a data-centric architecture that tries to bring computing and memory closer. Meanwhile, the processing-in-memory (PIM) architecture drew attention [4], due to the significant reduction in data movement overhead. In the early PIM designs, logic and memory were designed on the same die, causing practical challenges to the cost-sensitive memory industry. Therefore, recent PIM studies rely on 3D stacking memory (e.g., hybrid memory cube (HMC) [29]), where the logic and memory are decoupled by die stacking.

The aim is to take advantage of the 3D IC-based PIM's ultra-high bandwidth, massive parallelism, and high energy efficiency to mitigate or release the performance and energy overhead for memory security enhancement. For example, memory authentication leads to 6X bandwidth overhead [43], while 3D-based PIM can potentially provide 80X more bandwidth [2], which totally offsets the performance degradation paid for the memory security. There is an opportunity to integrate secure processors or security protocol accelerators in the logic die in the same stack with the memory dies. Gundu *et al.* [3] already proposed the Security DIMM architecture that leverages PIM for memory security. Their work targeted merkle tree authentication and expected 4.5X speedup, which reduced the overhead from 6X to 2.1X.

4. CONCLUSION

Security challenges have gained considerable attention from academia and industries as sensitive information and intellectual property may be compromised by the increasing power and number of hardware attacks. Existing countermeasures may induce design overhead, which degrades the performance and adds extra cost. 3D die-stacking and 2.5D-interposer design are promising technologies that provide improvements to existing hardware security schemes and include further security features due to the enhancement of integration density, improvement in performance and reduction in cost. This paper summarizes recent studies on hardware security designs based on 3D technology and proposes four opportunities: (i) a 3D architecture for shielding side-channel information; (ii) split fabrication using active interposers; (iii) circuit camouflage on monolithic 3D IC, and (iv) 3D IC-based security PIM. Advantages and challenges of these designs are discussed and analysed.

5. REFERENCES

[1] AMD Fury X GPU. http://www.amd.com/en-us/innovations/software-technologies/hbm.

[2] J. Ahn et al. A scalable processing-in-memory accelerator for parallel graph processing. In *Proc. 42nd Annu. Int. Symp. Comput. Archit.*, pages 105–117. ACM Press, 2015.

[3] Akhila Gundu Ali Shafiee Ardestani et al. A Case for Near Data Security. In *WoNDP 2nd Work. Near-Data Process. Int. Symp. Microarchitecture*, 2014.

[4] R. Balasubramonian et al. Near-Data Processing: Insights from a MICRO-46 Workshop. In *IEEE Micro*, 2014.

[5] C. Bao et al. A secure algorithm for task scheduling against side-channel attacks. In *Proc. Int. Workshop on Trustworthy Embedded Devices*, 2014.

[6] C. Bao et al. 3D Integration: New opportunities in defense against cache-timing side-channel attacks. In *IEEE Int. Conf. Comput. Des.*, 2015.

[7] M. Bilzor. 3D Execution Monitor (3D-EM): Using 3D Circuits to Detect Hardware Malicious Inclusions in General Purpose Processors. In *Proc. 6th Int. Conf. Inf. Warf. Secur.*, 2011.

[8] L.-W. Chow et al. Integrated circuits protected against reverse engineering and method for fabricating the same using an apparent metal contact line terminating on field oxide, 2007.

[9] R. P. Cocchi et al. Building block for a secure CMOS logic cell library, 2012.

[10] R. P. Cocchi et al. Circuit camouflage integration for hardware IP protection. In *Des. Autom. Conf. (DAC)*, 2014.

[11] R. Cochran et al. Post-silicon power characterization using thermal infrared emissions. In *Int. Symp. on Low Power Electronics and Design*, 2010.

[12] B. DiMarzio et al. Method and apparatus for camouflaging a standard cell based integrated circuit with micro circuits and post processing, 2013.

[13] M. S. Ebrahimi et al. Monolithic 3D integration advances and challenges: From technology to system levels. In *SOI-3D-Subthreshold Microelectron. Technol. Unified Conf.*, 2014.

[14] P. Emma et al. Is 3d chip technology the next growth engine for performance improvement? *IBM journal of research and development*, 52(6):541–552, 2008.

[15] P. Emma et al. 3d system design: A case for building customized modular systems in 3d. In *Interconnect Technology Conference (IITC)*, pages 1–3. IEEE, 2010.

[16] J. Ferrigno et al. When aes blinks: introducing optical side channel. *Information Security, IET*, 2008.

[17] M. Floyd et al. Adaptive energy-management features of the ibm power7 chip. *IBM Journal of Research and Development*, 2011.

[18] B. Hill et al. A split-foundry asynchronous FPGA. In *Proc. IEEE 2013 Cust. Integr. Circuits Conf.*, 2013.

[19] T. Huffmire et al. Hardware trust implications of 3-D integration. In *Proc. 5th Work. Embed. Syst. Secur.*, 2010.

[20] M. Hutter et al. The temperature side channel and heating fault attacks. In *Smart Card Research and Advanced Applications*. 2014.

[21] T. Iakymchuk et al. Temperature-based covert channel in fpga systems. In *6th International Workshop on Reconfigurable Communication-centric Systems-on-Chip (ReCoSoC)*, 2011.

[22] F. Imeson et al. Securing computer hardware using 3D integrated circuit (IC) technology and split manufacturing for obfuscation. In *Proc. 22nd USENIX Conf. Secur.*, 2013.

[23] A. Kannan et al. Enabling interposer-based disintegration of multi-core processors. In *Proc. of the 48th Int. Symp. on Microarchitecture (MICRO)*, 2015.

[24] J. Knickerbocker et al. 2.5 d and 3d technology challenges and test vehicle demonstrations. In *IEEE 62nd Electronic Components and Technology Conference (ECTC)*, 2012.

[25] P. Kocher et al. Differential power analysis. In *Advances in Cryptology*, 1999.

[26] W. Li et al. Reverse engineering circuits using behavioral pattern mining. In *Hardware-Oriented Secur. Trust (HOST)*, 2012.

[27] R. J. Masti et al. Thermal covert channels on multi-core platforms. *arXiv preprint arXiv:1503.07000*, 2015.

[28] D. Megas et al. Data Transformation in a Three Dimensional Integrated Circuit Implementation. In *DTIC Doc.*, 2012.

[29] J. T. Pawlowski. Hybrid memory cube (HMC). In *Hot Chips*, 2011.

[30] J. Rajendran et al. Is Split Manufacturing Secure? In *Des. Autom. Test Eur. Conf. Exhib.*, 2013.

[31] J. Rajendran et al. Security Analysis of Integrated Circuit Camouflaging. In *Proc. 2013 ACM SIGSAC Conf. Comput. Commun. Secur.*, 2013.

[32] J. Rajendran et al. VLSI testing based security metric for IC camouflaging. In *Test Conf. (ITC), IEEE Int.*, 2013.

[33] M. M. Shulaker et al. Monolithic 3D integration of logic and memory: Carbon nanotube FETs, resistive RAM, and silicon FETs. In *Int. Electron Devices Meet. (IEDM)*, 2014.

[34] R. Torrance et al. The State-of-the-Art in IC Reverse Engineering. In *Proc. 11th Int. Work. Cryptogr. Hardw. Embed. Syst.*, 2009.

[35] P. Tuyls et al. Read-proof hardware from protective coatings. In *Cryptographic Hardware and Embedded Systems (CHES)*. 2006.

[36] K. Vaidyanathan et al. Efficient and secure intellectual property (IP) design with split fabrication. In *IEEE Int. Symp. Hardware-Oriented Secur. Trust*, 2014.

[37] J. Valamehr et al. Hardware assistance for trustworthy systems through 3-D integration. In *Proc. 26th Annu. Comput. Secur. Appl. Conf.*, 2010.

[38] J. Valamehr et al. A Qualitative Security Analysis of a New Class of 3-D Integrated Crypto Co-processors. 2012.

[39] J. Valamehr et al. A 3-D Split Manufacturing Approach to Trustworthy System Development. *IEEE Trans. Comput. Des. Integr. Circuits Syst.*, 2013.

[40] M. Vinet et al. Monolithic 3D integration: A powerful alternative to classical 2D scaling. In *SOI-3D-Subthreshold Microelectron. Technol. Unified Conf. (S3S)*, 2014.

[41] M. Wordeman et al. A 3d system prototype of an edram cache stacked over processor-like logic using through silicon vias. In *IEEE International Solid-State Circuits Conference Digest of Technical Papers (ISSCC)*, 2012.

[42] Y. Xie et al. Security-Aware Design Flow for 2.5D IC Technology. In *Proc. 5th Int. Work. Trust. Embed. Devices*, 2015.

[43] C. Yan et al. Improving cost, performance, and security of memory encryption and authentication. In *Proc. 33rd Annu. Int. Symp. Comput. Archit.*, 2006.

[44] J. Zhao et al. Overview of 3d architecture design opportunities and techniques. *IEEE Design Test*, 2015.

[45] Y. Zhou et al. Side-channel attacks: Ten years after its publication and the impacts on cryptographic module security testing. *IACR Cryptology ePrint Archive*, 2005.

FCM: Towards Fine-Grained GPU Power Management for Closed Source Mobile Games

Jiachen Song[1], Xi Li[1,2], Beilei Sun[1,2], Zhinan Cheng[1], Chao Wang[1,2] and Xuehai Zhou[1,2]
[1]Dept. of Computer Science and Technology, University of Science and Technology of China (USTC)
Hefei, 230027, China
[2]Suzhou Institute for Advanced Study, USTC, Suzhou, 215123, China
{jchsong, sasbl, chinam}@mail.ustc.edu.cn, {llxx, cswang, xhzhou}@ustc.edu.cn

ABSTRACT

Contemporary mobile platforms employ embedded graphic processing units (GPUs) for graphics-intensive games, and dynamic voltage and frequency scaling (DVFS) policies are used to save energy without sacrificing quality. However, current GPU DVFS policies result in unnecessary power waste due to defective workload estimations of embedded GPUs during game play. In this paper, we propose the *Frame-Complexity Model (FCM)*, a fine-grained estimation of the GPU workload in a game frame, to quantify the GPU workload with the real runtime demand for GPU computing resources of a game frame. In FCM, three constituents of a game frame (i.e., structure, textures and computation) are quantified without modification of mobile games. Preliminary experiments show that, compared with the default policy, the FCM-directed GPU DVFS policy can reduce more power consumption of games (11.3% to 25.8%) with good Quality of Service (QoS).

Keywords

GPU Workload Model; DVFS; Mobile Games; Fine-grained; Power Management

1. INTRODUCTION

3D mobile games compete for computing resources of both CPUs and GPUs in mobile phones. Recently, GPUs have been launched with increasing frequency to satisfy graphics-intensive games [1]. Basically, high frequency leads to high power consumption. Efficient power management of embedded GPUs has become a critical problem [4, 7], especially during game play [6].

DVFS is introduced as the main technique for power management of embedded GPUs on mobile platforms [8]. However, most of current policies [3, 6, 8], including the default DVFS policy for embedded GPUs in smart phones, borrow the CPU-like workload estimation, in which the workload is estimated with the utilization of underlying GPUs in previous sampling intervals [7]. Unfortunately, in this historical utilization-based technique, mistaken and lagged estimations result in unnecessary power waste or performance loss. These defects become even worse in highly interactive mobile games: On the one hand, the GPU workload changes harshly from frame to frame due to the unpredictable input by players. On the other hand, the current workload is estimated with the information in previous frames, which may be outdated and wrong. Though more accurate models, such as PID [3] and LMS [2], are applied to improve the estimation, they can not eliminate the inherent defects of this historical utilization-based estimation. Besides, the open-source-based estimation in [3] can hardly be applied as most mobile games are closed source games. The game-state-based method in [2] fails to provide a fine-grained estimation since the GPU workload changes a lot in the same state (e.g., gaming). Thus, policies mentioned above lack of feasibility in the design of efficient GPU DVFS policies for closed-source mobile games. A different method of GPU workload estimation is required.

We find that, in modern graphics-intensive mobile games, a game frame mainly consists of three different kinds of GPU workloads, including the structural, the textural and the computational workloads. Each of them can be well quantified by specific parameter in the data flow from the CPU to the GPU. Besides, all the parameters can be easily traced without modification of games in Android system. These observations motivate us to build an accurate GPU workload model for runtime mobile games, which can be used to direct the GPU DVFS for closed-source mobile games in a fine-grained way. Totally, this paper makes the following contributions:

- Find out quantifications (the number of vertices, the size of textures and the amount of OpenGL|ES commands) for main constituents of GPU workload (the structural, textural and computational complexity) in a game frame.
- Build the Frame-Complexity Model (FCM) for runtime GPU workload estimation with found quantifications. Based on FCM, we propose the FCM-directed GPU DVFS policy (FGDP).
- Realize FGDP on our smartphone-like platform. Experiments show that FGDP saves more power (11.3%-25.8%) than the default utilization-based policy without obvious user-experience reduction.

The rest of this paper is organized as follows: In Section 2, we describe the design of FCM and FGDP in detail, followed by the experimental evaluation and analysis in Section 3. We conclude our work and plan the future work in Section 4.

GLSVLSI '16, May 18-20, 2016, Boston, MA, USA
© 2016 ACM. ISBN 978-1-4503-4274-2/16/05...$15.00
DOI: http://dx.doi.org/10.1145/2902961.2902989

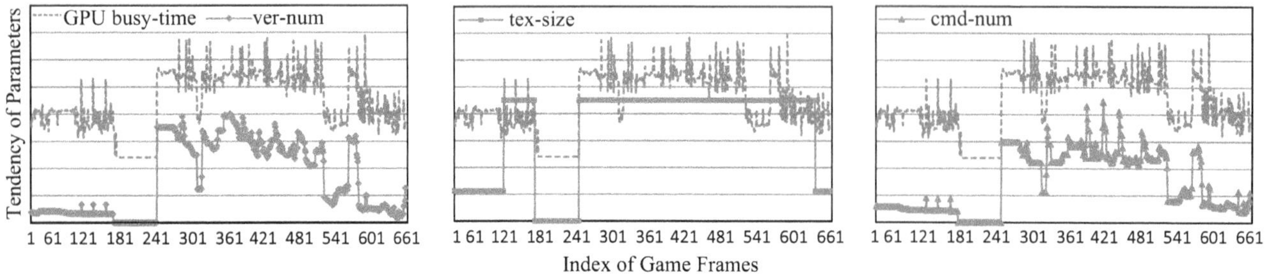

Fig. 1: Relationship between Each Parameter (Vertices, Textures, Commands) and GPU Busy-time in Quake-II.

2. DESIGN

2.1 Frame-Complexity Model

Game frames are generated from three kinds of data, including vertex data, texture data and command data. They can be well quantified by the following three parameters in our observations.

1. *Number of Vertices.* Vertex data composes the structure of a frame. The LoD (Level of Detail) defined as the number of triangles in a frame [5] has similar consideration. Since not every vertex is one of the three points of a triangle, we replace a triangle with a vertex.
2. *Size of Textures.* Textures have significant influence on the power consumption of GPU. Our former work [7] estimates the GPU workload with the number of function calls to *glBindTexture()*. We make it further to use the size of textures to quantify the textual complexity since not all the workloads of calls are equal.
3. *Number of Commands.* OpenGL|ES commands are used for providing flag information and controlling the GPU rendering pipeline. The number of commands indicates the complexity of control and computation.

Since these three kinds of data contribute to the main GPU workload, it is feasible for us to define the Frame-Complexity Model (FCM), as Equation (1) shows, to estimate the GPU workload with the quantifications above:

$$FC_{tot}(v,t,c) = \sum W_j * FC_j(x_j), (j = v,t,c) \quad (1)$$

where x_j $(j = v, t, c)$ represents the value of each parameter. The frame complexity (FC_{tot}) can be expressed as a weighted sum of the structural complexity (FC_v), the textural complexity (FC_t) and the computational complexity (FC_c) with the weight coefficient W_v, W_t and W_c.

2.2 Model Refinement

In FCM shown in Equation (1), FC_j $(j = v, t, c)$ will be built and W_j $(j = v, t, c)$ will be decided in this subsection, both of them are kept low-cost to avoid consuming much computation in our design.

FC_j $(j = v, t, c)$ follows the basic facts that the more vertices, textures or commands there are, the more complex each constituent is. To conveniently qualify the parameters, we define FC_j $(j = v, t, c)$ as the normalization of each parameter to [0, 255], as shown in Equation (2):

$$FC_j(x_j) = 255 * (\frac{x_j}{X_j}), \quad (j = v,t,c) \quad (2)$$

where the variable x_j is normalized to [0, 1] by X_j, it is set as the maximum number of each parameter respectively. The result is adjusted to [0, 255] by the constant 255.

Table 1: Correlation Coefficients of Parameters with GPU Busy-time in Different Games

Game	Parameter	r (with GPU busy-time)
FishJoy3	Vertex-num	0.890532404
	Texture-size	0.836408242
	Command-num	0.914506208
Quake-II	Vertex-num	0.863219856
	Texture-size	0.697975074
	Command-num	0.941740764
Jetpack	Vertex-num	0.799181952
	Texture-size	0.784825705
	Command-num	0.799086695

When it comes to W_j $(j = v, t, c)$, we carry out experiments to find out how these three resources contribute to the whole GPU workload. Since we can not measure only the power consumed by GPU for electrical specifications, we alternately employ GPU busy time in a frame, t in Equation (3), to measure the tendency of energy consumption. This is reasonable because we fix GPU to its max frequency (F) and voltage (V) to get the constant power P. The parameters α and C do not change since they are only decided by the physical properties of chips.

$$E = P * t = \alpha CV^2F * t \quad (3)$$

Three typical popular games (classic Quake-II, popular Jetpack and FishJoy3) are chosen. We trace the parameters (v, t and c) as well as the GPU busy time during game play, aiming at finding out the relationship of the energy consumption with each parameter. The correlation coefficients (rs) are calculated with Equation (4) and shown in Table 1:

$$r = \frac{\sum_{i=1}^{n}(x_i - \overline{x})(y_i - \overline{y})}{\sqrt{\sum_{i=1}^{n}(x_i - \overline{x})^2 \cdot \sum_{i=1}^{n}(y_i - \overline{y})^2}} \quad (4)$$

where $\overline{x}$ and $\overline{y}$ are mathematical expectations of x and y. If r is bigger than 0.6, x and y have a strong relationship of positive correlation [7].

High correlation coefficients (greater than 0.6, up to 0.94) in Table 1 verifies the correctness of each parameter, but we should not use single one parameter of the three to estimate the GPU workload. Actually, they affect the workload from different angles. In Fig.1, though the three lines (tex-size, ver-num and cmd-num) keep the consistent tendency with the GPU busy-time, their values vary a lot. Experiments with other games show similar results.

This paper simply assumes the contribution of each parameter is equal before more detailed experimental analysis of the relationship between them. The constants W_j $(j = v, t, c)$ are all set to 1/3 for the high correlation coefficient of each parameter. We believe the relationship is determined by the cooperation mechanism of the three-kind data in the construction of a game frame. Equation (5) shows our simple but efficient model.

$$FC_{tot} = 255 * \frac{1}{3} * [(\frac{x_v}{X_v}) + (\frac{x_t}{X_t}) + (\frac{x_c}{X_c})] \quad (5)$$

FCM is an abstraction of the GPU workload built from the quantifications of key constituents in a game frame. It does not rely on any specific platform or game.

2.3 FCM-directed GPU DVFS Policy

Based on FCM, we propose the FCM-directed GPU DVFS Policy (FGDP). Fig.2 shows the framework of FGDP.

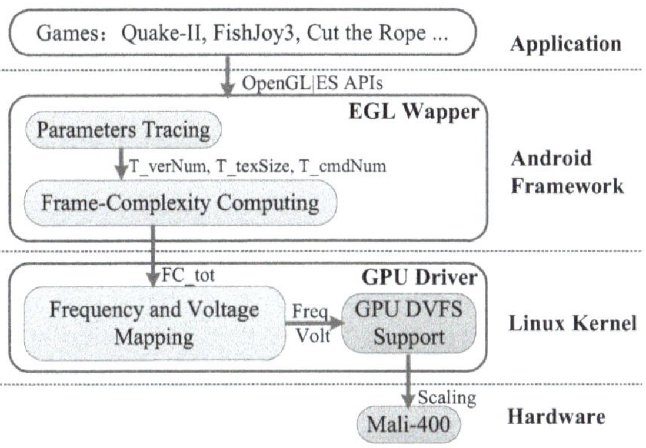

Fig. 2: Framework of FCM-directed GPU DVFS Policy

During game play, all OpenGL|ES APIs will pass through the EGL wrapper employed to manage the local window for OpenGL|ES in Android Framework. Here we start the FGDP consisting of the following three steps:

Step 1. The *Parameters Tracing* module traces the number of vertices (T_verNum), the size of textures ($T\_texSize$) and the number of OpenGL|ES APIs (T_cmdNum) in each frame. This is convenient for closed source games with the help of the tracing mechanism in Android system.

Step 2. The *Frame-Complexity Computing* module normalizes each parameter by X_v, X_t, X_c and calculates FC_{tot} with all parameters and W_v, W_t, W_c. This module is also placed in the EGL Wrapper for lower overhead of the data transmission. The result of FCM (FC_{tot}) is passed to the next module of FGDP along with an added system call which is designed only to deliver an integer down to the Linux kernel. Alg.1 shows the details of Step 2.

Step 3. The *Frequency and Voltage Mapping* module decides the frequency and voltage of GPU with FC_{tot}. We replaces the workload estimation with the FC_{tot} in the default and only DVFS policy in our platform. The scaling strategy relies on two thresholds: when FC_{tot} is higher (lower) than the upper (lower) bound, GPU is scaled to run at the high (low) frequency. Otherwise, GPU runs at the current frequency. The thresholds are set to specific percentages of FC_{tot} shown in Table 2.

FGDP performs per-frame estimation with FCM, but the frequency scaling is performed only when necessary In this way, the FGDP can stay stable and sensitive, reducing the thrashing phenomenon.

Table 2: Levels with Thresholds of Mali-400 DVFS

level	clk(MHz)	vol(V)	upthreshold(%)	downthreshold(%)
L1	266	1.00	–	30
L0	160	0.95	65	–

Alg. 1 Normalization and Frame-Complexity Computing

```
Input: double T_verNum, T_texSize, T_cmdNum;
Output: int FC_tot;
int FC_tot = 255;
if (T_verNum > X_v)
    v_forModel = 1.0;
else
    v_forModel = T_verNum/X_v;
if (Trace_texSize > X_t)
    t_forModel = 1.0;
else
    t_forModel = T_texSize/X_t;
if (Trace_cmdNum > X_c)
    c_forModel = 1.0;
else
    c_forModel = T_cmdNum/X_c;

FC_tot = (int)(255/3 * (v_forModel
                + t_forModel + c_forModel));
syscall(__NR_onframe, FC_tot, 0);
```

3. EXPERIMENTAL EVALUATION

All experiments are performed on our ODROID platform. It is equipped with a Samsung Exynos4210 ARM Cortex-A9 (dual-core) processor and a Mali-400 MP GPU, it offers a two-level scaling scheme between 160MHz and 255MHz with thresholds shown in Table 2. The operating system is Android 4.0.4 with Linux 3.0. All power measurements exclude any network interfaces and external hardware peripherals and the CPU clock and the bus frequency are fixed to a high level to ensure minimum interference.

3.1 Power Management: FGDP vs. UGDP

To compare FGDP with the default and only utilization-based GPU DVFS policy (UGDP), we recorded FC_{tot} and the GPU utilization, as well as the frequency levels mapped by FGDP and UGDP during the same game play. What should be mentioned is that, the driver of the GPU did not really perform the scaling in any policy and it ran at the low frequency level through the experiment. The result of popular game Fishjoy3 is shown by Fig.3(a), in which *Uti_org* represents the GPU utilization, *Lvl_uti* means the frequency level mapped by UGDP. *FC_tot* is the output of FCM, and *Lvl_fcm* is the frequency level mapped by FGDP.

Fig.3(a) shows that *FC_tot* keeps a consistent tendency with *Uti_org* except for some situations, e.g., when the game enters the menu state (around frame 161), *Uti_org* is high while *FC_tot* is low, resulting the high *Lvl_uti* and the low *Lvl_fcm*. Usually, game menus are simple scenes which should run with a low frequency to reduce the power consumption [2]. But UGDP scales the frequency to a high level. This phenomenon is probably caused by neglect of the FPS control in menu states. Generally, games with uncontrolled FPS run as fast as a device can afford, resulting in the high GPU utilization and the power waste under UGDP. FGDP works well because FCM estimates the real demand for GPU computation of current game frames.

In addition, FGDP is more sensitive to the changes of the GPU workload than UGDP. FCM estimates the GPU workload from the materials of the current game frame. But in UGDP, the historical utilization contains too much outdated information and fails to feel the harshly change of the GPU workload. We can tell this from the frames around 475 in Fig.3(a), where FGDP scales down the frequency and voltage because of harshly degradation of workload. However, UGDP remains the level of high frequency and voltage.

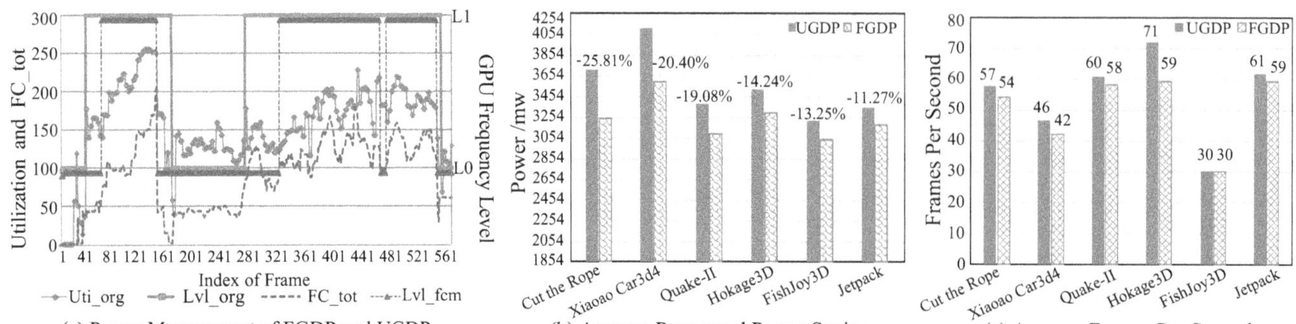

(a) Power Management of FGDP and UGDP (b) Average Power and Power Saving (c) Average Frames Per Second

Fig. 3: Results of Experiments: Comparison between FGDP and UGDP in Power Management and QoS.

From the analysis above, we can conclude that FGDP is superior to UGDP for at least two reasons: (i) Avoiding the power waste in frames with low complexity like menus in games. (ii) Improving the accuracy of power management with the high sensitivity to the changes between frames.

3.2 Power Saving and QoS of FGDP

In this part, six popular commercial mobile games are chosen to evaluate FGDP in the aspect of the power saving and the QoS. FPS (Frames Per Second) is used for the evaluation of QoS as most researchers do.

Fig.3(b) shows that FGDP reduces more power waste of games (-11.27% to -25.81%) than UGDP with the average power consumption of idle platform being 1854 mw. For most games, we do not see significant FPS drops (-2 on average) from Fig.3(c), indicating a guaranteed QoS of FGDP. For game Hokage3D, the FPS drop from 71 to 59 (-12) is reasonable, because FGDP reduces the high uncontrolled FPS of simple frames in situation like menu as analyzed in Sec.3.1. And it causes little user experience reduction since 60 is the max value of FPS after Project Butter. The overhead of the computation and data transmission in FCM is low, which can be neglected with the power reduced.

Different games achieve different amount of power reduction with FGDP. As expected, games with more simple frames like menu (e.g., Cut the Rope and Xiaoao Car3d4) gain more power reduction (-25.81% and -20.40%), because FGDP avoids the unnecessary high frequency caused by uncontrolled FPS. Meanwhile, interaction-intensive games (e.g., Quake-II) also achieve a better power reduction (-19.08%) due to the high sensitivity of FGDP. However, less power is reduced by 2D games like Jetpack (-11.27%)in our experiment, since they demand less computation of GPU compared with CPU [2]. Other games get a stable power reduction (-14.24% and -13.25%) without obviously impacting the user experience.

4. CONCLUSION AND FUTURE WORK

This paper provides a fine-grained GPU workload model for efficient GPU DVFS design during game play on mobile platforms. The proposed Frame-Complexity Model (FCM) quantifies the three main constituents of the GPU workload (i.e., the operations of vertices, textures and the computations) in a game frame. Preliminary experimental evaluation shows that, FCM is highly accurate and efficient, and FCM-directed GPU DVFS policy can reduce more power consumption (up to 25.81%) than the default utilization-based GPU DVFS policy with good QoS.

In the future, the combination of different parameters and auto-obtaining of constants in FCM will be carried forward. We will design a frame complexity oriented DVFS policy for mobile GPU power management.

Acknowledgments

This work was supported by National Science Foundation of China under grants (No.61379040, No.61272131 and No.61202053), Jiangsu Provincial Natural Science Foundation (No.-SBK201240198), Open Project of State Key Laboratory of Computer Architecture, Institute of Computing Technology, Chinese Academy of Sciences (No.CARCH201407).

References

[1] https://en.wikipedia.org/wiki/Mali_(GPU).

[2] B. Dietrich, D. Goswami, S. Chakraborty, A. Guha, and M. Gries. Time series characterization of gaming workload for runtime power management. *Computers, IEEE Transactions on*, 64(1):260–273, 2015.

[3] Y. Gu and S. Chakraborty. A hybrid dvs scheme for interactive 3d games. In *Real-Time and Embedded Technology and Applications Symposium, 2008. RTAS'08. IEEE*, pages 3–12. IEEE, 2008.

[4] J. Ji, C. Wang, and X. Zhou. System-level early power estimation for memory subsystem in embedded systems. In *Fifth IEEE International Symposium on Embedded Computing*, pages 370–375. IEEE, 2008.

[5] B. Mochocki, K. Lahiri, and S. Cadambi. Power analysis of mobile 3d graphics. In *Proceedings of the conference on Design, automation and test in Europe: Proceedings*, pages 502–507. European Design and Automation Association, 2006.

[6] A. Pathania, A. E. Irimiea, A. Prakash, and T. Mitra. Power-performance modelling of mobile gaming workloads on heterogeneous mpsocs. In *Design Automation Conference (DAC), 2015 52nd IEEE/ACM*. IEEE, 2015.

[7] B. Sun, X. Li, J. Song, Z. Cheng, Y. Xu, and X. Zhou. Texture-directed mobile gpu power management for closed-source games. In *High Performance Computing and Communications(HPCC), 2014 IEEE Intl Conf on*, pages 348–354. IEEE, 2014.

[8] D. You and K.-S. Chung. Dynamic voltage and frequency scaling framework for low-power embedded gpus. *Electronics letters*, 48(21):1333–1334, 2012.

Quality of Service-Aware, Scalable Cache Tuning Algorithm in Consumer-based Embedded Devices

Mohamad Hammam Alsafrjalani and Ann Gordon-Ross
Department of Electrical and Computer Engineering University of Florida (UF), Gainesville, FL, USA
E-mail: mha8@ufl.edu, ann@ece.ufl.edu

Abstract—To meet energy and quality of service (QoS) constraints in consumer/user-based embedded devices (CEDs), configurable caches can be tuned to a *best* configuration that consumes the least amount of energy while adhering to QoS expectations. However, due to disparate consumer QoS expectations and a myriad of unknown, third-party CED applications, tuning caches in CEDs is very challenging. In this paper, we propose a quality of service-aware, scalable tuning algorithm for configurable caches, which requires no a priori knowledge of applications or design-time efforts.

I. INTRODUCTION AND BACKGROUND

Consumer-based embedded devices (CEDs) (e.g., smartphones, tablets, wearable computing, etc.) have quality of service (QoS) expectations, which is the user-expected system performance (e.g., expected response time to user touch-input, global positioning system (GPS) accuracy, etc.). CEDs executing applications, such as drawing, audio compression and recording, video frame decoding, heartrate reading/monitoring, speech-to-text/text-to-speech translation, GPS route tracking, etc. can be viewed as soft real time systems, wherein the application's execution-time constraints are tightly coupled with the QoS (i.e., missed deadlines degrade the user's satisfaction with system performance). Due to increasing consumer demands for these applications, and the proliferation of increasingly performance-capable multicore CEDs with limited battery reserves, reducing energy consumption while meeting QoS expectations is a key design challenge, since reducing the energy consumption trades off performance capabilities and potentially degrades QoS.

QoS degradation occurs when an application executes below an expected performance level—a performance threshold—which may be evaluated as slower-than-expected response to consumer/user touch-input, GPS route updates, choppy video playback, etc. Thus, the key challenge is to reduce the CED's energy consumption by as much as possible without falling below this performance threshold, which is highly user-subjective.

One of the most effective way to regulate energy consumption while maintaining acceptable QoS is optimizing system components that have high impacts on both energy and QoS; the cache/memory hierarchy [3][9][10][11]. Configurable caches [10] enable adherence to an application's unique locality requirements using configurable parameters. Configurable parameters' values can be tuned/adjusted to the *best configuration* that most closely adheres to locality requirements, and thus most closely adheres to the energy and QoS expectations. However, determining the best configuration imposes tuning overhead [6] that degrades QoS or requires static application profiling [9] that may not scale to unknown applications, which limits applicability to the rapidly expanding number of, largely third-party, applications.

To address these challenges, we propose a quality of service-aware, scalable cache tuning algorithm for multicore CEDs with configurable caches that maintains user-expected QoS expectations while reducing energy consumption. We architect a dynamic, general purpose CED cache-tuning algorithm that *requires no a priori knowledge* or *static profiling* of the applications. To accommodate our tuning algorithm's hardware requirement, we build our work based on hardware cache tuners [1] and design a low hardware overhead tuning table to hold the required tuning information used by our algorithm.

Our results reveal disjointed trends for energy savings and tuning-time QoS degradation, which allows our tuning algorithm to prioritize QoS or energy savings. Our algorithm exploited this flexibility using two tuning modes and achieved average energy savings as high as 20.68% and 25.14%, for the data and instruction caches, respectively, and imposed average tuning-time QoS degradation as low as 0.7 occurrences on average, as compared to an off-the-shelf, base configuration commonly found on CEDs. Compared to our results, prior work could reveal additional energy savings, however, prior required a priori knowledge of the applications to avoid a high QoS degradation of 7.7 on average.

II. HARDWARE LAYOUT AND REQUIREMENTS

Without loss of generality, we illustrate our methods using a quad core system with configurable cache size, line size, and associativity, and a runtime cache tuner, as depicted in Figure 1. To limit runtime intrusion, we use a global hardware cache tuner connected to all cores. For a quad core system, this tuner imposes 322 cycles overhead [1], which negligible considering the number of cycles to execute 1 million instructions. Prior work shows that this tuning interval is long enough to warm up and stabilize the caches [2].

The cache tuner monitors the cores' states (busy, idle, etc.) and reads the application's execution characteristics (e.g., cache miss rate, number of instructions, cycle count) at the end of each *tuning interval*. Tuning intervals are the length of time that the core executes in a particular configuration in order to determine that configuration's execution characteristics. Tuning decisions guide how the design space is explored (i.e., the order and number of configurations evaluated), and the cache tuner makes a tuning decision at the end of each tuning interval using a dynamic tuning algorithm (Section III), the application's execution characteristics, and the application's performance threshold. We assume the performance threshold can be

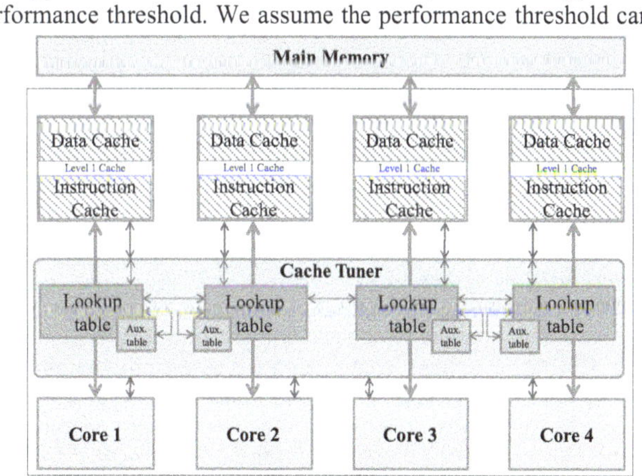

Figure 1: Quad core system with configurable caches and a global cache tuner.

GLSVLSI '16, May 18 - 20, 2016, Boston, MA, USA

ACM 978-1-4503-4274-2/16/05…$15.00
DOI: http://dx.doi.org/10.1145/2902961.2902987

relayed to the tuner by the operating system using memory mapped I/O, special instructions, etc. depending on the implementation details [2].

Our tuner stores the tuning information for tuning decisions in lookup tables, with one entry per application, which includes: the *energy consumption* of the best configuration explored thus far and *configuration characteristics*, which contain per-configuration information. The per-configuration lookup table includes: *explored*, *lowest energy*, and *QoS adherence*, which flag whether or not that configuration has been previously explored, is the lowest energy configuration explored thus far, and adheres to the application's QoS expectations, respectively. The per-application tuning information storage requirement *m* in bits is:

$$m = e + b * \lceil log_2(c) \rceil \qquad (1)$$

where *e* and *b* are the number of bits required to store the energy consumption and configuration characteristic information, respectively, and *c* is the number of configurations in the design space. To evaluate the storage requirements as compared to prior work, we assume that *e* is 32 bits, similarly to [1], and *b* is 3 bits, one for each configuration's characteristic flag.

To limit area overhead, this complete tuning information is only stored for an application during tuning. After the best configuration is determined, only that configuration is retained in a smaller auxiliary lookup table. To enable scalability to an arbitrary number of applications we utilize a least recently used replacement policy to govern the auxiliary table's information. Thus, given *a* applications, the total tuning information storage requirement *M* in bits is:

$$M = \log_2(a) * \lceil log_2(c) \rceil * m \qquad (2)$$

III. DYNAMIC TUNING ALGORITHM

A. Overview

Algorithm 1 depicts our dynamic tuning algorithm's finite state machine, which contains three states (Section III.B): *information input*, *exploration*, and *evaluation*. For each application, the algorithm explores the design space, one configuration per tuning interval, based on the tuning mode. Tuning is complete when the algorithm meets the tuning mode's stop-tuning condition (e.g., the conservative mode evaluates one cache parameter only) (Section III.B.iii).

B. Algorithm States

(i) Information Input State: When an application is scheduled to a core, either at inception or resumption, the algorithm begins in the *information input state*. First, the algorithm checks the auxiliary table to determine if this application's best configuration has already been determined. If the application is in the auxiliary table, the algorithm tunes the cache directly to the application's best configuration. Otherwise, the algorithm checks if the application is tuned for another core, and if so copies the tuning information from the other core's table to the current core's table, before tuning resumption. Otherwise, the algorithm attempts to the application's *read the tuning information* from the core's lookup table, and begins/resumes design space exploration in the *exploration state*.

(ii) Exploration state: The application's lookup table information provides the algorithm with information about all of the previously explored configurations. Using this information, the algorithm determines the next configuration to explore, and the application executes in that configuration for one tuning interval, after which the algorithm transitions to the *evaluation* state.

If there is no tuning information, design space exploration begins in the *base* configuration, which is a configuration that is guaranteed to meet QoS expectations. Even though the base configuration could be any of the CED's configurations, we select the configuration with the largest cache size, line size, and associativity as the base configuration since this configuration has the best potential for being the highest performance configuration. Considering the cache behavior and requirements for our test applications, and to compare our work to prior work [10], our base configuration is an 8KB, 4-way associativity cache with a 32B line size.

If there is tuning information, the algorithm resumes design space exploration using this information. Since the lookup table contains per-configuration information for only configurations that have already been explored, denoted with a set *explored* flag, the algorithm can determine the next parameter and value to explore by traversing the exploration ordering and locating the first configuration that does not have *explored* set. This configuration becomes the *current* configuration to evaluate.

Exploration ordering determines the order in which the configurable parameters and parameter values are explored. To minimize tuning-time QoS degradation, the algorithm traverses the design space in the reverse order of the parameters' impacts on performance [11] (i.e., lower impact to higher impact). This reverse parameter-performance-impact ordering reduces QoS degradation incurred during design space exploration. Since the base configuration is set to the largest parameter values, the algorithm explores configurations similar to the base configuration first.

In order to attain better energy savings, the algorithm will explore configurations with higher energy savings potential, but these configurations also have a higher risk of larger QoS degradation during tuning—extremist configurations that have energy consumptions extremely higher than the base configuration [3]. The algorithm regulates energy savings to QoS degradation using two tuning modes: moderate and conservative modes. Additionally, since larger parameter values have higher performance capabilities as compared to smaller parameter values [11], the algorithm traverses the parameters' values from largest to smallest.

The *exploration state* begins design space exploration with all parameters set to the parameters' largest values. Starting with the associativity, the algorithm evaluates the associativity values from largest to smallest. After the algorithm explores all of the associativity values, the algorithm reduces the line size value, and re-explores all of the associativity values (largest to smallest) for that line size, and repeats this process until all line size values have been explored. Similarly, once all of the line size values have been explored, the algorithm reduces the cache size, and re-explores all of the line size values (largest to smallest), and repeats this process until all cache size values have been explored. After each explored configuration, the algorithm sets the application's configuration's *explored* flag and proceeds to the *evaluation* state.

(iii) Evaluation state: In the evaluation state, the algorithm evaluates the current configuration's energy consumption and adherence to QoS expectations. Based on this evaluation's outcome, the tuning mode, and any prior tuning information, the algorithm makes tuning decisions.

If this is the first tuning interval, the algorithm does not have any tuning information in the lookup table. The algorithm adds a new entry to the lookup table for this application, the current configuration's energy consumption is stored in the *energy consumption* (i.e., this is the lowest energy configuration thus far), and the current configuration's *lowest energy* flag is set.

If this is not the first tuning interval, the algorithm compares the current configuration's energy consumption to the lowest energy configuration explored thus far. If the current configuration's energy is lower, the algorithm sets the current configuration's *lowest energy* flag, and proceeds to evaluate the configuration's QoS adherence before invalidating the prior lowest energy configuration's *lowest energy* flag or updating the *energy consumption* field (i.e., the configuration must both reduce energy as compared to the prior lowest energy configuration and adhere to QoS).

The algorithm evaluates QoS adherence by comparing the current configuration's execution characteristics to the application's performance threshold. If the current configuration meets the

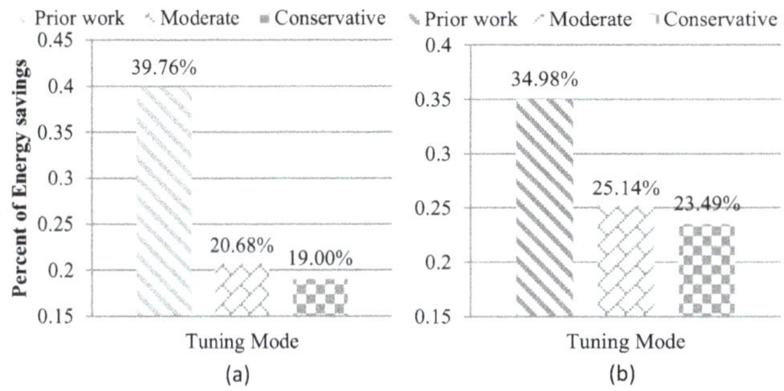

Figure 2. Average best configurations' energy consumptions normalized to the base configuration for all applications and tuning mode for the (a) data and (b) instruction caches

application's performance threshold, then the current configuration adheres to QoS expectations, and the algorithm sets the current configuration's *QoS adherence* flag, invalidates the prior lowest energy configuration's *lowest energy* flag, and updates the *energy consumption* field to the current configuration's energy consumption.

After this comparison, the algorithm makes tuning decisions, which uses the explored configurations' flags' values and the mode's stop-tuning stopping condition. The moderate mode limits tuning-time QoS degradation by only exploring one configuration that degrades QoS. Thus, moderate mode stops tuning as soon as the algorithm explores *one* configuration with the *adherence to QoS* flag unset (i.e., that configuration did not adhere to QoS requirements). To further limit tuning-time QoS degradation, not only does the conservative mode stop tuning as soon as a configuration with an unset *adherence to QoS* flag is explored, but also as soon as the algorithm explores all parameters with low performance impacts—associativity or line size, whichever comes first. Since high-performance-impact parameters have a higher possibility of degrading QoS, this additional stopping condition reduces the *probability* of exploring QoS-degrading configurations.

If the algorithm stops tuning, the best configuration has been determined, which is the configuration with the *lowest energy* and *adherence to QoS* flags set. The algorithm removes the application from the lookup table and stores the application's best configuration in the auxiliary table (Section II).

IV. EXPERIMENTAL RESULTS

A. Experimental Setup

To quantify our tuning algorithm's efficacy, we selected ten applications, from MiBench [7] suite, that represent consumer applications typically execute on CED systems. Our applications included audio (adpcm code/decode), image (jpeg code/decode), networking (dijkstra, patricia), security (sha), office (string search), and telecomm (gsm code/decode) applications.

We test our algorithm's ability to save energy while maintaining QoS expectations by designating a minimum performance threshold for our applications. Since these applications do not have/require defined QoS expectations, we determined reasonable performance thresholds based on the execution times for the configurations in the design space (Section II). To ensure that a reasonable number of configurations are able to meet QoS expectations (i.e., our algorithm would not be rigorously tested if *all* configurations could meet QoS expectations), for each application, we calculated the average performance across all of the configurations, and used that average as the application's performance threshold. Given $m = 10$ and $c = 18$ and Equations (1) and (2), our tuner and auxiliary table required 940 bits. For comparison, a prior work's hardware cache tuner with more storage requirements as compared to our design (e.g., per-configuration energy consumption was also stored) imposed only a 4.7% area overhead in a very small MIPS M4K processor [1], thus our tuner's area overhead will be less than 4.7%. Our tuner and auxiliary table imposed less than 0.5% power overhead for our experimental system (Figure 1), which we based on our extrapolations from [1] and the tuner size.

Since our system has private, dedicated L1 data and instruction caches that connect directly to main memory, we can assume that there are no tuning dependencies between the data and instruction caches, and the caches can be tuned simultaneously and evaluated independently. Our algorithm could also explore design spaces with multiple levels of caches in a similar manner, however, since the L1 cache interdependencies introduced through a shared level-two cache vastly increases the design space, multi-cache, multi-pass evaluation heuristics can be used for efficient exploration [6]. We executed our applications using cycle-accurate simulator, gem5 [5] to obtain performance values, and McPAT [8] to calculate the energy values for contemporary 40nm technology.

B. Evaluation Methodology

We evaluate our algorithm's energy savings for each tuning mode by normalizing our algorithm's determined configurations' energy consumptions to a base, non-configurable quad-core system's energy consumption (largest parameter values). We quantify the tuning energy overhead by normalizing the application's energy consumption during tuning to the application's energy consumption while executing with the base configuration for the same execution time as tuning required.

We evaluated the adaptability of each tuning mode to meet disparate QoS expectations during tuning by counting the number of times the algorithm explored a QoS-degrading configuration. Since QoS-degrading configurations have disparate execution times, QoS degradation varied in severity based on the configuration's performance. Since the severity of QoS degradation varies between configurations and we plan to quantify this severity in future work.

To compare our algorithm to prior work [11], we modified our algorithm analogously to [11]. We incorporated an *exhaustive* mode to search the complete design space, regardless of QoS degradations. Additionally, the exhaustive mode reveals the energy savings that would be obtained using prior work [9]. However, that prior work required a priori knowledge of the applications to alleviate tuning overhead. Since the exhaustive mode does not require a priori application knowledge, and imposes tuning overhead, our results for the exhaustive mode provides insights on the tradeoffs between energy savings and a priori application knowledge requirements.

C. Results and Analysis

(i) Energy Savings: Figure 2 depicts the percentage of average energy savings achieved by the algorithm's best

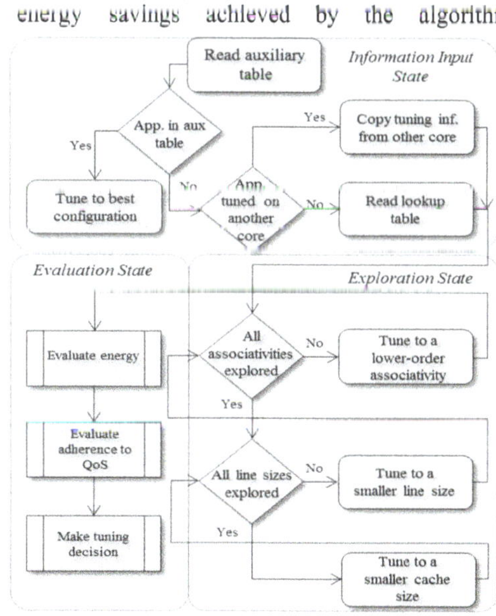

Algorithm 1: Dyanamic tuning algorithm's finite state machine

configurations for our ten applications, with respect to the base configuration's energy consumption for each tuning mode for the (a) data and (b) instruction caches.

The tuning modes exhibit similar trends for both the data and instruction caches. As expected, the aggressive mode (as in prior work [9][11]) achieved the highest average energy savings of 39.76% and 34.98% for the data and instruction caches, respectively. Even though the moderate and conservative modes explored fewer configurations, these modes still achieved average energy savings of 20.68% and 25.14%, and 19.00% and 23.49%, respectively.

Our energy overhead analysis revealed that all tuning modes imposed tuning overhead while exploring inferior, non-best configurations. However these overheads are amortized while the algorithm explored configurations that resulted in energy savings, as compared to the base configurations. Furthermore, the aggressive mode imposed more energy overhead, as compared to the moderate and conservative mode. However, the aggressive mode also explored more energy saving configurations, as compared to the moderate and aggressive mode. Since the moderate and conservative modes explored fewer configurations, these modes had a lower probability of exploring extreme configurations, while also exploring energy-saving configurations without exhaustively exploring the design space.

Since our algorithm explores configurations with large parameter values first, the moderate and conservative modes have a lower probability of exploring configurations with small parameter values, which can lead to QoS degradation. The energy and overhead results and our algorithm's parameter and value exploration ordering reveal that high-energy-saving configurations tend to have smaller parameter values. However, extreme configurations also tend to have small parameter values, thus leading to high-risk/high-reward design space exploration methods. Our different tuning modes enable users/designers to moderate this decision.

Since an application's execution time and execution frequency in CED's is subjective to costumer usage, the three tuning modes' beneficence is contingent on consumer usage patterns. Applications that execute frequently, or for extended periods of continuous operation, benefit more from high energy savings over these periods, and thus can tolerate high tuning overhead (i.e., the moderate mode). Alternatively, applications that are expected to execute for a short period of time benefit more from tuning modes that incur lower tuning overhead (i.e., the conservative mode). These short-executing applications do not benefit from the aggressive mode since these applications will not execute for a period of time long enough to amortize the high tuning overhead.

(ii) Adherence to QoS: Since prior work explored the entire design space, prior work had the highest number of QoS degradation occurrences, with an average of 7.7 tuning-time QoS degradations. Alternatively, since the moderate mode stopped tuning as soon as the algorithm explored one QoS-degrading configuration, the moderate mode had one QoS degradation occurrence regardless of the cache hierarchy. Since the conservative mode stopped tuning as soon as the algorithm finished exploring all of the low-performance-impact parameters, the conservative mode had the lowest number of QoS degradation occurrences, with an average of 0.7. These averages are low because the conservative mode only explored configurations with large cache sizes, which typically have higher performance capabilities, and thus lower QoS degradation potential.

Even though the conservative mode limits tuning-time QoS degradation, the conservative mode did not guarantee that the best configuration found adheres to QoS expectations. This suggests that not only configuration design space size, but also the number of configurations with low/high performance-impact parameters impact both tuning-time QoS degradation and post-tuning QoS adherence. A design space that has a low percentage of configurations with large parameter values leads to a high number of tuning-time QoS degradation occurrences for the aggressive mode. Alternatively, since high-energy-saving configurations tend to be small parameter value configurations, a design space that has a high percentage of configurations with large parameter values leads to less energy savings.

The difference between the numbers of tuning-time QoS degradation occurrences for the different tuning modes provides the algorithm with the flexibility to adhere to disparate user QoS expectations, which is a necessity for CEDs. Since user expectations vary based on the user's mood, experience level, location (e.g., work, commute, home, etc.), usage (e.g., naval, space, entertainment, etc.), gender, age, environment, time of day, etc. [4], our algorithm is capable of adhering to disparate QoS expectations for different user-defined experiences.

V. CONCLUSIONS AND FUTURE WORK

In this work, we proposed a tuning algorithm, which determined the best cache configuration while considering tuning-time QoS degradation and energy consumption. Our algorithm requires no a priori application information, profiling information, or design time effort, and tunes the cache during runtime while avoiding tuning-time QoS degradation using two tuning mode options that trade off these competing constraints. Our results revealed average energy savings as high as 20.68% and 25.14%, for the data and instruction caches, respectively, and average tuning-time QoS degradation as low as 0.7. Future work will extend our algorithm to multi-level cache optimization for CEDs, additional tuning heuristics, and disparate QoS and energy savings tradeoffs.

VI. ACKNOWLEDGEMENT

This work was supported by the National Science Foundation (CNS-0953447). Any opinions, findings, and conclusions or recommendations expressed in this material are those of the author(s) and do not necessarily reflect the views of the National Science Foundation.

VII. REFERENCES

[1] Adegbija, T.; Gordon-Ross, A.; Rawlins, M. "Analysis of cache tuner architectural layouts for multicore embedded systems," *Int. Con. on Performance Computing and Communications,* 2014.

[2] Adegbija, T., Gordon-Ross, A. "Energy-efficient phase-based cache tuning for multimedia applications in embedded systems," *IEEE Consumer Communications and Networking Conference*, 2014.

[3] Alsafrjalani, M.H.; Gordon-Ross, A. "Dynamic Scheduling for Reduced Energy in Configuration-Subsetted Heterogeneous Multicore Systems," *Int. Con. on Embedded and Ubiquitous Computing,* 2014.

[4] Amin, R., Jackson, F., Gilbert, J, Martin, J., Shaw, T. "Assessing the Impact of Latency and Jitter on the Perceived Quality of Call of Duty Modern Warfare 2," *Int. Con. on Human Computer Interaction,* 2013.

[5] Binkert, N.; Beckmann, B.; Black, G.; et al. "The gem5 simulator," SIGARCH Comput. Archit. News 39, 2 (August 2011), 1-7.

[6] Gordon-Ross, A., Viana, P., Vahid, F., Najjar W. Barros, E. "A One-Shot Configurable-Cache Tuner for Improved Energy and Performance," *IEEE/ACM Design, Automation and Test in Europe.* 2007

[7] Guthaus, M., Ringenberg, J., Ernst, D., Austin, T., Mudge, T., and Brown, R., "MiBench: a free, commercially representative embedded benchmark suite," Int. Workshop on Workload Characterization, 2001

[8] Li, S.; Ahn, Jung Ho; Strong, R.D.; et al. "McPAT: An integrated power, area, and timing modeling framework for multicore and manycore architectures," IEEE/ACM Int. Symp. on Microarchitecture, Dec. 2009

[9] Wang, W., Mishra, P., Gordon-Ross, A. "SACR: Scheduling-Aware Cache Reconfiguration for Real-Time Embedded Systems," *Int. Con. on VLSI Design,* 2009.

[10] Zhang, C., Vahid, F., Najjar, W. "A highly configurable cache architecture for embedded systems," *In Proc. of International Symposium on Computer Architecture,* 2003.

[11] Zhang, C., Vahid, F. "Cache configuration exploration on prototyping platforms," *IEEE International Workshop on Rapid Systems Prototyping,* 20

Temperature-aware Dynamic Voltage Scaling for Near-Threshold Computing

Saman Kiamehr
kiamehr@kit.edu

Mojtaba Ebrahimi
mojtaba.ebrahimi@kit.edu

Mehdi Tahoori
mehdi.tahoori@kit.edu

Karlsruhe Institute of Technology (KIT)
Karlsruhe, Germany

ABSTRACT

Power/energy reduction is of uttermost importance for applications with stringent power/energy budget such as ultra-low power and energy-harvested systems. Aggressive voltage scaling and in particular *Near-Threshold Computing* (NTC) is a promising approach to reduce the power and energy consumption. However, reducing the supply voltage leads to drastic performance variation induced by process and runtime variation. Temperature variation is one of the major sources of performance variation. In this paper, we study the impact of temperature variation on the circuit behavior at near threshold region and show that the ambient temperature has a huge impact on the metrics such as circuit delay, power and energy consumption. We also propose a low-cost, ambient temperature-aware voltage scaling technique to reduce the unnecessary energy overhead caused by temperature variation. Simulation results show that our proposed approach reduces the energy consumption by more than 3X.

Keywords

Near Threshold Computing, Low Power, Temperature, Voltage Scaling

1. INTRODUCTION

By technology downscaling deep into the nano meter era, power and energy have become major design constraints [8, 11]. This is much more pronounced for many emerging application domains with low power and energy budget such as ultra-low power and energy-harvested systems. Therefore, power and energy reduction are high priority objectives of today electronic design specially in embedded processors, remote sensors and implantable devices for applications such as *Internet of Things* (IoT). Aggressive supply voltage scaling is one of the most efficient ways of reducing the power and energy of digital circuits [8, 17]. It is shown that *Near-Threshold Computing* (NTC), in which the supply voltage is close to the threshold voltage of the transistor, provides a very high energy efficiency (10X or higher) compared to the traditional *Super Threshold* (ST) region at the cost of about 10X performance penalty [8].

The excellent energy-frequency trade-off of NTC makes it very beneficial specially for applications with relaxed performance requirements [15]. However, NTC brings many challenges such as *increased functional failure*, *performance loss*, and *performance variation*. One important challenge of NTC is increased functional failure of circuit elements such as SRAM cell. For instance, the failure rate of a typical 65 nm SRAM cell increases by approximately five orders of magnitude with scaling the voltage to the *Near-Threshold* (NT) region [8]. This issue could be effectively mitigated by exploiting alternative SRAM cell designs [3, 4], SRAM robustness analysis techniques [5] or reconfigurable cache designs [7]. The significant *performance loss* of around 10X is another important challenge for NTC. To address this challenge architecture level techniques such as NTC-based parallelism [21] and device level optimization techniques [19] are proposed.

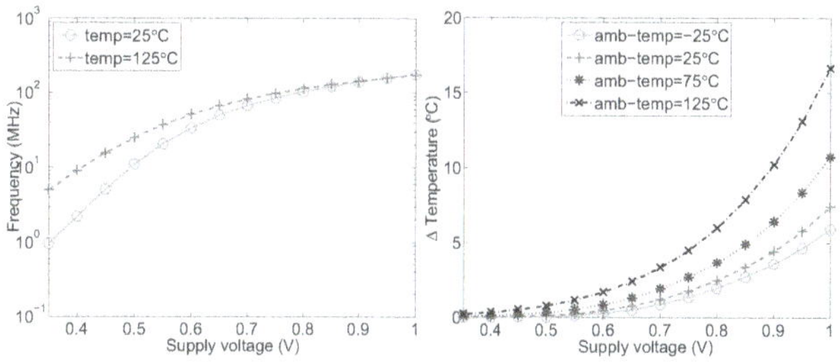

(a) (b)

Figure 1: a) Sensitivity of frequency of b19 benchmark circuit to temperature variation at different supply voltage values b) The difference between the ambient temperature and the circuit temperature (ΔTemperature) for different supply voltage values

Performance variation is one of the most important challenges of NTC [11]. It is shown that performance variation, due to process and runtime variations, in NT region is 5X larger than that of the ST region [8]. Therefore, addressing such a huge performance variation by additional timing margins can significantly affect the energy efficiency of the system. Soft edge clocking [10, 20] and body biasing [9] are two well-known approaches to deal with the performance variation at NTC.

Temperature variation is a major source of performance variation at NTC. Although the temperature-induced performance variation is as small as $\pm 5\%$ in ST region, it can become as high as $\pm 2X$ at NTC across the temperature range of 0-110°C [11]. The higher sensitivity of circuit performance to temperature at NTC is also shown in Figure 1(a).

Temperature-induced variation in memory arrays could be addressed by dynamically adapting the memory latency [2]. However, the effect of temperature variation on the perfor-

GLSVLSI '16, May 18-20, 2016, Boston, MA, USA

DOI: http://dx.doi.org/10.1145/2902961.2902997

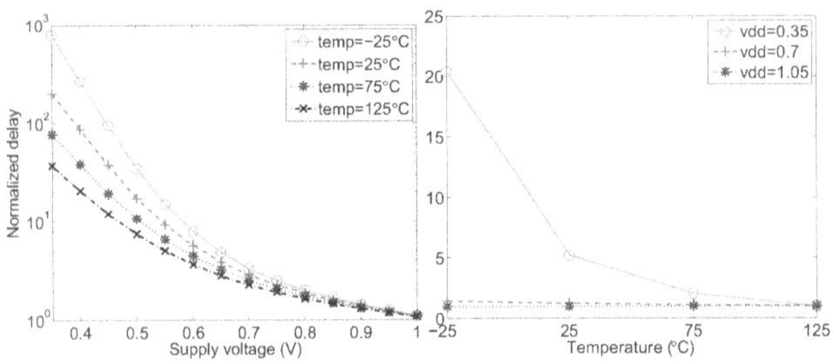

(a) (b)

Figure 2: a) Delay vs. supply voltage for different temperature values b) Normalized delay vs. temperature for different supply voltage values for b19 benchmark circuit

mance of logic units is higher compared to that of memory components, because the supply voltage of the logic core can be more aggressively reduced than that of the memory and hence the performance sensitivity to variation is larger [5, 6]. The reason behind using higher supply voltage for memories at NTC is twofold. The first reason is that in memory the leakage power is dominant and the optimum value of supply voltage for energy is obtained at higher values. The second reason is to avoid excessive memory functional failures at very low supply voltages. Although the impact of temperature variation on the performance of logic units is very large at NTC, this issue is not well studied yet.

In this paper, we first study the impact of ambient temperature on the chip temperature at different supply voltage ranges. Our results show that in the NT region, the chip temperature is very close to the ambient temperature. Afterwards, we comprehensively study the effect of ambient temperature variation on delay, power and energy consumption of the circuit operating at the NT and ST regions. According to our analysis, a circuit designed to work on high ambient temperature might fail in lower ambient temperatures due to the large circuit delay increase at lower temperature ranges. Therefore, the operating frequency has to be set according to the worst case delay (lower temperature). According to these observations, we propose a low-cost, ambient temperature-aware dynamic voltage scaling technique to leverage the huge performance variation at NTC for reducing the energy consumption of the circuit at higher temperature ranges. Simulation results show that, with a fixed performance constraint, the power/energy consumption of the chip can be reduced by more than 3X.

2. EFFECT OF AMBIENT TEMPERATURE ON CIRCUIT BEHAVIOR

2.1 Simulation setup

All the experiments in this paper were performed on the largest circuits of the ISCAS'89 and ITC'99 benchmark circuits. These circuits were synthesized using Synopsys Design Compiler with respect to the SAED 32 nm standard cell library. The place & route operation is performed by Cadence SoC Encounter. The temperature of the circuits were computed using Hotspot [1] according to the given ambient temperature and the circuit power profile.

To accurately obtain the circuit delay across different supply voltages, the target standard cell library has to be characterized for each supply voltage. In this regard, we exploited Liberate to generate a standard cell library for each target supply voltage and temperature. This tool performs SPICE characterization to build such libraries. For each supply voltage, the circuit is synthesized with respect to the corresponding standard cell library. All delay and power numbers are also obtained with respect to that library.

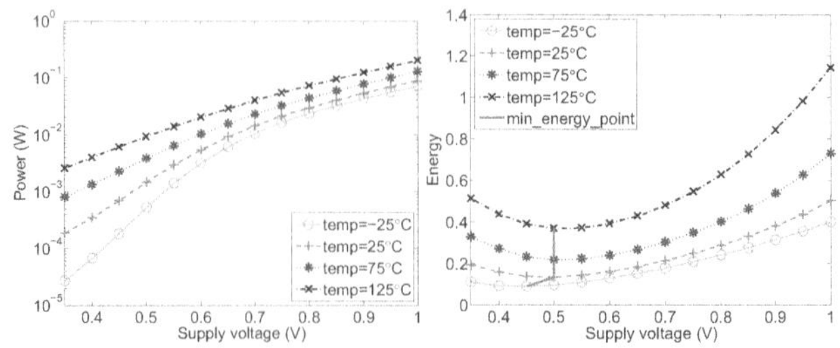

(a) (b)

Figure 3: a) The power consumption of b19 b) The energy consumption of b19

2.2 Chip temperature

Figure 1(b) shows the average chip temperature vs. ambient temperature for different supply voltage values. As shown, the gap between ambient temperature and circuit temperature reduces by scaling the voltage to the NT region. According to the figure, the chip temperature is approximately equal to the ambient temperature for the supply voltage values below 0.6 V. This means that for NTC applications, the chip temperature is equal to the ambient temperature and any change in the ambient temperature is reflected in the chip temperature. This can eventually lead to a huge variation in chip behavior (performance, power and energy).

2.3 Circuit delay

Given the fact that the chip temperature is almost equal to the ambient temperature in the NT region, it is very important to analyze the effect of the ambient temperature on the circuit delay. Figure 2 depicts the delay of the b19 benchmark circuit for different supply voltage values with the ambient temperature range of -25°C to 125°C. We analyzed all benchmark circuits and the trends are the same and the results are shown only for one circuit here. According to our analysis, the following points can be concluded:

- The circuit delay increases exponentially by decreasing the supply voltage value (see Figure 2(a)).
- The circuit delay sensitivity to temperature increases for lower supply voltage values (see Figure 2(a) and 2(b)).
- The circuit delay is much larger at lower temperatures.

The most important point here is that, if a chip is designed to work at NTC in an environment with high temperature variations, it might fail to meet the timing constraint when used in environments with lower temperatures due to the huge sensitivity of the circuit delay to temperature. This means that the timing constraint (operational frequency) has to be set according to the timing of the lowest possible ambient temperature.

2.4 Circuit power

Figure 3(a) shows the power consumption of the b19 benchmark circuit for different supply voltage and temperature ranges. As shown, the power reduces exponentially by supply voltage reduction. Moreover, the ambient temperature also impacts the power exponentially. As shown in this figure, the power of the circuit is much less for lower ranges of the ambient temperature. This is due to the fact that, the temperature impacts the leakage power exponentially and for larger temperature ranges the contribution of leakage power in the total power is more.

2.5 Circuit energy

Figure 3(b) shows the energy of the b19 benchmark circuit. Here the energy is defined as the product of the circuit power consumption and the circuit delay. According to the figure, the energy consumption of the circuit is much less at lower temperature ranges. This is because at lower temperature ranges, although the delay is larger, the power is much less (orders of magnitudes) compared to higher temperature ranges. As a result, the product of power and delay (energy) at lower temperature ranges is less than that of higher temperature ranges. Moreover, according to the figure, the minimum energy point (the supply voltage which gives the best energy consumption) is shifted to the left for lower temperature values. This means that, for lower temperature ranges, the best energy is obtained with lower supply voltage values.

It should be noted that we have shown the results of the analysis for one benchmark circuit, but the trends and conclusions hold for all other benchmark circuits as well.

3. PROPOSED TEMPERATURE-AWARE VOLTAGE SCALING

A chip at NTC might be used in environments with different ambient temperatures. A chip which is used in remote sensing (e.g. in IoT applications) could be used in places where the ambient temperature is as low as ~-50°C or in places where in the summer the ambient temperature is more than 50 °C. If the chip is used in a car near the engine, the temperature might increase beyond 100 °C.

According to the results presented in Section 2, the chip temperature at the NT region is approximately equal to the ambient temperature. The circuit delay is very sensitive to the ambient temperature at NTC and it increases for lower ranges of ambient temperature. This means that the timing constraint (frequency) has to be set according to the timing of the chip at the lowest possible ambient temperature in order to avoid any timing failure. However, if the chip is used in an environment with higher ambient temperature, the chip delay is much smaller which causes a large energy overhead. This means that, for an environment with higher ambient temperature, the voltage can be scaled down in order to reduce the unnecessary energy consumption with no performance penalty.

The idea here is to adjust the supply voltage of the chip according to the ambient temperature. For this purpose, an off-chip temperature sensor is used to obtain the chip temperature which is equal to the ambient temperature. This information is given to a voltage scaling module to adjust the supply voltage accordingly. In this scenario, the operation frequency is assumed to be constant and the supply voltage is the knob that is used to decrease the energy consumption. The supply voltage is scaled down if the ambient

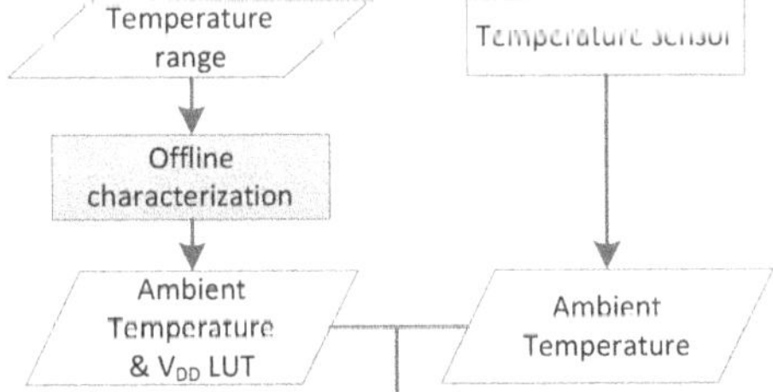

Figure 4: The flow of proposed approach

temperature is higher and for lower ranges of ambient temperature, the supply voltage is increased to compensate the delay increase at these temperature ranges.

Figure 4 shows the flow of our proposed approach. First, the temperature range is discretized to different sub-ranges. An offline characterization is performed to obtain a suitable supply voltage for each temperature sub-range which meets the timing constraint and has the best energy efficiency. These temperature sub-ranges and the corresponding supply voltages are stored in a *look-up table* (LUT). During the chip operation time, a temperature sensor obtains the ambient temperature and the voltage scaling module adjusts the supply voltage according to the sensed (ambient) temperature and LUT.

It should be noted that our approach is different from temperature-aware dynamic voltage scaling (DVFS) techniques applied for the ST region. In the ST region, the power density is rather high which could lead to hotspots. Therefore, temperature-aware DVFS techniques are proposed in order to avoid hotspots or minimize the peak temperature and energy consumption within the *Thermal Design Power* (TDP) [12, 16, 18]. However, at NTC, the power consumption is much lower and the temperature is close to the ambient temperature and hence the applied supply voltage has no effect on the chip temperature. Therefore, our approach is to get the ambient temperature as an input and adapt the supply voltage accordingly to minimize the energy.

Another benefit of our proposed technique is its low cost which is indispensable specially for IoT applications. Since the chip temperature is close to the ambient temperature in the NT region, instead of a costly on-chip temperature sensor, an off-chip temperature sensor is enough to obtain the ambient/chip temperature. Moreover, unlike the ST region, in which the chip temperature profile changes frequently, the chip/ambient temperature will change at a much larger time scale. Therefore, the temperature sampling frequency and its corresponding overhead will be much lower. Moreover, our voltage scaling technique is LUT-based and it does not require sophisticated monitoring circuits, such as *Critical Path Monitors* (CPM) [13, 14], with large area and power overheads.

3.1 Offline characterization

In order to perform offline characterization, for a given timing constraint and for each temperature range, the minimum supply voltage, with which the timing constraint is met, is obtained and stored in an LUT. In this part, we obtain the temperature-supply voltage LUT for different ITC'99 and ISCAS'89 benchmark circuits. The timing constraint here is set according to the timing of the circuit for $V_{DD} = 0.5$ at temperature equal to -25°C. Then for a range of temperature between -25°C to 125°C, the ambient temperature vs. supply voltage is obtained and the results are shown in Table 1. According to the table, the minimum supply voltage to meet the timing constraint is less for higher temperature ranges. This means that for higher ambient temperatures we can reduce the supply voltage in order to decrease the power/energy consumption.

The other observation is that, the obtained supply voltage for all benchmark circuits is almost the same because the supply voltage and ambient temperature affect all types of cells in the same manner, therefore the obtained supply voltage value is almost independent of the circuit structure.

Although the supply voltage points are almost the same for all benchmark circuits, however, the results for another

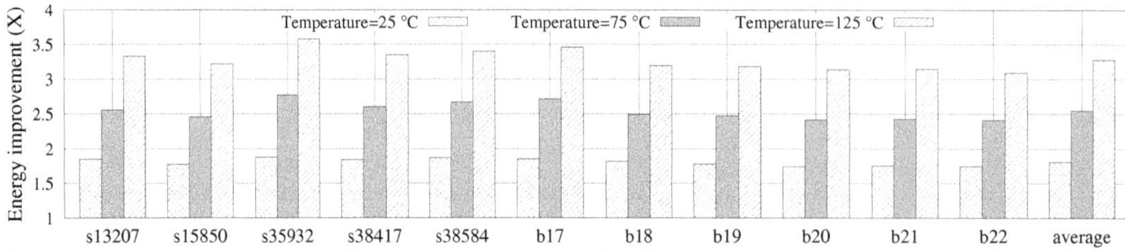

Figure 5: The energy improvement of proposed approach. The results are normalized to the case in which the ambient temperature is -25°C.

technology node (standard cell library) could change. Hence, for each library, the offline characterization has to be done only once for a representative circuit and then the results could be used for all other circuits synthesized with the same library.

3.2 Online voltage scaling

As shown earlier, for higher ambient temperature, the supply voltage can be scaled down to save the power/energy. Figure 5 shows the amount of energy improvement for different ambient temperature using our approach. These results are obtained for a case in which the chip is designed for the ambient temperature of -25°C. According to the results depicted in the figure, using our proposed voltage scaling approach, the energy consumption can be reduced and the energy improvement will increase for higher temperature ranges. The results show that the energy consumption can be reduced by more than 3X if the chip is used in an environment with 125°C ambient temperature.

The slight difference among the power improvements of various benchmark circuits is due to the different contributions of the dynamic and static power on the total power. For the circuits with a higher dynamic to static power ratio, the power improvement of our voltage scaling approach is higher because voltage scaling has a higher impact on the dynamic power.

These results are obtained for a case in which the operation frequency is fixed. The same approach can be used to adjust the frequency in order to improve the performance of the chip for the case in which the supply voltage is assumed to be constant.

4. CONCLUSION

Power and energy are the major design constraints specially for applications with stringent power and energy budget such as ultra-low power systems. To reduce the power and energy consumption, aggressive supply voltage scaling such as Near Threshold Computing (NTC) is a promising approach. However, in NTC, the circuit behavior is very sensitive to process and runtime variation and in particular temperature variation. In this paper, we comprehensively investigated the effect of temperature variation on circuit power, performance and energy. We showed that the circuit temperature is very close to the ambient temperature in NTC. Based on this observation, we proposed a low-cost, ambient temperature-aware voltage scaling in order to reduce the unnecessary energy overhead caused by the ambient temperature variation. Simulation results show that, using our proposed approach, the energy consumption is reduced by 3X with no effect on the circuit performance.

Table 1: The minimum supply voltage to meet timing constraint for different ambient temperature

	V_{DD}(V)			
Benchmark	T=-25°C	T=25°C	T=75°C	T=125°C
s13207	0.500	0.457	0.411	0.360
s15850	0.500	0.457	0.410	0.359
s35932	0.500	0.458	0.412	0.363
s38417	0.500	0.458	0.411	0.362
s38584	0.500	0.457	0.409	0.360
b17	0.500	0.459	0.413	0.364
b18	0.500	0.456	0.409	0.359
b19	0.500	0.458	0.412	0.361
b20	0.500	0.459	0.412	0.362
b21	0.500	0.458	0.412	0.361
b22	0.500	0.459	0.413	0.363

References

[1] "Hotspot," http://lava.cs.virginia.edu/HotSpot/.

[2] D. Bortolotti *et al.*, "An ambient temperature variation tolerance scheme for an ultra low power shared-l1 processor cluster," in *Digital System Design (DSD), Euromicro Conference on.* IEEE, 2013, pp. 625–632.

[3] B. H. Calhoun *et al.*, "A 256-kb 65-nm sub-threshold sram design for ultra-low-voltage operation," *Solid-State Circuits, IEEE Journal of*, vol. 42, no. 3, pp. 680–688, 2007.

[4] L. Chang *et al.*, "A 5.3 ghz 8t-sram with operation down to 0.41 v in 65nm cmos," in *VLSI Circuits*, 2007.

[5] G. Chen *et al.*, "Yield-driven near-threshold sram design," *Very Large Scale Integration (VLSI) Systems, IEEE Transactions on*, vol. 18, no. 11, pp. 1590–1598, 2010.

[6] H. Chen *et al.*, "Opportunistic turbo execution in ntc: exploiting the paradigm shift in performance bottlenecks," in *DAC*, 2015.

[7] R. G. Dreslinski *et al.*, "Reconfigurable energy efficient near threshold cache architectures," in *Microarchitecture, 2008. MICRO-41. 2008 41st IEEE/ACM International Symposium on.* IEEE, 2008, pp. 459–470.

[8] R. G. Dreslinski *et al.*, "Near-threshold computing: Reclaiming moore's law through energy efficient integrated circuits," *Proceedings of the IEEE*, vol. 98, no. 2, pp. 253–266, 2010.

[9] G. Gammie *et al.*, "A 45nm 3.5 g baseband-and-multimedia application processor using adaptive body-bias and ultra-low-power techniques," in *ISSCC*, 2008.

[10] V. Joshi *et al.*, "Soft-edge flip-flops for improved timing yield: design and optimization," in *ICCAD*, 2007.

[11] H. Kaul *et al.*, "Near-threshold voltage (ntv) design: opportunities and challenges," in *DAC*, 2012.

[12] J. Lee *et al.*, "Optimizing throughput of power-and thermal-constrained multicore processors using dvfs and per-core power-gating," in *DAC*, 2009.

[13] C. R. Lefurgy *et al.*, "Active guardband management in power7+ to save energy and maintain reliability," *Micro, IEEE*, vol. 33, no. 4, pp. 35–45, 2013.

[14] C. R. Lefurgy *et al.*, "Active management of timing guardband to save energy in power7," in *MICRO*, 2011.

[15] X. Lin *et al.*, "Joint sizing and adaptive independent gate control for finfet circuits operating in multiple voltage regimes using the logical effort method," in *ICCAD*, 2013.

[16] Y. Liu *et al.*, "Thermal vs energy optimization for dvfs-enabled processors in embedded systems," in *ISQED*, 2007.

[17] D. Marković *et al.*, "Ultralow-power design in near-threshold region," *Proceedings of the IEEE*, vol. 98, no. 2, pp. 237–252, 2010.

[18] T. S. Muthukaruppan *et al.*, "Hierarchical power management for asymmetric multi-core in dark silicon era," in *DAC*, 2013.

[19] B. Paul *et al.*, "Device optimization for ultra-low power digital sub-threshold operation," in *ISLPED*, 2004.

[20] M. Wieckowski *et al.*, "Timing yield enhancement through soft edge flip-flop based design." in *CICC*, 2008, pp. 543–546.

[21] B. Zhai *et al.*, "Energy efficient near-threshold chip multi-processing," in *Proceedings of the 2007 international symposium on Low power electronics and design.* ACM, 2007, pp. 32–37.

Leakage Power Minimization in Deep Sub-Micron Technology by Exploiting Positive Slacks of Dependent Paths

Tuhin Subhra Chakraborty¥, Santanu Kundu, Deepak Agrawal, Sanjay Tanaji Shinde, Jacob Mathews
Broadcom Limited, Bangalore - 560103, INDIA
Email: {Tuhin.Chakraborty, Santanu.Kundu, Deepak.Agrawal, Sanjay.Shinde, Jacob.Mathews}@broadcom.com

Rekha K. James
School of Engineering,
Cochin University of Science & Technology,
Kochi – 682022, INDIA
Email: rekhajames@cusat.ac.in

ABSTRACT

Leakage power minimization is one of the key aspects of modern multi-million low power system-on-chip (SoC) design. In post timing-closure phase, leakage-in-place-optimization (LIPO) is generally adopted to reduce leakage power by swapping high-leaky cells in the timing-data-paths by low-leaky ones of the same footprint. The traditional LIPO does not touch the clock network for leakage recovery. This paper investigates the opportunity to reduce leakage power further of an already leakage-power-minimized (by LIPO), timing closed design by minimally altering the balanced clock tree. The proposed method, *Opportunistic LIPO*, intends to borrow unused positive-slack from downstream (and/or upstream) paths, may or may not be at immediate neighborhood, and provide a "positive skew" (and/or "negative skew") at the capture (and/or launch) clock edge of the current path. In this way, the proposed scheme creates an *opportunity* in the current path to increase the low-leaky cells distribution. Experimental results, computed over some practical duration (less than 48 hours), on some industry-standard design based on 28nm technology, of having around 50 million gates, shows that the proposed algorithm, "*Opportunistic LIPO*", achieves 10-30% better leakage power as compared to traditional LIPO without increasing the number of timing violations and having no significant impact on overall area.

Keywords

Leakage power reduction; leakage-in-place-optimization (LIPO); slack margin; skew propagation; Opportunistic LIPO.

1. INTRODUCTION AND MOTIVATION

Today's SoCs and the applications are highly integrated, performance intensive, and very power conscious. In 40nm and smaller geometries, leakage is a significant component in the overall chip power and it varies significantly with process, voltage, temperature, and basic device level parameters – channel length, threshold voltage (V_t), oxide thickness, etc. [1]. For a typical 50 million gate SoC at 28nm technology, we have observed that leakage power consumption can be as high as ~60% of overall chip power at worst case. To keep optimal balance between speed, area, and power, all modern SoCs are designed at multiple threshold voltages (V_t). In multi-V_t design, a cell of specific footprint can have different leakage characteristics based on its threshold voltage and channel length. It is well known that as the channel length reduces in a particular V_t type, its performance increases at the cost of more leakage power. Similarly, if we move from High Vt (HVT) to Standard Vt (SVT), Low Vt (LVT), and so on, the performance improves at the cost of more leakage power. Another conventional method to reduce leakage power is to reduce the width of transistor. Channel width reduction results in a 1:1 leakage reduction. Cutting the channel width in half reduce the leakage current by half and also reduces the cell footprint area [2].

When a CAD tool tries to optimize a design in terms of timing, it faces a complex optimization problem to solve, due to large size of design and interdependency of various timing paths. A greedy, intelligent approach to solve the problem would be to balance the clock tree prior to routing and timing closure. This is rightly practiced by conventional CAD flow as shown in Fig. 1. In a multi-million gate SoC, there exists billions of timing paths. The design houses cannot ensure uniform slack availability to all the paths even after timing closure. In order to reduce leakage power in a timing-closed design, these unused positive slacks available can be utilized. Leakage-in-place-optimization (LIPO) aims to do that focusing on each individual path at a time. In traditional LIPO, if an individual timing-path has positive setup-slack, the high-leaky-cells in that path can be replaced by lower-leaky cells (having more delay), of the same foot-print until the positive slack gets exhausted or until all the low leaky cells in that path are swapped by some lower leaky one. This process does not introduce any new timing violation and also does not alter any existing physical routing including the clock network [3-8].

In post LIPO phase, every *individual* data-path having positive slack, preferably more than some small amount of specified slack margin, is expected to be exhausted in terms of leakage reduction. However, it is expected that multi-million SoCs will have non-uniform logic-depths across various pipeline stages. Hence, even after LIPO, there will be many non-critical paths with considerable positive setup-slack, although there is no opportunity of reducing the leakage further as all the cells might be of low leaky ones. At the same time, there will be many paths where leaky cells are used to meet timing. Hence, in one hand, there are paths where slack is not available, but leaky cells are present, and on the other hand, there are paths where slack is available, but it is fully optimized in terms of leakage. We want to create a bridge between this two extremes by minimally altering the balanced clock-tree. *Fig. 2 depicts that if all the cells in a typical 50 million gate SoC (in 28HP technology) are replaced by HVT35 type (lowest leaky cell in the library), the leakage power saving can be ~87.66% of the leakage power of pre-LIPO netlist. But we achieved only ~28.67% reduction after conventional LIPO. Hence in post LIPO timing closed design with balanced clock tree, there is scope to reduce the total positive slack further and hence reduce leakage power which we could not achieve currently due to balanced clock tree.*

GLSVLSI '16, May 18 - 20, 2016, Boston, MA, USA

ACM 978-1-4503-4274-2/16/05 $15.00
DOI: http://dx.doi.org/10.1145/2902961.2902991

This work was done in Data Controller Division of Avago Technologies, currently Broadcom Limited, Bangalore, India.
¥ Tuhin was with Avago Technologies when the work was conducted and now is currently with Qualcomm India Pvt. Ltd, Bangalore.
(Email: tchakrab@qti.qualcomm.com, tuhinsubhra1978@gmail.com)

This motivates us to investigate the opportunity to reduce leakage power further by minimally altering the balanced clock tree in search of an optimal skew distribution and propagates the skew from one node to another, *may or may not be at immediate neighborhood,* in view of increasing lower leaky cells distribution across the design.

Rest of the paper is organized as follow. In Section 2, we describe our proposed method – "opportunistic LIPO" in two subsections. In first sub-section, we describe the overall flow while in the second sub-section we describe the proposed skew-distribution algorithm running in the core of "opportunistic LIPO". The algorithm is further illustrated with the help of an example graph in the same sub-section. In Section 3, we show our experimental results. Finally, in Section 4, we draw the conclusions of the paper.

2. OPPORTUNISTIC LIPO

2.1 Basic Flow

In conventional balanced clock tree based flow, if any timing path has very less positive slack, LIPO cannot swap any cell in the data path to its higher V_t cell as it will cause setup time violation in that path. But at the same time, a significant positive slack might be present in the downstream or upstream timing paths even after LIPO which is currently unused. Fig. 3 shows our proposed method, *Opportunistic LIPO*, which can borrow the unused positive slack from the downstream paths and provide a "positive skew" at the capture clock edge of the current path; and/or borrow the unused positive slack from upstream timing paths and providing "negative skew" in the launch clock edge of the current path. Thus the algorithm creates an opportunity in the current path to swap lower V_t cells by a higher V_t ones. As opportunity propagates from downstream (or upstream) paths to the current path, we termed the current path as "opportunistic path" and the method as "opportunity propagation". As this new skew distribution will relax the timing in the opportunistic path, *incremental* CTS should be done to facilitate the same. With the new timing-relaxed database, one can perform LIPO again to reduce leakage power promised by the opportunity propagation. The authors believe that this approach will always be better or in the worst case will have similar performance over traditional LIPO.

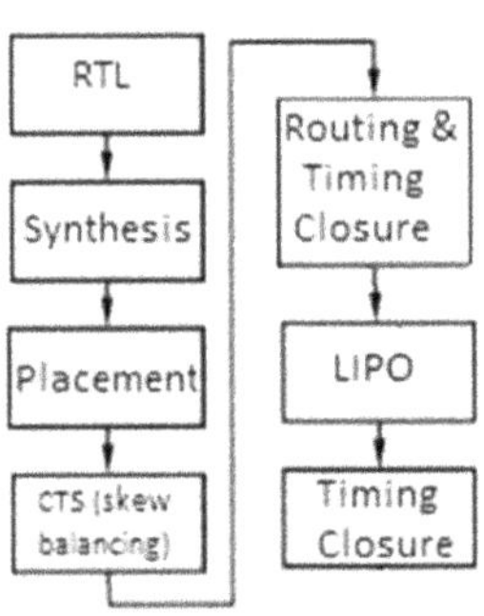

Fig. 1: Conventional CAD flow to reduce leakage power

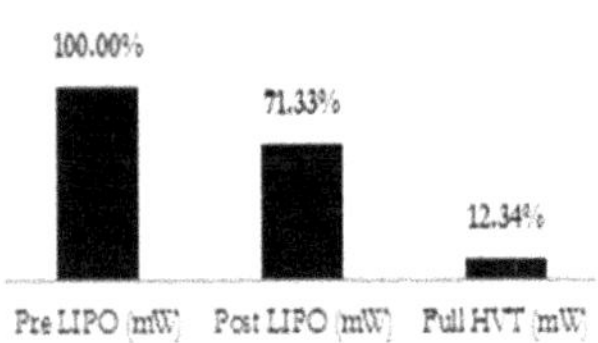

Fig. 2: Logic leakage power of a 50 M gate SoC

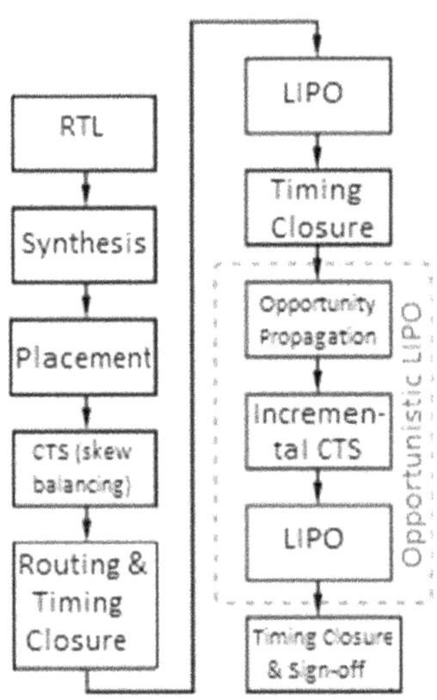

Fig. 3: Proposed "opportunistic LIPO" based leakage power minimization in a post timing-closed database

2.2 Proposed skew distribution algorithm

In the above section, we mentioned that "opportunistic LIPO" requires a new intelligent algorithm to propagate the "opportunities" created across the design. This section describes the algorithm. The connectivity information in digital circuits can be viewed as a graph. In view of that, we define the following parameters.

Node (R_m): A register or an IO port.

Edge ($E_{m,p}$): Nodes are connected by directed edges, where the arrow is in the direction of data flow. $E_{m,p}$ refers that data flow is from R_m to R_p.

Slack (SLK_{mp}): this is the worst set-up slack in the path m to p.

Delay (d_{mp}): worst delay between node m to p including setup time of node p. SLK_{mp} and d_{mp} are considered as weight of edges.

Skew (SK_m): this is the clock skew at node m.

Opportunistic Path (OP): A node to node timing path is called as Opportunistic Path, if there exist a chance of improving leakage power by swapping high leaky cells by some lower leaky cells, while the slack availability does not permit to do so.

Target Opportunity Propagated Value (TOPV): A predefined skew desired to satisfy sufficient leakage reduction in an OP.

Opportunity Receiver Node (ORN): The nodes associated with OP are called "opportunity receiver nodes (ORN)". The capture node is called the right ORN (**ORN_R**), and the launch node is called as the left ORN (**ORN_L**).

Opportunity Propagator Node (OPN): A capture node associated with a path which is not an OP type, but having positive setup-slack available greater than some pre-defined margin.

Opportunity Propagated Value (OPV): Amount of skew finally propagated to ORN. OPV at ORN_R is called as OPV_R, and OPV at ORN_L is called as OPV_L.

Path (P_{mp}): The worst setup timing path between nodes m and p.

Opportunity Propagation Path (OPP): This is a collection of nodes, each pair connected by single edge, forming a path trace between two end nodes – OPN and ORN. This is the path trace through which the proposed algorithm will propagate the opportunity from OPN to ORN.

Intermediate Nodes (IMN): The intermediate nodes other that OPN and ORN associated with an OPP.

Maximum Distance of Opportunity Propagation (D_{max}): D_{max} = Maximum number of edges allowed in an OPP by assumption of the algorithm.

Hard Skew Node (HSN): Nodes where the skew is fixed. The algorithm or a specific run of the algorithm cannot alter/update the skew value of that node.

Soft Skew Node (SSN): Nodes where the algorithm can alter/update the skew value.

SSM: This is the **setup slack margin** of any specific timing path.

HSM: This is the **hold slack margin** of any specific timing path.

Fig. 4 shows the input and output of the "proposed skew optimization algorithm" performing the following steps.

1. Identify all the OPs in the design and a corresponding TOPV for the same.
2. For all the OPs perform the following steps.
3. First consider ORN_R, and build the connectivity graph in its fan-out side as shown in Fig. 5.
   a. This graph is in the right neighbor-hood of ORN_R and is limited within some assumed D_{max} from ORN_R.
   b. Colour all the D_{max} nodes as HSN.
   c. Rest of the IMNs can be declared as SSN except those IMNs which were part of any OP covered in previous run. They are declared as HSN for all subsequent runs.

d. For all the SSNs at D_{max} -1, update skew values and setup slacks (SSLK) as following.

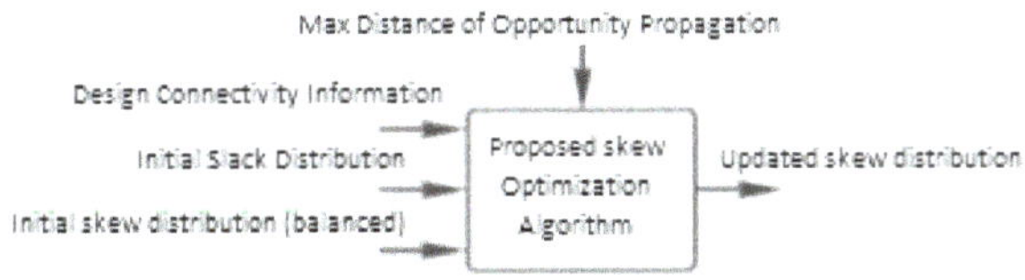

Fig. 4: Input-output of the proposed algorithm

i. SK_{Dmax-1}(new) =SK_{Dmax-1} (old)+min{SSM(all_fanout paths of that SSN), (β*T – SSLK (old)), HSM(all_fanin paths of that SSN)}; where T is clock period; $\beta \leq 1$, but very close to 1.

ii. SSLK(new) = SSLK(old) + SK_{Dmax-1}(new)

e. Once all SSNs of D_{max}-1 got covered, then repeat the above step for all the SSNs of D_{max}-2 and similarly proceed until we reach to the D=0 node, i.e. the ORN_R itself.

f. Calculate OPV_R = final skew value of the ORN_R.

g. If the OPV_R > TOPV, then skip step 4 and proceed to step 5 directly. Otherwise go to step 4.

4. Once we traverse the complete graph which is RHS of ORN_R, and we are not satisfied in terms of OPV, we consider ORN_L, and build the graph in its fan-in side as shown in Fig. 6.
   a. This graph is in the left neighbor-hood of ORN_L and is limited within D_{max} from ORN_L.
   b. Colour all the D_{max} nodes as HSN.
   c. Rest of the IMNs can be declared as SSN except those IMNs which were part of any OP covered in previous run. They are declared as HSN for all subsequent runs.
   d. For all the SSNs at D_{max} -1, update skew values and setup slacks as following.
      i. SK_{Dmax-1}(new) = - [SK_{Dmax-1} (old) + min{SSM(all_fanin paths of that SSN), (β*T – SSLK (old)), HSM(all_fanout paths of that SSN)}]
      ii. SSLK(new) = SSLK(old) - SK_{Dmax-1}(new)
   e. Once all SSNs of D_{max}-1 got covered, then repeat the above step for all the SSNs of D_{max}-2 and similarly proceed until we reach to the D = 0 node, i.e. the ORN_L itself.
   f. Calculate OPV_L = final skew value provided to ORN_L.
5. So, the final OPV of the OP = SLK (old) + OPV_R + OPV_L.
6. Color the ORN_R and ORN_L and declare them as **permanent HSN** for subsequent runs. Note that other IMNs in the run are not declared as permanent HSN. They may be declared as SSNs in some subsequent runs.
7. Then repeat the steps 3-6 until all the OPs get covered. Use updated skew distribution for the runs.
8. Output the final skew distribution of all the nodes. This goes as an input to the incremental CTS step of "opportunistic LIPO" as described in the previous sections.

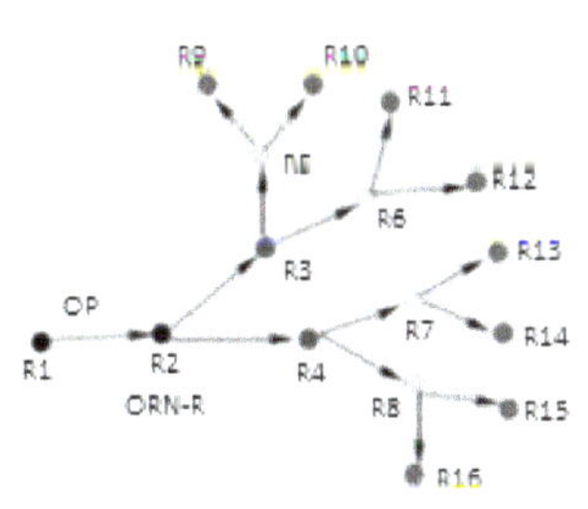

Fig. 5: A simple RHS graph formed within D_{max} = 3 from ORN_R. Red colored nodes (R9 – R16) are at D =3, and hence they all are HSN. Green nodes (R5 – R8) are at D = 2, and hence they are SSN. Blue nodes (R3 – R4) are at D = 1, and hence they are also SSN. R2 is at D = 0 and here it is ORN_R.

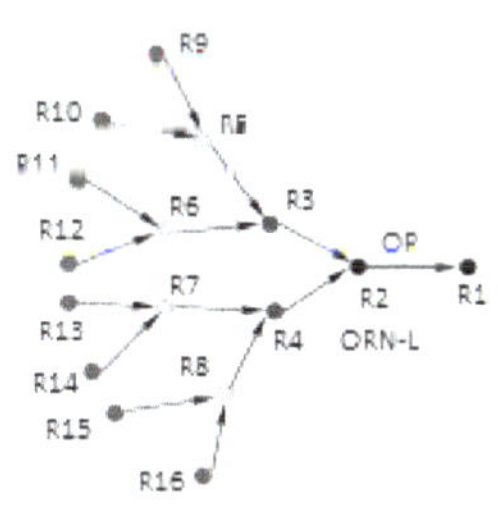

Fig. 6: A simple LHS graph formed within D_{max} = 3 from ORN_L. Red colored nodes (R9 – R16) are at D = 3, and hence they all are HSN. Green nodes (R5 – R8) are at D = 2, and hence they are SSN. Blue nodes (R3 – R4) are at D = 1, and hence they are also SSN. R2 is at D = 0 and here it is ORN_L.

The following scenarios should be noted for the above algorithm.

- There can be self-loop. That is a path whose source and sync node is same. These loops should be ignored completely as while updating the skew, it affects the launch and capture clock edge in same way.
- While we build the graph (RHS or LHS), there can be nodes (from D = 0 to D_{max}) which can be associated with multiple D. Infact, that is the general case. Fig. 7 shows a complicated graph; where nodes cannot be associated with a single D, and hence the following steps should be performed while the algorithm covers all the nodes associated with one D. Without loss of any generality, we use Fig. 7, which is a graph formed in RHS of ORN_R, to explain the detailed steps involved while parsing from various stage to stage in order to propagate the opportunity. It should be noted that the steps for LHS graph would be similar, only the sense of propagation gets reversed.

Detailed steps while parsing the algorithm (an example: elaboration of step 3.a to 3.f mentioned in the above section)

Ground Rule: At any pass of the algorithm, opportunity can propagate only from an HSN (temporary or permanent) to SSN, and all the immediate OPNs corresponding to that "opportunity" receiver node (i.e. for this example, all the fan-out nodes of the receiver node) must be HSN.

Step1 (Forming the graph): Start with D = 0 node (i.e. ORN), trace all the fan-out nodes, and associate them with D = 1. Then for each nodes associated with D = 1, trace all the fan-out nodes, and associated them with D = 2. Similarly, one can get the list of all the nodes associated with any D = d, by tracing all the fan-out nodes emanating from the nodes at D = d – 1. Table 1 shows the step1 result for the graph.

Step2 (Colouring the first set of HSN starting with D_{max}): As in this example, D_{max} = 3, so we stopped at D = 3 while forming Table 1. In this step, we will keep only those nodes at D = D_{max}, which can be considered as HSN for maximal benefit. We see the 1st node at D = 3 is R5, its fan-in nodes are not part of the other nodes in that column i.e. {R6, R8, R9, and R10}. We come to the next node, i.e. R6, and see that one of its fan-in node, R5, is a member of this column. So, we discard R5 from D = 3. Note that, R10 is also a fan-in node of R6, but atleast in this step we can't discard R10 as if we consider R10 to R6 edge, then the associativity of R6 should have been with D = 4 > D_{max}. So, the current list for D = 3 is {R6, R8, R9, R10}. Now, we come to R8, and it does not discard any node, and hence we move to R9. As R8 is fan-in node of R9, so R8 gets discarded, and we are with the list {R6, R9, R10}. Finally we come to R10, and see that R6 is one of its fan-in node. So, we discard R6 and finally declare R9 and R10 as the HSN to start the opportunity propagation. Table 2 shows the result of step2. Note that this particular cancellation step (i.e. step2) is run only to find out HSN associated with D = D_{max}. In case, if all the nodes associated with D_{max}, gets cancelled out and we don't find any HSN associated with that D, then we come D = D_{max} – 1 and repeat step 2 until we find some HSN to start the "opportunity propagation", as that is the ground rule mentioned above. It should be also highlighted that, while we are associating nodes with various D, and some of them we are declaring as HSN, if the graph size becomes too huge to consider due to run-time etc., in that case one may limit the number of nodes in each stage and those nodes being not considered should be treated as HSN.

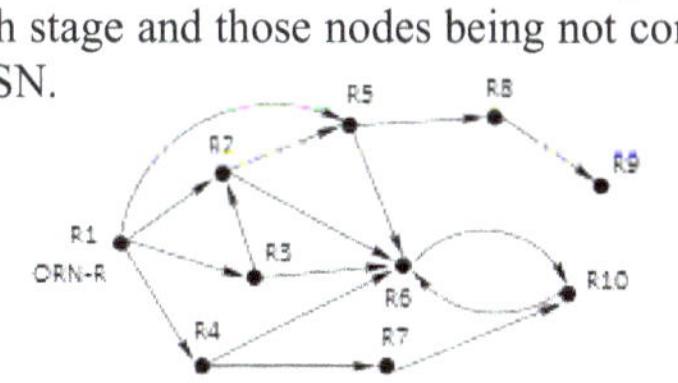

Fig. 7: A complicated generic graph with 10 nodes at the RHS of ORN_R, where nodes may not be associated with a single D.

Table 1: Formed graph as per Step1 by associating each node to one or multiple "D"

Distance from ORN (D)			
0	1	2	3
R1 (ORN)	R2	R2	R5
	R3	R5	R6
	R4	R6	R8
	R5	R7	R9
		R8	R10

Table 2: Results of Step2

Distance from ORN (D)			
0	1	2	3
R1 (ORN)	R2	R2	
	R3	R5	
	R4	R6	
	R5	R7	R9 (HSN)
		R8	R10 (HSN)

Table 3: Results of Step3 – pass1

Distance from ORN (D)			
0	1	2	3
R1 (ORN)	R2	R2	
	R3	R5	
	R4	R6 (HSN)	
	R5	R7 (HSN)	R9 (HSN)
		R8 (HSN)	R10 (HSN)

Table 4: Results of Step3 – pass2

Distance from ORN (D)			
0	1	2	3
R1 (ORN)	R2	R2	
	R3	R5 (HSN)	
	R4	R6 (HSN)	
	R5	R7 (HSN)	R9 (HSN)
		R8 (HSN)	R10 (HSN)

Table 5: Results of Step3 – pass3

Distance from ORN (D)			
0	1	2	3
R1 (ORN)	R2	R2 (HSN)	
	R3	R5 (HSN)	
	R4	R6 (HSN)	
	R5	R7 (HSN)	R9 (HSN)
		R8 (HSN)	R10 (HSN)

Table 6: Results of Step4

Distance from ORN (D)			
0	1	2	3
R1 (ORN)	R2 (HSN)	R2 (HSN)	
	R3 (HSN)	R5 (HSN)	
	R4 (HSN)	R6 (HSN)	
	R5 (HSN)	R7 (HSN)	R9 (HSN)
		R8 (HSN)	R10 (HSN)

Table 7: Results after step5, the final step, where ORN receives opportunity propagated

Distance from ORN (D)			
0	1	2	3
R1 (ORN) (permanent HSN)	R2 (SSN)	R2 (SSN)	
	R3 (SSN)	R5 (SSN)	
	R4 (SSN)	R6 (SSN)	
	R5 (SSN)	R7 (SSN)	R9 (SSN)
		R8 (SSN)	R10 (SSN)

Table 8: Experimental results in some industry standard chips having different initial skew distribution

Design Name	Gate Count	Max frequency of timing closure (MHz)	Leakage power reduction by the proposed method over traditional LIPO (%)
A	50M	400	11.22
		300	17.34
		200	28.92
B	60M	400	8.92
		300	14.65
		200	24.34

Step3 (Opportunity propagation across stages): At this time, we are ready to propagate opportunity to the previous stage, i.e. D = 2 in this example. We start with the first node of D = 2, i.e. R2. Its fan-out nodes are not HSN, so move to the next node, R5. Its fan-out nodes are not yet hard (declared HSN), so we move on to the next node R6. As R10 is hard, so we propagate opportunity to R6 and discard $E_{6,10}$. As there are no more fan-out edges from R6, so we declare R6 as HSN (temporarily only for this particular run of OP). Similarly, R7 gets opportunity from R10 and we discard $E_{7,10}$. Again this becomes hard, as there are no more fan-out edges from this node. Following the same logic, R8 also becomes hard. So, while we were passing through the columns of D = 2, R6, R7, R8 becomes hard, but still R2 and R5 left, so, we go for another pass.

The fan-out nodes of R2 are R5 and R6. But, at this time, only R6 is hard, not R5. So, R2 is not yet ready to receive opportunity. We move to the next node R5, and see that all the fan-out nodes of R5 is hard. So, we propagate opportunity to R5 and declare R5 as hard. As R2 is still left for D = 2, we go for another pass (i.e. pass3) and propagate opportunity to R2 as R5 and R6 both are hard after pass2. Table 3 – 5 explains the result after three passes.

Step4 (Opportunity propagation across stages): In step4, we move to D = 1 column, as all the nodes in D = 2 column has been declared as HSN and hence exhaustively covered. We start with R2 and see that this is already HSN, so we discard that and move to R3. As all the fan-out nodes of R3 are hard, so it receives opportunity as per the formulas mentioned in the "proposed algorithm" section and we declare it as hard after that. Similarly R4 also receives opportunity and gets declared as hard. Next R5 is already declared as hard, so we exhaustively covered all the nodes for D = 1, and done with this step. Table 6 shows the status of the nodes after this step. Note that all the nodes of D =1 got covered in single pass only.

Step5 (Final Step): This is the final step for this ORN. As all the fan-out nodes of R1 (ORN) are hard, so opportunity propagates to R1, and we declare R1 as "permanently hard" for all sub-sequent runs for other ORNs, may or may not be for the same OP.

Eventually we see that that opportunity propagated from R9, R10 to R1 which are separated by D = D_{max}. We declare other nodes i.e. R2 to R10 as SSNs for the sub-sequent runs corresponding to the other ORNs in the design. Table 7 shows this status flow.

3. EXPERIMENTAL RESULTS

The above algorithm is implemented using "tcl" and applied on some standard design using 28 nm technology. Table 8 shows that the algorithm is tried over two industry standard designs and it enhances leakage reduction ~10-30% over traditional LIPO based on the initial opportunity available in the design chosen. It should be noted that the benefit in terms of leakage reduction is expected to vary based on the design and the opportunity we have in the design, and hence the authors do not claim any generalized performance benchmark of the proposed algorithm.

4. CONCLUSIONS

We have presented a novel method to reduce leakage power in a timing-closed design by exploiting positive slacks available across the design while minimally disturbing a balanced clock-tree. The algorithm will definitely benefit in terms of leakage power unless we mess up in the CTS at post skew optimization phase. For this reason, the CTS should be handled intelligently.

REFERENCES

[1] S. Narendra and A. Chandrakasan, "Leakage in nanometer CMOS technologies," *Springer*, 2006.

[2] M. F. Turner, J. W. Byrn, and J. S. Brown, "Cell library management for power optimization," *Us patent – US 7,496,867 B2*, 2009.

[3] L. Wei *et. al.*, "Design and optimization of dual-threshold circuits for low-voltage low-power applications," *IEEE Trans. on VLSI Systems*, vol. 7, no. 1, pp. 16-24, 1999.

[4] S. Sirichotiyakul *et. al.*, "Stand-by power minimization through simultaneous threshold voltage selection and circuit sizing," *Proc. 36th ACM/IEEE Conf. of Design Automation,* 436, June 21-25, 1999.

[5] Y. Ho and T. Hwang, "Low power design using dual threshold voltage," *Proc. of the Conference on Asia South Pacific Design Automation*, pp. 205-208, 2004.

[6] P. Pant, R. K. Roy, and A. Chatterjee, "Dual-threshold voltage assignment with transistor sizing for low power CMOS circuits," *IEEE Trans. on VLSI Systems*, pp. 390-394, 2001.

[7] H. Abrishami *et. al.*, "Post sign-off leakage power optimization," *Design Automation Conference*, pp. 453-458, 2011.

[8] J. S. Brown, J. W. Byrn, and M. F. Turner, "Granular channel width for power optimization," US patent – US 8196086 B2, 2012.

An Enhanced Analytical Electrical Masking Model for Multiple Event Transients

Adam Watkins and Spyros Tragoudas
Department of Electrical and Computer Engineering
Southern Illinois University, Carbondale, IL 62901
watkins@engr.siu.edu, spyros@engr.siu.edu

ABSTRACT

Due to the reducing transistor feature size, the susceptibility of modern circuits to radiation induced errors has increased. This, as a result, has increased the likelihood of multiple transients affecting a circuit. An important aspect when modeling convergent pulses is the approximation of the gate output. Thus, in this paper, a model that approximates the output pulse shape for convergent inputs is proposed. Extensive simulations showed that the proposed model matched closely with HSPICE and provides a speed-up of 15X.

Keywords

Soft Errors; Transient Pulses; Transient Errors; Radiation Induced Errors; Multiple Event Transients; Multiple Event Upsets

1. INTRODUCTION

A soft error occurs when a neutron particle from cosmic radiation or an alpha particle from packaging hits the diffusion region of a transistor. This strike causes a temporary flow of current through the transistor causing a change on the gate output voltage. If the strike is sufficiently severe, the change will manifest into a voltage pulse commonly referred to as a single event upset (SEU). This SEU may propagate through the circuit and cause an observable error at the output.

As the transistor size has continued to decrease, the probability of a SEU occurring has continued to greatly increase. This, in effect, has created a need for accurate and efficient SEU simulators. The SEU problem has been investigated deeply [1], [2], [3]. However, due to the close proximity of transistors and the increase in transistor error sensitivity, the probability of a single or multiple radiation strikes producing multiple voltage pulses has become a concern. The authors in [4] investigated a 65 nm 3x3 inverter matrix and found that 40% of all single radiation strikes resulted in the generation multiple significant voltage pulses. Considering the possibility that a modern circuit is also vulnerable to multiple simultaneous strike, there is a significant concern for multiple transients. This creates the need for either the enhancement of existing SEU tools or the development of new tools which can consider the single event multiple transient (SEMT) and multiple even multiple transient (MEMT) effect.

Previous work in SEU's have shown that combinational circuits are vulnerable to 3 types of error masking effects: logical masking, electrical masking and temporal masking. Accurate estimation of the soft error rate requires consideration of all masking factors for not only SEU's but also the SEMT and MEMT cases. In this paper, the focus is on the consideration of the electrical masking effect. There have been many approaches to the electrical masking problem for the SEU case [5], [6], [7]. However, a major drawback with these approaches is that they do not accurately consider the effect of multiple pulses occurring on the gate input (referred to as convergent pulses). Since, in the SEMT and MEMT cases, there are many pulses generated, the occurrence of convergent pulses is much higher. To model these cases, an accurate electrical masking model must consider convergent pulses.

This research has been supported in part by grants NSF IIP 1432026, and NSF IIP 1361847 from the NSF I/UCRC for Embedded Systems at SIUC. Any opinions, findings, and conclusions or recommendations expressed in this material are those of the authors and do not necessarily reflect the views of the National Science Foundation

GLSVLSI '16, May 18-20, 2016, Boston, MA, USA

DOI: http://dx.doi.org/10.1145/2902961.2903007

There has been a few attempts at modeling the effect multiple transient pules, however all approaches suffer from inaccurate estimation of electrical masking. The authors in [8], [9] both proposed a simulation tool to determine the soft error rate (SER) of a combinational circuit in the presence of multiple transients, however, they calculate the output transient of a gate with a convergent input through the simple superposition of the pulse widths. As stated in [6], this is insufficient since accurate electrical masking modeling requires the inclusion of the pulse amplitude and non-linear portions of the glitch.

An additional possible solution to the pulse convergence problem is the simple extension of [6] for convergent pulses. In [6] an accurate iterative model for the single pulse case is proposed. Their model can easily be extended by generating larger look-up tables. However, since they characterize stacked transistors using look-up tables, gates with more than 2-inputs require tables with 125,000 entries for 3-input gates and over 7 million for 4-input gates. Thus our model provides an enhancement to [6] by allowing the characterization of stacked transistors using a look-up tables for the transistor and the Miller capacitance between the gate and drain terminals.

Based on the above discussion, there is a lack of accurate and fast methods to consider convergent pulses. This provides the motivation of this work. To the author's knowledge, the proposed model is the first masking model that accurately and efficiently approximates the entire output pulse shape for convergent input pulses. Through extensive experimentation, the proposed model has been shown to be robust for various input shapes and process technologies while providing a 15X speed-up over HSPICE.

The rest of this paper is organized as follows. In Section II, a background discussing the premise for the model is given. Section III details the derivation of the model's equations. Section IV provides the results and Section V concludes the paper.

2. PULSE APPROXIMATION MODEL

As in [6], an important aspect of the proposed model is the accurate approximation of the transistor drain to source current (I_{DS}). To consider the I_{DS} current, a look-up table for each transistor is created by sweeping both the gate-source voltage (V_{GS}) and the drain-source voltage (V_{DS}).

Additionally, as in [6], the effects of pulse overshoot and undershoot are considered through the use of a Miller capacitor. In contrast to [6], however, we consider the MOS parasitic effects on each individual transistor through the inclusion of a Miller capacitance between the gate and drain terminals. Fig. 1 demonstrates the proposed model for a NMOS and a PMOS transistor.

As stated in [6], it was observed that the value of the Miller capacitance varied over the range of drain-source (V_{DS}) and gate-source (V_{GS}) voltages. To consider this effect, it is proposed to generate a look-up table with each entry pertaining to the Miller capacitance at each specific V_{DS} and V_{GS} bias. The Miller capacitance look-up tables can be characterized using HSPICE by sweeping the V_{DS} and V_{GS} voltages and measuring the current flowing through the gate node of the transistor (i_m). Using the current i_m, the derivative of the difference between the gate and drain voltages and equation (1), the capacitance C_{Miller} can be calculated.

$$C_{Miller} = \frac{i_m}{\frac{d(V_{DS} - V_{GS})}{dt}} \quad (1)$$

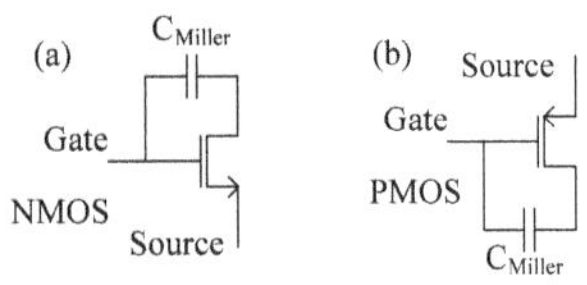

Fig. 1. (a) The transistor model used for a NMOS. (b) The transistor model for a PMOS.

As stated before, the I_{DS} current and the Miller capacitance for both the PMOS and NMOS transistors are characterized. Using this data, each transistor is modeled as a current source and its Miller capacitor. Any given gate can then be represented by replacing each transistor with a current source and a Miller capacitor connected between the drain and gate terminals. At the output of the gate, a load capacitance is added to consider the gate loading effects and to calibrate the model. Fig. 2. demonstrates the conversion to the proposed model on a 2-input NAND gate.

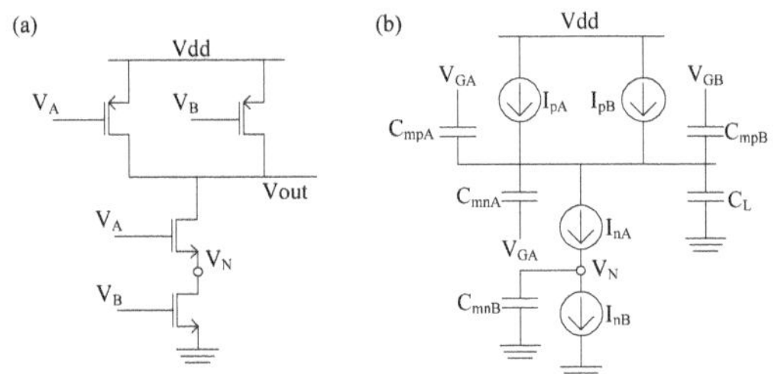

Fig. 2. (a) A standard 2-input CMOS NAND gate. (b) The NAND gate converted to the proposed model.

Before beginning the discussion on the equation derivation it is important to note that this model is general for all types of gates but for the sake of this discussion, the derivation will focus on CMOS NAND and NOR gates.

The proposed gate modeling for a given gate, as in Fig.2b, can be generalized for an *i* number of inputs as in Fig. 3. where a single current source represents the current for the pull-up network and a second current source represents the pull-down network. This is based on the assumption that the gate is a CMOS gate in which one network consists of parallel current sources and the equivalent current is equal to the sum of each parallel transistor current. The other current source represents the current flowing through series connected transistors which ideally have a single constant current. However, in practice, due to parasitic effects, the current in each stacked transistor varies. It was found through many simulations that the best approximation for this current was by taking the average between each transistor current in the stack. For example, if we have the circuit in Fig. 2b, the current on the stacked transistors can be calculated using the following equation:

$$I_{pd} = \frac{I_{nA} + I_{nB}}{2} \quad (2)$$

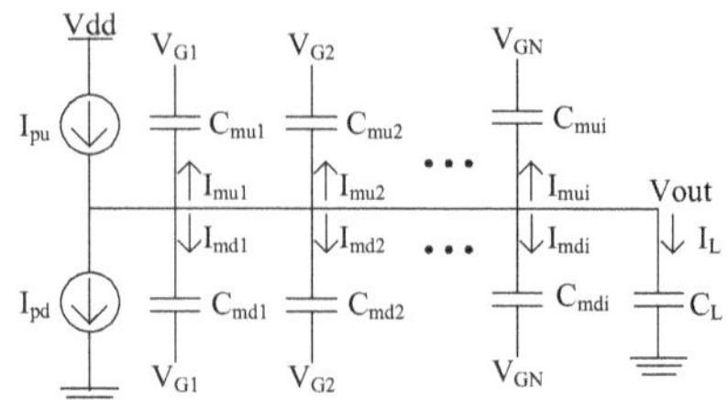

Fig. 3. A generalized representation for the gate model.

To derive the output equation for the node V_{out} in Fig. 3., we first use Kirchoff's Current Law (KCL) at the node V_{out}. Assuming that I_{mu_i} and I_{md_i} are the currents through the *i*-th Miller capacitor, I_L is the current through the load capacitor and I_{pu} and I_{pd} represent the pull-up and pull-down current respectively, KCL will result in the following:

$$I_{pu} = I_{pd} + I_L + \sum_{i=1}^{N} I_{mu_i} + \sum_{i=1}^{N} I_{md_i} \quad (3)$$

For our model, we discretize the time into time steps with the variable t_{step}. Additionally, we represent each variable in the current time instant with the subscript *i* and each variable in the previous time instant with the subscript *i-1*. Lastly, we represent the change in a value between two time instances using Δ (i.e. $V_i - V_{i-1} = \Delta V$).

According to the charge conservation law, we get equation (4) for each Miller capacitor C_{m_i} connected between V_{out} and the input voltage V_{G_i}.

$$I_{m_i} = \frac{[\Delta V_{out} - \Delta V_{G_i}]C_{m_i}}{t_{step}} \quad (4)$$

Next, consideration of the load capacitance C_L gives the following equation:

$$I_L = \frac{(\Delta V_{out})C_L}{t_{step}} \quad (5)$$

By substituting into equation (3) the current I_{m_i} from (4) for the currents I_{mu_i} and I_{md_i} and replacing the current I_L with equation (5), we get the following for a N_u number of Miller capacitors connected between V_{out} and the *i*-th input in the pull-up network (denoted by C_{mu_i}) and a N_d number of Miller capacitors connected to V_{out} and the *i*-th input on the pull-down network (denoted by C_{md_i}):

$$I_{pu} = I_{pd} + \frac{\Delta V_{out} C_L}{t_{step}} + \sum_{i=1}^{N_u} \frac{[\Delta V_{out} - \Delta V_{G_i}]C_{mu_i}}{t_{step}} + \sum_{i=1}^{N_d} \frac{[\Delta V_{out} - \Delta V_{G_i}]C_{md_i}}{t_{step}} \quad (6)$$

Rearranging (6) and solving for ΔV_{out} gives the following:

$$\Delta V_{out} = \frac{(I_{pu} - I_{pd})t_{step} + \sum_{i=1}^{N_u} \Delta V_{G_i} - C_{mu_i} + \sum_{i=1}^{N_d} \Delta V_{G_i} - C_{md_i}}{C_L + \sum_{i=1}^{N_u} C_{mu_i} + \sum_{i=1}^{N_d} C_{md_i}} \quad (7)$$

Assuming that ΔV_{out_i} equals $V_{out_i} - V_{out_{i-1}}$ we get

$$V_{out_i} = \Delta V_{out} + V_{out_{i-1}} \quad (8)$$

As can be observed in equations (7) and (8) an important aspect of the proposed model is the accurate consideration of both the pull-up and pull-down currents. As stated before, cases where the pull-up or pull-down transistors are composed of parallel connected transistors the current can simply be found through the sum of the drain to source currents. However, in cases where the transistors are in series, the determination of the equivalent current is more complicated.

In Fig. 2a. the pull-down branch consists of series connected NMOS transistors which will be used to demonstrate the derivation. Note that using the same method, the equations for stacked PMOS devices can be easily derived. Within the stack there is an intermediate node voltage *Vn* which is crucial for the determination of the drain to source currents in the transistors. Through many simulations using the transistor drain to source current look-up tables, it was found that accurate approximation of the node voltages provided accurate current values for each transistor in the stack.

To calculate the intermediate voltage, it is proposed to first convert each transistor to the representations in Fig. 1a and 1b. which results in the circuit in Fig. 2b. In Fig. 2b. the intermediate node voltage *Vn* is connected to a static capacitor representing the loading effect of the subsequent transistor stack. Next, we will look at how to derive the node voltage equation.

Similar to equation (7), the node voltage *Vn* is modeled using discrete time steps. Using KCL at *Vn* in Fig. 2b we get the following equation:

$$I_{D1} = I_{D2} + I_m \tag{9}$$

As in equation (4), the current through the static capacitor can be determined using the charge conservation law resulting in the following for the current I_m.

$$I_m = \frac{C_{m1}\left(V_{n_i} - V_{n_{i-1}}\right)}{t_{step}} \tag{10}$$

By substituting (10) into (9) and solving for V_{n_i}, we get the equation for the node voltage *Vn* at the time instant *i*.

$$V_{n_i} = \frac{(I_{D1} - I_{D2})t_{step}}{C_{m1}} + V_{n_{i-1}} \tag{11}$$

In cases where there are more than 2 stacked transistors, the described model is directly extendable for each intermediate node. Fig. 4a and b provides the conversion for 3 stacked NMOS transistors to our model. The node voltages V_{N1} and V_{N2} can be found in any order using equation (11) and by considering the currents flowing into the node. For example, if we wanted to solve for the node voltage V_{N2} the currents I_{D2} and I_{D3} would be used in equation (11) since they are directly connected to the node. Additionally, the order for solving the node equations does not matter since the node voltages from the previous step (step *i-1*) are used.

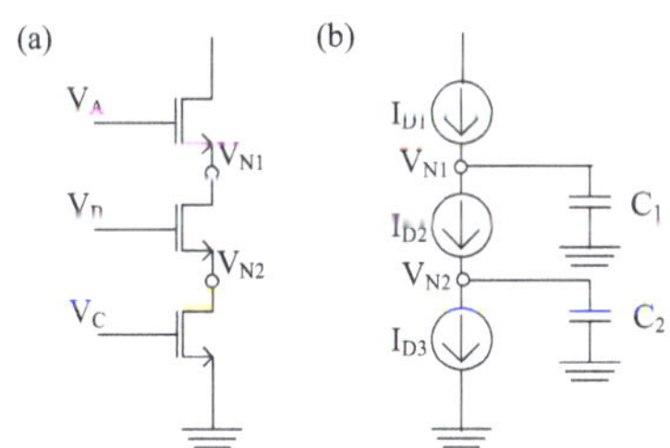

Fig. 4. (a) Three stacked NMOS transistors with two intermediate node *Vn1* and *Vn2*. (b) The transistors converted to the proposed circuit model.

3. EXPERIMENTAL RESULTS

The proposed algorithm was implemented in Matlab and characterized using the 32 nm and 45 nm PTM library and the 65 nm IBM library. To test the proposed model, we created 3 benchmark circuits for each process library to test two convergent pulses on a 2 and 3 input NAND gate and a 2 input NOR gate. The first two benchmark circuits denoted by NAND2R and NAND2F in column 1 of Table 1, consists of two NAND gate chains with each off-input held to a non-controlling value. The chains contain two gates and the R and F in the benchmark names represent either a rising (R) or falling (F) pulse on the convergent gate's inputs. Each chain is then connected to an input of the NAND gate. The benchmark circuits NOR2R and NOR2F are constructed similarly but the chains consist of NOR gates and are connected to the input of a 2 input NOR gate. The last benchmark circuits constructed, NAND3R and NAND3F, were created with 2 2 gate chains connected to the first and second input of the 3-input NAND gate. The remaining off-input was held to a non-controlling value.

Next, to accurately model the injected pulse shape, we represented the injection current as a current source located at the output of the first gate in the chain. We then used the function for the pulse shape given in [10] to relate the strike current to a given charge. The equation is given below with Q_o representing the charge resulting from a strike, τ representing a technology dependent pulse shaping parameter and t being the variable for time.

$$I(t) = \frac{2Q_o}{\tau\sqrt{\pi}}\sqrt{\frac{t}{\tau}}e^{\frac{-t}{\tau}} \tag{12}$$

Using equation (12), Q_o was varied over a range of charge values that results in an observable error. For our test cases, we found that a charge ranging from 3-16 fC for a τ of $90\text{x}10^{-12}$ provided an observable output shape for all processes tested. We then propagated the pulses through the gate chains to gate of interest and compared the generated outputs using the proposed model and the model in [6] to HSPICE. Table 1 details the average error for 30 cases per gate and transition type for the 32, 45 and 65 nm processes using 2400 data points over a range of 0 to 1.2 pico-seconds. The first column gives the benchmark name. All subsequent columns provide the MSE error for each test case for the proposed method and the method in [6]. Assuming that N represents the number of calculated points, V_i^H represents the pulse voltage at point i on the signal from HSPICE and V_i^C is the voltage calculated by the proposed model, the MSE was calculated using the following equation:

$$MSE = \frac{\sum_{i=0}^{N}(V_i^H - V_i^C)^2}{N} \tag{13}$$

As can be seen from Table 1, the proposed model is much more accurate over the model proposed in [6]. In all tested cases, the method in [6] predicted there would be an output pulse. However, they only propagate the pulse with the largest width which fails to consider the effect of multiple pulses and provides a pulse with a much smaller width. For this reason, their method tends to underestimate the severity of the pulse in the presence of convergent pulses. According to Table 1, our method closely predicts the output pulse shape.

Next, we run a simulation to observe how the number of points selected relates to the speed and accuracy. In this simulation, we used the NAND2F and NAND3F benchmark and applied a pulse to each input of the terminating NAND gate. We then varied the number of output data points for the terminating NAND gate in both HSPICE and the proposed model. Table 2 provides the results of this simulation.

The first column provides the number of simulation points used to calculate the result. Columns 2 and 3 provide the error of the proposed model and [6] for the given number of points. Columns 4, 5 and 6 gives the execution time of the proposed method, the method in [6] and HSPICE respectively. As can be seen from Table 2, the reduction in simulation time scales linearly to the reduction in simulation points.

In Fig. 5, we provide the output waveform of the simulation in Table 2 for 900 and 300 points respectively. As can be observed in Fig. 5a, the result for the proposed model closely matches the result obtained in HSPICE when 900 simulation points are used. If a higher accuracy is desired, the proposed model provides a near perfect match with 2400 points. For both the 900 and 300 point cases, it can be observed that the method in [6] greatly underestimates the resulting pulse thus providing a high MSE. The proposed model provides an accurate result with an MSE of 7.40×10^{-3} while still providing a speed-up of 15X compared to HSPICE for this benchmark. In general we have observed a speed-up of 15X for any 2-input gate using 900 points while maintaining a high accuracy

In Fig. 6a and 6b, we provide the output waveforms for the NAND3F simulation for 900 and 300 points respectively. Similar to the NAND2F benchmark, a simulation with 900 points provides a close waveform approximation. However, if a lower accuracy is tolerable, the number of points can be reduced further providing a faster simulation time as demonstrated in Table 2 and Fig. 6b. As can be observed in Table 2, proposed model provides a speed-up of 12X for the 900 point case. In general for any 3-input gate, we have observed a speed-up of 12X using 900 points while maintaining a high accuracy

Table 1. Proposed and [6] compared to HSPICE for 2400 points

Circuit	MSE [65nm] ($\times 10^{-3}$)		MSE [45nm] ($\times 10^{-3}$)		MSE [32nm] ($\times 10^{-3}$)	
	Proposed	[6]	Proposed	[6]	Proposed	[6]
NAND2R	0.760	108	0.453	35.6	0.190	45.6
NAND2F	1.000	110	0.550	67.8	0.467	50.9
NOR2R	0.220	23.0	0.345	133.0	0.402	146.2
NOR2F	0.986	103	0.678	42.5	0.493	33.9
NAND3R	0.887	115	0.785	55.6	0.352	39.2
NAND3F	0.998	98.9	0.467	39.8	0.465	30.8

Table 2. Execution Time vs Accuracy ($\times 10^{-3}$)

Points	Error Proposed	Error [6]	Execution Time Proposed	Execution Time [6]	Execution Time HSPICE
NAND2F					
2400	0.486	85.7	8.39	8.03	100
1200	3.90	92.0	4.34	4.01	60
900	7.40	97.8	3.43	3.05	50
300	41.1	115.9	1.23	1.18	20
NAND3F					
2400	0.529	37.5	12.1	11.4	120
1200	6.40	38.7	6.40	5.90	70
900	13.0	42.8	4.90	4.50	60
300	60.9	85.0	1.91	1.50	30

4. CONCLUSION

In this paper, we proposed a model that improves SEMT and MEMT error simulation by calculating the output pulse shape in the presence of convergence with an MSE of less than 7.40×10^{-3} for 2-input gates and 13×10^{-3} for 3-input gates using 900 points and a speed-up of 15X and 12X respectively compared to HSPICE. Future work with our model includes the study of the number of points effect the simulation result on large benchmarks and the study of SEMT and MEMT on large standard benchmark circuits using the proposed model.

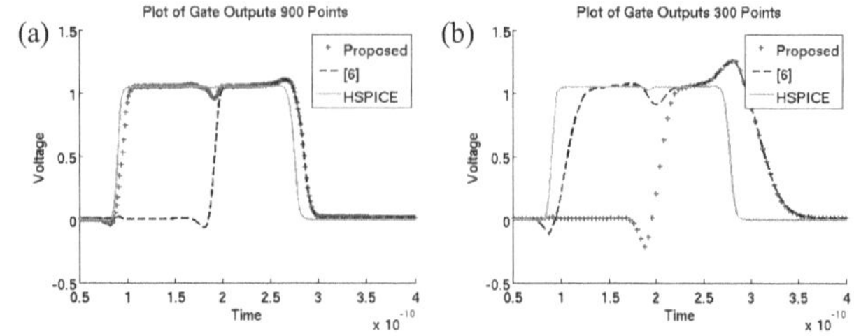

Fig. 5. (a) Output of NAND2F with 900 points. (b) Output of NAND2F with 300 points.

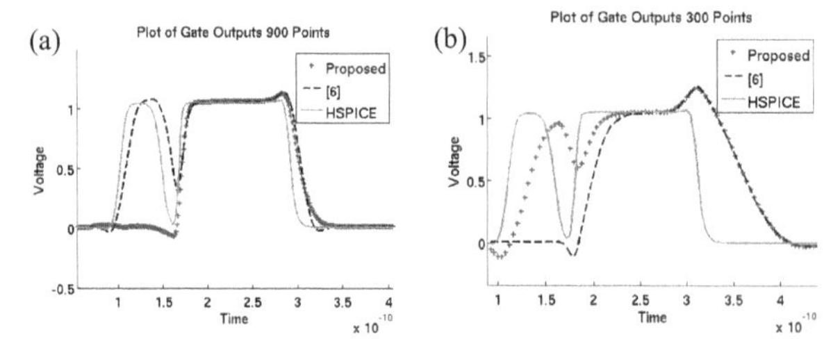

Fig. 6. (a) Output of NAND3F with 900 points. (b) Output of NAND3F with 300 points.

5. REFERENCES

[1] Miskov-Zivanov, N.; Marculescu, D.; , "MARS-C: modeling and reduction of soft errors in combinational circuits," Design Automation Conference, 2006 43rd ACM/IEEE , vol., no., pp.767-772, 0-0 0

[2] Ming Zhang; Shanbhag, N.R.; , "Soft-Error-Rate-Analysis (SERA) Methodology," Computer-Aided Design of Integrated Circuits and Systems, IEEE Transactions on , vol.25, no.10, pp.2140-2155, Oct. 2006

[3] Bin Zhang; Wei-Shen Wang; Orshansky, M.; , "FASER: fast analysis of soft error susceptibility for cell-based designs," Quality Electronic Design, 2006. ISQED '06. 7th International Symposium on , vol., no., pp.6 pp.-760, 27-29 March 2006

[4] Harada, R.; Mitsuyama, Y.; Hashimoto, M.; Onoye, T., "Neutron induced single event multiple transients with voltage scaling and body biasing," in *Reliability Physics Symposium (IRPS), 2011 IEEE International* , vol., no., pp.3C.4.1-3C.4.5, 10-14 April 2011

[5] Omana, M.; Papasso, G.; Rossi, D.; Metra, C.; , "A model for transient fault propagation in combinatorial logic," On-Line Testing Symposium, 2003. IOLTS 2003. 9th IEEE , vol., no., pp. 111- 115, 7-9 July 2003

[6] Feng Wang; Yuan Xie; , "Soft Error Rate Analysis for Combinational Logic Using an Accurate Electrical Masking Model," Dependable and Secure Computing, IEEE Transactions on , vol.8, no.1, pp.137-146, Jan.-Feb. 2011

[7] Watkins, A.; Tragoudas, S., "Transient pulse propagation using the Weibull distribution function," in *Defect and Fault Tolerance in VLSI and Nanotechnology Systems (DFT), 2012 IEEE International Symposium on* , vol., no., pp.109-114, 3-5 Oct. 2012

[8] Miskov-Zivanov, Natasa; Marculescu, D., "Multiple Transient Faults in Combinational and Sequential Circuits: A Systematic Approach," in *Computer-Aided Design of Integrated Circuits and Systems, IEEE Transactions on* , vol.29, no.10, pp.1614-1627, Oct. 2010

[9] Fazeli, M.; Ahmadian, S.N.; Miremadi, S.G.; Asadi, H.; Tahoori, M.B., "Soft error rate estimation of digital circuits in the presence of Multiple Event Transients (METs)," in *Design, Automation & Test in Europe Conference & Exhibition (DATE), 2011* , vol., no., pp.1-6, 14-18 March 2011

[10] J. Ziegler, "Terrestrial cosmic rays," IBM J. Res. Develop., vol. 40, no. 1, pp. 19–39, Jan 1996

Capturing True Workload Dependency of BTI-induced Degradation in CPU Components

Dimitrios Stamoulis[1,2] Simone Corbetta[2,3] Dimitrios Rodopoulos[3,4] Pieter Weckx[2,3]
Peter Debacker[2] Brett H. Meyer[1] Ben Kaczer[2] Praveen Raghavan[2]
Dimitrios Soudris[4] Francky Catthoor[2,3] Zeljko Zilic[1]

[1] McGill University, Montréal, Canada [2] imec vzw, Leuven, Belgium
[3] Katholieke Universiteit Leuven, Belgium [4] NTUA, Athens, Greece

ABSTRACT

Atomistic-based approaches accurately model Bias Temperature Instability phenomena, but they suffer from prolonged execution times, preventing their seamless integration in system-level analysis flows. In this paper we present a comprehensive flow that combines the accuracy of Capture Emission Time (CET) maps with the efficiency of the Compact Digital Waveform (CDW) representation. That way, we capture the true workload-dependent BTI-induced degradation of selected CPU components. First, we show that existing works that assume constant stress patterns fail to account for workload dependency leading to fundamental estimation errors. Second, we evaluate the impact of different real workloads on selected CPU sub-blocks from a commercial processor design. To the best of our knowledge, this is the first work that combines atomistic property and true workload-dependency for variability analysis.

CCS Concepts

•**Hardware → Aging of circuits and systems;** *Electronic design automation;*

Keywords

Bias Temperature Instability (BTI); Variability Analysis; Workload Dependency

1. INTRODUCTION

Bias Temperature Instability is important for digital system reliability, and EDA techniques have been proposed to model and mitigate the BTI-induced variability [12]. However, the aggressive scaling towards deca-nanometer nodes has significantly changed the modeling perception of BTI and the underlying simulation requirements. Recent literature shows that older models inherently fail to capture BTI phenomena at deeply-scaled technology nodes [18]. Previously, an atomistic approach has been proposed which concentrates on the charge-level activity of gate-stack defects [1]. It attributes the manifestation of BTI to a variable number of defects, each one with a specific temporal behavior (modeled using time constants) and a certain contribution to the overall V_{th} degradation of a transistor. Recent EDA literature supports a paradigm shift to defect-centric modeling [18] and a variety of atomistic implementations already capture BTI-induced degradation over arbitrary circuit lifetime intervals [14], or in a transient way.

More recent approaches are based on the analytical modeling of defect activity using Capture/Emission Time (CET) maps [17]. CET maps describe the probability density function of defect capture and emission times, as well as their correlations at high and low digital operating voltages [10]. However, monitoring the activity of several defects per transistor throughout the design lifetime poses severe restrictions on the circuit size, the amount of time samples (and hence the granularity of the workload stimuli), and simulation time. Consequently, existing works limit their exploration to simple gates [2,8], SRAM cells [14,15], and simple logic blocks [5,9].

Our goal is to employ the atomistic CET-based models for variability analysis along with the efficiency of CDW approximation to efficiently capture the time-varying BTI-induced path delay degradation on the *true* workload, i.e. without assuming distributed or constant profiles of the stress load. In this paper we adapt the analytical CET map modeling method to the system level, in such a way that we are able to achieve accurate yet efficient atomistic workload-dependent variability analysis for potentially any reference design and desired workload. We then provide examples which demonstrate this simulation capability on realistic CPU components and benchmark applications.

2. RELATED WORK & MOTIVATION

To the best of our knowledge, this is the *first study* that employs complete atomistic variability analysis of realistic CPU subsystems, while retaining the true workload dependency under different reference applications. A large body of previous works has focused on either simple CMOS logic gates [2,8], SRAMs [4,14,15], or larger netlists of repetitive blocks with reduced functional complexity [5,7]. Rodopoulos et al. have implemented atomistic models on top of transient SPICE simulators [3,5]. Although significant accuracy is achieved, the use of SPICE-based solvers is not scalable to larger circuits, resulting in prolonged execution times up to 100 hours even for a simple circuit with few gates. Weckx

GLSVLSI '16, May 18-20, 2016, Boston, MA, USA

DOI: http://dx.doi.org/10.1145/2902961.2902992

et al. have enabled atomistic analysis for SRAM cells with numerical methods [14,15]. Nonetheless, the formulation is bound to the given 6T topology and might be complicated to extend to arbitrary topologies with more transistors. Consequently, these approaches are not applicable to larger netlists due to scalability issues.

Moreover, only two existing works enable atomistic BTI analysis at the subsystem level, similarly to our approach. Kukner et al. have applied CET map modeling methodologies to enable workload-dependent analysis for several logic blocks [9]. Nonetheless, the evaluation is limited to only synthetic workloads. Relatively short varying patterns are randomly assigned to the input pins of each block and such activity information is propagated to the inner nodes. Instead, in the current paper we demonstrate the usability of our approach for several realistic test cases. Stamoulis et al. have recently enabled pseudo-transient atomistic simulations for an entire CPU data-path [6]. Nevertheless, the impact of workload-dependence is completely neglected and the same stress pattern is assumed for all the transistors, regardless of their relative position in the netlist and the activity factors of the inner nodes. Such an assumption is questionable, since these signal attributes are not constant in modern complex circuits, and poses a limitation to the desired BTI estimation. 4, we show that such assumption leads to fundamental estimation errors that cannot be neglected in future design for reliability.

3. PROPOSED FLOW

The purpose of our approach is to enable variability analysis that retains both the atomistic property and workload memory at an early stage of the standard ASIC design process, thus facilitating BTI-aware design of digital circuits. Figure 1 shows the overall flow, which is based on a number of well-defined steps: first, the true workload at the primary inputs of the circuit is traced; these input stress patterns are propagated to the inner nodes of the circuit, and then the workload-dependent degradation is carried out for each single transistor; last, Static Timing Analysis (STA) at transistor level is used to compute the paths delay degradation. The flow is based on commercial ASIC design tools.

3.1 Approximation for long waveforms

Monitoring the occupancy of several defects per transistor in a transient fashion imposes severe restrictions on scalability [2]. We employ an accurate yet efficient method to capture the evolution of stress patterns throughout the circuit lifetime. In previous work, a novel signal waveform representation has been proposed, namely Compact Digital Waveform (CDW) [4]. The analysis of the reference workload is reduced to a set of hyphenated CDW points; they represent the regions of a signal in which the impact of the workload on the BTI-induced variation will be computed. For each region with duration Δt, the CDW point is expressed by means of the frequency f and duty factor α of the stress signal across the region. The number of CDW points over which the BTI analysis is performed is dictated either by the methodology introduced in [4], or selected by the user. In the latter approach, the estimation points are equally spaced in time.

In general, the choice of the number and position of these points can play an important role, since it determines the accuracy of the estimation and the simulation overhead. In general, a higher number of CDW points makes the analysis more accurate at the cost of simulation time, while a more crude analysis suffers from averaging out the signal activity. This trade-off analysis is beyond the scope of the current paper, and the interested reader is referred to the literature [4]. Nevertheless, we can exploit proposed flow to estimate the relative divergence of the BTI estimation as a function of the number of selected CDW points.

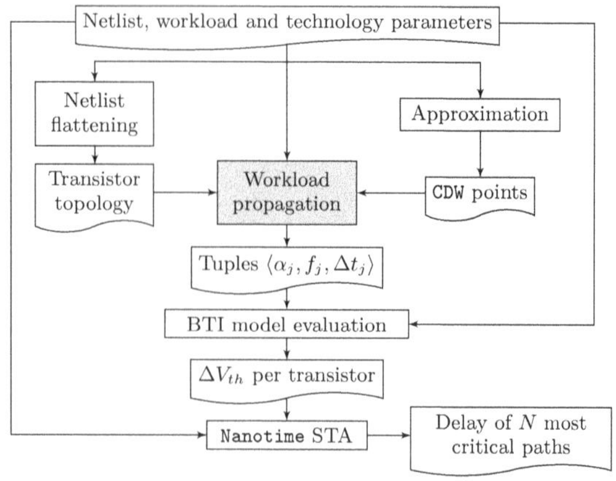

Figure 1: Proposed BTI flow overview.

3.2 Workload propagation

In order to retain the realistic workload dependency across all the nodes of the circuit, the stress activity patters needs to be propagated throughout all the transistors of the digital block in terms of $\langle f, \alpha, \Delta t \rangle$. Furthermore, we need to cope with the space requirements for complex circuits and large waveforms; tracing activity factors for all the internal nodes from RTL simulation would be unmanageable. For this reason, we collect complet waveforms at the primary inputs of the desired circuit abstraction, and flatten the standard cells of the gate-level design to their equivalent transistor topology (based on their SPICE-level descriptions from the reference technology library). We then automatically translate it to a second Verilog circuit description that is topologically equivalent to the SPICE-level one, but that can be still simulated using digital simulation tools. Based on this we then perform switch-level simulation over consecutive CDW points using Cadence NCSIM, and compute the signal activities at each transistor from activity TCF data instead of keeping complete VCD waves. Based on the resulting activity files for each region with duration Δt, we can easily compute the α and f values at each transistor. The resulting CDW representation captures the V_{gs} stress voltage at the transistor-level for all the nodes of the netlist under test, as required by the CET maps model.

3.3 Atomistic CET-based BTI modeling

Once the stress patterns of each transistor are known, we employ atomistic BTI modeling over all the CDW points to accurately evaluate the BTI-induced degradation of each transistor in terms of threshold voltage shift ΔV_{th}. By combining the features of both the CDW and CET-map methodologies for representative workloads on full processor components, we then formulate our BTI evaluation based on the model presented in [14]. For each trap of each transistor, the occupancy probability is evaluated, depending on the applied stress waveform specified by the current CDW point, to compute the contribution to the overall V_{th} shift.

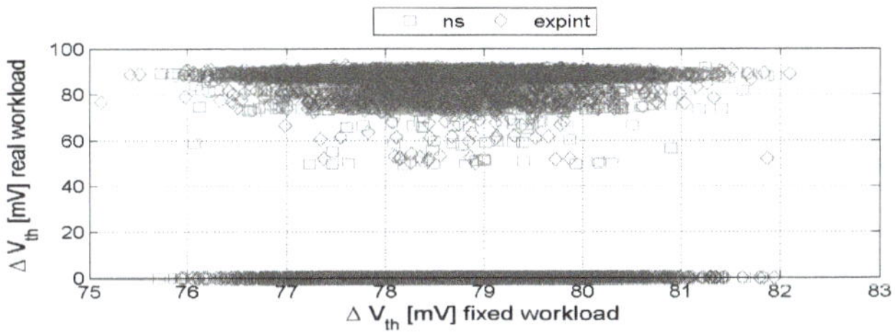

Figure 2: Dispersion plot comparing data samples from constant duty-factor case and simulated cases.

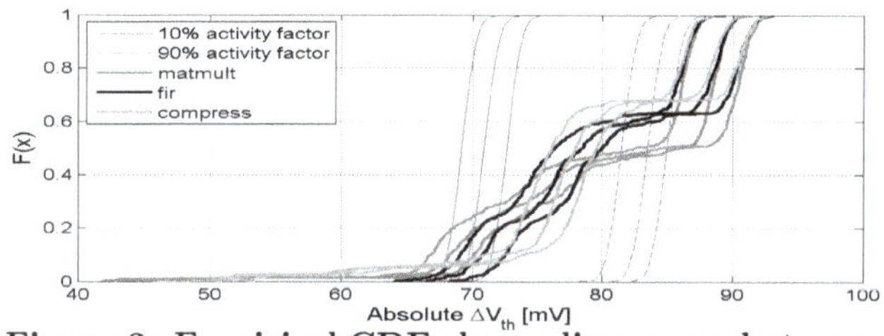

Figure 3: Empirical CDF shows divergence between constant and real workload.

We repeat this process over all the CDW points and derive the workload-dependent ΔV_{th} per transistor. Finally, by employing a transistor-level STA tool, namely Synopsys NanoTime, we computer the BTI-aware delay values, keeping track of its evolution throughout the duration of the reference application.

4. EXPERIMENTAL RESULTS

We substantiate the validity of our flow as a useful aid for early-stage BTI analysis and BTI-aware design techniques, by capturing the workload-dependent delay degradation for selected CPU modules. We provide an analysis of a few reference circuits taken from a representative commercial design. During our evaluation, the workload is generated through RTL simulation using simple, but real-world applications. An extensive experimental campaign has been conducted to capture workload dependency of BTI-induced aging in an accurate way and reasonable turnaround time.

For our experiments, we selected a number of applications from the `WCET` benchmark suite [11], to capture a convenient set of diverse use-cases. We then took digital subcircuits from the OpenSPARC T1 processor, whose design and verification environment is freely available [13]. This processor is representative of a complex and commercial full-chip design. As reference technology, we used the 40 nm standard-cell library from TSMC. We then focused our analysis on selected modules from the integer and floating-point (IEEE-754 2008 double-precision standard compliant) data-path, ranging from 6k equivalent gates (or 22k transistors) of the integer ALU to 36k equivalent gates (or 143k transistors) of the floating-point multiplier.

In the following subsections, the integer add/sub component will be used as main test vehicle to discuss on results, and few additional results will be shown for other components as well. The electrical and physical parameters employed in the transistor-level analysis are then taken directly from the modelcard of bulk CMOS nodes of TSMC technology. Calibration has been performed against available silicon measurements [16].

4.1 Constant versus real activity factors

In this subsection we demonstrate that an invalid assumption about the stress load profile to PMOS and NMOS transistors can lead to an erroneous degradation estimation. We compare our results that retain workload-dependent attribute against the results with the state-of-the-art proposal in [6], in which the authors assumed a constant activity factor and frequency across all transistors. We then adapted our flow to resemble this experimental setup, assuming a 50% duty-factor and 1 GHz frequency at each transistor and one single CDW point (that is placed exactly at the end of the workload). In this way, each transistor will be subject to the same exact stress, irrespective of the application generating the workload.

We perform variability analysis for an overall stress duration of three years, as in [6]. To perform this analysis we started from the CDW points computed by the flow for a number of applications, and we then scaled the duration of each CDW interval in such a way that the sum of all of them equals the desired wall-clock time. In each case, we maintained the original ratio among each CDW intervals.

For the integer add/sub circuit, we compare the ΔV_{th} at each transistor, computed based on the constant duty-factor case and the simulated one in Figure 2. It shows the dispersion plot of the ΔV_{th} values in two different applications: each point represents the threshold voltage shift at the end of the workload of each single transistor. The scatter plots highlights the mismatch of homonym transistors in the two scenarios. Two clouds are evident. First of all, the top-most cloud expresses a mismatch due to the assumed workload even for non-constant stresses. The bottom cloud, on the other hand, highlights the presence of non-stressed transistors in the circuit. These transistors will be however computed as degrading assuming a constant factor as in [6], thus providing a fundamental estimation error. Samples here are reported just for two different applications (**`ns`** and **`expint`**) for space reasons, but similar results have been obtained for the other applications as well.

The importance of the mismatch can also be evaluated by comparing the empyrical Cumulative Distribution Function (CDF) of the real stress case with constant stress case (i.e., 10% and 90%) and a wider time range (i.e., 1, 3 and 5 years of operation), for three different applications **`matmult`**, **`fir`** and **`compress`**. The empirical cumulative distribution function F(x) of the collected samples ΔV_{th} are shown in Figure 3. Lines are grouped according to the scenario, either of a constant workload or of a simulated one. The analyzed wall-clock time values are denoted by the curves shifting toward the right. The results show that the low (10%) and the high (90%) constant duty-factor (unchanged frequency) assumptions enclose the real aging evolution up to a certain degree. Beyond a certain interval, the estimation is basically erroneous. Also, the shape of the functions differs from the real case. It is worth observing that a higher stress time moves the curves toward the right-end side of the axis. For instance, assuming a ΔV_{th} degradation equal to 80 mV, the 10% assumption would over-constrain the design, since the cumulative probability at this point has already reached 1; for the 90% case, on the other hand, the design would be under-constrained, even for 12 months reference time. It is therefore evident that, we cannot avoid the workload-dependency analysis if we are to deliver cost-effective design solutions.

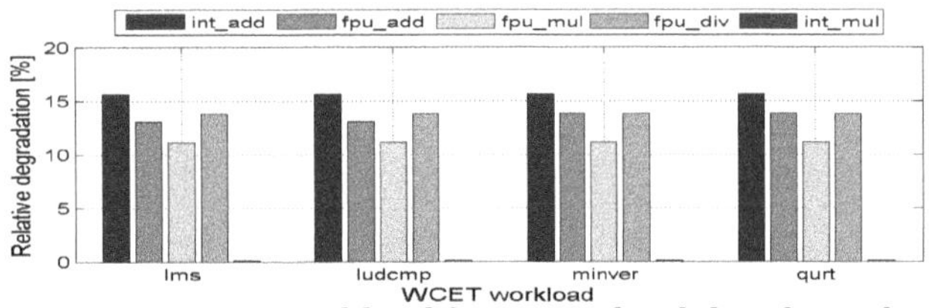

Figure 4: How workload impacts the delay degradation on different CPU modules.

4.2 Workload impact on path degradation

In a real use-case, a given application is using, at any time, only a portion of the processor's functionality. For instance, floating-point applications are expected to stress the FPU more than integer applications. To demonstrate such property, we consider a number of circuit/application pairs for the floating-point intensive cases. Figure 4 reports the delay relative degradation of the most critical path computed at the end of the workload, with respect to the time-0 value. Notice that the most critical path might have changed by the end of the workload. Indeed, aging-induced degradation determines also the reordering of paths, i.e. non-critical paths becoming critical paths and/or viceversa. Results have shown that this process continues over time (according to the workload), and in any case reordering is relevant already at the very beginning of the aging process.

The results demonstrate that the same workload accounts for a different path degradation on different circuits. For instance, the maximum difference is experienced when comparing the floating-point multiplier against the integer add/sub where the difference can be as high as 4%. In any case, the observed degradation is shown after 3 years of operation. Notice that even for floating-point applications such as `lms`, the integer portion of the circuitry is still degrading. This is due to the fact that integer operations are always in place in these benchmarks. On the contrary, these applications do not make use of the parallel hardware multiplier, and as such the degradation of the `int_mul` circuit is consistently 0.

5. CONCLUSIONS

In this paper, we propose a comprehensive flow that exploits the accuracy of CET maps with the efficiency of the CDW signal representation. Prior art on atomistic BTI modeling exhibits reduced scalability or accuracy issues, by either limiting the models to the circuit level or by assuming constant stress patterns at the system level. To the best of our knowledge, this is the *first* work that retains both the atomistic property and true workload-dependent aging attribute. That way, we enable variability analysis for several CPU subsystems, showing the importance of workload in BTI-induced aging analysis. First, we prove that worst-case margin-based proposals assuming constant workload (i.e., activity factor and frequency of the stress signal independent of the application) lead to over- or under-constrained designs. Moreover, we assess the impact of true workload dependency on different circuits, since the same applications result in different overall degradation among different CPU modules. Thus, we fully demonstrate the usability of our tool for efficiently capturing the workload-dependent BTI-induced degradation of CPU components under real applications.

Acknowledgments

The work presented herein is partially supported by project FP7-612069-HARPA of the European Commission.

6. REFERENCES

[1] B. Kaczer et al. Origin of NBTI variability in deeply scaled pFETs. In *IEEE IRPS*, pages 26–32, May 2010.

[2] B. Kaczer et al. Atomistic approach to variability of bias-temperature instability in circuit simulations. In *IEEE IRPS*, pages XT.3.1–XT.3.5, April 2011.

[3] D. Rodopoulos et al. Time and workload dependent device variability in circuit simulations. In *IEEE ICICDT*, pages 1–4, May 2011.

[4] D. Rodopoulos et al. Atomistic pseudo-transient BTI simulation with inherent workload memory. *IEEE TDMR*, 14(2):704–714, June 2014.

[5] D. Rodopoulos et al. Understanding timing impact of BTI/RTN with massively threaded atomistic transient simulations. In *IEEE ICICDT*, pages 1–4, May 2014.

[6] D. Stamoulis et al. Efficient reliability analysis of processor datapath using atomistic bti variability models. In *25th ACM GLSVLSI*, May 2015.

[7] J. Fang and S. Sapatnekar. Understanding the impact of transistor-level BTI variability. In *IEEE IRPS*, pages CR.2.1–CR.2.6, Apr. 2012.

[8] H. Kukner et al. Comparison of reaction-diffusion and atomistic trap-based BTI models for logic gates. *IEEE TDMR*, 14(1):182–193, Mar. 2014.

[9] H. Kukner et al. Degradation analysis of datapath logic subblocks under NBTI aging in FinFET technology. In *15th ISQED*, pages 473–479, Mar. 2014.

[10] H. Reisinger et al. The statistical analysis of individual defects constituting nbti and its implications for modeling dc- and ac-stress. In *IEEE IRPS*, pages 7–15, May 2010.

[11] J. Gustafsson et al. The mälardalen WCET benchmarks: Past, present and future. In *WCET 2010, 2010, Brussels, Belgium*, pages 136–146, 2010.

[12] H. Kufluoglu and M. Alam. A generalized reaction–diffusion model with explicit h–h_2 dynamics for negative-bias temperature-instability (nbti) degradation. *IEEE TED*, 54(5):1101–1107, May 2007.

[13] OpenSPARC, Oracle. http://www.oracle.com.

[14] P. Weckx P. et al. Defect-based methodology for workload-dependent circuit lifetime projections - Application to SRAM. In *IEEE IRPS*, pages 3A.4.1–3A.4.7, Apr. 2013.

[15] P. Weckx et al. Non-monte-carlo methodology for high-sigma simulations of circuits under workload-dependent BTI degradation – application to 6t SRAM. In *IEEE IRPS*, pages 5D.2.1–5D.2.6, 2014.

[16] Y. Reis, Ricardo; Cao and G. Wirth, editors. *Circuit Design for Reliability*. Springer, 2015.

[17] T. Grasser et al. Analytic modeling of the bias temperature instability using capture/emission time maps. In *IEEE IEDM*, pages 27.4.1–27.4.4, Dec 2011.

[18] T. Grasser et al. The paradigm shift in understanding the bias temperature instability: From reaction–diffusion to switching oxide traps. *IEEE TED*, 58(11):3652–3666, Nov. 2011.

Performance Constraint-Aware Task Mapping to Optimize Lifetime Reliability of Manycore Systems

Vijeta Rathore
School of Computer Engineering
Nanyang Technological University
Singapore
vijeta001@e.ntu.edu.sg

Vivek Chaturvedi
School of Computer Engineering
Nanyang Technological University
Singapore
vchaturvedi@ntu.edu.sg

Thambipillai Srikanthan
School of Computer Engineering
Nanyang Technological University
Singapore
astsrikan@ntu.edu.sg

ABSTRACT

Negative bias temperature instability (NBTI) has emerged as a critical challenge to lifetime reliability of computing systems. Traditionally, temperature-aware methodologies are used to mitigate the impact of NBTI on aging and degradation of computing systems. However, in the presence of process variation, which is the norm in manycore processors, temperature-aware techniques are inefficient in improving lifetime reliability and can result in poor performance. In this paper, we propose a novel performance constraint-aware task mapping technique to improve lifetime reliability by mitigating NBTI considering on-chip process variation. Our approach consists of two phases, namely design-time and run-time. During design time, we generate Pareto-optimal mappings. Following which, our run-time technique judiciously intervenes to perform workload migration to save the weakest processing core. We compare our approach with performance-greedy and thermal-aware task mapping techniques. The experiment results demonstrate that our approach outperforms other two techniques and improves lifetime reliability of a manycore system as much as 54% without violating the throughput constraint.

Keywords

Lifetime reliability; negative bias temperature instability (NBTI); manycore systems; task mapping

1. INTRODUCTION

Continuous technology scaling has enabled the design of manycore processors to provide higher computing performance with lower energy consumption. However, large integration of processing cores results in higher power density and soaring chip temperature. This not only increases the cooling and packaging costs but also makes the system highly vulnerable to failure mechanisms, such as negative bias temperature instability (NBTI).

NBTI has attracted considerable attention of the research community over the past decade [10, 9, 7]. As NBTI has a strong association with temperature, most of the previous works rely upon temperature-aware techniques to mitigate the impact of NBTI on system performance degradation and operational lifetime [11, 4]. Several other works employ guardbanding to tolerate degradation caused by NBTI. However, both temperature conscious approaches and gaurdbanding approaches are insufficient in improving the system reliability without causing negative impact on system performance, especially in the presence of process variation (PV).

Runtime approaches such as in [7, 9] respond to variations in core aging during actual execution. Most of the runtime approaches do not leverage on any offline/design-time analysis. Information obtained from offline analysis can make the runtime approaches light-weight.

In this work, we propose design-time/runtime hybrid approach to optimize lifetime reliability of the manycore system in the presence of PV while satisfying given performance constraint. The design-time phase employs Threshold Accepting Simulated Annealing (TASA) [5] algorithm to find a Pareto-optimal mapping with maximum mean time to failure (MTTF). During runtime our approach proactively migrates tasks to recover aging hotspots to healthy cores that can accommodate them while meeting the performance constraint. As compared to performance-greedy and thermal-aware task mapping techniques, our approach outperforms both and improves system lifetime reliability by as much as 54%.

The remainder of this paper is organized as follows. Section 2 discusses the preliminaries and related work. Section 3 gives the problem definition. Section 4 describes the solution approach. Section 5 presents the experiment details and results. Section 6 concludes and discusses future work.

2. PRELIMINARIES AND RELATED WORK

NBTI is a wearout phenomenon affecting PMOS transistors when the gate is negatively biased i.e. input is 0. It occurs due to the accumulation of positive charge at the oxide-substrate interface and in the oxide layer, which manifests as an increase in the threshold voltage. The degradation leads to increase of circuit delay, deteriorates performance and eventually leads to failure. NBTI also shows recovery on

GLSVLSI '16, May 18-20, 2016, Boston, MA, USA
© 2016 ACM. ISBN 978-1-4503-4274-2/16/05...$15.00
DOI: http://dx.doi.org/10.1145/2902961.2902996

Table 1: Long-term threshold voltage degradation due to NBTI

$\lvert\Delta Vth\rvert$
$\lvert\Delta Vth\rvert = \left[\frac{\sqrt{K_v{}^2 \alpha T_{clk}}}{1-\beta_t^{1/2n}}\right]^{2n}$
$\beta_t = 1 - \frac{2\xi_1 t_e + \sqrt{\xi_2 C(1-\alpha)T_{clk}}}{2t_{ox}+\sqrt{Ct}}$ $K_v = \left(\frac{q t_{ox}}{\epsilon_{ox}}\right)^3 K^2 C_{ox}(V_{gs} - V_{th})\sqrt{C}\exp\left(\frac{2Eox}{E_0}\right)$

removal of stress which partially lowers the increased threshold voltage [6].

We use reaction-diffusion (R-D) based device level NBTI model presented in [3] to estimate threshold voltage degradation under multiple cycles of stress and recovery, as given in Table 1. The values of the constants are defined in [3] and the technology related parameters are taken from Predictive Technology Model (PTM) [1]. We consider a transistor to fail when its threshold voltage increases to 0.34 V which is used as a failure definition in [2]. We find the mean time to failure (MTTF) of a core by solving the relation given in Table 1 for time for an increase in the *representative* threshold voltage[1] of the core to 0.34 V. We define MTTF of a manycore system as minimum of MTTF of all cores.

Guardbanding is traditionally used to mitigate NBTI, however, it is pessimistic as it considers worst-case operating conditions to calculate design margins leading to higher cost and performance loss towards beginning of life. Work presented in [9] is closely related to ours. These works use fractional recovery NBTI model to assign *capacity rate (CR)* to cores indicating how much more workload a core can take without getting stressed. They characterize applications in terms of their workload capacity, which is the ratio of execution times of worst-case execution path tasks and total execution time. As execution requests arrive, they map tasks of an application to a set of dynamically chosen cores, called *zone*, such that communication energy is minimized and performance requirement is matched. This approach attributes aging to execution time of the task. However, there are other factors as well that affect aging caused by a running task. We account for stress in terms of the worst-case duty cycles in the core owing to different task, which can be obtained through offline analysis.

3. PROBLEM DEFINITION

Task mapping agnostic of the degree of aging caused by a task can lead to excessive degradation of an already weak core limiting the lifetime reliability of the manycore system. We intend to find optimal task to core mappings to improve the lifetime reliability by mitigating NBTI while meeting the performance constraint.

We consider manycore systems with N cores, $C = \{c_0, c_1, c_2, \ldots, c_{N-1}\}$. A core c_i is represented as a tuple of maximum operation frequency, threshold voltage and oxide thickness *i.e.* $\{f_i, t_{oxi}, V_{thi}\}$. We consider chip to be affected by PV, thus, cores have different maximum frequency of operation, threshold voltage and oxide thickness. We also consider uniform supply voltage throughout the chip.

[1]We define representative threshold as the threshold voltage of the weakest transistor of the core

Algorithm 1: Design-time mapping exploration

```
Input: C, T, Th, H
Output: mapping m
Parameter : NUM_ROUNDS, NUM_STEPS, H
Arrange T in decreasing order of execution time e;
Arrange C in decreasing order of frequency f;
Generate a random initial mapping m that satisfies Th;
flagFirst ← 1;
for r ← 1 to NUM_ROUNDS do
    for i ← 1 to NUM_STEPS do
        Get m' from m such that m' meets Th;
        if For thousand tries it cannot find a mapping that meets Th then
            ThUnaware ← 1;
        end if
        △MTTF = MTTF_m' − MTTF_m;
        if △MTTF > −η_r & !ThUnaware & Th'_m < Th then
            Accept m' i.e. m = m';
            if flagFirst then
                Best_mapping = m;
                MTTF_Best_mapping = MTTF_m;
                flagFirst ← 0;
                break;
            else
                if (MTTF_m' > MTTF_Best_mapping) & ThUnaware & Th'_m < Th then
                    MTTF_Best_mapping = MTTF_m';
                end if
            end if
        end if
        if a multiple of thousand mappings are explored then
            if any strong or normal core is free while any weak core is assigned a task then
                continue exploration;
            else
                break;
            end if
        end if
    end for
end for
```

We consider workload consisting of periodic tasks. Specifically, the workload consists set of M tasks represented as $T = \{\tau_0, \tau_1, \ldots \tau_{M-1}\}$. A task τ_i is, in turn, represented as tuple $\{p_i, e_i, \alpha_i, \rho_i\}$. Here, p_i is the period, e_i is the execution time at normal core frequency, α_i is the average switching activity, and ρ_i is the worst-case duty cycle, *i.e.*, probability of the gate input to be 0 for the most stressed critical path. These parameters can be obtained through offline profiling. We define throughput constraint as time in which exactly one execution of each application should complete. We assume the cores to support multi-tasking i.e. more than one task can be executed on a core, in a sequence.

4. SOLUTION APPROACH

The solution approach consists of two phases, namely design-time and runtime. In design-time phase, we find mapping to achieve maximal MTTF of many-core system for a periodic workload while satisfying a throughput constraint. It uses an approximate optimization algorithm namely *Threshold Accepting (TA) simulated annealing* [5], in a modified form, as shown in Algorithm 1, to find Pareto-optimal solutions. We chose TA simulated annealing over Simulated Annealing (SA) approach since it is computationally less intensive and yet gives solutions of similar quality to SA.

Inputs to algorithm are set of cores C, set of tasks T, throughput constraint Th, and margins H. Output is a

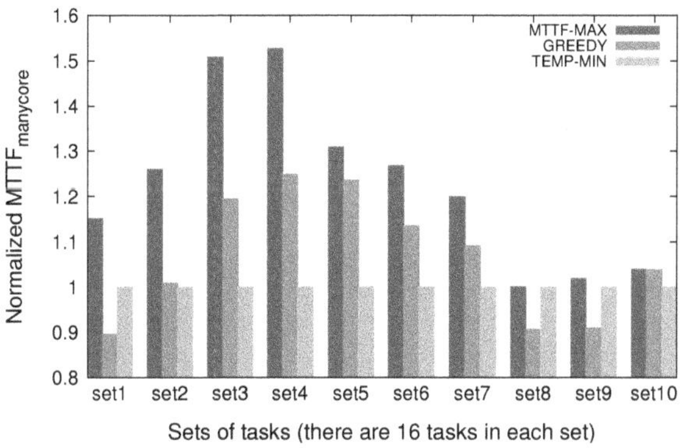

(a) Normalized MTTF for 10 sets

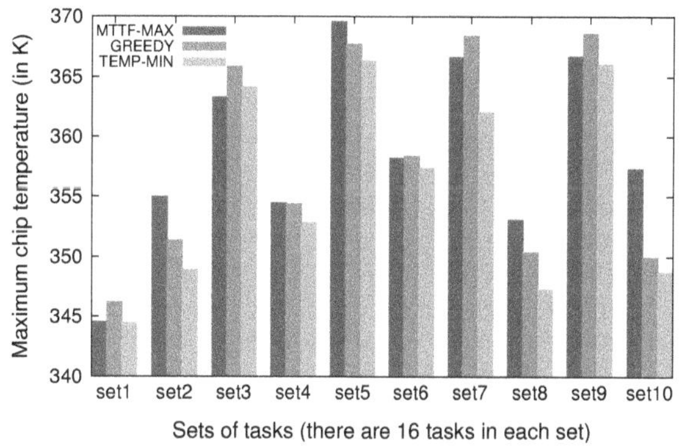

(b) Maximum chip temperature for 10 sets

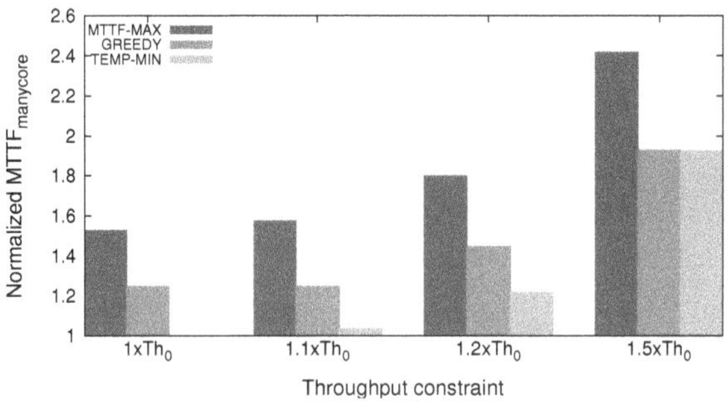

(c) Normalized MTTF for varying Th

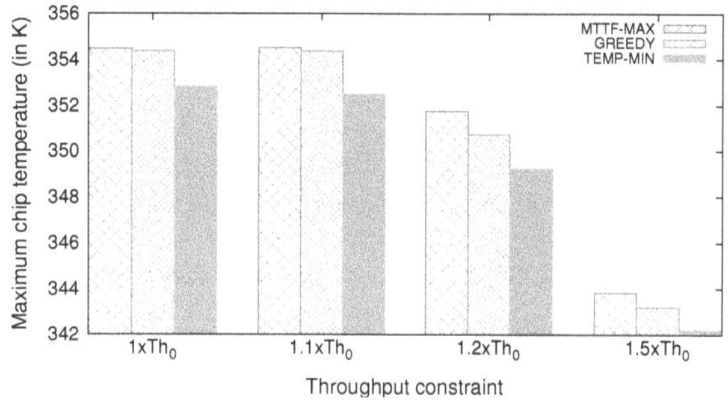

(d) Maximum chip temperature for varying Th

Figure 1: Design-time results

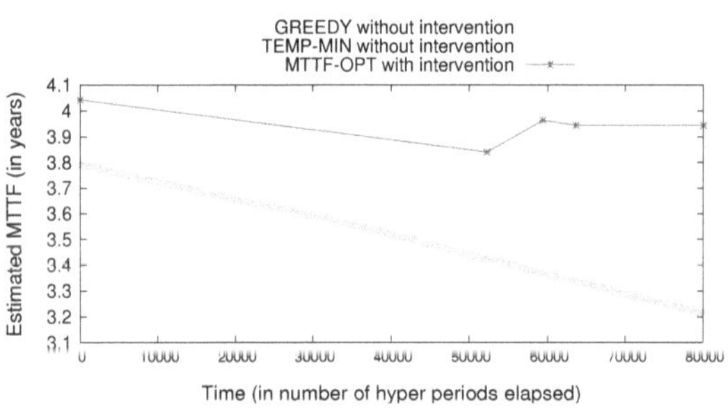

(a) RT-I – MTTF

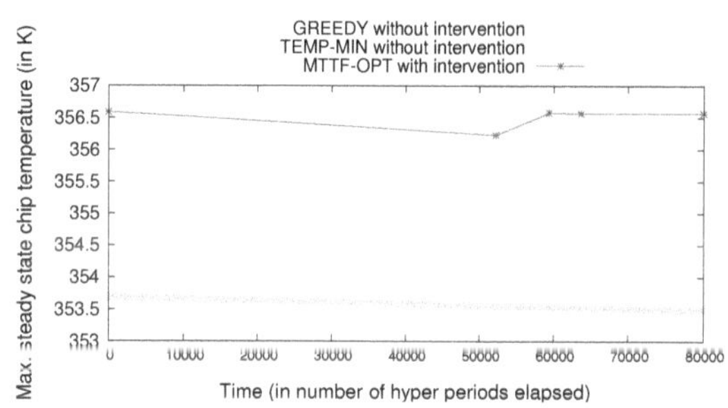

(b) RT-I – Maximum chip temperature

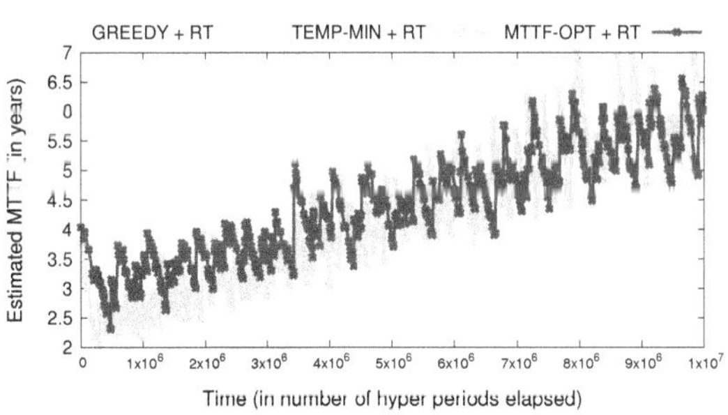

(c) RT-II – MTTF

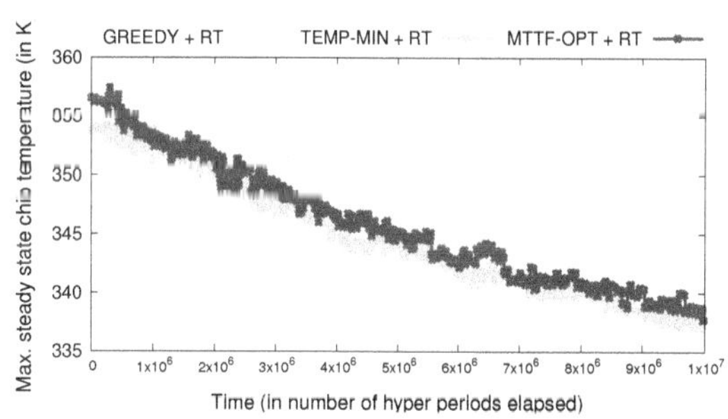

(d) RT-II – Maximum chip temperature

Figure 2: Runtime results

near-optimal task-to-core mapping that maximizes MTTF while meeting throughput constraint.

During runtime phase, we execute tasks, periodically sense threshold voltage degradation and intervene by migrating tasks, if needed. It starts by executing tasks as per mapping obtained from design-time phase and monitors core aging due to NBTI. The monitoring can be done using in-situ sensors as described in [8]. When a core becomes weak, as per a predefined *weakness-criterion*, the approach migrates tasks to healthier cores and recovers weak cores.

The runtime intervention algorithm checks if there are any weak cores as per the weakness-criterion. If there are any weak cores, it checks if any spare cores are available. If there are spare cores (say there are k spare cores), it migrates workload from k weakest cores to spare cores such that stronger cores get heavier workload and workload is distributed to all spare cores. We consider task's execution time for normal frequency core to define its heaviness. Next, if there are still any weak cores that are not freed yet, it either migrates to or swaps with the strong cores while meeting performance constraint. It frees weak cores, allows them to relax until recovery, and once fit, again uses them. The time complexity of runtime phase is $O(n.w)$, here n is total number of cores and w is number of weak cores.

5. EXPERIMENTS AND RESULTS

We compared our approach with two design-time mapping approaches, namely performance greedy (*GREEDY*) and thermal minimization (*TEMP-MIN*). The performance greedy approach generates mapping by assigning heavier tasks to faster cores. The thermal minimization approach aims at minimizing the maximum chip temperature.

All experiments were done for 16 core manycore system with PV. The representative threshold voltage for higher, normal and lower frequency cores were 0.235 V, 0.245 V and 0.255 V, respectively.

To evaluate the design-time phase (we call it *MTTF-OPT*) we compared it against GREEDY and TEMP-MIN for 10 sets of workloads $T_1, T_2, \ldots, T_{10}$ each consisting of 16 tasks. Figures 1a and 1b show the results. Figure 1a shows MTTF values normalized against $MTTF_{TEMP-MIN}$ in each case. Importantly, the cores with minimum MTTF and maximum chip temperature are different. The results show that MTTF-OPT improves the MTTF over both TEMP-MIN and GREEDY for all the sets – upto 54% over TEMP-MIN for set4, even though the corresponding maximum chip temperature for MTTF-OPT is higher than that of TEMP-MIN by 2 K. Results for sets $2-7$ and set 10 in Figure 1a indicate that TEMP-MIN performs worse than GREEDY in improving MTTF. This means that only minimizing temperature is not sufficient to improve lifetime reliability, as other factors such as duty cycle also affect it. Figures 1c and 1d indicate improved benefits with relaxed throughput constraint.

We evaluated the entire approach by taking the design-time solutions from MTTF-OPT, GREEDY, and TEMP-MIN for set 4 and performed two runtime experiments namely RT-I and RT-II. In RT-I, for mappings from GREEDY and TEMP-MIN approaches we did not intervene at runtime and intervened only for mapping from MTTF-OPT. Figure 2a shows that RT improved MTTF over the other two. Figure 2b shows maximum chip temperature. In RT-II we used RT with all. Figures 2c and 2d show MTTF and maximum chip temperature, respectively, for 10^7 hyperperiods. Figure 2c indicates that RT is able to maintain MTTF above a level for all the cases. Thus, RT is beneficial even if used independent of initial mapping. Figure 2d shows that RT also achieved reduction in temperature.

6. CONCLUSION

This paper presents a novel task mapping strategy for manycore systems to improve lifetime reliability by mitigating NBTI. The proposed approach consists of two phases, namely design-time and runtime. Design-time uses TA simulated annealing heuristic to find near-optimal mappings and the runtime phase is light-weight and involves adjustments to the mapping to account for aging and relax the stressed cores. The results indicate that the design-time phase achieves improvements upto 54% and runtime phase maintains the MTTF above what is achieved at design-time.

7. REFERENCES

[1] Predictive Technology Model (PTM). http://ptm.asu.edu/. [accessed 14-March-2016].

[2] M. Basoglu, M. Orshansky, and M. Erez. Nbti-aware dvfs: a new approach to saving energy and increasing processor lifetime. In *ISPLED*, pages 253–258. ACM, 2010.

[3] S. Bhardwaj, W. Wang, R. Vattikonda, Y. Cao, and S. Vrudhula. Predictive modeling of the nbti effect for reliable design. In *CICC*, pages 189–192. IEEE, 2006.

[4] A. Das, R. A. Shafik, G. V. Merrett, B. M. Al-Hashimi, A. Kumar, and B. Veeravalli. Reinforcement learning-based inter-and intra-application thermal optimization for lifetime improvement of multicore systems. In *DAC*, pages 1–6. IEEE, 2014.

[5] G. Dueck and T. Scheuer. Threshold accepting: a general purpose optimization algorithm appearing superior to simulated annealing. *JCoPh*, 90(1):161–175, 1990.

[6] M. Ershov, S. Saxena, H. Karbasi, S. Winters, S. Minehane, J. Babcock, R. Lindley, P. Clifton, M. Redford, and A. Shibkov. Dynamic recovery of negative bias temperature instability in p-type metal–oxide–semiconductor field-effect transistors. *Appl. Phys. Lett*, 83(8):1647–1649, 2003.

[7] P. Mercati, A. Bartolini, F. Paterna, T. S. Rosing, and L. Benini. Workload and user experience-aware dynamic reliability management in multicore processors. In *DAC*, page 2. ACM, 2013.

[8] P. Singh, E. Karl, D. Blaauw, and D. Sylvester. Compact degradation sensors for monitoring nbti and oxide degradation. *VLSI*, 20(9):1645–1655, August 2012.

[9] J. Sun, R. Lysecky, K. Shankar, A. Kodi, A. Louri, and J. Roveda. Workload assignment considering nbti degradation in multicore systems. *JETC*, 10(1):4, 2014.

[10] A. Tiwari and J. Torrellas. Facelift: Hiding and slowing down aging in multicores. In *MICRO-41*, pages 129–140. IEEE, 2008.

[11] Y. Wang, H. Luo, K. He, R. Luo, H. Yang, and Y. Xie. Temperature-aware nbti modeling and the impact of input vector control on performance degradation. In *DATE*, pages 1–6. IEEE, 2007.

ASIC Implementation of An All-digital Self-adaptive PVTA Variation-aware Clock Generation System

Jordi Pérez-Puigdemont
Universitat Politècnica de Catalunya
Dept. d'Eng. Electrònica, Barcelona
jordi.perez-puigdemont@upc.edu

Francesc Moll
Universitat Politècnica de Catalunya
Dept. d'Eng. Electrònica, Barcelona
francesc.moll@upc.edu

ABSTRACT

An all-digital self-adaptive clock generation system capable of autonomously adapt the clock frequency to compensate the effects of static spatially heterogeneous (SSHet) PVTA variations is presented. The design uses time-to-digital converters (TDCs) as delay sensors and a variable length ring oscillator (VLRO) as clock generator. The VLRO naturally adapts its frequency to the PVTA variations suffered by its logic gates while the TDCs are used to track these variations across the chip and modify the VLRO length in order to allocate them. The proposed system has been implemented in a silicon chip using a 65nm process. The fabricated chip has been used to test the system adaptive capabilities under SSHet voltage variations. Measurement results show that it effectively adapts the VLRO length, and hence the clock frequency, to the supply voltage variations.

1. INTRODUCTION

As transistor technology scales down the effects of process, voltage, temperature and ageing (PVTA) variations impact substantially on the integrated circuit (IC) performance, reliability and power consumption [1]. The rise in the transistor characteristics uncertainty added to the rising complexity of the ICs leads to an increment of the effort needed to determine the main circuit parameters, such as the maximum operation frequency or supply voltage, that result in the desired IC yield. This effort increment is translated finally as more design cost and time. Until now this problem has been treated by adding extra margins to the IC parameters [3], e. g. lowering the clock frequency or rising the supply voltage, but now this margins may undermine the technology scaling gains [8].

In the recent years, to tackle the variability issue, researchers have proposed to adapt the clock frequency to the PVTA variations suffered by the IC. Some propose to detect timing in the datapath and to then correct them and/or adapt IC performance [2] but this technique implies a high architectural complexity. Other authors propose to

GLSVLSI '16, May 18 - 20, 2016, Boston, MA, USA

ISBN 978-1-4503-4274-2/16/05...$15.00

DOI: http://dx.doi.org/10.1145/2902961.2903006

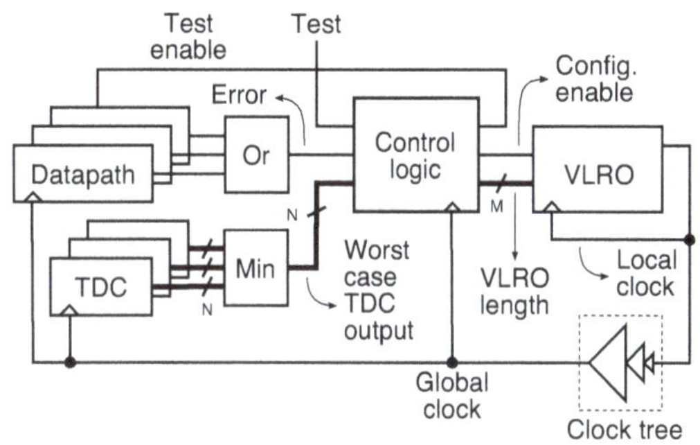

Figure 1: Self-adaptive system scheme.

use PVTA or delay sensors to adapt the clock frequency [5]. In the same line others propose to use sensors to detect fast PVTA variations to stop the clock until the perturbation ends [2] but, if the variation lasts, the system could be stopped for a long time.

In this article we propose a closed loop self-adaptive clock generation system capable of adapting the clock frequency to accommodate the PVTA variations that take place along the die. The proposed system is fully autonomous since it calibrates itself during the startup phase with no need of any external action. The system is based on a time-to-digital converter (TDC) as delay sensor and a variable length ring oscillator (VLRO) as clock source. The proposed system has been implemented and tested using a 65nm UMC process using exclusively digital standard cells proving the system fully portable to different technologies and fabrication processes.

The article is organised as follows: in section 2 we show in a detailed way the proposed design for the self-adaptive system. In section 3, we describe the system implementation on 65nm UMC process. In section 4 we present the measurements of the self-adaptive system and the analysis of its responses to SSHet voltage variations. Finally conclusions are drawn in section 5.

2. SYSTEM DESCRIPTION

An adaptive system can be described as three step process: sensing a physical magnitude, comparing the sensor output with a reference and performing the actions needed to reduce the difference between the measure and the reference.

The proposed system is based on three different blocks that perform the adaptive process sequentially: a time-to-digital converter (TDC) combined with a datapath with timing error detection capabilities, a control block and a vari-

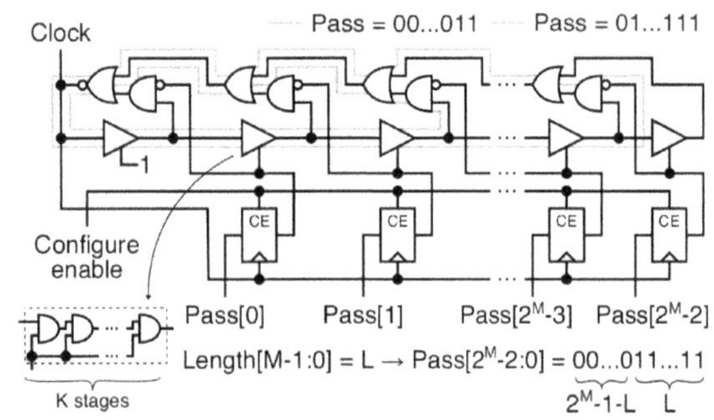

Figure 2: Variable length ring oscillator (VLRO).

able length ring oscillator (VLRO). First the TDCs sense the propagation length (τ), it is how deep a transition can travel through the logic path during one clock cycle, at different parts of the die. This logic depth is directly related with the clock period and inversely related with the logic gates propagation delay. After that the control block compares the worst of the TDC readings ($\tau_{\min}$) coming from different locations with the setpoint or objective value (τ_{obj}) and decides the new VLRO length (λ) that should minimize the adaptation error ($\varepsilon = \tau_{\text{obj}} - \tau_{\min}$). Finally the VLRO length is updated and consequently the clock period changes. The generated clock signal is then routed through the global clock tree and therefore the control loop is closed. The setpoint value is determined during the calibration phase that takes place at the system start-up. Fig. 1 shows the self-adaptive clock generation system.

The different adaptive system components will be discussed in detail in the next subsections.

2.1 VLRO

A variable length ring oscillator (VLRO) is a ring oscillator (RO) which its effective length (λ) can be varied, therefore the frequency of the generated oscillation signal can be changed. The VLRO scheme is depicted in Fig. 2 where two different effective length configurations are highlighted.

A VLRO acting as a clock generator has been chosen because it naturally adapts its oscillating frequency to the PVTA variations suffered by its logic gates. The VLRO used in the adaptive system is a fully-digital glitch-free VLRO similar to the one presented by us in [7].

2.2 TDC

The TDC used in the adaptive system is a circuit that outputs the number of stages (τ) in a delay line traversed by a positive transition within the positive part of the clock signal [4]. It is similar to the one we presented in [6]. The TDC sensor schematic is depicted in Fig. 3.

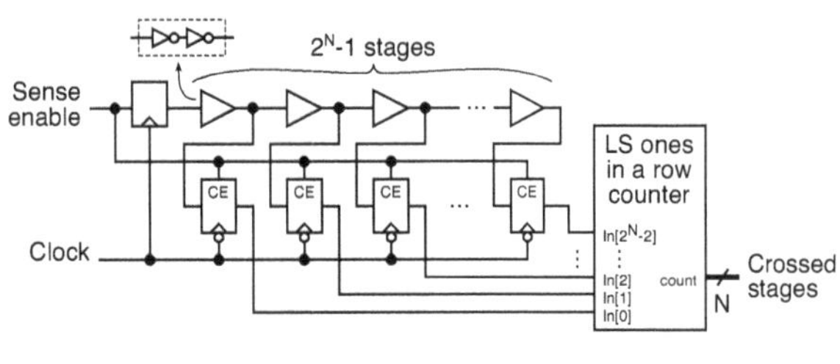

Figure 3: Time to digital converter (TDC).

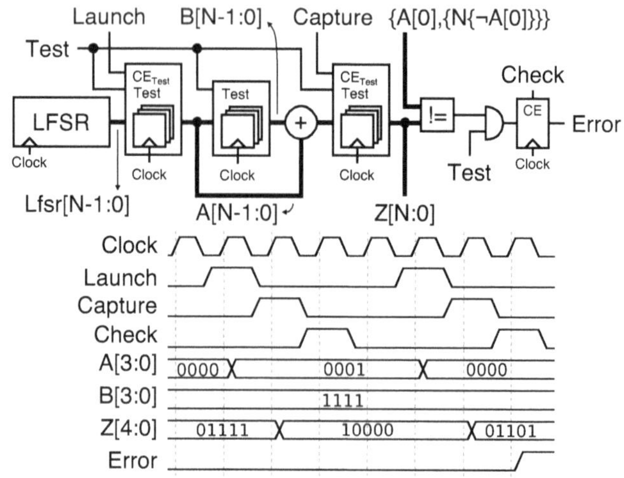

Figure 4: Datapath and test operation ($N = 4$).

The TDC consists in $2^N - 1$ stages, each one consisting of two inverters and a register that captures the state of the delay stage output at the clock falling edge. Then the register values are fed to a logic block that counts the number of positive bits in a row starting from the LSB and encodes it as a binary number of N bits.

Every TDC has a finite state machine (FSM) that is used to control its operation: injecting a pulse into the delay line, enabling the registers in the same clock cycle and waiting a given number of cycles until the process start again.

As we stated before, the TDC output will be proportional to the clock signal period and inversely proportional to the logic delay, as we presented in [6].

2.3 Datapath

The datapath used to test the self-adaptive system implementation is a ripple carry adder (RCA) where its two inputs are the two consecutive states of a linear feedback shift register (LFSR). Fig. 4 shows the datapath scheme.

In order to calibrate the system, *i.e.* determine the setpoint value τ_{obj}, the datapath has to able to detect timing errors. To do so a three clock cycle test procedure, which only excites the RCA critical path, has been implemented (Fig. 4) although any other error detection mechanism would work correctly. The synchronization signals used during the calibration phase are taken from the FSM of the TDC paired with datapath.

2.4 Control logic

The control block of the system is in charge of two different duties: a) calibrate the self-adaptive system at the start-up and b) estimate the VLRO length, from the TDC outputs, that minimizes the adaptation error ($\varepsilon = \tau_{\text{obj}} - \tau_{\min}$).

The objective of the calibration phase is to obtain the setpoint value. To do so, every time the reset signal is deactivated, the control logic puts the system into test mode by setting the test signal to one and the length of the VLRO to its maximum value. After that the length of the VLRO is progressively reduced in one unit every predefined number of cycles until an error is detected at any of the datapaths.

The setpoint value is determined as the minimum obtained TDC output value plus one ($\tau_{\text{obj}} = \tau_{\min} + 1$) when the error is detected. Now with τ_{obj} determined the TDCs can operate as approximate copies of the datapaths: if the output of some TDC is less than τ_{obj} is probable that a timing error will occur. After this, the control logic takes the system out of test mode and puts it into adaptive mode.

In the adaptive mode the control logic has the duty to determine the VLRO length λ that minimizes the adaptive error ε. To assure the stability and the convergence of the adaptive loop the λ value is determined by incrementing it by a function of its last value, the TDCs worst output ($\tau_{\min}$) and the setpoint value (τ_{obj}):

$$\lambda_{i+1} = \lambda_i + f(\lambda_i, \tau_{\min}, \tau_{\text{obj}}) \quad (1)$$

The synchronization of the control logic is based on an exact copy of the FSM used in the TDC-datapath pair. The LSB of the FSM output is used to trigger the changes of the control logic finite state machine and to enable the loading of the VLRO and control logic registers.

3. CHIP OVERVIEW

As we stated in Sec. 1 the presented self-adaptive clock generation system has been implemented and tested using a 65nm UMC process. We have used high, standard and low Vt standard cells in order to reduce the power consumption without reducing the performance.

In order to have flexibility testing homogeneous and heterogeneous PVTA variations we decided to place four RCA, each one paired with a TDC sensor, in four different power domains (PD_0 to PD_3) each one with independent VDD connections. The VLRO and the control logic, as well as the auxiliary output logic, are place in an other power domain (PD_{VLRO}) with its independent VDD source.

We decided to not place any decoupling capacitance on the internal supply voltage lines on the PCB or on the die. The reason for this decision is that the chip will be used in the future to test the ability of the system to adapt to fast dynamic voltage variations. Therefore the voltage on the different core VDD lines will be less stable than one would expect due to the switching noise.

4. MEASUREMENTS

The proposed system capacity to adapt the clock period value is tested under SSHet voltage variations under different calibration supply voltages values. We present and study the system calibration phase in Sec. 4.1 while system response to SSHet voltage variations is analyzed in Sec. 4.2.

4.1 System calibration

The system calibration is measured under the nominal voltage conditions, *i.e.* 1.2V, for all the power domains. The clock evolution during the calibration is depicted in Fig. 5. It shows the reduction of the clock period, progressively decrementing the VLRO length by one unit, until the error signal goes to one. At this moment the setpoint is set and the adaptive operation starts. Ideally after the error signal is asserted the clock period should be stabilized at approximately the last clock period value before the error signal became true. This is not the case because, once the system starts its normal operation, the number of toggling registers and its changing rate rise leading to an increment

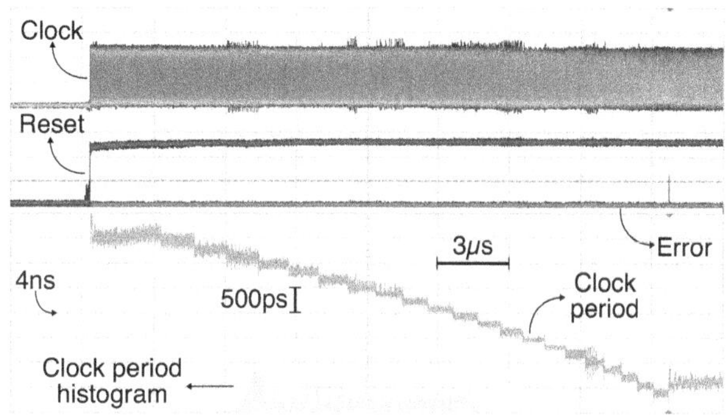

Figure 5: Oscilloscope capture of the self-adaptive system calibration phase.

in the dI/dt switching noise as well as a slight decrement of the supply voltage due to IR-drop. Therefore the clock period uncertainty and mean value are higher than expected, showing that the clock system effectively adapts to on-chip voltage conditions.

We also measured the clock period after calibration when the PD_0 supply voltage (VDD_0) is varied in a given number of steps from 0.9V to 1.3V while the VDD voltage for the other power domains is kept at nominal voltage (1.2V). Once the PD_0 supply voltage is set ($VDD_0 = V_{\text{cal}}$) the system is put to calibration mode. After that the clock period is measured obtaining its mean value for the VDD_0 value under which the calibration is performed ($\mu_{T_{\text{cal}}}(V_{\text{cal}})$). We can consider that $\mu_{T_{\text{cal}}}$ is the smallest period that the proposed system can produce without generating timing errors under these voltage conditions. $\mu_{T_{\text{cal}}}$ is represented in the four plots of Fig. 6 as red dots, its value increases as VDD_0 voltage is reduced.

4.2 Response to SSHet voltage variations

During runtime the clock is adjusted based on the setpoint obtained in the calibration phase. In this subsection we evaluate the influence of the voltage at calibration on the quality of clock adaptation to static spatially heterogeneous voltage (SSHet) variations. To do so after calibrating the system under $VDD_0 = V_{\text{cal}}$, as we explained in Sec. 4.1, the VDD_0 voltage is varied from 0.9V to 1.3V in a given number of steps. After each step of VDD_0 variation the clock period

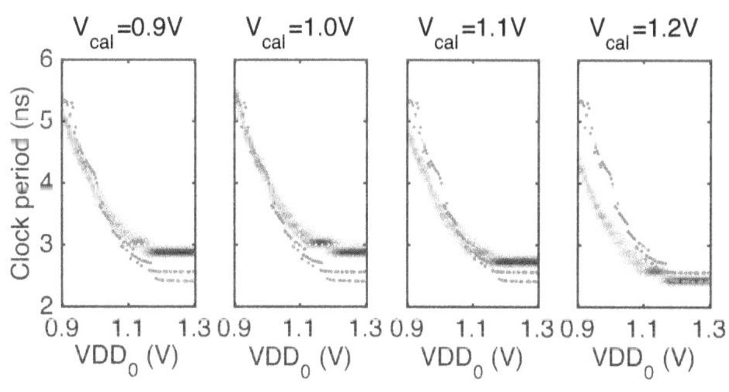

Figure 6: Clock period PDF_T as function of VDD_0 for four calibration voltage values. Also $\mu_{T_{\text{cal}}}$ is shown on each plot (·).

is analyzed obtaining its mean value $\mu_T(V_{cal}, VDD_0)$ and probability distribution $PDF_T(V_{cal}, VDD_0)$.

Fig. 6 depicts the $PDF_T(V_{cal}, VDD_0)$ under the whole studied VDD_0 range for four different calibration voltages along with the mean period value after calibration $\mu_{T_{\rm cal}}$ superposed in each plot. Fig. 6 shows that for low calibration voltages, the clock adaptation at runtime results in periods longer than the minimum (shown as red dots), while the opposite happens for high calibration voltages. In the former case timing errors are consequently likely to occur. Mean miss-adaptation (MMA) can be calculated for a given calibration voltage (V_{cal}) as:

$$MMA(V_{\rm cal}, VDD_0) = \mu_{T_{\rm cal}}(V_{\rm cal}) - \mu_T(V_{\rm cal}, VDD_0) \quad (2)$$

MMA for four different calibration voltages is depicted in Fig. 7 left graph along with the MMA for a fixed clock with a period value of 2.43 ns corresponding to $\mu_{T_{\rm cal}}(1.2{\rm V})$. MMA results for the proposed system are near zero for VDD_0 close to the calibration voltage and are always smaller or equal to the fixed clock value for all the measured scenarios.

It is also interesting to study the minimum clock period margin,Δ T, needed to counteract the MMA. It can be calculated for a given Calibration voltage ($V_{\rm cal}$) as:

$$\Delta T(V_{cal}) = \max_{VDD_0} MMA(V_{\rm cal}, VDD_0) \quad (3)$$

ΔT for the adaptive and the fixed clock are shown in Fig. 7 right graph. The adaptive system needs a smaller clock period marginΔ T than the fixed clock in order to assure a timing error free operation.

5. CONCLUSIONS

In this article we demonstrated an all-digital self-adaptive clock generation system that autonomously adapts the clock frequency to allocate the delay variations on the datapaths along the die induced by a static spatially heterogeneous PVTA variation. The self-adaptive systems is built using only digital blocks. The adaptive system all-digital nature makes it easily portable between different technologies. The test chip, implemented using UMC 65nm technology, measurements for different calibration and supply voltages leads us to state that the proposed system reduces the MMA compared with a fixed clock although it still could lead the datapaths to timing errors. To prevent this the system should be calibrated at the expected minimum supply voltage but then the system will operate at a performance lower than the possible maximum. Or, if the voltage can not be changed at will during the calibration phase, the clock period should be increased by a fixed amount equal to the correspondingΔ T value.Δ T margin is much smaller for the proposed adaptive system compared to the needed with the fixed clock leading to a sensible gain in the clock frequency under the same supply voltage variability scenario.

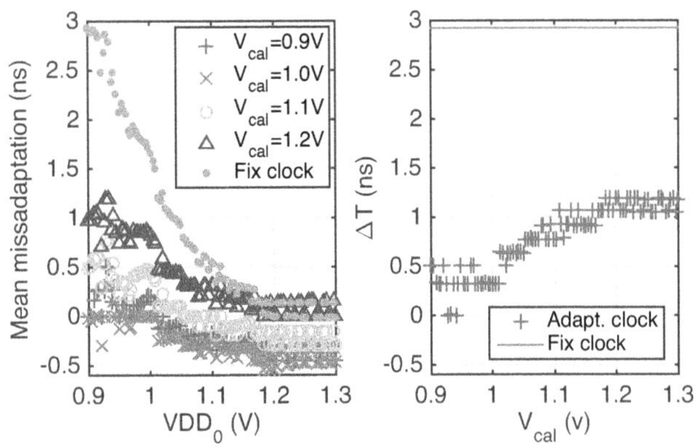

Figure 7: Left: Mean miss-adaptation $(\mu_{T_{var}} - \mu_{T_{\bf cal}})/\mu_{T_{\bf cal}}$ for VDD_0. Right: Mean period increment $\Delta T = (\mu_{T_{\bf cal}} - \mu_{T_{var}})/\mu_{T_{var}}$.

Acknowledgment

This work has been partially funded by the Spanish MINECO and ERDF funds through project TEC2013-45638-C3-2-R (Maragda).

6. REFERENCES

[1] K. Bowman, S. Duvall, and J. Meindl. Impact of die-to-die and within-die parameter fluctuations on the maximum clock frequency distribution for gigascale integration. *IEEE Journal of Solid-State Circuits*, 37(2):183–190, 2002.

[2] K. Bowman, J. Tschanz, S. Lu, P. Aseron, M. Khellah, A. Raychowdhury, B. Geuskens, C. Tokunaga, C. Wilkerson, T. Karnik, and V. De. A 45 nm resilient microprocessor core for dynamic variation tolerance. *Solid-State Circuits, IEEE Journal of*, 46(1):194–208, Jan 2011.

[3] K. A. Bowman, S. G. Duvall, and J. D. Meindl. Impact of die-to-die and within-die parameter fluctuations on the maximum clock frequency distribution for gigascale integration. *IEEE Journal of Solid State Circuits*, 37(2):183–190, 2002.

[4] A. Drake, R. Senger, H. Singh, G. Carpenter, and N. James. Dynamic measurement of critical-path timing. In *Integrated Circuit Design and Technology and Tutorial, 2008. ICICDT 2008. IEEE International Conference on*, pages 249 –252, june 2008.

[5] C. R. Lefurgy, A. J. Drake, M. S. Floyd, M. S. Allen-Ware, B. Brock, J. A. Tierno, and J. B. Carter. Active management of timing guardband to save energy in power7. In *Proceedings of the 44th Annual IEEE/ACM International Symposium on Microarchitecture*, MICRO-44, pages 1–11, New York, NY, USA, 2011. ACM.

[6] J. Perez-Puigdemont, A. Calomarde, and F. Moll. All-digital self-adaptive PVTA variation aware clock generation system for dfs. In *CMOS Variability (VARI), 2014 5th European Workshop on*, pages 1–4, Sept 2014.

[7] J. Perez-Puigdemont, F. Moll, and A. Calomarde. All-digital simple clock synthesis through a glitch-free variable-length ring oscillator. *Circuits and Systems II: Express Briefs, IEEE Transactions on*, 61(2):90–94, Feb 2014.

[8] X. Wang, A. Brown, N. Idris, S. Markov, G. Roy, and A. Asenov. Statistical threshold-voltage variability in scaled decananometer bulk HKMG MOSFETs: A full-scale 3-d simulation scaling study. *Electron Devices, IEEE Transactions on*, 58(8):2293–2301, Aug 2011.

Ultra-Low Energy Reconfigurable Spintronic Threshold Logic Gate

Deliang Fan
University of Central Florida
Orlando, FL, 32816
+1 407 823 4476
dfan@ucf.edu

ABSTRACT
This paper introduces a novel design of reconfigurable Spintronic Threshold Logic Gate (STLG), which employs spintronic weight devices to perform current mode weighted summation of binary inputs, whereas, the low voltage spintronic threshold device carries out the thresholding operation in an energy efficient manner. The proposed STLG can operate at a small terminal voltage of ~50mV, resulting in ultra-low energy consumption. The device-circuit simulation results for common benchmarks show that the proposed STLG circuit can achieve 87.5% and 11.1% energy reduction compared with state-of-the-art CMOS look-up-table (LUT) and Memristive Threshold Logic Gate (MTLG) respectively. The ultra-low programming energy of spintronic weight device also leads to three orders lower reconfiguration energy of STLG compared with MTLG design.

Keywords
Magnetic domain wall strip; Reconfigurable logic; Threshold logic; Magnetic tunnel junction; Spintronic

1. INTRODUCTION
A threshold logic gate (TLG) essentially constitutes of summation of weighted inputs, followed by a threshold operation as shown in Fig. 1, where IN_i*'s* are multiple binary inputs, W_i*'s* are scalar weights with which the corresponding inputs are multiplied and θ is the threshold [1]. The same TLG circuit can implement different Boolean functions by reconfiguring the weights, threshold, or both. In previous research, TLG has been implemented in CMOS and other bulk semiconductor technologies, such as CMOS look-up-tables (LUT) [1][3], single electron transistors [4] and resonant tunneling diode [5]. Such hardware implements suffer from power, delay and area overhead. Recent discovery of nano-scale memristor, whose resistance can be programmed with an applied electric field, has led to proposal of energy-efficient reconfigurable memristive TLG (MTLG) [2][3][6]. Compared with CMOS LUT based TLG design, such MTLG designs can potentially provide two orders lower energy consumption and high area density [3][11]. However, due to the intrinsic high energy consumption and long programming delay of memristor (Ag-Ch[2], TiO2[3]), the memristor based TLG suffers from high power and long delay in reconfiguration operation, thereby eschewing the benefits of reconfigurable logic computing.

Recent experiments on spintronic devices have demonstrated high speed switching of nano-scale magnets with spin polarized currents [7][14]. Together with other characteristics, including non-volatility, zero leakage current and high integration density, spintronic devices have been explored to design compact, low power memory [13], Boolean logic [8][11], analog and neuromorphic computing [9][10][12][13]. In this work, we propose a spintronic weight device (SWD) based on magnetic domain wall strip and magnetic tunnel junction. The continuous conductance of SWD can be programmed using a small current (~30μA) pulse within 2 ns. We then propose an ultra-low voltage (~50mV) spintronic TLG (STLG) design that employs SWD to perform current mode weighted summation of binary inputs, whereas, the low voltage spintronic threshold device carries out the threshold operation in an energy efficient manner. Spintronic device-circuit simulations for common benchmarks show that the proposed STLG achieves ultra-low energy consumption for both computation and reconfiguration operations compared with CMOS LUT and MTLG designs.

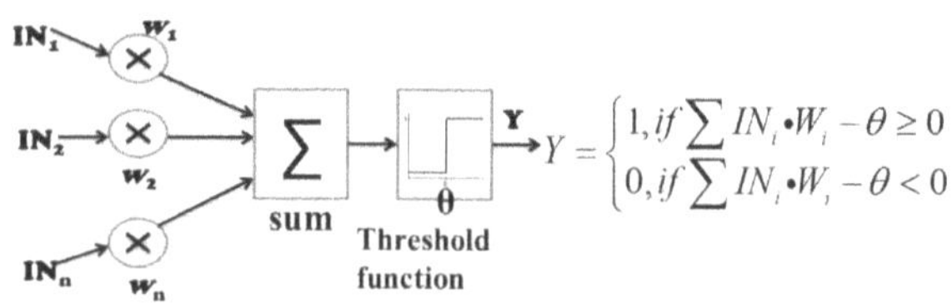

Figure 1. A schematic representation of threshold logic gate (TLG) and its mathematical expression

The rest of this paper is organized as follows. Section-2 presents the proposed spintronic weight device structure and circuit model. In section-3, the spintronic threshold device in TLG is introduced. The proposed circuit design of spintronic threshold logic gate is presented in section-4. Section-5 discusses the device-circuit co-simulation of the proposed STLG and performance comparison with CMOS LUT and MTLG. Section-6 concludes the paper.

2. SPINTRONIC WEIGHT DEVICE
A TLG can be divided into three steps, i.e. *weighing*, *summation* and *thresholding* as shown in Fig.1. In this section, we present the device structure and operation of the proposed spintronic weight device (SWD). The SWD has a programmable continuous conductance range, which can be employed to implement the first step (weighing) of a TLG.

The proposed SWD is based on a composite device structure consisting of a Domain Wall Motion (DWM) magnetic strip and a magnetic tunnel junction (MTJ) as shown in Fig. 2a. The MTJ consists of two ferromagnetic layers with an insulator (MgO) barrier sandwiched between them. The 'free' ferromagnetic layer (d4) connects laterally to two anti-parallel fixed magnetic domains - d1 and d2 [9][15][16]. The transition area between these two domains is called *domain wall* (DW). The larger thickness at the edges of the free layer is used to stabilize the DW at an

GLSVLSI '16, May 18-20, 2016, Boston, MA, USA
© 2016 ACM. ISBN 978-1-4503-4274-2/16/05…$15.00
DOI: http://dx.doi.org/10.1145/2902961.2902994

intermediate position within the free layer [15]. Recent experiments have shown that the steady DWM can be induced using current injection along the magnetic nano-strip [14][17]. For example, in Fig. 2a, when the electrons are injected into d2, they become spin-polarized and exert a Spin-Transfer Torque (STT) on the DW. If the STT is large enough to overcome the pinning field, it leads to steady DWM (to d1 in this case). The authors in [14] demonstrate steady DWM critical current density of ~6×10^{11}A/m^2 and ~60m/s DW velocity for 20nm-wide magnetic nano-strips. A *Neel* type DW is formed due to the small strip width (20nm) [14].

The proposed SWD device can be treated as a four terminal device with lateral and vertical current paths. For the lateral path (d1 to d2, $\pm$ x direction), d1 forms the input programming port, assuming d2 is supplied with a constant voltage. The DW can be moved along the free layer depending on the lateral current pulse magnitude, direction and duration [14][17], leading to a continuous resistance/ conductance change of the MTJ in the vertical direction.

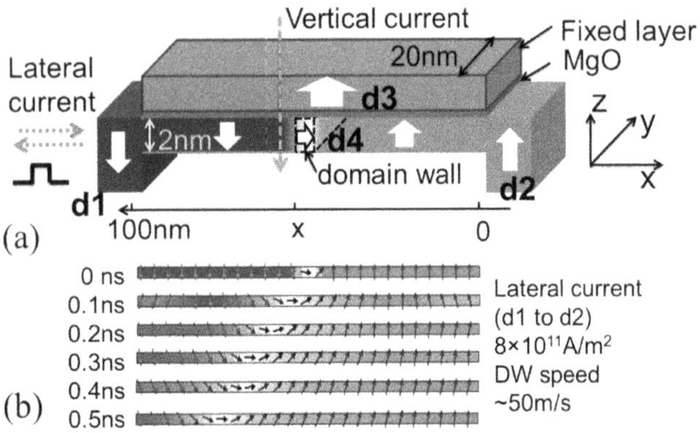

Figure 2. (a) The proposed spintronic weight device structure, (b) micro-magnetic simulation of free layer DW motion with 8×10^{11} A/m^2 lateral current injection from d1 to d2

The transient micro-magnetic simulation plot of the free layer using *mumax*^{3} [18] is shown in Fig. 2b, where a 0.5ns current pulse with magnitude of 8×10^{11}A/m^2 is applied from d1 to d2. The device parameters used in the simulation are listed in table-1[9]. We benchmarked the micro-magnetic simulation with the experimental data in [14] (the same nano-strip width of 20nm is fabricated) and it shows a good match as shown in Fig. 3a.

The vertical path (from d3 to d4, $\pm$ z direction) is used for sensing the position of DW in terms of MTJ vertical conductance. MTJ conductance is a function of voltage, tunneling oxide thickness (t_{MgO}) and the angle between free layer and pinned layer magnetizations. The atomistic level simulation framework based on Non-Equilibrium Green's Function (NEGF) formalism [19] is used to evaluate the MTJ resistance. In order to simulate the proposed device with CMOS interface circuits in HSPICE, SWD is modeled as three parallel MTJs with variable conductance

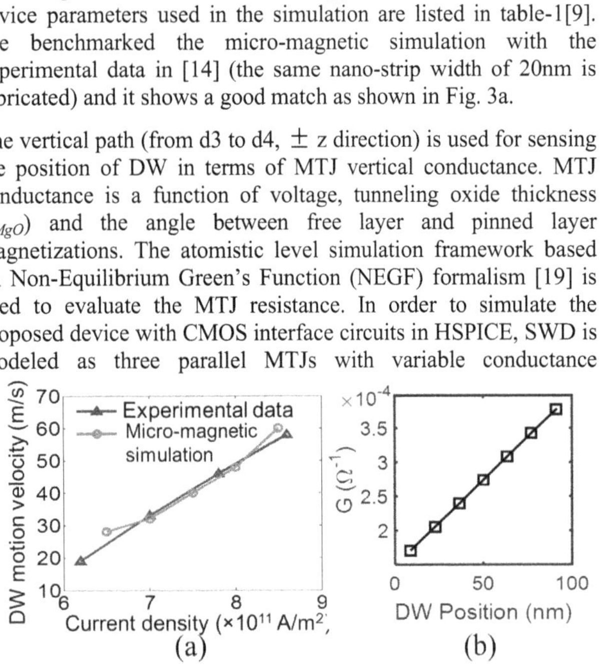

Figure 3. (a) Simulated DW motion velocity vs. lateral current density, (b) SWD conductance vs. DW position in the free layer

Table 1. SWD device parameters

Symbol	Quantity	Values
α	Damping coefficient	0.02
Ku	Uniaxial anisotropy constant	3.5×10^5 J/m3
Ms	Saturation magnetization	6.8×10^5 A/m
A_{ex}	Exchange stiffness	1.1×10^{-11} J/m
P	Polarization	0.6
t_{MgO}	MgO thickness of SWD	1.1nm

depending on DW positions.

$$G_L = \left(W\left(L - x - 0.5L_{DW}\right)\right)/RA_{AP} \quad (1)$$

$$G_R = \left(W\left(x - 0.5L_{DW}\right)\right)/RA_P \quad (2)$$

$$G_{DW} = \left(WL_{DW}\right)/RA_{DW} \quad (3)$$

where, G_L, G_{DW} and G_R are respectively the vertical conductance of left anti-parallel, domain wall and right parallel equivalent MTJ conductance; x is DW position (middle point), L is the length of free layer (100nm), L_{DW} is the domain wall length, W is the width of free layer, RA_{AP}, RA_{DW} and RA_P are respectively MTJ resistance-area product for anti-parallel, DW and parallel configurations obtained in the NEGF based MTJ model [19]. The conductance of the SWD can then be computed as:

$$G_{SWD} = G_L + G_{DW} + G_R \quad (4)$$

Fig. 3b shows the SWD conductance is linearly proportional to the DW positions in the free layer (with t_{MgO}=1.1nm). Thus, this device can be employed as weights at the inputs of a TLG by programming to a specific conductance. Based on our micro-magnetic simulation, the conductance of SWD can be programmed from minimum to maximum using a 30μA-2ns current pulse, which leads to low reconfiguration energy of the proposed TLG.

3. SPINTRONIC THRESHOLD DEVICE

In this section a spintronic threshold device (STD) is described. It will serve as the third step (thresholding) of a TLG.

The device structure of STD is shown in Fig. 4a. It constitutes of a thin and short nano-magnet domain-d3 connecting two anti-parallel fixed magnetic domains, i.e. d1 and d2. Domain-1 forms the input port and domain-2 is grounded. The magnetization of free layer (d3) can be written parallel to d2 by injecting a current (larger than critical current) along it from d1 to d2 and vice-versa [11][14]. A fixed small magnet m1 and d3 form a MTJ to read the state of d3. Unlike in SWD, the fixed layer of sense MTJ in STD is very small (20nm×20nm). The resistance states are binary, i.e. either high (AP) or low (P).

The threshold of STD, i.e. the minimum current magnitude required to switch the free layer magnetization (move DW from one end to the other end), is determined by the critical current density and DW velocity. Based on our micro-magnetic simulation and device dimension as shown in Fig. 4a, the STD current threshold is ~30μA for 1ns switching, corresponding to DW velocity of ~50m/s. Recently, application of spin orbital coupling has been explored for reducing the critical current and increasing DWM velocity [20]. The threshold current can be

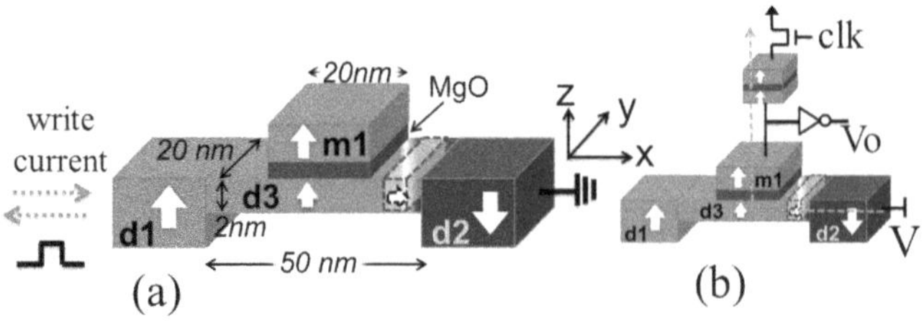

Figure 4. (a) STD device structure, (b) STD sense circuit

further reduced to be less than 10μA. The effective resistance of the MTJ formed between m1 and d3 is smaller when they have the same magnetization and vice versa. The ratio of the two resistances is defined in terms of tunneling magnetoresistance (TMR). As shown in Fig. 4b, STD forms a voltage divider with a fixed reference MTJ to sense the resistance state. Static current in the voltage divider can be minimized by increasing the MTJ oxide thickness. Note that in the detection circuit, the transient current with short duration (1ns) and low magnitude (~2μA) flows from d2 to m1, which will not disturb the state of d3. In summary, the circuit in Fig. 4b can detect the polarity of the current flow at its input node, acting as an ultra-low voltage and compact current comparator that can be employed in the following STLG design.

4. DESIGN OF SPINTRONIC THRESHOLD LOGIC GATE

Fig. 5 shows the circuit realization of a single Spintronic Threshold Logic Gate (STLG). In this section, we use two input STLG as an example to explain the design. Larger number of fan-ins can also be implemented and will be analyzed in section-5. This design mainly consists of three components, corresponding to three steps of a TLG, namely *weighing*, *summation* and *thresholding* as shown in Fig. 5. In STLG, SWD conductance can be pre-programmed to specific values (listed in Table-3) for different Boolean functions. Since the weights and threshold of a TLG can be either positive or negative, two SWDs combined as one *weight unit* are used to represent one input weight. For example, in Fig. 5, the difference of G_{1+} and G_{1-} represents the weight for input-1(i.e. $W_1=G_{1+}-G_{1-}$), which can be positive, negative or zero. Note that, in the proposed design the threshold is treated as the weight of an extra reference input whose value is always high (V_{ref} in Fig.5). Thus, the TLG function can be rewritten as *output*= $sign(\sum IN_i*W_i-1*W_r)$, where IN_i is the Binary input, W_i is the corresponding weight and W_r is the threshold value. Note that, in Table-2, $Ref=-W_r$. The input voltage signal to STLG is received through CMOS transistors with source terminals connected to a potential $V+\Delta V$ (for positive SWD) and $V-\Delta V$ (for negative SWD) where ΔV can be $\sim 50mV$. These input transistors act as deep triode region current sources (DTCS) [11]. The STD is connected to a DC supply-V. The static current therefore flows across a small terminal voltage of ΔV, resulting in small static power consumption. Moreover, the dynamic power dissipation is also largely reduced due to ultra-small voltage swing. Due to the small resistance of magneto metallic STD, the current flowing through out of each weigh unit is approximately $V_i\Delta V(G_{i+}-G_{i-})$, where V_i is binary value (0 or 1) indicating input state, G_{i+} and G_{i-} are the corresponding SWD conductance. Thus the current out of each weight unit can be either positive ($G_{i+}>G_{i-}$ & $V_i=1$), negative ($G_{i+}<G_{i-}$ & $V_i=1$) or zero ($G_{i+}=G_{i-}$ or $V_i=0$). Thus the positive or negative weights of each input is encoded as the conductance difference of G_{i+} and G_{i-}. The current flowing into the input of STD is expressed as $I_{STD}=\sum[V_i\Delta V(G_{i+}-G_{i-})+1*\Delta V(G_{r+}-G_{r-})]$. The direction of current flowing at the input of a STD, and hence the output of a TLG, would depend upon the input data and the corresponding weights. Table-2 and Table-3 list the detailed resistance values of weights and references for different Boolean functions. The output of the STD detection circuit associated with each TLG, in turn, drives the fan-out TLGs. Due to the non-volatility of the STD, the proposed STLG design can be easily extended to realize a pipelined architecture without inserting the CMOS latches.

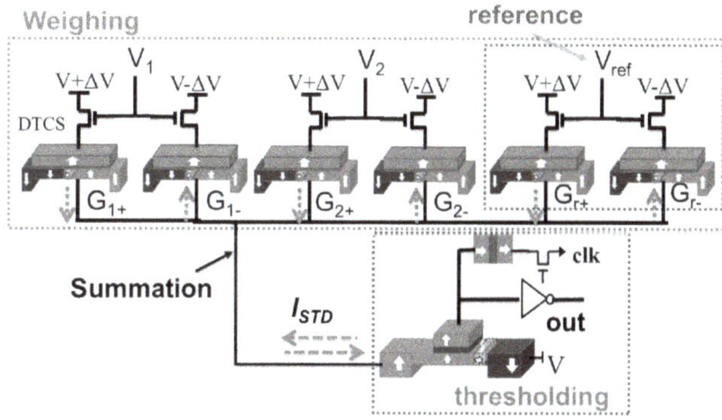

Figure 5. Proposed spintronic threshold logic gate

Table 2. Different Boolean function weights

Function	Weight				Function	Weight			
	A	B	C	Ref		A	B	C	Ref
AB	2	2	-	-3	A+B	2	2	-	-1
ABC	1	1	1	-3	A+B+C	1	1	1	-1
AB+BC+CA	1	1	1	-2	A+BC	2	1	1	-2
AB+AC	2	1	1	-3					

5. SIMULATION AND PERFORMANCE

In this section, we discuss circuit simulation and performance of the proposed STLG. 45nm NCSU Product Development Kit (PDK) library is used in HSPICE circuit simulation [21].

In this work, 2-input and 3-input linearly separable Boolean functions [3] are employed to demonstrate the functionality and performance of the proposed design. Table-2 lists few samples of TLG Boolean functions with their weights and references (negative value of threshold). Table-3 lists the SWD resistance values for different Boolean functions. Fig. 6 shows the HSPICE transient simulation plots for STLG implementing 2-input "AND" Boolean functions. Three complementary clocks are used in the circuit simulation. The first clock is "reset" clock, which is used to reset the STD. A -32μA current is applied at the input terminal of STD, leading to shift of DW to the right end of domain-3. The initial state of STD sense MTJ is in parallel state. When "Clk1" is on ('computation' cycle in Fig.6), the input voltages are applied in the corresponding DTCS transistors and the net current flowing into the STD is determined by the weighted summation of inputs. When the net current is greater than the threshold current, DW will be moved to the left (i.e. sense MTJ in AP state), or the sense MTJ still remains in P state (initial state). For input "A" and "B" with values of (11, 10, 01, 00), the corresponding net current flowing into STD is (31, 26, 26, 21)μA. Since the threshold current of STD is ~30 μA, it can be seen in Fig. 6 that the sense MTJ resistance (R_MTJ) is (high, low, low, low). When "Clk2" is on ('sense' cycle), the STD sense circuit read the state of MTJ and sends the binary voltage output to next TLG through an inverter.

Fig. 7a presents the computation energy consumption of STLG compared with CMOS LUT and MTLG [3] for linearly separable Boolean functions. It can be seen that both STLG and MTLG are much more energy efficient than CMOS LUT. On average, STLG

Table 3. Different STLG weights and energy

Function	A+ (KΩ)	A- (KΩ)	B+ (KΩ)	B- (KΩ)	C+ (KΩ)	C- (KΩ)	Ref+ (KΩ)	Ref- (KΩ)	Energy (fJ)
AB	3.24	5.85	3.24	5.85	-	-	5.85	2.65	5.7066
A+B	3.24	5.85	3.24	5.85	-	-	5.85	4.17	6.3231
ABC	4.17	5.85	4.17	5.85	4.17	5.85	5.85	2.65	6.8544
A+B+C	4.17	5.85	4.17	5.85	4.17	5.85	5.85	4.17	6.4848
AB+BC+CA	4.17	5.85	4.17	5.85	4.17	5.85	5.85	3.24	6.6726
A+BC	3.24	5.85	4.17	5.85	4.17	5.85	5.85	3.24	6.6726
AB+AC	3.24	5.85	4.17	5.85	4.17	5.85	5.85	2.65	6.8544

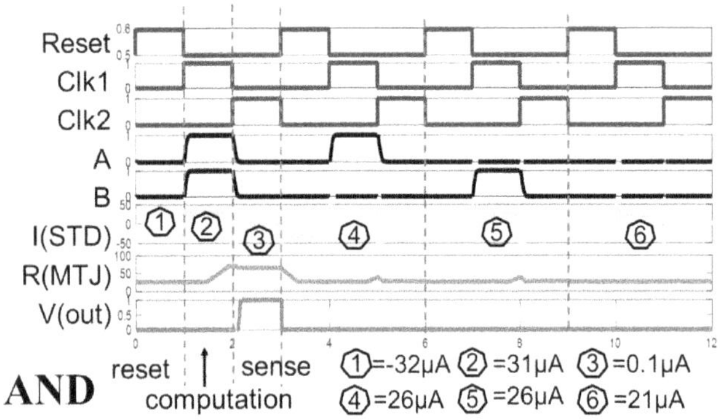

Figure 6. HSPICE simulation results of STLG implementing "AND" Boolean functions

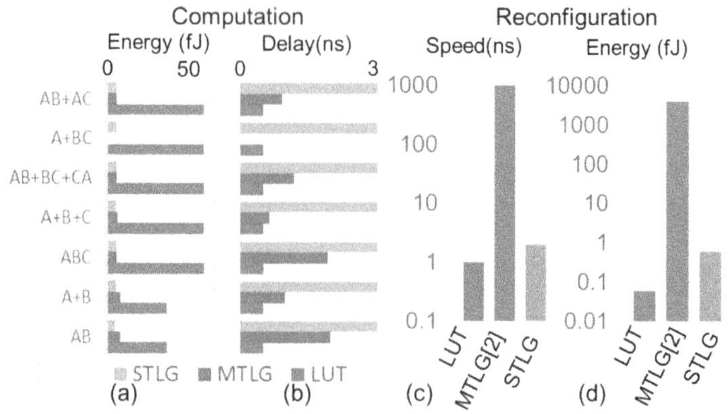

Figure 7. Comparison of (a) computation energy, (b) delay; comparison of TLG reconfiguration (c) speed and (d) energy

consumes 87.5% and 11.1% less energy compared to LUT and MTLG respectively. Such large energy saving mainly due to 1): ultra-low voltage (~50mV) across STLG 2): low STD current 3): DTCS transistors working in deep triode region. As for delay of TLG design, STLG is the worst due to three step operations, namely reset, computation and sense.

Recent proposed MTLG attracts a lot of interests due to the non-volatility, programmability and high area density of memristors [2][3]. However, MTLG suffers from high reconfiguration energy consumption due to high programming voltage (0.6V in Ag-Ch memristor[2] and 1.3V in TiO_2 memristor[3]) and long programming time (few μs [2]). Our proposed SWD conductance can be programmed much more energy efficiently and faster, greatly lowering the reconfiguration energy consumption in TLG design. In this work, we define the *reconfiguration energy* as the averaged energy of programming the weight from minimum to maximum and from maximum to minimum. For CMOS LUT, it is the averaged energy of writing "0" and writing "1". For Ag-Ch memristor, authors in [2] used 0.3V~1μs and -0.6V~1μs voltage pulses to program memristance between 10KΩ to 100KΩ. While in spintronic weight device, a ±30μA~2ns current pulse can move the DW from one end to the other, thus programming the weight from minimum to maximum or maximum to minimum. Fig. 7c and 7d present the reconfiguration speed and energy consumption of LUT, memristor (Ag-Ch) and SWD. It can be seen that the CMOS LUT consumes least energy and has the fastest programming speed. SWD reconfiguration energy and delay are slightly larger than CMOS LUT, however, it is almost three orders lower in energy consumption and three orders faster in programming speed compared with memristors (Ag-Ch) [2].

6. CONCLUSION

In this paper, we propose a spintronic weight device that can be combined with spintronic threshold device to design spintronic threshold logic gate. Ultra-low energy is achieved due to low voltage (~50mV), low current computing facilitated by the spintronic devices. Such spin-CMOS hybrid hardware can achieve 87.5% and 11.1% energy reduction compared with state-of-the-art CMOS LUT and memristor based threshold logic gate designs respectively. Moreover, the spintronic weight device also leads to low power and fast speed in reconfiguration operation of the proposed design. Compared with reconfigurable MTLG design, the proposed STLG consumes three orders lower reconfiguration energy, opening a new door for future post-CMOS, ultra-low energy reconfigurable computing era.

7. REFERENCES

[1] V. Beiu, J. Quintana and M. Avedillo, "VLSI Implementations of Threshold Logic - A Comprehensive Survey," *IEEE TNN*, vol. 14, pp. 1217-1243, 2003.

[2] A. Rothenbuhler, et. al, "Reconfigurable Threshold Logic Gates using Memristirve Devices", *JLPEA*, vol.3, pp.174-193, 2013

[3] J. Rajendra, H. Manem, R. Karri and G.S. Rose, "An Energy-Efficient Memristive Threshold Logic Circuit." *IEEE Trans. On Comp.*, vol. 61, No. 4, pp. 474-487, 2012

[4] C. Moffat, "A Survey of Nanoelectronics," Univ. College, London, U.K., http://ipga.phys.ucl.ac.uk/papers/rep94-2.pdf, 1994.

[5] K. Chen, et. al., "Monolithic Integration of Resonant Tunneling Diodes and FET's for Monostable-Bistable Transition Logic Elements (MOBILE's)," *IEEE EDL*, vol. 16, no. 2, pp. 70-73, 1995.

[6] T. Tran, et. al., "Reconfigurable Threshold Logic Gates Using Memristive Devices." *IEEE SubVT*, pp. 1-3, 2012.

[7] Y. Huai, et. al., "Observation of spin-transfer switching in deep submicron-sized and low-resistance magnetic tunnel junctions," *Appl. Phys. Lett.*, vol. 84, no. 16, p. 3118, 2004.

[8] C. Augustine, et. al., "Low-power functionality enhanced computation architecture using spin-based devices," in Proc. *IEEE/ACM Int. Symp. Nanoscale Arch.*, Jun. 2011, pp. 129–136.

[9] D. Fan, Y. Shim, A. Raghunathan and K. Roy, "STT-SNN: A Spin-Transfer-Torque Based Soft-Limiting Non-Linear Neuron for Low-Power Artificial Neural Networks", *IEEE Trans. On Nanotechnology*, vol. 14, no.6, pp1013-1023, 2015

[10] D. Fan, M. Sharad and K. Roy, "Hierarchical Temporal Memory Based on Spin-Neurons and Resistive Memory for Energy-Efficient Brain-Inspired Computing", *IEEE Trans. Neural Network and Learning Systems*, 2015. DOI=10.1109/TNNLS.2015.2462731

[11] D. Fan, M. Sharad and K. Roy, "Design and Synthesis of Ultralow Energy Spin-Memristor Threshold Logic", *IEEE Tran. On Nanotechnology*, vol. 13, no. 3, pp.574-583, 2014

[12] K. Roy, D. Fan, et. al. "Exploring Spin Transfer Torque Devices for Unconventional Computing", *JETCAS*, vol.5, no.1, pp.5-16, 2015

[13] X. Fong, Y. Kim, K. Yoendra, D. Fan, A. Sengupta and K. Roy, "Spin-Transfer Torque Devices for Logic and Memory Applications: Prospects and Perspectives", *IEEE Trans. On Computer-Aided Design of Integrated Cir. and Sys.*, vol. 25, no.1, pp.1-22, Jan. 2016

[14] S. Fukami, et. al., "20-nm magnetic domain wall motion memory with ultralow-power operation," *IEEE IEDM*, Washington, DC, Dec. 2013, pp. 3.5.1-3.5.4.

[15] A. Chanthbouala, et.al., "Vertical-current-induced domain-wall motion in MgO-based magnetic tunnel junctions with low current densities," *Nature Physics* vol. 7, no. 8, pp. 626-630, Apr. 2011

[16] X. Wang, Y. Chen, H. Xi, H. Li, and D. Dimitrov, "Spintronic memristor through spin-torque-induced magnetization motion," *IEEE Electron Device Letters*, Vol. 30, no. 3, pp.294-297, Feb. 2009

[17] C. Lim, et. al., "Domain wall displacement induced by subnanosecond pulsed current," *Applied Physics Letters*, vol. 84, no. 15, pp. 2820-2822, Apr. 2004

[18] [online] mumax.github.io

[19] X. Fong, et. al., "KNACK: A hybrid spin-charge mixed-mode simulator for evaluating different genres of spin-transfer torque MRAM bit-cells," In *SISPAD*, Osaka, Japan, Sept. 2011, pp. 51-54.

[20] M. Sharad, D. Fan, and K. Roy, "Spin-neurons: A possible path to energy-efficient neuromorphic computers," *Journal of Applied Physics*, vol. 114, no. 23, pp. 234906, Dec. 2013.

[21] [online] http://www.eda.ncsu.edu/wiki/FreePDK45:Contents

Red-Shield: Shielding Read Disturbance for STT-RAM Based Register Files on GPUs

Hang Zhang[†‡], Xuhao Chen[‡], Nong Xiao[†‡], Fang Liu[†‡], Zhiguang Chen[†‡]
[†]State Key Laboratory of High Performance Computing, College of Computer,
National University of Defense Technology
[‡]College of Computer, National University of Defense Technology
Changsha, Hunan 410073, China
{hangzhang, xuhaochen, nongxiao, liufang, chenzhiguang@nudt.edu.cn}

ABSTRACT

To address the high energy consumption issue of SRAM on GPUs, emerging Spin-Transfer Torque (STT-RAM) memory technology has been intensively studied to build GPU register files for better energy-efficiency, thanks to its benefits of low leakage power, high density, and good scalability. However, STT-RAM suffers from a reliability issue, read disturbance, which stems from the fact that the voltage difference between read current and write current becomes smaller as technology scales. The read disturbance leads to high error rates for read operations, which cannot be effectively protected by SECDEC ECC on large-capacity register files of GPUs.

Prior schemes (e.g. read-restore) to mitigate the read disturbance usually incur either non-trivial performance loss or excessive energy overhead, thus not applicable for the GPU register file design which aims to achieve both high performance and energy-efficiency. To combat the read disturbance on GPU register files, we propose a novel software-hardware co-designed solution, i.e. *Red-Shield*, which consists of three optimizations to overcome limitations of the existing solutions. First, we identify dead reads at compiling stage and augment instructions to avoid unnecessary restores. Second, we employ a small read buffer to accommodate register reads with high access locality to further reduce restores. Third, we propose an adaptive restore mechanism to selectively pick the suitable restore scheme, according to the busy status of corresponding register banks. Experimental results show that our proposed design can effectively mitigate the performance loss and energy overhead caused by restore operations, while still maintaining the reliability of reads.

Keywords

GPU, STT-RAM, Register File, Read Disturbance

1. INTRODUCTION

General-purpose graphics processing units (GPGPUs) have been widely adopted for high performance computing during the last decade, owing to its high throughput and energy-efficiency [14]. Its single instruction multiple thread (SIMT) architecture enables thousands of threads running concurrently to hide long latency of memory operations and hence achieve high throughput. To maintain hardware contexts of a huge number of threads, GPGPUs usually employ a large-capacity register file for seamlessly context switching. Unfortunately, large-capacity register files also consume a large portion of power that usually accounts for 15-20% of total power in modern GPUs [7], as the register files are currently built with SRAM technology that has high leakage power in submicron technology nodes. To combat the high energy consumption of SRAM, there have been extensive studies on replacing SRAM with emerging STT-RAM to build energy-efficient register files of GPUs, due to its benefits of low leakage power, high density, and good scalability [6, 8, 9].

However, `read disturbance` issue has become a major design challenge for STT-RAM based on-chip memory [16, 17] recently. The read disturbance lies in the decreasing difference between write current and read current that are applied to read/write STT-RAM cells. Due to performance concerns, GPU register files usually employ simple ECC protections against SRAM errors [11], however it is not sufficient to shield the high error rate caused by the read disturbance issue [17]. Therefore, how to cope with the read disturbance issue is a key concern that decides whether the emerging STT-RAM can be employed to build energy-efficient register files on GPUs, and it has not been addressed well by prior works.

Restoring data after each read can be a simple yet effective solution to suppress the read disturbance on GPU register files [16, 17]. However, this restore operations lead to unaccepted performance loss and energy overhead. Consequently, it is imperative to judiciously tackle the read disturbance for STT-RAM based register file while preserving the high throughput and energy-efficiency of GPUs. To this end, we propose a novel software-hardware co-design, namely ***Red-shield*** (***Re***ad ***D***isturbance ***Shield***), to alleviate the performance loss and extra energy consumption incurred by the read disturbance issue on GPUs. In summary, we make the following contributions in this work.

- We devise a compiler assisted dead read identification scheme to identify dead reads that do not need restores, and remove unnecessary restore operations related to these reads.
- Since successive reads to the same register lead to temporal locality, we employ a small SRAM read buffer to accommodate the reads with high locality.
- We propose an adaptive restore mechanism to selectively pick the optimal restore scheme, according to the status of register banks.

GLSVLSI '16, May 18-20, 2016, Boston, MA, USA

DOI: http://dx.doi.org/10.1145/2902961.2902988

Table 1: Read Disturbance Error Rate

Tech(nm)	45	32	22	15	11
BER	1.38E-8	3.38E-7	3.07E-6	2.16E-5	1.2E-4
LER	1.42E-5	3.50E-4	3.17E-3	2.21E-2	1.17E-1
LER SECDEC	1.02-10	6.12E-8	5.04E-6	2.46E-4	7.11E-3

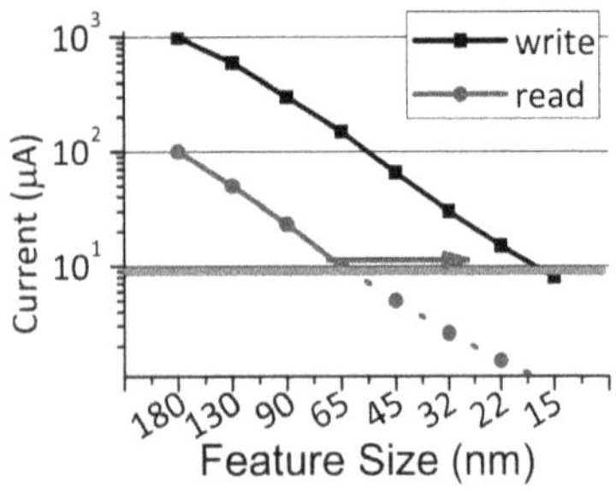

Figure 1: The scaling of read and write currents [17]

To the best of our knowledge, this is the first work to address the read disturbance issue for large-scale STT-RAM based register files on GPUs.

2. MOTIVATION

A STT-RAM read operation have the same operating mechanism as a write operation but with smaller voltage. Fig. 1 illustrates the current amplitude comparison between write current and read current at different technology nodes.

The decreasing difference between read current and write current leads to read operations with a high error rate. Therefore, the read disturbance has become a major design concern for STT-RAM based register files. We use the model from [17] to calcuate the read disturbance error rate. The 1024-bit register entry is evaluated as a whole block. Due to performance concerns, GPUs usually employ SECDEC ECC to protect register files [12]. The modeled error rate is shown in Table 1. The BER denotes the raw bit error rate, the LER denotes the line error rate, and the LER SECDEC denotes the line error rate after adopting SECDEC ECC. We can see that LER SECDEC is so high that it cannot guarantee the reliability of reading a register entry. For instance, the LER SECDEC at 22mm is about 5.04E-6, which is much greater than 2.5E-11, the acceptable error rate of DRAM [17, 13].

Additionally, the state-of-the-art design [17] that aims to suppress the read disturbance issue is not applicable to GPU register file design, because it is specifically designed for STT-RAM based LLC (L2 cache) whose features are quite different from those of the register file. It requires help information from the upper-level memory hierarchy (L1 cache), and however there is no such upper-level layer above register files on GPUs. Therefore, it is necessary to devise effective mechanisms to obviate the read disturbance issue on STT-RAM based GPU register files while not incurring much performance and energy overhead.

3. RED-SHIELD DESIGN

In this section, we present our proposed design, ***Red-shield***, which incorporates several software and hardware optimizations to address the read disturbance issue of STT-RAM based register files.

3.1 Dead Read Identification

To understand the characteristic of accessed register values on GPUs, we conduct program profiling on different benchmarks. The

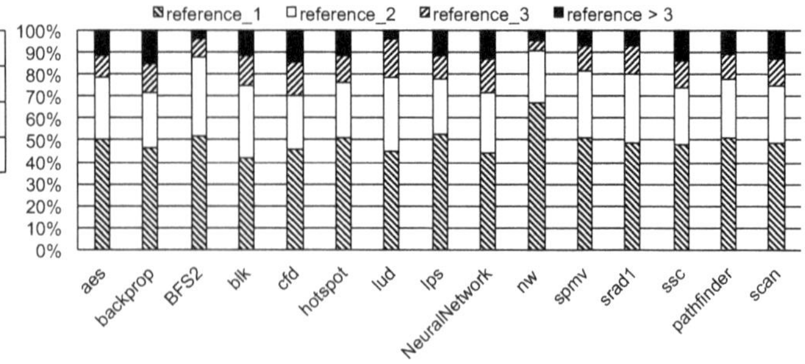

Figure 2: Register read access count distribution. It shows the number of read accesses to registers.

result is shown in Fig. 2. Most of these benchmarks have similar distributions. On average, nearly 49.3% of the generated register values are referenced (read) only once, while nearly 27.9% and 11.6% of them are referenced twice and three times, respectively. Those are referenced more than threes times only constitute 0.09% of total references. A similar result has been observed in previous work [5]. In fact, it implies that we do not need to restore those register values that will not be re-referenced in the future.

Furthermore, for a register value that will be re-referenced several times, the last reference also does not need to be restored, since there is no more read after the last reference. For instance, if we know the register value A will be referenced three times in total after it is generated, the 3rd read operation on A does not need a restore operation. Here, we refer to the last read operation as the ***dead read***, since the register value is not useful anymore after the last read operation. Apparently, the only read operation to the register value that has only one reference is also a ***dead read***.

If we can identify these dead reads before run-time, then the unnecessary restore operations to these dead reads can be avoided and both performance and energy-efficiency can be improved. To this end, we propose a dead read identification scheme that can effectively recognize dead reads at the compiling stage. The standard register analysis algorithm [1] is employed to analyze register liveness coverage.

3.2 Read Buffer Promotion

Although the dead read identification scheme can effectively reduce the number of unnecessary restore operations, for register values that have multiple references, it is still necessary to restore the data after each read operation (except for the last one). An example of the register liveness analysis result of `backprop` is shown in Fig. 3. 'R' denotes a register read; 'W' denotes a register write; 'L' indicates a register is alive. For instance, r_2 is referenced three times (line 2,4,8) in this snippet code. Though the last read operation can be identified as a dead read, there is still a need to restore the first two read operations after reading.

For the register values that have many references (e.g. more than 3 times), if the reference count information is available, we can devise smart schemes to leverage this temporal locality. To further reduce the number of restore operations, we propose a read buffer promotion scheme to make full use of this observed high temporal locality. To be specific, we build a reference tracking algorithm by leveraging the register liveness analysis. Based on the liveness information, this algorithm collects the reference count for each read operand of each instruction. The reference count for a specific register is re-collected only if the corresponding operand is dead or written. This reference count is also encoded into instructions. We

```
                      register number-> 0 1 2 3 4 5 6
cvt.u32.u16 $r2, $r0.hi;                  R L W L L
mul.half.lo.u16 $r5,$r3.lo,$r2.hi;        L L R R L W
mul.half.lo.u16 $r6,$r4.lo,$r1.hi;        L R L L R L W
mad.wide.u16 $r5,$r3.hi,$r2.lo,$r5;       L L R R L W L
mad.wide.u16 $r6,$r4.hi,$r1.lo,$r6;       L R L L R L W
shl.u32 $r5,$r5,0x00000010;               L L L L L W L
shl.u32 $r6,$r6,0x00000010;               L L L L L L W
mad.wide.u16 $r3,$r3.lo,$r2.lo,$r5;       L L R W L R L
```

Figure 3: A snippet of the PTX source code for the backprop benchmark

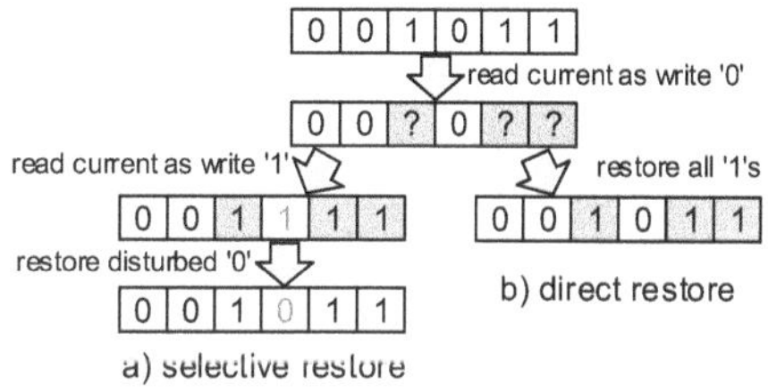

Figure 4: Comparison between the previous restore operation and our fast-restore operation

then deploy a small SRAM read buffer to store these register values with high temporal locality (e.g. reference count > 3).

3.3 Adaptive Restore Design

A STT-RAM read operation is similar to a write operation except that the read voltage is smaller than write voltage. To restore a data value in STT-RAM cells in an efficient way, people propose the selective restore (SR) [17] that involves two read operations and one write operation. After first read operation, SR requires another read that employs a current with an opposite direction compared to the first read. This second read operation aims to identify which specific cells have been disturbed. Then a successive write operation can write only the cells that have been destructed at the first read. The SR scheme is shown in Fig. 4(a). The SR can effectively reduce the number of restored data bits, and therefore save energy consumption caused by unnecessary restores. However, since SR requires extra operation and causes non-trivial performance overhead, it can not be naively applied to the STT-RAM based register file design on which performance is more critical.

On the other hand, the direct restore (DR) [16] can be also employed in our STT-RAM register file design. The idea is to skip the second read operation and restore all the "1"s, regardless whether each of these "1"s is disturbed or not. Thus we can save the time for performing one read operation for each restore. The downside of this scheme is that it might write the "1"s that are not disturbed and might consume unnecessary energy. However, this downside is not a problem because of two reasons: 1) Our previous dead read identification and read buffer promotion schemes can effectively reduce the number of restores. Thus, the number of required direct restores are relatively smaller compared to the baseline that employs SR scheme. 2) as technology scales, the read current and write current are getting closer, and therefore the direct restore (under the inversion optimization) only consumes a reasonable amount of energy close to the second read operation in the SR scheme.

Furthermore, we introduce an adaptive restore scheme that combines the benefits of the selective restore and the direct restore together, and can selectively choose to use SR or DR, according to the serving state of register banks. To be specific, the operand collector only performs DR when there is a bank conflict, since in this situation the latency of read operations has a dominant impact on performance; If there is no bank conflict, SR is preferred to minimize the energy consumption of restore operations.

4. EXPERIMENTAL EVLUATION

In this section, we present the simulation configuration, and evaluate our proposed design in terms of performance and energy. Then we give a brief estimation on the hardware area.

4.1 Simulation Configuration

We use a cycle accurate GPGPU simulator, GPGPU-Sim v3.2 [2], to model the detailed GPU architecture. We augment the simulator with the STT-RAM hybrid register file, with respect to the circuit level parameters of both SRAM and STT-RAM. Our baseline GPU is configured as NVIDIA Fermi GTX480. We modify the PTX parser to perform dead read identification.

We select 18 representative benchmarks from Rodina [3], Parboil [15], Mars [4] and NVIDIA CUDA SDK [10] benchmark suites to evaluate our proposed design. These benchmarks cover a wide range of applications with various characteristics.

We compare different configurations as follows.

- base: the baseline register file built with SRAM.
- STT: the register file design built with STT-RAM.
- WB: the STT-RAM based register file with a SRAM write buffer, configured as in previous work [9]. Since there is no read disturbance protection in this scheme, the line error rate is so high that it is not a feasible for GPUs.
- RD: the STT-RAM based register file design with the selective restore scheme [17].
- CO: Configured similar with RD, but with the dead read identification technique.
- CORB: Configured similar with CO, but with the read buffer promotion design.
- CORBAR: Configured similar with CORB, but with the adaptive restore scheme.

4.2 Performance Evaluation

Fig. 5 shows the GPU throughput under different configurations, all normalized to the baseline. It is clear to see that employing the selective restore scheme (RD) to suppress read disturbance incurs unacceptable performance loss, achieving only 83.4% of the SRAM baseline performance on average. This is because longer read operations (plus restore time) significantly increases the probability of stalling pipelines. Fortunately, our proposed dead read identification scheme (CO) can effectively improve throughput and achieve 90.6% of the baseline performance, due to the capability of avoiding unnecessary restore operations. For some applications, such as BAC, NEU and MON, CO can even alleviate the performance loss to achieve 96.26% of the baseline performance. Moreover, CORB further improves performance to 91.9% of the baseline on average, due to the capability of accommodating read request with multiple accesses. Some benchmarks like LAV, LPS and LUD can significantly benefit from the high temporal locality. Finally, CORBAR achieves 93.1% of the baseline performance on average, since it can adaptively choose when to use DR or SR according to whether the corresponding bank is busy or not. This adaptive feature is especially helpful for benchmarks like LPS, SRA and PAT, which have higher number of bank conflicts.

5. CONCLUSION

STT-RAM has been explored as a promising alternative for SRAM

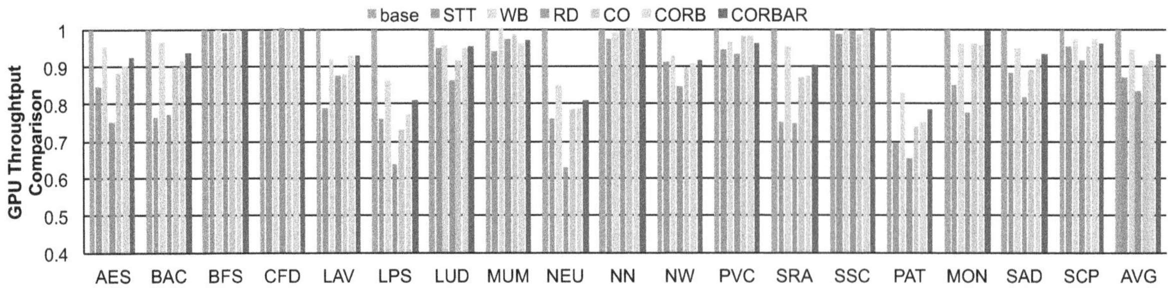

Figure 5: GPU throughput comparison between different configurations

to build the large-capacity register file on GPUs due to the advantage of high energy-efficiency. However, the read disturbance issue of STT-RAM imposes great challenges for register file design as technology further scales. To address the read disturbance issue, we present a novel design, *Red-shield*. It employs complier optimization to filter out short-lifetime reads so as to mitigate the performance and energy overhead incurred by the read-restore operations. Coupled with the read buffer promotion design as well as the optimized read-restore scheme, *Red-shield* can effectively alleviate pipeline stalls caused by read disturbance and improve the energy-efficiency. In total, our design can promote STT-RAM based GPU register files to become a feasible and effective solution for future GPU architectures.

6. ACKNOWLEDGEMENTS

We are grateful to our anonymous reviewers for their suggestions to improve this paper. This work is supported by National Natural Science Foundation of China, under grant Nos. 61433019, U1435217, 61232003, 61502514, 61402503, 61402501, 61120106005 and 61303073; National High Technology Research and Development 863 Program of China, under grant 2015AA015305.

7. REFERENCES

[1] A. W. Appel. *Modern compiler implementation in C.* Cambridge university press, 1997.

[2] A. Bakhoda, G. L. Yuan, W. W. L. Fung, H. Wong, and T. M. Aamodt. Analyzing CUDA workloads using a detailed GPU simulator. In *Proceedings of the International Symposium on Performance Analysis of Systems and Software (ISPASS)*, ISPASS, pages 163–174, 2009.

[3] S. Che, J. W. Sheaffer, M. Boyer, L. G. Szafaryn, L. Wang, and K. Skadron. A characterization of the Rodinia benchmark suite with comparison to contemporary CMP workloads. In *Proceedings of IEEE International Symposium on Workload Characterization (IISWC)*, IISWC, 2010.

[4] W. Fang, B. He, Q. Luo, and N. K. Govindaraju. Mars: Accelerating MapReduce with graphics processors. *IEEE Transactions on Parallel and Distributed Systems*, 22(4):608–620, 2011.

[5] M. Gebhart, S. W. Keckler, and W. J. Dally. A compile-time managed multi-level register file hierarchy. In *Proceedings of the 44th Annual IEEE/ACM International Symposium on Microarchitecture (MICRO)*, MICRO, 2011.

[6] N. Goswami, B. Cao, and T. Li. Power-performance co-optimization of throughput core architecture using resistive memory. In *Proceedings of the IEEE 19th International Symposium on High Performance Computer Architecture (HPCA)*, HPCA, 2013.

[7] J. Leng, T. Hetherington, A. ElTantawy, S. Gilani, N. S. Kim, T. M. Aamodt, and V. J. Reddi. GPUWattch: enabling energy optimizations in GPGPUs. In *Proceedings of the 40th Annual International Symposium on Computer Architecture (ISCA)*, ISCA, page 487, 2013.

[8] G. Li, X. Chen, G. Sun, H. Hoffmann, Y. Liu, Y. Wang, and H. Yang. A STT-RAM-based low-power hybrid register file for GPGPUs. In *Proceedings of the 52nd Annual Design Automation Conference (DAC)*, DAC, pages 1–6, 2015.

[9] X. Liu, M. Mao, X. Bi, H. Li, and Y. Chen. An efficient STT-RAM-based register file in GPU architectures. In *Proceedings of the 20th Asia and South Pacific Design Automation Conference (ASP-DAC)*, ASP-DAC, pages 490–495, 2015.

[10] NVIDA. GPU Computing SDK.

[11] D. J. Palframan, N. S. Kim, and M. H. Lipasti. Precision-aware soft error protection for GPUs. In *The IEEE 20th International Symposium on High Performance Computer Architecture (HPCA)*, HPCA, pages 49–59, 2014.

[12] D. Rossi, N. Timoncini, M. Spica, and C. Metra. Error Correcting Code Analysis for Cache Memory High Reliability and Performance. In *Design, Automation, and Test in Europe (DATE)*, HPCA, pages 1–6, 2011.

[13] B. Schroeder, E. Pinheiro, and W.-D. Weber. DRAM errors in the wild: a large-scale field study. In *Proceedings of the eleventh international joint conference on Measurement and modeling of computer systems (SIGMETRICS)*, SIGMETRICS, 2009.

[14] M. J. Schulte, M. Ignatowski, G. H. Loh, B. M. Beckmann, W. C. Brantley, S. Gurumurthi, N. Jayasena, I. Paul, S. K. Reinhardt, and G. Rodgers. Achieving Exascale Capabilities through Heterogeneous Computing. *IEEE Micro*, 35(4):26–36, jul 2015.

[15] J. A. Stratton, C. Rodrigues, I.-J. Sung, N. Obeid, L.-W. Chang, N. Anssari, G. D. Liu, and W.-M. W. Hwu. Parboil: A revised benchmark suite for scientific and commercial throughput computing. *IMPACT Technical Report*, 2012.

[16] Z. Sun, H. Li, and W. Wu. A dual-mode architecture for fast-switching STT-RAM. In *Proceedings of the 2012 ACM/IEEE international symposium on Low power electronics and design (ISLPED)*, ISLPED, pages 45–50, 2012.

[17] R. Wang, L. Jiang, Y. Zhang, L. Wang, and J. Yang. Selective restore: an energy efficient read disturbance mitigation scheme for future STT-MRAM. In *Proceedings of the 52nd Annual Design Automation Conference (DAC)*, DAC, pages 1–6, 2015.

Modeling and Study of Two-BDT-Nanostructure based Sequential Logic Circuits

Poorna Marthi, Sheikh Rufsan Reza,
Nazir Hossain, Jean-François Millithaler,
Martin Margala
Department of Electrical & Computer Engineering
University of Massachusetts Lowell,
+1978-934-2986
Poorna_Marthi@student.uml.edu

Ignacio Iñiguez-de-la-Torre, Javier Mateos,
Tomás González
Department of Applied Physics,
Universidad de Salamanca,Spain
Indy@usal.es

ABSTRACT

In this paper, study of different digital logic circuits developed using two-BDT ballistic nanostructure is presented. New D flip-flop (DFF) based on the same nanostructure is also proposed. The logic structure comprises two ballistic deflection transistors (BDTs) that are experimentally proven to operate at Terahertz frequencies. The non-linear behavior of the BDT's transfer characteristic has been perfectly reproduced by means of Monte Carlo simulations, where a specific attention has been devoted to surface charges. An analytical model built on the results of advanced MC simulations has been integrated into a behavioral Verilog AMS module to confirm the functionality of the circuit design. The module is used to analyze operating conditions of different combinational circuits and to investigate the feasibility of DFF design using BDT nanostructure. The simulation results indicate successful operation of both combinational and sequential circuits developed using two-BDT logic structure under proper biasing of gate and source terminals. The operating voltages of the proposed DFF are estimated to be $\pm$ 225mV.

Keywords

Ballistic Deflection Transistors (BDTs); Monte Carlo (MC) simulations; D-Flip Flop (DFF); Verilog-AMS model.

1. INTRODUCTION

Ballistic deflection transistor, usually referred as BDT, is a recent entrant among the ballistic devices that promises Terahertz speeds at room temperature [1]. An overview of emerging devices with a special emphasis on BDTs been presented in [2]. BDT is a six terminal device, comprising a grounded electron source, two gates and three output drains; and has been fabricated in an InGaAs-InAlAs heterostructure with an indium phosphide (InP) substrate. The SEM image of a BDT with channel width of 300nm and dielectric trench of 80nm is shown in Figure 1. Electrons, upon entering into the BDT from source terminal, will be pulled towards the top drain terminal. When gate terminals are properly biased, they induce a steering effect, assisted by a central deflector, to bounce electrons towards their respective drain terminals. However, high gate voltages will pinch off channels thus making BDT transfer characteristics nonlinear [3]. It was suggested that to achieve an optimum device performance and low leakage currents, the deflector should be placed 25% below the exact center of the device [4, 5]. After a thorough investigation on the experimental characteristics of BDT devices at room temperature, it was concluded that these devices are suitable for both analog and digital applications [6, 7, 8]. This paper presents the feasibility of D-Flip Flop developed using two-BDT logic structure.

GLSVLSI '16, May 18-20, 2016, Boston, MA, USA
 ISBN 978-1-4503-4274-2/16/05...$15.00
DOI: http://dx.doi.org/10.1145/2902961.2903001

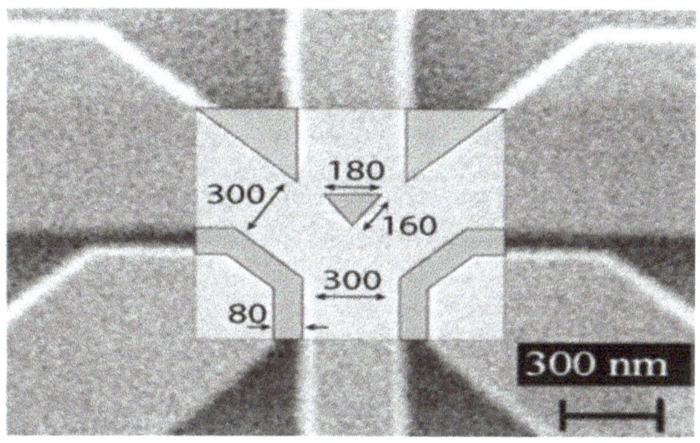

Figure 1. SEM image of BDT with channel width 300nm and trench of 80nm. The design for MC simulations has been drawn directly over, keeping all dimensions identical.

2. MC Simulations

The modeling tool is an ensemble MC simulator of electron dynamics coupled with a 2D Poisson Solver and based on finite differences approach [9]. It was used to simulate the exact replica, except for the access regions, of a real BDT shown on Figure 1. The fitting of the non-linear transfer characteristic of the 300 nm channel width BDT, presented on Figure 2., was possible by allowing the surface charges present at the interface semiconductor-dielectic to self-consistently adapt themselves with the surrounding carrier concentration. This special model improves the depletion mechanism and is able to correctly estimate the carrier concentration as well as the output current (Figure 2.). The only limitation is too let enough time to the model to stabilize. More informations can be found in [10]. MC simulations are also useful to predict the behavior of a smaller device, with a channel of 100 nm width, under the influence of different dielectric. The very high frequency response of the BDT can be studied by looking the time delay occuring when the device changes from one logic state to another. These two logic states are selected where the current's difference is the highest. On Figure 2, the logic high state can be found at V_{LG}=-2 V with a right drain current I_{Dhigh}=13 µA. The transfer characteristic being symmetric, by switching the gate bias from -2 to 2 V, the current will becoming lower with a value I_{Dlow}=5 µA. As said previously, surface charges need time to reach a steady state and to provide the correct behavior of the BDT. Little is know about the speed of increase or decrease of the surface so we are considering two limit or extrem cases. The first one, or model 1. suggests that these charges are following instantaneously the change of gate bias, while the second one, or model 2, implies that they aren't changing at all, remaining with the same value

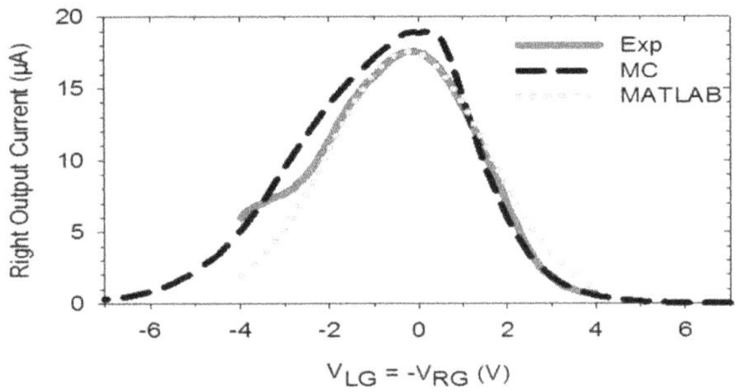

Figure 2. Comparison of experimental, Monte Carlo and MATLAB results of right drain current of BDT with channel width of 300nm.

Figure 3. shows the current history of the right drain with a gate bias switching occuring at 3 ps. For the case of the 300 nm channel BDT, the delay, or transient, last between 2 (Model 1) to 3 ps (Model 2). This would provide a theoretical frequency of operation of about 200 GHz. The peak of current at the transition can be explained by the drain channel being opened for a short period of time, allowing an excess of electrons to pass. Results for a smaller device of 100 nm channel width shows a time delay of less than 1 ps, providing a frequency of operation at 1 THz.

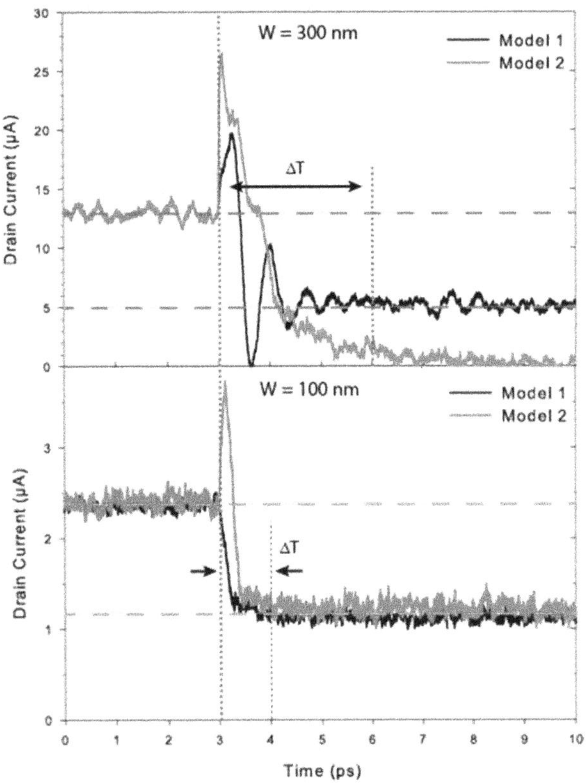

Figure 3. Current level transition between high to low state, for the two MC models and for two devices, 300 and 100 nm channel width

3. BDT Universal Combinational Circuits

Two-BDT logic structure has been used to demonstrate a variety of combinational logic functions [11]. In this structure, the output is the current in the common arms of the two BDTs as shown in Figure 4. Although the first proof of concept is evaluated using Monte Carlo simulations, the cascading logic with this structure has similar limitations as the normal BDTs. In order to obtain differential functionalities and to eliminate extra inverters in the circuits, two-BDT structure has been extended to three-BDT structure [11]. However, this study suggests that the two-BDT structure itself provides complementary outputs, thus eliminating the necessity of three-BDT structure. This study finds some important operating parameters such as gate voltage, output voltage, and power consumption of the circuits developed using two-BDT logic structure. Table 1 and Figure 5 show the logic functions realized using two-BDT nanostructure along with their respective biasing and output voltages.

Generally the logic low and logic high for input, gate and output terminals of logic circuits are of similar values. However, in case of BDTs, logic low and logic high values are different for source, gate and output drain terminals. The output voltage values can be made alike to that of the gate voltage ones using the proper values of the resistors but source voltages will be different when compared to gate and output voltages. This is because, when source voltage is logic low (0 V), the electrons will be pulled up towards top drain terminal and when it acts as logic high (V_{TD}, 650mV), no electrons will be pulled since there is no potential difference between source and drain. However, on other hand, gate voltages are in push-pull configuration and they can never be greater than a certain value (200mV when considered for this logic structure) because BDT will be pinched off for too high gate voltages.

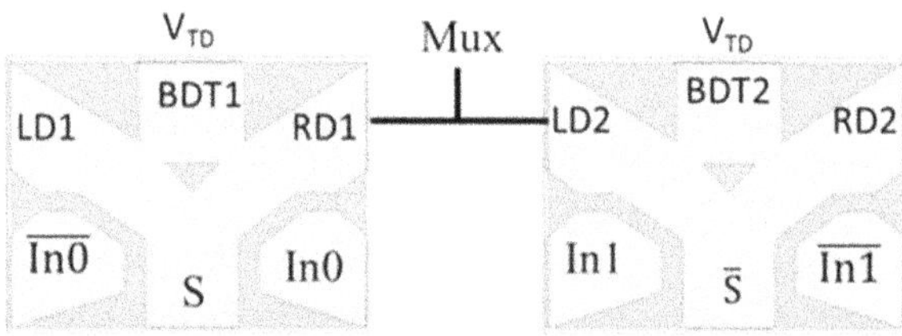

Figure 4. Two-BDT mux structure. The output terminals of two BDTs are shorted and connected as a common output

We studied the behavior of logic functionality of two-BDT logic structure under different biasing conditions. Table 1 indicates the required biasing voltages for different logic functions. '0' indicates logic low state and '1' indicates logic high state.

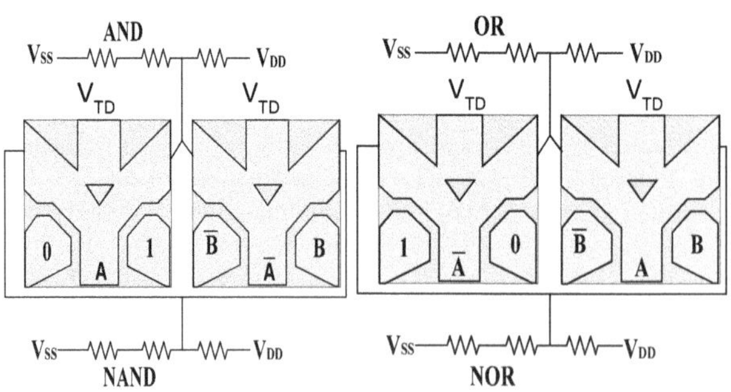

Figure 5. Universal combinational circuits NAND/NOR and their complementary signals AND/OR realized using two-BDT mux structure.

Table. 1 Bias voltage range and Power Consumption of Combinational circuits developed with two-BDT nanostructure

Gate Function	BDT Input signals			Biasing Voltages			Output Voltage Range				Power Consumed (μW)
	In0	In1	S	In0 (mV)	In1 (mV)	S (mV)	F(mV)		$\overline{F}$(mV)		
						'0'----'1'	'0'	'1'	'0'	'1'	
NAND	1	$\overline{B}$	A	225	±225	0---650	-212	+232	-212	+232	7.804
AND	B	0	$\overline{A}$	±225	-225	0---650	-212	+232	-212	+232	7.804
NOR	0	B	A	-225	±225	0---650	-212	+232	-212	+232	7.806
OR	0	$\overline{B}$	$\overline{A}$	-225	±225	0-650	-212	+232	-212	+232	7.806

4. Sequential circuits

A basic latch using BDT on the concept of back-to-back inverters has been presented recently [12]. In this paper we study the DFF developed using the two-BDT logic structure. A level sensitive D latch has been proposed [13]. It comprises of two BDTs namely BDT1 and BDT2. For a positive level-sensitive D latch, *Clk* acts as source of BDT2 and $\overline{Clk}$ as source to BDT1. When *Clk* is high, the *Q* is set to *D* and when *Clk* is low, *Q* will remain in its state by holding is data. Similarly, when $\overline{Clk}$ is connected to source of BDT2 and *Clk* is connected to source of BDT1, the circuit acts a negative level-sensitive D latch.

DFF developed with BDT structure is the combination of two level sensitive D latches as shown in Figure 6 and is similar to conventional silicon CMOS DFF. It uses master-slave approach, which is the most commonly used in ICs to realize FF.

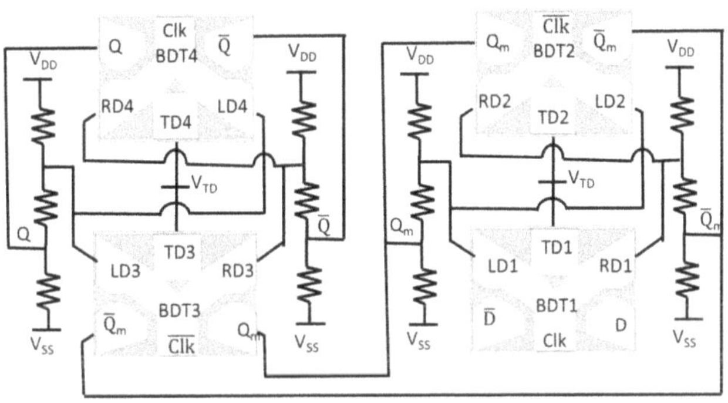

Figure 6. Proposed DFF using Ballistic Deflection Transistors

The DFF constructed acts as an edge triggered register and has two cases of triggering namely positive edge and negative edge triggering. In case of a positive triggered DFF, the negative level-sensitive D latch output Q_m follows the *D* inputs while slave positive level-sensitive D latch holds its previous value when *Clk* is low. When the *Clk* transitions from 0 to 1, the master latch holds its previous value and slave latch follows the master latch value. In case of negative edge triggered FF, the master acts as a positive level-sensitive D latch and the slave is negative level-sensitive D latch. In our study, a positive edge triggered DFF was built in Cadence AMS simulator, which was integrated with analytical model of single BDT.

5. Simulation Results and Discussion

Figure 7 shows the BDT DFF simulation results and are explained as follows: Master latch comprises of BDT1 and BDT2 whereas slave latch is BDT3 and BDT4. *Clk* signal is connected to source terminals of BDT1 and BDT4 whereas $\overline{Clk}$ is connected to BDT2 and BDT3.

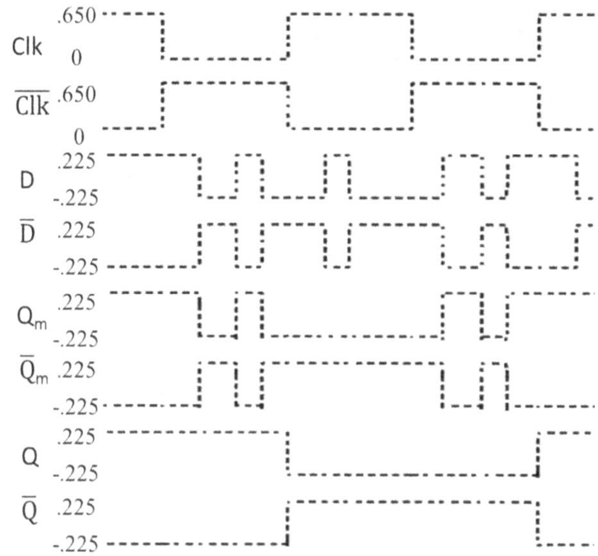

Figure 7. Simulation results of proposed DFF developed using Cadence AMS.

When *Clk* is logic 0 state (0V) and data signal *D* is in logic 0 state (-225mV), the electrons from the source of BDT1 enter into LD1, making Q_m logic 0 with a voltage value of -214mV. As the voltage at the top drain V_{TD} of BDT2 is equal to Vss of BDT2 ($\overline{Clk}$ = 650mV), there will not be flow of electrons in BDT2. Since there is no electron flow into terminals RD1/RD2, the $\overline{Q_m}$ stays in logic 1 state with a voltage value of +232mV. On the other hand, electrons from source terminal of BDT4 will be entering into respective drain terminal whose input gate voltage is high and thus maintaining the same voltage values at *Q* and $\overline{Q}$. Thus when clock signal *Clk* is in logic 0 state (0V), the master latch is accessing the data *D* and slave latch is holding its previous value. When *Clk* goes high and $\overline{Clk}$ goes low, the electrons from the source of BDT2 will be steered into LD2 as $\overline{Q_m}$ and Q_m remain to be in logic 1 and logic 0 states with voltage values of +232mV and -214mV respectively. It has been observed that both Q_m and $\overline{Q_m}$ output values are degraded with change in *Clk* signal but still remained in their previous logic states. However, slave latch will be accessing data in master latch and *Q* and $\overline{Q}$ also achieves logic 0 and logic1 states correspondingly. Thus when *Clk* goes from 0 to 1, slave latch access data from master latch whereas master latch holds its previous value. Hence, the DFF stores *D* value of logic 0 at *Q* when *Clk* goes from 0 to 1. Similarly, it can store logic 1 at output *Q* if data signal *D* is at logic 1 when *Clk* is in transition from 0 to 1, as indicated in simulation results. Therefore, the DFF stores the input *D* value at its output *Q* at a positive edge of the *Clk* signal.

5.1 Delay Estimation

Important delay parameters for proposed DFF with different sizes are estimated using MC simulations and shown in Table 2. Since the *Clk* signals act as source, the proposed DFF has very less Clk-to-Q delay. The D-to-Q delay in the worst case is estimated to 3ps and less than 1ps in DFF developed using BDT of channel width 300nm and 100nm respectively. The setup time will be similar to that of D to Q delay and hold time will be very much less compared to setup time. On the whole, the clock period of the proposed DFF is estimated to be twice the setup time (considering the worst case, T_H + $T_{Clk\text{-}Q}$ equals T_S). Thus, the operating frequencies of proposed DFFs are expected to range from 200GHz to 500GHz depending on size of the BDTs.

$$T_P \geq T_S + T_H + T_{Clk-Q}$$

$$T_P \geq 2 * T_S$$

Where T_P is clock period, T_S is setup time, T_H is hold time, $T_{Clk\text{-}Q}$ is clock to Q delay.

From Figure 3 mentioned in Section 2 of this paper, MC simulations have estimated D-to-Q delay for a 300nm and 100nm sized BDTs. The Clk-to-Q Delay is small compared to D-to-Q delay. The setup time for the proposed DFF would be D-to-Q delay of a single BDT.

Table 2. Timing parameters estimated for proposed D-FF

Delay Parameters	Time	
	BDT_300nm	BDT_100nm
Clk to Q	«1ps	«1ps
D to Q	2ps to 3ps	<1ps
Setup time	2ps to 3ps	<1ps
Hold time	«1ps	«1ps
Clock Period	5ps	< 2ps

6. Conclusion

In conclusion, this paper has presented the modeling of Ballistic Deflection Transistor using analytical model that is integrated with Verilog AMS and used to study the behavior of combinational circuits developed with two-BDT nanostructure under different biasing conditions. MC simulations coupled with a self-consistently adapting surface charge model, are able to reproduce the single BDT experimental results properly, and Terahertz frequency response has been evaluated. A new DFF using logic structure has been proposed. The simulated results, developed using Cadence AMS simulator, have indicated accurate functionality of DFF.

Acknowledgments

This research is supported by NSF ENG grant EECS 1546011.

7. References

[1] Diduck, Q., Margala, M., Feldman, M., 2006. A TeraHertz Transistor Based on Geometrical Deflection of Ballistic Current. *Microwave Symposium Digest IEEE MTT-S International*, pp. 345-347. DOI = http://dx.doi.org/10.1109/MWSYM.2006.249522

[2] Wolpert, D., Irie. H., Sobolweski, R., Ampadu, P., Diduck, Q., and Margala, M. 2009. Ballistic deflection transistors and emerging nanoscale era. *in Proc. ISCAS*, May 27, pp. 61-64. DOI = http://dx.doi.org/10.1109/ISCAS.2009.5117685

[3] Kaushal, V., Yu, Q., Ampadu, P., Guarino, G., and Sobolweski, R, and Margala, M. 2010. A study of Geometry effects on the performance of ballistic deflection transistor. *IEEE Trans. Nanotechnol.*, Vol.9, no. 6, pp. 723 – 733, November. DOI = http://dx.doi.org/10.1109/TNANO.2010.2050069

[4] Kaushal, V., Margala, M., Yu, Q., Ampadu, P., Guarino, G., and Sobolweski, R.2009. Current Transport modeling and experimental study of THz room temperature ballistic deflection transistors, *J. Phs., Conf. ser.*, vol. 193, pp. 012092-1-012092-4. DOI = http://dx.doi.org/10.1088/1742-6596/193/1/012092

[5] Kaushal, V., Diduck, Q., Margala, M. 2009. Study of Leakage Current Mechanisms in ballistic deflection transistors. *Proc. of ACM 19th Great Lakes Symposium on VLSI.* (GLSVLSI 2009). pp 165- 168. DOI = http://dx.doi.org/10.1145/1531542.1531584

[6] Torre, I., Mateos, J., Gonzalez, T., Kaushal, V., and Margala, M. 2013. Ballistic Deflection Transistors : geometry dependence and Boolean operations. *2013 Spanish Conference on Electron Devices (CDE)*, pp. 187 – 190. DOI = http://dx.doi.org/10.1109/CDE.2013.6481374

[7] Wolpert, D., Diduck, Q.,and Ampadu, P.2011. NAND gate Design for Ballistic Deflection Transistors. *IEEE Trans. Nanotechnol.*, Vol. 10, no. 1, pp.150 – 154, Jan.2 DOI = http://dx.doi.org/10.1109/TNANO.2009.2034962

[8] Wolpert, D., Torre, I., Kaushal, V., Margala, M., Ampadu, P., General purpose logic gate using ballistic nanotransistors. *2011 IEEE Conference on Nanotechnology (IEEE-Nano)*, pp. 1171-1176. DOI = http://dx.doi.org/10.1109/NANO.2011.6144451

[9] Mateos. J, Vasallo. B.G., Pardo, D., Gonzalez, T., Galloo, J.S., Roelens, Y., Bollaert, S., and Cappy.A. 2003. Ballistic Nanodevices for TeraHertz data processing : Monte Carlo Simulations. *Nanotechnology*, vol. 14, pp. 117 – 122. DOI = http://dx.doi.org/10.1088/0957-4484/14/2/303.

[10] Millithaler, J.F, Iñiguez-de-la-Torre, I., Mateos, J., Gonzalez T, Margala, M., 2015. Study of surface charges in ballistic deflection transistors. *IOP Nanotechnology*, DOI = http://dx.doi.org/10.1088/0957-4484/26/48/485202.

[11] Torre, I., Purohit, S., Kaushal, V., Margala, M., Gong, M., Sobolweski, R., Wolpert, D., Ampadu, P., Gonzalez, T., and Mateos. J.2011. Exploring Digital Logic Design using Ballistic Deflection Transistors through Monte Carlo simulations. *IEEE Transactions on Nanotechnology*, Vol. 10, No. 6, November. DOI =http://dx.doi.org/10.1109/TNANO.2011.2142321

[12] Marthi, P., Millithaler, J.F, Iñiguez-de-la-Torre, I., Mateos, J., Gonzalez T, Margala, M., 2015, "Exploration of digital latch design using ballistic deflection transistors- modeling and simulation", NMDC 2015.

[13] Marthi, P., Hossain, N., Millithaler, J.F, Margala, M., A New Level Sensitive D Latch using Ballistic Nanodevices, ISCAS, May, 2016.

Exploring Main Memory Design Based on Racetrack Memory Technology

Qingda Hu[1], Guangyu Sun[2], Jiwu Shu[1*], Chao Zhang[2]
[1]Department of Computer Science and Technology, Tsinghua University, Beijing, China
[2]CECA, Peking University, Beijing, China
hqd13@mails.tsinghua.edu.cn, gsun@pku.edu.cn,
shujw@tsinghua.edu.cn, zhang.chao@pku.edu.cn

ABSTRACT

Emerging non-volatile memories (NVMs), which include PCRAM and STT-RAM, have been proposed to replace DRAM, mainly because they have better scalability and lower standby power. However, previous research has demonstrated that these NVMs cannot completely replace DRAM due to either lifetime/performance (PCRAM) or density (STT-RAM) issues. Recently, a new type of emerging NVM, called Racetrack Memory (RM), has attracted more and more attention of memory researchers because it has ultra-high density and fast access speed without the write cycle issue. However, there lacks research on how to leverage RM for main memory. To this end, we explore main memory design based on RM technology in both circuit and architecture levels. In the circuit level, we propose the structure of the RM based main memory and investigate different design parameters. In the architecture level, we design a simple and efficient shift-sense address mapping policy to reduce 95% shift operations for performance improvement and power saving. At the same time, we analyze the efficiency of existing optimization strategies for NVM main memory. Our experiments show that RM can outperform DRAM for main memory, in respect of density, performance, and energy efficiency.

Keywords

Main Memory; Racetrack; Shifts; Performance; Energy

1. INTRODUCTION

As we move into the era of Big Data, various modern applications (i.e. in-memory computing/database) keep increasing demand for larger memory capacity and better memory performance. However, due to the fact that the progress of DRAM technology is slower than that of CMOS process technology, the gap between on-chip computing logic and off-chip memory subsystem keeps increasing. In addition, the high static power consumption of DRAM further obstacles the development of main memory. Thus, memory researchers have been seeking for alternatives of DRAM for future main memory design [8, 9, 10, 16, 25].

*Jiwu Shu is the corresponding author.

GLSVLSI '16, May 18 - 20, 2016, Boston, MA, USA

ISBN 978-1-4503-4274-2/16/05... $15.00
DOI: http://dx.doi.org/10.1145/2902961.2902967

Several emerging non-volatile memory technologies (NVMs) have been extensively investigated for future main memory design. These NVMs include Phase Change Memory (PCRAM), Spin-Transfer Torque RAM (STT-RAM), etc. Prior research has been proposed to improve performance, energy saving, and reliability of these NVMs for main memory [8, 9, 10, 16, 25]. However, it is still difficult to completely replace DRAM with these NVMs due to their own limitations. For example, STT-RAM can achieve better performance than DRAM. But, its storage density is several times smaller than that of DRAM [9]. Similarly, though MLC PCRAM can provide potential higher storage density and lower leakage power consumption, its limited lifetime and poor write performance become major obstacles [8]. Thus, these NVMs are preferred being combined with DRAM for hybrid main memory design as a compromise.

Recently, a new type of non-volatile memory called Racetrack Memory (RM) has attracted more and more attention. Through integrating multiple bits in a tape-like nanowire, RM can provide ultra-high storage density, SRAM-comparable access speed and high write endurance [5, 12, 17, 18, 19, 20, 22, 24]. Previous works focus on using RM as a replacement of SRAM for on-chip memory design, such as cache and registers. There still lacks research on how to leverage RM for main memory. In fact, there exists a difference between on-chip memory and main memory in the design parameters, organization and optimizing strategies. Simply replacing DRAM cells with RMs may result in an inefficient solution.

In this paper, we review the RM based main memory designs in different layers and explore the potential of using RM to completely replace DRAM in main memory. First, we propose the RM based main memory architecture and study design configurations of implementing RM in the chip level, to exploit trade-off among area, performance, and energy. Second, in the architecture level, we design a simple shift-sense address mapping to reduce 95% shift operations to achieve a great performance improvement and energy saving. Third, we analyze the efficiency of applying existing optimization techniques for NVM main memory on RM based design. Our experiments indicate that it is feasible to replace DRAM with RM for improvement of main memory, in respect of storage density, performance, and energy saving.

2. RACETRACK MEMORY

Racetrack memory (RM) is a new generation of spintronic-technology based memory [5, 12, 17, 18, 19, 20, 22, 24]. As shown in Figure 1(a)(i), one RM cell mainly includes a tape-like ferromagnetic wire for data storage, and access ports for data read/write operations. Multiple domains are stored in the wire to share a smaller set of access ports. Each domain can independently store one bit according to its magnetization direction. Thus, RM can achieve ultra-high

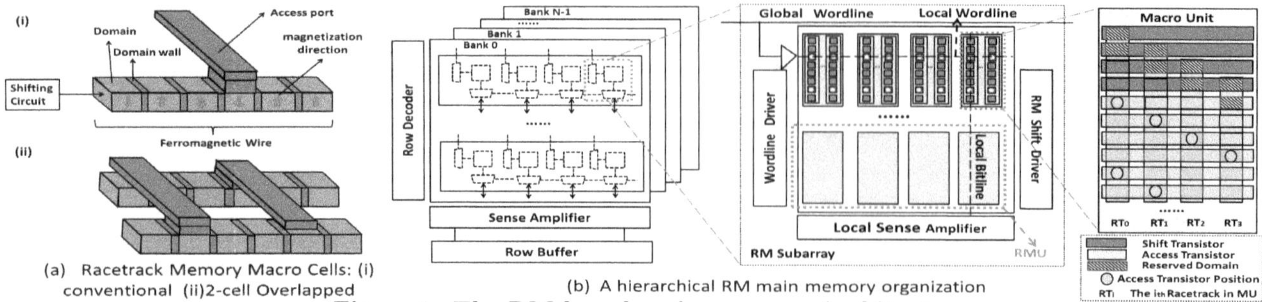

(a) Racetrack Memory Macro Cells: (i) conventional (ii)2-cell Overlapped

(b) A hierarchical RM main memory organization

Figure 1: The RM based main memory Architecture

storage density. Because a single domain and an access port form a MTJ (Magnetic Tunnel Junctions) structure similar to that in a STT-RAM cell, it can achieve fast operation speed and low energy consumption like STT-RAM.

RM typically has three basic operations. Read operations are performed by measuring the magneto-resistance of the bit through access ports. Write operations are completed by issuing a large current to change magnetization direction via access ports. Because multiple domains share several ports, the desired bit is required to be aligned with the port before being accessed. Shift operations are implemented by driving a spin-polarized current pulse via shifting circuit through the entire ferromagnetic wire, to shift domains in lock step.

Because a racetrack is longer and narrower compared to an access transistor, it is more area-efficient to overlap RM cells to improve storage density. Figure 1(a)(i) shows that the unused space of one conventional RM cell is dominating. Figure 1(a)(ii) shows that two transistors are stacked on the top of two racetracks, which can reduce the blank space to improve area efficiency. Thus, prior works [18, 20, 24] propose such an organization with overlapped RM cells, called Macro Unit (MU), as a basic building block for RM array.

The layout of MU is determined by three parameters: the number of racetracks in a MU (N_R), the number of bits (domains) in each racetrack (N_B), and the number of access ports in a MU (N_P). As the sample MU shown in Figure 1(a)(ii), N_R=2, N_B=6 and N_P=2. Without increasing the layout area, they are limited by some factors: (1) The maximum N_B is determined by the length of racetrack and domain, (2) The maximum N_R is limited by the width of transistor and racetrack. (3) The maximum N_P is determined by the length of racetrack and transistor. For a detailed introduction to MU, we refer the reader to [24]. In Section 4, we will study how to make choice of MU.

3. THE RM MAIN MEMORY DESIGN

In this section, we propose the RM based main memory architecture with its basic operations and timing restrictions, which differs from traditional DRAM design in the following respects. (1) Its basic building blocks are MUs, (2) varying latency and energy consumption induced by shift operations.

3.1 Main Memory Architecture

A single rank of main memory consists of multiple memory chips, which typically has 4, 8 or 16 data output pins [6, 15, 21]. As shown in Figure 1(b), a RM based chip consists of multiple banks. We use the decoupled sense amplifier and row buffer structure like in prior work [10], which supports multiplexed sense amplifiers, has greater flexibility for row buffer organization. Thus, the data is copied to the row buffer once it is sensed by sense amplifiers.

In order to reduce high latency for driving long bitlines /wordlines and keeping reliable sensing [3, 10], a RM bank is typically divided into a two-dimensional array of subarrays. Each subarray typically includes (1) an array of MUs organized as rows and columns, (2) wordline drivers to strength global wordline signals on the local wordlines, (3) local sense-amplifiers to sense low perturbation from local bitlines and amplify it on the global bitlines, (4) a unique RM shift driver to shift the desired rows to align with access ports.

MUs are the basic building blocks of RM array. The additional domains are reserved on the both ends of MUs to avoid data loss when shifting. Each row of data is stored in a bit-interleaved fashion over a row of MUs [22]. We abstract such a "Row of MUs" as a RMU. When a request arrives, the row decoder selects the RMU which contains the desired row, and shifts the row to align with access ports.

3.2 Basic Operations and Timing Restrictions

The RM based main memory typically has following fundamental operations and timing restrictions.

- Shift operations (ST) shift the desired row to align with access ports before activate operations.
- Activate operations (ACT) sense and latch the desired data into the row buffer.
- Read (RD) and write (WR) operations are issued by reading data from or writing data to the row buffer in a block granularity. The separate sense amplifier and buffer structure enables write-back operations (WB) [9]: the data is written solely on the row buffer, and flushed to the array only when a buffer conflict occurs and the content is dirty.
- Precharge (PRE) operations disconnect the activated row with the bitlines to prepare for another activation row.

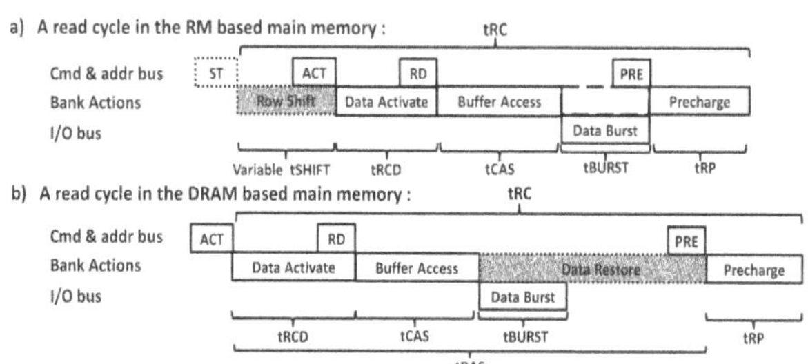

Figure 2: A read cycle of main memory

Using a read cycle as an example, as shown in Figure 2, the RM based main memory differs from DRAM in the following respects. (1) Before activates, if the desired row is not aligned with access ports, the memory controller sends ST operations to the corresponding bank. The time period that it takes to do shift operations is labelled as tSHIFT, which is variable because it is proportional to shift distance. (2) Since DRAM uses charge-based capacitor to store data, its read operations are destructive so that data must be restored back to arrays during each read cycle. The data restoration time (tRAS) is always high [15]. On the contrary, a read cycle of RM is not required to be restored to arrays because it is not read destructive. (3) DRAM must periodically do refresh operations to avoid data lost.

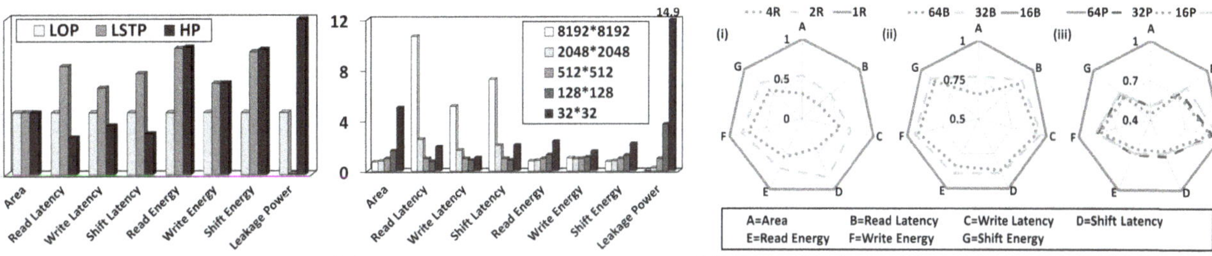

(a) The impact of device type (normalized to the LOP devices) (b) The impact of sub-array size (normalized to 512*512) (c) Effect on the area, latency and power induced by MU parameters: (i) N_R, (ii) N_B and (iii) N_P

Figure 3: The Chip-level exploration of RM

4. CHIP LEVEL EXPLORATION

In this section, we address several important configurations in the RM based chip design. In addition, we provide a comparison of RM with other NVMs in the chip level.

4.1 Chip Design Exploration of RM

The previous literature [24] extends a circuit-level simulator - NVSim [3] to develop a RM modeling model, which provides area, performance and power estimation of racetrack memory. In this work, according to Microns data sheet [14], we carefully extend this model to simulate a 128MB RM memory chip with eight banks, eight data output pins, and 256B row buffer in 45nm technology. Typical RM device-level parameters (include physical parameters of single racetrack and peripheral circuit) in this paper are similar to the previous work [24]. We select 45nm technology node because it is the most advanced one we can obtain. We believe that the similar trend is kept for other technology nodes.

4.1.1 Device Type

NVSim supports three types of devices defined by ITRS [3, 25]: low standby power (LSTP), low operating power (LOP) and high performance (HP). These devices have a significant impact on the design target because they are used in the both global support and peripheral circuitry. As shown in Figure 3(a), The HP devices are designed for the fastest access speed but they have highest dynamic/leakage power. The LOP devices are designed for the lowest dynamic power and their performance are between LSTP and HP devices. The LSTP devices are designed for lowest leakage power but they have lowest speed and higher dynamic power. Fortunately, all peripheral circuitry in the RM main memory can be powered down without losing any stored data when it is idle, because RM has non-volatility characteristics. Thus, we use the LOP devices to achieve a best energy delay product.

4.1.2 Sub-Array Size

The subarray size is a critical parameter for memory chip design. We study the subarray size from 32*32 to 8192*8192. As shown in Figure 3(b), smaller subarrays are designed for latency-optimized target because they decrease bitline (BL) and wordline (WL) latency. However, they result in more complex global interconnects for more sophisticated H-tree organization, increasing energy consumption of the H-tree. Moreover, when the size is further decreased below 32*32, the extra latency caused by more complex H-tree has offset reduction from shorter BL/WL. On the contrary, larger subarrays are designed for area-optimized target as they significantly amortize the peripheral circuitry area. However, they bring higher latency caused by longer BL/WL. Thus, the subarray size should neither be too small or too large.

4.1.3 Macro Unit

As shown in Figure 3(c), we analyze the effect on the area, latency and power induced by MU parameters. We find that increasing N_R and N_B can improve the efficiency of the layout significantly, which gets a lower latency and energy consumption due to its smaller layout. Thus, we use the maximal N_R and N_B to perform further analysis in the rest of this paper. Each macro cell has four racetrack stripes, and each racetrack has 64 data bits [18, 24].

Figure 3(c)(iii) shows the effect of increasing N_P. Considering the length of racetrack, transistor, and the gap distance between two transistor, when N_P is large (> 16), the area increases with the increasing number of ports, dominated by the transistor size, bringing higher latency and power. However, when N_P is small (< 16), the area decreases with the increasing number of ports, because overhead bits reserved on the both ends of MUs decrease greatly. When $N_P = 16$, it is more area efficient to overlap multiple RM stripes as a MU structure. Thus, we use 16 access ports per MU to reduce shifts without increasing latency/power/area significantly. In Section 5, we will provide the sensitivity of the number of shift operations to N_P in the system level.

4.2 Comparison of RM Characteristics with Other Memory Technologies

We compare the characteristics of a RM based memory chip with other memory technologies, including DRAM, PCM and STTRAM. Their device-level parameters come from previous works [3, 21] and are also simulated by modified NVSim. Because DRAM has high leakage power, we use commodity DRAM and LSTP peripheral devices to obtain a best energy-delay product like in related literature [21, 25].

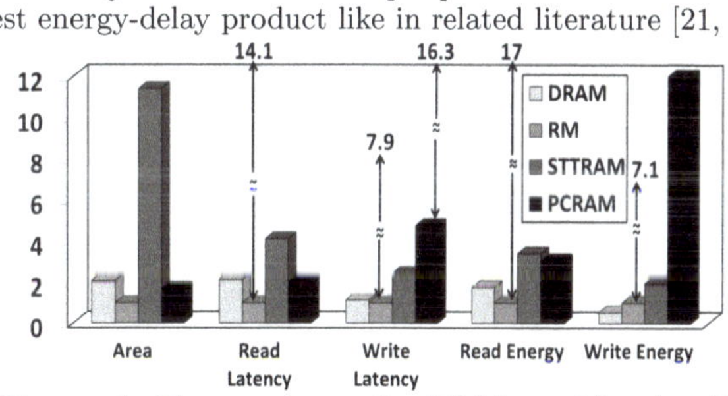

Figure 4: Comparison of a RM based bank with other memory technologies

Figure 4 shows that RM has 2.1X storage density compared with DRAM, which means that a RM chip can store two times capacity than DRAM with the same area size. Also, RM has the lowest read/write latency and read energy due to its smallest layout area. However, due to the effect of variable shifts, the shift plus read latency/energy is 14.1/17 times higher than the baseline read and the shift plus write latency/energy is 7.9/7.1 times higher than the baseline write in the worst case. So optimization for shifts reduction is needed.

5. ARCHITECTURE LEVEL EXPLORATION

In this section, we first propose a simple address mapping technique for shift intensity reduction. Then, we evaluate several existing optimization methods for other NVMs to study their efficiency for the RM based main memory.

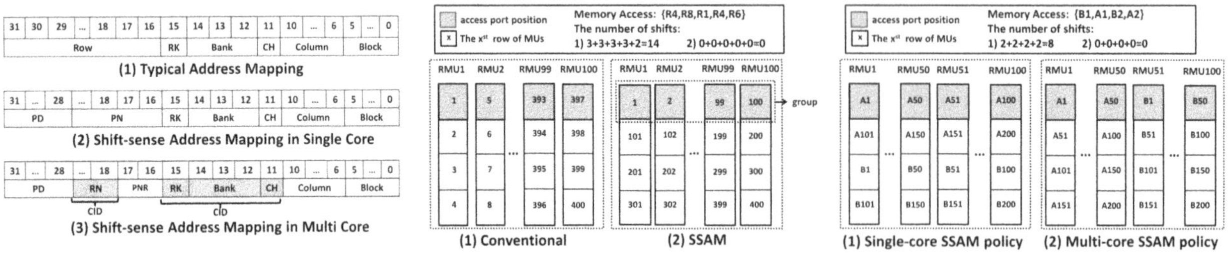

(a) Memory Address Mappings (Example system in figure has 2 Channels, 2 Ranks per Channel, 8 Banks and 64B Cache-lines)

(b) One example showing the advantage of replacing the conventional address mapping policy with SSAM in single-core

(c) One example showing the advantage of replacing Single-core SSAM policy with Multi-core SSAM policy in multi-core

Figure 5: Shift-sense Address Mapping in Single-core and Multi-Core

5.1 Experimental Setup

We modify the main memory simulator - NVMain [15] to simulate the basic operations and timing restrictions, and integrate it into gem5 [1] as our simulation platform. Table I shows our major processor and memory parameters. We use the methodology from NVMain to estimate the overall energy consumption via calculating the occurrences of different memory operations. For RM and other NVMs, the timing and energy parameters are output from the extended NVSim. For DRAM, they are obtained from Micron data sheet [14]. Note that although RM can provide higher capacity with the same area constraint, the workloads used in this work with limited memory usage cannot leverage this advantage. Thus, we just use the same capacity for different technologies to simplify the following discussion.

Table 1: Major processor and memory parameters

Processor	4 single Alpha cores, out-of-order, 3GHz,
L1 Caches	32KB I-cache, 32KB D-cache, 4-way, 2-cycle latency
L2 Caches	4MB, 8-way, 10-cycle latency 64B-lines
Memory	DDR3-1600, 4GB, 64bit I/O, FR-FCFS, 8 banks(x8) 1/2 channels(@1-core/4-core), 1/2 ranks per channel(@1-core/4-core)
DRAM	Memory Timing and Energy Parameters from [14]
RM Latency	Read: 5ns Write: 9.3ns Shift: 4.3ns
RM Energy	Read: 10.6nJ Write: 28nJ Shift: 11.3nJ (2KB row)

We use a representative subset of benchmarks from the SPEC CPU2006 suite [4], STREAM [13] and SPLASH [23]. Specific benchmarks in each benchmark suite are selected for their memory intensity. We also randomly choose from these benchmarks to form 10 multiprogrammed workloads, which has four applications and each of which is bound to one processing core. We execute all target benchmarks for five billion instructions to cover enough large working set.

5.2 Shift-Sense Address Mapping

Address mapping has a significant impact on the memory system behavior. As shown in Figure 5(a), conventional memory systems normally use a typical open-page address mapping policy [6, 7, 11, 15], mapping all adjacent columns of the same row to a sequential region, which maximizes the spatial locality to minimize activates. Also, it interleaves memory address among ranks and banks in the granularity of the row size to pipeline memory requests.

However, the conventional mapping treats every row activation equally without considering the shift issue, which distributes all adjacent rows continuously over all RMUs. As shown in Figure 5(b), 400 rows are distributed sequentially from the first RMU to the last RMU (assuming one bank has 100 RMUs and each RMU has one racetrack, four bits, one port to simplify discussion). However, this mapping may result in frequent shifts among a much small set of RMUs, because memory access always has high spatial locality. Figure 5(b) illustrates an example that one application generates an access sequence {R4,R8,R1,R4,R6}. These requests are mapped to only two RMUs, leading to high frequent shift operations (the total shifts is 14). In consideration of large storage capacity of main memory and strong spatial locality of memory access, we propose the Shift-Sense Address Mapping (SSAM) policy to reduce shifts significantly.

Single Core. We first explain How SSAM works in the single core scenario. SSAM divides row address bits (bit16-bit31) into two parts: PD and PN (Figure 5(a)). PD (Port Distance) indicates the gap distance between the row and its access port. PN (Port Number) indicates the serial number of the port. More specifically, assuming that every x bits share one port, SSAM divides all rows into x groups based on PD, and distributes adjacent row address to the same group. If the entire space of one group is used up, SSAM allocates subsequent rows to the next group.

SSAM reduces shift intensity greatly mainly because of two reasons. (1) Intra-group. Assuming that the capacity of main memory is 2GB and every 16 rows share one wordline, each group is as large as 128MB (2GB/16) to reduce frequent shifts caused by spatial locality of several small regions. (2) Inter-group. Because latency and energy of shift operations are proportional to shift distance, decreasing distance can improve performance and energy. SSAM reduces distance of most shifts to nearly one, because the difference between two adjacent row address in the same RMU is larger (128MB).

Multi Core. When multiple threads share the same DRAM devices, the single-core SSAM policy may produce inter-thread interference, because memory address of all threads is mapped evenly across all RMUs. As shown in Figure 5(c), when adopting single-core SSAM policy, two threads A and B may be mapped to the same RMUs simultaneously. When they generate an access sequence {B1, A1, B2, A2}, they will conflict with each other, increasing the amount of extra shifts. The probability of the inter-core interference grows with the number of cores. When different cores are not mapped to the same RMUs, this type of interference cannot happen. Thus, we further divide the PN bits into RN and PNR (Figure 5(a)). RN (RMU Number) indicates the serial number of the RMU. PNR (Port Number in RMU) indicates the serial number of the access port within the RMU. The multi-core SSAM policy utilizes RMU partitioning to map different cores to different RMUs, via dividing bit11-bit15 and bit18-bit27, labelled as CID (Color ID). As shown in Figure 5(c), core A and core B are allocated to disjoint RMUs to avoid interference.

Implementation. The operating system can use a buddy system to manage physical pages, and form a hierarchy lists of free pages based on different orders and different colors (based on CIDs), like page-coloring technique used in [7, 11], which allocates different CIDs to specific applications depending on the application's need for memory capacity, can be designed to allocate a sequential region as much as possible. Thus, for single-core SSAM, it can be designed

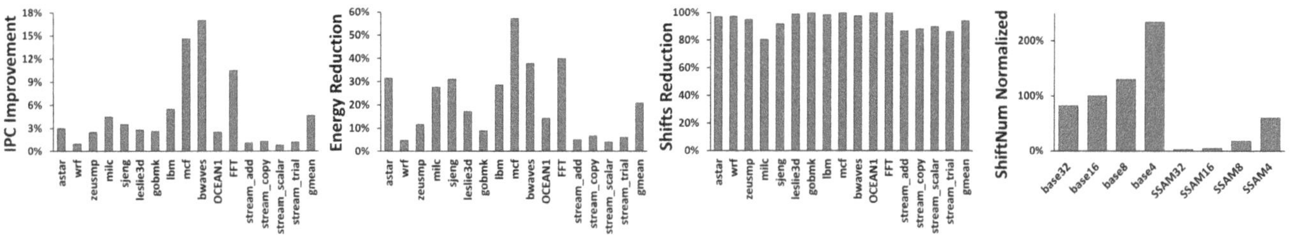

(a) IPC improvement over baseline after using SSAM (b) Energy reduction over baseline after using SSAM (c) Shift intensity reduction over baseline after using SSAM (d) Effect of access ports per MU on SSAM (normalized to base16)

Figure 6: The IPC improvement, energy reduction and shifts reduction when adopting SSAM in single-core

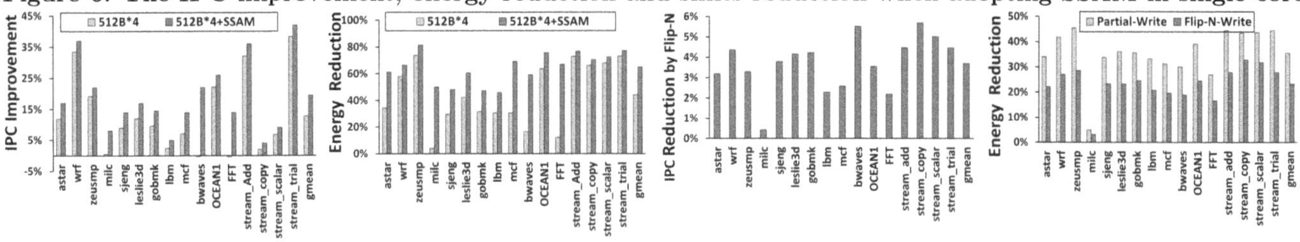

(a) IPC improvement over baseline after using 512B*4 and 512B*4-SSAM (b) Energy consumption reduction over baseline after using 512B*4 and 512B*4-SSAM (c) IPC degradation over baseline after using Flip-N-Write (d) Energy consumption reduction over baseline after using Flip-N-Write and Partial-Write

Figure 7: Comparison of energy and performance across different existing methods

as a static physical address mapping, which can be implemented in the memory controller or inside RM chips, does not change the existing memory interface, has negligible implementation overhead. For multi-core SSAM, RMU partitioning can be entirely managed via the virtual to physical address mapping of the OS. However, in this paper, we adopt a static partition scheme to allocate an equal number of CID to each core, because it does not need profiling of workloads and we find that it is robust to dynamic workload changes. The strategy of dynamically assigning CIDs to cores can be further explored, but is beyond the scope of this paper.

Results. For single-core, Figure 6 shows that SSAM significantly reduces energy consumption by 21% and improves IPC by 5% over the conventional address mapping (baseline) on average. The reason is that SSAM greatly reduces shifts by 95% (Figure 6(c)). For multi-core, as the resource competition becomes more severe, the multi-core experiments in Figure 8(c) shows that SSAM reduces running time by 18% and energy by 50% compared to the baseline. As shown in Figure 6(d), we also evaluate the sensitivity to the number of shared ports per MU. When adopting the traditional policy, shift operations grow significantly with decreasing ports. When using SSAM, shift operations can still be reduced greatly even using less ports. Note that shifts can be reduced more via SSAM if considering that the RM-based main memory has higher storage density.

Comparison with the existing methods. Numerous works [17, 20, 22] propose to address the shift problem. However, these works need complex control logic and large hardware cost, industrial venders of main memory may have some hesitation in adopting them. In contrast, SSAM reduces shifts with simple control logic and negligible hardware cost. In addition, [19] adjusts the associativity of RM cache to reduce shifts. [12] uses the warp register remapping to place registers around ports to decrease the max shift distance. However, they are designed for targeted on-chip cache or GPU registers, do not consider different characteristics of main memory, such as much greater capacity and stronger spatial locality. SSAM not only uses large capacity of each group to reduce the average shift distance (inter-group), but also to reduce frequent shifts induced by strong spatial locality of several small regions (intra-group). Moreover, SSAM reduces shifts in both single-core and multi-core scenarios.

5.3 Efficiency of Existing Strategies

There exists a lot of prior works about the NVM main memory. They have proposed some novel methods to reduce energy and performance degradation. However, because relatively symmetric read/write operations of the RM based memory are faster than PCRAM/STTRAM, and RM has a unique shift operation, the existing methods may be not appropriate for it. Thus, we analyze the efficiency of the existing popular methods on the RM based main memory.

5.3.1 *Performance Optimization*

Prior work [10] proposes the separate sense amplifier and buffer structure to enable the multiplexing of sense amplifiers. Then, it utilizes the saving area to replace a single conventional row buffer with multiple narrower buffers. Narrower buffer can reduce dynamic read/write energy, and multiple buffers can mitigate performance and energy penalties caused by row buffer miss. However, its benefits may be reduced on the RM based main memory for two reasons: (1) Multiple buffers may bring extra shifts. For example, if $(i+1)_{th}$ buffer is required to activate one row, the system shifts access ports with the desired row. But when i_{th} buffer needs to be written back to array, the system may need to shift ports back. (2) Reads and writes of RM are faster, which may decrease the benefits from multiple row buffers.

We replace a single row buffer with four 512B buffer as in Ref.[10]. As shown in Figure 7(a)(b), we find that the buffer organization can still improve IPC by 13% and reduce energy consumption by 44% on average. But we also observe that its benefits for the RM based main memory is smaller than being used in PCRAM/STTRAM. In addition, the combination of the buffer organization and SSAM can greatly reduce shift operations, improves IPC by 20% and reduces energy by 65%, because we find that the buffer organization without SSAM brings 29% extra shifts on average.

5.3.2 *Write Energy Reduction*

Because writes are much slower and consume much more energy than reads for PCRAM and STT-RAM, prior work has proposed various read-modify write based techniques to reduce write energy, such as the representative work Flip-N-Write (FNW) [2]. Before each write, FNW reads the original row of data to make a bit-by-bit comparison, and decides whether to flip or not. FNW aligns each block with a single

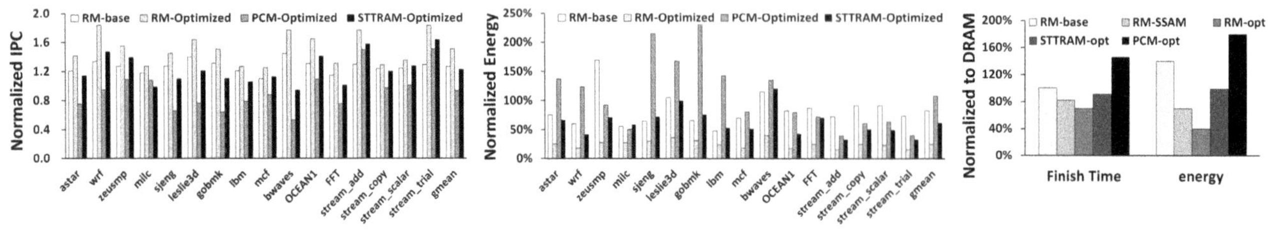

(a) The IPC normalized to DRAM in single-core (b) The Energy normalized to DRAM in single-core (c) Finish time, Energy normalized to DRAM in multi-core

Figure 8: Comparison of energy and performance across different memory technologies

bit to indicate whether the data was flipped or not. Therefore, FNW can reduce write bits of dirty blocks by half to save write energy. However, FNW brings severe read latency and energy in the RM based main memory, because both read and write operations of RM are much faster and consume relatively close energy. Thus, we compare FNW with Partial Write (PW) [9, 10]. PW assigns each block with a dirty bit and tracks dirty data from cache to main memory, which aims to write only dirty blocks back to array. Note that PW does not affect system performance.

We consider both PW and FNW at a cache line granularity. Although FNW can reduce more write energy, Figure 7(d) shows that PW reduces more total energy compared than FNW (36% to 23%), because FNW results in extra read energy consumption. In addition, Figure 7(c) shows that FNW reduces IPC by 4% due to the latency of extra read operations.

6. SYSTEM-LEVEL COMPARISON

In this section, we compare the baseline RM main memory (RM-base), the RM main memory with all optimization options (SSAM, PW and buffers organization) (RM-Optimized) with other memory technologies: the DRAM main memory, the PCRAM main memory with all the same optimization options (PCM-Optimized) and the STTRAM main memory with all the same options (STTRAM-Optimized).

In single-core comparison, Figure 8(a)(b) shows that RM-Optimized achieves best performance and lowest energy consumption over all other memory technologies. Compared to DRAM, RM-Optimized improves system IPC by 49% and reduces energy consumption by 75% on average.

In multi-core comparison, Figure 8(c) shows that RM-Optimized also provides significantly best performance and lowest energy consumption over all other technologies. Compared to DRAM, RM-Optimized design reduces the execution time by 31% and reduces energy consumption by 59%.

7. CONCLUSION

RM has potential to replace DRAM for future main memory design. In this work, we provide a holistic research on this topic by investigating some important design factors and issues in the RM based memory. In the chip layer, we explore the design choices to exploit trade-off among area, performance, and energy. In the architecture layer, we design a new shift-sense address mapping policy to reduce 95% shifts. Moreover, we analyze and study the efficiency of applying existing optimization techniques for NVM main memory on RM based design. Our experiments indicate that the optimized RM based main memory can improve IPC by 49% and reduce energy consumption by 75% compared to DRAM.

8. ACKNOWLEDGMENTS

We would like to thank the anonymous GLSVLSI reviewers for their comments that helped improve this paper. This work is supported by the National Natural Science Foundation of China (Grant No.61232003, 61433008), the Beijing Municipal Science and Technology Commission of China (Grant No.D151100000815003), the National High Technology Research and Development Program of China (Grant No.2013AA013201).

9. REFERENCES

[1] N. Binkert et al. The gem5 simulator. *ACM SIGARCH Computer Architecture News*, 39(2), 2011.
[2] S. Cho and H. Lee. Flip-n-write: a simple deterministic technique to improve pram write performance, energy and endurance. In *MICRO*, 2009.
[3] X. Dong et al. Nvsim: A circuit-level performance, energy, and area model for emerging nonvolatile memory. *IEEE Transactions on Computer-Aided Design of Integrated Circuits and Systems*, 31(7), 2012.
[4] J. L. Henning. Spec cpu2006 benchmark descriptions. *ACM SIGARCH Computer Architecture News*, 34(4), 2006.
[5] A. Iyengar and S. Ghosh. Modeling and analysis of domain wall dynamics for robust and low-power embedded memory. In *DAC*, 2014.
[6] B. Jacob et al. *Memory systems: cache, DRAM, disk*. Morgan Kaufmann, 2010.
[7] M. K. Jeong et al. Balancing dram locality and parallelism in shared memory cmp systems. In *HPCA*, 2012.
[8] M. Joshi and T. Li. Mercury: A fast and energy-efficient multi-level cell based phase change memory system. In *HPCA*, 2011.
[9] E. Kultursay et al. Evaluating stt-ram as an energy-efficient main memory alternative. In *ISPASS*, 2013.
[10] B. C. Lee et al. Architecting phase change memory as a scalable dram alternative. In *ISCA*, 2009.
[11] L. Liu et al. A software memory partition approach for eliminating bank-level interference in multicore systems. In *PACT*, 2012.
[12] M. Mao et al. Exploration of gpgpu register file architecture using domain-wall-shift-write based racetrack memory. In *DAC*, 2014.
[13] J. McCalpin. Stream benchmark. *www.cs.virginia.edu/stream/ref.html*, 1995.
[14] Micron. *8Gb: x4, x8, x16 DDR3L SDRAM Description*. www.micron.com, 2015.
[15] M. Poremba and Y. Xie. Nvmain: An architectural-level main memory simulator for emerging non-volatile memories. In *ISVLSI*, 2012.
[16] M. K. Qureshi et al. Scalable high performance main memory system using phase-change memory technology. *ISCA*, 2009.
[17] A. Ranjan et al. Dyrectape: a dynamically reconfigurable cache using domain wall memory tapes. In *DATE*, 2015.
[18] G. Sun et al. From device to system: cross-layer design exploration of racetrack memory. In *DATE*, 2015.
[19] Z. Sun et al. Design exploration of racetrack lower-level caches. In *ISLPED*, 2014.
[20] Z. Sun and H. Li. Cross-layer racetrack memory design for ultra high density and low power consumption. In *DAC*, 2013.
[21] S. Thoziyoor et al. A comprehensive memory modeling tool and its application to the design and analysis of future memory hierarchies. In *ISCA*, 2008.
[22] R. Venkatesan et al. Stag: Spintronic-tape architecture for gpgpu cache hierarchies. In *ISCA*, 2014.
[23] S. C. Woo et al. The splash-2 programs: Characterization and methodological considerations. In *ACM SIGARCH Computer Architecture News*, volume 23, 1995.
[24] C. Zhang et al. Quantitative modeling of racetrack memory, a tradeoff among area, performance, and power. In *ASP-DAC*, 2015.
[25] P. Zhou et al. A durable and energy efficient main memory using phase change memory technology. In *ISCA*, 2009.

An Offline Frequent Value Encoding for Energy-Efficient MLC/TLC Non-volatile Memories

Ali Alsuwaiyan Kartik Mohanram
Department of Electrical and Computer Engineering, University of Pittsburgh, Pittsburgh
asa78@pitt.edu kartik.mohanram@gmail.com

ABSTRACT

This paper describes a low overhead, offline frequent value encoding (FVE) solution to reduce the write energy in multi-level/triple-level cell (MLC/TLC) non-volatile memories (NVMs). The proposed solution, which does not require any runtime software support, clusters a set of general-purpose applications according to their data frequency profiles and generates a dedicated offline FVE that minimizes write energy for each cluster. Results show that the write energy reduction of evaluation sets—using FVEs generated for training sets—are close (equal) to the best known solution for MLC (TLC) NVM encoding; however, our solution incurs a memory overhead that is 16× (5.7×) less than the best comparable scheme in the literature for MLC (TLC) NVMs.

Categories and Subject Descriptors: B.3.2 [Hardware]: Primary Memory
Keywords: Non-volatile Memories, Encoding, Energy

1. Introduction

It is acknowledged that DRAM scalability will slow beyond the 22nm feature size due to its considerable static and dynamic power requirements [1]. Non-volatile memory (NVM) technologies, such as phase change memory (PCM) [2] and resistive RAM (RRAM) [3], are being actively investigated to replace DRAM. Such technologies are highly scalable, have extended data retention times, and consume negligible static power. NVM technologies, however, have their own limitations, e.g., higher write energy, higher write latency, and limited endurance in comparison to DRAM [2,4,5].

Data encoding solutions (e.g., [6–8]) explicitly reduce write energy in NVM technologies. They also implicitly improve NVM endurance [9], and (in some cases) improve access latency [10]. Frequent value encoding (FVE) was originally introduced to encode data and address buses [11–13]. FVE can achieve high reductions in NVM write energy by mapping frequent values (words) into low energy codewords. Recently, FVE has been proposed to encode single-level cell (SLC) memory words in PCM [14]. The authors investigated both static (offline) and dynamic (online) encoding. They report that although offline encoding (originally introduced as "find-once for a given program" in [11]) achieves higher energy reductions on average, it requires compiler and operating system support, which is not desirable in practice. In contrast, online encoding may be better, but it requires a non-trivial online profiling effort that may impact system performance. However, to the best of our knowledge, FVE has not been applied to MLC/TLC NVMs, where a single physical cell can store more than one logical bit to realize density and cost advantages [15,16]. Since MLC/TLC NVMs have higher write energy and access latency as well as lower endurance in comparison to SLC NVMs, there is strong motivation to develop data encoding and wear-leveling techniques for MLC/TLC NVMs [9,10,17–19].

In this paper, we present an offline FVE for MLC/TLC NVMs that achieves an average write energy reduction approaching, and sometimes exceeding, that of optimal offline encoding [11]. The proposed method, which does not require compiler or operating system support, is based on finding multiple optimal FVEs. Each FVE is derived by aggregating the data frequency profiles of a group of compatible applications. To the best of our knowledge, this is the first work that presents a feasible version of an offline FVE approaching the average energy reductions of optimal offline FVE. This work makes the following contributions:

- It describes the use of k-medoids algorithm [20] to cluster a set of general-purpose benchmark applications (SPEC CPU2006 [21])into k compatible groups. The applications are represented as an observation matrix consisting of rows of feature sets that are essential inputs to the k-medoids algorithm (Section 3.1).
- We process the output of the k-medoids algorithm to produce offline, low overhead, energy-efficient FVEs. The objective is to reach the write energy of optimal offline FVE while avoiding its disadvantages (Section 3.2). The proposed codec (coder/decoder) architecture uses read-only memories (ROMs) that are known to consume low power/energy in comparison to lookup tables (LUTs) and content-addressable memories (CAMs) (Section 3.3).

We divide the set of SPEC CPU2006 benchmarks into training and evaluation sets. The training set is used to derive the k offline FVE mappings, which are then used to encode the applications in the evaluation set. We evaluate the proposed solution for the MLC PCM prototype in [22] and the TLC RRAM prototype in [16]. Results (Section 4) indicate that average write energy in the MLC case is only 5% more than that of optimal offline FVE. The result is even better in the TLC case, where the average write energy of the proposed technique is 1% less than that of optimal offline FVE. In comparison to the write energies of MLC and TLC data comparison write (DCW) [23], the proposed solution achieves 39% and 35% energy savings, respectively, while the memory overhead in both cases does not exceed 3.5%. We report results for different values of k (the number of clusters), and for some values, our method results in average write energy that is only 4% more than that of the state-of-the-art MLC PCM encoding technique in [24]. However, [24] requires 50% NVM overhead, which is 16× in comparison to the proposed solution. Whereas the 50% overhead of [24] can be reduced, we argue that such a reduction will result in exponentially larger sizes of LUTs in comparison to the codec ROMs required by our solution. For TLC RRAM, our method results in the same average write energy as incomplete data mapping (IDM) [10]. However, IDM has a memory overhead of 20%, i.e., 5.7× the overhead of the solution proposed in this paper.

This research was supported by King Fahd University of Petroleum and Minerals and NSF Award CCF-1217738.

GLSVLSI '16, May 18–20, 2016, Boston, MA, USA

ISBN 978-1-4503-4274-2/16/05...$15.00
DOI: http://dx.doi.org/10.1145/2902961.2902979

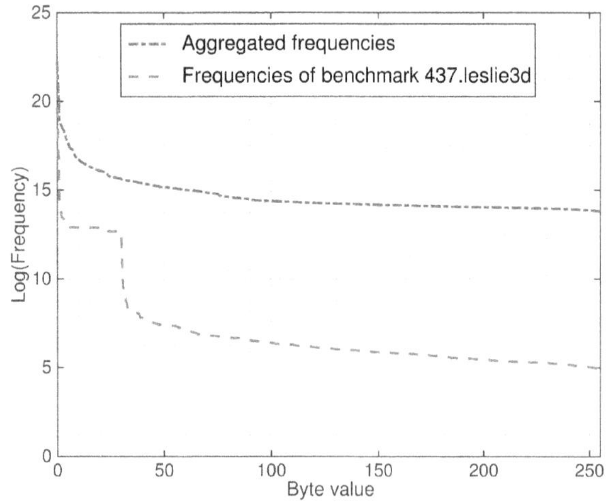

Figure 1: **In this plot, the x-axis is all the possible values (bytes) and the y-axis is the frequency of the corresponding value in logarithmic scale. Clearly, the frequency profile of benchmark 437.leslie3d exhibits good skew that supports the locality of frequent values. But aggregating the frequency profiles of 32 benchmarks results in a relatively flat plot, suggesting that more than 98% of the values are almost equally likely.**

2. Background and Motivation

This section provides an illustrative overview of offline FVE [11] and highlights its potential advantages. Motivated by the fact that most computer applications have high data locality, FVE encodes frequent values such that they are assigned to the least energy codewords. It has been reported that these frequent values may account for 32% of all the values written to memory by a specific application [12]. Consider an example where an application has only four possible values: A, B, C, and D:

Value	A	B	C	D
Frequency	20	5	10	4
Energy (pJ)	36	307	547	20

In this table, the 1st row is the possible value, 2nd is the corresponding frequency of occurrence of that value, and 3rd is the corresponding write energy for each value. Therefore, the total energy consumed by this application is 7,805 pJ. The following value-codeword assignment:

Value	A	C	B	D
Codeword	D	A	B	C

reduces the total energy to 4,483 pJ, i.e., 43%. The assignment ranks the values in decreasing frequencies and codewords in increasing energies, and assigns values with high frequency to codewords with low energy in the order of the ranking. For example, A has the highest frequency and D has the lowest energy, we assign value A the codeword D. This optimal offline code assignment will only be good if used for this specific application (or a similar one), and therefore it is referred to as *optimal perfect knowledge* assignment, i.e., find-once for a given program [11]. Henceforth, we simply refer to this method as the perfect knowledge method.

In practice, if we have more than one application, we aggregate their frequency profiles and generate a combined code assignment resulting in lower energy. However, combining frequencies of incompatible applications may eliminate skew that is essential to achieve high energy reductions, as illustrated in Fig. 1. The plots show (1) the aggregate frequency plot of 32 distinct benchmark applications (28 SPEC CPU2006 [21] and four Splash-2 [25]) and (2) the frequency plot of the leslie3d benchmark. Even though most offline frequency profiles of individual applications are skewed in favor of FVE, aggregating frequency profiles may eliminate skew and plateaus the graph for almost 98% of possible values. This is in comparison to the individual frequency plot of the benchmark leslie3d, in which the last elbow in the plot appears after 23% of possible values, implying high energy reduction.

Most applications have skewed frequency profiles in favor of perfect knowledge FVE. A primary motivation for this work is the careful aggregation of the frequency profiles of applications to derive multiple encodings, in which each encoding is still a result of a skewed aggregate frequency profile.

The authors in [14] evaluated perfect knowledge FVE on SLC PCM. While they reported that average write energy is greatly reduced, perfect knowledge FVE requires profiling support during the compilation process, implying a long compilation time for most applications. Another disadvantage of perfect knowledge FVE is that it requires operating system support, since for every application, we need to store the code assignment specific to that application in its executable. Perfect knowledge FVE is therefore expensive in practice.

On the other hand, online profiling occurs during application execution, e.g., [14]. Frequent values are identified on the fly and may also be replaced by other more frequent values. Although online profiling provides adaptive write energy reduction, it requires significant hardware and may affect overall system performance.

3. Contributions

The main contribution of this paper is the integration of an offline FVE solution for the purpose of MLC/TLC NVM write energy reduction approaching the reductions of perfect knowledge FVE without its disadvantages: the need for operating system and compiler support. Specifically, this work makes the following contributions:

- We use the k-medoids algorithm to cluster a set of applications into k compatible subsets. Precisely, our contribution is encoding the input applications as an observation matrix that consists of rows of feature sets, which is an essential input to the k-medoids algorithm (Section 3.1).
- We process the output of the k-medoids algorithm to derive a set of offline frequent value encodings. The objective is to achieve an average write energy that is as close as possible to the average write energy of perfect knowledge FVE (Section 3.2). We propose a codec architecture that utilizes ROMs that are known to consume low dynamic power in comparison to LUTs and CAMs (Section 3.3).

The proposed solution requires a slight modification to the traditional NVM memory word structure. This modified word structure is only internal to our codec and does not require any architectural changes outside the boundaries of the codec. As in Fig. 2a, an NVM word is composed of one or two tag cells, followed by a number of fixed length data slices. Each slice stores a frequent value in one of k encoded forms, and the tag cell(s) helps in the decoding process. The logical width of a data slice is referred to as frequent value length (FVL), and is equal to $\lceil log_2 v_{max} \rceil$, where v_{max} is the maximum possible frequent value. The FVL parameter and the number of possible frequent values to be encoded (FVN) characterize FVE. In this work, we fix FVL to 8 logical bits in the MLC case (Fig. 2b) and 9 logical bits in the TLC case (Fig. 2c). For FVN, however, the obvious choice would be 2^{FVL}, and this is used in this work. It is possible, however, that FVN $< 2^{FVL}$, and this can be combined with compression to lower the number of bit writes,

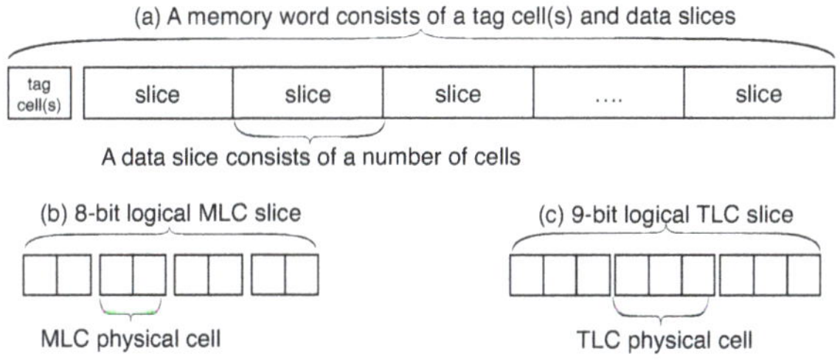

Figure 2: **(a) A memory word in the proposed scheme consists of one or two tag cells and a number of data slices, which varies for MLC and TLC as shown in Table 1. Throughout this paper: (b) an MLC data slice consists of 4 physical MLC cells or 8 logical bits and (c) a TLC data slice consists of 3 physical TLC cells or 9 logical bits.**

e.g., [14]. However, the cells in which the compressed values are written will potentially wear out faster. Hence, in this work, FVN is fixed to 2^{FVL}, i.e., 256 for MLC and 512 for TLC, to avoid biased wear of the memory cells.

3.1 Memory Trace Clustering

Finding data clusters is an unsupervised learning process in which data is divided into a given number of subgroups. Classical clustering algorithms include k-means [26] and k-medoids [20]. Clustering has played an important role in many areas, including artificial intelligence, pattern recognition, medical research, business intelligence, psychology, and political science [26, 27].

We utilize the k-medoids algorithm to cluster 32 memory traces of SPEC CPU2006 [21] and Splash-2 [25] benchmarks. These benchmarks represent a wide range of real user applications, and it is expected that most applications will have similar workloads. The k-medoids algorithm takes the following inputs: the number of clusters k, an observation matrix, and a similarity distance metric. For this work, the observation matrix consists of 32 rows (one row per benchmark), while the number of columns equals the feature set size, which is 256 for MLC and 512 for TLC.

Feature set extraction: The first step in generating the feature set of a given application is to extract its frequency information. Let $f(v)$ be a function returning the frequency of value v in the given application, where $0 \leq v < \text{FVN}$. Using this function, we form a set of pairs $\{(v, f(v)) : 0 \leq v < \text{FVN}\}$ and sort it in decreasing order with respect to $f(v)$ to generate an ordered list of these pairs. Each pair in the ordered list is composed of two entries: a value v and its frequency $f(v)$. Augmenting all the first entries of the pairs in the ordered list results in the feature set row vector $\vec{v_d}$. This feature set vector uniquely characterizes the given application. Two applications have the same vector *iff* they share similar, if not identical, frequency profiles. The rows of the observation matrix are constructed from these feature set vectors for all the 32 benchmarks. Note that a feature set vector is a permutation of all the values from 0 to FVN-1.

The similarity metric provides a means of measuring the distance between two applications, or more precisely, two feature sets or observations. It helps assign an observation to a cluster. In this work, since the rows of the observation matrix are permutations of the same set, a rank-based metric (Spearman rank correlation) was adopted. However, in most cases (see Section 4), other classic metrics, which are not rank correlated, perform equally well, i.e., the cosine and square Euclidean metrics.

As illustrated in Fig. 3, given k, an observation matrix, and a similarity metric, the k-medoids algorithm assigns a cluster ID (ranging from 0 to $k-1$) to every observation. Obviously, the size of the clusters may not be equal. Also, some of the clusters may have

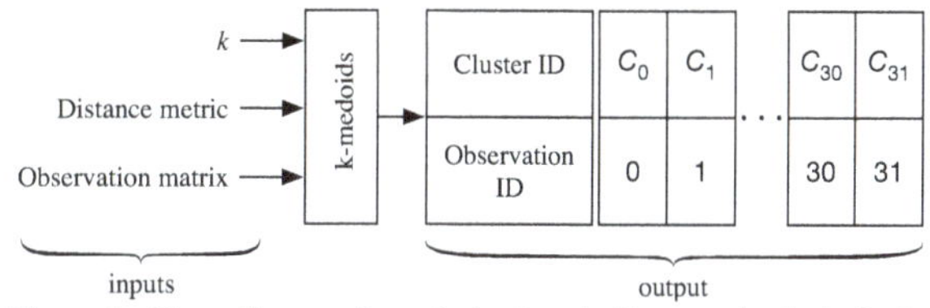

Figure 3: **Given the number of clusters k, the required similarity metric, and the observation matrix, the k-medoids algorithm divides the 32 observations (applications) into k clusters ($0 \leq C_i < k$ and $0 \leq i < 32$, where C_i is the cluster ID of observation i.)**

a single observation. For the sake of separating training data from evaluation data, we split the output of the k-medoids algorithm into a training set and an evaluation set. This strategy is widely used in the literature and its purpose is to measure and compare the quality of clustering in both sets. A good clustering results in relatively close qualities, provided that the right number of clusters is chosen.

Since the size of the clusters may be different, and some clusters may contain an odd number of observations, we cannot always choose half the observations in each cluster to construct the training set. Instead, we create k lists, $L[i]$, where each list is initially identical to the corresponding cluster. We remove one observation at a time from the list containing the largest number of observations until the number of observations in the lists is halved. We assume that L is available as input to the code generation algorithm.The observations in the cluster lists represent the training set and the remaining observations represent the evaluation set.

3.2 Code Generation

Consider a function $e(v)$ that calculates the energy of frequent value v as the sum of the write energies of the cells composing v. For example, with respect to the PCM MLC prototype in [22], if $v = 0$ and FVL=8, then $e(0) = 36 \times 4 = 144$ pJ, since the value 0 is composed of 4 MLCs whose values are all 00. Another example is $e(0) = 2 \times 3 = 6$ pJ in case of RRAM TLC [16].

Next, we form a set of pairs $\{(v, e(v)) : 0 \leq v < \text{FVN}\}$ and sort it in increasing order by $e(v)$ to generate an ordered list of these pairs. Augmenting the first entries of all these ordered pairs, i.e., the v portion of the pairs, results in the vector $\vec{v_e}$. Similar to $\vec{v_d}$, the elements of $\vec{v_e}$ form a permutation of the integers in the range 0 to FVN-1. Note that $\vec{v_e}$ depends on the underlying MLC/TLC NVM technology and not on the application. It is a list of all the codewords ordered in increasing order by their energies. In the code generation algorithm, this vector is referenced item-wise, i.e., $\vec{v_e}[i]$ refers to the ith element in the vector. Also, in the same algorithm, we assume that the function $F_p(o, v)$ returns the perfect knowledge frequency of value v in observation (application) o. Further, $L[i]$ is the ith cluster list introduced earlier.

Algorithm 1 outlines the process of code generation. The final output of the algorithm is a two dimensional mapping $M(i, v)$, where $0 \leq i < k$ and $0 \leq v < \text{FVN}$ are the encoding number and the value-to-be-encoded, respectively. Each cluster list generates one code as follows. First, the perfect knowledge frequency profiles of the applications in the cluster are aggregated, resulting in a set of pairs $\{(v, f(v)) : \forall v\}$. This set is sorted in decreasing order by frequency. The sorted list is stored in structure P, where $P[j]$ is the jth pair with respect to the sort order, and $P[j].v$ refers to the v entry of the pair. The final step to build the ith dictionary, $M(i, v)$, for all v. This is achieved by associating $P[j].v$ with the jth codeword, $\vec{v_e}[j]$. These steps are repeated to build the codes for each of the other cluster lists.

Algorithm 1: Generating the k codes for the k clusters

Output : $M(i, v), 0 \leq i < k, 0 \leq v <$ FVN, the ith codeword of value v
for $i = 0$ *to* $k - 1$ **do**
    Initialize $f(v) = 0, \forall v$
    for *each observation o in* $L[i]$ **do**
        for $v = 0$ *to FVN* $- 1$ **do**
            $f(v) \leftarrow f(v) + F_P(o, v)$
    Sort the pairs $\{(v, f(v)) : \forall v\}$ in descending order by $f(v)$, and let $P[i]$ be the ith pair of this list. Further, let $P[i].v$ is the value part of the pair
    for $j = 0$ *to FVN-1* **do**
        $M(i, P[j].v) \leftarrow \vec{v_e}[j]$

3.3 Hardware Realization

The resulting codes from algorithm 1 are used to program k ROMs, one ROM per cluster. ROM i is programmed with the portion of the mapping tables corresponding to cluster i. Each slice of the incoming memory word is associated with its own encoding ROM, and the incoming memory word is encoded k times, one time per code. Then, the encoded version that results in minimum energy is selected for writing, taking into account the current content of the target address. Fig. 4 shows the encoding path for $k = 2$. Since we have two clusters, the code assignment algorithm will result in two mappings. Tag cell T_0 (T_1) takes the value 0 (1) to indicate that the word is encoded using the 0th (1st) mapping. The encoding overhead in bits due to using ROMs equals the size of one encoding ROM $\times$ the number of slices per word $\times$ the number of words in the memory line $\times$ k. Note that all encoding ROMs have the same size which is FVN $\times$ FVL bits.

For decoding, we invert the mapping tables into ROMs as shown in the decoding architecture in Fig. 5. To avoid extra delay in the read path, the same ROM is duplicated in each slice across the whole memory line. One or more tag cells store the cluster number to decode the encoded slices inside the NVM array. Given a tag cell and an encoded slice, a decoding ROM outputs the decoded frequent value. Despite the duplication, the overhead is low in practice. The decoding overhead equals the size of one ROM $\times$ the number of slices per word $\times$ the number of words in the memory line, and ROM size is $k \times$ FVN $\times$ FVL bits.

In Fig. 4 and 5, encoders and decoders are duplicated across all the slices in the memory line for simplicity. If this design is not affordable, an alternative lower overhead design is also possible using multiplexers and pipelining.

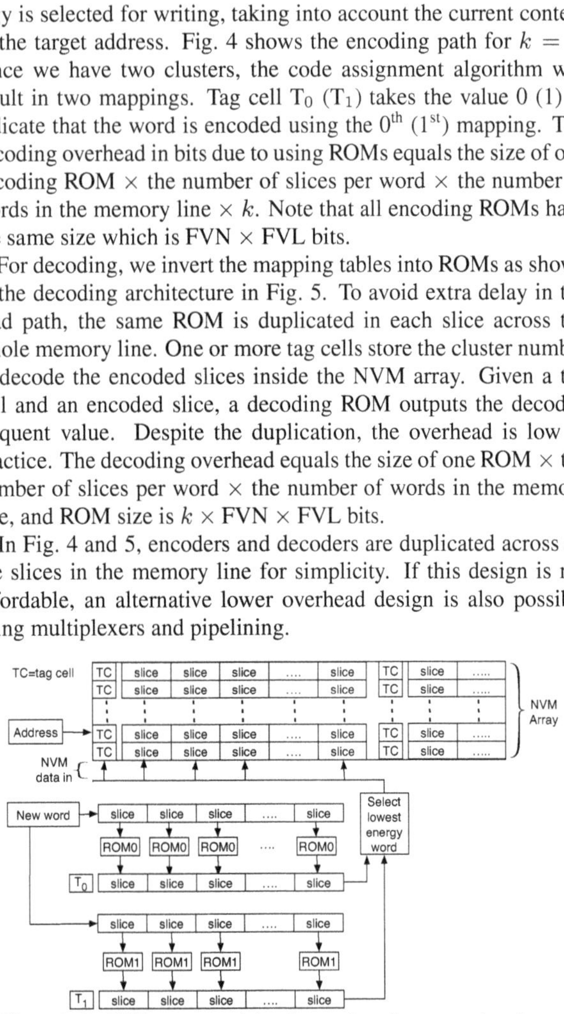

Figure 4: **An NVM array consists of a number of rows, and each row contains words that are organized as in Fig. 2a. An unencoded new word from the CPU is received along with a target address. Then k encoded versions are generated and the word with the lowest energy (with respect to the current word at the target address) is selected for writing. For decoding purposes, each encoded version is associated with a tag value that is stored with the lowest energy version.**

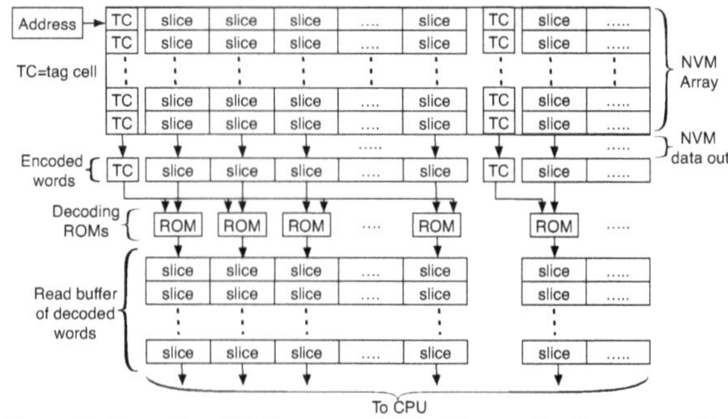

Figure 5: **Decoding ROMs are replicated for each slice across the memory line. ROMs are addressed by slice value augmented with tag value.**

4. Evaluation and Results

In this section, we present the simulation results of the proposed solution for the 4-state MLC PCM prototype in [22] and the 8-state TLC RRAM prototype in [16]. For brevity, we refer to these prototypes in this section as MLC and TLC, respectively.

Simulation setup: We evaluated the proposed solution using a trace-driven memory simulator. We used the Pin binary instrumentation tool [28] to extract the memory traces of 32 distinct applications: 28 SPEC CPU2006 [21] benchmarks and 4 Splash-2 [25] benchmarks. Table 1 lists the simulation configuration and the memory overhead due to using the tag cell(s). The number of logical bits in the memory line is 512 bits for MLC and 513 bits in TLC due to padding. In MLC, a 64-bit logical word is constructed from 32 physical cells. To avoid unnecessary padding in the TLC case, we chose a word size of 57 physical cells (171 logical bits). Note that this word size is local to the memory controller and does not imply a change to the word size of the CPU.

	MLC	TLC
Logical bits per memory line	512	513
Slice width or FVL (in logical bits)	8	9
Slices per word	8 / 16	19
Words per memory line	8 / 4	3
Tag cell(s) per word	1 / 2	1 / 2
NVM overhead	3.1%	1.8% / 3.5%

Table 1: **MLC/TLC memory line organization and NVM overhead**

Memory overhead: As indicated in Table 1, NVM overhead due to tag cell(s) is always 3.1% in MLC, since the ratio between the number of tag and data cells in the word is fixed. In TLC, the number of slices per word is constant, but the number of tag cells is one or two, and therefore, the overhead is 1.8% or 3.5%, respectively. The number of tag cells in the MLC and TLC cases is $\lceil log_2 k \rceil$, where k is the number of clusters. Further, Table 2 reports the overhead for the codec ROMs for different values of k. Clearly, the codec overhead is negligible in comparison to the sizes of state-of-the-art NVMs.

k	2	4	8	16
MLC (KBytes)	8	16	64	128
TLC (KBytes)	43	86	171	342

Table 2: **Assuming one codec is shared among all the words in a memory line, we show the ROM overhead for MLC/TLC NVMs for different values of k.**

Hardware and latency overheads: We implemented Verilog modules for our codec circuitry. In our design, we avoid replicating the codec across all the words of the memory line, since this results in higher area. Instead, a single codec instance is shared (and pipelined to avoid latency penalty) among all the memory words across the memory line. Using Design Compiler, we synthesize these modules on a 45nm technology node [29]. Since $k = 8$ provides best results for MLC, we chose to synthesize this case to examine the overheads. We implement the codec ROMs using `case` statements and the the cosine metric.

The area of the synthesized codec is 0.23 mm^2, which is negligible in comparison to the area of the state-of-the-art PCM memories, e.g., less than 0.4% the area of the 8Gb PCM in [30]. The latencies (energies) of the decoder and encoder paths are 1.93 ns (1.1 pJ/cell) and 3.91 ns (2.3 pJ/cell), which is also negligible in comparison to the PCM program-and-verify (P&V) write latencies (energies) [22]. Assuming P&V writes 34 cells at once, we can reduce the total memory line latency to a single word latency, since by the time the P&V modules complete writing one PCM word, the encoder will have encoded the entire line. But the decoding latency of the complete memory line equals the number of words per line times the word latency, i.e., 15.44 ns. If this is high, the decoder can be replicated to achieve a read latency that is as low as 1.93 ns for the memory line. Although this replication results in tripling the codec area (0.62 mm^2), it also reduces the read latency by 8×.

Energy reductions: Fig. 6 compares state-of-the-art methods to the proposed solution for MLC PCM. The bars represent the geometric mean (GM) of the write energy for each method across all the 32 applications. GMs are normalized to the GM energy consumed by DCW [23]. The methods from left to right are: DCW, the 50% overhead method [24], MFNW [18], cell remapping [9], and perfect knowledge FVE [11]. NVM overheads of these methods are 0%, 50%, 3.1%, 3.1%, and 0%, respectively. The following bars belong to the proposed solution, labeled by the number of clusters, followed by a comma, followed by the distance metric used, which is either cosine, square Euclidean, or Spearman rank correlation (denoted by cos, sqeuc, and spearman, respectively). The first bar assumes no clustering, i.e., a metric is not required. It is clear that clustering is beneficial as k increases from 2 to 16. Clearly, as k increases, energy reductions also increase. $k = 8$ results in more or equal energy reduction in comparison to 16 clusters.

Although the GM of the write energy of the proposed solution is measured across all the 32 applications, the training set, which is used to generate the k FVE mappings, is only composed of 16 applications. Fig. 7 compares the GM energy of the proposed solution across all applications, training set applications, and evaluation set applications. Energy reduction across the evaluation set for $k = 1$ is almost equivalent to DCW. As k increases, the reduction across the evaluation set improves. Although energy reduction across all the applications for $k = 8$ is better than $k = 16$, the energy reduction across the evaluation sets is marginally better ($\approx 1\%$) for $k = 16$ in comparison to $k = 8$.

Fig. 8 is the TLC equivalent of Fig. 6. The methods from left to right are: DCW, MFNW for TLC, incomplete data mapping (IDM) [10], and perfect knowledge FVE. NVM overheads of these methods are 0%, 1.8%, 20%, and 0%, respectively. Similar to the MLC case, as k increases, the energy reduction also improves. To compare energy reductions across the training and evaluation sets, we also provide a break down of this result in Fig. 9. Similar to MLC, when no clustering is performed ($k = 1$), energy reduction is only 5% better than DCW across the evaluation set. As k increases, the energy reduction across evaluation set improves. NVM overheads of the proposed solution are 1.8% for $k \leq 4$, and 3.5% for $k = 8$ and 16.

In all the previous charts, we divide the 32 applications into two halves: training set and evaluation set. To show the robustness of the clustering, we re-run the simulations using a training set size of

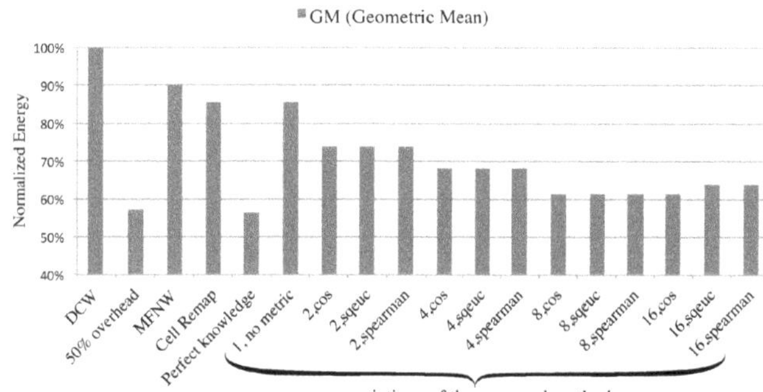

Figure 6: **The x-axis lists state-of-the-art MLC PCM encoding techniques followed by our proposed method. The y-axis is the geometric mean (GM) write energy normalized to data comparison write (DCW) [23]. From left to right, the encodings are: DCW, 50% overhead encoding [24], MFNW [18], cell remapping [9], and perfect knowledge FVE [11]. This is followed by aggregate FVE without clustering (1,no metric), and variations of our method, broken down by the number of clusters and distance metric, e.g., (2,cos) to indicate two clusters with the cosine metric.**

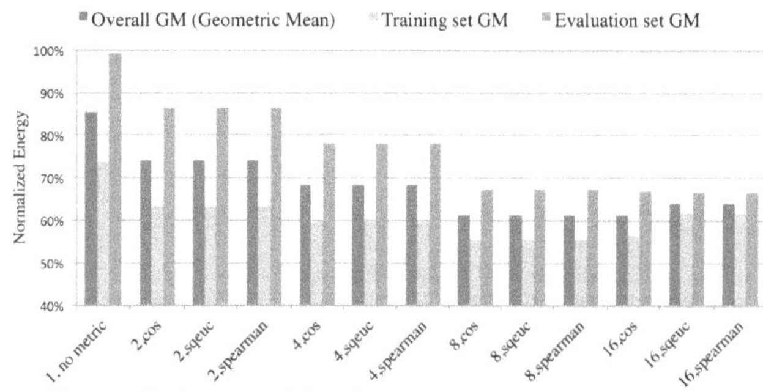

Figure 7: **Each group of three bars represent the overall geometric mean (GM), training set GM, and evaluation set GM of MLC write energies. Similar to Fig. 6, write energies are normalized to DCW. As the number of clusters increases, the gap between write energies of the training set and evaluation set reduces.**

8 applications and evaluation set size of 24 applications. Since we use only 8 benchmarks for training, a cluster size of 16 is no longer possible, and therefore, we only show the result for k =2, 4, and 8. Fig. 10 shows the robustness chart in the MLC case. Clearly, the clustering is robust and the energy of the 25% training set size case (8 applications) is only 3.34% more on average in comparison to the 50% training set size (16 applications). The result is similar in the TLC case (Fig. 11), as the average energy is only 3.5% more.

In Fig. 6, the 50% overhead method produces the lowest MLC write energy, which is almost identical to perfect knowledge, but costs 50% NVM overhead, which is about 16× more than our overhead. Moreover, the average write energy of the proposed solution is only 5% more than that of perfect knowledge when using 8 clusters. In comparison to MFNW and cell remapping, the proposed method consumes 29% and 24% lower energy, respectively.

For the TLC result in Fig. 8, IDM results in marginally better energy reduction over perfect knowledge ($\approx 1\%$). Note that our proposed solution is comparable to IDM when $k = 16$ for the square Euclidean and Spearman metrics. However, IDM has NVM overhead of 20% $\approx 5.7\times$ the proposed solution NVM overhead.

5. Conclusions

This paper proposed an energy efficient, low overhead offline FVE for MLC/TLC NVMs that approaches the performance of perfect knowledge FVE. The main idea is to cluster the perfect knowledge frequency profiles of a broad set of general-purpose applications to generate combined FVE mappings for each cluster. Results show that the average write energy for MLC PCM of the proposed

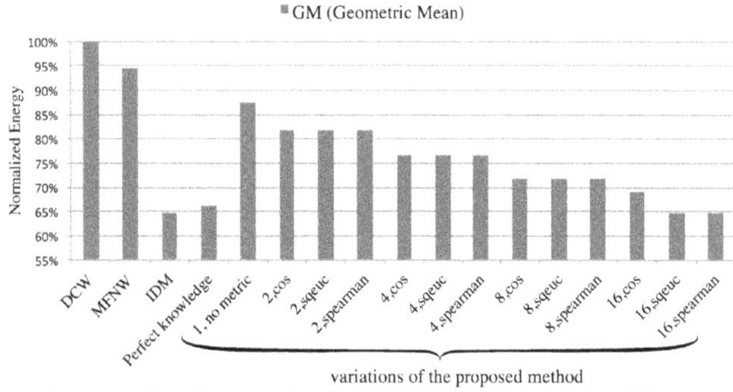

Figure 8: **Results, organized similar to Fig. 6, for state-of-the-art TLC encoding solutions (left to right): MFNW for TLC, incomplete data mapping (IDM) [10], and perfect knowledge FVE. Again, write energies are normalized to DCW.**

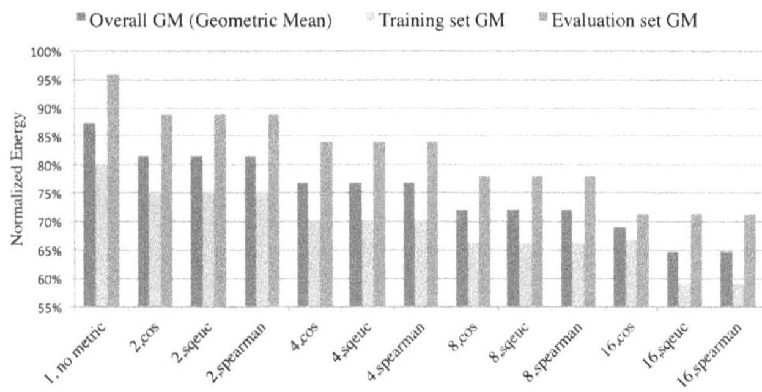

Figure 9: **Results for TLC RRAM, organized similar to Fig. 7. The gap between write energies of the training and evaluation sets consistently decreases as k increases, except for the case from $k = 8$ to $k = 16$ for the square Euclidean and Spearman metrics (12% in both cases).**

method is only 5% more than the average write energy of perfect knowledge FVE. For TLC RRAM, the average write energy of the proposed solution is better by 1%. Furthermore, the low NVM and codec overheads makes the proposed method easy to implement and integrate into modern memory controllers.

6. References

[1] "International Technology Roadmap for Semiconductors," 2011.

[2] B. C. Lee *et al.*, "Architecting phase change memory as a scalable DRAM alternative," in *Proc. Intl. Symposium on Computer Architecture*, 2009.

[3] I. Baek *et al.*, "Highly scalable nonvolatile resistive memory using simple binary oxide driven by asymmetric unipolar voltage pulses," in *Proc. Intl. Electron Devices Meeting*, 2004.

[4] H.-S. Wong *et al.*, "Metal–oxide RRAM," *Proceedings of the IEEE*, vol. 100, no. 6, 2012.

[5] J. Yue and Y. Zhu, "Accelerating write by exploiting PCM asymmetries," in *Proc. Intl. Symposium on High Performance Computer Architecture*, 2013.

[6] J. Li and K. Mohanram, "Write-once-memory-code phase change memory," in *Proc. Design, Automation and Test in Europe Conference*, 2014.

[7] D. Dgien *et al.*, "Compression architecture for bit-write reduction in non-volatile memory technologies," in *Proc. Intl. Symposium Nanoscale Architectures*, 2014.

[8] A. Mirhoseini *et al.*, "Coding-based energy minimization for phase change memory," in *Proc. Design Automation Conference*, 2012.

[9] J. Wang *et al.*, "Energy-efficient multi-level cell phase-change memory system with data encoding," in *Proc. Intl. Conference on Computer Design*, 2011.

[10] D. Niu *et al.*, "Low power multi-level-cell resistive memory design with incomplete data mapping," in *Proc. Intl. Conference on Computer Design*, 2013.

[11] J. Yang and R. Gupta, "Frequent value locality and its applications," *ACM Trans. Embed. Comput. Syst.*, vol. 1, no. 1, 2002.

[12] J. Yang *et al.*, "Frequent value encoding for low power data buses," *ACM Trans. Des. Autom. Electron. Syst.*, vol. 9, no. 3, 2004.

[13] D. Suresh *et al.*, "Energy-efficient encoding techniques for off-chip data buses," *ACM Trans. on Embedded Computing Systems*, vol. 8, no. 2, 2009.

[14] G. Sun *et al.*, "A frequent-value based PRAM memory architecture," in *Proc. Asia and South Pacific Design Automation Conference*, 2011.

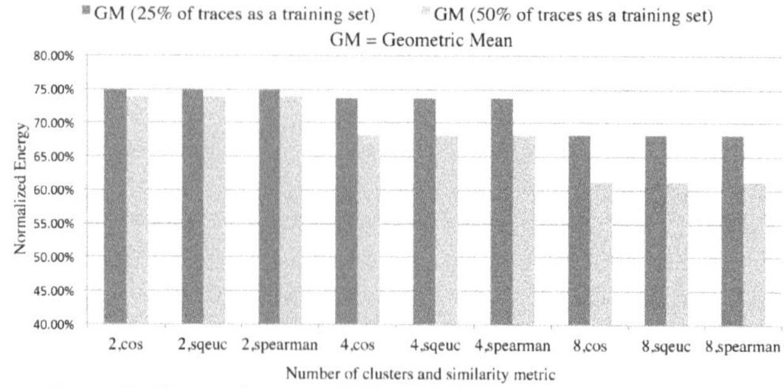

Figure 10: **Geometric mean (GM) of MLC write energies, normalized to DCW. The two cases are training on 50% of the applications and evaluation on 50% versus training on 25% and evaluation on 75%. By training on 25% of the applications, write energy increases by only 3.34% on average.**

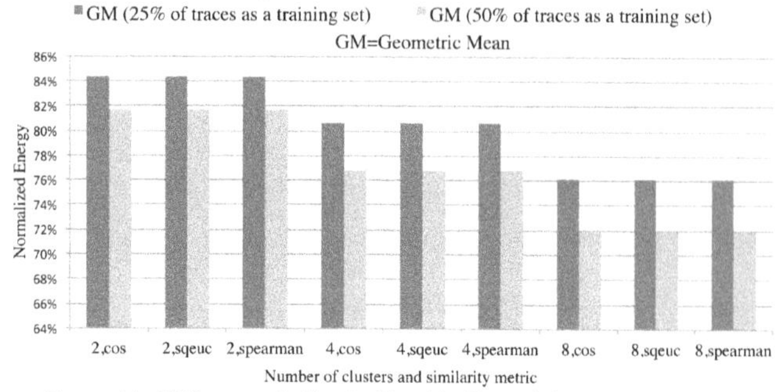

Figure 11: **TLC case similar to Fig. 10. By training on 25% of the applications, write energy increases by only 3.5% on average in comparison to training on 50% of the applications.**

[15] D.-H. Kang *et al.*, "Two-bit cell operation in diode-switch phase change memory cells with 90nm technology," in *Proc. Symposium on VLSI Technology*, 2008.

[16] C. Xu *et al.*, "Understanding the trade-offs in multi-level cell ReRAM memory design," in *Proc. Design Automation Conference*, 2013.

[17] W. Wen *et al.*, "State-restrict MLC STT-RAM designs for high-reliable high-performance memory system," in *Proc. Design Automation Conference*, 2014.

[18] A. Alsuwaiyan and K. Mohanram, "MFNW: A flip-n-write architecture for multi-level cell non-volatile memories," in *Proc. Intl. Symposium on Nanoscale Architectures*, 2015.

[19] L. Jiang *et al.*, "ER: Elastic RESET for low power and long endurance MLC based phase change memory," in *Proc. Intl. Symposium on Low Power Electronics and Design*, 2012.

[20] H.-S. Park and C.-H. Jun, "A simple and fast algorithm for K-medoids clustering," *Expert Systems with Applications*, vol. 36, no. 2, Part 2, 2009.

[21] "SPEC CPU2006," 2006.

[22] F. Bedeschi *et al.*, "A bipolar-selected phase change memory featuring multi-level cell storage," *IEEE Journal of Solid-State Circuits*, vol. 44, no. 1, 2009.

[23] B.-D. Yang *et al.*, "A low power phase-change random access memory using a data-comparison write scheme," in *Proc. Intl. Symposium on Circuits and Systems*, 2007.

[24] A. Mirhoseini *et al.*, "Phase change memory write cost minimization by data encoding," *IEEE Journal on Emerging and Selected Topics in Circuits and Systems*, vol. 5, no. 1, 2015.

[25] J. M. Arnold *et al.*, "Splash 2," in *Proc. Parallel algorithms and architectures*, 1992.

[26] J. Wu, *Cluster Analysis and K-means Clustering: An Introduction*, 2012.

[27] L. Kaufman and P. J. Rousseeuw, *Finding groups in data: An introduction to cluster analysis*. New York: Wiley, 1990.

[28] C.-K. Luk *et al.*, "Pin: Building customized program analysis tools with dynamic instrumentation," in *Proc. Conference on Programming Language Design and Implementation*, 2005.

[29] J. E. Stine *et al.*, "Freepdk: An open-source variation-aware design kit," in *Microelectronic Systems Education*, 2007.

[30] Y. Choi *et al.*, "A 20nm 1.8v 8gb PRAM with 40mb/s program bandwidth," in *Proc. Intl. Solid-State Circuits Conference*, 2012.

Low-Power Multi-Port Memory Architecture based on Spin Orbit Torque Magnetic Devices

Rajendra Bishnoi, Fabian Oboril and Mehdi B. Tahoori
Chair of Dependable Nano Computing (CDNC), Karlsruhe Institute of Technology (KIT), Karlsruhe, Germany
{rajendra.bishnoi, fabian.oboril, mehdi.tahoori}@kit.edu

ABSTRACT

Multi-port memories are widely used as shared memory, such as register files, in a microprocessor system, and its number of ports and capacities are significantly increasing with every product generation. However, with technology advancements, multi-port memories are facing severe challenges due to their bit-cell leakage and scalability, as well as reliability issues due to increase in design complexity. In this paper, we design a novel multi-port memory architecture in which we employ emerging *Spin Orbit Torque* (SOT) magnetic devices as a storing component because of its several beneficial attributes such as non-volatility, scalability, zero-leakage, almost infinite endurance, low access latency, low area and immunity to soft-errors. Moreover, due to separate read and write current paths in these devices, simultaneous read and write operations can be performed on the same cell while maintaining data integrity. In our proposed architecture, we have demonstrated that with this characteristic of SOT, the read-write contention can be resolved inherently at the device-level, which can simplify the overall multi-port design. Experimental results show that our proposed multi-port design has low access latency, and high energy efficiency with negligible area overhead.

Keywords

Spin Orbit Torque, multi-port non-volatile memory

1. INTRODUCTION

The rapid pace of technology advancement and a high throughput demand lead to a massive parallel data processing in a microprocessor, especially for communication and multimedia applications [1]. Multi-port memory is the key element in providing such a high throughput because it allows simultaneous array accesses. Since system designers continue strive to increase the performance of a microprocessor, a trend of increasing the number of ports, registers and/or their capacity has been growing significantly [2]. For instance, the total register capacity of NVIDIA Kepler GK210 is around 7.7 MByte [3]. In general, multi-port memories are designed based on SRAM based bit-cell, which are highly affected due to leakage and scalability issues, and the addition of memory ports and/or capacity make the matter worse [4]. Emerging spintronics magnetic memory technologies, such as *Spin Orbit Torque* (SOT) and *Spin Transfer Torque* (STT), have a potential to overcome these challenges because their storing devices are having features of zero-leakage and scalability. Additionally, these technologies also have several other beneficial attributes such as almost infinite endurance, high-density, CMOS compatibility and immunity to radiation-induced soft-errors [5, 6]. The SOT is the latest spintronic technology, which is much faster, energy efficient and reliable compared to STT [7–9], hence it is better suited for a multi-port memory design.

Recently, a dual port bit-cell architecture using an SOT is proposed in [10]. However, the sneaky current path during operational mode is overlooked in this architecture, which can easily result in read and write failures. Additionally, in this architecture, a level converter is also required for each write circuitry that significantly contributes to the total area and energy. Another dual-port bit-cell architecture is proposed in [11], and a multi-level cell based structure for a Graphic Processor Unit architecture is proposed in [12]. Nevertheless, both use STT memory technology that has a high switching latency and energy, due to which the overall multi-port design becomes slow and energy inefficient. Therefore, a reliable low-cost multi-port architecture which has latency and energy efficiency, is still missing.

In this paper, we have utilized a fact about SOT-MTJ cell that it can inherently perform simultaneous read and write operations. In an SOT device, since read and write currents have isolated paths, both can flow at the same time through the same bit-cell without affecting each other functionality. In this way, the read-write contention can be resolved at the bit-cell level. We exploit this feature of SOT-MTJ to design a unique multi-port memory architecture in which we have modified the standard SOT bit-cell structure. Overall, the simultaneous read and write feature of the SOT simplifies the multi-port design. Additionally, two low-power schemes, namely, *Unnecessary Write Termination* and *Unnecessary Write Avoidance*, are introduced on the top of our proposed multi-port memory architecture for further energy improvements. Our simulation results show that our proposed multi-port design is overall beneficial for read operations as well as leakage reduction. In addition, integration of avoiding redundant write schemes, its energy efficiency can be increased upto 68 %.

The rest of the paper is organized as follows. In Sec 2, the background of SOT technology is discussed. Sec 3 presents the implementation of our proposed architecture. Sec 4 shows the simulation results, followed by conclusions in Sec 5.

2. BACKGROUND

2.1 Spin Orbit Torque

The storing devices in *Magnetic Random Access Memory* (MRAM) are *Magnetic Tunnel Junction* (MTJ) cells in which data is stored as a resistance state value. An SOT

GLSVLSI '16, May 18-20, 2016, Boston, MA, USA
© 2016 ACM. ISBN 978-1-4503-4274-2/16/05...$15.00
DOI: http://dx.doi.org/10.1145/2902961.2903022

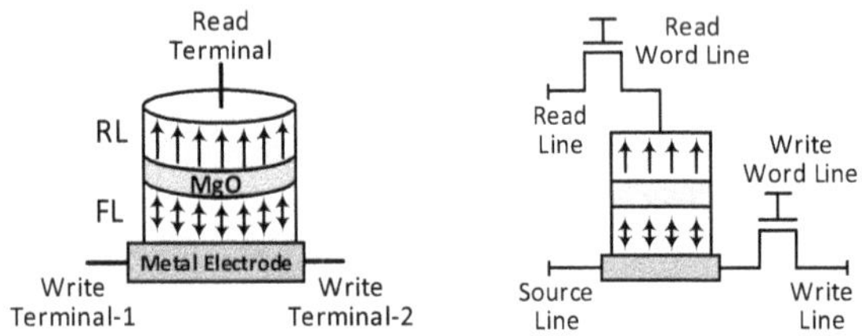

(a) SOT-MTJ device (b) Standard bit-cell

Figure 1: SOT-MRAM storing device and bit-cell

based MTJ cell, as shown in Figure 1(a), consists of two ferromagnetic layers separated by a thin (a few nm) *barrier oxide layer* such as *magnesium oxide* (MgO). Out of these two ferromagnetic layers, one has always fixed magnetic orientation, that is known as *Referenced Layer* (RL) or *Pinned Layer*. In contrast, the magnetic orientation of the other ferromagnetic layer can be rotated freely based on the direction of the current flow, which is referred to as *Free Layer* (FL). As described in the figure, the SOT-MTJ device comprises of total three terminals, out of which two are write terminals and one is read terminal. The write current flows between the two write terminals through a metal electrode, that generates a torque on the magnetization of the FL. This results in the change in the magnetization state of the FL which in turn changes the resistance state of the device (write operation). The *Rasbha effect* [13] or the *Spin Hall Effect* [14] are responsible for such switching phenomenon. When the magnetic orientation of both layers are in the same ('P' magnetization state) and opposite ('AP' magnetization state) directions, it exhibits a low and a high resistance state, respectively. On the other hand, a low read current flows through the MTJ layer stacks between the read terminal and any one of the write terminal. This read current is sensed using a sense amplifier to read a value.

A typical bit-cell architecture for an SOT-MRAM is shown in Figure 1(b). It consists of two access transistors and an MTJ cell [9]. Here separate read and write transistors have to be considered in order to avoid any sneaky current path during operational periods. During read and write operations, the corresponding access transistors are on by activating their respective *word lines*. The read current flows through a *read line* (which is connected to a sense amplifier) to a *source line*. The write current, which has a bidirectional path, flows between *source line* and *write line*.

The switching of SOT-MTJ device is much faster with lower energy than that of the STT based MTJ cell due to the absence of the incubation delay [7, 9]. Also, a permanent magnet is fixed on SOT-MTJ cell which not only further improves the switching latency and energy, but also delivers deterministic switching. Moreover, read and write have isolated current paths, which means these two can be optimized independently and the possibility of read disturb is almost zero. This also implies that the read and write current can be increased to provide additional benefits for latency improvements with the energy trade-off. The reason is that the switching delay of the SOT device is inversely proportional to the applied switching current. In addition, SOT-MTJ cell possesses high endurance compared to STT-MTJ cell because write current, which is relatively higher than the read current, does not flow through the oxide layer.

3. MULTI-PORT MEMORY USING SOT

The device structure of SOT-MTJ can support simultaneous read and write operations with a negligible influence on each other. With this attribute, the read and write contention of multi-port memories can be inherently resolved at the bit-cell level and delivers a dual-port characteristic. In this section, first we explain the overview of the SOT based multi-port memory and the concept of simultaneous read-write, followed by the bit-cell architecture and the corresponding array organization. At the end, memory port enhancements and redundant write avoidance techniques for our proposed multi-port design are discussed.

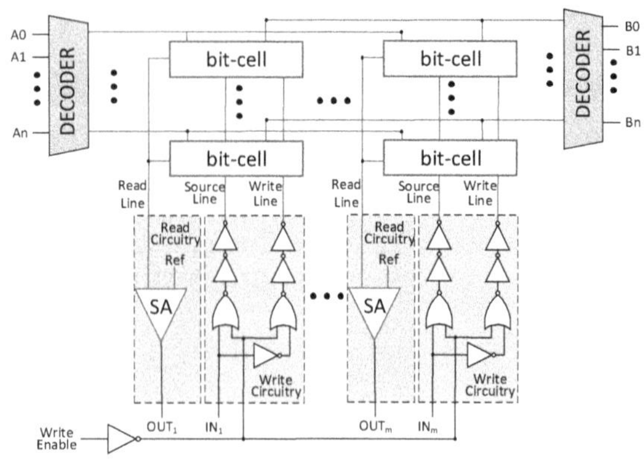

Figure 2: Block diagram of 1R1W multi-port memory using SOT bit-cell.

3.1 Overview of multi-port memories

Multi-port memories are extensively used as shared bit-cell array for microprocessor as it can provide data access parallelism to enhance the overall performance. A block diagram of a typical two-port memory (1R1W: one read and one write) using SOT bit-cell, is shown in Figure 2. It consists of two decoders to facilitate the two different addresses to access the bit-cell array and read-write periphery circuitry to perform necessary memory operations, as shown in the figure. Here read-write circuits are the same as the ones employed for the standard SOT-MRAM design. In general, our proposed multi-port design is implemented on the top of the single-port SOT-MRAM with the modification of just additional accessibility to the bit-cell. This is done since the bit-cell inherently provides the characteristics for simultaneous read and write operations, which simplifies the overall multi-port memory architecture design. In order to utilize this feature and to enhance the bit-cell accessibility, the bit-cell architecture has to be altered, which is explained in next subsection. Please note that the proposed architecture is demonstrated for 1R1W memory port, however, the number of ports can be easily extended by adding access lines and introducing corresponding bitlines in the design.

3.2 Simultaneous read-write concept

In standard single-port SOT-MRAM, the read current flows from the read terminal to any one of the write terminals (source-line as illustrated in Figure 1(a)) through the oxide layer. In reality, this read current can pass through either of the two write terminals due to the symmetric struc-

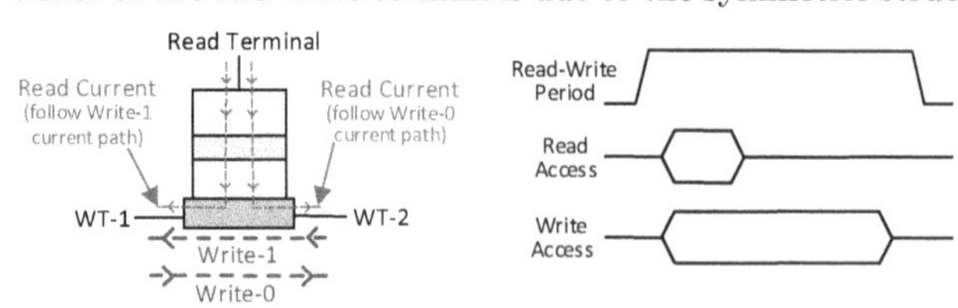

(a) Simultaneous read-write (b) Read and write access

Figure 3: Demonstration of simultaneous read and write concept on SOT-MTJ.

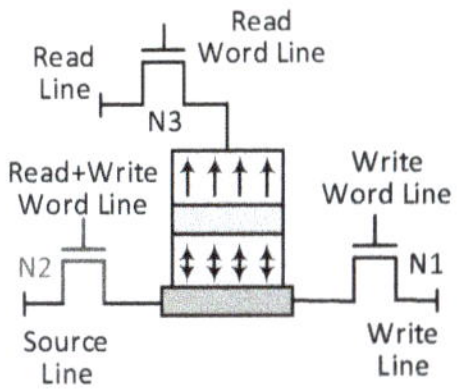

Access transistors			Operations
N1	N2	N3	
ON	ON	OFF	Write only
OFF	ON	ON	Read only
ON	ON	ON	Read + Write

Figure 4: Modified bit-cell architecture

ture of the SOT-MTJ cell. We exploit this fact about the SOT-MTJ cell, in which the read current is directed to follow the write current path in the case of simultaneous read-write operations as described in Figure 3(a). In other words, the conventional write current always flows from a high potential terminal to the one at a low potential, and hence, the read current can also flow through the same path after passing through the oxide layer. In addition, as illustrated in Figure 3(b), the read access is significantly faster than (around 5 X in our setup) the write access. Therefore, always old data can be read without any conflicts in the case of simultaneous read-write operations on the same bit-cell.

3.3 Bit-cell architecture modification

As mentioned earlier, due to symmetric structure of the SOT device, a read current can flow through either of the write terminals. However, in the present bit-cell structure, there is a dissimilarity in the two read current paths. One of the paths has an additional NMOS transistor (write access transistor) in the bit-cell, whereas the other path has no such transistor. Because of this, a disproportionate amount of read current flows, which can disturb the distinguishability of the two read values. This is due to the reason that the bit-cell read current value has to be compared with a reference current value which is always fixed. To avoid such scenario and to develop a symmetric read current path for better readability, we introduce an additional NMOS transistor to the other write terminal as well (connecting to the sourceline as shown in Figure 4). The new bit-cell architecture also serves an additional purpose that it eliminates the asymmetry in the write currents which is essentially because of the potential degradation due to the existing single NOMS transistor [15]. The addition of another NMOS transistor balances the write current, which in turn balances the write latency. This extra access transistor is activated when either (or both) read or write word line is activated. In other words, this transistor is required to be on for both read and write memory operations. Therefore, we ORed the read and write word lines, and the gate of the newly added access transistor is connected to the resulting output. The bit-cell operations with respect to their access transistors are illustrated in the table shown in Figure 4. The functionality of this bit-cell architecture is further explained next.

3.4 Array organization

In this section, the functionality of memory operations in term of memory array organization is explained. All the four possible scenarios for the proposed multi-port memory array accesses are described below:

3.4.1 *When only write is performed*

For the write operation, a bi-directional current path is established using write circuitry as illustrated in Figure 2. The two directions of the write current are decided based on the input data value. With the modified bit-cell architecture, the directions of the current for writing respective values are demonstrated in Figure 5(a). Here, we have shown the final inverters in order to illustrate the complete current source and sink paths through the bit-cell. These two inverters are the part of the write block that drives the source and write lines. During the write operation, these two inverters have always opposite output values. In order to establish the complete current path, the two access transistors, which are connected to the write terminals, are always on during the write operation. Note that the access transistors connected to the read terminal should be off when only write operation is performed, to avoid any sneaky current path.

3.4.2 *When only read is performed*

For read only operations, the write access is disabled by setting write enable signal to '0'. Therefore, both inputs of the inverters of the write block become '1', which make source-line and write-line '0'. Since, only the read operation is performed, access transistor 'N3' and 'N2' are on. Therefore, a read current path is established as illustrated in Figure 5(b). In our implementation, we have employed a pre-charge based *sense amplifier* (SA) similar to one proposed in [16]. In this SA architecture, one end of the MTJ is connected to the amplifier component and the other end is connected to ground, so that an appropriate read current, which is evoked using SA, can flow through the MTJ device.

3.4.3 *Simultaneous read-write on the same bit-cell*

When both read and write operations are performed on the same cell, all three access transistors (namely, 'N1', 'N2' and 'N3') of the bit-cells are on. In such scenarios, the write current behaves same as illustrated in Figure 5(a). However, the read current path has to be altered based on the write current flow directions, as shown in Figure 5(c). In other words, the read current always follows the write current path after passing through the oxide layer of the MTJ cell. For instance, if write '1' is performed, the read current flows through the transistor 'N2'. Otherwise, it flows through the transistor 'N1' in the case of write '0'. Please note that, the sneaky write current path cannot be established in such scenarios because either source line or write line has to be at the '0' potential and the potential developed at the read terminal is always more than that. In addition, the metal electrode of the SOT device, through which the write current flows, is made up of tantalum bearing very low resistance compared to the resistance value of the MTJ device itself. Hence, the resistance value of metal electrode has negligible impact on the overall read current and readability.

In SOT-MRAM, in general, the read operation is performed much faster than write, which means there is a significant delay margin (of around 5 X in our implementation) between the read and write latencies. Therefore, during simultaneous read and write operations on the same value, the previous value in the bit-cell is always read first, before writing a new value into the bit cell. Furthermore, the margin between read and write latency is significant enough to maintain the impact of process variation, i.e., to gurantee that read always finishes before write. In case, if there is any overlap between the slow read and fast write due to extreme influence of the process variation, the read and write circuitries can be easily tuned to make them fast and slow, respectively. Since read and write latencies are inversely proportional to their respective current values, increasing read current and decreasing write current can make read and write circuitries fast and slow, respectively.

3.4.4 *Simultaneous read-write on different bit-cell*

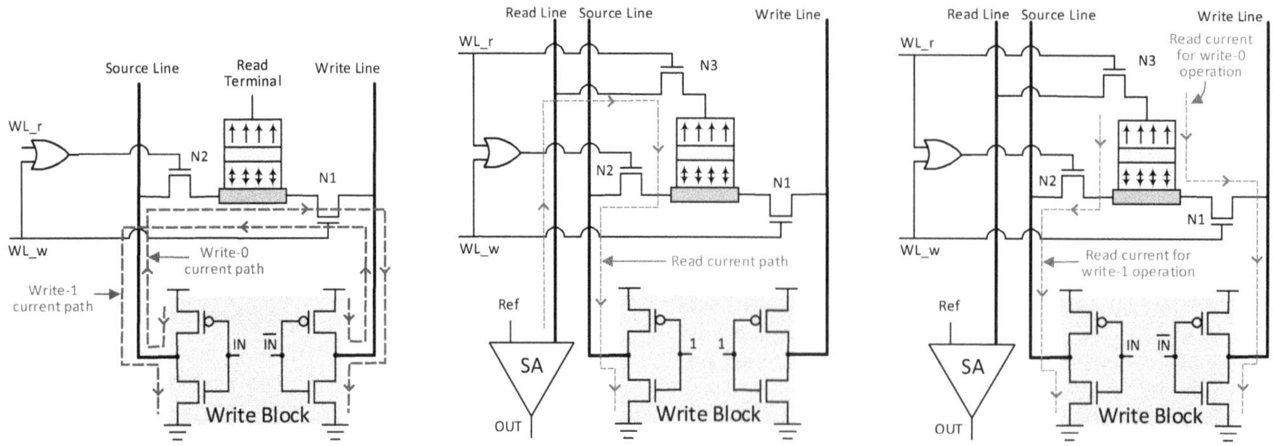

(a) Write only operation (b) Read only operation (c) Simultaneous read-write on same bit-cell

Figure 5: Demonstration of write and read current flow path for write only, read only and simultaneous read-write on the same cell.

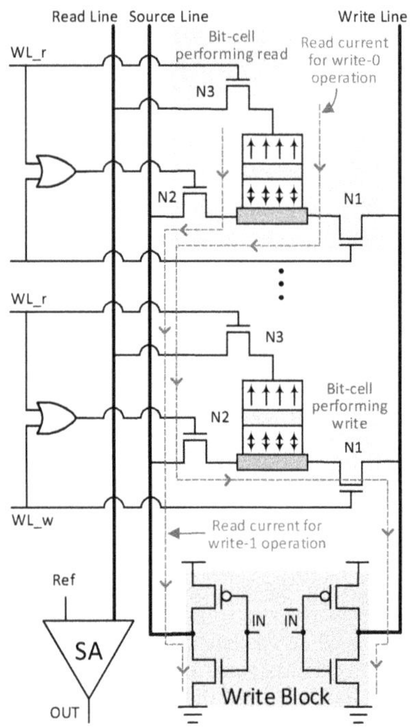

Figure 6: Demonstration of write and read currents for simultaneous read-write on different bit-cells.

In this case, simultaneous read and write operations are performed on different bit-cells, nevertheless they share common bitlines in the same column. Bit-cells with the two independent read and write operations on the same column are illustrated in Figure 6. Similar to the read-only and write-only operations, the access transistors 'N2' and 'N3' are on for the bit-cell where read is performed. On the other hand, access transistors 'N1' and 'N2' are on for the bit-cell where write is performed. Therefore, the read current flows through the oxide layer of the MTJ cell whose value needs to read and follows the same current path as the write current of the MTJ on which the write operation is performed. The read current path with respect to the two write current path cases are shown in the figure.

3.5 Memory ports enhancement

In general, communication applications require multiple read-write ports in order to obtain high throughput in a processor. In this paper, our focus is 1R1W multi-port memory architecture, nevertheless extra read-write ports can be easily added to our implementation just by expanding the bit-cell accessibility and increasing corresponding read, source and write lines. Similar to the conventional multi-port architecture, multiple read through the same bit-cell are possible. Moreover, read and write operations on the same cell (r-w contention) can be addressed in a similar way as explained previously. Furthermore, with the addition of ports, the read currents from different ports can follow the write current in the similar way as described earlier. Otherwise, when no write operation is performed, there has to be a dedicated source-line access through which potential '0' can be provided. On the other hand, write-write contention can be resolved based on prioritizing the signals similar to the conventional methods.

3.6 Avoiding redundant writes

An SOT storing device requires a constant current value (around 130 uA in our implementation setup) to switch its magnetization, resulting in significant write access energy consumption. For an energy efficient design, we need to make sure that this architecture consumes energy only when it is necessary. Therefore, in our implementation, we have classified the write operation for each bit into the *necessary* and *unnecessary* categories, which are defined as:

- Unnecessary operations: When the value to be written in the bit-cell is already stored. In this case, the magnetic switching in SOT device does not happen.
- Necessary operations: When the value to be written in the bit-cell is different from the stored one. In this case, the magnetic switching in the SOT device actually happens.

To distinguish between the necessary and unnecessary operations, it is required to know the content of the bit-cell in which the write operation has to be performed. To do so, a read has to be performed prior every write and the write operation is performed after comparing it with the value to be written, similar to the one proposed in [17]. Unlike this technique, we require a dedicated sense amplifier and read-line in our design implementation. In this paper, we term this scheme as an *Unnecessary Write Avoidance* (UWA). With the UWA scheme, considerable energy is saved, nevertheless there is a timing penalty as the circuit delays of the read

Table 1: SOT-MTJ parameters

Parameters	Value
Damping factor	0.5
Bias magnetic field [18]	0.1 T
Saturation Magnetization	1.1×10^6 A/m
Metal Electrode [19]	100 nm × 50 nm × 2.5 nm
Critical current	59 uA
'AP'/'P' resistance	10 KΩ/5 KΩ

and comparator are added to the write latency. This timing penalty can be completely eliminated if the read and write operations are performed concurrently (similar to the one explained in the Section 3.4), which we term as an *Unnecessary Write Termination* (UWT) scheme.

4. EXPERIMENTAL RESULTS

We have performed a detailed circuit-level analysis for our proposed simultaneous read-write multi-port memory architecture. In this section, we first explain the simulation setup, followed by the bit-cell analysis in which the design behavior of our proposed multi-port memory with respect to the standard single-port bit-cell design is illustrated. At the end, a multi-port memory architecture-level analysis is presented to demonstrate a comprehensive comparison of our proposed design with the conventional CMOS-based multi-port design.

4.1 Simulation setup

For the circuit-level implementation, we employed the SOT based MTJ model proposed in [20]. The MTJ parameters used for our work are depicted in Table 1. We used TSMC 65 nm general purpose SPICE model for the simulation of CMOS components. Simulations were performed using Cadence Spectre tool with a power supply voltage of 1.2 V and temperature of 27° C.

4.2 Bit-cell analysis

To demonstrate the efficiency of our proposed multi-port memory architecture, we performed a bit-cell analysis using SPICE simulations. In this analysis, we have compared the behavior of the standard single-port SOT-MRAM design versus our proposed multi-port design. For the standard single-port design, we considered 2T1MTJ (two access transistor and one MTJ cell) type of bit-cell design. On the other hand, the modified 3T1MTJ (3 access transistor and 1 MTJ) type bit-cell, as described in Section 3.3, was used for our proposed multi-port design. Note that, similar read and write circuitries were used for both of these designs. For the proposed multi-port design, the circuit-level analysis was performed in two phases: (1) Independent operation, i.e, when only one operation (either read or write) is performed. (2) Simultaneous operation, i.e., when both read-write operations are performed at the same time.

The results for the independent and simultaneous operations for our proposed multi-port design along with the standard single-port design are summarize in Table 2. As shown in the table, the read latency and energy of our proposed independent operation are slightly increased compared to the standard single-port design. This is due to the addition of an extra NMOS transistor in the bit-cell of the proposed multi-port design. Note that, we have used pre-charged based sense amplifier in which only a peak of current is generated (due to a short-circuit) during a read evaluation. On the other hand, the read latency of our proposed multi-port simultaneous operations is considerably higher compared to

Table 2: Proposed simultaneous read-write 3T1MTJ design versus standard single-port 2T1MTJ design

Design parameters		Standard single-port 2T1MTJ	Proposed 3T1MTJ Independent operation	Proposed 3T1MTJ Simultaneous operation
Read	Latency (ps)	28	30	46
	Energy (fJ)	0.26	0.34	31.44
Write	Latency (ps)	266	266	266
	Energy (fJ)	31.23	31.43	31.44
# Cycle requires for a read and a write operation		Two	One	

both standard single-port and proposed multi-port independent read operations. The reason for the same is that the write current which is relatively very high compared to the read current, slows the read process. Furthermore, the write latency and energy are same for all three cases because the addition of a low read current for a very short duration has almost no impact on a high write current value. Please note that, the read and write latencies are inversely proportional to their respective current values, which means, an increase in the current value can be used for the latency reduction for both read and write operations. In our implementation, both read and write latencies are optimized for the minimum energy consumption, however, these latencies can be further improved by passing higher current, at the cost of more energy.

4.3 Multi-port memory architecture analysis

We have developed a 32 × 32 1R1W multi-port memory for our proposed architecture together with the two proposed avoiding unnecessary write schemes presented in Section 3.6. Moreover, we also implemented conventional CMOS-based multi-port memory with a single-ended read and a double-ended write architecture for the same configuration. The results for the latency and energy comparisons are presented in Table 3. In this table, the results for Unnecessary Write Termination (UWT) and Unnecessary Write Avoidance (UWA) schemes are illustrated for both necessary and unnecessary write operations.

The read latency and energy in our proposed multi-port design are smaller compared to the conventional CMOS design. This is because, in our implementation, we employed pre-charged based SA which is fast and energy efficient. On the other hand, the write latency and energy is relatively high in our proposed multi-port design. This is due to the fact that the SOT device requires a constant current value (around 130 uA in our setup) for a specified duration to switch its magnetization. The switching latency, as mentioned earlier, can be improved with the increase in the write current value. Moreover, the energy efficiency can be significantly improved in the case of unnecessary writes using avoiding unnecessary write schemes with our proposed multi-port design. For instance, compared to proposed multi-port design, the energy in UWT and UWA can be saved for unnecessary writes by around 28 % and 68 %, respectively. The reason of such a high energy saving for UWA scheme is that the write operation is not performed at all for the case of unnecessary writes. In that case, the energy is only consumed by a read and comparator circuitry during the write operation. Nevertheless, there is a timing penalty of 25 % compared to our proposed multi-port design. Whereas, for UWT scheme, the write operation is performed along with the read and the comparison. Hence, for UWT scheme, there is no timing penalty, but the energy saving is less compared to that of UWA. In general, more than 75 %

Table 3: Comparison of conventional CMOS based 32X32 1R1W multi-port memory with our proposed simultaneous read-write architecture

Parameters	CMOS 1R1W multi-port design	Proposed 1R1W multi-port design	Proposed multi-port design with Unnecessary Write Termination		Proposed multi-port design with Unnecessary Write Avoidance	
			Necessary writes	Unnecessary writes	Necessary writes	Unnecessary writes
Read Latency (ps)	263	253	253	253	253	253
Write Latency (ps)	241	431	431	431	539	539
Read Energy (pJ)	1.3	1.1	1.1	1.1	1.1	1.1
Write Energy (pJ)	1.3	2.5	2.6	1.8	2.6	0.8
Leakage (mW)	19.5	8.5	9.8	9.8	9.8	9.8

of the write operations are the unnecessary writes [21, 22]. Since our proposed multi-port design with UWT and UWA are bit-wise technique, the overall energy savings for these approaches can be significantly high at the application-level. Moreover, our proposed architecture is very effective for the leakage reduction because its bit-cell has zero-leakage unlike CMOS design. In our proposed design, the leakage is only contributed by the periphery circuitries such as decoder, read-write circuitry, drivers, etc. Moreover, for the write avoidance schemes, leakage energy is more because of the additional read and comparator circuitry.

We have also analyzed the area for the multi-port design. The proposed multi-port architecture requires three vertical and three horizontal metal lines and the integration of UWT and/or UWA schemes adds one extra vertical metal line as illustrated in Figure 7. The SOT-MTJ cell, which is small in size, is fabricated in different technology layer and its bit-cell comprises of at most four NMOS transistors for 1R1W multi-port design. Hence, the overall SOT based bit-cell is small in area, and the metal pitch of the metal lines for both rows and columns decide the total array area. We estimated the area of a 32 × 32 1R1W multi-port memory using TSMC standard cell library layouts for appropriate sizes. With the addition of write avoidance scheme, due to an extra read and a comparator circuitry, the overall area is increased by 12.7 % compared to our proposed multi-port design.

In summary, our proposed SOT based multi-port memory design has less read latency and energy, and also provide significant leakage reduction. Moreover, the integration of UWT and/or UWA makes the design more energy efficient, especially for applications where switching activity is relatively low.

5. CONCLUSIONS

Spin Orbit Toque is an emerging non-volatile magnetic memory technology which has several advantageous features such as scalability, low area, high endurance, no leakage and immunity to soft-errors. In addition, this device has a capability to perform simultaneous read and write operations on the same cell without affecting each other functionality. In this paper, we propose a novel multi-port memory architecture by exploiting the simultaneous read-write attribute along with its other benefits. We demonstrated the functionality of 1R1W multi-port architecture in all scenarios. Experimental results show that our proposed multi-port design is highly beneficial for read operations and leakage reduction. Furthermore, addition of avoiding redundant write schemes can increase its energy efficiency up to 68 %.

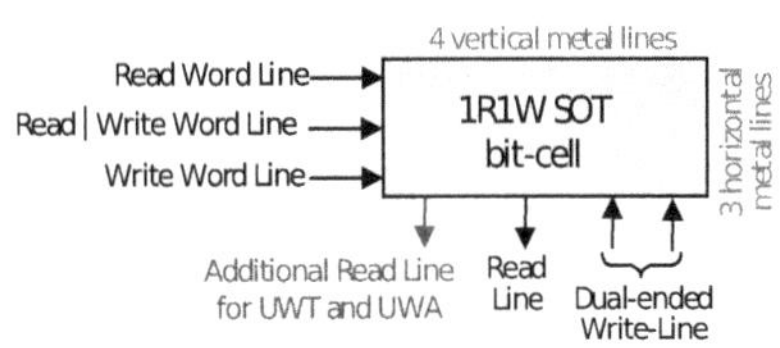

Figure 7: Word-line and bitlines metal tracks for 1R1W bit-cells of proposed multi-port architecture.

6. ACKNOWLEDGEMENT

This work was partly supported by the European Commission under the Seventh Framework Program as part of the spOt project (http://www.spot-research.eu/).

References

[1] J. Owens, et al. Gpu computing. *Proceedings of the IEEE*, 96(5):879–899, 2008.
[2] M. Arora. The architecture and evolution of cpu-gpu systems for general purpose computing. *By University of California, San Diago*, 27, 2012.
[3] NVIDIA Whitepaper: Kepler GK110/210 GPU Computing Architecture. Available: http://international.download.nvidia.com/pdf/kepler/NVIDIA-Kepler-GK110-GK210-Architecture-Whitepaper.pdf.
[4] M. Gebhart, et al. Unifying primary cache, scratch, and register file memories in a throughput processor. *International Symposium on Microarchitecture*, pages 96–106, 2012.
[5] International Technology Roadmap for Semiconductors. Available: http://www.itrs.net, 2013.
[6] F. Oboril, et al. Evaluation of Hybrid Memory Technologies using SOT-MRAM for On-Chip Cache Hierarchy. *TCAD*, 34(3):367–380, March 2015.
[7] Garello, et al. Ultrafast magnetization switching by spin-orbit torques. *Applied Physics Letters*, 105(21), 2014.
[8] R. Bishnoi, et al. Non-Volatile Non-Shadow Flip-Flop using Spin Orbit Torque for Efficient Normally-off Computing. *ASPDAC*, 2016.
[9] Z. Wang, et al. Magnetic non-volatile flip-flop with spin-Hall assistance. *Rapid Research Letters*, 9:375–378, 2015.
[10] Y. Seo, et al. Spin-hall magnetic random-access memory with dual read/write ports for on-chip caches. *Magnetics Letters*, 6:1–4, 2015.
[11] X. Bi, et al. STT-RAM designs supporting dual-port accesses. In *DATE*, pages 853–858, 2013.
[12] X. Liu, et al. An efficient STT-RAM-based register file in GPU architectures. *ASP-DAC*, pages 490–495, 2015.
[13] P. Gambardella and I. M. Miron. Current-induced spin–orbit torques. *Philosophical Transactions of the Royal Society of London A: Mathematical, Physical and Engineering Sciences*, 369(1948):3175–3197, 2011.
[14] L. Liu, et al. Spin-torque switching with the giant spin hall effect of tantalum. *Science*, 336(6081):555–558, 2012.
[15] Y. Kim, et al. Write-optimized reliable design of STT MRAM. *ISLPED*, pages 3–8, 2012.
[16] W. Zhao, et al. Design considerations and strategies for high-reliable STT-MRAM. *Microelectronics Reliability*, 51(9):1454–1458, 2011.
[17] R. Bishnoi, et al. Avoiding unnecessary write operations in STT-MRAM for low power implementation. *ISQED*, pages 548–553, 2014.
[18] K. Jabeur, et al. Ultra-energy-efficient CMOS/magnetic nonvolatile flip-flop based on spin-orbit torque device. *Electronics Letters*, 50(8):585–587, 2014.
[19] K. Jabeur, et al. Spin orbit torque non-volatile flip-flop for high speed and low energy applications. *Electron Device Letters*, 35(3):408–410, 2014.
[20] K. Jabeur, et al. Compact Modeling of a Magnetic Tunnel Junction Based on Spin Orbit Torque. *Transactions on Magnetics*, 50(7):1–8, 2014.
[21] P. Zhou, et al. Energy reduction for STT-RAM using early write termination. *ICCAD*, pages 264–268, 2009.
[22] R. Bishnoi, et al. Asynchronous Asymmetrical Write Termination (AAWT) for a low power STT-MRAM. *DATE*, pages 1–6, 2014.

Optimizing the Operating Voltage of Tunnel FET-Based SRAM Arrays Equipped with Read/Write Assist Circuitry

Hassan Afzali-Kusha, Alireza Shafaei, and Massoud Pedram
Department of Electrical Engineering, University of Southern California, Los Angeles, CA 90089
{afzaliku, shafaeib, pedram}@usc.edu

ABSTRACT

This paper deals with obtaining the minimum operating voltage of memory arrays based on TFET SRAM cells. First, we compare the I-V characteristics of two TFETs and one FDSOI using SPICE simulations. The results reveal that TFET devices exhibit high ON/OFF current ratios at different power supply voltage levels. This observation suggests a higher stability for SRAM cells based on these devices. Next, the characteristics of 6T SRAM cells implemented using minimum sized transistors based on these three device structures are compared. The comparison, which considers two TFET cell structures, i.e., inward and outward SRAMs, is performed at different supply voltages. The results for the hold static noise margin show that at low supply voltages (i.e., below 300mV), the FDSOI SRAM cell cannot hold data whereas both the inward and outward structures of TFET have acceptable noise margins at all supply voltages. Among the two TFET structures, the outward cell is selected because of higher speed especially for the write operation. TFET SRAMs suffer from long read access latency at ultra-low supply voltages (e.g., 150mV). The problem, however, may be overcome by using the negative GND read-assist technique. The results show that for a 32×32 TFET outward SRAM array, the minimum energy consumption (energy-delay product) may be achieved at the supply voltage of 200mV (300mV) with 1.32GHz (4.55GHz) as the read access frequency.

CCS Concepts

• **Hardware~Static memory** • **Hardware~Circuits power issues**

Keywords

SRAM Cells, TFET, FDSOI, Negative GND Technique, Read and Write Assist Techniques

1. INTRODUCTION

SRAM arrays occupy a large portion of the state-of-the-art digital circuits such as microprocessors and systems-on-chips [1]. Accordingly, the power consumption of these large memory arrays constitute a large portion of the chip power consumption.

The main component of the power consumption of the SRAM array is the leakage power [3]. There are different knobs to decrease the SRAM leakage power consumption. One of the effective ones is reducing the power supply voltage (V_{dd}) level [4][5]. The technique, which can minimize the energy consumption and/or the energy-delay product, should be performed carefully. In fact, an aggressive V_{dd} scaling for a noticeable leakage power reduction, may degrade the reliability and speed of SRAM cells [4].

Among the structures which can be used for implementing SRAM cells, FinFET or FDSOI devices may work at lower V_{dd} levels compared to bulk CMOS counterparts. This is due to the improved gate control over the channel reducing the short channel effects. This improves the energy efficiency of SRAM arrays. Aggressive supply voltage scaling, however, is a major challenge even in such devices. At ultra-low supply voltages, it is difficult for an SRAM cell to reliably hold the data. To make this possible, devices with satisfactory ON/OFF current ratio under ultra-low V_{dd} levels are required.

Recently steep subthreshold-slope devices such as Tunnel FETs (TFETs) whose operation is based on the principle of inter-band tunneling of electrons, have gained attention [15]. TFET has been shown as a power efficient switch for logic circuits [6]. The authors of [6], also, have discussed the unidirectionality of the TFET and its deterioration effect on the performance of the standard 6T SRAM cell. Modifications at the circuit level may be used to compensate for the weakness of TFET devices [8][12][17]. In the case of SRAMs, read and write assist techniques, which have small area and energy overheads, are among the circuit techniques that have received attention [7].

In this paper, we focus on obtaining the minimum operating voltage of a TFET SRAM array with assist techniques. The memory array is fabricated using the standard 6T SRAM cells based on minimum sized transistors, which is the state-of-the-art in order to achieve area efficient cells [21][22]. In addition to two existing TFET device structures based on homojunction InAs double-gate, we consider an independent-gate FDSOI structure. Both of the TFET devices have gate length of 20nm and the FDSOI has a gate length of 30nm. TFETs show high ON/OFF current ratios even at the supply voltage of 100mV. The study includes reliability, performance (speed), and power characteristics of the SRAM cells at different supply voltages. The FDSOI-based SRAM cell has zero read static noise margin (RSNM) because of its weak pull-down transistors compared to its access transistors. In addition, it cannot hold data below 300mV. On the other hand, the TFET SRAMs enjoy from higher hold SNM (HSNM) and RSNM values and much smaller power consumption in the hold state (three orders of magnitude lower than that of the FDSOI SRAM). They, however, suffer from lower write margin (WM) values. In addition, the TFET SRAMs have larger read and write access latencies.

GLSVLSI '16, May 18-20, 2016, Boston, MA, USA
© 2016 ACM. ISBN 978-1-4503-4274-2/16/05…$15.00
DOI: http://dx.doi.org/10.1145/2902961.2903031

Next, we investigate the characteristics of the SRAM cells at low supply voltages to explore the suitability of using TFET devices for low-power memory arrays. The investigation reveals that the reliability and power consumption requirements for the SRAM cells are met when TFET devices are used. Also, with the aid of read and write assist circuits, the performance of the SRAM array may be improved. More precisely, for the read operation, the negative GND and for the write operation, the negative bit-line techniques are adopted with an overhead of about ~15% for each assist technique. Using read assist technique in a 32×32 SRAM array, 65% lower read latencies is achieved when averaged over different voltages (from 100mV to 500mV). Furthermore, for the 32×32 SRAM array, the minimum operating voltage for the minimum energy consumption (energy-delay product) is determined to be 200mV (300mV) with 1.32GHz (4.55GHz) as the access frequency.

The rest of the paper is organized as follows. Section 2 presents the basic structures and characteristics of TFET and FDSOI devices as well as the SRAM cell designs. In Section 3, different parameters of the SRAM designs at the nominal supply voltage are studied. The impacts of aggressive voltage scaling on the SRAM parameters are investigated in Section 4. In Section 5, the minimum operating voltages of a 32×32 SRAM array which provide the minimum energy and energy-delay product are determined. Finally, Section 6 concludes the paper.

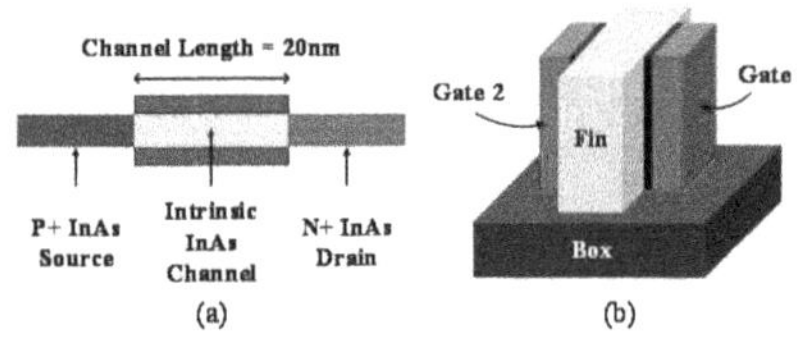

Figure 1. The structures of the (a) Homojunction InAs double gate nTFET and (b) FDSOI.

2. DEVICES AND SRAM DESIGNS

2.1 Device Structures and Characteristics

In recent years, several research works have concentrated on the operation and characteristics of inter-band TFETs (see, e.g., [6-9]). Due to their potentials for sub-KT/q subthreshold-slope operation, one can consider them for very low power digital circuits by aggressively scaling down the supply voltage. In this section, the structures and characteristics of two TFET are compared with an independent multi-gate FDSOI (IMG-FDSOI). An N-type (P-type) TFET structure consists of a P+ (N+) source, an intrinsic channel, and an N+ (P+) drain. The structures of an N-type TFET and FDSOI are schematically drawn in Figure 1.

For the simulations, the TFET transistors are studied through two models of III-V TFET Model (T1) [11] and Universal TFET Model (T2) [13]. The former has both heterogeneous and homogeneous structures where we choose the homogeneous one due to the fact that the device with minimum size in low voltages may be used [10]. The latter contains four structures of double-gate, single-gate, high-performance, and low-power TFET models. To make the conditions of devices similar, we choose the double-gate structure. In the case of the FDSOI device, we adopt the independent multi-gate FDSOI (IMG-FDSOI) model of [14]. In this paper, the channel lengths of TFETs are set to 20nm, whereas a channel length of 30nm is adopted for the FDSOI device. Moreover, in all devices, the width (W) is assumed to be equal to the channel length.

To compare the I-V characteristics of these three structures for the design of SRAM cells, we have plotted the ON current to OFF current ratios (I_{on}/I_{off}) for a wide range of the supply voltage in Figure 2. The results includes both the n-type and p-type devices. As is evident from the figures, for both device types, the ratio is higher for the TFET structures. Since the stability of the SRAM cell depends on this ratio, one may expect a higher stability for the cells based on the TFET devices. Next, we compare the parameters of the 6T SRAM cells designed based on these device structures.

2.2 SRAM Cell Structures

The SRAM cell designed based on the IMG-FDSOI is denoted by 6T-FDSOI. For TFET SRAM cells, we have two standard structures of *inward* and *outward* due to the unidirectional effect of the TFET current. This effect impacts the access transistor. The access transistor of the SRAM cell is used for both of the read and write operations. The access transistor should be able to direct the current in both directions (toward the cell and outward form the cell). Due to the unidirectional effect, the access transistor can direct the ON current only in one direction, and hence, the bit line and bit-line bar (*BL* and *BLB*) voltages in the hold and read states should be assigned such that the stability of the cell can be achieved. We have depicted the structures in Figure 3(a) and (b). For each of these inward and outward structures, the two device models of T1 and T2 are used for implementing the SRAM cells. These cells are denoted by 6Tin-T1, 6Tout-T1, 6Tin-T2, and 6Tout-T2 where the names are self-explanatory.

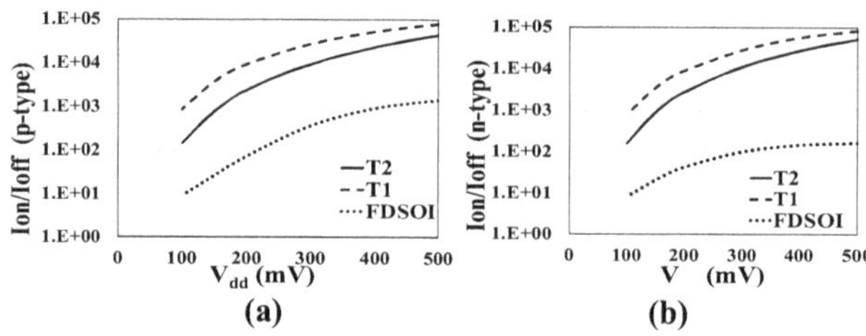

Figure 2. The *Ion/Ioff* ratio of the (a) n-type devices and (b) p-type devices versus the supply voltage.

3. SRAM PARAMETERS AT THE NOMINAL SUPPLY VOLTAGE

3.1 Hold State

In large array cells, most of the cells are in the hold state, and hence, it is important that the cells hold their data during this state. A parameter which can measure the stability of the cell during the hold state is called Hold SNM (HSNM). In Figure 4(a), we have plotted the parameter for these five types of SRAM cells at the nominal supply voltage of 500mV. For the TFET SRAM cells, the HSNM parameter was evaluated for both cases of bit line and bit-line bar voltages of 0 and V_{dd} (i.e., $BL = BLB = 0$ and $BL = BLB = V_{dd}$) for the inward and outward structures. The results showed that for the outward structures 0 and for the inward structures V_{dd} provide higher HSNM values. As is observed from the figures, the HSNM values of the outward and inward structures of each TFET SRAM cell are the same. This is originated from the fact that the access transistors are in the OFF state during the hold state making these two types having almost the same HSNM values. The SRAM cells based on T2 structure provide the highest HSNM values.

In large SRAM arrays, most of the cells are very often in the hold state where the static (leakage) power dissipation is the only cause of the power loss [3]. Hence, the static power of the cells should be minimized to decrease the total power consumption.

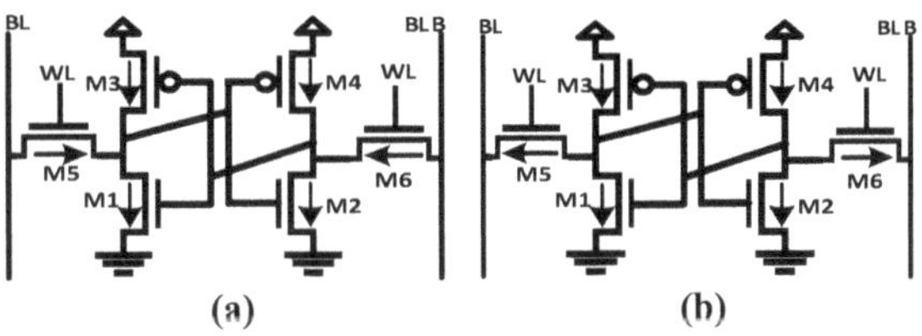

Figure 3. The (a) inward and (b) outward 6T TFET SRAM cells.

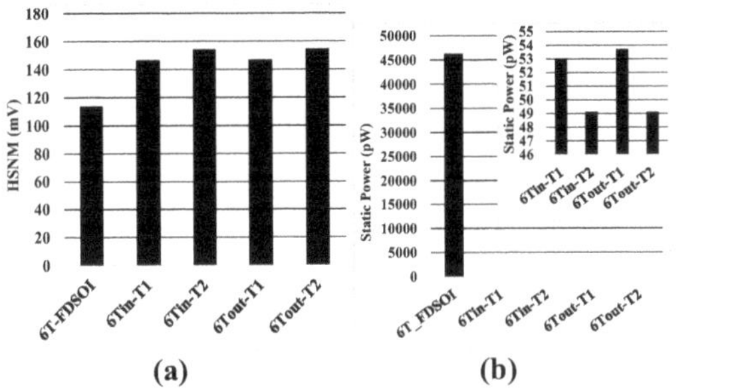

Figure 4. The (a) HSNM and (b) Static Power (SP) of the structures for V_{dd} = 500mV (results are shown for one SRAM cell).

We have shown this parameter for the five structures at the nominal supply voltage of 500mV in Figure 4 (b). The TFET SRAM cells exhibit the lowest leakage power values due to their low off current (see the inset). The inward and outward structures have the same power consumptions due to the voltages that have been assigned to the *BL* and *BLB* lines in this state. The static power of the FDSOI is very high due to its relatively very high OFF current. The T1 based SRAM cells have slightly better power consumptions compared to the corresponding T2 based cells due to the higher I_{on}/I_{off}.

3.2 Read State

3.2.1 Read SNM

In the conventional 6T cell, when Q = "0", during the read operation, the voltage of the node Q rises. If this voltage becomes larger than the trip voltage of the right inverter (M2-M4), the data that is in the cell will flip. The stability of the cell during the read operation may be measured through the read SNM (RSNM) parameter. For measuring the RSNM, again, both cases of 0 and V_{dd} for the *BL* and *BLB* voltages were considered. The results reveal that using 0 for the *BL* and *BLB* in the inward structures and the V_{dd} for the outward structures provide more stability during the read operation for the cells. For instance in outward structure, when V_{dd} = 500mV, RSNMs are 19mV and 103mV for *BL* = *BLB* = 0 and *BL* = *BLB* = V_{dd}, respectively. For the case with *BL* = *BLB* = V_{dd}, the access transistor is reverse biased, but still provides a current between OFF and ON current regardless of the V_{gs} (e.g., for V_{dd} = 500mV, this current is 500× larger than the OFF current and 160× smaller than the ON current). Hence, we can read from the cell with higher delay. To mitigate this, read-assist techniques will be adopted.

The RSNM parameter for all the five SRAM cells are presented in Figure 6. As is evident from the figure, the FDSOI structure has zero RSNM value due to the fact that all the transistors (also pull-down transistor) are minimum sized [21][22]. One may increase the sizes of some of transistors to obtain acceptable RSNM for this cell. This, however, achieved at the price of increasing the SRAM area which is undesired. In the case of the TFET structures, however, the large subthreshold slope (SS) and high I_{on}/I_{off} provide high enough RSNM values.

3.2.2 Read Time

In this part, the read times of the SRAM structures are investigated. The definition of the read time considered here is based on measuring the time that the word line (WL) reaches 50% of V_{dd} until the sense amplifier senses the voltage. The definition for sensing the voltage by the sense amplifier is based on the time that the difference of the two outputs become equal to the half of V_{dd} [15]. It should be noted that the read time parameter depends on the number of the cells in each column. In this work, the results are presented for SRAM array structure of 32×32.

Also, for measuring the read time more accurately, the pre-charge and sense amplifier circuits also were considered. For the FDSOI structures, the usual pre-charge circuit was used. In the case of the TFET SRAM arrays, however, due to the unidirectional effect of the TFETs, we had to add an extra TFET transistor to mitigate the effect. These two pre-charge circuits are depicted in Figure 5(a) and (b). For this circuit, the sizes (*W*/*L*) of M1 and M2 are 40 and M3 (clamp transistor) is 1. The TFET structure has an extra clamp transistor with the size of 1.

We have also considered a latch type sense amplifier made of seven transistors (7T) as shown in Figure 5 (c). The sense amplifier contains two isolating transistors (M1 and M4), two cross-coupled inverters composed of two pull up (M2 and M3) and two pull down (M5 and M6) transistors and a footer transistors. All of the transistors have the minimum size of 1. The sense enable (SE) signal becomes activated when the word line becomes active. When a voltage difference of ΔV is established between *BL* and *BLB*, it triggers the positive feedback provided by the cross-coupled inverters in order to rapidly generate the proper outputs.

The results for read time has been depicted in the Figure 6(b). The smallest read time belongs to the FDSOI cell while the largest time is for the outward structures based on T1 model.

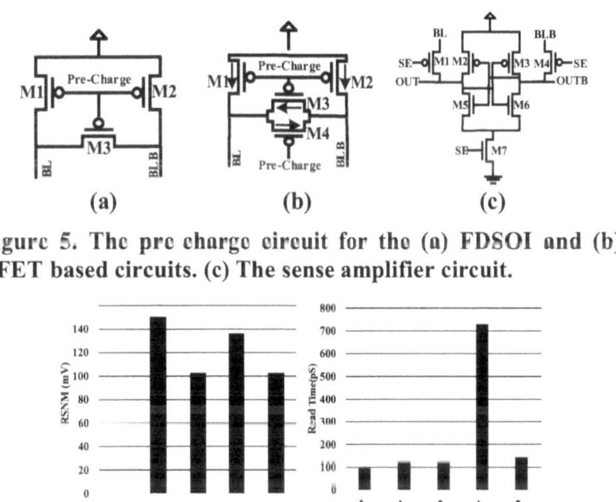

Figure 5. The pre charge circuit for the (a) FDSOI and (b) TFET based circuits. (c) The sense amplifier circuit.

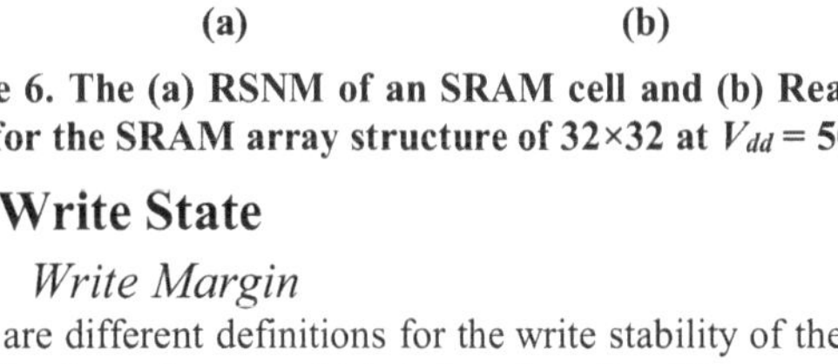

Figure 6. The (a) RSNM of an SRAM cell and (b) Read Time (RT) for the SRAM array structure of 32×32 at V_{dd} = 500 mV.

3.3 Write State

3.3.1 Write Margin

There are different definitions for the write stability of the SRAM cell. We chose the one which is based on the difference between

V_{dd} and the minimum word line (*WL*) voltage that can cause a successful write. This is called the combined word line margin (CWLM) [2]. The results for this parameter for all the structures are given in Figure 7 (a). Since there is no possibility for writing into the inward structures, their write margin is zero. This originates from the fact that the access transistors are inward making impossible to write to the cell [8]. The results indicate the largest value for the 6T-FDSOI (thanks to its high ON current) while the 6Tout-T1 has the lowest value.

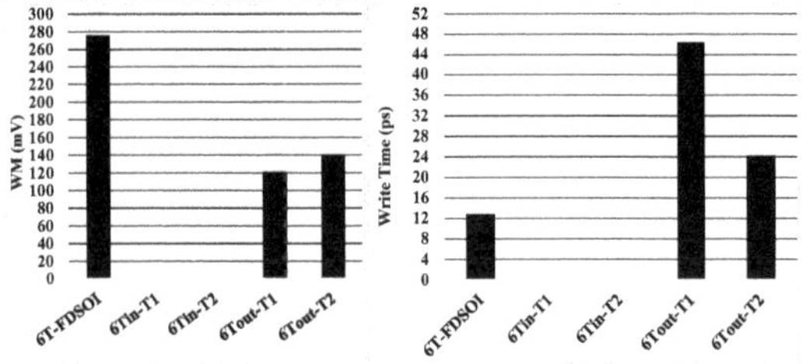

(a) (b)

Figure 7. The (a) Write Margin and (b) Write Time for the SRAM array structures of 32×32 at V_{dd} = 500 mV.

3.3.2 Write Time

Another important metric in the write state is the write time (WT) which may be measured from the time that the word line reaches 50% of the V_{dd} during its activation until the internal nodes *Q* and *QB* reaches each other. The results for this metric have been provided in Figure 7(b) for all the structures in the case of a 32×32 array. As is obvious form the figure, the FDSOI structure has the lowest write time due to its high ON current and also lower capacitance.

4. SRAM PARAMETERS VERSUS THE SUPPLY VOLTAGE

In this section, we explore the SRAM parameters as the supply voltage scales down. While lowering the voltage reduces the energy consumption of the SRAM, one should make sure that the stability and performance requirements are met.

4.1 Hold State

In Figure 8(a), we have plotted the HSNM parameter for the five structures at different supply voltages. As is shown, the FDSOI structures does not have any HSNM at voltages below 300mV preventing its use for ultra-low power SRAM arrays with minimum areas. Again, by the proper selection of the *BL* and *BLB* voltages, the inward and outward structures provide the same HSNM values for the same devices where all the four structures have acceptable (about 20% of V_{dd}) HSNM values. Next, we have drawn the static power of the structures at different voltages in Figure 8(b) which reveals ultra-low static powers for the TFET structures.

4.2 Read State

The RSNM parameter at different supply voltages has been plotted in Figure 9 (a). As we had observed before, the FDSOI structure does not have read stability. This excludes its use for minimum area ultra-low power SRAM arrays. Again, by selecting proper values for the *BL* and *BLB* voltages, for a given device, the inward and outward structures provide the same levels of stability. The T1 based SRAM cells provide larger RSNM (more than 0.3 V_{dd} even at 100mV). In the case of T2 based SRAM cell, the RSNM value is acceptable (about 20% of V_{dd}) for voltages down to 150mV.

Next, the read time at different voltages has been plotted in Figure 9(b). For the supply voltages below 300mV, the FDSOI cell cannot be read. Also, among the TFET structures, the inward structures, can be read faster. The T1 based SRAM cells can be read faster than the T2 based cells. In summary, the TFET structures can be read in ultra-low voltages, however the read times are in the range of ns for ultra-low voltages.

4.3 Write State

Now, we consider the impact of the supply voltage scaling on the write margin parameter. The parameter has been plotted in Figure 10 (a) which reveals that below 300mV, the FDSOI structure does not have any WM.

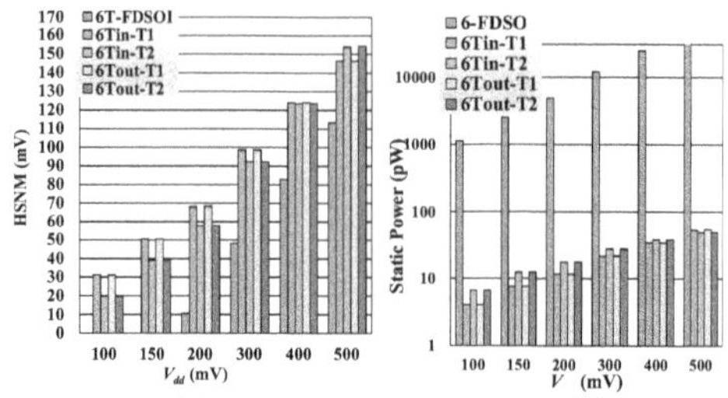

(a) (b)

Figure 8. The (a) HSNM and (b) Static Power of the five structures versus the supply voltage. Vertical axis in (b) is in logarithmic (base 10) scale.

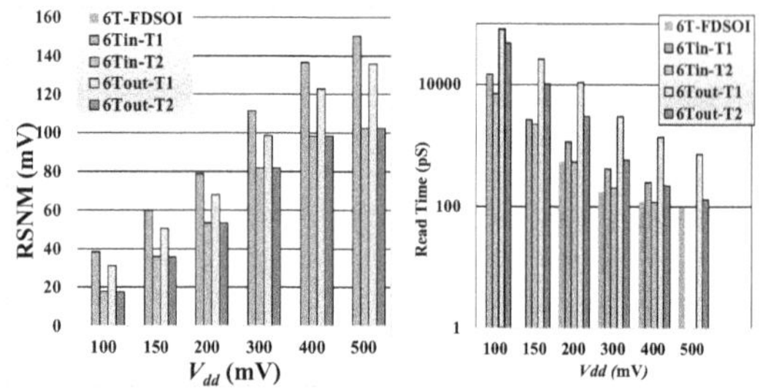

(a) (b)

Figure 9. The (a) RSNM and (b) Read Time of the five structures versus the supply voltage. Vertical axis in (b) is in logarithmic (base 10) scale.

In the case of the inward TFET structures, since the cell cannot be written, there is no positive WM value at any of the voltages. While the 6ToutT2 enjoys from acceptable (about 20% of V_{dd}) WM values even at voltages below 200mV, the 6ToutT1 does not have acceptable WM at voltages below 200mV. Next, we present the results for the write time which are presented in Figure 10 (b). The figure indicates a fast write operation for the FDSOI structure (below 60ps even at 100mV). Since the inward TFET structures may not be written, no write time has been shown for these cells. For the outward TFET structures, the write operation may be performed at supply voltages below 200 mV but taking a long time. The 6ToutT2 structure has a smaller write time in comparison to that of the 6ToutT1.

5. OBTAINING THE MINIMUM OPERATING VOLTAGE FOR THE 32×32 SRAM ARRAY

As was shown above, reducing the supply voltage causes different characteristics for the SRAM designs. From the reliability perspective, the 6ToutT2 SRAM cell satisfied the reliability parameters including HSNM, RSNM, and WM. On the other hand, the outward structure can successfully write data. Therefore, 6ToutT2 SRAM cell is selected for TFET array. This cell, however, may not meet the speed requirement. To solve this problem of the 6ToutT2 SRAM cell, one may invoke some circuit techniques as will be explained next. It should be noted that we consider an array of 32×32 in this section (wiring capacitance has not been considered for both TFET and FDSOI arrays).

5.1 Improving the Read Time

For improving the read time, there are three techniques that can be used. The techniques which include negative cell GND [2], word line boost [19], and cell V_{dd} boost [20] have different area overheads and efficiencies. Our study showed that the negative cell GND was the more efficient one and hence we used this scheme.

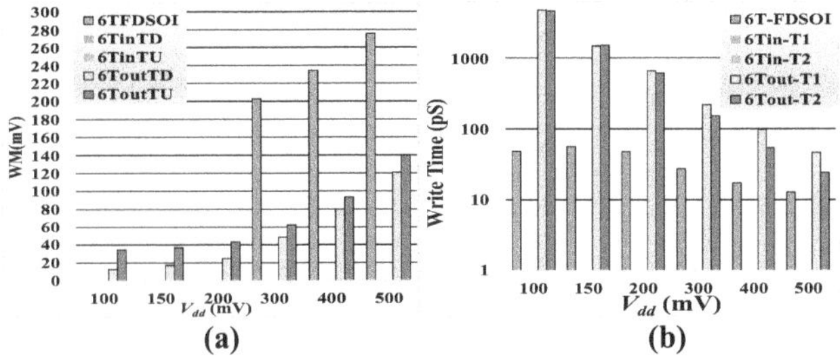

Figure 10. The (a) Write Margin and (b) Write Time versus the supply voltage. Vertical axis in (b) is in logarithmic (base 10) scale.

5.1.1 The Negative Cell GND Technique

Reducing the GND voltage of the cell improves the reading time [8]. In this technique, the V_{gs} of pull down transistor as well as the V_{ds} values of the pull down and access transistors of the cell are increased. To explore this technique, here, we consider a low V_{dd} of 150mV. In Figure 12(a), the read time of the 6ToutT2 cell has been plotted at different negative voltages (in a fraction of Vdd) for the GND. As expected, when the negative bias during the read operation increases, the read time may decrease up to about 90%. The technique will affect the energy efficiency of the whole SRAM array which will be discussed later in this section.

5.1.2 The Negative Voltage Generator

For generating the negative voltage, we utilize the circuit proposed in [2] (shown in Figure 11). A proper value is used for Cc. The buffer shape is an inverter that is sized minimum (the INV$_{PMOS}$ W/L= 1 and INVN$_{MOS}$$W/L$=1). Also the transistor were sized as M1$_{W/L}$ = 13, M2$_{W/L}$ = 1 and M3$_{W/L}$ = 2, to provide the minimum delay such that lower read times are obtained.

For reducing the area overhead of this technique, the negative voltage generator is shared between cells on the same row. The output of this circuit has the load of two source-to-gate capacitances of the pull down transistors of each cell in the row. The sizing scheme and proper value of Cc provided us with the minimum circuit delay at negative supply voltage of -66% V_{dd}. The read time obtained is about 2.5nS which corresponds to a 75% improvement. The SNM of half-selected cells as a result of using this technique is significantly improved (due to stronger cross-coupled inverters). For instance, V_{dd} = 500mV (V_{dd} = 200mV), the HSNM is 154mV (57mV) whereas the SNM of a half-selected cell is 236mV (92mV).

5.1.3 Exploring the Total Energy and Energy-Delay Product

Now, to determine to total energy of the array, we consider the array structure with the negative GND circuit when V_{dd} ranges from 100mV to 500mV. The read times and energy of reading the cell are studied. In addition, the static power of the SRAM array was calculated to determine the total energy of the array based on the following equation:

$$E_{total} = \alpha \cdot E_{acess} + (1 - \alpha) \cdot t_{access} \cdot P_{static} \quad (1)$$

where α denotes the activity factor, which is assumed to be 0.3 in this paper. Based on this, we have plotted the total energy versus V_{dd} in the Figure 13(a).

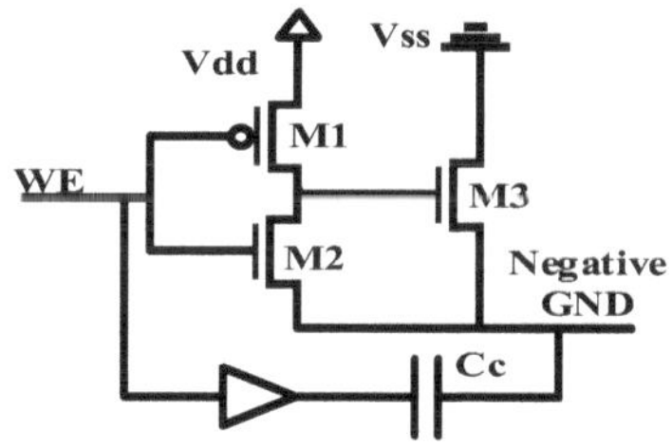

Figure 11. The circuit for generating the negative voltages for the GND of cells in each row.

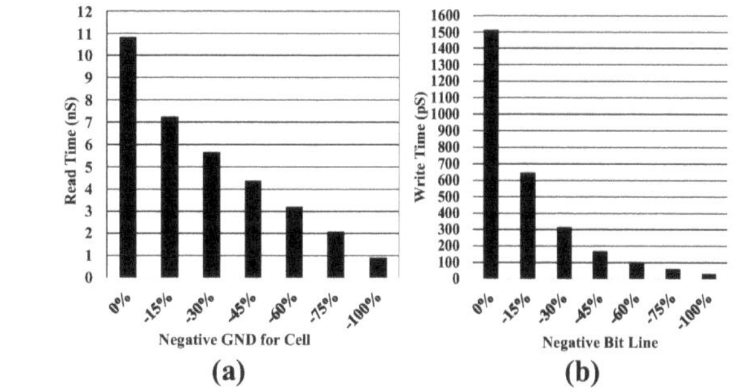

Figure 12. The effects of different negative voltages for (a) the GND of cell on the read time for the 32×32 SRAM array, and (b) the bit line on the write time of each cell at V_{dd} = 150mV. Both figures are obtained using 6ToutT2 SRAM cell.

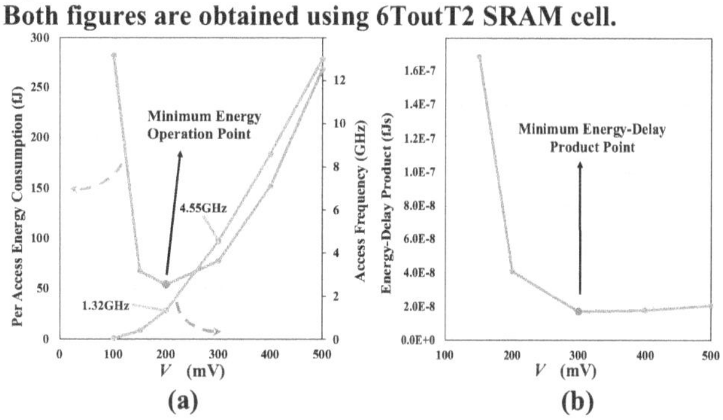

Figure 13. The (a) total energy and (b) energy-delay product for the 32×32 6ToutT2 SRAM array with the read assist circuit versus the supply voltage.

As this figure suggests, the minimum operating voltage for obtaining the minimum total energy consumption is 200mV. Obviously, higher voltages lead to higher energy consumption of the array while lower voltages lead to more energy consuming for the read operation and hence the minimum supply voltage occurs somewhere in between 100mV and 500 mV. It is imperative to mention that the access frequency at this voltage is about 1.32GHZ. Next, the total energy is used to calculate the total energy-delay product whose results are given in Figure 13-(b). The supply voltage corresponding to the minimum energy-delay product occurs at 300mV. This voltage corresponds to the access frequency of 4.55GHz. Finally, note that we also considered the activity factor of 0.5 obtaining the same minimum voltages for the minimum total energy and total energy-delay product.

5.2 Improving the Write Time

For improving the write time, the following four techniques may be used: boosted cell GND [2], negative bit line, word line boost [19], and cell V_{dd} collapse [18]. Again, there are area overheads associated with these techniques, and hence, one need to choose the more efficient one with less area overhead. After evaluating these techniques, we found the bit line negative method as the better technique to be used in this work. In this technique, by decreasing the bit line to negative values which increases the V_{gs} and V_{ds} of access transistors, the write ability is improved. This is due to stronger dependence of the TFET ON current on the V_{ds} which discharges the internal node voltages (VQ or VQB) faster. For generating the negative voltage, we use the circuit of Figure 11. The results for the read time of the 32×32 array with 6ToutT2 structure for different negative voltages are given in Figure 12(b). The supply voltage was assumed to be 150mV. As the negative voltage increases, the write time decreases.

It should be noted that when the bit line is decreased from zero to a negative value, the gate-to-source voltages (V_{gs}) of the access transistors of the other cells in the column (of the cell in which we intend to write) become positive. This makes these cells susceptible to unintentional writing. To make sure that this does not occur in our SRAM arrays, we simulated a cell with the same condition (bit line with a negative voltage and bit line bar at V_{dd}). The result of the simulation showed that there was no unintended writing of the cells. Finally, to minimize the area overhead, the circuit should be shared with all the cells in each column. Connecting the output of the negative voltage generator to the GND of all the cells in a column induces a large load on the circuit due to the capacitances of the source of the pull down transistor of each cell. Therefore, the sizes of the transistors and Cc capacitance should be determined carefully.

6. Conclusion

In this work, we studied the possibility of using TFET devices for realizing SRAM cells at low supply voltages. The study also included a comparison with the FDSOI based SRAM cells. First, the ratios of ON to OFF currents of two type of devices were compared. Then, based on these devices, four minimum sized TFET based 6T cells were compared with a FDSOI based cell in terms of different SRAM parameters at the nominal supply voltage of 0.5V. The four TFET cells consisted of two different TFET models as well as two inward and outward access transistors for each TFET model. To investigate the possibility of using these cells at low supply voltages, the impact of the supply voltage scaling on these parameters were studied for voltages as low as 0.1V. The comparison showed that at low supply voltages (i.e., below 300mV) the minimum sized FDSOI SRAM cell could not hold data whereas both the inward and outward structures had acceptable noise margins at all supply voltages. Also, it was observed that Among the TFET structures, the outward cells had higher speeds especially for the write operation. Also, lowering the supply voltage increased the read access time of the TFET SRAMs especially at very low supply voltages. To overcome the problem, we suggested using the negative GND read-assist technique. Finally, for a 32×32 TFET SRAM array, the minimum operating voltages for the minimum energy consumption and energy-delay product were determined.

7. ACKNOWLEDGMENTS

This research is sponsored by the Software and Hardware Foundations of the National Science Foundation.

8. References

[1] International Technology Roadmap for Semiconductors," 2012. [Online]. Available: http://www.itrs2.net/itrs-reports.html

[2] M. Yabuuchi, K. Nii, Y. Tsukamoto, S. Ohbayashi, and et. al., "A 45 nm 0.6 V cross-point 8T SRAM with negative biased read/write assist," in Proc. IEEE *Symp. VLSI Circuits*, 2009.

[3] S.W. Chang, P.W. Chou, W.C. Wu, "A 130mV SRAM with expanded write and read margins for subthreshold applications," IEEE JSSC, vol. 46, no. 2, pp. 520-529, Feb. 2011.

[4] A.-R. Ahmadimehr, B. Ebrahimi, A. Afzali-Kusha, "A high speed subthreshold SRAM cell design," in Proc. *ASQED*, 2009.

[5] B. Calhoun and A. Chandrakasan, "A256kb sub-threshold SRAM in 65nm CMOS," in Proc. *ISSCC*, 2006, pp.480–481.

[6] W. M. Reddick and G. A. J. Amaratunga, "Silicon surface tunnel transistor," *Applied Physics Letters*, vol. 67, no. 4, pp. 494–496, Jul. 1995.

[7] R. W. Mann, J. Wang, S. Nalam, and et. al, "Impact of circuit assist methods on margin and performance in 6T SRAM," *Solid State Electron.*, vol. 54, no. 11, pp. 1398–1407, Nov. 2010.

[8] D. Kim, Y. Lee, J. Cai, I. Lauer, and et. Al., "Low power circuit design based on heterojunction tunneling transistors (hetts)," in Proc. *ISLPED*. 2009.

[9] K. Bhuwalka, S. Sedlmaier, A. Ludsteck, and et. Al., "Vertical tunnel field-effect transistor," IEEE Transactions on Electron Devices, vol. 51, no. 2, pp. 279–282, Feb. 2004.

[10] P. F. Wang, "Complementary tunneling fets (ctfet) in cmos technology," Ph.D. dissertation, TU Munchen, Munich, Germany, May 2003.

[11] S. Mookerjea and S. Datta, "Comparative study of Si, Ge and InAs basedsteep subthreshold slope tunnel transistors for 0.25v supply voltagelogic applications," in Proc. *DRC*, June 2008.

[12] V. Saripalli, S. Datta, V. Narayanan, and et. al., "Variation-tolerant ultra-low-power heterojunction tunnel FET SRAM design," *IEEE/ACM International Symposium on Nanoscale Architectures*, vol. 1, pp. 45-52, Jun. 2011.

[13] H. Lu, J. W. Kim, D. Esseni, and et. Al., "Continuous semiempirical model for the current-voltage characteristics of tunnel FETs," in Proc. *Int. Conf. ULIS*, 2014.

[14] http://www-device.eecs.berkeley.edu/bsim/?page=BSIMIMG

[15] A.-T. Do, Z.-H. Kong, K.-S. Yeo, and et. al., "Design and sensitivity analysis of a new current-mode sense amplifier for low-power sram," IEEE TVLSI, vol. 19, no. 2, pp. 196–204, Feb. 2011.

[16] S. Mookerjea, D. Mohata, R. Krishnan, and et. al., "Experimental demonstration of 100nm channel length In0.53Ga0.47As-based vertical inter-band tunnel field effect transistors (TFETs) for ultra low-power logic and SRAM applications," in Proc. *IEDM*, pp. 1-3, 7-9 Dec. 2009

[17] X. Yang and K. Mohanram, "Robust 6T Si tunneling transistor SRAM design," in Proc. *DATE*, pp. 1–6, March 2011.

[18] K. Zhang, K. Mistry, and M. Bohr, "A 4.6 GHz 162 Mb SRAM design in 22 nm tri-gate CMOS technology with integrated active VMIN-enhancing assist circuitry," in Proc. *ISSCC*, Feb. 2012.

[19] C. C. Wang et al, "A Boosted Wordline Voltage Generator for Low Voltage Memories," in Proc. *ICECS*, Dec. 2003, pp. 806 - 809.

[20] M. Yamaoka , K. Osada, and K. Ishibashi "0.4-V logic-library-friendly SRAM array using rectangular-diffusion cell and delta-boosted-array voltage scheme," IEEE JSSCC, vol. 39, no. 6, pp. 934 - 940, June 2004.

[21] T. Song et al., "A 14nm FinFET 128Mb 6T SRAM with VMIN enhancement techniques for low-power applications," *ISSCC*, Feb 2014.

[22] E. Karl et al., "A 0.6V 1.5GHz 84Mb SRAM Design in 14nm FinFET CMOS Technology," *ISSCC*, Feb 2015.

Approximate Differential Encoding for Energy-Efficient Serial Communication

Daniele Jahier Pagliari
daniele.jahier@polito.it

Enrico Macii
enrico.macii@polito.it

Massimo Poncino
massimo.poncino@polito.it

Department of Control and Computer Engineering
Politecnico di Torino, Turin, Italy

ABSTRACT

Embedded computing systems include several off-chip serial links, that are typically used to interface processing elements with peripherals, such as sensors, actuators and I/O controllers. Because of the long physical lines of these connections, they can contribute significantly to the total energy consumption. On the other hand, many embedded applications are *error resilient*, i.e. they can tolerate intermediate approximations without a significant impact on the final quality of results. This feature can be exploited in serial buses to explore the trade-off between data approximations and energy consumption.

We propose a simple yet very effective approximate encoding for reducing dynamic energy in serial buses. Our approach uses *differential encoding* as a baseline scheme, and extends it with bounded approximations to overcome the intrinsic limitations of differential encoding for data with low temporal correlation. We show that encoder and decoder for this algorithm can be implemented in hardware with no throughput loss and truly marginal power overheads. Nonetheless, our approach is superior to state-of-the-art approximate encodings, and for realistic inputs it reaches up to 95% power reduction with <1% average error on decoded data.

Keywords

Low Power; Interfaces; Serial Communication; Bus Encoding; Approximate Computing

1. INTRODUCTION

Serial off-chip communication links are popular in embedded systems, due to a number of advantages over parallel interfaces. They offer higher signaling frequencies, thanks to the absence of skew and jitter issues, and to the reduction of crosstalk. Moreover, they reduce costs thanks to the lower pin count, smaller wire area, and easier routing [12]. Off-chip serial buses are most commonly used to connect processing elements (e.g. SoCs) with sensors, actuators and I/O controllers [12]. Typical protocols for these connections include *SPI*, *I2C*, *CAN*, etc.

The consumption due to off-chip serial links can be a significant fraction of the total system energy budget. In fact, physical off-chip interconnects have very large capacitive loads that have not scaled with the same trend as IC technology during the years [11]. Moreover, a typical system often contains tens of these buses operating concurrently (e.g., to interface with multiple sensors). Therefore, the optimization of communication energy costs is a key aspect for the efficiency of an embedded system.

The main source of consumption in long off-chip connections is dynamic energy due to transitions between electrical levels. At the logic level, these transitions correspond to bit value changes. Therefore, most techniques proposed in literature to save energy in serial connections focus on reducing the number of value changes, by *encoding* the data sent on the bus [4, 7–11, 13].

Most encoding algorithms for off-chip serial buses are *lossless*, meaning that the input data can be recovered exactly at the decoder's end, assuming that there are no channel errors [4, 7, 9, 10, 13]. However, many applications that involve serial connections are *error resilient*, i.e. they can tolerate some approximations without a significant impact on the final output quality [3]. This property can be exploited to construct a *lossy* encoding, that can reach larger energy saving at the expense of non-exact decoding.

For instance, error resilience is typical in applications that process data sampled from analog sensors. In this case, approximations can be tolerated as long as they are negligible with respect to the environmental noise and A/D conversion errors. Similarly, resilience is also present when outputs are intended for human consumption, as in multimedia, where the limited perception of human sense organs allows small approximations without a sensible quality loss. Both sensors and multimedia peripherals (e.g. displays) are commonly interfaced serially with the processing subsystem.

The idea of accepting approximations in order to improve other design metrics (and in particular energy efficiency) has been formalized in the Approximate Computing paradigm [6]. Most techniques in this context focus on approximating *computations*, but the same ideas have been recently applied also to *communication* interfaces [11].

One simple yet effective lossless encoding for serial buses is the one proposed by [7], which is based on word-level *differential encoding (DE)*, i.e. sending on the bus the bitwise differences between subsequent words. The effectiveness of this method is due to the strong (positive or negative) *cor-*

GLSVLSI '16, May 18-20, 2016, Boston, MA, USA

DOI: http://dx.doi.org/10.1145/2902961.2902974

relation between subsequent words, for many realistic input sets. However, pure differential encoding does not provide savings when data are uncorrelated, and may even incur in a total energy increase.

In this paper we propose a new difference-based encoding that, by allowing approximations, overcomes the limitations of lossless DE. Moreover, for the same inputs, it reaches significantly larger energy saving with respect to state-of-the-art algorithms, both accurate and approximate, with minimal impact on quality. We show the effectiveness of our method for realistic bus traces generated by error resilient applications, as well as for random data with different distributions. Finally, we propose a hardware implementation of our algorithm, showing that it introduces minimal power overheads and no throughput loss.

2. BACKGROUND AND RELATED WORK

Due to the large pitch of PCB lines, off-chip serial connections can be considered as purely capacitive loads [4,7,8,10, 11]. Thus, the total power consumption is approximately equal to the dynamic power, and can be computed as:

$$P_{chan} = P_{dyn} = \alpha \cdot C_{tot} \cdot V_{DD} \cdot V_{swing} \cdot f \quad (1)$$

where C_{tot} is the total channel capacitance, accounting for contributions due to the driver, the pin and the wire, V_{DD} is the driver supply voltage, and V_{swing} is the voltage swing between electrical levels. f is the clock frequency used for transmitting, and $\alpha \in [0, 1]$ is the *switching activity factor*, that accounts for the probability of occurrence of a value change in each clock cycle.

The vast majority of techniques for optimizing energy consumption in off-chip buses focuses on lowering α, reducing the number of intra-word and inter-word bit toggles by means of a proper *encoding* algorithm [4,7–11,13]. We refer to the total sum of bit value changes during the operation of a bus as the *Transition Count* (TC).

The literature on bus encodings for low power focuses prevalently on parallel buses, while serial buses did not receive as much attention. This is partly due to the fact that a *single* physical line offers less opportunities for optimization. However, serial interconnects are becoming extremely popular in modern computing systems, for both off-chip and on-chip links. Therefore, in the last years, interest on low power serial bus encodings has grown significantly [4,7–11,13]. In general, encoding algorithms can be divided in two categories: *lossless* or *accurate* encodings, for which in absence of channel errors the transmitted data can be decoded *exactly* at the receiver's end, and *lossy* or *approximate* encodings, which sacrifice total accuracy in the transmission, in order to reach larger TC reductions.

Lossless algorithms can be used in all types of I/O buses, i.e. data, addresses, and instructions. Most of them have been proposed in the context of Network on Chip (NoC) links [4, 7,9,10,13], but they are also applicable to off-chip buses. A common characteristic of lossless approaches is to leverage *a priori assumptions* on the nature of the data to be encoded, in order to achieve TC reduction. The most common feature exploited is *temporal correlation*, i.e. dependence among subsequent words.

For example, the authors of [7] propose a simple scheme called SILENT based on *differential encoding*, i.e., transmitting the bitwise difference between subsequent words; this solution allows to reduce the transition count when data are strongly correlated, both positively (same sign) and negatively (opposite signs). However, when data are uncorrelated, pure differential encoding can even lead to an *increase* of the power consumption in the bus.

Several other lossless encodings try overcome this issue. In [9], a hybrid encoding is proposed, that transmits either the bitwise difference between consecutive words or the one between every other word, depending on a prediction of data correlation. The authors of [13], instead, propose to invert the bit values only in the even positions of a word, when the intra-word transition count is more than half the length of the word. In [4], TC reduction is achieved by swapping the positions of some bits within words.

All three of these algorithms, however, suffer from the major drawback of requiring *redundant* bits, which are extremely costly in serial connections. In fact, if these ancillary bits are transmitted on an additional physical line, the total cost of the connection in terms of area, wiring, etc. is doubled. Instead, if they are sent on the same line as the data there is a latency overhead, as a fraction of the bus bandwidth is "wasted" for transmitting the redundant information.

Finally, the work of [10] is specifically targeted at *display interfaces*, and it exploits the locality of data in images. To this end, pixel *differences*, rather than pixel values, are sent on the bus, and a look-up-table is used to map the most common differences, i.e. the smallest ones, to low transition count codewords.

Lossy encodings, on the other hand, cannot be used for addresses and instruction, but only for *data* buses. However, for the latter type of connection, they allow greater power savings at the expense of non-exact decoding. An early work in this field is found in [8], again in the context of display interfaces. The authors propose approximate encodings for two LCD serial protocols, based on a smart rounding with bounded error of some LSBs of the transmitted pixels, which accounts also for inter-pixel transitions. More recently, the *Rake* algorithm has been introduced in [11]. Rake has linear complexity in the bit-width of the transmitted words, and heuristically attempts to minimize the TC, under a maximum value deviation constraint. In practice, Rake approximates each word by inverting some of its bits, in order to generate long sequences of ones and zeros. Interestingly, Rake does not exploit data correlation to reduce the TC.

3. PROPOSED METHOD

3.1 Differential Encoding

Word-level Differential Encoding (DE) is a simple yet effective way to reduce the transition count, and consequently the power consumption in serial buses, for many realistic case studies [7]. The basic idea of this technique is to transmit on the bus the *bitwise difference* between consecutive words. Accordingly, codeword bits are generated as follows:

$$B_i[t] = b_i[t] \oplus b_i[t-1], \ \forall i \in [1, n] \quad (2)$$

where $\oplus$ indicates the binary XOR operator, $b_i[t]$ is the i-th bit of the input word at time t, and $B_i[t]$ is the corresponding bit of the DE codeword. The decoding operation is equally simple, and is achieved as:

$$b_i[t] = B_i[t] \oplus b_i[t-1], \ \forall i \in [1, n] \quad (3)$$

The rationale of DE is that many realistic bus traces (from sensors, multimedia applications, etc.) contain data with

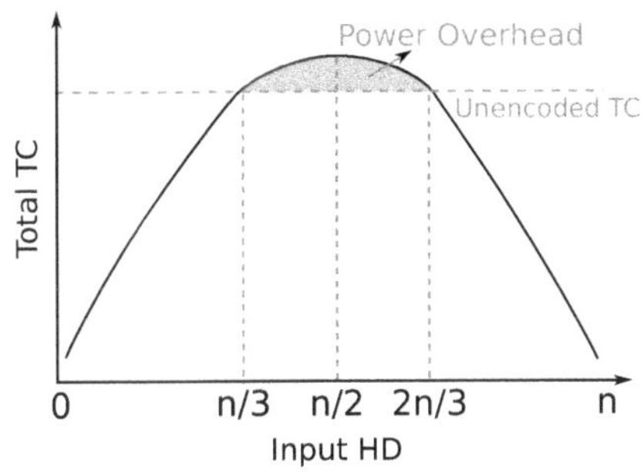

Figure 1: Input Hamming Distance versus Transition Count for accurate Differential Encoding.

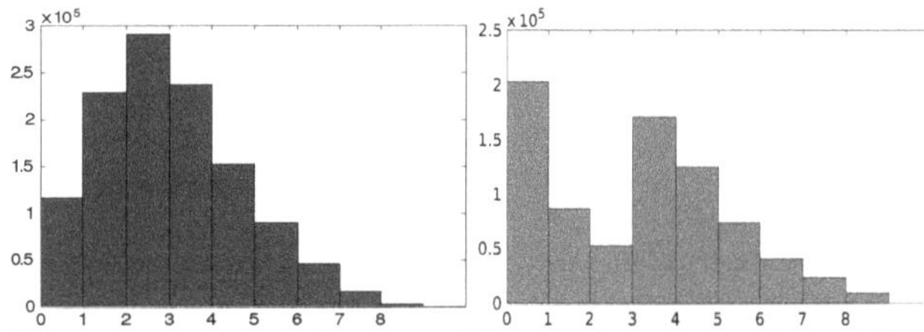
(a) HD histogram in the original bus trace. (b) HD histogram after 3-LSB-saturation.

Figure 2: Hamming Distance histogram of the bus trace produced by an image, before and after LSB-saturation.

a strong *temporal correlation*, i.e. a strong dependence between subsequent words. In common binary formats, two strongly correlated words most probably also have either a very small or a very large *Hamming Distance* (HD), defined as the number of different bits in corresponding positions. For example, let us consider two's complement representation. If two consecutive numbers in a bus trace are similar and have the same sign (strong *positive* correlation), then *in most cases* they only differ in some of the Least Significant Bits (LSBs), hence they have a small HD. On the contrary, if they have opposite sign, but still similar magnitude (strong *negative* correlation), the majority of the Most Significant Bits (MSBs) will be different, due to sign extension, resulting in a large HD.
By encoding words as bitwise differences, DE reduces the transition count in both these conditions. In fact, according to Eq.2, the codewords will be dominated by 0s when the HD is very small, and by 1s when it is very large. Hence, in both cases, the probability of a value transition will be lowered. More details on using differential encoding for TC reduction in serial buses can be found in [7].

3.2 Motivation

Fig. 1 shows the *qualitative* dependence between the total TC (and consequently the power consumption) achieved by pure differential encoding and the average HD of the input data, as reported in [7]. Consistently with the analysis of Sec. 3.1, the largest savings are obtained for very small or very large HDs. However, when the HD is about half of the word length n, DE fails to reduce the TC, and actually incurs in a power overhead.
As mentioned in Sec. 3.1, many realistic input traces are characterized by strong temporal correlation, which favors small or large average HD values. However, data transmitted on off-chip serial buses, e.g. from/to sensors and actuators to/from processing elements, often have a relatively short bitwidth (8-12 bits) [12]. Thus, despite correlation, many word pairs have a HD that falls in the region for which DE savings are small, or even negative. An example is displayed in Fig. 2a, which contains the HD histogram of the trace of words generated when transmitting on a serial bus the 512x512 image *Lena* [1], represented as 24-bit RGB. The spatial correlation of pixel values in the image translates into a marked temporal correlation between consecutive bus words. The most probable HD is 2, but many pairs of words have HD= 3 or HD= 4. Due to the fact that pixels are represented with only 8 bits (per color channel), and considering Fig. 1, it is evident that these HD values are not optimal for pure differential encoding.

3.3 Approximate Differential Encoding

The traces that exhibit the data correlation property exploited by differential encoding are often related to error resilient applications [6]. For example, data from sensors are often characterized by phases of idleness, in which words are approximately constant (hence correlated), alternated with phases of intense information content [5]. Similarly, data from multimedia applications also exhibit a strong correlation, due to their intrinsic features (e.g. the already mentioned spatial correlation between image pixels) [1]. The error tolerance property can be exploited to slightly modify the data, in order to reshape the histogram of Hamming Distances, in a way that favors differential encoding.
To this end, we propose a new lossy serial bus encoding, called Approximate Differential Encoding (ADE). ADE preprocesses the words before encoding them as explained in Sec. 3.1. In particular, some of the LSBs are rounded (i.e. saturated either to 11..1 or 00..0), in a way similar to [8]. By doing so, when the bitwise difference among two consecutive words is computed, the LSB-part of the resulting codeword will consist either of all ones or of all zeros, and will not generate any intra-word transition.
From the HD perspective, LSB rounding reshapes its distribution by skewing it towards the extreme values, i.e., those for which DE performs well. This can be observed in Fig. 2b, which contains the HD histogram of the same trace of Fig. 2a, but in which 3 LSBs have been rounded. Notice how the probability of HD $= 0$ increases dramatically, while the occurrence of HD values between 2 and 4 is reduced. When differential encoding is applied to this second set of data, TC reduction, and consequently power saving will be significantly larger than when transmitting the original exact values. Notice that, by saturating 3-LSBs, ADE implicitly accepts a maximum error on each pixel of just $\frac{7}{256} \approx 2.7\%$ [8]. As we will show in Sec. 4, this error constraint produces a minimal degradation in quality.
The complete ADE encoding phase is reported in Algorithm 1 in form of pseudo-code. Thanks to properties of boolean logic, it can be proved that performing the saturation phase after the bitwise difference phase does not alter the resulting codewords.
The number of LSBs that are saturated (denoted as l) is an input parameter of our algorithm. This allows to change the quality level of the encoding at runtime, for example in response to a change in the system status, such as the percentage of battery charge in a mobile device, or the environmental conditions. Moreover, ADE decoding (which is identical to DE decoding, expressed by Eq. 3) does not need to be aware of the quality parameter l. Thanks to this,

Algorithm 1 ADE encoding algorithm.

```
input:
    w: input word
    l: number of saturated bits
output:
    B: codeword
procedure ADE ALGORITHM
    ▷ Saturation Phase
    for i ∈ [1, l] do
        tmp_i[t] = w_{l+1}[t]
    end for
    for i ∈ [l + 1, n] do
        tmp_i[t] = w_i[t]
    end for
    ▷ Bitwise Difference Phase
    for i ∈ [1, n] do
        B_i[t] = tmp_i[t] ⊕ tmp_i[t − 1]
    end for
end procedure
```

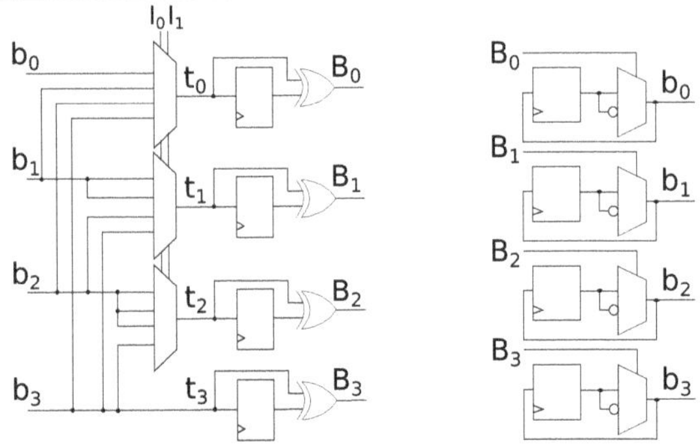

(a) Encoder. (b) Decoder.

Figure 3: Hardware implementation of 4-bit ADE.

ADE is more flexible than just reducing the bitwidth of the transmitted data and then performing accurate DE.

3.4 Example of Operation

Table 1 reports an example of operation of ADE on 8-bit data. Besides the input words and the ADE outputs, with the corresponding total transition counts (TC), the table also reports the outcomes of accurate differential encoding (DE), and of LSB-saturation (LSBS) without differential encoding. In both LSBS and ADE, three LSBs are saturated, which corresponds to a maximum allowed error of 2.7%, as in the example of Sec. 3.3. For the computation of the total TC, we considered both intra-word and inter-word transitions, and we assumed LSB-first transmission.

ADE performs better than both other algorithms, by combining their features; the principle of LSBS is used to force similar subsequent words to become identical (inputs 2-4), so that when they are encoded with DE they produce a TC of 0. The column labeled |E| for LSBS and ADE refers to the introduced error (assuming that the words represent unsigned integers). Obviously, it is identical for both lossy algorithms. On average, the error per word is $\frac{11}{6} = 1.83 < 1\%$.

3.5 Hardware Implementation

Fig. 3 contains the schematic of the hardware implementation of the ADE algorithm. For simplicity, the diagram refers to a 4-bit realization. The encoder is exactly equivalent to Algorithm 1: multiplexers allow a variable number of saturated bits, depending on the value of l (l_0 and l_1 in the figure), whereas flip-flops and XOR gates realize differential encoding. The decoder is even simpler and bit-sliced: for each bit, a multiplexer selects between the asserted and the negated value from the last decoded word, depending on the corresponding codeword bit.

Both hardware units have a single clock cycle latency, and 1-word/cycle throughput. Therefore, they do not introduce any performance overhead. Moreover, as confirmed by the experiments in Sec. 4, the area and power overheads are also minimal. In fact, each hardware block is composed of a single register plus a small number of logic gates.

Input			DE		
Word	TC	|E|	Word	TC	|E|
00001011	3	-	00001011	3	-
00001111	5	-	00000100	5	-
00001100	7	-	00000011	7	-
00001101	11	-	00000001	9	-
00010111	15	-	00010111	13	-
00100011	19	-	00110100	17	-
LSBS			**ADE**		
Word	TC	|E|	Word	TC	|E|
00001000	2	3	00001000	2	3
00001111	4	0	00000111	4	0
00001111	6	3	00000000	4	3
00001111	8	2	00000000	4	2
00010111	12	0	00011000	6	0
00100000	14	3	00110111	10	3

Table 1: Example of operation of the DE, LSBS and ADE algorithms for a trace of 8-bit unsigned data.

4. EXPERIMENTAL RESULTS

4.1 Experimental Setup

We tested ADE on different input sets, some taken from realistic error resilient applications and some others randomly generated:

- A set of images from the Kodak online database [1], represented as 24-bit (8-bit per channel) RGB. They are representative of multimedia applications, which involve various types of serial buses, for instance in the connection to a display panel, or in the interface with an image sensor (e.g., using the MIPI CSI-2 camera interface [2]).
- A set of Electrocardiogram (ECG) data on 11-bit unsigned binary, taken from the Physionet online database [5], as representatives of biomedical sensors.
- A third set of realistic input data coming from the axes of an accelerometer IC, used in a shock detection application. These data are represented on 12-bit two's complement.
- To show the generality of our method, we also tested it with Gaussian and uniform randomly generated data. In this case, we used 12-bit unsigned format. For Gaussian data, we set the mean value μ of the distribution to half of the full-scale (2^{11}), and we tried different values for the standard deviation σ. Uniform inputs span the entire range $[0 : 2^{12} - 1]$.

For each input set, we simulated a LSB-first serial transmission, and evaluated the total transition count (TC), including both intra-word and inter-word transitions. As explained in Sec. 2, TC is directly proportional to power consumption in the bus. The relatively small bitwidth of all considered

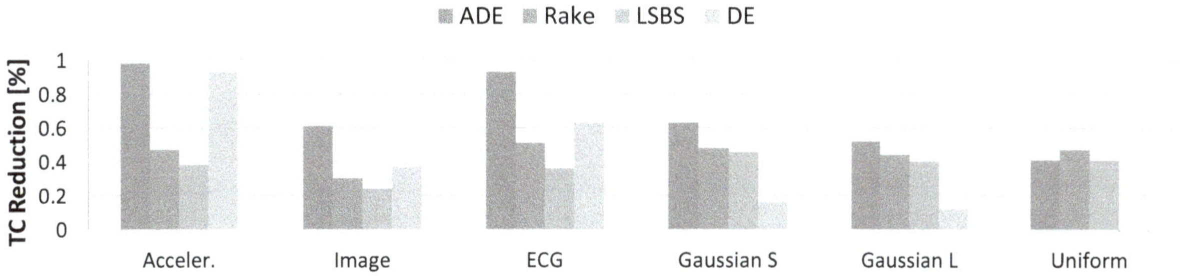

Figure 4: Comparison between ADE and state of the art serial encodings, with a maximum relative error of 1%.

input sets reflects the one used in real applications. In fact, most analog-to-digital converters connected to sensors provide 8-12-bit outputs, and 24-bit RGB is the most common format used in real displays [8].

4.2 Comparison with the State of the Art

We compared the ADE algorithm with accurate Differential Encoding (DE) [7], as well as with Least Significant Bit Saturation (LSBS) [8]. As explained in Sec. 3, these algorithms are used as an inspiration for ADE. Moreover, as a representative of state of the art approximate encodings for serial buses, we considered also *Rake*, proposed in [11]. The bar chart in Fig. 4 reports the TC reduction obtained with these algorithms for the inputs described in Sec. 4.1. Two Gaussian sets are considered, with small (S) and large (L) standard deviations of $\sigma = 2^7$ and $\sigma = 2^9$ respectively. For approximate encodings, the maximum allowed error constraint is set to $\epsilon_r = 1\%$ of the full-scale value (FS) of the considered input set. In ADE and LSBS, the number of saturated bits is obtained as: $l = \lfloor \log_2(\epsilon_r \cdot FS) \rfloor$, so that the constraint is never violated.

ADE performs better than all other algorithms but for the uniformly distributed data set. In particular, for the Image and ECG inputs, the TC reduction obtained with ADE is remarkably over 20% better with respect to all other algorithms. The largest savings are obtained for the ECG and accelerometer data due to the long "almost-constant" (highly correlated) sections in the bus traces produced by these inputs. Furthermore, ADE *always* achieves greater savings with respect to accurate DE. Even for the uniform set (i.e., a fully random uncorrelated signal) ADE is still able to reduce the TC of ≈ 40%, while DE causes a slight increase in TC. This is an important property, that justifies the presence of approximations in ADE. Notice that, for some inputs, this property is not achieved by LSBS and Rake.

The Pareto curve generated by the four algorithms in the error vs power saving space is shown in Fig. 5 for some of the tested input sets. In this experiment, the number of saturated bits in ADE and LSBS (l) has been varied from 1 to 5. The maximum error constraint of Rake [11] has been set to the value $2^l - 1$, to compare it fairly with the other two algorithms. In the plots, the x axis reports the average *absolute* error per word obtained at the output of the decoder, whereas the y axis shows the TC reduction. For ADE, Rake and LSBS, different points in the curves correspond to different error constraints. The horizontal line, instead, represent the TC reduction obtained with accurate DE, which does not make any error.

The plots clearly show that ADE dominates other approximate encodings: for a given average error, it reaches significantly larger power savings. The advantages of ADE are particularly marked for ECG and Image data, but they area also present for random inputs. Moreover, as mentioned, ADE is always superior to DE, differently from Rake and LSBS. For ECG data, our encoding reaches more than 95% power reduction, if an average absolute error of 10 is accepted (less than 0.5% of the full scale value $FS = 2^{11} - 1 = 2047$). In the same quality conditions, both Rake and LSBS savings are still inferior to DE (which reduces TC of ≈ 63%).

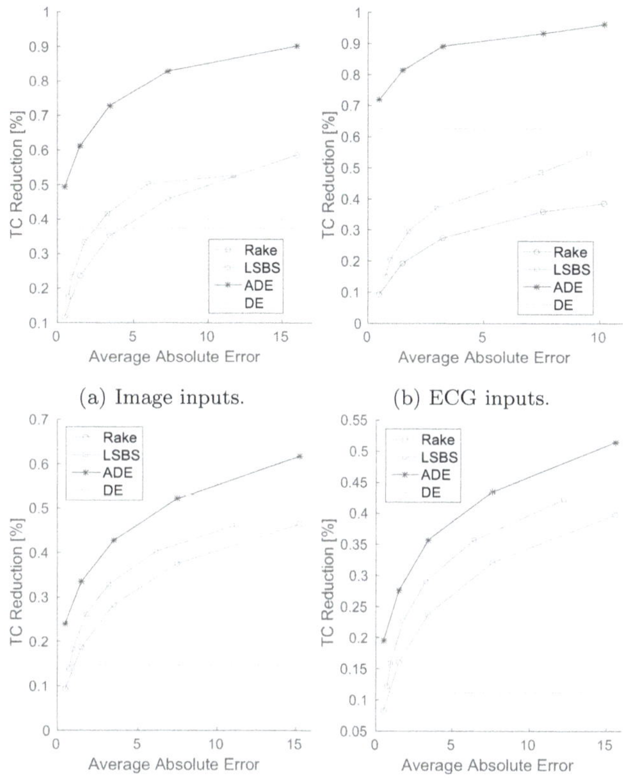

(a) Image inputs.

(b) ECG inputs.

(c) Gaussian S inputs.

(d) Gaussian L inputs.

Figure 5: Absolute error versus TC reduction Pareto curve for different serial encodings.

4.3 Results Analysis

The results shown in Sec. 4.2 are explained considering the discussion of Sec. 3. The saturation of LSBs performed in ADE *favors* differential encoding, by reshaping the distribution of Hamming Distances. Thanks to this reshaping, our algorithm outperforms both LSBS and accurate DE. This phenomenon has already been shown in Fig. 2 for image inputs. In Fig. 6, original (left) and "saturated" (right) HD distributions are shown for ECG inputs and for one of the

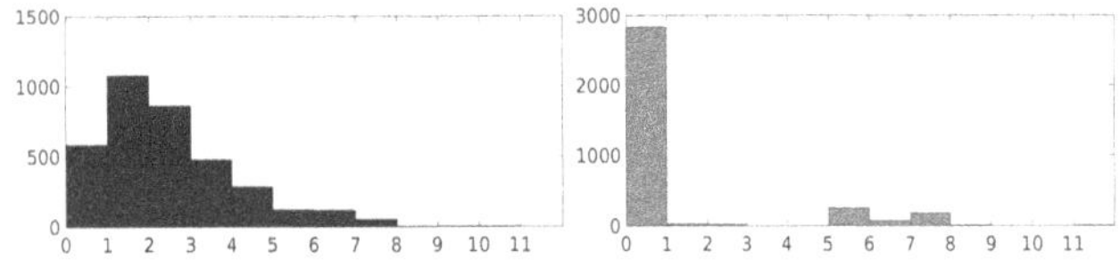

(a) ECG inputs ($n = 11$, $l = 4$).

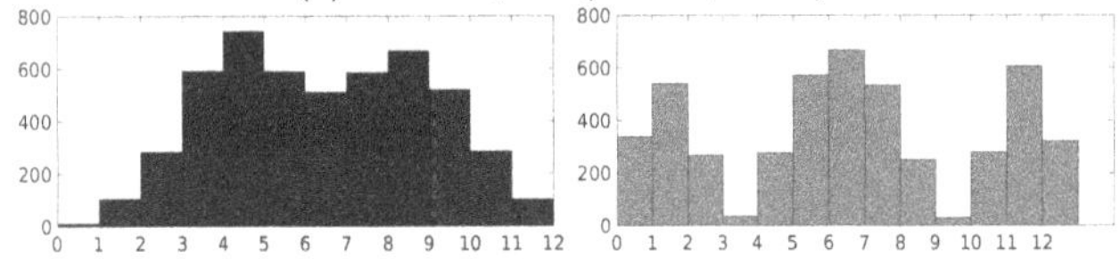

(b) Gaussian S inputs ($n = 12$, $l = 5$).

Figure 6: HD histogram reshaping due to LSB saturation.

(a) Input. (b) ADE Decoding Output.

Figure 7: Example of ADE decoding output with $l = 2$, for an image. Power reduction $\approx 65\%$.

two Gaussian sets. The allowed error is $< 1\%$ for both inputs; the corresponding number of saturated bits l is reported in the figures, and depends on the data bitwidth.
Finally, Fig. 7 shows one of test images used in our experiments [1], before and after a simulated serial transmission using ADE. In this simulation, l has been set to 2, which corresponds to a maximum allowed error of $\frac{3}{256} \approx 1.1\%$, and causes a TC reduction of $\approx 65\%$ on the bus. Notice that despite this significant power reduction, the two images look extremely similar; the output of ADE decoding is slightly more noisy due to the errors introduced by saturation, but this does not impact the visual quality. This qualitative analysis is also confirmed by quantitative measures. In fact, the structural similarity index (SSIM) between the two images is 98.8%.

4.4 Hardware Overheads

As a final experiment, we synthesized the hardware implementations of ADE encoder and decoder, shown in Fig. 3a and 3b, targeting a 45nm CMOS standard cell library from ST Microelectronics. The two designs have been specified at RTL in VHDL, and synthesized using Synopsys DC K-2015.06. To verify the correctness of the implementations both at RTL and post synthesis, we leveraged timing simulation in Mentor Questa Simulator v10.4, with random inputs. During post synthesis simulations, we also annotated switching activity data, which we then loaded in Synopsys PT J-2014.12 to accurately estimate power.
Synthesis results for a 12-bit implementation are shown in Table 2. This bitwidth has been chosen to match the typical accuracy of many sensor ICs. Area and power information in the table refer to implementations at f_{max}, and the latter includes both leakage and dynamic contributions. Evidently, encoder and decoder overheads are negligible, even at very high operating frequencies.

Circuit	f_{max} $[GHz]$	Area $[\mu m^2]$	Power $[mW]$
Encoder	1.67	170.40	0.33
Decoder	2.50	101.61	0.60

Table 2: Synthesis results for 12-bit ADE encoder and decoder on 45nm CMOS.

5. CONCLUSIONS

Energy optimization in communication interfaces, and especially in long off-chip serial connections, is an important design problem for modern embedded systems. In this paper, we have proposed Approximate Differential Encoding (ADE), a novel approximate encoding for reducing power consumption in serial buses.
ADE is based on simple approximation mechanisms, that leverage the correlation properties, as well as the error tolerance exhibited by many realistic input sets. Thanks to this, it is able to significantly reduce the Transition Count, and therefore the power consumption on the bus, with negligible implementation overheads. The savings obtained with ADE are superior to both accurate and approximate encodings existing in literature for this type of buses. Moreover, ADE allows to set different quality constraints at runtime, in order to respond to changes in the application requirements or in the system status. In conclusion, this encoding configures as a very promising way to tackle consumption in serial buses.

6. REFERENCES

[1] Kodak image database. http://r0k.us/graphics/kodak.

[2] MIPI Camera Interface Specifications, 2015 http://mipi.org/specifications/camera-interface.

[3] V. Chippa et al. Analysis and characterization of inherent application resilience for approximate computing. Proc. *DAC 2013* pp 1–9.

[4] S. Ghosh et al. Data correlation aware serial encoding for low switching power on-chip communication. Proc. *ISVLSI 2014*, pp. 124–129.

[5] A. Goldberger et al. Physiobank, physiotoolkit, and physionet: Components of a new research resource for complex physiologic signals. *Circulation*, 101(23):e215–e220, 2000.

[6] J. Han and M. Orshansky. Approximate computing: An emerging paradigm for energy-efficient design. Proc. *ETS 2013*, pp. 1–6.

[7] K. Lee et al. Silent: serialized low energy transmission coding for on-chip interconnection networks. Proc. ICCAD 2004, pp. 448–451.

[8] M. Poncino and E. Macii. Low-energy rgb color approximation for digital lcd interfaces. *IEEE Trans. on Consum. Electron.*, 52(3):1004–1012, 2006.

[9] X. Ren et al. Adaptive low-power transmission coding for serial links in network-on-chip. *Procedia Engineering*, 29:1618–1624, 2012.

[10] S. Salerno et al. Limited intra-word transition codes: an energy-efficient bus encoding for lcd display interfaces. Proc *ISLPED '04*, pp. 206–211, 2004.

[11] P. Stanley-Marbell and M. Rinard. Value-deviation-bounded serial data encoding for energy-efficient approximate communication. Technical Report MIT-CSAIL-TR-2015-022, MIT, 2015.

[12] F. Vahid and T. Givargis. *Embedded System Design: A Unified Hardware/Software Introduction.* Wiley, 2001.

[13] J. Zeng et al. Transition inversion coding with parity check for off-chip serial transmission. Proc. *ICECS, 2014*, pp. 634–637, 2014.

Fast Thermal Simulation using SystemC-AMS*

Yukai Chen, Sara Vinco, Enrico Macii and Massimo Poncino
Department of Control and Computer Engineering, Politecnico di Torino, Torino, Italy
name.surname@polito.it

ABSTRACT

Out of the many options available for thermal simulation of digital electronic systems, those based on solving an RC equivalent circuit of the thermal network are the most popular choice in the EDA community, as they provide a reasonable tradeoff between accuracy and complexity. HotSpot, in particular, has become the de-facto standard in these communities, although other simulators are also popular. These tools have many benefits, but they are relatively inefficient when performing thermal analysis for long simulation times, due to the occurrence of a large number of redundant computations intrinsic in the underlying models.

This work shows how a standard description language, namely SystemC and its analog and mixed-signal (AMS) extension, can be used to successfully simulate the equivalent thermal network,by achieving accuracy comparable to existing simulators, yet with much better performance. Results show that SystemC-AMS thermal simulation can outpace HotSpot simulation by 10X to 90X, with speedup improving as the size of the thermal network increases, and negligible estimation error. As a further advantage, the adoption of the same language to describe functionality and temperature allows the simultaneous simulation of both dimensions with no co-simulation overhead, thus enhancing the overall design flow.

Keywords

Thermal analysis; Thermal estimation; Simulation; SystemC-AMS

1. INTRODUCTION

Temperature is a critical dimension in embedded system design, as it heavily impacts performance, power consumption and reliability of the final system [2]. This has led to the use of a variety of tools for estimating temperature (both transient and steady-state), with the goal of enhancing the design flow with increased reliability and knowledge of the underlying physical mechanisms.

*This work was supported by the EC co-funded CONTREX (Design of embedded mixed-criticality CONTRol systems under consideration of EXtra-functional properties) project Grant Agreement FP7-ICT- 611146

GLSVLSI '16, May 18-20, 2016, Boston, MA, USA

DOI: http://dx.doi.org/10.1145/2902961.2902975

All these tools solve the same problem (i.e., a 2D or 3D heat diffusion equation) and basically differ in terms of their granularity and of the type of solver employed, with the latter aspect affecting their accuracy [7, 9, 10, 15, 16, 19]. In the EDA and computer architecture community, the de-facto standard for thermal simualtion is HotSpot, a tool based on the circuit-equivalent of a thermal network, which achieves a good trade-off between granularity and accuracy [16]. HotSpot uses the chip floorplan and thermal package information to build an equivalent circuit description, that is solved over time on given traces of power dissipation.

A few approaches have been proposed to speed up the underlying equation solving mechanisms of HotSpot [8, 10, 17, 20]. However, all such solutions are relatively inefficient when performing thermal analysis for long simulation times, due to a large number of redundant computations intrinsic in the underlying models.

As a further limitation, all tools are designed to work standalone, thus making the integration with other embedded system design tools, *e.g.*, for functional or power simulation, extremely challenging. Executing the thermal simulators on traces produced offline by power simulation tools prevents the possibility of evaluating the mutual influence of temperature and power [5, 18]. This limitation is overcome by the construction of co-simulation frameworks, that integrate dedicated simulators through complex synchronization and data exchange mechanisms [3, 6]. However, co-simulation introduces a significant overhead, together with possible errors or timing misalignments.

This work shows how a standard functional description language, namely SystemC and its Analog and Mixed Signal extension (AMS) [1], can be successfully used to simulate the equivalent thermal network. The AMS extension provides electrical linear network constructs, thus allowing the straightforward implementation of the electrical circuit equivalent thermal model. The AMS solver proves to guarantee a high level of accuracy *w.r.t.* existing simulators, coupled with speedups of up to 90X *w.r.t.* HotSpot simulation, that increase with the size of the thermal network.

As a further advantage, the adoption of a functional language allows to simulate the thermal network simultaneously *w.r.t.* the system functional and power models, thus enhancing the overall embedded system desi gn flow.

2. BACKGROUND AND RELATED WORK

2.1 Thermal modeling

When referring to silicon chips, temperature estimation amounts to solving the heat diffusion equation in 3D, which is typically used to describe heat conduction in a chip and to calculate the temperature profile [11]:

$$\nabla^2 T + \frac{\dot{q}}{k} = \frac{1}{\alpha}\frac{\partial T}{\partial t} \quad (1)$$

where T is the temperature, q is the heat flux (in W/m^2), k is thermal conductivity of the material (in $W/(mK)$), and $\alpha = \frac{k}{\rho c}$ is the thermal diffusivity, corresponding to the ratio between the thermal conductivity and volumetric heat capacity (density ρ times specific heat capacity c). $\nabla^2 T$ is the Laplacian of T and corresponds in 3D to $\frac{\partial T^2}{\partial x} + \frac{\partial T^2}{\partial y} + \frac{\partial T^2}{\partial z}$.

Equation 1 can be solved using numerical methods such as Finite Difference Method (FDM), Finite Element Method (FEM), or methods based on the Green function [13]. Both FDM and FEM methods discretize the entire chip according to some granularity and construct a system of linear equations, thus handling complicated material structures with different thermal properties in different layers. Methods based on Green function, conversely, provide a semi-analytical approach that analyzes only layers of interest. This reduces the problem size compared to FDM or FEM, but results in less accurate estimates due to the simplified two dimensional modeling of the thermal problem.

2.2 Related Work on Thermal Simulation

A number of methods for solving Equation 1 rely on the well-known *duality between thermal and electrical networks*, *i.e.*, they represent heat flow as a current passing through a thermal resistance and leading to a temperature difference, analogous to voltage. Such methods rely on existing circuit-level simulators like SPICE to solve the steady-state or transient voltage of the nodes of the equivalent circuit [9, 19].

Among the thermal simulators based on an electrical circuit equivalent, HotSpot [16] is the most popular one, particularly in the computer architecture and EDA communities. The equivalent circuit of the chip is built from a given floorplan and from the essential features of the thermal package. HotSpot solves Equation 1 at each time step by using an adaptive solver of Runge-Kutta equations, based on a given trace of power dissipation values. It can model both steady-state and transient cases, and it supports two levels of granularity (*i.e.*, block-level and grid-level) with obvious tradeoff between accuracy and speed. Other approaches try to reduce the overhead of the HotSpot equation solver by implementing some context-specific optimizations; for instance, the authors of [8] exploit periodicity in the power trace to speed up the solution of transient analysis, whereas [20] uses spatially and temporally adaptive techniques to reduce computation time.

SESCTherm [10] is a thermal modeling infrastructure based on finite-difference analysis, that adopts the same underlying equation solver as HotSpot, but adopts a mix of grid and block modes.

DTTEM [17] uses a similar interface as HotSpot (*i.e.*, conductance and capacitance matrices). The main difference between DTTEM and HotSpot lies in the temperature evaluation mechanism; by sampling power values at small and constant time intervals, transient temperature evaluation can be discretized, thus simplifying the solution of the heat transfer differential equation.

Except for the solutions based on SPICE simulations, all these approaches basically try to implement different strategies to speed up the solution of the differential heat diffusion equation by optimizing either time sampling or analysis granularity. However, they are relatively inefficient when performing thermal analysis for long simulation times, due to the occurrence of a large number of redundant computations intrinsic in the underlying models. Moreover, all approaches are based on pre-built power simulation traces, which implies that multiple runs correspond to multiple constructions of the equations and/or of the thermal network.

In this work we show that a standard circuit solver like the one provided by SystemC-AMS can result in comparable if not better speed/accuracy tradeoffs than those optimized solutions, while achieving the benefit of a concurrent simulation of functionality, power and temperature within a single simulation run.

2.3 Introduction to SystemC-AMS

SystemC-AMS extends SystemC with constructs for modelling analog and mixed-signal systems (AMS) [1]. To cover a wide variety of domains, SystemC-AMS defines three different abstraction levels, supporting different communication styles and representations *w.r.t.* the physical domain. *Timed Data-Flow* (TDF) models are scheduled statically by considering their producer-consumer dependencies in the discrete time domain. *Linear Signal Flow* (LSF) supports the modelling of continuous time through a library of pre-defined primitive modules (*e.g.*, integration, delay), each associated with a linear equation. Finally, the *Electrical Linear Network* (ELN) level models electrical networks through the instantiation of predefined primitives, *e.g.*, resistors or capacitors, associated with electrical equations.

SystemC-AMS is supported by an internal solver, that analyzes the ELN and LSF components to derive the equations modelling system behaviour. The equations are solved numerically over time to determine the evolution of system state, by adopting numerical solvers, *e.g.*, Euler and trapezoidal methods. The internal solver also guarantees that ELN descriptions are conservative, *i.e.*, the set of equations derived from ELN is extended with the application of conservation laws.

3. A SYSTEMC-AMS THERMAL SIMULATOR FOR SOC

The construction of the SystemC-AMS thermal model relies on electrical circuit equivalent models, as they allow to reduce a phenomenon that can not be natively represented in SystemC-AMS (*i.e.*, temperature) to linear networks, that have a dedicated abstraction level. The RC network is built by following state-of-the-art methods, and in particular the method used by HotSpot [16]. The novelty of the current work lies in the code generation process. HotSpot provides a stand-alone tool that explicitly solves circuit equations modeled as matrices. On the contrary, the proposed approach exploits the native support of SystemC-AMS for electric network primitives to map the RC network elements one-to-one to SystemC-AMS constructs (*e.g.*, resistors and capacitors). Circuit equations are then automatically derived and solved by the SystemC-AMS internal solver.

The resulting methodology is as depicted in Figure 1:

- *construction of the RC network* by reproducing the method used by HotSpot (Section 3.1);
- *SystemC-AMS code generation*, achieved by mapping the RC network elements to SystemC-AMS primitives (Section 2.3);
- simulation of the RC network by using the SystemC-AMS simulation kernel as a circuit solver (Section 3.3). Inputs are provided by a dedicated testbench, either (a) as *power dissipation traces* (á la HotSpot), or (b) by simulating the thermal model *in parallel w.r.t. functional and power models*.

3.1 Construction of the RC network

The algorithm to construct the RC network reproduces the method followed by HotSpot. In the current version of the methodology, we support only block-level simulation, *i.e.*, the simulator estimates one temperature value for each component. Finer granularity, *i.e.*, the grid-level of HotSpot, will be supported as part of future work. Both steady-state and transient simulation are supported.

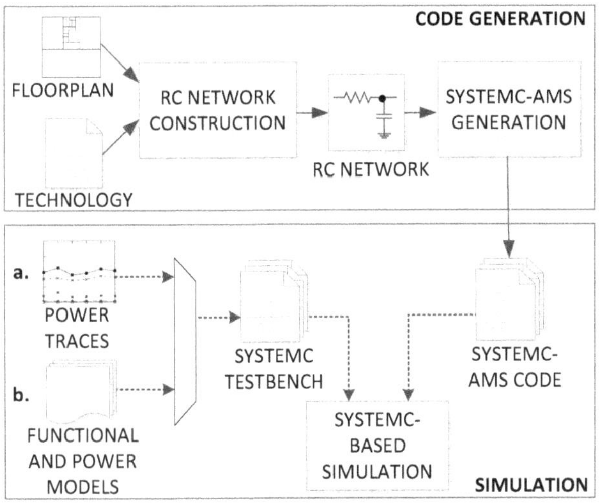

Figure 1: Proposed methodology for the construction of the SystemC-AMS thermal simulator.

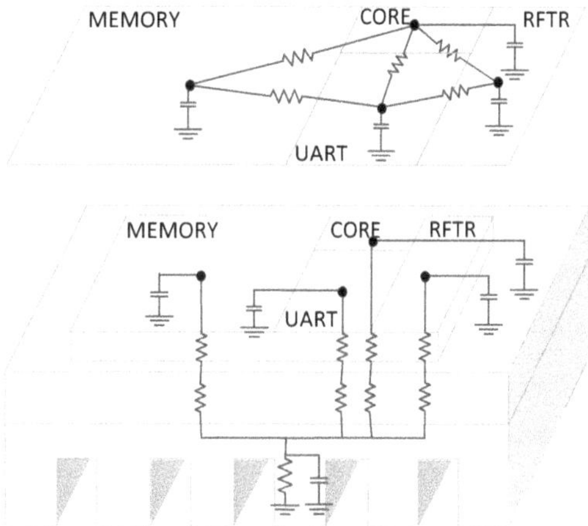

Figure 2: Example of electrical circuit equivalent model: the RC network is decomposed in a lateral model (top), representing heat transfers that occur horizontally between adjacent components, and a vertical model (bottom), that sketches the heat spread across the package layers.

Figure 2 exemplifies the application to a simple case study consisting of a core, a memory, a RF transceiver and a UART device. The construction of the RC network heavily depends on the input information: chip floorplan, necessary to determine which components are adjacent, and technology information (*e.g.*, number of layers, materials, thermal characteristics).

Each chip component is mapped to a *RC network node*, whose current represents power consumption and whose voltage represents temperature. Additional nodes are used to represent the underlying package layers (*i.e.*, heat spreader and heat sink). Heat transfer flow between adjacent nodes is represented by a *resistor*, whose thermal resistance is proportional to the thickness of the material and inversely proportional to the cross-sectional area and to the thermal conductivity. Resistance values are stored in a matrix whose lines and columns are circuit nodes. If the RC network is used for transient simulation, *capacitors* are connected to each node, to capture the delay before a change in power determines a change in temperature. Thermal capacitance is proportional to both thickness and area, and it depends on the thermal capacitance per unit volume. Capacitance values are stored in a dedicated array.

3.2 SystemC-AMS code generation

The second step is the implementation of the computed RC network in SystemC-AMS. Figure 3 exemplifies the proposed approach by showing how the lateral model depicted on top of Figure 2 is implemented in SystemC-AMS[1].

Interface modeling.

The electrical circuit equivalent model is instantiated as a single SystemC module (`SC_MODULE`, line 1), encapsulating the entire RC network. The interface of the module is made of two ports for each chip component: one input port to gather the evolution of power consumption over time, and one output port to convey the corresponding value of temperature.

The flexibility of SystemC-AMS and its support for multiple levels of abstraction allows to decouple the semantics of the interface from the semantics of the actual behavior implementation. For this reason, the abstraction level adopted for ports is TDF, that determines a fixed timestep at which input ports are read, RC network is evaluated and output ports are updated. This reflects the behavior of HotSpot, that assumes that the power traces contain samples collected at fixed time steps. Ports are thus declared as `sca_tdf::sca_in` and `sca_tdf::sca_out` ports of type double (lines 2–3).

Body implementation.

The body of the `SC_MODULE` includes the implementation of the RC network, by reproducing the model computed as in Section 3.1. This is realized by adopting the ELN level of abstraction, that natively supports electrical network elements. The construction of the SystemC-AMS thermal model is thus a one-to-one mapping of circuit elements into SystemC-AMS primitives.

Each circuit node is implemented as a SystemC-AMS ELN node (`sca_node`, lines 6–7), despite of ground, that is represented with an ad-hoc primitive (`sca_node_ref`, line 5).

Resistors are mapped to instances of the `sca_r` primitive, that represents SystemC-AMS resistors (line 12). The resistance value is extracted from the resistance matrix computed in the previous methodology step (Section 3.1); *e.g.*, the snapshot of code in Figure 3 shows that the resistance modeling the heat flow between the core and the memory is 215.48Ω (lines 27–30).

Capacitors are mapped to an instance of the `sca_c` primitive, that represents SystemC-AMS capacitors (line 11). The capacitance value is extracted from the computed capacitance array; *e.g.*, the core capacitance is 874 10^{-5}F (lines 23–26).

The input power ports are connected to the ELN circuit via current source primitives, that transform a numerical value into a current (`sca_isource` primitive, lines 9 and 15–18). In the pictorial representation in Figure 3, TDF ports are represented by the white square terminals of the primitive blocks.

Conversely, the temperature of each chip component is extracted through a voltage sink, that extrapolates a voltage value and makes it available on the output ports. Voltage sinks are represented with instances of the `sca_vsink` primitive, whose output terminal is connected to the corresponding output temperature port (the black square terminals, lines 10 and 19–22).

3.3 Stimuli Generation

The final step is the generation of input stimuli. The SystemC-AMS thermal simulator is connected to a *testbench module* through

[1]Note that this constitutes only a subset of the complete RC network. Symbols adopted for the primitives are as standardized in the SystemC-AMS standard [1].

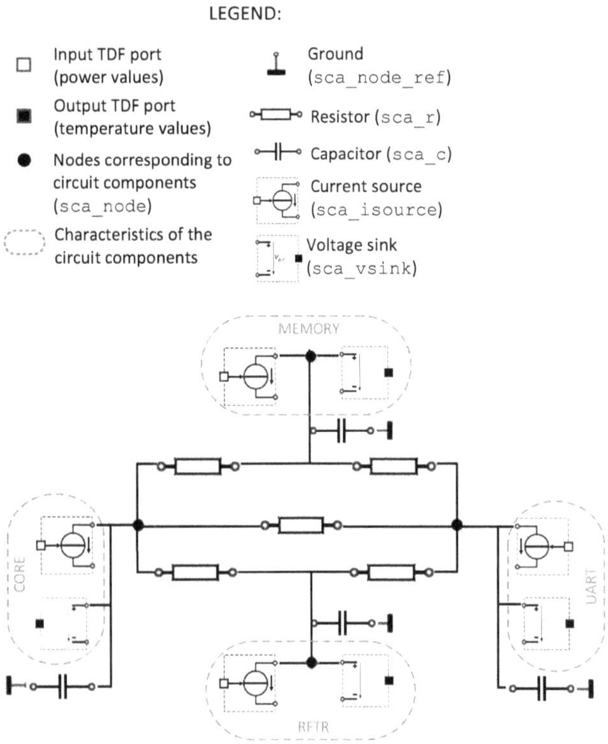


```
SC_MODULE (thermal_network){
  sca_tdf::sca_in<double> p_CORE ;
  sca_tdf::sca_out<double> t_CORE ;
  ...
  sca_eln::sca_node_ref gnd;
  sca_eln::sca_node node_CORE;
  sca_eln::sca_node node_MEMORY;
  ...
  sca_eln::sca_tdf::sca_isource* iCORE;
  sca_eln::sca_tdf::sca_vsink* vCORE;
  sca_eln::sca_c* c_CORE;
  sca_eln::sca_r* r_MEM_CORE;
...

SC_CTOR(thermal_network){
  i_CORE = new sca_eln::sca_tdf::sca_isource("i_CORE");
  i_CORE->p(gnd);
  i_CORE->n(node_CORE);
  i_CORE->inp(p_CORE);

  v_CORE = new sca_eln::sca_tdf::sca_vsink("v_CORE");
  v_CORE->p(node_CORE);
  v_CORE->n(gnd);
  v_CORE->outp(t_CORE);

  c_CORE = new sca_eln::sca_c("c_CORE");
  c_CORE->p(node_CORE);
  c_CORE->n(gnd);
  c_CORE->value=0.00008741;

  r_MEM_CORE= new sca_eln::sca_r("r_MEM_CORE");
  r_MEM_CORE->p(node_MEMORY);
  r_MEM_CORE->n(node_CORE);
  r_MEM_CORE->value = 215.48122572;
  ...
} };
```

Figure 3: Example of implementation of the lateral model of Figure 2 in SystemC-AMS: implementation of the RC network with ELN primitives (left) and excerpt of SystemC-AMS code (right).

a complementary interface: power ports are in output, and temperature ports are in input. The testbench generates stimuli over time for the thermal simulator, by adopting two possible strategies.

The first option is to load *dissipation power traces* from files previously generated by a power simulator (option *a* in Figure 1). The estimated temperature values are then dumped to a thermal trace file for future elaborations. This corresponds to the simulation semantics of all thermal simulators, including HotSpot.

The second option consists of simulating the RC network on *dynamically generated power information* (option b in Figure 1). In this scenario, the testbench wraps SystemC processes implementing power models, or functional models enriched with power information [4, 12]. This approach is made possible by the adoption of a functional language for thermal simulation. A major advantage is that power information is generated dynamically, depending on the evolution of functionality, and that the mutual effects of power and temperature can be reproduced at runtime.

An example of this strategy is sketched in Figure 4. The testbench includes both a functional model and a power model: the `pause` functional signal is used to determine the evolution of the power state machine, that dynamically updates the power values written in output to the thermal model.

It is important to note that this second scenario provides a novelty *w.r.t.* the current state-of-the-art. Simultaneous simulation is indeed achieved by simulating all aspects in a single simulation run and by adopting a single simulation kernel, *i.e.*, SystemC with its AMS extension. Comparing this solution with approaches such as [3, 6], we avoid the overhead and the criticality of building a

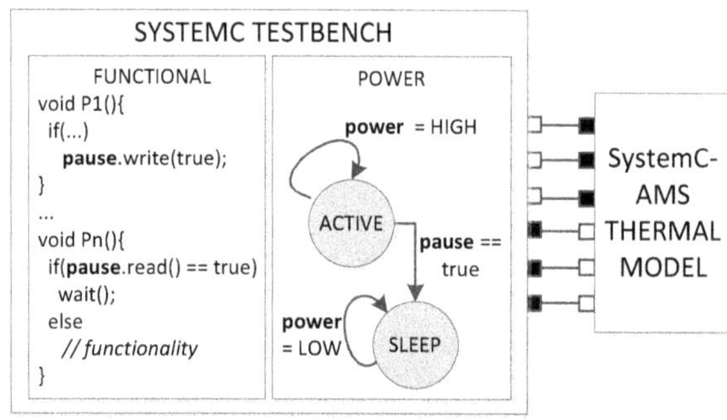

Figure 4: Example of how functional and power models can influence thermal simulation through simultaneous simulation.

co-simulation framework, thus achieving faster simulation and an enhanced guarantee of correctness.

4. EXPERIMENTAL RESULTS

4.1 Simulation Setup

The proposed methodology has been automated in a C++ tool, that takes in input two files, modeling floorplan and technology information. The tool builds the RC network and saves the generated code to a SystemC file, named by default `RCnetwork.h`. Furthermore, the tool generates the interface of the testbench module, while its implementation is left to the designer. Table 1 summarizes the technology values. Air is always set to a fixed ambient tempera-

Layers	Thickness	Thermal Conductivity
Die	1.5e-04 m	100.0 W/m-K
TIM	2.0e-05 m	4.000 W/m-K
Heat-spreader	1.0e-03 m	400.0 W/m-K
Heat-sink	6.9e-03 m	400.0 W/m-K

Table 1: Technology parameters.

ture of 40°C. Convection capacitance *w.r.t.* ambient is $140.4\frac{J}{K}$, and convection resistance is $0.1\ \frac{K}{W}$.

4.2 Case Studies

To compare our methodology to HotSpot, we used five benchmarks of different sizes and complexity: the example in Figure 2 (benchmark 1), two built-in examples of HotSpot (benchmark 2 and 3), and two synthetic benchmarks (4 and 5). The latter two do not correspond to any functionality, and are only used to prove effectiveness and scalability of the proposed simulation approach. The benchmarks have been generated by replicating a number of cores, caches and memories, with typical power consumption traces. The corresponding floorplans have been derived by using the HotSpot thermal-aware floorplanning tool.

To ensure a fair comparison, we fed both HotSpot and our tool with the same power traces and floorplan and technology files.

4.3 Correctness of the Computed RC Network

To test the correctness of our approach, we compared the RC network built by our approach for each benchmark with the one built by HotSpot. Table 2 reports the main characteristics of the RC networks.

Since our RC network construction algorithm is based on HotSpot, it is no surprise that the RC networks are identical, in terms of both number of nodes, resistors and capacitors. This guarantees that both SystemC-AMS and HotSpot solve the same equations, and that any inaccuracy lies in the solver, rather than in the constructed thermal model.

Benchmark	Components (#)	Nodes (#)	Resistors (#)	Capacitors (#)
1	4	28	64	28
2	18	84	288	84
3	30	132	442	132
4	40	172	586	172
5	86	356	1,206	356

Table 2: Characteristics of the computed RC networks.

4.4 Simulation Time

To evaluate the temporal performance of SystemC-AMS simulations, we compare separately the time to generate the RC thermal model and the time to simulate the network. Table 3 reports *generation times*, and shows that the time necessary to build the thermal model is similar for HotSpot and SystemC-AMS, since both the approaches rely on the same algorithm for RC network construction. The time is slightly higher for our approach, since it requires a further step to map the resistor and capacitor matrices to SystemC-AMS primitives, and to print the generated code onto a file. To overcome this limitation, we could avoid the dump of the RC on a file and rely on some interprocess communication facility to exchange the data structure representing the netlist with SystemC-AMS. In any case, generation times are truly negligible, as shown in Table 3.

Table 4 completes the analysis with the most relevant information, i.e., the comparison of *simulation times*. Data refers to a

Benchmark	SystemC-AMS (s)	HotSpot (s)
1	0.002	0.001
2	0.004	0.001
3	0.011	0.002
4	0.016	0.003
5	0.120	0.020

Table 3: Comparison of RC Network Generation Time.

1000ms trace with timestep 1ms. SystemC-AMS proves to be much faster than HotSpot, with a speedup of up to 96X. The interesting aspect is that speedup scales linearly with the size of the netlist. This proves that the improved performance is due to the SystemC-AMS simulation kernel, that handles more efficiently the RC network equations. Note that the achieved simulation speedup compensates for the slightly longer generation time (Table 3). These results allow us to claim that our approach is competitive also *w.r.t.* optimized variants of HotSpot, that achieve speedups around 4X over standard HotSpot [21], thus far lower than our experienced performance.

Benchmark	SystemC-AMS (s)	HotSpot (s)	Speedup
1	0.101	1.472	14.55
2	0.536	17.446	32.55
3	0.983	40.609	41.31
4	1.425	72.591	50.94
5	3.343	321.397	96.14

Table 4: Comparison of Simulation Time.

4.5 Accuracy

To prove the accuracy of our simulator, we determine the relative error *w.r.t.* HotSpot, by analyzing the traces of each component. The relative error is computed as in Equation 2:

$$Err_{relative} = (T_{AMS} - T_{HotSpot})/(T_{HotSpot} - T_{Ambient}) \quad (2)$$

We first compared SystemC-AMS and HotSpot on *steady-state scenarios*. The input power traces consist of a single power value per component, corresponding to the average power dissipation of the component over time. SystemC-AMS proved to be extremely accurate, as we got a 0% error on all benchmarks. This can be explained by the similar underlying solvers, and by the fact that steady-state evaluation does not require iterations, thus avoiding the accumulation of approximations.

Case Study	Avg. error (%)
1	0.034
2	0.052
3	0.140
4	0.160
5	0.015

Table 5: Accuracy of transient temperature estimation.

The *transient scenario* is more interesting, as the RC network includes also capacitors and multiple iterations are necessary to compute the thermal trace. Table 5 shows that the average error committed on all benchmarks is far below 1%. This proves that the SystemC-AMS solver is extremely accurate *w.r.t.* the HotSpot simulation kernel. Figure 5 proves the high level of accuracy by showing that the temperature curves computed by SystemC-AMS and HotSpot for benchmark 1 are overlapped (top), and that the error becomes visible only by zooming in on very small time windows (bottom).

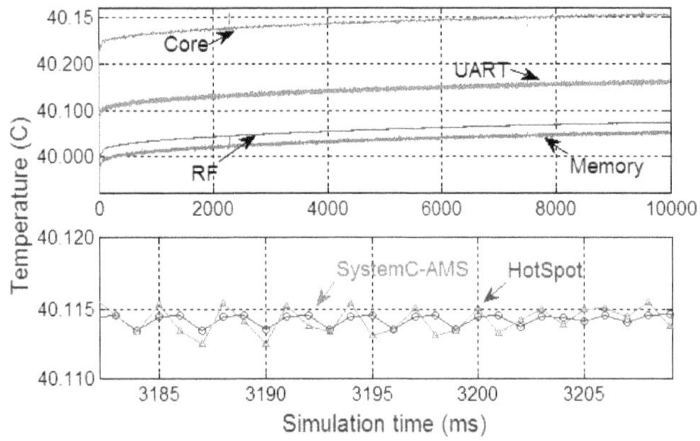

Figure 5: Transient temperature profile from SystemC-AMS and HotSpot applied to benchmark 1 (top) and zoomed view of the memory transient temperature profiles (bottom).

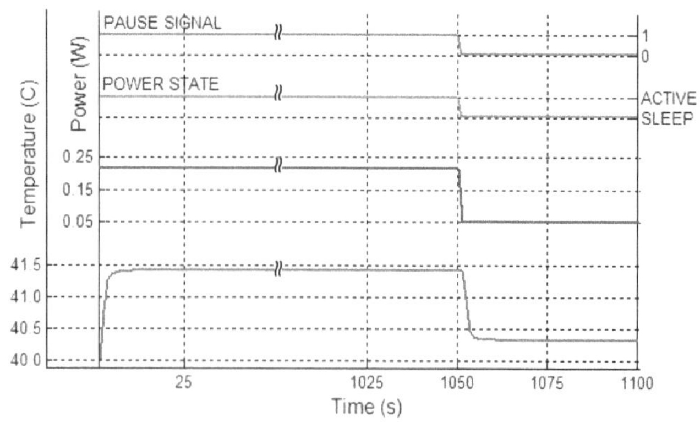

Figure 6: Effect of simultaneous simulation of functional and power models with the SystemC-AMS thermal model.

By zooming in the curves, we observed that the maximum error always happens at inflection points of the temperature profiles. This is caused by the electrical characteristics of SystemC-AMS capacitors and resistors, that result in slightly different time constants. The inspection of the traces suggests however that the less abrupt transitions resulting by SystemC-AMS simulation are more realistic than the discontinuous sawtooth profile computed by the solver in HotSpot.

4.6 Simultaneous simulation with functional and power models

As a final experiment, we implemented a scenario in which the SystemC-AMS thermal simulation of benchmark 1 (Figure 2) is run concurrently with functional and power models. To this extent, we enriched the testbench by implementing the functional and power models sketched in Figure 4 as SystemC processes. Our goal was to dynamically derive power information for the digital core from its functional evolution [14], to determine the influence of the executed application on the thermal profile.

Figure 6 traces the evolution of the resulting simulation. As soon as the `pause` signal is set to 0, the power model reacts and performs the transition from $ACTIVE$ to $SLEEP$, thus lowering power dissipation from 0.2314W to 0.0500W. This is detected by the thermal simulator, that gradually decreases the core temperature from 41.42°C to 40.33°C. Overall simulation lasted 6.302s and was performed in a single run with the sole support of the SystemC simulation kernel. Building the same scenario with HotSpot, or with any other custom thermal simulator, would have required the construction of a co-simulation infrastructure with an architectural or a circuit simulator.

5. CONCLUSIONS

This work demonstrated that SystemC-AMS can be used to successfully simulate thermal evolution by modeling the equivalent thermal network through ELN primitives without the need of implementing custom circuit simulators. Experimental results showed that our SystemC-AMS-based approach reaches a high level of accuracy *w.r.t.* HotSpot, with an average error lower that 1% on all tested benchmarks, while achieving speedup of up to 90X, that scales linearly with the size of the thermal network. Given this latter nice scalability feature, we are confident that the speedup will be even larger for grid-level simulation, where the number of electrical elements and circuit nodes is much larger. This will be our future work on this subject.

6. REFERENCES

[1] Accellera. *SystemC-AMS*. www.systemc-ams.org.
[2] A. H. Ajami, K. Banerjee, and M. Pedram. Modeling and analysis of nonuniform substrate temperature effects on global ULSI interconnects. *IEEE TCAD*, 24(6):849–861, 2005.
[3] B. Beckmann, Y. Eckert, et al. A comprehensive timing, power, thermal, and reliability model for exascale node architectures. In *Proc. of DOE MODSIM*, 2013.
[4] L. Benini, R. Hodgson, and P. Siegel. System-level power estimation and optimization. In *Proc. of ACM/IEEE ISLPED*, pages 173–178, 1998.
[5] N. Hatami, R. Baranowski, et al. Multilevel simulation of nonfunctional properties by piecewise evaluation. *ACM TODAES*, 19(4):37:1–37:21, 2014.
[6] M. Hsieh, K. Pedretti, J. Meng, et al. SST + Gem5 = a scalable simulation infrastructure for high performance computing. In *Proc. of ACM SIMUTOOLS*, pages 196–201, 2012.
[7] T. Kemper, Y. Zhang, Z. Bian, and A. Shakouri. Ultrafast temperature profile calculation in IC chips. In *IEEE THERMINIC*, pages 133–137, 2006.
[8] P. Liu, Z. Qi, H. Li, L. Jin, W. Wu, S. Tan, and J. Yang. Fast thermal simulation for architecture level dynamic thermal management. In *IEEE ICCAD*, pages 639–644, 2005.
[9] W. Liu, A. C. A., A. Macii, et al. Layout-driven post-placement techniques for temperature reduction and thermal gradient minimization. *IEEE TCAD*, 32(3):406–418, 2013.
[10] J. Nayfach and J. Renau. SOI, interconnect, package, and mainboard thermal characterization. *IEEE ISLPED*, pages 327–330, 2009.
[11] M. Ozisik. *Boundary Value Problems of Heat Conduction*. Oxford University Press, 1968.
[12] X. Pan, J. Molina, and C. Grimm. Modeling power consumption at system-level for design of power integrity-aware AMS-circuits. In *Proc. of ECSI/IEEE FDL*, pages 1–8, 2015.
[13] M. Pedram and S. Nazarian. Thermal modeling, analysis, and management in VLSI circuits: Principles and methods. *Proc. of the IEEE*, 94(8):1487–1501, 2006.
[14] S. Rhoads. Plasma CPU Core, 2001. opencores.org.
[15] K. Skadron, M. Stan, W. Huang, et al. Temperature-aware computer systems: Opportunities and challenges. *IEEE Micro*, 23(6):52–61, 2003.
[16] K. Skadron, M. R. Stan, B. Huang, S. Velusamy, K. Sankaranarayanan, and D. Tarjan. Temperature-aware microarchitecture: Extended discussion and results. Technical Report CS-2003-08, Univ. of Virginia Dept. of CS, 2003.
[17] L. Thiele, L. Schor, H. Yang, and I. Bacivarov. Thermal-aware system analysis and software synthesis for embedded multi-processors. In *ACM/EDAC/IEEE DAC*, pages 268–273, 2011.
[18] A. Viehl, B. Sander, O. Bringmann, and W. Rosenstiel. Integrated requirement evaluation of non-functional system-on-chip properties. In *ECSI/IEEE FDL*, pages 105–110, 2008.
[19] T.-Y. Wang and C. Chen. SPICE-compatible thermal simulation with lumped circuit modeling for thermal reliability analysis based on modeling order reduction. In *IEEE ISQED*, pages 357–362, 2004.
[20] Y. Yang, Z. Gu, C. Zhu, R. Dick, and L. Shang. ISAC: Integrated space-and-time-adaptive chip-package thermal analysis. *IEEE TCAD*, 26(1):86–99, 2007.
[21] A. Ziabari, E. Ardestani, J. Renau, and A. Shakouri. Fast thermal simulators for architecture level integrated circuit design. In *IEEE SEMI-THERM*, pages 70–75, 2011.

Learning-Based Near-Optimal Area-Power Trade-offs in Hardware Design for Neural Signal Acquisition

Cosimo Aprile
LIONS and LSM, EPFL
Lausanne, Switzerland
cosimo.aprile@epfl.ch

Luca Baldassarre
LIONS, EPFL
Lausanne, Switzerland

Vipul Gupta
LIONS, EPFL
Lausanne, Switzerland

Juhwan Yoo
Broadcom
United States of America

Mahsa Shoaran
MICS, Caltech
United States of America

Yusuf Leblebici
LSM, EPFL
Lausanne, Switzerland

Volkan Cevher
LIONS, EPFL
Lausanne, Switzerland

ABSTRACT

Wireless implantable devices capable of monitoring the electrical activity of the brain are becoming an important tool for understanding and potentially treating mental diseases such as epilepsy and depression. While such devices exist, it is still necessary to address several challenges to make them more practical in terms of area and power dissipation. In this work, we apply Learning Based Compressive Subsampling (LBCS) to tackle the power and area trade-offs in neural wireless devices. To this end, we propose a low-power and area-efficient system for neural signal acquisition which yields state-of-art compression rates up to 64× with high reconstruction quality, as demonstrated on two human iEEG datasets. This new fully digital architecture handles one neural acquisition channel, with an area of $210 \times 210 \mu m$ in $90nm$ CMOS technology, and a power dissipation of only $1 \mu W$.

Keywords

Neural signals, Compressive Sensing, digital signal processing, area-efficient, low-power, signal recovery

1. INTRODUCTION

The microelectromechanical (MEMS) technology is opening new venues of applications in health-care with significant new possibilities. In recent years MEMS facilitated advances in wireless implantable devices and have enabled monitoring of biological signals in the human body, such as blood pressure, electrical activity of heart and brain, and so on. In particular, the capability of monitoring the brain activity captured the interest of many scientists for decades and from the 90s clinicians have begun to use implantable devices to observe the activity of the neurons [1]. Being able to efficiently interface the electrical system with the biological environment would enable patients with brain diseases (such as epilepsy or Parkinson) to be monitored and treated with minimally invasive systems.

According to the US National Institute of Neurological Disorders and Stroke, more than 50 million people worldwide [2] are affected by epilepsy and 25% of the patients are pharmaco-resistant. Since 1997, the usage of prostheses has been approved to provide medical treatments for some brain diseases, such as Parkinson and epilepsy, and in 2005 also for depression [3]. Data compression is needed for reducing the power consumption of data telemetry and favouring the biocompatibility of a small wireless implantable device.

In order to reduce the power requirements of data transmission, compressive sensing (CS) [4, 5] has been exploited in many recent approaches (e.g., [6, 7, 8] and references therein). In a nutshell, CS consists in taking fewer linear samples than dictated by the Shannon-Nyquist theorem, while still allowing robust off-line signal reconstruction. This is possible by exploiting the fact that the information content of a signal is often much lower than its raw data content.

In this work, we design a digital encoder for neuronal signals based on Learning Based Compressive Subsampling (LBCS) [9], which allows to reduce the chip's power and area requirements, while improving on the reconstruction performance. Such method is based on the simple idea of sampling a fixed set of coefficients that preserve as much of the signal's energy as possible. The set of indices is learnt from a training set of fully sampled signals, by selecting the ones that capture most of the signals' average energy. LBCS offers a pair of highly efficient linear encoder and decoder, thus challenging the conventional recovery approach in CS, where non-linear decoding procedures such as basis pursuit are necessary for reliable signal reconstructions.

In few words, our learning-based digital encoder scheme leverages the benefits of structured linear sampling and linear recovery to yield state-of-the-art compression perfor-

GLSVLSI '16, May 18-20, 2016, Boston, MA, USA

DOI: http://dx.doi.org/10.1145/2902961.2903028

mance, maintaining a high signal reconstruction quality up to 64× compression, as quantitatively demonstrated on two human iEEG datasets.

The paper is organized as follows. We introduce the main concepts of Compressive Sensing and Learning Based Compressive Subsampling in Section 2, and in Section 3 we describe the digital architecture tailored for LBCS. Numerical experiments are reported in Section 4, while in Section 5 we analyse and describe our circuit design. Section 6 concludes the paper.

2. COMPRESSION ALGORITHM

In this section, we first introduce the basics of Compressive Sensing, reviewing three recent approaches applied to neuronal signals. We then discuss non-linear structured recovery, before discussing Learning-Based Compressive Subsampling.

2.1 Compressive Sensing

The main tenet of Compressive Sensing states that a signal $\mathbf{x} \in \mathbb{R}^N$ which has K non-zero coefficients can be robustly recovered from only $M = \mathcal{O}(K \log \frac{N}{K})$ samples $\mathbf{y} \in \mathbb{R}^M$,

$$\mathbf{y} = \mathbf{A}\mathbf{x} + \mathbf{w} \;, \tag{1}$$

where $\mathbf{A}$ is a linear operator that either satisfies the Restricted Isometry Property (RIP) or is incoherent [10], and $\mathbf{w}$ accounts for measurement noise. Obviously, $\mathbf{y}$ offers a compressed version of $\mathbf{x}$. If we are able to directly sample $\mathbf{y}$, we save both on storage and communication power. Recovering $\mathbf{x}$, though, usually requires to solve a non-linear optimization problem. Nonetheless, recent advances in optimization have provided efficient algorithms that can scale to very large signals [11].

Theoretically, i.i.d. sub-Gaussian matrices are incoherent and also satisfy the RIP. Furthermore, they are universal, i.e., given an ortho-normal basis $\mathbf{\Phi}$ which allows for a sparser representation of a signal $\mathbf{x}$, the RIP or the incoherence of $\mathbf{A\Phi}$ is the same as of the original $\mathbf{A}$ [10]. However, sub-Gaussian matrices are prohibitively expensive to use in practice, since they require $\mathcal{O}(MN)$ space and time.

More efficient types of sampling are being successfully used in real applications, such as subsampled fast transforms, like the Fast Fourier (FFT), the Discrete Cosine (DCT) or the Fast Walsh-Hadamard (FWHT) Transforms, which can be computed in $\mathcal{O}(N \log N)$ time.

The following three randomized sampling approaches, recently proposed for the compression of neural signals are very efficient on the sampling side, but require solving non-linear optimization problems to reconstruct the original signals.

- Bernoulli (BERN): uses a random Bernoulli $\{\pm 1\}$ matrix to sample each channel independently [7].
- Multi-Channel Sampling (MCS): the idea behind MCS [8] consists in taking random Bernoulli $\{0, 1\}$ combinations of the samples across all channels at a given time point i, that is

  $$\mathbf{y}_i = \mathbf{A}\mathbf{x}_i \;, \tag{2}$$

  where $\mathbf{A}$ is a $M \times \#ch$ Bernoulli matrix, with $\#ch$ being the number of channels, and $\mathbf{x}_i$ contains the values at time i for all channels. This allows to design a relatively simple encoder scheme, but requires the channels to be fairly correlated in order to faithfully reconstruct the signals, as further discussed in [12].
- Structured Hadamard Sampling (SHS): the method presented in [12] randomly samples the indices of the Fast Walsh-Hadamard Transform (FWHT) of each channel according to a probability function that favors low frequencies, which seem to carry most of signal's energy.

2.2 Structured recovery

Additional structures in the signal $\mathbf{x}$, such as interdependencies between its non-zero coefficients or constraints on its support, allow to reduce the number of samples required for exact or stable recovery (see [13] and [14]). Many of these structures can be encoded via linear inequalities that admit tight and tractable convex relaxations [15]. Interestingly, natural signals are often characterized by sparse and structured representations in time-frequency (or space-frequency) domains, such as provided by wavelets [16].

In order to reconstruct the original signal $\mathbf{x}$ from its compressive samples $\mathbf{y}$, most structured-sparsity methods resort to solving the following optimization problem on the wavelet coefficients $\boldsymbol{\alpha}$,

$$\begin{aligned} \underset{\boldsymbol{\alpha} \in \mathcal{A}}{\text{minimize}} \quad & f(\boldsymbol{\alpha}) \\ \text{subject to} \quad & \mathbf{A\Phi}\boldsymbol{\alpha} - \mathbf{y} \in \mathcal{K} \end{aligned} \tag{3}$$

where f is a Gauge function that promotes the structure we expect in $\boldsymbol{\alpha}$, $\mathcal{K}$ encodes our information about the noise and $\mathcal{A}$ is a constraint set that specifies further assumptions about the signal, e.g. boundedness. We reconstruct the signal as $\widetilde{\mathbf{x}} = \mathbf{\Phi}\widetilde{\boldsymbol{\alpha}}$, where $\widetilde{\boldsymbol{\alpha}}$ is the solution to (3) and $\mathbf{\Phi}$ is the wavelet transformation matrix.

In [12], three different structured-sparsity recovery methods have been compared for reconstructing iEEG signals sampled via the SHS, MCS and BERN approaches. The best performance was obtained using a Gauge function that exploits the natural tree representation of the wavelets coefficients in order to penalize the coefficients closer to the tree leaves. Such an approach is called Hierarchical Group Lasso (HGL). In particular, they considered the above problem with $\mathcal{K} = \{0\}$, $\mathcal{A} = \mathbb{R}^N$ and

$$\|\mathbf{x}\|_{\mathcal{T}} := \sum_{\mathcal{G} \in \mathcal{T}} \|\mathbf{x}_{|\mathcal{G}}\|, \tag{4}$$

where $\mathcal{T} = \{\mathcal{G}_1, \ldots, \mathcal{G}_N\}$ is a collection of index sets, each set $\mathcal{G}_i \subseteq \{1, \ldots, N\}$ containing the node i in the tree and all its descendants, see [17] for more details.

2.3 Learning Based Compressive Subsampling

The compression architecture that we propose in this paper is based on the idea of Learning-Based Compressive Subsampling (LBCS)[9], which consists on *linear encoding* and *linear decoding* with respect to a given orthonormal basis, resulting in a much simpler and faster solution compared to the approaches described in Section 2.1.

LBCS can be summarized as follows. Given a signal $\mathbf{x} \in \mathbb{R}^N$, we consider the compression model

$$\mathbf{y} = \mathbf{P}_\Omega \mathbf{\Psi} \mathbf{x} \;, \tag{5}$$

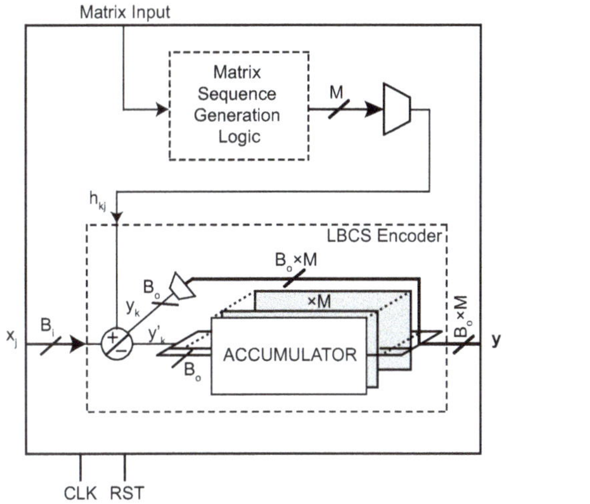

Figure 1: One channel block diagram showing the LBCS encoder and the matrix sequence generation logic.

where $\mathbf{\Psi} \in \mathbb{R}^{N\times N}$ is an orthonormal basis and $\mathbf{P}_\Omega \in \mathbb{R}^{M\times N}$ is a subsampling matrix whose rows are canonical basis vectors. The effect of applying $\mathbf{P}_\Omega$ to $\mathbf{\Psi x}$ is to retain only the coefficients indexed by the set Ω, also known as the *subsampling map*. The vector $\mathbf{y} \in \mathbb{R}^M$ is the compressed version of $\mathbf{x}$, with a nominal compression rate (CR) of $\frac{N}{M}$. The signal $\mathbf{x}$ is then approximately recovered via the fast linear decoder

$$\hat{\mathbf{x}} = \mathbf{\Psi}^* \mathbf{P}_\Omega^T \mathbf{y}\ . \tag{6}$$

Given a training set $\mathcal{D} = \{\mathbf{x}_1, \dots, \mathbf{x}_m\}$ of m fully sampled signals of unit norm, we learn the optimal subsampling map Ω by choosing the indices that capture most of the average energy in the transform domain:

$$\hat{\Omega} = \arg\max_{\Omega, |\Omega|=M} \frac{1}{m} \sum_{j=1}^{m} \sum_{i\in\Omega} |\langle \boldsymbol{\psi}_i, \mathbf{x}_j\rangle|^2, \tag{7}$$

where $\boldsymbol{\psi}_i$ is the i-th row of $\mathbf{\Psi}$. $\hat{\Omega}$ can be exactly found by selecting the M indices whose values of $\frac{1}{m}\sum_{j=1}^{m} |\langle \boldsymbol{\psi}_i, \mathbf{x}_j\rangle|^2$ are the largest [9]. The learnt sampling scheme is then used to directly sample only those transform coefficients indexed by $\hat{\Omega}$ for all signals $\mathbf{x}$.

2.4 Adaptive encoding

Given a basis $\mathbf{\Psi}$ and a desired number of samples M, the optimal linear encoding of each $\mathbf{x}$ is given by retaining only the M largest coefficients of $\mathbf{\Psi x}$ in absolute value. However, this adaptive encoding requires to first compute all the coefficients $\mathbf{\Psi x}$, which is prohibitive with small area and power consumption, as discussed in Section 5.1.

3. SYSTEM ARCHITECTURE

In this section, we propose the architecture to allow an embedded sampling and compression of the neural input signal based on the LBCS approach described in Section 2.3.

In the following, we fix $\mathbf{\Psi}$ equal to the Hadamard matrix $\mathbf{H}$ which has the advantage of only requiring a single bit to represent each matrix entry and also minimizes the matrix multiplication operations. Let $\mathbf{H}_\Omega = \mathbf{P}_\Omega \mathbf{H}$ be the matrix composed of the rows of $\mathbf{H}$ indexed by Ω. We sequentially compute $\mathbf{y} = \mathbf{H}_\Omega \mathbf{x}$: looking at each component of $\mathbf{y}$, we have

$$y_k = \sum_{j=1}^{N} h_{kj} x_j,\ k \in \{1, \dots, M\}, \tag{8}$$

where h_{kj} is the (k, j)-entry of $\mathbf{H}_\Omega$.

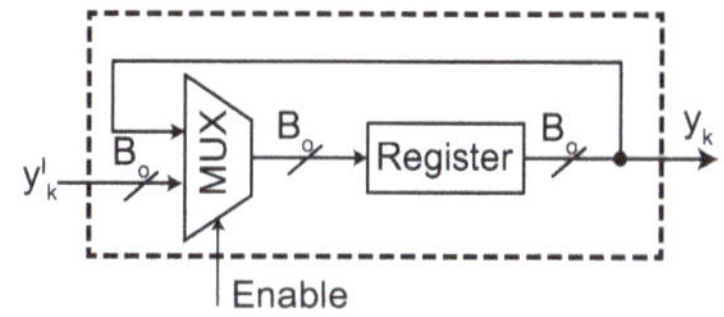

Figure 2: Accumulator block diagram.

3.1 Sampling procedure

Figure 1 shows the block diagram of the LBCS architecture proposed in this work for one-channel sampling. The *Matrix Sequence Generator Logic* is a chip memory that stores the entries of $\mathbf{H}_\Omega$ that are used for the sub-sampling procedure performed by the *LBCS Encoder* block. The entries are stored into the chip memory in a sequential fashion through the *Matrix Input*. The sampling procedure starts once the memory is loaded and a *serializer* is used to sequentially send the h_{kj} weights to the summation node.

The input signal x_j is the digital output of an A/D converter with a resolution of B_i bits. At the beginning of each window of length N, we set $\mathbf{y} = 0$ and then, at each time step j, x_j is summed or subtracted to the B_o-bit accumulator value y_k depending on the one-bit Hadamard entry h_{kj}, updating each component via the rule:

$$y'_k = y_k + h_{kj} x_j,\ k \in \{1, \dots, M\}, \tag{9}$$

Instead of performing the subtraction through a subtractor, the B_o-bit signal y'_k is formed with a single B_o-bit ripple carry adder, and the h_{kj} input defines the polarity of y_k. This also allows to avoid any multipliers in the weighting phase when y_k is fed-back to the summation node. Each accumulator has to be updated before the next sample x_j arrives, therefore we use an *enable* signal to drive the multiplexer of the accumulator block, shown in Figure 2, in order to update only one register per time. With this design choice, we avoid having one adder per accumulator lane, but require an internal digital clock frequency

$$f_{encoder} = M \times f_s, \tag{10}$$

where f_s is the signal sampling frequency[1].

When $M = \frac{N}{CR}$ is large, the internal clock frequency may become a limiting factor, requiring additional digital blocks to synchronize the clock. However, as further described in Section 4, the sampling frequency is 5kHz for the considered datasets, choosing $N = 256$ and a hypothetical compression rate of 16×, the LBCS encoder freqcncy results to be 5kHz×$\frac{256}{16}$ = 80kHz, which is still in a relatively low frequency range.

[1]The h_{kj}-serializer works at frequency $f_{encoder}$ too.

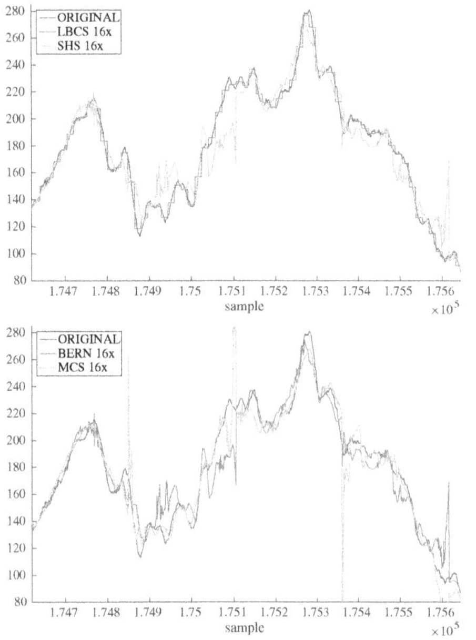

Figure 3: `I001-P034-D01` Reconstruction example for channel `Grid28` on four windows of length 256 each.

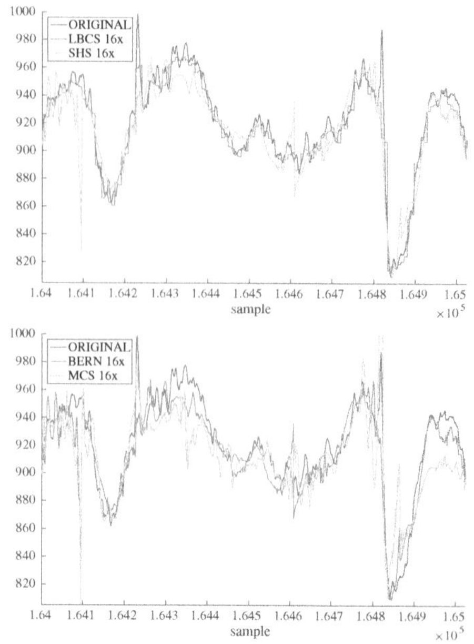

Figure 4: `Study 040` Reconstruction example for channel `LG50` on four windows of length 256 each.

4. SIMULATIONS

In this section, we first give the details related to the human iEEG datasets used in the experiments and then we compare the numerical results obtained applying the LBCS encoder against the other approaches described in Section 2.1.

4.1 Dataset details

The **`iEEG.org`** portal contains several datasets of EEG and iEEG data which are manually annotated by expert clinicians. We focus on the following two datasets.

4.1.1 `I001-P034-D01`

The `I001-P034-D01` dataset consists of approximately 1 day, 8 hours and 10 minutes of recordings at 5kHz, or approximately $6 \cdot 10^8$ samples. In order to reduce the dataset size, we use samples only from the 12th and 13th seizure, and an equal number of samples before the seizure onset, for training and testing respectively.

We consider the 32 active grid electrodes which, from a first visual inspection, more clearly show significant changes between the samples annotated as seizures from the rest. In order to better compare to the sampling strategy that combines samples across the channels (MCS), we consider only a sub-grid of 4×4 electrodes.

4.1.2 `Study 040`

The `Study 040` dataset consists of approximately 2 days, 23 hours and 50 minutes of recordings at 5kHz, or approximately $1.3 \cdot 10^9$ samples. In order to reduce the dataset size, we use samples only from the 1st and the 3rd seizure and an equal number of samples before the seizure onset, for training and testing respectively. We consider all the 64 active grid electrodes.

4.2 Experimental protocol

The training set of both datasets are used to learn the sampling pattern for the LBCS approach and also to tune the variable density parameters for the SHS method. Once the sampling pattern is fixed, LBCS uses it to compress all the signal windows in the test set. The reconstruction is then performed with the linear decoder (6). For the randomized methods, MCS, BERN and SHS, we draw 20 different sampling patterns from the relative distributions for each signal window in the test and reconstruct using the tree-based HGL norm (4), which was shown in [12] to yield the best results.

4.3 Performance Evaluation

We concatenate all reconstructed windows for each channel j together, forming the entire reconstructed signal, $\hat{\mathbf{x}}_j$ for the test seizure. We then compute the SNR for each channel as $\text{SNR}_j = 20 \log_{10}\left(\frac{\|\mathbf{x}_j\|_2}{\|\mathbf{x}_j - \hat{\mathbf{x}}_j\|_2}\right)$, where $\mathbf{x}_j$ is the recorded signal for channel j, and average these SNRs to obtain our final measure of performance, $\text{SNR} = \frac{1}{\#ch}\sum_{i=1}^{\#ch}\text{SNR}_j$. For the randomized methods, we also average over the 20 draws.

4.4 Numerical results

We conducted numerical experiments with all the methods described in this paper on both datasets. We varied the length of the signal window N, the number of bits, B_i, of the input A/D converter and the compression rate CR. We observed that the LBCS approach is not very sensitive to the window length N, therefore, for the sake of space, we present only results for $N = 256$ and $B_i = 10$ bits, which seemed to offer the best trade-off between reconstruction quality and area-power consumption, as further discussed in Section 5.1.

Tables 1 and 2 report the reconstruction quality, in dB, obtained on the `I001-P034-D01` and the `Study 040` datasets respectively. As expected, adaptive compression sets the upper limit on the achievable performance. LBCS offers the best reconstruction quality at any compression rate, with an

Table 1: I001-P034-D01 **N = 256,** $B_i = 10$

Method	Compression rate					
	2	4	8	16	32	64
Adaptive	41.60	39.86	36.38	31.40	25.42	19.43
LBCS	**40.79**	**37.64**	**33.27**	**28.48**	**23.27**	**18.06**
SHS HGL	36.92	27.96	23.89	20.26	18.53	14.49
BERN HGL	37.48	26.69	20.49	16.87	13.53	11.15
MCS HGL	28.96	24.40	20.92	17.48	n.a.	n.a.

Table 2: Study 040 **N = 256,** $B_i = 10$

Method	Compression rate					
	2	4	8	16	32	64
Adaptive	40.79	40.05	38.11	35.28	32.07	28.61
LBCS	**40.55**	**38.90**	**35.77**	**33.09**	**30.28**	**27.28**
SHS HGL	37.58	33.67	31.75	29.21	27.73	24.75
BERN HGL	38.23	33.57	29.59	26.62	24.03	22.08
MCS HGL	37.20	34.22	30.82	27.03	23.00	18.45

increase in the SNR of several dBs compared to the other methods. The SHS approach offers the second best performance, as its variable density is adapted to the signals, but still fails at capturing as much structure as LBCS. The BERN and MCS methods offer a much inferior performance at high compression rates, because imposing structure only during reconstruction does not fully compensate the limitations of their structure-unaware sampling mechanisms. Figures 3 and 4 show some reconstructions obtained with each method on both datasets. The LBCS reconstructions are much smoother and better follow the original signal.

The linear decoder (6) yields reconstructions at a fraction of the computational cost of the other methods. Indeed, solving a single optimization problem with the HGL norm, using `DecOpt` [11], requires on average approximately 0.1s, while the linear decoder requires only approximately 10^{-5}s for a 256 samples signal.

5. CIRCUIT DESIGN AND VALIDATION

In this section, we first analyze the difference in terms of area and power consumption between Hadamard-based adaptive and LBCS encoding. Afterwards we describe the implemented circuit.

5.1 Adaptive vs LBCS encoders

Section 2.4 describes that the best linear encoder, for a fixed compression rate, is given by adaptively sampling the coefficients that capture most of the energy of each signal. We now analyze the power and area costs for LBCS and adaptive encoding respectively.

5.1.1 LBCS Power and Area analysis

- *Power cost*: as shown in Figure 1, M B_o-bit accumulators are used to store the Hadamard coefficients. This leads to a dynamic power consumption of:

$$P_{LBCS} \propto M \cdot B_o \cdot f_s \cdot V_{DD}^2 \cdot C_{ref}, \quad (11)$$

  where V_{DD} is the operating voltage of the digital block and C_{ref} is the reference capacitance defined by the technology.

- *Area cost*: since a single adder is used for sampling, the area of the digital encoder block is proportional to the number M of accumulators:

$$Area_{LBCS} \propto M. \quad (12)$$

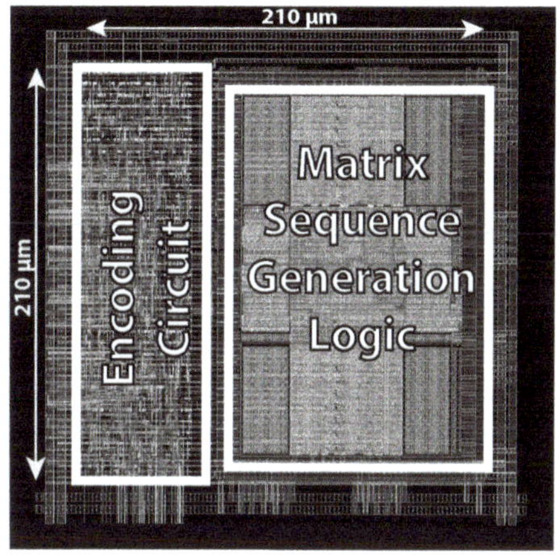

Figure 5: One channel encoder layout showing the LBCS encoding circuit and the matrix sequence generation logic for $N = 256$ and $CR = 16$.

5.1.2 Adaptive Power and Area analysis

- *Power cost*: considering a similar architecture, the adaptive encoder requires N accumulators, leading to a dynamic power consumption:

$$P_{Adaptive} \propto N \cdot B_o \cdot f_s \cdot V_{DD}^2 \cdot C_{ref}. \quad (13)$$

- *Area cost*: the area cost is proportional to the number of accumulators used to store all the the Hadamard coefficients:

$$Area_{Adaptive} \propto N. \quad (14)$$

5.1.3 Comparison

Comparing the area-power costs of the two approaches, we obtain

$$\frac{P_{Adaptive}}{P_{LBCS}} \geq \frac{N}{M} = CR,$$
$$\frac{Area_{Adaptive}}{Area_{LBCS}} \geq \frac{N}{M} = CR.$$

Combining these observations with Tables 1 and 2, we conclude that LBCS yields reconstructions almost as good as the ones obtained with the adaptive encoder, but at a fraction of its power and area cost. The advantage is more significant the higher the compression ratio.

5.2 Circuit implementation

To implement the proposed architecture, we have defined our target signal quality close to 30dB. Then, considering a sampling time window of 256 samples and assuming an ADC resolution $B_i = 10$ bits, we have set the compression ratio $CR = 16$ following the numerical results reported in Tables 1 and 2. The internal encoder core clock frequency is then $f_{encoder} = M \times f_s = 80$kHz and the accumulator resolution is set as $B_o = B_i + \log_2(N)$ to avoid overflow.

The architecture shown in Figure 1 has been implemented in a 1P9M 90 nm CMOS technology. The design is fully

Table 3: Comparison With Published Work

Parameter	[12]	[8]	[12]	This Work
Compression Method	MCS	BERN	SHS	LBCS
Compression Rate	16	10	16	16
Technology [μm CMOS]	0.18	0.09	-	0.09
Compr. Power Cost [μW]	0.95[a]	1.9	-	1.0
Compr. Area Cost [mm^2]	0.008[a]	0.090	-	0.044
Recovered Signal [dB][b]	22.2	21.7	24.7	30.8

[a] Compression power and area cost per channel.
[b] Average SNR calculated from Tables 1 and 2, considering CR=16 for all the compression methods.

digital and the layout of a one-channel encoder is shown in Figure 5. To verify the functionality of the digital encoder, the digitized neuronal data is directly given as input to the LBCS block. A post place-and-route simulation has verified that the M outputs given by the encoder are equal to the expected values computed in Matlab. The simulation has been run considering a worst case scenario with slow-slow process corner operating at 0.9V, which results in an estimated power consumption of the LBCS encoder around $1\mu W$. The silicon area of the encoder block is $210 \times 210\mu m$. Considering the fact that the electrode pitch in a typical Utah-MEA is $400\mu m$, the resulting size of the encoder is fully suitable for such embedded applications.

6. CONCLUSIONS

This work shows the application of LBCS to address the reduction of area and power costs for neural signal encoding and data telemetry in wireless implantable devices. The proposed scheme enables *on-the-fly* data compression with faster off-line recovery and higher reconstruction quality than random Bernoulli [7], multi-channel [8] or Structured Hadamard Sampling [12]. In Table 3 there is the performance summary and comparison with published works.

In the proposed design, the memory that stores the sub-sampled Hadamard matrix entries occupies a relative large area. In a multichannel implementation, the memory content is shared among all the channels, reducing the impact of the storage area over the overall chip area. Furthermore, we are currently studying how to generate the desired matrix entries directly in the chip.

LBCS is a general approach applicable to any sparse data acquisition system for which fully sampled signals are available. Our future work will focus on designing digital encoders for other applications like image processing.

Acknowledgment

This work was supported in part by the European Commission under grant ERC Future Proof and by the Swiss Science Foundation under grants SNF 200021-146750 and SNF CRSII2-147633. The authors would like to thank Jonathan Narinx for useful discussions on the system design.

7. REFERENCES

[1] A. C. Hoogerwerf and K. D. Wise, "A three-dimensional microelectrode array for chronic neural recording," *Biomedical Engineering, IEEE Transactions on*, vol. 41, no. 12, pp. 1136–1146, 1994.

[2] M. Leonardi and T. B. Ustun, "The global burden of epilepsy," *Epilepsia*, vol. 43, no. s6, pp. 21–25, 2002.

[3] C. B. Nemeroff, H. S. Mayberg, S. E. Krahl, J. McNamara, A. Frazer, T. R. Henry, M. S. George, D. S. Charney, and S. K. Brannan, "Vns therapy in treatment-resistant depression: clinical evidence and putative neurobiological mechanisms," *Neuropsychopharmacology*, vol. 31, no. 7, pp. 1345–1355, 2006.

[4] E. J. Candès, "Compressive sampling," in *Proceedings oh the International Congress of Mathematicians: Madrid, August 22-30, 2006: invited lectures*, 2006, pp. 1433–1452.

[5] D. Donoho, "Compressed sensing," *IEEE Transactions on Information Theory*, vol. 52, no. 4, pp. 1289–1306, 2006.

[6] J. N. Laska, S. Kirolos, M. F. Duarte, T. S. Ragheb, R. G. Baraniuk, and Y. Massoud, "Theory and implementation of an analog-to-information converter using random demodulation," in *IEEE International Symposium on Circuits and Systems*, 2007, pp. 1959–1962.

[7] F. Chen, A. P. Chandrakasan, and V. M. Stojanovic, "Design and analysis of a hardware-efficient compressed sensing architecture for data compression in wireless sensors," *IEEE Journal of Solid-State Circuits*, vol. 47, no. 3, pp. 744–756, 2012.

[8] M. Shoaran, M. H. Kamal, C. Pollo, P. Vandergheynst, and A. Schmid, "Compact low-power cortical recording architecture for compressive multichannel data acquisition," *IEEE Transactions on Biomedical Circuits and Systems*, vol. 8, no. 6, pp. 857–870, December 2014.

[9] L. Baldassarre, Y.-H. Li, J. Scarlett, B. Gözcü, I. Bogunovic, and V. Cevher, "Learning-based compressive subsampling," *arXiv preprint arXiv:1510.06188*, 2015.

[10] S. Foucart and H. Rauhut, *A mathematical introduction to compressive sensing*. Springer, 2013.

[11] Q. Tran-Dinh and V. Cevher, "A primal-dual algorithmic framework for constrained convex minimization," *arXiv preprint arXiv:1406.5403*, 2014.

[12] L. Baldassarre, C. Aprile, M. Shoaran, Y. Leblebici, and V. Cevher, "Structured sampling and recovery of ieeg signals," in *6th IEEE International Workshop on Computational Advances in Multi-Sensor Adaptive Processing (CAMSAP)*, 2015.

[13] R. Baraniuk, V. Cevher, M. Duarte, , and C. Hegde, "Model-based compressive sensing," *IEEE Transactions on Information Theory*, vol. 56, no. 4, pp. 1982–2001, 2010.

[14] A. Kyrillidis, L. Baldassarre, M. El Halabi, Q. Tran-Dinh, and V. Cevher, "Structured sparsity: Discrete and convex approaches," in *Compressed Sensing and its Applications*. Springer, 2015, pp. 341–387.

[15] M. E. Halabi and V. Cevher, "A totally unimodular view of structured sparsity," in *AISTATS*, 2015.

[16] S. Mallat, *A wavelet tour of signal processing*. Academic press, 1999.

[17] R. Jenatton, J. Mairal, G. Obozinski, and F. Bach, "Proximal methods for hierarchical sparse coding," *Journal of Machine Learning Reasearch*, vol. 12, pp. 2297–2334, 2011.

Load Balanced On-Chip Power Delivery for Average Current Demand

Divya Pathak
Drexel University
divya.pathak@drexel.edu

Mohammad Hossein Hajkazemi
George Mason University
mhajkaze@gmu.edu

Mohammad Khavari Tavana
George Mason University
mkhavari@gmu.edu

Houman Homayoun
George Mason University
hhomayoun@gmu.edu

Ioannis Savidis
Drexel University
isavidis@coe.drexel.edu

ABSTRACT

A dynamic power management system for homogeneous chip multi-processors (CMP) is proposed. Each core of the CMP includes on chip DC-DC switching buck converters that are interconnected through a switch network. The peak current rating of the buck converter is selected to meet only the average current demand of the load circuit. A real-time load balancing algorithm is developed which reconfigures the power delivery network by combining the output of multiple buck converters when the workload demand exceeds the peak current rating. Simulation results for the proposed power delivery method indicate up to a 44% reduction in the energy consumption of the CMP system. In addition, the on-chip footprint of the power delivery network, including the on-chip voltage regulators and the switching network, is reduced by at least 23%.

1. INTRODUCTION

With the paradigm shift in computing systems from performance oriented design to energy efficiency, considerable research effort has focused on optimizing the core configuration by reducing the over-provisioning of the core resources. Little attention, however, is given to the reduction in the over-provisioning of the circuits delivering power to the cores. Conventionally, the voltage regulator and power conditioning circuits are off-chip. The power consumption and the footprint of the voltage regulators and the conditioning circuits is therefore not a concern while optimizing the power delivery to the core(s). The introduction of chip multi-processors (CMPs) resulted in new challenges in the delivery of power to the multiple cores. Providing low latency, per-core dynamic voltage and frequency scaling (DVFS) is challenging with off-chip voltage regulators [1]. The power supply voltage regulation is also reduced due to longer on-chip interconnects connecting the off-chip VR to the multiple load circuits. On chip voltage regulators (OCVRs) have been extensively researched and successfully introduced in commercial multi-core systems in Intel 4th generation processors [2] as well as IBM POWER8 servers [3]. The choice of OCVR topology is dependant on several factors including system level parameters such as the optimal power conversion efficiency and maximum load current consumption as well as the physical design of the passive components. System level tools such as a power virus [4] or McPAT [5] are used to determine a first order estimate of the peak power consumption of the cores, which is typically overestimated. As a result, the OCVR and the power delivery network are over-provisioned to support a peak load current larger than what is consumed by the cores.

In this paper, an interconnected on-chip power distribution network is modeled. Rather than a static configuration designed for the worst case power consumption of the cores, a work load aware reconfigurable power delivery system is developed. A detailed statistical analysis of the cycle accurate power consumption profile of workloads executed on a CMP system is performed. Each OCVR is designed to support a peak current rating equal to the average load current I_{avg} consumed across all workloads. SPICE simulations indicate that by reducing the peak current rating of the OCVRs to support I_{avg}, the energy efficiency of the CMP improves and the on-chip area occupied by the OCVRs is reduced. A load balancing algorithm is developed for dynamic power management. The algorithm is executed on the on-chip power management unit (PMU), and is capable of reconfiguring the power delivery network (PDN) to combine the outputs of multiple OCVRs to support load currents in excess of I_{avg}.

The rest of the paper is organized as follows: Prior work exploring reconfigurable power delivery networks (RPDN) are discussed in Section 2. The system level simulation and the power consumption profile of multi-application workloads are described in Section 3. The proposed power delivery methodology is discussed in Section 4. Simulated results indicating an improvement in the energy efficiency of the CMP system are also included in Section 4. Concluding remarks are provided in Section 5.

2. RELATED WORK

Recent work has attempted to improve the energy efficiency of multi-core and many-core systems by reconfiguring the power delivery network according to the power demand of the work load. An RPDN using switched capacitor volt-

GLSVLSI '16, May 18-20, 2016, Boston, MA, USA

DOI: http://dx.doi.org/10.1145/2902961.2903030

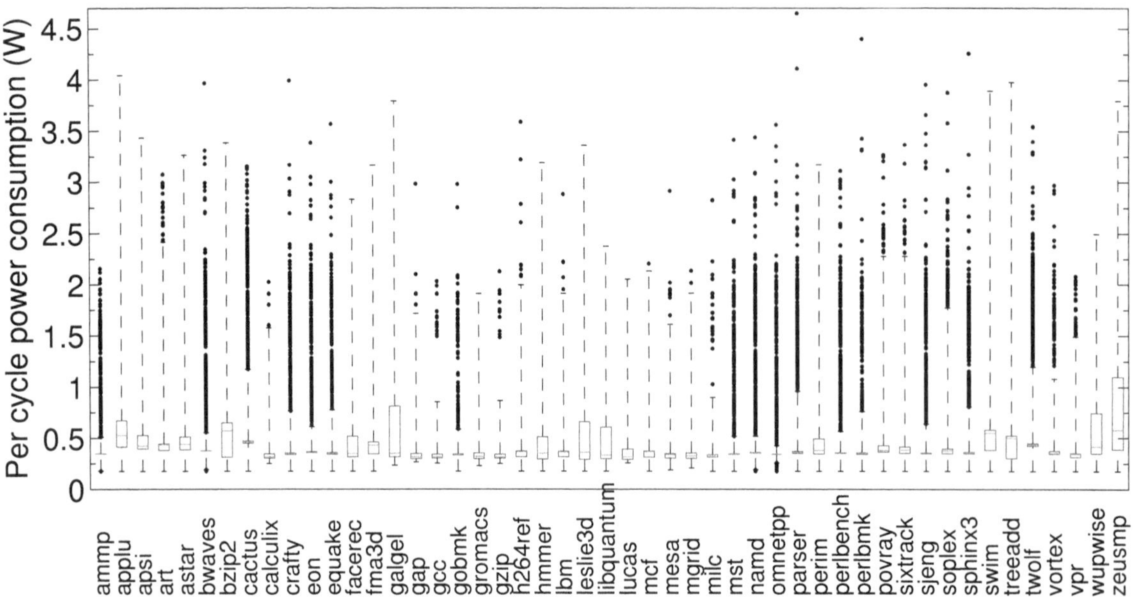

Figure 1: Statistical analysis of the per cycle power consumption of the SPEC CPU 2000 and SPEC CPU 2006 benchmarks.

Table 1: Architectural parameters of the core.

Parameter	Value
Core clock frequency	2.4 GHz
Power supply voltage (V_{dd})	1 V
Issue, Commit width	2
INT and FP Instruction Queue	16 entries
Load and Store Queue	16 entries
INT and FP Physical Register File	48 entries
ROB size	48
L1 cache	32 KB, 4-way
L2 cache	256 KB

age regulators (SCVRs) and cross bar switches to serve 8 cores is proposed in [6]. The RPDN consists of 32 cells, where each cell is an SCVR capable of supporting two voltage step down conversions (2:1 and 3:2). The simulation results indicate that the reconfigurable power delivery network offers 40% energy savings as compared to a configuration with per core voltage regulators. The switched capacitor voltage regulators offer 80% power conversion efficiency. The work does not address the inferior voltage regulation offered by the SCVRs.

A run time reconfigurable voltage regulator network of buck converters is described in [7]. The lowest energy consumption across various DVFS levels is determined by solving an integer linear programming (ILP) problem. The timing penalty to set the switching network is not quantified and the ILP is solved for discrete DVFS timing penalties ranging from 5% to 15%. An off-chip buck converter (LTC3816) SPICE model is used instead of an OCVR model, although the OCVR offers an order of magnitude faster voltage response time under DVFS [1].

An RPDN for 3-D many-core systems is proposed in [8]. Single input multiple output buck converters supply power to the many-core system. The energy optimization problem across DVFS operating points (voltage and frequency pairs) is solved through ILP formulation.

Clustering of voltage regulators to boost the energy efficiency of the system is proposed in [9], but the work ignores the variation in the power conversion efficiency (PCE) of the voltage regulators due to dynamic voltage and frequency scaling. As shown in [10], ignoring the PCE variation of the voltage regulators leads to suboptimal workload mapping and therefore a large penalty on the energy savings possible with DVFS.

Recent work on RPDNs does not offer an analysis of the deterioration in the response time of the power delivery system due to the search and decision time needed to flip the requisite number of switches and reconfigure the connections between the cores [6, 7, 8]. In addition, prior work consider over-provisioned voltage regulators designed for worst case power consumption. The RPDN proposed in this paper is novel as the power network is designed to supply the average power demand of the cores and is adaptable to support peak power demands. The RPDN configuration is managed dynamically without the overhead of solving an off-line or on-line linear or nonlinear programming optimization problem.

3. POWER DISSIPATION BEHAVIOR OF APPLICATIONS ON A CMP SYSTEM

The cycle dependant power dissipation of the workloads executing on a CMP system provide insight to optimize the design of the PDN. Workloads which are computation intensive consume higher power during CPU bound phases of the application, but the maximum power consumed is considerably lower than the peak power consumption of a well developed power virus. A detailed power trace analysis of the SPEC2000 and SPEC2006 benchmark suite is performed to obtain realistic power consumption statistics of the workloads. A 16-core CMP in 45 nm technology is modeled using a processor architectural simulator [11]. McPAT [5] is integrated in the simulator to analyze the power consumption of the core. Each core has a 2-way issue and out-of-order execution unit. The micro-architectural parameters of the core used in the simulations are summarized in Table 1.

Each of the 49 benchmarks from the SPEC benchmark suite are simulated at four different timing intervals to cover multiple execution phases. The simulations are run for 10K cycles per time interval. The dynamic and static power consumption is sampled cycle by cycle through McPAT. The statistical dispersion of the per cycle power consumption of different SPEC benchmarks with single phase forwarding is shown through a box plot in Fig. 1. The interquartile range for all the studied benchmarks falls approximately an order of magnitude below the peak power (P_{peak}) consumption of 5.73 W reported through McPAT simulations. The number of outliers beyond 5σ coverage for each benchmark is an insignificant fraction of the sample size. The combined power dissipation characteristics of all the 49 benchmarks are as follows: The minimum, average, and maximum power consumption is, respectively, 0.175 W, 0.555 W, and 4.755 W. The power dissipation of the applications is between 0.3 W and 0.5 W for approximately 65% of the execution time. The minimum, average, and maximum power dissipation variation per clock cycle is, respectively, 0 W, 0.195 W, and 4.333 W. The power variation is less than 0.1 W for 90% of the time. The studied benchmarks spend 78% of the run-time consuming less than the average power. The maximum power consumption of 4.75 W across all benchmarks is consumed for a very small percentage of the run-time (7.5×10^{-5}%).

4. PROPOSED DESIGN OF THE POWER DELIVERY NETWORK

Significant work has been done to optimize the core configuration, work load mapping, and dynamic/static clustering of the cores in a CMP system, but the energy and area loss incurred due to the integration of over-provisioned VRs has been overlooked. In the proposed power delivery system, the loadline of the OCVR serving each core or cluster of cores is designed for the average current (I_{avg}) consumed. Designing the OCVR loadline around I_{avg} reduces the peak voltage demand on the OCVR and significantly decreases the maximum supported load current. The block representation of the power delivery network is shown in Fig. 2. For a CMP system consisting of N cores or core clusters, N OCVRs provide the regulated power. In the proposed PDN, if the OCVR serves a cluster of n identical cores, the power rating of the OCVR is $n{\cdot}I_{avg}$. The output of each OCVR is connected to the inputs of a high-speed switching (HSS) fabric. The N outputs of the HSS fabric are connected to the local PDN grid of the N cores or core clusters. The HSS fabric is controlled by the power management unit (PMU). The interconnected power delivery network shown in Fig. 2 provides increased service reliability as compared to conventional on-chip power distribution with a single OCVR serving a single core. In addition, the interconnected network provides opportunity to balance load currents through reconfiguration of the switches.

4.1 Load balancing through run-time OCVR clustering

A technique to deliver currents higher than I_{avg} is described in this section. The current sensors placed in each core are constantly monitored by the PMU. When the sum of the currents sensed from all cores within a cluster (I_{sense}) reaches a threshhold ($\triangle I$) below I_{avg}, the PMU configures

---

Algorithm 1 Load balanced power delivery with run-time OCVR clustering to support higher than average load current consumption.

Inputs:
Current consumption sensed from the core: I_{sense_x}
Current threshhold: $\triangle I$
Voltage level applied to the core: $V_x \in [V_{dd\_1}, V_{dd\_2}, ..., V_{dd\_m}]$ where x $\in$ [1,...,n], m = number of DVFS levels, n = number of OCVRs/Cores
Switch matrix: $Switch_{n,n-1}$
Constraints:
$t_{switch} + t_{PMU} < t_{core}$
$\sum_{i=1}^{n} V_x{\cdot}I_{sense\_x} <$ n$\cdot V_{dd_m}{\cdot}I_{avg}$

Append array *CORE_RED* with core id x where $I_{sense\_x} \geq I_{avg}$ - $\triangle I$
Append array *CORE_GREEN* with core id y where $I_{sense\_y} < I_{avg}$ - $\triangle I$
if *length(CORE_RED)* > 0 **then**
  call *OCVR_CLUSTER* ▷ Reconfigure the PDN by clustering the output of OCVRs
else
  call *OCVR_DECLUSTER* ▷ Reconfigure the PDN by de-clustering the output of OCVRs
end if
procedure OCVR_CLUSTER
  for each i in min(length(*CORE_RED*), length(*CORE_GREEN*)) **do**
    Demand(i) ← $CORE\_RED(I_{sense\_i})$ + $CORE\_GREEN(I_{sense\_i})$
    if *Demand(i)* $\leq 2{\cdot}$ I_{avg} **then**
      $V_{CORE\_RED(i)} \leftarrow V_{CORE\_GREEN(i)}$ ▷ Align the V_{dd} levels of the two cores whose OCVR outputs are being combined
      $Switch_{CORE\_RED(i),CORE\_GREEN(i)} \leftarrow 1$ ▷ Close the switch so that *CORE_RED(i)* is served by the OCVR connected to *CORE_GREEN(i)*
      Delete *CORE_RED(i)* and *CORE_GREEN(i)* from the respective arrays
    end if
  end for
end procedure
procedure OCVR_DECLUSTER
  for each nonzero element in sparse matrix *Switch* **do**
    if $I_{sense\_i} + I_{sense\_j} < 2{\cdot}I_{avg}$ - $\triangle I$ **then**
      $Switch_{i,j} \leftarrow 0$ ▷ Open the switch connecting core i with OCVR j
    end if
  end for
end procedure

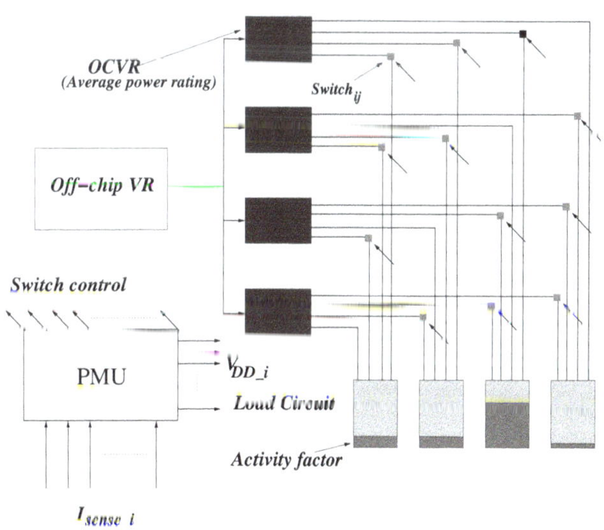

Figure 2: Proposed interconnected on-chip power delivery network with run-time voltage regulator clustering through a switching fabric.

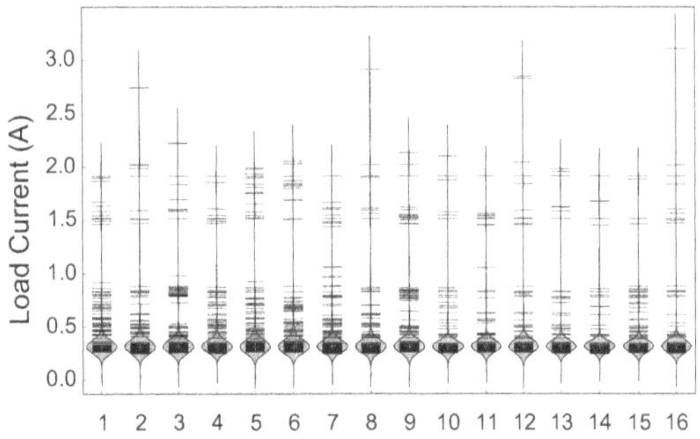

(a)

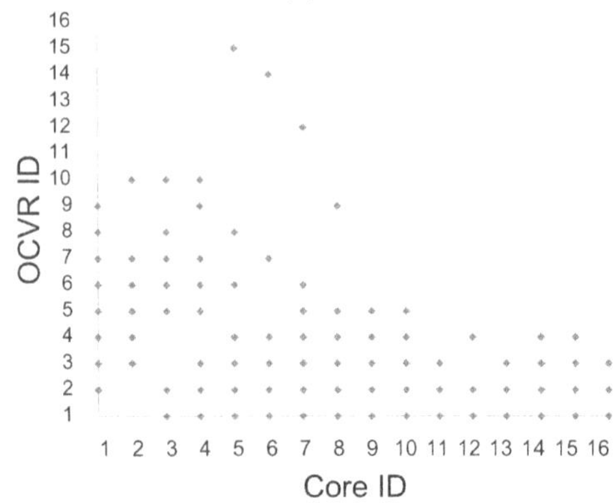

(b)

Figure 3: Simulated results of the implementation of Algorithm 1 for a 16-core CMP system with 16 OCVRs each with a peak rating of 0.6 A. (a) Load current variation per core and (b) cumulative configuration of the switches for 1000 CPU cycles.

the HSS to source additional current from the OCVRs which are located nearest to the cluster and are sourcing current less than I_{avg}. The logic controlling the HSS fabric within the PMU operates on two system parameters; the V_{dd} levels and the total load current sensed from each core cluster. The analysis of the power consumption provided in Section 3 indicates that the probability of the load current demand exceeding I_{avg} is 22%. As a result, there is always more than one core operating at or below I_{avg}. The PMU is provisioned to add at least one additional OCVR to serve a core requiring current higher than I_{avg}. The sum of the decision time of the PMU and the time to reconfigure the switches must be less than or equal to the load current transient response time (current slew-rate) of an OCVR with a current rating of I_{peak} to ensure an uninterrupted power supply to the core cluster.

The switching control of the HSS fabric is described by Algorithm 1. Algorithm 1 is implemented in the Python programming language and is analyzed with the parameters summarized in Table 2. A stochastic model of the current consumption of the cores in a CMP system is developed based on the statistical parameters captured from the per cycle power consumption analysis of the SPEC benchmarks. The load current obtained from the stochastic model for 1000 CPU cycles across 16 cores is shown in Fig. 3(a). The peak current rating of each OCVR is set to 0.6 A (I_{peak}), which is one order of magnitude less than the I_{peak} obtained through McPAT. The active switches required to support the run-time load current variation on each core for 1000 CPU cycles are shown in Fig. 3(b). A generic statistical load current model is also analyzed through Monte Carlo simulations with a maximum possible value of I_{peak}. Four DVS levels, listed in Table 2, are selected corresponding to the core configuration provided in Table 1.

Table 2: Simulation parameters for Algorithm 1.

Parameter	Value
Number of Cores	8, 16, 32, 64, 128
DVS levels	0.7 V, 0.8 V, 0.9 V, 1 V
OCVR current rating (I_{avg})	0.6 A
Current threshold ($\triangle I$)	0.1 A
Load current variation	SPEC benchmark power consumption statistics
Execution duration	10 million CPU cycles

4.2 Energy efficiency of CMP system

The switching DC-DC buck converter offers superior power supply voltage regulation and is therefore an optimum choice to power the cores. The circuit implementation of a buck converter consists of a switching network and a passive low pass filter. The inductor in the low pass filter acts as a low-loss energy transfer device which improves the power conversion efficiency. In this section, the PCE of the buck converter is analyzed for changes with the peak load current rating. The goal is to analyze the impact on the energy efficiency of the CMP when designing the OCVRs to support only the average load current demand of the cores.

4.2.1 Power conversion efficiency

The power consumed by the buck converter (P_{buck}) is given by (1) [12]. The P_{mos}, P_{ind}, P_{cap}, and P_{pwm} are the power loss in, respectively, the MOS power transistors and the cascaded buffers driving them, the inductor and capacitor of the filter circuit, and the pulse width modulator circuit. The detailed mathematical formulae of each of the components which contribute to P_{buck} are given in [12].

$$P_{buck} = P_{mos} + P_{ind} + P_{cap} + P_{pwm} \tag{1}$$

The power consumed by the filter circuit, power transistors, and the buffers driving them increases with the maximum supported output current of the buck converter. Alternatively, multiple phases are used to drive higher output currents. The circuit schematic of a buck converter with multiple phases of the filter circuit, MOS power transistors, and cascaded buffers is shown in Fig. 4. Two custom buck converters with maximum output current ratings of 6 A and 0.6 A are implemented [13]. The two converters represent voltage regulators that support the I_{peak} and I_{avg} currents of a CMP with core parameters as listed in Table 1. The circuit characteristics and power consumption of the components of the buck converters are listed in Table 3. The buck converter with a maximum output current rating of 0.6 A consumes 22.65 mW, which is 3.3% of the power consumed by the over-provisioned buck converter. The on-chip implementation of the two buck converters yields similar ratios between the power consumed by each passive component, although at a higher switching frequency to reduce the size of the filter inductor and capacitor.

Table 3: Circuit parameters and power consumption for two peak load currents of DC-DC switching buck converters [13].

Parameter	Maximum output current of 6 A	Maximum output current of 0.6 A
Peak to peak inductor ripple current	1.65 A	182.5 mA
Switching frequency	368.25 kHz	100.02 kHz
Duty cycle	43.4%	40.16%
Peak-to-peak output ripple voltage	1.924 mV	2.281 mV
Inductor power dissipation	260.83 mW	675 µW
Output capacitor power dissipation	368.91 µW	13.56 µW
Total power dissipation	688.99 mW	22.65 mW
Footprint	209 mm^2	161 mm^2

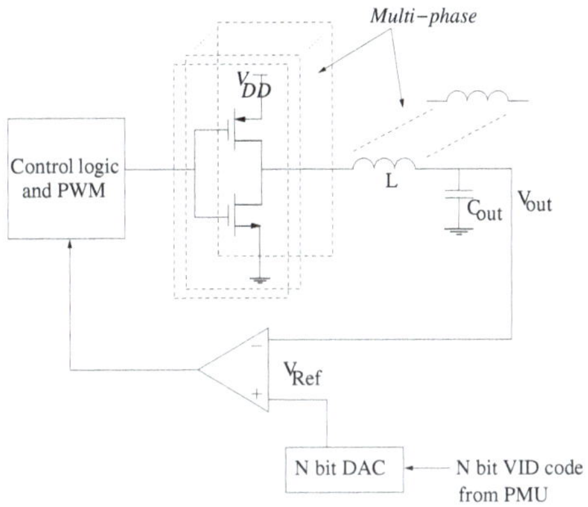

Figure 4: Schematic of a multi-phase DC-DC switching buck converter.

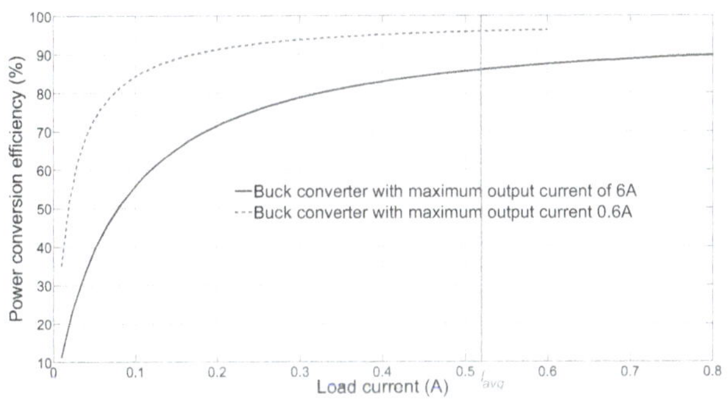

Figure 5: Power conversion efficiency with load current for two DC-DC buck converters with a maximum load current rating of 6 A and 0.6 A.

The large reduction in the power dissipation of the buck converter achieved by reducing the peak load current rating results in an improvement in the PCE. Although the over-provisioned buck converter offers a peak PCE of 89.7% at an output current of 6 A, the reduction in the PCE with decreasing output current is significant. The variation in the PCE with the output current for the two buck converters is shown in Fig. 5. The typical workloads executed on the CMP (with the core configuration listed in Table 1) consume currents in the range of I_{avg} and therefore the buck converter with an output rating of 0.6 A offers a higher average PCE for a majority of the run-time of the workloads.

4.2.2 *Improvement in energy efficiency*

The total energy consumption of a CMP system implemented with a conventional PDN for a given execution time T_{epoch} with N cores and N OCVRs is given by (2). The cores are served by over-provisioned OCVRs identical to the buck converter with a maximum output current of 6 A. The dynamic and static power consumed by the cores in the presence of DVFS are given by $P_{dynamic}$ and P_{static}, respectively. PCE_1 represents the power conversion efficiency of the over-provisioned OCVR. At low load currents close to I_{avg}, the PCE_1 offered by the over-provisioned buck converter is 87%. Alternatively, if the power delivery system is designed with each core supported by a buck converter that supplies a maximum output current of 0.6 A, the achieved PCE_2 at I_{avg} is 96.36%. In addition, the static power consumed by idle cores or core clusters is close to zero as power gating through the HSS fabric is performed. The HSS fabric, however, imposes an additional switching loss P_{switch}, which is the dynamic power consumed by the PMOS transistors while switching, and a conduction loss $P_{conduction}$ while in the ON state and passing the average current I_{avg}.

$$E_{CMP,conventional} = \{\sum_{i=1}^{N} \frac{(P_{dynamic\_i} + P_{static})}{PCE_1}\} \cdot T_{epoch} \quad (2)$$

The total energy consumed by the CMP with N OCVRs, where each OCVR is designed for an I_{avg} rating, and Nx(N-1) PMOS switches is given by (3). The parameters j, k, and l are, respectively, the number of active cores consuming current below I_{avg}, the number of active core(s) consuming current above I_{avg}, and the number of idle core(s) power gated through the HSS network. In the case of idle cores, the power consumed by the OCVRs ($P_{OCVR,leakage}$) is the only component contributing to the system energy. As described in Section 3, applications consume current less than I_{avg} for about 78% of the time. The P_{switch} loss is therefore incurred for 22% of the execution time of the workloads when the load current demand exceeds I_{avg}.

$$E_{CMP,proposed} = \sum_{t=1}^{T_{epoch}} \{\sum_{i=1}^{j} \frac{(P_{dynamic\_i} + P_{static})}{PCE_2} + \sum_{i=1}^{k} \frac{(P_{dynamic\_i} + P_{static} + P_{switch} + P_{conduction})}{PCE_2} + \sum_{i=1}^{l} P_{OCVR,leakage}\}; \quad j+k+l=N \quad (3)$$

Circuit simulations of a PDN designed to support the I_{avg} for each of the 16 cores are performed to determine the energy consumption as given by (3). The 16 cores are simulated as piecewise constant current sinks. The current variation with time for the 16 current sinks is shown in Fig.

Table 4: Parameters of the PDN determined through SPICE simulation.

Parameter	Value
PMOS Width	800 µm
PMOS switching time	160 ps
Area occupied by 16x15 switching network	9600 μm^2
Per core maximum switching capacitance	2.4 nF
Piecewise constant load current variation	Stochastic model
P_{switch}	0.1 W
$P_{conduction}$	0.06 W
P_{static} (obtained through McPAT)	0.175 W

3(a). A 16x15 PMOS switching network is implemented in a 45 nm technology. The gates of the PMOS switches are controlled through time varying voltage signals. The P_{switch} and $P_{conduction}$ for the PMOS switch with an output capacitance provided by a single core is determined through SPICE simulations. The P_{static} and $P_{dynamic}$ of a core is measured through McPAT. The $P_{dynamic}$ for each core is overestimated as the power consumption per clock cycle is captured at the highest supported DVS level of 1 V. The parameter values of the switching network and the PDN are summarized in Table 4.

The additional switching and conduction losses due to the PMOS switches are an insignificant fraction of the total power consumed by the CMP as both are only consumed when the PDN is reconfigured to combine the outputs of the OCVRs. The energy consumption of the proposed power delivery system is up to 44% less than the energy consumed by the CMP with over-provisioned OCVRs and PDN. On average, there is a 15% reduction in the energy consumption as shown through simulations of the proposed PDN with a stochastic load current modeled on the SPEC benchmark power traces shown in Fig.1. By reducing the maximum rating of the OCVR (buck converter), the percentage reduction in the energy consumed for a core sinking current less than I_{avg} is 36%. The reduction in energy is due to the optimal PCE offered by the buck converter at the maximum output current supported. The energy efficiency of the CMP is therefore improved significantly by designing the power delivery system to support the average current demand of the cores. In addition, if a system level workload mapping technique is applied to distribute identical workloads on a cluster of cores, serving the core cluster with one OCVR that implements DVFS is advantageous to further reduce the energy consumption [6, 10].

4.3 Technique to prevent system failure

The power consumption analysis of the different workloads provided in Section 3 and the construction of the PDN in Section 4 ensure that there is always an OCVR available in the CMP system to support core(s) demanding higher than the average current(s). In the unlikely event that an OCVR is not located to support the higher than average current requirement of a core, the core is stalled by the PMU until an OCVR becomes available for clustering. The probability of not finding an OCVR for clustering is low when an efficient workload mapping technique is implemented. The performance penalty due to stalling the core is therefore negligible.

5. CONCLUSIONS

A load balanced circuit technique to deliver average power through on-chip voltage regulators (OCVRs) is developed. The current rating of each OCVR is reduced to support only the average current demands of typical workloads executed on the CMP system. The reduction in the maximum output current of the OCVRs improves the power conversion efficiency, reduces the footprint of the PDN (voltage regulator and switch fabric) by at least 23%, and improves the energy efficiency of the CMP system by at most 44%. The simulated results indicate that the optimum OCVR configuration for a CMP system depends on the average load current requirement per core. The proposed inter-connected power delivery system is applicable to any OCVR circuit topology and offers higher reliability through a run-time clustering technique that prevents system failure when the current demand of the core exceeds the maximum output current supported by a single OCVR.

6. REFERENCES

[1] W. Kim et al, "System Level Analysis of Fast, Per-Core DVFS Using On-chip Switching Regulators," *Proceedings of the International Symposium on High Performance Computer Architecture*, pp. 123–134, February 2008.

[2] E.A. Burton et al, "FIVR–Fully Integrated Voltage Regulators on 4th Generation Intel Core SoCs," *IEEE Applied Power Electronics Conference and Exposition*, pp. 432–439, March 2014.

[3] E.J. Fluhr et al, "The 12-Core POWER Processor With 7.6 Tb/s IO Bandwidth, Integrated Voltage Regulation, and Resonant Clocking," *IEEE Journal of Solid-State Circuits*, Vol. 50, No. 1, pp. 10–23, January 2015.

[4] mersenne.org, "Great Internet Mersenne Prime Search," http://www.mersenne.org/download/#stresstest.

[5] S. Li et al, "McPAT: an integrated power, area, and timing modeling framework for multicore and manycore architectures," *IEEE/ACM International Symposium on Microarchitecture*, pp. 469–480, 2009.

[6] W. Godycki et al, "Enabling Realistic Fine-Grain Voltage Scaling with Reconfigurable Power Distribution Networks," *Proceedings of the IEEE/ACM International Symposium on Microarchitecture (MICRO)*, pp. 381–393, December 2014.

[7] W. Lee et al, "Optimizing a Reconfigurable Power Distribution Network in a Multicore Platform," *IEEE Transactions on Computer-Aided Design of Integrated Circuits and Systems*, Vol. 34, No. 7, pp. 1110–1123, July 2015.

[8] M. Sai et al, "3D Many-core Microprocessor Power Management by Space-Time Multiplexing based Demand-supply Matching," *IEEE Transaction on Computers*, Vol. 64, No. 11, pp. 3022–3036, November 2015.

[9] I. Vaisband and E.G. Friedman, "Energy efficient adaptive clustering of on-chip power delivery systems," *INTEGRATION, The VLSI Journal*, Vol. 48, pp. 1–9, January 2015.

[10] M. Tavana et al, "Realizing Complixity-Effective On-Chip Power Delivery for Many-Core Platforms by Exploiting Optimized Mapping," *Proceedings of the International Conference on Computer Design*, pp. 581–588, October 2015.

[11] D.M. Tullsen, "Simulation and Modeling of a Simultaneous Multithreading Processor," *Proceedings of the International Conference for the Resource Management & Performance Evaluation of Enterprise Computing Systems, CMG. Part 2(of 2)*, pp. 819–828, 1996.

[12] E. Salman and E.G. Friedman, *High Performance Integrated Circuit Design*, McGraw Hill, 2012.

[13] Texas Instruments, "WEBENCH Design Center," http://webench.ti.com.

Author Index